Kernel Methods and Machine Learning

Offering a fundamental basis in kernel-based learning theory, this book covers both statistical and algebraic principles. It provides over 30 major theorems for kernel-based supervised and unsupervised learning models. The first of the theorems establishes a condition, arguably necessary and sufficient, for the kernelization of learning models. In addition, several other theorems are devoted to proving mathematical equivalence between seemingly unrelated models.

With nearly 30 closed-form and iterative algorithms, the book provides a step-by-step guide to algorithmic procedures and analyzing which factors to consider in tackling a given problem, enabling readers to improve specifically designed learning algorithms and to build models for new application paradigms such as green IT and big data learning technologies.

Numerous real-world examples and over 200 problems, several of which are MATLAB-based simulation exercises, make this an essential resource for undergraduate and graduate students in computer science, and in electrical and biomedical engineering. It is also a useful reference for researchers and practitioners in the field of machine learning. Solutions to some problems and additional resources are provided online for instructors.

S. Y. Kung is a Professor in the Department of Electrical Engineering at Princeton University. His research areas include VLSI array/parallel processors, system modeling and identification, wireless communication, statistical signal processing, multimedia processing, sensor networks, bioinformatics, data mining, and machine learning. He is a Fellow of the IEEE.

Kernel Methods and Machine Learning

S. Y. KUNG
Princeton University

CAMBRIDGE
UNIVERSITY PRESS

CAMBRIDGE
UNIVERSITY PRESS

University Printing House, Cambridge CB2 8BS, United Kingdom

One Liberty Plaza, 20th Floor, New York, NY 10006, USA

477 Williamstown Road, Port Melbourne, VIC 3207, Australia

314-321, 3rd Floor, Plot 3, Splendor Forum, Jasola District Centre, New Delhi - 110025, India

103 Penang Road, #05-06/07, Visioncrest Commercial, Singapore 238467

Cambridge University Press is part of the University of Cambridge.

It furthers the University's mission by disseminating knowledge in the pursuit of education, learning and research at the highest international levels of excellence.

www.cambridge.org
Information on this title: www.cambridge.org/9781107024960

First published 2014

A catalogue record for this publication is available from the British Library

Library of Congress Cataloging in Publication data
Kung, S. Y. (Sun Yuan)
Kernel methods and machine learning / S.Y. Kung, Princeton University, New Jersey.
pages cm
ISBN 978-1-107-02496-0 (hardback)
1. Support vector machines. 2. Machine learning. 3. Kernel functions. I. Title.
Q325.5.K86 2014
006.3′10151252–dc23 2014002487

ISBN 978-1-107-02496-0 Hardback

Additional resources for this publication at www.cambridge.org/9781107024960

To Jaemin, Soomin, Timmy, and Katie, who have been our constant source of joy and inspiration

Contents

Preface *page* xvii

Part I Machine learning and kernel vector spaces 1

1 Fundamentals of kernel-based machine learning 3

1.1 Introduction 3
1.2 Feature representation and dimension reduction 4
1.2.1 Feature representation in vector space 6
1.2.2 Conventional similarity metric: Euclidean inner product 8
1.2.3 Feature dimension reduction 8
1.3 The learning subspace property (LSP) and "kernelization" of learning models 9
1.3.1 The LSP 9
1.3.2 Kernelization of the optimization formulation for learning models 13
1.3.3 The LSP is necessary and sufficient for kernelization 14
1.4 Unsupervised learning for cluster discovery 15
1.4.1 Characterization of similarity metrics 15
1.4.2 The LSP and kernelization of K-means learning models 16
1.4.3 The LSP and kernelization of ℓ_2 elastic nets 18
1.5 Supervised learning for linear classifiers 19
1.5.1 Learning and prediction phases 20
1.5.2 Learning models and linear system of equations 21
1.5.3 Kernelized learning models for under-determined systems 23
1.5.4 The vital role of the ℓ_2-norm for the LSP 24
1.5.5 The LSP condition of one-class SVM for outlier detection 25
1.6 Generalized inner products and kernel functions 25
1.6.1 Mahalanobis inner products 26
1.6.2 Nonlinear inner product: Mercer kernel functions 27
1.6.3 Effective implementation of kernel methods 30
1.7 Performance metrics 31
1.7.1 Accuracy and error rate 31
1.7.2 Sensitivity, specificity, and precision 32
1.7.3 The receiver operating characteristic (ROC) 33

1.8 Highlights of chapters 35
1.9 Problems 38

2 **Kernel-induced vector spaces** 44
2.1 Introduction 44
2.2 Mercer kernels and kernel-induced similarity metrics 45
2.2.1 Distance axioms in metric space 45
2.2.2 Mercer kernels 46
2.2.3 Construction of Mercer kernels 50
2.2.4 Shift-invariant kernel functions 50
2.3 Training-data-independent intrinsic feature vectors 50
2.3.1 Intrinsic spaces associated with kernel functions 52
2.3.2 Intrinsic-space-based learning models 56
2.4 Training-data-dependent empirical feature vectors 60
2.4.1 The LSP: from intrinsic space to empirical space 61
2.4.2 Kernelized learning models 63
2.4.3 Implementation cost comparison of two spaces 66
2.5 The kernel-trick for nonvectorial data analysis 67
2.5.1 Nonvectorial data analysis 68
2.5.2 The Mercer condition and kernel tricks 70
2.6 Summary 72
2.7 Problems 72

Part II Dimension-reduction: PCA/KPCA and feature selection 77

3 **PCA and kernel PCA** 79
3.1 Introduction 79
3.2 Why dimension reduction? 79
3.3 Subspace projection and PCA 81
3.3.1 Optimality criteria for subspace projection 81
3.3.2 PCA via spectral decomposition of the covariance matrix 82
3.3.3 The optimal PCA solution: the mean-square-error criterion 83
3.3.4 The optimal PCA solution: the maximum-entropy criterion 87
3.4 Numerical methods for computation of PCA 89
3.4.1 Singular value decomposition of the data matrix 90
3.4.2 Spectral decomposition of the scatter matrix 90
3.4.3 Spectral decomposition of the kernel matrix 91
3.4.4 Application studies of the subspace projection approach 94
3.5 Kernel principal component analysis (KPCA) 95
3.5.1 The intrinsic-space approach to KPCA 95
3.5.2 The kernelization of KPCA learning models 99
3.5.3 PCA versus KPCA 105
3.5.4 Center-adjusted versus unadjusted KPCAs 106
3.5.5 Spectral vector space 110

3.6 Summary 113
3.7 Problems 113

4 **Feature selection** 118
4.1 Introduction 118
4.2 The filtering approach to feature selection 119
4.2.1 Supervised filtering methods 120
4.2.2 Feature-weighted linear classifiers 122
4.2.3 Unsupervised filtering methods 124
4.2.4 Consecutive search methods 124
4.3 The wrapper approach to feature selection 127
4.3.1 Supervised wrapper methods 127
4.3.2 Unsupervised wrapper methods 129
4.3.3 The least absolute shrinkage and selection operator 130
4.4 Application studies of the feature selection approach 131
4.5 Summary 134
4.6 Problems 134

Part III Unsupervised learning models for cluster analysis 139

5 **Unsupervised learning for cluster discovery** 141
5.1 Introduction 141
5.2 The similarity metric and clustering strategy 141
5.3 K-means clustering models 144
5.3.1 K-means clustering criterion 144
5.3.2 The K-means algorithm 146
5.3.3 Monotonic convergence of K-means 148
5.3.4 The local optimum problem of K-means 151
5.3.5 The evaluation criterion for multiple trials of K-means 152
5.3.6 The optimal number of clusters 152
5.3.7 Application examples 152
5.4 Expectation-maximization (EM) learning models 153
5.4.1 EM clustering criterion 153
5.4.2 The iterative EM algorithm for basic GMM 155
5.4.3 Convergence of the EM algorithm with fixed σ 156
5.4.4 Annealing EM (AEM) 158
5.5 Self-organizing-map (SOM) learning models 159
5.5.1 Input and output spaces in the SOM 161
5.5.2 The SOM learning algorithm 162
5.5.3 The evaluation criterion for multiple-trial SOM 165
5.5.4 Applications of SOM learning models 166

5.6 Bi-clustering data analysis 169
5.6.1 Coherence models for bi-clustering 170
5.6.2 Applications of bi-clustering methods 171
5.7 Summary 173
5.8 Problems 174

6 Kernel methods for cluster analysis 178
6.1 Introduction 178
6.2 Kernel-based K-means learning models 179
6.2.1 Kernel K-means in intrinsic space 180
6.2.2 The K-means clustering criterion in terms of kernel matrix 181
6.3 Kernel K-means for nonvectorial data analysis 183
6.3.1 The similarity matrix for nonvectorial training datasets 184
6.3.2 Clustering criteria for network segmentation 185
6.3.3 The Mercer condition and convergence of kernel K-means 187
6.4 K-means learning models in kernel-induced spectral space 190
6.4.1 Discrepancy on optimal solution due to spectral truncation 191
6.4.2 Computational complexities 193
6.5 Kernelized K-means learning models 194
6.5.1 Solution invariance of spectral-shift on the kernel matrix 194
6.5.2 Kernelized K-means algorithms 195
6.5.3 A recursive algorithm modified to exploit sparsity 197
6.6 Kernel-induced SOM learning models 201
6.6.1 SOM learning models in intrinsic or spectral space 201
6.6.2 Kernelized SOM learning models 202
6.7 Neighbor-joining hierarchical cluster analysis 204
6.7.1 Divisive and agglomerative approaches 204
6.7.2 An NJ method that is based on centroid update 206
6.7.3 Kernelized hierarchical clustering algorithm 207
6.7.4 Case studies: hierarchical clustering of microarray data 212
6.8 Summary 213
6.9 Problems 215

Part IV Kernel ridge regressors and variants 219

7 Kernel-based regression and regularization analysis 221
7.1 Introduction 221
7.2 Linear least-squares-error analysis 222
7.2.1 Linear-least-MSE and least-squares-error (LSE) regressors 223
7.2.2 Ridge regression analysis 225
7.3 Kernel-based regression analysis 225
7.3.1 LSE regression analysis: intrinsic space 227
7.3.2 Kernel ridge regression analysis: intrinsic space 228

7.3.3 The learning subspace property (LSP): from intrinsic to empirical space 228
7.3.4 KRR learning models: empirical space 228
7.3.5 Comparison of KRRs in intrinsic and empirical spaces 230
7.4 Radial basis function (RBF) networks for regression analysis 230
7.4.1 RBF approximation networks 230
7.4.2 The Nadaraya–Watson regression estimator (NWRE) 232
7.4.3 Back-propagation neural networks 234
7.5 Multi-kernel regression analysis 240
7.6 Summary 244
7.7 Problems 244

8 Linear regression and discriminant analysis for supervised classification 248
8.1 Introduction 248
8.2 Characterization of supervised learning models 249
8.2.1 Binary and multiple classification 249
8.2.2 Learning, evaluation, and prediction phases 250
8.2.3 Off-line and inductive learning models 251
8.2.4 Linear and nonlinear learning models 252
8.2.5 Basic supervised learning strategies 252
8.3 Supervised learning models: over-determined formulation 253
8.3.1 Direct derivation of LSE solution 254
8.3.2 Fisher's discriminant analysis (FDA) 258
8.4 Supervised learning models: under-determined formulation 263
8.5 A regularization method for robust classification 266
8.5.1 The ridge regression approach to linear classification 266
8.5.2 Perturbational discriminant analysis (PDA): an extension of FDA 268
8.5.3 Equivalence between RR and PDA 269
8.5.4 Regularization effects of the ridge parameter ρ 270
8.6 Kernelized learning models in empirical space: linear kernels 273
8.6.1 Kernelized learning models for under-determined systems 273
8.6.2 Kernelized formulation of KRR in empirical space 276
8.6.3 Comparison of formulations in original versus empirical spaces 277
8.7 Summary 278
8.8 Problems 278

9 Kernel ridge regression for supervised classification 282
9.1 Introduction 282
9.2 Kernel-based discriminant analysis (KDA) 284
9.3 Kernel ridge regression (KRR) for supervised classification 287
9.3.1 KRR and LS-SVM models: the intrinsic-space approach 287
9.3.2 Kernelized learning models: the empirical-space approach 288

9.3.3 A proof of equivalence of two formulations 289
9.3.4 Complexities of intrinsic and empirical models 290
9.4 Perturbational discriminant analysis (PDA) 290
9.5 Robustness and the regression ratio in spectral space 292
9.5.1 The decision vector of KDA in spectral space 293
9.5.2 Resilience of the decision components of KDA classifiers 293
9.5.3 Component magnitude and component resilience 298
9.5.4 Regression ratio: KDA versus KRR 299
9.6 Application studies: KDA versus KRR 300
9.6.1 Experiments on UCI data 300
9.6.2 Experiments on microarray cancer diagnosis 301
9.6.3 Experiments on subcellular localization 302
9.7 Trimming detrimental (anti-support) vectors in KRR learning models 303
9.7.1 A pruned-KRR learning model: pruned PDA (PPDA) 304
9.7.2 Case study: ECG arrhythmia detection 306
9.8 Multi-class and multi-label supervised classification 307
9.8.1 Multi-class supervised classification 307
9.8.2 Multi-label classification 310
9.9 Supervised subspace projection methods 313
9.9.1 Successively optimized discriminant analysis (SODA) 313
9.9.2 Trace-norm optimization for subspace projection 318
9.9.3 Discriminant component analysis (DCA) 325
9.9.4 Comparisons between PCA, DCA, PC-DCA, and SODA 331
9.9.5 Kernelized DCA and SODA learning models 333
9.10 Summary 335
9.11 Problems 336

Part V Support vector machines and variants 341

10 Support vector machines 343
10.1 Introduction 343
10.2 Linear support vector machines 344
10.2.1 The optimization formulation in original vector space 345
10.2.2 The Wolfe dual optimizer in empirical space 345
10.2.3 The Karush–Kuhn–Tucker (KKT) condition 348
10.2.4 Support vectors 349
10.2.5 Comparison between separation margins of LSE and SVM 351
10.3 SVM with fuzzy separation: roles of slack variables 353
10.3.1 Optimization in original space 354
10.3.2 The learning subspace property and optimization in empirical space 354
10.3.3 Characterization of support vectors and WEC analysis 356

10.4 Kernel-induced support vector machines 358
10.4.1 Primal optimizer in intrinsic space 359
10.4.2 Dual optimizer in empirical space 359
10.4.3 Multi-class SVM learning models 361
10.4.4 SVM learning softwares 362
10.5 Application case studies 362
10.5.1 SVM for cancer data analysis 362
10.5.2 Prediction performances w.r.t. size of training datasets 364
10.5.3 KRR versus SVM: application studies 364
10.6 Empirical-space SVM for trimming of support vectors 365
10.6.1 ℓ_1-Norm SVM in empirical space 365
10.6.2 ℓ_2-Norm SVM in empirical space 365
10.6.3 Empirical learning models for vectorial and nonvectorial data analysis 367
10.6.4 Wrapper methods for empirical learning models 369
10.6.5 Fusion of filtering and wrapper methods 373
10.7 Summary 374
10.8 Problems 375

11 Support vector learning models for outlier detection 380
11.1 Introduction 380
11.2 Support vector regression (SVR) 381
11.3 Hyperplane-based one-class SVM learning models 383
11.3.1 Hyperplane-based ν-SV classifiers 383
11.3.2 Hyperplane-based one-class SVM 385
11.4 Hypersphere-based one-class SVM 389
11.5 Support vector clustering 392
11.6 Summary 393
11.7 Problems 393

12 Ridge-SVM learning models 395
12.1 Introduction 395
12.2 Roles of ρ and C on WECs of KRR and SVM 396
12.2.1 Roles of ρ and C 396
12.2.2 WECs of KDA, KRR, and SVM 397
12.3 Ridge-SVM learning models 399
12.3.1 Ridge-SVM: a unifying supervised learning model 401
12.3.2 Important special cases of Ridge-SVM models 401
12.3.3 Subset selection: KKT and the termination condition 402
12.4 Impacts of design parameters on the WEC of Ridge-SVM 404
12.4.1 Transition ramps and the number of support vectors 404
12.4.2 Effects of ρ and C_{min} on the transition ramp 404
12.4.3 The number of support vectors w.r.t. C_{min} 408

12.5 Prediction accuracy versus training time 408
12.5.1 The tuning of the parameter C 409
12.5.2 The tuning of the parameter $C_{\min}$ 409
12.5.3 The tuning of the parameter ρ 411
12.6 Application case studies 412
12.6.1 Experiments on UCI data 412
12.6.2 Experiments on microarray cancer diagnosis 413
12.6.3 Experiments on subcellular ocalization 414
12.6.4 Experiments on the ischemic stroke dataset 415
12.7 Summary 416
12.8 Problems 417

Part VI Kernel methods for green machine learning technologies 419

13 Efficient kernel methods for learning and classification 421
13.1 Introduction 421
13.2 System design considerations 423
13.2.1 Green processing technologies for local or client computing 423
13.2.2 Cloud computing platforms 423
13.2.3 Local versus centralized processing 424
13.3 Selection of cost-effective kernel functions 424
13.3.1 The intrinsic degree J 426
13.3.2 Truncated-RBF (TRBF) kernels 428
13.4 Classification complexities: empirical and intrinsic degrees 430
13.4.1 The discriminant function in the empirical representation 432
13.4.2 The discriminant function in the intrinsic representation 433
13.4.3 Tensor representation of discriminant functions 436
13.4.4 Complexity comparison of RBF and TRBF classifiers 438
13.4.5 Case study: ECG arrhythmia detection 438
13.5 Learning complexities: empirical and intrinsic degrees 439
13.5.1 Learning complexities for KRR and SVM 439
13.5.2 A scatter-matrix-based KRR algorithm 440
13.5.3 KRR learning complexity: RBF versus TRBF kernels 440
13.5.4 A learning and classification algorithms for big data size N 440
13.5.5 Case study: ECG arrhythmia detection 442
13.6 The tradeoff between complexity and prediction performance 444
13.6.1 Comparison of prediction accuracies 444
13.6.2 Prediction–complexity tradeoff analysis 446
13.7 Time-adaptive updating algorithms for KRR learning models 447
13.7.1 Time-adaptive recursive KRR algorithms 448
13.7.2 The intrinsic-space recursive KRR algorithm 449
13.7.3 A time-adaptive KRR algorithm with a forgetting factor 452

13.8 Summary 453
13.9 Problems 453

Part VII Kernel methods and statistical estimation theory 457

14 Statistical regression analysis and errors-in-variables models 459
14.1 Introduction 459
14.2 Statistical regression analysis 460
14.2.1 The minimum mean-square-error (MMSE) estimator/regressor 461
14.2.2 Linear regression analysis 462
14.3 Kernel ridge regression (KRR) 463
14.3.1 Orthonormal basis functions: single-variate cases 463
14.3.2 Orthonormal basis functions: multivariate cases 466
14.4 The perturbation-regulated regressor (PRR) for errors-in-variables models 467
14.4.1 MMSE solution for errors-in-variables models 468
14.4.2 Linear perturbation-regulated regressors 470
14.4.3 Kernel-based perturbation-regulated regressors 471
14.5 The kernel-based perturbation-regulated regressor (PRR): Gaussian cases 472
14.5.1 Orthonormal basis functions: single-variate cases 472
14.5.2 Single-variate Hermite estimators 473
14.5.3 Error–order tradeoff 475
14.5.4 Simulation results 477
14.5.5 Multivariate PRR estimators: Gaussian distribution 480
14.6 Two-projection theorems 482
14.6.1 The two-projection theorem: general case 483
14.6.2 The two-projection theorem: polynomial case 485
14.6.3 Two-projection for the PRR 486
14.6.4 Error analysis 486
14.7 Summary 487
14.8 Problems 488

15 Kernel methods for estimation, prediction, and system identification 494
15.1 Introduction 494
15.2 Kernel regressors for deterministic generation models 495
15.3 Kernel regressors for statistical generation models 500
15.3.1 The prior model and training data set 500
15.3.2 The Gauss–Markov theorem for statistical models 501
15.3.3 KRR regressors in empirical space 507
15.3.4 KRR regressors with Gaussian distribution 509
15.4 Kernel regressors for errors-in-variables (EiV) models 510
15.4.1 The Gauss–Markov theorem for EiV learning models 511
15.4.2 EiV regressors in empirical space 515
15.4.3 EiV regressors with Gaussian distribution 517
15.4.4 Finite-order EiV regressors 518

15.5 Recursive KRR learning algorithms 521
15.5.1 The recursive KRR algorithm in intrinsic space 522
15.5.2 The recursive KRR algorithm in empirical space 524
15.5.3 The recursive KRR algorithm in intrinsic space with a forgetting factor 525
15.5.4 The recursive KRR algorithm in empirical space with a forgetting factor and a finite window 527
15.6 Recursive EiV learning algorithms 529
15.6.1 Recursive EiV learning models in intrinsic space 529
15.6.2 The recursive EiV algorithm in empirical space 530
15.7 Summary 531
15.8 Problems 531

Part VIII Appendices 537

Appendix A Validation and testing of learning models 539
A.1 Cross-validation techniques 539
A.2 Hypothesis testing and significance testing 541
A.2.1 Hypothesis testing based on the likelihood ratio 542
A.2.2 Significance testing from the distribution of the null hypothesis 545
A.3 Problems 547

Appendix B *k*NN, PNN, and Bayes classifiers 549
B.1 Bayes classifiers 550
B.1.1 The GMM-based-classifier 551
B.1.2 The basic Bayes classifier 552
B.2 Classifiers with no prior learning process 554
B.2.1 *k* nearest neighbors (*k*NN) 554
B.2.2 Probabilistic neural networks (PNN) 555
B.2.3 The log-likelihood classifier (LLC) 557
B.3 Problems 559

References 561
Index 578

Preface

Machine learning is a research field involving the study of theories and technologies to adapt a system model using a training dataset, so that the learned model will be able to generalize and provide a correct classification or useful guidance even when the inputs to the system are previously unknown. Machine learning builds its foundation on linear algebra, statistical learning theory, pattern recognition, and artificial intelligence. The development of practical machine learning tools requires multi-disciplinary knowledge including matrix theory, signal processing, regression analysis, discrete mathematics, and optimization theory. It covers a broad spectrum of application domains in multimedia processing, network optimization, biomedical analysis, etc.

Since the publication of Vapnik's book entitled *The Nature of Statistical Learning Theory* (Springer-Verlag, 1995) and the introduction of the celebrated support vector machine (SVM), research on kernel-based machine learning has flourished steadily for nearly two decades. The enormous amount of research findings on unsupervised and supervised learning models, both theory and applications, should already warrant a new textbook, even without considering the fact that this fundamental field will undoubtedly continue to grow for a good while.

The book first establishes algebraic and statistical foundations for kernel-based learning methods. It then systematically develops kernel-based learning models both for unsupervised and for supervised scenarios.

- The secret of success of a machine learning system lies in finding an effective representation for the objects of interest. In a basic representation, an object is represented as a feature vector in a finite-dimensional vector space. However, in numerous machine learning applications, two different types of modified representations are often employed: one involving dimension reduction and another involving dimension expansion.

  Dimension reduction. Dimension reduction is vital for visualization because of humans' inability to see objects geometrically in high-dimensional space. Likewise, dimension reduction may become imperative because of a machine's inability to process computationally demanding data represented by an extremely huge dimensionality. Subspace projection is a main approach to dimension reduction. This book will study principal component analysis (PCA) and discriminant component analysis (DCA), two such projection methods for unsupervised and supervised learning scenarios, respectively.

Dimension expansion. In other application scenarios, the dimensionality of the original feature space may be too small, which in turn limits the design freedom of any linear methods, rendering them ineffective for classifying datasets with complex data distributions. In this case, dimension expansion offers a simple and effective solution. One of the most systematic approaches to dimension expansion is the kernel methods, which are based on polynomial or Gaussian kernels. The higher the order of the kernel functions the more expanded the new feature space.

As shown later, the kernel methods, when applied to PCA or DCA, will lead to kernel PCA and kernel DCA, respectively. Likewise, the same methods may be used to derive various kernelized learning models both for unsupervised and for supervised scenarios.

- **Unsupervised learning models.** The book presents conventional unsupervised learning models for clustering analysis. They include K-means, expectation-maximization (EM), self-organizing-map (SOM), and neighbor-joining (NJ) methods. All these unsupervised learning models can be formulated as ℓ_2-based optimizers, thus they satisfy a critical learning subspace property (LSP). This in turn assures the existence of their kernelized counterparts, i.e. kernelized learning models. The latter models are formulated in terms of pairwise similarities between two objects, as opposed to the representative feature vectors for individual objects. Hence kernelized learning models are naturally applicable to non-vectorial data analysis, such as network segmentation.
- **Supervised learning models.** The book also presents conventional supervised learning models for classfication. They include least-squares error (LSE), Fisher discriminant analysis (FDA), ridge regression (RR) and linear SVM. All these supervised learning models can be formulated as ℓ_2-based optimizers, thus they satisfy the LSP condition, which in turn leads to their respective kernelized formulations, such as kernel RR (KRR) and kernel SVM. The combination of KRR and SVM further yields a hybrid classifier, named Ridge-SVM. The Ridge-SVM is endowed with a sufficient set of design parameters to embrace existing classifiers as its special cases, including KDA, KRR, and SVM. With properly adjusted parameters, again, all these kernelized supervised learning models are naturally applicable to nonvectorial data analysis, such as subcellular protein-sequence prediction.

In the book, the presentation of these topics and their extensions will be subdivided into the following parts:

(i) Part I: Machine learning and kernel vector spaces
(ii) Part II: Dimension-reduction: PCA/KPCA and feature selection
(iii) Part III: Unsupervised learning models for cluster analysis
(iv) Part VI: Kernel ridge regressors and variants
(v) Part V: Support vector machines and variants
(vi) Part VI: Kernel methods for green machine learning technologies
(vii) Part VII: Kernel methods for statistical estimation theory
(viii) Part VIII: Appendices.

The table of contents provides a more detailed description of the scope of the book.

From the perspective of new feature representation

The study of kernel-based machine learning involves a natural extension of the linear methods into their nonlinear counterparts. This book starts by devoting much of the discussion to establishing formally the linear learning models so as to make sure that students are given an opportunity to acquire a solid grasp of the underlying linear algebra and statistical principles of the learning models. The mathematical principle of kernel methods, instead of linear methods, hinges upon replacing the conventional pairwise similarity metric by a nonlinear kernel function. This ultimately leads to the nonlinear (and more flexible) decision boundaries for pattern classification. In summary, this basic mapping approach is conceptually simple. It involves (1) mapping the original representative vectors to the (dimension-expanded) intrinsic space, resulting in a training-data-independent feature representation; and (2) applying the same linear methods to the new and higher-dimensional feature vectors to yield a kernel-based learning model, which is defined over the intrinsic space.

From the perspective of the kernel trick

If the LSP holds, the above two-step mapping procedure can ultimately lead to a kernelized learning model, defined over the "empirical space" with a training-data-dependent feature representation. In the literature, the tedious two-step re-mapping process has often been replaced by a shortcut, nicknamed the "kernel trick." Most authors present the kernel trick as an elegant and simple notion. However, as evidenced by the following two aspects, a deeper understanding will prove essential to fully appreciating the limitation/power of the kernel trick.

- **The pre-requisite of applying the kernel trick.** First of all, note that not all linear learning models are amenable to the kernel trick. Let us briefly explain the precondition for applying the kernel trick. Conceptually, machine learning methods are built upon the principle of learning from examples. Algebraically, the range of the training vectors forms a learning subspace prescribing the subspace on which the solution is most likely to fall. This leads to a formal condition named the learning subspace property (LSP). It can be shown that the kernel trick is applicable to a linear learning model if and only if the LSP holds for the model. In other words, the LSP is the pre-requisite for the kernelizability of a linear learning model.
- **The interplay between two kernel-induced representations.** Given the kernelizability, we have at our disposal two learning models, defined over two different kernel-induced vector spaces. Now let us shift our attention to the interplay between two kernel-induced representations. Even though the two models are theoretically equivalent, they could incur very different implementation costs for learning and prediction. For cost-effective system implementation, one should choose the lower-cost representation, irrespective of whether it is intrinsic or empirical. For example, if the dimensionality of the empirical space is small and manageable, an empirical-space learning model will be more appealing. However, this will not be so if the number of

training vectors is extremely large, which is the case for the "big-data" learning scenario. In this case, one must give serious consideration to the intrinsic model, whose cost can be controlled by properly adjusting the order of the kernel function.

Presentation style and coverage of the book

For an introductory textbook, it would be wise to keep the mathematics to a minimum and choose materials that are easily accessible to beginning students and practitioners. After all, one of the overriding reasons for my undertaking of this project is because the original book by Vapnik is mathematically so deep that it is accessible only to the most able researchers.

Moreover, an editor keenly reminded me of the famous cliché that "for every equation in the book the readership would be halved." To be fair, my original intention was indeed to write a mathematically much simpler textbook. The book can hardly be considered a success by this measure – having included nearly a thousand equations, thirty or so algorithms, and almost as many theorems.

From another viewpoint, however, such heavy use of equations does serve some very useful purposes.

- This book includes nearly sixty numerical examples, many with step-by-step descriptions of an algorithmic procedure. Concrete examples with numerical equations may go a long way towards clarifying the mathematical algorithm or theorem. They provide a tangible, and much less abstract, illustration of the actual procedure.
- This book contains equations specifying the bounds of computational complexities or estimates of prediction performance associated with a learning model, each of which could serve as a preliminary and quantitative guideline on the effectiveness of the learning model for specific applications.
- The book aims at demonstrating how machine learning models can be integrated into a recognition application system. Some theorems and equations in the book are devoted to establishing connections between equivalent learning models, paving a way to avoid redundant experiments on equivalent (and thus predictable) models. In short, the mathematical equivalence both improves the understanding of the models and prevents repetitive coding efforts.
- Compared with natural language or computer language (e.g. pseudocodes), the mathematics and equations provide a more concise descriptive language. With somewhat casual mathematical language, the semi-formal presentation style of this book should help beginning readers to more easily appreciate the power of the linear algebra and statistical theory behind the machine learning tools.

Comprehensiveness versus cohesiveness

Since machine learning covers a vast range of subjects, the selection of materials for this book inevitably involves a tradeoff between comprehensiveness and cohesiveness. Admittedly, the coverage of the book is far from being comprehensive. The constraint on space was certainly an important factor. On the other hand, there is already a large volume of publications on SVM and its variants. In order to save space, it was necessary to leave out many SVM-related subjects, knowing that several excellent presentations of SVM are already available in textbook form.

What sets the book apart from others is unlikely to be its scope of coverage; rather, it may very well be the cohesive presentation and novel results.

- **Cohesive presentation.** The book aims at offering a cohesive, organized, and yet balanced presentation with natural flow between sections. This streamlined approach facilitates the presentation of key ideas in a single flow, without digression into the analytical details. Moreover, the streamlined approach also reflects a personal (and subjective) viewpoint on how to relate the loosely connected subjects.
- **Novel results.** Some significant novel results have been introduced here for the first time in textbook form. For example, under the supervised scenario, DCA for optimal subspace projection will outperform PCA, which is meant for use in unsupervised scenarios. A hybrid learning model of KRR and SVM, named Ridge-SVM, covers many existing classifiers as special cases, including KDA, KRR, and SVM. With properly adjusted parameters, it has been shown to deliver improved generalization and prediction capability. The book also establishes the theoretical foundation linking kernel methods and the rich theory in estimation, prediction, and system identification. Curiously, the presentation of these novel ideas seemed to fall naturally into appropriate places in their respective chapters.

Finally, due to its emphasis being placed on a cohesive and streamlined presentation of key ideas, the book necessarily had to forgo some otherwise important research results. I would like to take this opportunity to express my most sincere apologies and profound regret to researchers whose contributions have inadvertently been omitted here.

Readership of the book

The book was designed for senior and graduate students with a diversity of educational experiences in computer science, electrical engineering, financial engineering, applied statistics, etc. The main focus of the book aims at taking a beginning student, with some prior exposure to linear algebra, statistical theory, and convex optimization, through an integrated understanding of the underlying principles and potential applications of kernel-based learning models. In addition, the book should provide enough material for it to be used either as a textbook for classroom instruction or as a reference book for self-study.

- **As a textbook for machine learning course.** The book may be adopted for one-semester senior or graduate courses in machine learning in, say, electrical engineering and computer science departments. For example, by carefully picking some fundamental materials from Chapters 1 through 13, it should be possible to find enough material to be organized into a one-semester course that covers feature representations, and unsupervised and supervised learning models, with balanced yet rigorous treatments in statistics and linear algebra.

Just like in other textbooks, exercises are included at the end of each chapter. They should be useful for self-study and for probing into some of the more intricate aspects of the subjects treated in the text.

- **As a recommended or supplementary reference for courses on artificial intelligence.** The scope of the materials covered here is sufficiently broad to allow it to be re-structured for many other educational purposes. For example, the book may be adopted as a recommended reference for artificial intelligence and machine learning. It may also be adopted as a textbook/reference for a two-semester course. In this case, the first semester can be devoted to fundamental concepts, with the second semester covering advanced research areas such as big-data learning and kernel-based statistical estimation. For the latter area, Chapters 14 and 15 present statistical estimation techniques with errors-in-variables methods, Gauss–Markov theorems, and kernel methods for time-series analysis.
- **As a reference book for research and development.** The book is also intended for professional engineers, scientists, and system integrators who want to learn systematic ways of implementing machine learning systems. Throughout the book, application examples are provided to motivate the learning model developed. The book provides practitioners with basic mathematical knowledge so that they know how to apply off-the-shelf machine learning codes to solve new problems. In addition, efforts have been made to make the book relatively self-contained. For example, some basic matrix algebra and statistical theory are included in the book, making the book more accessible to newcomers from other fields and to those who have become rusty with some aspects of their undergraduate curriculum.

Acknowledgements

I found this writing project to be expectedly difficult at the beginning, but surprisingly enjoyable towards the end. It was truly rewarding seeing so many old and new results fall so nicely into place together. I also came to the realization that I had been so very fortunate to be surrounded by many fine people, professors, colleagues, students, and friends. The emotional parting with a seven-year-long project is somewhat offset by the pleasure of being able to finally acknowledge this unique group of people who made it possible.

I am pleased to acknowledge the generous support of a gift grant from Mitsubishi (MERL), a research grant from Motorola, multiple research grants from the Hong Kong Research Grants Council, and the DARPA Research Program on active authentication. The project was also indirectly supported by various fellowships, received by some of my collaborators, from Princeton University, the Canadian Government, and Microsoft Inc.

I was fortunate to benefit from the outstanding professional support of many fine people at Cambridge University Press (CUP), including Phil Meyler, Sarah Marsh, Elizabeth Horne, Kirsten Bot, Jessica Murphy, Dr. Steven Holt, and numerous others. I wish to thank the anonymous CUP reviewer who kindly suggested the current title of the book.

During the period of the book project, I was a Distinguished Visiting Professor at the EEE Department of the University of Hong Kong for several summers. I am grateful for the kind hospitality, warm friendship, and stimulating exchange with C. Q. Chang, Fei Mai, Y. S. Hung, and many others.

This book was an outgrowth of many years of teaching and research on neural networks, biometric authentication, and machine learning. I am grateful to the Department of Electrical Engineering of Princeton University and my fellow colleagues for having created such a scholarly environment for teaching and research. In particular, I would like to acknowledge Sarah McGovern, Stacey Weber, and Lori Baily for their cheerful spirit and generous assistance.

I am much indebted to my Ph.D. students, former and current, for their participation in building my understanding of machine learning. They include Xinying Zhang, Yunnan Wu, C. L. Myers, Ilias Tagkopoulos, Yuhui Luo, Peiyuan Wu, and Yinan Yu (Princeton University), as well as Jian Guo, Shibiao Wan, and F. Tobar (outside Princeton University). Their research studies have provided an important foundation for this book. Moreover, they have helped develop this book in various ways.

I would like to acknowledge the invaluable contributions of all of the students in my class during the past six years, undergraduate and graduate, for their invaluable contribution to examples and exercises. In particular, I would like to mention Tiffany Tong, Chun-Yi Lee, Chia-Chun Lin, Dan Li, K. H. Lee, Si Chen, Yang Yang, Clement Canonne, Pei-yuan Wu, Zhang Zhuo, Xu Chen, Pingmei Xu, Shang Shang, Rasmus Rothe, Vincent Pham, and Jintao Zhang.

I express my sincere gratitude to my visiting professors for stimulating discussions and for their proofreading of numerous versions of the previous drafts when they visited Princeton University. They are Young-Shik Moon, Shang-Hung Lai, Shaikh Fattah, Jie Lin, Wei-Kuang Lai, Xiao-Dong Gu, Yu Liu, and K. Diamantaras. I also benefited greatly from the enlightening exchanges with many external collaborators, in particular, Professors J. Morris Chang, Y. K. Chen, Y. B. Kan, T. S. Lin, Mahesan Niranjan, D. Mandic, T. McKelvery, Jin-Shiuh Taur, Yue Wang, and Juan Zhou.

There is little doubt that I must have missed some important names of people whom I would like to thank, and to whom I wish to offer my most sincere apologies and profound regret in that regard.

It is always fun and brings back fond memories recalling my Stanford years, so I must express my special appreciation of Professor Thomas Kailath, my advisor and life-time mentor, for his constant inspiration and friendship. I am proud to be closely associated with a group of outstanding scholars including Professors Patrick DeWilde, Lenart Ljung, Bernard Levy, George Verghese, and Erik Verriest, among many others. Moreover, my first exposure to machine learning was a course taught by none other than Professor R. O. Duda, which was based on his now classical book *Pattern Classification and Scene Analysis* (John Wiley, 1973).

Their mention so far does not fully acknowledge the measure of the contributions by Professor Man-Wai Mak, Mr. Peiyuan Wu, and Miss Yinan Yu. For their invaluable and indispensable roles, they could conceivably have been named as co-authors of the book.

Finally, a book project of such scale would not have been possible without strong support from my parents, my wife, and all our children. In recent years, the center of attention of my (much extended) family seems to have been focused upon our four grandchildren. It is only fitting that the book is dedicated to them.

S. Y. KUNG
Princeton

Part I

Machine learning and kernel vector spaces

Chapter 1 provides an overview of the broad spectrum of applications and problem formulations for kernel-based unsupervised and supervised learning methods. The dimension of the original vector space, along with its Euclidean inner product, often proves to be highly inadequate for complex data analysis. In order to provide more effective similarity metrics of any pairs of objects, in the kernel approach one replaces the traditional Euclidean inner product by more sophisticated and kernel-induced inner products associated with the corresponding kernel-induced vector spaces. Among the most useful such spaces are the (primal) intrinsic and (dual) empirical spaces.

The interplay between the formulations of learning models in the primal/dual spaces plays a key role both in the theoretical analysis and in the practical implementation of kernel methods. Chapter 1 shows that a vital condition for kernelization of a learning model is the LSP condition, which is often verifiable via Theorem 1.1. In fact, the optimization formulation prescribed in Theorem 1.1 covers most, if not all, of the ℓ_2-based learning models treated in this book – both unsupervised and supervised.

Chapter 2 starts with the vital Theorem 2.1, which states that Mercer's condition of the kernel function used will be imperative for the existence of the kernel-induced vector spaces. For vectorial data analysis, in the first stage, the original vector space can be mapped to the kernel-induced intrinsic vector space. Here, every individual object is represented by a (possibly high-dimensional) feature vector in intrinsic space. The intrinsic-space approach is conceptually simpler because, once the mapping has been done, the rest of the mathematical and/or algorithmic developments can just follow exactly what was used in the conventional learning models. There are, however, fundamental limitations on the use of the intrinsic feature representation. More specifically, they fail to be applicable to the following two circumstances.

- If a Gaussian kernel is used for vectorial data analysis, the intrinsic-based learning models are not computationally implementable since the dimension of the corresponding intrinsic space is infinite.
- Since the intrinsic vector space is undefinable for nonvectorial objects, the intrinsic-space approach is obviously unapplicable to nonvectorial data analysis.

Fortunately, both problems can be avoided if the learning formulation may be kernelized, an approach better known as the kernel-trick. Kernelization refers to the process of converting an optimizer in the intrinsic space into one formulated in the empirical space. With kernelized learning models, all we need is to have the pairwise relationship clearly defined, making it amenable to both vectorial and nonvectorial data analyses. This is why it is actually much more popular than its counterpart in the intrinsic space.

1 Fundamentals of kernel-based machine learning

1.1 Introduction

The rapid advances in information technologies, in combination with today's internet technologies (wired and mobile), not only have profound impacts on our daily lifestyles but also have substantially altered the long-term prospects of humanity. In this era of *big data*, diversified types of raw datasets with huge data-size are constantly collected from wired and/or mobile devices/sensors. For example, in Facebook alone, more than 250 million new photos are being added on a daily basis. The amount of newly available digital data more than doubles every two years. Unfortunately, such raw data are far from being "information" useful for meaningful analysis unless they are processed and distilled properly. The main purpose of machine learning is to convert the wealth of raw data into useful knowledge.

Machine learning is a discipline concerning the study of adaptive algorithms to infer from training data so as to extract critical and relevant information. It offers an effective data-driven approach to data mining and intelligent classification/prediction. The objective of learning is to induce optimal decision rules for classification/prediction or to extract the salient characteristics of the underlying system which generates the observed data. Its potential application domains cover bioinformatics, DNA expression and sequence analyses, medical diagnosis and health monitoring, brain–machine interfaces, biometric recognition, security and authentication, robot/computer vision, market analysis, search engines, and social network association.

In machine learning, the learned knowledge should be represented in a form that can readily facilitate decision making in the classification or prediction phase. More exactly, the learned decision-making parameters should be stored and efficiently used by the deployed classifier for fast or low-power identification of new patterns or detection of abnormal events.

Neural networks and kernel methods are two important pillars to machine learning systems theory. Neural networks have for a long time been a dominant force in machine learning [20, 95, 141, 220, 226]. In the past two decades, however, kernel-based techniques for supervised and unsupervised learning have received growing attention and have been extensively covered in many machine learning and pattern recognition textbooks [22, 239, 244, 267, 280, 281].

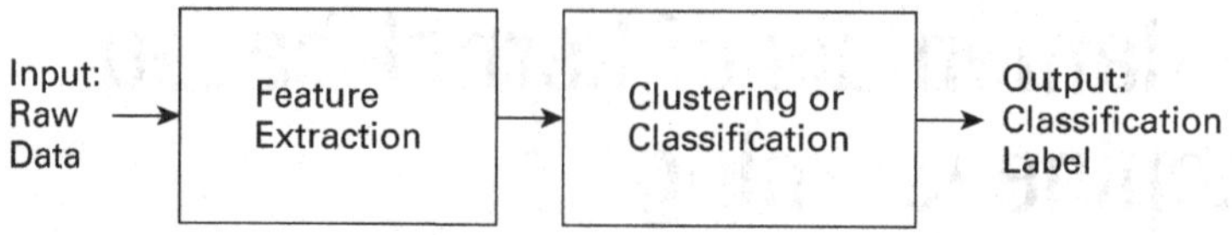

Fig. 1.1. A typical machine learning system consists of two subsystems: feature extraction and clustering/classifier.

Machine learning systems

As depicted in Figure 1.1, two subsystems for machine learning must be jointly considered: (1) feature extraction and (2) clustering/classification. The former involves how to effectively represent the data while the latter concerns how to classify them correctly.

- **Feature extraction subsystem.** Feature extraction is critical to the success of data analysis. It is vital to find an appropriate interpretation of the given raw data so as to extract useful features for the subsequent data analysis. After the feature extraction stage, each of the raw data is assumed to be represented as a point (or a vector) in a properly defined Hilbert vector space.
- **Clustering/classification subsystem.** The objective of learning is to distill the information from the training dataset so that the learned rule can be used to facilitate expedient and accurate detection/classification in the deployed application systems. From the perspective of learning, machine learning tools fall largely into two major categories: unsupervised clustering and supervised classification. The class labels of the training data are unknown/known in advance in the unsupervised/supervised learning scenarios. The former can facilitate clustering of data and the latter leads to the prediction of new and unknown objects (e.g. tumor versus normal cells).

Machine learning builds its foundation on inter-disciplinary fields including statistical learning theory, linear algebra, pattern recognition, neural networks, and artificial intelligence [53, 54, 119, 181, 259, 281]. The development of practical machine learning tools requires multi-disciplinary knowledge from regression analysis, discrete mathematics, matrix algebra, signal processing, and optimization theory.

For practical implementation of machine learning application systems, a major emphasis of the system design methodology should be placed on the software/hardware implementation and co-design of the total system. In particular, it is imperative to consider the combined cost (including e.g. processing time and processing power) and the integrated performance of the two above-mentioned subsystems.

1.2 Feature representation and dimension reduction

Figures 1.2(a) and (b) depict two different types of dataset, each being popular in its own right.

- *Static data.* For many applications, the input raw data are given in the format of a data matrix. For example, the dataset collected for N different samples, each being

(a)

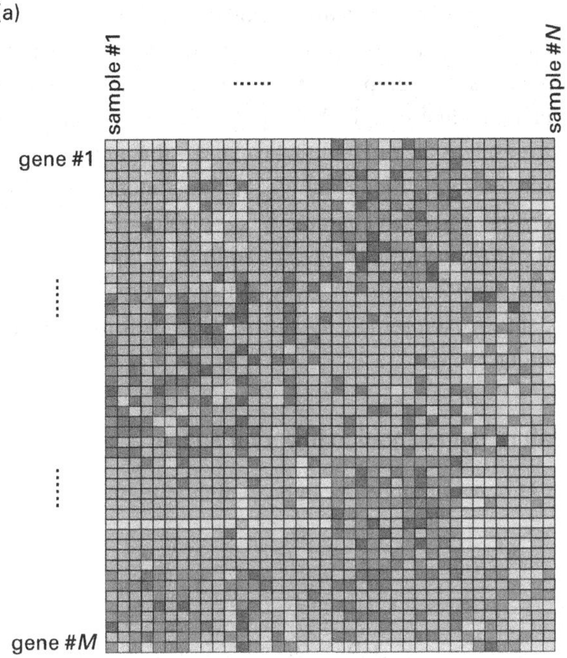

(b)

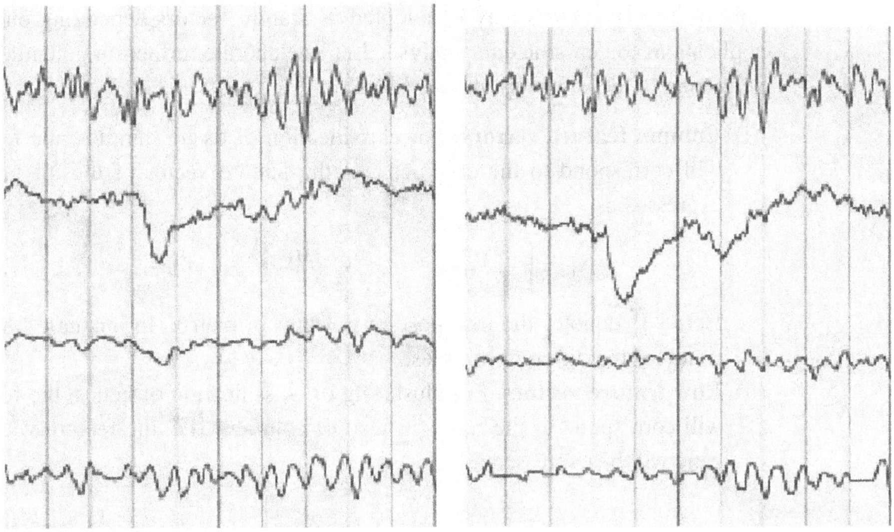

Fig. 1.2. (a) An example of a static microarray data matrix. Sample/gene clustering of microarray data, the raw data can be represented in a matrix form. (b) Example of temporal signals. Temporal signals represent a very different type of dataset. Shown here are eight different kinds of EEG waveforms. (Adapted from Opensource EEG libraries and toolkits [156].)

represented by an M-dimensional *feature vector*, can be organized into an $M \times N$ *data matrix*. An element of the data matrix represents a feature value. For microarray data analysis, as exemplified by Figure 1.2(a), it represents the expression level of a gene in an individual sample. More precisely, N is the number of microarray experiments (one for each tissue or condition) and M is the number of genes per microarray. Consider a second application example, e.g. documentation analysis, where there are N different documents, each characterized by a set of M keywords. In this case, a feature value (or attribute) would correspond to the frequency of a keyword in a document.

- *Temporal signals.* A very different type of dataset is represented by temporal data as exemplified by the ECG waveforms for arrythmia detection displayed in Figure 1.2(b).

1.2.1 Feature representation in vector space

An $M \times N$ *data matrix* can be explicitly expressed as follows:

$$\mathbf{X} = \begin{bmatrix} x_1^{(1)} & x_2^{(1)} & \ldots & x_N^{(1)} \\ x_1^{(2)} & x_2^{(2)} & \ldots & x_N^{(2)} \\ \ldots & \ldots & \ldots & \ldots \\ x_1^{(M)} & x_2^{(M)} & \ldots & x_N^{(M)} \end{bmatrix} = [\mathbf{x}_1\ \mathbf{x}_2\ \ldots\ \mathbf{x}_N] = \begin{bmatrix} \mathbf{y}^{(1)} \\ \mathbf{y}^{(2)} \\ \vdots \\ \mathbf{y}^{(M)} \end{bmatrix}. \tag{1.1}$$

As exemplified by the microarray data matrix shown in Figure 1.3(a), either its column or its row vectors may be adopted as feature vectors depending on the intended applications to genomic data analysis. Let us elaborate further on potential applications pertaining to these two options.

(i) **Column feature vectors.** For classification of tissue samples, the feature vectors will correspond to the columns, i.e. the feature vector of the ith sample will be expressed as

$$\mathbf{x}_i = \left[\ x_i^{(1)}\ \ x_i^{(2)}\ \ \ldots\ \ x_i^{(M)}\ \right]^{\mathrm{T}} \quad \text{for} \quad i = 1, \ldots, N. \tag{1.2}$$

Here $[\cdot]^{\mathrm{T}}$ denotes the transpose of a vector or matrix. In this case, the N columns stand for the different samples.

(ii) **Row feature vectors.** For clustering or classification of genes, the feature vectors will correspond to the rows (instead of columns), i.e. the feature vector of the jth gene will be expressed as

$$\mathbf{y}^{(j)} = \left[\ x_1^{(j)}\ \ x_2^{(j)}\ \ \ldots\ \ x_N^{(j)}\ \right] \quad \text{for} \quad j = 1, \ldots, M. \tag{1.3}$$

We shall adopt the convention that a feature vector will often be represented by an M-dimensional vector formed by M real values. Consequently, a data vector corresponds to a data point in the vector space of the real field: $\mathbb{R}^M$.

Vector space

Linear algebra provides the basic theory for manipulating the patterns in vector spaces. The basic vector algebra covers the ideas of linear independence, subspaces and their

(a)

	Normal Sample	Cancer Sample
Gene A	2.0	0.3
Gene B	2.0	0.1
Gene C	2.5	3.0

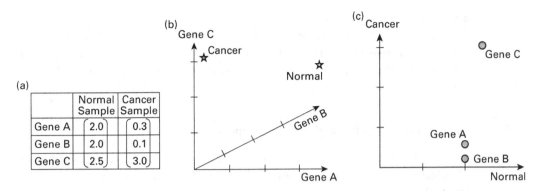

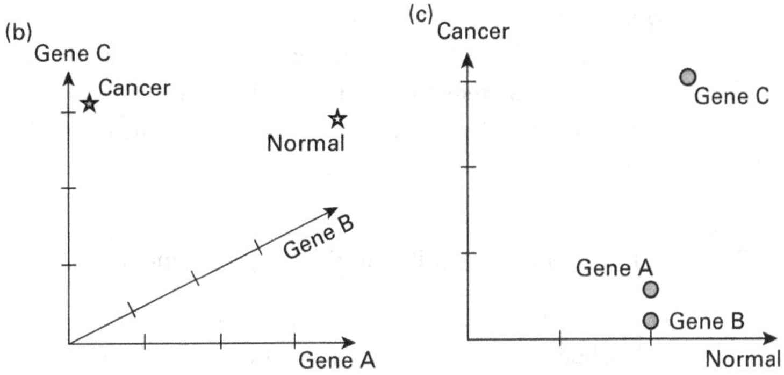

Fig. 1.3. A dataset may be represented either by a table or by its corresponding vector spaces. (a) A data matrix describing a gene–sample relationship is shown as a table here. The first column shows three gene features pertaining to a normal tissue sample, while the second column shows gene features for a cancer sample. (b) There are two possible vector space representations. Shown here is a three-dimensional vector space, in which each gene represents one of the three axes of the vector space. In this case, the training data are represented by two vectors: one for the normal sample and one for the cancer sample. (c) Alternatively, the training data may also be represented by three vectors in a two-dimensional vector space, for which each condition represents one of the two axes. In this case, the three genes are represented as the three vectors shown. Note that genes A and B exhibit high similarity manifested by their close distance in the Cartesian coordinates. Consequently, they are more likely to be grouped into the same cluster.

spans, norm and inner product, and linear transformations. The fundamental concept of the vector space (or linear space) plays a key role in most mathematical treatments in machine learning.

Basis

A set of linear independent vectors that spans the entire vector space is called a **basis**. In other words, every vector in the space can be represented as a linear combination of the basis vectors. Moreover, this representation is unique due to the linear independence of the basis vectors.

Span

In machine learning study, *linear combination* of a set of given feature vectors, say $S = \{\mathbf{x}_1, \mathbf{x}_2, \ldots, \mathbf{x}_k\}$, is commonly used. Such a vector can be expressed as

$$a_1\mathbf{x}_1 + a_2\mathbf{x}_2 + \cdots + a_k\mathbf{x}_k,$$

where the scalars ($a_1, a_2, \ldots, a_k \in \mathbb{R}$) are called the **coefficients** of the combination. The **span** of $S = \{\mathbf{x}_1, \mathbf{x}_2, \ldots, \mathbf{x}_k\}$ is the set of all linear combinations of those vectors and it is denoted by

$$\mathtt{span}(S) = \{a_1\mathbf{x}_1 + a_2\mathbf{x}_2 + \cdots + a_k\mathbf{x}_k,\ a_1, a_2, \ldots, a_k \in \mathbb{R}\}.$$

For any set S, the set $U \equiv \mathtt{span}(S)$ is a linear space. We sometimes also write $\mathtt{span}(\mathbf{x}_1, \ldots, \mathbf{x}_k)$ to denote $\mathtt{span}(S)$, and we say that the vectors $\mathbf{x}_1, \ldots, \mathbf{x}_k$ span U.

Subspace

If a space V has a finite number of basis vectors, the number of the basis vectors is called the **dimension** of V, denoted by dim(V). A subset U of a vector space V, which is in itself a vector space over the same scalar field as V, is called a **subspace** of V. For example, the set $U = \{[x,\ 0]^{\mathrm{T}},\ x \in \mathbb{R}\}$ is a one-dimensional subspace of $\mathbb{R}^2$.

1.2.2 Conventional similarity metric: Euclidean inner product

Traditional metrics, such as distance and correlation measures, are usually defined on a Euclidean vector space of the real field: $\mathbb{R}^M$, where M is the dimension of the vector space. The Euclidean vector space is synonymous with finite-dimensional, real, positive definite, inner product space.

Vector norm

For a real M-dimensional vector $\mathbf{x}$, the most commonly used is the Euclidean norm (or ℓ_2-norm):

$$\|\mathbf{x}\| \equiv \|\mathbf{x}\|_2 = \left(\sum_{i=1}^{M} x_i^2\right)^{1/2}.$$

Euclidean inner product

A popular similarity metric for a pair of vectors, say $\mathbf{x}$ and $\mathbf{y}$, in a vector space over the real field R is the Euclidean *inner product* (or dot product):

$$\langle \mathbf{x}, \mathbf{y}\rangle \equiv \mathbf{x}\cdot\mathbf{y} \equiv \mathbf{x}^{\mathrm{T}}\mathbf{y} = x^{(1)}y^{(1)} + x^{(2)}y^{(2)} + \cdots + x^{(M)}y^{(M)}.$$

From the subspace span's perspective, the more parallel the two vectors the smaller the angle. On the other hand, two vectors $\mathbf{x}$ and $\mathbf{y}$ are called **orthogonal** if $\langle \mathbf{x}, \mathbf{y}\rangle = 0$, in which case we write $\mathbf{x} \perp \mathbf{y}$, or $\theta = \pi/2$, i.e. they are geometrically perpendicular. Given two vectors, the smaller the magnitude of their inner product the less similar they are.

Euclidean distance

The Euclidean distance between two vectors is

$$\|\mathbf{x} - \mathbf{y}\| = \sqrt{\sum_i (x_i - y_i)^2}.$$

The higher the Euclidean distance, the more divergent (i.e. dissimilar) the two vectors are. Note also that the distance and inner product are related as follows:

$$\|\mathbf{x} - \mathbf{y}\| = \sqrt{\mathbf{x}\cdot\mathbf{x} + \mathbf{y}\cdot\mathbf{y} - 2\mathbf{x}\cdot\mathbf{y}}.$$

1.2.3 Feature dimension reduction

For many applications encountered by machine learning, the extreme dimensionality of the feature space may cause a problem for the development of learning models. For example, a microarray may simultaneously record the gene expressions for an extremely large number (thousands or more) of different genes. For classification of tissue samples, cf. Eq. (1.1), the associated feature vectors will have an extremely huge dimensionality. In this case, it is advantageous to reduce the feature dimension to reduce the computational burden to a manageable level. There are two common approaches to feature-dimension reduction.

- **Feature selection.** A basic dimension-reduction technique is via feature selection, where a subset of useful features is retained from the original features. Both supervised and unsupervised learning techniques for feature selection have been developed. The techniques fall into two major categories: (1) filter methods and (2) wrapper methods. In filter methods, features are selected according to individual scores of the features. In wrapper methods, features are selected according to the classification results of a specific classifier.
- **Subspace projection.** New features are constructed as linear combinations of the original features. A popular subspace approach to dimension reduction is known as *principal component analysis* (PCA). The principal subspace is theoretically the optimal solution under many information-preserving criteria. The PCA may be effectively computed via singular value decomposition (SVD) on the data matrix.

1.3 The learning subspace property (LSP) and "kernelization" of learning models

Both unsupervised and supervised learning strategies are based on the fundamental principle of *learning from examples*.

(i) The class labels of the training data are known in advance in the supervised learning scenario. This is depicted in Figure 1.4(a). The supervised learning strategy is usually much more effective if the learning software can make full use of a teacher's guidance.
(ii) The unsupervised learning scenario is illustrated in Figure 1.4(b), where a set of training samples is made available, but the class labels of the training samples are unknown. This scenario arises in many cluster discovery application problems.

1.3.1 The LSP

This section formally establishes the *learning subspace property* (LSP), which is applicable to most unsupervised and supervised learning models. The property serves to connect two kernel-based learning models, one in the intrinsic space and another in empirical spaces. The interplay between the two types of learning models dominates the machine learning analysis.

In the original space, the decision vector is characterized by $\mathbf{w}$ and the discrminant function by $f(\mathbf{x}) = \mathbf{w}^{\mathrm{T}}\mathbf{x}_i + b$, where b is a proper threshold. For over-determined

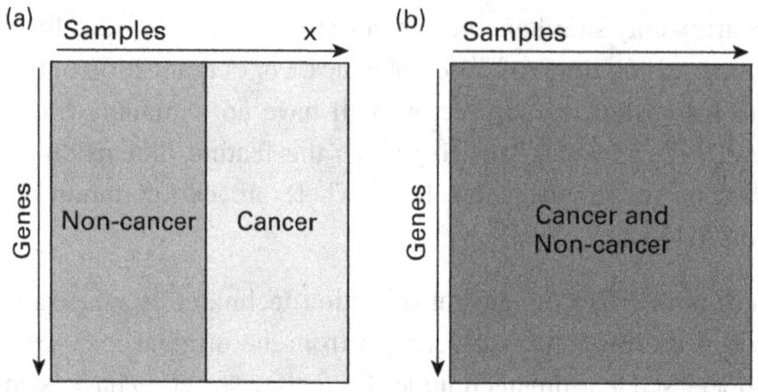

Fig. 1.4. There are two types of training data in machine learning: (a) supervised learning data, where the class labels of the training vectors are known in advance; and (b) unsupervised learning data, where no class labels are provided.

systems, i.e. $N > M$, $\texttt{span}[\mathbf{X}]$ will generically cover the full-dimensional space $\mathbb{R}^M$, making the LSP trivial and obvious. For under-determined systems, i.e. $M \geq N$, N training vectors can at best span an N-dimensional subspace, denoted by $\texttt{span}[\mathbf{X}]$.

For most ℓ_2-norm-based unsupervised and supervised learning models, the optimal solution vector will satisfy a so-called LSP:

$$\mathbf{w} \in \texttt{span}[\mathbf{X}].$$

In matrix notation,

$$\mathbf{w} = \mathbf{Xa}, \tag{1.4}$$

for an N-dimensional vector $\mathbf{a}$.

As far as the original space is concerned, the LSP is meaningful only for under-determined systems, i.e. $M \geq N$. Let us provide a brief explanation of why the LSP is very critical to kernel-based learning models. It can be shown that, for Gaussian kernels (see Eq. (1.46)), the corresponding dimension of the intrinsic space is infinite, see Eq. (1.50), i.e. $J \to \infty$. This automatically renders almost all kernel-based learning models under-determined systems, since it is obvious that $J \gg N$. Note that a kernel-based learning model can (theoretically) be formulated in its intrinsic vector space, with finite or indefinite dimension. From a practical standpoint, however, it becomes problematic computationally if the space has an infinite dimensionality. In this case, it is necessary to resort to a kernelized formulation, aiming at solving for a decision vector represented in the empirical space whose dimension is guaranteed to be finite (N).

A basic optimizer formulation for learning models

Given a set of N training vectors $\{\mathbf{x}_j \in \mathbb{R}^M, j = 1, \ldots, N\}$, many supervised and unsupervised learning models adopt an ℓ_2-norm-based optimization formulation with the *objective function* expressed in the following form:

$$\mathcal{E}\left(\left\{\mathbf{w}_k^{\mathrm{T}}\mathbf{x}_j,\ k = 1, \ldots, K,\ j = 1, \ldots, N\right\}, \left\{\left\|\sum_{k=1}^{K} \beta_k^{(\ell)} \mathbf{w}_k\right\|, \ell = 1, \ldots, L\right\}\right),$$

in which both the training vectors and the weighting coefficients,

$$\{\mathbf{x}_j,\ j = 1,\ldots,N\} \text{ and } \{\beta_k^{(\ell)},\ k = 1,\ldots,K, \ell = 1,\ldots,L\},$$

are known and given. The problem is that of finding the optimal solution for

$$\{\mathbf{w}_k \in R^M,\ k = 1,\ldots,K\},$$

which represent *node vectors* (in the case of unsupervised learning models) or *decision vectors* (in the case of supervised learning models). Note that there are in total $K \times N + L$ variables in the cost function. For example, if $K = 2$, $N = 3$, and $L = 1$, then the cost function has $2 \times 3 + 1 = 7$ variables:

$$\mathcal{E}\left(\mathbf{w}_1^{\mathrm{T}}\mathbf{x}_1, \mathbf{w}_1^{\mathrm{T}}\mathbf{x}_2, \mathbf{w}_1^{\mathrm{T}}\mathbf{x}_3, \mathbf{w}_2^{\mathrm{T}}\mathbf{x}_1, \mathbf{w}_2^{\mathrm{T}}\mathbf{x}_2, \mathbf{w}_2^{\mathrm{T}}\mathbf{x}_3, ||\beta_1\mathbf{w}_1 + \beta_2\mathbf{w}_2||^2\right).$$

For most learning models, there will be additional (equality and/or inequality) constraints imposed on the optimizer. The LSP will hold for the constrained optimizer if the conditions prescribed in the following theorem can be met.

THEOREM 1.1 (Learning subspace property (LSP)) *Consider an optimizer aiming at finding*

$$\arg\min_{\{\mathbf{w}_k \in \mathbb{R}^M,\ \forall k\}} \mathcal{E}\left(\mathbf{w}_k^{\mathrm{T}}\mathbf{x}_j,\ \forall k,j;\quad \left\|\sum_{k=1}^{K}\beta_k^{(\ell)}\mathbf{w}_k\right\|^2,\ \forall \ell\right) \tag{1.5}$$

subject to the equality constraints

$$c_p\left(\mathbf{w}_k^{\mathrm{T}}\mathbf{x}_j,\ \forall k,j\right) = 0, \quad p = 1,\ldots,P, \tag{1.6}$$

and inequality constraints

$$d_q\left(\mathbf{w}_k^{\mathrm{T}}\mathbf{x}_j, \forall k,j; \left\|\sum_{k=1}^{K}\beta_k^{(\ell)}\mathbf{w}_k\right\|^2,\ \forall \ell\right) \leq 0, \quad q = 1,\ldots,Q. \tag{1.7}$$

Here $\forall k$, $\forall j$, *and* $\forall \ell$ *stand for* $k = 1,\ldots,K$, $j = 1,\ldots,N$, *and* $\ell = 1,\ldots,L$, *respectively.*

Suppose further that $\mathcal{E}(\cdot)$ *and* $\{d_q(\cdot), q = 1,\ldots,Q,\}$ *are all monotonically increasing functions w.r.t.* $||\sum_{k=1}^{K}\beta_k^{(\ell)}\mathbf{w}_k||$ *for* $\ell = 1,\ldots,L$. *Then, under the given constraints,*

$$\min_{\mathbf{w}_k \in \mathbb{R}^M,\ \forall k} \mathcal{E} = \min_{\mathbf{w}_k = \mathbf{X}\mathbf{a}_k, \mathbf{a}_k \in \mathbb{R}^N,\ \forall k} \mathcal{E}. \tag{1.8}$$

This equivalence guarantees an equally good result even if the solution is restricted to the learning subspace property (LSP):

$$\mathbf{w}_k \in \mathtt{span}[\mathbf{X}], \textit{ equivalently, } \mathbf{w}_k = \mathbf{X}\mathbf{a}_k, \textit{ for some } \mathbf{a}_k \in \mathbb{R}^N,\ \forall k. \tag{1.9}$$

□

Proof. Note that any decision vector $\mathbf{w}'_k$, $k = 1,\ldots,K$, may be subdivided into two components, namely $\mathbf{w}'_k = \mathbf{w}_k + \tilde{\mathbf{w}}_k$, in which the first component $\mathbf{w}_k \in \mathtt{span}[\mathbf{X}]$, while the second component $\tilde{\mathbf{w}}_k$, is orthogonal to that subspace.

- Note that, in terms of $\mathbf{w}_k'^{\mathrm{T}}\mathbf{x}_j$, taking $\mathbf{w}_k'$ or $\mathbf{w}_k$ makes no difference, since

$$\mathbf{w}_k'^{\mathrm{T}}\mathbf{x}_j = \mathbf{w}_k^{\mathrm{T}}\mathbf{x}_j.$$

- In terms of the ℓ_2-norm, however, $\mathbf{w}_k$ enjoys a net advantage over $\mathbf{w}_k'$, because

$$\left\|\sum_{k=1}^{K}\beta_k^{(\ell)}\mathbf{w}_k'\right\|^2 = \left\|\sum_{k=1}^{K}\beta_k^{(\ell)}\mathbf{w}_k + \sum_{k=1}^{K}\beta_k^{(\ell)}\tilde{\mathbf{w}}_k\right\|^2$$
$$= \left\|\sum_{k=1}^{K}\beta_k^{(\ell)}\mathbf{w}_k\right\|^2 + \left\|\sum_{k=1}^{K}\beta_k^{(\ell)}\tilde{\mathbf{w}}_k\right\|^2 \geq \left\|\sum_{k=1}^{K}\beta_k^{(\ell)}\mathbf{w}_k\right\|^2.$$

The proof for Eq. (1.8) can be accomplished by showing that the inclusion of any orthogonal component (to the *learning subspace*) into $\mathbf{w}$ may only work against the optimizer. It can be divided into two parts.

- First, any orthogonal component can only increase the value of $\mathcal{E}(\cdot)$.
- Second, any orthogonal component can only make it harder to meet the inequality constraint prescribed by Eq. (1.7).

□

Theorem 1.1 establishes a formal condition for the LSP. Complex though it appears, the cost function in Eq. (1.6) can hardly cover all kernelizable models.[1] On the other hand, even though the current form is somewhat conservative, it does embrace all the kernelizable learning models covered by the book. Some prominent examples are listed here.

- **Unsupervised learning models:** kernel PCA, kernel K-means, kernel SOM (self-organizing-map), and elastic nets. While some illustrative examples are provided in Section 1.4, the full treatment will be deferred to Chapter 6.
- **Supervised learning models:** kernel discriminant component analysis (DCA), kernel ridge regressor (KRR), support vector machine (SVM), support vector regression (SVR), and support vector clustering (SVC). While some illustrative examples are provided in Section 1.5, the full treatment will be deferred to Chapters 9–11.

In summary, the optimization formulation prescribed in Theorem 1.1 covers most, if not all, of the ℓ_2-based learning models treated in this book (both unsupervised and supervised). Some concrete examples for the LSP can be found in Example 1.1 for unsupervised learning applications and Examples 1.2, 1.3, and 1.5 for supervised learning applications. Nevertheless, as demonstrated by Example 1.4, the LSP is invalid for some prominent learning models, including LASSO regularizer, ℓ_1-norm SVMs, ℓ_1-norm elastic nets, and the doubly regularized SVMs [268, 288, 320, 321].

[1] For advanced unsupervised learning models, such as expectation maximization (EM), the unknowns could also include the membership function, denoted by $h_{k,j}$, with $k = 1, \ldots, K$ and $j = 1, \ldots, N$.

1.3.2 Kernelization of the optimization formulation for learning models

Kernelization refers to the process of converting an optimizer originally in the original space (or intrinsic space) into a formulation in the empirical space. Let us now further show that the LSP is vital for kernelization of the optimization formulation of a learning model.

If the LSP holds over the original vector space, i.e.

$$\mathbf{w}_k \in \mathtt{span}[\mathbf{X}],\ k = 1, \ldots, K.$$

In matrix notation, it means that there always exists a vector $\mathbf{a}_k \in R^N$ such that

$$\mathbf{w}_k = \mathbf{X}\mathbf{a}_k, \quad k = 1, \ldots, K. \tag{1.10}$$

It follows that

$$\mathbf{w}_k^{\mathrm{T}}\mathbf{x}_j = \mathbf{a}_k^{\mathrm{T}}\vec{\mathbf{k}}(\mathbf{x}_j),$$

where we denote the kernel-induced *empirical feature vector* associated with $\mathbf{x}$ to be

$$\vec{\mathbf{k}}(\mathbf{x}) = \begin{bmatrix} \mathbf{x}_1^{\mathrm{T}}\mathbf{x} \\ \mathbf{x}_2^{\mathrm{T}}\mathbf{x} \\ \vdots \\ \mathbf{x}_N^{\mathrm{T}}\mathbf{x} \end{bmatrix} = \begin{bmatrix} \mathbf{x}_1^{\mathrm{T}} \\ \mathbf{x}_2^{\mathrm{T}} \\ \vdots \\ \mathbf{x}_N^{\mathrm{T}} \end{bmatrix} \mathbf{x} = \mathbf{X}^{\mathrm{T}}\mathbf{x}. \tag{1.11}$$

In addition, let the *kernel matrix* associated with the training dataset $\mathcal{X}$ be

$$\mathbf{K} = \begin{bmatrix} \mathbf{x}_1^{\mathrm{T}}\mathbf{x}_1 & \mathbf{x}_1^{\mathrm{T}}\mathbf{x}_2 & \ldots & \mathbf{x}_1^{\mathrm{T}}\mathbf{x}_N \\ \mathbf{x}_2^{\mathrm{T}}\mathbf{x}_1 & \mathbf{x}_2^{\mathrm{T}}\mathbf{x}_2 & \ldots & \mathbf{x}_2^{\mathrm{T}}\mathbf{x}_N \\ \vdots & \vdots & \ldots & \vdots \\ \mathbf{x}_N^{\mathrm{T}}\mathbf{x}_1 & \mathbf{x}_N^{\mathrm{T}}\mathbf{x}_2 & \ldots & \mathbf{x}_N^{\mathrm{T}}\mathbf{x}_N \end{bmatrix} = \mathbf{X}^{\mathrm{T}}\mathbf{X}. \tag{1.12}$$

In other words, the kernel matrix is formed from the $N \times N$ pairwise inner products among the N training vectors:

$$\mathbf{K} = \{K_{ij}\},\ \text{where } K_{ij} = \mathbf{x}_i^{\mathrm{T}}\mathbf{x}_j, \quad i = 1, \ldots, N,\ j = 1, \ldots, N.$$

The quadratic term

$$\left\| \sum_{k=1}^{K} \beta_k^{(\ell)} \mathbf{w}_k \right\|^2 = \sum_{k=1}^{K}\sum_{k'=1}^{K} \beta_k^{(\ell)}\beta_{k'}^{(\ell)} \mathbf{w}_k^{\mathrm{T}}\mathbf{w}_{k'} = \sum_{k=1}^{K}\sum_{k'=1}^{K} \beta_k^{(\ell)}\beta_{k'}^{(\ell)} \mathbf{a}_k^{\mathrm{T}}\mathbf{K}\mathbf{a}_k$$

may be expressed as function of $\mathbf{a}_k$ and the kernel matrix $\mathbf{K}$.

Kernelized learning model

The model aims at finding

$$\underset{\{\mathbf{a}_k \in \mathbb{R}^N,\ \forall k\}}{\arg\min}\ \mathcal{E}\left(\mathbf{a}_k^{\mathrm{T}}\vec{\mathbf{k}}(\mathbf{x}_j), \forall k, j; \sum_{k=1}^{K}\sum_{k'=1}^{K} \beta_k^{(\ell)}\beta_{k'}^{(\ell)} \mathbf{a}_k^{\mathrm{T}}\mathbf{K}\mathbf{a}_k,\ \forall \ell \right) \tag{1.13}$$

subject to the equality constraints

$$c_p\left(\mathbf{a}_k^{\mathrm{T}}\vec{\mathbf{k}}(\mathbf{x}_j),\ \forall k,j\right) = 0, \quad p = 1,\ldots,P, \tag{1.14}$$

and inequality constraints

$$d_q\left(\mathbf{a}_k^{\mathrm{T}}\vec{\mathbf{k}}(\mathbf{x}_j),\ \forall k,j;\ \sum_{k=1}^{K}\sum_{k'=1}^{K}\beta_k^{(\ell)}\beta_{k'}^{(\ell)}\mathbf{a}_k^{\mathrm{T}}\mathbf{K}\mathbf{a}_k,\ \forall \ell\right) \geq 0, \quad q = 1,\ldots,Q. \tag{1.15}$$

We call this new formulation a kernelized learning model because the optimizer is now fully characterized by the $N \times N$ pairwise inner products among the N training vectors. Such a kernelization procedure is commonly known as the *kernel trick* [64]. The formulation significantly expands the domain of machine learning applications. In this regard, there are two main aspects.

- *Vectorial data analysis.* Note that the notion of the LSP can be naturally extended to kernel-induced vector spaces when nonlinear kernels are adopted. (See Problem 1.14.) In the extreme case, it may cope with nonlinear functions of indefinite order such as Gaussian RBF kernels, since its learning complexity is dominated by N (the data size) instead of the dimension of the feature vector or the degree of nonlinearity of the kernel functions adopted.
- *Nonvectorial data analysis.* The kernelized optimizer basically circumvents the need to explicitly specify the vector space used for data analysis, making it amenable to nonvectorial data analysis.

1.3.3 The LSP is necessary and sufficient for kernelization

Let us now establish that the LSP is a necessary and sufficient condition for the kernelizability of such optimizers that are originally formulated in the original space.

Sufficiency

According to Eq. (1.9), with the LSP held to be valid, then the kernelized learning model (Eqs. (1.13)–(1.13)) may be used to learn $\mathbf{a}_k$, $\forall k$, which then in turn leads us to the final optimal solution: $\mathbf{w}_k = \mathbf{X}\mathbf{a}_k$, $\forall k$. This establishes the sufficiency of the LSP for kernelization.

Necessity

The proof for necessity is almost by inspection. Note that the kernelized learning model can only solve for $\mathbf{a}_k$, $\forall k$, which reveals no information concerning any orthogonal components that may exist. This means that if the LSP is invalid, then the kernelized learning models cannot fully recover $\mathbf{w}_k$ by means of $\mathbf{w}_k = \mathbf{X}\mathbf{a}_k$, $\forall k$. Thus the LSP is necessary in order for the kernelized optimizer to fully replace the original optimizer.

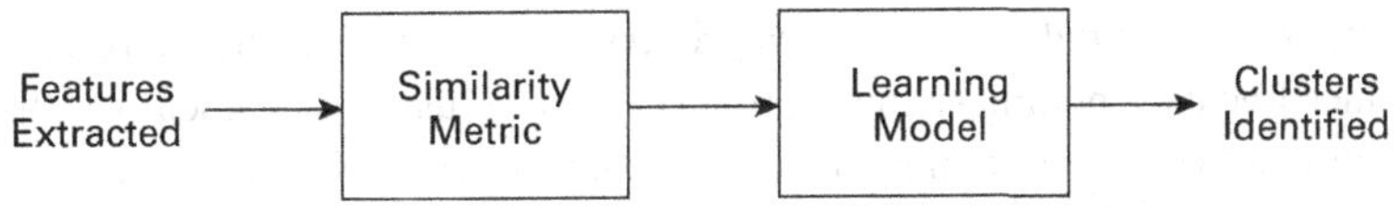

Fig. 1.5. Two characteristic components of unsupervised cluster discovery are (1) the similarity metric and (2) the learning model.

1.4 Unsupervised learning for cluster discovery

It is a major challenge to design unsupervised learning algorithms to reveal underlying cluster structures embedded in the dataset, which potentially consists of a large number of high-dimensional training vectors. Various kinds of useful information may be extracted from the raw data, even though their class labels are not made available. For example, key statistical properties (e.g. the density distribution) of the training dataset may be estimated. Alternatively, their underlying generating models may be postulated or estimated. The distilled information may facilitate the analysis or classification of newly observed data.

There are several tutorial papers providing comprehensive surveys of clustering algorithms and applications. (See e.g. [307].) They include algorithms based on parametric models (e.g. the K-means[2] algorithm [164]), graph-theoretic models (e.g. [48, 117]), and density-estimation models (e.g. [73]).

As illustrated by Figure 1.5, there are two pivotal design stages for unsupervised clustering analysis.

- **How to select a proper similarity metric?** The question boils down to whether two training vectors are sufficiently similar to be grouped together. The similarity metrics must be specified before unsupervised learning models may be derived. Consequently, a suitable similarity metric is vital for effective clustering.
- **How to choose an efficient learning model?** The clustering results also depend on the specific learning model adopted. Some popular clustering models include the K-means algorithm, the expectation-maximization (EM) clustering algorithm, and the self-organizing map (SOM).

1.4.1 Characterization of similarity metrics

Given a set of N training vectors in the vector space of the real field, R^M,

$$\{\mathbf{x}_1, \mathbf{x}_2, \ldots, \mathbf{x}_N\},$$

the objective of unsupervised cluster discovery is to partition them into K subgroups according to their similarity. Regarding what would constitute a proper similarity metric, there are two perspectives worth considering.

[2] The notation k-means is used in many books, instead of K-means.

- **Linear versus nonlinear similarity metrics.** Depending on the data cluster structure, either linear or nonlinear inner products may be used to characterize the similarity metric between two training vectors. The linear metric would be adequate if the data distribution is relatively simple or when the feature dimension is relatively high (compared with the size of the training dataset). To handle more complex data distributions, it is often necessary to adopt nonlinear inner products prescribed by nonlinear kernel functions, e.g. the polynomial functions or the Gaussian *radial basis function* (RBF), or simply Gaussian kernel.
- **Shift-invariance.** By shift-invariance, we mean that the similarity function is independent of translation of the coordinate system. While shift-invariance holds for the Gaussian kernel function, it is not valid for linear or polynomial kernel functions. Without the shift-invariance property, the coordinate system chosen may affect the results; therefore, it is common to adopt a mass-center pre-adjusted coordinate system.

1.4.2 The LSP and kernelization of K-means learning models

One of the most prominent unsupervised learning models is K-means. Let us denote the training dataset as $\mathcal{X} = \{\mathbf{x}_1, \mathbf{x}_2, \ldots, \mathbf{x}_N\}$, each sample of which is assumed to be generated by one (and only one) of the K clusters, denoted by $\{C_1, C_2, \ldots, C_K\}$, and represented by the respective probabilistic models $\Theta = \{\Theta_1, \Theta_2, \ldots, \Theta_K\}$. K-means aims at finding

$$\arg\min_{\{\mathbf{w}_k, \forall k\}} \left\{ \sum_{k=1}^{K} \sum_{\mathbf{x}_t \in C_k} ||\mathbf{x}_t - \mathbf{w}_k||^2 \right\}, \tag{1.16}$$

where $\mathbf{w}_k$ denotes the kth cluster's centroid.

As will be shown presently, the LSP holds for the K-means learning model, since it is based on an ℓ_2-norm clustering criterion that satisfies Theorem 1.1. Moreover, as will be elaborated on in Section 1.4.3, the LSP holds also for many other prominent unsupervised clustering algorithms, e.g. the SOM and elastic nets, both being based on the ℓ_2-norm criterion.

In an optimal K-means solution, the centroid, say $\mathbf{w}_k$, associated with a training vector $\mathbf{x}_j$ must be the one yielding the minimum distance among all the centroids. Therefore, when the optimality is reached, the cost function in Eq. (1.16) can be equivalently expressed as

$$\mathcal{E}\left(\mathbf{w}_k^{\mathrm{T}}\mathbf{x}_j, k = 1, \ldots, K, j = 1, \ldots, N;\ ||\mathbf{w}_k||, k = 1, \ldots, K\right)$$

$$= \sum_{j=1}^{N} \min_{k=1,\ldots,K} \{||\mathbf{x}_j - \mathbf{w}_k||^2\} \tag{1.17}$$

$$= \sum_{j=1}^{N} \min_{k=1,\ldots,K} \{||\mathbf{x}_j||^2 - 2\mathbf{w}_k^{\mathrm{T}}\mathbf{x}_j + ||\mathbf{w}_k||^2\}, \tag{1.18}$$

then the function $\mathcal{E}(\cdot)$ is a monotonically increasing function of $\|\mathbf{w}_k\|^2$, $k = 1, \ldots, K$, and, according to Theorem 1.1, the LSP condition holds for the K-means learning model.

Let us now look into a numerical example.

Example 1.1 (Unsupervised learning example) *Given the training dataset*

$$\mathbf{x}_1 = \begin{bmatrix} 0 \\ 0 \\ 0 \\ 0 \end{bmatrix}, \quad \mathbf{x}_2 = \begin{bmatrix} 0 \\ 0 \\ 2 \\ 0 \end{bmatrix}, \quad \mathbf{x}_3 = \begin{bmatrix} 2 \\ 2 \\ 0 \\ 1 \end{bmatrix}, \quad \mathbf{x}_4 = \begin{bmatrix} 3 \\ 3 \\ 2 \\ 1 \end{bmatrix},$$

find two centroids $\mathbf{w}_1$ *and* $\mathbf{w}_2$ *that minimize the cost function in Eq. (1.17).*

Solution: *By inspection, the optimal centroids are*

$$\mathbf{w}_1 = \begin{bmatrix} 0 \\ 0 \\ 1 \\ 0 \end{bmatrix} \in \mathtt{span}[\mathbf{X}], \quad \mathbf{w}_2 = \begin{bmatrix} 2.5 \\ 2.5 \\ 1 \\ 1 \end{bmatrix} \in \mathtt{span}[\mathbf{X}].$$

Note that both optimal centroids fall within the learning subspace.

Kernelized formulation for K*-means*

As explained below, the LSP assures that K-means have a kernelized formulation. Thanks to the LSP, the optimal solution for K-means can be expressed as

$$\mathbf{w}_k \in \mathtt{span}[\mathbf{X}], \; k = 1, \ldots, K.$$

In matrix notation, it is assured that there always exists a vector $\mathbf{a}_k \in \mathbb{R}^N$ such that

$$\mathbf{w}_k = \mathbf{X}\mathbf{a}_k, \quad k = 1, \ldots, K. \tag{1.19}$$

Recall the denotation of the kernel-induced *empirical feature vector* $\vec{\mathbf{k}}(\mathbf{x})$ and the *kernel matrix* $\mathbf{K}$ associated with the training dataset $\mathcal{X}$ in Eqs. (1.11) and (1.12), respectively. On substituting Eq. (1.19) into Eq. (1.17), we arrive at

$$\begin{aligned}
&\mathcal{E}\left(\mathbf{w}_k^{\mathrm{T}}\mathbf{x}_j,\; k = 1, \ldots, K,\; j = 1, \ldots, N;\; ||\mathbf{w}_k||, k = 1, \ldots, K\right) \\
&\quad = \sum_{j=1}^{N} \min_{k=1,\ldots,K} \{\|\mathbf{x}_j\|^2 - 2\mathbf{w}_k^{\mathrm{T}}\mathbf{x}_j + \|\mathbf{w}_k\|^2\}, \\
&\quad = \sum_{j=1}^{N} \min_{k=1,\ldots,K} \{\|\mathbf{x}_j\|^2 - 2\mathbf{a}_k^{\mathrm{T}}\vec{\mathbf{k}}(\mathbf{x}_j) + \mathbf{a}_k^{\mathrm{T}}\mathbf{K}\mathbf{a}_k\}.
\end{aligned} \tag{1.20}$$

Note that the new kernel-based optimizer formulation is fully characterized by the kernel matrix

$$\mathbf{K} = \{K_{ij}\}, \text{where } K_{ij} = \mathbf{x}_i^{\mathrm{T}}\mathbf{x}_j, \quad i = 1, \ldots, N,\; j = 1, \ldots, N.$$

It is vital that the kernel matrix must be a positive semi-definite matrix – a critical condition for the quadratic optimizer to be meaningful.

1.4.3 The LSP and kernelization of ℓ_2 elastic nets

Let us study another unsupervised learning model with closed-form optimization criterion, i.e. the ℓ_2-norm *elastic net*. The elastic net learning model, proposed by Durbin and Willshaw [57], is closely related to the active contour model presented by Kass, Witkin, and Terzopoulos [121].

ℓ_2 elastic nets

The objective function of the ℓ_2 elastic net may be simplified to

$$\mathcal{E}\{\mathbf{w}\} = -\sigma^2 \sum_{j=1}^{N} \log\left[\sum_{k=1}^{K} \exp(-||\mathbf{x}_j - \mathbf{w}_k||^2/(2\sigma^2))\right] + \frac{\kappa}{2}\sum_{k=1}^{K-1} ||\mathbf{w}_{k+1} - \mathbf{w}_k||^2, \quad (1.21)$$

where $\mathbf{w}$ denotes the set of node vectors $\{\mathbf{w}_k, \forall k\}$ and $\mathbf{x}_j$ and $\mathbf{w}_k$ represent the training vector j and node k, respectively. Here σ dictates the effective radius of the region covered by a node vector and the constraint parameter κ is chosen to assure that the consecutive nodes are kept within a reasonable proximity.

By applying the gradient method to the cost function in Eq. (1.21), we obtain the following updating rule for $\mathbf{w}_k, k = 2, \ldots, K-1$:

$$\Delta\mathbf{w}_k = \eta \sum_{j=1}^{N} \Lambda_j(k)(\mathbf{x}_j - \mathbf{w}_k) + \kappa(\mathbf{w}_{k+1} - 2\mathbf{w}_k + \mathbf{w}_{k-1}),$$

where η is a small and positive learning rate and $\Lambda_j(k)$ is the neighborhood sensitivity function (see Chapter 5) defined as

$$\Lambda_j(k) = \frac{\exp(-|\mathbf{x}_j - \mathbf{w}_k|^2/(2\sigma^2))}{\sum_i \exp(-|\mathbf{x}_j - \mathbf{w}_i|^2/(2\sigma^2))}. \quad (1.22)$$

Note that the optimizer formulation, given in Eq. (1.21), is an ℓ_2-norm-based criterion. Let us define

$$\beta_k^{(\ell)} = \begin{cases} +1 & \text{if } k = \ell + 1 \\ -1 & \text{if } k = \ell \\ 0 & \text{otherwise} \end{cases} \quad (1.23)$$

for $\ell = 1, \ldots, K-1$, then

$$\left|\left|\sum_{k=1}^{K} \beta_k^{(\ell)} \mathbf{w}_k\right|\right| = ||\mathbf{w}_{\ell+1} - \mathbf{w}_\ell|| \quad \text{for} \quad \ell = 1, \ldots, K-1.$$

Note that the incorporation of the regularization term $||\sum_{k=1}^{K} \beta_k^{(\ell)} \mathbf{w}_k||$ into the cost function Eq. (1.5) facilitates the achievement of topological and neighborhood sensitivity in the elastic net. It follows that we can now further denote

$$\mathcal{E}\{\mathbf{w}\} \equiv -\sigma^2 \sum_{t} \log\left[\sum_{k=1}^{K} \exp\left(-\frac{||\mathbf{x}_j - \mathbf{w}_k||^2}{2\sigma^2}\right)\right] + \frac{\kappa}{2}\sum_{\ell=1}^{K-1} ||\mathbf{w}_{\ell+1} - \mathbf{w}_\ell||^2,$$

$$\equiv -\sigma^2 \sum_t \log \left[\sum_{k=1}^{K} \exp \left(-\frac{\|\mathbf{x}_j\|^2 - 2\mathbf{w}_k^{\mathrm{T}}\mathbf{x}_j + \|\mathbf{w}_k\|^2}{2\sigma^2} \right) \right]$$
$$+ \frac{K}{2} \sum_{k=1}^{K-1} ||\mathbf{w}_{k+1} - \mathbf{w}_k||^2, \tag{1.24}$$

It can easily be seen that $\mathcal{E}(\cdot)$ is a monotonically increasing function w.r.t. $\{||\mathbf{w}_k||, k = 1, \ldots, K\}$ and w.r.t. $\{|| \sum_{k=1}^{K} \beta_k^{(\ell)} \mathbf{w}_k||, \ \ell = 1, \ldots, K-1\}$. Consequently, Theorem 1.1 is good for the ℓ_2 elastic net learning model.

Kernelized formulation for ℓ_2 elastic nets

It is important to note that the LSP condition assures the existence of the kernel-matrix-based variant of the learning model,

$$\mathcal{E}\{\mathbf{w}\} \equiv -\sigma^2 \sum_t \log \left[\sum_{k=1}^{K} \exp \left(-\frac{K_{jj} - 2\mathbf{a}_k^{\mathrm{T}} \vec{\mathbf{k}}(\mathbf{x}_j) + ||\mathbf{a}_k||_{\mathbf{K}}^2}{2\sigma^2} \right) \right]$$
$$+ \frac{K}{2} \sum_{k=1}^{K-1} ||\mathbf{a}_{k+1} - \mathbf{a}_k||_{\mathbf{K}}^2, \tag{1.25}$$

where $|| \cdot ||_{\mathbf{K}}$ denotes the Mahalanobis distance (see Eq. (1.43)), i.e.

$$||\mathbf{a}_k||_{\mathbf{K}}^2 \equiv \mathbf{a}_k^{\mathrm{T}}\mathbf{K}\mathbf{a}_k \quad \text{and} \quad ||\mathbf{a}_{k+1} - \mathbf{a}_k||_{\mathbf{K}}^2 \equiv [\mathbf{a}_{k+1} - \mathbf{a}_k]^{\mathrm{T}}\mathbf{K}[\mathbf{a}_{k+1} - \mathbf{a}_k].$$

ℓ_1 elastic nets

In contrast, the ℓ_1 elastic nets proposed by Zou and Hastie adopt a LASSO (i.e. ℓ_1-norm) regularization term [268, 321]. As demonstrated in Example 1.4, such learning models fail the LSP condition and, consequently, they are not kernelizable.

1.5 Supervised learning for linear classifiers

Supervised machine learning builds its foundation on the powerful paradigm of "*learning from examples*." More specifically, a supervised model learns from the training dataset to learn a prediction function, which may be used subsequently in the prediction phase to classify newly observed patterns. Given the training vectors

$$\mathcal{X} = \{\mathbf{x}_1, \mathbf{x}_2, \ldots, \mathbf{x}_N\},$$

each belonging to one of the K classes, denoted by $C = \{C_1, C_2, \ldots, C_K\}$. The class label of each training pattern is usually encoded into a teacher value prescribed by a real number. For example, for a training vector $\mathbf{x}_t$, the teacher value will be denoted as y_t, where $y_t \in \mathbb{R}$.

For supervised classification, the class labels of all the training vectors are known in advance. In short, the complete training dataset is

$$[\mathcal{X}, \mathcal{Y}] = \{[\mathbf{x}_1, y_1], [\mathbf{x}_2, y_2], \ldots, [\mathbf{x}_N, y_N]\}.$$

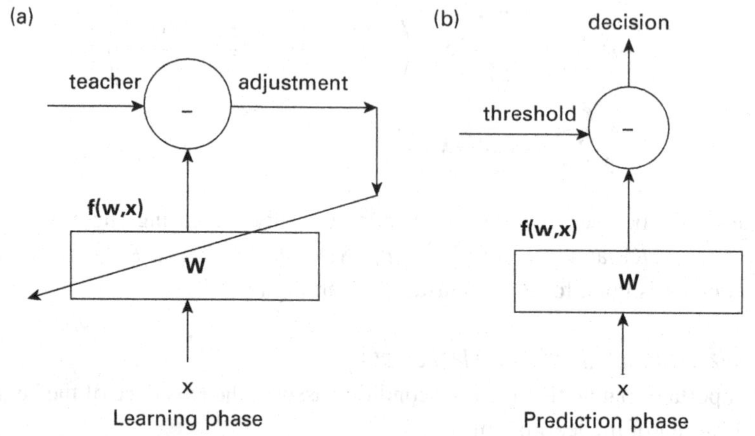

Fig. 1.6. Supervised training for binary classification consists of learning and testing phases. (a) The objective in the learning phase is to find the parameters **w** that can not only achieve a high classification accuracy but also behave robustly amidst possible perturbations. The input **x** will be drawn from the given training dataset. (b) In the testing phase, the **w** learned during the learning phase will be used for prediction. In this phase, **w** is treated as a constant and can no longer be adjusted. Moreover, the input **x** will be a new pattern that has not been used by the learning model before. Namely, it is drawn from a separate test dataset that has no overlap with the training dataset.

In most introductory treatments, it is customary to place the focus of discussion exclusively on linear classification of two classes, i.e. $K = 2$ with $C = \{\mathcal{C}_+, \mathcal{C}_-\}$. The methods developed for linear binary classification can then be naturally extended to nonlinear and multi-class classification.

1.5.1 Learning and prediction phases

For supervised classification, the focus is placed on the so-called *discriminant function*,

$$f(\mathbf{w}, \mathbf{x}), \tag{1.26}$$

and, for notational convenience, we often simply denote $f(\mathbf{x}) = f(\mathbf{w}, \mathbf{x})$. It follows that a decision boundary can be formed as

$$f(\mathbf{x}) = f(\mathbf{w}, \mathbf{x}) = 0,$$

which divides the data space into two regions: one positive and one negative.

The study of supervised classification can be divided into several phases.

- **Learning phase.** Figure 1.6(a) depicts the flow chart associated with the learning phase. The learning objective is to find an optimal solution for **w** so that the response $f(\mathbf{w}, \mathbf{x})$ can best match the training vectors with their respective teacher values. In the basic training strategy, the first concern is to find **w** such that

$$\begin{cases} \text{if } \mathbf{x}_i \in \mathcal{C}_+ \text{ then } f(\mathbf{w}, \mathbf{x}_i) \geq 0 \\ \text{if } \mathbf{x}_i \in \mathcal{C}_- \text{ then } f(\mathbf{w}, \mathbf{x}_i) < 0 \end{cases} \tag{1.27}$$

for as many training samples as possible.

- **Testing/evaluation phase.** In practice, the learning performance must also take into account the generalization capability of the trained discriminant function. This is often the task conducted in the evaluation phase. As depicted in Figure 1.6(b), the test data used in the testing phase are brand new patterns, i.e. they are drawn from a separate pool that does not overlap with the training dataset. The decision rule for a test vector $\mathbf{x}$ is as follows:

$$\mathbf{x} \in \begin{cases} \mathcal{C}_+ & \text{if } f(\mathbf{w}, \mathbf{x}) \geq 0 \\ \mathcal{C}_- & \text{if } f(\mathbf{w}, \mathbf{x}) < 0, \end{cases} \tag{1.28}$$

  where $\mathbf{w}$ is derived during the learning phase.
- **Prediction phase.** Finally, in the so-called prediction phase, the classifier showing the best evaluation result will be deployed for the field application.

Training and testing accuracies

The *training accuracy* is a common metric used to calibrate how well the learned classifier can differentiate the positive and negative data drawn from the training dataset. In contrast, the *testing accuracy* reflects the classification accuracy of the learned classifier on the testing dataset, which has no overlap with the training dataset. It should be of no surprise that the training and testing accuracies are in general very different. This means that a high training accuracy does not necessarily lead to a high testing/prediction accuracy, and vice versa. Especially, if a learned model is heavily overtrained so as to strive for a super-high training performance, it is likely to suffer from a side effect of having a poor and downgraded testing accuracy. Therefore, it is vital to take measures to make the trained classifier more robust and error-resilient. For example, an effective supervised learning method is to find classifiers that can provide the widest possible margin to separate positive and negative training data.

Testing and prediction accuracies

It is commonly accepted that the *testing accuracy* serves as a reasonable indicator of the prediction performance. Therefore, all the learned classifiers must undergo the evaluation process during the testing phase. The classifier receiving the best cross-validation will be deployed for real-world applications. Ideally, the *prediction accuracy* should be reasonably consistent with the *testing accuracy*. However, this is contingent upon the conditions that (1) a large set of statistically consistent testing data is assumed to be made available to the learner; and (2) the testing and predicting data share the same data acquisition environment.

1.5.2 Learning models and linear system of equations

The training dataset contains input/teacher pairs:

$$[\mathcal{X}, \mathcal{Y}] = \{[\mathbf{x}_1, y_1], [\mathbf{x}_2, y_2], \ldots, [\mathbf{x}_N, y_N]\},$$

where

(i) N denotes the number of training data, $\mathbf{x}_i \in \mathbb{R}^M$, where M is the dimension of the feature vectors, and
(ii) for any positive training vector $\mathbf{x}_i$, we set its teacher value to $y_i = +1$, and for any negative training vector $\mathbf{x}_j$, we set $y_j = -1$.

Let us now momentarily focus on solving either exactly or approximately for the optimal solution for an M-dimensional decision vector $\mathbf{w}$ such that[3]

$$\mathbf{x}_n^{\mathrm{T}}\mathbf{w} = y_i, \text{ for } n = 1, \ldots, N. \tag{1.29}$$

Once the optimal solution for $\mathbf{w}$ has been found, we can derive a linear decision boundary,

$$f(\mathbf{x}) = \mathbf{x}^{\mathrm{T}}\mathbf{w} = 0, \tag{1.30}$$

which will subsequently be used for classification of a newly observed vector $\mathbf{x}$.

On cascading all the N equations in matrix form, we have

$$\begin{bmatrix} \mathbf{x}_1^{\mathrm{T}} \\ \mathbf{x}_2^{\mathrm{T}} \\ \vdots \\ \mathbf{x}_N^{\mathrm{T}} \end{bmatrix} \mathbf{w} = \begin{bmatrix} y_1 \\ y_2 \\ \vdots \\ y_N \end{bmatrix}. \tag{1.31}$$

In matrix notation, we have

$$\mathbf{X}^{\mathrm{T}}\mathbf{w} = \mathbf{y}, \tag{1.32}$$

where

$$\mathbf{X} = [\mathbf{x}_1\, \mathbf{x}_2 \ldots \mathbf{x}_N] \quad \text{and} \quad \mathbf{y} \equiv \left[y_1\, y_2\, \ldots\, y_N\right]^{\mathrm{T}}.$$

This leads to the following two distinctive problem formulations.

- **Over-determined scenario:** $N > M$. In this case, the learning model can be treated as an approximation problem and thus mathematically formulated as an over-determined linear system. Denote the least-squared error (LSE) as

$$\mathcal{E}(\mathcal{X}, \mathbf{w}) = \sum_{n=1}^{N} \left(\mathbf{x}_n^{\mathrm{T}}\mathbf{w} - y_n\right)^2 = \left\|\mathbf{X}^{\mathrm{T}}\mathbf{w} - \mathbf{y}\right\|^2. \tag{1.33}$$

In this case, the *scatter matrix*,

$$\mathbf{S} = \mathbf{X}\mathbf{X}^{\mathrm{T}},$$

is generically nonsingular, and thus the optimal decision vector $\mathbf{w}$ can be derived as

$$\arg\min_{\mathbf{w}\in\mathbb{R}^M} \mathcal{E}(\mathcal{X}, \mathbf{w}),$$

[3] As shown in Problem 1.6 the optimal linear solution has this special form assuming that (1) the numbers of positive and negative training vectors are the same, thus $\sum_{n=1}^{N} y_n = 0$; and (2) the whole dataset is mass-centered (i.e. $\sum_{n=1}^{N} \mathbf{x}_n = \mathbf{0}$).

which leads to the following closed-form solution:

$$\mathbf{w} = (\mathbf{X}\mathbf{X}^{\mathrm{T}})^{-1}\mathbf{X}\mathbf{y} = \mathbf{S}^{-1}\mathbf{X}\mathbf{y}.$$

- **Under-determined scenario:** $M > N$. In this case, the scatter matrix $\mathbf{S} = (\mathbf{X}\mathbf{X}^{\mathrm{T}})$ will be singular, implying that there exist multiple non-unique solutions for Eq. (1.32). For such under-determined problems, the learning model should be reformulated. Among the many possible solutions for Eq. (1.32), the best choice would be the one providing the widest separation margin (i.e. $2/\|\mathbf{w}\|$). This leads to a new optimizer aiming at finding

$$\arg\min_{\mathbf{w}\in\mathbb{R}^M} \|\mathbf{w}\|^2, \quad \text{subject to } \mathbf{x}_i^{\mathrm{T}}\mathbf{w} = y_i, \text{ for } i = 1, \ldots, N. \tag{1.34}$$

1.5.3 Kernelized learning models for under-determined systems

Theorem 1.1 is apparently valid for both the optimization formulations Eqs. (1.33) and (1.34). As a result, the optimal solution for $\mathbf{w}$ must satisfy the LSP. Let us discuss the procedure for the kernelization of the optimizer given in Eq. (1.34) whose LSP assures the existence of a kernelized reformulation. More precisely, it assures that there exist coefficients $\{a_n, n = 1, \ldots, N\}$, such that

$$\mathbf{w} = \sum_{n=1}^{N} a_n \mathbf{x}_n = \mathbf{X}\mathbf{a}, \tag{1.35}$$

where $\mathbf{a} \equiv [a_1\ a_2\ \ldots\ a_N]^{\mathrm{T}}$. In matrix notation,

$$\mathbf{X}^{\mathrm{T}}\mathbf{w} = \mathbf{X}^{\mathrm{T}}\mathbf{X}\mathbf{a} = \mathbf{K}\mathbf{a} = \mathbf{y}, \tag{1.36}$$

where the *kernel matrix* associated with the linear kernel function,

$$K(\mathbf{x}, \mathbf{x}') = \mathbf{x}^{\mathrm{T}}\mathbf{x}',$$

is defined as follows

$$\mathbf{K} = \{K_{ij}\}, \text{ with its}(i, j)\text{th entry } K_{ij} = \mathbf{x}_i^{\mathrm{T}}\mathbf{x}_j.$$

Assuming that $\mathbf{K}$ is nonsingular, then we have a unique solution for $\mathbf{a}$,

$$\mathbf{a} = \mathbf{K}^{-1}\mathbf{y}, \tag{1.37}$$

which in turn leads to the following discriminant function expressed in the kernel function:

$$f(\mathbf{x}) = \mathbf{x}^{\mathrm{T}}\mathbf{w} = \sum_{n=1}^{N} (\mathbf{x} \cdot \mathbf{x}_n) a_n = \sum_{n=1}^{N} K(\mathbf{x}, \mathbf{x}_n) a_n. \tag{1.38}$$

Example 1.2 (Kernel trick for the under-determined problem) *Consider a supervised training dataset $[\mathcal{X}, \mathcal{Y}]$, with $M = 3 > N = 2$:*

$$\mathbf{x}_1 = \begin{bmatrix} 1 \\ 2 \\ 0 \end{bmatrix}, \ y_1 = +1, \qquad \mathbf{x}_2 = \begin{bmatrix} 0 \\ 0 \\ -1 \end{bmatrix}, \ y_2 = -1.$$

From Eq. (1.37), we obtain

$$\begin{aligned}\mathbf{a} &= \mathbf{K}^{-1}\mathbf{y}\\ &= [\mathbf{X}^{\mathrm{T}}\mathbf{X}]^{-1}\mathbf{y}\\ &= \left(\begin{bmatrix} 1 & 2 & 0\\ 0 & 0 & -1\end{bmatrix}\begin{bmatrix} 1 & 0\\ 2 & 0\\ 0 & -1\end{bmatrix}\right)^{-1}\begin{bmatrix} +1\\ -1\end{bmatrix} = \begin{bmatrix} 5 & 0\\ 0 & 1\end{bmatrix}^{-1}\begin{bmatrix} +1\\ -1\end{bmatrix} = \begin{bmatrix} \frac{1}{5}\\ -1\end{bmatrix}.\end{aligned} \tag{1.39}$$

Thus $a_1 = \frac{1}{5}$ *and* $a_2 = -1$. *According to the LSP, we can obtain*

$$\mathbf{w} = \sum_{n=1}^{N} a_n\mathbf{x}_n = a_1\mathbf{x}_1 + a_2\mathbf{x}_2 = [\tfrac{1}{5}\ \tfrac{2}{5}\ 1]^{\mathrm{T}}, \tag{1.40}$$

which should be the same as the solution derived directly from Eq. (1.34).

1.5.4 The vital role of the ℓ_2-norm for the LSP

As established previously, the LSP is a necessary and sufficient condition for the kernelizability of many optimization formulations. Let us now use some numerical examples to accentuate the close relationship between the LSP and the use of ℓ_2-norm.

Example 1.3 (ℓ_2-norm-based learning models) *Consider a supervised training dataset* $[\mathcal{X}, \mathcal{Y}]$, *with* $M = 3 > N = 2$:

$$\mathbf{x}_1 = \begin{bmatrix} 1\\ 2\\ 0\end{bmatrix}, \ y_1 = +1, \qquad \mathbf{x}_2 = \begin{bmatrix} 0\\ 0\\ -1\end{bmatrix}, \ y_2 = -1.$$

For many regularization problems, it is effective to incorporate an ℓ_2*-norm ridge penalty into the sum-of-squared-errors yielding the following objective function [99, 112, 275]:*

$$\arg\min_{\mathbf{w}\in\mathbb{R}^M}\left(\sum_{i=1}^{2}\|\mathbf{w}^{\mathrm{T}}\mathbf{x}_i - y_i\|^2 + \|\mathbf{w}\|^2\right), \tag{1.41}$$

where $\|\mathbf{w}\| = \|\mathbf{w}\|_2$ *stands for the* ℓ_2*-norm of* $\mathbf{w}$. *The optimal solution is* $\mathbf{w} = [\frac{1}{6}\ \frac{1}{3}\ \frac{1}{2}]^{\mathrm{T}}$, *which falls within the learning subspace.*

The use of the ℓ_2-norm is critical for the development of kernel methods. Most prominent supervised learning models, such as the kernel ridge regressor (KRR) and the support vector machine (SVM), are based on the ℓ_2-norm. Consequently, the LSP holds valid for both of them, implying that both learning models are kernelizable. See Chapters 9 and 10.

Example 1.4 (ℓ_1-norm-based learning models) *Consider the same training dataset* $[\mathcal{X}, \mathcal{Y}]$, *with* $M = 3 > N = 2$. *Now, in contrast, assume that the LASSO (i.e.* ℓ_1*-norm)* *penalty is used in the cost function. This leads to a LASSO-type optimizer [268] aiming at finding*

$$\arg\min_{\mathbf{w}\in\mathbb{R}^M}\left(\sum_{i=1}^{2}\|\mathbf{w}^{\mathrm{T}}\mathbf{x}_i - y_i\|^2 + \|\mathbf{w}\|_1\right), \tag{1.42}$$

The optimal solution now becomes $\mathbf{w} = [0\ \frac{3}{8}\ \frac{1}{2}]^{\mathrm{T}}$, *and fails to observe the LSP. Since it fails the LSP condition, the optimizing formulation is no longer kernelizable.*

By the same token, it can similarly be shown that the LSP is not observed by other ℓ_1*-norm formulations, including* ℓ_1*-norm SVMs [320], the* ℓ_1*-norm elastic net [321], doubly regularized SVMs [288], and numerous LASSO-type optimization formulations [27, 253, 321]. Since they fail the vital LSP condition, all of them are not kernelizable. (See Problem 1.12.)*

1.5.5 The LSP condition of one-class SVM for outlier detection

Note that, in Theorem 1.1, the inequality constraint (cf. Eq. (1.7)) is somewhat more flexible than the equality constraint (cf. Eq. (1.6)). Such flexibility is needed in order to make the formulation amenable to some important learning models. On such example is the hypersphere-based SVM outlier detection, whose treatment will be deferred to Section 11.4. Here we shall briefly describe the formulation from the perspective of the LSP.

Example 1.5 (Outlier-detecting learning models) *An outlier can be characterized by the distance between a training vector and the centroid of the class associated with it. More precisely, a vector with a distance greater than a specified radius, denoted by R, can be viewed as an outlier. With the details omitted here, eventually such an outlier-detecting optimizer aims at finding*

$$\begin{aligned} &\underset{\mathbf{w},R,\boldsymbol{\xi}\in\mathbb{R}^N}{\text{minimize}} \quad \tau(\mathbf{w},R,\boldsymbol{\xi}) = R^2 + C\sum\nolimits_{i=1}^{N}\xi_i \\ &\textit{subject to } ||\mathbf{w}||^2 + ||\mathbf{x}_i||^2 - 2\mathbf{w}^{\mathrm{T}}\mathbf{x}_i - R^2 - \xi_i \le 0 \\ &\qquad \textit{and } -\xi_i \le 0. \end{aligned}$$

In this case, with reference to the inequality Eq. (1.7), note that there is only one type of constraint (i.e. $Q = 1$*):*

$$d(\mathbf{w}^{\mathrm{T}}\mathbf{x}_i; ||\mathbf{w}||^2) = ||\mathbf{w}||^2 + ||\mathbf{x}_i||^2 - 2\mathbf{w}^{\mathrm{T}}\mathbf{x}_i - R^2 - \xi_i, \quad \forall i.$$

Since $d(\cdot)$ *is a monotonically increasing function of* $||\mathbf{w}||^2$*, Theorem 1.1 can be used to show that the LSP holds. The LSP in turn will lead to a kernelized learning model. For more detail, see Algorithm 11.3.*

1.6 Generalized inner products and kernel functions

In order to handle situations that involve complex and nonlinear classification, the role of the Euclidean inner product must be taken over by a more versatile nonlinear kernel function [64, 181, 280, 281]. This motivates the adoption of the nonlinear kernel-based learning models introduced in the present section.

In Section 1.3, the LSP condition described in Theorem 1.1 can be applied to the original vector space, which is implicitly associated with the scenarios when linear kernels are adopted. The same concept can be naturally extended and applied to kernel-induced vector spaces. It has a vital significance in the development of kernel methods because the LSP condition in the new feature space assures the existence of the kernelizability of numerous unsupervised and supervised learning models using ℓ_2-norm criteria.

Machine learning analysis depends very much on the specific metric used to characterize the similarity between two vectors in a Hilbert space. Conventionally, the Euclidean linear inner product is used as the default choice of the similarity metric. However, many (big) training datasets are often too complex to be effectively clustered and/or classified in terms of the simple Euclidean metric. Consequently, it compels the extension of the traditional Euclidean inner product to a more versatile similarity metric. There is a great diversity of similarity metrics and they all share an important common attribute, namely that the more similar the two objects are the greater the value of the generalized inner product should be. If the two objects are represented in a vectorial form, then nonlinear inner products are usually deemed to be more amenable to complex and big data learning than their linear counterparts.

1.6.1 Mahalanobis inner products

In order to take into account various weighting factors and correlation among different features, the Euclidean inner product can be extended to a more general inner product shown as follows:

$$K(\mathbf{x}, \mathbf{x}') = \langle \mathbf{x}, \mathbf{x}' \rangle_{\mathbf{M}} = \mathbf{x}^{\mathrm{T}} \mathbf{M} \mathbf{x}',$$

where $\mathbf{M}$ is a positive semi-definite matrix. Such a generalized inner product is sometimes referred to as *Mahalanobis inner product* [165]. In fact, in statistics, the matrix $\mathbf{M}$ often represents the inverse of the covariance matrix of the training dataset.

Three types of Mahalanobis inner product are worth considering.

- **Mutually independent and isotropic features.** The Euclidean inner product is a special case of the Mahalanobis inner product with $\mathbf{M} = \mathbf{I}$. The use of such an inner product implicitly assumes that
  (i) all the features are equally weighted and
  (ii) there exists no inter-feature dependence.
- **Mutually independent but non-isotropic features.** When the features are mutually independent, but not isotropic, then it is suitable to adopt a diagonal Mahalanobis matrix,

$$\mathbf{M} = \mathrm{Diag}\{\, w_i\}, \; i = 1, \ldots, M,$$

  where the weights $\{w_i, \; i = 1, \ldots, M\}$ reflect the importance of the respective features. For example, if the second feature is twice as important as the first feature, it is appropriate to set

$$\mathbf{M} = \begin{bmatrix} 1 & 0 \\ 0 & 2 \end{bmatrix}.$$

- **Mutually correlated features.** For many practical applications, it is common to assume inter-feature dependence. In this case, it is necessary to adopt a non-diagonal Mahalanobis matrix. For example, with

$$\mathbf{M} = \begin{bmatrix} 1 & 0.5 \\ 0.5 & 2 \end{bmatrix},$$

the nonzero off-diagonal elements reflect inter-feature dependence/correlation.

The Mahalanobis inner product naturally leads to the following *Mahalanobis distance* between $\mathbf{x}$ and $\mathbf{x}'$:

$$||[\mathbf{x} - \mathbf{x}']||_{\mathbf{M}} \equiv \sqrt{[\mathbf{x} - \mathbf{x}']^{\mathrm{T}}\mathbf{M}[\mathbf{x} - \mathbf{x}']}. \tag{1.43}$$

Example 1.6 *Given a pair of two-dimensional vectors,* $\mathbf{x} = [1\ 0]^{\mathrm{T}}$ *and* $\mathbf{x}' = [0\ 1]^{\mathrm{T}}$, *their Euclidean distance is*

$$\textit{Euclidean distance} = \sqrt{\mathbf{x}^{\mathrm{T}}\mathbf{x} + \mathbf{x}'^{\mathrm{T}}\mathbf{x}' - 2\mathbf{x}^{\mathrm{T}}\mathbf{x}'} = \sqrt{1 + 1 - 2 \times 0} = \sqrt{2}.$$

However, when the features are known to be mutually dependent, the definition of the corresponding distance metric should take such dependence into account. For example, in a two-dimensional vector space, if

$$\mathbf{M} = \begin{bmatrix} 2 & 1 \\ 1 & 4 \end{bmatrix},$$

then the Mahalanobis distance between $\mathbf{x}$ *and* $\mathbf{x}'$ *is now defined to be*

$$\sqrt{[\mathbf{x} - \mathbf{x}']^{\mathrm{T}}\mathbf{M}[\mathbf{x} - \mathbf{x}']} = \sqrt{\mathbf{x}^{\mathrm{T}}\mathbf{M}\mathbf{x} + \mathbf{x}'^{\mathrm{T}}\mathbf{M}\mathbf{x}' - 2\mathbf{x}^{\mathrm{T}}\mathbf{M}\mathbf{x}'} \tag{1.44}$$

$$= \sqrt{2 + 4 - 2 \times 1} = 2. \tag{1.45}$$

1.6.2 Nonlinear inner product: Mercer kernel functions

Since linear inner products are often inadequate to handle complex or big data analysis, one must adopt an inner product expressed by nonlinear kernel functions:

$$\langle \mathbf{x}, \mathbf{x}' \rangle = K(\mathbf{x}, \mathbf{x}').$$

The purpose is to achieve a greater flexibility in learning and prediction capabilities. Two prominent kernel functions are as follows.

(i) A Gaussian function of the Euclidean distance between $\mathbf{x}$ and $\mathbf{x}'$ is

$$K(\mathbf{x}, \mathbf{x}') = \exp\left\{-\frac{\|\mathbf{x} - \mathbf{x}'\|^2}{2\sigma^2}\right\}, \tag{1.46}$$

for a pre-specified standard deviation σ. It represents the statistical similarity/ambiguity between the two vectors. In other words, under Gaussian distribution, this function reflects the likelihood that a vector $\mathbf{x}$ may be mistaken for another vector $\mathbf{x}'$.

(ii) A polynomial function of the Euclidean inner product of the two vectors:

$$K(\mathbf{x}, \mathbf{x}') = \left(1 + \frac{\mathbf{x} \cdot \mathbf{x}'}{\sigma^2}\right)^p, \tag{1.47}$$

where p is a positive integer, for a pre-specified normalization parameter σ.

The Mercer condition assures that there is a Hilbert vector space, endowed with a Euclidean-like distance metric – a property that is vital for many learning models [42, 43, 175].

According to Mercer's theorem, see Theorem 2.1, a Mercer kernel is a function that can be decomposed into

$$K(\mathbf{x}, \mathbf{x}') = \sum_{k=1}^{J} \phi^{(k)}(\mathbf{x})\phi^{(k)}(\mathbf{x}'), \tag{1.48}$$

for a certain set of basis functions $\{\phi^{(k)}(\mathbf{x}), k = 1, 2, \ldots, J\}$, where J may be finite or indefinite. In vector notation, a Mercer kernel can be expressed in an inner-product format:

$$K(\mathbf{x}, \mathbf{x}') = \vec{\phi}(\mathbf{x})^{\mathrm{T}}\vec{\phi}(\mathbf{x}'), \tag{1.49}$$

where

$$\vec{\phi}(\mathbf{x}) = [\phi^{(1)}(\mathbf{x}) \;\; \phi^{(2)}(\mathbf{x}) \;\; \ldots \;\; \phi^{(J)}(\mathbf{x})]^{\mathrm{T}}. \tag{1.50}$$

This induces the reproducing kernel Hilbert spaces (RKHSs) [8, 126, 284] for which the basis functions $\{\phi^{(k)}(\mathbf{x}), k = 1, 2, \ldots\}$ serve as the bases. In other words, any vector in the original space $\mathcal{O} = \mathbb{R}^M$ may be mapped to a reproducing kernel vector space via the following nonlinear mapping:

$$\mathbf{x} \to \vec{\phi}(\mathbf{x}).$$

As such, the new inner product is represented by the Euclidean inner product in the new feature space of dimension J, which may be either finite or indefinite. Moreover, it adopts the following kernel-induced *distance metric* between $\mathbf{x}$ and $\mathbf{x}'$:

$$\begin{aligned}&\sqrt{K(\mathbf{x}, \mathbf{x}) + K(\mathbf{x}', \mathbf{x}') - 2K(\mathbf{x}, \mathbf{x}')}\\ &= \sqrt{||\vec{\phi}(\mathbf{x})||^2 + ||\vec{\phi}(\mathbf{x}')||^2 - 2\vec{\phi}(\mathbf{x})^{\mathrm{T}}\vec{\phi}(\mathbf{x}')}.\end{aligned}$$

Applications to unsupervised clustering and visualization

The introduction of kernel-induced vector spaces may facilitate visualization of the distribution of complex data patterns. As depicted in Figure 1.7(a), three ring-shaped clusters are highly non-separable in the original space. In hunting for a greater separability between the three clusters, a nonlinear Gaussian kernel is adopted and the original vectors are mapped to their kernel-induced representations, resulting in the three separable cluster structures exhibited in Figure 1.7(b).

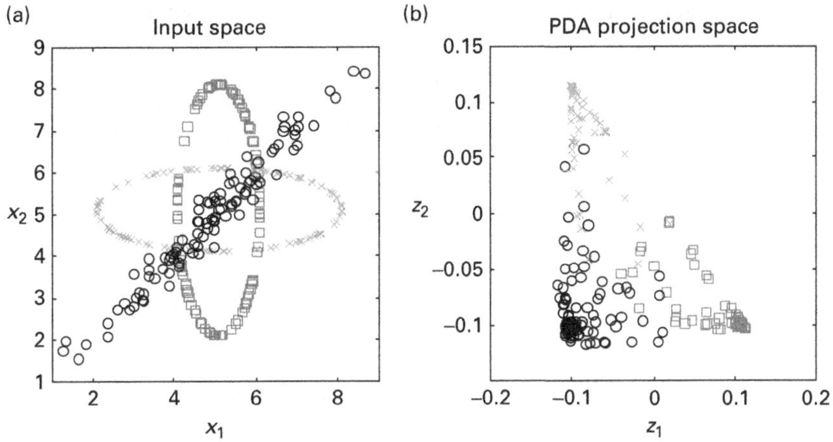

Fig. 1.7. Effect of kernel-induced mapping exemplified by a dataset consisting of three rings. (a) Visualization via PCA in the original space. (b) Visualization via kernel PCA (using Gaussian kernel) with supervised learning. (Courtesy of M.W. Mak.)

Applications to supervised classification

The introduction of kernel-induced vector spaces may play a vital role in the derivation of nonlinear boundaries for successful classification of complex data patterns. This may be illustrated by the following numerical example.

Example 1.7 (Kernel method facilitates derivation of nonlinear decision boundaries) *Consider a supervised training dataset* $[\mathcal{X}, \mathcal{Y}]$, *with* $M = 2$ *and* $N = 8$*:*

$$\mathbf{X} = \begin{bmatrix} +1 & +1 & -1 & -1 & +1 & 0 & -1 & 0 \\ +1 & -1 & -1 & +1 & 0 & -1 & 0 & +1 \end{bmatrix}$$

and

$$\mathbf{y} = \begin{bmatrix} +1 & +1 & +1 & +1 & -1 & -1 & -1 & -1 \end{bmatrix}.$$

The training data are not linearly separable in the original space. However, if the kernel function is particularly chosen to be

$$K(\mathbf{x}, \mathbf{x}') = x^{(1)^2} x'^{(1)^2} + x^{(2)^2} x'^{(2)^2}, \tag{1.51}$$

then the kernel-induced intrinsic space will be represented by

$$\vec{\boldsymbol{\phi}}(\mathbf{x}) = \begin{bmatrix} x^{(1)^2} \\ x^{(2)^2} \end{bmatrix}.$$

Let $\mathbf{u} = [1 \quad 1]^{\mathrm{T}}$, *then*

$$\mathbf{u}^{\mathrm{T}} \vec{\boldsymbol{\phi}}(\mathbf{x}_i) - 3 = y_i, \; i = 1, 2, \ldots, 8.$$

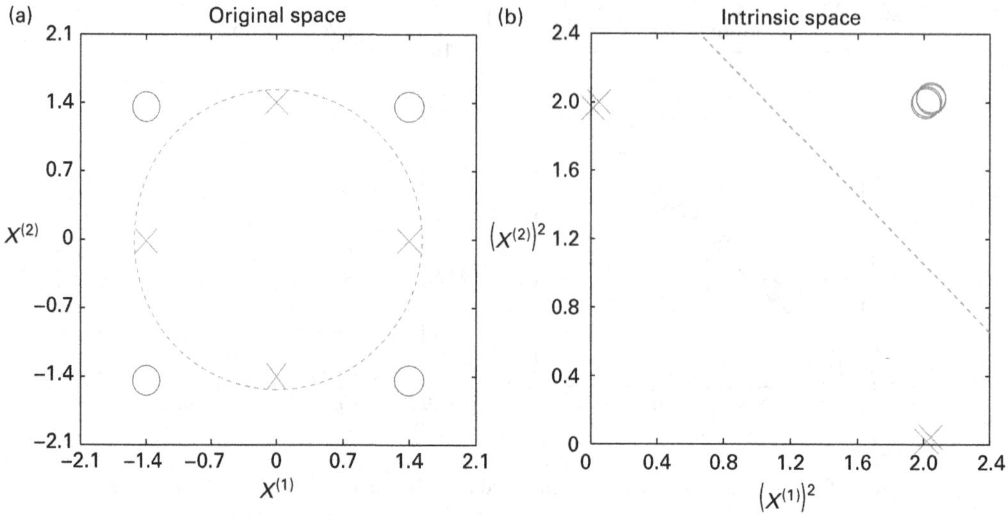

Fig. 1.8. A linear decision boundary in the intrinsic space may correspond to a nonlinear decision boundary after being re-mapped back to the original vector space. (a) The training dataset in the original space with the nonlinear decision boundary shown as a dashed circle. (b) The training dataset in the intrinsic space separable by a linear decision boundary shown as a dashed line.

This means that the training data will be linearly separable in the intrinsic space with an optimal decision boundary:

$$f(\mathbf{x}) = \mathbf{u}^{\mathrm{T}} \overrightarrow{\phi}(\mathbf{x}) - 3 = \left(x^{(1)}\right)^2 + \left(x^{(2)}\right)^2 - 3 = 0.$$

It is worth noting that, although the decision boundary is linear in the intrinsic space, see Figure 1.8(b), it corresponds to a nonlinear decision boundary when re-mapped back to the original vector space, see Figure 1.8(a).

1.6.3 Effective implementation of kernel methods

The kernel-based learning models may be based on either of the following two representations.

- **Intrinsic-space representation.** This approach is conceptually simpler and more straightforward to explain. It involves a full process with explicit feature mapping to the intrinsic space. The learning model will treat the intrinsic dataset just as if it were the original dataset. In other words, there will be no need for any new algorithms.
- **Empirical-space representation.** The LSP condition assures the existence of the kernelized learning models defined in the kernel-induced empirical space. For many application scenarios, the kernelized formulation is often simpler than its intrinsic counterpart.

Implementation cost comparison of two spaces

Just imagine that we are offered by an airliner a choice of paying for the luggage-shipping either (1) by the total weight or (2) by the total number of pieces. The obvious choice will be whichever comes with the lower final cost. The selection between the two kernel approaches is very much the same idea. With the LSP condition, both intrinsic-space and kernelized learning models will be available at our disposal. It is now beneficial to note that the cost for the intrinsic-space approach is dominated by the intrinsic degree J while that for the empirical approach is dominated by the empirical degree N. Evidently, for an effective implementation, the one with the lower cost should be adopted.

Section 2.4.3 will provide a full exploration of both kernel approaches. The corresponding procedures both in the training phase and in the testing phase will also be further elaborated upon.

1.7 Performance metrics

Numerous metrics have been proposed to evaluate the performance of machine learning models. For ease of discussion, let us first introduce a hypothetical accuracy table summarizing the key statistics of a fictitious HIV study concerning 40 samples in the test set:

	True	False
$N = 15$	TN = 10	FP = 5
$P = 25$	TP = 12	FN = 13

Here, $P = 15$ and $N = 25$ respectively denote the numbers of positive and negative cases in the test set, meaning that 40% and 60% of the test samples are actually negative and positive, respectively. (The total number of samples is $40 = N + P = 15 + 25$.)

Let TN, TP, FN, and FP denote "true negatives," "true positives," "false negatives," and "false positives," respectively. The first row of the table above shows that $N = 15 = \text{TN} + \text{FP} = 10 + 5$. Likewise, the second row of the table shows that $P = 25 = \text{TP} + \text{FN} = 12 + 13$.

1.7.1 Accuracy and error rate

Two common performance metrics are the *error rate* and the *classification accuracy*.

- The *error rate* is the ratio of misclassified cases among all the tests conducted:

$$\text{Error Rate} = \frac{\text{Errors}}{\text{Total}} = \frac{\text{FP} + \text{FN}}{P + N}.$$

In the HIV table, there are two types of misclassifications. There are in total $18 = 5 + 13$ errors, including 5 negatives being identified as positive by mistake and

13 positives failing to be identified. This translates into an error rate of $(13+5)/(25+15) = 45\%$.

- The **classification accuracy** is

$$\text{Accuracy} = 1 - \text{Error Rate} = \frac{\text{TP} + \text{TN}}{P+N}. \tag{1.52}$$

In the HIV table, the classification accuracy is $1 - 45\% = 55\%$.

The accuracy alone can hardly reveal a full picture of performance, especially when there is a population imbalance between the positives and negatives. For example, if $P \ll N$, then both P and TP will be relatively small; thus

$$\text{Accuracy} = \frac{\text{TP} + \text{TN}}{P+N} \approx \frac{\text{TN}}{N}.$$

In this case, an arbitrarily high accuracy can be artificially created by increasing the acceptance threshold so as to artificially attain a large number of putative negative cases, yielding in turn a high TN and, consequently, a high accuracy. However, such a high accuracy has no practical meaning by itself.

1.7.2 Sensitivity, specificity, and precision

A performance metric is practically useful only when the costs both of false-positives and of errors are jointly taken into account. In practice, there often exists a significant disparity between the two types of costs, compelling us to consider more than one metric simultaneously. Three key performance metrics are specificity, sensitivity, and precision.

- **Specificity.** The false-positive rate (FPR), $\text{FPR} = \text{FP}/N$, is the percentage of negatives (i.e. uninfected persons) that are detected as positives (i.e. those with the infection). Likewise, the true-negative rate (TNR) is

$$\text{TNR} = \frac{\text{TN}}{N} = \frac{\text{TN}}{\text{FP} + \text{TN}} = 1 - \frac{\text{FP}}{N} = 1 - \text{FPR}, \tag{1.53}$$

which reflects the ability to correctly classify negative samples. In fact, the true-negative rate (TNR) is often known as the *specificity*. More precisely,

$$\text{Specificity} = \text{TNR} = \frac{\text{TN}}{N}. \tag{1.54}$$

A perfect specificity implies that no uninfected person may be erroneously identified as infected. In our hypothetical HIV table, 10 (TN) out of 15 (N) are predicted to be negative, so the specificity of the test is merely 67%. Equivalently, $\text{FPR} = 5/(10+5) = 33\%$, because 5 of the 15 negative cases are identified by mistake.

- **Sensitivity.** The false-negative rate, or miss probability, is the percentage of positive cases falsely missed by the test: $\text{FNR} = \text{FN}/P$. Likewise, the true-positive rate (TPR) is

$$\text{TPR} = \frac{\text{TP}}{P} = \frac{\text{TP}}{\text{TP} + \text{FN}} = 1 - \text{FNR}, \tag{1.55}$$

which indicates the capability to correctly classify positive cases. The TPR is also known as the *sensitivity*. More precisely,

$$\text{Sensitivity} = \text{TPR} = \frac{\text{TP}}{P}. \tag{1.56}$$

A perfect sensitivity implies that every HIV-positive patient will be successfully identified. In the HIV table, only 12 (TP) out of 25 (P) HIV-positive cases are successfully identified, so the sensitivity is merely 48%. In other words, FNR $= 13/(12 + 13) =$ 52%, because 13 of the 25 positive cases are missed by the test.

- **Precision.** The false-discovery rate (FDR) is defined as

$$\text{FDR} = \frac{\text{FP}}{\text{TP} + \text{FP}}.$$

The FDR is closely related to a notion called *precision*, which is defined as the ratio between the truly and putatively positive samples:

$$\text{Precision} = \frac{\text{TP}}{\text{TP} + \text{FP}} = 1 - \text{FDR}.$$

In the HIV table, the precision is 60%, because 12 among the 20 positively identified cases are true positives.

1.7.3 The receiver operating characteristic (ROC)

The tradeoff between specificity and sensitivity depends closely on how the decision threshold is set. The higher the acceptance threshold, the higher the specificity and the lower the sensitivity. Conversely, the lower the acceptance threshold, the lower the specificity and the higher the sensitivity. Mathematically, it is easy to show that

$$\min\left\{\frac{\text{TP}}{P}, \frac{\text{TN}}{N}\right\} \le \frac{\text{TP} + \text{TN}}{P + N} \le \max\left\{\frac{\text{TP}}{P}, \frac{\text{TN}}{N}\right\}. \tag{1.57}$$

So the *accuracy* always lies in between the *sensitivity* and the *specificity*. For the HIV example, the classification accuracy 55% is between the sensitivity (48%) and the specificity (66.66%).

Since the *accuracy* is a weighted average of the *sensitivity* and the *specificity*, if the *sensitivity* is much higher than the *accuracy*, then the *specificity* has to fall much below the *accuracy*. On the other hand, the *specificity* can be improved at the expense of a reduced *sensitivity*. The tradeoff between the specificity and the sensitivity can best be described by means of a receiver operating characteristic (ROC), which is defined as a curve comprising sensitivity and specificity for the entire range of the acceptance threshold. One such ROC curve is exemplified in Figure 1.9(a).

Conversion between ROCs

Suppose that the ratio of the total numbers of negative and positive samples is known in advance and denoted as $r = N/P$. In this case, the sensitivity (denoted as s), precision (denoted as ρ), and specificity (denoted as σ) are related as follows:

$$\rho = \frac{s}{s + r(1 - \sigma)}. \tag{1.58}$$

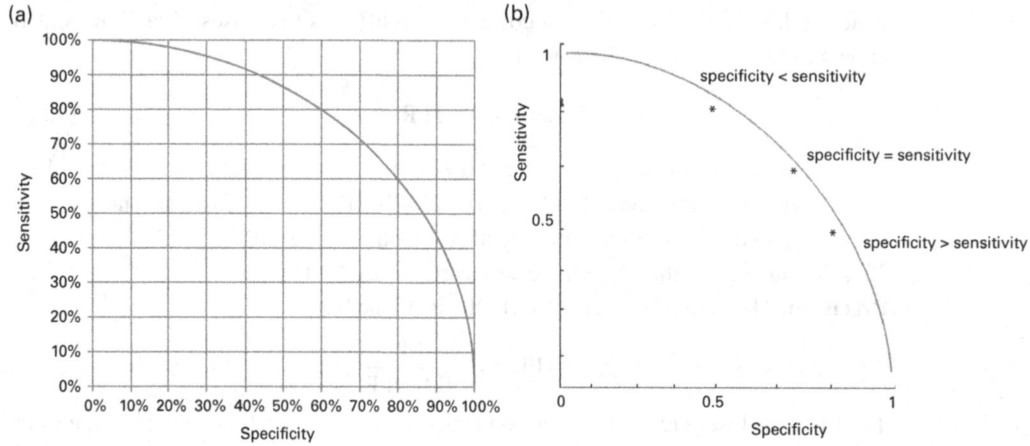

Fig. 1.9. (a) An example ROC: sensitivity versus specificity. (b) Three operating conditions are marked. The asterisks ($*$) show locations where the specificity is less than, equal to, and greater than the sensitivity. Note that the point where accuracy = sensitivity = specificity is at the middle.

(See Problem 1.18.) This provides a simple formula to link the precision-versus-sensitivity and specificity-versus-sensitivity ROCs. In other words, given knowledge of r, it will be straightforward to convert one ROC into the other.

Equal error rate

When the FPR and the FNR are of almost equivalent importance, it is common to adjust the decision threshold such that FPR $=$ FNR, i.e. $\mathrm{FN}/P = \mathrm{FP}/N$. This is called the *equal error rate* (EER). Under this circumstance, according to Eqs. (1.52), (1.54), and (1.56),

$$\text{accuracy} = \text{specificity} = \text{sensitivity}.$$

See Figure 1.9(b). Note also that, when the test performs well on both *specificity* and *sensitivity*, then a high accuracy can be fully guaranteed.

The area under the curve (AUC)

In addition to the EER, another single-parameter performance index is the *area under the curve* (AUC). By examining ROCs closely, as with Figure 1.9, it should be evident that the larger the AUC the better the performance. Moreover, the AUC reaches 1.0 only when a perfect performance is attained. (See Problem 1.16.)

Hypothesis and significance tests

There exist numerous useful hypothesis tests and validation techniques. The reader is referred to Appendix A for more discussion.

1.8 Highlights of chapters

The book aims at establishing theoretical foundations for kernel-based learning methods. It covers statistical and algebraic theories essential to kernel-based analysis, develops kernel-based learning models (both unsupervised and supervised), and explores a broad spectrum of application domains of machine learning in multimedia and biomedical problems.

The book is systematically organized into eight distinctive and yet related parts, highlighted as follows.

(i) **Part I: Machine learning and kernel vector spaces.** Chapter 1 provides an overview of the broad spectrum of applications and problem formulations for kernel-based unsupervised and supervised learning methods. In order to provide a more effective similarity metric of any pair of objects, the kernel approach replaces the traditional Euclidean inner product by more sophisticated and kernel-induced inner products associated with the corresponding kernel-induced vector spaces. Two such most useful spaces are the (primal) intrinsic and (dual) empirical spaces. The interplay between the formulations of learning models in the primal/dual spaces plays a key role both in the theoretical analysis and in the practical implementation of kernel methods.

Chapter 2 starts with the vital Theorem 2.1, which states that the use of the Mercer kernel function will be imperative for the existence of the kernel-induced Hilbert vector spaces. For vectorial data analysis, at the first stage, the original vector space can be mapped to the kernel-induced intrinsic vector space. Hence, every individual object is represented by a (possibly high-dimensional) feature vector in intrinsic space. The intrinsic-space approach is conceptually simpler because, once the mapping has been done, the rest of the mathematical and/or algorithmic developments can just follow exactly what was used in the conventional learning models.

Kernelization, better known as the kernel trick, refers to the process of converting an optimizer in the intrinsic space into one formulated in the empirical space. A vital condition for kernelizability of a learning model is the LSP condition. Theorem 1.1 characterizes the optimization formulation which satisfies the LSP condition. With kernelized learning models, all we need is to have the pairwise relationship clearly defined, making it amenable to both vectorial and nonvectorial data analyses. This is why it is actually much more popular than its counterpart in the intrinsic space.

(ii) **Part II: Dimension-reduction: PCA/KPCA and feature selection.** This part contains two chapters concerning reduction of the dimensionality of the feature space. Chapter 3 covers the most prominent subspace projection approach, namely the classical *principal component analysis* (PCA)indexsubspace projection methods!principal component analysis (PCA). The optimal error and entropy attainable by PCA are given in a closed-form formula. When a nonlinear kernel is adopted, it further extends to the kernel-PCA (KPCA) learning model. Chapter 4 explores various aspects of feature selection methods for supervised and unsupervised learning scenarios. It presents several filtering-based and wrapper-based methods for feature selection.

(iii) **Part III: Unsupervised learning models for cluster analysis.** Unsupervised cluster discovery is instrumental for data analysis in many important applications. It involves a process of partitioning training datasets into disjoint groups. The performance of cluster discovery depends on several key factors, including the number of clusters, the topology of node vectors, the objective function for clustering, iterative learning algorithms (often with multiple initial conditions), and, finally, the evaluation criterion for picking the best result among multiple trials. This part contains two chapters: Chapter 5 covers unsupervised learning models that are based on the conventional Euclidean metric for vectorial data analysis while Chapter 6 focuses on the use of kernel-induced metrics as well as kernelized learning models, which may be equally applied to nonvectorial data analysis. For example, kernel K-means may be applied to network segmentation of large-scale networks, where the use of sparsity will be vital for computational feasibility.

(iv) **Part IV: Kernel ridge regressors and variants.** This part contains three chapters, covering learning models that are closely related to the kernel ridge regressor (KRR).

Chapter 7 discusses applications of the KRR to regularization and approximation problems. If a Gaussian RBF kernel is adopted, the KRR learning model can be shown to be intimately related to several prominent regularization models. The chapter also shows that, if the LSP condition is satisfied, then some multi-kernel problems effectively warrant a mono-kernel solution.

Chapter 8 covers a broad spectrum of conventional linear classification techniques. The chapter establishes their mathematical relationship with respect to the *ridge regression* (RR).

Chapter 9 extends the linear classification to kernel methods for nonlinear classifiers that are closely related to the KRR. The robustness analysis of the KRR model would be best conducted in the *spectral space* because the spectral components are mutually orthogonal, and, consequently, the perturbation effect on each of the components can be isolated componentwise to facilitate individual sensitivity analysis. It can be shown that ridge regularization tends to redistribute the weight so as to suppress the weaker (i.e. more sensitive) components more and thus, relatively speaking, enhance the stronger (i.e. more resilient) components. Consequently, the regularization can effectively alleviate over-fitting problems, thus improving the generalization capability of the learned models.

According to the KRR's weight–error curve (WEC), there is a linear relationship between the error and weight, implying that the greater the error the higher the weight. This problem is rectified by the somewhat *ad hoc* pruned-PDA (PPDA) algorithm, described in Algorithm 9.2, where the anti-support vectors are removed from the future learning process so as to circumvent their detrimental effect and improve the performance.

Chapter 9 also extends the binary classification formulation to multi-class, and, moreover, to multi-label, classification formulations. Finally, it explores several trace-norm optimization formulations for subspace projection designed for class discrimination. DCA and SODA are presented, both of which may be viewed as hybrid learning models of PCA and FDA.

(v) **Part V: Support vector machines and variants.** This part contains three chapters, namely chapters 10, 11, and 12, all closely related to the subject of support vector machines (SVMs).

Chapter 10 focuses on the basic SVM learning theory, which lies in the identification of a set of "support vectors" via the well-known Karush–Kuhn–Tucker (KKT) condition. The "support vectors" are solely responsible for the formation of the decision boundary. The LSP is obviously valid for SVM learning models, and the kernelized SVM learning models (cf. Algorithm 10.1) have exactly the same form for linear and nonlinear problems.

Chapter 11 covers support-vector-based learning models aiming at outlier detection. The technique of support vector regression (SVR), see Algorithm 11.1, aims at finding an approximating function to fit the training data under the guidance of teacher values. The chapter explores, in addition, several SVM-based learning models for outlier detection, including hyperplane-OCSVM (Algorithm 11.2), hypersphere OCSVM (Algorithm 11.3), and SVC. For Gaussian kernels, it can be shown that all of these three algorithms coincide with each other and, moreover, the fraction of outliers can be analytically estimated.

Chapter 12 introduces the notion of the weight–error curve (WEC) for characterization of kernelized supervised learning models, including KDA, KRR, SVM, and Ridge-SVM. Given a learned model, each training vector is endowed with two parameters: weight and error. These parameters collectively form the so-called WEC. The WEC analysis leads to a hybrid classifier, named the Ridge-SVM, which is endowed with an array of design parameters, and, consequently, it covers many existing classifiers as special cases, including KDA, KRR, and SVM. With properly adjusted parameters, the Ridge-SVM is promising for learning robust classifiers with improved generalization capability.

(vi) **Part VI: Kernel methods for green machine learning technologies.** The traditional curse of dimensionality is often focused on the extreme dimensionality of the feature space, i.e. M. However, for kernelized learning models, the concern is naturally shifted to the extreme dimensionality of the kernel matrix, N, which is dictated by the size of the training dataset. For example, in some biomedical applications, the sizes may be hundreds of thousands. In social media and big data applications, the sizes could be easily on the order of millions. This creates a new large-scale learning paradigm that calls for a new level of computational tools, both in hardware and in software.

Chapter 13 explores cost-effective design of kernel-based machine learning and classification. The chapter also develops time-adaptive KRR learning models that are critical for applications to time-series analysis. The recursive algorithms for time-adaptive KRR learning models may be derived from either deterministic or statistical formulations.

(vii) **Part VII: Kernel methods for statistical estimation theory.** Linear prediction and system identification has been a well-established field in information sciences. On the other hand, kernel methods have become popular in the past two decades, thus having a relatively short history. It is vital to establish a theoretical foundation linking kernel methods and the rich theory in estimation, prediction, and system identification. This part contains two chapters addressing this important issue.

Chapter 14 focuses on a statistical analysis that is based on knowledge of the (joint) density functions of all the input and output variables and their respective noises.

Chapter 15 focuses on estimation, prediction, and system identification starting from the observed samples and prior knowledge of the first- and second-order statistics of the system parameters.

(viii) **Part VIII: Appendices.** Appendix A reviews useful validation techniques and test schemes for learning models. Appendix B covers supervised classifiers without an explicit learning process and the popular and fundamental Bayes classifiers.

1.9 Problems

Problem 1.1 (Rank and span) *You are given a data matrix*

$$\mathbf{X} = \begin{bmatrix} 1 & 0.5 & 2 \\ 0.5 & 2 & 0 \\ 1 & 1 & 1 \\ 1 & 0 & 1 \\ 0 & 0 & 1 \end{bmatrix}.$$

(a) *What is the rank of* $\mathbf{X}$*?*

(b) *What is the (column) span of* $\mathbf{X}$*?*

Problem 1.2 (Mahalanobis inner product) *If we choose a special Mahalanobis inner product with*

$$\mathbf{M} = \begin{bmatrix} 2 & 0 \\ 0 & 4 \end{bmatrix},$$

it has a simple interpretation, namely that the second feature is twice as important as the first feature. Can you provide a simple interpretation if

$$\mathbf{M} = \begin{bmatrix} 2 & 1 \\ 1 & 4 \end{bmatrix}?$$

Problem 1.3 (Clustering of three vectors) *Consider the following two closeness criteria for a pair of vectors.*

- *Euclidean inner product: the greater the inner product the closer the pair.*
- *Euclidean distance: the shorter the distance the closer the pair.*

(a) *Consider the dataset*

$$\begin{bmatrix} 0.1 \\ 0 \end{bmatrix}, \begin{bmatrix} 1 \\ 0 \end{bmatrix}, \begin{bmatrix} 0 \\ 2 \end{bmatrix},$$

Find the closest pair for each of the two closeness criteria. Show that the two different criteria result in the same closest pair.

(b) *Repeat the same problem for a new dataset:*

$$\begin{bmatrix} 0 \\ 0.1 \end{bmatrix}, \begin{bmatrix} 1 \\ 0 \end{bmatrix}, \begin{bmatrix} 0 \\ 2 \end{bmatrix},$$

Show that, in this case, the two metrics have different closest pairs.

Problem 1.4 (Cosine function as kernel function) *Suppose that the kernel function between* $\mathbf{x}$ *and* $\mathbf{x}'$ *is defined as*

$$\cos(\theta_{\mathbf{x},\mathbf{x}'}) \equiv \frac{\langle \mathbf{x}, \mathbf{x}' \rangle}{\langle \mathbf{x}, \mathbf{x}' \rangle^{1/2} \langle \mathbf{x}', \mathbf{x}' \rangle^{1/2}}, \tag{1.59}$$

where $\theta_{\mathbf{x},\mathbf{x}'}$ *denotes the angle between the vectors* $\mathbf{x}$ *and* $\mathbf{x}'$.

(a) *Does the Mercer condition hold if the cosine function (Eq. (1.59)) is used as the inner product?*

(b) *Do the distance axioms hold for the distance metric induced by this inner product?*

Problem 1.5 *Given a training dataset of four vectors:*

$$\begin{bmatrix} 0 \\ 0 \end{bmatrix}, \begin{bmatrix} 1 \\ 0 \end{bmatrix}, \begin{bmatrix} 0 \\ 2 \end{bmatrix}, \begin{bmatrix} -1 \\ -1 \end{bmatrix}, \begin{bmatrix} +1 \\ +1 \end{bmatrix}.$$

Find the most similar pair of vectors, based on

(a) *the similarity induced from a Gaussian kernel function (Eq. (1.46));*

(b) *the similarity induced from a polynomial kernel function (Eq. (1.47)); and*

(c) *the similarity induced from* $\cos(\theta_{\mathbf{x},\mathbf{x}'})$ *defined in Problem 1.4.*

Problem 1.6 *Assume that* $\sum_{n=1}^{N} \mathbf{x}_n = \mathbf{0}$ *and* $\sum_{n=1}^{N} y_n = 0$*, and that the learning objective is to minimize the least-squared error (LSE)*

$$E(\mathcal{X}, \mathbf{w}) = \sum_{n=1}^{N} (f(\mathbf{x}) - y_n)^2 = \sum_{n=1}^{N} \left(\mathbf{x}_n^{\mathrm{T}}\mathbf{w} + b - y_n\right)^2. \tag{1.60}$$

Show that the threshold value $b = 0$ *for the optimal discriminant function* $f(\mathbf{x}) = \mathbf{x}^{\mathrm{T}}\mathbf{w} + b$.

Hint: *Zero the first-order derivative of* $E(\mathcal{X}, \mathbf{w})$ *with respect to* b.

Problem 1.7 (Supervised learning: square and invertible matrix) *You are given a* 3×3 *training data matrix and the corresponding teacher vector:*

$$\mathbf{X} = \begin{bmatrix} 1 & 1 & 0 \\ 0 & 1 & 1 \\ 0 & 0 & 1 \end{bmatrix} \quad \text{and} \quad \mathbf{y} = \begin{bmatrix} +1 \\ +1 \\ -1 \end{bmatrix}.$$

(a) *Find a valid solution for the decision vector by simply solving for the given linear system of equations prescribed by* $\mathbf{X}^{\mathrm{T}}\mathbf{w} = \mathbf{y}$.

(b) *What is the width of the separation zone?*

Problem 1.8 (Supervised learning: over-determined system) *Consider an over-determined linear system of equations* $\mathbf{X}^{\mathrm{T}}\mathbf{w} = \mathbf{y}$*, with* $N = 4$ *and* $M = 3$

$$\mathbf{X} = \begin{bmatrix} 1 & 1 & -2 & 0 \\ -2 & 2 & 0 & 0 \\ 1 & 0 & 1 & -2 \end{bmatrix} \quad \text{and} \quad \mathbf{y} = \begin{bmatrix} +1 \\ +1 \\ -1 \\ -1 \end{bmatrix}.$$

Show that the optimal LSE solution for the decision vector $\mathbf{w}$ *can be obtained as follows:*

$$\mathbf{w} = (\mathbf{X}\mathbf{X}^{\mathrm{T}})^{-1}\mathbf{X}\mathbf{y}.$$

Find the optimal decision vector using this formulation.

Problem 1.9 (Supervised learning: under-determined system) *Study and compare the following two under-determined supervised datasets with* $N = 2$ *and* $M = 3$.

(a) *Consider the first under-determined supervised dataset:*

$$\mathbf{X} = \begin{bmatrix} 0.5 & -0.5 \\ -2 & 2 \\ 1 & -1 \end{bmatrix} \quad \text{and} \quad \mathbf{y} = \begin{bmatrix} +1 \\ -1 \end{bmatrix}.$$

The objective is to find an optimal decision vector $\mathbf{w}$ *that can create a maximal margin of separation. Show that the optimal linear discriminant function for this dataset can be simply expressed as* $f(\mathbf{x}) = \mathbf{w}^{\mathrm{T}}\mathbf{x}$*, with the optimal decision vector*

$$\mathbf{w} = \mathbf{X}(\mathbf{X}^{\mathrm{T}}\mathbf{X})^{-1}\mathbf{y}.$$

Find the optimal decision vector using this formulation. Does the solution satisfy the LSP condition, i.e. is it true that $\mathbf{w} \in \mathtt{span}[\mathbf{X}]$*?*

(b) *Now consider a second supervised dataset:*

$$\mathbf{X} = \begin{bmatrix} 0.5 & -0.5 \\ -2 & 2 \\ 1 & -1 \end{bmatrix} \text{ and } \mathbf{y} = \begin{bmatrix} +2 \\ -1 \end{bmatrix}.$$

Show that now the optimal discriminant function requires a more general expression: $f(\mathbf{x}) = \mathbf{w}^{\mathrm{T}}\mathbf{x} + b$*. Compute the optimal solution. Does the solution satisfy the LSP condition?*

Problem 1.10 (Feature representation in kernel-based intrinsic space) *The XOR dataset comprises four training vectors:*

$$\mathbf{x}_1 = \begin{bmatrix} +1 \\ +1 \end{bmatrix}, \quad \mathbf{x}_2 = \begin{bmatrix} -1 \\ -1 \end{bmatrix}, \quad \mathbf{x}_3 = \begin{bmatrix} +1 \\ -1 \end{bmatrix}, \quad \mathbf{x}_4 = \begin{bmatrix} -1 \\ +1 \end{bmatrix}.$$

For a second-order polynomial kernel function $K(\mathbf{x}, \mathbf{x}') = \left(1 + \mathbf{x} \cdot \mathbf{x}'\right)^2$*.*

(a) *What is the intrinsic degree* J*?*
(b) *Find the representative vectors in the intrinsic space for the four vectors.*
(c) *What are the pairwise distances of the training vectors in the original space?*
(d) *What are the pairwise distances in the intrinsic space?*

Problem 1.11 *Show that, for any kernel function, the number of independent basis functions for the empirical space can be no higher than* $\min\{J, N\}$*. This means that the true degree of freedom associated with a kernel-induced vector space is (generically) equal to* $\min\{J, N\}$*, i.e. the rank of the kernel matrix will be* $\min\{J, N\}$*.*

Problem 1.12 (LSP and kernelization of ℓ_2- and ℓ_1-norm optimization problems) *Consider the same (under-determined) supervised training dataset given in Example 1.3.*

(a) *Show that, for an* ℓ_2*-norm-based cost function*

$$\underset{\mathbf{w}\in\mathbb{R}^M}{\text{minimize}} \|\mathbf{w}\|^2 \quad \textit{subject to} \quad \mathbf{w}^{\mathrm{T}}\mathbf{x}_i - y_i = 0, \; i = 1, 2, \tag{1.61}$$

the optimal solution is $\mathbf{w} = [\frac{1}{5}\ \frac{2}{5}\ 1]^{\mathrm{T}}$*. Verify that the solution falls within the learning subspace. Kernelize the problem, in terms of the linear kernel, and solve the problem in the kernel domain. Show that the solution is the same as that derived from the original optimization formulation.*

(b) *Show that, for an optimizer with* ℓ_1*-norm cost function [268]*

$$\min_{\mathbf{w}\in\mathbb{R}^M} \|\mathbf{w}\|_1 \quad \textit{subject to} \quad \mathbf{w}^{\mathrm{T}}\mathbf{x}_i - y_i = 0, \; i = 1, 2, \tag{1.62}$$

the optimal solution is $\mathbf{w} = [0\ \frac{1}{2}\ 1]^{\mathrm{T}}$*. Verify that this solution no longer falls within the learning subspace.*

Why is it impossible to kernelize the problem?

Problem 1.13 (Learning subspace property of ℓ_2-norm elastic mesh) *Show that the cost function in Eq. (1.21) for a one-dimensional elastic grid may be naturally extended to a modified cost function that is valid for a two-dimensional elastic mesh. Prove that the LSP remains valid for the elastic mesh learning model.*

Problem 1.14 (Learning subspace property: linear versus nonlinear kernels) *Consider an supervised training dataset $[\mathcal{X}, \mathcal{Y}]$, with M and N denote the feature dimension and training data size, respectively.*

(a) *Show that, generically speaking, the span of* $\mathbf{X}$ *has a full dimension of M, for an over-determined problem (i.e. $M < N$), rendering the LSP meaningless. On the other hand, show why the LSP is a very useful property for an under-determined problem, i.e. $M > N$.*

(b) *Show why the LSP becomes a meaningful property for an over-determined problem (i.e. $M < N$) when a kernel method using a nonlinear kernel function is adopted.*

Problem 1.15 (Learning subspace property: ℓ_1-norm versus ℓ_2-norm) *Consider an (under-determined) supervised training dataset $[\mathcal{X}, \mathcal{Y}]$, with $M > N$.*

(a) *Show that an ℓ_2-norm-based optimization problem,*

$$\min_{\mathbf{w}\in\mathbb{R}^M} ||\mathbf{w}||^2 + \sum_{i=1}^{N} ||\mathbf{w}^{\mathrm{T}}\mathbf{x}_i - y_i||^2, \tag{1.63}$$

satisfies the condition for the LSP.

(b) *Show that an ℓ_1-norm-based optimization problem,*

$$\min_{\mathbf{w}\in\mathbb{R}^M} \|\mathbf{w}\|_1 + \sum_{i=1}^{N} \|\mathbf{w}^{\mathrm{T}}\mathbf{x}_i - y_i\|^2, \tag{1.64}$$

fails the condition for the LSP.

Problem 1.16 (Range of the AUC) *Show that the value of the area under the curve (AUC) has a range of* [0.5 1.0], *with* 1.0 *being perfect and* 0.5 *being poorest. More specfically, design a classification scheme, without any learning at all, which yields an AUC of* 0.5.

Problem 1.17 *The tradeoff between specificity and sensitivity depends on the specific application needs.*

(a) *Construct two specificity-versus-sensitivity ROCs satisfying the following application description: the first classifier is designed for applications emphasizing high precision, while the second classifier is for applications emphasizing high sensitivity.*

(b) *Which of the two ROCs yields a superior AUC?*

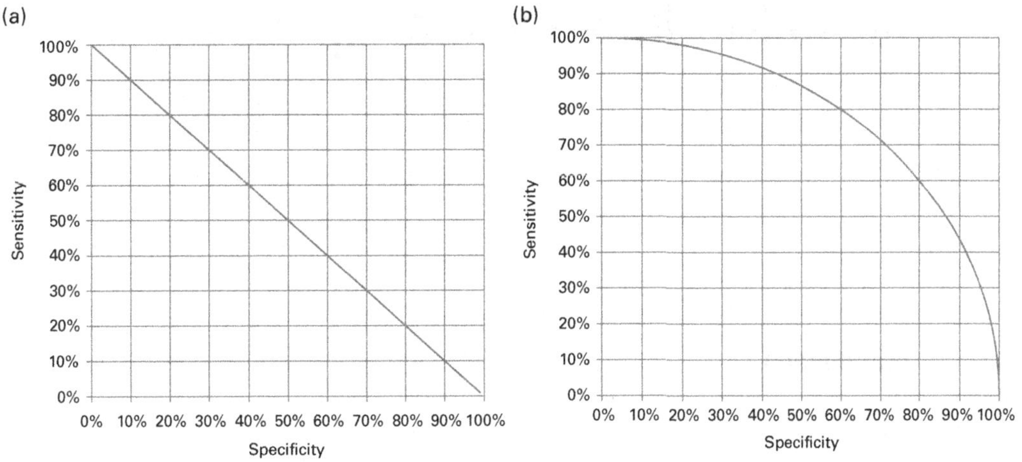

Fig. 1.10. Two ROCs for specificity versus sensitivity.

Problem 1.18 (Conversion of ROCs)
Suppose that it is known that $r = N/P = 2$.

(a) *Show that the relationship among the sensitivity, specificity, and precision may be characterized by Eq. (1.58).*
(b) *Derive the precision-versus-sensitivity ROCs from the two specificity-versus-sensitivity ROCs shown in Figure 1.10.*
(c) *Explain why a specificity-versus-precision curve is of little practical use.*

2 Kernel-induced vector spaces

2.1 Introduction

The notion of kernel-induced vector spaces is the cornerstone of kernel-based machine learning. Generalization of the traditional definition of a similarity metric plays a vital role in facilitating the analysis of complex and big data. It is often necessary to generalize the traditional Euclidean inner product to the more flexible and nonlinear inner products characterized by properly chosen kernel functions. The new inner product leads to a new distance metric, allowing the data analysis to be effectively performed in a higher-dimensional vector space. The topics addressed in this chapter are as follows.

- Section 2.2 introduces Mercer's fundamental theorem stating the necessary and sufficient condition for a function be a Mercer kernel. It will examine several prominent kernel functions, including the polynomial and Gaussian kernel functions.
- Section 2.3 introduces the notion of intrinsic space associated with a kernel function. The intrinsic space is so named because it is independent of the training dataset. The dimension of the space is denoted by J and will be referred to as the *intrinsic degree*. This degree, whether finite or infinite, dictates the training efficiency and computational cost.
- Section 2.4 introduces a finite-dimensional kernel-induced vector space, known as *empirical space*, which is jointly determined by the kernel function and the training dataset. The dimension of the empirical space is equal to the data size N. With the LSP condition, both the intrinsic-space and the kernelized learning model will be at our disposal. However, the cost for the intrinsic-space approach is dominated by the intrinsic degree J, while that for the empirical approach is dominated by the empirical degree N. Therefore, kernelized learning models may sometime offer a more cost-effective implementation. Even when the intrinsic degree J is indefinite, e.g. for Gaussian kernel functions, a kernelized learning model remains computationally feasible since it is defined over the empirical space, which always has a finite dimensionality.
- Section 2.5 demonstrates that the kernel approach allows us to go beyond the framework of vectorial representation. In the kernel approach to nonvectorial data analysis, the role of the *kernel matrix* is substituted by a *similarity matrix*. In this sense, the kernelized learning model provides a unifying platform for both vectorial and nonvectorial applications.

2.2 Mercer kernels and kernel-induced similarity metrics

This section will formally address the necessary and sufficient condition for Mercer kernels.

2.2.1 Distance axioms in metric space

Let us briefly review the three fundamental axioms on a distance metric. A set $\mathbf{X}$ is called a *metric space* if a distance metric for its elements can be defined such that

(i) for all $\mathbf{x}$ and $\mathbf{y}$, $d(\mathbf{x}, \mathbf{y}) > 0$, unless $\mathbf{x} = \mathbf{y}$, in which case $d(\mathbf{x}, \mathbf{x}) = 0$;
(ii) for all $\mathbf{x}$ and $\mathbf{y}$, $d(\mathbf{x}, \mathbf{y}) = d(\mathbf{y}, \mathbf{x})$; and
(iii) for all $\mathbf{x}$, $\mathbf{y}$, and $\mathbf{z}$, $d(\mathbf{x}, \mathbf{y}) \leq d(\mathbf{x}, \mathbf{z}) + d(\mathbf{z}, \mathbf{y})$.

In a (Hilbert) vector space, the similarity score of a pair of vectors $\mathbf{x}$ and $\mathbf{y}$ may be represented by the inner product associated with the space. Traditionally, the Euclidean inner product is adopted. Namely,

$$\langle \mathbf{x}, \mathbf{y} \rangle = \mathbf{x}^{\mathrm{T}}\mathbf{y} = \mathbf{x} \cdot \mathbf{y}.$$

Since the distance metric is dictated by the inner product, it follows that the *Euclidean distance* is

$$||\mathbf{x} - \mathbf{y}|| = \sqrt{\mathbf{x} \cdot \mathbf{x} + \mathbf{y} \cdot \mathbf{y} - 2\mathbf{x} \cdot \mathbf{y}}.$$

It can be verified that the traditional Euclidean distance satisfies all three of the distance axioms. Furthermore, the axioms hold also for the following extended distance metrics.

- The Mahalanobis distance satisfies all three of the distance axioms if and only if the Mahalanobis matrix $\mathbf{M}$ is positive semi-definite.
- When the inner product is characterized by a nonlinear kernel function, the induced distance metric observes the distance axioms if and only if the kernel function is a Mercer kernel.

Given a pair of one-dimensional vectors, $\mathbf{x} = 1.0$ and $\mathbf{y} = 10.0$, their distance depends on the kernel function used. The following are some illustrative numerical examples.

(i) If the Euclidean inner product is used, then their Euclidean distance is

$$\sqrt{\mathbf{x} \cdot \mathbf{x} + \mathbf{y} \cdot \mathbf{y} - 2\mathbf{x} \cdot \mathbf{y}} = \sqrt{1 + 100 - 2 \times 10} = 9.$$

(ii) For the second-order polynomial kernel

$$K(\mathbf{x}, \mathbf{y}) = (1 + \mathbf{x} \cdot \mathbf{y})^2$$

the distance (associated with its intrinsic space) is

$$\sqrt{K(\mathbf{x}, \mathbf{x}) + K(\mathbf{y}, \mathbf{y}) - 2K(\mathbf{x}, \mathbf{y})} = \sqrt{4 + 10\,201 - 2 \times 121} = 100.42.$$

(iii) For the Gaussian kernel

$$K(\mathbf{x},\mathbf{y}) = \exp\left\{-\frac{\|\mathbf{x}-\mathbf{y}\|^2}{2}\right\}$$

the distance is

$$\begin{aligned}\sqrt{K(\mathbf{x},\mathbf{x}) + K(\mathbf{y},\mathbf{y}) - 2K(\mathbf{x},\mathbf{y})} &= \sqrt{1.0 + 1.0 - 2 \times 2.6 \times 10^{-18}} \\ &= \sqrt{2}(1 - 1.3 \times 10^{-18}) \approx \sqrt{2}.\end{aligned}$$

(iv) For a sigmoid function,

$$K(\mathbf{x},\mathbf{y}) = \frac{1}{1 + e^{-\mathbf{x}\cdot\mathbf{y}}}, \tag{2.1}$$

it is no longer be possible to use $\sqrt{K(\mathbf{x},\mathbf{x}) + K(\mathbf{y},\mathbf{y}) - 2K(\mathbf{x},\mathbf{y})}$ to characterize the distance because

$$\begin{aligned}K(\mathbf{x},\mathbf{x}) + K(\mathbf{y},\mathbf{y}) - 2K(\mathbf{x},\mathbf{y}) &= \frac{1}{1+e^{-1}} + \frac{1}{1+e^{-100}} - \frac{2}{1+e^{-10}} \\ &= 0.7311 + 1.0 - 2.0 = -0.2689 < 0.\end{aligned}$$

This provides convincing evidence that the sigmoidal function is not a Mercer kernel.

2.2.2 Mercer kernels

In kernel methods, the conventional Euclidean inner product can be extended to a versatile nonlinear inner product, represented by a Mercer kernel $K(\mathbf{x},\mathbf{y})$ of two vectors $\mathbf{x}$ and $\mathbf{y}$. Such a generalized inner product will be much more amenable to complex and big data analysis.

Let $\mathcal{X}$ be the original space, which can be assumed to be a subset of $\mathbb{R}^M$. In functional analysis, a Mercer kernel is a function $K(\cdot,\cdot)$ from $\mathcal{X} \times \mathcal{X}$ to $\mathbb{R}$ that satisfies the Mercer condition [42, 175, 280, 281].

The Mercer condition

Let $K(\mathbf{x},\mathbf{y})$ be a continuous symmetric kernel that is defined in a closed interval for $\mathbf{x}$ and $\mathbf{y}$. The function $K(\mathbf{x},\mathbf{y})$ is called a Mercer kernel if it meets the Mercer condition that

$$\int K(\mathbf{x},\mathbf{y})h(\mathbf{x})h(\mathbf{y})d\mathbf{x}\, d\mathbf{y} \geq 0, \tag{2.2}$$

for any squarely integrable function $h(\mathbf{x})$, i.e. $\int h(\mathbf{x})^2\, d\mathbf{x}$ is finite.

Mercer's theorem[175] states that there exists a reproducing kernel Hilbert space $\mathcal{H}$ and a mapping

$$\boldsymbol{\phi} : \mathbf{x} \rightarrow \boldsymbol{\phi}(\mathbf{x}),\ \boldsymbol{\phi}(\mathbf{x}) \in \mathcal{H},$$

such that the inner product for $\mathcal{H}$ is represented by $K(\mathbf{x},\mathbf{y})$, i.e. $K(\mathbf{x},\mathbf{y}) = \boldsymbol{\phi}(\mathbf{x})^{\mathrm{T}}\boldsymbol{\phi}(\mathbf{y})$.

THEOREM 2.1 (Mercer's theorem) *The Mercer condition is necessary and sufficient for $K(\mathbf{x}, \mathbf{y})$ to be expandable into an absolutely and uniformly convergent series*

$$K(\mathbf{x}, \mathbf{y}) = \sum_{i=1}^{\infty} c_i \tilde{q}_i(\mathbf{x}) \tilde{q}_i(\mathbf{y}), \tag{2.3}$$

with positive coefficients $\{c_i > 0\}$, i.e. it may be factorized as

$$K(\mathbf{x}, \mathbf{y}) = \overrightarrow{q}(\mathbf{x})^{\mathrm{T}} \overrightarrow{q}(\mathbf{y}), \tag{2.4}$$

where we denote

$$\overrightarrow{q}(\mathbf{x}) \equiv [\sqrt{c_1}\tilde{q}_1(\mathbf{x})\sqrt{c_2}\tilde{q}_2(\mathbf{x})\ldots]^{\mathrm{T}}.$$

□

Proof of sufficiency. For notational simplicity, we shall first focus on the proof for the scalar case only. Note that every symmetric, continuous, and positive definite function $K(x, y)$, defined in the square $a \le x, y \le b$ (a, b, finite), can be expanded in the absolutely and uniformly convergent series

$$K(x, y) = \sum_{k=1}^{\infty} \lambda_k e_k(x) e_k(y),$$

where $e_k(x)$ and λ_k are the *eigenfunctions* and *eigenvalues* of the homogeneous integral equation

$$\lambda e(x) = \int_a^b K(x, y) e(y) dy, \ x \in [a, b].$$

Note also that the proof can be carried through to high-dimensional vector space, i.e. any continuous, symmetric, positive semi-definite kernel function $K(\mathbf{x}, \mathbf{y})$, where $\mathbf{x} \in \mathbb{R}^M$ and $\mathbf{y} \in \mathbb{R}^M$, can be expressed as a dot product in a high-dimensional space.

Proof of necessity. Note that, if $K(\mathbf{x}, \mathbf{y})$ can be factorized into $K(\mathbf{x}, \mathbf{y}) = \overrightarrow{q}(\mathbf{x})^{\mathrm{T}} \overrightarrow{q}(\mathbf{y})$ for any vector function

$$\overrightarrow{q}(\mathbf{x}) = [q_1(\mathbf{x}) q_2(\mathbf{x}) \ldots \ q_J(\mathbf{x})]^{\mathrm{T}},$$

then

$$\begin{aligned}\int K(\mathbf{x}, \mathbf{y}) h(\mathbf{x}) h(\mathbf{y}) d\mathbf{x} \, d\mathbf{y} &= \int h(\mathbf{x}) \overrightarrow{q}(\mathbf{x})^{\mathrm{T}} \overrightarrow{q}(\mathbf{y}) h(\mathbf{y}) d\mathbf{x} \, d\mathbf{y} \\ &= \sum_{i=1}^{J} \left[\int q_i(\mathbf{x}) h(\mathbf{x}) d\mathbf{x} \right]^2 \ge 0.\end{aligned}$$

for any squarely integrable function $h(\mathbf{x})$.

In short, $K(\mathbf{x}, \mathbf{y})$ is a Mercer kernel if and only if it is factorizable. Moreover, for a Mercer kernel, a distance metric can be defined as

$$\sqrt{K(\mathbf{x}, \mathbf{x}) + K(\mathbf{y}, \mathbf{y}) - 2K(\mathbf{x}, \mathbf{y})}.$$

THEOREM 2.2 (Mercer kernels) *This theorem formally establishes that the Mercer condition holds for some important kernel functions, qualifying them as Mercer kernels.*

(a) *Denote a kernel function as*

$$K(\mathbf{x},\mathbf{y}) = \sum_{i=1}^{J} c_i \tilde{q}_i(\mathbf{x})\tilde{q}_i(\mathbf{y}), \tag{2.5}$$

where

$$q_i(\mathbf{x}) = \prod_{j=1}^{M} x_j^{r_j}, \tag{2.6}$$

where $\{r_j, \forall j\}$ are natural numbers, is expressed as functions of the elements of the vector $\mathbf{x}$*. The function $K(\mathbf{x},\mathbf{y})$ is a Mercer kernel if and only if all its defining coefficients $\{c_i, \forall i\}$ are non-negative.*

(b) *A typical polynomial kernel function,*

$$K(\mathbf{x},\mathbf{y}) = \left(1 + \frac{\mathbf{x}\cdot\mathbf{y}}{\sigma^2}\right)^p, \tag{2.7}$$

where p is a positive integer, is always a Mercer kernel.

(c) *A Gaussian RBF kernel function,*

$$K(\mathbf{x},\mathbf{y}) = \exp\left\{-\frac{\|\mathbf{x}-\mathbf{y}\|^2}{2\sigma^2}\right\}, \tag{2.8}$$

is always a Mercer kernel. □

Proof of part (a). The sufficiency part is a direct consequence of Mercer's theorem, Theorem 2.1. The necessity is due to the fact that, if any one of the coefficients $\{c_i\}$ is negative, there always exists a squarely integrable function $h(\mathbf{x})$ such that

$$\int K(\mathbf{x},\mathbf{y})h(\mathbf{x})h(\mathbf{y})d\mathbf{x}\, d\mathbf{y} < 0.$$

Proof of part (b). A typical polynomial kernel function, see Eq. (2.7), can be expanded into the following form:

$$K(\mathbf{x},\mathbf{y}) = \sum_{q=0}^{p} d_q(\mathbf{x}\cdot\mathbf{y})^q, \tag{2.9}$$

where $d_q \geq 0$. Burges [30] further showed that a function $(\mathbf{x}\cdot\mathbf{y})^p$ has the following multinomial expansion:

$$(\mathbf{x}\cdot\mathbf{y})^p = \sum_i c_i q_i(\mathbf{x})q_i(\mathbf{y}),$$

where the coefficients $\{c_i\}$ are positive and, more importantly, the polynomial functions $q_i(\mathbf{x})$ can be spelled out as functions of the elements of the vector $\mathbf{x}$ as shown in Eq. (2.6). Therefore, a typical polynomial kernel function satisfies the Mercer condition.

Consider as an example a second-order polynomial function $(\mathbf{x}\cdot\mathbf{y})^2$ on a two-dimensional vector space, i.e. $\mathbf{x} = [x^{(1)}\ x^{(2)}]^{\mathrm{T}}$ and $\mathbf{y} = [y^{(1)}\ y^{(2)}]^{\mathrm{T}}$. Its binomial expansion is

$$(\mathbf{x}\cdot\mathbf{y})^2 = \left(x^{(1)}y^{(1)} + x^{(2)}y^{(2)}\right)^2$$
$$= \left(x^{(1)}(y^{(1)}\right)^2 + \left(x^{(2)}y^{(2)}\right)^2 + 2x^{(1)}x^{(2)}y^{(1)}y^{(2)}.$$

In this case,

$$q_1(\mathbf{x})q_1(\mathbf{y}) = \left(x^{(1)}\right)^2\left(y^{(1)}\right)^2,$$
$$q_2(\mathbf{x})q_2(\mathbf{y}) = \left(x^{(2)}\right)^2\left(y^{(2)}\right)^2,$$
$$q_3(\mathbf{x})q_3(\mathbf{y}) = x^{(1)}x^{(2)}y^{(1)}y^{(2)}.$$

Note that all the coefficients are positive: $c_1 = 1$, $c_2 = 1$, and $c_3 = 2$.

Proof of part (c). A Gaussian kernel function, see Eq. (2.8), can be expanded into the following power series:

$$K(\mathbf{x},\mathbf{y}) = \exp\left\{-\frac{\|\mathbf{x}\|^2}{2\sigma^2}\right\}\left(\sum_{q=0}^{\infty} d_q\left(\frac{\mathbf{x}\cdot\mathbf{y}}{\sigma^2}\right)^q\right)\exp\left\{-\frac{\|\mathbf{y}\|^2}{2\sigma^2}\right\},$$

where all the coefficients are positive. In fact, $d_q = (q!)^{-1} > 0$. Therefore, it is obviously a Mercer kernel.

Remark

The Mahalanobis inner product is a Mercer kernel if and only if the Mahalanobis matrix $\mathbf{M}$ is symmetric and positive semi-definite. To show this, we note that, if the Mahalanobis matrix $\mathbf{M}$ is symmetric and positive semi-definite, there exists a real matrix $\tilde{\mathbf{M}}$ such that $\mathbf{M} = \tilde{\mathbf{M}}\tilde{\mathbf{M}}^{\mathrm{T}}$. It follows that we have the following factorization:

$$K(\mathbf{x},\mathbf{y}) = \mathbf{x}^{\mathrm{T}}\mathbf{M}\mathbf{y} = \vec{q}(\mathbf{x})^{\mathrm{T}}\vec{q}(\mathbf{y}),$$

where $\vec{q}(\mathbf{x}) = \tilde{\mathbf{M}}\mathbf{x}$. Thus Eq. (2.4) can be validated.

Note that the polynomial and Gaussian kernel functions may be further extended to functions of a Mahalanobis inner product of $\mathbf{x}$ and $\mathbf{y}$. For example, a polynomial extension has the following form:

$$K(\mathbf{x},\mathbf{y}) = \left(1 + \mathbf{x}^{\mathrm{T}}\mathbf{R}^{-1}\mathbf{y}\right)^p,$$

where p is a positive integer, while a Gaussian extension is

$$K(\mathbf{x},\mathbf{y}) = \frac{1}{\sqrt{(2\pi)^M|\mathbf{R}|}}\exp\left\{-\frac{1}{2}(\mathbf{x}^{\mathrm{T}}\mathbf{R}^{-1}\mathbf{y})\right\}. \tag{2.10}$$

It can be shown that both extended functions are Mercer kernels. (Proof omitted.)

2.2.3 Construction of Mercer kernels

Given known Mercer kernels, there are several efficient ways to construct new Mercer kernels. For example, given two Mercer kernels $g(\mathbf{x},\mathbf{y})$ and $h(\mathbf{x},\mathbf{y})$, the following are also Mercer kernels:

(i) $k_1(\mathbf{x},\mathbf{y}) = g(\mathbf{x},\mathbf{y}) + h(\mathbf{x},\mathbf{y})$,
(ii) $k_2(\mathbf{x},\mathbf{y}) = g(\mathbf{x},\mathbf{y})h(\mathbf{x},\mathbf{y})$, and
(iii) $k_3(\mathbf{x},\mathbf{y}) = q(\mathbf{x})g(\mathbf{x},\mathbf{y})q(\mathbf{y})$,

where $q(\mathbf{x})$ is an arbitrary squarely integrable function. Moreover, the new *intrinsic degrees* may be analytically derived. (See Problem 2.5.)

2.2.4 Shift-invariant kernel functions

It is sometimes of practical use to examine the shift-invariance property of the kernel functions chosen [235]. A kernel function is shift-invariant if it has the following form:

$$K(\mathbf{x},\mathbf{y}) = K(\mathbf{x} - \mathbf{y}).$$

An RBF kernel is a function of $\|\mathbf{x} - \mathbf{y}\|$, so it is apparently shift-invariant. In particular, the Gaussian kernel is shift-invariant; consequently, the similarity metric and classifiers based on RBF kernels will be coordinate-independent. However, this property is not shared by polynomial kernels. More exactly, the similarity metric associated with polynomial kernels will be coordinate-dependent, and the coordinate of the vector space must be carefully chosen. (See Problem 2.14.) A common choice of the coordinate system is one whose origin coincides with the center of mass of the training dataset.

2.3 Training-data-independent intrinsic feature vectors

When a kernel function satisfies the Mercer condition, this assures the existence of a Hilbert vector space endowed with a kernel-induced distance metric. The corresponding vector space will be called the *intrinsic space*, so named because the space is *independent* of the training dataset.

Consider a finite-decomposable kernel function:

$$K(\mathbf{x},\mathbf{y}) = \sum_{j=1}^{J} \phi^{(j)}(\mathbf{x})\phi^{(j)}(\mathbf{y}),$$

for a finite integer J, where $\phi^{(1)}(\mathbf{x})$ is often (although not necessarily always) a constant, e.g. $\phi^{(1)}(\mathbf{x}) = 1$. The dimension of the space, J, will be referred to as the *intrinsic degree*. The foundation of the kernel methods hinges upon a nonlinear mapping from the *original vector space* $\mathbb{R}^M$ to an *intrinsic vector space* $\mathcal{H}$, i.e.

$$\mathbf{x} \rightarrow \vec{\boldsymbol{\phi}}(\mathbf{x}),$$

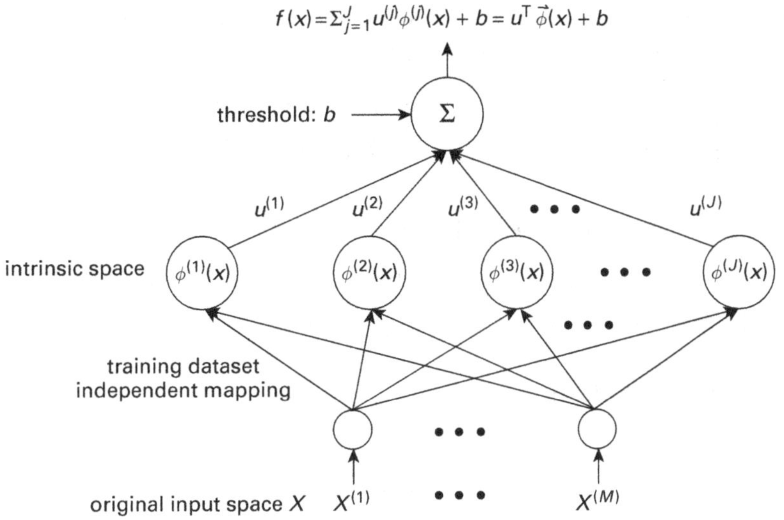

Fig. 2.1. For the intrinsic representation, a two-layer network is often adopted in order to model nonlinear score/discriminant functions, in which a layer of representative nodes ϕ is inserted between the input nodes and output nodes. The intrinsic space is of dimension J, which may be finite or indefinite. The basis function of $\mathcal{H}$ is uniquely determined by the kernel function and is independent of the training vectors. That is why the name *intrinsic* space is used. Consequently, its lower network requires no learning because it is uniquely specified by the kernel function.

where

$$\vec{\boldsymbol{\phi}}(\mathbf{x}) \equiv [\phi^{(1)}(\mathbf{x}), \phi^{(2)}(\mathbf{x}), \ldots, \phi^{(J)}(\mathbf{x})]^{\mathrm{T}}. \tag{2.11}$$

The *intrinsic vector space* $\mathcal{H}$ has the following properties.

- It is a Hilbert space endowed with an inner product defined as follows:

$$K(\mathbf{x}, \mathbf{y}) = \sum_{j=1}^{J} \phi^{(j)}(\mathbf{x})\phi^{(j)}(\mathbf{y}) = \vec{\boldsymbol{\phi}}(\mathbf{x})^{\mathrm{T}}\vec{\boldsymbol{\phi}}(\mathbf{y}). \tag{2.12}$$

- The basis functions of the vector space are independent of the training dataset. That is why the name *intrinsic* space is used. In a supervised classification scenario, such an induced vector space can be represented by a two-layer network as depicted in Figure 2.1.
- *Lower layer.* In this layer, a vector in the original M-dimensional space is (nonlinearly) mapped to a new representation vector:

$$\mathbf{x} = [x^{(1)}, x^{(2)}, \ldots, x^{(M)}]^{\mathrm{T}} \to \vec{\boldsymbol{\phi}}(\mathbf{x}) = [\phi^{(1)}(\mathbf{x}), \phi^{(2)}(\mathbf{x}), \ldots, \phi^{(J)}(\mathbf{x})]^{\mathrm{T}}.$$

  Figure 2.1 depicts this new representation space, which will be called the *intrinsic space* and denoted as $\mathcal{H}$. The dimension J will be referred to as the *intrinsic degree*, which may be either finite or indefinite.

- *Upper layer.* In this layer, the nonlinear representative vector $\overrightarrow{\phi}(\mathbf{x})$ undergoes a linear mapping to yield a discriminant function:

$$f(\mathbf{x}) = \mathbf{u}^{\mathrm{T}}\overrightarrow{\phi}(\mathbf{x}) + b, \tag{2.13}$$

where $\mathbf{u}$ is the intrinsic-space decision vector and b is a bias threshold.

2.3.1 Intrinsic spaces associated with kernel functions

Several prominent Mercer kernels and their corresponding intrinsic representations will be introduced in this section.

2.3.1.1 Linear kernel functions

The basic linear kernel function is

$$K(\mathbf{x}, \mathbf{y}) = \mathbf{x}^{\mathrm{T}}\mathbf{y}.$$

In this case, $\overrightarrow{\phi}(\mathbf{x}) \equiv \mathbf{x}$, i.e. the intrinsic space for the basic linear kernel function is the original vector space itself.

2.3.1.2 Polynomial kernel functions

The typical formulation for a polynomial kernel of order p (POLY_p) is

$$K(\mathbf{x}_i, \mathbf{x}_j) = \left(1 + \frac{\mathbf{x}_i \cdot \mathbf{x}_j}{\sigma^2}\right)^p, \quad \text{where } p \text{ is a positive integer.}$$

It can be shown that the intrinsic degree of the POLY_p kernel function is

$$J = J^{(p)} = \begin{pmatrix} M+p \\ p \end{pmatrix} = \frac{(M+p)!}{M!p!}, \tag{2.14}$$

To provide an illustrative example, let us focus on the case study of mapping a two-dimensional ($M = 2$) vector space to its induced intrinsic space associated with a second-order ($p = 2$) kernel function, as is graphically depicted in Figure 2.2.

We shall from now on denote a two-dimensional input vector as

$$\mathbf{x} = [x^{(1)}\ x^{(2)}]^{\mathrm{T}} \equiv [u\ v]^{\mathrm{T}}.$$

A basic second-order polynomial kernel function,

$$K(\mathbf{x}, \mathbf{y}) = (1 + \mathbf{x}\cdot\mathbf{y})^2,$$

can be expressed as

$$K(\mathbf{x}, \mathbf{y}) = (1 + \mathbf{x}\cdot\mathbf{y})^2 = \overrightarrow{\phi}(\mathbf{x})^{\mathrm{T}}\overrightarrow{\phi}(\mathbf{y}),$$

where, according to the definition in Eq. (2.11),

$$\overrightarrow{\phi}(\mathbf{x}) = [1 \sqrt{2}u \sqrt{2}v \sqrt{2}uv\ u^2\ v^2]^{\mathrm{T}}. \tag{2.15}$$

As depicted in Figure 2.2, the newly induced intrinsic space has a dimensionality ($J = 6$) much higher than the original dimensionality ($M = 2$). The higher-dimensional space offers extra flexibility for both unsupervised and supervised learning applications.

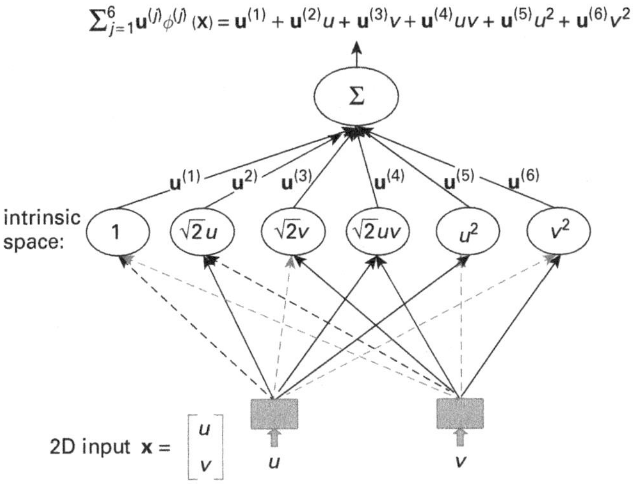

Fig. 2.2. The second-order polynomial kernel is a finite-decomposable kernel. Therefore, the discriminant function can be represented by a linear combination of a finite number ($J = 6$) of polynomial basis functions.

Example 2.1 (Expanded feature space) *In the XOR dataset, see Figure 2.3, the training data are*

$$\mathbf{x}_1 = \begin{bmatrix} +1 \\ +1 \end{bmatrix}, \quad \mathbf{x}_2 = \begin{bmatrix} -1 \\ -1 \end{bmatrix}, \quad \mathbf{x}_3 = \begin{bmatrix} +1 \\ -1 \end{bmatrix}, \quad \mathbf{x}_4 = \begin{bmatrix} -1 \\ +1 \end{bmatrix}.$$

If $K(\mathbf{x}, \mathbf{y}) = (1 + \mathbf{x} \cdot \mathbf{y})^2$, then, according to Eq. (2.11), the four original vectors can be mapped to their corresponding intrinsic vectors:

$$\vec{\boldsymbol{\phi}}(\mathbf{x}_1) = \begin{bmatrix} +1 \\ +\sqrt{2} \\ +\sqrt{2} \\ +\sqrt{2} \\ +1 \\ +1 \end{bmatrix}, \quad \vec{\boldsymbol{\phi}}(\mathbf{x}_2) = \begin{bmatrix} +1 \\ -\sqrt{2} \\ -\sqrt{2} \\ +\sqrt{2} \\ +1 \\ +1 \end{bmatrix},$$
$$\vec{\boldsymbol{\phi}}(\mathbf{x}_3) = \begin{bmatrix} +1 \\ +\sqrt{2} \\ -\sqrt{2} \\ -\sqrt{2} \\ +1 \\ +1 \end{bmatrix}, \quad \vec{\boldsymbol{\phi}}(\mathbf{x}_4) = \begin{bmatrix} +1 \\ -\sqrt{2} \\ +\sqrt{2} \\ -\sqrt{2} \\ +1 \\ +1 \end{bmatrix}. \tag{2.16}$$

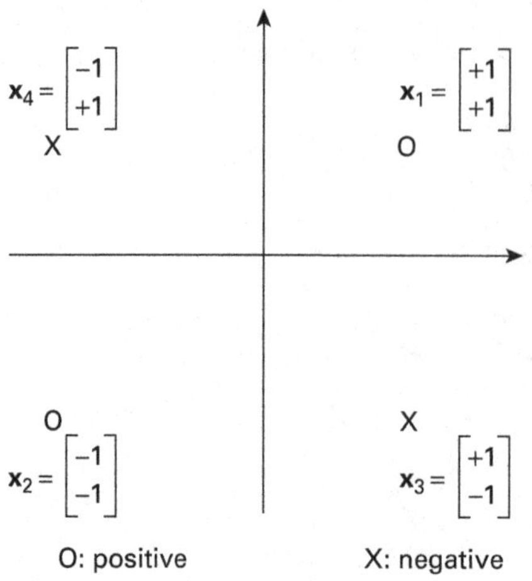

Fig. 2.3. The XOR problem. There are four training patterns (two positive and two negative) in a two-dimensional space. Clearly, the positive and negative classes are not linearly separable in the original vector space. This problem can be easily resolved via mapping the original vectors to the intrinsic vectors, cf. Eq. (2.16).

Intrinsic data matrix

All the training vectors will be mapped to the intrinsic vector space. As a result, the data matrix $\mathbf{X}$ is mapped to an intrinsic space, denoted by $\mathbf{\Phi}$, which has the following form:

$$\mathbf{\Phi} = \begin{bmatrix} \phi^{(1)}(\mathbf{x}_1) & \phi^{(1)}(\mathbf{x}_2) & \dots & \phi^{(1)}(\mathbf{x}_N) \\ \phi^{(2)}(\mathbf{x}_1) & \phi^{(2)}(\mathbf{x}_2) & \dots & \phi^{(2)}(\mathbf{x}_N) \\ \vdots & \vdots & \dots & \vdots \\ \phi^{(J)}(\mathbf{x}_1) & \phi^{(J)}(\mathbf{x}_2) & \dots & \phi^{(J)}(\mathbf{x}_N) \end{bmatrix}. \tag{2.17}$$

Factorization of kernel matrix

The kernel matrix is jointly determined by both the kernel function *and* the training vectors:

$$\mathbf{K} = \begin{bmatrix} K(\mathbf{x}_1, \mathbf{x}_1) & K(\mathbf{x}_1, \mathbf{x}_2) & \dots & K(\mathbf{x}_1, \mathbf{x}_N) \\ K(\mathbf{x}_2, \mathbf{x}_1) & K(\mathbf{x}_2, \mathbf{x}_2) & \dots & K(\mathbf{x}_2, \mathbf{x}_N) \\ \vdots & \vdots & \dots & \vdots \\ K(\mathbf{x}_N, \mathbf{x}_1) & K(\mathbf{x}_N, \mathbf{x}_2) & \cdots & K(\mathbf{x}_N, \mathbf{x}_N) \end{bmatrix}. \tag{2.18}$$

According to Eq. (2.12), the (i, j)th element of the kernel matrix is

$$K(\mathbf{x}_i, \mathbf{x}_j) = \overrightarrow{\boldsymbol{\phi}}(\mathbf{x}_i)^{\mathrm{T}} \overrightarrow{\boldsymbol{\phi}}(\mathbf{x}_j).$$

The kernel matrix and the intrinsic data matrix are related by the following factorization linking:

$$\mathbf{K} = \mathbf{\Phi}^{\mathrm{T}} \mathbf{\Phi}, \tag{2.19}$$

where

$$\mathbf{\Phi} = \begin{bmatrix} \vec{\phi}(\mathbf{x}_1) & \vec{\phi}(\mathbf{x}_2) & \dots & \vec{\phi}(\mathbf{x}_N) \end{bmatrix}. \tag{2.20}$$

For any Mercer kernel, its corresponding kernel matrix is always semi-positive definite and symmetric, for an arbitrary finite set of inputs $\{\mathbf{x}_i\}_{i=1}^N$.

Example 2.2 (Factorization of kernel matrix) *Let us revisit the previous XOR dataset with the same kernel function: $K(\mathbf{x}, \mathbf{y}) = (1 + \mathbf{x} \cdot \mathbf{y})^2$. For the four training vectors, the 4×4 kernel matrix of Eq. (2.18) becomes*

$$\mathbf{K} = \begin{bmatrix} 9 & 1 & 1 & 1 \\ 1 & 9 & 1 & 1 \\ 1 & 1 & 9 & 1 \\ 1 & 1 & 1 & 9 \end{bmatrix},$$

which has the following factorization:

$$\begin{aligned}\mathbf{K} &= \mathbf{\Phi}^{\mathrm{T}}\mathbf{\Phi} \\ &= \begin{bmatrix} +1 & +\sqrt{2} & +\sqrt{2} & +\sqrt{2} & +1 & +1 \\ +1 & -\sqrt{2} & -\sqrt{2} & +\sqrt{2} & +1 & +1 \\ +1 & +\sqrt{2} & -\sqrt{2} & -\sqrt{2} & +1 & +1 \\ +1 & -\sqrt{2} & +\sqrt{2} & -\sqrt{2} & +1 & +1 \end{bmatrix} \\ &\times \begin{bmatrix} +1 & +1 & +1 & +1 \\ +\sqrt{2} & -\sqrt{2} & +\sqrt{2} & -\sqrt{2} \\ +\sqrt{2} & -\sqrt{2} & -\sqrt{2} & +\sqrt{2} \\ +\sqrt{2} & +\sqrt{2} & -\sqrt{2} & -\sqrt{2} \\ +1 & +1 & +1 & +1 \\ +1 & +1 & +1 & +1 \end{bmatrix}.\end{aligned}$$

2.3.1.3 Gaussian kernel functions

In general, a nonlinear kernel function may not be finitely decomposable and the kernel has an indefinite number of basis functions. A typical example is the Gaussian kernel function:

$$K(\mathbf{x}, \mathbf{y}) = \exp\left\{-\frac{\|\mathbf{x} - \mathbf{y}\|^2}{2\sigma^2}\right\}.$$

Note that

$$K(\mathbf{x}, \mathbf{y}) = \exp\left\{-\frac{\|\mathbf{x}\|^2}{2\sigma^2}\right\}\left(\sum_{q=0}^{\infty}\frac{(\mathbf{x} \cdot \mathbf{y})^q}{(q!)\sigma^{2q}}\right)\exp\left\{-\frac{\|\mathbf{y}\|^2}{2\sigma^2}\right\}.$$

In this case, the intrinsic vector will assume the following form:

$$\vec{\phi}(\mathbf{x}) = \exp\left\{-\frac{\|\mathbf{x}\|^2}{2\sigma^2}\right\}\vec{\omega}(\mathbf{x}), \tag{2.21}$$

where

$$\vec{\omega}(\mathbf{x}) \equiv [\tilde{\omega}^{(1)}(\mathbf{x})\ \tilde{\omega}^{(2)}(\mathbf{x})\ \ldots]^{\mathrm{T}} \tag{2.22}$$

with each entry $\tilde{\omega}^{(i)}(\mathbf{x})$ being a simple multi-variable polynomial scaled by a proper positive coefficient. More exactly, each basis function has the same form as that prescribed in Eq. (2.23),

$$\exp\left\{-\frac{\|\mathbf{x}\|^2}{2\sigma^2}\right\}\left(x^{(1)}\right)^{d_1}\cdots\left(x^{(M)}\right)^{d_M}\left(x^{(M+1)}\right)^{d_{M+1}} \tag{2.23}$$

modulo a scaling factor. (Note that such a basis function is non-polynomial.) For example, assuming $\mathbf{x} = [\,u\ v]^{\mathrm{T}}$, a simple multi-variable polynomial could be $1, u, v, uv, u^2, v^2, uv^2, u^3, v^3, \ldots$. In other words, it has an infinite number of basis functions.

2.3.1.4 Truncated-RBF kernel functions

A truncated-RBF (TRBF) kernel of order p (TRBF_p),

$$K(\mathbf{x},\mathbf{y}) = \exp\left\{-\frac{\|\mathbf{x}\|^2}{2\sigma^2}\right\}\left[\sum_{k=0}^{p}\frac{1}{k!}\left(\frac{\mathbf{x}\cdot\mathbf{y}}{\sigma^2}\right)^k\right]\exp\left\{-\frac{\|\mathbf{y}\|^2}{2\sigma^2}\right\}, \tag{2.24}$$

also has a finite intrinsic degree, just like polynomial kernels. For the TRBF_p kernel, each basis function has exactly the same form as that prescribed in Eq. (2.23). Note that the TRBF has a finite intrinsic degree and yet it represents a good approximation of the Gaussian kernel. More precisely, the intrinsic degree of TRBF_p is

$$J = J^{(p)} = \begin{pmatrix} M+p \\ p \end{pmatrix} = \frac{(M+p)!}{M!p!}, \tag{2.25}$$

i.e. it is exactly the same as the degree of its polynomial counterpart, POLY_p kernel.

As discussed in Section 2.2.3, given a Mercer kernel $g(\mathbf{x},\mathbf{y})$, we have that $k_3(\mathbf{x},\mathbf{y}) = q(\mathbf{x})g(\mathbf{x},\mathbf{y})q(\mathbf{y})$ will also be a Mercer kernel for any function $q(\mathbf{x})$. Therefore, we simply need to set

$$g(\mathbf{x},\mathbf{y}) = \sum_{k=0}^{p}\frac{1}{k!}\left(\frac{\mathbf{x}\cdot\mathbf{y}}{\sigma^2}\right)^k$$

and

$$q(\mathbf{x}) = \exp\left\{-\frac{\|\mathbf{x}\|^2}{2\sigma^2}\right\},$$

in order to prove that TRBF_p is a Mercer kernel.

2.3.2 Intrinsic-space-based learning models

For kernel methods implemented in the intrinsic space, the approach is conceptually straightforward. Figure 2.4 shows such a full process both for the training and for the

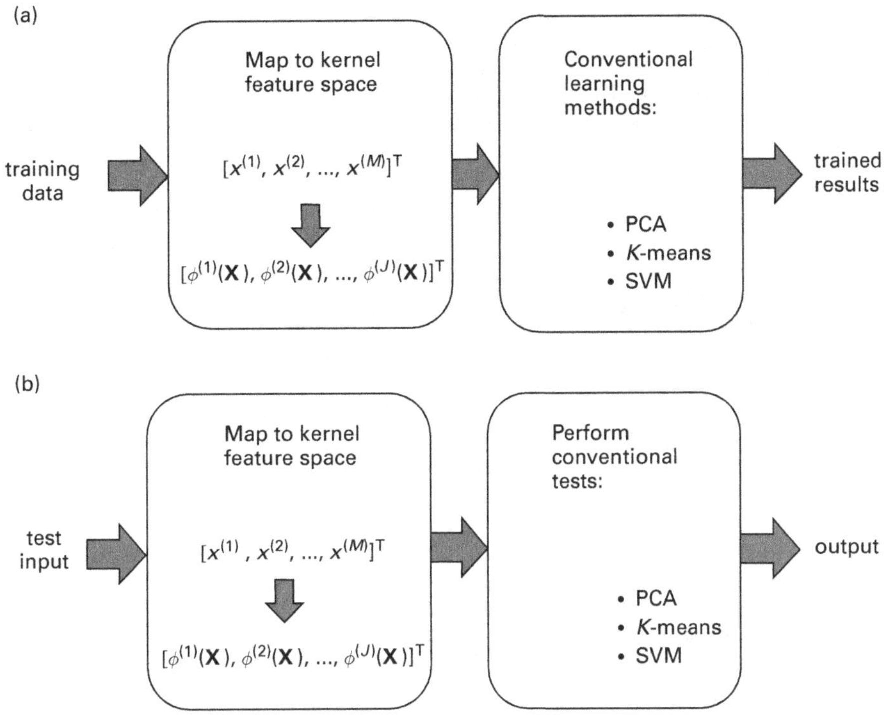

Fig. 2.4. The intrinsic-space approach involves explicit mapping of the original vectors to their kernel-induced intrinsic representations: (a) training phase and (b) testing/prediction phase.

testing phase. It involves (1) an explicit mapping step from the original vector space to the intrinsic vector space, and then (2) the conventional learning optimizer can be directly applied to the newly mapped dataset.

2.3.2.1 Kernel processing with intrinsic representation (training phase)

As depicted in Figure 2.4(a), the learning process contains two steps.

- First, as shown in Figure 2.5(a), map the original dataset onto the kernel-induced intrinsic vector. Given $K(\mathbf{x}, \mathbf{y}) = \overrightarrow{\boldsymbol{\phi}}(\mathbf{x})^{\mathrm{T}} \overrightarrow{\boldsymbol{\phi}}(\mathbf{y})$, a vector $\mathbf{x}$ in the original space may be mapped to a point $\overrightarrow{\boldsymbol{\phi}}(\mathbf{x})$ in the kernel-induced intrinsic vector space (see Figure 2.1):

$$\mathbf{x} = [x^{(1)}, x^{(2)}, \ldots, x^{(M)}]^{\mathrm{T}} \rightarrow \overrightarrow{\boldsymbol{\phi}}(\mathbf{x}) = [\phi^{(1)}(\mathbf{x}), \phi^{(2)}(\mathbf{x}), \ldots, \phi^{(J)}(\mathbf{x})]^{\mathrm{T}}, \tag{2.26}$$

  where the kernel-induced basis functions $\{\phi^{(k)}(\mathbf{x}), k = 1, 2, \ldots\}$ serve as the bases for the new feature space. All these basis functions are pre-determined by the kernel function and, consequently, they are independent of the training dataset.
- Next, a conventional learning optimizer (whether LSP-based or not) can be directly applied to the newly mapped training dataset. An LSP-based optimizer, for unsupervised or supervised learning, may be exemplified by the following Algorithm 2.1.

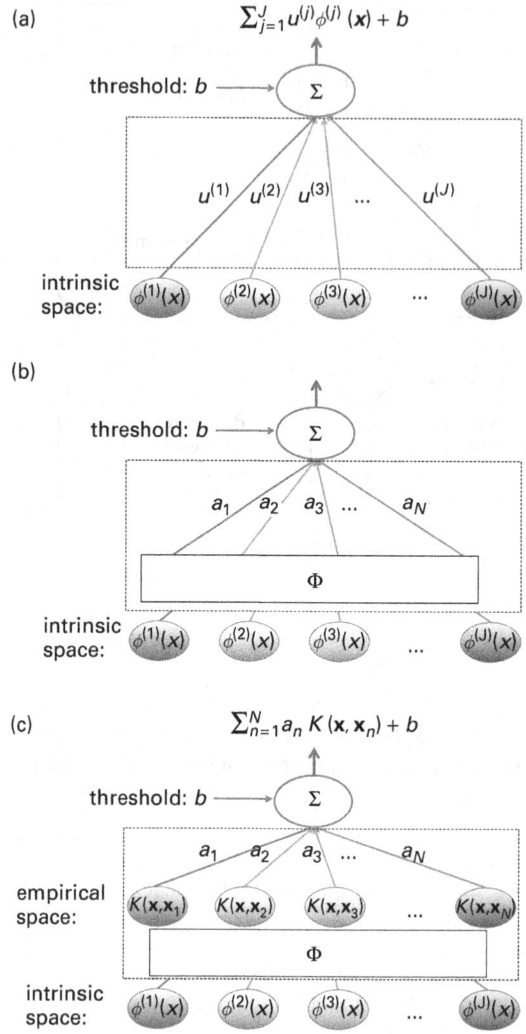

Fig. 2.5. The intrinsic-space approach will *not* be applicable to nonvectorial data processing or to kernel methods using Gaussian kernels, whose corresponding intrinsic space $\mathcal{H}$ is of infinite dimension, i.e. $J \to \infty$. The LSP enables the conversion of the intrinsic representation into a manageable empirical representation. (a) The intrinsic representation if feasible. (b) Under the LSP condition, the decision vector $\mathbf{u}$ can be expressed by a linear combination of all the training vectors in the intrinsic space. In terms of the network configuration, this equivalence amounts to the insertion of an extra matrix-multiplication layer for the mapping $\mathbf{u} = \mathbf{\Phi a}$, which is assured to exist under the LSP condition. (c) Consequently, the role of intrinsic representation may be equivalently taken over by its corresponding representation in the empirical space – a process referred to as *kernelization*.

ALGORITHM 2.1 (LSP-based learning models in intrinsic space) *The learning model aims at finding the optimal solution*

$$\arg\min_{\{\mathbf{u}_k \in \mathbb{R}^M,\ \forall k\}} \mathcal{E}\left(\mathbf{u}_k^{\mathrm{T}} \overrightarrow{\boldsymbol{\phi}}(\mathbf{x}_j),\ \forall k,j;\ \left\| \sum_{k=1}^{K} \beta_k^{(\ell)} \mathbf{u}_k \right\|^2,\ \forall \ell \right) \tag{2.27}$$

subject to the equality constraints

$$c_p\left(\mathbf{u}_k^{\mathrm{T}} \overrightarrow{\boldsymbol{\phi}}(\mathbf{x}_j),\ \forall k,j \right) = 0, \quad p = 1,\ldots,P,$$

and inequality constraints

$$d_q\left(\mathbf{u}_k^{\mathrm{T}} \overrightarrow{\boldsymbol{\phi}}(\mathbf{x}_j), \forall k,j;\ \left\| \sum_{k=1}^{K} \beta_k^{(\ell)} \mathbf{u}_k \right\|^2,\ \forall \ell \right) \le 0, \quad q = 1,\ldots,Q.$$

Here $\forall k$, $\forall j$, *and* $\forall \ell$ *stand for* $k = 1,\ldots,K, j = 1,\ldots,N$, *and* $\ell = 1,\ldots,L$, *respectively.*

According to Theorem 1.1, if $\mathcal{E}(\cdot)$ *and* $\{d_q(\cdot), q = 1,\ldots,Q\}$ *are monotonically increasing functions w.r.t.* $\|\sum_{k=1}^{K} \beta_k^{(\ell)} \mathbf{u}_k\|$ *for* $\ell = 1,\ldots,L$, *then, under the given constraints,*

$$\min_{\mathbf{u}_k \in \mathbb{R}^M,\ \forall k} \mathcal{E} = \min_{\mathbf{u}_k = \boldsymbol{\Phi}\mathbf{a}_k, \mathbf{a}_k \in \mathbb{R}^N,\ \forall k} \mathcal{E}. \tag{2.28}$$

This equivalence guarantees an equally good result even if the solution is restricted to the LSP:

$$\mathbf{u}_k \in \mathtt{span}[\boldsymbol{\Phi}],\ \textit{equivalently},\ \mathbf{u}_k = \boldsymbol{\Phi}\mathbf{a}_k,\ \textit{for some}\ \mathbf{a}_k \in \mathbb{R}^N,\ \forall k.$$

□

2.3.2.2 Kernel processing with intrinsic representation (prediction phase)

As depicted in Figure 2.4(b), the prediction process contains two steps.

- First, map a test vector, denoted by $\mathbf{x}$, in the original space to the kernel-induced intrinsic vector.
- Next, apply a conventional prediction method to the new feature vector to produce the desired output. For example, for supervised classification, the learned vector can produce the inner product $\mathbf{u}^{\mathrm{T}} \overrightarrow{\boldsymbol{\phi}}(\mathbf{x})$ to be used for the final prediction or classification.

2.3.2.3 Under-determined supervised classification

As an example, let us study an intrinsic-space learning model for under-determined supervised classification. In this case, the optimizer aims at finding

$$\arg\min_{\mathbf{w} \in \Re^M} \|\mathbf{u}\|^2 \ \text{ subject to } \mathbf{u}^{\mathrm{T}} \overrightarrow{\boldsymbol{\phi}}(\mathbf{x}_j) - y_j = 0,\ j = 1,\ldots,N. \tag{2.29}$$

According to Theorem 1.1, this is an LSP-based learning model – a fact verifiable by the following numerical example.

Example 2.3 (A learning model formulated in intrinsic space) *Consider an (underdetermined) supervised training dataset* $[\mathcal{X}, \mathcal{Y}]$, *with*

$$M = 3 > N = 2: \quad \mathbf{x}_1 = \begin{bmatrix} 1 \\ 2 \\ 0 \end{bmatrix}, y_1 = +1, \quad \mathbf{x}_2 = \begin{bmatrix} 0 \\ 0 \\ -1 \end{bmatrix}, y_2 = -1.$$

Suppose that the kernel function is

$$K(\mathbf{x}, \mathbf{y}) = \left(1 + \frac{\mathbf{x} \cdot \mathbf{y}}{\sigma^2}\right)^2. \tag{2.30}$$

then the kernel-induced intrinsic representation becomes

$$\overrightarrow{\phi}(\mathbf{x}) = [\, 1 \; \sqrt{2}x^{(1)} \sqrt{2}x^{(2)} \; \sqrt{2}x^{(3)} \; \sqrt{2}x^{(1)}x^{(2)} \; \sqrt{2}x^{(1)}x^{(3)} \; \sqrt{2}x^{(2)}x^{(3)} \; (x^{(1)})^2 \; (x^{(2)})^2 \; (x^{(3)})^2 \,]^{\mathrm{T}}. \tag{2.31}$$

The mapped training vectors in the intrinsic space are

$$\overrightarrow{\phi}(\mathbf{x}_1) = \begin{bmatrix} 1 & \sqrt{2} & 2\sqrt{2} & 0 & 2\sqrt{2} & 0 & 0 & 1 & 4 & 0 \end{bmatrix}^{\mathrm{T}},$$
$$\overrightarrow{\phi}(\mathbf{x}_2) = \begin{bmatrix} 1 & 0 & 0 & -\sqrt{2} & 0 & 0 & 0 & 0 & 0 & 1 \end{bmatrix}^{\mathrm{T}}.$$

It can be shown that the unique and optimal solution for Eq. (2.29) is

$$\mathbf{u} = \begin{bmatrix} -0.224 & 0.049 & 0.099 & -0.366 & 0.099 & 0 & 0 & 0.035 & 0.14 & -0.259 \end{bmatrix},$$

which falls within the learning subspace from the intrinsic space's perspective. The optimal solution for **u** *leads to the following (nonlinear) decision boundary:*

$$f(\mathbf{x}) = \mathbf{u}^{\mathrm{T}}\overrightarrow{\phi}(\mathbf{x}) = 0.035(1 + u + 2v)^2 - 0.259(1 - w)^2, \tag{2.32}$$

which is useful for the decision making in the prediction phase.

Note that, while the decision boundary is linear in the intrinsic space, it corresponds to a nonlinear decision boundary when mapped back to the original data space.

2.4 Training-data-dependent empirical feature vectors

The intrinsic representation enjoys the simplicity of being independent of the training dataset. However, its practical usage may be cast into doubt if a Gaussian kernel is used. In this case, the intrinsic-space-based learning model is no longer computationally feasible since the intrinsic degree associated with a Gaussian kernel is infinite, i.e. $J \to \infty$. Fortunately, even with $J \to \infty$, it is still feasible to adopt a finite-dimensional kernel-induced vector space, known as *empirical space*. The empirical vector space is jointly defined by the kernel function and the particular training dataset. The kernelized learning models characterized in the empirical space have found many promising applications in the context of machine learning.

2.4.1 The LSP: from intrinsic space to empirical space

For LSP-based learning models, an equivalent and feasible optimizer can be formulated for Gaussian kernels. More exactly, the curse of an infinite dimension of J can be effectively circumvented by the finite-dimensional empirical representation.

As illustrated by Figure 2.5, the LSP enables the conversion of the intrinsic representation into a new empirical representation. The full conversion may be subdivided into the following three stages.

(i) As shown in Figure 2.5(a), during the learning phase, the original training dataset will be mapped to a new set of induced training vectors

$$\{\vec{\boldsymbol{\phi}}(\mathbf{x}_1), \vec{\boldsymbol{\phi}}(\mathbf{x}_2), \ldots, \vec{\boldsymbol{\phi}}(\mathbf{x}_N)\}.$$

(ii) Under the LSP condition, it is known that the *intrinsic decision vector* $\mathbf{u}$ can be expressed as a linear combination of all the training vectors in the intrinsic space, i.e.

$$\mathbf{u} = \sum_{i=1}^{N} \vec{\boldsymbol{\phi}}(\mathbf{x}_i) a_i$$

for some coefficients a_i. In matrix notation,

$$\mathbf{u} = \boldsymbol{\Phi}\mathbf{a}, \tag{2.33}$$

where the training data matrix in the intrinsic space is denoted as

$$\boldsymbol{\Phi} \equiv [\vec{\boldsymbol{\phi}}(\mathbf{x}_1), \vec{\boldsymbol{\phi}}(\mathbf{x}_2), \ldots, \vec{\boldsymbol{\phi}}(\mathbf{x}_N)]. \tag{2.34}$$

This relationship is depicted in Figure 2.5(b).

(iii) The inner product $\vec{\boldsymbol{\phi}}(\mathbf{x})^{\mathrm{T}}\mathbf{u}$ can now be rewritten as

$$\vec{\boldsymbol{\phi}}(\mathbf{x})^{\mathrm{T}}\mathbf{u} = \vec{\boldsymbol{\phi}}(\mathbf{x})^{\mathrm{T}}\boldsymbol{\Phi}\mathbf{a} = \vec{\mathbf{k}}(\mathbf{x})^{\mathrm{T}}\mathbf{a},$$

where the empirical representation is defined as

$$\begin{aligned}\vec{\mathbf{k}}(\mathbf{x}) &\equiv \boldsymbol{\Phi}^{\mathrm{T}}\vec{\boldsymbol{\phi}}(\mathbf{x}) \\ &= \begin{bmatrix} \vec{\boldsymbol{\phi}}(\mathbf{x}_1)^{\mathrm{T}} \\ \vdots \\ \vec{\boldsymbol{\phi}}(\mathbf{x})_N^{\mathrm{T}} \end{bmatrix} \vec{\boldsymbol{\phi}}(\mathbf{x}) = \begin{bmatrix} \vec{\boldsymbol{\phi}}(\mathbf{x}_1)^{\mathrm{T}}\vec{\boldsymbol{\phi}}(\mathbf{x}) \\ \vdots \\ \vec{\boldsymbol{\phi}}(\mathbf{x}_N)^{\mathrm{T}}\vec{\boldsymbol{\phi}}(\mathbf{x}) \end{bmatrix} \\ &= \begin{bmatrix} K(\mathbf{x}_1, \mathbf{x}) \\ \vdots \\ K(\mathbf{x}_N, \mathbf{x}) \end{bmatrix},\end{aligned} \tag{2.35}$$

with the *empirical degree* N defined as the size of the training dataset. In short, as depicted in Figure 2.5(c), the role of the intrinsic representation, $\vec{\boldsymbol{\phi}}(\mathbf{x})$, may be substituted by its counterpart $\vec{\mathbf{k}}(\mathbf{x})$.

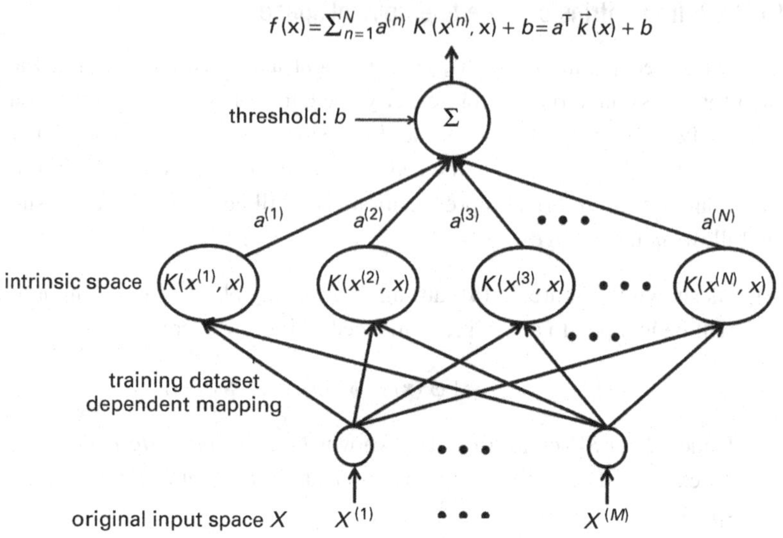

Fig. 2.6. The two-layer network configuration for the representation in the empirical space. The new N-dimensional vector space is denoted by $\mathcal{K}$, and its N basis functions of the vector space are dependent on the N training vectors. More precisely, the basis functions are jointly determined by the kernel function $K(\mathbf{x}, \mathbf{y})$ and the N training vectors.

Empirical vector space

Given a training dataset $\{\mathbf{x}_1, \mathbf{x}_2, \ldots, \mathbf{x}_N\}$ and a specific kernel function $K(\mathbf{x}, \mathbf{y})$, any new vector $\mathbf{x}$ can be represented by the following *empirical feature vector*, or simply *empirical vector*:

$$\vec{\mathbf{k}}(\mathbf{x}) \equiv \begin{bmatrix} K(\mathbf{x}_1, \mathbf{x}) \\ K(\mathbf{x}_2, \mathbf{x}) \\ \vdots \\ K(\mathbf{x}_N, \mathbf{x}) \end{bmatrix}. \tag{2.36}$$

As depicted in Figure 2.6, the mapping $\mathbf{x} \to \vec{\mathbf{k}}(\mathbf{x})$ maps the original vector space $\mathbb{R}^M$ onto a new N-dimensional *empirical vector space*, denoted by $\mathcal{K}$. The *empirical vector space* has the following properties.

- It is an N-dimensional Hilbert space endowed with an inner-product:

$$\vec{\mathbf{k}}(\mathbf{x})^{\mathrm{T}} \vec{\mathbf{k}}(\mathbf{y}).$$

- The definitions of the basis functions of the vector space are dependent on the N training vectors. More precisely, the basis functions are jointly determined by the kernel function $K(\mathbf{x}, \mathbf{y})$ and the N training vectors. That is why the name *empirical space is used.* Note that the dimension of the *empirical feature vector* is equal to the *empirical degree* N.

Degree of design freedom

Note that $\vec{\mathbf{k}}(\mathbf{x}) = \mathbf{\Phi}^{\mathrm{T}} \vec{\boldsymbol{\phi}}(\mathbf{x})$ (see Eq. (2.35)) and that $\mathbf{\Phi}$ is a $J \times N$ matrix; therefore, the rank of the kernel matrix is upper bounded by $\min\{J, N\}$, and therefore so is the degree of design freedom. Therefore, no matter how large N may grow – say in a big data problem – the N basis functions $\{K(\mathbf{x}, \mathbf{x}_n), n = 1, \ldots, N\}$ can never have more than J linearly independent bases. This can be demonstrated by a simple numerical example. In other words, the degree of design freedom is limited by J.

Example 2.4 (Linearly dependent basis functions in empirical space) *Now the dataset contains seven training vectors:*

$$\begin{bmatrix} 0 \\ 0 \end{bmatrix}, \begin{bmatrix} +1 \\ +1 \end{bmatrix}, \begin{bmatrix} -1 \\ -1 \end{bmatrix}, \begin{bmatrix} +1 \\ -1 \end{bmatrix}, \begin{bmatrix} -1 \\ +1 \end{bmatrix}, \begin{bmatrix} +1 \\ 0 \end{bmatrix}, \begin{bmatrix} +2 \\ 0 \end{bmatrix}.$$

With the second-order polynomial kernel $K(\mathbf{x}, \mathbf{y}) = (1 + \mathbf{x}^{\mathrm{T}}\mathbf{y})^2$, *the seven basis functions are displayed in the following empirical feature vector:*

$$\vec{\mathbf{k}}(\mathbf{x}) = \begin{bmatrix} K(\mathbf{x}_1, \mathbf{x}) \\ K(\mathbf{x}_2, \mathbf{x}) \\ K(\mathbf{x}_3, \mathbf{x}) \\ K(\mathbf{x}_4, \mathbf{x}) \\ K(\mathbf{x}_5, \mathbf{x}) \\ K(\mathbf{x}_6, \mathbf{x}) \\ K(\mathbf{x}_7, \mathbf{x}) \end{bmatrix} = \begin{bmatrix} 1 \\ (1+u+v)^2 \\ (1-u-v)^2 \\ (1+u-v)^2 \\ (1-u+v)^2 \\ (1+u)^2 \\ (1+2u)^2 \end{bmatrix}.$$

Note that for the coefficients

$$c_1 = 6, \quad c_2 = 1, \quad c_3 = -1, \quad c_4 = 1, \quad c_5 = -1, \quad c_6 = -8, \quad c_7 = 2,$$

it can easily be verified that $\sum_{i=1}^{7} c_i K(\mathbf{x}, \mathbf{x}_i) = 0$. *Therefore, the* $N = 7$ *basis functions* $\{K(\mathbf{x}, \mathbf{x}_i), i = 1, \ldots, 7\}$ *are linearly dependent. This in turn means that the degree of freedom is less than* $N = 7$.

2.4.2 Kernelized learning models

The LSP condition assures the existence of a kernelized learning model characterized by the empirical space. Figure 2.7 shows the empirical space approach (also known as the kernel trick) for both the learning and prediction phases.

During the learning phase, the original training dataset $\{\mathbf{x}_1, \mathbf{x}_2, \ldots, \mathbf{x}_N\}$ is used to generate an $N \times N$ *kernel matrix*:

$$\mathbf{K} = \begin{bmatrix} K(\mathbf{x}_1, \mathbf{x}_1) & K(\mathbf{x}_1, \mathbf{x}_2) & \ldots & K(\mathbf{x}_1, \mathbf{x}_N) \\ K(\mathbf{x}_2, \mathbf{x}_1) & K(\mathbf{x}_2, \mathbf{x}_2) & \ldots & K(\mathbf{x}_2, \mathbf{x}_N) \\ \vdots & \vdots & \ldots & \vdots \\ K(\mathbf{x}_N, \mathbf{x}_1) & K(\mathbf{x}_N, \mathbf{x}_2) & \ldots & K(\mathbf{x}_N, \mathbf{x}_N) \end{bmatrix}, \qquad (2.37)$$

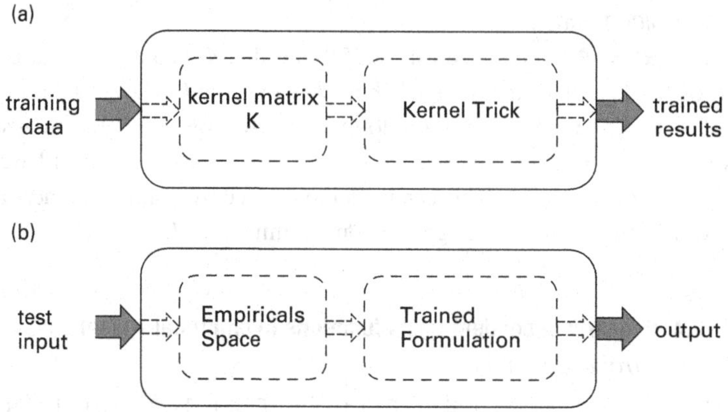

Fig. 2.7. The empirical-space approach to machine learning will not involve explicit feature mapping to the intrinsic space. Its learning is based primarily on the kernel matrix formed from the training dataset. (a) The training phase: the kernel matrix is formed from the training dataset. The learning of system parameters often makes use of the so-called "kernel-trick." (b) The testing phase: the trained system parameters will be used for testing or prediction conducted in the representation on the empirical space.

and $\vec{\mathbf{k}}(\mathbf{x}_j)$ is the jth column of $\mathbf{K}$, i.e.

$$\vec{\mathbf{k}}(\mathbf{x}_j) = \left[\, K(\mathbf{x}_1, \mathbf{x}_j) \quad K(\mathbf{x}_2, \mathbf{x}_j) \quad \ldots \quad K(\mathbf{x}_N, \mathbf{x}_j) \,\right]. \tag{2.38}$$

In other words, $\mathbf{K} = [\, \vec{\mathbf{k}}(\mathbf{x}_1), \vec{\mathbf{k}}(\mathbf{x}_2), \ldots, \vec{\mathbf{k}}(\mathbf{x}_N)]$.

2.4.2.1 Kernelized optimizer formulation (training phase)

According to Eq. (2.33), $\mathbf{u} = \mathbf{\Phi}\mathbf{a}$; thus

$$\|\mathbf{u}\|^2 = ||\mathbf{a}_k||^2_{\mathbf{K}}, \tag{2.39}$$

and then, as shown below, the intrinsic-space optimizer can be reformulated in the empirical space, a procedure known as the *kernelization process.*

ALGORITHM 2.2 (Kernelized learning model in empirical space) *Algorithm 2.1 can be reformulated into an optimizer characterized by the empirical-space representation. The new optimizer aims at finding*

$$\underset{\{\mathbf{a}_k \in \mathbb{R}^N,\ \forall k\}}{\arg\min}\ \mathcal{E}\left(\mathbf{a}_k^{\mathrm{T}} \vec{\mathbf{k}}(\mathbf{x}_j),\ \forall k, j;\ \left\| \sum_{k=1}^{K} \beta_k^{(\ell)} \mathbf{a}_k \right\|_{\mathbf{K}},\ \forall \ell \right) \tag{2.40}$$

subject to the equality constraints

$$c_p\left(\mathbf{a}_k^{\mathrm{T}}\overrightarrow{\mathbf{k}}(\mathbf{x}_j),\ \forall k,j\right)=0,\quad p=1,\ldots,P,$$

and inequality constraints

$$d_q\left(\mathbf{a}_k^{\mathrm{T}}\overrightarrow{\mathbf{k}}(\mathbf{x}_j),\ \forall k,j;\ \left\|\sum_{k=1}^{K}\beta_k^{(\ell)}\mathbf{a}_k\right\|_{\mathbf{K}},\ \forall\ell\right)\le 0,\quad q=1,\ldots,Q.$$

Here $\forall k$, $\forall j$, *and* $\forall \ell$ *stand for* $k=1,\ldots,K, j=1,\ldots,N$, *and* $\ell=1,\ldots,L$, *respectively.* □

After kernelization, the learning model is fully characterized by the kernel matrix, and such an approach is commonly known as the *kernel trick* [64]. This is directly related to the *representer theorem*, which was proposed by Kimeldarf and Wahba [126] and Schölkopf, Herbrich, Smola, and Williamson [236].

2.4.2.2 Kernelized classification formulation (prediction phase)

As shown in Figure 2.7(b), in the prediction phase, the kernelization process contains the following two steps.

- First, the test vector $\mathbf{x}$ in the original space will be mapped to a new representation in the *empirical space*:

$$\mathbf{x}=[x^{(1)},x^{(2)},\ldots,x^{(M)}]^{\mathrm{T}}\rightarrow\overrightarrow{\mathbf{k}}(\mathbf{x})=[K(\mathbf{x},\mathbf{x}_1),K(\mathbf{x},\mathbf{x}_2),\ldots,K(\mathbf{x},\mathbf{x}_N)]^{\mathrm{T}}.\quad(2.41)$$

- During the learning phase, the optimal solution for $\mathbf{a}$ should presumably have been learned from Algorithm 2.2. The optimal vector $\mathbf{a}$ and the empirical representation $\overrightarrow{\mathbf{k}}(\mathbf{x})$ together yield the following (nonlinear) decision boundary:

$$f(\mathbf{x})=\mathbf{a}^{\mathrm{T}}\overrightarrow{\mathbf{k}}(\mathbf{x})+b=0,\quad(2.42)$$

  for use in the prediction phase.

2.4.2.3 A kernelized learning model for under-determined systems

Given the LSP, the optimizer prescribed by Eq. (2.29) can be reformulated into a kernelized learning model, which aims at finding

$$\arg\min_{\mathbf{a}\in\Re^M}\|\mathbf{a}\|_{\mathbf{K}}^2,\quad\text{subject to }\overrightarrow{\mathbf{k}}(\mathbf{x}_j)^{\mathrm{T}}\mathbf{a}=y_j,\quad\text{for}\quad j=1,\ldots,N.\quad(2.43)$$

where $\mathbf{K}$ and $\overrightarrow{\mathbf{k}}(\mathbf{x}_j)$ are defined in Eqs. (2.37) and (2.38), respectively.

To demonstrate the fact that the intrinsic and empirical approaches reach the same solution, let us now revisit a previous numerical example.

Example 2.5 (Kernelization of under-determined supervised learning models)

For the training dataset given in Example 2.3, the optimal solution for the kernelized learning formulation can be solved as follows.

With reference to Eq. (2.43), for $j = 1$, we have

$$\vec{\mathbf{k}}(\mathbf{x}_1)^{\mathrm{T}}\mathbf{a} = [K(\mathbf{x}_1,\mathbf{x}_1)\; K(\mathbf{x}_1,\mathbf{x}_2)]\mathbf{a} = y_1 = +1.$$

For $j = 2$, on the other hand, we have

$$\vec{\mathbf{k}}(\mathbf{x}_2)^{\mathrm{T}}\mathbf{a} = [K(\mathbf{x}_2,\mathbf{x}_1)\; K(\mathbf{x}_2,\mathbf{x}_2)]\mathbf{a} = y_2 = -1.$$

Combining the above, the unique and optimal solution for **a** *can be solved as*

$$\begin{aligned}\mathbf{a} &= \begin{bmatrix} K(\mathbf{x}_1,\mathbf{x}_1) & K(\mathbf{x}_1,\mathbf{x}_2) \\ K(\mathbf{x}_2,\mathbf{x}_1) & K(\mathbf{x}_2,\mathbf{x}_2) \end{bmatrix}^{-1} \begin{bmatrix} +1 \\ -1 \end{bmatrix} \\ &= \begin{bmatrix} 36 & 1 \\ 1 & 4 \end{bmatrix}^{-1} \begin{bmatrix} +1 \\ -1 \end{bmatrix} = \begin{bmatrix} +0.035 \\ -0.259 \end{bmatrix}. \end{aligned} \tag{2.44}$$

Thus $a_1 = +0.035$ and $a_2 = -0.259$. The solution leads to the following discriminant function:

$$\begin{aligned} f(\mathbf{x}) &= 0.035K(\mathbf{x}_1,\mathbf{x}) - 0.259K(\mathbf{x}_2,\mathbf{x}) \\ &= 0.035(1 + u + 2v)^2 - 0.259(1 - w)^2, \end{aligned}$$

which is exactly the same as the intrinsic-space solution, see. Eq. (2.32).

2.4.3 Implementation cost comparison of two spaces

The curse of dimensionality represents a major hurdle to be overcome for cost-effective implementation of learning models [13]. For kernel methods, the dimensions of concern include the intrinsic degree (J) for the intrinsic space and the empirical degree (N) for the empirical space. The cost for the intrinsic-space approach is dominated by the intrinsic degree J, while that for the empirical approach is dominated by the empirical degree N. As a specific example, the so-called KRR learning models in the intrinsic and empirical spaces (see Eqs. (9.31) and (9.25), respectively) require $O(J^3)$ and $O(N^3)$ operations, respectively. With the LSP condition, both the intrinsic-space and the kernelized learning models are at our disposal. Since they lead to equivalent results, the one with the lower cost should be implemented in practical applications.

In summary, as long as one of the two degrees is kept reasonably low, a cost-effective implementation should be feasible. On the other hand, if both degrees are extremely large, it becomes compelling to consider a reduction of the original feature dimension. Discussions on dimension-reduction methods can be found in Chapters 3 and 4 as well as Section 9.9.

- **When to use the intrinsic-space formulation.** The basis functions of the intrinsic vector space are independent of the training dataset. Hence its dimension (i.e. the intrinsic degree J) depends only on the original feature dimension M *and* the kernel function used. Most importantly, it is independent of the size of the dataset.

  Listed below are some scenarios for which the intrinsic approach would be much more preferable than its empirical counterpart. (See Chapter 13.)

- There are important learning models that are not LSP-based, implying that empirical variants of them simply do not exist. In this case, the intrinsic approach becomes the sole option.
- The intrinsic approach may enjoy very significant computational advantage over its empirical-space counterpart when $J \ll N$, e.g. for applications involving big-data machine learning.
- The formulation given in the intrinsic space may be somewhat simpler for the implementation of time-adaptive learning algorithms.

Cherry-picking kernel functions

Since the cost for the intrinsic-space approach is dominated by the intrinsic degree J, there is a strong motivation to lower the intrinsic degree J as much as the performance allows. In Example 1.7, the kernel function was carefully chosen to be $K(\mathbf{x}, \mathbf{y}) = \left(x^{(1)}\right)^2\left(y^{(1)}\right)^2 + \left(x^{(2)}\right)^2\left(y^{(2)}\right)^2$. With a low intrinsic degree $J = 2$, the induced space is adequate to linearly separate the four positive and four negative training samples. However, such a clever and "cherry-picking" kernel function does not come about naturally, and it often has to be carefully learned from the training dataset. Several learning methods have been proposed for just such a purpose, including e.g. LASSO-type classifiers [268] and kernel-SODA feature extractors [311b].

- **When to use the empirical-space formulation.** The basis functions of the empirical vector space are jointly determined by the training dataset *and* the kernel function used. The dimension of the empirical space, i.e. the empirical degree N, is equal to the size of the dataset. The formulation enjoys substantial computational savings when the empirical degree N is relatively small, compared with the intrinsic degree J.

  Listed below are three important scenarios for which the kernel trick is vital:

- The first is when a Gaussian kernel is used, i.e. when $J \to \infty$.
- Another case is when the application scenario involves nonvectorial data analysis.
- It is also a natural approach to incomplete data analysis, c.f. Problem 6.14.

2.5 The kernel-trick for nonvectorial data analysis

In multimedia and biomedical applications, it is common to encounter vectorial as well as nonvectorial datasets. Kernelized learning models provide a unifying paradigm for both vectorial and nonvectorial data processing applications. In the kernel approach to nonvectorial data analysis, the role of the *kernel matrix* is substituted by a *similarity matrix*. However, a suitable similarity metric depends heavily on the applications, and there exists no systematic formulation to effectively characterize the similarity metrics for various types of applications.

More seriously, the numerical property of kernel methods depends closely on the condition that the kernel matrix be *positive semi-definite*. Unfortunately, for most real-world applications, the initial similarity matrices are not likely to satisfy the condition. Consequently, they must be first converted into a positive semi-definite matrix before kernelized learning models can safely be applied.

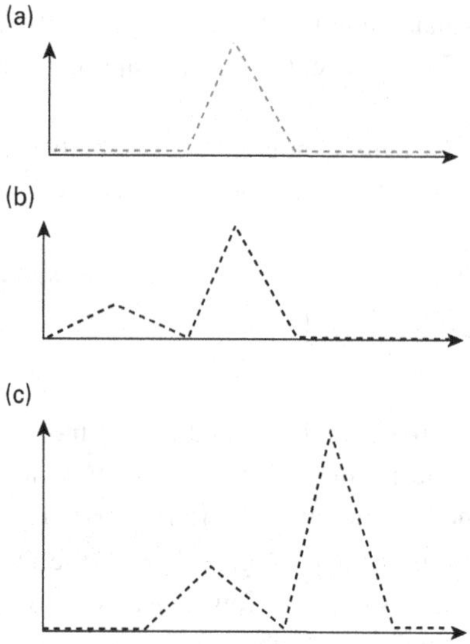

Fig. 2.8. Three temporal waveforms are shown here. Whether a pair of waveforms should be viewed as similar or dissimilar can be quantitatively expressed in terms of a similarity metric, if such a metric may be properly defined for the intended applications. In contrast to the vectorial case, it is usually very complex and highly non-trivial to define a proper similarity metric for nonvectorial objects. Just like for its vectorial counterpart, the general rule is that the metric should be so defined that the higher the value the higher the similarity.

2.5.1 Nonvectorial data analysis

Note that the major difference between the intrinsic and empirical representations lies in the fact that the former is a representation of each individual object, while the latter stems from the pairwise relationship (such as similarity) between a pair of objects. In other words, there exists no empirical representation for any single object.

Similarity metrics for sequences, time series, and temporal waveforms

In genomic applications, each row vector in a time-course microarray data matrix represents a set of continuous measurements of the expression levels of genes associated with *in vivo* experiments using microarrays. The time-course data may not be meaningfully interpreted as static vectors. They can be more meaningfully interpreted as a time series. In this case, it will be highly inappropriate to measure the similarity between two temporal signals $\mathbf{x}_i$ and $\mathbf{x}_j$ by either a linear inner product $\mathbf{x}_i^{\mathrm{T}}\mathbf{x}_j$ or, for that matter, even by any kernel-induced inner product $K_{ij} = K(\mathbf{x}_i, \mathbf{x}_j)$. For example, consider the two waveforms shown in Figures 2.8(a) and (b), for which a direct vector inner product would yield a value higher than the inner product of the two waveforms represented by Figures 2.8(b) and (c), i.e. from the inner product's perspective, $S_{ab} > S_{bc}$. This would have suggested there a higher mutual resemblance within the pair $\{ab\}$ than within the pair $\{bc\}$.

However, as can easily be visualized, the waveform in Figure 2.8(c) is really a time-shifted representation of that in Figure 2.8(b). Therefore, it may be logically argued that

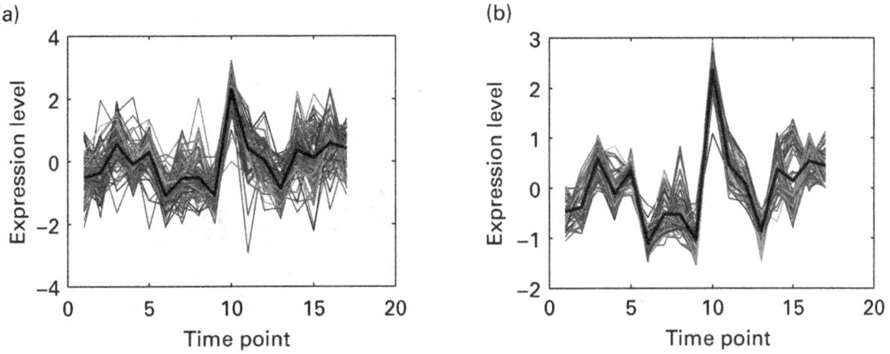

Fig. 2.9. Expression levels of a set of ribosomal genes and their mean: (a) before and (b) after applying median filtering.

the pair $\{bc\}$ bears more mutual resemblance than does the pair $\{ab\}$. This means that there should exist a different similarity metric, say $S'(\mathbf{x}_i, \mathbf{x}_j)$, which is more amenable to the comparison of waveforms. In the literature, scaling-type and alignment-type pre-processing methods are often used for matching waveforms. After proper scaling and alignment, the pair $\{bc\}$ can in fact be perfectly matched. Hence, for a temporally senstive similarity metric, we should have $S'_{ab} < S'_{bc}$, reversing the verdict from the inner product's perspective.

This example emphasizes the vital importance of applying pre-processing for achieving a more suitable definition for similarity metric. In the signal processing literature, there are several well-known pre-processing methods that work well for such a purpose, including lowpass filtering for noise reduction and highpass filtering for detection of abrupt changes [189, 190]. As an example, Figure 2.9(a) shows highly noisy time-course microarray data associated with a set of genes from the ribosomal gene group. Figure 2.9(b) demonstrates that, after lowpass filtering, the processed waveforms exhibit a more compact cluster. This highlights the promising roles of signal processing techniques in facilitating cluster analysis for temporal waveforms.

Similarity metrics for network segmentation

Graphic techniques are vital for analysis of biological networks, such as protein–protein interactions or metabolic/signalling pathways. Another important application scenario involves analysis of social networks based in terms of users' profiles and/or social contacts. In this case, graphic processing tools (such as graph segmentation) will be a vital part of data mining and machine learning applications, including e.g. protein functional classification, user-profile-based search engines, epidemic links, mass surveillance, etc.

Graphs are often denoted as $G = (V, E)$, where V is the vertex set and E is the edge set. For network applications, rich information is naturally embedded in link network graphs, exemplified by Figure 2.10. The similarity matrix of a graph is represented by the affinity matrix $\mathbf{A} = \{A_{ij}\}$, where A_{ij} specifies the adjacency between two vertices $\mathbf{x}_i$ and $\mathbf{x}_j$. The objective of network segmentation to divide the vertices of the graph into

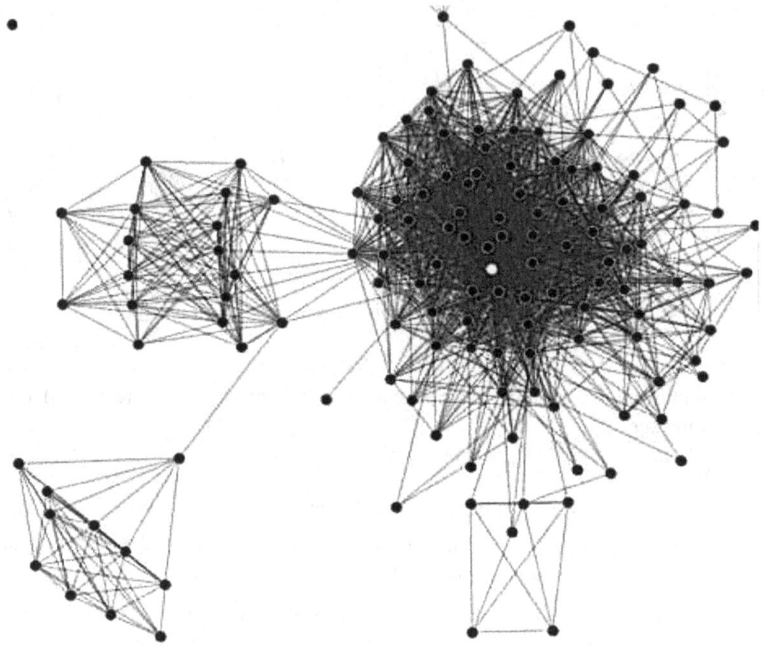

Fig. 2.10. An example of the graphic representation of a social network.

joint or disjoint subsets. One popular approach is to find a partition by maximizing some graph-theoretical criteria, such as the *ratio association*, *ratio cut*, and *normalized cut* [48]. In particular, for the ratio association criterion, the affinity matrix **A** will assume the role of the kernel matrix **K** (see Chapter 6).

2.5.2 The Mercer condition and kernel tricks

Kernelized learning models provide a unified platform for both vectorial and nonvectorial data mining applications. For example, kernel K-means is known to be viable for clustering of temporal signals or graphic nodes. The optimizer has a formulation similar to Eq. (1.20), with the kernel matrix being replaced by the similarity matrix. In other words, the entries of the kernel matrix should be substituted by the pairwise similarity values, i.e.

$$K_{ij} = \begin{cases} S_{ij} & \text{for clustering of temporally adjusted waveforms} \\ A_{ij} & \text{for partitioning graphs by the associative-ratio criterion.} \end{cases} \quad (2.45)$$

However, kernel methods are theoretically valid only for a Mercer kernel matrix, i.e. a positive semi-definite matrix. Such a condition is computationally vital for both unsupervised and supervised learning models.

- **Unsupervised learning models.** When applying kernel K-means to a nonvectorial dataset, the optimizer's cost function is

$$\sum_{j=1}^{N} \min_{k=1,\ldots,K} \{S_{jj} - 2\mathbf{a}_k^{\mathrm{T}} \overrightarrow{\mathbf{k}}_j + \mathbf{a}_k^{\mathrm{T}} \mathbf{S} \mathbf{a}_k\},$$

where $\mathbf{S}$ is the $N \times N$ similarity matrix and $\overrightarrow{\mathbf{k}}_j$ denotes the jth column of $\mathbf{S}$. For the optimizer to have a meaningful solution, it is necessary for $\mathbf{S}$ to be a Mercer matrix, i.e. a positive semi-definite matrix.

- **Supervised learning models.** As an example, for prediction of the subcellular location of proteins, profile alignment SVMs may be applied [166]. The cost function for the SVM optimizer aims at solving for the empirical *decision vector* $\mathbf{a}$:

$$\max_{\mathbf{a}} L(\mathbf{a}) = \mathbf{a}^{\mathrm{T}}\mathbf{y} - \frac{1}{2}\mathbf{a}^{\mathrm{T}}\mathbf{S}\mathbf{a},$$

amidst some equality and inequality constraints. In this case, the matrix $\mathbf{S}$ is derived from the pairwise profile alignment scores between the N training protein sequences. Note again that, for the optimizer to have a meaningful solution, it is necessary for $\mathbf{S}$ to be a Mercer matrix.

As shown below, different strategies for assuring that one has a positive semi-definite kernel matrix or similarity matrix are used for vectorial and nonvectorial data analyses.

- **Mercer kernel assures positive semi-definite kernel matrix for vectorial data.** The adoption of a Mercer kernel, e.g. a polynomial or Gaussian kernel, assures that the kernel matrix is positive semi-definite.
- **A similarity matrix need not be positive semi-definite.** There exists no theoretical assurance that a similarity matrix given in Eq. (2.45) will be positive semi-definite. Generally speaking, the condition fails more often than it is met. To combat this problem, a common approach is to first convert the similarity matrix into a Mercer matrix before applying any kernelized learning models.

A case study: Subcelluar protein sequence analysis

The vital importance of using a positive semi-definite similarity matrix was demonstrated by a previous study on protein subcellular classification [88, 166].

Example 2.6 (Profile alignment SVMs for subcelluar localization) *In this experiment, profile alignment SVMs [166] are applied to predict the subcellular location of proteins in a eukaryotic protein dataset provided by Reinhardt and Hubbard [216]. The dataset comprises 2427 annotated sequences extracted from SWILSPROT 33.0, including those for 684 cytoplasm, 325 extracellular, 321 mitochondrial, and 1097 nuclear proteins. Five different kernels were derived from the similarity matrix obtained via profile alignment of protein sequences of four different subcellular functions.*

The classification accuracies obtained via each of the five kernel matrices are displayed in the following table. Note that the highest accuracy (99.1%) is attained by the only positive semi-definite kernel matrix ($\mathbf{K}_5$) out of the five matrices. Note also that

	Profile alignment kernel				
	$K_1^{\rm pro}$	$K_2^{\rm pro}$	$K_3^{\rm pro}$	$K_4^{\rm pro}$	$K_5^{\rm pro}$
Accuracy (%)	*45.9*	*73.6*	*77.1*	*82.9*	*99.1*
Proportion of negative eigenvalues in $K^{\rm pro}$ *(%)*	*8.5*	*6.2*	*0.3*	*0.2*	*0.0*
Meeting Merecer's condition	*No*	*No*	*No*	*No*	*Yes*

the classification accuracy deteriorates drastically with increasing negativeness of the kernel matrix (as measured by the number of negative eigenvalues), i.e. in the sequence $\mathbf{K}_4$, $\mathbf{K}_3$, $\mathbf{K}_2$, $\mathbf{K}_1$. *This provides clear evidence of the vital importance of the positive semi-definiteness of kernel or similarity matrices.*

2.6 Summary

The kernel approach makes use of a kernel-induced inner product, instead of the traditional Euclidean inner product, to measure the similarity metric of two vectors. This amounts equivalently to the use of the Euclidean inner product in a kernel-induced Hilbert space. Theoretically, Mercer's condition (Theorem 2.1) is imperative for the existence of such a space. Two typical kernel-induced spaces are intrinsic space and empirical space. The chapter provides a formal treatment of the learning models and prediction rules characterized by the two spaces. As such, it establishes an important theoretical footing for all of the subsequent chapters.

2.7 Problems

Problem 2.1 (Distance axioms) *Show that the three distance axioms hold for the* l_p *norms, where* $p = 1$, $p = 2$, *and* $p = \infty$.

Problem 2.2 (Distance axioms and Mahalanobis distance) *Supposing that the Mahalanobis matrix* $\mathbf{M}$ *is a symmetric and positive semi-definite matrix, show that the three distance axioms hold for the Mahalanobis distance defined as follows:*

$$MD(\mathbf{x}, \mathbf{y}) = \sqrt{[\mathbf{x} - \mathbf{y}]^{\rm T}\mathbf{M}[\mathbf{x} - \mathbf{y}]}. \tag{2.46}$$

Problem 2.3 *Consider the following training dataset:*

$$\begin{bmatrix} 0 \\ 0 \end{bmatrix}, \begin{bmatrix} 1 \\ 0 \end{bmatrix}, \begin{bmatrix} 0 \\ 2 \end{bmatrix}, \begin{bmatrix} -1 \\ -1 \end{bmatrix}.$$

(a) *Find the most similar pair of vectors based on the Mahalanobis distance metric for the Mahalanobis matrix*

$$\mathbf{M} = \begin{bmatrix} 4 & 0 \\ 0 & 2 \end{bmatrix}.$$

(b) *Repeat (a) for*

$$\mathbf{M} = \begin{bmatrix} 2 & 1 \\ 1 & 1 \end{bmatrix}.$$

Problem 2.4 (Mercer kernels) *In Eq. (2.21), the intrinsic feature vector is given as*

$$\vec{\phi}(\mathbf{x}) = \exp\left\{-\frac{\|\mathbf{x}\|^2}{2\sigma^2}\right\}\vec{\omega}(\mathbf{x}).$$

An alternative useful intrinsic representation may be defined as follows:

$$\vec{\phi}(\mathbf{x}) = \vec{\omega}(\mathbf{x}). \tag{2.47}$$

This corresponds to the following kernel function:

$$K'(\mathbf{x}, \mathbf{y}) = \vec{\omega}(\mathbf{x})^{\mathrm{T}}\vec{\omega}(\mathbf{x}) = \exp\left\{\frac{\mathbf{x}\cdot\mathbf{y}}{\sigma^2}\right\}.$$

Prove that $K'(\mathbf{x}, \mathbf{y}) = \exp\left\{(\mathbf{x}\cdot\mathbf{y})/\sigma^2\right\}$ *is a Mercer kernel.*

Problem 2.5 (Induced Mercer kernels) *Consider two Mercer kernels* $g(\mathbf{x}, \mathbf{y})$ *and* $h(\mathbf{x}, \mathbf{y})$*, with intrinsic degrees* J_g *and* J_h*, respectively.*

(a) *Show that* $K_1(\mathbf{x}, \mathbf{y}) = g(\mathbf{x}, \mathbf{y}) + h(\mathbf{x}, \mathbf{y})$ *is a Mercer kernel with intrinsic degrees* $J_1 \leq J_g + J_h$.

(b) *Show that* $K_2(\mathbf{x}, \mathbf{y}) = g(\mathbf{x}, \mathbf{y})h(\mathbf{x}, \mathbf{y})$ *is a Mercer kernel with intrinsic degrees* $J_2 \leq J_g \times J_h$.

(c) *Show that* $K_3(\mathbf{x}, \mathbf{y}) = q(x)g(\mathbf{x}, \mathbf{y})q(y)$ *is a Mercer kernel with intrinsic degrees* $J_3 = J_g$.

(d) *Show that* $K_4(\mathbf{x}, \mathbf{y}) = \exp\{g(\mathbf{x}, \mathbf{y})\}$ *will also be a Mercer kernel. Is the intrinsic degree of* $K_4(\mathbf{x}, \mathbf{y})$ *finite or infinite?*

Problem 2.6 (Exponential kernel) *Show that the exponential kernel function (also known as the Laplacian kernel)*

$$K(\mathbf{x}, \mathbf{y}) = \exp\left(-\frac{\|\mathbf{x} - \mathbf{y}\|}{\sigma}\right)$$

is a Mercer kernel.

Problem 2.7 (The sigmoidal function is NOT a Mercer kernel) *Prove that the sigmoidal function is not a Mercer kernel by showing that, when the sigmoidal function is expressed as an expansion of powers of* $\mathbf{x}\cdot\mathbf{y}$*, i.e.* $(\mathbf{x}\cdot\mathbf{y})^q$ *(cf. Eq. (2.9)), there exist some coefficients that are negative.*

Problem 2.8 *Use the property developed in Problem 2.9 to prove that the sigmoidal function is not a Mercer kernel.*

Hint: *Note that the pairwise kernel matrix for two points,* (1.0, 1.0) *and* (1.0, 10.0), *in two-dimensional space is*

$$\mathbf{K} = \begin{bmatrix} K(1.0, 1.0) & K(1.0, 10.0) \\ K(10.0, 1.0) & K(10.0, 10.0) \end{bmatrix} = \begin{bmatrix} 1/(1+e^{-1}) & 1/(1+e^{-10}) \\ 1/(1+e^{-10}) & 1/(1+e^{-100}) \end{bmatrix},$$

which has a negative eigenvalue.

Problem 2.9 *Mercer's condition implies that a kernel function is a Mercer kernel if and only if all the pairwise kernel matrices induced by the kernel function exhibit positive semi-definiteness.*

(a) *As a special case, show that Mercer's condition can be satisfied only if*

$$K(\mathbf{x}, \mathbf{x}) + K(\mathbf{y}, \mathbf{y}) - 2K(\mathbf{x}, \mathbf{y}) = [1 \quad -1]\mathbf{K}_{2\times 2}[1 \quad -1]^{\mathrm{T}} > 0,$$

which in turn implies the existence of the generalized distance

$$d(\mathbf{x}, \mathbf{y}) = \sqrt{K(\mathbf{x}, \mathbf{x}) + K(\mathbf{y}, \mathbf{y}) - 2K(\mathbf{x}, \mathbf{y})}.$$

(b) *Show that*

$$K(\mathbf{x}, \mathbf{x}) + K(\mathbf{y}, \mathbf{y}) - 2K(\mathbf{x}, \mathbf{y}) \geq 0$$

for any Gaussian kernel $K(\mathbf{x}, \mathbf{y})$.

Problem 2.10 (Positive semi-definiteness of kernel matrix) *The following are two important properties regarding the positive semi-definiteness of the kernel matrix.*

(a) *Show that, if* $K(\mathbf{x}, \mathbf{y})$ *is a Mercer kernel, then its corresponding kernel matrix will be positive semi-definite.*

(b) *Show that a non-Mercer kernel* $K(\mathbf{x}, \mathbf{y})$ *may sometimes produce a positive semi-definite kernel matrix for some dataset.*

Problem 2.11 *Show that any symmetric matrix is positive semi-definite if and only if all its eigenvalues are non-negative.*

Problem 2.12 *The eigenfunction decomposition property can be verified by the following equality:*

$$\int_{-a}^{a} \cdots \int_{-a}^{a} K(\mathbf{x}, \mathbf{x}')\phi(\mathbf{x}')d\mathbf{x}' = \lambda\phi(\mathbf{x}).$$

Consider a linear kernel,

$$K(\mathbf{x}, \mathbf{x}') = \mathbf{x}^{\mathrm{T}}\mathbf{x}',$$

for the two-dimensional vectors $\mathbf{x} = [u\ v]^{\mathrm{T}}$ *and* $\mathbf{x}' = [u'\ v']^{\mathrm{T}}$.

(a) *Is $\phi(\mathbf{x}) = u$ an eigenfunction?*
(b) *Is $\phi(\mathbf{x}) = u + v$ an eigenfunction?*

Problem 2.13 *Consider a second-order polynomial kernel,*

$$K(\mathbf{x}, \mathbf{x}') = (1 + \mathbf{x} \cdot \mathbf{x}')^2,$$

for the two-dimensional vectors $\mathbf{x} = [u\ v]^{\mathrm{T}}$ and $\mathbf{x}' = [u'\ v']^{\mathrm{T}}$.

(a) *Is $\phi(\mathbf{x}) = u$ an eigenfunction?*
(b) *Is $\phi(\mathbf{x}) = u + v$ an eigenfunction?*
(c) *Show that $\phi(\mathbf{x}) = u^2$ is generally not an eigenfunction.*

Problem 2.14 (Shift-invariance property) *Some questions concerning the shift-invariance of kernel functions are as follows.*

(i) *Show that the Euclidean distance is shift-invariant, i.e. it is coordinate-independent.*
(ii) *Show that the Euclidean inner product, $\langle \mathbf{x}, \mathbf{y} \rangle = \mathbf{x}^{\mathrm{T}}\mathbf{y}$, is not shift-invariant, i.e. it is coordinate-dependent.*
(iii) *Show that a polynomial kernel with finite order cannot be shift-invariant.*

Problem 2.15 (Transformation-invariance property) *This problem explores some invariance properties under unitary transformation. (A unitary matrix $\mathbf{U}$ satisfies the condition that $\mathbf{U} * \mathbf{U}^{\mathrm{T}} = I$.)*

(i) *Show that Euclidean distance is invariant under unitary transformation.*
(ii) *Show that Euclidean inner product is invariant under unitary transformation. More specifically, if $\mathbf{y}_1 = \mathbf{U}\mathbf{x}_1$ and $\mathbf{y}_2 = \mathbf{U}\mathbf{x}_2$, then $\mathbf{y}_1^{\mathrm{T}}\mathbf{y}_2 = \mathbf{x}_1^{\mathrm{T}}\mathbf{x}_2$.*

Problem 2.16 (Intrinsic degree of polynomial kernels) *It is known that the intrinsic degree for a pth-order polynomial kernel is $J = J^{(p)} = (M + p)!/(M!p!)$, where M is the feature dimension.*

(a) *Show that the intrinsic dimension of the first-order kernel function $K(\mathbf{x}, \mathbf{y}) = (1 + \mathbf{x} \cdot \mathbf{y})$ is $M + 1$.*
(b) *Considering training vectors in a two-dimensional vector space, what is the intrinsic degree for $p = 2$? What is the intrinsic degree for $p = 3$?*

Problem 2.17 *Show that the following two second-order polynomial kernel functions do not have the same intrinsic degree:*

(i) $K_1(\mathbf{x}, \mathbf{y}) = (1 + \mathbf{x} \cdot \mathbf{y})^2,$
(ii) $K_2(\mathbf{x}, \mathbf{y}) = 1 + (\mathbf{x} \cdot \mathbf{y})^2.$

Part II

Dimension-reduction: PCA/KPCA and feature selection

This part contains two chapters concerning reduction of the dimension of the feature space, which plays a vital role in improving learning efficiency as well as prediction performance.

Chapter 3 covers the most prominent subspace projection approach, namely the classical *principal component analysis* (PCA), cf. Algorithm 3.1. Theorems 3.1 and 3.2 establish the optimality of PCA for both the minimum reconstruction error and maximum entropy criteria. The optimal error and entropy attainable by PCA are given in closed form. Algorithms 3.2, 3.3, and 3.4 describe the numerical procedures for the computation of PCA via the data matrix, scatter matrix, and kernel matrix, respectively.

Given a finite training dataset, the PCA learning model meets the LSP condition, thus the conventional PCA model can be kernelized. When a nonlinear kernel is adopted, it further extends to the kernel-PCA (KPCA) learning model. The KPCA algorithms can be presented in intrinsic space or empirical space (see Algorithms 3.5 and 3.6). For several real-life datasets, visualization via KPCA shows more visible data separability than that via PCA. Moreover, KPCA is closely related to the kernel-induced spectral space, which proves instrumental for error analysis in unsupervised and supervised applications.

Chapter 4 explores various aspects of feature selection methods for supervised and unsupervised learning scenarios. It presents several filtering-based and wrapper-based methods for feature selection, a popular method for dimension reduction. For some applications, even if the size of the original feature dimension is computationally handleable, there is an independent need to identify a good set of features, or linear combinations of them, so as to improve the prediction performance.

3 PCA and kernel PCA

3.1 Introduction

Two primary techniques for dimension-reducing feature extraction are *subspace projection* and *feature selection*. This chapter will explore the key subspace projection approaches, i.e. PCA and KPCA.

(i) Section 3.2 provides motivations for dimension reduction by pointing out (1) the potential adverse effect of large feature dimensions and (2) the potential advantage of focusing on a good set of highly selective representations.
(ii) Section 3.3 introduces subspace projection approaches to feature-dimension reduction. It shows that the well-known PCA offers the optimal solution under two information-preserving criteria: least-squares error and maximum entropy.
(iii) Section 3.4 discusses several numerical methods commonly adopted for computation of PCA, including singular value decomposition (on the data matrix), spectral decomposition (on the scatter matrix), and spectral decomposition (on the kernel matrix).
(iv) Section 3.5 shows that spectral factorization of the kernel matrix leads to both kernel-based spectral space and kernel PCA (KPCA) [238]. In fact, KPCA is synonymous with the kernel-induced spectral feature vector. We shall show that nonlinear KPCA offers an enhanced capability in handling complex data analysis. By use of examples, it will be demonstrated that nonlinear kernels offer greater visualization flexibility in unsupervised learning and higher discriminating power in supervised learning.

3.2 Why dimension reduction?

In many real-world applications, the feature dimension (i.e. the number of features or attributes in an input vector) could easily be as high as tens of thousands. Such an extreme dimensionality could be very detrimental to data analysis and processing. For example, consider the following.

- **Computational cost.** A high dimensionality in feature spaces usually means high computational complexity and power consumption both in the (off-line) learning and in the (online) prediction phases.

- **Performance degradation due to suboptimal search.** An extreme feature dimension may cause the numerical process to converge prematurely to a suboptimal solution.
- **Data over-fitting.** In *supervised learning*, when the vector dimension (M) far exceeds the number of training samples (N), data over-fitting becomes highly likely, and this could in turn jeopardize the generalization capability. Feature-dimension reduction offers an effective remedy to mitigate the above-mentioned problems.

In addition, it is worth noting that a vital application of dimension reduction is for visualization purposes. A great variety of techniques has been proposed for dimension reduction [44b, 100, 129].

Feature subspace and feature selection

For notational consistency, throughout the book, a subscript t, as in $\mathbf{x}_t$, denotes the tth sample, while a superscript (j), as in $x^{(j)}$, denotes the jth feature of the vector $\mathbf{x}$.

Suppose that there are in total N training samples, each of which is denoted by an M-dimensional vector:

$$\mathbf{x}_t = \begin{bmatrix} x_t^{(1)} \\ x_t^{(2)} \\ \vdots \\ x_t^{(M)} \end{bmatrix}, \quad t = 1, \ldots, N.$$

Then a *data matrix* can be explicitly expressed as follows:

$$\mathbf{X} = [\mathbf{x}_1 \; \mathbf{x}_2 \; \ldots \; \mathbf{x}_N] \tag{3.1}$$

$$= \begin{bmatrix} x_1^{(1)} & x_2^{(1)} & \ldots & x_N^{(1)} \\ x_1^{(2)} & x_2^{(2)} & \ldots & x_N^{(2)} \\ \ldots & \ldots & \ldots & \ldots \\ x_1^{(M)} & x_2^{(M)} & \ldots & x_N^{(M)} \end{bmatrix}. \tag{3.2}$$

A (linear) dimension-reduction method aims at finding the matrix $\mathbf{W} = [\mathbf{w}_1 \ldots \mathbf{w}_m]$ such that the mapping

$$\mathbf{x} \rightarrow \mathbf{W}^{\mathrm{T}}\mathbf{x} = \mathbf{y}$$

creates an optimal lower-dimensional representation of $\mathbf{x}_t$:

$$\mathbf{y} = [y^{(1)}, y^{(2)}, \ldots, y^{(m)}]^{\mathrm{T}}. \tag{3.3}$$

Two prominent approaches to dimension reduction are (1) subspace projection and (2) feature selection.

- **Subspace projection.** The most powerful and popular approach to dimension reduction is via subspace projection. In this case, each of the new representations $y_t^{(i)}$, $i = 1, \ldots, m$, will be a linear combination of the original features.
- **Feature selection.** Feature selection chooses m most useful features from the original M features. For feature selection, each of the new representations $y_t^{(i)}$, $i = 1, \ldots, m$, will be simply one of the original features.

To summarize, while the subspace-projection approach uses linear combinations of the original features to construct new representations, the feature-selection approach merely retains a subset of the original features for the subsequent data analysis. Each of the two approaches has its own merits and is appealing in its own suitable application domains.

3.3 Subspace projection and PCA

Statistically, a training dataset is commonly modeled as multivariate stochastic observations with a Gaussian distribution. In this case, the optimal subspace can be obtained via PCA, which exploits the statistical dependence and inherent redundancy embedded in the multivariate training dataset to obtain a compact description of the data. Pearson [201] proposed PCA in 1901 as a methodology for fitting planes in the least-squares sense (what is called *linear regression*). Subsequently, it was Hotelling (in 1933) [100] who adopted PCA for the analysis of the correlation structure between many random variables. Some interesting applications may be found in some recent books, e.g. [50, 115].

Assuming Gaussian distributed data, PCA is well known to be optimal under both mean-square-error (MSE) and maximum-entropy criteria. PCA can be computed by several numerically stable algorithms, including eigenvalue decomposition and singular value decomposition (SVD) [79, 80]. Moreover, the optimal performances achieved by PCA can be expressed in closed form. Consequently, PCA is commonly adopted as a convenient tool for feature extraction and/or visualization.

3.3.1 Optimality criteria for subspace projection

The optimization criterion is usually based on how well the full information may be reconstructed from the reduced-dimension partial information. Two optimality criteria for information preservation are as follows.

- **Mean-square-error criterion.** The objective is to determine how well the partial information $\mathbf{y}$ can reconstruct the full-dimensional vector $\mathbf{x}$. The criterion is usually based on the following **reconstruction error**:

$$\epsilon(\mathbf{x}|\mathbf{y}) \equiv \min_{\mathbf{y}\in\mathbb{R}^m} \|\mathbf{x} - \hat{\mathbf{x}}_{\mathbf{y}}\|, \tag{3.4}$$

  where the M-dimensional vector $\hat{\mathbf{x}}_{\mathbf{y}}$ denotes the best estimate of the M-dimensional vector $\mathbf{x}$ from the reduced m-dimensional vector $\mathbf{y}$.
- **Maximum-entropy criterion.** The second criterion is based on the amount of **mutual information**, i.e. how much information (relevant to the original data $\mathbf{x}$) is retained by the reduced-dimension vector $\mathbf{y}$. In this case, an effective design criterion is to maximize the **entropy** $H(\mathbf{y})$.

Under the Gaussian distribution assumption, the second-order statistics (i.e. the covariance matrix) alone suffices to determine the optimal projection subspace. We shall show below that PCA delivers the optimal subspace solution in closed form. More precisely, the optimal subspace is often characterized by the "principal" eigenvectors of the covariance matrix.

3.3.2 PCA via spectral decomposition of the covariance matrix

Suppose that the M-dimensional training vectors $\mathbf{x}_t = [x_t^{(1)}, x_t^{(2)}, \ldots, x_t^{(M)}]^{\mathrm{T}}$ have the following zero-mean and Gaussian distribution function:

$$p(\mathbf{x}) = \frac{1}{\sqrt{(2\pi)^M |\mathbf{R}|}} \exp\left\{-\frac{1}{2}(\mathbf{x}^{\mathrm{T}}\mathbf{R}^{-1}\mathbf{x})\right\}, \tag{3.5}$$

where $\mathbf{R}$ is the $M \times M$ covariance matrix

$$\mathbf{R} = \{r_{ij}\},$$

and $r_{ij} = E[x_t^{(i)\mathrm{T}} x_t^{(j)}]$ is an *inter-feature* covariance between the ith and jth features.

PCA transforms the original coordinate of the vector space into a new coordinate that can showcase the statistical independence associated with the data distribution. Such a transformation is often computable via spectral decomposition of the (estimated) covariance matrix $\mathbf{R}$:

$$\mathbf{R} = \mathbf{V}\boldsymbol{\Lambda}\mathbf{V}^{\mathrm{T}}, \tag{3.6}$$

where $\boldsymbol{\Lambda}$ is a diagonal matrix

$$\boldsymbol{\Lambda} = \mathrm{Diag}\{\lambda_1, \lambda_2, \ldots, \lambda_M\},$$

with the eigenvalues arranged in a monotonically decreasing order, i.e.

$$\lambda_1 \geq \lambda_2 \geq \ldots \geq \lambda_M,$$

and $\mathbf{V}$ is a unitary matrix,

$$\mathbf{V} = \begin{bmatrix} \mathbf{v}_1 & \mathbf{v}_2 & \ldots & \mathbf{v}_M \end{bmatrix}.$$

The bases of the new coordinate are characterized by the column of the unitary matrix $\mathbf{V}$.

Principal components

Note that any vector $\mathbf{x}_t$ can be transformed to its representation in the *spectral vector space* via the following linear mapping:

$$\mathbf{x}_t \rightarrow \mathbf{V}^{\mathrm{T}}\mathbf{x}_t.$$

As a result of transformation, all the new components become statistically independent. The variance of a new component reflects its signal power, which is equal to the corresponding eigenvalue.

Estimation of the covariance matrix

Practically speaking, the second-order statistics or the covariance matrix of the random vector $\mathbf{x}$ is rarely given in advance. It is often estimated from the training dataset. A common formula for the estimated covariance matrix is as follows:

$$\hat{r}_{ij} = \frac{1}{N}\sum_{t=1}^{N} x_t^{(i)} x_t^{(j)}, \quad i = 1, \ldots, M, \quad \text{and} \quad j = 1, \ldots, M. \tag{3.7}$$

This leads to the following PCA algorithm.

ALGORITHM 3.1 (PCA unsupervised learning model) *From the training dataset* $\{\mathbf{x}_1\ \mathbf{x}_2\ \ldots\ \mathbf{x}_N\}$, *we first compute the (estimated) covariance matrix* $\mathbf{R} = \{\hat{r}_{ij}\}$, *where*

$$\hat{r}_{ij} = \frac{1}{N}\sum_{t=1}^{N} x_t^{(i)} x_t^{(j)}, \quad i = 1, \ldots, M, \quad \text{and} \quad j = 1, \ldots, M. \tag{3.8}$$

Apply spectral decomposition on $\mathbf{R}$*:*

$$\mathbf{R} = \mathbf{V}\Lambda\mathbf{V}^{\mathrm{T}} \tag{3.9}$$

For PCA, we retain the m highest principal components

$$y_t^{(i)} = \mathbf{v}_i^{\mathrm{T}}\mathbf{x}_t \quad i = 1, 2, \ldots, m, \tag{3.10}$$

where $\mathbf{v}_i$ *denotes the ith (column) eigenvector of the covariance matrix* $\mathbf{R}_\mathbf{x}$ *corresponding to the ith largest eigenvalue* λ_i. □

In matrix notation, the first m principal components of the vector $\mathbf{x}_t$ is

$$\mathbf{y}_t = \begin{bmatrix} \mathbf{v}_1^{\mathrm{T}} \\ \mathbf{v}_2^{\mathrm{T}} \\ \vdots \\ \mathbf{v}_m^{\mathrm{T}} \end{bmatrix} \mathbf{x}_t = [\mathbf{V}_m]^{\mathrm{T}}\mathbf{x}_t. \tag{3.11}$$

A two-dimensional vector space PCA is exemplified in Figure 3.1(a). In this example, the original dimension is $M = 2$, so there are two components: the principal component is $\mathbf{v}_1^{\mathrm{T}}\mathbf{x}_t$, while the minor component is $\mathbf{v}_2^{\mathrm{T}}\mathbf{x}_t$. The projection along the principal component provides a viewing direction that yields the widest possible spread of data in the projected subspace, increasing the chance of retaining the greatest possible amount information useful for the (subsequent) recovery of the original data.

3.3.3 The optimal PCA solution: the mean-square-error criterion

This section establishes the theoretical proof that PCA is optimal under the minimum-error criteria. Note that the reconstruction error is defined as

$$||\mathbf{x} - \hat{\mathbf{x}}_\mathbf{y}||^2. \tag{3.12}$$

The least-mean-squares estimate is the optimal solution which minimizes the reconstruction error. In the linear estimation theory [120, 151, 230], under the assumption of Gaussian distribution of the original data x, such an optimal estimate of x given y has a closed-form formula (see Chapter 14):

$$\hat{\mathbf{x}}_\mathbf{y} = E[\mathbf{x}|\mathbf{y}] = \mathbf{R}_{\mathbf{xy}}[\mathbf{R}_\mathbf{y}]^{-1}\mathbf{y},$$

where $\mathbf{R}_{\mathbf{xy}}$ denotes the cross-covariance matrix of $\mathbf{x}$ and $\mathbf{y}$, $\mathbf{R}_\mathbf{y}$ denotes the covariance matrix of $\mathbf{y}$, and $E[\cdot]$ denotes the expectation.

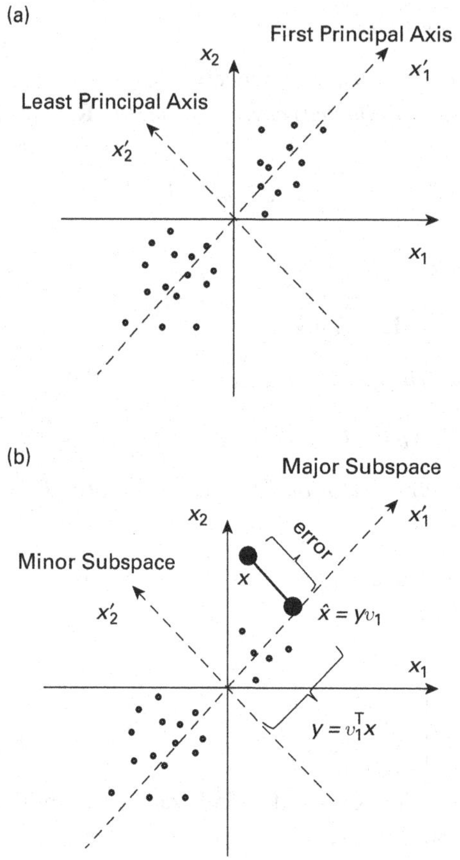

Fig. 3.1. PCA for a two-dimensional data space. (a) The data distribution dictates the two orthogonal components. The dataset has statistically a wider spread along the first (and principal) component, $x^{(1)\prime}$, than along the second (minor) component $x^{(2)\prime}$. (b) For any vector $\mathbf{x}$, its principal component statistically carries more "entropy" and results in less reconstruction error. The reconstructed estimate $\hat{\mathbf{x}}_{\mathbf{y}}$ is equivalent to the projection $\mathbf{y}$ onto $x^{(1)\prime}$. The associated reconstruction error $(\mathbf{x} - \hat{\mathbf{x}}_{\mathbf{y}})$ is also displayed graphically.

Since the m highest principal components (corresponding to the eigenvalues $\{\lambda_i, i = 1, \ldots, m\}$) are represented by $\mathbf{y}$, the m-dimensional (principal) subspace of $\mathbf{x}$ is fully covered. This implies that the reconstruction error is all contributed by the remaining minor components, i.e. those corresponding to the minor eigenvalues $\{\lambda_i, i = m+1, \ldots, M\}$. This leads to the optimality of PCA formally stated as follows [50].

THEOREM 3.1 (Optimality of PCA in reconstruction error) *PCA offers an optimal subspace projection with the minimal expected value of reconstruction error:*

$$E[||\mathbf{x} - \hat{\mathbf{x}}_{\mathbf{y}}||^2] = \mathtt{tr}\{\, \mathbf{R}_{\mathbf{X}}\} - \sum_{i=1}^{m} \lambda_i = \sum_{i=m+1}^{M} \lambda_i,$$

where the trace $\mathtt{tr}\{\cdot\}$ *denotes the sum of all the diagonal elements of the matrix.*

Proof. We shall derive the full proof for the simpler two-dimensional special case first and then extend it to the general case. □

Derivation for the two-dimensional case

Assume for simplicity that the original vector space (denoted by $\mathcal{O}$) is two-dimensional. Our objective is to find the optimal one-dimensional subspace projection.

As illustrated in Figure 3.1(a), the major and minor subspaces are determined by the distribution of the original data. Figure 3.1(b) displays the projection **y**, the reconstructed estimate $\hat{\mathbf{x}}_{\mathbf{y}}$, and the error $(\mathbf{x} - \hat{\mathbf{x}}_{\mathbf{y}})$ for any individual vector **x**. Mathematically, $\mathbf{R}_{\mathbf{x}}$ can be spectrally decomposed as

$$\begin{aligned}\mathbf{R}_{\mathbf{x}} &= \mathbf{V}\boldsymbol{\Lambda}\mathbf{V}^{\mathrm{T}} \\ &= [\mathbf{v}_1\ \mathbf{v}_2]\begin{bmatrix} \lambda_1 & 0 \\ 0 & \lambda_2 \end{bmatrix}\begin{bmatrix} \mathbf{v}_1^{\mathrm{T}} \\ \mathbf{v}_2^{\mathrm{T}} \end{bmatrix},\end{aligned}$$

where $\mathbf{v}_1$ and $\mathbf{v}_2$ represent the projection vectors for the major and minor subspaces, respectively. In other words, $\mathbf{v}_1 = \mathbf{v}_{\mathrm{major}}$ and $\mathbf{v}_2 = \mathbf{v}_{\mathrm{minor}}$. In this case, the optimal PCA projection is

$$\mathbf{y} = \mathbf{v}_1^{\mathrm{T}}\mathbf{x}.$$

In this special case, it can be shown that

$$\begin{aligned}\mathbf{R}_{\mathbf{xy}} &= E[\mathbf{x}\mathbf{y}^{\mathrm{T}}] = E[\mathbf{x}\mathbf{x}^{\mathrm{T}}]\mathbf{v}_1 \\ &= \mathbf{R}_{\mathbf{x}}\mathbf{v}_1 = \lambda_1\mathbf{v}_1\end{aligned}$$

and that

$$\begin{aligned}\mathbf{R}_{\mathbf{y}} &= E[\mathbf{y}\mathbf{y}^{\mathrm{T}}] = \mathbf{v}_1^{\mathrm{T}}E[\mathbf{x}\mathbf{x}^{\mathrm{T}}]\mathbf{v}_1 \\ &= \mathbf{v}_1^{\mathrm{T}}\mathbf{R}_{\mathbf{x}}\mathbf{v}_1 = \lambda_1.\end{aligned} \tag{3.13}$$

From the last two equations, we have

$$\hat{\mathbf{x}}_{\mathbf{y}} = E(\mathbf{x}|\mathbf{y}) = \mathbf{R}_{\mathbf{xy}}[\mathbf{R}_{\mathbf{y}}]^{-1}\mathbf{y} = \mathbf{v}_1\mathbf{y}$$

and that

$$\mathbf{x} - \hat{\mathbf{x}}_{\mathbf{y}} = (\mathbf{I} - \mathbf{v}_1\mathbf{v}_1^{\mathrm{T}})\mathbf{x} = \mathbf{v}_2\mathbf{v}_2^{\mathrm{T}}\mathbf{x} = \mathbf{v}_2\epsilon,$$

where

$$\epsilon = \mathbf{v}_2^{\mathrm{T}}\mathbf{x}.$$

Following a derivation similar to Eq. (3.13), we can show that

$$E[\epsilon^2] = \mathbf{v}_2^{\mathrm{T}}\mathbf{R}_{\mathbf{x}}\mathbf{v}_2 = \lambda_2.$$

It follows that

$$E[\|\mathbf{x} - \hat{\mathbf{x}}_{\mathbf{y}}\|^2] = ||\mathbf{v}_2||^2E[\epsilon^2] = E[\epsilon^2] = \lambda_2.$$

In other words, the reconstruction error is dictated by the minor component.

Derivation for the general case

For the general M-dimensional case, we shall only briefly outline the derivation as follows:

$$\mathbf{R} = \mathbf{R_x} = \mathbf{V}\mathbf{\Lambda}\mathbf{V}^{\mathrm{T}}$$
$$= \left[\mathbf{V}_{\text{major}}\ \mathbf{V}_{\text{minor}}\right] \begin{bmatrix} \mathbf{\Lambda}_{\text{major}} & 0 \\ 0 & \mathbf{\Lambda}_{\text{minor}} \end{bmatrix} \begin{bmatrix} \mathbf{V}^{\mathrm{T}}_{\text{major}} \\ \mathbf{V}^{\mathrm{T}}_{\text{minor}} \end{bmatrix},$$

where

$$\mathbf{\Lambda}_{\text{major}} = \text{Diag}\{\lambda_1, \lambda_2, \ldots, \lambda_m\}$$

and

$$\mathbf{\Lambda}_{\text{minor}} = \text{Diag}\{\lambda_{m+1}, \lambda_{m+2}, \ldots, \lambda_M\}.$$

The PCA solution is

$$\mathbf{y} = \mathbf{V}^{\mathrm{T}}_{\text{major}}\mathbf{x}. \tag{3.14}$$

It follows that

$$\begin{aligned} \hat{\mathbf{x}}_{\mathbf{y}} &= \mathbf{R_{xy}}[\mathbf{R_y}]^{-1}\mathbf{y} = \mathbf{V}_{\text{major}}\mathbf{V}^{\mathrm{T}}_{\text{major}}\mathbf{x}, \\ \mathbf{x} - \hat{\mathbf{x}}_{\mathbf{y}} &= \mathbf{V}_{\text{minor}}\mathbf{V}^{\mathrm{T}}_{\text{minor}}\mathbf{x}. \end{aligned} \tag{3.15}$$

Finally, we have

$$E[\|\mathbf{x} - \hat{\mathbf{x}}_{\mathbf{y}}\|^2] = \mathtt{tr}\{\mathbf{\Lambda}_{\text{minor}}\} = \sum_{i=m+1}^{M} \lambda_i. \tag{3.16}$$

Proof of optimality

As depicted in Figure 3.2, the computation of PCA may be represented by a two-layer network. The M-dimensional input vectors are reduced to m-dimensional vectors $\mathbf{y} = \mathbf{W}^{\mathrm{T}}_{\text{lower}}\mathbf{x}$, where the columns of $\mathbf{W}_{\text{lower}}$ form an orthogonal basis for an m-dimensional subspace.

The original input vectors can be reconstructed from $\mathbf{y}$ as

$$\hat{\mathbf{x}}_{\mathbf{y}} = \mathbf{W}_{\text{upper}}\mathbf{y}.$$

Some simple algebra shows that the optimal two-layer network must obey a vital symmetrical property, namely that

$$\mathbf{W}_{\text{upper}} = \mathbf{W}_{\text{lower}} = \mathbf{W},$$

where $\mathbf{W}^{\mathrm{T}}\mathbf{W} = \mathbf{I}_{m\times m}$. Hence the PCA problem can be reformulated as one of finding the optimal $M \times m$ matrix $\mathbf{W}$ such that the reduced-dimension vector

$$\hat{\mathbf{x}}_{\mathbf{y}} = \mathbf{W}\mathbf{y} = \mathbf{W}\mathbf{W}^{\mathrm{T}}\mathbf{x} \tag{3.17}$$

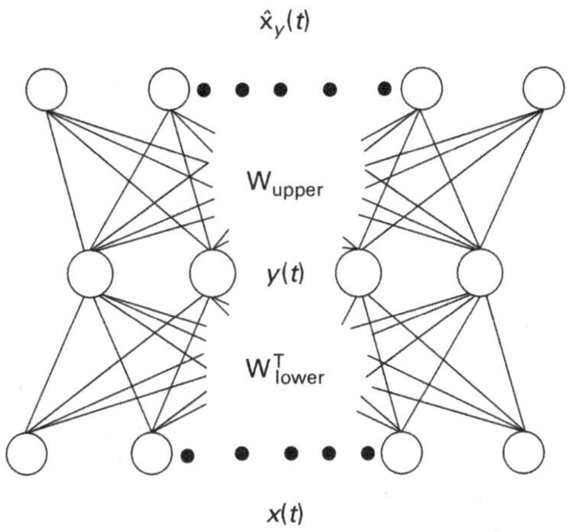

Fig. 3.2. The computation of PCA may be represented by a two-layer network. The M-dimensional input vectors are compressed into m-dimensional representation vectors $\mathbf{y} = \mathbf{W}_{\text{lower}}^{\mathrm{T}}\mathbf{x}$. Then the input vectors are reconstructed from $\mathbf{y}$ via $\hat{\mathbf{x}}_{\mathbf{y}} = \mathbf{W}_{\text{upper}}\mathbf{y}$. The PCA analysis discussed in the text proves that the optimal solution is when $\mathbf{W}_{\text{upper}} = \mathbf{W}_{\text{lower}} = \mathbf{W} = \mathbf{V}_m$. Note that $\mathbf{W}^{\mathrm{T}}\mathbf{W} = \mathbf{I}_{m\times m}$.

can lead to a reconstruction with the least *mean-square reconstruction error*:

$$E\{\|\mathbf{x} - \hat{\mathbf{x}}_{\mathbf{y}}\|^2\} = \mathtt{tr}(\mathbf{R}_{\mathbf{x}}) - \mathtt{tr}(\mathbf{W}^T\mathbf{R}_{\mathbf{x}}\mathbf{W}^{\mathrm{T}}) = \mathtt{tr}(\mathbf{R}_{\mathbf{x}}) - \mathtt{tr}(\mathbf{R}_{\mathbf{y}}).$$

(See Problem 3.2.)

According to Eq. (3.16), by setting $\mathbf{W} = \mathbf{V}_{\text{major}} = \mathbf{V}_m$, i.e. the matrix formed from the first m columns of the unitary matrix $\mathbf{V}$, we arrive at the optimal reconstruction error, see Eq. (3.4). (See Problem 3.3 and Ref. [50] for more details.)

3.3.4 The optimal PCA solution: the maximum-entropy criterion

In information theory, the entropy is often used to measure the amount of information contained by a random vector. The entropy of a random process $\mathbf{x}$ is defined as

$$H(\mathbf{x}) \equiv -\int \mathrm{p}(\mathbf{x})\log \mathrm{p}(\mathbf{x})d\mathbf{x},$$

where the integration is taken over the M-dimensional vector space.

Let the vector formed by a subset of features be denoted by $\mathbf{y}$. As illustrated by Figure 3.3(a), the *mutual information* between $\mathbf{x}$ and $\mathbf{y}$ can be expressed as

$$I(\mathbf{x}|\mathbf{y}) = H(\mathbf{y}) - H(\mathbf{y}|\mathbf{x}).$$

This is graphically depicted in Figure 3.3(a). Since $\mathbf{y}$ contains no new information beyond $\mathbf{x}$, we have that $H(\mathbf{y}|\mathbf{x}) = 0$. It follows that

$$I(\mathbf{x}|\mathbf{y}) = H(\mathbf{y}). \tag{3.18}$$

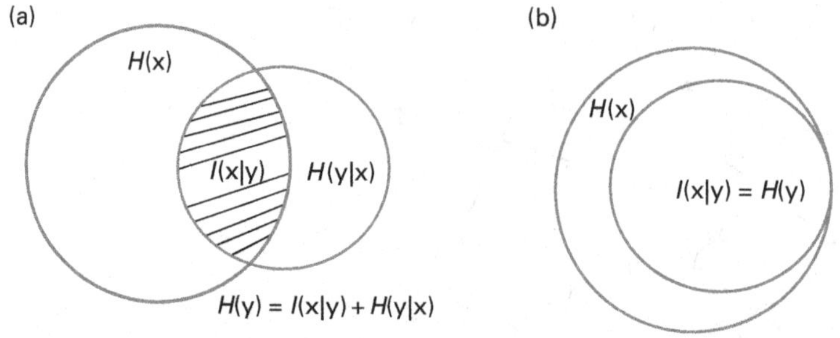

Fig. 3.3. Illustration of the entropies $H(\mathbf{x})$ and $H(\mathbf{y})$, and mutual information. (a) When $\mathbf{x}$ and $\mathbf{y}$ have their own sources, showing $H(\mathbf{x})$ (large disk), $H(\mathbf{y})$ (small disk), and mutual information $I(\mathbf{x}|\mathbf{y}) = I(\mathbf{y}|\mathbf{x})$ (overlap region). In this case, $\text{H}(\mathbf{y}) = I(\mathbf{x}|\mathbf{y}) + H(\mathbf{y}|\mathbf{x})$. (b) If $\mathbf{y}$ is extracted from $\mathbf{x}$, then $H(\mathbf{y}|\mathbf{x}) = 0$ since it contains no new information beyond $\mathbf{x}$. As a result, the mutual information $I(\mathbf{x}|\mathbf{y}) = H(\mathbf{y})$. Note also that $H(\mathbf{x}, \mathbf{y}) = H(\mathbf{x})$.

This is shown in Figure 3.3(b). Therefore, maximizing the **mutual information** $I(\mathbf{x}|\mathbf{y})$ is equivalent to maximizing the **entropy** $H(\mathbf{y})$. Put simply, the best reduced-dimension vector $\mathbf{y}$ is one that delivers the maximal **entropy** $H(\mathbf{y})$.

The fact that maximum mutual information is equivalent to maximum entropy (for subspace projection) has a simple explanation. Let $H(\mathbf{x}, \mathbf{y})$ and $H(\mathbf{y})$ denote the entropies of $(\mathbf{x}, \mathbf{y})$ and $\mathbf{y}$, respectively. If $\mathbf{y}$ is from a subspace of $\mathbf{x}$, $\mathbf{y}$ cannot contain any information beyond $\mathbf{x}$. Consequently, $H(\mathbf{x}, \mathbf{y}) = H(\mathbf{x})$. It follows that

$$H(\mathbf{y}) \leq H(\mathbf{x}, \mathbf{y}) = H(\mathbf{x}).$$

In order for $\mathbf{y}$ to retain as much information as possible, it is clear that we want $H(\mathbf{y})$ to be as close to $H(\mathbf{x})$ as possible.

Since $\mathbf{x}_t$ has a Gaussian distribution, $\mathbf{y}_t = \mathbf{W}\mathbf{x}_t$ has a Gaussian distribution too. By Eq. (3.5),

$$p(\mathbf{y}) = \frac{1}{\sqrt{(2\pi)^m |\mathbf{R}_\mathbf{y}|}} \exp\left\{-\frac{1}{2}(\mathbf{y}^\mathrm{T}\mathbf{R}_\mathbf{y}^{-1}\mathbf{y})\right\},$$

where $\mathbf{R}_\mathbf{y} = \mathbf{W}\mathbf{R}_\mathbf{x}\mathbf{W}^\mathrm{T}$ is the covariance matrix of $\mathbf{y}$. It follows that the entropy of $\mathbf{y}_t$ is given by the following expression [50]:

$$I(\mathbf{x}|\mathbf{y}) = H(\mathbf{y}) = \frac{1}{2}\log_2(|\mathbf{R}_\mathbf{y}|) + \frac{m}{2}\log_2(2\pi e). \tag{3.19}$$

This leads to another optimality property of PCA.

THEOREM 3.2 (Optimality of PCA in Mutual Information) *PCA offers an optimal subspace projection with maximal mutual information between* $\mathbf{x}$ *and* $\mathbf{y}$*:*

$$I(\mathbf{x}|\mathbf{y}) = \frac{1}{2}\sum_{i=1}^{m}\log_2(2\pi e\lambda_i).$$

□

Proof. The optimal PCA solution is $\mathbf{y} = \mathbf{V}^\mathrm{T}_{\text{major}}\mathbf{x}$. It follows that

$$\begin{aligned}\mathbf{R}_\mathbf{y} &= E[\mathbf{V}^\mathrm{T}_{\text{major}}\mathbf{x}\mathbf{x}^\mathrm{T}\mathbf{V}_{\text{major}}] = \mathbf{V}^\mathrm{T}_{\text{major}}E[\mathbf{x}\mathbf{x}^\mathrm{T}]\mathbf{V}_{\text{major}} \\ &= \mathbf{V}^\mathrm{T}_{\text{major}}\mathbf{R}_\mathbf{x}\mathbf{V}_{\text{major}} = \mathbf{\Lambda}_{\text{major}},\end{aligned}$$

and therefore $|\mathbf{R}_\mathbf{y}| = \prod_{i=1}^{m} \lambda_i$. According to Eq. (3.19), the maximum mutual information is

$$I(\mathbf{x}|\mathbf{y}) = \frac{1}{2}\sum_{i=1}^{m} \log_2(\lambda_i) + \frac{m}{2}\log_2(2\pi e)$$
$$= \frac{1}{2}\sum_{i=1}^{m} \log_2(2\pi e\lambda_i).$$

3.4 Numerical methods for computation of PCA

This section describes several numerically efficient methods for computation of PCA, including singular value decomposition (of the data matrix), spectral decomposition (of the scatter matrix), and spectral decomposition (of the kernel matrix).

First, let us note that the true covariance matrix of the input variable is often unavailable in practice. Instead, one usually has a set of training vectors,

$$\{\mathbf{x}_n,\ n = 1, \ldots, N\},$$

from which an $M \times N$ *data matrix* can be formed:

$$\mathbf{X} = [\mathbf{x}_1\ \mathbf{x}_2 \ldots\ \mathbf{x}_N].$$

Recall that the optimal reconstruction of $\mathbf{x}$ from $\mathbf{y}$ is given by Eq. (3.17), i.e.

$$\hat{\mathbf{x}} = \hat{\mathbf{x}}_\mathbf{y} = \mathbf{W}\mathbf{y} = \mathbf{W}\mathbf{W}^{\mathrm{T}}\mathbf{x},$$

where $\mathbf{W} \in \mathbb{R}^{M\times m}$ and $\mathbf{W}^{\mathrm{T}}\mathbf{W} = \mathbf{I}_{m\times m}$.

In this case, the PCA formulation aims at finding the optimal $M \times m$ matrix $\mathbf{W}$ to minimize a "sum of squared errors" (SSE):

$$\mathrm{SSE} = \sum_{n=1}^{N} ||\mathbf{x}_n - \hat{\mathbf{x}}_n||^2 = \sum_{n=1}^{N} ||\mathbf{x}_n - \mathbf{W}\mathbf{W}^{\mathrm{T}}\mathbf{x}_n||^2. \tag{3.20}$$

By noting that $\mathbf{W}^{\mathrm{T}}\mathbf{W} = \mathbf{I}_{m\times m}$ and that

$$||\mathbf{W}\mathbf{W}^{\mathrm{T}}\mathbf{x}_n||^2 = \mathbf{x}_n^{\mathrm{T}}\mathbf{W}\mathbf{W}^{\mathrm{T}}\mathbf{W}\mathbf{W}^{\mathrm{T}}\mathbf{x}_n = \mathbf{x}_n^{\mathrm{T}}\mathbf{W}\mathbf{W}^{\mathrm{T}}\mathbf{x}_n,$$

we arrive at

$$||\mathbf{W}\mathbf{W}^{\mathrm{T}}\mathbf{x}_n||^2 = \mathtt{tr}\left(\mathbf{x}_n^{\mathrm{T}}\mathbf{W}\mathbf{W}^{\mathrm{T}}\mathbf{x}_n\right) = \mathtt{tr}\left(\mathbf{W}^{\mathrm{T}}\mathbf{x}_n\mathbf{x}_n^{\mathrm{T}}\mathbf{W}\right).$$

It follows that

$$\mathrm{SSE} = \sum_{n=1}^{N} ||\mathbf{x}_n - \mathbf{W}\mathbf{W}^{\mathrm{T}}\mathbf{x}_n||^2$$
$$= \sum_{n=1}^{N} ||\mathbf{x}_n||^2 - \mathtt{tr}\left(\sum_{n=1}^{N} \mathbf{W}^{\mathrm{T}}\mathbf{x}_n\mathbf{x}_n^{\mathrm{T}}\mathbf{W}\right)$$

$$= \sum_{n=1}^{N} ||\mathbf{x}_n||^2 - \mathtt{tr}\left(\mathbf{W}^{\mathrm{T}}\mathbf{X}\mathbf{X}^{\mathrm{T}}\mathbf{W}\right)$$

$$= \sum_{n=1}^{N} ||\mathbf{x}_n||^2 - \mathtt{tr}\left(\mathbf{W}^{\mathrm{T}}\mathbf{S}\mathbf{W}\right),$$

since the first sum term is a constant w.r.t. $\mathbf{W}$. The optimizer aims at finding

$$\underset{\{\mathbf{W}\in\mathbb{R}^{M\times m},\mathbf{W}^{\mathrm{T}}\mathbf{W}=\mathbf{I}_{m\times m}\}}{\arg\max} \quad \mathtt{tr}\left(\mathbf{W}^{\mathrm{T}}\mathbf{S}\mathbf{W}\right), \quad \text{where} \quad \mathbf{S} = \mathbf{X}\mathbf{X}^{\mathrm{T}}. \tag{3.21}$$

It is well known that one way to find the optimal solution which maximizes the trace norm is via applying eigenvalue (or spectral) decomposition to the scatter matrix $\mathbf{S} = \mathbf{X}\mathbf{X}^{\mathrm{T}}$. This will be elaborated in the subsequent discussion.

3.4.1 Singular value decomposition of the data matrix

Another efficient method to compute PCA is by applying singular value decomposition (SVD) [80, 272] directly to the data matrix $\mathbf{X}$.

ALGORITHM 3.2 (PCA algorithm based on SVD of the data matrix) *The SVD-based PCA algorithm is as follows.*

(i) Construct the data matrix:

$$\mathbf{X} = [\mathbf{x}_1\ \mathbf{x}_2 \ldots\ \mathbf{x}_N].$$

(ii) Apply SVD to the data matrix $\mathbf{X}$*:*

$$\mathbf{X} = \begin{cases} \mathbf{V}\,[\mathbf{D}\quad \mathbf{0}]\,\mathbf{U} & \text{if } N \geq M \\ \mathbf{V}\begin{bmatrix}\mathbf{D}\\ \mathbf{0}\end{bmatrix}\mathbf{U} & \text{if } M > N. \end{cases} \tag{3.22}$$

Here $\mathbf{V}$ *and* $\mathbf{U}$ *denote* $M \times M$ *and* $N \times N$ *unitary matrices, respectively, and* $\mathbf{D}$ *denotes a diagonal matrix of size* $M \times M$ *or* $N \times N$*, whichever is smaller, i.e. the diagonal matrix* $\mathbf{D}$ *is formed by the* $\min\{M, N\}$ *(generically nonzero) nonsingular values of* $\mathbf{X}$*.*

(iii) Let $\mathbf{y}$ *denote the reduced-dimension (m-dimensional) PCA representation formed from the first m principal components of a test vector* $\mathbf{x}$*, i.e.*

$$\mathbf{y} = \mathbf{V}_m^{\mathrm{T}}\mathbf{x}, \tag{3.23}$$

where $\mathbf{V}_m$ *is the* $m \times N$ *matrix formed from the first m rows of the unitary matrix* $\mathbf{V}$*.*

□

3.4.2 Spectral decomposition of the scatter matrix

It can be shown that, except for a scaling factor, the (estimated) covariance matrix is equivalent to the following matrix:

$$\mathbf{S} = \mathbf{X}\mathbf{X}^{\mathrm{T}}.$$

The matrix $\mathbf{S}$ is named the *scatter matrix* [53, 54]. Therefore, given the *data matrix* $\mathbf{X}$, its PCA may also be computed from its *scatter matrix* $\mathbf{S}$, as opposed to the (statistically estimated) *covariance matrix* $\mathbf{R_x}$. In fact, from now on, our PCA discussion will be exclusively focused on $\mathbf{S}$ or its center-adjusted variant, denoted by $\bar{\mathbf{S}}$.

For the *over-determined scenario*, i.e. $N \geq M$, the PCA may be efficiently computed via spectral decomposition of the scatter matrix.

ALGORITHM 3.3 (PCA algorithm based on scatter matrix) *The scatter-matrix based PCA algorithm is as follows.*

(i) Construct the data matrix $\mathbf{X}$ *from the training dataset.*
(ii) Construct the scatter matrix: $\mathbf{S} = \mathbf{X}\mathbf{X}^{\mathrm{T}}$.
(iii) Compute the spectral decomposition:

$$\mathbf{S} = \mathbf{V}\mathbf{\Lambda}_M\mathbf{V}^{\mathrm{T}}, \tag{3.24}$$

where $\mathbf{\Lambda}_M = \mathbf{D}^2$ *is an* $M \times M$ *matrix.*

(iv) The subspace-projected vector $\mathbf{y}$ *can be obtained as*

$$\mathbf{y} = \mathbf{V}_m^{\mathrm{T}}\mathbf{x}, \tag{3.25}$$

where $\mathbf{V}_m$ *is the* $M \times m$ *matrix formed from the first* m *columns of the unitary matrix* $\mathbf{V}$.

Note that this result is basically equivalent to Eq. (3.11), except for a scaling factor of $\sqrt{N}$. □

3.4.3 Spectral decomposition of the kernel matrix

PCA may also be computed from the (linear) kernel matrix $\mathbf{K}$.[1] This may be computationally appealing when $M > N$, since the kernel matrix will then have a smaller dimension than that of the scatter matrix.

ALGORITHM 3.4 (PCA algorithm based on kernel matrix) *The kernel-matrix-based PCA algorithm is as follows.*

(i) Construct the data matrix $\mathbf{X}$ *from the training dataset.*
(ii) Construct the kernel matrix:

$$\mathbf{K} = \mathbf{X}^{\mathrm{T}}\mathbf{X} = \begin{bmatrix} \mathbf{x}_1^{\mathrm{T}}\mathbf{x}_1 & \mathbf{x}_1^{\mathrm{T}}\mathbf{x}_2 & \dots & \mathbf{x}_1^{\mathrm{T}}\mathbf{x}_N \\ \mathbf{x}_2^{\mathrm{T}}\mathbf{x}_1 & \mathbf{x}_2^{\mathrm{T}}\mathbf{x}_2 & \dots & \mathbf{x}_2^{\mathrm{T}}\mathbf{x}_N \\ \vdots & \vdots & \dots & \vdots \\ \mathbf{x}_N^{\mathrm{T}}\mathbf{x}_1 & \mathbf{x}_N^{\mathrm{T}}\mathbf{x}_2 & \dots & \mathbf{x}_N^{\mathrm{T}}\mathbf{x}_N \end{bmatrix}, \tag{3.27}$$

associated with a linear kernel function $K(\mathbf{x}, \mathbf{x}') = \mathbf{x}^{\mathrm{T}}\mathbf{x}'$.

[1] It is well known that the scatter matrix $\mathbf{S} = \mathbf{X}\mathbf{X}^{\mathrm{T}}$ and the (linear) kernel matrix $\mathbf{K} = \mathbf{X}^{\mathrm{T}}\mathbf{X}$ always have the same nonzero eigenvalues. When $M > N$, the eigenvalue decomposition of the scatter matrix $\mathbf{S}$ has a new expression:

$$\mathbf{S} = \mathbf{V}\mathbf{\Lambda}_M\mathbf{V}^{\mathrm{T}} = \mathbf{V}\begin{bmatrix} \mathbf{\Lambda}_{N\times N} & \mathbf{0} \\ \mathbf{0} & \mathbf{0}_{(M-N)\times(M-N)} \end{bmatrix}\mathbf{V}^{\mathrm{T}}. \tag{3.26}$$

(iii) Apply the spectral decomposition:

$$\mathbf{K} = \mathbf{U}^{\mathrm{T}}\mathbf{\Lambda}\mathbf{U}. \tag{3.28}$$

Note that

$$\mathbf{K} = \mathbf{X}^{\mathrm{T}}\mathbf{X} = \mathbf{U}^{\mathrm{T}}\left[\mathbf{D} \quad \mathbf{0}\right]\mathbf{V}^{\mathrm{T}}\mathbf{V}\begin{bmatrix}\mathbf{D}\\ \mathbf{0}\end{bmatrix}\mathbf{U} = \mathbf{U}^{\mathrm{T}}\mathbf{D}^{2}\mathbf{U}.$$

Now we obtain

$$\mathbf{\Lambda} = \mathbf{D}^{2}. \tag{3.29}$$

(iv) Let the first $m \times m$ principal minor of the diagonal matrix $\mathbf{D}$ be denoted as $\mathbf{D}_m$, i.e.

$$\mathbf{D}_m \equiv \mathrm{Diag}[\sqrt{\lambda_1}, \sqrt{\lambda_2}, \ldots, \sqrt{\lambda_m}].$$

It follows that the highest m ($m \leq \min\{M, N\}$) principal components of $\mathbf{x}$ can be expressed as

$$\mathbf{y} = \mathbf{D}_m^{-1}\mathbf{U}_m\mathbf{X}^{\mathrm{T}}\mathbf{x} = \mathbf{D}_m^{-1}\mathbf{U}_m\overrightarrow{\mathbf{k}}(\mathbf{x}), \tag{3.30}$$

where $\mathbf{U}_m$ denotes the $m \times N$ matrix formed from the first m rows of the unitary matrix $\mathbf{U}$ and $\overrightarrow{\mathbf{k}}(\mathbf{x})$ denotes the empirical feature vector,

$$\overrightarrow{\mathbf{k}}(\mathbf{x}) = \mathbf{X}^{\mathrm{T}}\mathbf{x},$$

induced by the basic linear kernel function. □

Equivalence between Eq. (3.25) and Eq. (3.30)

The proof can be separately treated as follows.

- When $N \geq M$,

$$\begin{aligned}\mathbf{D}_m^{-1}\mathbf{U}_m\mathbf{X}^{\mathrm{T}} &= \mathbf{D}_m^{-1}\mathbf{U}_m\mathbf{U}^{\mathrm{T}}\begin{bmatrix}\mathbf{D}\\ \mathbf{0}_{M\times(N-M)}\end{bmatrix}\mathbf{V}^{\mathrm{T}}\\ &= [\mathbf{D}_m \quad \mathbf{0}_{m\times(N-m)}]\begin{bmatrix}\mathbf{D}\\ \mathbf{0}_{M\times(N-M)}\end{bmatrix}\mathbf{V}^{\mathrm{T}}\\ &= [\mathbf{I}_m \quad \mathbf{0}_{m\times(M-m)}]\mathbf{V}^{\mathrm{T}} = \mathbf{V}_m^{\mathrm{T}}.\end{aligned}$$

- When $M > N$,

$$\begin{aligned}\mathbf{D}_m^{-1}\mathbf{U}_m\mathbf{X}^{\mathrm{T}} &= \mathbf{D}_m^{-1}\mathbf{U}_m\mathbf{U}^{\mathrm{T}}[\mathbf{D} \quad \mathbf{0}]\mathbf{V}^{\mathrm{T}}\\ &= \mathbf{D}_m^{-1}[\mathbf{D}_m \quad \mathbf{0}_{m\times(M-m)}]\mathbf{V}^{\mathrm{T}} = [\mathbf{I}_m \quad \mathbf{0}_{m\times(M-m)}]\mathbf{V}^{\mathrm{T}} = \mathbf{V}_m^{\mathrm{T}}.\end{aligned}$$

Thus the equivalence between Eq. (3.25) and Eq. (3.30) is now formally established.

Example: XOR dataset

As depicted in Figure 2.3, the XOR dataset contains four training vectors,

$$\mathbf{x}_1 = \begin{bmatrix} +1 \\ +1 \end{bmatrix}, \quad \mathbf{x}_2 = \begin{bmatrix} -1 \\ -1 \end{bmatrix}, \quad \mathbf{x}_3 = \begin{bmatrix} +1 \\ -1 \end{bmatrix}, \quad \mathbf{x}_4 = \begin{bmatrix} -1 \\ +1 \end{bmatrix}.$$

Obviously, there exists no classifier that may linearly separate the positive and negative vectors. Hence it provides a simple case study demonstrating the need to employ the extra discriminating capability of kernel PCA induced by nonlinear kernel functions.

Traditional PCA The scatter matrix is

$$\mathbf{S} = \mathbf{X}\mathbf{X}^{\mathrm{T}}, \tag{3.31}$$

and

$$\mathbf{S} = \mathbf{V}\mathbf{\Lambda}_{2\times 2}\mathbf{V}^{\mathrm{T}} = \begin{bmatrix} 4 & 0 \\ 0 & 4 \end{bmatrix} = \begin{bmatrix} 1 & 0 \\ 0 & 1 \end{bmatrix}\begin{bmatrix} 4 & 0 \\ 0 & 4 \end{bmatrix}\begin{bmatrix} 1 & 0 \\ 0 & 1 \end{bmatrix}, \tag{3.32}$$

which by itself is already in a spectrally decomposed form. Its two eigenvalues are 4 and 4. Since $\mathbf{\Lambda}_{2\times 2} = \mathbf{D}^2$,

$$\mathbf{D} = \begin{bmatrix} 2 & 0 \\ 0 & 2 \end{bmatrix}.$$

For this particular example $\mathbf{V} = \mathbf{I}$, so the two-component PCA of a test vector $\mathbf{x}$ (see Eq. (3.33)) will just be the vector $\mathbf{x}$ itself:

$$\mathbf{y} = \mathbf{V}_2^{\mathrm{T}}\mathbf{x} = \mathbf{V}^{\mathrm{T}}\mathbf{x} = \begin{bmatrix} u \\ v \end{bmatrix} = \mathbf{x}. \tag{3.33}$$

Kernel PCA (with a linear kernel) For comparison, we now take a look at the derivation via kernel PCA. The (linear) kernel matrix $\mathbf{K}$ is

$$\mathbf{K} = \begin{bmatrix} 2 & -2 & 0 & 0 \\ -2 & 2 & 0 & 0 \\ 0 & 0 & 2 & -2 \\ 0 & 0 & -2 & 2 \end{bmatrix},$$

which has the following spectral decomposition:

$$\mathbf{K} = \mathbf{U}^{\mathrm{T}}\mathbf{\Lambda}\mathbf{U}$$
$$= \begin{bmatrix} +\frac{1}{2} & +\frac{1}{2} & +\frac{1}{2} & +\frac{1}{2} \\ -\frac{1}{2} & -\frac{1}{2} & +\frac{1}{2} & +\frac{1}{2} \\ +\frac{1}{2} & -\frac{1}{2} & +\frac{1}{2} & -\frac{1}{2} \\ -\frac{1}{2} & +\frac{1}{2} & +\frac{1}{2} & -\frac{1}{2} \end{bmatrix}\begin{bmatrix} 4 & 0 & 0 & 0 \\ 0 & 4 & 0 & 0 \\ 0 & 0 & 0 & 0 \\ 0 & 0 & 0 & 0 \end{bmatrix}\begin{bmatrix} +\frac{1}{2} & -\frac{1}{2} & +\frac{1}{2} & -\frac{1}{2} \\ +\frac{1}{2} & -\frac{1}{2} & -\frac{1}{2} & +\frac{1}{2} \\ +\frac{1}{2} & +\frac{1}{2} & +\frac{1}{2} & +\frac{1}{2} \\ +\frac{1}{2} & +\frac{1}{2} & -\frac{1}{2} & -\frac{1}{2} \end{bmatrix}.$$

Note that the kernel matrix has exactly the same nonzero eigenvalues as before, i.e. 4 and 4.

Solution via Eq. (3.30) For the XOR dataset, $M = 2$ and $N = 4$, so $\mathbf{\Lambda}$ has only two nonsingular eigenvalues and so does

$$\mathbf{\Lambda}_M = \mathbf{\Lambda}_{2\times 2} = \begin{bmatrix} 4 & 0 \\ 0 & 4 \end{bmatrix}.$$

Supposing that $m = 2$ components are to be extracted, this means that

$$\mathbf{D}_m = \mathbf{D}_M = \begin{bmatrix} 2 & 0 \\ 0 & 2 \end{bmatrix},$$

and Eq. (3.30) can be applied to derive

$$\begin{aligned} \mathbf{y} &= \mathbf{D}_m^{-1}\mathbf{U}_m \vec{\mathbf{k}}(\mathbf{x}) \\ &= \begin{bmatrix} \frac{1}{2} & 0 \\ 0 & \frac{1}{2} \end{bmatrix} \begin{bmatrix} +\frac{1}{2} & -\frac{1}{2} & +\frac{1}{2} & -\frac{1}{2} \\ +\frac{1}{2} & -\frac{1}{2} & -\frac{1}{2} & +\frac{1}{2} \end{bmatrix} \begin{bmatrix} u+v \\ -u-v \\ u-v \\ -u+v \end{bmatrix} = \begin{bmatrix} u \\ v \end{bmatrix}, \end{aligned}$$

which is identical to the conventional PCA given in Eq. (3.33).

Comparison of computational complexities

Note that the cost of spectral decomposition for an $M \times M$ scatter matrix $\mathbf{S}$ is around $O(M^3)$. Likewise, the cost of decomposition of an ($N \times N$ matrix) kernel matrix $\mathbf{K}$ is $O(N^3)$ [79].

- For the scenario in which $M \ll N$, the PCA solution will be more effectively computed via spectral decomposition of the relatively small-sized scatter matrix $\mathbf{S}$, as opposed to the (larger) kernel matrix $\mathbf{K}$.
- On the other hand, when $M \gg N$, the empirical-space approach is computationally advantageous because it is faster to do spectral factorization of the (smaller) $N \times N$ matrix kernel matrix $\mathbf{K}$ rather than the (larger) $M \times M$ scatter matrix $\mathbf{S}$ in Eq. (3.24).

3.4.4 Application studies of the subspace projection approach

There exists a rich literature on the wide spectrum of applications of PCA, embracing the fields of signal, image, multimedia, and biomedical processing. Here we shall just use one case study to highlight its potential applications. In the ischemic stroke study [311], given the (complex) scattering parameters [211] of microwave signals (around $0.1 - 3.0$ GHz), the objective is to discriminate patients suffering from ischemic strokes from healthy volunteers. Vectorization of the raw feature space results in about 30,000 complex numbers, thus the final feature vector has a dimension of 62,556. It would be very useful if such a high-dimensional data structure could be visualized by a two-dimensional display. Figure 3.4(a) shows the first two principal components of 27 ischemic stroke samples and 45 samples from healthy control subjects. Note that, according to Figure 3.4(a), the two classes are visibly linearly non-separable, pointing to the need to engage nonlinear kernels in order to achieve an enhanced separability.

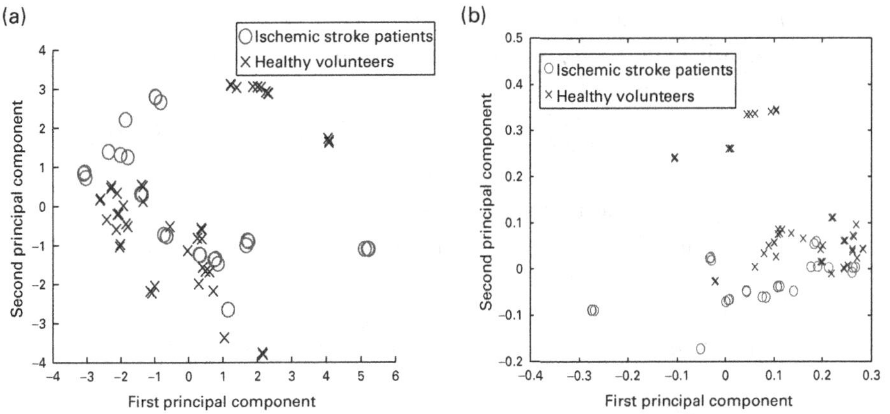

Fig. 3.4. KPCA clearly yields a higher separability than PCA, for the ischemic stroke microwave dataset [211]. (a) Visualization via two PCA components; and (b) visualization via two principal KPCA components with Gaussian kernel and center-adjustment, $\sigma = 15$.

Indeed, as shown in Figure 3.4(b), the visualization provided by a more powerful kernel PCA offers a much enhanced separability. The kernel-PCA theory will be fully treated in Section 3.5.

3.5 Kernel principal component analysis (KPCA)

The principal components in the kernel-induced vector space can be determined in a fashion very similar to the conventional PCA [100]. Again, there are two approaches to the computation of nonlinear kernel PCA (KPCA) [238].

- The first involves explicit mapping of the original training vectors onto their intrinsic representation, then applying the conventional PCA to the newly induced vectors to produce kernel PCA. in the intrinsic space. However, this approach is computationally infeasible if a Gaussian kernel is used due to its infinite intrinsic degree, i.e. $J = \infty$.
- The second method is via the kernel matrix, which is computationally feasible both for a finite and for an infinite intrinsic degree J.

3.5.1 The intrinsic-space approach to KPCA

Similarly to Eq. (3.20), the optimizer in the intrinsic space can be formulated as one finding the optimal $m \times M$ matrix $\mathbf{W}$ which minimizes the following SSE:

$$\text{SSE} = \sum_{n=1}^{N} ||\vec{\phi}_n - \hat{\vec{\boldsymbol{\phi}}}_n||^2 = \sum_{n=1}^{N} ||\vec{\phi}_n - \mathbf{W}\mathbf{W}^{\mathrm{T}}\vec{\phi}_n||^2, \tag{3.34}$$

where we used a simplifying denotation that $\vec{\phi}_n \equiv \vec{\phi}(\mathbf{x}_n), n = 1, \ldots, N$.

Trace-norm optimization formulation

Similarly to Eq. (3.21), the SSE-based optimizer in the intrinsic space can be converted into a trace-based optimizer aiming at finding

$$\underset{\{\mathbf{W}\in\mathbb{R}^{J\times m},\mathbf{W}^{\mathrm{T}}\mathbf{W}=\mathbf{I}_{m\times m}\}}{\arg\max} \quad \mathtt{tr}\left(\mathbf{W}^{\mathrm{T}}\mathbf{S}\mathbf{W}\right), \quad \text{where } \mathbf{S}=\mathbf{\Phi}\mathbf{\Phi}^{\mathrm{T}}. \tag{3.35}$$

It will become clear presently that the number of nontrivial principal components is upper bounded by $\min\{J,N\}$. Supposing that $m = \min\{J,N\}$, the KPCA can be derived via the standard PCA procedure in the intrinsic space. To better illustrate the detailed steps involved in this approach, we shall now look into a numerical example based on the XOR dataset. The first four principal components will be of interest because $m = \min\{J,N\} = \min\{6,4\} = 4$.

It is well known that the optimal solution for maximizing the trace norm can be obtained via eigenvalue decomposition of the scatter matrix. This is formally stated below.

ALGORITHM 3.5 (Intrinsic-space approach to KPCA) *The intrinsic-space approach contains three steps.*

(i) Given a nonlinear kernel function, the intrinsic data matrix $\mathbf{\Phi}$ *can be induced from the original data set. This leads to a new scatter matrix in the intrinsic space:*

$$\mathbf{S}=\mathbf{\Phi}\mathbf{\Phi}^{\mathrm{T}}.$$

(ii) By applying spectral decomposition to the scatter matrix $\mathbf{S}$, *we obtain*

$$\mathbf{S}=\mathbf{V}\mathbf{\Lambda}\mathbf{V}^{\mathrm{T}}. \tag{3.36}$$

(iii) Assuming that $m \leq \min\{J,N\}$, *the optimal solution for Eq. (3.35) is*

$$\mathbf{W}=\mathbf{V}_m, \tag{3.37}$$

and the KPCA for the m principal components can be computed as

$$\mathbf{y}=\mathbf{V}_m^{\mathrm{T}}\vec{\phi}(\mathbf{x})=\begin{bmatrix}\mathbf{v}_1^{\mathrm{T}}\\ \mathbf{v}_2^{\mathrm{T}}\\ \vdots\\ \mathbf{v}_m^{\mathrm{T}}\end{bmatrix}\vec{\phi}(\mathbf{x}). \tag{3.38}$$

The optimal trace norm (see Eq. (3.35)) can be derived as follows:

$$\begin{aligned}\mathtt{tr}\left(\mathbf{W}^{\mathrm{T}}\mathbf{S}\mathbf{W}\right) &= \mathtt{tr}\left(\mathbf{V}_m^{\mathrm{T}}\mathbf{V}\mathbf{\Lambda}\mathbf{V}^{\mathrm{T}}\mathbf{V}_m\right)\\ &= \mathtt{tr}\left([\mathbf{I}_m\ \mathbf{0}_{m\times(N-m)}]\mathbf{\Lambda}[\mathbf{I}_m\ \mathbf{0}_{m\times(N-m)}]^{\mathrm{T}}\right)\\ &= \mathtt{tr}(\mathbf{\Lambda}_{m\times m})=\sum_{i=1}^{m}\lambda_i.\end{aligned} \tag{3.39}$$

□

Example: Polynomial-kernel KPCA for XOR dataset (intrinsic approach)

The procedure contains three steps.

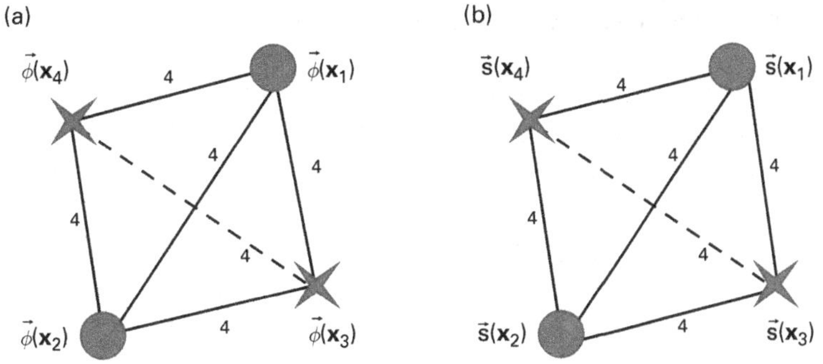

Fig. 3.5. The feature vectors for the XOR dataset in (a) the kernel-induced intrinsic space and (b) the kernel-induced spectral space. While the four original vectors have different distances in the original vector space, the distances between any two training vectors are all the same (i.e. 4) in the intrinsic space. For example, in the intrinsic space, the distance between the first two intrinsic feature vectors can be computed as $\left[(1-1)^2 + \left(\sqrt{2}-\left(-\sqrt{2}\right)\right)^2 + \left(\sqrt{2}-\left(-\sqrt{2}\right)\right)^2 + \left(\sqrt{2}-\sqrt{2}\right)^2 + (1-1)^2 + (1-1)^2\right]^{1/2} = 4$. By the same token, the distances for the other pairs can be computed and are verifiably identical. Consequently, the four vectors are pushed towards the four corners of a pyramid structure shown here. This phenomenon of the training vectors being pushed towards corners of a high-dimensional space is commonly observed in many KPCA applications [136].

(i) **Construct the 6×4 intrinsic data matrix $\boldsymbol{\Phi}$.** Let $K(\mathbf{x}, \mathbf{x}') = (1 + \mathbf{x}\cdot\mathbf{x}')^2$, where $\mathbf{x} = [u\ v]^{\mathrm{T}}$ and $\mathbf{x}' = [u'\ v']^{\mathrm{T}}$. As previously derived in Eq. (2.16), the newly mapped data matrix $\boldsymbol{\Phi}$ is

$$\boldsymbol{\Phi} = \left[\ \vec{\phi}(\mathbf{x}_1)\ \ \vec{\phi}(\mathbf{x}_2)\ \ \vec{\phi}(\mathbf{x}_3)\ \ \vec{\phi}(\mathbf{x}_4)\ \right] = \begin{bmatrix} +1 & +1 & +1 & +1 \\ +\sqrt{2} & -\sqrt{2} & +\sqrt{2} & -\sqrt{2} \\ +\sqrt{2} & -\sqrt{2} & -\sqrt{2} & +\sqrt{2} \\ +\sqrt{2} & +\sqrt{2} & -\sqrt{2} & -\sqrt{2} \\ +1 & +1 & +1 & +1 \\ +1 & +1 & +1 & +1 \end{bmatrix}. \tag{3.40}$$

Since all four induced vectors have the same distance in the intrinsic space, they form a pyramid structure in the intrinsic space as depicted in Figure 3.5(a).

The intrinsic data matrix $\boldsymbol{\Phi}$ leads to a new scatter matrix in the intrinsic space:

$$\mathbf{S} = \boldsymbol{\Phi}\boldsymbol{\Phi}^{\mathrm{T}} = \begin{bmatrix} \sqrt{\frac{4}{3}} & 0 & 0 & 0 & \sqrt{\frac{4}{3}} & \sqrt{\frac{4}{3}} \\ 0 & 2\sqrt{2} & 0 & 0 & 0 & 0 \\ 0 & 0 & 2\sqrt{2} & 0 & 0 & 0 \\ 0 & 0 & 0 & 2\sqrt{2} & 0 & 0 \\ \sqrt{\frac{4}{3}} & 0 & 0 & 0 & \sqrt{\frac{4}{3}} & \sqrt{\frac{4}{3}} \\ \sqrt{\frac{4}{3}} & 0 & 0 & 0 & \sqrt{\frac{4}{3}} & \sqrt{\frac{4}{3}} \end{bmatrix}. \tag{3.41}$$

(ii) **Compute the eigenvalue decomposition of S.**

$$\mathbf{S} = \mathbf{V}\mathbf{\Lambda}\mathbf{V}^{\mathrm{T}}$$

$$= \begin{bmatrix} \sqrt{\frac{1}{3}} & 0 & 0 & 0 & 0 & 0 \\ 0 & 0 & 1 & 0 & 0 & 0 \\ 0 & 0 & 0 & 1 & 0 & 0 \\ 0 & 1 & 0 & 0 & 0 & 0 \\ \sqrt{\frac{1}{3}} & 0 & 0 & 0 & \sqrt{\frac{1}{2}} & \sqrt{\frac{1}{2}} \\ \sqrt{\frac{1}{3}} & 0 & 0 & 0 & \sqrt{\frac{1}{2}} & -\sqrt{\frac{1}{2}} \end{bmatrix}$$

$$\times \begin{bmatrix} 2\sqrt{3} & 0 & 0 & 0 & 0 & 0 \\ 0 & 2\sqrt{2} & 0 & 0 & 0 & 0 \\ 0 & 0 & 2\sqrt{2} & 0 & 0 & 0 \\ 0 & 0 & 0 & 2\sqrt{2} & 0 & 0 \\ 0 & 0 & 0 & 0 & 0 & 0 \\ 0 & 0 & 0 & 0 & 0 & 0 \end{bmatrix}$$

$$\times \begin{bmatrix} \sqrt{\frac{1}{3}} & 0 & 0 & 0 & \sqrt{\frac{1}{3}} & \sqrt{\frac{1}{3}} \\ 0 & 0 & 0 & 1 & 0 & 0 \\ 0 & 1 & 0 & 0 & 0 & 0 \\ 0 & 0 & 1 & 0 & 0 & 0 \\ 0 & 0 & 0 & 0 & \sqrt{\frac{1}{2}} & \sqrt{\frac{1}{2}} \\ 0 & 0 & 0 & 0 & \sqrt{\frac{1}{2}} & -\sqrt{\frac{1}{2}} \end{bmatrix}. \tag{3.42}$$

(iii) **Compute KPCA.** According to Eq. (2.11), a test vector $\mathbf{x}$ is mapped to the following intrinsic feature vector:

$$\vec{\phi}(\mathbf{x}) = [1\ \sqrt{2}u\ \sqrt{2}v\ \sqrt{2}uv\ u^2\ v^2]^{\mathrm{T}}.$$

Using Eq. (3.38), the spectral feature vector is represented by the first $m = 4$ KPCA components of $\mathbf{x}$. It can be computed as

$$\vec{s}(\mathbf{x}) = [\mathbf{V}^{(4)}]^{\mathrm{T}}\vec{\phi}(\mathbf{x})$$

$$= \begin{bmatrix} \sqrt{\frac{1}{3}} & 0 & 0 & 0 & \sqrt{\frac{1}{3}} & \sqrt{\frac{1}{3}} \\ 0 & 0 & 0 & 1 & 0 & 0 \\ 0 & 1 & 0 & 0 & 0 & 0 \\ 0 & 0 & 1 & 0 & 0 & 0 \end{bmatrix} \begin{bmatrix} 1 \\ \sqrt{2}u \\ \sqrt{2}v \\ \sqrt{2}uv \\ u^2 \\ v^2 \end{bmatrix}$$

$$= \begin{bmatrix} 1/\sqrt{3} + (1/\sqrt{3})u^2 + (1/\sqrt{3})v^2 \\ \sqrt{2}uv \\ \sqrt{2}u \\ \sqrt{2}v \end{bmatrix}. \tag{3.43}$$

3.5.2 The kernelization of KPCA learning models

In order to convert KPCA to a formulation of the kernel-trick type, it is necessary that we first validate the LSP for KPCA.

The learning subspace property (LSP)

The following proof of the LSP makes use of the formulation based on minimization of the SSE, see Eq. (3.34). The procedure is very similar to that used in Theorem 1.1.

Let us first assume that the best solution within the learning subspace is $\mathbf{W}$, i.e. $\mathbf{W} \in \mathtt{span}[\mathbf{\Phi}]$. Now we shall modify $\mathbf{W}$ by any additive and orthogonal component, denoted by $\tilde{\mathbf{W}}$, i.e. $\tilde{\mathbf{W}}$ is orthogonal to the subspace $\mathtt{span}[\mathbf{\Phi}]$. This results in a modified candidate solution:

$$\mathbf{W}' = \mathbf{W} + \tilde{\mathbf{W}}.$$

Since $\tilde{\mathbf{W}}^{\mathrm{T}}\overrightarrow{\phi}_n = 0$, it is known that $\mathbf{W}'^{\mathrm{T}}\overrightarrow{\phi}_n = \mathbf{W}^{\mathrm{T}}\overrightarrow{\phi}_n$. Moreover,

$$\begin{aligned} ||\overrightarrow{\phi}_n - \mathbf{W}'\mathbf{W}'^{\mathrm{T}}\overrightarrow{\phi}_n||^2 &= ||\overrightarrow{\phi}_n - \mathbf{W}'\mathbf{W}^{\mathrm{T}}\overrightarrow{\phi}_n||^2 \\ &= ||\overrightarrow{\phi}_n - \mathbf{W}\mathbf{W}^{\mathrm{T}}\overrightarrow{\phi}_n||^2 + ||\tilde{\mathbf{W}}\mathbf{W}^{\mathrm{T}}\overrightarrow{\phi}_n||^2 \\ &\geq ||\overrightarrow{\phi}_n - \mathbf{W}\mathbf{W}^{\mathrm{T}}\overrightarrow{\phi}_n||^2. \end{aligned}$$

Hence the additive modification will not improve the SSE, and thus the LSP condition is established.

Recall that the optimizer in the intrinsic space aims to maximize the trace norm in Eq. (3.35). Since the LSP condition is established, this means that there exists an $N \times m$ matrix $\mathbf{A}$ such that

$$\mathbf{W} = \mathbf{\Phi}\mathbf{A}.$$

Then it follows that

$$\begin{aligned} \mathbf{W}^{\mathrm{T}}\mathbf{S}\mathbf{W} &= \mathbf{A}^{\mathrm{T}}\mathbf{\Phi}^{\mathrm{T}}\mathbf{S}\mathbf{\Phi}\mathbf{A} \\ &= \mathbf{A}^{\mathrm{T}}\mathbf{\Phi}^{\mathrm{T}}\mathbf{\Phi}\mathbf{\Phi}^{\mathrm{T}}\mathbf{\Phi}\mathbf{A} = \mathbf{A}^{\mathrm{T}}\mathbf{K}^2\mathbf{A} \end{aligned}$$

and

$$\mathtt{tr}\left(\mathbf{W}\mathbf{S}\mathbf{W}^{\mathrm{T}}\right) = \mathtt{tr}\left(\mathbf{A}^{\mathrm{T}}\mathbf{K}^2\mathbf{A}\right) \tag{3.44}$$

The constraint on $\mathbf{W}$ may also be re-expressed in terms of $\mathbf{A}$, i.e.

$$\begin{aligned} \mathbf{I}_{m\times m} &= \mathbf{W}^{\mathrm{T}}\mathbf{W} = \mathbf{A}^{\mathrm{T}}\mathbf{\Phi}^{\mathrm{T}}\mathbf{\Phi}\mathbf{A} \\ &= \mathbf{A}^{\mathrm{T}}\mathbf{\Phi}^{\mathrm{T}}\mathbf{\Phi}\mathbf{A} = \mathbf{A}^{\mathrm{T}}\mathbf{K}\mathbf{A}. \end{aligned}$$

In summary, the trace optimizer in the intrinsic space can be converted into the following kernelized optimizer in the empirical space aiming at finding

$$\underset{\{\mathbf{A}\in\mathbb{R}^{N\times m}:\mathbf{A}^{\mathrm{T}}\mathbf{K}\mathbf{A}=\mathbf{I}_{m\times m}\}}{\arg\max} \quad \mathtt{tr}\left(\mathbf{A}^{\mathrm{T}}\mathbf{K}^2\mathbf{A}\right), \quad \text{where} \quad \mathbf{K} = \mathbf{\Phi}^{\mathrm{T}}\mathbf{\Phi}. \tag{3.45}$$

The kernelized model, characterized by the kernel matrix, which is better known as the *kernel trick* [64], can effectively circumvent the need for explicit mapping to kernel-induced intrinsic feature space. The optimal solution for maximizing the trace norm can be obtained via eigenvalue decomposition of the kernel matrix. This is formally stated below.

ALGORITHM 3.6 (Empirical-space approach to KPCA) *The empirical-space approach contains three steps.*

(i) Given a nonlinear kernel function, the kernel matrix is

$$\mathbf{K} = \begin{bmatrix} K(\mathbf{x}_1,\mathbf{x}_1) & K(\mathbf{x}_1,\mathbf{x}_2) & \dots & K(\mathbf{x}_1,\mathbf{x}_N) \\ K(\mathbf{x}_2,\mathbf{x}_1) & K(\mathbf{x}_2,\mathbf{x}_2) & \dots & K(\mathbf{x}_2,\mathbf{x}_N) \\ \vdots & \vdots & \dots & \vdots \\ K(\mathbf{x}_N,\mathbf{x}_1) & K(\mathbf{x}_N,\mathbf{x}_2) & \dots & K(\mathbf{x}_N,\mathbf{x}_N) \end{bmatrix}. \tag{3.46}$$

(ii) Apply spectral decomposition to the kernel matrix **K**, *we obtain*

$$\mathbf{K} = \mathbf{U}^{\mathrm{T}}\boldsymbol{\Lambda}\mathbf{U}.$$

(ii) Denote the empirical feature vector $\vec{\mathbf{k}}(\mathbf{x})$ *as follows:*

$$\vec{\mathbf{k}}(\mathbf{x}) \equiv \begin{bmatrix} K(\mathbf{x}_1,\mathbf{x}) \\ K(\mathbf{x}_2,\mathbf{x}) \\ \vdots \\ K(\mathbf{x}_N,\mathbf{x}) \end{bmatrix}. \tag{3.47}$$

Assume that $m \le \min\{J, N\}$. *Then the optimal solution for Eq. (3.45) is*

$$\mathbf{A}^{\mathrm{T}} = \mathbf{D}_m^{-1}\mathbf{U}_m. \tag{3.48}$$

In conclusion, the highest m principal components of **x** *may be computed as*

$$\mathbf{y} = \mathbf{D}_m^{-1}\mathbf{U}_m\vec{\mathbf{k}}(\mathbf{x}), \tag{3.49}$$

where $m \le \min\{J, N\}$. *If* $J < N$, *then its spectral feature vector is*

$$\vec{\mathbf{s}}(\mathbf{x}) = \boldsymbol{\Lambda}^{-\frac{1}{2}}\mathbf{U}\vec{\mathbf{k}}(\mathbf{x}).$$

□

To verify the algorithm, let us first show that the constraint is satisfied, i.e.

$$\begin{aligned} \mathbf{A}^{\mathrm{T}}\mathbf{K}\mathbf{A} &= \mathbf{D}_m^{-1}\mathbf{U}_m\boldsymbol{\Phi}^{\mathrm{T}}\boldsymbol{\Phi}\mathbf{U}_m^{\mathrm{T}}\mathbf{D}_m^{-1} \\ &= \mathbf{D}_m^{-1}\mathbf{U}_m\mathbf{K}\mathbf{U}_m^{\mathrm{T}}\mathbf{D}_m^{-1} \\ &= \mathbf{D}_m^{-1}\mathbf{U}_m\mathbf{U}^{\mathrm{T}}\boldsymbol{\Lambda}\mathbf{U}\mathbf{U}_m^{\mathrm{T}}\mathbf{D}_m^{-1} \\ &= \mathbf{D}_m^{-1}\boldsymbol{\Lambda}_{m\times m}\mathbf{D}_m^{-1} \\ &= \mathbf{D}_m^{-1}\mathbf{D}_m^{2}\mathbf{D}_m^{-1} = \mathbf{I}_{m\times m}. \end{aligned}$$

Note further that

$$\begin{aligned}
\mathbf{A}^{\mathrm{T}}\mathbf{K}^2\mathbf{A} &= \mathbf{D}_m^{-1}\mathbf{U}_m\mathbf{\Phi}^{\mathrm{T}}\mathbf{\Phi}\mathbf{\Phi}^{\mathrm{T}}\mathbf{\Phi}\mathbf{U}_m^{\mathrm{T}}\mathbf{D}_m^{-1} \\
&= \mathbf{D}_m^{-1}\mathbf{U}_m\mathbf{K}^2\mathbf{U}_m^{\mathrm{T}}\mathbf{D}_m^{-1} \\
&= \mathbf{D}_m^{-1}\mathbf{U}_m\mathbf{U}^{\mathrm{T}}\mathbf{\Lambda}^2\mathbf{U}_m^{\mathrm{T}}\mathbf{D}_m^{-1} \\
&= \mathbf{D}_m^{-1}\mathbf{\Lambda}_{m\times m}^2\mathbf{D}_m^{-1} \\
&= \mathbf{\Lambda}_{m\times m}.
\end{aligned}$$

This implies that the optimal trace norm obtained by the algorithm is, cf. Eq. (3.44),

$$\mathtt{tr}\left(\mathbf{W}^{\mathrm{T}}\mathbf{S}\mathbf{W}\right) = \sum_{i=1}^{m}\lambda_i,$$

which is consistent with Eq. (3.39) derived via the intrinsic-space approach. Thus the kernelized KPCA is now validated.

KPCA and spectral feature vectors

When $m = \min\{J, N\}$, Eq. (3.49) yields exactly the same solution as the kernel-induced spectral feature vector derived in Eq. (3.59), i.e.

$$y^{(i)} = \mathbf{s}^{(i)}(\mathbf{x}), \quad i = 1, 2, \ldots, \min\{J, N\}.$$

Note that the spectral feature vectors are basically the same as KPCA and can be directly derived via the kernel matrix $\mathbf{K}$.

Let us provide a numerical example to illustrate the steps involved in the kernel-trick approach to KPCA.

Example: Polynomial-kernel KPCA for XOR dataset (empirical approach)

For the four XOR training vectors, the 4×4 kernel matrix associated with $K(\mathbf{x}, \mathbf{x}') = (1 + \mathbf{x}^{\mathrm{T}}\mathbf{x}')^2$ is

$$\mathbf{K} = \begin{bmatrix} 9 & 1 & 1 & 1 \\ 1 & 9 & 1 & 1 \\ 1 & 1 & 9 & 1 \\ 1 & 1 & 1 & 9 \end{bmatrix}.$$

By the spectral decomposition of $\mathbf{K}$, we obtain

$$\mathbf{K} = \mathbf{U}^{\mathrm{T}}\mathbf{\Lambda}\mathbf{U} = \begin{bmatrix} \frac{1}{2} & \frac{1}{2} & \frac{1}{2} & \frac{1}{2} \\ \frac{1}{2} & \frac{1}{2} & -\frac{1}{2} & -\frac{1}{2} \\ \frac{1}{2} & -\frac{1}{2} & \frac{1}{2} & -\frac{1}{2} \\ \frac{1}{2} & -\frac{1}{2} & -\frac{1}{2} & \frac{1}{2} \end{bmatrix} \begin{bmatrix} 12 & 0 & 0 & 0 \\ 0 & 8 & 0 & 0 \\ 0 & 0 & 8 & 0 \\ 0 & 0 & 0 & 8 \end{bmatrix} \begin{bmatrix} \frac{1}{2} & \frac{1}{2} & \frac{1}{2} & \frac{1}{2} \\ \frac{1}{2} & \frac{1}{2} & -\frac{1}{2} & -\frac{1}{2} \\ \frac{1}{2} & -\frac{1}{2} & \frac{1}{2} & -\frac{1}{2} \\ \frac{1}{2} & -\frac{1}{2} & -\frac{1}{2} & \frac{1}{2} \end{bmatrix}.$$

The *empirical feature vector* of a test vector $\mathbf{x}$ is

$$\vec{\mathbf{k}}(\mathbf{x}) = \begin{bmatrix} K(\mathbf{x}_1,\mathbf{x}) \\ K(\mathbf{x}_2,\mathbf{x}) \\ K(\mathbf{x}_3,\mathbf{x}) \\ K(\mathbf{x}_4,\mathbf{x}) \end{bmatrix} = \begin{bmatrix} (1+u+v)^2 \\ (1-u-v)^2 \\ (1+u-v)^2 \\ (1-u+v)^2 \end{bmatrix}. \tag{3.50}$$

Let us set $m = \min\{J, N\} = 4$. According to Eq. (3.49), $\mathbf{A}^{\mathrm{T}} = \mathbf{D}_4^{-1}\mathbf{U}_4$, it follows that the KPCA can be computed as

$$\begin{aligned} \mathbf{y} &= \mathbf{A}^{\mathrm{T}}\vec{\mathbf{k}}(\mathbf{x}) = \mathbf{D}_4^{-1}\mathbf{U}_4\vec{\mathbf{k}}(\mathbf{x}) = \mathbf{\Lambda}_4^{-\frac{1}{2}}\mathbf{U}\vec{\mathbf{k}}(\mathbf{x}) \\ &= \begin{bmatrix} 1/\sqrt{3} + (1/\sqrt{3})u^2 + (1/\sqrt{3})v^2 \\ \sqrt{2}uv \\ \sqrt{2}u \\ \sqrt{2}v \end{bmatrix}, \end{aligned} \tag{3.50$'$}$$

which is identical to the *spectral feature vector* obtained via the intrinsic-space approach, see Eq. (3.43).

It follows that the four training spectral feature vectors (without center-adjustment) are

$$\vec{\mathbf{s}}(\mathbf{x}_1) = \begin{bmatrix} +\sqrt{3} \\ +\sqrt{2} \\ +\sqrt{2} \\ +\sqrt{2} \end{bmatrix}, \quad \vec{\mathbf{s}}(\mathbf{x}_2) = \begin{bmatrix} +\sqrt{3} \\ +\sqrt{2} \\ -\sqrt{2} \\ -\sqrt{2} \end{bmatrix},$$

$$\vec{\mathbf{s}}(\mathbf{x}_3) = \begin{bmatrix} +\sqrt{3} \\ -\sqrt{2} \\ +\sqrt{2} \\ -\sqrt{2} \end{bmatrix}, \quad \vec{\mathbf{s}}(\mathbf{x}_4) = \begin{bmatrix} +\sqrt{3} \\ -\sqrt{2} \\ -\sqrt{2} \\ +\sqrt{2} \end{bmatrix}.$$

As displayed in Figure 3.5(b), the four equally distanced spectral feature vectors form a pyramid data structure. Moreover, their first two KPCA components are shown in Figure 3.6(a).

Example: Gaussian-kernel KPCA for XOR dataset (empirical approach)

When the intrinsic degree J is finite, e.g. for polynomial kernels, then either the intrinsic-space approach (Eq. (3.43)) or the kernel matrix method (Eq. (3.49)) may be adopted for the computation of KPCA. However, when the intrinsic degree J is indefinite, e.g. for Gaussian kernels, then the intrinsic-space approach (Eq. (3.43)) is no longer computationally viable. In this case, only the empirical-space approach (Eq. (3.49)) still remains applicable.

As an example, let us now re-derive the kernel PCA for the XOR dataset with the Gaussian kernel function (setting $\sigma = \sqrt{1/2}$):

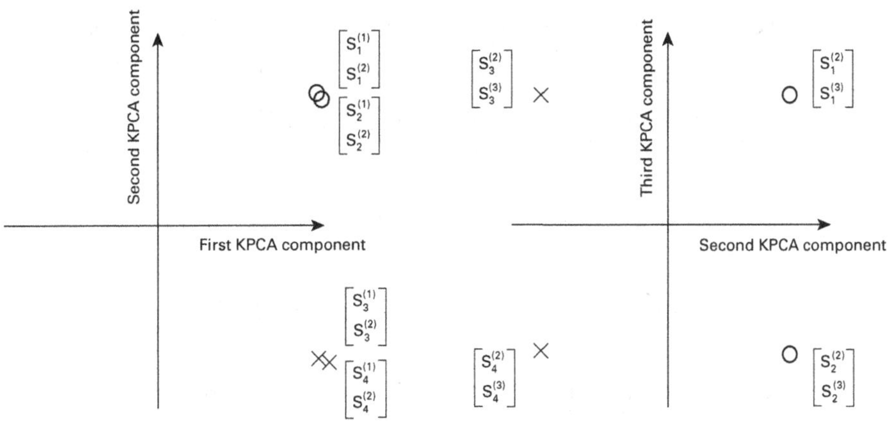

Fig. 3.6. KPCA components can be selected to visualize the separation between two classes of data. Note that the two classes, $(\mathbf{x}_1, \mathbf{x}_2)$ versus $(\mathbf{x}_3, \mathbf{x}_4)$, are clearly separated by the second component. (a) Display of the first and second components based on center-unadjusted KPCA. (b) Display of the second and third components based on center-unadjusted KPCA, which is equivalent to display of the first and second components based on center-adjusted KPCA.

$$K(\mathbf{x}, \mathbf{x}') = \exp\left\{-\|\mathbf{x} - \mathbf{x}'\|^2\right\}. \tag{3.51}$$

From the four XOR training vectors, the 4×4 kernel matrix can be constructed as

$$\mathbf{K} = \begin{bmatrix} 1 & 0.0003 & 0.0183 & 0.0183 \\ 0.0003 & 1 & 0.0183 & 0.0183 \\ 0.0183 & 0.0183 & 1 & 0.0003 \\ 0.0183 & 0.0183 & 0.0003 & 1 \end{bmatrix}.$$

By spectral decomposition, we obtain

$$\begin{aligned} \mathbf{K} &= \mathbf{U}^{\mathrm{T}} \mathbf{\Lambda} \mathbf{U} \\ &= \begin{bmatrix} \frac{1}{2} & \frac{1}{2} & \frac{1}{2} & \frac{1}{2} \\ \frac{1}{2} & -\frac{1}{2} & \frac{1}{2} & -\frac{1}{2} \\ \frac{1}{2} & -\frac{1}{2} & -\frac{1}{2} & \frac{1}{2} \\ \frac{1}{2} & \frac{1}{2} & -\frac{1}{2} & -\frac{1}{2} \end{bmatrix} \\ &\times \begin{bmatrix} 0.9637 & 0 & 0 & 0 \\ 0 & 0.9997 & 0 & 0 \\ 0 & 0 & 0.9997 & 0 \\ 0 & 0 & 0 & 1.0370 \end{bmatrix} \\ &\times \begin{bmatrix} \frac{1}{2} & \frac{1}{2} & \frac{1}{2} & \frac{1}{2} \\ \frac{1}{2} & -\frac{1}{2} & -\frac{1}{2} & \frac{1}{2} \\ \frac{1}{2} & -\frac{1}{2} & \frac{1}{2} & -\frac{1}{2} \\ \frac{1}{2} & \frac{1}{2} & -\frac{1}{2} & -\frac{1}{2} \end{bmatrix}. \end{aligned}$$

The empirical feature vector of any test vector $\mathbf{x} = [u\ v]^{\mathrm{T}}$ may be expressed as

$$\vec{\mathbf{k}}(\mathbf{x}) = \begin{bmatrix} K(\mathbf{x}_1, \mathbf{x}) \\ K(\mathbf{x}_2, \mathbf{x}) \\ K(\mathbf{x}_3, \mathbf{x}) \\ K(\mathbf{x}_4, \mathbf{x}) \end{bmatrix} = \begin{bmatrix} e^{-(1-u)^2} \cdot e^{-(1-v)^2} \\ e^{-(1+u)^2} \cdot e^{-(1+v)^2} \\ e^{-(1-u)^2} \cdot e^{-(1+v)^2} \\ e^{-(1+u)^2} \cdot e^{-(1-v)^2} \end{bmatrix}$$

$$= e^{-(u^2+v^2+2)} \begin{bmatrix} e^{2u} \cdot e^{2v} \\ e^{-2u} \cdot e^{-2u} \\ e^{2u} \cdot e^{-2u} \\ e^{-2u} \cdot e^{2u} \end{bmatrix}. \tag{3.52}$$

According to Eq. (3.49), the spectral feature vector can be computed as

$$\vec{\mathbf{s}}(\mathbf{x}) = \mathbf{D}_4^{-1}\mathbf{U}_4\vec{\mathbf{k}}(\mathbf{x})$$

$$= \boldsymbol{\Lambda}^{-\frac{1}{2}}\mathbf{U}\vec{\mathbf{k}}(\mathbf{x}) = e^{-(u^2+v^2+2)} \begin{bmatrix} 0.491\left(e^{2u}+e^{-2u}\right)\left(e^{2v}+e^{-2v}\right) \\ 0.500\left(e^{2u}+e^{-2u}\right)\left(e^{2v}-e^{-2v}\right) \\ 0.50\left(e^{2u}-e^{-2u}\right)\left(e^{-2v}+e^{2v}\right) \\ 0.509\left(e^{2u}-e^{-2u}\right)\left(e^{2v}-e^{-2v}\right) \end{bmatrix}.$$

Application to supervised classification

In supervised classification, the decision boundaries are determined by the (induced) training vectors:

$$\vec{\mathbf{s}}(\mathbf{x}_1) = \begin{bmatrix} +0.4908 \\ +0.4999 \\ +0.4999 \\ +0.5092 \end{bmatrix}, \quad \vec{\mathbf{s}}(\mathbf{x}_2) = \begin{bmatrix} +0.4908 \\ -0.4999 \\ -0.4999 \\ +0.5092 \end{bmatrix},$$

$$\vec{\mathbf{s}}(\mathbf{x}_3) = \begin{bmatrix} +0.4908 \\ -0.4999 \\ +0.4999 \\ -0.5092 \end{bmatrix}, \quad \vec{\mathbf{s}}(\mathbf{x}_4) = \begin{bmatrix} +0.4908 \\ +0.4999 \\ -0.4999 \\ -0.5092 \end{bmatrix}.$$

By inspection, it is obvious that

$$\mathbf{v} = [0\,0\,0\,1]^{\mathrm{T}}$$

is the optimal spectral-space *decision vector* since it leads to the maximum separation margin (i.e. $0.5092 - (-0.5092) = 1.184$) between the positive and negative training data. In other words, the decision component is the fourth component. This leads to the following optimal decision boundary:

$$f(\mathbf{x}) = 0.509e^{-(u^2+v^2+2)}\left(e^{2u} - e^{-2u}\right)\left(e^{2v} - e^{-2v}\right) = 0. \tag{3.53}$$

For a specific test pattern, say $\mathbf{x}_t = [1 \quad 0.1]^{\mathrm{T}}$, the corresponding spectral feature vector is

$$\vec{\mathbf{s}}(\mathbf{x}_t) = [0.3708\ 0.0747\ 0.3647\ 0.0733]^{\mathrm{T}}. \tag{3.54}$$

Its discriminant function is equal to the value of its fourth component, i.e. $f(\mathbf{x}_t) = 0.0733 > 0$. Therefore, $\mathbf{x}_t$ is identified to be a positive pattern by Eq.(3.53).

3.5.3 PCA versus KPCA

Since PCA can be viewed a special case of KPCA when the linear kernel function is adopted, nonlinear kernels offer a greater degree of freedom in handling complex data analysis. The enhanced capability can be attributed to two important changes in the kernel-induced representation: (1) the dimension of the new vector space is usually higher than the original dimension M; and (2) the induced vectors tend to be more distant from each other and thus more favorably redistributed in the new vector space. (See Problem 3.13.) This is an advantageous property for both unsupervised and supervised machine learning. More exactly, as shown in the examples below, nonlinear kernels offer greater visualization flexibility in unsupervised learning and higher discriminating power in supervised learning.

Unsupervised learning example

As an example showing that KPCA offers improved visualization for unsupervised learning applications, let us take a close look at the three-ring dataset depicted in Figure 3.7(a). It can be shown that the original coordinate system by itself already provides a PCA representation, which shows that all three rings are intertwined and highly non-separable. Figure 3.7(b) shows that an improved separability is being achieved by its KPCA representation based on a Gaussian kernel function.

It is recognized that KPCA offers improved data separability for many real-world application examples. Figure 3.4 compares PCA and KPCA visualization for the ischemic stroke dataset [211, 311]. KPCA clearly offers a much greater separability between the two classes of datasets than does its PCA counterpart. As another example, a similar advantage has been reported in texture classification, see e.g. Kim *et al.* [125].

Supervised learning example

Classification of an XOR dataset offers an illuminating example showing that a nonlinear kernel has a higher discrimination power than its linear counterpart. It is well known that the XOR classification problem does not admit a linear solution in the original space. In contrast, we have just shown that a perfect linear classification solution does exist in the spectral space using a Gaussian kernel.

It is worth noting that the four spectral feature vectors of the XOR dataset all have a mutual distance approximately equal to 4, so they basically form a pyramid data structure as displayed in Figure 3.5(b). Such a well-separated data structure allows a perfect linear classification of the training vectors, even with an arbitrary regrouping. More precisely, by randomly changing the class labels of the XOR training vectors, three variants of XOR-type problems may be constructed, each of which has its own linear solution in the spectral space.

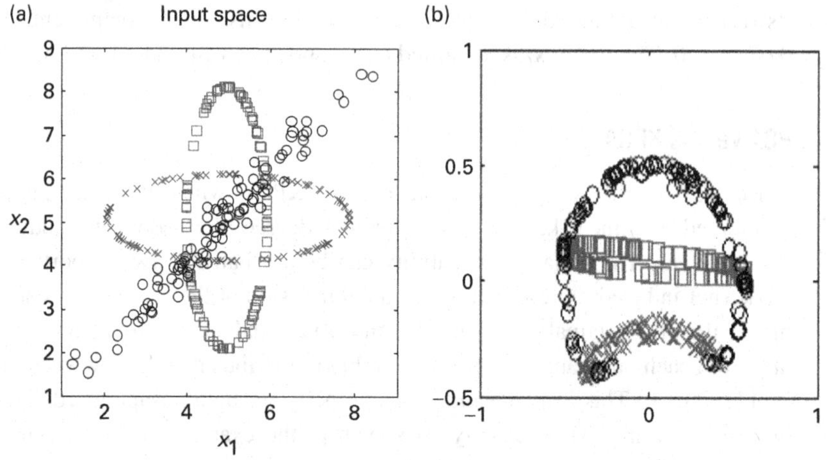

Fig. 3.7. Representations of a three-ring dataset: (a) PCA representation and (b) KPCA representation. KPCA clearly yields a higher separability than PCA. (Courtesy of M. W. Mak.)

- For the original XOR classification problem, we have just demonstrated that the fourth component alone is sufficient to provide a perfect classification between $(\mathbf{x}_1, \mathbf{x}_2)$ and $(\mathbf{x}_3, \mathbf{x}_4)$. Namely, the optimal *decision vector* in the spectral space is $\mathbf{v} = [0\,0\,0\,1]^{\mathrm{T}}$.
- The second variant involves supervised classification between $(\mathbf{x}_1, \mathbf{x}_4)$ and $(\mathbf{x}_2, \mathbf{x}_3)$. It can be shown that the second component is the *decision component* in this case. Thus, the optimal *decision vector* will be $\mathbf{v} = [0\,1\,0\,0]^{\mathrm{T}}$.
- The second variant involves separating $(\mathbf{x}_1, \mathbf{x}_3)$ from $(\mathbf{x}_2, \mathbf{x}_4)$. The optimal solution now hinges upon the third component. In other words, the optimal *decision vector* now becomes $\mathbf{v} = [0\,0\,1\,0]^{\mathrm{T}}$.

Note that the numerical sensitivities pertaining to the different *decision component(s)* can be very different and will play a major role in determining the robustness of the classification, especially for the *kernel ridge regressor* (KRR) to be discussed in Chapter 9.

3.5.4 Center-adjusted versus unadjusted KPCAs

It is worth noting that the data matrix in the intrinsic space is usually not center-adjusted [238]. As a result, the first KPCA component is usually dominated by the effect of the coordinate system rather than the cluster structure itself. We shall illustrate this point by using the XOR dataset as an example again.

Center-unadjusted kernel PCA: XOR dataset

Let us first revisit the center-unadjusted KPCA of the XOR dataset, the first and second components of which are displayed in Figure 3.6(a). Note that it not center-adjusted, its centroid being $[1\ 0\ 0\ 0\ 1\ 1]^{\mathrm{T}}$ in the intrinsic space. As a result, the first component in Eq. (3.40) is completely attributed to the mass centroid.

Figure 3.6(b), on the other hand, displays the second and third KPCA components of the center-unadjusted data matrix, which actually play the role of the two principal components for best visualization of the data structure. In fact, they correspond to the first and second components of the center-adjusted KPCA representation, i.e. the principal KPCA components after the removal of any influence of coordinate translation.

Center-adjusted kernel PCA: XOR dataset

In order to remove the influence of any coordinate translation, our focus is now placed upon a center-adjusted matrix $\bar{\mathbf{\Phi}}$ from the matrix $\mathbf{\Phi}$. More exactly,

$$\bar{\mathbf{\Phi}} = \left[I - \frac{1}{N}\mathbf{e}^{\mathrm{T}}\mathbf{e} \right] \mathbf{\Phi}, \tag{3.55}$$

where $\mathbf{e} \equiv \begin{bmatrix} 1 & 1 & \ldots & 1 \end{bmatrix}^{\mathrm{T}}$. Let us again revisit the XOR example. Note that the matrix $\mathbf{\Phi}$ in Eq. (3.40) needs to be center-adjusted and the intrinsic data matrices before and after the adjustment are, respectively,

$$\mathbf{\Phi} = \begin{bmatrix} +1 & +1 & +1 & +1 \\ +\sqrt{2} & -\sqrt{2} & +\sqrt{2} & -\sqrt{2} \\ +\sqrt{2} & -\sqrt{2} & -\sqrt{2} & +\sqrt{2} \\ +\sqrt{2} & +\sqrt{2} & -\sqrt{2} & -\sqrt{2} \\ +1 & +1 & +1 & +1 \\ +1 & +1 & +1 & +1 \end{bmatrix} \rightarrow \bar{\mathbf{\Phi}} = \begin{bmatrix} 0 & 0 & 0 & 0 \\ +\sqrt{2} & -\sqrt{2} & +\sqrt{2} & -\sqrt{2} \\ +\sqrt{2} & -\sqrt{2} & -\sqrt{2} & +\sqrt{2} \\ +\sqrt{2} & +\sqrt{2} & -\sqrt{2} & -\sqrt{2} \\ 0 & 0 & 0 & 0 \\ 0 & 0 & 0 & 0 \end{bmatrix}.$$

The four newly induced training vectors in the intrinsic space can again be represented by the pyramid shown in Figure 3.5(a).

Now apply SVD to the new data matrix $\bar{\mathbf{\Phi}}$:

$$\bar{\mathbf{\Phi}} = \mathbf{V} \begin{bmatrix} \bar{\mathbf{D}} \\ \mathbf{0} \end{bmatrix} \mathbf{U}$$

$$= \begin{bmatrix} \sqrt{\frac{1}{3}} & 0 & 0 & 0 & 0 & 0 \\ 0 & 0 & 1 & 0 & 0 & 0 \\ 0 & 0 & 0 & 1 & 0 & 0 \\ 0 & 1 & 0 & 0 & 0 & 0 \\ \sqrt{\frac{1}{3}} & 0 & 0 & 0 & \sqrt{\frac{1}{2}} & \sqrt{\frac{1}{2}} \\ \sqrt{\frac{1}{3}} & 0 & 0 & 0 & \sqrt{\frac{1}{2}} & -\sqrt{\frac{1}{2}} \end{bmatrix}$$

$$
\times \begin{bmatrix} 0 & 0 & 0 & 0 \\ 0 & 2\sqrt{2} & 0 & 0 \\ 0 & 0 & 2\sqrt{2} & 0 \\ 0 & 0 & 0 & 2\sqrt{2} \\ 0 & 0 & 0 & 0 \\ 0 & 0 & 0 & 0 \end{bmatrix}
\times \begin{bmatrix} \frac{1}{2} & \frac{1}{2} & \frac{1}{2} & \frac{1}{2} \\ \frac{1}{2} & \frac{1}{2} & -\frac{1}{2} & -\frac{1}{2} \\ \frac{1}{2} & -\frac{1}{2} & \frac{1}{2} & -\frac{1}{2} \\ \frac{1}{2} & -\frac{1}{2} & -\frac{1}{2} & \frac{1}{2} \end{bmatrix}.
$$

On comparing the SVD of $\mathbf{\Phi}$ and that of $\bar{\mathbf{\Phi}}$ (see Eq. (3.55)), they share exactly the same values in three of the four KPCA components.

Center-adjusted kernel PCA: kernel-matrix based approach

The center-adjusted kernel PCA may be directly derived via a center-adjusted kernel matrix [238]. From Eq. (3.55), we have

$$
\begin{aligned}
\bar{\mathbf{K}} &= \bar{\mathbf{\Phi}}\bar{\mathbf{\Phi}}^{\mathrm{T}} \\
&= \left[I - \frac{1}{N}\mathbf{e}^{\mathrm{T}}\mathbf{e}\right] \mathbf{\Phi}\mathbf{\Phi}^{\mathrm{T}} \left[I - \frac{1}{N}\mathbf{e}^{\mathrm{T}}\mathbf{e}\right] \\
&= \left[I - \frac{1}{N}\mathbf{e}^{\mathrm{T}}\mathbf{e}\right] \mathbf{K} \left[I - \frac{1}{N}\mathbf{e}^{\mathrm{T}}\mathbf{e}\right].
\end{aligned} \tag{3.56}
$$

Therefore, center-adjustment may be directly implemented on the kernel matrix without the explicit mapping to the intrinsic space.

Example 3.1 (Center-adjusted kernel matrix: XOR dataset) *Let us illustrate of the effect of center-adjustment by means of the XOR example. First, we shall derive the center-adjusted kernel matrix for the XOR-dataset. Recall that the* 4×4 *kernel matrix is*

$$
\mathbf{K} = \begin{bmatrix} 9 & 1 & 1 & 1 \\ 1 & 9 & 1 & 1 \\ 1 & 1 & 9 & 1 \\ 1 & 1 & 1 & 9 \end{bmatrix}.
$$

By use of Eq. (3.56), we obtain

$$
\bar{\mathbf{K}} = \left[I - \frac{1}{N}\mathbf{e}^{\mathrm{T}}\mathbf{e}\right] \begin{bmatrix} 9 & 1 & 1 & 1 \\ 1 & 9 & 1 & 1 \\ 1 & 1 & 9 & 1 \\ 1 & 1 & 1 & 9 \end{bmatrix} \left[I - \frac{1}{N}\mathbf{e}^{\mathrm{T}}\mathbf{e}\right] = \begin{bmatrix} 6 & -2 & -2 & -2 \\ -2 & 6 & -2 & -2 \\ -2 & -2 & 6 & -2 \\ -2 & -2 & -2 & 6 \end{bmatrix}.
$$

By spectral decomposition, we obtain

$$\bar{\mathbf{K}} = \mathbf{U}^{\mathrm{T}}\bar{\boldsymbol{\Lambda}}\mathbf{U} = \begin{bmatrix} +\frac{1}{2} & +\frac{1}{2} & +\frac{1}{2} & +\frac{1}{2} \\ +\frac{1}{2} & -\frac{1}{2} & -\frac{1}{2} & +\frac{1}{2} \\ -\frac{1}{2} & +\frac{1}{2} & -\frac{1}{2} & +\frac{1}{2} \\ -\frac{1}{2} & -\frac{1}{2} & +\frac{1}{2} & +\frac{1}{2} \end{bmatrix} \begin{bmatrix} 8 & 0 & 0 & 0 \\ 0 & 8 & 0 & 0 \\ 0 & 0 & 8 & 0 \\ 0 & 0 & 0 & 0 \end{bmatrix} \times \begin{bmatrix} +\frac{1}{2} & +\frac{1}{2} & -\frac{1}{2} & -\frac{1}{2} \\ +\frac{1}{2} & -\frac{1}{2} & +\frac{1}{2} & -\frac{1}{2} \\ +\frac{1}{2} & -\frac{1}{2} & -\frac{1}{2} & +\frac{1}{2} \\ +\frac{1}{2} & +\frac{1}{2} & +\frac{1}{2} & +\frac{1}{2} \end{bmatrix}.$$

The four training spectral feature vectors (after center-adjustment) are

$$\vec{\mathbf{s}}(\mathbf{x}_1) = \begin{bmatrix} +\sqrt{2} \\ +\sqrt{2} \\ +\sqrt{2} \\ 0 \end{bmatrix}, \quad \vec{\mathbf{s}}(\mathbf{x}_2) = \begin{bmatrix} +\sqrt{2} \\ -\sqrt{2} \\ -\sqrt{2} \\ 0 \end{bmatrix},$$

$$\vec{\mathbf{s}}(\mathbf{x}_3) = \begin{bmatrix} -\sqrt{2} \\ +\sqrt{2} \\ -\sqrt{2} \\ 0 \end{bmatrix}, \quad \vec{\mathbf{s}}(\mathbf{x}_4) = \begin{bmatrix} -\sqrt{2} \\ -\sqrt{2} \\ +\sqrt{2} \\ 0 \end{bmatrix}.$$

The data structure of the kernel PCA can be effectively visualized by displaying the first, second, and third components of the center-adjusted KPCA, resulting in the pyramid structure shown in Figure 3.5(b).

Example 3.2 (Kernel PCA: ischemic stroke microwave dataset) *The effect of center-adjustment can be further illuminated by a case study based on the ischemic stroke microwave dataset [211, 311]. Figure 3.8(a) shows that, for the unadjusted case, the two most useful components are the second and third KPCA components. We purposefully skipped the use of the first component, which is dictated by the centroid's location and thus irrelevant to revelation of the data cluster structure. Consequently, the second and third KPCA components are adopted here for best visualization effect. Figure 3.8(b) shows that, for the center-adjusted case, the two most useful components are the first and second KPCA components. We note the striking resemblance between Figures 3.8(a) and (b), even though one of them is derived from the original kernel matrix and the other is center-adjusted.*

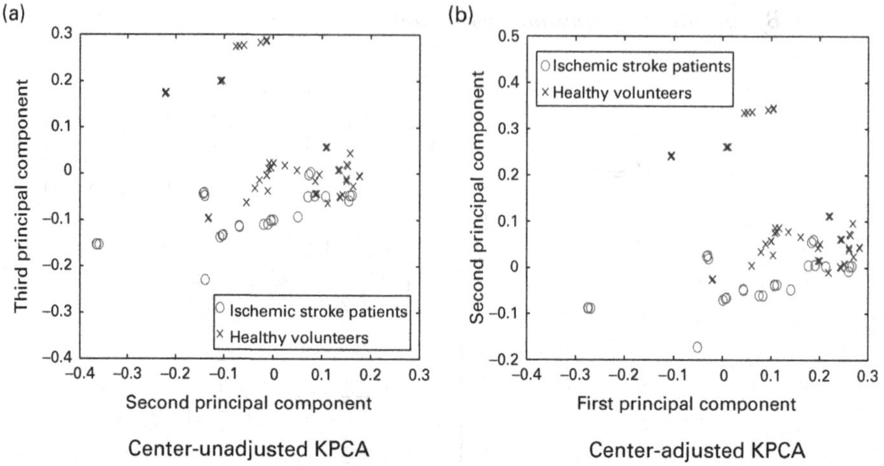

Fig. 3.8. A comparison between the original and center-adjusted kernel PCAs for the ischemic stroke microwave dataset [211, 311]. (a) For the unadjusted case, the second and third components of the kernel PCA are displayed. (b) In contrast, for center-adjusted Kernel PCAs, the first and second components are used here for visualization. Note the strong resemblance between the two displays.

3.5.5 Spectral vector space

Another finite-dimensional vector space is the *spectral space* derived below. By eigenvalue decomposition of the kernel matrix $\mathbf{K}$, we have

$$\mathbf{K} = \mathbf{U}^{\mathrm{T}}\mathbf{\Lambda}\mathbf{U} = \mathbf{U}^{\mathrm{T}}\mathbf{\Lambda}^{\frac{1}{2}}\mathbf{\Lambda}^{\frac{1}{2}}\mathbf{U}. \tag{3.57}$$

This leads to the spectral factorization of $\mathbf{K}$:

$$\mathbf{K} = \mathbf{E}^{\mathrm{T}}\mathbf{E}, \quad \text{where} \quad \mathbf{E} = \mathbf{\Lambda}^{\frac{1}{2}}\mathbf{U}. \tag{3.58}$$

For simplicity, we shall assume that $\mathbf{\Lambda}$ is invertible. In this case, $\mathbf{E}$ will also be invertible. For any test vector $\mathbf{x}$, its representation in the kernel-PCA space can be expressed as

$$\vec{\mathbf{s}}(\mathbf{x}) \equiv \mathbf{E}^{-\mathrm{T}}\vec{\mathbf{k}}(\mathbf{x}) = \mathbf{\Lambda}^{-\frac{1}{2}}\mathbf{U}\vec{\mathbf{k}}(\mathbf{x}), \tag{3.59}$$

where $\mathbf{E}^{-\mathrm{T}}$ denotes the transpose of the inverse $\mathbf{E}^{-1}$. Equation (3.59) defines the *spectral vector space*, denoted by $\mathcal{S}$. The two-layer network representation of the spectral vector space is illustrated in Figure 3.9. The spectral vector space has the following properties.

- It is an N-dimensional Hilbert space endowed with the conventional (linear) inner product:

$$\langle \mathbf{x}, \mathbf{x}' \rangle = \vec{\mathbf{s}}(\mathbf{x})^{\mathrm{T}}\vec{\mathbf{s}}(\mathbf{x}') = K(\mathbf{x}, \mathbf{x}').$$

- The basis functions of the vector space are dependent on the training dataset. More precisely, the basis functions are jointly determined by the kernel function $K(\mathbf{x}, \mathbf{x}')$ and the kernel matrix $\mathbf{K}$ formed from the training dataset.

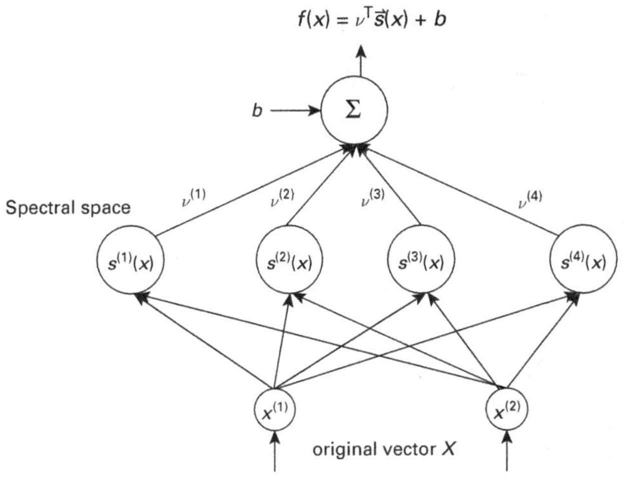

Fig. 3.9. Kernel PCA can be obtained by mapping the original training vectors to a kernel-based orthogonal spectral space. The mapping of an original vector $\mathbf{x}$ to a new representation in the spectral space can be illustrated by a two-layer network as shown here.

- Insofar as the training dataset is concerned, it has the data-dependent orthogonality shown below:

$$\sum_{n=1}^{N} s^{(k)}(\mathbf{x}_n)s^{(j)}(\mathbf{x}_n) = \begin{cases} 0 & \text{if } k \neq j, \\ \lambda_k & \text{if } k = j. \end{cases} \tag{3.60}$$

  The proof is left as an exercise.

Comparison of three kernel-induced spaces

Let us now compare the three vector spaces induced by the kernel function: the intrinsic space, empirical space, and spectral space. The intrinsic space associated with a kernel function is conveniently independent of the training dataset. Its vector dimension is called the intrinsic degree, and is denoted by J. Both the *empirical space* and the *spectral space* are of dimension N and are determined both by the kernel function and by the particular training dataset.

The kernel-based methods may be formulated as in various kernel vector spaces, including the intrinsic space $\mathcal{H}$, empirical space $\mathcal{K}$, and the spectral space $\mathcal{S}$. Let the projection or decision vectors corresponding to the three kernel spaces be denoted by $\mathbf{u}$, $\mathbf{a}$, and $\mathbf{v}$, respectively.

The relationship between $\mathbf{u}$ and $\mathbf{a}$ can be formally established as follows:

$$\vec{\mathbf{k}}(\mathbf{x}) = \begin{bmatrix} K(\mathbf{x}_1, \mathbf{x}) \\ K(\mathbf{x}_2, \mathbf{x}) \\ \vdots \\ K(\mathbf{x}_N, \mathbf{x}) \end{bmatrix} = \begin{bmatrix} \vec{\phi}(\mathbf{x}_1)^{\mathrm{T}}\vec{\phi}(\mathbf{x}) \\ \vec{\phi}(\mathbf{x}_2)^{\mathrm{T}}\vec{\phi}(\mathbf{x}) \\ \vdots \\ \vec{\phi}(\mathbf{x}_N)^{\mathrm{T}}\vec{\phi}(\mathbf{x}) \end{bmatrix} = \mathbf{\Phi}^{\mathrm{T}}\vec{\phi}(\mathbf{x}). \tag{3.61}$$

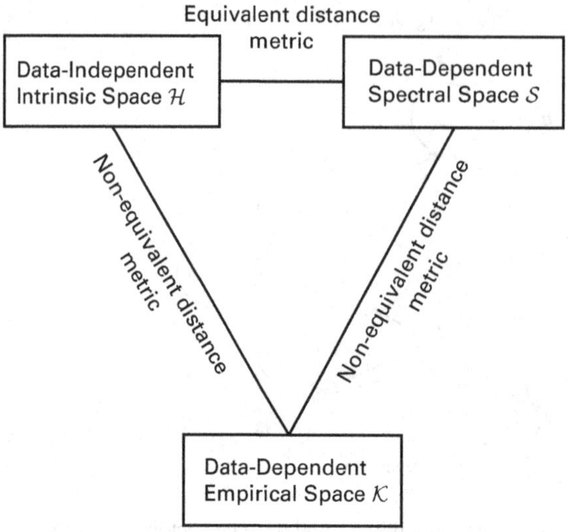

Fig. 3.10. Distance metrics associated with three Hilbert spaces: $\mathcal{H}$, $\mathcal{S}$, and $\mathcal{K}$. Note that the intrinsic space $\mathcal{H}$ and the empirical space $\mathcal{K}$ have different inner products, and thus induce different metrics. In contrast, the intrinsic space $\mathcal{H}$ and the spectral space $\mathcal{S}$ do share the same inner products (within the training dataset), i.e. they lead to identical distances between any two training vectors. In short, the intrinsic space $\mathcal{H}$ and the spectral space $\mathcal{S}$ are basically interchangeable for most unsupervised and supervised learning problems.

On pre-multiplying it by $\mathbf{a}^{\mathrm{T}}$, we have

$$\mathbf{a}^{\mathrm{T}}\vec{\mathbf{k}}(\mathbf{x}) = \mathbf{a}^{\mathrm{T}}\mathbf{\Phi}^{\mathrm{T}}\vec{\phi}(\mathbf{x}) = \mathbf{u}^{\mathrm{T}}\vec{\phi}(\mathbf{x}), \tag{3.62}$$

which leads to $\mathbf{u} = \mathbf{\Phi}\mathbf{a}$. Similarly, noting that $\vec{\mathbf{s}}(\mathbf{x}) \equiv \mathbf{\Lambda}^{-\frac{1}{2}}\mathbf{U}\vec{\mathbf{k}}(\mathbf{x})$, we can show that

$$\vec{\mathbf{k}}(\mathbf{x}) = \mathbf{U}^{\mathrm{T}}\mathbf{\Lambda}^{\frac{1}{2}}\vec{\mathbf{s}}(\mathbf{x}) = \mathbf{E}^{\mathrm{T}}\vec{\mathbf{s}}(\mathbf{x}).$$

It follows that

$$\mathbf{a}^{\mathrm{T}}\vec{\mathbf{k}}(\mathbf{x}) = \mathbf{a}^{\mathrm{T}}\mathbf{E}^{\mathrm{T}}\vec{\mathbf{s}}(\mathbf{x}) = \mathbf{v}^{\mathrm{T}}\vec{\mathbf{s}}(\mathbf{x}), \tag{3.63}$$

which implies that $\mathbf{v} = \mathbf{E}\mathbf{a}$. In summary, as depicted in Figure 3.10, all three projection vectors are intimately related:

$$\mathbf{u}^{\mathrm{T}}\vec{\phi}(\mathbf{x}) = \mathbf{a}^{\mathrm{T}}\vec{\mathbf{k}}(\mathbf{x}) = \mathbf{v}^{\mathrm{T}}\vec{\mathbf{s}}(\mathbf{x}). \tag{3.64}$$

Some of their similarities and dissimilarities are summarized below:

- **Intrinsic space $\mathcal{H}$ versus spectral space $\mathcal{S}$.** It is easy to show that $\mathbf{E}^{\mathrm{T}}\mathbf{E} = \mathbf{\Phi}^{\mathrm{T}}\mathbf{\Phi}$ ($= \mathbf{K}$). That has the following implication: for the N training vectors, the distances between any two vectors in the intrinsic space $\mathcal{H}$ and in the spectral space $\mathcal{S}$ are equal. (This equality does not extend beyond the training dataset.) This is the vital interchangeability between $\mathcal{H}$ and $\mathcal{S}$ during the learning phase during which the data processing is restricted exclusively to the training dataset.
- **Empirical space $\mathcal{K}$ versus spectral space $\mathcal{S}$.** Both the empirical space and the spectral space are useful for practical applications. The advantage of the spectral

space lies in its orthogonality property allowing the vector dimension to be effectively reduced. Its disadvantage lies in the (substantial) computational cost incurred for the spectral decomposition. In contrast, the empirical space offers a representation that is easily available. However, it is important to note that its induced inner product and distance metric are different from that of the intrinsic or spectral space. In other words, we cannot assume the convenience of interchangeability between $\mathcal{K}$ and $\mathcal{H}$, or between $\mathcal{K}$ and $\mathcal{S}$.

3.6 Summary

Dimension-reduction could have a great effect on learning efficiency and/or prediction performance. PCA has been the most prominent and popular technique for optimal subspace projection and visualization. This chapter first covers the fundamental theory of PCA. Theorems 3.1 and 3.2 establish the optimality of PCA both for the minimum reconstruction error and for maximum entropy criteria; moreover, the optimal error and entropy attainable by PCA can be derived in a closed-form formula.

Given a finite training dataset, various numerical methods have been proposed for the computation of PCA. Note that PCA is an LSP-based learning model, so a kernelized PCA learning model can be developed. For a thorough algorithmic comparison between the original and kernelized PCA learning models, Algorithms 3.2, 3.3, and 3.4 provide three possible procedures for the computation of PCA, namely via the original data matrix $\mathbf{X}$, the scatter matrix $\mathbf{S}$, and the kernel matrix $\mathbf{K}$, respectively. Depending on the sizes of M and N associated with the intended application, the user can compare the three procedures and choose the most cost-effective approach.

As a final note, online time-adaptive PCA learning models may have a special appeal for scenarios where new data are continuously arriving. Various adaptive-learning PCA models have been proposed [196, 227]. For example, Kung and Diamantaras proposed an APEX learning model, based on a modified version of Oja's learning rule, for adaptively learning multiple principal components. Moreover, the convergence property and the optimal learning rate have been analyzed by Kung and Diamantaras [50, 135, 137].

3.7 Problems

Problem 3.1 (Optimal estimate of x given y) *Show that the optimal estimate of* $\mathbf{x}$ *given* $\mathbf{y}$, *minimizing* $E\{\|\mathbf{x} - \hat{\mathbf{x}}_\mathbf{y}\|^2\}$, *has a closed-form formula*

$$\hat{\mathbf{x}}_\mathbf{y} = E[\mathbf{x}|\mathbf{y}] = \mathbf{R}_{\mathbf{xy}}[\mathbf{R}_\mathbf{y}]^{-1}\mathbf{y}.$$

Problem 3.2 *Suppose that* $\mathbf{y} = \mathbf{W}\mathbf{x}$, *where* $\mathbf{W}$ *is an* $m \times N$ *matrix with orthonormal rows, i.e.* $\mathbf{W}^{\mathrm{T}}\mathbf{W} = \mathbf{I}$.

(a) *Show that the optimal estimate of* $\mathbf{x}$ *given* $\mathbf{y}$, *minimizing* $E\{\|\mathbf{x} - \hat{\mathbf{x}}_\mathbf{y}\|^2\}$, *has the following symmetric form:*

$$\hat{\mathbf{x}}_\mathbf{y} = \mathbf{W}\mathbf{y} = \mathbf{W}\mathbf{W}^{\mathrm{T}}\mathbf{x}.$$

Hint: *By virtue of the principle of orthogonality in linear estimation theory [120], an optimal estimate must satisfy that* $(\mathbf{x} - \hat{\mathbf{x}}_\mathbf{y}) \perp \mathbf{y}$. *It follows that*

$$\begin{aligned} E\left[\mathbf{y}^{\mathrm{T}}\left(\mathbf{x} - \hat{\mathbf{x}}_\mathbf{y}\right)\right] &= E\left[\mathbf{y}^{\mathrm{T}}(\mathbf{x} - \mathbf{W}\mathbf{W}^{\mathrm{T}}\mathbf{x})\right] \\ &= E\left[\mathbf{x}^{\mathrm{T}}\mathbf{W}\mathbf{W}^{\mathrm{T}}\mathbf{x} - \mathbf{x}^{\mathrm{T}}\mathbf{W}\mathbf{W}^{\mathrm{T}}\mathbf{W}\mathbf{W}^{\mathrm{T}}\mathbf{x})\right] \\ &= E\left[\mathbf{x}^{\mathrm{T}}\mathbf{W}\mathbf{W}^{\mathrm{T}}\mathbf{x} - \mathbf{x}^{\mathrm{T}}\mathbf{W}\mathbf{W}^{\mathrm{T}}\mathbf{x})\right] = 0. \end{aligned}$$

(b) *Show that the mean-squared error (Eq. (3.4)) is*

$$\begin{aligned} E\{\|\mathbf{x} - \hat{\mathbf{x}}_\mathbf{y}\|^2\} &= E\{\mathtt{tr}(\mathbf{x} - \hat{\mathbf{x}}_\mathbf{y})(\mathbf{x} - \hat{\mathbf{x}}_\mathbf{y})^{\mathrm{T}}\} \\ &= \mathtt{tr}(\mathbf{R}_\mathbf{x}) - \mathtt{tr}(\mathbf{W}^{\mathrm{T}}\mathbf{R}_\mathbf{x}\mathbf{W}). \end{aligned}$$

Problem 3.3 (MSE of optimal estimate of x given y) *Prove that* $\mathbf{V}_{\text{major}}\mathbf{x}$, *see Eq. (3.14), yields the optimal PCA solution, with the optimal mean-squared error (MSE) being* $\sum_{i=m+1}^{M} \lambda_i$.

(a) *Show that*

$$\mathbf{W}^{\mathrm{T}}\mathbf{R}_\mathbf{x}\mathbf{W} = \mathbf{W}^{\mathrm{T}}\mathbf{V}\boldsymbol{\Lambda}\mathbf{V}^{\mathrm{T}}\mathbf{W} = \mathbf{W}'^{\mathrm{T}}\boldsymbol{\Lambda}\mathbf{W}',$$

where $\boldsymbol{\Lambda}$ *is a diagonal matrix,* $\mathbf{V}$ *is a unitary matrix, and* $\mathbf{W}'^{\mathrm{T}} \equiv \mathbf{W}^{\mathrm{T}}\mathbf{V}$.

(b) *Denote* $\mathbf{P} \equiv \mathbf{W}'\mathbf{W}'^{\mathrm{T}}$ *and show that*

$$\mathtt{tr}(\mathbf{W}^{\mathrm{T}}\mathbf{R}_\mathbf{x}\mathbf{W}) = \sum_{i=1}^{m} p_{ii}\lambda_i.$$

(c) *By noting the fact that* $\mathbf{W}'$ *is a submatrix of a unitary matrix, show that*

$$p_{ii} \le 1 \quad \text{and} \quad \sum_{i=1}^{m} p_{ii} = m.$$

(d) *Finally, show that the optimal solution can be obtained by setting*

$$\mathbf{W}' = [\mathbf{I}_{m\times m} \quad \mathbf{0}_{m\times(M-m)}]^{\mathrm{T}},$$

i.e. $\mathbf{W} = \mathbf{V}_{\text{major}}$.

Problem 3.4 (PCA via spectral decomposition of S and K) *You are given the data matrix*

$$\mathbf{X} = \begin{bmatrix} 3 & 6 \\ 3 & -6 \\ 0 & 6 \\ 3 & 0 \end{bmatrix}.$$

(a) *Compute the eigenvalue decomposition of* $\mathbf{S} = \mathbf{X}\mathbf{X}^{\mathrm{T}}$.
(b) *Compute the eigenvalue decomposition of* $\mathbf{K} = \mathbf{X}^{\mathrm{T}}\mathbf{X}$.
(c) *Compare the eigenvalues of* $\mathbf{S}$ *and* $\mathbf{K}$.
(d) *Verify the following formula:*

$$\mathbf{X}\mathbf{U}^{\mathrm{T}}\boldsymbol{\Lambda}^{-\frac{1}{2}}\boldsymbol{\Lambda}\boldsymbol{\Lambda}^{-\frac{1}{2}}\mathbf{U}\mathbf{X}^{\mathrm{T}} = \mathbf{X}\mathbf{X}^{\mathrm{T}} = \mathbf{S}. \tag{3.65}$$

Problem 3.5 *With reference to Eq. (3.28), show that*

$$\mathbf{\Lambda}^{-\frac{1}{2}}\mathbf{U}_{M\times(N-M)}\mathbf{X}^{\mathrm{T}}\mathbf{X} = \mathbf{\Lambda}^{\frac{1}{2}}\mathbf{U}_{M\times(N-M)}.$$

Problem 3.6 (PCA for optimal reconstruction error) *Given Eq. (3.15), show that* $\mathbf{x} - \hat{\mathbf{x}}_{\mathbf{y}} = \mathbf{V}_{\text{minor}}\mathbf{V}^{\mathrm{T}}_{\text{minor}}\mathbf{x}$*, and that*

$$E[(\mathbf{x} - \hat{\mathbf{x}}_{\mathbf{y}})^2] = \mathtt{tr}\{\Lambda_{\text{minor}}\} = \sum_{i=m+1}^{N} \lambda_i.$$

Hint: *(1)* $\mathtt{tr}(\mathbf{AB}) = \mathtt{tr}(\mathbf{BA})$*; and (2) if* $\mathbf{A}$ *is formed from random variables, then* $E[\mathtt{tr}(\mathbf{A})] = \mathtt{tr}(E[\mathbf{A}])$.

Problem 3.7 (PCA: Major and minor subspaces) *Given three features* $x^{(1)}$, $x^{(2)}$, *and* $x^{(3)}$ *with a zero-mean Gaussian distribution and the covariance matrix*

$$\mathbf{R}_{\mathbf{x}} = \begin{bmatrix} 500 & 420 & 200 \\ 420 & 450 & 0 \\ 200 & 0 & 400 \end{bmatrix},$$

the objective is to find the two-dimensional PCA subspace. Determine Λ_{major}, Λ_{minor}, $\mathbf{V}_{\text{major}}$, *and* $\mathbf{V}_{\text{minor}}$.

Problem 3.8 (Information loss w.r.t. dimension of PCA) *Suppose that*

$$\mathbf{R}_{\mathbf{x}} = \begin{bmatrix} 36 & 24 & 18 & 10 & 9 \\ 24 & 28 & 12 & 10 & 4 \\ 18 & 12 & 18 & 6 & 8 \\ 10 & 10 & 6 & 13 & 4 \\ 9 & 4 & 8 & 4 & 10 \end{bmatrix}.$$

(a) *What is the minimum dimension m for which the*

$$\text{Relative error} = \frac{e[\|\mathbf{x} - \hat{\mathbf{x}}_{\mathbf{y}}\|^2]}{e[\|\mathbf{x}\|^2]} = \frac{\sum_{i=m+1}^{M} \lambda_i}{\sum_{i=1}^{M} \lambda_i} \tag{3.66}$$

is no higher than 10%?

(b) *What is the minimum dimension m for which the*

$$\text{Entropy ratio} = \frac{\sum_{i=1}^{m} \log_2(2\pi e\lambda_i)}{\sum_{i=1}^{M} \log_2(2\pi e\lambda_i)} \tag{3.67}$$

is no less than 90%?

Problem 3.9 *Consider kernel PCA for the XOR dataset using the second-order polynomial kernel function.*

(a) *Verify that the empirical feature vector (see Eq. (3.50)) for* $\mathbf{x} = [1 \quad 0]^{\mathrm{T}}$ *is*

$$\vec{\mathbf{k}}(\mathbf{x}) = \begin{bmatrix} K(\mathbf{x}_1, \mathbf{x}) \\ K(\mathbf{x}_2, \mathbf{x}) \\ \vdots \\ K(\mathbf{x}_N, \mathbf{x}) \end{bmatrix} = \begin{bmatrix} 4 \\ 0 \\ 4 \\ 0 \end{bmatrix}.$$

and that its spectral feature vector (see Eq. 3.50′) is

$$\vec{\mathbf{s}}(\mathbf{x}) = \mathbf{\Lambda}^{-\frac{1}{2}}\mathbf{U}\vec{\mathbf{k}}(\mathbf{x}). = \begin{bmatrix} \frac{2}{\sqrt{3}} \\ 0 \\ \sqrt{2} \\ 0 \end{bmatrix}. \tag{3.68}$$

(b) *Repeat* **(a)** *for a new vector* $\mathbf{x} = [2 \quad 0]^{\mathrm{T}}$.

Problem 3.10 (Kernel-induced Cholesky space) *By the Cholesky decomposition, a kernel matrix* $\mathbf{K}$ *can be factorized into the following product:*

$$\mathbf{K} = \mathbf{C}^{\mathrm{T}}\mathbf{C},$$

where $\mathbf{C}$ *is a lower triangular matrix. An original vector* $\mathbf{x}$ *may be mapped to a representative vector in the Cholesky space:*

$$\mathbf{x} \rightarrow \vec{\mathbf{c}}(\mathbf{x}) \equiv \mathbf{C}^{-\mathrm{T}}\vec{\mathbf{k}}(\mathbf{x}). \tag{3.69}$$

The mapped training vectors in the Cholesky space may then be used to learn a decision vector, denoted as $\mathbf{d}$*, defined in the Cholesky space, which in turn leads to the following (nonlinear) decision boundary:*

$$f(\mathbf{x}) = \mathbf{d}^{\mathrm{T}}\vec{\mathbf{c}}(\mathbf{x}) + b = 0.$$

(a) *Compare the computational costs of the Cholesky decomposition versus the spectral factorization.*

(b) *Show that any two representative vectors in the Cholesky space have exactly the same distance as their counterparts in the spectral space. As an example, consider the XOR dataset with the second-order polynomial kernel function. Show that the Cholesky factorization yields*

$$\mathbf{K} = \begin{bmatrix} 3 & 0 & 0 & 0 \\ 0.333 & 2.981 & 0 & 0 \\ 0.333 & 0.298 & 2.967 & 0 \\ 0.333 & 0.298 & 0.270 & 2.954 \end{bmatrix} \begin{bmatrix} 3 & 0.333 & 0.333 & 0.333 \\ 0 & 2.981 & 0.298 & 0.298 \\ 0 & 0 & 2.967 & 0.270 \\ 0 & 0 & 0 & 2.954 \end{bmatrix}.$$

Show that the distance between any two of the mapped training vectors is 4.

Problem 3.11 (KPCA for XOR dataset) *The choice of* σ *may affect kernel analysis based on the Gaussian kernel function*

$$K(\mathbf{x}, \mathbf{x}') = \exp\left\{-\frac{\|\mathbf{x} - \mathbf{x}'\|^2}{2\sigma^2}\right\}.$$

This problem compares kernel PCAs corresponding to different Gaussian kernels.

(a) *Compute the kernel PCA for the XOR dataset with the Gaussian kernel function (setting $\sigma = 1$):*

$$K'(\mathbf{x}, \mathbf{x}') = \exp\left\{-\frac{\|\mathbf{x} - \mathbf{x}'\|^2}{2}\right\}.$$

Compare the result with Eq. (3.51), the solution obtained for the kernel function: $K(\mathbf{x}, \mathbf{x}') = \exp\left\{-\|\mathbf{x} - \mathbf{x}'\|^2\right\}$.

(b) *Find the optimal decision boundary for $K'(\mathbf{x}, \mathbf{x}')$ and compare the result with the solution given in Eq. (3.53).*

Problem 3.12 (Center-adjusted KPCA for XOR dataset) *Compute the center-adjusted kernel PCA for the XOR dataset with the Gaussian kernel function*

$$K'(\mathbf{x}, \mathbf{x}') = \exp\left\{-\frac{\|\mathbf{x} - \mathbf{x}'\|^2}{2}\right\}.$$

Problem 3.13 *By setting $\sigma \to 0$ in the Gaussian kernel*

$$K(\mathbf{x}, \mathbf{x}') = \exp\left\{-\frac{\|\mathbf{x} - \mathbf{x}'\|^2}{2\sigma^2}\right\},$$

we obtain

$$\sqrt{K(\mathbf{x}, \mathbf{x}) + K(\mathbf{x}', \mathbf{x}') - 2K(\mathbf{x}, \mathbf{x}')} \to \sqrt{1 + 1 - 2 \times 0} = \sqrt{2}. \tag{3.70}$$

This means that all pairs of vectors have approximately an equal distance of around $\sqrt{2}$, which in turn implies that all the induced training vectors are being relocated to the corners of a high-dimensional cube in the intrinsic space.

(a) *Explain why such a "cornerized" data structure may be beneficial to supervised learning applications.*

(b) *Explain why such a data structure could be detrimental to unsupervised learning applications.*

Problem 3.14 (Distance in spaces $\mathcal{H}$ and $\mathcal{S}$) *Show that the distance between any two induced training vectors in $\mathcal{H}$ will always be identical to the distance between their counterparts in $\mathcal{S}$. Verify the result using the dataset given in Problem 2.3 with a second-order polynomial kernel.*

Problem 3.15 (MATLAB simulation: PCA for expression data) *Download from http://www.genome.wi.mit.edu/mpr and create a 7192×72 microarray data matrix.*

(a) *Calculate eigenvalues and eigenvectors of the scatter matrix $\mathbf{S}$ and plot the eigenvalues for $m = 1, 2, \ldots, 72$.*

(b) *For $m = 1, 2, \ldots, 18$, plot the reconstruction errors $E[||\mathbf{x} - \hat{\mathbf{x}}_{\mathbf{y}}||^2]$ for different values of m. Compare the results with the theoretical numbers $\sum_{i=1}^{m} \lambda_i$.*

(c) *For $m = 1, 2, \ldots, 18$, plot the entropy $H(\mathbf{y})$ (or mutual information $I(\mathbf{x}|\mathbf{y})$) for each individual feature. Compare the results with the theoretical values $\frac{1}{2} \sum_{i=1}^{m} \log_2(2\pi e \lambda_i)$.*

4 Feature selection

4.1 Introduction

Two primary techniques for dimension-reducing feature extraction are *subspace projection* and *feature selection*. Compared with subspace projection, feature selection has the following advantages.

- Owing to its simplicity, feature selection can quickly and effectively weed out a large fraction of the insignificant features and yield a manageable vector dimension for subsequent data analysis.
- Feature selection is appealing from the perspective of online processing. Processing speed and power consumption are usually the major concerns for online processing. Feature selection results in a reduced number of selected features. This means that fewer features will need to be acquired in the input acquisition phase, thus saving processing power in the raw-data acquisition phase. This saving does not apply to the subspace projection approach, for which all of the original features must be acquired first before proper linear combinations can be computed to generate principal components.
- There are application-specific roles of feature selection, which simply could not be replaced by subspace projection. For example, gene selection is vital to genomic study. It is known that a few genes are often responsible for the cause or cure of tumors while most of the remaining genes are just "housekeeping" genes that have no functional roles and should be discarded for the sake of performance. Moreover, if a specific subset of genes is specially effective for accurate prediction of certain tumors, those genes are also most likely to be the biomarkers for the design of effective drugs to cure the tumors.

Under this circumstance, feature selection may not only save computation by reducing the dimension of feature vectors but also retain satisfactory prediction performance. As an example, for microarray gene expression data analysis, features correspond to genes that are often co-expressed, resulting in a great deal of inter-gene redundancy. Exploitation of *inter-feature* redundancy permits a significant dimension reduction without compromising the prediction information.

Figure 4.1 shows a subcellular functional prediction performance curve. It shows that the performance deteriorates when either too many or too few features are used,

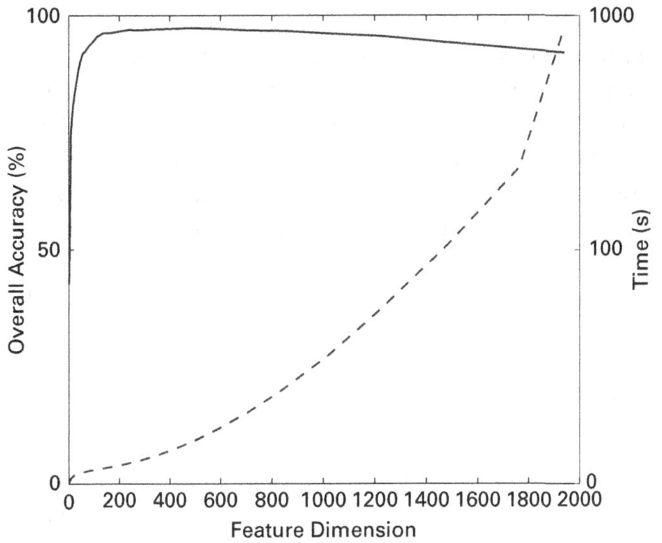

Fig. 4.1. The accuracy and testing time for different numbers of features selected by a Fisher-based method [200], for the eukaryotic protein dataset published by Reinhardt and Hubbard [216]. The non-monotonic performance curve indicates that the performance deteriorates when either too many or too few features are used. The solid curve shows that the performance reaches a peak when the correct number of well-selected features is adopted. The dashed curve shows that the computational time grows (at a more than linear rate) as the number of features increases. The dataset comprises 2427 annotated sequences extracted from SWILSPROT 33.0, including those for 684 cytoplasm, 325 extracellular, 321 mitochondrial, and 1097 nuclear proteins. In this experiment, profile alignment SVMs [166] are applied to predict the subcellular location of proteins and fivefold cross-validation was used to obtain the prediction accuracy.

suggesting that the optimal prediction can be reached when the correct number of well-selected set of features is adopted for training and, subsequently, for prediction.

This chapter introduces two major approaches to feature selection: filtering methods and wrapper methods.

(i) Section 4.2 introduces several filtering methods for feature selection, both unsupervised and supervised.
(ii) Section 4.3 covers several wrapper methods for feature selection, both unsupervised and supervised.
(iii) Section 4.4 highlights an application case study of the feature selection techniques introduced in the chapter.

4.2 The filtering approach to feature selection

Diverse feature selection methods have been proposed, and they are often subdivided into two major categories [89, 128].

- **Filtering approach.** Each of the features is assigned a score to reflect its individual discriminative power. A feature will be selected if it scores higher than a certain threshold. On the other hand, it will be dropped only if it scores below the threshold. This approach provides a simple and effective tool to quickly weed out irrelevant or unimportant features when the initial feature size is enormously huge.
- **Wrapper approach.** The wrapper approach is tightly coupled with the classifier adopted for post-processing. In contrast to its filtering counterpart, this approach requires the actual classification to be conducted using the full feature set. The feature selection depends on the role of the features in the classification result [89, 128].

4.2.1 Supervised filtering methods

In this approach, each feature is assigned an individual score and its selection/elimination is determined by whether its score is above/below an acceptance threshold. The filtering approach may be applied both to unsupervised and to supervised learning scenarios. However, very different types of selection criteria will have to be applied to the different scenarios.

- *Supervised filtering criteria.* For a supervised learning scenario, the known class labels may be used to define the score of individual features. Such (supervised) scores can effectively reflect the feature's capability in discriminating positive and negative classes.
- *Unsupervised filtering criteria.* For an unsupervised learning scenario, we do not know in advance the class labels of the training vectors. In this case, the feature score is often represented by the degree of information embedded in the individual feature.

In the supervised scenario, a feature's score can be effectively represented by its signal-to-noise ratio (SNR). The SNR is defined as the ratio of signal (inter-class distinction) and noise (intra-class) perturbation.

- *Signal.* The signal is characterized as the distance between the mean values of the positive and negative classes.
- *Noise.* The noise, on the other hand, can be defined as the sum (or the average) of the class-conditional standard deviations of the positive and negative classes.

Such an SNR provides a measurement of how effectively the feature may be used to differentiate the two classes. There are many variants of SNR-type ranking criteria, such as the signed SNR [66], Fisher discriminative ratio (FDR) [200], t-test [110], Bayesian technique [9, 71], BSS/WSS [56], and TNom [15]. All these scores reflect how significantly each feature is differentially expressed.

Signed-SNR test

For any single feature, we adopt $\{\mu^+, \mu^-\}$ and $\{\sigma^+, \sigma^-\}$ to denote respectively the class-conditional means and standard deviations of the (positive/negative) classes. The most popular test criterion is the *signed-SNR score* [66]:

$$\text{Signed SNR}(j) = \frac{\mu_j^+ - \mu_j^-}{\sigma_j^+ + \sigma_j^-}. \tag{4.1}$$

SNR test

The SNR test is based on the absolute value of the signed SNR.

FDR test

The Fisher discriminant ratio (FDR) [200] is given by

$$\text{FDR}(j) = \frac{\left(\vec{\mu}_j^+ - \vec{\mu}_j^-\right)^2}{(\sigma_j^+)^2 + (\sigma_j^-)^2}. \tag{4.2}$$

Symmetric divergence (SD) test

Another SNR-type metric is the symmetric divergence (SD) [167]:

$$\text{SD}(j) = \frac{1}{2}\left(\frac{(\sigma_j^+)^2}{(\sigma_j^-)^2} + \frac{(\sigma_j^-)^2}{(\sigma_j^+)^2}\right) + \frac{1}{2}\left(\frac{\left(\mu_j^+ - \mu_j^-\right)^2}{(\sigma_j^+)^2 + (\sigma_j^-)^2}\right) - 1. \tag{4.3}$$

where $\vec{\mu}_j^+$, $\vec{\mu}_j^-$, σ_j^+, and σ_j^- represent the class-conditional means and standard derivations of the jth feature, respectively.

Two-sample t*-statistics*

The two-sample t-test, which was introduced by Gosset,[1] shares the same SNR-type principle. The t-test can be used to assess the confidence on judgments made on small samples generated.

Let $x^{(i)}$ and $y^{(i)}$ denote the measured expression levels of a feature under two different classes. Our goal is to determine whether the mean of $x^{(i)}$ is significantly different from that of $y^{(i)}$. The *test statistic* is

$$t_s = \frac{\bar{x} - \bar{y}}{\sqrt{s_x^2/N_x + s_y^2/N_y}}, \tag{4.4}$$

where $(\bar{x}, \bar{y})$, (s_x^2, s_y^2), and (N_x, N_y) are the means, variances, and sizes of the respective samples.

For a two-sample t-test, if $|t_s|$ exceeds a certain threshold, the feature can be deemed to be differentially expressed enough to discriminate two different classes, and thus it can be selected. Otherwise, the feature will be weeded out.

Example 4.1 (Applications of SNR-type tests) *There are many successful applications of supervised filtering approaches to microarray data. In Figure 4.2(a), the FDR values*

[1] Gosset devised the t-test as a way to cheaply monitor the quality of beer. He published the test in *Biometrika* in 1908, under the pen name "Student."

(a)

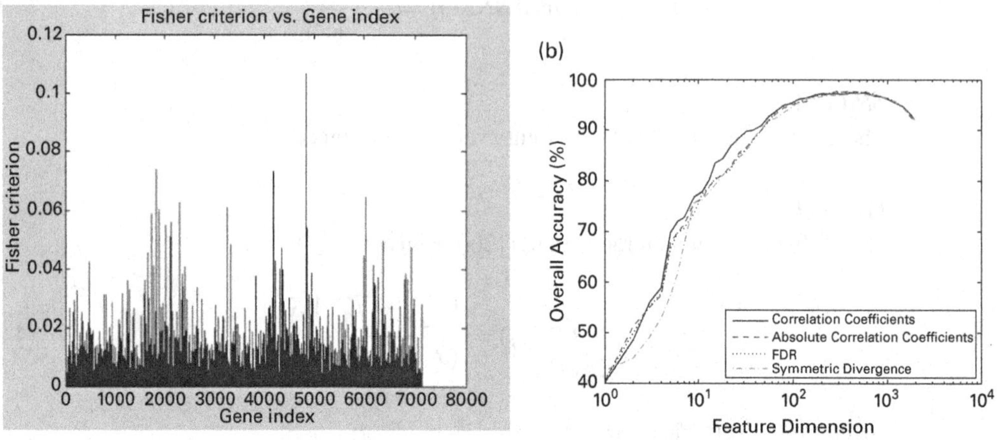

Fig. 4.2. (a) The SNR (or FDR) values for 6817 human genes recorded in the microarray data [82]. (Here FDR stands for Fisher discriminant ratio.) (b) Accuracy based on features selected by SNR, signed SNR, symmetric divergence, and correlation coefficients. Note that all these SNR-type criteria yield similar performance.

of about 7000 genes are displayed. For example, as shown in Figure 4.2(b), the top 100 of the genes (those above 0.03 in FDR) are already fairly adequate for effective classification. In fact, all the SNR-Type tests produce comparable performance. As exemplified by a simulation study shown in Figure 4.2(b), the performances corresponding to signed SNR, SNR, and FDR are fairly close [168].

In the simulation study on microarray data conducted by Ma and Huang [162], the expression levels of 22 normal colon tissues and 40 tumor tissues were measured using the Affymetrix gene chip containing the probes of 6500 human genes. In a pre-filtering step, 2000 genes were selected, taking the highest minimal intensity across the samples. Then, 34 biomarkers were found based on the t-statistics obtained from the normal and tumor tissues. It was found that many of the biomarkers are biologically relevant, for example, the gene MYL6 was found to be relevant to colon tumors. It is expressed in smooth muscle tissues, and its expression is correlated with the colon tumor found in a previous experiment [5]. □

4.2.2 Feature-weighted linear classifiers

As set of training vectors in $\mathbb{R}^M$ is said to be *linearly separable* into positive and negative classes if the two classes can be divided by an $(M-1)$-dimensional *decision hyperplane*, characterized by $f(\mathbf{w}, \mathbf{x}) = 0$. In other words, the decision boundary is given by a linear function defined as

$$f(\mathbf{w}, \mathbf{x}) = \mathbf{w}^{\mathrm{T}}\mathbf{x} + b = \sum_{j=1}^{M} w^{(j)}x^{(j)} + b,$$

where $\mathbf{w} = [w^{(1)}\ w^{(2)}\ \ldots\ w^{(M)}]^{\mathrm{T}} \in \mathbb{R}^M$, $\mathbf{x} = [x^{(1)}\ x^{(2)}\ \ldots\ x^{(M)}]^{\mathrm{T}} \in \mathbb{R}^M$, and $b \in \mathbb{R}$ are the parameters of the discriminant function.

In the filtering approach to feature selection, each feature has its own individual SNR, which reflects its effectiveness for differentiating the two classes. Consequently, a weighted-voting linear classifier can be derived as a natural extension of the filtering method. The design of a feature-weighted classifier contains three steps.

(i) *SNR as weight.* The voting weights ($\{w^{(i)}\}$) are set to be the same as the (signed) SNR:

$$w^{(i)} = \frac{\mu_i^+ - \mu_i^-}{\sigma_i^+ + \sigma_i^-}, \tag{4.5}$$

where $\{\mu_i^+, \sigma_i^+\}$ and $\{\mu_i^-, \sigma_i^-\}$ respectively represent the positive and negative means and standard deviations pertaining to the ith feature.

(ii) *Local score: independent feature evaluation and selection.* The feature-voting classifier is a (feature-wise) independently trained classifier, each feature being evaluated and assigned a local score:

$$v^{(i)} = x^{(i)} - \mu^{(i)},$$

where $\mu^{(i)}$ is the mean of N values corresponding to the ith feature of all the N training samples.

The local score contributes a local vote (on positive versus negative decision) as viewed from one single feature. More precisely, if $w^{(i)} > 0$, a score with $x^{(i)} - \mu^{(i)} \geq 0$ votes for a positive decision and a score with $x^{(i)} - \mu^{(i)} < 0$ counts for a negative decision. In contrast, if $w^{(i)} < 0$, a positive score votes for a negative decision and a negative score for a positive decision.

(iii) *Discriminant function.* Note that different features deserve different weights. This leads to the following linear discriminant function:

$$f(\mathbf{w}, \mathbf{x}) = \sum_{j=1}^{M} w^{(j)}(x^{(j)} - \mu^{(j)}) + \theta = \mathbf{w}^{\mathrm{T}}\mathbf{x} + b, \tag{4.6}$$

where $\mathbf{w} = [w^{(1)}\ w^{(2)}\ \ldots\ w^{(M)}]^{\mathrm{T}}$, $b = -\sum_j w^{(j)}\mu^{(j)} + \theta$, and θ is an acceptance threshold.

Example 4.2 (Application of feature-weighted classifiers) *In the experiment conducted by Golub et al. [82], the discriminant function was adopted to classify two categories of human acute leukemias: one class is acute lymphoblastic leukemia (ALL) and the other class is acute myeloid leukemia (AML).*

There are in total 72 samples, 38 for training and 34 for testing. The dataset comprises expression profiles on 6817 genes obtained from Affymetrix GeneChip. First, the SNR scores of the 6817 genes were rank ordered using the SNRs according to 38 training samples. In the filtering stage, only the 50 top-scored genes were kept for *subsequent analysis, i.e. $M = 50$ in Eq. (4.6). The linear discriminant function based on the weighted score was applied, resulting in successful classification of all 34 testing samples.* □

4.2.3 Unsupervised filtering methods

For unsupervised learning data, the usefulness of a feature depends on its data distributions. The possible selection criteria include variance, entropy, or density of each feature. In practical applications, the variance is the most popular metric to judge a feature's relevance. For example, genes with relatively flat expression levels over time (i.e. those with low variance) are unlikely to reveal useful information.

Variance

Using the variance criterion, irrelevant features may be effectively weeded out. A "gene shaving" approach [93] is one which seeks subsets of genes with large variations across samples (or conditions) that have similar expression patterns by iteratively discarding the genes with the smallest variations was proposed. It was successfully applied to data from patients (with diffuse large B-cell lymphoma) to identify genes that are indicative of survival. As another example, Figure 4.3 shows the histogram of the variances of the gene profiles before and after the filtering for the yeast cell cycle data [263]. Note that many low-variance genes are successfully removed by this simple filtering process.

4.2.4 Consecutive search methods

A major weakness of the filter approach is due to the fact that the selection is completely dictated by the ranking of the features and thus fails to pay proper attention to inter-feature redundancy. The latter is omnipresent and plays a vital role in many real applications.

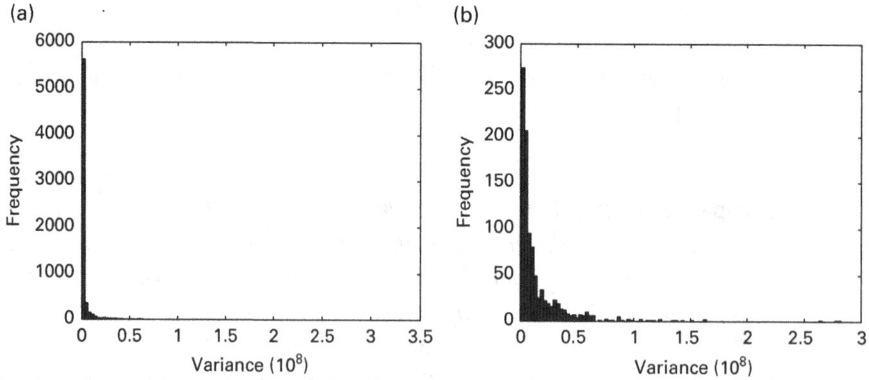

Fig. 4.3. Histograms of the variances of the gene profiles of Tamayo *et al.*'s [263] yeast cell cycle data (un-normalized): (a) before filtering and (b) after filtering.

One solution is to adopt a selection scheme that is based on the collective relevance measure of a group of features, called a *group score*. Unfortunately, such a scheme is extremely costly in computation, since it involves exhaustive computation of the group scores for all possible combinations of features. The exhaustive search procedure would entail a good fraction of all the 2^M possible combinations – a prohibitive cost if M is large. The scheme is useful only when there exists a lot of computational resources during the off-line learning phase.

Forward search and backward elimination

We need a more efficient strategy to account for the inter-feature redundancy. The following two consecutive search methods offer a good balance between computation and performance.

(i) **Forward search.** Forward search is usually effective when a relative small number of features (from a much larger feature set) are to be selected and retained. The search begins at an empty feature set, and gradually adds newly selected features. The new member is selected based on how much new information it may add to the existing subset. *Once a feature is admitted, it cannot be discarded in the future.*

(ii) **Backward elimination** Backward elimination is usually preferred when relative few features are to be eliminated from the original feature set. This approach begins with the full feature set. One by one, it eliminates the features whose absence causes the least loss of information. *Once a feature has been eliminated, it cannot be restored in the future.*

Both schemes have reasonably taken into account inter-feature redundancy – unlike the filter approach – yet they have somewhat avoided the enormous computational complexity associated with the *group ranking* approach.

Case study

For a better understanding of inter-feature redundancy and its role on feature selection, let us study a simple case where the original raw data are represented by zero-mean Gaussian-distributed three-dimensional random vectors with the following covariance matrix:

$$\mathbf{R_x} = \begin{bmatrix} 500 & 420 & 200 \\ 420 & 450 & 0 \\ 200 & 0 & 400 \end{bmatrix}.$$

Figure 4.4 depicts the entropy "Venn diagram" associated with the three features from $x^{(1)}$, $x^{(2)}$, and $x^{(3)}$.

It will be straightforward if the task is to find only one of the three features to deliver the maximum entropy. Recall that the mutual information is equal to the entropy: $I(\mathbf{x}|\mathbf{y}) = H(\mathbf{y})$.

For example, if just the first feature $x^{(1)}$ is selected, $\mathbf{y} = x^{(1)}$. From the covariance matrix $\mathbf{R_x}$, we note that $E[{x^{(1)}}^2] = 500$. According to Eq. (3.19), $H(\mathbf{y}) = H(x^{(1)}) = 6.53$. By the same token, we can show that $H(x^{(2)}) = 6.45$ and $H(x^{(3)}) = 6.37$. Since $H(x^{(1)}) > H(x^{(2)}) > H(x^{(3)})$, the optimal single-feature choice is $\mathbf{y} = x^{(1)}$.

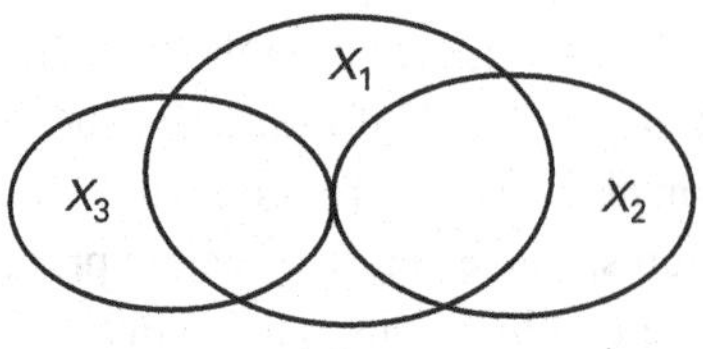

Fig. 4.4. The "Venn diagram" for three features with inter-feature redundancy. In the Venn diagram, such redundancy is reflected by the existence of overlaps among the three areas. For optimal feature selection, inter-feature redundancy must be taken into account.

Now the task is to select *two* features to represent the original vector. It is illuminating to compare the four approaches introduced previously.

- **Optimal selection: ranking based on group scores.** To compute all the group scores, i.e. group entropies, the joint entropy for the pairs $\{x^{(1)}, x^{(2)}\}$, $\{x^{(1)}, x^{(3)}\}$, and $\{x^{(2)}, x^{(3)}\}$ should be computed. Let us first work on $\mathbf{y} = [x^{(1)}\ x^{(2)}]^{\mathrm{T}}$:

$$R_{\mathbf{y}} = \begin{bmatrix} 500 & 420 \\ 420 & 450 \end{bmatrix}.$$

According to Eq. (3.19),

$$H([x^{(1)}\ x^{(2)}]^{\mathrm{T}}) = \frac{1}{2}\log_2(|R_{\mathbf{y}}|) + \frac{2}{2}\log_2(2\pi e) = 11.88. \tag{4.7}$$

It can be shown that $H([x^{(1)}\ x^{(2)}]^{\mathrm{T}}) = 11.88$, $H([x^{(1)}\ x^{(3)}]^{\mathrm{T}}) = 12.74$, and $H([x^{(2)}\ x^{(3)}]^{\mathrm{T}}) = 12.82$. Since $H([x^{(2)}\ x^{(3)}]^{\mathrm{T}}) > H([x^{(1)}\ x^{(3)}]^{\mathrm{T}}) > H([x^{(1)}\ x^{(2)}]^{\mathrm{T}})$, the (optimal) selection is clearly $\mathbf{y} = [x^{(2)}\ x^{(3)}]^{\mathrm{T}}$.[2]
- **Selection based on the filtering approach.** Since $H(x^{(1)}) > H(x^{(2)}) > H(x^{(3)})$, the choice is now $\mathbf{y} = [x^{(1)}\ x^{(2)}]^{\mathrm{T}}$ according to the ranking of individual scores. This is different from the optimal solution obtained previously via group ranking.
- **Forward search approach.** As discussed previously, $x^{(1)}$ will be chosen if just one feature is used in the first round. According to the forward search rule, $x^{(1)}$ cannot be dropped when we move into the second round of selection. Now we search for a feature that can best pair up with $x^{(1)}$. In this sense, $x^{(3)}$ is a better choice because $H([x^{(1)}\ x^{(3)}]^{\mathrm{T}}) > H([x^{(1)}\ x^{(2)}]^{\mathrm{T}})$. Therefore, $\mathbf{y} = [x^{(1)}\ x^{(3)}]^{\mathrm{T}}$ will be the solution, which is not an optimal choice.
- **Backward elimination approach.** Owing to its high inter-feature redundancy as indicated by r_{12} and r_{13}, $x^{(1)}$ has substantial overlaps with $x^{(2)}$ and $x^{(3)}$, as depicted by the "Venn diagram" in Figure 4.4. Consequently, elimination of $x^{(1)}$ will result in the least loss in entropy. So $x^{(1)}$ is the most dispensable and should be the first to be eliminated. The remaining two features are $\{x^{(2)}, x^{(3)}\}$, leading to an optimal selection.

[2] Note that the fact that $11.88 < 6.53 + 6.45$ and $12.74 < 6.53 + 6.37$ is due to the presence of inter-feature redundancy. Graphically, in the Venn diagram in Figure 4.4, such redundancy is reflected by the overlapping regions between $(x^{(1)}, x^{(2)})$ and $(x^{(1)}, x^{(3)})$, respectively. The Venn diagram also shows that there is no inter-feature redundancy between $x^{(2)}$ and $x^{(3)}$. This is also reflected by the fact that there is zero correlation between the two features, i.e. $r_{23} = 0$. Therefore, the joint entropy is just the sum of $H(x^{(2)})$ and $H(x^{(3)})$. That is $H(\mathbf{y}) = 6.45 + 6.37 = 12.82$ if $\mathbf{y} = [x^{(2)}\ x^{(3)}]^{\mathrm{T}}$, which represents the optimal two-feature selection.

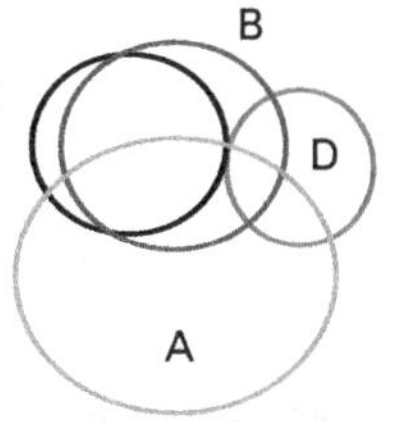

	Filtering	FS	BE	Optimal
One feature	A	A	A	A
Two features	AB	AB	AC	AC
Three features	ABC	ABD	ACD	ABD

Fig. 4.5. A Venn diagram showing the entropy of four features. The different selection results are tabulated.

However, if just one feature is to be selected, the backward elimination will lead to the final choice of $x^{(2)}$ – which is no longer optimal. (In the second round of elimination, $x^{(3)}$ is eliminated because $H(x^{(3)}) < H(x^{(2)})$.)

Example 4.3 *Consider four features whose entropy and mutual information are graphically depicted by the Venn diagram shown in Figure 4.5. The results of feature selection via the filtering method, forward search (FS), backward elimination (BE), and group score (optimal) are summarized in the table in Figure 4.5.*

4.3 The wrapper approach to feature selection

The wrapper method makes use of the classification results to determine how well the candidate feature subsets may perform so as to make the best selection of the features [89, 128].

4.3.1 Supervised wrapper methods

As shown in Figure 4.6, the features selected via the wrapper approach depend on the classifier adopted [89, 318]. A basic wrapper procedure involves feeding a set of features into the algorithm and evaluating their quality from the learner's output. It contains two steps.

(i) An optimal linear classifier is first learned from the full-feature (supervised) training vectors in $\mathbb{R}^M$. (For the detailed learning schemes, see Chapters 8 and 9.) The decision boundary is characterized by the decision vector $\mathbf{w}$:

$$\mathbf{w}^{\mathrm{T}}\mathbf{x} + b = \sum_{i=1}^{M} w^{(i)}x^{(i)} + b = 0,$$

where b is a constant threshold.

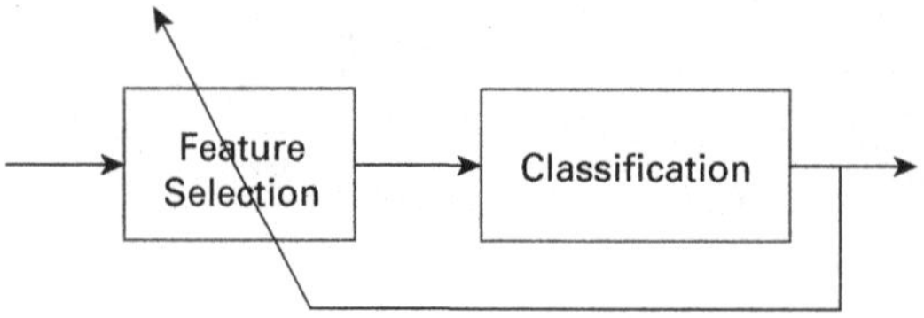

Fig. 4.6. The wrapper approach makes use of the feedback from a designated classifier to evaluate the importance of features in terms of their classification capability. The most influential features will be selected.

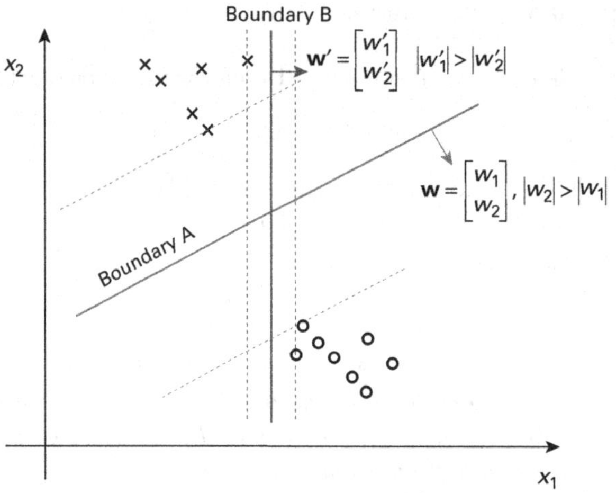

Fig. 4.7. Selecting one out of two features by SVM-RFE. A linear SVM will use "boundary A" for classification and therefore feature $x^{(2)}$ will be selected because $|w^{(2)}| > |w^{(1)}|$ for this decision boundary.

(ii) The magnitude of the coefficients of the decision vector **w**, i.e. $\{|w^{(i)}|\}_{i=1}^{M}$, can be used to measure the relevance of their corresponding features. More exactly, the features $\{x^{(i)}\}_{i=1}^{M}$ can be ranked according to their scores $\{|w^{(i)}|\}_{i=1}^{M}$.

To illustrate this principle of feature selection, let us use the simple example in Figure 4.7. Note that the linear "boundary A" is clearly better than "boundary B" in terms of their separation margin. It is assumed that the "boundary A," with the weight vector $\mathbf{w} = [w^{(1)}\ w^{(2)}]^{\mathrm{T}}$, is indeed the optimal linear decision boundary derived from the learning method adopted. The fact that $|w^{(2)}| > |w^{(1)}|$ suggests that $x^{(2)}$ is a more effective feature than $x^{(1)}$ for the purpose of classification.

In the backward elimination approach, the features with lower scores will be eliminated. Guyon *et al.* [89] proposed a wrapper approach combining the SVM with recursive feature elimination (RFE). The RFE algorithm eliminates unimportant features recursively using the linear decision hyperplane. Its flowchart is shown in Figure 4.8 and its procedure is summarized below.

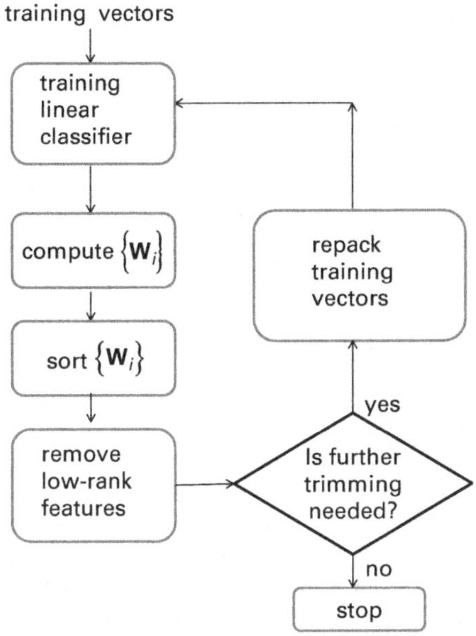

Fig. 4.8. The flowchart for RFE. The procedure is applicable to linear SVM as well as to any other linear classifier.

Initiation. Initially, all the features are used to learn an optimal linear classifier.

Iteration. During each iteration, train an optimal linear classifier using the remaining features. Then these features are ranked in descending order according to the magnitudes of the linear classifierąęs weights $w^{(i)}$, and a small fraction of lowest-ranked features will be eliminated.

Termination. If more features need to be eliminated, continue the next iteration with the remaining features. Otherwise, the iterative process will terminate. The remaining features form the final set to be selected.

Application examples

SVM-RFE was adopted to select informative mass points from two cancer datasets, concerning ovarian and lung cancer, from Rajapakse *et al.* [212]. Another application to gene selection based on microarray data will be discussed later.

4.3.2 Unsupervised wrapper methods

The wrapper approach is conventionally viewed as a supervised technique as it relies on the known class labels of the training vectors. However, it can be naturally extended to unsupervised scenarios. The originally unsupervised dataset can be first divided into subgroups. Once each of the subgroups has artificially been assigned a class label, the wrapper method can readily be applied. This process is illustrated in Figure 4.9. As an example, CLIFF [305] was successfully applied to select features from the leukemia dataset [66], and predicted the class of the test samples with a high accuracy.

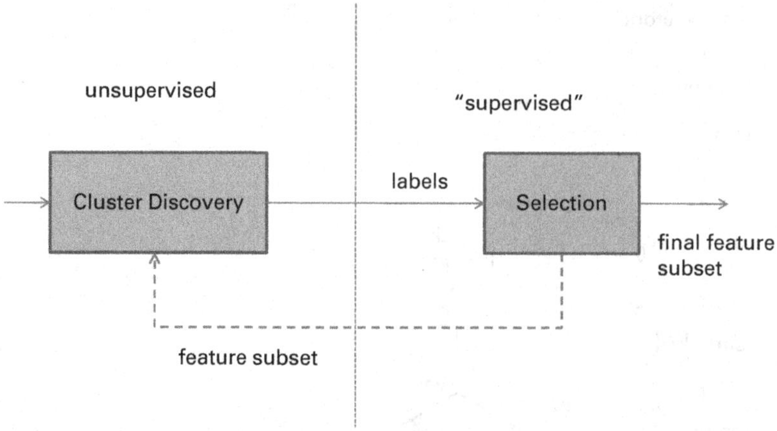

Fig. 4.9. The typical procedure for the unsupervised wrapper approach, where a feature subset is fed into a clustering algorithm whose results are used to perform feature selection. On the left, an unsupervised cluster discovery procedure is performed, generating "class labels" for each cluster. Once we have these class labels, we can solve the feature selection problem using a "supervised" feature approach (as shown on the right). The dashed feedback line represents the possibility of using an iterative process, such as that in [305], where the features can be further pruned.

Laplacian linear discriminant analysis-based recursive feature elimination (LLDA-RFE), which was proposed by Niijima and Okuno [194], is a multivariate feature selection technique that is closely related to the Laplacian score [96] and the Q–α algorithm [300]. The idea behind LLDA-RFE hinges upon a notion of soft clustering, which avoids the need to explicitly subdivide training vectors into distinctive subsets. LLDA-RFE reportedly [194] has a favorable performance edge over Laplacian score and SVD entropy in experiments conducted on seven microarray datasets [5, 7, 11, 66, 124, 208, 277].

4.3.3 The least absolute shrinkage and selection operator

Many machine learning applications have naturally been formulated as optimization problems. For feature selection, it is desirable to incorporate the number of features selected into the optimization criterion. Specifically, features may be selected using a regression technique known as the least absolute shrinkage and selection operator (LASSO), which was proposed by Tibshirani [268], whereby the ℓ_1-norm of the decision vector is incorporated into the objective function. It can be shown that this new optimization formulation, which involves minimizing the ℓ_1-norm, an augmented cost function, can effectively suppress the irrelevant or redundant features. Consequently, many of the regression coefficients $w^{(j)}$ will be coerced to become 0. In practice, the features corresponding to zero-valued coefficients may be removed while compromising very little the optimality. This is why LASSO has been adopted as a popular feature reduction method.

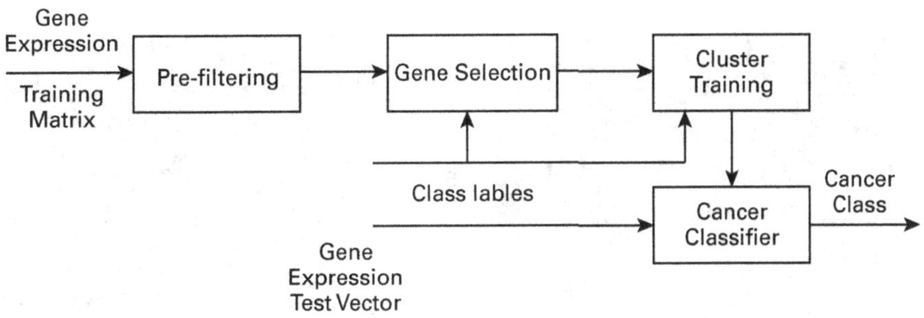

Fig. 4.10. The configuration of a cancer classification system based on gene expression data. The normalized gene expression matrices at various stages of the system building process are also shown.

4.4 Application studies of the feature selection approach

In [82], the microarray dataset contains 47 samples of acute lymphoblastic leukemia (ALL) and 25 samples of acute myeloid leukemia (AML). (The dataset can be downloaded from http://www.genome.wi.mit.edu/mpr.) For each sample, the expression levels of 7192 genes (of which 6817 human genes are of interest; the others are the controls) are measured, forming an expression matrix of size 7192×72. The matrix is further divided into a training set (containing 27 ALL and 11 AML cases) and a test set (containing 20 ALL and 14 AML cases). Since many (housekeeping) genes are irrelevant to the biological process related to acute leukemia, most of them may be filtered out without affecting the performance. In fact, as explained below, only 50 genes were required to yield a high classification/prediction performance [82].

As shown in Figure 4.10, the selection process is divided into two stages.

(i) **Stage 1: Unsupervised gene pre-filtering.** Of the 7129 genes in Golub's dataset, most were found to be irrelevant to the classification task. In fact, many genes have expression values well below or beyond the meaningful level. Therefore, it is advantageous to weed out those genes with insignificant variation and extremely large values. Following Dudoit *et al.* [55], a variation filter was adopted to identify and then remove gene i satisfying any of the following conditions:
(1) $\max_j g_{ij} - \min_j g_{ij} \leq 500$
(2) $\max_j g_{ij} > 16{,}000$
(3) $\left|\max_j g_{ij}/\min_j g_{ij}\right| \leq 5$
where g_{ij} is the expression level of gene i for training sample j. The correlation matrix in Figure 4.11(b) shows that, after this pre-filtering step, the two-class pattern begins to emerge. After this step, only 2729 genes survive the pre-filtering process. Namely, the matrix size is now reduced to 2729×38. Nevertheless, because the pre-filtering step does not make use of the class labels for selecting genes, there remain many irrelevant genes in the expression matrix. Thus, there is a need to resort to the (more effective) supervised selection schemes.

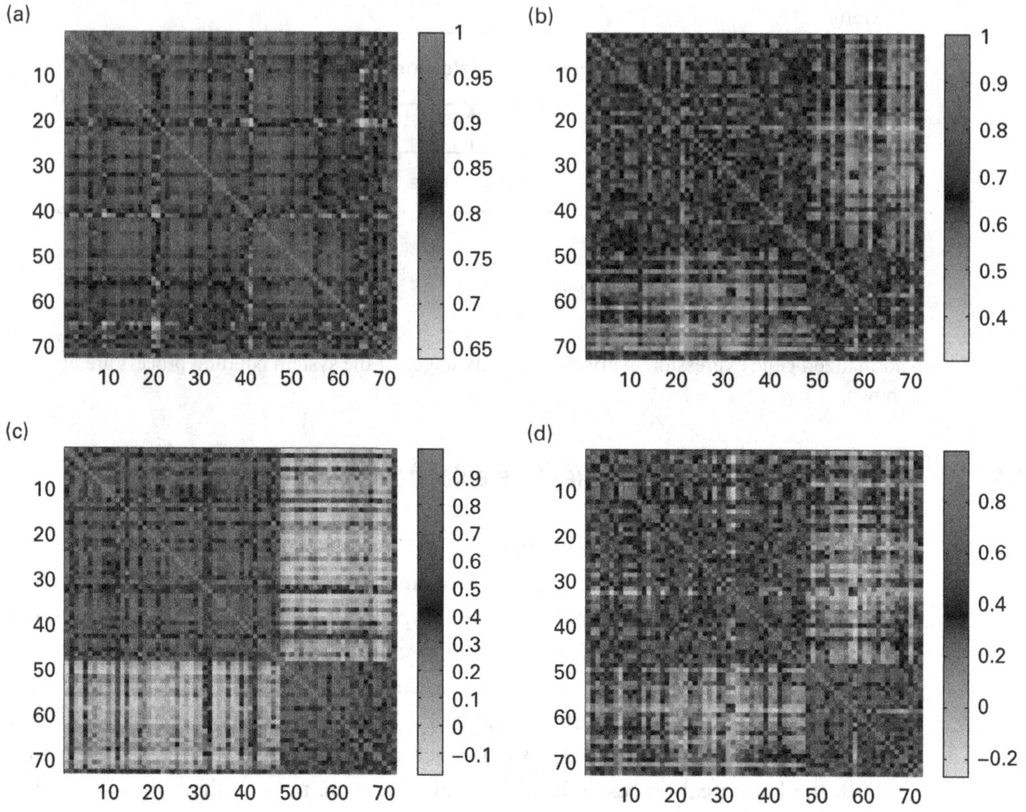

Fig. 4.11. The correlation matrix of the leukemia dataset based on (a) raw data, (b) genes after filtering, (c) genes after signed-SNR selection, and (d) genes after SVM-RFE selection.

(ii) **Stage 2: Supervised gene selection.** More irrelevant genes can be weeded out by either the *filter* or the *wrapper* approach (c.f. Section 4.2).

Once a subset of (say, m) genes has been selected from the total set, the two-class pattern in Figure 4.11 becomes apparent, suggesting that the selected features ($m = 50$) are relevant for the classification task.

Figure 4.12 shows the scores obtained by the SVMs together with the decision thresholds that lead to maximum accuracy. Confirming Golub's result, the accuracy is 100% for the SVM that employs signed-SNR-selected genes.

The number of genes selected could greatly impact the classification accuracy, as illuminated by the following comparative study.

- **A wide range of gene selection.** To have a more detailed comparison between the capability of FDR and SVM-RFE in selecting relevant genes, Figure 4.13 plots the accuracy against the number of selected genes. Evidently, signed SNR is superior to SVM-RFE for a wide range of feature dimensions.

Table 4.1. The accession numbers of the genes selected by signed SNR and SVM-RFE when the maximum number of genes to be selected is set to 5. All genes, except for the one with an asterisk, are part of the gene set selected by Golub *et al.*

Rank	FDR (signed SNR)	SVM-RFE
1	U22376	X04085
2	M55150	M19507*
3	U50136	M28130
4	X95735	U46751
5	U82759	X17042

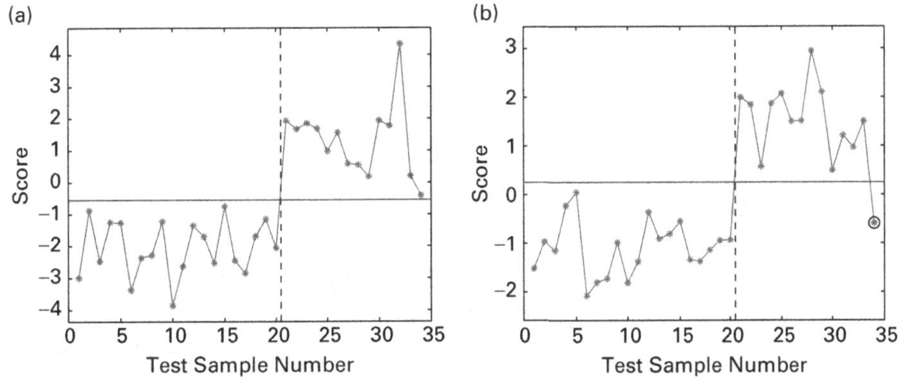

Fig. 4.12. Prediction scores and decision threshold (horizontal line) of SVM classifiers using 50 genes selected by (a) FDR, with perfect classification accuracy, and (b) SVM-RFE. On the left (right) of the vertical dashed line are 20 ALL (14 AML) test samples. The sole incorrect prediction is highlighted by the extra circle.

- **Selection of subsets of adequate size.** Fifty-input linear SVMs were used to classify the AML against ALL patterns, i.e. one SVM for classifying features selected by signed SNR and another for classifying features selected by SVM-RFE. (See Figure 4.13.) Just like Golub's result, the genes selected by signed SNR yielded a perfect (100%) accuracy with an SVM classifier, while the accuracy for the SVM-RFE subset was somewhat lower (97.1%).
- **Selection of a very small subset of critical genes.** Now we study the case where the number of allowable genes is very small. To this end, FDR (signed SNR) and SVM-RFE were used to find the top five genes for the classification task. The accession numbers of the selected genes are shown in Table 4.1. Although the genes found by the two selection methods are very different, these two sets of genes lead to the same prediction accuracy, which is 94.1%. Note that there exists no single overlap between the FDR and SVM-RFE selection pools. Moreover, we note that four of the five selected genes from the SVM-RFE can be found from the set of 50 highest-SNR genes selected by Golub *et al.* [82].

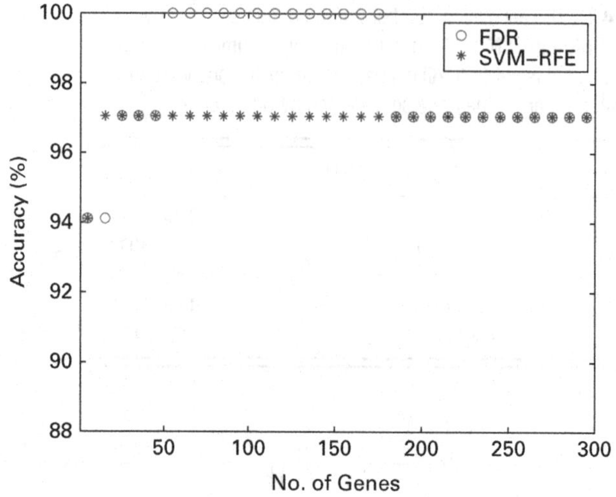

Fig. 4.13. Prediction accuracy of SVM classifiers for different numbers of genes selected by FDR and SVM-RFE.

4.5 Summary

Dimension-reduction is critical in enhancing learning efficiency and/or improving prediction performance. There are two popular feature extraction approaches, namely subspace projection and feature selection, both being popular for dimension-reduction of feature vectors. This chapter presents various feature selection techniques via either filtering or the wrapper approach, covering both supervised and unsupervised scenarios.

4.6 Problems

Problem 4.1 (PCA versus feature selection) *Suppose that*

$$\mathbf{R_x} = \begin{bmatrix} 5 & 3 & 0 \\ 3 & 5 & 3 \\ 0 & 3 & 5 \end{bmatrix}$$

Find the eigenvector corresponding to the first principal component of $\mathbf{R}$.

Perform feature selection on $x^{(1)}$, $x^{(2)}$, *and* $x^{(3)}$ *using the maximum-entropy criterion.*

(a) *If the reduced dimension is* $m = 1$, *determine the entropy obtained by the optimal PCA solution. Compare it with the entropy obtained by the optimal one-feature selection.*

(b) *If the reduced dimension is* $m = 2$, *determine the entropy obtained by the optimal PCA solution. Compare it with the entropy obtained by the optimal two-feature selection.*

Problem 4.2 (Filtering approach to feature selection) *Consider a dataset with six training vectors:*

$$\begin{aligned}
\mathbf{x}_1 &= [0.3\ 0.6\ 0.1]^{\mathrm{T}}, & y_1 &= +1,\\
\mathbf{x}_2 &= [0.8\ 0.3\ 0.6]^{\mathrm{T}}, & y_2 &= +1,\\
\mathbf{x}_3 &= [0.6\ \ -0.8\ 0.5]^{\mathrm{T}}, & y_3 &= +1,\\
\mathbf{x}_4 &= [-0.2\ 0.7\ 0.9]^{\mathrm{T}}, & y_4 &= -1,\\
\mathbf{x}_5 &= [0.1\ \ -0.2\ 0.7]^{\mathrm{T}}, & y_5 &= -1,\\
\mathbf{x}_6 &= [-0.1\ \ -0.3\ 1]^{\mathrm{T}}, & y_6 &= -1.
\end{aligned}$$

(a) *Rank order the features according to their signed-SNR scores.*
(b) *Rank order the features according to their FDR scores.*

Problem 4.3 (Feature-weighted linear classifier) *Consider the dataset given in Problem 4.2.*

(a) *Design the feature-weighted classifier using the top two features based on the signed-SNR score.*
(b) *Design the classifier using all three of the features based on the signed-SNR score.*
(c) *Design the classifier using the top two features based on the FDR score.*
(d) *Design the classifier using all three of the features based on the FDR score.*

Problem 4.4 *Consider four features whose entropy and mutual information are graphically represented by the following Venn diagram:*

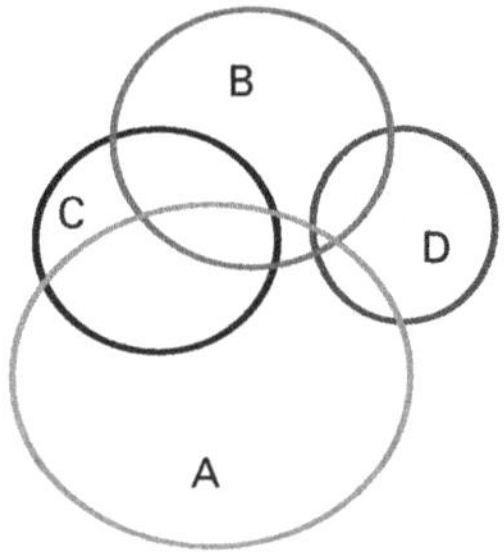

Select one, two, or three features by the filtering approach and the group-score method, as well as by forward search and backward elimination.

Problem 4.5 (Entropy of Gaussian variables) *You are given the covariance matrix, $\mathbf{R}_{\mathbf{y}}$, of a zero-mean Gaussian distributed vector variable $\mathbf{y}$. Show that the entropy of the variable $\mathbf{y}$ is*

$$H(\mathbf{y}) = \frac{1}{2}\log_2((2\pi)^m|\mathbf{R}_{\mathbf{y}}|) + \frac{m}{2}\log_2 e \tag{4.8}$$

Hints: *Show that*

$$H(\mathbf{y}) = -E\{\log p(\mathbf{y})\}$$

and

$$E\{\mathbf{y}^{\mathrm{T}}\mathbf{R}_{\mathbf{y}}^{-1}\mathbf{y}\} = \mathtt{tr}\ E\{\mathbf{R}_{\mathbf{y}}^{-1}\mathbf{y}\mathbf{y}^{\mathrm{T}}\}.$$

Problem 4.6 *You are given three features with the following covariance matrix:*

$$\mathbf{R}_{\mathbf{x}} = \begin{bmatrix} 100 & 80 & 0 \\ 80 & 100 & 0 \\ 0 & 0 & \delta \end{bmatrix}.$$

Using the entropy criterion, select the best single feature (Select 1). Find the second feature to best complement (in the entropy sense) the first feature (Select 2). Fill in the following table:

	Select 1	Select 2
$180 \le \delta$		
$100 \le \delta < 180$		
$36 \le \delta < 100$		
$\delta < 36$		

Problem 4.7 *You are given three features with the following covariance matrix*

$$\mathbf{R}_{\mathbf{x}} = \begin{bmatrix} 1 & 0.9 & 0.4 \\ 0.9 & 1 & 0 \\ 0.4 & 0 & 0.8 \end{bmatrix}.$$

Use the maximum-entropy criterion with (a) forward search and (b) backward elimination to select one or two features. Comment on the optimality (optimal or incorrect) of the selected features. Describe your results in the following table:

	Maximum-entropy forward search	Maximum-entropy backward elimination
One feature		
Two features		

Problem 4.8 (Entropy of innovation components) *You are given three features statistically modeled by zero-mean random variables with the following covariance matrix:*

$$\mathbf{R}_{\mathbf{x}} = \begin{bmatrix} 500 & 420 & 200 \\ 420 & 450 & 0 \\ 200 & 0 & 400 \end{bmatrix}.$$

Under the maximum-entropy criterion, the best single feature selected is $x^{(1)}$. Which of the two remaining features, $x^{(2)}$ or $x^{(3)}$, would best complement $x^{(1)}$ so as to yield the maximum joint entropy?

Hint: *An innovation-based forward search is presented below.*

- *In order to select the best feature to pair up with $x^{(1)}$, the innovation component of $x^{(2)}$ w.r.t. to $x^{(1)}$ can be computed as*

$$\nu_2 = x^{(2)} - 0.84x^{(1)}, \quad \textit{where} \quad 0.84 = r_{12} = \frac{420}{500}. \tag{4.9}$$

  According to Eq. (3.19), the entropy of ν_1 and ν_2 can be obtained as

$$H(\nu_2) = \frac{1}{2}\log_2(E[\nu_2^2]) + \frac{m}{2}\log_2(2\pi e) = 5.35.$$

- *On the other hand, the innovation component of $x^{(3)}$ w.r.t. to $x^{(1)}$ can be computed as*

$$\nu_3 = x^{(3)} - 0.4x^{(1)}, \quad \textit{where} \quad 0.4 = r_{13} = \frac{200}{500}, \tag{4.10}$$

  and it follows that

$$H(\nu_3) = \frac{1}{2}\log_2(E[\nu_3^2]) + \frac{m}{2}\log_2(2\pi e) = 6.21.$$

Because $H(\nu_2) < H(\nu_3)$, the best feature to pair up with $x^{(1)}$ should be $x^{(3)}$, even though $x^{(2)}$ has higher entropy than $x^{(3)}$, i.e. $H(x^{(2)}) = 6.45 > H(x^{(3)}) = 6.37$.

Problem 4.9 (Filter versus wrapper approaches) *Consider an over-determined linear system of equations $\mathbf{X}^{\mathrm{T}}\mathbf{w} = \mathbf{y}$, with $N = 4$ and $M = 3$:*

$$\mathbf{X} = \begin{bmatrix} 1 & 1 & -2 & 0 \\ -2 & 2 & 0 & 0 \\ 1 & 0 & 1 & -2 \end{bmatrix} \quad \textit{and} \quad \mathbf{y} = \begin{bmatrix} +1 \\ +1 \\ -1 \\ -1 \end{bmatrix}.$$

(a) *Select two out of the three features via the filter approach.*
(b) *Select two out of the three features via the wrapper approach.*

Problem 4.10 (Embedded methods) *One of the first embedded methods proposed for feature selection is the ℓ_0-norm SVM [296], which optimizes the following objective function:*

$$\min_{\mathbf{w}\in\mathbb{R}^M, b} \|\mathbf{w}\|_0 + C\|\boldsymbol{\xi}\|_0 \tag{4.11}$$

subject to

$$y_i(\mathbf{w}\cdot\mathbf{x}_i + b) \geq 1 - \xi_i, \quad i = 1, \ldots, N,$$

where $\|\mathbf{w}\|_0$ *is the number of nonzero elements in* $\mathbf{w}$, *N is the number of training vectors, C is a penalty factor, and* $\xi_i \geq 0$ *are slack variables. Another effective method considered for feature selection is selection via an* ℓ_1*-norm SVM [27], which is based on the following LASSO-type constraint optimization:*

$$\min_{\mathbf{w}\in\mathbb{R}^M, b} \|\mathbf{w}\|_1 + C\|\boldsymbol{\xi}\|_1 \tag{4.12}$$

subject to

$$y_i(\mathbf{w}\cdot\mathbf{x}_i + b) \geq 1 - \xi_i, \quad i = 1, \ldots, N,$$

where $\|\mathbf{w}\|_1 = \sum_{j=1}^{M} |w^{(j)}|$.

(a) *Explain why minimizing the* ℓ_0*-norm augmented cost function provides a direct way of combining feature selections and classifier design in a single objective function.*

(b) *Explain why minimizing the* ℓ_1*-norm augmented cost function can indirectly suppress the irrelevant or redundant features.*

Problem 4.11 (Soft-clustering-based wrapper approach: LLDA-RFE algorithm) *The LLDA-RFE algorithm [194], a soft-clustering-based wrapper method, is briefly described as follows.*

(i) *A normalized similarity matrix,* $\mathbf{S}$, *can be derived in two stages. A similarity matrix can be constructed from the pairwise similarity scores of the given (zero-mean) training vectors. Then the matrix is normalized so that the sum of the entries in each column is 1. Owing to the symmetry of the matrix, the sum of the entries in each row is also normalized.*

(ii) *In terms of* $\mathbf{S}$, *a score function is given as follows:*

$$\mathbf{W}^* = \arg\max_{\mathbf{W}} J(\mathbf{W}) = \arg\max_{\mathbf{W}} \mathtt{tr}\{\mathbf{W}^{\mathrm{T}}\mathbf{X}[2\mathbf{S} - \mathbf{I}]\mathbf{X}^{\mathrm{T}}\mathbf{W}\}, \tag{4.13}$$

where $\mathbf{W}$ *is a* $d \times M$ *projection matrix designed for mapping an M-dimensional space to a d-dimensional space.*

(iii) *The score associated with a feature, say* x_j, *can be computed as follows:*

$$\sum_{i=1}^{\gamma} \sqrt{\lambda_i}\left|\mathbf{W}^*_{ji}\right|, \tag{4.14}$$

where $\{\lambda_i, i = 1, \ldots, N\}$ *denote the (monotonically decreasing) eigenvalues of* $\Delta = \mathbf{X}[2\mathbf{S} - \mathbf{I}]\mathbf{X}^{\mathrm{T}}$, *and* γ *is the number of positive eigenvalues. The features with the lowest weights are removed recursively.*

(a) *Explain the potential applications of soft-clustering approaches.*

(b) *Study the difference between the hard-clustering and soft-clustering approaches, exemplified by LLDA-RFE.*

Part III

Unsupervised learning models for cluster analysis

Unsupervised cluster discovery is instrumental for data analysis in many important applications. It involves a process of partitioning the training dataset into disjoint groups. The performance of cluster discovery depends on several key factors, including the number of clusters, the topology of node vectors, the objective function for clustering, iterative learning algorithms (often with multiple initial conditions), and, finally, an evaluation criterion for picking the best result among multiple trials. This part contains two chapters: Chapter 5 covers unsupervised learning models employing the conventional Euclidean metric for vectorial data analysis while Chapter 6 focuses on the use of kernel-induced metrics and kernelized learning models, which may be equally applied to nonvectorial data analysis.

Chapter 5 covers several conventional unsupervised learning models for cluster discovery, including K-means and expectation-maximization (EM) learning models, which are presented in Algorithms 5.1 and 5.2, along with the respective proofs of the monotonic convergence property, in Theorems 5.1 and 5.2. By imposing topological sensitivity on the cluster (or node) structure, we can extend the basic K-means learning rule to the SOM learning model presented in Algorithm 5.3. Finally, for biclustering problems, where features and objects are simultaneously clustered, several useful coherence models are proposed.

Chapter 6 covers kernel-based cluster discovery, which is useful both for vectorial and for nonvectorial data analyses. For vectorial data analysis, a basic kernel K-means learning model involves (1) mapping the original training vectors to their representations in the intrinsic vector space $\mathcal{H}$, and then subsequently (2) applying the conventional K-means procedure to partition the new feature vectors. Usually, the feature dimension in the new space is much higher, providing much greater design flexibility, especially for supervised learning. Without the teacher's guidance, unfortunately, there is no clear and assertible advantage for unsupervised learning to be gained merely by substituting the Euclidean metric with a kernel-induced metric. In other words, from the perspective of performance, kernel-induced metrics offer much more tangible benefits to supervised learning models than do their unsupervised counterparts.

On the other hand, we note that the LSP condition holds for most ℓ_2-norm-based learning models, including K-means and the self-organizing map (SOM). The LSP is vital for kernelization, i.e. converting the optimizer into one characterized by the kernel matrix $\mathbf{K}$ associated with the training vectors. For K-means, the equivalence between two cost functions, one given in the intrinsic space and another in the empirical space, is established in Theorem 6.1.

Under the kernelized formulation, which is informally known as the kernel trick, all we need is to have the pairwise relationship clearly defined. In other words, there will be no need to have an explicit definition of a vector space or even an explicit quantification of each of the individual objects. Moreover, it is important to recognize that, for some applications, a pairwise similarity between two objects is more naturally quantifiable than each of the individual objects. For nonvectorial objects, such pairwise similarities may naturally assume the role of kernel functions of two vectors. This is why kernelized unsupervised learning models are especially amenable to nonvectorial data analysis.

However, the numerical property of kernel methods depends closely on the assumption that the kernel matrix is a Mercer matrix, defined as a matrix that is *positive semi-definite*. For vectorial data analysis, a Mercer matrix is assured as long as a Mercer kernel is adopted. Unfortunately, for nonvectorial analysis, there is no such equivalent theorem to assure a similarity matrix being a Mercer matrix. On the contrary, for most real-world applications, the raw similarity matrices do not meet the condition, and thus must be first converted to Mercer matrices before kernel learning models may be safely applied. Two prominent approaches to such conversion are spectral truncation and spectral shift.

- Spectral truncation involves dropping the spectral components associated with the negative eigenvalues and constructing a lower-rank Mercer matrix. This conversion, however, could result in performance degradation. Theorem 6.3 provides a quantitative analysis tradeoff between the dimension reduction and the clustering accuracy.
- Any symmetric matrix may be converted to a Mercer matrix by a spectral shift, which does not affect the optimal solution, as stated in Theorem 6.4.

The spectral shift approach has a promising application to network segmentation in large-scale (e.g. social) networks, where the use of sparsity will be vital for computational feasibility. Algorithm 6.3 presents a fast kernel K-means method via the recursive kernel trick on the kernel matrix. The procedure expedites the learning by fully exploiting the sparsity inherent in many real-life network applications.

As mentioned previously, the SOM is also an ℓ_2-norm-based learning model, making it amenable to kernelization. This eventually leads to Algorithm 6.4, a kernelized SOM learning model. By the same token, Algorithm 6.5 presents a kernelized *neighbor-joining* (NJ) learning model.

5 Unsupervised learning for cluster discovery

5.1 Introduction

The objective of cluster discovery is to subdivide a given set of training data, $\mathcal{X} \equiv \{\mathbf{x}_1, \mathbf{x}_2, \ldots, \mathbf{x}_N\}$, into a number of (say K) subgroups. Even with unknown class labels of the training vectors, useful information may be extracted from the training dataset to facilitate pattern recognition and statistical data analysis. Unsupervised learning models have long been adopted to systematically partition training datasets into disjoint groups, a process that is considered instrumental for classification of new patterns. This chapter will focus on conventional clustering strategies with the Euclidean distance metric. More specifically, it will cover the following unsupervised learning models for cluster discovery.

- Section 5.2 introduces two key factors – the similarity metric and clustering strategy – dictating the performance of unsupervised cluster discovery.
- Section 5.3 starts with the basic criterion and develops the iterative procedure of the K-means algorithm, which is a common tool for clustering analysis. The convergence property of the K-means algorithm will be established.
- Section 5.4 extends the basic K-means to a more flexible and versatile expectation-maximization (EM) clustering algorithm. Again, the convergence property of the EM algorithm will be treated.
- Section 5.5 further considers the topological property of the clusters, leading to the well-known self-organizing map (SOM).
- Section 5.6 discusses bi-clustering methods that allow simultaneous clustering of the rows and columns of a data matrix.

5.2 The similarity metric and clustering strategy

Let $\mathcal{X}$ denote the complete set of the training data

$$\mathcal{X} \equiv \{\mathbf{x}_1, \mathbf{x}_2, \ldots, \mathbf{x}_N\},$$

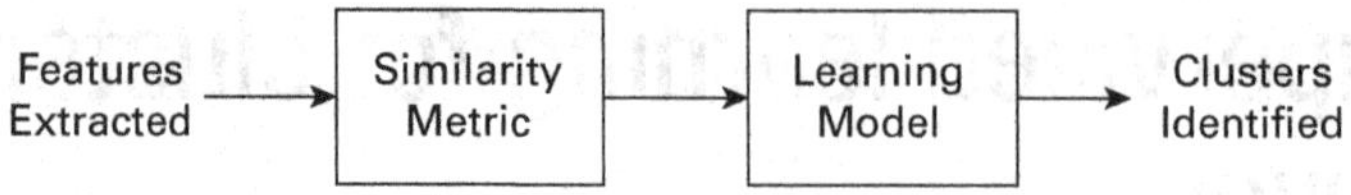

Fig. 5.1. Two key factors for unsupervised cluster discovery are (1) the similarity metric and (2) the clustering strategy.

where $\mathbf{x}_i \in \mathbb{R}^M$:

$$\mathbf{x}_i = \begin{bmatrix} x_i^{(1)} \\ x_i^{(2)} \\ \vdots \\ x_i^{(M)} \end{bmatrix}.$$

Cluster discovery is to divide these N training vectors into K groups. Such a partition explicitly specifies which of these vectors should be placed into the same group.

As shown in Figure 5.1, the performance of unsupervised cluster discovery is dictated by two key factors: (1) the similarity metric and (2) the clustering strategy.

Similarity metric

Whether a pair of training vectors should be assigned to the same group depends very much on the specific similarity metric used to measure the closeness of the objects. As to what constitutes a good similarity metric, it hinges upon a good understanding of the statistical properties of the dataset, e.g. the data distribution and cluster structures. In particular, very different metrics apply to vectorial versus nonvectorial data analysis.

(i) For vectorial objects, we often adopt one of the following types of similarity metrics.
  - *Euclidean and Mahalanobis distance metrics in the original vector space.* (See Section 1.2.2.)
  - *Generalized distance metric in the kernel-induced vector space.* (See Section 2.2.)

(ii) For nonvectorial cases, the *similarity metric* depends very much on the types of objects, which may be temporal or graphic. (See Section 2.5.1.)

The emphasis in this chapter is placed on clustering of vectorial data and, in particular, the traditional Euclidean linear product and its induced distance. The Euclidean inner product (or dot product) is $\mathbf{x} \cdot \mathbf{y} = \mathbf{x}^{\mathrm{T}}\mathbf{y}$, which induces the popular Euclidean distance which is also known as the 2-norm: $\|\mathbf{x} - \mathbf{y}\|$. In Chapter 6, the conventional clustering methods will be extended to generalized inner products and distances for vectorial and nonvectorial samples.

Clustering strategy

Any unsupervised clustering problem starts with a given training dataset $\mathcal{X}$ that denotes the complete set of the training vectors:

$$\mathcal{X} \equiv \{\mathbf{x}_1, \mathbf{x}_2, \ldots, \mathbf{x}_N\}.$$

Its clustering performance obviously depends on the data distribution. In addition, it also depends on several factors in the procedure used for cluster discovery.

- **The number of clusters K.** The task of clustering is to divide these N training vectors into K disjoint clusters, where K denotes the number of clusters. More exactly, $\mathcal{X} = \{\mathcal{X}_1 \bigcup \mathcal{X}_2 \cdots \bigcup \mathcal{X}_K\}$. The value of K is usually *pre-assigned* and is to remain unchanged throughout the learning process. The question is that of how to select K. Ideally, it may be determined via some information-theoretical criterion. (See Section 5.3.6.) However, in practice, the value of K is more often empirically determined.
- **Node vectors.** Each cluster, sometimes known as a cluster node, is assigned a representative *node vector* denoted by $\mathbf{w}_k,\ k = 1, \ldots, K$. The main task of clustering involves finding an optimal set of K node vectors, i.e. $\{\mathbf{w}_k,\ k = 1, \ldots, K\}$.
- **Topology of node vectors.** A basic objective function of clustering is just a function of $\mathcal{X}$ and $\{\mathbf{w}_k,\ k = 1, \ldots, K\}$. K-means is a typical example. However, advanced clustering schemes are likely to take other factors into consideration; a typical example is the topology of node vectors. In this case, node vectors are organized on a topologically ordered grid. For example, such topologies are a defining characteristic of a prominent clustering algorithm known as the SOM. The SOM represents data by means of nodes (one node for each cluster) organized on a grid with fixed topology. In this case, the objective function of clustering must consider $\mathcal{X}$, $\{\mathbf{w}_k,\ k = 1, \ldots, K\}$, and the overall distances of the topologically adjacent node vectors.
- **The objective function of unsupervised optimizers.** Ideally, the objective function of clustering is pre-specified, which sets the foundation of the learning rule. In general, the objective function includes both intra-cluster and inter-cluster metrics, as exemplified below.
  - (i) *Minimum intra-cluster compactness or maximum inter-cluster separation.* Heuristically, vectors assigned to the same cluster should exhibit a certain mutual proximity. This is typically exemplified by the K-means clustering criterion shown in Eq. (5.7). On the other hand, vectors from different clusters should have greater distances. A modified K-means criterion, given in Eq. (6.4), explicitly shows such a preference.
  - (ii) *Topologically adjusted inter-cluster criteria.* A typical example is the SOM, which has a delicate inter-cluster requirement. In fact, for two topologically neighboring nodes (nodes with adjacent indices), it becomes actually preferable to have their respective node vectors close to each other – as opposed to being far apart. Such a preference may be incorporated into the objective function as exemplified by Eq. (5.30).
- **Iterative learning procedures.** Given a pre-specified objective function, now the question is that of how to find its optimal solution. To find an optimum, one typically

resorts to an iterative procedure, in which two different sets of parameters are updated alternately:

(i) the membership of the (disjoint) clusters, i.e. $\{\mathcal{X}_1, \mathcal{X}_2, \ldots, \mathcal{X}_K\}$; and

(ii) the node vectors of the clusters, i.e. $\{\mathbf{w}_k,\ k = 1, \ldots, K\}$.

- **Evaluation criterion for selection among multiple-trials.** Because the clustering performance of any iterative method depends heavily on the initial condition, it is advisable to (1) execute multiple copies of the same procedure, each time with a randomized initial condition; and (2) evaluate and find the best solution. The question is how one should conduct such an evaluation. The answer hinges upon the establishment of an evaluation criterion to compare and assess various clustering results.

5.3 *K*-means clustering models

A basic and popular clustering algorithm is the K-means [53, 54, 70, 164]. Assuming that the number of clusters K is fixed, the K-means algorithm subdivides N training vectors, $\mathcal{X} = \{\mathbf{x}_1, \mathbf{x}_2, \ldots, \mathbf{x}_N\}$, into K disjoint clusters. More exactly, $\mathcal{X} = \{\mathcal{X}_1 \bigcup \mathcal{X}_2 \ldots \bigcup \mathcal{X}_K\}$. For notational convenience, let the K clusters be respectively labeled by $\mathcal{C} = \{\mathcal{C}_1, \mathcal{C}_2, \ldots, \mathcal{C}_K\}$.

Maximum likelihood clustering criterion

The K-means algorithm can be formulated from a likelihood optimization perspective. Assume that the training dataset $\mathcal{X}$ is generated from a set of K locally distributed probabilistic models, parameterized by $\Theta = \{\Theta_1, \Theta_2, \ldots, \Theta_K\}$. The K-means' objective is to find a model Θ^* that has statistically the highest (log-)likelihood to generate the observed data. More exactly, the objective is to find

$$\Theta^* = \arg\max_{\Theta} \log p(\mathcal{X}|\Theta). \tag{5.1}$$

5.3.1 *K*-means clustering criterion

Under the assumption of independent distribution,

$$p(\mathcal{X}|\Theta) = \prod_{t=1}^{N} p(\mathbf{x}_t|\Theta). \tag{5.2}$$

Let us now focus on a specific vector, say $\mathbf{x}_t$, shown in Figure 5.2(a). The question at hand is that of how to evaluate its individual likelihood. To maximize the likelihood, note that $\mathbf{x}_t$ is most likely to be generated by the model $\mathcal{C}_k$, where

$$k = \arg\max_{j} p(\mathbf{x}_t|\Theta_j)\ \forall j = 1, \ldots, K.$$

It follows that the optimal individual likelihood is

$$p(\mathbf{x}_t|\Theta) = p(\mathbf{x}_t|\Theta_k). \tag{5.3}$$

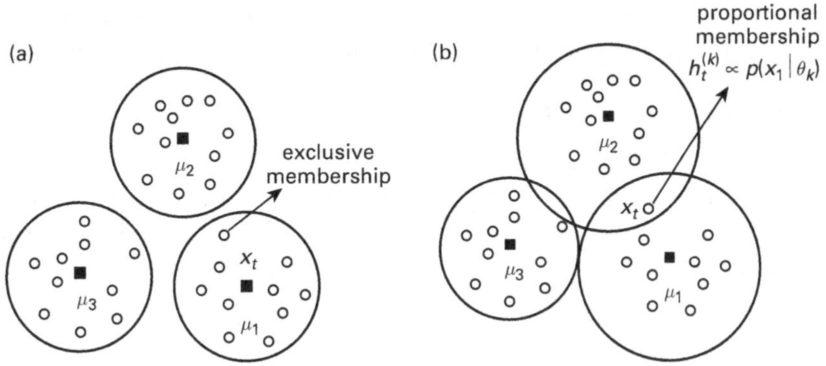

Fig. 5.2. The difference between K-means and EM is emphasized by their membership assignments. (a) K-means adopts a hard membership (i.e., as shown in Eq. (5.3), any vector $\mathbf{x}_t$ is exclusively associated with one cluster only). (b) EM allows each vector to have soft membership, i.e. straddling multiple clusters.

Under the assumption of independent distribution, the overall likelihood is

$$p(\mathcal{X}|\Theta) = \prod_{k=1}^{K} \prod_{\mathbf{x}_t \in \mathcal{C}_k} p(\mathbf{x}_t|\Theta_k). \tag{5.4}$$

Let us further assume that each cluster is governed by the following Gaussian distribution with isotropic covariance:

$$p(\mathbf{x}_t|\Theta_k) = \frac{1}{\sqrt{(2\pi\sigma)^M}} \exp\left\{-\frac{\|\mathbf{x}_t - \vec{\mu}_k\|^2}{2\sigma^2}\right\}, \tag{5.5}$$

where $\vec{\mu}_k$ and σ denote respectively the centroid and standard deviation of the kth cluster node. Then Eq. (5.4) becomes

$$-\log p(\mathcal{X}|\Theta) \propto -\sum_{k=1}^{K} \sum_{\mathbf{x}_t \in \mathcal{C}_k} \log p(\mathbf{x}_t|\Theta_k) = \sum_{k=1}^{K} \sum_{\mathbf{x}_t \in \mathcal{C}_k} \|\mathbf{x}_t - \vec{\mu}_k\|^2 + \text{constant}, \tag{5.6}$$

where all the non-critical terms are summarily represented by a single *constant*. Thus, maximizing the log-likelihood function basically amounts to minimizing a new criterion in terms of a sum-of-squared distances (SSD). This result is now summarized as follows. Under the basic Gaussian distribution model, the objective of the K-means is to find K centroids to best minimize the following SSD cost function:

$$E_{\text{SSD}} = \sum_{k=1}^{K} \sum_{\mathbf{x}_t \in \mathcal{C}_k} \|\mathbf{x}_t - \vec{\mu}_k\|^2. \tag{5.7}$$

In summary, for the basic K-means algorithm, the clusters $\{\mathcal{C}_j,\ j = 1, \ldots, K\}$ are parameterized by the cluster centroids. More exactly,

$$\Theta = \{\Theta_1, \Theta_2, \ldots, \Theta_K\} = \{\ \vec{\mu}_j,\ j = 1, \ldots, K\}.$$

Hence, the Euclidean inner product (or Euclidean distance) can be adopted as an effective similarity metric for the development of the K-means algorithms.

5.3.2 The K-means algorithm

Joint optimization formulation

The most direct formulation is to minimize the cost function jointly with respect to both $\{\vec{\mu}_k, k = 1, \ldots, K\}$ and $\{\mathcal{X}_k, k = 1, \ldots, K\}$. Mathematically, the optimization problem can be expressed as

$$\min_{\{\vec{\mu}_k, \mathcal{X}_k\}, k=1,\ldots,K} E_{\text{SSD}}. \tag{5.8}$$

Iterative optimization formulation

The solution of such a direct joint optimization problem is very difficult and highly impractical. Fortunately, the joint optimization problem can be naturally divided into the following two simple optimization formulations and iterative methods may be developed to progressively improve the cost function.

(i) In the *winner-identification* step, we shall fix the centroid parameters $\{\vec{\mu}_k\}, k = 1, \ldots, K$, and focus on updating the membership parameters $\{\mathcal{X}_k\}, k = 1, \ldots, K$, to best minimize the SSD cost.
(ii) In the *centroid-update* step, we shall fix the membership parameters $\{\mathcal{X}_k\}$ and focus on updating the centroid parameters $\{\vec{\mu}_k\}$ to best minimize the SSD cost.

Pursuant to this guideline, we can now present formally the (iterative) K-means algorithm.

Initialization

There are two possible schemes to initialize the K-means iterative procedure.

(i) The K initial centroids, $\vec{\mu}_k$ for $k = 1, \ldots, K$, are randomly assigned.
(ii) Alternatively, at the very beginning, each training vector, say $\mathbf{x}_t$, is randomly assigned to an arbitrary cluster, say $\mathcal{C}_k$.

The two initialization schemes are basically interchangeable. Using the K centroids, the membership association can be uniquely derived by Eq. (5.9). Using the membership assignment, on the other hand, the K centroids can be immediately obtained according to Eq. (5.10).

ALGORITHM 5.1 (K-means iterative learning algorithm) *As illustrated in Figure 5.3, once properly initialized, the K-means iterative procedure alternately updates the memberships and centroids in each iteration.*

(i) **Winner identification.** *For every pattern* $\mathbf{x}_t$, $\mathbf{x}_t \in \mathcal{X}=\{\mathbf{x}_1, \mathbf{x}_2, \ldots, \mathbf{x}_N\}$, *its distance to each of the K centroids will be computed and compared. The winning cluster, say the kth, with the closest centroid,*

$$k = \arg\min_{\{j:j=1,\cdots,K\}} \|\mathbf{x}_t - \vec{\mu}_j\|, \tag{5.9}$$

will be referred to as the "winner." Consequently, in the updated membership, $\mathbf{x}_t \in \mathcal{C}_k$.

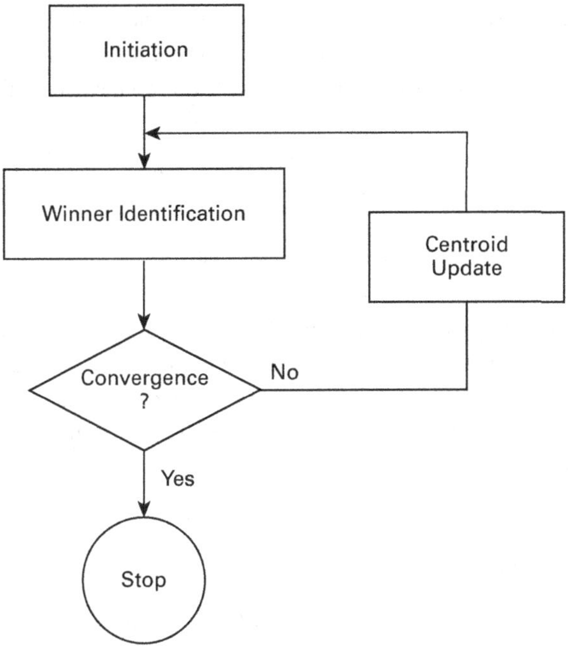

Fig. 5.3. The flowchart of the K-means algorithm.

(ii) **Centroid update.** *When a new vector $\mathbf{x}_t$ is added to a cluster, say C_k, the old centroid of that cluster (denoted by $\vec{\mu}_k^{\text{old}}$) will be updated as follows:*

$$\vec{\mu}_k^{\text{old}} \quad \rightarrow \quad \vec{\mu}_k = \frac{1}{N_k} \sum_{\mathbf{x}_t \in C_k} \mathbf{x}_t, \tag{5.10}$$

where N_k denotes the total number of vectors in C_k (including $\mathbf{x}_t$). □

Computational costs for K*-means*

The computational costs for the two substeps are estimated as follows.

(i) **Winner identification.** In each membership updating for one training vector, say $\mathbf{x}_t$, the incurred computation amounts to $O(KM)$ operations, mostly spent on computing the K distances to $\mathbf{x}_t$, i.e. $\|\mathbf{x}_t - \vec{\mu}_j\|$, $j = 1, \ldots, K$. It means $O(KMN)$ per epoch to cover all the N training vectors in one entire round.

(ii) **Centroid update.** This substep requires a computational cost of order $O(MN_k)$, where M and N_k are respectively the dimension and size of the cluster C_k. It amounts to roughly $O(MN^2/K)$ per epoch, after an approximation of $N_k \approx N/K$.

This suggests that most of the computation is spent on the *centroid update* substep. This motivates the development of a more efficient updating scheme. Indeed, the centroid can be more efficiently updated as follows:

$$\vec{\mu}_k^{\text{old}} \quad \rightarrow \quad \vec{\mu}_k = \frac{(N_k - 1)\vec{\mu}_k^{\text{old}} + \mathbf{x}_t}{N_k}, \tag{5.11}$$

where N_k denotes the new size of the updated cluster C_k, x_t included. We note that the same computational saving can be applied to the cluster where its old member is leaving, instead of joining. If $\mathbf{x}_t$ is removed from, say, the cluster C_p, we have a similar updating formula:

$$\vec{\mu}_p^{\text{old}} \quad \rightarrow \quad \vec{\mu}_p = \frac{(N_p)\vec{\mu}_p^{\text{old}} - \mathbf{x}_t}{N_p - 1}, \tag{5.12}$$

where N_p denotes the new size of the updated cluster C_p, with x_t no longer included.

In summary, the computational cost associated with addition/removal of a member to/from a cluster is $O(M)$ per training pattern. For the entire epoch of N training data, it amounts to a total of $O(MN)$ operations, significantly fewer than for *winner identification*. The latter, incurring $O(KMN)$ operations per epoch, now dominates the overall computational complexity.

5.3.3 Monotonic convergence of K-means

K-means guarantees a monotonic convergence to a (local) optimum as formally stated below.

THEOREM 5.1 (Monotonic convergence of K-means) *The K-means iterative procedure monotonically converges to a (local) optimum in terms of the SSD criterion.*

□

Proof. Let us now establish the monotonically decreasing property of the objective function in each of the updating steps.

(i) First, let us demonstrate the monotonic reduction of the cost function in the *winner-identification* step while keeping the node vectors (i.e. centroids) fixed. Let $\{C_k^{\text{old}}\}$ and $\{C_k\}$ denote the old and new clusters. Note that the distance to the new winner has to be shorter than that to the old one, thus reducing the cost function in Eq. (5.7). Mathematically,

$$\sum_{k=1}^{K} \sum_{\mathbf{x}_t \in C_k} \|\mathbf{x}_t - \vec{\mu}_k^{\text{old}}\|^2 \le \sum_{k=1}^{K} \sum_{\mathbf{x}_t \in C_k^{\text{old}}} \|\mathbf{x}_t - \vec{\mu}_k^{\text{old}}\|^2, \tag{5.13}$$

where $\{\vec{\mu}_k^{\text{old}}\}$ denotes the centroid before the centroid update.

(ii) We can also show the monotonic reduction of the cost function in the *centroid-update* step, while keeping the membership fixed. It is easy to verify that the new centroid is the optimal solution for minimizing the sum of the squared errors: $\sum_{\mathbf{x}_t \in C_k} \|\mathbf{x}_t - \vec{\mu}_k\|^2$, when the memberships remain fixed. Note that the gradients of the objective function are taken with respect to the centroids and they are twice continuously differentiable (with a positive semi-definite Hessian). Then the gradient of the objective function vanishes at a local minimizer. This means that the local minimizer $\vec{\mu}_k$ can be obtained by taking the first-order gradient of the objective function with respect to $\vec{\mu}_k$ and equating it to zero:

$$0 = \frac{\partial\left(\sum_{\mathbf{x}_t \in \mathcal{C}_k} \|\mathbf{x}_t - \vec{\mu}_k\|^2\right)}{\partial \vec{\mu}_k} = -\sum_{\mathbf{x}_t \in \mathcal{C}_k} (\mathbf{x}_t - \vec{\mu}_k) = N_k \vec{\mu}_k - \sum_{\mathbf{x}_t \in \mathcal{C}_k} \mathbf{x}_t,$$

which directly leads to Eq. (5.10), i.e.

$$\vec{\mu}_k = \frac{1}{N_k} \sum_{\mathbf{x}_t \in \mathcal{C}_k} \mathbf{x}_t.$$

Consequently,

$$\sum_{k=1}^{K} \sum_{\mathbf{x}_t \in \mathcal{C}_k} \|\mathbf{x}_t - \vec{\mu}_k\|^2 \leq \sum_{k=1}^{K} \sum_{\mathbf{x}_t \in \mathcal{C}_k^{\text{old}}} \|\mathbf{x}_t - \vec{\mu}_k^{\text{old}}\|^2. \tag{5.14}$$

Namely, the new cost function Eq. (5.7) can only be lower or at least the same as before.

On combining Eqs. (5.13) and (5.14), it is obvious that the total cost function monotonically decreases in every iteration, i.e.

$$\sum_{k=1}^{K} \sum_{\mathbf{x}_t \in \mathcal{C}_k} \|\mathbf{x}_t - \vec{\mu}_k\|^2 \leq \sum_{k=1}^{K} \sum_{\mathbf{x}_t \in \mathcal{C}_k^{\text{old}}} \|\mathbf{x}_t - \vec{\mu}_k^{\text{old}}\|^2.$$

In summary, the iterative algorithm of K-means progressively improves the clustering accuracy. Since the cost function $E(\mathcal{X})$ cannot be negative, the iterative procedure must terminate at some point.

□

Now let us illustrate the iterative process of K-means by means of a simple example.

Example 5.1 (Case study: K-means and global optimality) *As shown in Figure 5.4, the training dataset consists of five one-dimensional vectors* $\{\mathbf{x}_1 = 2.0,\ \mathbf{x}_2 = 4.0,\ \mathbf{x}_3 = 6.0,\ \mathbf{x}_4 = 7.0,\ \mathbf{x}_5 = 8.0\}$, *which are to be clustered into two groups* ($K = 2$) *by applying a K-means iterative updating scheme. For this simple example, K-means will always converge to a global optimal solution no matter how the model is initialized.*

Initialization

As shown in Figure 5.4(a1), four members $\{\mathbf{x}_1, \mathbf{x}_2, \mathbf{x}_3, \mathbf{x}_5\}$ *are initially assigned to the first (dark-shading) cluster and the remaining one* $\{\mathbf{x}_4\}$ *to the second (light-shading) cluster. As shown in Figure 5.4(a2), the two centroids can be computed as* $\vec{\mu}_1 = 5.0$ *and* $\vec{\mu}_2 = 7.0$.

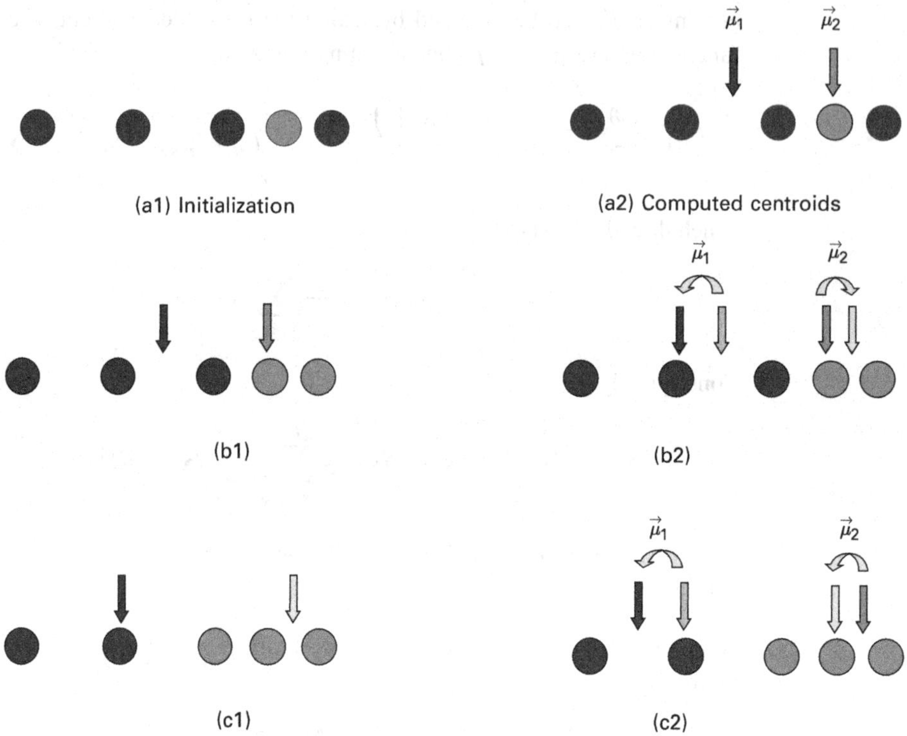

Fig. 5.4. A simple example of K-means iterations. (a1) Initially, cluster 1 has four members and cluster 2 has one member. (a2) Given such memberships, two centroids can be computed, for cluster 1 and cluster 2. (b1) Membership update via the centroids in (a2). (b2) Centroid update: both centroids are updated via the newly updated memberships. (c1) Membership update via the newly updated centroids in (b2). (c2) The two centroids are again updated. The iterations will continue until termination.

First epoch

- *Figure 5.4(b1). Winner identification: the rightmost member* $\mathbf{x}_5$ *switches its membership from the first cluster to the second cluster.*
- *Figure 5.4(b2). Centroid update: the three remaining members* $\{\mathbf{x}_1, \mathbf{x}_2, \mathbf{x}_3\}$ *of the first cluster vote to relocate the centroid to the new location* $\vec{\mu}_1 = 4.0$*. The two members* $\{\mathbf{x}_4, \mathbf{x}_5\}$ *of the second cluster vote to relocate the centroid to the new location* $\vec{\mu}_2 = 7.5$.

Second epoch

- *Figure 5.4(c1). Winner identification: the center member* $\mathbf{x}_3$ *switches its membership from the first cluster to the second cluster. Now the two leftmost nodes* $\{\mathbf{x}_1, \mathbf{x}_2\}$ *form one cluster and the rightmost three* $\{\mathbf{x}_3, \mathbf{x}_4, \mathbf{x}_5\}$ *form another.*
- *Figure 5.4(c2). Centroid update: the two members* $\{\mathbf{x}_1, \mathbf{x}_2\}$ *of the first cluster vote to relocate the centroid to the new location* $\vec{\mu}_1 = 3.0$*. The three members* $\{\mathbf{x}_3, \mathbf{x}_4, \mathbf{x}_5\}$

of the second cluster vote to relocate the centroid to the new location $\vec{\mu}_2 = 7.0$. *Now the sum-squared-error, see Eq. (5.7), has reached its minimum and convergence has been attained.*

5.3.4 The local optimum problem of K-means

Unfortunately, K-means often converges to a local optimum and, consequently, the performance of each K-means depends closely on the initial condition. This can be illustrated by the following numerical example.

Example 5.2 (Example of local optimum) *Consider three training vectors in* $\mathbb{R}^2$ *as depicted in Figure 5.5:*

$$\mathbf{x}_1 = \begin{bmatrix} 1 \\ 0 \end{bmatrix}, \quad \mathbf{x}_2 = \begin{bmatrix} 0 \\ 0 \end{bmatrix}, \quad \mathbf{x}_3 = \begin{bmatrix} 0 \\ 1 \end{bmatrix}.$$

There are two global optima. One is the partition $(\mathbf{x}_1, \mathbf{x}_2)(\mathbf{x}_3)$*, for which* $||\mathbf{x}_1 - \vec{\mu}_1||^2 = ||\mathbf{x}_2 - \vec{\mu}_1||^2 = 0.25$ *and* $E_{\text{SSD}} = 0.25 + 0.25 + 0 = 0.5$. *The other is the partition* $(\mathbf{x}_2, \mathbf{x}_3)(\mathbf{x}_1)$*, again for which* $E_{\text{SSD}} = 0.25 + 0.25 + 0 = 0.5$.

If the iteration is initiated with the partition $(\mathbf{x}_1, \mathbf{x}_3)(\mathbf{x}_2)$*, then the two centroids are* $\vec{\mu}_1 = [0.5 \quad 0.5]^{\text{T}}$ *and* $\vec{\mu}_2 = [0 \quad 0]^{\text{T}}$. *As explained below, the iteration should be terminated since it has already reached convergence.*

- *The first vector* $\mathbf{x}_1$ *is closer to* $\vec{\mu}_1$ *than it is to* $\vec{\mu}_2$*, so it will continue to belong to the first cluster.*
- *Likewise,* $\mathbf{x}_3$ *is also closer to* $\vec{\mu}_1$ *than it is to* $\vec{\mu}_2$*, so it will also stay with the first cluster.*
- *Obviously,* $\mathbf{x}_2$ *is closer to* $\vec{\mu}_2$ *than it is to* $\vec{\mu}_1$.

Note that, when the centroids are fixed as they are, it is impossible to reduce the cost function $E(\mathcal{X})$ *merely by updating the membership of any of the three training vectors. By application of the K-means learning rule, the iteration is stuck at its beginning*

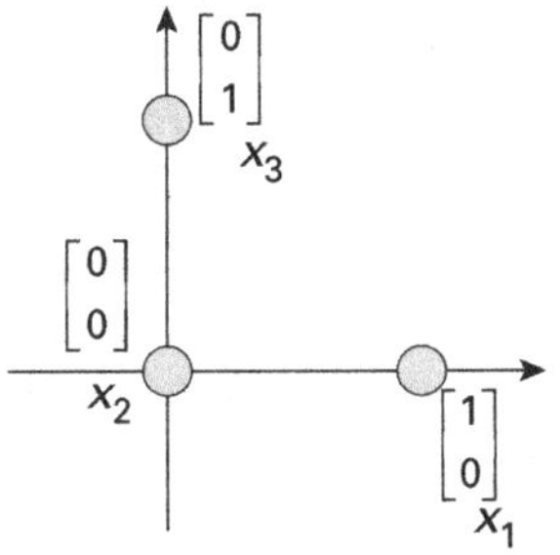

Fig. 5.5. A simple K-means clustering problem involves only three training vectors.

point. In other words, it has already converged and, by definition, the initial partition $(\mathbf{x}_1, \mathbf{x}_3)(\mathbf{x}_2)$ *qualifies as a local minimum. However, it is not a global optimum because its cost function,* $E_{\text{SSD}} = 0.5 + 0.5 + 0 = 1.0$*, is greater than the global minimum* (0.5).

□

5.3.5 The evaluation criterion for multiple trials of *K*-means

One way to solve the local minimum problem is by performing K-means multiple times, each time starting with a newly randomized initial condition. Then, from the multiple clustering results, we can choose the one with the lowest E_{SSD}.[1] In summary, for the multi-trial K-means, a good evaluation criterion is E_{SSD} given in Eq. (5.7), i.e. the SSD.

5.3.6 The optimal number of clusters

If the number of clusters, K, is unknown a priori, then we need to design a method to estimate K. Several estimation criteria have been proposed for this purpose, such as the Akaike information criterion (AIC), the Bayesian information criterion (BIC), and the minimum description length (MDL) [3, 218, 242]. The MDL criterion aims at finding an integer K that minimizes

$$\text{MDL}(K) = -\log \mathcal{L}_{\text{ML}} + 0.5(6K - 1)\log N,$$

where $\log \mathcal{L}_{\text{ML}}$ is the log maximum likelihood (given in Eq. (5.1)) and N is the number of training patterns.

5.3.7 Application examples

Among numerous examples of successful application of K-means, let us highlight just the one case study presented below.

Example 5.3 (K-means for gene clustering analysis) *Figure 5.6(a) shows the nine centers (thick black lines) and the profiles of each cluster (thin lines) found by applying K-means clustering to the 421 normalized gene profiles extracted from the yeast dataset by Tamayo et al. Intuitively, genes that exhibit the same up and down patterns over time are likely to be co-regulated by the same cellular process, thus sharing a common or similar function. Figure 5.6(b) shows the visualization of the clusters' centroids for a set of training vectors, projected onto two principal components.*

[1] In MATLAB, the instruction code [IDX,C] = kmeans(X^T, K, 'distance', 'correlation', 'replicates', number of times you want to operate Kmeans) returns the K cluster centroid locations in the $K \times M$ matrix C.

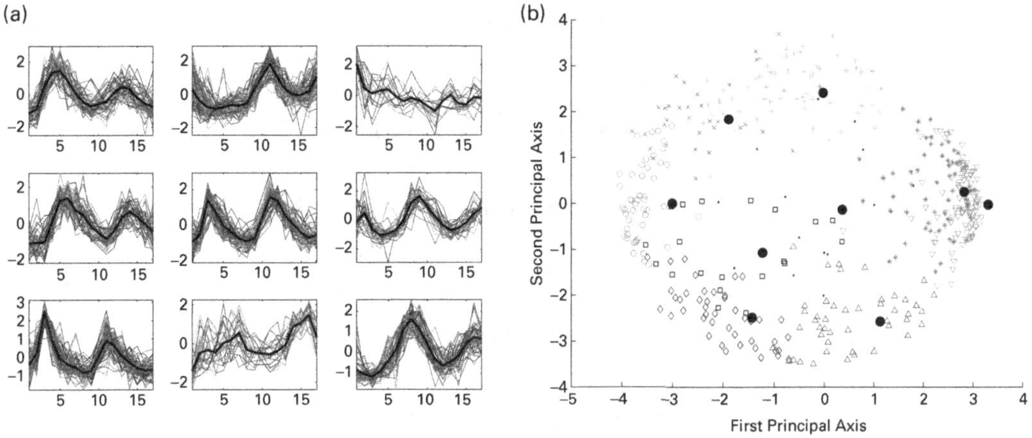

Fig. 5.6. (a) Centroids (thick black lines) and the profiles of each cluster (thin lines) found by applying K-means clustering to the (normalized) gene profiles of Tamayo *et al.*'s yeast cell cycle data [263]. (b) Projection of 421 gene profiles and nine centers (large •) found by K-means clustering onto two principal components. (The nine clusters are denoted by different symbols.) This display is meant to be compared with Figure 5.15(b).

Note that co-expressed genes are likely to be co-regulated and functionally related. Therefore, gene clustering analysis may be critical to prediction of functions of new genes which could in turn facilitate identification of critical biomarkers.

5.4 Expectation-maximization (EM) learning models

The K-means algorithm can be extended to the more general expectation-maximization (EM) algorithm proposed by Dempster, Laird, and Rubin in 1977 [47]. This is a versatile technique for parameter estimation that is applicable to most statistical models and has been a popular algorithm for many optimization problems.

In EM, just like with K-means, the model parameters (denoted by $\Theta = \{\Theta_1, \Theta_2, \ldots, \Theta_K\}$) are trained to best fit the data under a statistical model. As illustrated by Figure 5.2, EM and K-means differ in their ways of assigning membership to a training pattern, say $\mathbf{x}_t$, as follows.

- *K-means uses hard membership assignment.* As depicted in Figure 5.2(a), a training vector $\mathbf{x}_t$ must be exclusively assigned to one and only one cluster in K-means.
- *EM uses soft membership assignment.* As shown in Figure 5.2(b), the membership of $\mathbf{x}_t$ may be proportionally assigned to all the clusters.

5.4.1 EM clustering criterion

Just like K-means, EM aims to find the optimal parameter Θ^{opt} which maximizes the log-likelihood function

$$\Theta^{\text{opt}} = \arg\max_{\Theta} \log p(\mathcal{X}|\Theta). \tag{5.15}$$

Note that

$$p(\mathbf{x}_t|\Theta) = \sum_k p(\mathbf{x}_t|\Theta_k)P(\Theta_k).$$

Assume all equal prior probabilities, i.e. $P(\Theta_k) = 1/K$ for $k = 1, \ldots, K$. Then

$$p(\Theta_k|\mathbf{x}_t) = \frac{p(\mathbf{x}_t|\Theta_k)}{K\, p(\mathbf{x}_t|\Theta)}. \tag{5.16}$$

Under the assumption of independent distribution, it follows that

$$\begin{aligned}\log p(\mathcal{X}|\Theta) &= \sum_t \log p(\mathbf{x}_t|\Theta) = \sum_t \left(\sum_k P(\Theta_k|\mathbf{x}_t)\right) \log p(\mathbf{x}_t|\Theta)\\ &= \sum_t \sum_k P(\Theta_k|\mathbf{x}_t) \left\{\log\left(\frac{p(\mathbf{x}_t|\Theta_k)}{K}\right) - \log\left(\frac{p(\mathbf{x}_t|\Theta_k)}{K\, p(\mathbf{x}_t|\Theta)}\right)\right\}\\ &= \sum_t \sum_k P(\Theta_k|\mathbf{x}_t) \left\{\log\left(\frac{p(\mathbf{x}_t|\Theta_k)}{K}\right) - \log p(\Theta_k|\mathbf{x}_t)\right\}.\end{aligned}$$

Noting that $\sum_k \{p(\Theta_k|\mathbf{x}_t)\log(1/K)\} = -\log K$, we arrive at

$$\begin{aligned}\log p(\mathcal{X}|\Theta) = &\sum_t \sum_k \{P(\Theta_k|\mathbf{x}_t)\log p(\mathbf{x}_t|\Theta_k) - P(\Theta_k|\mathbf{x}_t)\log P(\Theta_k|\mathbf{x}_t)\}\\ &- N \log K.\end{aligned}$$

Denote the membership proportion of $\mathbf{x}_t$ alloted to the kth cluster $h_t^{(k)}$. From Eq. (5.16),

$$h_t^{(k)} = P(\Theta_k|\mathbf{x}_t) = \frac{p(\mathbf{x}_t|\Theta_k)}{\sum_{j=1}^{K} p(\mathbf{x}_t|\Theta_j)}.$$

Note that, by definition, $h_t^{(k)}$ must be normalized such that

$$\sum_{k=1}^{K} h_t^{(k)} = 1.$$

For example, if $p(\mathbf{x}_t|\Theta_1) = 0.015$, $p(\mathbf{x}_t|\Theta_2) = 0.006$, and $p(\mathbf{x}_t|\Theta_3) = 0.004$,

$$\begin{aligned}h_t^{(1)} &= \frac{0.015}{0.015 + 0.006 + 0.004} = 0.6,\\ h_t^{(2)} &= \frac{0.006}{0.015 + 0.006 + 0.004} = 0.24,\\ h_t^{(3)} &= 0.16,\end{aligned}$$

then the log-likelihood becomes

$$\log p(\mathcal{X}|\Theta) = \sum_t \sum_k \{h_t^{(k)} \log p(\mathbf{x}_t|\Theta_k) - h_t^{(k)} \log h_t^{(k)}\} - N \log K. \tag{5.17}$$

The EM criterion for the basic GMM model

The EM algorithm is versatile and applicable to many statistical distribution models, including the popular Gaussian mixture model (GMM). Each of the mixed clusters in a GMM has a Gaussian density distribution parameterized by both the centroid $\vec{\mu}$ and the covariance $\mathbf{\Sigma}$. More exactly,

$$p(\mathbf{x}_t|\Theta_k) = \mathcal{N}(\vec{\mu}_k, \mathbf{\Sigma}_k), \quad k = 1, \ldots, K.$$

For illustration convenience, we shall focus on a basic GMM with the following simplifying assumptions:

- We assume that we have an isotropic (i.e. circularly symmetric) Gaussian distribution. Then the conditional density function of $\mathbf{x}_t$ will become

$$p(\mathbf{x}_t|\Theta_k) = \frac{1}{\sqrt{2\pi}\sigma} \exp\left\{-\frac{\|\mathbf{x}_t - \vec{\mu}_k\|^2}{2\sigma^2}\right\}, \quad \forall k = 1, \ldots, K. \tag{5.18}$$

- Further assume that all clusters have an isotropic distribution with $\mathbf{\Sigma} = \sigma \mathbf{I}$, which is to remain fixed throughout the EM iteration process.

Under such assumptions, the optimization criterion given in Eq. (5.17) can be further simplified to

$$\log p(\mathcal{X}|\Theta) = -\frac{1}{2\sigma^2}\sum_t\sum_k h_t^{(k)}\|\mathbf{x}_t - \vec{\mu}_k\|^2 - \sum_t\sum_k h_t^{(k)} \log h_t^{(k)} \\ - N\log(\sqrt{2\pi}\sigma K).$$

SSD-and-entropy criterion

The optimization objective can be obviously reformulated as one minimizing an SSD-and-entropy criterion, which is formally defined as follows:

$$E_{\text{EM}}(\mathcal{X}, \Theta) = \sum_t\sum_k h_t^{(k)}\|\mathbf{x}_t - \vec{\mu}_k\|^2 + 2\sigma^2\sum_t\sum_k h_t^{(k)} \log h_t^{(k)}. \tag{5.19}$$

5.4.2 The iterative EM algorithm for basic GMM

The EM optimizer aims at minimizing $E_{\text{EM}}(\mathcal{X}, \Theta)$ with respect to $\{\vec{\mu}_k, k = 1, \ldots, K\}$ and $\{\mathcal{C}_k, k = 1, \ldots, K\}$. It is more practical, and faster, to apply an iterative method to find the optimal solution which minimizes the SSD-and-entropy criterion in Eq. (5.19).

ALGORITHM 5.2 (EM iterative learning algorithm) *As illustrated by the EM flowchart shown in Figure 5.7, once properly initialized, the EM iterative procedure alternately updates the memberships and centroids in each iteration.*

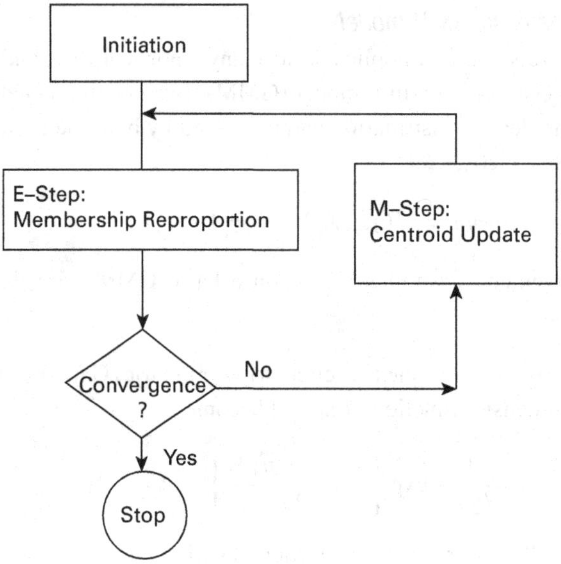

Fig. 5.7. The EM iterative updating basically follows the same flowchart as that for K-means. Note that the "winner identification" is replaced by "membership reproportion," since there is no longer an exclusive winner.

(i) **E-step: Membership reproportion.** *In the E-step, the node vector (i.e. the centroids $\{\overrightarrow{\mu_k}\}$) are fixed. The membership proportion of $\mathbf{x}_t$ allotted to the kth cluster can be updated as*

$$h_t^{(k)} = \frac{p(\mathbf{x}_t|\Theta_k)}{\sum_{j=1}^{K} p(\mathbf{x}_t|\Theta_j)} = \frac{\exp\left\{-\|\mathbf{x}_t - \overrightarrow{\mu_k}\|^2/(2\sigma^2)\right\}}{\sum_k \exp\left\{-\|\mathbf{x}_t - \overrightarrow{\mu_k}\|^2/(2\sigma^2)\right\}}, \tag{5.20}$$

Note that $\sum_{k=1}^{K} h_t^{(k)} = 1$.

(ii) **M-Step: Centroid update.** *In the M-step, the membership proportions $\{h_t^{(k)}\}$, $k = 1, \ldots, K$, are fixed. The node vector $\{\overrightarrow{\mu_k}\}$ can be updated as a weighted centroids of all the N training vectors:*

$$\mu_k' = \frac{\sum_{t=1}^{N} h_t^{(k)} \mathbf{x}_t}{\sum_{t=1}^{N} h_t^{(k)}}, \quad \text{for} \quad k = 1, \ldots, K. \tag{5.21}$$

This resembles closely the centroid-update step in K-means. □

Just like the animation we provided for the K-means algorithm, we again adopt an self-explanatory animation in Figure 5.8 to illustrate the first few EM iterations of the same dataset.

5.4.3 Convergence of the EM algorithm with fixed σ

THEOREM 5.2 (Monotonic convergence of EM) *The EM iterative procedure monotonically converges to a (local) optimum in terms of the SSD-and-entropy criterion.* □

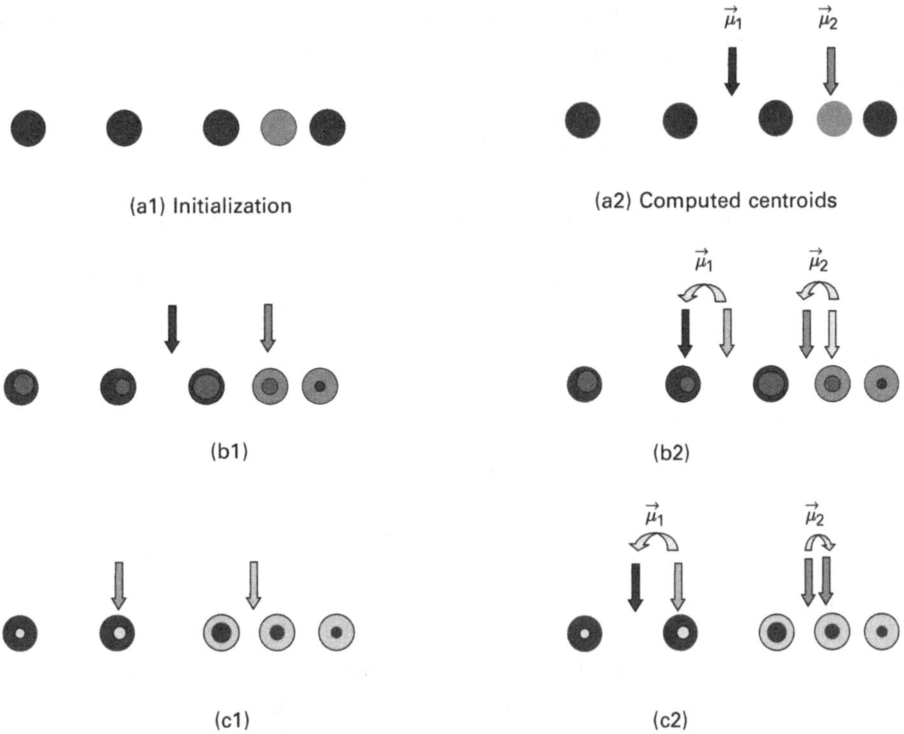

Fig. 5.8. A simple example of EM iterations. (a1) Initially, cluster 1 has four members and cluster 2 has one member. (a2) Given such memberships, two centroids can be computed, for Cluster 1 and Cluster 2. (b1) E-step: membership-reproportion based on the centroids in (a). (b2) M-step: centroid update: both centroids are updated based on the reproportioned memberships. (c1) E-step: membership-reproportion based on the newly updated centroids in (b2). (c2) M-step: the two centroids are again updated.

Proof. Let us now establish the monotonically decreasing property of the SSD-and-entropy cost, see Eq. (5.19), in each of the updating steps.

(a) *Monotonically decreasing property in the E-step.* In the E-step, while fixing $\{\vec{\mu}_k,\ 1 \le k \le K\}$, we aim to (locally) minimize SDD-and-entropy function in Eq. (5.19) with respect to $\{h_t^{(k)},\ 1 \le k \le K\}$ for any arbitrary t that $1 \le t \le N$. The following proof shows that the updated solution prescribed by Eq. (5.20) does indeed provide a constrained optimization of the cost function with respect to $\{h_t^{(k)},\ 1 \le k \le K\}$.

Note that

$$E_{\mathrm{EM}}(\mathcal{X}, \Theta) = \sum_{t=1}^{N}\sum_{k=1}^{K} h_t^{(k)}\|\mathbf{x}_t - \vec{\mu}_k\| + 2\sigma^2 \sum_{t=1}^{N}\sum_{k=1}^{K} h_t^{(k)} \log h_t^{(k)}.$$

In order to minimize E_{EM} w.r.t. $\{h_t^{(k)},\ 1 \le k \le K\}$, we construct the following Lagrangian function:

$$\sum_{k=1}^{K} h_t^{(k)} \|\mathbf{x}_t - \vec{\mu}_k\| + 2\sigma^2 \sum_{k=1}^{K} h_t^{(k)} \log h_t^{(k)} + \lambda \left(\sum_{k=1}^{K} h_t^{(k)} - 1 \right).$$

On taking its first-order derivative w.r.t. $h_t^{(k)}$, we obtain its zero-gradient point as

$$\|\mathbf{x}_t - \vec{\mu}_k\|^2 + 2\sigma^2 h_t^{(k)} + 2\sigma^2 + \lambda = 0,\ 1 \le k \le K$$

which implies that

$$h_t^{(k)} \propto \exp\left\{ -\frac{\|\mathbf{x}_t - \vec{\mu}_k\|^2}{2\sigma^2} \right\}$$

Since $\sum_{k=1}^{K} h_t^{(k)} = 1$, it follows that

$$h_t^{(k)} = \frac{\exp\left\{-\|\mathbf{x}_t - \vec{\mu}_k\|^2/(2\sigma^2)\right\}}{\sum_{j=1}^{k} \exp\left\{-\|\mathbf{x}_t - \vec{\mu}_k\|^2/(2\sigma^2)\right\}}$$

Since the updated value has now been shown to be a local minimum, the cost function must be monotonically decreasing in the E-step. Thus we have the proof.

(b) *Monotonically decreasing property in the M-step.* In the M-step, while fixing $\{h_t^{(k)}\}$, we aim to (locally) minimize the SDD-and-entropy function with respect to $\{\vec{\mu}_k\}$. The fact that $\{h_t^{(k)}\}$ is fixed means that the second term (ie. the entropy term) in Eq. (5.19) can be regarded as constant. Hence the updated solution in Eq. (5.21) yields a zero gradient of the cost function with respect to $\{\vec{\mu}_k\}$. This implies that the updated value represents a local minimizer, and therefore the cost function is monotonically decreasing.

5.4.4 Annealing EM (AEM)

While EM may still often converge to a local optimum, it generally delivers a more favorable solution than that offered by K-means. This improvement may be attributed to the soft membership criterion adopted by EM, which tends to mitigate the influence of how the algorithm is initiated. Usually, the ultimate goal of EM is to obtain a hard-clustering result, just like with K-means. This may be achieved by gradually reducing the standard deviation σ. In fact, EM will gradually approach K-means when σ becomes infinitesimal. This is related to the principle of *simulated annealing* proposed by Kirkpatrick *et al.* [127].

In the *simulated-annealing* approach, the "entropy" or uncertainty of a solution is controlled by a temperature parameter. The higher the temperature the higher the entropy. The *standard deviation* σ in a Gaussian distribution (Eq. (5.5)) is reminiscent of the temperature parameter in *simulated annealing*. More exactly, the larger the *standard deviation* σ the fuzzier the membership. Therefore, σ can effectively substitute for the role of the temperature parameter to achieve an annealing effect. This leads to the "annealing EM" (AEM) algorithm proposed below.

The AEM starts with a large value of the σ parameter and gradually lowers it during the iterations. At the beginning, the membership proportions for the K clusters will be approximately equal due to the large σ parameter. In other words, the membership of $\mathbf{x}_t$ is almost evenly distributed over all the clusters, regardless of the initialization. (For the extreme case that $\sigma \to \infty$, $h_t^{(k)} \approx 1/K, \forall k$, according to Eq. (5.20).) This serves to mitigate the influence of the initial condition.

Ultimately, the standard deviation σ will diminish to an infinitesimal value, i.e. $\sigma \to 0$. In this case, EM's SSD-and-entropy criterion, Eq. (5.19), essentially converges to the SSD criterion of K-means, Eq. (5.7).

Each vector will now be exclusively assigned to one and only one winner (just like with K-means):

$$\lim_{\sigma \to 0} h_t^{(k)} = \begin{cases} 1, & \text{if } k = \arg\min_{j=1,\ldots,K} \|\mathbf{x}_t - \vec{\mu}_j\| \\ 0, & \text{otherwise.} \end{cases} \tag{5.22}$$

In other words, the inner loop of AEM will gradually converge to K-means when $\sigma \to 0$.

The AEM updating algorithm

As illustrated in Figure 5.9, the AEM updating procedure involves two loops of iterations.

(a) *Inner loop: EM updating.* Within the same epoch, perform the traditional EM iterations shown as the inner loop in Figure 5.9. For a fixed σ, monotonic convergence was established in Section 5.4.3

(b) *Outer loop: temperature reduction.* The success of AEM depends intimately on a well-planned annealing schedule inherent in the simulated annealing scheme. After the EM updating for a fixed σ has converged to a local minimum, the temperature parameter σ should be adjusted to a lower value before a new epoch starts. This corresponds to the outer-loop update depicted in Figure 5.9.

5.5 Self-organizing-map (SOM) learning models

In order to establish the neighborhood relationship between clusters, it is necessary to label the clusters according to a well-coordinated grid structure. Figure 5.10 provides a simple illustration highlighting the difference between neighborhood-insensitive versus -sensitive node structures. While the class labels are arbitrarily ordered in Figure 5.10(a), they are coordinated in an orderly manner in Figure 5.10(b)..

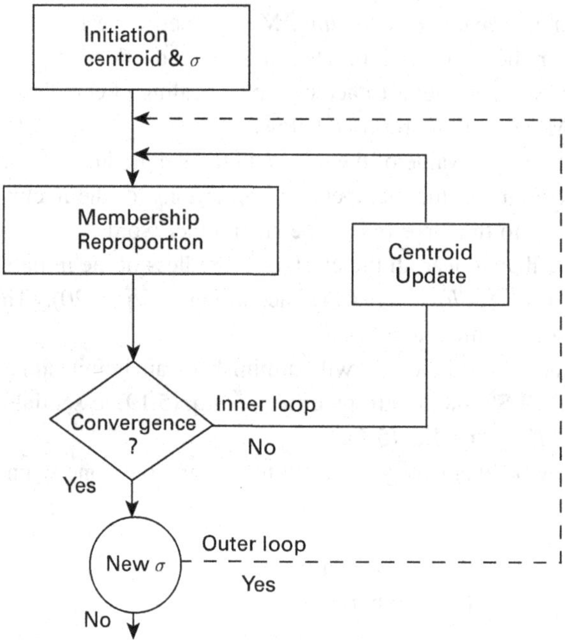

Fig. 5.9. The flowchart for "annealing EM" (AEM) and "neighborhood-sensitive" AEM (NAEM) algorithms. A simulated annealing schedule may be used to help reach the global optimum by EM. By successively cooling down the temperature (represented by σ here), the EM algorithm can be naturally extended to an "annealed" EM variant named AEM. NAEM is an extension of AEM by incorporating **topological order** into the initial indexing of the nodes. The neighborhood sensitivity during the iterative learning process is a natural property embedded in EM. Thus, there is no need for any special modification.

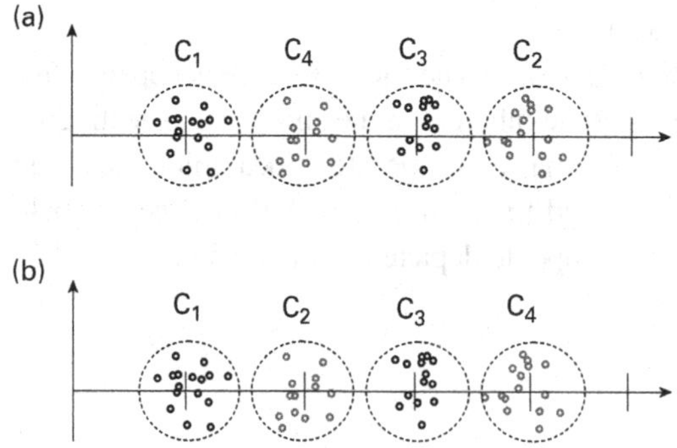

Fig. 5.10. The main difference between K-means and SOM lies in their topological sensitivity. (a) K-means clustering can be labeled in random order. (b) SOM requires a topologically sensitive order of the class labels. In this example, two-dimensional input vectors are mapped to a one-dimensional grid. (In this case, $M = 2$, $k = 1$, and $L_1 = 4$. For distance-related computation, the grid interval equals 1.)

- K-means is indifferent to the labeling of the clusters. Thus Figure 5.10(a) or (b) will represent equally acceptable solutions for K-means. Consequently, it lacks the capability of exploiting neighborhood sensitivity among the cluster nodes.
- To compensate for such a shortcoming, neighborhood sensitivity must be incorporated into the learning process. This is exemplified by the well-known SOM clustering algorithm proposed by Kohonen [129, 130, 131]. For the SOM, it is vital to establish a node topology characterized by well-coordinated node indices. As a result, the configuration in Figure 5.10(b) is deemed to be topologically well ordered.

5.5.1 Input and output spaces in the SOM

Both SOM and K-means aim at finding clusters so that intra-cluster data distributions are as compact as possible. The difference lies in the fact that SOM imposes an additional condition on neighborhood sensitivity, which requires topologically adjacent nodes (represented by the node centroids) to exhibit some proximity when mapped back to the original vector space. Accordingly, the learning/adaptation of a node must be allowed to propagate to adjacent nodes in the grid according to a given neighborhood sensitivity function [67].

An SOM learning model can be configured as a mapping network exemplified by Figure 5.11(a), which shows the higher-dimensional (three-dimensional) original data at the lower layer are mapped to a lower-dimensional (two-dimensional) mesh at the upper layer.

- The input space is represented by the lower layer. We shall denote the tth input sample, which is drawn randomly from the training dataset, as $\mathbf{x}_t$, where $t = 1, 2, \ldots, N$. The entire input dataset is represented by

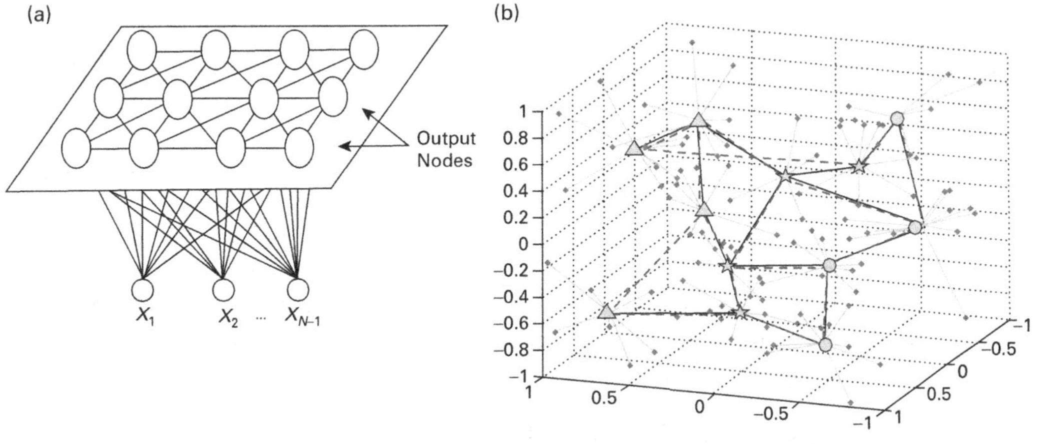

Fig. 5.11. The SOM input–output mapping. (a) Mapping from the original input space to a topologically well-arranged grid structure. Here data from a three-dimensional input space ($M = 3$) are mapped to a two-dimensional mesh ($k = 2$). (b) In the 4×3 two-dimensional SOM mesh, the 12 nodes are arranged into three shape-coded columns, symbolized by triangles, stars, and circles respectively. The neighboring nodes are connected by dashed lines. The original training vectors are represented by small dots, each of which is assigned to one of the 12 SOM nodes.

$$\{\mathbf{x}_t, t = 1, 2, \ldots, N\}.$$

- The output space is represented by the upper layer, which is arranged as a k-dimensional grid/mesh comprising $L_1 \times L_2 \times \cdots \times L_k$ nodes. Each node represents a cluster denoted by C_i, where $i \in I^{L_1 \times L_2 \times \cdots \times L_k}$ and the integers $L_1, L_2, \ldots, L_k$ usually depend on specific applications. The nodes are parameterized by their *node vectors*:

$$\vec{\mu}_i, \quad \text{where} \quad i \in I^{L_1 \times L_2 \times \cdots \times L_k}.$$

Just like K-means, for vectorial data, the node vector is usually represented by its "centroid" in the input vector space. For nonvectorial data, the node vector is usually represented by the most "centrally located" training sample in the same cluster. Typically, $k = 1, 2,$ or 3, so that the trained SOM may be easily visualized, thus serving as a tool to display (originally high-dimensional) data samples. As an example, for a two-dimensional mesh, each output node will be double-indexed and represented by its *node vector*:

$$\vec{\mu}_i, \quad \text{where} \quad i = (i_1, i_2), \text{ and } i_1 = 1, \ldots, L_1; i_2 = 1, \ldots, L_2.$$

The objective of SOM learning is to train collectively the node vectors $\{\vec{\mu}_i\}$ of all the nodes in the mesh so that the mesh can best represent the original training dataset. In order for SOM to serve as an effective visualization tool, the mapped clusters must be topologically organized into a low-dimensional mesh or grid, exemplified by Figure 5.11(a). In our simulation study, the input vector space is three-dimensional ($M = 3$) and the output nodes are represented by a 4×3 grid, i.e. $L_1 = 4$ and $L_2 = 3$. The SOM mapping result is displayed in Figure 5.11(b). This allows the original three-dimensional data distribution to be visualized by a two-dimensional display.

5.5.2 The SOM learning algorithm

Initialization

The initialization for SOM is very different from that for K-means, where random initialization is often adopted. For SOM, initially, the node vectors $\{\vec{\mu}_i, \; i \in I^{L_1 \times L_2 \times \cdots \times L_k}\}$ (usually represented by centroids of the members in the same node) are placed in an orderly manner in a small region near the center of all the training vectors.

The iterative learning process of SOM is more complicated than that of K-means. As shown in Figure 5.12, SOM involves a two-loop training procedure, elaborated in the following algorithm.

ALGORITHM 5.3 (SOM iterative learning algorithm) *SOM involves a two-loop learning algorithm: in the inner-loop the centroids of the clusters are updated and multiple epochs are to be executed in each inner loop before it exits to the outer loop. In the outer loop the effective range of the neighborhood function is reduced before returning to the inner loop again for further updating. The details are as follows.*

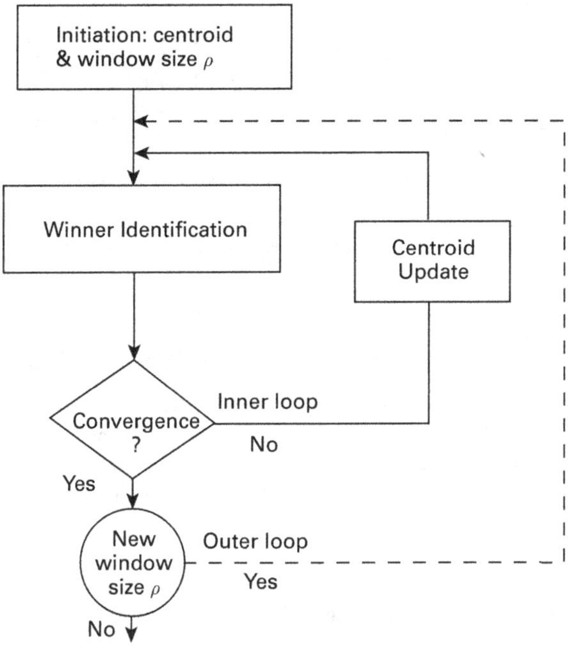

Fig. 5.12. The flowchart of the SOM algorithm. Neighborhood-sensitive centroid updates are performed in the inner-loop iterations, while the size of learning window ρ is gradually reduced in the outer-loop updates.

- **Inner loop: centroid updates.** *In the inner loop, each training pattern* $\overrightarrow{\mathbf{s}}_t$, *for all* $t = 1, \ldots, N$, *will be sequentially processed with the following updating process.*
  - *(i) Identification of winner.* *Just like with K-means, see Eq. (5.9), the cluster whose centroid is nearest to* $\mathbf{x}_t$ *will be identified as the winner:*

$$i^* = \arg \min_{i \in I^{L_1 \times L_2 \times \cdots \times L_k}} \|\mathbf{x}_t - \overrightarrow{\boldsymbol{\mu}}_i\|. \tag{5.23}$$

  - *(ii) Update of winner's node vector.* *The node centroid of the* i^**th node vector (i.e. the winner) is additively modified by the following amount:*

$$\Delta \overrightarrow{\boldsymbol{\mu}}_{i^*} = \eta \left(\mathbf{x}_t - \overrightarrow{\boldsymbol{\mu}}_{i^*}\right), \tag{5.24}$$

    where η *is a small positive learning rate.*
  - *(iii) Centroid update of the neighboring nodes (co-winners).* *Let the co-winners be the nodes in a certain neighborhood around the winner* i^*, *denoted by* I^*. *The node centroid of each co-winner is additively modified by the following amount*

$$\Delta \overrightarrow{\boldsymbol{\mu}}_k = \eta \Lambda(k, i^*) \left(\mathbf{x}_t - \overrightarrow{\boldsymbol{\mu}}_{i^*}\right) \quad \text{for all} \quad k \in I^*, \tag{5.25}$$

    where $\Lambda(k, i^*)$ *is a pre-specified neighborhood sensitivity function that will be further elaborated on presently.*

  Continue with the next training data until the entire epoch has been completed.

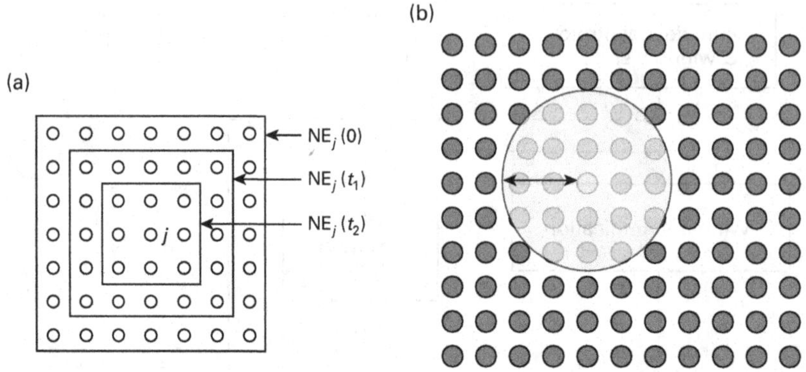

Fig. 5.13. (a) The sizes of the square windows shrink over time. This effectively reduces the size of the neighborhood, denote as "NE". (Note that the winning node may change at each iteration.) (b) The sizes of circular windows shrink over time. The center of the big circle represents the winning node, the arrow represents the radius, and the big circle represents the current neighborhood.

- **Outer-loop updating: gradual shrinking of learning windows.** *A broader neighborhood is commonly adopted initially, so as to assure a higher neighborhood sensitivity. In the outer loop, the effective range of the neighborhood is gradually shrunk by either (1) reducing the widow size w (see Eqs. (5.26) and (5.27) or (2) decreasing the range parameter r (see Eqs. (5.28) and (5.29)). For example, reduction in a two-dimensional square and circular windows is shown in Figure 5.13(a).* □

Centroid update of the neighboring nodes (co-winners)

Recall that a primary goal of SOM is to learn a neighborhood-sensitive and topologically structured SOM grid. Such sensitivity may be attained by coercing the "co-winners" to adapt in a similar fashion to the winner. Such a co-learning strategy is designed to retain the physical proximity between topologically adjacent nodes, e.g. C_i and C_{i+1} in Figure 5.10.

Let i^* denote the index of the winner and let I^* denote the set of co-winners neighboring the i^*th node. The amount of adaptation for the co-winners will be made proportional to a certain neighborhood sensitivity function $\Lambda(k, i^*)$. This is elaborated next.

(i) *The neighborhood sensitivity function* $\Lambda(k, i^*)$ *is a function of the window shape and size.* Both square and circular windows are popular choices.
   - A square window centered at the winner node is often adopted; see Figure 5.13(a). For example, for a two-dimensional SOM, we usually adopt a (roughly $d \times d$) square window as the neighborhood function:

$$\Lambda(k, i^*) = \begin{cases} 1 & \text{if} \quad \max(2|k_1 - i_1^*|, 2|k_2 - i_2^*|) \leq d \\ 0 & \text{if} \quad \max(2|k_1 - i_1^*|, 2|k_2 - i_2^*|) > d. \end{cases} \tag{5.26}$$

- Sometimes, a circular window (with radius d) may be adopted:

$$\Lambda(k, i^*) = \begin{cases} 1 \text{ if } \|k - i^*\| \leq d \\ 0 \text{ if } \|k - i^*\| > d. \end{cases} \tag{5.27}$$

  This is depicted in Figure 5.13(b).

  All co-winners within the window will receive the same updates [129, 219].

(ii) *The neighborhood sensitivity function* $\Lambda(k, i^*)$ *is a function of node indices.*[2]

  The amplitude of $\Lambda(k, i^*)$ decreases monotonically with increasing lateral distance $\|k - i^*\|$ controlled by a range factor r [95, 159, 160, 219]:

$$\Lambda(k, i^*) = \exp\left\{-\frac{\|k - i^*\|^2}{r}\right\}. \tag{5.29}$$

Why is gradual shrinking of learning windows employed?

For the discussion on the outer-loop updating, let us denote an epoch as the updating process for one entire of block of N data $\{\mathbf{x}_1, \mathbf{x}_2, \ldots, \mathbf{x}_N\}$. Usually the SOM training requires a large number of epochs, i.e. the same training data need to be recycled many times.

The purpose of a neighborhood sensitivity function is to make sure the index-adjacent nodes can co-learn together. However, a legitimate concern is that one may be unable to distinguish two adjacent nodes from each other if the window size continues to remain wide. To overcome this problem, it is advisable to gradually reduce the window size d or the range parameter r during the learning process.

5.5.3 The evaluation criterion for multiple-trial SOM

The SOM learning results depend on the initial iterate as well as the window-shrinking schedule. It will be very appealing to resort to multi-trial SOM, where various initial conditions and window shrinking schedules may be tried and only the best result needs to be retained. The catch lies in deciding how to determine the best result, for which one needs a good evaluation criterion.

An important merit of K-means is that it is based on a well-formulated objective function for optimality, making the evaluation criterion easily available. Relatively, the derivation of SOM is somewhat *ad hoc* and there is no analytically derived objective function.

As a simple example, assuming a two-dimensional grid, one *ad hoc* evaluation criterion involves a tradeoff between the following two kinds of cost function:

[2] Another interesting variant is when the neighborhood sensitivity function $\Lambda(k, i^*)$ is defined a function of node vectors (see Problem 5.6). More precisely, the amplitude of $\Lambda(k, i^*)$ decreases monotonically with increasing distance between the node vectors $\vec{\mu}_k$ and $\vec{\mu}_{i^*}$:

$$\Lambda(k, i^*) = \exp\left\{-\frac{\|\vec{\mu}_k - \vec{\mu}_{i^*}\|^2}{r}\right\}. \tag{5.28}$$

- **Intra-cluster compactness: E_1.** E_1 is the sum of the variances, which reflects the overall intra-cluster compactness:

$$E_1 = E_{K\text{-means}} = \sum_i^{L_1} \sum_j^{L_2} \sum_{\mathbf{x}_t \in C_{i,j}} \|\mathbf{x}_t - \vec{\mu}_{i,j}\|^2, \tag{5.30}$$

where $C_{i,j}$ ($\vec{\mu}_{i,j}$) denotes the (i,j)th node (centroid) in the mesh, where $i = 1, \ldots, L_1$ and $j = 1, \ldots, L_2$.

- **Topologically sensitive inter-cluster relationship: E_2.** E_2 represents the total link distance in the mesh, which can be computed as

$$E_2 = E_{\text{neighborhood-sensitivity}} = \sum_{i=2}^{L_1-1} \sum_{j=2}^{L_2-1} \sum_{m=-1}^{1} \sum_{n=-1}^{1} \|\vec{\mu}_{i+m,j+n} - \vec{\mu}_{i,j}\|^2. \tag{5.31}$$

Note that K-means and SOM have the same intra-cluster compactness, as exemplified by Figures 5.10(a) and (b), respectively. However, they have different requirements in terms of inter-cluster distances because K-means is concerned only about E_1, not about E_2.

With reference to Figure 5.10, assuming that the distance between two (logically) adjacent nodes is approximately 1.0, for the random-ordered cluster structure obtained by K-means $E_2 = \|\vec{\mu}_2 - \vec{\mu}_1\|^2 + \|\vec{\mu}_3 - \vec{\mu}_2\|^2 + \|\vec{\mu}_4 - \vec{\mu}_3\|^2 = (4-1)^2 + (3-4)^2 + (2-3)^2 = 11$. In contrast, for the neighborhood-sensitive SOM, $E_2' = (2-1)^2 + (3-2)^2 + (4-3)^2 = 3$, which is much smaller than E_2. This reflects the fact that SOM places emphasis on the inter-cluster distances between the neighboring node, whereas K-means does not.

Numerical simulation results for SOM applied to real data are shown in Figures 5.14(a) and (b), where E_1 decreases but E_2 increases throughout the iterations. This helps highlight the inherent tradeoff between E_1 and E_2 in SOM learning.

In summary, the following evaluation criterion is useful for selecting the best SOM from multiple copies of learned SOMs:

$$\begin{aligned} E &= E_1 + \rho E_2 \\ &= \sum_i^{L_1} \sum_j^{L_2} \sum_{\mathbf{x}_t \in C_{i,j}} \|\mathbf{x}_t - \vec{\mu}_{i,j}\|^2 + \rho \sum_{i=2}^{L_1-1} \sum_{j=2}^{L_2-1} \sum_{m=-1}^{1} \sum_{n=-1}^{1} \|\vec{\mu}_{i+m,j+n} - \vec{\mu}_{i,j}\|^2, \end{aligned} \tag{5.32}$$

where ρ is a positive weighting factor.

5.5.4 Applications of SOM learning models

Compared with K-means, SOM offers some unique and appealing properties.

- SOM can provide an "executive summary" of a massive set of samples. Thanks to its topological sensitivity, SOM can facilitate visualization of massive data sets, thus allowing more insightful data analysis and interpretation. Note that the neighborhood relationship is preserved after the vectors have been mapped to the mesh

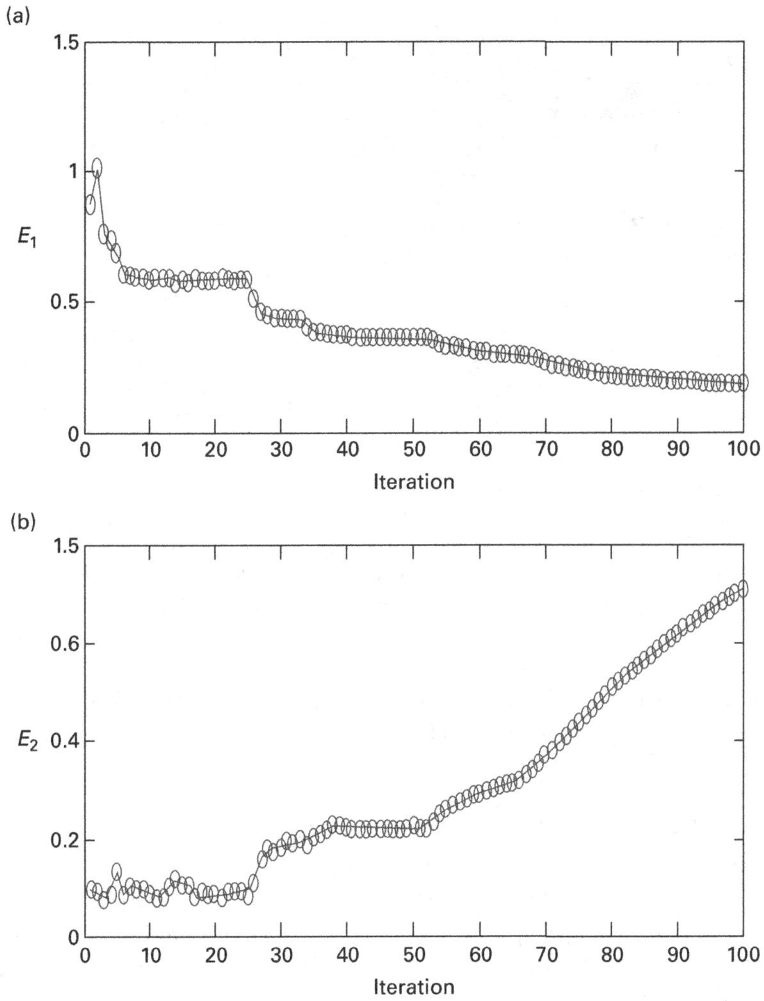

Fig. 5.14. SOM simulation results show trends of E_1 (intra-cluster compactness) and E_2 (topologically sensitive inter-cluster distance) over 100 epochs. (a) decreasing E_1 and (b) increasing E_2.

structure. Namely, the neighborhood-sensitive SOM grid structure is reflected by the fact that the (logically) adjacent nodes will be proximally located in the original vector space. This is exemplified by Figure 5.15(b), in sharp contrast to Figure 5.6(b).

- SOM is less sensitive to cluster size in that it allows over-sized clustering (setting the number of clusters larger than the actual number of clusters). For example, an inherently four-class dataset can be mapped to a much larger number of cluster say 25. For K-means, the clustering result would not be too useful. For SOM, rich information may still be extracted to help the final data analysis. For example, if the 25 clusters can be systematically organized into a 5×5 mesh, the additional topological information (i.e. the node index) can provide very useful information for the categorization of the data.

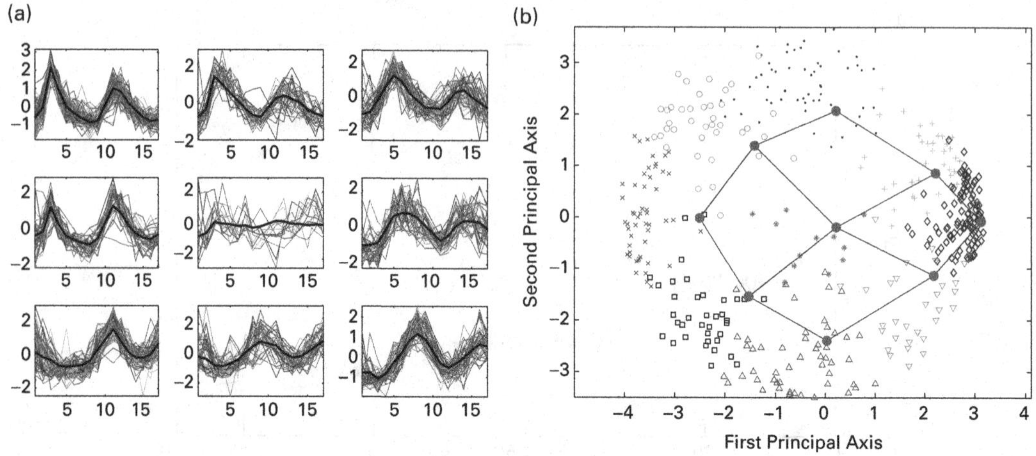

Fig. 5.15. (a) Centroids (thick black lines) and the profiles of each cluster (thin lines) found by applying SOM clustering to the gene profiles of Tamayo *et al.*'s [263] yeast cell cycle data (normalized). (b) Projection of 421 gene profiles and nine centers (large •) found by SOM clustering onto two principal components. The nine clusters are denoted by different symbols. Note that the K-means, cf. Figure 5.6(b), and SOM clustering results are very different.

SOMs have successfully been applied to genomic cluster discovery and data analysis. Two examples will be highlighted below.

Example 5.4 (Tissue sample clustering analysis) *Figure 5.15 shows the gene clusters in Tamayo et al.'s gene expression data using the SOM. Figure 5.15(a) shows the clusters of the yeast gene expression profiles. Note that the neighboring clusters exhibit a strong similarity of the expression patterns. For better visualization, the input vectors and the centroids of the SOM clusters are projected onto two principal components in Figure 5.15(b).*

Sample clustering is an effective means for cancer cluster discovery. In particular, the SOM has proven effective for identifying cancer classes. For example, in Ref. [82], the SOM was applied to automatically discover acute myeloid leukemia (AML) and acute lymphoblastic leukemia (ALL) from DNA microarray data without previous knowledge of these classes. The 38 leukemia test samples were successfully divided into two classes on the basis of the expression pattern of all 6817 genes.

Example 5.5 (Gene cluster discovery) *Gene clustering provides an effective means for biomarker discovery. More specifically, the SOM has been successfully applied to discover biologically significant gene expression patterns. For example, in Tamayo* et al.*'s experiment, the yeast cell cycle data were first preprocessed to obtain 828 most relevant genes, which were subsequently normalized over each of the two 90-minute runs. A software package called "GeneCluster" was applied to map the yeast genes onto a*

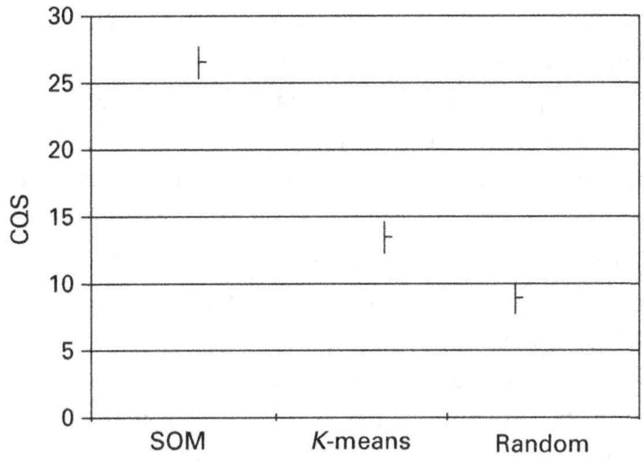

Fig. 5.16. In terms of the processes in GO annotation, Gat-Viks *et al.* [75] demonstrated that the SOM clustering solutions outperform K-means clustering and random clustering in terms of the clustering quality score (CQS). (Adapted from Ref. [75].)

6×5 SOM grid [215]. In other words, the yeast genes were represented by the 30 SOM nodes. Tamayo et al. *[263] reported that the SOM clusters matched well with the prior known gene functions. In fact, in Tamayo* et al. *[263], the SOM was applied to three different types of gene expression analysis: yeast cell cycles, macrophage differentiation in HL-60 cells, and hematopoietic differentiation across four cell lines.*[3] *In each case, the derived gene clusters are compared with known classification labels to verify the effectiveness of the SOM for identification of predominant gene expression patterns.*

In addition, according to Gibbons and Roth [77], the SOM reportedly holds advantages over K-means when the number of clusters is large. Moreover, Gat-Viks *et al.* [75] compared various clustering results for the processes in gene ontology (GO) annotation and SOM outperformed K-means and random clustering in terms of the clustering quality score (CQS). This is illustrated in Figure 5.16.

5.6 Bi-clustering data analysis

Bi-clustering analysis is a data mining technique that allows simultaneous clustering of the rows and columns of a data matrix. It is also known by a number of other synonyms such as co-clustering, two-mode clustering, etc. [92, 180, 276]. It has promising applications to a diversity of multimedia and biological applications.

[3] The application software adopted was GeneCluster [263], which is useful for organizing genes into biologically relevant clusters that suggest novel hypotheses about hematopoietic differentiation. It can help highlight certain genes and pathways that are involved in the "differentiation therapy" used in the treatment of acute promyelocytic leukemia.

(i) For biological applications, a good example is gene/condition clustering analysis using microarray data. The gene expression data are arranged as an $M \times N$ matrix of real numbers $A = [a_{ij}]$, where M is the number of row vectors and N is the number of column vectors. Each entry a_{ij} represents the logarithm of the relative abundance of the mRNA of the ith gene under the jth condition. The gene expression profile of each condition (sample) is described as an M-dimensional vector in which each element represents the expression level of one gene. Similarly, the profile of each gene is described as an N-dimensional vector in which each element represents the expression level of one condition.

(ii) As to multimedia applications, a good example is word/document clustering analysis, where the M words data are arranged as M row vectors, while the N documents are arranged as N column vectors. Taken together, they form an $M \times N$ data matrix.

Bi-clustering algorithms can be applied to discover blocks in the data matrix that correspond to a subset of rows (genes or words) and a subset of columns (conditions or documents).

5.6.1 Coherence models for bi-clustering

Given a data matrix and a clustering criterion, a subset of rows that exhibit similar behavior across a subset of columns, or vice versa, can be identified. This process is referred to as bi-clustering, whose results depend upon what we consider as a good bi-cluster. A quantitative criterion for biclustering is often a deviation function of the rows and columns in a sub-matrix, denoted as **A**, to reflect how the sub-matrix deviates from a desired form. Such a metric is often represented by a matrix norm of the data matrix of **A**. The most commonly used matrix norm is the Frobenius norm, denoted by $\|\mathbf{A}\|_{\mathrm{F}}$, which is defined as the square root of the sum of squares of all elements in the sub-matrix.

Basic bi-cluster criterion: constant-value matrix norm

Hartigan [92] proposed a constant-value matrix norm that has a very broad application spectrum. In the definition, a perfect bi-cluster is one with a constant value, denoted by c, in every matrix entry. The bi-clustering criterion is defined as the amount of its deviation from a constant-valued matrix:

$$\|\mathbf{A}\|_{\text{constant-value}} \equiv \min_{c} \left\| \mathbf{A} - \begin{bmatrix} c & c & \ldots & c \\ c & c & \ldots & c \\ \vdots & \vdots & \vdots & \vdots \\ c & c & \ldots & c \end{bmatrix} \right\|_{\mathrm{F}}, \tag{5.33}$$

where $\|\cdot\|_{\mathrm{F}}$ denotes the Frobenius norm. Figure 5.17 shows an example in which the constant-value matrix norm of a subset of row vectors and column vectors becomes very small after reshuffling a data matrix.

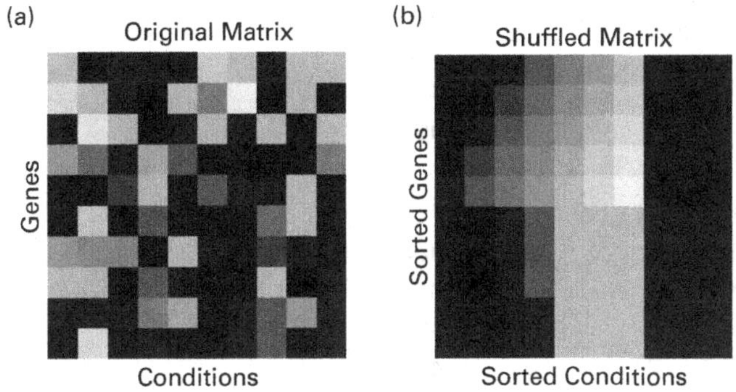

Fig. 5.17. Bi-clustering using the constant-value coherence model. (a) Given a random gene expression data matrix, all possible ways to sort row and column vectors may be tried. (b) If a contiguous and constant-valued block can be identified, then the block of row and column vectors is likely to represent a meaningful bi-cluster.

Coherence models with additive and/or multiplicative adjustments

However, in many practical situations, the constant-value matrix norm is simply not rich enough to handle the true underlying process leading to the data matrix. The similarity measure should be adjusted to reflect the true coherence of the row vectors and column vectors in the bi-cluster. Two coherence models worthy of consideration are additive and multiplicative models.

(i) **Additive coherence model**. In the "additive model," a shift relation between two vectors in the same family can be tolerated [38]. Mathematically, two feature vectors **a** and **b** are said to belong to the same family if and only if they are are related by

$$\mathbf{b} = \alpha + \mathbf{a},$$

where α is the additive adjustment that is allowed in order to bring **a** and **b** closer to each other.

(ii) **Multiplicative coherence model**. In addition to a constant shift, this model also allows a scaling relation between two vectors in the same family. Mathematically, two feature vectors **a** and **b** are said to belong to the same family if and only if they are related by

$$\mathbf{b} = \gamma \times \mathbf{a}$$

or, more generally,

$$\mathbf{b} = \alpha + \gamma \times \mathbf{a}.$$

Figure 5.18 shows the effect on the family of genes of applying additive and multiplicative coherence models to the expression data.

5.6.2 Applications of bi-clustering methods

Bi-clustering provides a viable approach to simultaneous clustering of both genes and conditions in that it reveals gene sets that are co-expressed within a subset of conditions.

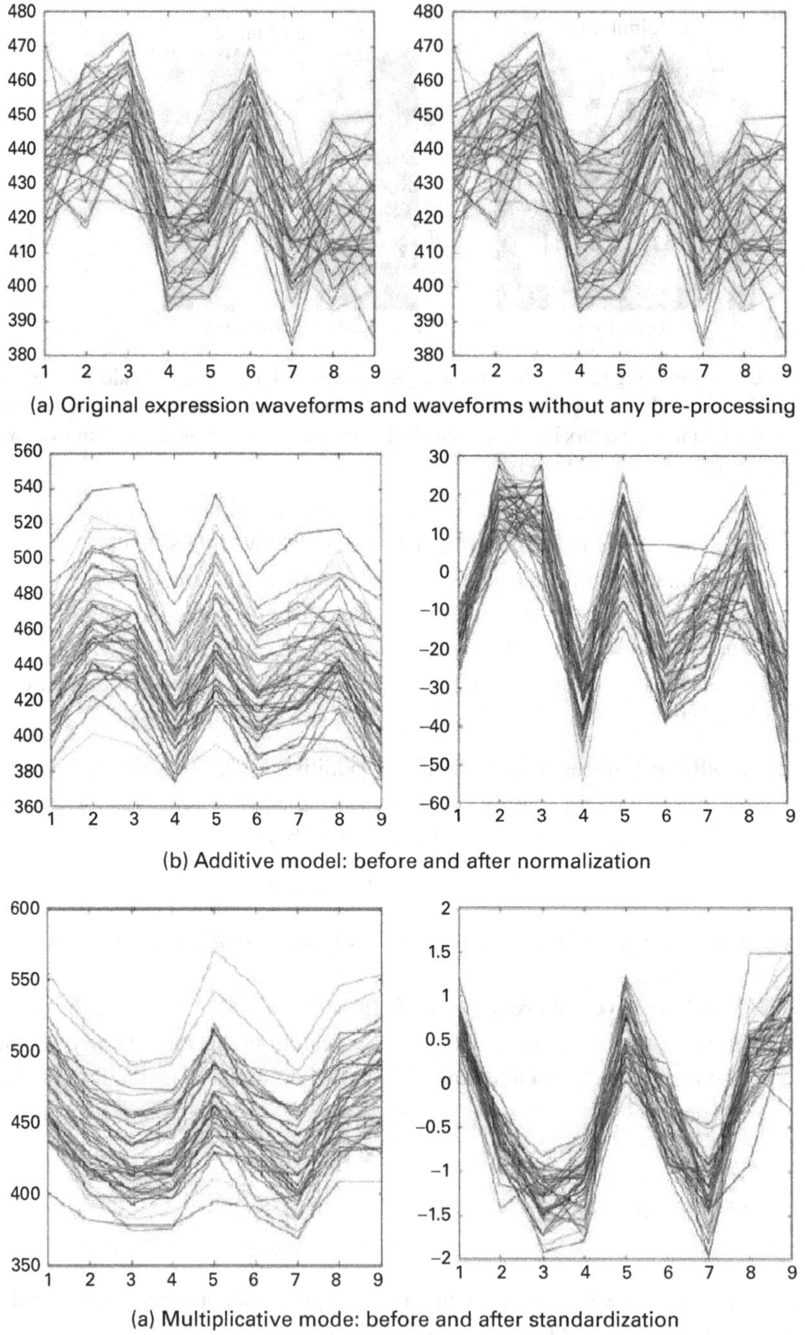
(a) Original expression waveforms and waveforms without any pre-processing
(b) Additive model: before and after normalization
(a) Multiplicative mode: before and after standardization

Fig. 5.18. Effects of applying normalization pre-processing (additive coherence model) and standardization pre-processing (multiplicative coherence model) to gene expression data. Each curve represents the expression level of one gene across nine samples in the yeast dataset. Three different time-course gene groups are shown in parts (a)–(c), each representing clustering results from a different coherent model. At first glance, the genes in group (a) appear to be most coherent in terms of the conventional distance metric. However, the genes in group (b) become more compact after all the gene expression levels have been adjusted by normalization. In fact, the genes in group in (c) are by far the most compact after adjustment by standardization.

However, because bi-clustering involves simultaneous clustering both of row vectors and of column vectors, the corresponding coherence models are consequently becoming more complex. Moreover, the exact suitable models for a gene/condition group are usually unknown a priori. For gene expression analysis, both additive and multiplicative coherence models have been adopted for bi-clustering by a number of researchers [38, 148, 180, 264].

In addition, comprehensive coherence models to cover an array of representations of gene expression data have been proposed [142, 143, 262]. Supervised machine learning techniques may prove much more effective as a means to pinpoint the most suitable model or models. For example, a supervised bi-clustering strategy was proposed for condition selection in clustering analysis of yeast genes using microarray data. The strategy begins with a core set of vectors, then similar vectors are admitted to the group on a one-by-one basis. A proper criterion for expansion has to be designed so that it will first admit the candidate gene (or condition) that bears closest resemblance to the current subgroup. The process continues until all of the candidate vectors have received a proper evaluation and most (if not all) similar vectors have been admitted to the group. The bi-cluster which is ultimately formed depends on the tradeoff between a maximum size (in terms of the number of row vectors/column vectors) and a closest intra-group proximity.

Liang *et al.* [155] performed bi-clustering on a microarray data set of MDA231 sublines to identify co-expressed gene sets, e.g. gene clusters with sizes of at least 20 that were co-expressed in at least 60 (80%) of the cellular conditions. The identification of co-expressed gene sets may further facilitate the subsequent transcriptional network analysis.

Finally, Alizadeh *et al.* [4] obtained bi-clustering results for microarray data analysis via hierarchical clustering of a microarray data matrix consisting of 96 normal and malignant lymphocytes samples measured at more than 10,000 cDNA clones. Via simultaneous grouping of genes (row-wise clustering) and normal/malignant lymphocytes (column-wise clustering), bi-clustering helps facilitate the identification of diffuse large B-cell lymphomas.

5.7 Summary

Unsupervised learning models have long been adopted to systematically partition training datasets into disjoint groups, a process that is instrumental for facilitating many applications in pattern recognition and statistical data analysis. This chapter introduces several conventional unsupervised learning models for cluster discovery including the popular K-means and expectation-maximization (EM) learning models, which are presented respectively in Algorithms 5.1 and 5.2. For the purpose of establishing their theoretical foundation, and further enhancing their practical appeal, the monotonic convergence of K-means and EM algorithms models is given formally in Theorems 5.1 and 5.2.

The basic K-means learning rule can be further extended to a very important variant by imposing topological sensitivity on the cluster (or node) structure. This leads to the prominent SOM learning model presented in Algorithm 5.3. For vectorial data analysis, the topological sensitivity of the cluster structure may be characterized by the proximity either in the node space or in the original input space. However, for nonvectorial data analysis, the node-space approach becomes the only option since the original vector space is not defined for nonvectorial data.

Finally, the chapter also presents the basic coherence models which are useful for bi-clustering applications. Bi-cluster learning models have recently received increasing attention in many new applications such as document and microarray data analysis. For example, bi-clustering can be adopted for simultaneous clustering of both genes and conditions so that it reveals gene sets that are co-expressed within a subset of conditions. Hence, it serves as a promising learning model for facilitating transcriptional network analysis. The challenge lies in finding computationally effective bi-clustering methods for large-size data arrays. This is a research topic worthy of further exploration.

5.8 Problems

Problem 5.1 *You are given the following training dataset:*

$$\begin{bmatrix} 0 \\ 0 \end{bmatrix}, \begin{bmatrix} 1 \\ 0 \end{bmatrix}, \begin{bmatrix} 0 \\ 2 \end{bmatrix}, \begin{bmatrix} -1 \\ -1 \end{bmatrix}.$$

Partition the four vectors into two clusters according to the Euclidean metric.

(a) *Show three different ways of partitioning them into two pairs. Which way yields the best partition result?*

(b) *Show four different ways of partitioning them into two groups: one group with a single vector and the other with the remaining three vectors. Which way yields the best partition result? How does it compare with the best pairwise partition?*

Problem 5.2 *Consider the following one-dimensional dataset:*

$$\mathcal{X} = \{1,\ 3,\ 4.5,\ 5,\ 6.5,\ 7,\ 8,\ 10\}.$$

Apply K-means to partition the dataset into three clusters, assuming the initial cluster centers to be 1.0 *and* 10.0*, respectively. How many updating steps are required before the algorithm converges?*

Problem 5.3 *Consider the following training vectors:* $\mathbf{x}_1 = (4, 3)$, $\mathbf{x}_2 = (4, 4)$, $\mathbf{x}_3 = (4, 5)$, $\mathbf{x}_4 = (0, 4)$, $\mathbf{x}_5 = (8, 0)$, $\mathbf{x}_6 = (3, 4)$, *and* $\mathbf{x}_7 = (5, 4)$.

(a) *Apply K-means to partition the dataset into three clusters, assuming the initial cluster centers to be:* $\vec{\mu}_1 = \mathbf{x}_1$, $\vec{\mu}_2 = \mathbf{x}_4$, *and* $\vec{\mu}_3 = \mathbf{x}_5$. *How many updating steps are required before the algorithm converges?*

(b) *Apply EM to partition the dataset into three clusters with the same centers initially.*

Problem 5.4 *Let N denote the number of patterns, M the feature dimension, and K the number of mixtures. Show that computational complexity (in terms of multiplications) for each epoch in the E-step in the EM algorithm is* $O(NMK + NK)$ *and that in the M-step is* $O(2NMK)$.

Problem 5.5 (Updating centroid and covariance matrix) *Assume that an individual cluster in a GMM has a Gaussian density distribution parameterized by* $\Theta = \{\vec{\mu}, \Sigma\}$ *containing both centroid* $\vec{\mu}$ *and covariance* Σ. *This problem derives the updating algorithms for covariance matrices.*

(a) *For the K-means algorithm, show that the covariance of the jth cluster can be estimated as:*

$$\Sigma_j = \frac{\sum_{t=1}^{N}[\mathbf{x}_t - \vec{\mu}_j][\mathbf{x}_t - \vec{\mu}_j]^{\mathrm{T}}}{N_j}, \tag{5.34}$$

where N_j *stands for the number of members in the jth cluster.*

(b) *For the EM algorithm, show that the covariance of the jth cluster can be estimated as*

$$\Sigma_j = \frac{\sum_{t=1}^{N} h_t^{(k)}\, [\mathbf{x}_t - \vec{\mu}_j][\mathbf{x}_t - \vec{\mu}_j]^{\mathrm{T}}}{\sum_{t=1}^{N} h_t^{(k)}}. \tag{5.35}$$

Problem 5.6 (Physical-space sensitivity for SOM learning) *The neighborhood sensitivity function may be defined in the physical space, as exemplified by Eq. (1.22), as opposed to a function defined in the index space. More precisely, the neighborhood sensitivity function* $\Lambda(j, i^*)$ *will then be substituted by* $\Lambda(\vec{\mu}_j, \mathbf{x}_t)$, *e.g.*

$$\Lambda(j, i^*) = \exp\left\{-\frac{\| \vec{\mu}_j - \mathbf{x}_t \|^2}{r}\right\},$$

which is a function that decreases monotonically with the distance between the node vector $\vec{\mu}_j$ *and the training vector* $\mathbf{x}_t$.

Compare these two types of neighborhood sensitivity functions.

Problem 5.7 (LSP condition for SOM) *Given an unsupervised training dataset, let the learning objective be finding a two-dimensional mesh that minimizes the SOM-type criterion function given in Eq. (5.32). Show that this problem formulation meets the LSP condition prescribed in Theorem 1.1.*

Problem 5.8 *Develop a scheme that may effectively incorporate prior information into the EM clustering algorithm.*

Problem 5.9 *Explain the distinction between K-means, EM, AEM, and SOM, from different aspects listed in the following table:*

	K-means	EM	AEM	SOM
Node topology	–	–	–	Grid
Initialization	Random	Random	Random	Ordered on grid
Nodes to be updated	Winner-only	Co-winners	Co-winners	Co-winners
Neighborhood sensitivity	–	–	–	Shrink window

Problem 5.10 (Bi-clustering) *Using Cheng and Church's additive coherence model, find two consistent rectangular blocks (with maximum possible size) for the following data matrix:*

$$\mathbf{X} = \begin{bmatrix} 1 & 1 & 2 & 2 & 3 \\ 1 & 4 & 2 & 2 & 1 \\ 4 & 3 & 5 & 4 & 6 \\ 1 & 3 & 5 & 1 & 1 \\ 0 & 1 & 1 & 1 & 2 \end{bmatrix}.$$

Problem 5.11 (MATLAB simulation: clustering of GMM dataset) *Conduct the following simulation study.*

(a) *Create a synthetic database for GMM as follows: randomly generate four ten-dimensional vectors: $\vec{\mu}_1$, $\vec{\mu}_2$, $\vec{\mu}_3$, and $\vec{\mu}_4$, which will be used as the centroids of the GMM model. Compute the shortest distance between the centroids, which will be used as the variance of the Gaussian distribution (σ) of the GMM model.*

(b) *Create 100, 200, 300, and 400 data points respectively centered at $\vec{\mu}_1$, $\vec{\mu}_2$, $\vec{\mu}_3$, and $\vec{\mu}_4$, for the Gaussian distribution with variance σ^2.*

(c) *What is the distribution of the total dataset of 1000 points?*

(d) *Apply K-means to divide the dataset into three groups. What is the minimum energy function?*

(e) *Apply K-means and the EM algorithm to divide the dataset into four groups. Compare the minimum energy functions of (c) and (d).*

Problem 5.12 (MATLAB simulation) *Use MATLAB to create a mixture density function with three Gaussian component densities, with their prior probabilities known to be as follows:*

(a) $P(\Omega_1) = 0.2$, $P(\Omega_2) = 0.3$, *and* $P(\Omega_3) = 0.5$;

(b) $P(\Omega_1) = 0.1$, $P(\Omega_2) = 0.1$, *and* $P(\Omega_3) = 0.8$.

Use two-mean, three-mean, and four-mean K-means algorithms. Compute the likelihood between the data distribution and your estimate.

Repeat the problem with the EM clustering algorithm.

Problem 5.13 (MATLAB simulation: clustering of expression data) *Download from "http://www.genome.wi.mit.edu/mpr" and create a* 7192×72 *microarray data matrix.*

(a) *Apply K-means and partition the genes into six clusters.*
(b) *Apply SOM and partition the genes into* 2×3 *clusters.*
(c) *Apply K-means and partition the samples (rather than genes) into six clusters;*
(d) *Apply SOM and partition the samples into* 2×3 *clusters.*

Problem 5.14 (MATLAB simulation on image database) *An image database containing ten categories, each with 100 JPG images, can be found at http://wang.ist.psu.edu/docs/related/. Apply K-means and SOM clustering techniques to the dataset and subdivide* 1000 *images into nine K-means clusters and* 3×3 *SOM clusters, respectively.*

6 Kernel methods for cluster analysis

6.1 Introduction

The various types of raw data encountered in real-world applications fall into two main categories, vectorial and nonvectorial types. For vectorial data, the Euclidean distance or inner product is often used as the similarity measure of the training vectors: $\{\mathbf{x}_i, i = 1, \ldots, N\}$. This leads to the conventional K-means or SOM clustering methods. This chapter extends these methods to kernel-based cluster discovery and then to nonvectorial clustering applications, such as sequence analysis (e.g. protein sequences and signal motifs) and graph partition problems (e.g. molecular interactions, social networks). The fundamental unsupervised learning theory will be systematically extended to nonvectorial data analysis.

This chapter will cover the following kernel-based unsupervised learning models for cluster discovery.

- Section 6.2 explores kernel K-means in intrinsic space. In this basic kernel K-means learning model, the original vectors are first mapped to the basis functions for the intrinsic vector space $\mathcal{H}$, and the mapped vectors will then be partitioned into clusters by the conventional K-means. Because the intrinsic-space approach will *not* be implementable for some vectorial and all nonvectorial applications, alternative representations need to be pursued. According to Theorem 1.1, the LSP condition holds for K-means. According to Eq. (1.20), this means that the problem formulation may be fully and uniquely characterized by the kernel matrix $\mathbf{K}$ associated with the training vector, i.e. without a specific vector space being explicitly defined. In short, the original vector-based clustering criterion is converted to a vector-free clustering criterion. Theorem 6.1 establishes the equivalence between the intrinsic-space-based and the kernel-matrix-based K-means algorithms. The latter approach, also known as the *kernel trick*, extends K-means' application domain to clustering of nonvectorial objects. A prominent example is network segmentation.
- Section 6.3 explores criteria suitable for clustering of nonvectorial data. For nonvectorial data, an object is not originally given in vector form, so it does not have an intrinsic-space representation. Consequently, the intrinsic-space approach is not applicable to cluster discovery of nonvectorial objects. In order for kernel K-means to remain applicable, the notion of similarity needs to be extended to nonvectorial objects. This leads to the development of kernel K-means methods that can be applied

to the similarity matrix (substituting the formal kernel matrix) formed from nonvectorial training data. For the network segmentation problem, we shall establish the equivalence between the partition criteria for network segmentation and the kernel-matrix based K-means clustering criterion. This assures that kernel K-means may serve as an effective tool for network segmentation. This section also establishes the fact that the positive semi-definiteness is a critical condition for monotonic convergence of kernel K-means; see Theorem 6.2. In order to safely apply kernel K-means, the similarity matrix (or kernel matrix) must be converted to one that satisfies the convergence condition. Two popular methods for such conversion are via applying to the kernel matrix either (1) a spectral-truncation operation (Section 6.4) or (2) a spectral-shift operation (Section 6.5). The former benefits from the orthogonality inherently found in the spectral space, while the latter has theoretical support from Theorem 6.4, which establishes the fact that the optimal clustering solution is invariant with respect to the spectral shift.

- Section 6.4 shows how the orthogonality inherently found in the spectral space can facilitate dimension reduction for possible computational saving in a clustering discovery algorithm such as kernel K-means. However, there is a tradeoff between the dimension reduction and the accuracy. To this end, Theorem 6.3 provides a closed-form analysis linking the approximation error and the dimension reduction, which may be used to determine the best tradeoff.
- Section 6.5 proposes the adoption of a recursive kernel trick for network segmentation. Algorithm 6.3 presents a fast kernel K-means method employing recursive updating of the pattern–centroid similarity, which may expedite the learning processing by exploiting the sparsity in many network segmentation problems.
- In Section 6.6, the kernel methods are similarly applied to the SOM learning model. According to Theorem 1.1, the LSP condition holds for the SOM's 2-norm-based formulation. Algorithm 6.4 presents the kernel-matrix (or kernel-trick)-based SOM learning algorithm.
- Section 6.7 considers a typical hierarchical clustering method, more specifically, the neighbor-joining algorithm.

6.2 Kernel-based K-means learning models

The objective of traditional clustering methods is to partition training vectors by using similarity criteria applied on the basis of Euclidean metrics. More precisely, the Euclidean distance or inner product is used to measure the similarity between the training vectors in the original vector space, $\{\mathbf{x}_i, i = 1, \ldots, N,\}$. With reference to Figure 1.5, the performance of cluster discovery is dictated by the similarity metric adopted.

For complex data analysis, the Euclidean inner product and its corresponding Euclidean distance are often highly inadequate for many unsupervised or supervised learning scenarios. The kernel approach makes use of a more sophisticated kernel-induced inner product, instead of the traditional Euclidean inner product, to measure the similarity metric of two vectors. Many kernel-based K-means clustering methods have been proposed in the literature [31, 85, 303, 315, 317]. For a general survey, as well as additional references, see [67].

This section shows that, on switching to the kernel-induced space, all of the conventional techniques for unsupervised clustering, including K-means, have very natural kernel-based extensions. In the kernel approach, the pair-wise similarity between two training samples, say $\mathbf{x}$ and $\mathbf{y}$, is characterized by the kernel function $K(\mathbf{x}, \mathbf{y})$ [78, 187].

6.2.1 Kernel K-means in intrinsic space

The use of the kernel-induced inner product (as the similarity metric) amounts equivalently to the use of the Euclidean inner product in a kernel-induced Hilbert space. As depicted in Figure 2.4, the basis functions for the original vector space will be substituted by a new set of basis functions representing the intrinsic vector space $\mathcal{H}$, i.e.

$$\mathbf{x} = [x^{(1)}, x^{(2)}, \ldots, x^{(M)}]^{\mathrm{T}} \rightarrow \vec{\boldsymbol{\phi}}(\mathbf{x}) = [\phi^{(1)}(\mathbf{x}), \phi^{(2)}(\mathbf{x}), \ldots, \phi^{(J)}(\mathbf{x})]^{\mathrm{T}}.$$

This has an effect on the formulations both for the learning phase and for the prediction phase. The original training vectors are first mapped to their new representations in the intrinsic space. The mapped vectors will then be partitioned into clusters by the conventional K-means. This implies that the new similarity metric is equivalent to the Euclidean inner product in the intrinsic vector space $\mathcal{H}$. The kernel-based clustering algorithm is summarized as follows.

ALGORITHM 6.1 (K-means learning models in intrinsic space)

Learning phase

Following the procedure shown in Figure 2.4, the K-means learning algorithm in the intrinsic space contains two steps.

(i) First, the original M-dimensional training vectors $\{\mathbf{x}_i, i = 1, \ldots, N\}$ *are mapped to a set of J-dimensional intrinsic vectors;* $\{\vec{\boldsymbol{\phi}}(\mathbf{x}_j), j = 1, \ldots, N\}$.

(ii) Then, apply the conventional K-means to partition the N intrinsic vectors. The objective is to minimize the following criterion function:

$$\sum_{k=1}^{K} \sum_{\mathbf{x}_t \in \mathcal{C}_k} \| \vec{\boldsymbol{\phi}}(\mathbf{x}_t) - \vec{\mu}_{\mathcal{H}}^{(k)} \|^2, \tag{6.1}$$

where $\vec{\mu}_{\mathcal{H}}$ *denotes the node vector (i.e. the centroid in this case) in* $\mathcal{H}$ *for the cluster* $\mathcal{C}_k$.

Prediction phase

The prediction phase can follow a procedure similar to that described in Figure 2.4. It contains two steps.

(i) First, the new input vector $\mathbf{x}$ *is mapped to a J-dimensional intrinsic vector,* $\vec{\phi}(\mathbf{x})$.

(ii) Then, find one "centroid" in the intrinsic space that is closest to $\vec{\phi}(\mathbf{x})$. *Naturally, the test vector should be assigned to the cluster with the closest node vector. Namely,*

$$\mathbf{x} \in \mathcal{C}_k \text{ if } k = \arg \min_{j=1,\cdots,K} \| \vec{\phi}(\mathbf{x}) - \vec{\mu}_{\mathcal{H}}^{(k)} \|. \tag{6.2}$$

□

Pros and cons

Note that the traditional K-means involves clustering of M-dimensional vectors, while intrinsic-space K-means involves J-dimensional vectors. In general, the latter will be computationally more costly, since $J \gg M$ usually.

In the intrinsic vector space $\mathcal{H}$, we usually enjoy a better separability between data clusters, exemplified by the three-ring dataset depicted in Figure 3.7. This improved separability is often attributed to the higher dimensionality of the space $\mathcal{H}$.

6.2.2 The K-means clustering criterion in terms of kernel matrix

Two examples below indicate clearly that the intrinsic-space approach will *not* be universally applicable.

- The intrinsic-space approach is not applicable to Gaussian kernels, whose corresponding intrinsic space $\mathcal{H}$ has an infinite dimension, i.e. $J \to \infty$. This makes the intrinsic-space approach infeasible for Gaussian kernels. Section 3.5.5 shows that the intrinsic space $\mathcal{H}$ and the spectral space $\mathcal{S}$ share the same pairwise distance/similarity for all the training vectors. It means that the spectral space offers a computationally feasible alternative.
- The intrinsic-space approach is not applicable to cluster discovery of nonvectorial objects. If the kernel K-means approach is to be useful for clustering nonvectorial objects, a clustering criterion in terms of kernel matrix will be critical. Moreover, the notion of similarity needs to be further extended to data analysis for nonvectorial objects. Moreover, the role of the kernel matrix will be assumed by the similarity matrix.

Fortunately, according to Theorem 1.1, the LSP condition holds for K-means. According to Eq. (1.20), this means that the problem formulation may be fully and uniquely characterized by the kernel matrix $\mathbf{K}$ associated with the training vector, i.e. without a specific vector space being explicitly defined. Such a formulation is also known as the *kernel trick.*

The centroid-based clustering criterion in intrinsic space

Assuming that the kernel satisfies the Mercer condition, the clustering criterion for K-means performed on the intrinsic vector space is

$$E_{\text{kernel}} = \sum_{k=1}^{K} \sum_{\mathbf{x}_t \in \mathcal{C}_k} \| \vec{\phi}(\mathbf{x}_t) - \vec{\mu}_{\mathcal{H}}^{(k)} \|^2, \tag{6.3}$$

where $\vec{\phi}(\mathbf{x}_t)$ and $\vec{\mu}_{\mathcal{H}}^{(k)}$ respectively denote the training vectors and cluster centroids in the intrinsic space. This requires the explicit derivation of the locations of all the centroids and therefore is referred to as a *centroid-based* objective function.

The centroid-free clustering criterion in intrinsic space

It has been known [53, 54] that the centroid-based criterion given in Eq. (6.3) may be reformulated into a new "centroid-free" criterion function as follows:

$$\begin{aligned} E_{\text{kernel}} &= \sum_{k=1}^{K} \sum_{\mathbf{x}_t \in \mathcal{C}_k} \| \vec{\phi}(\mathbf{x}_t) - \vec{\mu}_{\mathcal{H}}^{(k)} \|^2 \\ &= \sum_{k=1}^{K} \frac{1}{2N_k} \sum_{\vec{\phi}(\mathbf{x}_i)\in \mathcal{C}_k} \sum_{\vec{\phi}(\mathbf{x}_j)\in \mathcal{C}_k} \| \vec{\phi}(\mathbf{x}_i) - \vec{\phi}(\mathbf{x}_j) \|^2, \end{aligned} \tag{6.4}$$

where N_k denotes the number of objects in the cluster $\mathcal{C}_k$.

The kernelized or vector-free clustering criterion

In order to obviate the need for explicit computation of the centroids and furthermore avoid the need for any explicitly defined vector space, we would like to have a versatile and vector-free representation of the objective function:

$$\begin{aligned} E_{\text{kernel}} &= \sum_{k=1}^{K} \frac{1}{2N_k} \sum_{\vec{\phi}(\mathbf{x}_i)\in \mathcal{C}_k} \sum_{\vec{\phi}(\mathbf{x}_j)\in \mathcal{C}_k} \| \vec{\phi}(\mathbf{x}_i) - \vec{\phi}(\mathbf{x}_j) \|^2 \\ &= \sum_{k=1}^{K} \frac{1}{2N_k} \sum_{\vec{\phi}(\mathbf{x}_i)\in \mathcal{C}_k} \sum_{\vec{\phi}(\mathbf{x}_j)\in \mathcal{C}_k} \| \vec{\phi}(\mathbf{x}_i)\|^2 + \| \vec{\phi}(\mathbf{x}_j) \|^2 - 2\vec{\phi}(\mathbf{x}_i)\cdot\vec{\phi}(\mathbf{x}_j) \\ &= \sum_{k=1}^{K} \sum_{\vec{\phi}(\mathbf{x}_i)\in \mathcal{C}_k} \| \vec{\phi}(\mathbf{x}_i)\|^2 - \sum_{k=1}^{K} \frac{1}{N_k} \sum_{\vec{\phi}(\mathbf{x}_i)\in \mathcal{C}_k} \sum_{\vec{\phi}(\mathbf{x}_j)\in \mathcal{C}_k} \vec{\phi}(\mathbf{x}_i)\cdot\vec{\phi}(\mathbf{x}_j) \\ &= \sum_{i=1}^{N} K_{ii} - \sum_{k=1}^{K} \left\{ \frac{1}{N_k} \sum_{\vec{\phi}(\mathbf{x}_i)\in \mathcal{C}_k} \sum_{\vec{\phi}(\mathbf{x}_j)\in \mathcal{C}_k} K_{ij} \right\}. \end{aligned} \tag{6.5}$$

This will be referred to as a *vector-free* objective function. Note that, both for linear and for nonlinear kernels, the *vector-free* criterion is expressed in terms of the kernel matrix.

THEOREM 6.1 (Equivalence of clustering criteria) *The following three clustering criteria are equivalent.*

- **Centroid-based clustering criteria in intrinsic space:**

$$E_{\text{kernel}} = \sum_{k=1}^{K} \sum_{\mathbf{x}_t \in \mathcal{C}_k} \| \vec{\phi}(\mathbf{x}_t) - \vec{\mu}_{\mathcal{H}}^{(k)} \|^2. \tag{6.6}$$

- **Centroid-free clustering criteria in intrinsic space:**

$$E_{\text{kernel}} = \sum_{k=1}^{K} \frac{1}{2N_k} \sum_{\vec{\phi}(\mathbf{x}_i)\in\mathcal{C}_k} \sum_{\vec{\phi}(\mathbf{x}_j)\in\mathcal{C}_k} \|\vec{\phi}(\mathbf{x}_i) - \vec{\phi}(\mathbf{x}_j)\|^2. \tag{6.7}$$

- **Kernelized clustering criteria in terms of the kernel matrix:**

$$E_{\text{kernel}} = \sum_{i=1}^{N} K_{ii} - \sum_{k=1}^{K} \left\{ \frac{1}{N_k} \sum_{\vec{\phi}(\mathbf{x}_i)\in\mathcal{C}_k} \sum_{\vec{\phi}(\mathbf{x}_j)\in\mathcal{C}_k} K_{ij} \right\}. \tag{6.8}$$

Proof. The equivalence is based on Eqs. (6.3)–(6.5). □

The *vector-free* criterion works for any algorithm that depends solely on the kernel matrix, thus forgoing the need for an explicit definition of a vector space. Hence, the kernel K-means can be carried out by the kernel matrix itself. In this sense, the kernel matrix may be viewed as the common platform for clustering analysis both of vectorial and of nonvectorial data. As a result, it allows a kernel-trick-based method for K-means (Section 6.5).

Note further that the term $\sum_{i=1}^{N} K_{ii}$ may be dropped without affecting the clustering criterion, since it remains constant with respect to any clustering. Therefore, K-means can be converted into a maximization problem with a new objective function:

$$D(\mathbf{K}) = \sum_{k=1}^{K} \left\{ \frac{1}{N_k} \sum_{\vec{\phi}(\mathbf{x}_i)\in\mathcal{C}_k} \sum_{\vec{\phi}(\mathbf{x}_j)\in\mathcal{C}_k} K_{ij} \right\}. \tag{6.9}$$

6.3 Kernel K-means for nonvectorial data analysis

For nonvectorial data, an object is not originally given in vector form, so it does not have an intrinsic-space representation. Consequently, the intrinsic-space approach is not applicable to cluster discovery of nonvectorial objects. In the kernelized formulation, informally known as the kernel trick, all we need is to have the pairwise relationship clearly defined. In other words, there will be no need to have an explicit definition of a vector space or even an explicit quantification of each of the individual objects. Moreover, it is important to recognize that, for some applications, pairwise similarity between two objects is more naturally quantifiable than each of the individual objects. For nonvectorial objects, such pairwise similarities may naturally assume the role of kernel functions of two vectors. This is why kernelized unsupervised learning models are especially amenable to nonvectorial data analysis.

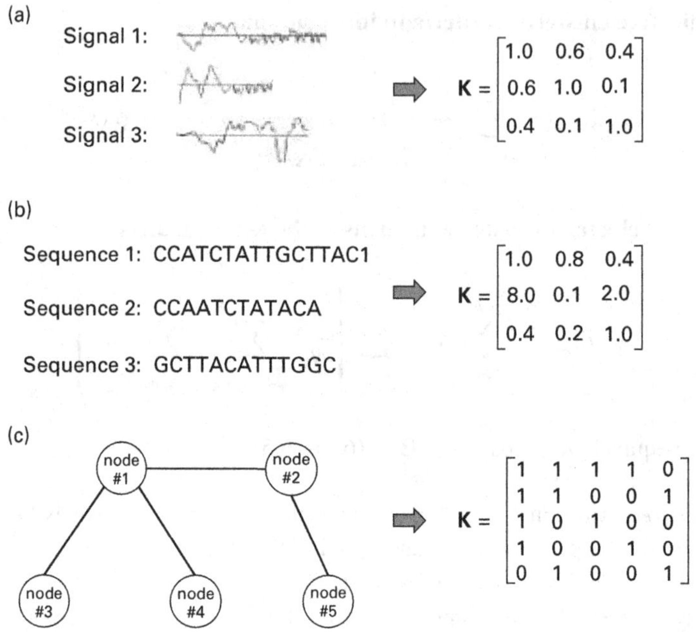

Fig. 6.1. For nonvectorial objects, the role of kernel functions is replaced by pairwise similarity metrics. Therefore, the entries of the kernel matrix are the similarity scores between two objects. Shown here are examples for (a) time series, (b) sequences, and (c) graphs.

6.3.1 The similarity matrix for nonvectorial training datasets

The general rule is that the greater the likeness of the pair the higher the similarity score. In addition, the similarity metric must adequately reflect the underlying "physical" or "genetic" resemblance between two samples. Of course, the exact choice of similarity score must be application-specific. Moreover, as depicted in Figure 6.1, there is a variety of nonvectorial data, including time series, sequences, and graphs. In general, the derivation of their similarity scores is much more complex than that for the vectorial data. For example, the characterization of the similarity of two protein sequences, say VDPRIQGELEKLNQ and QDPRIDGVLQKLNVV, usually involves sophisticated alignments of the sequences.

The similarity matrix for nonvectorial data

The *similarity matrix* for a nonvectorial training dataset, $\mathcal{X} \equiv \{\mathbf{x}_1, \mathbf{x}_2, \ldots, \mathbf{x}_N\}$, can be constructed as

$$\mathbf{S} = \{S_{ij}\} = \begin{bmatrix} S(\mathbf{x}_1, \mathbf{x}_1) & S(\mathbf{x}_1, \mathbf{x}_2) & \ldots & S(\mathbf{x}_1, \mathbf{x}_N) \\ S(\mathbf{x}_2, \mathbf{x}_1) & S(\mathbf{x}_2, \mathbf{x}_2) & \ldots & S(\mathbf{x}_2, \mathbf{x}_N) \\ \vdots & \vdots & \ldots & \vdots \\ S(\mathbf{x}_N, \mathbf{x}_1) & S(\mathbf{x}_N, \mathbf{x}_2) & \ldots & S(\mathbf{x}_N, \mathbf{x}_N) \end{bmatrix}, \quad (6.10)$$

where S_{ij} denotes the similarity between two nonvectorial objects $\mathbf{x}_i$ and $\mathbf{x}_j$. If the kernel-based clustering approach is adopted, then the $N \times N$ matrix will play the same role as the kernel matrix, i.e. $\mathbf{K} = \mathbf{S}$.

6.3.2 Clustering criteria for network segmentation

An important sub-category of nonvectorial data analysis is network segmentation, which has a diversity of applications. For example, some multimedia application examples include social network analysis, sensor networks, etc. In the biological domain, as another example, proteins that interact are likely to have similar localization or functions. Graphs of interactions between the proteins of an organism can be acquired via many modern high-throughput technologies. Dividing protein interaction networks into modular subgraphs may facilitate prediction of biological functions for proteins within the same submodules, thereby facilitating investigation of the location or functions of proteins in a cell.

The objective of network segmentation is to obtain disjoint subnetworks such that the nodes within the same subnetwork are densely connected among themselves while being loosely connected to the nodes in the other subnetworks.

A network can be represented by a graph denoted as $G = (V, E)$, where V is the vertex set and E is the edge set. For example, in the graph depicted in Figure 6.2(a), V consists of eight nodes and E of 11 edges. Quantitatively, a graph is often represented by an adjacency matrix $\mathbf{A} = \{A_{ij}\}$. When A_{ij} is binary-valued, it can be used to represent the adjacency or "direct connectivity" of two nodes $\mathbf{x}_i$ and $\mathbf{x}_j$. When A_{ij} is real, then it may be used to characterize the similarity between the two nodes. Moreover, various clustering algorithms can be applied to the partitioning of the graph. The objective criterion is often given as a function of the adjacency matrix $\mathbf{A}$.

Criteria for K-means on graph partition

Network segmentation may be regarded as a special type of cluster discovery. Its goal is to identify highly connected groups in a network. Popular criteria for evaluating the segmentation of a graph include *ratio association*, *ratio cut*, and many others. The criteria for *ratio association* and *ratio cut* are elaborated below.

- *Ratio association: intra-cluster similarity.* Define the intra-cluster degree pertaining to specific vertex as the number of edges linking the vertex to itself or another vertex within the same cluster. One plausible criterion for graph partitioning is expressed in terms of intra-cluster degrees. The higher the better, thus the optimal solution is the one maximizing the ratio association.

  As shown below, the kernel matrix suitable for the ratio association criterion is the adjacency matrix $\mathbf{A}$. Namely, the best partition is the one which maximizes the so-called *ratio association*:

$$\max \sum_{k=1}^{K} \left\{ \frac{1}{N_k} \sum_{\mathbf{x}_i \in \mathcal{C}_k} \sum_{\mathbf{x}_j \in \mathcal{C}_k} A_{ij} \right\},$$

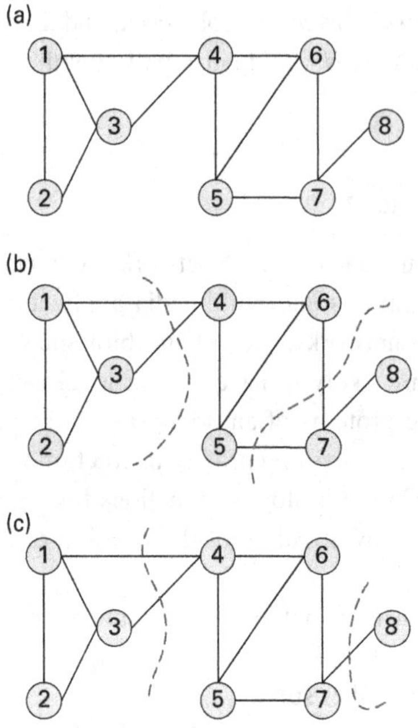

Fig. 6.2. (a) The original graph. (b) An optimal ratio-association solution. (c) An optimal ratio-cut solution.

whose optimal solution can be obtained by applying K-means and assuming that the role of the kernel matrix is played by the adjacency matrix $\mathbf{A}$.

- *Ratio cut: inter-cluster distance.* An alternative partitioning criterion is expressed as an average inter-cluster degree (i.e. the edges linking two vertices from different clusters). The lower the inter-cluster linkage the better. It was shown that [48] the optimal solution is the one maximizing the so-called *ratio cut*:

$$\max \sum_{k=1}^{K} \left\{ \frac{1}{N_k} \sum_{\mathbf{x}_i \in \mathcal{C}_k} \sum_{\mathbf{x}_j \in \mathcal{C}_k} A'_{ij} \right\},$$

where A'_{ij} are the elements of the matrix $\mathbf{A}'$ defined as

$$\mathbf{A}' \equiv \mathbf{A} - \mathrm{Diag}\{d_{ii}\},$$

with $d_{ii} = \sum_{j=1}^{N} A_{ij}$. The solution for the optimal ratio cut can be obtained by applying K-means to the modified kernel matrix: $\mathbf{A}'$.

As evidenced by the following example, the *ratio-association* and *ratio-cut* criteria usually lead to different optimal solutions. Different applications will call for different kernel matrices. For example, a combined association/cut criterion may call for a formulation which applies Eq. (6.9) to the following kernel matrix:

$$\mathbf{K} = \alpha\mathbf{A} + \alpha'\mathbf{A}',$$

where α and α' can be adjusted to reflect whether the association or cut should be more emphasized.

Example 6.1 (Graph partitioning) *Figure 6.2(a) shows a graph with eight nodes whose inter-node connectivity is characterized by the following adjacency matrix:*

$$\mathbf{A} = \begin{bmatrix} 1 & 1 & 1 & 1 & 0 & 0 & 0 & 0 \\ 1 & 1 & 1 & 0 & 0 & 0 & 0 & 0 \\ 1 & 1 & 1 & 1 & 0 & 0 & 0 & 0 \\ 1 & 0 & 1 & 1 & 1 & 1 & 0 & 0 \\ 0 & 0 & 0 & 1 & 1 & 1 & 1 & 0 \\ 0 & 0 & 0 & 1 & 1 & 1 & 1 & 0 \\ 0 & 0 & 0 & 0 & 1 & 1 & 1 & 1 \\ 0 & 0 & 0 & 0 & 0 & 0 & 1 & 1 \end{bmatrix}. \tag{6.11}$$

Partition it into three subgraphs using the ratio-association criterion, leads to an optimal partition shown in Figure 6.2(b).

For the ratio-cut criterion, however, the corresponding kernel matrix becomes

$$\mathbf{A}' = \begin{bmatrix} -3 & 1 & 1 & 1 & 0 & 0 & 0 & 0 \\ 1 & -2 & 1 & 0 & 0 & 0 & 0 & 0 \\ 1 & 1 & -3 & 1 & 0 & 0 & 0 & 0 \\ 1 & 0 & 1 & -4 & 1 & 1 & 0 & 0 \\ 0 & 0 & 0 & 1 & -3 & 1 & 1 & 0 \\ 0 & 0 & 0 & 1 & 1 & -3 & 1 & 0 \\ 0 & 0 & 0 & 0 & 1 & 1 & -3 & 1 \\ 0 & 0 & 0 & 0 & 0 & 0 & 1 & -1 \end{bmatrix}. \tag{6.12}$$

The ratio-cut criterion will result in a different optimal solution, which is shown in Figure 6.2(c).

These optimal solutions can be computed via many optimization tools, including the kernel methods to be elaborated in the discussion.

6.3.3 The Mercer condition and convergence of kernel K-means

Note that Eq. (6.9) suggests that it is possible to kernelize the optimizer, i.e. the formulation can be exclusively based on the kernel matrix and, more importantly, can proceed without any vector space being explicitly defined.

However, the numerical property of kernel methods depends closely on the assumption that the kernel matrix is a Mercer matrix, defined as a matrix that is *positive semi-definite*. For vectorial data analysis, a Mercer matrix is assured as long as a Mercer kernel is adopted. Unfortunately, for nonvectorial analysis, there is no such equivalent theorem to assure a similarity matrix being a Mercer matrix. On the contrary, for most real-world applications, the raw similarity matrices do not satisfy the condition. (For example, this is so for the similarity matrix $\mathbf{A}$ in Eq. (6.11) or $\mathbf{A}'$ in Eq. (6.12).) Those similarity matrices must be first converted to Mercer matrices before kernel learning models may be safely applied.

6.3.3.1 Monotonic convergence condition

As shown in Section 5.3, the convergence of the conventional K-means depends critically on the monotonic decrease of the cost function. More exactly, the convergence claim is based on the monotonically decreasing properties given in Eq. (5.13) and Eq. (5.14). Unfortunately, as demonstrated by the following counterexample, the latter might no longer hold if the Mahalanobis matrix (or kernel matrix) is not positive semi-definite.

Example 6.2 (Counter example to monotonically decreasing property) *Let us consider the training dataset,* $\mathcal{X} = \{\mathbf{x}_1, \mathbf{x}_2, \ldots, \mathbf{x}_N\}$, *with the first two elements of the dataset known to be*

$$\mathbf{x}_1 = \begin{bmatrix} 0 \\ 0 \end{bmatrix}, \ \mathbf{x}_2 = \begin{bmatrix} 0 \\ 1 \end{bmatrix}.$$

Moreover, the kernel function is given as

$$K(\mathbf{x}, \mathbf{y}) \equiv \mathbf{x}^{\mathrm{T}}\mathbf{M}\mathbf{y}, \quad \textit{where} \quad \mathbf{M} = \begin{bmatrix} 1 & 0 \\ 0 & -1 \end{bmatrix},$$

which obviously fails the Mercer condition. Assume that, in the first iteration, we have that $\mathbf{x}_1 = [0 \quad 0]^{\mathrm{T}}$ *forms a cluster all by itself and the centroid is* $\vec{\mu} = [0 \quad 0]^{\mathrm{T}}$. *Suppose further that, in the next iteration, it is somehow decided that* $\mathbf{x}_2 = [0 \quad 1]^{\mathrm{T}}$ *should join* $\mathbf{x}_1 = [0 \quad 0]^{\mathrm{T}}$ *to form a new cluster with two members. The new centroid is obviously the average of the two training vectors:* $\vec{\mu}' = (\mathbf{x}_1 + \mathbf{x}_2)/2 = [0 \quad 0.5]^{\mathrm{T}}$. *Note, however, that*

$$\|\mathbf{x}_1 - \vec{\mu}'\|^2_{\mathbf{M}} + \|\mathbf{x}_2 - \vec{\mu}'\|^2_{\mathbf{M}} = -0.5 > \|\mathbf{x}_1 - \vec{\mu}\|^2_{\mathbf{M}} + \|\mathbf{x}_2 - \vec{\mu}\|^2_{\mathbf{M}} = -1.$$

This means that updating the centroid actually increases the cost compared with leaving the original centroid intact. This violates Eq. (5.14) and thus contradicts the monotonically decreasing property.

It is evident from the example that the failure of the Mercer condition voids the assurance on the monotonically decreasing property and, consequently, the convergence of K-means can no longer be fully guaranteed.

In summary, we have established two conditions:

- The positive semi-definiteness of the kernel function is a necessary condition for a full assurance on the monotonic convergence of kernel K-means.
- The positive semi-definiteness of the kernel function is also a sufficient condition for the monotonic convergence of kernel K-means (Eqs. (5.13) and (5.14)).

On combining the necessary and sufficient conditions, we reach the following conclusion.

THEOREM 6.2 (Condition for monotonic convergence of kernel K-means) *The monotonic convergence of kernel K-means can always be assured if and only if the kernel matrix (or similarity matrix)* **K** *is a Mercer matrix, i.e. it is a positive semi-definite matrix.*

6.3.3.2 Conversion into positive semi-definite kernel matrices

To assure the monotonic convergence of iterative algorithms such as kernel K-means, it is advisable to first convert a non-Mercer matrix (denoted **K**) into a Mercer matrix (denoted **K**′).

Note that the (positive and negative) eigenvalues of the kernel matrix **K** are derivable by spectral decomposition:

$$\mathbf{K} = \mathbf{U}^{\mathrm{T}}\boldsymbol{\Lambda}\mathbf{U},$$

where $\boldsymbol{\Lambda} = \mathrm{Diag}\{\lambda_i\}$. Let all the eigenvalues be arranged in decreasing order:

$$\lambda_1 \geq \lambda_2 \geq \ldots \geq \lambda_m \geq 0 > \lambda_{m+1} \geq \ldots \geq \lambda_N.$$

Two prominent approaches to such conversion are spectral truncation and spectral shift.

- **The spectral-truncation approach.** Spectral truncation involves dropping the spectral components associated with negative eigenvalues and constructing a lower-rank Mercer matrix [65, 223]. In other words, the new eigenvalues become

$$\boldsymbol{\Lambda}' = \mathrm{Diag}\{\lambda'_i\}, \quad \text{where } \lambda'_i = \max\{\lambda_i, 0\},$$

and the new kernel is

$$\mathbf{K}' = \mathbf{U}^{\mathrm{T}}\boldsymbol{\Lambda}'\mathbf{U}.$$

Therefore, $\lambda'_i \geq 0$, and the new kernel matrix is now guaranteed to be positive semi-definite.

This conversion, however, could result in performance degradation. Theorem 6.3 provides a quantitative analysis tradeoff between the dimension reduction and the clustering accuracy [136], in which it is shown that the discrepancy between the modified and original cost functions (see Eq. (6.9)) is as follows:

$$D(\mathbf{K}') - D(\mathbf{K}) \leq k|\lambda_N|, \tag{6.13}$$

where k is the number of clusters. Therefore, as depicted in Figure 6.3(a), spectral truncation results in a respectable approximation when $|\lambda_N|$ is relatively small. The full discussion will be deferred to Section 6.4.

- **The spectral-shift approach.** Any symmetric matrix may be converted to a Mercer matrix by a spectral shift, which does not affect the optimal solution, as stated in Theorem 6.4. The conversion can be expressed as

$$\mathbf{K}' = \mathbf{K} + s\mathbf{I}, \tag{6.14}$$

where s is a positive constant resulting in a positive semi-definite matrix via an eigenshift. It follows that $\mathbf{K}' = \mathbf{K} + s\mathbf{I} = \mathbf{U}^{\mathrm{T}}[\mathbf{\Lambda} + s\mathbf{I}]\mathbf{U}$. In other words, the new eigenvalues become

$$\lambda_i' = \lambda_i + s.$$

If $s = -\lambda_N \geq 0$, then $\lambda_i' \geq 0$.

6.4 *K*-means learning models in kernel-induced spectral space

Two kernel K-means methods may effectively circumvent the computational problem of having to map the original training vectors to (possibly infinite-dimensional) intrinsic space $\mathcal{H}$. They are *spectral K-means* and *kernelized K-means* algorithms, see Section 6.5.

There are two stages in the so-called *spectral K-means*. First, the N original training vectors are mapped to the N-dimensional spectral space. Then, the conventional K-means can be applied to determine the K best clusters. Recall that the mapping from each training vector, say $\mathbf{x}_i$, to the kernel-induced spectral space has the following formula (see Eq. (3.59)):

$$\vec{\mathbf{s}}(\mathbf{x}_i) = \mathbf{\Lambda}^{-\frac{1}{2}}\mathbf{U}\vec{\mathbf{k}}(\mathbf{x}_i),$$

where $\mathbf{\Lambda}$ and $\mathbf{U}$ are derived via the spectral decomposition

$$\mathbf{K} = \mathbf{U}^{\mathrm{T}}\mathbf{\Lambda}\mathbf{U} = \mathbf{E}^{\mathrm{T}}\mathbf{E}.$$

Recall that

$$\mathbf{E} = \mathbf{\Lambda}^{\frac{1}{2}}\mathbf{U},$$

where the *jth* column of the matrix $\mathbf{E}$ is exactly $\vec{\mathbf{s}}(\mathbf{x}_j)$. It follows that

$$K_{ij} = \vec{\mathbf{s}}(\mathbf{x}_i)^{\mathrm{T}}\vec{\mathbf{s}}(\mathbf{x}_j). \tag{6.15}$$

Recall that

$$K_{ij} = \vec{\boldsymbol{\phi}}(\mathbf{x}_i)^{\mathrm{T}}\vec{\boldsymbol{\phi}}(\mathbf{x}_j) = \vec{\mathbf{s}}(\mathbf{x}_i)^{\mathrm{T}}\vec{\mathbf{s}}(\mathbf{x}_j).$$

This implies that the intrinsic space $\mathcal{H}$ or the spectral space $\mathcal{S}$ are interchangeable in any 2-norm-based clustering learning formulations, including e.g. K-means and SOM.

ALGORITHM 6.2 (Spectral K-means learning models)

Learning phase

Following the procedure shown in Figure 2.7, the K-means learning algorithm in the spectral space contains two steps.

(i) *First, the original M-dimensional training vectors* $\{\mathbf{x}_i, i = 1, \ldots, N\}$ *are mapped to a set of N-dimensional spectral vectors:* $\{\vec{\mathbf{s}}(\mathbf{x}_j), j = 1, \ldots, N\}$.

(ii) Then, apply the conventional K-means to partition the N spectral vectors. The objective is to minimize the criterion in Eq. (6.1):

$$\sum_{k=1}^{K} \sum_{\mathbf{x}_t \in \mathcal{C}_k} \| \vec{\mathbf{s}}(\mathbf{x}_t) - \vec{\mu}_S^{(k)} \|^2, \tag{6.16}$$

where $\vec{\mu}_S$ denotes the node vector (i.e. the centroid in this case) in $\mathcal{S}$ for the cluster $\mathcal{C}_k$.

Prediction phase

The prediction phase can follow a procedure similar to that described in Figure 2.7. The prediction phase contains two steps.

(i) First, the new input vector $\mathbf{x}$ *is mapped to an N-dimensional spectral vector:*

$$\vec{\mathbf{s}}(\mathbf{x}) = \mathbf{\Lambda}^{-\frac{1}{2}} \mathbf{U} \vec{\mathbf{k}}(\mathbf{x}).$$

(ii) Then, find the "centroid" in the spectral space which is closest to $\vec{\mathbf{s}}(\mathbf{x})$. *Naturally, the test vector should be assigned to the cluster with the closest node vector. Namely,*

$$\mathbf{x} \in \mathcal{C}_k \text{ if } k = \arg \min_{j=1,\cdots,K} \| \vec{\mathbf{s}}(\mathbf{x}) - \vec{\mu}_S^{(k)} \|. \tag{6.17}$$

□

6.4.1 Discrepancy on optimal solution due to spectral truncation

Note that the components of the transformed vectors $\{\vec{\mathbf{s}}(\mathbf{x}_j), j = 1, \ldots, N\}$ are orthogonal to each other. This prompts a spectral subspace approach to dimension reduction. Since the principal subspace is theoretically the most representative, it is possible to retain only the highest (say m) principal components without severely affecting the clustering result. This will be referred to as the *spectral-truncation* approach.

There are pros and cons associated with the reduced-dimension spectral subspace methods. There is a clear advantage in terms of the computational cost, which can now be reduced by a factor of m/N. The down-side is that the resulting clustering may suffer from some loss of accuracy since $N - m$ minor components are dropped. In other words, there is a tradeoff between the dimension reduction and the accuracy. In this section, in order to better assess the best tradeoff, we shall provide a closed-form analysis showing how the approximation error may depend on the reduced dimension.

Fortunately, for the spectral K-means, there exists a vector-free criterion that can be exclusively characterized by the associated kernel matrices, i.e. $\mathbf{K}$ and $\mathbf{K}'$, before and after the dimension reduction, respectively. In fact, as derived in Eq. (6.5), the vector-free criterion is

$$E_{\text{kernel}} = \sum_{i=1}^{N} K_{ii} - \sum_{k=1}^{K} \left\{ \frac{1}{N_k} \sum_{\vec{\phi}(\mathbf{x}_i) \in \mathcal{C}_k} \sum_{\vec{\phi}(\mathbf{x}_j) \in \mathcal{C}_k} K_{ij} \right\}. \tag{6.18}$$

Consequently, a closed-form error analysis can be developed to assess the discrepancy. First, let us compare the original and reduced-dimension kernel matrices:

$$\mathbf{K} = \mathbf{E}^{\mathrm{T}}\mathbf{E} = \mathbf{U}^{\mathrm{T}}\mathbf{\Lambda}\mathbf{U} \text{ and } \mathbf{K}' = \mathbf{E}'^{\mathrm{T}}\mathbf{E}' = \mathbf{U}^{\mathrm{T}}\mathbf{\Lambda}'\mathbf{U},$$

and let the difference be denoted as

$$\tilde{\mathbf{K}} \equiv \mathbf{K} - \mathbf{K}' = \mathbf{U}^{\mathrm{T}}\tilde{\mathbf{\Lambda}}\mathbf{U},$$

where $\tilde{\mathbf{\Lambda}} \equiv \mathbf{\Lambda} - \mathbf{\Lambda}'$. The approximation error will be dictated by $\tilde{\mathbf{K}}$.

THEOREM 6.3 (Discrepancy on optimal solution of kernel K-means due to spectral truncation) *It is obvious that the greater the matrix $\tilde{\mathbf{K}}$, the higher the discrepancy. Quantitatively, we can establish the following upper bound [136].*

- *If the kernel matrix $\mathbf{K}$ is positive semi-definite and*

$$\lambda_1 \geq \lambda_2 \geq \ldots \geq \lambda_N \geq 0,$$

then

$$\text{discrepancy} = \sum_{k=1}^{K} \left\{ \frac{1}{N_k} \sum_{\mathbf{x}_i \in \mathcal{C}_k} \sum_{\mathbf{x}_j \in \mathcal{C}_k} \tilde{K}_{ij} \right\} \leq K\lambda_{m+1}. \tag{6.19}$$

- *If the kernel matrix $\mathbf{K}$ is not positive semi-definite and*

$$\lambda_1 \geq \lambda_2 \geq \ldots \geq \lambda_m \geq \ldots \geq \lambda_{m'} \geq 0 \geq \ldots \geq \lambda_N,$$

then

$$\text{discrepancy} = \sum_{k=1}^{K} \left\{ \frac{1}{N_k} \sum_{\mathbf{x}_i \in \mathcal{C}_k} \sum_{\mathbf{x}_j \in \mathcal{C}_k} \tilde{K}_{ij} \right\} \leq K \max\{|\lambda_{m+1}|, |\lambda_N|\}. \tag{6.20}$$

Note that Eq. (6.13) is a special case of Eq. (6.20).

Proof. The derivation used the fact that $(1/N_k) \sum_{\mathbf{x}_i \in \mathcal{C}_k} \sum_{\mathbf{x}_j \in \mathcal{C}_k} \tilde{\mathbf{K}}_{ij}$ is upper bounded by $\tilde{\mathbf{K}}$'s largest eigenvalue. □

Tightness of the upper bound

The above upper bound can be shown to be tight by constructing a kernel matrix whose discrepancy is exactly $K\lambda_{m+1}$. The following construction procedure leads to a kernel matrix whose discrepancy is exactly $K\lambda_{m+1}$.

First, we note that the following kernel matrix has $m + 1$ nonzero eigenvalues:

$$\mathbf{K} = \mathbf{U}_m^{\mathrm{T}} \mathbf{\Lambda}_{m\times m} \mathbf{U}_m^{\mathrm{T}} + \mathbf{u}_{m+1}^{\mathrm{T}} \boldsymbol{\lambda}_{m+1} \mathbf{u}_{m+1}.$$

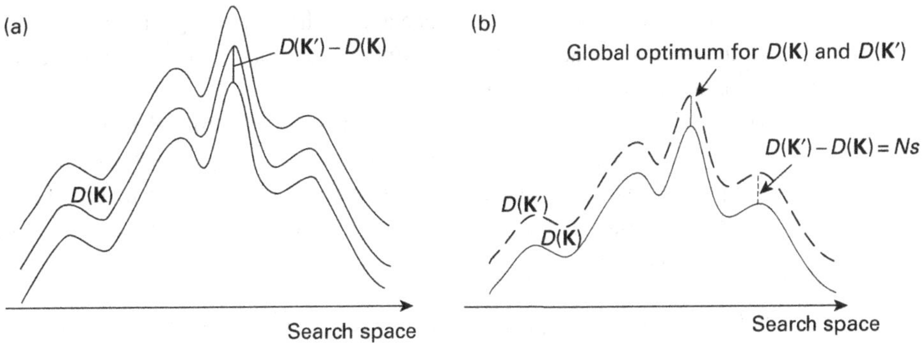

Fig. 6.3. (a) Spectral truncation (i.e. eigen truncation) causes a discrepancy bounded by $K|\lambda_N|$. This is because the objective function associated with the eigen truncated kernel matrix falls between the two dashed curves. (b) Shift invariance: the optimal solution is not affected by the spectral shift (i.e. eigen shift) because the two curves (as shown) share the same peak location.

Then, we can prove that the eigentruncated kernel matrix has m nonzero eigenvalues and that

$$\tilde{\mathbf{K}} \equiv \mathbf{K} - \mathbf{K}' = \mathbf{u}_{m+1}^{\mathrm{T}} \boldsymbol{\lambda}_{m+1} \mathbf{u}_{m+1}.$$

Finally, by setting the normalized vector

$$\mathbf{u}_{m+1} = \frac{1}{\sqrt{K}} \left[\frac{1}{\sqrt{N_1}}, \ldots, \frac{1}{\sqrt{N_1}}, \frac{1}{\sqrt{N_2}}, \ldots, \frac{1}{\sqrt{N_2}}, \ldots, \frac{1}{\sqrt{N_K}}, \ldots, \frac{1}{\sqrt{N_K}} \right]^{\mathrm{T}},$$

we can derive the exact bound shown below:

$$\text{discrepancy} = \sum_{k=1}^{K} \left\{ \frac{1}{N_k} \sum_{\mathbf{x}_i \in C_k} \sum_{\mathbf{x}_j \in C_k} \tilde{K}_{ij} \right\} = K\lambda_{m+1}.$$

Implication of the upper bound

The discrepancy is illustrated by Figure 6.3(a). It has several practical implications.

- If m is sufficiently large that the error $K\lambda_{m+1}$ is less than a tolerable level, then the m-dimensional kernel K-means should suffice for yielding a satisfactorily close clustering result.
- If the global optimum w.r.t. $D(\mathbf{K})$ holds a margin over any local optimum by a gap greater than $2K\lambda_{m+1}$, then the optimum w.r.t. $D(\mathbf{K}')$ is exactly the same as that w.r.t. $D(\mathbf{K})$, with the worst scenario taken into account.

6.4.2 Computational complexities

Some disadvantages associated with the spectral-truncation approach are listed below.

(i) The spectral decomposition itself is computationally expensive, adding an extra cost of $O(N^3)$ or higher. This makes the approach less appealing from the computational perspective.

(ii) If $N > J$, then the spectral-space approach incurs a higher computational cost than the intrinsic-space K-means. Moreover, it requires the additional cost needed for obtaining spectral decomposition.
(iii) Sometimes, for large and sparse networks, it is critical to preserve the sparsity during the iterations. The proposed *kernel trick* meets this requirement, but the spectral-truncation approach tends to ruin the sparsity structure. This renders the spectral-truncation approach less attractive for segmentation of large-scale but sparse networks.

On the other hand, the spectral K-means could sometimes be more computationally efficient than the intrinsic-space approach, especially when $N \leq J$. Even though the spectral K-means has to account for the extra cost on computing the spectral decomposition, the overhead could be more than compensated for by the saving due to the adoption of reduced-dimension spectral K-means.

6.5 Kernelized *K*-means learning models

As evidenced by the vector-free cost function in Eq. (6.5), the problem formulation of kernel K-means and its computation can be exclusively derived from the kernel matrix $\mathbf{K}$. The empirical-space approach (also known as *the kernel trick*) yields a result equivalent to that derived from other K-means algorithms that are based on the intrinsic or spectral representations. However, the former enjoys an important advantage in that it can fully preserve the sparsity structure (if any) of the original kernel matrix.

6.5.1 Solution invariance of spectral-shift on the kernel matrix

The proposed kernel trick may be applied to both of the following scenarios:

- the kernel matrix (or similarity matrix) is by itself already positive semi-definite, or
- the kernel matrix needs to be spectrally shifted via Eq. (6.14) to be converted into a Mercer matrix.

The spectral-shift approach has gained considerable popularity thanks to a very useful shift-invariance theorem that can be stated as follows.

THEOREM 6.4 (Solution invariance of spectral shift on the kernel matrix) *The new matrix $\mathbf{K}'$ will lead to the same optimal solution as the old matrix $\mathbf{K}$. More exactly, let $\mathbf{K}' = \mathbf{K}+s\mathbf{I}$, then the optimal solution for a norm-free objective function that is based on $\mathbf{K}'$ will be exactly the same as that for one that is based on $\mathbf{K}$. (See Figure 6.3(b).)* □

Proof. We shall demonstrate that the shift-invariance property is closely related to the trace-based derivation given by Dhillon *et al.* [48].

Let $\mathbf{K}' = \mathbf{K} + s\mathbf{I}$, then the optimal solution for a norm-free objective function that is based on $\mathbf{K}'$ will be exactly the same as that for one based on $\mathbf{K}$.

By Eq. (6.9), the cost functions before and after the spectral shift are

$$D(\mathbf{K}) = \sum_{k=1}^{K}\left\{\frac{1}{N_k}\sum_{\mathbf{x}_i\in\mathcal{C}_k}\sum_{\mathbf{x}_j\in\mathcal{C}_k} K_{ij}\right\} \quad \text{and} \quad D(\mathbf{K}') = \sum_{k=1}^{K}\left\{\frac{1}{N_k}\sum_{\mathbf{x}_i\in\mathcal{C}_k}\sum_{\mathbf{x}_j\in\mathcal{C}_k} K'_{ij}\right\}.$$

Note that

$$K'_{ij} = \begin{cases} K_{ij} & \text{if } \ i \neq j, \\ K_{ij} + s & \text{if } \ i = j. \end{cases} \tag{6.21}$$

It follows that

$$D(\mathbf{K}') - D(\mathbf{K}) = \sum_{k=1}^{K}\left\{\frac{1}{N_k}\sum_{\mathbf{x}_i\in\mathcal{C}_k}\sum_{\mathbf{x}_j\in\mathcal{C}_k}(K'_{ij} - K_{ij})\right\} = Ns,$$

which is a constant and thus will not affect the clustering preference.

In short, the (global or local) optimum of $D(\mathbf{K}')$ is also the (global or local) optimum of $D(\mathbf{K})$, and vice versa. This is pictorially illustrated by Figure 6.3(b). □

6.5.2 Kernelized K-means algorithms

For simplicity, let us just assume that $\mathbf{K}$ is a Mercer matrix, i.e. it is positive semi-definite.

6.5.2.1 The squared-centroid norm (SCN) and data–centroid similarity (DCS)

For a Mercer matrix $\mathbf{K}$, according to Eq. (6.15), there exist N (intrinsic or spectral) vectors, $\{\vec{\mathbf{s}}_i, i = 1, \ldots, N,\}$ in the spectral space such that $\vec{\mathbf{s}}_i \cdot \vec{\mathbf{s}}_j = K_{ij}$. Now let us apply the conventional K-means to the N spectral vectors so as to find a minimizing solution for the following clustering criterion function:

$$\sum_{k=1}^{K}\sum_{\vec{\boldsymbol{\phi}}_t\in\mathcal{C}_k}\|\vec{\mathbf{s}}_t - \vec{\boldsymbol{\mu}}_k\|^2,$$

where for notational convenience we shall re-denote

$$\vec{\boldsymbol{\mu}}_k = \vec{\boldsymbol{\mu}}_{\mathcal{S}}^{(k)} = \frac{\sum_{i\in\mathcal{C}_k}\vec{\mathbf{s}}_i}{N_k}.$$

For deriving an efficient K-means algorithm, a critical design step is to find a way to efficiently compute and update the squared value of the *pattern–centroid distance* between any training pattern $\vec{\boldsymbol{\phi}}_t$ and each centroid $\vec{\boldsymbol{\mu}}_k$:

$$\begin{aligned}\|\vec{\mathbf{s}}_t - \vec{\boldsymbol{\mu}}_k\|^2 &= \|\vec{\mathbf{s}}_t\|^2 + \|\vec{\boldsymbol{\mu}}_k\|^2 - 2\vec{\mathbf{s}}_t\cdot\vec{\boldsymbol{\mu}}_k \\ &= \|\vec{\mathbf{s}}_t\|^2 + \|\vec{\boldsymbol{\mu}}_k\|^2 - 2R_{tk},\end{aligned}$$

for $k = 1, \ldots, K$. Since $\|\vec{\mathbf{s}}_t\|^2$ is a constant with respect to clustering, it can be dropped without affecting the result of the winner selection. Therefore only the following two types of parameters need to be constantly updated:

- *the squared-centroid norm* (SCN) for the kth centroid, $\|\vec{\mu}_k\|^2$; and
- *the data–centroid similarity* (DCS) between the tth item of data and the kth centroid, R_{tk}.

Note that during the iterations in the kernel-matrix-based K-means, there is no need to explicitly compute the centroid $\vec{\mu}_k$, which may be undefined for nonvectorial data. Instead, $\|\vec{\mu}_k\|^2$ and R_{jk} will be explicitly computed.

The winning cluster will be identified as the cluster nearest to $\vec{\mathbf{s}}_t$, i.e.

$$k = \arg\min_{r=1,\ldots,K} \|\vec{\mu}_r\|^2 - 2R_{tr} \tag{6.22}$$

6.5.2.2 The direct kernelized K-means

Suppose that we are given the initial cluster membership $C_r^{(0)}$, and the initial number of members in the cluster $C_r^{(0)}$ is denoted $N_r^{(0)}$. Then

- $$\|\vec{\mu}_r^{(0)}\|^2 = \frac{1}{\left(N_r^{(0)}\right)^2} \sum_{i \in C_r^{(0)}} \sum_{j \in C_r^{(0)}} K_{ij}. \tag{6.23}$$

- $$\begin{aligned} R_{tk}^{(0)} &= \vec{\mathbf{s}}_t \cdot \vec{\mu}_r^{(0)} \\ &= \frac{1}{N_r^{(0)}} \sum_{i \in C_r^{(0)}} \vec{\mathbf{s}}_t \cdot \vec{\mathbf{s}}_i \\ &= \frac{1}{N_r^{(0)}} \sum_{i \in C_r^{(0)}} K_{ti}. \end{aligned} \tag{6.24}$$

Every training pattern $\vec{\mathbf{s}}_t$, $t = 1, \ldots, N$, is sequentially presented for the following iterative updating process. (An epoch means the updating process with one complete round of all the N training data.)

Direct update

The detailed updating schemes for the SCN and DCS are elaborated below. Note that, for every winning cluster, there is a losing cluster. Therefore, we let k represent the index of the cluster where x_t is added, and at the same time let p represent the index of the cluster from where x_t is removed. If $k = p$, then no updating is needed. If $k \neq p$, then we have to update the old SCN and DCS parameters. More precisely, $\|\vec{\mu}_k\|^2$, $\|\vec{\mu}_p\|^2$, R_{tk}, and R_{tp} have to be updated to their respective new parameters $\|\vec{\mu}_k'\|^2$, $\|\vec{\mu}_p'\|^2$, R_{tk}', and R_{tp}'.

(i) *Updating of the SCN.* For the winning cluster, $\vec{\mathbf{s}}_t$ is now a new member just added to the new cluster C_k', which now contains $N_k' = N_k + 1$ members, with its new centroid relocated to

$$\vec{\mu}_k' = \frac{1}{N_k'} \sum_{\vec{s}_i \in C'_k} \vec{s}_i. \tag{6.25}$$

The new SCN becomes

$$\|\vec{\mu}_k'\|^2 = \frac{N_k^2}{(N_k+1)^2}\|\vec{\mu}_k\|^2 + \frac{2N_k}{(N_k+1)^2}R_{tk} + \frac{1}{(N_k+1)^2}K_{tt}. \tag{6.26}$$

For the losing cluster, $\vec{s}_t$ is now being removed from the updated cluster C_p', which now contains $N_p' = N_p - 1$ members, and its new centroid is relocated to

$$\vec{\mu}_p' = \frac{1}{N_p'} \sum_{\vec{s}_i \in C'_k} \vec{s}_i. \tag{6.27}$$

In this case, the SCN may be updated as follows:

$$\|\vec{\mu}'_p\|^2 = \frac{N_p^2}{(N_p-1)^2}\|\vec{\mu}_p\|^2 - \frac{2N_p}{(N_p-1)^2}R_{tp} + \frac{1}{(N_p-1)^2}K_{tt}. \tag{6.28}$$

The computational expense is merely $O(1)$.

(ii) *Updating of data–centroid similarly (DCS).* If a direct method is used for updating the data–centroid similarities, then, for the winning cluster,

$$R_{jk}' = \frac{1}{N_k'} \sum_{i \in C'_k} K_{ji} = \frac{1}{N_k+1} \sum_{i \in C'_k} K_{ji}, \quad j = 1, \ldots, N, \tag{6.29}$$

and for the losing cluster,

$$R_{jp}' = \frac{1}{N_p'} \sum_{i \in C'_p} K_{ji} = \frac{1}{N_p-1} \sum_{i \in C'_p} K_{ji}, \quad j = 1, \ldots, N. \tag{6.30}$$

6.5.3 A recursive algorithm modified to exploit sparsity

The kernel trick can potentially yield an enormous computational saving for the partitioning of highly sparse networks. This section discusses why and how the traditional K-means algorithm is replaced by the (sparsity-preserving) kernel trick. (See also Ref. [146].)

In order to obtain extra computational saving, we propose to use a parameter-scaling scheme to effectively circumvent many operations being unnecessarily "wasted" on the scaling factors. To this end, let us introduce scaled SCN and scaled DCS elaborated as follows.

- *The scaled-SCN parameter.* The scaled-SCN (SSCN) parameter is

$$\|\tilde{\mu}_r\|^2 = (N_r)^2\,\|\vec{\mu}_r\|^2 \tag{6.31}$$

$$= \sum_{i \in C_r} \sum_{j \in C_r} K_{ij}. \tag{6.32}$$

- *The scaled-DCS parameter.* The scaled-DCS (SDCS) parameter is

$$\tilde{R}_{jr} \equiv N_k R_{jr} = \sum_{i \in C_k} K_{ti}. \tag{6.33}$$

which will be named the scaled DCS or, more simply, *sum of similarities* (SOS).

Accordingly, the rule for selecting the winner (see Eq. (6.22)) should be modified as follows:

$$k = \arg \min_{r=1,\ldots,K} \left\{ \frac{\|\tilde{\mu}_r\|^2}{N_r^2} - \frac{2\tilde{R}_{tr}}{N_r} \right\}, \tag{6.34}$$

This leads to the following modification of the updating algorithms.

Updating of scaled-squared-centroid-norm (SSCN) parameter

- Consider the winning cluster C_k. The pattern $\vec{\mathbf{s}}_t$ will be joining C'_k. According to Eq. (6.26),

$$\begin{aligned}\|\tilde{\mu}'_k\|^2 &= (N_k+1)^2 \|\vec{\mu}'_k\|^2 \\ &= N_k^2 \|\vec{\mu}_k\|^2 + 2N_k R_{tk} + K_{tt} \\ &= \|\tilde{\mu}_k\|^2 + 2\tilde{R}_{jk} + K_{tt}.\end{aligned}$$

This implies that

$$\Delta \|\tilde{\mu}_k\|^2 = \|\tilde{\mu}'_k\|^2 - \|\tilde{\mu}_k\|^2 = 2\tilde{R}_{jk} + K_{tt}, \quad j = 1, \ldots, N. \tag{6.35}$$

- Consider the losing cluster C_p. Now $\vec{\mathbf{s}}_t$ will be removed from C'_p. According to Eq. (6.28),

$$\begin{aligned}\|\tilde{\mu}'_p\|^2 &= (N_p-1)^2 \|\vec{\mu}'_p\|^2 \\ &= N_p^2 \|\vec{\mu}_p\|^2 - 2N_p R_{tp} + K_{tt} \\ &= \|\tilde{\mu}_p\|^2 - 2\tilde{R}_{jp} + K_{tt}.\end{aligned}$$

This implies that

$$\Delta \|\tilde{\mu}_p\|^2 = \|\tilde{\mu}'_p\|^2 - \|\tilde{\mu}_p\|^2 = -2\tilde{R}_{jp} + K_{tt}, \quad j = 1, \ldots, N. \tag{6.36}$$

Updating of the sum-of-similarities parameter (SOS)

- Consider the winning cluster C_k. The pattern $\vec{\mathbf{s}}_t$ will be joining C'_k. According to Eq. (6.29),

$$\begin{aligned}\tilde{R}'_{jk} &= (N_k+1)R'_{jk} \\ &= \sum_{i \in C'_k} K_{ji} = \sum_{i \in C_k} K_{ji} + K_{jt} \\ &= \tilde{R}_{jk} + K_{jt}, \text{ for } j = 1, \ldots, N.\end{aligned}$$

This implies that

$$\Delta \tilde{R}_{jk} = \tilde{R}'_{jk} - \tilde{R}_{jk} = K_{jt}, \quad j = 1, \ldots, N. \tag{6.37}$$

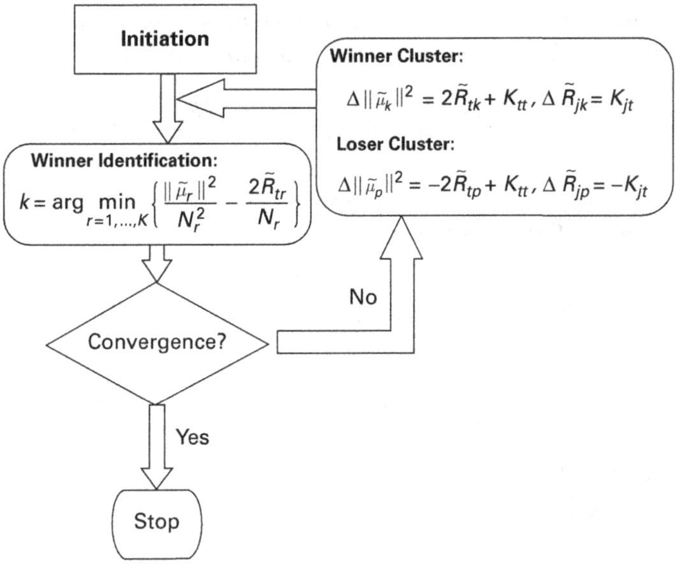

Fig. 6.4. This flowchart shows the recursive kernel trick which takes advantage of sparsity. In the kernel trick, two sets of parameters are updated: (1) *the scaled squared-centroid norm* (*SSCM*) for the rth centroid, $\|\tilde{\boldsymbol{\mu}}_r\|^2$, which can be computed from the kernel values; and (2) *the sum of similarities* (*SOS*) between the tth item of data and the rth centroid, $\tilde{R}_{jr} = \sum_{i\in C_k} K_{ti}$, see Eq. (6.33).

- Consider the losing cluster C_p. Now $\vec{\mathbf{s}}_t$ will be removed from C'_p. According to Eq. (6.30),

$$\begin{aligned}\tilde{R}'_{jp} &= (N_p - 1)R'_{jp} \\ &= \sum_{i\in C'_p} K_{ji} = \sum_{i\in C_p} K_{ji} - K_{jt} \\ &= \tilde{R}_{jp} - K_{jt}, \quad \text{for} \quad j = 1, \ldots, N.\end{aligned}$$

This implies that

$$\Delta\tilde{R}_{jp} = -K_{jt}, \quad j = 1, \ldots, N. \tag{6.38}$$

This leads to the modified kernelized K-means shown in Figure 6.4.

ALGORITHM 6.3 (Recursive kernelized K-means) *Assume that the kernel matrix formed by the N training data is positive semi-definite. Initially, assign each of the training patterns, say $\vec{\mathbf{s}}_t$, randomly to any cluster. Compute the initial values of the SSCN and SOS according to Eqs. (6.23) and (6.24). Then, each training pattern $\vec{\mathbf{s}}_t$, $t = 1, \ldots, N$ will be sequentially processed according to the following iterative updating procedure.*

(i) ***Winner identification.*** *Assume that the training pattern* $\vec{\mathbf{s}}_t$ *currently belongs to* C_p*, i.e. the pth cluster. The winner of* $\vec{\mathbf{s}}_t$ *is identified as follows:*

$$k = \arg \min_{r=1,\ldots,K} \left\{ \frac{\|\tilde{\boldsymbol{\mu}}_r\|^2}{N_r^2} - \frac{2\tilde{R}_{tr}}{N_r} \right\}, \tag{6.39}$$

If $k \neq p$*, perform the following updates.*

(ii) ***Updating of the SSCN parameter.***

- *For the winning cluster,*

$$\Delta\|\tilde{\boldsymbol{\mu}}_k\|^2 = 2\tilde{R}_{tk} + K_{tt},\ j = 1, \ldots, N. \tag{6.40}$$

- *For the losing cluster,*

$$\Delta\|\tilde{\boldsymbol{\mu}}_p\|^2 = -2\tilde{R}_{tp} + K_{tt},\ j = 1, \ldots, N. \tag{6.41}$$

(iii) ***Updating the SOS.***

- *For the winning cluster,*

$$\Delta\tilde{R}_{jk} = K_{jt},\ j = 1, \ldots, N. \tag{6.42}$$

- *For the losing cluster,*

$$\Delta\tilde{R}_{jp} = -K_{jt},\ j = 1, \ldots, N. \tag{6.43}$$

□

Computational saving by recursive methods

Note that, for each update of R_{jk} in Eq. (6.29), or R_{jk} in Eq. (6.30), the total cost will be $O(N_k \cdot N)$, since there are N vertices, i.e. $j = 1, \ldots, N$. Assuming that all clusters have approximately the same number of members, on average, the total cost can be roughly estimated to be $O(N^2/K)$. This number could be prohibitively high. Fortunately, via the recursive methods given in Eqs. (6.42) and (6.43), the cost can be reduced to merely $O(N)$ for updating the N SOS values $\tilde{R}_{jk}$ or $\tilde{R}_{jp}, j = 1, \ldots, N$. This means that, in terms of the order of magnitude, the saving ratio amounts to N^2/K to N, or equivalently, N/K to 1. For example, if $N = 10{,}000$ and $K = 10$, the computational saving due to the recursive method would be a factor of 1000.

Computational saving by sparsity

The *recursive kernel trick* in Algorithm 6.3 is especially appealing for analysis of sparsely connected networks. Note that no actual updating will be required in Eqs. (6.35) and (6.36) for most of the parameters. The actual updating takes places only for those (very few) which have nonzero entries K_{jt}.

For applications to the segmentation of highly sparse networks, the algorithm enjoys a substantial saving due to sparsity. (With dedicated hardware flagging nonzero elements, the processing speed-up may increase linearly with the degree of sparsity.) As shown in Table 6.1, the amount of computation required can be further reduced to $O(N_s)$, where N_s is the average number of nonzero elements per column in the kernel matrix. For highly sparse networks, it is expected that $N_s \ll N$, thus the extra saving can be very

Table 6.1. Savings per training pattern

	Direct update	Recursive update
Non-sparse	$O(N^2/K)$	$O(N)$
Sparsity	$O(NN_s/K)$	$O(N_s)$

substantial. In terms of the order of magnitude, the saving ratio amounts to N *to* N_s. For example, if $N = 10,000$ and $N_s = 100$, the computational saving would be roughly a factor of 100.

The computational saving achievable by using dedicated processing units

It is worth noting that the operations in the *recursive kernel trick* are mostly additions/substractions, as opposed to multiplications. This allows dedicated hardware processors to be used to further expedite the computation.

6.6 Kernel-induced SOM learning models

The same strategy has been applied to extend the traditional SOM learning algorithms to their kernel-based equivalents [6, 25, 108, 163, 283]. This section details the extension of SOM to several kernel-induced spaces, including the intrinsic, spectral, and empirical spaces.

6.6.1 SOM learning models in intrinsic or spectral space

The new training vectors in the intrinsic space are $\{\vec{\mathbf{s}}(\mathbf{x}_j), j = 1, \ldots, N\}$, each vector being J-dimensional. When J is finite, the conventional SOM learning algorithm may be applied directly to the new training dataset.

When $J \to \infty$, the intrinsic representation is no longer feasible. Likewise, when the objects are nonvectorial the intrinsic representation cannot be applied. One way out is to substitute the (uncomputable or infinite-dimensional) intrinsic representation by its spectral counterpart in $\mathcal{S}$. Computationally, we shall first perform the spectral decomposition:

$$\mathbf{K} = \mathbf{U}^{\mathrm{T}}\mathbf{\Lambda}\mathbf{U} = \mathbf{E}^{\mathrm{T}}\mathbf{E}.$$

Then the *jth* column of the matrix $\mathbf{E}$ is exactly the *jth* training vector $\vec{\mathbf{s}}_j$. The training dataset is now $\{\vec{\mathbf{s}}_j, j = 1, \ldots, N\}$, each of its members being a vector in the N-dimensional spectral space. Note that

$$K_{ij} = \vec{\mathbf{s}}(\mathbf{x}_i)^{\mathrm{T}}\vec{\mathbf{s}}(\mathbf{x}_j) = \vec{\mathbf{s}}_i^{\mathrm{T}}\vec{\mathbf{s}}_j,$$

for the intrinsic space $\mathcal{H}$ and spectral space $\mathcal{S}$. This implies that the two spaces are interchangeable for any 2-norm-based clustering formulations.

Obviously, the traditional SOM algorithm, Algorithm 5.3, can be applied to the induced training dataset, in the spectral space, $\{\vec{\mathbf{s}}_j, j = 1, \ldots, N\}$, or to the dataset in the intrinsic space, $\{\vec{\boldsymbol{\phi}}(\mathbf{x}_j), j = 1, \ldots, N\}$.

The SOM learning algorithm in intrinsic or spectral space

The learning phase contains two steps. First, the original M-dimensional vectors $\{\mathbf{x}_i, i = 1, \ldots, N\}$ are mapped to the set of N training vectors $\{\vec{\mathbf{s}}_j, j = 1, \ldots, N\}$. With reference to Figure 5.12, the SOM iterative learning process involves the following two-loop updating scheme.

- **Inner loop: centroid updates.** Every training pattern $\vec{\mathbf{s}}_t$, $t = 1, \ldots, N$, is sequentially presented for the following iterative updating process. (An epoch means the updating process with one complete round of all the N training data.)
  - (i) *Identification of the winner.* The winner is identified as the cluster nearest to $\vec{\mathbf{s}}_t$:
  $$i^* = \arg\min_{i \in I^{L_1 \times L_2 \times \cdots \times L_k}} \|\vec{\mathbf{s}}_t - \vec{\boldsymbol{\mu}}_i\|, \tag{6.44}$$
  where the node vector $\vec{\boldsymbol{\mu}}_i$ represents the centroid in the spectral space.
  - (ii) *Update of winner's node vector.* The centroid of the i^*th node (i.e. the winner) will be updated by the following amount:
  $$\Delta \vec{\boldsymbol{\mu}}_{i^*} = \eta \left(\vec{\mathbf{s}}_t - \vec{\boldsymbol{\mu}}_{i^*}\right), \tag{6.45}$$
  where η is a small positive learning rate.
  - (iii) *Centroid update of the neighboring nodes (co-winners).* Let the co-winners be the nodes in a certain neighborhood around the winner i^*, denoted by I^*. The node centroid of the co-winners will be additively modified by the following amount:
  $$\Delta \vec{\boldsymbol{\mu}}_k = \eta \Lambda(k, i^*) \left(\vec{\mathbf{s}}_t - \vec{\boldsymbol{\mu}}_{i^*}\right), \tag{6.46}$$
  where $\Lambda(k, i^*)$ is a pre-specified neighborhood sensitivity function.
- **Outer-loop updating: gradual shrinking of learning windows.** In the outer loop, the neighborhood sensitivity function $\Lambda(k, i^*)$ will be gradually reduced.

The *spectral SOM* algorithm in the spectral space requires the computationally costly spectral decomposition $\mathbf{K} = \mathbf{U}^{\mathrm{T}}\boldsymbol{\Lambda}\mathbf{U}$. This motivates the exploration of a (more direct) kernel matrix approach to kernel SOM learning. This subject will be elaborated on in the discussion.

6.6.2 Kernelized SOM learning models

It can be shown that the SOM-learned solutions always observe the learning subspace property (LSP), rendering it possible to characterize the SOM learning model in the empirical space. This leads to the following kernelized (or kernel-trick) SOM learning algorithm.

SOM learning algorithms in empirical space

The flowchart largely follows Figure 5.12, which was designed originally for the conventional SOM learning algorithm. In particular, the process of shrinking the learning window in the outer loop remains exactly the same as before. The inner loop for the kernelized learning contains the following steps.

- For nonvectorial data processing, the conventional winner identification formulation (Eq. (5.23)) must be substituted by the minimization of a vector-free formulation given in Eq. (6.22) that is based on the *proximity metric*:

$$\|\vec{\mu}_k\|^2 - 2R_{tk} \equiv \text{SCN} - 2 \times \text{DCS}. \tag{6.47}$$

  Recall that the abbreviations SCN and DCS mean squared-centroid norm and data–centroid similarity, respectively. By the same token, the updating on the centroid (Eq. (5.24)) is no longer suitable for nonvectorial data and it must be substituted by updating on the SCN and DCS, which are amenable to vector-free formulation.
- Likewise, centroid updating on the co-winners must also be must be substituted by updating on the SCN and DCS of the co-winners. Fortunately, the neighborhood sensitivity functions (Eqs. (5.26), (5.27), and (5.29)) are vector-free and can remain unchanged.

With all the above adjustments, we can derive the following.

ALGORITHM 6.4 (Kernelized SOM learning model) *The kernel-matrix based SOM learning model involves two loops.*

- **Inner loop: centroid updates.** *Every training pattern* $\vec{\mathbf{s}}_t$, $t = 1, \ldots, N$, *is sequentially presented for the following iterative updating process.*
  - *(i) Identification of the winner. The winner is identified as the cluster nearest to* $\vec{\mathbf{s}}_t$*:*

$$i^* = \arg\min_{r \in I^{L_1 \times L_2 \times \ldots \times L_k}} \{\|\vec{\mu}_r\|^2 - 2R_{tr}\}. \tag{6.48}$$

  - *(ii) Update of winner's node vector. The centroid of the* i^**th node (i.e. the winner) will be updated by the following amount:*

$$\begin{aligned}\Delta R_{ji^*} &= \Delta\{\vec{\mathbf{s}}_j^{\mathrm{T}}\vec{\mu}_{i^*}\} = \vec{\mathbf{s}}_j^{\mathrm{T}}\Delta\vec{\mu}_{i^*} \\ &\overset{\text{Eq. (6.45)}}{=} \eta\left(\vec{\mathbf{s}}_j^{\mathrm{T}}\vec{\mathbf{s}}_t - \vec{\mathbf{s}}_j^{\mathrm{T}}\vec{\mu}_{i^*}\right) \\ &= \eta\left(K_{ji^*} - R_{ji^*}\right) \ \forall j = 1, \ldots, N;\end{aligned}$$

  and

$$\begin{aligned}\Delta\|\vec{\mu}_{i*}\|^2 &\overset{\text{Eq. (6.45)}}{=} \|\vec{\mu}_{i^*} + \eta\left(\vec{\mathbf{s}}_t - \vec{\mu}_{i^*}\right)\|^2 - \|\vec{\mu}_{i^*}\|^2 \\ &= 2(\eta - \eta^2)R_{ti^*} + (\eta^2 - 2\eta)\|\vec{\mu}_{i*}\|^2 + \eta^2 K_{tt}^2.\end{aligned}$$

  With a very small learning rate η, *we have*

$$\Delta\|\vec{\mu}_{i*}\|^2 \approx 2\eta\left(R_{ti^*} - \|\vec{\mu}_{i*}\|^2\right). \tag{6.49}$$

(iii) *Centroid update of neighboring nodes (co-winners). The co-winners in the neighborhood $I*$ will be updated by the following amount:*

$$\Delta R_{jk} = \eta \Lambda(k, i^*) \left(K_{ji^*} - R_{ji^*}\right) \ \forall k \in I^*; \tag{6.50}$$

and, by following Eq. (6.49),

$$\Delta \|\vec{\mu}_k\|^2 \approx 2\eta \Lambda(k, i^*) \left(R_{ti^*} - \|\vec{\mu}_{i*}\|^2\right) \ \forall k \in I^*, \tag{6.51}$$

where $\Lambda(k, i^*)$ is a pre-specified neighborhood function.

- **Outer-loop updating: gradual shrinking of learning windows.** *In the outer loop, the effective range of the neighborhood sensitivity function $\Lambda(k, i^*)$ is gradually reduced.*

□

For sparse networks, kernelized SOM learning algorithms can potentially provide a great computational saving.

6.7 Neighbor-joining hierarchical cluster analysis

In addition to the mesh structure adopted by SOM learning, another popular clustering topology is a hierarchical structure featuring recursive subdivision into substructures [111, 252, 292]. A hierarchical tree is also known as a dendrogram. In a tree structure, the distances from the root to all the nodes (i.e. entities) on the same level are all identical. In biological study, this distance may reflect the stage of mutation (either evolution or cancer). More precisely, the length of the edge that connects the ancestral and descendant nodes represents the estimated evolutionary time between them.

The main purpose of constructing a dendrogram is to systematically organize the training dataset so as to facilitate assimilation of the relationship among the samples. In particular, it provides a convenient and effective platform for the purpose of establishing a homologous or evolutionary lineage of the data samples.

6.7.1 Divisive and agglomerative approaches

Hierarchical clustering techniques are often adopted to find a hierarchical (or tree) structure. The techniques fall into two general categories.

- The *divisive approach*, dividing the whole set of training objects into subgroups, see Section 6.7.1.1.
- The *agglomerative approach*, merging subgroups of training objects into supergroups, see Section 6.7.1.2.

6.7.1.1 Divisive hierarchical clustering methods

The divisive algorithm constructs a tree based on a top-down approach. At the beginning, a single node containing all the N elements $\mathcal{X} = \{\mathbf{x}_1, \mathbf{x}_2, \ldots, \mathbf{x}_N\}$ is divided

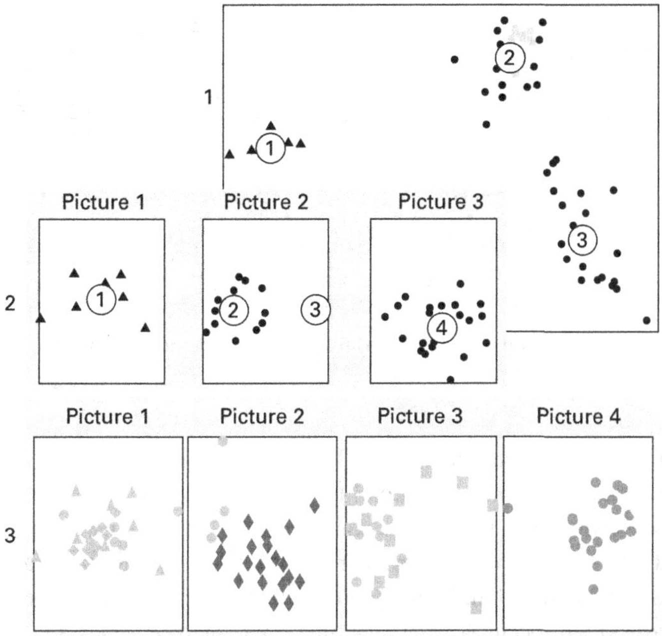

Fig. 6.5. Hierarchical data exploration on the NCI-SRBCT dataset, which contains four tumor subtypes, namely EWS, RMS, BL, and NB.

into two (or more) subgroups, each of which is then further subdivided into more sub-subgroups. Such division will go on until the lowest level units have reached a desired fine granularity.

As an example, VISDA is a software tool for hierarchical cluster discovery in high-dimensional data proposed by Wang *et al.* [290, 291]. In VISDA, a PCA-based K-means clustering algorithm is used to subdivide $\mathcal{X}$ into daughter nodes, which are then recursively subdivided into (grand)daughter nodes, and so on. The tool has successfully been applied to many microarray datasets, including leukemia and NCI-SBRCT datasets [82, 123], to detect previously unrecognized tumor subtypes. Figure 6.5 shows a three-level hierarchy constructed by VISDA to fully explore the four-cluster data structure in the NCI-SRBCT dataset [123].

6.7.1.2 Agglomerative approaches

One conceptually simple approach to the kernel-based neighbor-joining (NJ) hierarchical clustering is to map the training vector in the original space to its intrinsic (or spectral) space first, and then apply an agglomerative method to successively merge subgroups of training objects into supergroups according to their distances in the intrinsic (or spectral) space. The node vector of a merged node may be represented by the corresponding centroid of all the intrinsic (or spectral) training vectors associated with the node.

The agglomerative algorithm initially starts with N (leaf) nodes, each containing a single element of the training dataset: $\mathcal{X} = \{\mathbf{x}_1, \mathbf{x}_2, \ldots, \mathbf{x}_N\}$. Then, two of the nodes are

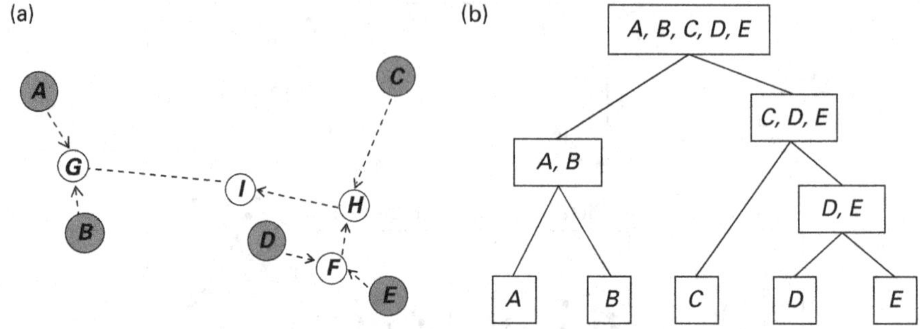

Fig. 6.6. An example of an agglomerative approach: (a) five original nodes and the merged nodes; and (b) the resultant tree structure.

selected to be combined into a new node, This reduces the number of nodes to $N - 1$. The same process can continue until all of the elements have been merged into a single (ancestor) node. Altogether, the process contains $N - 1$ pairwise merging steps.

As an example, let us apply an agglomerative method to cluster five training vectors $(A, B, C, D,$ and $E)$ as shown in Figure 6.6(a). This pairwise merging process (depicted as dashed arrows) will occur $N - 1 = 4$ times. The merged nodes are consecutively $(DE) \rightarrow F$, $(AB) \rightarrow G$, $(C, F) \rightarrow H$, and $(G, H) \rightarrow I$. More precisely, F is represented by the centroid of (DE) and H is the centroid of $(CF) = (CDE)$. The overall NJ algorithm (described below) runs as follows:

$$\begin{aligned}\{A, B, C, D, E\} &\Rightarrow \{A, B, C, F\} \Rightarrow \{G, C, F\} \\ &\Rightarrow \{G, H\} \Rightarrow \{I = (ABCDE)\}.\end{aligned} \tag{6.52}$$

The final tree structure is depicted in Figure 6.6(b).

6.7.2 An NJ method that is based on centroid update

A prominent method that is based on the agglomerative approach is the NJ algorithm. The NJ procedure starts with N nodes, and then two nearest nodes (i.e. with the shortest distance between them, or most similar) are identified. It follows that these two nearest nodes will merge into a single node, thus reducing the total number of nodes by one. Then the remaining $N - 1$ nodes will be further reduced to $N - 2$ nodes. The same process is continued until all the training objects have been merged into one common ancestor node.

For vectorial data, the pairwise (Euclidean) distance is the most popular metric and is easily computable. This leads to the following basic NJ algorithm.

(1) *Initiation.* Given N training data, the NJ algorithm initially starts with N nodes, each characterized as a point in an $\mathbb{R}^M$ space.
(2) *Iterations.* The NJ procedure is to carry out the following *merging and updating* iterative process $N - 1$ times. By this finite procedure, all the nodes will be merged into a single grand-ancestor node.

(i) *Node merger.* Identify the distance-wise nearest pair of the nodes, denoted as node A and node B, with respective centroids $\vec{\mu}_A$ and $\vec{\mu}_B$, and merge them into a new node. Now the total number of nodes is reduced by one.

(ii) *Centroid update.* The merged node will be represented by its new centroid, which can be efficiently updated as follows:

$$\vec{\mu}_{New} = \frac{N_A \vec{\mu}_A + N_B \vec{\mu}_B}{N_A + N_B}. \tag{6.53}$$

where N_A and N_B denote the numbers of patterns in the old node A and node B, respectively.

6.7.3 Kernelized hierarchical clustering algorithm

In order to avoid the cost required for mapping to the new space, a kernel-trick-based NJ clustering algorithm may be adopted. As explained below, explicit computation of the node vectors may be circumvented via the empirical-space approach.

ALGORITHM 6.5 (Kernelized NJ clustering algorithm) *Given N training data, the NJ algorithm initially starts with N nodes, characterized by an $N \times N$ similarity matrix* $\mathbf{S}$.

(i) Node merger. Identify the distance-wise nearest pair of nodes, denoted as node A and node B, and merge them into a new node. Now the total number of nodes is reduced by one.

(ii) Update. Compute the $(N-1) \times (N-1)$ similarity matrix for the new $(N-1)$ nodes.

The NJ procedure is to repeat the above merging and updating iterative process $N-1$ times (meaning that the process is carried out N times in total). The major complexity of the NJ algorithm lies in the iterative updating of the similarity matrix. □

Assume that the similarity matrix $\mathbf{S}$ is positive definite, so the entries of $\mathbf{S}$ can be formally regarded as the inner products of two vectors in a certain well-defined Hilbert space. In this case, the separation of any two objects, represented by their intrinsic vectors (say $\vec{\phi}(\mathbf{x})$ and $\vec{\phi}(\mathbf{y})$) can be derived from their inner products:

$$\|\vec{\phi}(\mathbf{x}) - \vec{\phi}(\mathbf{y})\| = \sqrt{\vec{\phi}(\mathbf{x})^{\mathrm{T}}\vec{\phi}(\mathbf{x}) + \vec{\phi}(\mathbf{y})^{\mathrm{T}}\vec{\phi}(\mathbf{y}) - 2\vec{\phi}(\mathbf{x})^{\mathrm{T}}\vec{\phi}(\mathbf{y})}.$$

Note that, once all the pairwise inner products are known, all the pairwise distances are readily computable, but not vice versa. This implies that the inner product offers richer information than the distance. This property provides a foundation for the kernel trick [64], which claims that the updating rule can be equivalently implemented via a series of operations on inner products – without explicitly computing the node vectors.

Elaborated below are two steps in one iteration of the kernel-trick-based NJ algorithm: (1) *identification and merger of the closest pair of nodes* and (2) *update of data-centroid similarities (DCSs).*

Identification and merger of two closest nodes

Given the training data $\{\vec{\phi}(\mathbf{x}_1), \vec{\phi}(\mathbf{x}_2), \ldots, \vec{\phi}(\mathbf{x}_N)\}$, we first compute the pairwise distance $d(\vec{\phi}(\mathbf{x}_i), \vec{\phi}(\mathbf{x}_j))$ from the similarity matrix $\mathbf{S} = \{S_{ij}\}$:

$$\begin{aligned} d(\vec{\phi}(\mathbf{x}_i), \vec{\phi}(\mathbf{x}_j)) &= \| \vec{\phi}(\mathbf{x}_i) - \vec{\phi}(\mathbf{x}_j) \| \\ &= \sqrt{\vec{\phi}(\mathbf{x}_i)^{\mathrm{T}}\vec{\phi}(\mathbf{x}_i) + \vec{\phi}(\mathbf{x}_j)^{\mathrm{T}}\vec{\phi}(\mathbf{x}_j) - 2\vec{\phi}(\mathbf{x}_i)^{\mathrm{T}}\vec{\phi}(\mathbf{x}_j)} \\ &= \sqrt{S_{ii} + S_{jj} - 2S_{ij}}, \quad \text{for} \quad i = 1, \ldots, N; j = 1, \ldots, N. \end{aligned}$$

Let the pair of closest nodes be denoted as $\{\vec{\alpha}, \vec{\beta}\}$. In the equation, the pair may be identified as

$$\{\vec{\alpha}, \vec{\beta}\} = \arg \min_{\{\vec{\phi}(\mathbf{x}_i), \vec{\phi}(\mathbf{x}_j)\}} d(\vec{\phi}(\mathbf{x}_i), \vec{\phi}(\mathbf{x}_j)).$$

The identified pair will then be merged into one node represented by the new centroid of the merged cluster, denoted by $\vec{\gamma}$:

$$\vec{\gamma} = \frac{N_\alpha}{N_\alpha + N_\beta}\boldsymbol{\alpha} + \frac{N_\beta}{N_\alpha + N_\beta}\boldsymbol{\beta} \tag{6.54}$$

where N_α and N_β are the respective cluster sizes for clusters $\boldsymbol{\alpha}$ and $\boldsymbol{\beta}$. (Although $N_\alpha = 1$ and $N_\beta = 1$ in the very first iteration, the sizes grow with the number of iterations.)

Update of the DCS

Without loss of generality, we shall assume that the last two objects happen to be the closest pair, i.e. $\boldsymbol{\alpha} = \vec{\phi}(\mathbf{x}_{N-1})$ and $\boldsymbol{\beta} = \vec{\phi}(\mathbf{x}_N)$. (For example, samples D and E are the first pair to be merged in the example shown in Figure 6.6.) The merged node $\vec{\gamma}$ is represented by

$$\vec{\gamma} = \frac{N_\alpha}{N_\alpha + N_\beta}\vec{\phi}(\mathbf{x}_{N-1}) + \frac{N_\beta}{N_\alpha + N_\beta}\vec{\tilde{\phi}}(\mathbf{x}_N). \tag{6.55}$$

Let the new $(N-1)$ vectors be denoted by $\vec{\tilde{\phi}}(\mathbf{x}_i), i = 1, 2, \ldots, N-1$. Then

$$\vec{\tilde{\phi}}(\mathbf{x}_i) = \begin{cases} \vec{\phi}(\mathbf{x}_i) & \text{if} \quad i = 1, 2, \ldots, N-2 \\ \vec{\gamma} & \text{if} \quad i = N-1. \end{cases} \tag{6.56}$$

Now let us discuss the computation of the $(N-1) \times (N-1)$ similarity matrix $\tilde{\mathbf{S}} = \{\tilde{S}_{ij}\}$, where

$$\tilde{S}_{ij} = \vec{\tilde{\phi}}(\mathbf{x}_i)^{\mathrm{T}}\vec{\phi}(\mathbf{x}_j), \ i = 1, \ldots, N-1; \ j = 1, \ldots, N-1.$$

Fortunately, the first $(N-2) \times (N-2)$ minor of $\tilde{\mathbf{S}}$ needs no updating since it remains exactly the same as the first $(N-2) \times (N-2)$ minor of $\mathbf{S}$. Namely,

$$\tilde{S}_{i,j} = S_{ij}, \ i = 1, \ldots, N-2; \ j = 1, \ldots, N-2. \tag{6.57}$$

The merged node is $\vec{\tilde{\phi}}(\mathbf{x}_{N-1}) = \vec{\gamma}$, which is in turn merely a weighted average of the two old nodes $\{\vec{\phi}(\mathbf{x}_{N-1}), \vec{\phi}(\mathbf{x}_N)\}$, see Eq. (6.55). This leads to a similar updating formulation for the DCS:

$$\begin{aligned}\tilde{S}_{i,N-1} &= \vec{\tilde{\phi}}(\mathbf{x}_i)^{\mathrm{T}}\vec{\tilde{\phi}}(\mathbf{x}_{N-1}) \\ &= \frac{N_\alpha}{N_\alpha+N_\beta}\vec{\tilde{\phi}}(\mathbf{x}_i)^{\mathrm{T}}\vec{\phi}(\mathbf{x}_{N-1}) + \frac{N_\beta}{N_\alpha+N_\beta}\vec{\tilde{\phi}}(\mathbf{x}_i)^{\mathrm{T}}\vec{\phi}(\mathbf{x}_N),\ \forall i.\end{aligned}$$

Considering $i = 1, \ldots, N-2$,

$$\tilde{S}_{i,N-1} = \frac{N_\alpha}{N_\alpha+N_\beta}S_{i,N-1} + \frac{N_\beta}{N_\alpha+N_\beta}S_{i,N},\ i = 1,\ldots,N-2. \tag{6.58}$$

In addition, the self-product of the newly created node $\vec{\tilde{\phi}}(\mathbf{x}_{N-1})$ can be computed as

$$\begin{aligned}\tilde{S}_{N-1,N-1} &= \vec{\tilde{\phi}}(\mathbf{x}_{N-1})^{\mathrm{T}}\vec{\tilde{\phi}}(\mathbf{x}_{N-1}) \\ &= \begin{bmatrix} N_\alpha/(N_\alpha+N_\beta) \\ N_\beta/(N_\alpha+N_\beta)\end{bmatrix} \\ &\quad \times \begin{bmatrix} \vec{\phi}(\mathbf{x}_{N-1})^{\mathrm{T}}\vec{\phi}(\mathbf{x}_{N-1}) & \vec{\phi}(\mathbf{x}_{N-1})^{\mathrm{T}}\vec{\phi}(\mathbf{x}_N) \\ \vec{\phi}(\mathbf{x}_N)^{\mathrm{T}}\vec{\phi}(\mathbf{x}_{N-1}) & \vec{\phi}(\mathbf{x}_N)^{\mathrm{T}}\vec{\phi}(\mathbf{x}_N)\end{bmatrix} \\ &= \begin{bmatrix} N_\alpha/(N_\alpha+N_\beta) \\ N_\beta/(N_\alpha+N_\beta)\end{bmatrix}\begin{bmatrix} S_{N-1,N-1} & S_{N-1,N} \\ S_{N,N-1} & S_{N,N}\end{bmatrix}\end{aligned} \tag{6.59}$$

By Eqs. (6.57)–(6.59), we have by now completed the updating of the new $(N-1) \times (N-1)$ similarity matrix $\tilde{\mathbf{S}}$ via the so-called kernel trick. It is important to note that the entire process does not involve any explicit derivation of the new centroid given in Eq. (6.54). Moreover, the weighted-averaging formula will be adopted throughout the remaining updating processes, with $\{\boldsymbol{\alpha}, \boldsymbol{\beta}, \vec{\gamma}, N_\alpha, N_\beta\}$ properly redefined for the specific iteration. We shall omit the detail here, instead we use a numerical example to illustrate the kernel-trick iterations (Figure 6.7).

Example 6.3 (NJ clustering of objects with a positive-definite similarity matrix) *Assume that there are five vectorial objects (A, B, C, D, E) with a positive-definite similarity matrix (kernel matrix):*

$$\mathbf{S} = \begin{bmatrix} S_{AA} & S_{AB} & S_{AC} & S_{AD} & S_{AE} \\ S_{BA} & S_{BB} & S_{BC} & S_{BD} & S_{BE} \\ S_{CA} & S_{CB} & S_{CC} & S_{CD} & S_{CE} \\ S_{DA} & S_{DB} & S_{DC} & S_{DD} & S_{DE} \\ S_{EA} & S_{EB} & S_{EC} & S_{ED} & S_{EE}\end{bmatrix} = \begin{bmatrix} 1.0 & 0.6 & 0.2 & 0.2 & 0.4 \\ 0.6 & 1.0 & 0.3 & 0.3 & 0.4 \\ 0.2 & 0.3 & 1.0 & 0.5 & 0.6 \\ 0.2 & 0.3 & 0.5 & 1.0 & 0.8 \\ 0.4 & 0.4 & 0.6 & 0.8 & 1.0\end{bmatrix}. \tag{6.60}$$

First merger

Note that the pairwise similarity $S_{DE} = 0.8$ is the highest and thus the corresponding pairwise distance $d_{DE} = \sqrt{1.0 + 1.0 - 2 \times 0.8}$ is the shortest. So (DE) will be merged

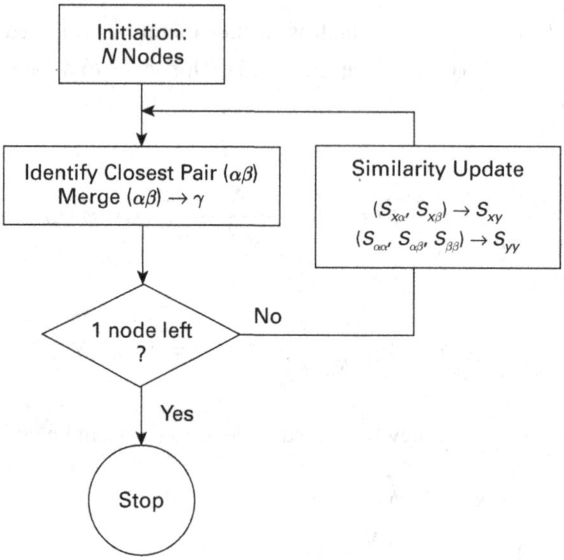

Fig. 6.7. The flowchart of the NJ hierarchical clustering algorithm.

into a new node: (DE) → F. In this case, both $\boldsymbol{\alpha} = D$ *and* $\boldsymbol{\beta} = E$ *contain only one member, i.e.* $N_\alpha = N_\beta = 1$.

Now we are down to four nodes (three old and one new). The new similarity matrix can be constructed by using Eqs. (6.57)–(6.59).

According to Eq. (6.58),

$$S_{AF} = \vec{\phi}(A)^T \vec{\phi}(F) = \frac{\vec{\phi}(A)^T \vec{\phi}(D) + \vec{\phi}(A)^T \vec{\phi}(E)}{2}$$
$$= \frac{S_{AD} + S_{AE}}{2} = \frac{0.2 + 0.4}{2} = 0.3. \tag{6.61}$$

Likewise, $S_{BF} = (S_{BD} + S_{BE})/2 = (0.3 + 0.4)/2 = 0.35$ *and* $S_{CF} = (S_{CD} + S_{CE})/2 = (0.1 + 0.6)/2 = 0.35$. *Finally, using Eq. (6.59),*

$$s_{FF} = \begin{bmatrix} 0.5 & 0.5 \end{bmatrix} \begin{bmatrix} S_{DD} & S_{DE} \\ S_{ED} & S_{EE} \end{bmatrix} \begin{bmatrix} 0.5 \\ 0.5 \end{bmatrix} = 0.9.$$

This leads to the following (4 × 4) similarity matrix ready for the next iteration:

$$\begin{bmatrix} S_{AA} & S_{AB} & S_{AC} & S_{AF} \\ S_{BA} & S_{BB} & S_{BC} & S_{BF} \\ S_{CA} & S_{CB} & S_{CC} & S_{CF} \\ S_{FA} & S_{FB} & S_{FC} & S_{FF} \end{bmatrix} = \begin{bmatrix} 1.0 & 0.6 & 0.2 & 0.3 \\ 0.6 & 1.0 & 0.3 & 0.35 \\ 0.2 & 0.3 & 1.0 & 0.35 \\ 0.3 & 0.35 & 0.35 & 0.9 \end{bmatrix}.$$

Second merger

To determine the next pair to merge, the pairwise distances among (A, B, C, F) *will be computed. The pair AB is then identified to be the closest and will be merged. The merger is denoted as (AB) → G. (In this case,* $\boldsymbol{\alpha} = A$, $\boldsymbol{\beta} = B$, *and* $N_\alpha = N_\beta = 1$.*)*

Now we are down to three nodes (G, C, F) and their similarity matrix can be derived as (details omitted)

$$\begin{bmatrix} S_{GG} & S_{GC} & S_{GF} \\ S_{CG} & S_{CC} & S_{CF} \\ S_{FG} & S_{FC} & S_{FF} \end{bmatrix} = \begin{bmatrix} 0.8 & 0.25 & 0.325 \\ 0.25 & 1.00 & 0.35 \\ 0.325 & 0.35 & 0.9 \end{bmatrix}.$$

Third merger

At this stage, (CF) is identified to be the closet pair to be merged: $(CF) \rightarrow H$. The similarity matrix of the two remaining nodes (G, H) can be derived as follows. Note that $\boldsymbol{\alpha} = C$ contains one member while $\boldsymbol{\beta} = F$ has two members, i.e. $N_\alpha = 1$ and $N_\beta = 2$. Since H is weighted average of C and F, with weights $\frac{1}{3}$ and $\frac{2}{3}$, respectively, it follows that

$$S_{GH} = \frac{1}{3} S_{GC} + \frac{2}{3} S_{GF} = 0.3 \tag{6.62}$$

and that

$$S_{HH} = \begin{bmatrix} \frac{1}{3} & \frac{2}{3} \end{bmatrix} \begin{bmatrix} S_{CC} & S_{CF} \\ S_{FC} & S_{FF} \end{bmatrix} \begin{bmatrix} \frac{1}{3} \\ \frac{2}{3} \end{bmatrix} = \frac{2}{3}.$$

This results in the following (2×2) similarity matrix:

$$\begin{bmatrix} S_{GG} & S_{GH} \\ S_{HG} & S_{HH} \end{bmatrix} = \begin{bmatrix} 0.8 & 0.3 \\ 0.3 & 0.667 \end{bmatrix}.$$

Fourth merger

Using Eq. (6.59), $N_\alpha = 2$ and $N_\beta = 3$,

$$S_{II} = \begin{bmatrix} \frac{2}{5} & \frac{3}{5} \end{bmatrix} \begin{bmatrix} 0.8 & 0.3 \\ 0.3 & 0.667 \end{bmatrix} \begin{bmatrix} \frac{2}{5} \\ \frac{3}{5} \end{bmatrix} = 0.512.$$

Summary

This pairwise merging process will occur $N - 1 = 4$ times. The overall NJ algorithm runs as follows:

$$\{A, B, C, D, E\} \Rightarrow \{A, B, C, F\} \Rightarrow \{G, C, F\} \\ \Rightarrow \{G, H\} \Rightarrow \{I = (ABCDE)\}, \tag{6.63}$$

with the corresponding similarity matrices:

$$\mathbf{S} \Rightarrow \begin{bmatrix} 1.0 & 0.6 & 0.2 & 0.3 \\ 0.6 & 1.0 & 0.3 & 0.35 \\ 0.2 & 0.3 & 1.0 & 0.35 \\ 0.3 & 0.35 & 0.35 & 0.9 \end{bmatrix} \Rightarrow \begin{bmatrix} 0.8 & 0.25 & 0.325 \\ 0.25 & 1.00 & 0.35 \\ 0.325 & 0.35 & 0.9 \end{bmatrix} \\ \Rightarrow \begin{bmatrix} 0.8 & 0.3 \\ 0.3 & 0.667 \end{bmatrix} \Rightarrow \begin{bmatrix} 0.512 \end{bmatrix}. \tag{6.64}$$

The final tree clustering structure is depicted in Figure 6.6(b). □

The role of Mercer's condition

Even if the original similarity matrix is not positive semi-definite, the NJ algorithm can still proceed and terminate after a finite number of steps. The slight inconvenience is that it may sometimes encounter negative values of the DCS and, in that case, the notion of a closest pair may be subject to a different interpretation. In short, for a simple theoretical justification and an ambiguity-free implementation of the NJ algorithm, the adoption of a spectral-shift conversion method (making the similarity matrix positive semi-definite) is highly recommended.

Pros and cons of the NJ algorithm

The pros and cons of the NJ algorithm, compared with K-means and SOM, are as follows.

(i) The NJ algorithm enjoys several advantages over K-means and SOM. (1) Because NJ is a finite algorithm, it is computationally much simpler than K-means, especially for large datasets. (2) There is no concern regarding the issue of convergence. (3) The solution of the NJ clustering algorithm is generically unique, obviating the need for multiple trials.

(ii) On the other hand, the downside of the NJ clustering method lies in the fact that there exists no formal criterion to calibrate the goodness of the clustering results. Its good performance has to be justified by means of independently obtained supporting evidence, such as biological validation or evolutionary traits.

6.7.4 Case studies: hierarchical clustering of microarray data

Hierarchical clustering analysis has been applied to a broad spectrum of genomic applications. It plays an important role in biological taxonomic studies, insofar as it establishes the tree-structural relationship among various organisms, which in turn facilitates interpretation of unknown objects. A phylogenetic tree or evolutionary tree is often adopted to show the evolutionary lineages among various biological entities and to infer the evolutionary history of an organism. In epidemiology, it is instrumental in discovering infectious diseases and studying the genetic roots of a defect or illness.

Gene cluster discovery

The cluster discovery tool can be applied to form gene groups from the expression data. It is instrumental for predicting functions of novel genes, since genetically similar genes/proteins often share a common evolutionary origin. Hierarchical clustering analysis has been applied to both time-course (e.g. yeast) and independent (e.g. lymphoma) microarray experiments. For example, cell cycle data were collected for the budding yeast *Saccharomyces cerevisiae*, and the yeast genes were assembled into a hierarchical tree (or dendrogram) by Eisen *et al.* [61]. The clustered genes in the dendrogram were found to have known similar function and demonstrated a strong tendency to share common roles in cellular processes. Even though the tree structure does not have a clearly defined clustering criterion, like K-means or SOM, it may still reveal an intriguing cluster structure. For example, the NJ hierarchical clustering algorithm was applied to the

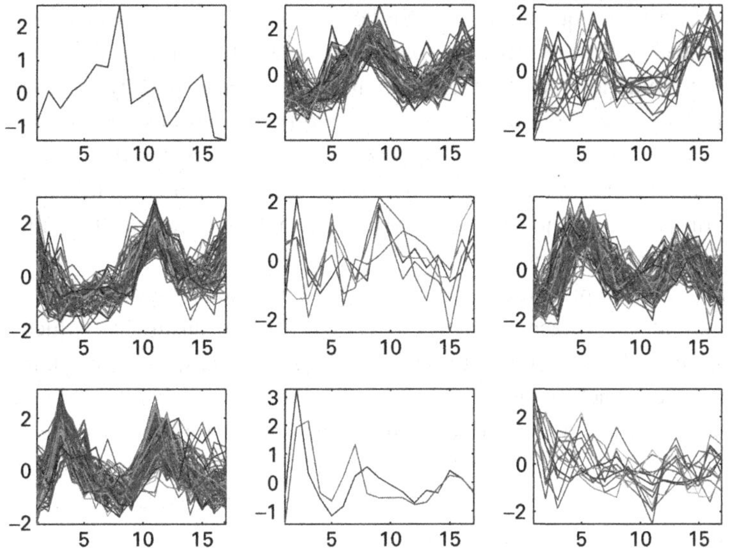

Fig. 6.8. With a defined boundary between clusters, a tree can be used to reveal the underlying cluster structure. Shown here is hierarchical clustering of the gene profiles of Tamayo *et al.*'s [263] yeast cell cycle data (normalized). (The maximum number of clusters was set to 9.)

421 normalized gene profiles extracted from Tamayo *et al.*'s yeast dataset [263]. The result is shown in Figure 6.8. Nine gene clusters are identified, with the profiles of each cluster displayed.

Tissue clustering analysis

Sørlie *et al.* [255] performed hierarchical clustering on 115 malignant breast tumors, each characterized by the expression level of 534 genes. The clustering results suggest that there exist several distinctive clusters of breast tumors: one basal-like, one ERBB2-overexpressing, two luminal-like, and one normal breast-tissue-like.

6.8 Summary

This chapter starts with the description of a basic kernel K-means learning model. In this case, the original vectors are first mapped to new represention in the intrinsic vector space $\mathcal{H}$ and then the mapped vectors will subsequently be partitioned by means of the conventional K-means. This approach, while conceptually straightforward, would not apply to two important situations: (1) when a Gaussian kernel is applied to vectorial data analysis; and (2) when the application is meant for nonvectorial data analysis. The reason in the former case is due to the infinite intrinsic degree J, while what counts against its validity in the latter is the fact that the original vector space is undefinable. To combat this problem, a simple solution presents itself if the LSP condition may be validated.

According to Theorem 1.1, the LSP condition holds for K-means, so it can be naturally extended to its kernel-matrix-based variant. Equation (1.20) implies that the problem formulation may be fully and uniquely characterized by the kernel matrix $\mathbf{K}$ associated with the given set of training vectors. Theorem 6.1 establishes the equivalence between the intrinsic-space-based versus the kernel-matrix-based K-means algorithms. In short, the original vector-based clustering criterion is converted to a vector-free clustering criterion. Consequently, under such a formulation, there will be no need to have an explicitly defined vector space.

An important implication is that the kernel-matrix learning models may fill the void where the intrinsic-space learning models are deemed unsuitable, which includes all the problems related to nonvectorial data analysis. There is, however, a major concern regarding the kernel methods for nonvectorial data analysis: a kernel matrix (or similarity matrix) formed from a nonvectorial dataset need not be positive semi-definite. As formally stated in Theorem 6.2, the positive semi-definiteness of the kernel matrix will be critical for assurance of its numerical performance, especially regarding the monotonic convergence of kernel K-means.

In order to assure a safe numerical implementation of kernel K-means learning models, the kernel matrix must be properly converted so as to meet the convergence condition. There are two prominent approaches.

(i) **The spectral-space approach.** The orthogonal basis vectors used in spectral space are amenable to dimension-reduction for achieving possible computational saving in kernel K-means algorithms. In addition, by dropping the components associated with the eigenvalues which are negative and/or have small positive values, a low-rank and positive semi-definite similarity matrix may be formed. However, there is a tradeoff between the dimension reduction and the accuracy. In order to better assess the best tradeoff, Theorem 6.3 provides a closed-form analysis showing how the approximation error may change with respect to the reduced dimension.

(ii) **The kernel-trick approach.** The kernelized learning model employing the kernel matrix, also known as the *kernel trick*, is very amenable to nonvectorial data analysis. In order to assure the convergence condition, in this case, the kernel matrix may be converted to an eligible kernel matrix by a spectral-shift operation. Theorem 6.4 establishes the invariance of the optimal solution before and after the spectral shift. The kernel trick has a promising application example for network segmentation for social network data analysis, where the preservation of sparsity is vital for computational savings. Algorithm 6.3 presents a fast and recursive kernel-matrix-based learning algorithm, i.e. the kernel trick, which may speed up the learning process by several orders of magnitude.

Self-organizing map (SOM) is by inspection an LSP-based learning model and, consequently, kernelized SOM learning models can be derived according to the typical conversion formula. Algorithm 6.4 describes one such kernelized SOM learning learning model. For completeness, another prominent kernel-matrix-based method, namely the *neighbor-joining* (NJ) learning model, is presented in Algorithm 6.5.

6.9 Problems

Problem 6.1 *For linear kernels, show that the three proposed K-means criteria, given in Eqs. (6.6)–(6.8), are mathematically equivalent.*

Problem 6.2 *Show that the optimization criterion proposed for kernel K-means may be reformulated as a trace-maximization problem. Work out the trace-based optimization formulation for the ratio-association and ratio-cut problems. (See Ref. [48].)*

Problem 6.3 (Different criteria for kernel K-means) *Consider the following training dataset:*

$$\mathbf{x}_1 = \begin{bmatrix} 0 \\ 0 \end{bmatrix}, \quad \mathbf{x}_2 = \begin{bmatrix} 1 \\ 0 \end{bmatrix}, \quad \mathbf{x}_3 = \begin{bmatrix} 0 \\ 2 \end{bmatrix}, \quad \mathbf{x}_4 = \begin{bmatrix} -1 \\ -1 \end{bmatrix},$$

and assume that a second-order polynomial kernel is adopted.

(a) *Map the four training vectors to the kernel-induced intrinsic space. Apply kernel K-means to find $K = 2$ optimal clusters.*

(b) *Repeat the same problem, but now with the original vectors mapped to the kernel-induced spectral space.*

(c) *Compare the two K-means results. Can you justify the theoretical equivalence between the two approaches. (Theoretically, they should lead to an identical solution, given the same initial condition.)*

Problem 6.4 (Dimension-reduced clustering) *Consider the following training dataset:*

$$\begin{bmatrix} 0 \\ 0 \end{bmatrix}, \begin{bmatrix} 1 \\ 0 \end{bmatrix}, \begin{bmatrix} 1 \\ 1 \end{bmatrix}, \begin{bmatrix} -1 \\ -1 \end{bmatrix}, \begin{bmatrix} 0 \\ 2 \end{bmatrix}, \begin{bmatrix} 2 \\ 2 \end{bmatrix}.$$

(a) *For the second-order polynomial kernel $K(\mathbf{x}, \mathbf{y}) = 1 + (\mathbf{x} \cdot \mathbf{y})^2$, the intrinsic degree is $J = 6$. Apply kernel K-means to find an optimal two-cluster partition based on the six-dimensional intrinsic vectors.*

(b) *Use KPCA to reduce the dimension from $J = 6$ to $m = 3$. Apply kernel K-means to the reduced-dimensional vectors. Compare the result with the full-dimensional case by computing their respective cost functions. Verify the bound on the discrepancy prescribed by Eq. (6.19).*

Problem 6.5 (Network segmentation) *An eight-node network is described by the following adjacency matrix:*

$$\mathbf{A} = \begin{bmatrix} 1 & 1 & 1 & 1 & 0 & 0 & 0 & 0 \\ 1 & 1 & 1 & 0 & 0 & 0 & 0 & 1 \\ 1 & 1 & 1 & 1 & 1 & 0 & 0 & 0 \\ 1 & 0 & 1 & 1 & 1 & 0 & 0 & 0 \\ 0 & 0 & 1 & 1 & 1 & 1 & 1 & 1 \\ 0 & 0 & 0 & 0 & 1 & 1 & 0 & 0 \\ 0 & 0 & 0 & 0 & 1 & 0 & 1 & 1 \\ 0 & 1 & 0 & 0 & 1 & 0 & 1 & 1 \end{bmatrix}. \tag{6.65}$$

(a) *Find the optimal graph partitioning using the ratio-association criterion, for* $K = 2$ *and* $K = 3$.

(b) *Find the optimal graph partitioning using the ratio-cut criterion, for* $K = 2$ *and* $K = 3$.

Problem 6.6 (Network segmentation via SOM or NJ) *Consider the eight nodes associated with the adjacency matrix given in Problem 6.5.*

(a) *Apply the kernel-matrix-based SOM algorithm to map the eight nodes onto a* 2×2 *mesh.*

(b) *Apply the NJ clustering algorithm to hierarchically cluster the eight nodes.*

Problem 6.7 (Link prediction) *An eight-node social network is described by the following incompletely specified adjacency matrix:*

$$\mathbf{A} = \begin{bmatrix} 1 & 1 & 1 & 1 & - & - & 0 & 0 \\ 1 & 1 & 1 & 0 & 0 & 0 & 0 & 0 \\ 1 & 1 & 1 & 1 & 1 & 0 & 0 & 0 \\ 1 & 0 & 1 & 1 & 1 & 0 & 0 & 0 \\ - & 0 & 1 & 1 & 1 & 1 & 1 & 1 \\ - & 0 & 0 & 0 & 1 & 1 & 0 & 0 \\ 0 & 0 & 0 & 0 & 1 & 0 & 1 & 1 \\ 0 & 0 & 0 & 0 & 1 & 0 & 1 & 1 \end{bmatrix},$$

where "1" denotes a "known link" and "–" an indicates "unknown" link.

(a) *Suppose that it is known that the first node is connected either to the fourth node or to the fifth node, but not to both. Which of the two links is more likely and why?*

(b) *Suppose that it is known that the first node may be connected to one or both of the fourth and fifth nodes or to neither of them. What is the most likely scenario and why?*

Problem 6.8 (Kernelized SOM learning models with consideration of sparsity) *Algorithm 6.4 for SOM learning fails to consider on the network sparsity. Is it possible to develop a sparsity-driven SOM learning model for sparse networks?*

Hint: *Apply the same idea as in Algorithm 6.3.*

Problem 6.9 *Consider the situation of the neighborhood sensitivity function* $\Lambda(k, i^*)$ *adopted in the kernelized SOM model described by Algorithm 6.4 if the sensitivity is characterized as a function of node vectors, e.g.*

$$\Lambda(k, i^*) = \exp\left\{-\frac{||\vec{\mu}_k - \vec{\mu}_{i^*}||^2}{r}\right\}. \tag{6.66}$$

Derive a vector-free formula as a substitute for Eq. (6.66) so that the learning model may be rendered amenable to nonvectorial data analysis.

Problem 6.10 (Kernel-matrix-based NJ learning model) *You are given five samples* $\{A, B, C, D, E\}$ *with the following (positive-definite) similarity matrix:*

$$\mathbf{S} = \begin{bmatrix} 1 & 0.4 & 0.2 & 0.1 & 0 \\ 0.4 & 1 & 0.6 & 0.3 & 0.2 \\ 0.2 & 0.6 & 1 & 0.2 & 0.1 \\ 0.1 & 0.3 & 0.2 & 1 & 0.5 \\ 0 & 0.2 & 0.1 & 0.5 & 1 \end{bmatrix}.$$

Build a hierarchical tree structure via the kernelized NJ approach.

Problem 6.11 (MATLAB simulation: reduced-dimension K-means) *Download from http://www.genome.wi.mit.edu/mpr and create a* 7192×72 *microarray data matrix. Assuming* $K = 3$*, what is the minimum dimension* m *guaranteeing that the clustering discrepancy (Eq. (6.19)) will remain within 5%, i.e.* $K\lambda_{m+1}/(\sum_{i=1}^{M} \lambda_i) \leq 5\%$.

Problem 6.12 (MATLAB simulation: clustering of expression data) *By downloading from http://www.genome.wi.mit.edu/mpr, create a* 7192×72 *microarray data matrix.*

(a) *Partition the genes via the NJ algorithm.*
(b) *Partition the samples by the NJ algorithm.*

Problem 6.13 (MATLAB simulation: social network) *The dataset for Zachary's karate club describes the social acclivities involving 34 members of a university social network. Download the dataset from the site http://www-personal.umich.edu/mejn/netdata/ and create a* 34×34 *adjacency matrix.*

(a) *Partition the dataset by applying the recursive kernelized K-means (Algorithm 6.3).*
(b) *Compare the derived clustering results with the following previously reported partition:*

cluster I: 1, 2, 3, 4, 5, 6, 7, 8, 9, 11, 12, 13, 14, 17, 18, 20, and 22;
cluster II: 10, 15, 16, 19, 21, 23, 24, 25, 26, 27, 28, 29, 30, 31, 32, 33, and 34.

Problem 6.14 (Kernel approach to incomplete data analysis) *This problem shows that kernel methods may be applicable to incomplete data analysis (IDA), where some entries of the data matrix are unknown. Namely, the data matrix is formed from "partial vectors" and the missing entries may vary from one column to another.*

(a) *Suppose first that the data matrix is fully specified, i.e. there are no missing data. Show that the following normalized inner-product*

$$K(\mathbf{x}, \mathbf{y}) = \frac{\mathbf{x}^T \mathbf{y}}{||\mathbf{x}||^2 \; ||\mathbf{y}||^2}$$

is a Mercer kernel function.

(b) *With missing data, the similarity function of two partial vectors may be redefined as the normalized inner-product based exclusively on the features found in both partial vectors. Show that, the Mercer condition may fail in this case. Consequently, it is* *essential to first convert the similarity matrix into a positive semi-definite matrix (cf. Section 6.3.3.2) before applying a kernel method.*

(c) *Modify the data matrix in Problem 6.11 by randomly removing 1% of its data entries (i.e. making them unknown) and then conduct unsupervised clustering analysis via the kernel trick, e.g. kernelized K-means or kernelized SOM.*

(d) *Show that the same kernel approach may be likewise extended to supervised learning applications.*

Part IV

Kernel ridge regressors and variants

This part contains three chapters, covering learning models closely related to the kernel ridge regressor (KRR).

(i) Chapter 7 discusses applications of the kernel ridge regressor (KRR) to regularization and approximation problems.
(ii) Chapter 8 covers a broad spectrum of conventional linear classification techniques, all related to ridge regression.
(iii) Chapter 9 extends the linear classification to kernel methods for nonlinear classifiers that are closely related to the kernel ridge regressor (KRR).

Chapter 7 discusses the role of ridge regression analysis in regularization problems. The optimization formulation for the kernel ridge regressor (KRR), in the intrinsic space, obviously satisfies the LSP condition in Theorem 1.1, implying the existence of a kernelized KRR learning model, see Algorithm 7.1.

If a Gaussian RBF kernel is adopted, the KRR learning model is intimately related to several prominent regularization models:

(i) the RBF approximation networks devised by Poggio and Girosi [207];
(ii) Nadaraya–Watson regression estimators [191, 293]; and
(iii) RBF-based back-propagation neural networks [198, 226, 294].

The chapter also addresses the role of the multi-kernel formulation in regression/classification problems. It shows that, if the LSP condition is satisfied, then some multi-kernel problems effectively warant a mono-kernel solution.

Chapter 8 covers a family of linear classifiers. The basic linear regression analysis leads to the classical least-squares-error (LSE) classifiers, see Algorithm 8.1. The derivation of Fisher's conventional linear discriminant analysis is based on finding the best projection direction which can maximize the so-called signal-to-noise ratio; see Algorithm 8.2. By shifting the focus onto the ratio between the so-called "signal" and "signal plus noise," a modified Fisher discriminant analysis (FDA) can be derived; see Algorithm 8.3. The two variants of FDA are equivalent. Theorem 8.1 further establishes the equivalence between the LSE learning model and two FDA learning models.

The robustness of the learned models has always been a central issue in the field of machine learning and statistics [105, 106]. A practical way to validate the robustness of a classifier is to test its resilience against input measurement errors. There are two learning models intended to make the learned regressors/classifiers resilient with respect to input measurement noise, also known as errors in variables [86, 233]. One model is to incorporate a ridge penalty into the LSE cost function, leading to the *ridge regressor* (RR). Another approach is to artificially perturb the training vectors by adding uncorrelated noise before conducting the discriminant analysis, leading to the so-called *perturbational discriminant analysis* (PDA).

Although the RR and PDA stem from very different roots, they are shown to be mathematically equivalent in Theorem 8.2. Algorithm 8.4 describes a scatter-matrix-based RR/PDA learning model (in the original space). Since the RR is LSP-based, the kernelized learning models (in the empirical space) can be derived; see Algorithm 8.5.

Chapter 9 extends the conventional linear classification to kernel-based nonlinear classification. The mathematical equivalence between *kernel ridge regression* (KRR) and nonlinear PDA is established. Moreover, kernelized KRR learning models can again be derived; see Algorithm 9.1.

KPCA and kernel-based spectral space prove useful for analytical assessment of the robustness of KRR classifiers. It can be shown that ridge regularization tends to redistribute the weight so as to suppress more of the weaker (i.e. more sensitive) components, thus, relatively speaking, enhancing the stronger (i.e. more resilient) components. Consequently, the regularization can effectively alleviate over-fitting problems, thus improving the generalization capability of the learned models.

According to KRR's WEC, there is a linear relationship between the error and weight, implying that the greater the error the higher the weight. This causes grave concern regarding the role of the training vectors (named anti-support vectors) located at the two extreme ends of the KRR WEC. More precisely, the anti-support vectors are potentially detrimental since they are assigned excessive voting weights in the decision rule. This problem is rectified by the somewhat *ad hoc* pruned-PDA (PPDA) algorithm described in Algorithm 9.2, where the anti-support vectors are removed from the future learning process so as to circumvent their detrimental effect and improve the performance.

Chapter 9 also extends the binary classification formulation to multi-class, and, moreover, multi-label classification formulations. Finally, it explores several trace-norm optimization formulations for subspace projection designed for class discrimination. DCA and SODA are presented, both of them may be viewed as hybrid learning models of PCA and FDA.

7 Kernel-based regression and regularization analysis

7.1 Introduction

In statistical regression analysis, the input is often represented as an *independent* variable $\mathbf{x}$, while the output is taken as a *dependent* variable y modeled by a nonlinear regression function of the input $\mathbf{x}$, corrupted by an additive noise ε. More precisely,

$$y = h(\mathbf{x}) + \varepsilon.$$

The objective of regression analysis is to find the optimal estimation of the *dependent* variable y from $\mathbf{x}$. The non-parametric MMSE estimator can be expressed in terms of the conditional probability distribution of y given $\mathbf{x}$, i.e.

$$\hat{h}(\mathbf{x}) = E[y|\mathbf{x}] = \int y p_{y|\mathbf{x}}(y|\mathbf{x}) dy$$

provides an optimal solution that minimizes the MSE

$$E[\|y - \hat{h}(\tilde{\mathbf{x}})\|^2].$$

It is important to note that this statistical formulation will require knowledge of the joint distribution functions of the input/output variables. In practice, unfortunately, such knowledge is rarely to be had. In real-world applications of supervised machine learning, what is made available is often merely a finite training dataset of the input $\mathbf{x}$ and output y, from which robust estimators/regressors are to be learned.

Given a finite training dataset, ridge regression (RR) is a popular technique that is useful for enhancing the robustness of linear regressors. The objective of this chapter is to extend RR to the kernel ridge regressor (KRR). Since KRR meets the LSP condition prescribed in Theorem 1.1, it facilitates the development of a kernel-matrix-based method for KRR. With the Gaussian kernels adopted, the KRR method bears a great similarity to some prominent techniques that are based on approximation theory, a windows approach, or neural networks.

The applications of kernel-based methods for regression and regularization basically fall into two categories.

- *Regression/approximation:* Starting from the classic theory on linear prediction and system identification, e.g. [2, 94, 120, 151, 158, 210, 232], kernel methods facilitate systematically identifying optimal nonlinear functions of the input vector $\mathbf{x}$ to best predict the likely response of a system to the input. This will be the subject of the current chapter.

- *Classification:* Kernel-based supervised learning models can be developed for training optimal decision boundaries to separate different classes of data samples. This subject will be treated in full in Chapter 9.

This chapter will address the following topics regarding kernel-based regularization techniques.

- Section 7.2 studies several linear regularization methods that are based on the training dataset, including the classical least-squares-error (LSE) and RR approaches.
- Section 7.3 extends the linear regression analysis to cases with nonlinear kernels. Formulations both in the intrinsic and in the empirical vector spaces will be developed. Once the nonlinear kernel has been specified, the intrinsic representation is already fully pre-specified, and only the parameters of the upper (and linear) network need to be learned. This basically covers the complete processes involved in the KRR learning model in the intrinsic space. Finally, since KRR meets the LSP condition, the intrinsic formulation can be converted into one with empirical representation.
- Section 7.4 reviews several regularization or estimation models using Gaussian RBF kernel functions, including
  (i) the RBF approximation networks devised by Poggio and Girosi [207];
  (ii) Nadaraya–Watson regression estimators [191, 293]; and
  (iii) RBF-based back-propagation neural networks [198, 226, 294].
  Section 7.4 also highlights the intimate relationships between these models and the RBF-based KRR learning model.
- Section 7.5 explores the flexibility and limitations of the adoption of multiple kernel functions for regression and classification problems.

7.2 Linear least-squares-error analysis

Statistical regression analysis

Regression analysis can be viewed as a system identification problem, where an unknown system is viewed as a black box characterized by its input $\mathbf{x}$ and the corresponding response y. A regression system is characterized by a deterministic but unknown function $h(\mathbf{x})$, where the output is commonly expressed as

$$y = h(\mathbf{x}) + \varepsilon.$$

Here $\mathbf{x} = [x_1, x_2, \ldots, x_M]^{\mathrm{T}}$ denotes the input vector, and ε is an independent zero-mean random noise.

In a basic regression learning model, see Figure 14.1(a), the observed output response is often assumed to be corrupted by statistically independent noise. Regression analysis involves determination of a nonlinear regressor function $f(\mathbf{x})$ to best estimate the original model $h(\mathbf{x})$ from the given statistical information on the *independent* variable $\mathbf{x}$ and *dependent* variable y.

7.2.1 Linear-least-MSE and least-squares-error (LSE) regressors

The MMSE regressor is a non-parametric method aiming at minimizing the so-called mean-squared error (MSE) [120, 151, 230]:

$$L = E[\|\epsilon\|^2] = E[\|y - f(\mathbf{x})\|^2].$$

Let us for simplicity assume that both the input and the output variables **x** and **y** have zero mean. A linear estimator has a simple formulation:

$$\hat{y} = f(\mathbf{x}) = \mathbf{x}^{\mathrm{T}}\mathbf{w}.$$

The objective is to find the best vector **w** to minimize the MSE:

$$E[\|y - \mathbf{w}^{\mathrm{T}}\mathbf{x}\|^2].$$

The optimizer can be expressed as

$$\underset{\hat{\mathbf{w}} \in \mathbb{R}^M}{\arg\min}\, E[\|y - \mathbf{w}^{\mathrm{T}}\mathbf{x}\|^2] \tag{7.1}$$

Linear-least-MSE regressor

The *linear-least-MSE* estimator aims at finding a linear solution $\mathbf{x}^{\mathrm{T}}\mathbf{w}$ that minimizes the MSE:

$$E[\|y - \mathbf{w}^{\mathrm{T}}\mathbf{x}\|^2] = E[y^2] + \mathbf{w}^{\mathrm{T}}E[\mathbf{x}\mathbf{x}^{\mathrm{T}}]\mathbf{w} - 2\mathbf{w}^{\mathrm{T}}E[\mathbf{x}y],$$

whose zero-gradient point with respect to **w** leads to a typical formulation for the optimal *linear-least-MSE* estimator [120]:

$$f(\mathbf{x}) = \mathbf{w}^{\mathrm{T}}\mathbf{x}, \quad \text{with} \quad \mathbf{w} = R_{\mathbf{x}}^{-1}R_{\mathbf{x}y}, \tag{7.2}$$

where we denote $R_{\mathbf{x}} = E[\mathbf{x}\mathbf{x}^{\mathrm{T}}]$ and $R_{\mathbf{x}y} = E[\mathbf{x}y]$.

Least-squares-error (LSE) solution: finite training dataset

This section will study various linear regression and regularization techniques given a finite training dataset. Let

$$\mathcal{X} \equiv \{\mathbf{x}_1, \mathbf{x}_2, \ldots, \mathbf{x}_N\}$$

denote the training input dataset, and let

$$\mathcal{Y} \equiv \{y_1, y_2, \ldots, y_N\}$$

denote the desired response values (or *teacher values*) associated with $\mathcal{X}$. Furthermore, let $[\mathcal{X}, \mathcal{Y}]$ denote the joint input/output training dataset. More exactly,

$$[\mathcal{X}, \mathcal{Y}] = \{(\mathbf{x}_1, y_1)(\mathbf{x}_2, , y_2) \ldots (\mathbf{x}_N, y_N)\}.$$

In the statistics literatures, linear regression is a commonly adopted technique for modeling the relationship between a dependent (output) variable **y** and one independent and multivariate (input) random vector **x**. Given a finite training dataset, linear regression analysis can be formulated as the classic linear LSE estimation problem.

More precisely, it involves finding a vector $\mathbf{w}$ and a threshold value b such that $\mathbf{w}^{\mathrm{T}}\mathbf{x}_i + b$ can best approximate the desired output y_i, i.e. $\mathbf{w}^{\mathrm{T}}\mathbf{x}_i + b \approx y_i$.

For simplicity, we shall for the time being assume that both the input and the output samples have zero mean, i.e. $\sum_{i=1}^{N} \mathbf{x}_i = \mathbf{0}$ and $\sum_{i=1}^{N} y_i = 0$. (If not, they can always be center-pre-adjusted by a proper coordinate translation.) Under this assumption, the role of the threshold value b is no longer useful. (See Problem 7.5.) Consequently, the linear LSE problem involves finding a vector $\mathbf{w}$ such that the estimation function $f(\mathbf{x}) = \mathbf{w}^{\mathrm{T}}\mathbf{x}_i$ can best approximate the desired output in LSE:

$$E_{\mathrm{LSE}}(\mathbf{w}) = \sum_{i=1}^{N} \epsilon_i^2, \tag{7.3}$$

where the *estimation error* is defined as

$$\epsilon_i \equiv \mathbf{w}^{\mathrm{T}}\mathbf{x}_i - y_i.$$

In matrix notation, we let $\mathbf{X}$ denote an $M \times N$ training *data matrix*

$$\mathbf{X} = [\mathbf{x}_1 \mathbf{x}_2 \ \ldots \ \mathbf{x}_N], \tag{7.4}$$

and let $\mathbf{S}$ denote an $M \times M$ *scatter matrix*

$$\mathbf{S} = \mathbf{X}\mathbf{X}^{\mathrm{T}},$$

In addition, let $\mathbf{y}$ denote an N-dimensional *teacher vector*: $\mathbf{y} \equiv \left[y_1 \ldots y_N\right]^{\mathrm{T}}$. Now the LSE cost function can be re-expressed by the following matrix notation:

$$\begin{aligned} E_{\mathrm{LSE}}(\mathbf{w}) &= \|\mathbf{X}^{\mathrm{T}}\mathbf{w} - \mathbf{y}\|^2 \\ &= \mathbf{w}^{\mathrm{T}}\mathbf{X}\mathbf{X}^{\mathrm{T}}\mathbf{w} - 2\mathbf{w}^{\mathrm{T}}\mathbf{X}\mathbf{y} + \|\mathbf{y}\|^2 \\ &= \mathbf{w}^{\mathrm{T}}\mathbf{S}\mathbf{w} - 2\mathbf{w}^{\mathrm{T}}\mathbf{X}\mathbf{y} + \|\mathbf{y}\|^2. \end{aligned} \tag{7.5}$$

On zeroing the first-order gradient with respect to $\mathbf{w}$, we have

$$\frac{\partial E_{\mathrm{LSE}}(\mathbf{w})}{\partial \mathbf{w}} = 2\mathbf{S}\mathbf{w} - 2\mathbf{X}\mathbf{y} = 0. \tag{7.6}$$

This leads to the optimal LSE solution:

$$\mathbf{w} = \mathbf{S}^{-1}\mathbf{X}\mathbf{y}. \tag{7.7}$$

The best unbiased linear estimator (BLUE)

For a model with deterministic and fixed $\mathbf{w}$, the Gauss–Markov theorem states that the LSE solution enjoys an important advantage by virtue of being a "best unbiased linear estimator" (BLUE). This means that the least-squares estimator has the minimum variance among all unbiased linear estimators.

7.2.2 Ridge regression analysis

A classic solution to overcome over-fitting or ill-posed problems in the regression analysis is so-called ridge regularization, also known as Tikhonov regularization, in which a *ridge* penalty term is imposed on the objective function in the optimizer so as to keep the regressor coefficients under control. This leads to the classic *ridge regression* (RR) methods which are commonly used in many regularization problems [99, 112, 275].

Given a finite training dataset, the objective of a linear regressor is to minimize the following cost function:

$$E_{\rm RR}(\mathbf{w}) = \sum_{i=1}^{N} \epsilon_i^2 + \rho\|\mathbf{w}\|^2, \tag{7.8}$$

where $\epsilon_i \equiv \mathbf{w}^{\rm T}\mathbf{x}_i - y_i$. It can be shown that the optimal decision vector is

$$\mathbf{w} = [\mathbf{X}\mathbf{X}^{\rm T} + \rho\mathbf{I}]^{-1}\mathbf{X}\mathbf{y} = [\mathbf{S} + \rho\mathbf{I}]^{-1}\mathbf{X}\mathbf{y}. \tag{7.9}$$

7.3 Kernel-based regression analysis

In this section, both learning formulations in the intrinsic and empirical spaces will be developed, and the best choice between the two options will be found to depend on the application intended.

- **The intrinsic-space approach.** Assume that the dimension of the intrinsic space is finite, i.e. $J < \infty$. Once the nonlinear kernel has been specified, the intrinsic representation is already fully pre-specified, and the parameters of the upper (and linear) network can be learned via the same LSE optimization formulation. This leads to the LSE learning model in the intrinsic space. With an additional ridge regularization incorporated, we can arrive at the KRR formulation in the intrinsic space.
- **The empirical-space approach.** If the intrinsic space is infinite, i.e. $J \to \infty$, the intrinsic-space KRR formulation will no longer be feasible. Fortunately, the KRR optimizer meets the LSP condition in the intrinsic space, allowing the conversion of the intrinsic formulation into an empirical formulation. The latter has the exclusive advantage that it is amenable to Gaussian kernels, or any other situations when $J \to \infty$.

Learning models in intrinsic space

The representative vector, $\vec{\boldsymbol{\phi}}(\mathbf{x})$, in the intrinsic space can be obtained via the following decomposition:

$$K(\mathbf{x}, \mathbf{x}') = \vec{\boldsymbol{\phi}}(\mathbf{x})^{\rm T}\vec{\boldsymbol{\phi}}(\mathbf{x}').$$

The intrinsic feature vector associated with the kernel is expressed as

$$\vec{\boldsymbol{\phi}}(\mathbf{x}) = \begin{bmatrix} \phi^{(1)}(\mathbf{x}) \\ \phi^{(2)}(\mathbf{x}) \\ \vdots \\ \phi^{(J)}(\mathbf{x}) \end{bmatrix},$$

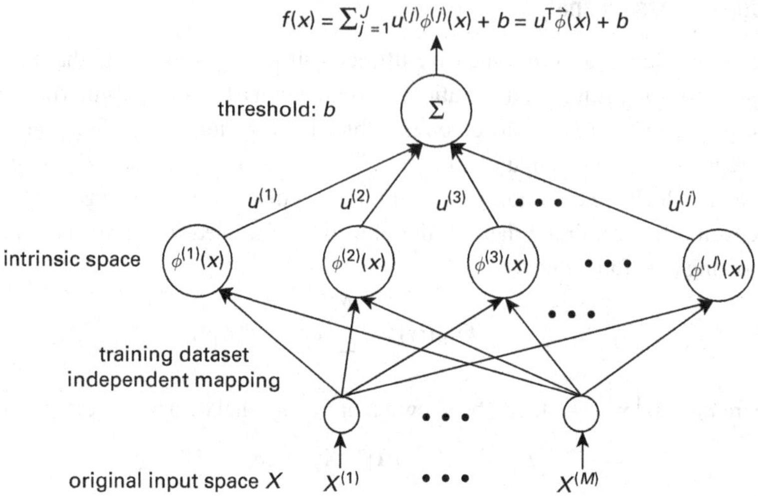

Fig. 7.1. This two-layer network shows how a vector $\mathbf{x}$ in the original space can be mapped to a new representative vector in its intrinsic space. For kernel-based regression analysis, the estimator is expressed as a linear combination of the new basis functions. The dimension of the intrinsic space is denoted by J, which may be finite or infinite.

where $\{\phi^{(j)}(\mathbf{x}), j = 1, \ldots, J\}$ form the set of basis functions for the kernel-induced intrinsic vector space. This is illustrated in Figure 7.1.

In kernel methods, the estimation function is most popularly expressed as a linear combination of $\{\phi^{(j)}(\mathbf{x}), j = 1, \ldots, J\}$, i.e.

$$f(\mathbf{x}) = \sum_{i=1}^{J} u^{(j)}\phi^{(j)}(\mathbf{x}) + b = \mathbf{u}^{\mathrm{T}}\overrightarrow{\boldsymbol{\phi}}(\mathbf{x}) + b. \tag{7.10}$$

As elaborated below, the threshold value b may sometimes be dropped without compromising the performance.

- **Regression formulation.** For regression problems, the output value $y \in \mathbb{R}$, so it is amenable to an arbitrary constant shift. Consequently, center-adjusting the coordinates can be regarded as being straightforward. Assuming that both the input feature vectors (in the intrinsic vector space) and the output values have zero mean, the threshold parameter b may conveniently be dropped. This condition can be easily met by a proper adjustment of the coordinate system in advance. Therefore, for notational simplicity in mathematical analysis, the threshold term b may be dropped, i.e. $b = 0$, without loss of generality. This approach will be adopted in the present chapter, whose focus is exclusively on regression analysis.
- **Classification formulation.** Here the adjustment is not so straightforward as regression problems, since we have commonly binary teacher values, e.g. $y \in \{+1, -1\}$, which is no longer amenable to such a shift. This will be the approach adopted in Chapters 10–13, where the focus of attention is exclusively on classification.

Basis vector with implicit bias

It is worth noting that there is, inherently, already a bias term included in the basis functions induced by a polynomial kernel function or a constant-augmented kernel function. (See Problems 7.6 and 7.7.)

The threshold term b may be dropped without compromising the performance when there is already an *implicit bias* [87] included in the basis functions induced by the kernel function. As an example, the difference between the linear kernel and a polynomial kernel of degree 1 is that the latter induces an *implicit bias* term, whereas the former does not. For more explanation, see Problems 7.4–7.7.

7.3.1 LSE regression analysis: intrinsic space

Let $f(\mathbf{x})$ denote the estimation function (or discriminant function when applied to classification) associated with $\mathbf{x}$. Then it is desirable to have $f(\mathbf{x}_i)$ as close as possible to y_i for $i = 1, \ldots, N$. The LSE optimizer aims at minimizing the following cost function:

$$\min_{\mathbf{u}} E_{\text{LSE}}(\mathbf{u}) = \sum_{i=1}^{N} \epsilon_i^2, \tag{7.11}$$

where $\epsilon_i \equiv f(\mathbf{x}_i) - y_i$ denotes the approximation error. By dropping the threshold term, the estimation function in Eq. (7.10) can be simplified to

$$f(\mathbf{x}) = \sum_{i=1}^{J} u^{(j)}\phi^{(j)}(\mathbf{x}) = \mathbf{u}^{\mathrm{T}}\overrightarrow{\boldsymbol{\phi}}(\mathbf{x}). \tag{7.12}$$

It follows that the LSE optimization becomes

$$\min_{\mathbf{u}} E_{\text{LSE}}(\mathbf{u}) = \sum_{i=1}^{N} \epsilon_i^2 = \sum_{i=1}^{N} \left(\mathbf{u}^{\mathrm{T}}\overrightarrow{\boldsymbol{\phi}}(\mathbf{x}_i) - y_i\right)^2. \tag{7.13}$$

In matrix notation, Eq. (7.13) can be expressed as

$$\min_{\mathbf{u}} E_{\text{LSE}}(\mathbf{u}) = \|\Phi^{\mathrm{T}}\mathbf{u} - \mathbf{y}\|^2, \tag{7.14}$$

where

$$\Phi = \left[\overrightarrow{\boldsymbol{\phi}}(\mathbf{x}_1)\,\overrightarrow{\boldsymbol{\phi}}(\mathbf{x}_2)\ldots\overrightarrow{\boldsymbol{\phi}}(\mathbf{x}_N)\right]$$

denotes the data matrix in the kernel-induced *intrinsic* space.

For the over-determined case, i.e. $J \le N$, $\mathbf{S}$ will likely be nonsingular. Then the kernel-based LSE solution shares the very same form as Eq. (7.7):

$$\mathbf{u} = \left[\Phi\Phi^{\mathrm{T}}\right]^{-1}\Phi\mathbf{y} = \mathbf{S}^{-1}\Phi\mathbf{y}.$$

Recall that we denote the scatter matrix in the intrinsic space as $\mathbf{S} \equiv \Phi\Phi^{\mathrm{T}}$.

The Gauss–Markov theorem states that if the output noises have zero mean, are uncorrelated, and have equal variance, then the LSE estimator is a "best linear unbiased estimator" (BLUE). In other words, the LSE estimator selects an estimator that minimizes the MSE on an arbitrary input distribution among all unbiased estimators. This subject will be elaborated on further in Chapter 15.

7.3.2 Kernel ridge regression analysis: intrinsic space

For the intrinsic space, the *kernel ridge regressor* (KRR) aims at minimizing the following objective function:

$$E_{\mathrm{KRR}}(\mathbf{u}) = \sum_{i=1}^{N} \epsilon_i^2 + \rho\|\mathbf{u}\|^2, \tag{7.15}$$

where $\epsilon_i \equiv \mathbf{u}^{\mathrm{T}}\vec{\boldsymbol{\phi}}(\mathbf{x}_i) - y_i = \mathbf{u}^{\mathrm{T}}\vec{\boldsymbol{\phi}}_i - y_i$. In matrix notation, this criterion function can be re-expressed as

$$E_{\mathrm{KRR}}(\mathbf{u}) = \|\Phi^{\mathrm{T}}\mathbf{u} - \mathbf{y}\|^2 + \rho\|\mathbf{u}\|^2. \tag{7.16}$$

It can be shown that Eq. (7.15) leads to the following optimal solution:

$$\mathbf{u} = [\Phi\Phi^{\mathrm{T}} + \rho\mathbf{I}]^{-1}\Phi\mathbf{y} = [\mathbf{S} + \rho\,\mathbf{I}]^{-1}\Phi\mathbf{y}. \tag{7.17}$$

It follows that the predicted output response can be expressed as

$$\hat{y} = f(\mathbf{x}) = \vec{\boldsymbol{\phi}}(\mathbf{x})^{\mathrm{T}}\mathbf{u} = \vec{\boldsymbol{\phi}}(\mathbf{x})^{\mathrm{T}}[\mathbf{S} + \rho\mathbf{I}]^{-1}\Phi\mathbf{y}. \tag{7.18}$$

7.3.3 The learning subspace property (LSP): from intrinsic to empirical space

The 2-norm formulation of Eq. (7.15) satisfies the condition prescribed by Theorem 1.1. For the KRR problem,

$$\begin{aligned} g\left(\{\mathbf{u}^{\mathrm{T}}\vec{\boldsymbol{\phi}}_j, j = 1,\ldots,N\}, \|\mathbf{u}\|^2\right) &= E_{\mathrm{LSE}}(\mathbf{u}) + \rho\|\mathbf{u}\|^2 \\ &= \sum_{j=1}^{N} ||\mathbf{u}^{\mathrm{T}}\vec{\boldsymbol{\phi}}_j - y_j||^2 + \rho\|\mathbf{u}\|^2, \end{aligned}$$

and there are no equality or inequality constraints.

Its optimal solution has the LSP in the intrinsic space:

$$\mathbf{u} = \Phi\mathbf{a}. \tag{7.19}$$

7.3.4 KRR learning models: empirical space

The regression problem may be reformulated in the empirical-space representation. Using the LSP, the criterion function in Eq. (7.16) can be written as

$$\begin{aligned} E_{\mathrm{KRR(kernel\ space)}}(\mathbf{a}) &= \|\mathbf{K}^{\mathrm{T}}\mathbf{a} - \mathbf{y}\|^2 + \rho\|\mathbf{u}\|^2 \\ &= \mathbf{a}^{\mathrm{T}}\mathbf{K}^2\mathbf{a} - 2\mathbf{a}^{\mathrm{T}}\mathbf{K}\mathbf{y} + \|\mathbf{y}\|^2 + \rho\mathbf{a}^{\mathrm{T}}\mathbf{K}\mathbf{a}, \end{aligned} \tag{7.20}$$

where $\mathbf{K} \equiv \Phi^{\mathrm{T}}\Phi$ is the $(N \times N)$-dimensional kernel matrix. Its zero gradient with respect to $\mathbf{a}$ leads to

$$2\mathbf{K}^2\mathbf{a} - 2\mathbf{K}\mathbf{y} + 2\rho\mathbf{K}\mathbf{a} = 0. \tag{7.21}$$

A solution of the regressor vector $\mathbf{a}$ in the *empirical space* can be solved as

$$\mathbf{a} = [\mathbf{K} + \rho\mathbf{I}]^{-1}\,\mathbf{y}. \tag{7.22}$$

Using the LSP again, the predicted output response can be expressed as

$$\begin{aligned} \hat{y} &= f(\mathbf{x}) = \vec{\boldsymbol{\phi}}(\mathbf{x})^{\mathrm{T}}\mathbf{u} = \vec{\boldsymbol{\phi}}(\mathbf{x})^{\mathrm{T}}\Phi\mathbf{a} \\ &= \vec{\mathbf{k}}(\mathbf{x})^{\mathrm{T}}\mathbf{a} = \sum_{i=1}^{N} a_i K(\mathbf{x}_i, \mathbf{x}), \end{aligned} \tag{7.23}$$

where we denote

$$\vec{\mathbf{k}}(\mathbf{x}) = \Phi^{\mathrm{T}}\vec{\boldsymbol{\phi}}(\mathbf{x}) = \begin{bmatrix} \vec{\boldsymbol{\phi}}(\mathbf{x}_1)^{\mathrm{T}}\vec{\boldsymbol{\phi}}(\mathbf{x}) \\ \vec{\boldsymbol{\phi}}(\mathbf{x}_2)^{\mathrm{T}}\vec{\boldsymbol{\phi}}(\mathbf{x}) \\ \vdots \\ \vec{\boldsymbol{\phi}}(\mathbf{x}_N)^{\mathrm{T}}\vec{\boldsymbol{\phi}}(\mathbf{x}) \end{bmatrix} = \begin{bmatrix} K(\mathbf{x}_1, \mathbf{x}) \\ K(\mathbf{x}_2, \mathbf{x}) \\ \vdots \\ K(\mathbf{x}_N, \mathbf{x}) \end{bmatrix}.$$

This is identical to the solution derived by the intrinsic space approach (Eq. (7.18)) while avoiding explicitly computing the intrinsic feature vectors $\{\vec{\boldsymbol{\phi}}(\mathbf{x})\}$.

The KRR method for regression analysis in the empirical space is now formally stated here.

ALGORITHM 7.1 (KRR learning models in empirical space) *The KRR regression algorithm with training dataset $[\mathcal{X}, \mathcal{Y}]$ contains the following steps.*

- *For a specific kernel function $K(\mathbf{x}, \mathbf{x}')$, compute the $N \times N$ symmetric kernel matrix:*

$$\mathbf{K} = \begin{bmatrix} K(\mathbf{x}_1, \mathbf{x}_1) & K(\mathbf{x}_1, \mathbf{x}_2) & \cdots & K(\mathbf{x}_1, \mathbf{x}_N) \\ K(\mathbf{x}_2, \mathbf{x}_1) & K(\mathbf{x}_2, \mathbf{x}_2) & \cdots & K(\mathbf{x}_2, \mathbf{x}_N) \\ \cdots & \cdots & \cdots & \cdots \\ K(\mathbf{x}_N, \mathbf{x}_1) & K(\mathbf{x}_N, \mathbf{x}_2) & \cdots & K(\mathbf{x}_N, \mathbf{x}_N) \end{bmatrix}, \tag{7.24}$$

- *Compute the empirical decision vector:*

$$\mathbf{a} = [\mathbf{K} + \rho\mathbf{I}]^{-1}\,\mathbf{y}, \tag{7.25}$$

- *The predicted output response is*

$$\begin{aligned} \hat{y} &= f(\mathbf{x}) = \vec{\mathbf{k}}(\mathbf{x})^{\mathrm{T}}\mathbf{a} \\ &= \sum_{i=1}^{N} a_i K(\mathbf{x}_i, \mathbf{x}), \quad \textit{where} \quad \mathbf{a} = [\mathbf{K} + \rho\mathbf{I}]^{-1}\,\mathbf{y}. \end{aligned} \tag{7.26}$$

□

7.3.5 Comparison of KRRs in intrinsic and empirical spaces

On comparing the two solutions, Eq. (7.17) and Eq. (7.28), it should be evident that

$$[\mathbf{S} + \rho\, \mathbf{I}_J]^{-1}\Phi = \Phi\, [\mathbf{K} + \rho \mathbf{I}_N]^{-1}, \tag{7.27}$$

where $\mathbf{I}_J$ and $\mathbf{I}_N$ denote the $J \times J$ and $N \times N$ identity matrices, respectively. It follows that

$$\mathbf{u} \underset{\text{Eq. (7.19)}}{=} \Phi\mathbf{a} \underset{\text{Eq. (7.22)}}{=} \Phi\, [\mathbf{K} + \rho \mathbf{I}_N]^{-1}\, \mathbf{y}. \tag{7.28}$$

For mathematically interested readers, we shall show below that Eq. (7.27) may also be directly established in simple steps. Note that

$$[\Phi\Phi^{\mathrm{T}} + \rho \mathbf{I}_J]\Phi = \Phi[\Phi^{\mathrm{T}}\Phi + \rho \mathbf{I}_N],$$

thus

$$[\mathbf{S} + \rho \mathbf{I}_J]\Phi = \Phi[\mathbf{K} + \rho \mathbf{I}_N]. \tag{7.29}$$

Equation (7.27) can be obtained by pre-multiplying and post-multiplying the above by $[\mathbf{S} + \rho \mathbf{I}]^{-1}$ and $[\mathbf{K} + \rho \mathbf{I}]^{-1}$, respectively.

Computational complexities

As before, Eq. (7.18) is computationally appealing for the over-determined case, i.e. $J \leq N$, while Eqs. (7.25) and (7.26) will be preferred for the under-determined case in which $J > N$.

7.4 Radial basis function (RBF) networks for regression analysis

With the Gaussian kernels adopted, the KRR method bears a great similarity to some prominent techniques that are based on approximation theory, a windows approach, or neural networks. This section will treat some of these regularization networks:

(i) the RBF approximation networks devised by Poggio and Girosi [207];
(ii) Nadaraya–Watson regression estimators; and
(iii) RBF back-propagation neural networks.

7.4.1 RBF approximation networks

The KRR solution may be obtained by a constrained regularization formulation, employing the Gaussian radial basis function (RBF) proposed by Poggio and Girosi [207].

Let dataset $[\mathcal{X}, \mathcal{Y}] = \{(\mathbf{x}_i, y_i) \in R^n \times R \,|\, i = 1, \ldots, N\}$ be the training set and let $f(\cdot)$ denote the prediction function. The learning phase of a regularization problem involves finding $f(\cdot)$ that minimizes the following energy function:

$$E[f] = \sum_{i=1}^{N} \epsilon_i^2 + \rho \|Pf\|^2 = \sum_{i=1}^{N} (y_i - f(\mathbf{x}_i))^2 + \rho \|P[f]\|^2, \tag{7.30}$$

where $\|\cdot\|$ denotes the L_2 norm in the function space. The constraint operator ($P[\cdot]$) in a regularization problem should be carefully selected to ensure the smoothness of the function $f(\mathbf{x})$; see Ref. [207]. The positive *regularization parameter* ρ dictates the strictness of the smoothness constraints. The larger the value of ρ the smoother the approximation function. Moreover, the constraint operator (P) is often assumed to be *linear* so that the solution $f(\mathbf{x})$ can be solved by applying the *variational principle*.

It is common to set the constraint operator P as a linear differential operator:

$$\|P[f]\|^2 = \int_{R^n} \left(\sum_{m=0}^{\infty} d_m (D_m f(\mathbf{x}))^2 \right) d\mathbf{x}, \tag{7.31}$$

where d_m are real positive coefficients. Let us define the operators $D_{2k} = \nabla^{2k} = (\partial^2/\partial x_1^2 + \cdots + \partial^2/\partial x_n^2)^k$ and $D_{2k+1} = \nabla\nabla^{2k} = (\partial/\partial x_1 \nabla^{2k}, \ldots, \partial/\partial x_n \nabla^{2k})$, where ∇^2 is the Laplacian operator and ∇ is the gradient operator.

Because the differential (constraint) operator P is linear and shift-invariant, the induced Green function associated with Eq. (7.30) has a special form,

$$G(\mathbf{x}, \mathbf{y}) = G(\mathbf{x} - \mathbf{y}).$$

In order for the regularization formulation to lead to the Gaussian kernel function, the coefficients in Eq. (7.31) must be chosen as follows [314]:

$$d_m = \frac{\sigma^{2m}}{m! 2^m}. \tag{7.32}$$

For the coefficients in Eq.(7.32), the corresponding Green function will be

$$G(\mathbf{x}) \propto \exp\left\{-\frac{\|\mathbf{x}\|^2}{2\sigma^2}\right\}.$$

On denoting $K(\mathbf{x}_i, \mathbf{x}_j) = G(\mathbf{x}_i - \mathbf{x}_j)$, it can be shown that

$$f(\mathbf{x}) = \sum_{i=1}^{N} a_i K(\mathbf{x}_i, \mathbf{x}) = \sum_{i=1}^{N} a_i \exp\left\{-\frac{\|\mathbf{x} - \mathbf{x}_i\|^2}{2\sigma^2}\right\}, \tag{7.33}$$

where the coefficients $\{a_i, i = 1, \ldots, N\}$ can be learned from the training dataset $[\mathcal{X}, \mathcal{Y}]$. Denote further that $\mathbf{K} = \{K(\mathbf{x}_i, \mathbf{x}_j)\}$, $\mathbf{y} = [y_1, \ldots, y_N]^{\mathrm{T}}$, and $\mathbf{a} = [a_1, \ldots, a_N]^{\mathrm{T}}$. The vector $\mathbf{a}$ can be solved by the following matrix equation [207]:

$$\mathbf{a} = (\mathbf{K} + \rho\mathbf{I})^{-1}\mathbf{y}. \tag{7.34}$$

(See Problem 7.8.) One possible derivation of this formulation can be based on the fact that, when a Gaussian kernel is used, the KRR solution is equivalent to an RBF regularization network. This is elaborated on below.

Comparison of KRR regressors and Poggio's approximation model

Let us consider a Gaussian kernel, $K(\mathbf{x}, \mathbf{y}) = \exp\{-\|\mathbf{x} - \mathbf{y}\|^2/(2\sigma^2)\}$, which can be expanded into a special Taylor series:

$$K(\mathbf{x}, \mathbf{y}) = \exp\left\{-\frac{\|\mathbf{x}\|^2}{2\sigma^2}\right\} \left[\sum_{k=1}^{\infty} \frac{1}{k!} \left(\frac{\mathbf{x} \cdot \mathbf{y}}{\sigma^2}\right)^k \right] \exp\left\{-\frac{\|\mathbf{y}\|^2}{2\sigma^2}\right\}.$$

For the scalar case, the intrinsic feature vector $\overrightarrow{\boldsymbol{\phi}}(\mathbf{x})$ has the following form

$$\overrightarrow{\boldsymbol{\phi}}(\mathbf{x}) = \exp\left\{-\frac{\|x\|^2}{2\sigma^2}\right\}\left[1 \; \frac{x}{\sigma} \; \frac{1}{2}\left(\frac{x}{\sigma}\right)^2 \; \cdots\right],$$

which contains an indefinite number of basis functions, i.e. $J = J^{(\text{RBF})} \to \infty$.

Assuming the LSP, $\mathbf{u} = \Phi\mathbf{a}$, and it follows that

$$\mathbf{a}^{\mathrm{T}}\overrightarrow{\mathbf{k}}(\mathbf{x}) = \mathbf{u}^{\mathrm{T}}\overrightarrow{\boldsymbol{\phi}}(\mathbf{x}).$$

In this case, we may replace the constraint term $\|Pf\|^2$ (in Eq. (7.30)) by a more familiar regularization term, i.e. $\|\mathbf{u}\|^2$, to yield a KRR-type regularization formulation, cf. Eq. (7.15):

$$E[\mathbf{u}] = \sum_{i=1}^{N} \epsilon^2 + \rho\|\mathbf{u}\|^2. \tag{7.35}$$

Starting from Eq. (7.15), the optimal solution can be obtained (cf. Eq. (7.22)) as

$$\hat{y} = f(\mathbf{x}) = \overrightarrow{k}(\mathbf{x})^{\mathrm{T}}\mathbf{a} = \sum_{i=1}^{N} a_i K(\mathbf{x}_i, \mathbf{x}), \quad \text{where} \quad \mathbf{a} = [\mathbf{K} + \rho\mathbf{I}]^{-1}\mathbf{y}. \tag{7.36}$$

On comparing Eq. (7.36) with the KRR solution (Eq. (7.26)), we conclude that Poggio's RBF approximation networks and KRR give exactly the same solution. Note also that both approaches make use of all the N empirical basis functions, each of which corresponds to one training sample. For more details on the theoretical connection between the two learning models, see Smola *et al.* [250].

7.4.2 The Nadaraya–Watson regression estimator (NWRE)

An alternative approach is via a non-parametric density estimation technique, e.g. the Parzen windows approach [199, 221, 222], in which the probability density function (pdf) of the population is inferred from a finite dataset. We shall show that a (normalized) RBF model may also be derived via an interpolation approach using RBF-based Parzen windows.

Given the joint pdf of $\mathbf{x}$ and y, $p_{X,Y}(\mathbf{x}, y)$, an estimate $\hat{y}$ of the output of the regression model can be expressed as the conditional mean of y given $\mathbf{x}$, i.e.

$$\hat{y} = E[y|\mathbf{x}] = \int y p_Y(y|\mathbf{x})dy, \tag{7.37}$$

where $p_Y(y|\mathbf{x})$ is the conditional pdf of y, given $\mathbf{x}$. It follows that

$$\hat{y} = E[y|\mathbf{x}] = \int_{-\infty}^{\infty} y p_Y(y|\mathbf{x})dy = \frac{\int_{-\infty}^{\infty} y p_{X,Y}(\mathbf{x}, y)dy}{p_X(\mathbf{x})}, \tag{7.38}$$

where $p_{X,Y}(\mathbf{x}, y)$ denotes the joint pdf of $\mathbf{x}$ and y and $p(\mathbf{x})$ the pdf of $\mathbf{x}$. In practice, the joint pdf $p_{X,Y}(\mathbf{x}, y)$ is unknown and can only be estimated from the training dataset $[\mathcal{X}, \mathcal{Y}]$.

Following the same concept as in the errors-in-variables model, we can assume that the true data must be a perturbed version of the observed training data, with the density function of the perturbation denoted by $p_{\Delta\mathbf{x}}(\Delta\mathbf{x})$. Likewise, the true teacher can be assumed to be a perturbed value of the given teacher values $\{y_i, i = 1, 2, \ldots, N\}$ with the density function of the perturbation denoted by $p_{\Delta y}(\Delta y)$. Furthermore, we assume that $\Delta\mathbf{x}$ and Δy are statistically independent and that both $p_{\Delta\mathbf{x}}(\Delta\mathbf{x})$ and $p_{\Delta y}(\Delta y)$ are zero mean. We can locally view the data around $\mathbf{x}_i$ as being perturbed by an amount $\Delta\mathbf{x}$, i.e. $\mathbf{x} - \mathbf{x}_i = \Delta\mathbf{x}$, and the teacher likewise by an amount $\Delta y = y - y_i$.[1] This justifies the adoption of the Parzen–Rosenblatt density estimator [199, 221, 222], which leads to an estimate of the joint pdf as follows:

$$\hat{p}_{X,Y}(\mathbf{x}, y) = c\sum_{i=1}^{N} p_{\Delta\mathbf{x}}(\mathbf{x} - \mathbf{x}_i)p_{\Delta y}(y - y_i),$$

where c is an appropriate normalization factor. Since $p_{\Delta y}(\Delta y)$ is zero mean, we have

$$\begin{aligned}\int_{-\infty}^{\infty} y p_{\Delta y}(y - y_i)dy &= \int_{-\infty}^{\infty} (y - y_i)p_{\Delta y}(y - y_i)d(y - y_i) \\ &\quad + y_i\int_{-\infty}^{\infty} p_{\Delta y}(y - y_i)d(y - y_i) \\ &= y_i.\end{aligned}$$

It follows that

$$\int_{-\infty}^{\infty} y\hat{p}_{X,Y}(\mathbf{x}, y)dy = c\sum_{i=1}^{N} y_i p_{\Delta\mathbf{x}}(\mathbf{x} - \mathbf{x}_i). \tag{7.39}$$

Similarly, we can obtain the estimate of the pdf as

$$\hat{p}_X(\mathbf{x}) = \int_{-\infty}^{\infty} \hat{p}_{X,Y}(\mathbf{x}, y)dy = c\sum_{i=1}^{N} p_{\Delta\mathbf{x}}(\mathbf{x} - \mathbf{x}_i). \tag{7.40}$$

On substituting for $p_{X,Y}(\mathbf{x}, y)$ and $p_X(\mathbf{x})$ in Eq. (7.38) their estimates in Eqs. (7.39) and (7.40), we can obtain the Parzen–Rosenblatt estimate of the output of the regression model as follows:

$$\hat{y} = \frac{\sum_{i=1}^{N} y_i p_{\Delta\mathbf{x}}(\mathbf{x} - \mathbf{x}_i)}{\sum_{i=1}^{N} p_{\Delta\mathbf{x}}(\mathbf{x} - \mathbf{x}_i)}. \tag{7.41}$$

The Nadaraya–Watson regression estimator

In practice, the perturbation's density function is often represented by a Gaussian function. For example, the ith interpolation function is usually represented by

$$p_{\Delta\mathbf{x}}(\mathbf{x} - \mathbf{x}_i) = \frac{1}{(\sqrt{2\pi} \times \sigma)^M} \exp\left\{-\frac{\|\mathbf{x} - \mathbf{x}_i\|^2}{2\sigma^2}\right\}.$$

[1] A subtle point regarding the notation is worth mentioning. Note that, for notational convenience, we use $\mathbf{x} \equiv \mathbf{x}_i + \Delta\mathbf{x}$ instead of $\tilde{\mathbf{x}} \equiv \mathbf{x}_i + \Delta\mathbf{x}$, which would be more explicitly consistent with the use of errors-in-variables models.

From Eq. (7.41), the Parzen–Rosenblatt estimate now becomes

$$\hat{y} = \frac{\sum_{i=1}^{N} y_i \exp\left\{-\|\mathbf{x} - \mathbf{x}_i\|^2/(2\sigma^2)\right\}}{\sum_{i=1}^{N} \exp\left\{-\|\mathbf{x} - \mathbf{x}_i\|^2/(2\sigma^2)\right\}}, \tag{7.42}$$

which is known as the Nadaraya–Watson regression estimator (NWRE) [191, 293].

Note that observations with inputs closer to $\mathbf{x}$ are weighted more heavily than the others, and the weights are adjustable by a width parameter σ. Indeed, if σ is small, only nearby neighbors of $\mathbf{x}$ contribute to the estimate at this point. This procedure is reminiscent of k-nearest-neighbor (kNN) methods when k is small. On the other hand, if σ is large, a greater number of neighbors will contribute collectively to the estimate. This is analogous to the situation when a large value of k is adopted in the kNN method. In this sense, the NWRE is closely related to nearest-neighbor estimators such as kNN.

Comparison of KRR and NWRE

On comparing Eq. (7.42) with Eq. (7.26) and Eq. (7.36), we note that all three estimators use the same N empirical RBF basis functions as the interpolation functions, each of which corresponds to one training sample. The main difference is that, while the optimal coefficients for the KRR and RBF networks need to be learned via, say, Eq. (7.25), the coefficients for the Nadaraya–Watson estimator are directly available from the teacher values. However, the Nadaraya–Watson regression estimator needs to be normalized, making it more involved when all the computations are taken into consideration. It is also interesting to note that while KRR is often referred to as a parametric method, the Nadaraya–Watson estimator is considered to be a non-parametric method.

7.4.3 Back-propagation neural networks

Neural networks [220] have long been a dominant force in machine learning. The most prominent learning model for training multi-layer neural networks is the back-propagation (BP) algorithm, which was independently proposed by Werbos [294], Parker [198], and Rumelhart *et al.* [226]. They have had many important applications, see e.g. [91, 118, 138, 289].

7.4.3.1 Architecture of RBF neural networks

In neural network learning paradigms, the manner in which "neural nodes" are trained is intimately related to how they are structured. For this reason, it is popular to structure the neural network as a multi-layer architecture, with two or more layers. In BP neural networks, the neural nodes are trained by back-propagating the teacher values from the top-layer downwards. In RBF neural networks, each node of the representation layer is represented by an RBF. As depicted in Figure 7.2, the basic architecture of RBF neural networks comprises two layers.

- *Lower layer (first layer).* The nonlinearity hinges upon the node functions $\{\phi^{(j)}(\mathbf{x}), j = 1, \ldots, L\}$ of the two-layer neural model. The choice of the function is critical since it affects the new representation of the input vector $\mathbf{x}$, which indirectly

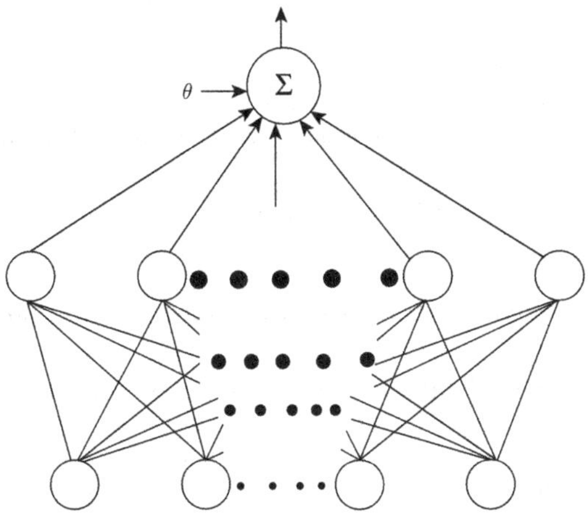

Fig. 7.2. A two-layer network is often adopted to model nonlinear score/discriminant functions, in which a layer of representative nodes ϕ is inserted between the input nodes and output nodes.

models the output response $f(\mathbf{x})$. In order to maintain some consistency with the RBF-based kernel methods, the node function may be chosen to be a Gaussian RBF:

$$\phi^{(j)}(\mathbf{x}) = \exp\left\{-\frac{\|\mathbf{x} - \vec{\mu}_j\|^2}{\sigma^2}\right\}, \tag{7.43}$$

whose centroids may be adaptively learned.[2]

- *Upper layer (second layer).* The network output can be represented by a linear combination of the nonlinear node functions, i.e.

$$\begin{aligned} f(\mathbf{x}) &= u^{(0)} + \sum_{j=1}^{J} u^{(j)}\phi^{(j)}(\mathbf{x}) \\ &= \sum_{j=0}^{J} u^{(j)}\phi^{(j)}(\mathbf{x}), \quad n = 1, \ldots, N, \end{aligned} \tag{7.44}$$

where $\mathbf{x}_n$ is the nth input vector, $u^{(0)}$ is a bias term, and $\phi^{(0)}(\cdot) \equiv 1$.

Denote the mean vector and covariance matrix of the jth kernel of a multi-layer RBF network as $\vec{\mu}_j = [\mu_{j1}, \ldots, \mu_{jM}]^{\mathrm{T}}$ and $\Sigma_j = \mathrm{Diag}\{\sigma^2, \ldots, \sigma^2\}$, respectively, where M is the input feature dimension. For the two-layer RBF network, we further denote the sum of squared errors for the entire training training dataset as

$$E = \frac{1}{2}\sum_{n=1}^{N}\left[f(\mathbf{x}_n) - y_n\right]^2 = \frac{1}{2}\sum_{n=1}^{N}\epsilon(\mathbf{x}_n)^2, \tag{7.45}$$

[2] Depending on the application scenario, the standard deviation σ may be considered either as a fixed constant or as an adaptively learnable parameter.

where

$$\epsilon(\mathbf{x}_n) \equiv f(\mathbf{x}_n) - y_n, \quad n = 1, \ldots, N, \tag{7.46}$$

denotes the error between the nth target output and the nth actual output, and $f(\mathbf{x}_n)$ is evaluated using Eq. (7.44).

The complete training process comprises the following *initialization* and *iteration* stages:

- determination of the initial weights both for the lower layer and for the upper layer in the network.
- updating the network weights by the BP learning algorithm, the upper layer first and then the lower layer.

They will be elaborated on later.

7.4.3.2 Determination of initial network weights

For the purpose of facilitating a fast convergence for the BP learning network, the network weights may initially be assigned as follows.

- *Lower layer.* Initially, the teacher values do not have to play a role for assigning the weights of the lower layer. An unsupervised learning strategy may be used to initialize the bottom network. A popular approach is to do it by means of unsupervised K-means algorithms, where by the data are first subdivided into K clusters with $\mathbf{x} \in X_j, j = 1, \ldots, K$. Then, for each cluster, the centroid may be computed as follows:

$$\vec{\mu}_j = \frac{1}{N_j} \sum_{\mathbf{x} \in X_j} \mathbf{x}. \tag{7.47}$$

  It may be advantageous to apply K-means separately to the positive and negative datasets, creating K_+ and K_- clusters, respectively. In this case, the total number of clusters will be $K = K_+ + K_-$.
- *Upper layer.* In contrast to the lower layer, the teacher values may be put to effective use for finding optimal initial weights for the upper layer. More precisely, the parameters of the upper layer may be obtained via an LSE-type supervised learning problem, which ultimately leads to a problem of solving an linear system of equations.

  In vector notation, Eq. (7.44) may be rewritten as

$$f(\mathbf{x}) = \mathbf{u}^{\mathrm{T}} \vec{\phi}(\mathbf{x}),$$

  where

$$\mathbf{u} = \begin{bmatrix} u^{(0)} \\ u^{(1)} \\ \vdots \\ u^{(J)} \end{bmatrix} \quad \text{and} \quad \vec{\phi}(\mathbf{x}) = \begin{bmatrix} \phi^{(0)}(\mathbf{x}) \\ \phi^{(1)}(\mathbf{x}) \\ \vdots \\ \phi^{(J)}(\mathbf{x}) \end{bmatrix}.$$

  Likewise, an *error vector* may be defined as

$$\vec{\epsilon} \equiv [\epsilon_1 \ \epsilon_2 \ \ldots \ \epsilon_N]^{\mathrm{T}} = \Phi^{\mathrm{T}} \mathbf{u} - \mathbf{y}, \tag{7.48}$$

where

$$\Phi = \begin{bmatrix} \phi^{(0)}(\mathbf{x}_1) & \phi^{(0)}(\mathbf{x}_2) & \dots & \phi^{(0)}(\mathbf{x}_N) \\ \phi^{(1)}(\mathbf{x}_1) & \phi^{(1)}(\mathbf{x}_2) & \dots & \phi^{(1)}(\mathbf{x}_N) \\ \vdots & \vdots & \ddots & \vdots \\ \phi^{(J)}(\mathbf{x}_1) & \phi^{(J)}(\mathbf{x}_2) & \dots & \phi^{(J)}(\mathbf{x}_N) \end{bmatrix} \text{ and } \mathbf{y} = \begin{bmatrix} y_1 \\ y_2 \\ \vdots \\ y_N \end{bmatrix}.$$

It follows that Eq. (7.45) can be rewritten in a vector/matrix notation:

$$E = \|\vec{\epsilon}\|^2 = \|\Phi^{\mathrm{T}}\mathbf{u} - \mathbf{y}\|^2$$

$$= (\Phi^{\mathrm{T}}\mathbf{u} - \mathbf{y})^{\mathrm{T}}(\Phi^{\mathrm{T}}\mathbf{u} - \mathbf{y}) \tag{7.49}$$

$$= \mathbf{u}^{\mathrm{T}}\Phi\Phi^{\mathrm{T}}\mathbf{u} - 2\mathbf{u}^{\mathrm{T}}\Phi\mathbf{y} - ||\mathbf{y}||^2. \tag{7.50}$$

When the training data size is sufficiently large, Φ has generically a full (row) rank of $J + 1$. This means that the matrix $\Phi\Phi^{\mathrm{T}}$ will be nonsingular. By zeroing the first-order gradient of E with respect to $\mathbf{w}$, the optimal solution may obtained as follows:

$$\mathbf{u} = (\Phi\Phi^{\mathrm{T}})^{-1}\Phi\mathbf{y}. \tag{7.51}$$

7.4.3.3 Recursive updating of network weights via BP learning

The BP learning method adopts a gradient-descent updating rule. Because of the layered network structure, the teacher values can directly be used only for the updating of the top layer. The name BP stems from the fact that it involves layer-by-layer downward propagation of the so-called *error signals*. Mathematically, the error signals pertaining to a layer are defined as the gradient of the cost function E with respect to each of the nodes in that layer.

More exactly, the error signals for the two layers of the RBF neural network in Figure 7.2 are described as follows.

(i) Let the error signal pertaining to the first layer, $\delta 1_j(\mathbf{x})$, be defined as the gradient of E with respect to the jth node of the first layer:

$$\delta 1_j(\mathbf{x}) \equiv \frac{\partial E}{\partial \phi_j(\mathbf{x})}. \tag{7.52}$$

(ii) Let the error signal of the second layer, $\delta 2(\mathbf{x})$, be defined as the gradient of E with respect to the response node in the output layer:

$$\delta 2(\mathbf{x}) \equiv \frac{\partial E}{\partial f(\mathbf{x})} = \epsilon(\mathbf{x}). \tag{7.53}$$

Note that the teacher values can be directly involved in the processing of the *error signal* only in the top layer. The *error signal* required for the lower layers will be made available indirectly by an error BP procedure. That is, starting from the top layer, the error signals are successively propagated downwards to the bottom layer.

Let us now elaborate the detailed procedures of a BP learning algorithm for an RBF two-layer network, as in Figure 7.2. Note that, in BP learning, the weights in the upper layer must be processed before the weights of the lower layer can be ready for updating.

- *Updating of the second-layer weights.* Note that, using Eq. (7.53), we have

$$\nabla_{\mathbf{u}} E = \frac{\partial E}{\partial f(\mathbf{x})} \cdot \nabla_{\mathbf{u}} f(\mathbf{x}) = \delta 2(\mathbf{x}) \cdot \overrightarrow{\boldsymbol{\phi}}(\mathbf{x}). \tag{7.54}$$

Upon presentation of the nth pattern in a particular epoch, the upper-layer weights are updated as follows:

$$\begin{aligned} \mathbf{u}^{(n+1)} &= \mathbf{u}^{(n)} + \Delta \mathbf{u}^{(n)} \\ &= \mathbf{u}^{(n)} - \eta (\nabla_{\mathbf{u}} E)^{(n)} \\ &\overset{\text{Eq. (7.54)}}{=} \mathbf{u}^{(n)} - \eta\, \delta 2(\mathbf{x}_n) \cdot \overrightarrow{\boldsymbol{\phi}}(\mathbf{x}_n) \\ &\overset{\text{Eq. (7.53)}}{=} \mathbf{u}^{(n)} - \eta \epsilon(\mathbf{x}_n) \overrightarrow{\boldsymbol{\phi}}(\mathbf{x}_n). \end{aligned} \tag{7.55}$$

- *Updating of the first-layer weights.* Note that

$$\begin{aligned} \left(\nabla_{\overrightarrow{\mu}_j} E\right) &= \left(\frac{\partial E}{\partial \phi_j(\mathbf{x})}\right) \cdot \left(\nabla_{\overrightarrow{\mu}_j} \phi_j(\mathbf{x})\right) \\ &= \delta 1_j(\mathbf{x}) \cdot \left(\nabla_{\overrightarrow{\mu}_j} \phi_j(\mathbf{x})\right), \end{aligned} \tag{7.56}$$

where the error signals of the first layer, $\delta 1_j(\mathbf{x})$, can be computed via the error signal of the second layer ($\delta 2(\mathbf{x})$):

$$\delta 1_j(\mathbf{x}) = \frac{\partial E}{\partial \phi_j(\mathbf{x})} = \frac{\partial E}{\partial f(\mathbf{x})} \cdot \frac{\partial f(\mathbf{x})}{\partial \phi_j(\mathbf{x})} = \delta 2(\mathbf{x}) u^{(j)}. \tag{7.57}$$

From Eq. (7.43), it can be derived that

$$\begin{aligned} \nabla_{\overrightarrow{\mu}_j} \phi_j(\mathbf{x}) &= -\frac{2 \exp\left\{-\|\mathbf{x} - \overrightarrow{\mu}_j\|^2/(2\sigma^2)\right\}}{\sigma^2} \cdot (\mathbf{x} - \overrightarrow{\mu}_j) \\ &= -\frac{2\phi^{(j)}(\mathbf{x})}{\sigma^2} \cdot \left(\mathbf{x} - \overrightarrow{\mu}_j\right). \end{aligned} \tag{7.58}$$

Weight updating rule:

Upon presentation of the nth training vector $\mathbf{x}_n$, assuming that the upper error signal $\delta 2(\mathbf{x})$ has already been processed, the lower-layer weights may be updated as follows:

$$\begin{aligned} \overrightarrow{\mu}_j^{(n+1)} &= \overrightarrow{\mu}_j^{(n)} + \Delta \overrightarrow{\mu}_j^{(n)} \\ &= \overrightarrow{\mu}_j^{(n)} + \eta \left(\nabla_{\overrightarrow{\mu}_j} E\right) \\ &= \overrightarrow{\mu}_j^{(n)} + \eta\, \delta 1(\mathbf{x}_n) \cdot \left(\nabla_{\overrightarrow{\mu}_j} \phi_j(\mathbf{x})\right) \\ &\overset{\text{Eq. (7.57)}}{=} \overrightarrow{\mu}_j^{(n)} + \eta \left(\delta 2(\mathbf{x}_n) u^{(j)}\right) \cdot \frac{-2\phi^{(j)}(\mathbf{x}_n)}{\sigma^2} \cdot \left(\mathbf{x}_n - \overrightarrow{\mu}_j^{(n)}\right) \\ &\overset{\text{Eq. (7.53)}}{=} \overrightarrow{\mu}_j^{(n)} - \frac{2\eta \epsilon(\mathbf{x}_n) u^{(j)} \phi^{(j)}(\mathbf{x}_n)}{\sigma^2} \cdot \left(\mathbf{x}_n - \overrightarrow{\mu}_j^{(n)}\right). \end{aligned} \tag{7.59}$$

Comparison of RBF approximation model and BPNN

With a Gaussian basis function being adopted, there exists a close relationship among KRR, the RBF approximation model, and neural networks.

- From Eq. (7.44), the neural network output is a linear combination of the node functions, each represented by a Gaussian basis function:

$$\phi_j(\mathbf{x}) = \exp\left\{-\frac{\|\mathbf{x} - \vec{\mu}_j\|^2}{2\sigma^2}\right\}, \quad j = 1, \ldots, J,$$

  Hence

$$f(\mathbf{x}) = u^{(0)} + \sum_{j=1}^{J} u^{(j)} \exp\left\{-\frac{\|\mathbf{x} - \vec{\mu}_j\|^2}{\sigma^2}\right\}\sigma^2. \tag{7.60}$$

- The output response functions of an RBF approximation network and an RBF KRR are basically the same, i.e.

$$f(\mathbf{x}) = \sum_{n=1}^{N} a_n K(\mathbf{x}, \mathbf{x}_n) = \sum_{n=1}^{N} a_n \exp\left\{-\frac{\|\mathbf{x} - \vec{\mu}_j\|^2}{2\sigma^2}\right\}. \tag{7.61}$$

  This result bears a great resemblance to the response functions of the RBF neural network given in Eq. (7.60).

Comparison between KRR and BPNN

Structurally, as evidenced by Figures 7.1 and 7.2, both KRR and BPNN adopt a two-layer network architecture. Both of them use the middle layer as a basis to form the decision boundary. However, there is a distinctive difference in the learning strategies for the lower network.

- For KRR, once the kernel is known, the lower network is already fully pre-specified, and the new feature vectors can be pre-computed for all the training vectors. Thus learning is no longer required for the lower layer. This is in sharp contrast to the case for a BPNN network, in which the lower layer has to be trained by the BP learning rule.
- Both for KRR and for BPNN, the upper (and linear) network can be learned in a similar and linear (e.g. LSE) formulation.

By comparing Eq. (7.60) and Eq. (7.61), we also note a main difference in terms of the number of middle-layer nodes for KRR and BPNN.

- *KRR's advantage.* Since KRR uses as many node functions as the number of training vectors, the node vectors will be the same as the training vectors. Hence, there will be no learning required for the first layer.
- *BPNN's advantage.* On the other hand, a neural network can use a small number of node functions, i.e. usually $J < N$. However, the node functions of a neural network need to be trained by the BP or other learning rule.

Number of node functions

The number of node functions or basis functions may influence some performance indicators, including the training time, prediction speed/power, and robustness and accuracy of the classifiers. For cost effectiveness, it may be desirable to have a reasonable number of node functions, that is neither too large nor too small. Some popular ways of choosing the number of basis functions are presented below.

(i) **Reduction of J.** In a neural network, the number of basis functions, J, is often chosen by trial and error. It is possible to reduce J by applying unsupervised clustering learning methods, such as K-means. In this case, the number of node functions can be reduced to the number of clusters, K. However, if K is chosen too small, the prediction performance of the network will likely be compromised.

(ii) **Reduction of N.** With some supervised learning methods, the number of active node functions may be much smaller than the empirical degree N. For example, using the SVM learning model, the number will be reduced to S, which represents the number of support vectors. (See Chapter 10.)

7.5 Multi-kernel regression analysis

Multi-kernel methods have recently been proposed for adaptive filtering and learning for nonlinear systems [269, 313]. In this approach, multiple kernel functions, $\{K_l(\mathbf{x}, \mathbf{y}),\ l = 1, \ldots, L\}$, are simultaneously used, each of them having its individual kernel-induced intrinsic sub-spaces. The basis functions of the subspaces are derived from factorization of their corresponding kernel functions:

$$K_l(\mathbf{x}, \mathbf{y}) = \overrightarrow{\phi}_l(\mathbf{x})^{\mathrm{T}} \overrightarrow{\phi}_l(\mathbf{y}), \quad l = 1, 2, \ldots, L.$$

The multi-kernel discriminant function has the following formulation:

$$f(\mathbf{x}) = \left(\sum_{l=1}^{L} \mathbf{u}_l^{\mathrm{T}} \overrightarrow{\phi}_l(\mathbf{x}) \right) + b. \tag{7.62}$$

The motivation for using multi-kernel regression lies in the hope that an improved learning/prediction performance will be brought about by its extra flexibility. This is the focus of our study below.

KRR formulation: equal regularization factors

A natural multi-kernel KRR formulation could be one aiming at minimizing the following criterion function:

$$E_{\mathrm{KRR(multi\text{-}kernel)}} = \sum_{i=1}^{N} \epsilon_i^2 + \rho \sum_{l=1}^{L} \|\mathbf{u}_l\|_2^2, \tag{7.63}$$

where $\epsilon_i \equiv f(\mathbf{x}_i) - y_i = \sum_{l=1}^{L} \mathbf{u}_l^{\mathrm{T}} \vec{\phi}_l(\mathbf{x}_i) \ + b - y_i$. We denote that

$$\mathbf{u} = \begin{bmatrix} \mathbf{u}_1 \\ \mathbf{u}_2 \\ \vdots \\ \mathbf{u}_L \end{bmatrix} \quad \text{and} \quad \vec{\phi}(\mathbf{x}) = \begin{bmatrix} \vec{\phi}_1(\mathbf{x}) \\ \vec{\phi}_2(\mathbf{x}) \\ \vdots \\ \vec{\phi}_L(\mathbf{x}) \end{bmatrix}, \tag{7.64}$$

and note that

$$\sum_{l=1}^{L} \mathbf{u}_l^{\mathrm{T}} \vec{\phi}_l(\mathbf{x}_i) = \mathbf{u}^{\mathrm{T}} \vec{\phi}(\mathbf{x}_i),$$

and the design freedom is LJ, i.e. the expanded dimension of the multi-kernel intrinsic space. Then we arrive at a more concise expression for the multi-kernel discriminant function:

$$f(\mathbf{x}) = \mathbf{u}^{\mathrm{T}} \vec{\phi}(\mathbf{x}) + b.$$

Now the multi-kernel KRR problem, given in Eq. (7.63), can be reformulated as one aiming at minimizing

$$E_{\text{KRR(multi-kernel)}} = \sum_{i=1}^{N} \epsilon_i^2 + \rho \|\mathbf{u}\|_2^2, \tag{7.65}$$

where $\epsilon_i = \mathbf{u}^{\mathrm{T}} \vec{\phi}(\mathbf{x}_i) + b - y_i$. According to Theorem 1.1, the LSP holds for this formulation and the optimal decision vector $\mathbf{u}$ in Eq. (7.65) has the following form:

$$\mathbf{u} = \Phi \mathbf{a} = \begin{bmatrix} \Phi_1 \\ \Phi_2 \\ \vdots \\ \Phi_L \end{bmatrix} \mathbf{a}. \tag{7.66}$$

Denote a new mono-kernel function as

$$K(\mathbf{x}, \mathbf{y}) = \sum_l K_l(\mathbf{x}, \mathbf{y}), \quad \text{with} \quad K_l(\mathbf{x}, \mathbf{y}) = \vec{\phi}_l(\mathbf{x})^{\mathrm{T}} \vec{\phi}_l(\mathbf{y}), \quad l = 1, 2, \ldots, L.$$

Denote that

$$\vec{\mathbf{k}}_l(\mathbf{x}) \equiv \Phi_l^{\mathrm{T}} \vec{\phi}_1(\mathbf{x}), \; l = 1, 2, \ldots, L.$$

It follows that

$$f(x) = \begin{bmatrix} \mathbf{u}^{\mathrm{T}} \end{bmatrix} \begin{bmatrix} \vec{\phi}(\mathbf{x}) \end{bmatrix} + b \tag{7.67}$$

$$= \mathbf{a}^{\mathrm{T}} \begin{bmatrix} \Phi_1^{\mathrm{T}} & \ldots & \Phi_L^{\mathrm{T}} \end{bmatrix} \begin{bmatrix} \vec{\phi}_1(\mathbf{x}) \\ \vdots \\ \vec{\phi}_L(\mathbf{x}) \end{bmatrix} + b \tag{7.68}$$

$$= \mathbf{a}^{\mathrm{T}} \left[\sum_{l=1}^{L} \vec{\mathbf{k}}_l(\mathbf{x}) \right] + b \tag{7.69}$$

$$= \mathbf{a}^{\mathrm{T}} \vec{\mathbf{k}}(\mathbf{x}) + b, \tag{7.70}$$

where we denote

$$\overrightarrow{\mathbf{k}}(\mathbf{x}) = \sum_{l=1}^{L} \overrightarrow{\mathbf{k}}_l(\mathbf{x}).$$

Now we obtain a compact discriminant function associated with the newly defined mono-kernel:

$$f(x) = \mathbf{a}^{\mathrm{T}} \overrightarrow{\mathbf{k}}(\mathbf{x}) + b. \tag{7.71}$$

Let $a_n,\ n = 1, \ldots, N$, denote the coefficient of the vector $\mathbf{a}$. Then the discriminant function can be expressed as

$$f(x) = \sum_{n}^{N} a_n K(\mathbf{x}_n, \mathbf{x}) + b, \quad \text{where} \quad K(\mathbf{x}_n, \mathbf{x}) \equiv \sum_{l}^{L} K_l(\mathbf{x}_n, \mathbf{x}).$$

Note that, with the LSP, the design freedom becomes N, i.e. the dimension of the mono-kernel empirical space.

The role of the LSP

The LSP plays a vital role here. Note that, if it were not for the use of the LSP, the multi-kernel discriminant function $f(\mathbf{x}) = \sum_{l=1}^{L} \mathbf{u}_l^{\mathrm{T}} \overrightarrow{\phi}_l(\mathbf{x}) + b$ (Eq. (7.62)) would have led to a more natural (and more general) formulation, namely

$$f(\mathbf{x}) = \sum_{l} \mathbf{a}_l^{\mathrm{T}} \overrightarrow{\mathbf{k}}_l(\mathbf{x}) + b, \tag{7.72}$$

where, in general,

$$\mathbf{a}_1 \neq \mathbf{a}_2 \neq \ldots \neq \mathbf{a}_L.$$

In this sense, it would appear that the design freedom is LN; however, the LSP assures that

$$\mathbf{a}_1 = \mathbf{a}_2 = \ldots = \mathbf{a}_L = \mathbf{a},$$

Thus, the vital implication of the LSP is that only one N-dimensional vector $\mathbf{a}$ needs to be learned, as opposed to L N-dimensional vectors $\{\mathbf{a}_1, \mathbf{a}_2, \ldots, \mathbf{a}_L\}$. In short, the true design freedom is only N instead of LN.

KRR formulation: non-equal regularization factors

In general, the multi-kernel KRR problem aims at minimizing the following cost function:

$$E_{\text{KRR(multi-kernel)}} = \sum_{i=1}^{N} \epsilon_i^2 + \sum_{l=1}^{L} \rho_l \|\mathbf{u}_l\|_2^2, \tag{7.73}$$

where $\epsilon_i \equiv \left(\sum_{l=1}^{L} \mathbf{u}_l^{\mathrm{T}} \overrightarrow{\phi}_l(\mathbf{x}_i) + b\right) - y_i$. If we define a new kernel function

$$K_l'(\mathbf{x}, \mathbf{y}) = \frac{\rho}{\rho_l} K_l(\mathbf{x}, \mathbf{y}), \tag{7.74}$$

then

$$\overrightarrow{\phi'}_l(\mathbf{x}_i)^{\mathrm{T}}\overrightarrow{\phi'}_l(\mathbf{x}_i) = \frac{\rho}{\rho_l}\overrightarrow{\phi}_l(\mathbf{x}_i)^{\mathrm{T}}\overrightarrow{\phi}_l(\mathbf{x}_i).$$

It is obvious that $\overrightarrow{\phi'}_l(\mathbf{x}_i) = \sqrt{\rho/\rho_l}\,\overrightarrow{\phi}_l(\mathbf{x}_i)$. On setting

$$\mathbf{u}_l = \sqrt{\frac{\rho}{\rho_i}}\mathbf{u}'_l,$$

we have

$$\mathbf{u}_l^{\mathrm{T}}\overrightarrow{\phi}_l(\mathbf{x}_i) = \mathbf{u}'^{\mathrm{T}}_l\overrightarrow{\phi'}_l(\mathbf{x}_i),$$

leading to a new cost function,

$$E_{\mathrm{KRR(multi\text{-}kernel)}} = \sum_{i=1}^{N}\epsilon_i^2 + \rho\sum_{l=1}^{L}\|\mathbf{u}'_l\|_2^2, \tag{7.75}$$

where $\epsilon_i = \mathbf{u}'^{\mathrm{T}}\overrightarrow{\phi}'(\mathbf{x}_i) + b - y_i$. The new (and normalized) cost function leads to a mono-kernel discriminant function (characterized by the new kernel $K'(\mathbf{x},\mathbf{y})$):

$$F(\mathbf{x}) = \sum_{n}^{N} a_n K'(\mathbf{x}_n,\mathbf{x}) + b, \quad \text{where} \quad K'(\mathbf{x}_n,\mathbf{x}) \equiv \sum_{l}^{L} K'_l(\mathbf{x}_n,\mathbf{x}).$$

From Eq. (7.74), the final optimal discriminant function is

$$f(x) = \sum_{n}^{N} a_n K(\mathbf{x}_n,\mathbf{x}) + b, \quad \text{where} \quad K(\mathbf{x},\mathbf{y}) \equiv \sum_{l}^{L}\frac{\rho}{\rho_l}K_l(\mathbf{x},\mathbf{y}), \tag{7.76}$$

which is again expressed in a mono-kernel formulation. Consequently, the optimal solution can be found by the conventional KRR, cf. Algorithm 9.1.

In summary, the improved learning/prediction performance brought about by the multi-kernel formulation relies exclusively on a proper choice of the multiple regularization parameters $\{\rho_l,\ l = 1,\ldots,L\}$ in Eq. (7.76).

Mono-kernel represented as a linear combination of sub-kernels

The mono-kernel solution holds for all optimization formulations that satisfy the condition in Theorem 1.1. These include some useful multi-kernel extensions of the SVM learning model. This is why we shall focus exclusively upon mono-kernel learning models in all subsequent treatments of supervised classifiers, including KRR and SVM.

In other words, under the LSP, a multi-kernel learning model can actually end up with an optimal mono-kernel solution. In this sense, for all the LSP-valid classification/regression problems, we have effectively obviated the need for explicit use of the multi-kernel formulation in Eq. (7.72), since we may substitute the more concise mono-kernel formulation Eq. (7.76), which is also indicative of the fact that the extra freedom lies in its flexibility in choosing the most suitable regularization parameters $\{\rho_l,\ l = 1,\ldots,L\}$.

7.6 Summary

What is usually made available to the users in real-world applications are various kinds of training datasets, so it is important to explore how to apply the regression techniques to a finite training data. This chapter develops a kernel ridge regressor (KRR) tailored to a finite training dataset, see Algorithm 7.1. It also explores the intimate relationships between RBF-based KRR and several prominent regularization models, including

(i) the RBF approximation networks devised by Poggio and Girosi [207];
(ii) Nadaraya–Watson regression estimators [191, 293]; and
(iii) RBF back-propagation neural networks [198, 226, 294].

The chapter also treats multi-kernel formulations for regression analysis. The role of the LSP proves vital for the derivation of a mono-kernel solution for multi-kernel classification problems that satisfy the LSP condition.

7.7 Problems

Problem 7.1 *In a basic LSE regression problem we aim at finding*

$$\arg\min_{\mathbf{w}\in\mathbb{R}^M}\left\{E(\mathbf{w})=\sum_{i=1}^{N}(\mathbf{w}^{\mathrm{T}}\mathbf{x}_i-y_i)^2\right\}.$$

(a) *Show that, by zeroing the first-order gradient of $E(\mathbf{w})$ with respect to $\mathbf{w}$, the optimal LSE solution can be derived as follows:*

$$\mathbf{w}=(\mathbf{X}\mathbf{X}^{\mathrm{T}})^{-1}\mathbf{X}\mathbf{y}.$$

(b) *What is the optimal LSE solution if*

$$\mathbf{X}=\begin{bmatrix}1 & 1 & -2 & 0\\ -2 & 2 & 0 & 0\\ 1 & 0 & 1 & -2\end{bmatrix}\quad \text{and}\quad \mathbf{y}=\begin{bmatrix}0\\-1\\-1\\2\end{bmatrix}?$$

Problem 7.2 *In a more general formulation of the LSE regression problem, the objective is to find an optimal $\mathbf{w}$ and b so as to minimize the following least-squares error:*

$$\arg\min_{\mathbf{w}\in\mathbb{R}^M,\,b\in\mathbb{R}}\left\{E(\mathbf{w},b)=\sum_{i=1}^{N}\left(\mathbf{w}^{\mathrm{T}}\mathbf{x}_i+b-y_i\right)^2\right\},\tag{7.77}$$

(a) *Show that, by zeroing the first-order gradient of $E(\mathbf{w},b)$ with respect to b and $\mathbf{w}$, the optimal LSE solution can be derived as follows:*

$$\mathbf{w}=\mathbf{S}^{-1}\mathbf{X}[\mathbf{y}-b\mathbf{e}],\quad \text{with}\quad b=\frac{\mathbf{y}^{\mathrm{T}}\mathbf{e}-(\mathbf{X}\mathbf{y})^{\mathrm{T}}\mathbf{S}^{-1}(\mathbf{X}\mathbf{e})}{\mathbf{e}^{\mathrm{T}}\mathbf{e}-(\mathbf{X}\mathbf{e})^{\mathrm{T}}\mathbf{S})^{-1}(\mathbf{X}\mathbf{e})}.\tag{7.78}$$

(b) *Find the optimal LSE solution for the dataset in Problem 7.1 and compare the two solutions.*

Problem 7.3 (Linear ridge regression analysis) *Find the optimal linear ridge regressor (RR) for the dataset in Problem 7.1, with the ridge factor set to* $\rho = 1.0$. *Compare the optimal LSE and RR solutions.*

Problem 7.4 (Kernels with and without implicit bias) *To illustrate the notion of implicit bias in kernel-induced basis functions, let us compare the linear kernel against a polynomial kernel of degree* 1. *The estimation function for the former is given as*

$$f(\mathbf{x}) = \mathbf{w}^{\mathrm{T}}\mathbf{x} + b, \tag{7.79}$$

while that for the latter is

$$f'(\mathbf{x}) = \tilde{\mathbf{w}}^{\mathrm{T}}\tilde{\mathbf{x}}. \tag{7.80}$$

Note that

$$\tilde{\mathbf{x}}^{\mathrm{T}} = [1 \quad \mathbf{x}^{\mathrm{T}}]^{\mathrm{T}},$$

i.e. embedded in $\tilde{\mathbf{w}}$ *is an implicit bias term that is absent from* $\mathbf{w}$.

(a) *Show that the following two optimization formulations yield fundamentally different solutions:*

$$\underset{\mathbf{w}\in\mathbb{R}^M}{\text{minimize}} \left\{ \sum_{i=1}^{N} \epsilon_i^2 + \rho\|\mathbf{w}\|^2 \right\}$$

and

$$\underset{\mathbf{w}\in\mathbb{R}^{M+1}}{\text{minimize}} \left\{ \sum_{i=1}^{N} \epsilon_i^2 + \rho\|\tilde{\mathbf{w}}\|^2 \right\}.$$

(b) *Show that the following two optimization formulations lead to basically equivalent solutions:*

$$\underset{\mathbf{w}\in\mathbb{R}^M}{\text{minimize}} \left\{ \sum_{i=1}^{N} \epsilon_i^2 + \rho\|\mathbf{w}\|^2 + \rho b^2 \right\}$$

and

$$\underset{\tilde{\mathbf{w}}\in\mathbb{R}^{M+1}}{\text{minimize}} \left\{ \sum_{i=1}^{N} \epsilon_i^2 + \rho\|\tilde{\mathbf{w}}\|^2 \right\}$$

Problem 7.5 (The case of using an explicit threshold term *b*) *Consider a given training dataset in the intrinsic space:*

$$\{(\vec{\phi}_1, y_1)\ (\vec{\phi}_2, , y_2)\ \ldots\ (\vec{\phi}_N, y_N)\}$$

It is common practice to first center-adjust the training dataset so as to create a new training dataset:

$$\{(\vec{\phi}'_1, y'_1)\,(\vec{\phi}'_2, , y'_2)\ \ldots\ (\vec{\phi}'_N, y'_N)\},$$

where

$$\vec{\phi}'_i = \vec{\phi}_i - \mu_{\vec{\phi}} \qquad \text{and} \qquad y'_i = y_i - \mu_{\mathbf{y}},$$

with

$$\mu_{\vec{\phi}} \equiv \frac{\sum_{i=1}^{N} \vec{\phi}_i}{N} \qquad \text{and} \qquad \mu_{\mathbf{y}} \equiv \frac{\sum_{i=1}^{N} y_i}{N}.$$

Since the new dataset has zero means on input and output, its optimal estimator has the following form: $f'(\mathbf{x}) = \hat{\mathbf{u}}^{\mathrm{T}} \vec{\phi}\,'(\mathbf{x})$.

Show that, by mapping back the original coordinate, the optimal estimator can be expressed as

$$f(\mathbf{x}) = \hat{\mathbf{u}}^{\mathrm{T}} \vec{\phi}(\mathbf{x}) + b, \tag{7.81}$$

and determine the threshold value b.

Problem 7.6 (Implicit bias induced by polynomial kernels) *Show that, for a polynomial kernel of pth order,* $K(\mathbf{x}, \mathbf{x}') = \left(1 + (\mathbf{x} \cdot \mathbf{x}')/\sigma^2\right)^p$, *the threshold parameter b can be dropped without incurring a performance loss.*
Hint: *Note that* $\phi^{(1)}(\mathbf{x}) = 1$ *in the intrinsic basis functions.*

Problem 7.7 (Constant-augmented RBF kernel function) *A constant-augmented RBF kernel function has the following form:*

$$K(\mathbf{x}, \mathbf{x}') = c^2 + e^{-\|\mathbf{x}-\mathbf{x}'\|^2/\sigma^2}.$$

Show that this artificially creates an implicit bias in the kernel-induced intrinsic space, obviating the need for another threshold term b.

Problem 7.8 (Find a_i coefficients of RBF approximating networks) *The coefficients of the RBF approximating networks may be derived in the following steps.*

(a) *Show that, if the coefficients in Eq. (7.31) have to be chosen as* $d_m = \sigma^{2m}/(m!2^m)$ *then the Green function for Eq. (7.30) is*

$$G(\mathbf{x}) \propto e^{-\|\mathbf{x}\|^2/(2\sigma^2)}.$$

(b) *Assuming that the matrix* $(\mathbf{K} + \rho\mathbf{I})$ *is nonsingular, there is a unique solution*

$$\mathbf{a} = (\mathbf{K} + \rho\mathbf{I})^{-1}\mathbf{y},$$

where $\mathbf{K} = \{K(\mathbf{x}_i, \mathbf{x}_j) = \{G(\mathbf{x}_i - \mathbf{x}_j)\}$ *is an* $N \times N$ *matrix and* $\mathbf{I}$ *is an* $N \times N$ *identity matrix. Show that such a result can be obtained by substituting the solution into Eq. (7.35).*

Problem 7.9 *Apply Poggio's RBF-based network to solve for the XOR classification problem. What are the basis functions for the lower-layer network? What are the optimal weights for the upper-layer network?*

Problem 7.10 (BP learning for three-layer neural networks) *A major advantage of BP learning is that the (error) BP learning algorithm may be naturally extended to multi-layer networks with an arbitrary number of layers. Generalize the BP learning procedure for two-layer RBF networks derived in Section 7.4.3 to a procedure valid for training three-layer RBF networks.*

Problem 7.11 *For multi-layer neural networks, a popular nonlinear activation function is the following sigmoid function:*

$$a_j(l) = f(u_j(l)) = \frac{1}{1 + e^{-u_j(l)}}.$$

Show that

$$f'(u_j) = a_j(1 - a_j).$$

Problem 7.12 (Total least-squares regression analysis) *The total-least-squares (TLS) method, which was proposed by Golub and van Loan [81], provides a learning model for situations where errors are present both in the teacher vector* $\mathbf{y}$ *and in the data matrix* $\mathbf{X}$.

(a) *Show that a closed-form TLS solution can be obtained by applying singular value decomposition to an expanded data matrix:*

$$\tilde{\mathbf{X}} \equiv \begin{bmatrix} \mathbf{X} \\ \mathbf{y}^{\mathrm{T}} \end{bmatrix},$$

which has the following singular-value-decomposition:

$$\tilde{\mathbf{X}} = \tilde{\mathbf{U}}\tilde{\Sigma}\tilde{\mathbf{V}}.$$

Let $\tilde{\mathbf{u}}_{M+1}$ *denote the smallest left-singular-vector (i.e. the last column) of the unitary matrix* $\tilde{\mathbf{U}}$. *Then the decision vector* $\mathbf{w}$ *can be derived from the following formulation:*

$$\begin{bmatrix} \mathbf{w} \\ -1 \end{bmatrix} \propto \tilde{\mathbf{u}}_{M+1}.$$

(b) *Is the TLS formulation LSP-based? Does the TLS formulation have a kernelized formulation?*

8 Linear regression and discriminant analysis for supervised classification

8.1 Introduction

With guidance from a teacher, a supervised machine learning system can effectively distill the information inherent in the training dataset and learn a simple *decision* rule, which will subsequently be used for unknown test data during the prediction/inference phase. The ultimate goal is to have a simple rule to predict the class labels of the test data with a high accuracy.

In supervised classification, the dataset consists of a set of N training vectors:

$$\{\mathbf{x}_1, \mathbf{x}_2, \ldots, \mathbf{x}_N\},$$

where $\mathbf{x}_i \in \mathbb{R}^M$. Moreover, let the class label of $\mathbf{x}_t$ be represented by y_t, and referred to as the teacher value. In short, the information available consists of a set of input/teacher pairs denoted as

$$[\mathcal{X}, \mathcal{Y}] = \{[\mathbf{x}_1, y_1], [\mathbf{x}_2, y_2], \ldots, [\mathbf{x}_N, y_N]\}.$$

The teacher values for all the training vectors are known beforehand. Note that regression analysis has been a major vehicle for supervised machine learning, where teacher values are often continuous real values. In contrast, for supervised classification problems, the teachers are often represented by discrete values. Apart from this relatively minor difference, the two types of problem are largely interchangeable.

In the present chapter, emphasis will be placed on the algebraic and optimization approach to supervised classification. In order to arrive at robust classification, various regression and regularization techniques will again prove very useful. Two approaches will be explored in this chapter.

- **Regression perspective:** Note that regression analysis is mathematically formulated as a curve-fitting problem, which leads to the LSE formulation.
- **Separability perspective:** The objective of classification is more naturally related to the separation of two different classes, which leads to Fisher's discriminant analysis (FDA).

Moreover, this chapter will establish the equivalence between the LSE and FDA formulations.

(i) Section 8.2 presents several aspects of the characterization of supervised learning models and highlights the vital roles of linear supervised learning models in machine learning.

(ii) Algebraically, linear supervised classification may be formulated as either an over-determined linear system or an under-determined linear system. Section 8.3 treats the scenario of over-determined systems ($M < N$), which covers two prominent classifiers: least-squares-error (LSE) classifiers, Section 8.3.1, and Fisher's discriminant analysis (FDA), Section 8.3.2. The Section 8.3 will also establish the fact that the two classifiers are basically equivalent.

(iii) Section 8.4 treats the scenario of under-determined systems of equations ($M \geq N$). In this case, the learning objective is to find a decision boundary that has a maximum safety margin from both classes of training data. This effectively creates a maximum margin to separate the two opposite classes.

(iv) In Section 8.5, the regression/regularization analysis is adopted as a unifying framework both for over-determined and for under-determined learning systems. More specifically, the regularization technique in effect leads to the design of the classical robust classifier known as the *ridge regressor* (RR). Via a perturbational analysis, we shall develop a perturbational-FDA learning model or simply *perturbational discriminant analysis* (PDA).

(v) Section 8.6 shows that, for most 2-norm-based supervised learning models, the optimal decision vector will satisfy a so-called *learning subspace property* (LSP). This ultimately leads to a kernel-domain solution referred to as the *kernel ridge regression* (KRR) classifier. The section also compares the algorithmic formulations and computational costs for original and empirical spaces.

8.2 Characterization of supervised learning models

8.2.1 Binary and multiple classification

The main idea here is to introduce a *discriminant function* of an input vector $\mathbf{x}$ for each class. Let $\{C_1, C_2, \ldots, C_L\}$ denote the L possible classes, where $L \geq 2$. In the learning phase, L *discriminant functions*, denoted as $f_j(\mathbf{x}), j = 1, 2, \ldots, L$, will be learned using the training dataset. In the testing phase, i.e. after the learning phase has been completed, a test pattern will be identified with the class which yields the maximum score of the discriminant function. A simple architecture for classification is depicted in Figure 8.1.

Given any new test vector $\mathbf{x}$, the class with the highest score of the discriminant function will be identified. More exactly, the test pattern will be identified as the kth class (i.e. $\mathbf{x} \in C_k$) when

$$k = \arg\max_j f_j(\mathbf{x}).$$

Discriminant function for binary classification

Binary classification (i.e. $L = 2$) is an important special case. For many applications, the objective is to identify whether a test sample should belong to a negative class (usually normal) or a positive class (usually abnormal). In this chapter, the positive and negative classes will be denoted as $\mathcal{C}_+$ and $\mathcal{C}_-$, with the corresponding teacher values set as $y_i = +1$ or $y_i = -1$, respectively. Given a pattern $\mathbf{x}$, we shall denote its scores for

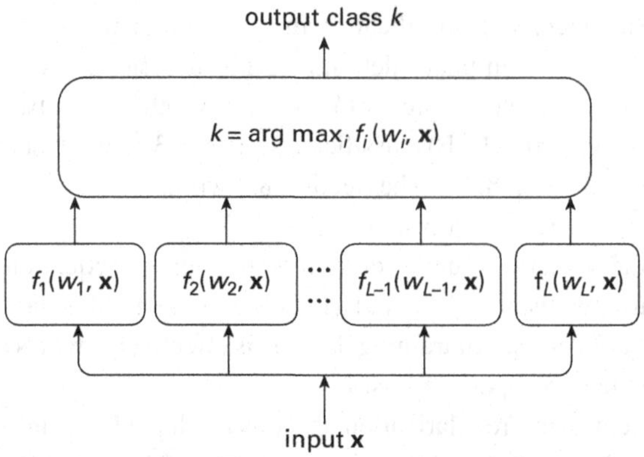

Fig. 8.1. A generic classifier architecture. There are L modules for the L classes, each represented by the discriminant functions for the corresponding class.

C_+ and C_- as $f_+(\mathbf{x})$ and $f_-(\mathbf{x})$, respectively. The *discriminant function* is defined as the difference between the two scores:

$$f(\mathbf{x}) = f_+(\mathbf{x}) - f_-(\mathbf{x}).$$

Decision rule

The class decision is determined by comparing $f(\mathbf{x})$ with a pre-set threshold value θ, i.e.

$$\mathbf{x} \in \begin{cases} C_+ & \text{if } f(\mathbf{x}) \geq \theta \\ C_- & \text{if } f(\mathbf{x}) < \theta. \end{cases} \tag{8.1}$$

Unless specified otherwise, the threshold value is often set to be $\theta = 0$ by default.

8.2.2 Learning, evaluation, and prediction phases

Machine learning for supervised classification contains three distinctive processing phases.

(i) *The learning phase.* The learning phase may sometimes be referred to as the training phase. In this phase, the discriminant function, parameterized by say $\mathbf{w}$, can be learned from the training dataset $[\mathcal{X}, \mathcal{Y}]$. Different learning models lead to different trained solutions. Most supervised learning models can be formulated as a kind of optimization problem. Mathematically, the learning objective is to find the parameters $\mathbf{w}$ which optimize the given objective function. The final result will be the learned *decision boundary* defined as

$$f(\mathbf{w}, \mathbf{x}) = 0.$$

(ii) *The evaluation phase.* The evaluation phase may also be called the testing phase. To create the testing dataset, a subset of the training dataset may be set aside beforehand so that it will be prohibited to use those vectors in the testing dataset in the learning phase. For example, in the K-fold cross-validation approach, one out of K parts of the known data is reserved as the testing dataset. Since the testing data do not participate in the training process, the teacher values of the testing dataset

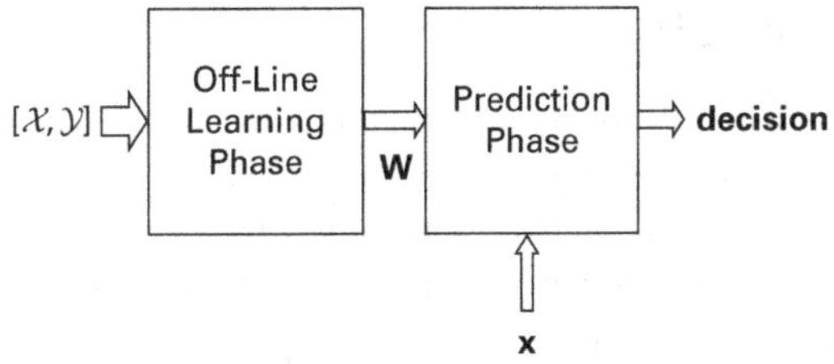

Fig. 8.2. The flowchart of supervised classification via explicit off-line learning. Two phases are explicitly shown in the diagram. (1) The off-line learning (training) phase: training data are distilled into a relatively simple decision rule, parameterized by $\mathbf{w}$. The objective of the supervised learning is to find $\mathbf{w}$ from the training data $[\mathcal{X}, \mathcal{Y}]$, i.e. the learning process precludes any knowledge concerning the test sample $\mathbf{x}$. (2) The on-field prediction (retrieval) phase: the sample $\mathbf{x}$ is known only during the retrieval phase. At that time both $\mathbf{x}$ and the learned parameter $\mathbf{w}$ are blended into the decision rule to obtain a prediction.

will never be used during the training phase. However, the teacher values have to be revealed in the testing phase in order to evaluate the accuracy. It is worth noting that it is during this evaluation phase that the best learning model(s) or classifier(s) will be compared and selected.

(iii) *The prediction phase.* The prediction phase may be more generally called the inference phase. In this phase, a new pattern (unseen before) can be identified by means of the learned decision boundary $f(\mathbf{w}, \mathbf{x}) = 0$.

Training accuracy versus prediction accuracy

The prediction accuracy is usually evaluated by means of the test dataset, as opposed to the training dataset. A high training accuracy does not necessarily imply a high testing accuracy. In particular, if a classifier is overtrained, it may achieve a high training accuracy, but will be likely to suffer from some undesirable side-effect (e.g. over-fitting) and thus compromise the testing performance.

8.2.3 Off-line and inductive learning models

When there is a preliminary learning phase, as shown in Figure 8.2, the learning approach contains two stages: (1) the off-line learning phase and (2) the online prediction phase. During the learning phase, the training dataset is used to train the decision parameter $\mathbf{w}$.[1]

Chapters 8–13 are all devoted to inductive and off-line learned models. The decision rule, trained under an *inductive* setting, must cover all the possible data in the entire vector space. More explicitly, $f(\mathbf{w}, \mathbf{x})$ can be trained by inductive learning. This approach can effectively distill the information inherent in the training dataset *off-line* into a simple set of decision parameters $\mathbf{w}$. Since $f(\mathbf{w}, \mathbf{x}) = 0$ is fully defined by the decision parameters $\mathbf{w}$, the inductive learning strategy has the promising potential of requiring low classification complexity and low computing power during the prediction phase.

[1] Appendix B explores several prominent supervised classifiers with no prior off-line learning process.

8.2.4 Linear and nonlinear learning models

The main objective of the (off-line) learning phase is to learn a decision boundary to separate the positive class from the negative class. More exactly, in the learning phase, the training data are distilled into a few decision parameters to be loaded into a (simple) classification model. With such a preliminary distilling process, classification or prediction of a new test pattern $\mathbf{x}$ can be executed expediently, especially in comparison with online classification methods. In addition to the advantage of speed, the off-line learning may also facilitate low-power processing in the prediction phase.

Why linear classification?

In supervised learning, the learned decision rule may be a linear or nonlinear function of $\mathbf{x}$ – the former corresponds to linear classification while the latter corresponds to nonlinear classification.

There are many reasons why linear classification has long been at the center of attention in the machine learning literature. Some primary reasons are as follows.

(i) Linear classifiers are in general more effective for high-dimensional feature vector space – the higher the better.
(ii) Linear classifiers are essential for both filtering and wrapper methods in feature selection. (See Chapter 4.)
(iii) Linear classifiers consume less processing time and power during the prediction phase than do their nonlinear counterparts.
(iv) The study of linear classification also lays the theoretical foundation of nonlinear kernel-based classification.

The emphasis of this chapter will be placed on linear classification. In the subsequent chapter, we shall explore how to systematically extend the basic linear techniques to nonlinear and kernel-based classification.

8.2.5 Basic supervised learning strategies

The training data are all represented by vectors in an M-dimensional real-valued vector space $\mathbb{R}^M$. As depicted in Figure 8.3(a), the positive and negative training vectors are *linearly separable* if they can be perfectly divided by an $(M-1)$-dimensional *decision hyperplane*, characterized by $f(\mathbf{w}, \mathbf{x}) = 0$. In other words, the decision boundary is dictated by the *linear discriminant function* defined as

$$f(\mathbf{w}, \mathbf{x}) = \mathbf{w}^{\mathrm{T}}\mathbf{x} + b = \sum_{j=1}^{M} w^{(j)}x^{(j)} + b, \tag{8.2}$$

where $\mathbf{w} = [w^{(1)}\ w^{(2)}\ \ldots\ w^{(M)}]^{\mathrm{T}} \in \mathbb{R}^M$, $\mathbf{x} = [x^{(1)}\ x^{(2)}\ \ldots\ x^{(M)}]^{\mathrm{T}} \in \mathbb{R}^M$, and $b \in \mathbb{R}$ are the parameters of the discriminant function.

If $\mathbf{w}$ is normalized, i.e. $\|\mathbf{w}\| = 1$, it may be used as a *projection vector*. As depicted in Figure 8.3(b), all samples in $\mathbb{R}^M$ may be projected onto a one-dimensional vector space. Via the projection, the entire decision hyperplane will be reduced to a single point, serving as the threshold for classification.

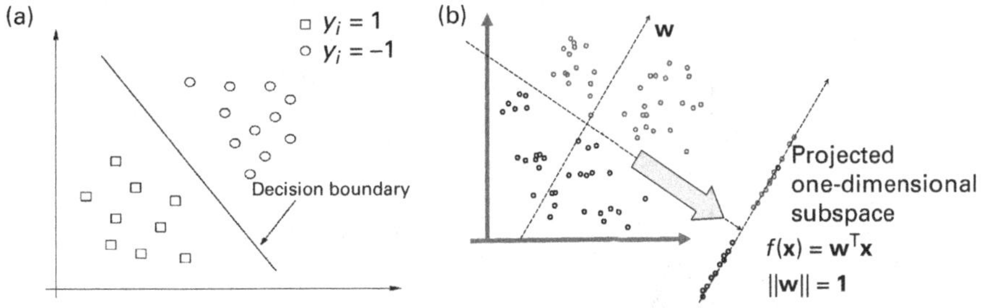

Fig. 8.3. (a) Linearly separable data and (b) vector-to-score mapping: $\mathbf{x} \to f(\mathbf{x})$.

Given a set of (say N) M-dimensional vectors, $\mathcal{X} = \{\mathbf{x}_1, \mathbf{x}_2, \ldots, \mathbf{x}_N\}$, the objective of linear classification is to find a linear discriminant function to best separate the two different classes of training data. There are numerous approaches to the development of linear classifiers. Some examples are given below.

(i) **Solving linear systems of equations.** Independent evaluation of individual features fails to take into account inter-feature dependence. This could significantly affect the classifier's performance. Alternatively, the learning problem can be formulated as solving a linear system of equations. In this case, the attributes of all the features will be collectively (instead of individually) assessed. Such an algebraic approach represents an important branch of supervised machine learning models.

(ii) **Maximizing separation margin between two classes.** It can be shown that the two classes have separation margin $2/\|\mathbf{w}\|$, which is often adopted as the cost function for many prominent optimizers e.g. (1) the learning models for under-determined systems, Section 8.4 and (2) the support vector machine (SVM), Section 10.2.

(ii) **Robust learning models.** Two major approaches to the development of robust learning models are discussed in Section 8.5.

 (a) *Regularization via ridge regression.* The principle of ridge regression (RR) lies in using a penalty-incorporated loss function so as to keep the regressor's l_2-norm, i.e. $\|\mathbf{w}\|$, under control.

 (b) *Learning with artificially added input-perturbation to the input training vectors.* Another approach is to artificially perturb the training vectors by adding uncorrelated noise before conducting the discriminant analysis, leading to the so-called *perturbational discriminant analysis* (PDA).

8.3 Supervised learning models: over-determined formulation

A general formula for a linear discriminant function is

$$f(\mathbf{x}) = \mathbf{w}^{\mathrm{T}}\mathbf{x} + b.$$

where $\mathbf{w} = [w^{(1)}w^{(2)} \ldots w^{(M)}]^{\mathrm{T}} \in \mathbb{R}^M$, $\mathbf{x} = [x^{(1)}x^{(2)} \ldots x^{(M)}]^{\mathrm{T}} \in \mathbb{R}^M$, and $b \in \mathbb{R}$ are the parameters of the discriminant function.

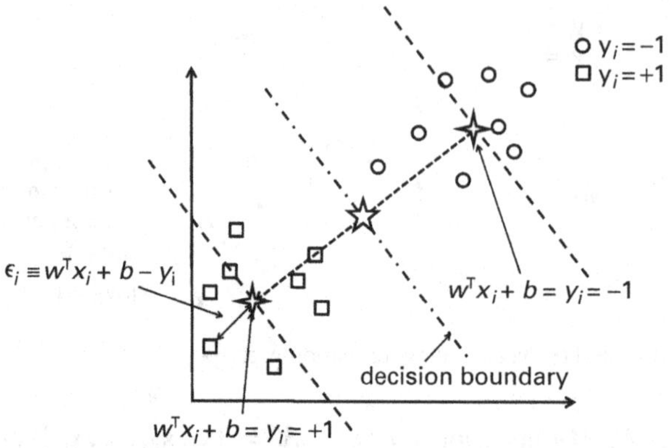

Fig. 8.4. In general, supervised classification can be formulated as a regression problem, where all the training data are approximated by two parallel hyperplanes, shown as dashed lines, one corresponding to $y_i = +1$ and another to $y_i = -1$.

Ideally, a basic linear system for learning the decision vector **w** will be guided by the following desired equality:

$$\mathbf{w}^{\mathrm{T}}\mathbf{x}_i + b = y_i, \quad i = 1, \ldots, N, \tag{8.3}$$

with $y_i = +1$ for positive training samples and $y_i = -1$ for negative training samples.

When $N > M$, this amounts to an over-determined linear system of equations, i.e. there are more equations than unknowns. We shall discuss two classical methods to cope with such an over-determined scenario. One is by means of least-squares analysis as proposed by Gauss, which which leads to the well-known LSE classifier. The other is Fisher's *linear discriminant analysis*, leading to the FDA classifier. Finally, we shall prove that the LSE and FDA classifiers are identical to each other.

8.3.1 Direct derivation of LSE solution

The objective of linear regression [19] is to best match the response $f(\mathbf{w}, \mathbf{x}_i)$ for an input $\mathbf{x}_i$ to a desired or supervised value y_i. Namely,

$$\mathbf{w}^T\mathbf{x}_i + b \approx y_i, \quad i = 1, \ldots, N. \tag{8.4}$$

As depicted in Figure 8.4, the *approximation error* is defined as

$$\epsilon_i \equiv \mathbf{w}^{\mathrm{T}}\mathbf{x}_i + b - y_i, \quad i = 1, \ldots, N.$$

The objective of the least-squares analysis is to find the decision vector **w** and the threshold b which minimize the following sum of squared errors:

$$E_{\mathrm{LSE}}(\mathbf{w}, b) = \sum_{i=1}^{N}(\epsilon_i)^2 = \sum_{i=1}^{N}(\mathbf{w}^{\mathrm{T}}\mathbf{x}_i + b - y_i)^2. \tag{8.5}$$

In the gradient method, the optimal solution can be obtained by taking the first-order gradient of $E(\mathbf{w}, b)$, with respect to b and **w**, and equalizing them to zero.

On taking the first-order gradient of $E(\mathbf{w}, b)$ with respect to b, we obtain

$$\frac{\partial E(\mathbf{w}, b)}{\partial b} = \sum_{i=1}^{N} 2(\mathbf{w}^{\mathrm{T}}\mathbf{x}_i + b - y_i) = 2\left(Nb + N_+ - N_- + \sum_{i=1}^{N} \mathbf{w}^{\mathrm{T}}\mathbf{x}_i\right) = 0,$$

leading to

$$b = -\mathbf{w}^{\mathrm{T}}\vec{\mu} + b', \tag{8.6}$$

where $\vec{\mu} = \sum_{i=1}^{N} \mathbf{x}_i/N$ is the mass center and $b' = (N_+ - N_-)/N$.

Denote the centroid-adjusted training vectors as:

$$\bar{\mathbf{x}}_i = \mathbf{x}_i - \vec{\mu},$$

and denote the *centroid-adjusted* scatter matrix as

$$\bar{\mathbf{S}} \equiv \sum_{i=1}^{N} [\mathbf{x}_i - \vec{\mu}][\mathbf{x}_i - \vec{\mu}]^{\mathrm{T}} = \sum_i \bar{\mathbf{x}}_i\bar{\mathbf{x}}_i^{\mathrm{T}} = \bar{\mathbf{X}}\bar{\mathbf{X}}^{\mathrm{T}}. \tag{8.7}$$

On plugging Eq. (8.6) into Eq. (8.5), we obtain

$$\begin{aligned}
E(\mathbf{w}, b) &= \sum_i (\epsilon_i)^2 \\
&= \sum_i (\mathbf{w}^{\mathrm{T}}\bar{\mathbf{x}}_i + b' - y_i)(\bar{\mathbf{x}}_i^{\mathrm{T}}\mathbf{w} + b' - y_i) \\
&= \mathbf{w}^{\mathrm{T}}\left(\sum_i \bar{\mathbf{x}}_i\bar{\mathbf{x}}_i^{\mathrm{T}}\right)\mathbf{w} - 2\mathbf{w}^{\mathrm{T}}\left(\sum_i \bar{\mathbf{x}}_i y_i\right) + \sum_i (y_i^2 + b'^2) \\
&= \mathbf{w}^{\mathrm{T}}\bar{\mathbf{S}}\mathbf{w} - 2\mathbf{w}^{\mathrm{T}}[N_+\vec{\mu}_+ - N_-\vec{\mu}_-] + N(1 + b'^2).
\end{aligned} \tag{8.8}$$

Now note that the mass center, positive centroid, and negative centroid. are always collinear. More exactly,

$$\frac{\vec{\mu}_+ - \vec{\mu}}{N_-} = \frac{\vec{\mu} - \vec{\mu}_-}{N_+} = \frac{\vec{\mu}_+ - \vec{\mu}_-}{N},$$

where $\vec{\mu}_+$ and $\vec{\mu}_-$ denote the positive and negative centroids, respectively. It follows that, denoting $\mathbf{\Delta} \equiv \vec{\mu}_+ - \vec{\mu}_-$,

$$N_+\vec{\mu}_+ - N_-\vec{\mu}_- = \frac{2N_+N_-}{N}(\vec{\mu}_+ - \vec{\mu}_-) = \frac{2N_+ - N_-}{N}\mathbf{\Delta}. \tag{8.9}$$

On plugging Eq. (8.9) into Eq. (8.8), we obtain

$$E(\mathbf{w}, b) = \mathbf{w}^{\mathrm{T}}\bar{\mathbf{S}}\mathbf{w} - \frac{4N_+N_-}{N}\mathbf{w}^{\mathrm{T}}\mathbf{\Delta} + N(1 + b'^2). \tag{8.10}$$

Taking the first-order gradient of $E(\mathbf{w}, b)$ in Eq. (8.10) with respect to $\mathbf{w}$, we can obtain the following optimal solution:

$$\mathbf{w}_{\mathrm{LSE}} = \frac{2N_+N_-}{N}\bar{\mathbf{S}}^{-1}\mathbf{\Delta}. \tag{8.11}$$

In summary, from Eqs. (8.6) and (8.11), the decision boundary of the LSE classifier is

$$\mathbf{w}^{\mathrm{T}}\mathbf{x} + b = 0,$$

where

$$\mathbf{w} = \frac{2N_+N_-}{N}\bar{\mathbf{S}}^{-1}(\vec{\mu}_+ - \vec{\mu}_-) \quad \text{and} \quad b = -\mathbf{w}^{\mathrm{T}}\vec{\mu} + \frac{N_+ - N_-}{N}. \tag{8.12}$$

More explicitly,

$$\mathbf{w} = \frac{2N_+N_-}{N}\bar{\mathbf{S}}^{-1}\mathbf{\Delta} \quad \text{and} \quad b = -\frac{2N_+N_-}{N}\vec{\mu}^{\mathrm{T}}\bar{\mathbf{S}}^{-1}\mathbf{\Delta} + \frac{N_+ - N_-}{N}. \tag{8.13}$$

A matrix formulation of the LSE problem

It is notationally simpler to work with Eq. (8.4) in matrix notation. Now the objective of the least-squares analysis is to find the decision vector **w** and the threshold b to best approximate the following matrix equation:

$$\mathbf{X}^{\mathrm{T}}\mathbf{w} + \mathbf{e}b \approx \mathbf{y}, \tag{8.14}$$

where we denote

$$\mathbf{X} = [\mathbf{x}_1\ \mathbf{x}_2\ \ldots\ \mathbf{x}_N]$$

and

$$\mathbf{y} \equiv \begin{bmatrix} y_1 \\ \vdots \\ y_N \end{bmatrix} \text{and } \mathbf{e} \equiv \begin{bmatrix} 1 \\ \vdots \\ 1 \end{bmatrix}.$$

Denote an *error vector*

$$\vec{\epsilon} \equiv [\epsilon_1\ \epsilon_2\ \ldots\ \epsilon_N]^{\mathrm{T}} = \mathbf{X}^{\mathrm{T}}\mathbf{w} + \mathbf{e}b - \mathbf{y}, \tag{8.15}$$

then the LSE criterion of Eq. (8.5) can be rewritten in a vector/matrix notation:

$$\begin{aligned} E_{\mathrm{LSE}}(\mathbf{w}, b) &= ||\vec{\epsilon}||^2 \\ &= ||\mathbf{X}^{\mathrm{T}}\mathbf{w} + b\mathbf{e} - \mathbf{y}||^2 \\ &= \mathbf{w}^{\mathrm{T}}\mathbf{X}\mathbf{X}^{\mathrm{T}}\mathbf{w} - 2\mathbf{w}^{\mathrm{T}}\mathbf{X}[\mathbf{y} - b\mathbf{e}] - ||\mathbf{y} - b\mathbf{e}||^2 \\ &= \mathbf{w}^{\mathrm{T}}\mathbf{S}\mathbf{w} - 2\mathbf{w}^{\mathrm{T}}\mathbf{X}[\mathbf{y} - b\mathbf{e}] - ||\mathbf{y} - b\mathbf{e}||^2. \end{aligned} \tag{8.16}$$

Using the gradient method, the optimal solutions are computed by simultaneously zeroing the first-order gradient of $E_{\mathrm{LSE}}(\mathbf{w}, b)$ with respect to b and **w**:

$$\frac{\partial E_{\mathrm{LSE}}(\mathbf{w}, b)}{\partial b} = 2\left(\mathbf{e}^{\mathrm{T}}\mathbf{X}^{\mathrm{T}}\mathbf{w} + b\mathbf{e}^{\mathrm{T}}\mathbf{e} - \mathbf{e}^{\mathrm{T}}\mathbf{y}\right) = 2\left(\mathbf{e}^{\mathrm{T}}\mathbf{X}^{\mathrm{T}}\mathbf{w} + Nb - \mathbf{e}^{\mathrm{T}}\mathbf{y}\right) = 0 \tag{8.17}$$

and

$$\frac{\partial E_{\mathrm{LSE}}(\mathbf{w}, b)}{\partial \mathbf{w}} = 2\mathbf{S}\mathbf{w} - 2\mathbf{X}[\mathbf{y} - b\mathbf{e}] = 0. \tag{8.18}$$

ALGORITHM 8.1 (Learning algorithm for LSE classifier) *Combining Eqs. (8.17) and (8.18), the LSE solution may be computed by solving the following matrix system:*

$$\begin{bmatrix} \mathbf{S} & \mathbf{X}\mathbf{e} \\ \mathbf{e}^{\mathrm{T}}\mathbf{X}^{\mathrm{T}} & N \end{bmatrix} \begin{bmatrix} \mathbf{w}_{\mathrm{LSE}} \\ b \end{bmatrix} = \begin{bmatrix} \mathbf{X}\mathbf{y} \\ \mathbf{e}^{\mathrm{T}}\mathbf{y} \end{bmatrix}. \tag{8.19}$$

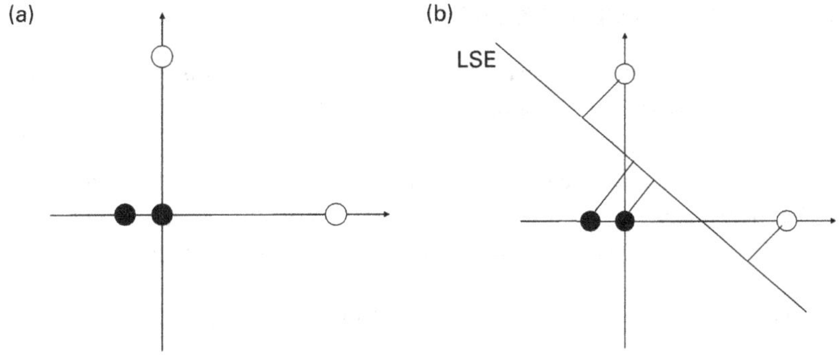

Fig. 8.5. The LSE classifier for four two-dimensional training vectors. (a) The dataset. (b) The decision boundary is jointly determined by all four of the training vectors.

After $\mathbf{w}$ *and* b *have been learned, the decision boundary can be obtained as*

$$f(\mathbf{x}) = \mathbf{w}^{\mathrm{T}}\mathbf{x} + b = 0. \qquad \square$$

Example 8.1 (Find LSE classifier via matrix system solver) *As shown in Figure 8.5(a), there are four training vectors:*

$$\begin{aligned} \mathbf{x}_1 &= [0.0 \quad 1.0]^{\mathrm{T}}, & y_1 &= +1, \\ \mathbf{x}_2 &= [1.0 \quad 0.0]^{\mathrm{T}}, & y_2 &= +1, \\ \mathbf{x}_3 &= [-0.2 \quad 0.0]^{\mathrm{T}}, & y_3 &= -1, \\ \mathbf{x}_4 &= [0.0 \quad 0.0]^{\mathrm{T}}, & y_4 &= -1. \end{aligned}$$

This is an over-determined scenario because the number of vectors is higher than the dimension of the feature space. The training data matrix is

$$\mathbf{X} = \begin{bmatrix} 0 & 1 & -0.2 & 0 \\ 1 & 0 & 0 & 0 \end{bmatrix},$$

and the scatter matrix is

$$\mathbf{S} = \mathbf{X}\mathbf{X}^{\mathrm{T}} = \begin{bmatrix} 1.04 & 0 \\ 0 & 1 \end{bmatrix}.$$

On solving the matrix system Eq. (8.19) for this dataset, we obtain

$$\mathbf{w}_{\mathrm{LSE}} = \begin{bmatrix} +1.774 \\ +1.806 \end{bmatrix} \text{ and } b = -0.806.$$

Thus, the decision boundary of the LSE classifier is prescribed by

$$1.774x^{(1)} + 1.806x^{(2)} - 0.806 = 0, \tag{8.20}$$

which is pictorially shown as the dashed line in Figure 8.5(b). $\square$

8.3.2 Fisher's discriminant analysis (FDA)

A classical approach to linear classification is Fisher's discriminant analysis (FDA), which is also known as linear discriminant analysis (LDA).

The objective function of the FDA classifier is based on a signal-to-noise ratio pertaining to the training vectors from each of the two classes. Let $\vec{\mu}$, $\vec{\mu}_+$, and $\vec{\mu}_-$ denote respectively the centroids of the total mass, the positive training set, and the negative training set. The signal and noise matrices are defined as follows [53, 54, 73, 174].

- The signal matrix is represented by the following *between-class* scatter matrix:

$$\begin{aligned}\mathbf{S}_\mathrm{B} &= N_+[\vec{\mu}_+ - \vec{\mu}][\vec{\mu}_+ - \vec{\mu}]^\mathrm{T} + N_-[\vec{\mu}_- - \vec{\mu}][\vec{\mu}_- - \vec{\mu}]^\mathrm{T} \\ &= \frac{N_+N_-}{N}[\vec{\mu}_+ - \vec{\mu}_-][\vec{\mu}_+ - \vec{\mu}_-]^\mathrm{T} = \frac{N_+N_-}{N}\mathbf{\Delta}\mathbf{\Delta}^\mathrm{T}.\end{aligned} \tag{8.21}$$

- The noise matrix is characterized by the following *within-class* scatter matrix:

$$\mathbf{S}_\mathrm{W} = \sum_{i:y_i=+1}[\mathbf{x}_i - \vec{\mu}_+][\mathbf{x}_i - \vec{\mu}_+]^\mathrm{T} + \sum_{i:y_i=-1}[\mathbf{x}_i - \vec{\mu}_-][\mathbf{x}_i - \vec{\mu}_-]^T.$$

The objective of FDA involves finding the projection vector $\mathbf{w}$ which maximizes the Fisher score defined by the following signal-to-noise ratio:

$$\tilde{J}(\mathbf{w}) = \frac{\text{signal}}{\text{noise}} = \frac{\mathbf{w}^\mathrm{T}\mathbf{S}_\mathrm{B}\mathbf{w}}{\mathbf{w}^\mathrm{T}\mathbf{S}_\mathrm{W}\mathbf{w}}.$$

Note that the *signal* here represents the distance between the two projected centroids, while the *noise* here is the variance of the intra-cluster data along the projection.

The FDA aims at finding

$$\arg\max_{\{\mathbf{w}\in\mathbb{R}^M\}} \tilde{J}(\mathbf{w}). \tag{8.22}$$

The optimal solution can be obtained by finding the zero-gradient point such that

$$\frac{\partial\tilde{J}(\mathbf{w})}{\partial\mathbf{w}} = 0.$$

It follows that

$$\frac{\partial\tilde{J}(\mathbf{w})}{\partial\mathbf{w}} = \left(\frac{2}{\mathbf{w}^\mathrm{T}\mathbf{S}_\mathrm{W}\mathbf{w}}\right)\mathbf{S}_\mathrm{B}\mathbf{w} - \left(\frac{2\mathbf{w}^\mathrm{T}\mathbf{S}_\mathrm{B}\mathbf{w}}{(\mathbf{w}^\mathrm{T}\mathbf{S}_\mathrm{W}\mathbf{w})^2}\right)\mathbf{S}_\mathrm{W}\mathbf{w} = 0.$$

By substituting $\mathbf{S}_\mathrm{B} = (N_+N_-/N)\,\mathbf{\Delta}\mathbf{\Delta}^\mathrm{T}$ into the above, we arrive at

$$\frac{\partial\tilde{J}(\mathbf{w})}{\partial\mathbf{w}} = \beta\mathbf{\Delta} - \gamma\mathbf{S}_\mathrm{W}\mathbf{w} = 0, \tag{8.23}$$

where we denote that

$$\mathbf{\Delta} \equiv \vec{\mu}_+ - \vec{\mu}_- \tag{8.24}$$

and that

$$\beta = \frac{2N_+N_-}{N} \frac{\mathbf{w}^{\mathrm{T}}\boldsymbol{\Delta}}{\mathbf{w}^{\mathrm{T}}\mathbf{S}_{\mathrm{W}}\mathbf{w}}$$

and

$$\gamma = \frac{2\mathbf{w}^{\mathrm{T}}\mathbf{S}_{\mathrm{B}}\mathbf{w}}{(\mathbf{w}^{\mathrm{T}}\mathbf{S}_{\mathrm{W}}\mathbf{w})^2}.$$

Let us assume further that $\mathbf{S}_{\mathrm{W}}$ is nonsingular. Then Eq. (8.23) can be satisfied by any solution with the following form:

$$\mathbf{w} \propto \mathbf{S}_{\mathrm{W}}^{-1}\boldsymbol{\Delta}. \tag{8.25}$$

Put simply, an optimal solution is

$$\tilde{\mathbf{w}}_{\mathrm{FDA}} = \mathbf{S}_{\mathrm{W}}^{-1}\boldsymbol{\Delta}.$$

ALGORITHM 8.2 (Conventional algorithm for Fisher's discriminant analysis (FDA)) *The conventional optimal FDA solution is*

$$\tilde{\mathbf{w}}_{\mathrm{FDA}} = \mathbf{S}_{\mathrm{W}}^{-1}\boldsymbol{\Delta}, \tag{8.26}$$

and it can be shown (details omitted) that the optimal threshold is

$$b = -\vec{\mu}^{\mathrm{T}}\mathbf{S}_{\mathrm{W}}^{-1}\boldsymbol{\Delta} + \frac{N_+ - N_-}{2N_+N_-(1-\alpha)}, \tag{8.27}$$

where

$$\alpha = \left(\frac{N}{N_+\,N_-} + \boldsymbol{\Delta}^{\mathrm{T}}\mathbf{S}_{\mathrm{W}}^{-1}\boldsymbol{\Delta}\right)^{-1} \boldsymbol{\Delta}^{\mathrm{T}}\mathbf{S}_{\mathrm{W}}^{-1}\boldsymbol{\Delta}.$$

After **w** *and b have been learned, the decision boundary is*

$$f(\mathbf{x}) = \mathbf{w}^{\mathrm{T}}\mathbf{x} + b = 0. \qquad \square$$

Figure 8.6 provides a pictorial interpretation of Eq. (8.26). Two kinds of intra-cluster data distributions will be considered.

(i) *Isotropic* $\mathbf{S}_{\mathrm{W}}$. Assuming that $\mathbf{S}_{\mathrm{W}}$ is isotropic means that all of the features are independent with equal variance (based on the within-class statistics), i.e. the decision vector will be proportional to $\boldsymbol{\Delta}$. This automatically leads to a decision boundary perpendicular to $\boldsymbol{\Delta}$. This is depicted in Figure 8.6(a).
(ii) *Non-isotropic* $\mathbf{S}_{\mathrm{W}}$. On the other hand, if $\mathbf{S}_{\mathrm{W}}$ is non-isotropic, the FDA solution given by Eq. (8.26) must take into account the variance difference and mutual correlation between the features. With such adjustment the decision boundary will no longer be perpendicular to $\boldsymbol{\Delta}$. This phenomenon is illustrated by Figure 8.6(b).

Recall that, in Eq. (8.7), the centered (i.e. center-adjusted) *scatter matrix* is defined as

$$\mathbf{S}_{\mathrm{C}} \equiv \bar{\mathbf{S}} \equiv \bar{\mathbf{X}}\bar{\mathbf{X}}^{\mathrm{T}} = \sum_{i=1}^{N}[\mathbf{x}_i - \vec{\mu}][\mathbf{x}_i - \vec{\mu}]^{\mathrm{T}}. \tag{8.28}$$

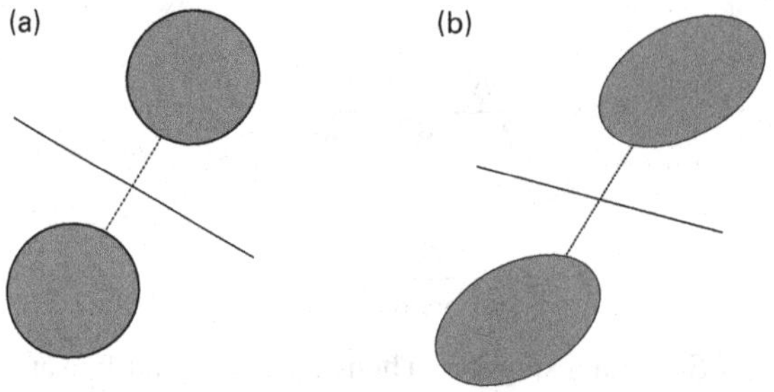

Fig. 8.6. A pictorial illustration of the optimal FDA solution. (a) For the special case that all the features are independent with equal variance, the decision boundary is perpendicular to $\mathbf{\Delta}$. Here the circular equipotential contour of the within-class data distribution is used to indicate an isotropic $\mathbf{S}_W$. (b) The fact that the matrix $\mathbf{S}_W$ is now more generic is manifested by an elliptic (instead of circular) equipotential contour. This results in a tilted decision boundary, which is no longer perpendicular to $\mathbf{\Delta}$.

It can be shown that [53, 54]

$$\mathbf{S}_C \equiv \bar{\mathbf{S}} = \mathbf{S}_W + \mathbf{S}_B. \tag{8.29}$$

Therefore, maximization of the conventional Signal-to-noise ratio (SNR) is identical to maximization of a modified Fisher score:

$$J(\mathbf{w}) = \frac{\text{signal}}{\text{signal} + \text{noise}} = \frac{\mathbf{w}^T\mathbf{S}_B\mathbf{w}}{\mathbf{w}^T(\mathbf{S}_B + \mathbf{S}_W)\mathbf{w}} = \frac{\mathbf{w}^T\mathbf{\Delta}\mathbf{\Delta}^T\mathbf{w}}{\mathbf{w}^T\bar{\mathbf{S}}\mathbf{w}}. \tag{8.30}$$

The optimal solution is again its zero-gradient point, i.e. $\partial J(\mathbf{w})/\partial \mathbf{w} = 0$. Assuming that $\bar{\mathbf{S}}$ is nonsingular (which should generically be the case for over-determined systems when $N > M$), we have

$$\mathbf{w}_{FDA} = \bar{\mathbf{S}}^{-1}[\vec{\mu}_+ - \vec{\mu}_-] = \bar{\mathbf{S}}^{-1}\mathbf{\Delta}. \tag{8.31}$$

ALGORITHM 8.3 (Modified algorithm for FDA) *An alternative solution for FDA is as follows:*

$$\mathbf{w}_{FDA} = \bar{\mathbf{S}}^{-1}\mathbf{\Delta} \tag{8.32}$$

and

$$b = -\vec{\mu}^T\bar{\mathbf{S}}^{-1}\mathbf{\Delta} + \frac{N_+ - N_-}{2N_+N_-}. \tag{8.33}$$

After $\mathbf{w}$ *and* b *have been learned, the decision boundary is*

$$f(\mathbf{x}) = \mathbf{w}^T\mathbf{x} + b = 0.$$ □

Equivalence between conventional and modified FDAs

Despite the difference in their appearances, $\mathbf{w}_{FDA}$ in Eq. (8.31) and $\tilde{\mathbf{w}}_{FDA}$ in Eq. (8.26) are basically equivalent. To prove this, let us rewrite Eqs. (8.26) and (8.31) as

$$\tilde{\mathbf{w}}_{FDA} = \mathbf{S}_W^{-1}\mathbf{\Delta} \quad \text{and} \quad \mathbf{w}_{FDA} = \bar{\mathbf{S}}^{-1}\mathbf{\Delta}.$$

By Woodbury's matrix identity [301], we have

$$\bar{\mathbf{S}}^{-1} = (\mathbf{S}_W + \mathbf{S}_B)^{-1} = \left(\mathbf{S}_W + \frac{N_+N_-}{N}\boldsymbol{\Delta}\boldsymbol{\Delta}^T\right)^{-1}$$
$$= \mathbf{S}_W^{-1} - \mathbf{S}_W^{-1}\boldsymbol{\Delta}\left(\frac{N}{N_+N_-} + \boldsymbol{\Delta}^T\mathbf{S}_W^{-1}\boldsymbol{\Delta}\right)^{-1}\boldsymbol{\Delta}^T\mathbf{S}_W^{-1}.$$

Let us denote

$$\alpha = \left(\frac{N}{N_+N_-} + \boldsymbol{\Delta}^T\mathbf{S}_W^{-1}\boldsymbol{\Delta}\right)^{-1}\boldsymbol{\Delta}^T\mathbf{S}_W^{-1}\boldsymbol{\Delta},$$

then

$$\mathbf{w}_{FDA} = \bar{\mathbf{S}}^{-1}[\vec{\mu}_+ - \vec{\mu}_-] = \bar{\mathbf{S}}^{-1}\boldsymbol{\Delta}$$
$$= \mathbf{S}_W^{-1}\boldsymbol{\Delta} - \mathbf{S}_W^{-1}\boldsymbol{\Delta}\left(\frac{N}{N_+N_-} + \boldsymbol{\Delta}^T\mathbf{S}_W^{-1}\boldsymbol{\Delta}\right)^{-1}\boldsymbol{\Delta}^T\mathbf{S}_W^{-1}\boldsymbol{\Delta}$$
$$= \mathbf{S}_W^{-1}\boldsymbol{\Delta}(1-\alpha) = (1-\alpha)\tilde{\mathbf{w}}_{FDA}. \tag{8.34}$$

Barring a scaling factor, the FDA solution $\mathbf{w}_{FDA}$ is equivalent to the conventional FDA solution $\tilde{\mathbf{w}}_{FDA}$. Note also that the new FDA solution in Eq. (8.31) is basically the same as the LSE solution in Eq. (8.11).

Equivalence between LSE and FDAs

Note that

$$\mathbf{w}_{LSE} \overset{\text{Eq. (8.11)}}{=} \frac{2N_+N_-}{N}\bar{\mathbf{S}}^{-1}\boldsymbol{\Delta}$$
$$\overset{\text{Eq. (8.31)}}{=} \frac{2N_+N_-}{N}\mathbf{w}_{FDA}$$
$$\overset{\text{Eq. (8.34)}}{=} \frac{2(1-\alpha)N_+N_-}{N}\tilde{\mathbf{w}}_{FDA}.$$

This establishes the equivalence between LSE and the new FDA. The equivalence can also be formally established by substituting Eq. (8.32) and (8.33) into the RR learning formulation in Eq. (8.19) and verifying the following matrix equality (see Problem 8.12):

$$\begin{bmatrix} \mathbf{S} & \mathbf{X}\mathbf{e} \\ \mathbf{e}^T\mathbf{X}^T & N \end{bmatrix}\begin{bmatrix} \mathbf{w}_{FDA} \\ b \end{bmatrix}$$
$$= \begin{bmatrix} \mathbf{S} & \mathbf{X}\mathbf{e} \\ \mathbf{e}^T\mathbf{X}^T & N \end{bmatrix}\begin{bmatrix} \bar{\mathbf{S}}^{-1}\boldsymbol{\Delta} \\ -\vec{\mu}^T\bar{\mathbf{S}}^{-1}\boldsymbol{\Delta} + (N_+ - N_-)/(2N_+N_-) \end{bmatrix}$$
$$= \kappa\begin{bmatrix} \mathbf{X}\mathbf{y} \\ \mathbf{e}^T\mathbf{y} \end{bmatrix}.$$

The discussion is now summarized by the equivalence theorem.

THEOREM 8.1 (Equivalence between LSE and FDA) *The optimal LSE and FDA classifiers are basically equivalent.* □

The following is a numerical example demonstrating the equivalence between LSE and FDA.

Example 8.2 (Equivalence between LSE and FDA: four two-dimensional training vectors) *Consider the dataset in Example 8.1:*

$$\begin{aligned} \mathbf{x}_1 &= [0.0 \quad 1.0]^{\mathrm{T}}, & y_1 &= +1, \\ \mathbf{x}_2 &= [1.0 \quad 0.0]^{\mathrm{T}}, & y_2 &= +1, \\ \mathbf{x}_3 &= [-0.2 \quad 0.0]^{\mathrm{T}}, & y_3 &= -1, \\ \mathbf{x}_4 &= [0.0 \quad 0.0]^{\mathrm{T}}, & y_4 &= -1. \end{aligned}$$

The data matrices before and after centroid-adjustment are respectively

$$\mathbf{X} = \begin{bmatrix} 0 & 1 & -0.2 & 0 \\ 1 & 0 & 0 & 0 \end{bmatrix} \textit{ and } \bar{\mathbf{X}} = \begin{bmatrix} -0.2 & 0.8 & -0.4 & -0.2 \\ 0.75 & -0.25 & -0.25 & -0.25 \end{bmatrix}.$$

The mass centroid, positive centroid, and negative centroid are respectively

$$\vec{\mu} = [0.2 \quad 0.25]^{\mathrm{T}}, \vec{\mu}_+ = [0.5 \quad 0.5]^{\mathrm{T}}, \textit{ and } \vec{\mu}_- = [-0.1 \quad 0]^{\mathrm{T}}.$$

The scatter matrix is

$$\bar{\mathbf{S}} = \bar{\mathbf{X}}\bar{\mathbf{X}}^{\mathrm{T}} = \begin{bmatrix} 0.88 & -0.2 \\ -0.2 & 0.75 \end{bmatrix}.$$

It follows that the FDA solution can be obtained as

$$\mathbf{w}_{\mathrm{FDA}} = \bar{\mathbf{S}}^{-1}(\vec{\mu}_+ - \vec{\mu}_-) = \begin{bmatrix} 0.88 & -0.2 \\ -0.2 & 0.75 \end{bmatrix}^{-1} \begin{bmatrix} 0.6 \\ 0.5 \end{bmatrix} = \begin{bmatrix} 0.887 \\ 0.903 \end{bmatrix},$$

and

$$b = -\mathbf{w}^{\mathrm{T}}\vec{\mu} + \frac{N_+ - N_-}{2N_+N_-} = -0.403.$$

The decision boundary of the FDA classifier is

$$0.887x^{(1)} + 0.903x^{(2)} - 0.403 = 0, \tag{8.35}$$

which is basically the same as the LSE classifier given by Eq. (8.20). The decision boundary is pictorially shown as the long solid line in Figure 8.5(b).

Connection between LSE and FDA solutions

If $\mathbf{S}$ is nonsingular (as is usually the case when $N > M$), then Eq. (8.18) leads to a useful formulation for the decision vector:

$$\mathbf{w} = \mathbf{S}^{-1}\mathbf{X}[\mathbf{y} - b\mathbf{e}]. \tag{8.36}$$

Since both Eq. (8.36) and Eq. (8.11) are valid solutions for the LSE problem, they have to be equivalent. The former serves as a useful link to the ridge regressor (see Eq. (7.9)), while the latter is closely linked to FDA (see Eq. (8.31)). This establishes the equivalence between LSE and FDA.

8.4 Supervised learning models: under-determined formulation

In order to design a statistically robust classifier, one usually requires a large number of training vectors. It is desirable to have a sufficiently large training data size to assure an invertible scatter matrix $\bar{\mathbf{S}}$ in Eq. (8.31). At the very minimum, it is necessary that $N > M$ in order for there to be a chance of having an invertible $\mathbf{S}$.

On the other hand, when there are insufficient training data, i.e. when $M \geq N$, the matrix equation in Eq. (8.14) becomes under-determined. The number of constraining equations becomes lower than that of the unknowns. This renders the conventional LSE and FDA formulations invalid. An alternative approach is proposed as follows.

The 2-norm criterion for maximum margin separation

When $M \geq N$, there always (generically speaking) exists a decision vector $\mathbf{w}$ that makes make all the training vectors "error-free," i.e.

$$\epsilon_i \equiv \mathbf{w}^{\mathrm{T}}\mathbf{x}_i + b - y_i = 0, \; i = 1, \ldots, N. \tag{8.37}$$

In this case, all the training vectors fall exactly on two parallel (EFP) hyperplanes characterized by $\mathbf{w}$:

$$\mathbf{w}^{\mathrm{T}}\mathbf{x}_i + b = y_i = +1$$

for the positive training vectors; and

$$\mathbf{w}^{\mathrm{T}}\mathbf{x}_i + b = y_i = -1$$

for the negative training vectors. The two hyperplanes are separated by a distance of $2/\|\mathbf{w}\|$, where $\|\mathbf{w}\| = \|\mathbf{w}\|_2$ denotes the 2-norm of $\mathbf{w}$. This distance provides a measure of the success achieved by the learned classifier – the wider the better. Note further that, if $M \geq N$, the error-free solution will be highly non-unique. To enforce uniqueness, it is natural to impose an additional learning objective (on top of the error-free condition) in requiring the decision vector $\mathbf{w}$ to deliver a minimum 2-norm: $\|\mathbf{w}\|$.

The augmented objective leads to the following optimization formulation:

$$\min_{\mathbf{w}} \left\{ \frac{1}{2}\|\mathbf{w}\|^2 \right\}$$
$$\text{subject to } \epsilon_i = 0 \; \forall i = 1, \ldots, N. \tag{8.38}$$

The Lagrangian function is

$$\begin{aligned} L(\mathbf{w}, b, \mathbf{a}) &= \frac{1}{2}\|\mathbf{w}\|^2 - \sum_{i=1}^{N} a_i \epsilon_i \\ &= \frac{1}{2}\|\mathbf{w}\|^2 - \sum_{i=1}^{N} a_i(\mathbf{w}^{\mathrm{T}}\mathbf{x}_i + b - y_i), \end{aligned} \tag{8.39}$$

where all the Lagrange multipliers a_i form an N-dimensional vector $\mathbf{a}$.

The optimal solution can be obtained by finding its zero-gradient point with respect to b, $\mathbf{w}$, and $\mathbf{a}$. This leads to the following observations.

- *The learning subspace property (LSP).* The zero gradient with respect to $\mathbf{w}$ implies that

$$\frac{\partial L(\mathbf{w}, b, \mathbf{a})}{\partial \mathbf{w}} = \mathbf{w} - \sum_{i=1}^{N} a_i \mathbf{x}_i = 0,$$

which in turn leads to

$$\mathbf{w} = \sum_{i=1}^{N} a_i \mathbf{x}_i. \tag{8.40}$$

Equivalently, in matrix notation,

$$\mathbf{w} = \mathbf{X}\mathbf{a}. \tag{8.41}$$

This establishes the LSP condition, i.e. $\mathbf{w} = \mathbf{X}\mathbf{a}$.

- *The orthogonal-hyperplane property (OHP).* Likewise, the zero gradient with respect to b leads to

$$\sum_{i=1}^{N} a_i = \mathbf{e}^{\mathrm{T}}\mathbf{a} = 0. \tag{8.42}$$

This establishes that the OHP ($\mathbf{e}^{\mathrm{T}}\mathbf{a} = 0$) is a necessary condition for the optimality.

A closed-form optimal solution

The "error-free" condition Eq. (8.37) can be expressed in matrix form:

$$\mathbf{X}^{\mathrm{T}}\mathbf{w} + \mathbf{e}b = \mathbf{y}. \tag{8.43}$$

On substituting the LSP in Eq. (8.41), i.e. $\mathbf{w} = \mathbf{X}\mathbf{a}$, into Eq. (8.43), we arrive at

$$\mathbf{X}^{\mathrm{T}}\mathbf{w} + \mathbf{e}b = \mathbf{X}^{\mathrm{T}}\mathbf{X}\mathbf{a} + \mathbf{e}b = \mathbf{y}. \tag{8.44}$$

On combining Eq. (8.44) and Eq. (8.42), the optimal solution for $\mathbf{a}$ may be obtained via the following matrix equation:

$$\begin{bmatrix} \mathbf{X}^{\mathrm{T}}\mathbf{X} & \mathbf{e} \\ \mathbf{e}^{\mathrm{T}} & 0 \end{bmatrix} \begin{bmatrix} \mathbf{a} \\ b \end{bmatrix} = \begin{bmatrix} \mathbf{y} \\ 0 \end{bmatrix}. \tag{8.45}$$

Once $\mathbf{a}$ has been obtained, the optimal decision vector can be derived as $\mathbf{w} = \mathbf{X}\mathbf{a}$. This formulation will be revisited in Section 8.6.1 when we re-derive the same model from a kernelization (or kernel-trick) perspective.

Why the name OHP?

For under-determined systems, i.e. $M \geq N$, there exists *a data hyperplane* characterized by a *normal vector*, denoted by $\mathbf{p}$, which can be derived as[2]

$$\mathbf{p} = \mathbf{U}^{\mathrm{T}} \begin{bmatrix} \mathbf{R}^{-1}\mathbf{e} \\ \mathbf{q} \end{bmatrix} \tag{8.46}$$

for any $(M - N)$-dimensional vector $\mathbf{q}$. It follows that

$$\mathbf{X}^{\mathrm{T}}\mathbf{p} = [\mathbf{R} \quad \mathbf{0}]\mathbf{U}\mathbf{p} = \mathbf{e}. \tag{8.47}$$

The OHP implies that the "data hyperplane" (characterized by $\mathbf{p}$) and the "separation hyperplane" (characterized by $\mathbf{w}$) must be orthogonal to each other. Mathematically, the OHP can be expressed as

$$\mathbf{w}^{\mathrm{T}}\mathbf{p} = 0. \tag{8.48}$$

By plugging Eq. (8.41) into Eq. (8.48), we obtain Eq. (8.42), i.e. $\mathbf{e}^{\mathrm{T}}\mathbf{a} = 0$.

As illustrated by Figure 8.7, the OHP is a necessary condition for attaining a maximal margin of separation between the two error-free hyperplanes.

Example 8.3 (The OHP property of two two-dimensional training vectors) *Let us consider the dataset shown in Figure 8.7, with $M = N = 2$, and*

$$\mathbf{X} = \begin{bmatrix} -1 & 3 \\ 1 & 5 \end{bmatrix} \text{ and } \mathbf{y} = \begin{bmatrix} +1 \\ -1 \end{bmatrix}$$

By Eq. (8.46), it follows that

$$\mathbf{p} = \begin{bmatrix} -0.5 \\ +0.5 \end{bmatrix}.$$

Note that

$$\mathbf{X}^{\mathrm{T}}\mathbf{p} = [1 \quad 1]^{\mathrm{T}} = \mathbf{e},$$

so we have verified Eq. (8.47). Moreover, it can be derived that (See Eq. (8.68))

$$\mathbf{w} = [-0.25 \quad -0.25]^{\mathrm{T}}.$$

Note that $\mathbf{w}^{\mathrm{T}}\mathbf{p} = 0$, so we have verified the OHP in the original space, i.e. Eq. (8.48).

---

2 The derivation of non-unique solutions for a normal vector $\mathbf{p}$ is outlined as follows. Take QR decomposition on $\mathbf{X}^{\mathrm{T}} = [\mathbf{R}\ \mathbf{0}]\mathbf{U}$, where $\mathbf{R}$ is an invertible lower-triangular matrix and $\mathbf{U}$ is a unitary matrix. On plugging the decomposition into Eq. (8.47), we have

$$[\mathbf{R} \quad \mathbf{0}]\mathbf{U}\mathbf{p} = \mathbf{e}.$$

Since $\mathbf{R}$ is invertible, it follows that

$$\mathbf{R}^{-1}[\mathbf{R} \quad \mathbf{0}]\mathbf{U}\mathbf{p} = [\mathbf{I} \quad \mathbf{0}]\mathbf{U}\mathbf{p} = \mathbf{R}^{-1}\mathbf{e},$$

i.e.

$$\mathbf{U}\mathbf{p} = \begin{bmatrix} \mathbf{R}^{-1}\mathbf{e} \\ \mathbf{q} \end{bmatrix},$$

for any $(M - N)$-dimensional vector $\mathbf{q}$. Thus Eq. (8.46).

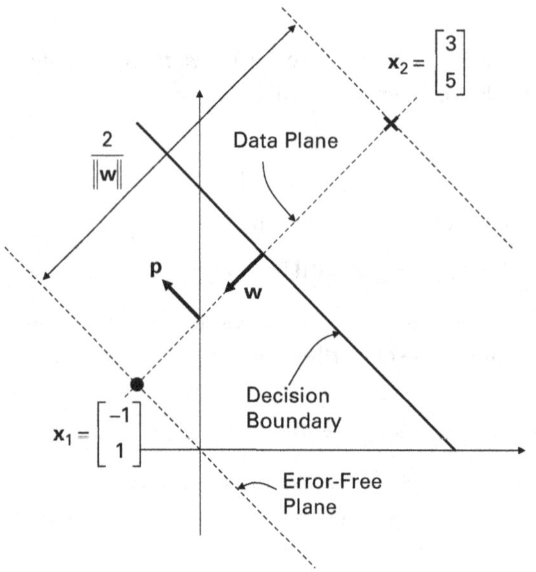

Fig. 8.7. An example (with $N = M = 2$) illustrating the orthogonal hyperplane property in which the error-free planes and decision boundary are orthogonal to the data hyperplane in an under-determined linear system.

8.5 A regularization method for robust classification

So far, the supervised learning models involving over- and under-determined systems have been treated separately with distinctive approaches in Sections 8.3 and 8.4, respectively. The regression/regularization techniques introduced in Chapter 7 provide a unifying framework in which to treat both over- and under-determined systems.

In this section, two approaches will be treated and their equivalence will be established.

(i) *Regression approach: the ridge regression (RR) formulation.* The principle of ridge regression involves the use of a penalty-incorporated loss function so as to keep the regressor coefficients under control. This may overcome possible over-fitting or ill-posed problems and enhance the robustness of the learned classifier [99, 112, 275].

(ii) *Separability approach: perturbational FDA formulation.* Starting from the error-in-variable models, we shall develop a learning model that can effectively cope with input measurement errors. This leads to a perturbational variant of FDA, also known as *perturbational discriminant analysis* (PDA).

8.5.1 The ridge regression approach to linear classification

In the ridge regression approach, both the vector norm and the error terms are included in the cost function (see Eq. (8.49)). The objective is to find the decision vector such that

$$\min_{\mathbf{w},b} E(\mathbf{w}, b) = \min_{\mathbf{w},b} \left\{ \sum_{i=1}^{N} \epsilon_i^2 + \rho \|\mathbf{w}\|^2 \right\}, \tag{8.49}$$

where

$$\epsilon_i = \mathbf{w}^{\mathrm{T}}\mathbf{x}_i + b - y_i \quad \forall i = 1, \ldots, N.$$

In the matrix notation,

$$E(\mathbf{w}, b) = \|\mathbf{X}^{\mathrm{T}}\mathbf{w} + \mathbf{e}b - \mathbf{y}\|^2 + \rho\|\mathbf{w}\|^2. \tag{8.50}$$

Solution in the original space

Using the gradient method, the optimal solutions are computed by simultaneously zeroing the first-order gradient of $E(\mathbf{w}, b)$ with respect to b and $\mathbf{w}$:

$$\frac{\partial E(\mathbf{w}, b)}{\partial b} = \mathbf{e}^{\mathrm{T}}\mathbf{X}^{\mathrm{T}}\mathbf{w} + b\mathbf{e}^{\mathrm{T}}\mathbf{e} - \mathbf{e}^{\mathrm{T}}\mathbf{y} = \mathbf{e}^{\mathrm{T}}\mathbf{X}^{\mathrm{T}}\mathbf{w} + Nb - \mathbf{e}^{\mathrm{T}}\mathbf{y} = 0 \tag{8.51}$$

and

$$\frac{\partial E(\mathbf{w}, b)}{\partial \mathbf{w}} = 2\mathbf{X}(\mathbf{X}^{\mathrm{T}}\mathbf{w} + \mathbf{e}b - \mathbf{y}) + 2\rho\mathbf{w} = 0. \tag{8.52}$$

The last equation alone leads to a useful formulation for the decision vector:

$$\mathbf{w} = [\mathbf{X}\mathbf{X}^{\mathrm{T}} + \rho\mathbf{I}]^{-1}\mathbf{X}[\mathbf{y} - b\mathbf{e}] = [\mathbf{S} + \rho\mathbf{I}]^{-1}\mathbf{X}[\mathbf{y} - b\mathbf{e}]. \tag{8.53}$$

ALGORITHM 8.4 (Scatter-matrix-based algorithm for linear ridge classification) *Combining Eqs. (8.51) and (8.52), the solution for the linear ridge classifier may be derived from the following matrix system:*

$$\begin{bmatrix} \mathbf{S} + \rho\mathbf{I} & \mathbf{X}\mathbf{e} \\ \mathbf{e}^{\mathrm{T}}\mathbf{X}^{\mathrm{T}} & N \end{bmatrix} \begin{bmatrix} \mathbf{w}_{\mathrm{RR}} \\ b \end{bmatrix} = \begin{bmatrix} \mathbf{X}\mathbf{y} \\ \mathbf{e}^{\mathrm{T}}\mathbf{y} \end{bmatrix}. \tag{8.54}$$

After $\mathbf{w}$ *and* b *have been learned, the decision boundary is*

$$f(\mathbf{x}) = \mathbf{w}^{\mathrm{T}}\mathbf{x} + b = 0.$$

□

Example 8.4 (Linear ridge regression classifier for four two-dimensional vectors) *Let us revisit the same dataset as in Example 8.1. Suppose that the regularization parameter* $\rho = 0.01$*, and the regularized scatter matrix is*

$$\mathbf{S} + \rho\mathbf{I} = \mathbf{X}\mathbf{X}^{\mathrm{T}} + \rho\mathbf{I} = \begin{bmatrix} 1.05 & 0 \\ 0 & 1.05 \end{bmatrix},$$

and

$$\mathbf{X}\mathbf{e} = \begin{bmatrix} 0 & 1 & -0.2 & 0 \\ 1 & 0 & 0 & 0 \end{bmatrix} \begin{bmatrix} 1 \\ 1 \\ 1 \\ 1 \end{bmatrix} = \begin{bmatrix} 0.8 \\ 0 \end{bmatrix}.$$

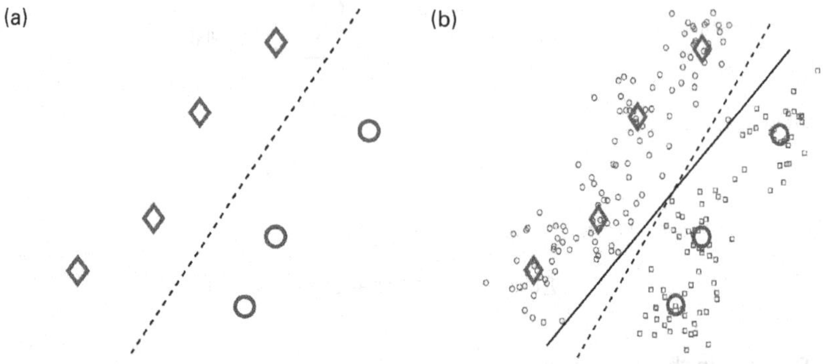

Fig. 8.8. (a) The observed training data. The (dashed-line) decision boundary is determined assuming that the training data are noise-free. (b) Possible distribution of the original noisy-free data. The (solid-line) decision boundary reflects the adjustment taking into account the knowledge that the training data are contaminated by additive noise.

The matrix system Eq. (8.54) becomes:

$$\begin{bmatrix} 1.05 & 0 & 0.8 \\ 0 & 1.05 & 1 \\ 0.8 & 1 & 4 \end{bmatrix} \begin{bmatrix} \mathbf{w} \\ b \end{bmatrix} = \begin{bmatrix} 0.8 \\ 1 \\ 0 \end{bmatrix}.$$

This leads to the optimal solution

$$\mathbf{w}_{\mathrm{RR}} = \begin{bmatrix} 1.747 \\ 1.7756 \end{bmatrix} \textit{and} \quad b = -0.793.$$

This leads to the final linear decision boundary:

$$1.747x^{(1)} + 1.7756x^{(2)} - 0.793 = 0.$$

8.5.2 Perturbational discriminant analysis (PDA): an extension of FDA

By incorporating perturbation into the input training dataset, we develop a learning model that is based on a perturbational discriminant analysis (PDA). With reference to Figure 8.8, such a learning model takes into account the likely input observation noise so as to enhance the resilience of the learned classifiers. It can be shown that the input noise power in PDA mathematically corresponds to the regularization parameter ρ used in the ridge regressor (RR) [21].

Recall that $\bar{\mathbf{X}}$ denotes the center-adjusted data matrix, and that its perturbed counterpart can be expressed as $\bar{\mathbf{X}} + \mathbf{N}$, where the "noise matrix" $\mathbf{N}$ represents random and uncorrelated additive noise terms. This leads to the following perturbed and center-adjusted scatter matrix:

$$(\bar{\mathbf{X}} + \mathbf{N})(\bar{\mathbf{X}} + \mathbf{N})^{\mathrm{T}} \approx \bar{\mathbf{X}}\bar{\mathbf{X}}^{\mathrm{T}} + \rho\mathbf{I} = \bar{\mathbf{S}} + \rho\mathbf{I}.$$

Let us denote

$$\mathbf{\Delta} \equiv \vec{\mu}_+ - \vec{\mu}_-,$$

where $\boldsymbol{\mu}_+$ and $\boldsymbol{\mu}_-$ are respectively the positive and negative centroids in the intrinsic space.

For noisy data, the modified Fisher score can be obtained as

$$J_{\text{PDA}} = \frac{\mathbf{w}^{\text{T}}\boldsymbol{\Delta}\boldsymbol{\Delta}^{\text{T}}\mathbf{w}}{\mathbf{w}^{\text{T}}[\bar{\mathbf{S}} + \rho\mathbf{I}]\mathbf{w}}. \tag{8.55}$$

Noting the close resemblance between Eq. (8.30) and Eq. (8.55), the optimal PDA solution for Eq. (8.55) should resemble Eq. (8.32), i.e. it should be of the following form:

$$\mathbf{w}_{\text{PDA}} = [\bar{\mathbf{S}} + \rho\mathbf{I}]^{-1}[\boldsymbol{\mu}_+ - \boldsymbol{\mu}_-] = [\bar{\mathbf{S}} + \rho\mathbf{I}]^{-1}\boldsymbol{\Delta} \tag{8.56}$$

and

$$b = -\overrightarrow{\boldsymbol{\mu}}^{\text{T}}[\bar{\mathbf{S}} + \rho\mathbf{I}]^{-1}\boldsymbol{\Delta} + \frac{N_+ - N_-}{2N_+N_-} = -\overrightarrow{\boldsymbol{\mu}}^{\text{T}}\mathbf{w}_{\text{PDA}} + \frac{N_+ - N_-}{2N_+N_-}. \tag{8.57}$$

Example 8.5 (PDA solution for classification of four two-dimensional vectors) *Let us revisit the same dataset as in Example 8.4. Supposing that the regularization parameter* $\rho = 0.01$, *it is easy to verify that by applying Eq. (8.56) we can obtain a PDA solution that is the same as the solution obtained via the scatter-matrix formulation in Example 8.4.*

More exactly, for this example,

$$\mathbf{w}_{\text{PDA}} = [\bar{\mathbf{S}} + \rho\mathbf{I}]^{-1}\boldsymbol{\Delta} = \begin{bmatrix} 0.88 & -0.2 \\ -0.2 & 0.75 \end{bmatrix}^{-1} \begin{bmatrix} 0.6 \\ 0.5 \end{bmatrix} = \begin{bmatrix} 0.8737 \\ 0.8878 \end{bmatrix} \tag{8.58}$$

and

$$b = -\overrightarrow{\boldsymbol{\mu}}^{\text{T}}\mathbf{w}_{\text{PDA}} + \frac{N_+ - N_-}{2N_+N_-} = -\begin{bmatrix} 0.2 & 0.25 \end{bmatrix} \begin{bmatrix} 0.8737 \\ 0.8878 \end{bmatrix} + 0 = -0.3967. \tag{8.59}$$

Note that here $\kappa = N/2N_+N_- = 0.5$ *and that*

$$\mathbf{w}_{\text{PDA}} = \kappa\mathbf{w}_{\text{RR}} = 0.5\mathbf{w}_{\text{RR}}.$$

See also Eq. (8.60).

8.5.3 Equivalence between RR and PDA

The equivalence between the two classifiers is summarized as follows:

THEOREM 8.2 (Equivalence Between RR and PDA) *When* $\rho > 0$, *the ridge regressor (RR) and perturbational discriminant analysis (PDA) have the same optimal solution. Moreover, the equivalence holds both for over-determined and for under-determined scenarios, including* $N > M$ *and* $M \geq N$. □

Proof. The equivalence between the RR (Eq. (8.54)) and PDA (Eq. (8.56)) can be formally established by substituting Eqs. (8.56) and (8.57) into Eq. (8.54) and showing that (see Problem 8.12)

$$\begin{bmatrix} \mathbf{S}+\rho\mathbf{I} & \mathbf{X}\mathbf{e} \\ \mathbf{e}^{\mathrm{T}}\mathbf{X}^{\mathrm{T}} & N \end{bmatrix} \begin{bmatrix} \mathbf{w}_{\mathrm{PDA}} \\ b \end{bmatrix}$$
$$= \begin{bmatrix} \mathbf{S}+\rho\mathbf{I} & \mathbf{X}\mathbf{e} \\ \mathbf{e}^{\mathrm{T}}\mathbf{X}^{\mathrm{T}} & N \end{bmatrix} \begin{bmatrix} [\bar{\mathbf{S}}+\rho\mathbf{I}]^{-1}\boldsymbol{\Delta} \\ -\vec{\mu}^{\mathrm{T}}[\bar{\mathbf{S}}+\rho\mathbf{I}]^{-1}\boldsymbol{\Delta}+(N_{+}-N_{-})/(2N_{+}N_{-}) \end{bmatrix}$$
$$= \kappa \begin{bmatrix} \mathbf{X}\mathbf{y} \\ \mathbf{e}^{\mathrm{T}}\mathbf{y} \end{bmatrix}, \tag{8.60}$$

where $\kappa = N/(2N_{+}N_{-})$.

8.5.4 Regularization effects of the ridge parameter ρ

In practice, the scatter matrix may be ill-conditioned and thus inevitably create numerical problems for LSE or FDA (i.e. LDA). Fortunately, these problems can generally be effectively solved by the RR (i.e. PDA). To illustrate this point, let us look into a couple of illuminating numerical examples.

Example 8.6 (Balance between two discriminant components) *Consider four training vectors:*

$$\mathbf{x}_1 = \begin{bmatrix} 1.0 \\ 0.1 \end{bmatrix}, \quad \mathbf{x}_2 = \begin{bmatrix} 0.8 \\ 0.1 \end{bmatrix}, \quad \mathbf{x}_3 = \begin{bmatrix} -0.8 \\ -0.1 \end{bmatrix}, \quad \mathbf{x}_4 = \begin{bmatrix} -1.0 \\ -0.1 \end{bmatrix},$$

with teacher values $y_1 = -1$, $y_2 = -1$, $y_3 = +1$, and $y_4 = +1$. The scatter matrix can be computed as

$$\mathbf{S} = \mathbf{X}\mathbf{X}^{\mathrm{T}} = \begin{bmatrix} 1.0 & 0.8 & -0.8 & -1.0 \\ 0.1 & 0.1 & -0.1 & -0.1 \end{bmatrix} \begin{bmatrix} 1.0 & 0.1 \\ 0.8 & 0.1 \\ -0.8 & -0.1 \\ -1.0 & -0.1 \end{bmatrix} = \begin{bmatrix} 3.28 & 0.36 \\ 0.36 & 0.04 \end{bmatrix}.$$

Since $\sum_{n=1}^{N} \mathbf{x}_n = \mathbf{0}$ and $\sum_{n=1}^{N} y_n = 0$, the optimal threshold value in Eq. (8.54) is already known, i.e. $b = 0$. (See Problem 1.6.) When $N_{+} = N_{-}$, it can be shown that $\mathbf{X}\mathbf{y} \propto \boldsymbol{\Delta}$. In this case,

$$\boldsymbol{\Delta} = [1.8 \quad 0.2]^{\mathrm{T}},$$

while

$$\mathbf{X}\mathbf{y} = [3.6 \quad 0.4]^{\mathrm{T}}.$$

It follows that the LSE solution is

$$\mathbf{w}_{\mathrm{LSE}} = [\mathbf{S}]^{-1}\mathbf{X}\mathbf{y} = [0 \quad 10.0]^{\mathrm{T}}.$$

In Figure 8.9, the linear decision boundary of LSE corresponds to the case with $\rho = 0$. Note that the discriminant function of the LSE classifier can be expressed by $x^{(2)}$ alone:

$$f(\mathbf{x}) = \mathbf{w}^{\mathrm{T}}\mathbf{x} = x^{(2)}.$$

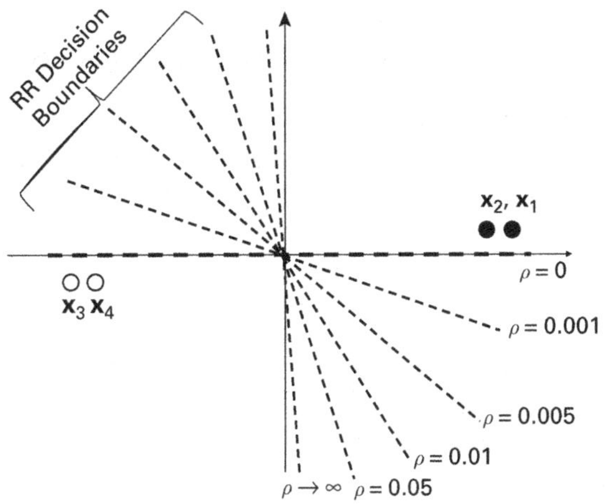

Fig. 8.9. Ridge-regression (RR)-based classifiers for a four-sample dataset. For different ridge factors $\rho = 0.0, 0.001, 0.005, 0.01,$ and 0.05, and, ultimately, $\rho \to \infty$, the optimal RR decision vectors are shown as dashed straight lines. Note that the decision component $\mathbf{x}^{(2)}$ is much weaker than the other decision component, $\mathbf{x}^{(1)}$. (The strength of a decision component can be quantitatively characterized by the PCA analysis, see Chapter 9.) The figure shows that, as the ridge factor ρ increases, the role of the weaker component $\mathbf{x}^{(2)}$ is gradually replaced by that of the stronger component $\mathbf{x}^{(1)}$.

For this simple dataset, the two classes may also be perfectly separated by $x^{(1)}$ by adopting an alternative discriminant function:

$$f'(\mathbf{x}) = \mathbf{w}'^T\mathbf{x} = x^{(1)}.$$

This example helps raise an important question: that of how to balance the two discriminant components so as to best cope with real-world application environments.

Robustness of learned models

From the perspective of the LSE, the second feature $x^{(2)}$ dominates the first feature $x^{(1)}$ in terms of the importance in decision making. Recall that the LSE is equivalent to the FDA, which is based on SNR. Therefore, in terms of the SNR metric, one would also conclude that $x^{(2)}$ dominates $x^{(1)}$ in decision making. However, $x^{(2)}$ is actually more sensitive to noise than $x^{(1)}$ and tends to be more problematic. In general, when the scatter matrix is ill-conditioned, there may exist serious sensitivity problems for some of the features. To design a robust classifier, it becomes practically important to take into account also the sensitivity of the components.

A large SNR may result from either a large signal or a small noise. If it is from the former, an SNR-optimal classifier will likely remain robust. If it is from the latter, however, the large SNR could merely be the result of dividing a small signal by an even smaller noise. In this case, the SNR-based learned model may be easily prone to noise or perturbation. In short, in order to assure a robust generalization, it is safest to have both a respectable SNR and a relatively high signal level. For this dataset, the sensitivity concern may significantly tip the balance towards to $x^{(1)}$. The signal metric can be characterized by a "post-projection centroid separation" as described below.

Post-projection centroid separation

Let $d = d_{\text{centroids}}$ denote the separation width between the positive and negative centroids, after they have been projected along the direction of the decision vector $\mathbf{w}$. Mathematically,

$$d = d_{\text{centroids}} = \frac{|f(\vec{\mu}_+) - f(\vec{\mu}_-)|}{||\mathbf{w}||}. \tag{8.61}$$

This means that any test pattern that deviates from its class centroid by $d/2$ or less may still be correctly classified by the learned classifier. A wider (narrower) separation margin indicates that the learned classifier will be more resilient (sensitive) with respect to the input perturbation.

For this dataset, the margins corresponding to the two features are very different. The separation margin associated with $x^{(1)}$ is

$$d_{\text{centroids}} = \frac{|f(\vec{\mu}_+) - f(\vec{\mu}_-)|}{||\mathbf{w}||} = 1.8,$$

while the separation margin associated with $x^{(2)}$ is merely

$$d_{\text{centroids}} = \frac{|f'(\vec{\mu}_+) - f'(\vec{\mu}_-)|}{||\mathbf{w}'||} = 0.2,$$

which is much narrower than that of $x^{(1)}$. Therefore, the first feature is considered to be more resilient than the second feature.

Note that a narrow separation margin means that the discrimination function is more vulnerable to any error incurred in its corresponding component(s). To design a robust classifier, it makes practical sense to also take into account the separation margin of a component in addition to its SNR.

Robustness of learned models w.r.t. ρ

As illustrated by the following numerical example, the balance between the SNR and the separation margin can be properly controlled by adjusting the value of ρ.

Example 8.7 (Separation margins w.r.t. different ρ) *It follows that the solution for the optimal decision vector has the simplified expression*

$$\mathbf{w} = [\mathbf{S} + \rho\mathbf{I}]^{-1}\mathbf{X}\mathbf{y}.$$

For different values of $\rho = 0, 0.001, 0.005, 0.01,$ *and* 0.05, *and, ultimately,* $\rho \to \infty$, *we have the following decision vectors and separation margins. For* $\rho = 0$, $\mathbf{w}_{\text{LSE}} = [\mathbf{S}]^{-1}\mathbf{X}\mathbf{y} = [0 \quad 10.0]^{\text{T}}$, *with* $d = 0.2$; *for* $\rho = 0.001$, $\mathbf{w} = [\mathbf{S} + 0.001\mathbf{I}]^{-1}\mathbf{X}\mathbf{y} = [0.7316 \quad 3.3327]^{\text{T}}$, *with* $d = 0.5812$; *for* $\rho = 0.005$, $\mathbf{w} = [\mathbf{S} + 0.005\mathbf{I}]^{-1}\mathbf{X}\mathbf{y} = [0.9877 \quad 0.9877]^{\text{T}}$, *with* $d = 0.4142$; *for* $\rho = 0.01$, $\mathbf{w} = [\mathbf{S} + 0.01\mathbf{I}]^{-1}\mathbf{X}\mathbf{y} = [1.0315 \quad 0.5731]^{\text{T}}$, *with* $d = 1.6706$; *for* $\rho = 0.05$, $\mathbf{w} = [\mathbf{S} + 0.05\mathbf{I}]^{-1}\mathbf{X}\mathbf{y} = [1.0582 \; 0.2116]^{\text{T}}$, *with* $d = 1.8042$; *and for* $\rho \to \infty$, $\mathbf{w} \to [\mathbf{S} + \rho\mathbf{I}]^{-1}\mathbf{X}\mathbf{y} \propto [0.36 \quad 0.04]^{\text{T}}$, *with a separation margin* $d = 1.8110$.

Robustness of learned classifiers

The decision vectors for different values of ρ are shown in Figure 8.9. At the beginning, we set $\rho = 0$, which corresponds to the LSE (or FDA) classifier. Its decision rule, i.e. $10\mathbf{x}^{(2)} = 0$, is exclusively dominated by the second feature. The separation margin is only $d = 0.2$, according to Eq. (8.61), thus the learned classifier is considered to be very vulnerable to input perturbation.

As ρ grows larger, the role of the resilient feature $x^{(1)}$ gradually gains more strength. Note that, as ρ increases from $\rho = 0$ to $\rho \to \infty$, the corresponding separation margin steadily goes up, from $d = 0.2$ to $d = 1.8110$. This means that the learned classifier becomes more robust with increasing ρ.

When $N_+ = N_-$, it can be shown that the product $\mathbf{Xy}$ is proportional to $\mathbf{\Delta}$. This means that the RR solution will gradually approach $\mathbf{\Delta}$ when $\rho \to \infty$. In that case, the RR solution yields the widest possible post-projection separation margin, i.e. $d_{\text{centroids}} = 1.8110$, see Eq. (8.61).

In summary, to strive for the best possible prediction accuracy, one must consider the features' SNR strength as well as their separation margin. For a more thorough quantitative analysis of the regularization effect of ρ, see Eq. (9.51) in Section 9.5. □

8.6 Kernelized learning models in empirical space: linear kernels

For both learning models for under-determined systems and for ridge regressors, the LSP condition holds. Consequently, they may be reformulated in terms of kernelized models represented by the empirical space.

8.6.1 Kernelized learning models for under-determined systems

Recall that the learning model for under-determined systems has the following optimization formulation:

$$\min_{\mathbf{w}} \left\{ \frac{1}{2}\|\mathbf{w}\|^2 \right\}$$
$$\text{subject to } \mathbf{w}^{\text{T}}\mathbf{x}_i + b = y_i \quad i = 1, \ldots, N. \tag{8.62}$$

The constraint can be expressed in matrix form:

$$\mathbf{X}^{\text{T}}\mathbf{w} + \mathbf{e}b = \mathbf{y}. \tag{8.63}$$

By substituting the LSP condition ($\mathbf{w} = \mathbf{Xa}$) into Eq. (8.63), we obtain

$$\mathbf{X}^{\text{T}}\mathbf{w} + \mathbf{e}b = \mathbf{X}^{\text{T}}\mathbf{Xa} + \mathbf{e}b = \mathbf{Ka} + \mathbf{e}b = \mathbf{y}, \tag{8.64}$$

where $\mathbf{K}$ is the (linear) kernel matrix ($K_{ij} = \mathbf{x}_i^{\text{T}}\mathbf{x}_j$). On combining Eq. (8.64) and Eq. (8.42), we have the following kernelized learning model:

$$\begin{bmatrix} \mathbf{K} & \mathbf{e} \\ \mathbf{e}^{\text{T}} & 0 \end{bmatrix} \begin{bmatrix} \mathbf{a} \\ b \end{bmatrix} = \begin{bmatrix} \mathbf{y} \\ 0 \end{bmatrix}. \tag{8.65}$$

Generally speaking, because $M \geq N$, the kernel matrix $\mathbf{K}$ should be nonsingular (see Example 8.8). Then the closed-form optimal solution can be derived as follows:

$$\mathbf{a} = \mathbf{K}^{-1}(\mathbf{y} - b\mathbf{e}), \text{ where } b = \frac{\mathbf{y}^{\mathrm{T}}\mathbf{K}^{-1}\mathbf{e}}{\mathbf{e}^{\mathrm{T}}\mathbf{K}^{-1}\mathbf{e}}. \tag{8.66}$$

The optimal solution $\mathbf{a}$ will then lead to the optimal decision vector,

$$\mathbf{w} = \mathbf{X}\mathbf{a} = \mathbf{X}\mathbf{K}^{-1}(\mathbf{y} - b\mathbf{e}),$$

and the optimal decision boundary,

$$f(\mathbf{x}) = \mathbf{w}^{\mathrm{T}}\mathbf{x} + b = 0.$$

Now let us use some numerical examples to illustrate the application of the kernelized formulation.

Example 8.8 (Kernelized formulation for dataset in Example 8.3) *It can be verified that the same solution of* $\mathbf{a}$ *and* b *may also be obtained by directly solving one matrix equation (Eq. (8.65)):*

$$\begin{bmatrix} 2 & 2 & 1 \\ 2 & 34 & 1 \\ 1 & 1 & 0 \end{bmatrix} \begin{bmatrix} a_1 \\ a_2 \\ b \end{bmatrix} = \begin{bmatrix} +1 \\ -1 \\ 0 \end{bmatrix}. \tag{8.67}$$

In this case, we may also apply Eq. (8.66) and obtain

$$b = \frac{\mathbf{y}^{\mathrm{T}}\mathbf{K}^{-1}\mathbf{e}}{\mathbf{e}^{\mathrm{T}}\mathbf{K}^{-1}\mathbf{e}} = 1.0$$

and

$$\mathbf{a} = \mathbf{K}^{-1}(\mathbf{y} - b\mathbf{e}) = \begin{bmatrix} +0.0625 \\ -0.0625 \end{bmatrix}.$$

It follows that

$$\mathbf{w} = \mathbf{X}\mathbf{a} = \begin{bmatrix} -1 & 3 \\ 1 & 5 \end{bmatrix} \begin{bmatrix} +0.0625 \\ -0.0625 \end{bmatrix} = \begin{bmatrix} -0.25 \\ -0.25 \end{bmatrix}, \tag{8.68}$$

just the same as before.

In the above example, the solution may be computed via either Eq. (8.65) or Eq. (8.66). In general, the former is more versatile and reliable, i.e. if Eq. (8.66) is computable then so will be Eq. (8.65) – but not vice versa. This difference is illustrated by the following example.

Example 8.9 (Classification of three two-dimensional training vectors) *As shown in Figure 10.2 later, the three training vectors are*

$$\begin{aligned}
\mathbf{x}_1 &= [0.0 \quad 0.0]^{\mathrm{T}}, \quad y_1 = -1, \\
\mathbf{x}_2 &= [1.0 \quad 0.0]^{\mathrm{T}}, \quad y_2 = +1, \\
\mathbf{x}_3 &= [0.0 \quad 1.0]^{\mathrm{T}}, \quad y_3 = +1.
\end{aligned}$$

The linear kernel matrix

$$\mathbf{K} = \mathbf{X}^{\mathrm{T}}\mathbf{X} = \begin{bmatrix} 0 & 0 & 0 \\ 0 & 1 & 0 \\ 0 & 0 & 1 \end{bmatrix}$$

is singular, rendering the solution via Eq. (8.66) invalid. However, the matrix system in Eq. (8.65), i.e.

$$\begin{bmatrix} 0 & 0 & 0 & 1 \\ 0 & 1 & 0 & 1 \\ 0 & 0 & 1 & 1 \\ 1 & 1 & 1 & 0 \end{bmatrix} \begin{bmatrix} a_1 \\ a_2 \\ a_3 \\ b \end{bmatrix} = \begin{bmatrix} -1 \\ +1 \\ +1 \\ 0 \end{bmatrix},$$

allows a valid solution:

$$\mathbf{a} = [-4 \quad +2 \quad +2]^{\mathrm{T}} \quad \text{and} \quad b = -1.$$

This leads to the final linear decision boundary:

$$2x^{(1)} + 2x^{(2)} - 1 = 0.$$

There are scenarios for which none of the kernel-space formulations is valid, i.e. the solution is NOT computable either via Eq. (8.65) or via Eq. (8.66). This is illustrated by the following example.

Example 8.10 (Classification of four two-dimensional training vectors) *For the same dataset as in Example 8.1, there are four training vectors:*

$$\begin{aligned}
\mathbf{x}_1 &= [0.0 \quad 1.0]^{\mathrm{T}}, \quad y_1 = +1, \\
\mathbf{x}_2 &= [1.0 \quad 0.0]^{\mathrm{T}}, \quad y_2 = +1, \\
\mathbf{x}_3 &= [-0.2 \quad 0.0]^{\mathrm{T}}, \quad y_3 = -1, \\
\mathbf{x}_4 &= [0.0 \quad 0.0]^{\mathrm{T}}, \quad y_4 = -1.
\end{aligned}$$

The linear kernel matrix

$$\mathbf{K} = \mathbf{X}^{\mathrm{T}}\mathbf{X} = \begin{bmatrix} 0 & 1 \\ 1 & 0 \\ -0.2 & 0 \\ 0 & 0 \end{bmatrix} \begin{bmatrix} 0 & 1 & -0.2 & 0 \\ 1 & 0 & 0 & 0 \end{bmatrix} = \begin{bmatrix} 1 & 0 & 0 & 0 \\ 0 & 1 & -0.2 & 0 \\ 0 & -0.2 & 0.04 & 0 \\ 0 & 0 & 0 & 0 \end{bmatrix} \tag{8.69}$$

is singular, rendering the solution via Eq. (8.64) invalid. In this example, the matrix system in Eq. (8.65) is

$$\begin{bmatrix} 1 & 0 & 0 & 0 & 1 \\ 0 & 1 & -0.2 & 0 & 1 \\ 0 & -0.2 & 0.04 & 0 & 1 \\ 0 & 0 & 0 & 0 & 1 \\ 1 & 1 & 1 & 1 & 0 \end{bmatrix} \begin{bmatrix} a_1 \\ a_2 \\ a_3 \\ a_4 \\ b \end{bmatrix} = \begin{bmatrix} +1 \\ +1 \\ -1 \\ -1 \\ 0 \end{bmatrix},$$

which is also not solvable. In this case, none of the kernel-matrix formulations is numerically feasible. We have to resort to scatter-matrix formulations to obtain a solution. As shown below, the numerical problem will no longer exist with a ridge factor ρ incorporated.

8.6.2 Kernelized formulation of KRR in empirical space

The empirical-space *kernel ridge regression* (KRR) algorithm based on linear Kernels is summarized as follows.

ALGORITHM 8.5 (Empirical-space KRR algorithm for linear classification) *The kernel-matrix-based algorithm contains the following steps.*

- *Given a training dataset $[\mathcal{X}, \mathcal{Y}]$, form the $N \times N$ symmetric kernel matrix:*

$$\mathbf{K} = \mathbf{X}^{\mathrm{T}}\mathbf{X}. \tag{8.70}$$

- *With the ridge factor ρ incorporated, the linear kernel-based learning formulation becomes*

$$\begin{bmatrix} \mathbf{K} + \rho\mathbf{I} & \mathbf{e} \\ \mathbf{e}^{\mathrm{T}} & 0 \end{bmatrix} \begin{bmatrix} \mathbf{a} \\ b \end{bmatrix} = \begin{bmatrix} \mathbf{y} \\ 0 \end{bmatrix}. \tag{8.71}$$

  Since $\mathbf{K} + \rho\mathbf{I}$ is always nonsingular if $\rho > 0$, Eq. (8.71) has another closed-form solution:

$$\mathbf{a} = [\mathbf{K} + \rho\mathbf{I}]^{-1}[\mathbf{y} - b\mathbf{e}], \text{ where } b = \frac{\mathbf{y}^{\mathrm{T}}[\mathbf{K} + \rho\mathbf{I}]^{-1}\mathbf{e}}{\mathbf{e}^{\mathrm{T}}[\mathbf{K} + \rho\mathbf{I}]^{-1}\mathbf{e}}. \tag{8.72}$$

- *The discriminant function can then be obtained as*

$$f(\mathbf{x}) = \vec{\mathbf{k}}(\mathbf{x})^{\mathrm{T}}\mathbf{a} + b = \sum_{i=1}^{N} a_i K(\mathbf{x}_i, \mathbf{x}) + b, \tag{8.73}$$

  where

$$\vec{\mathbf{k}}(\mathbf{x}) = \begin{bmatrix} K(\mathbf{x}_1, \mathbf{x}) \\ K(\mathbf{x}_2, \mathbf{x}) \\ \vdots \\ K(\mathbf{x}_N, \mathbf{x}) \end{bmatrix} = \begin{bmatrix} \mathbf{x}_1^{\mathrm{T}}\mathbf{x} \\ \mathbf{x}_2^{\mathrm{T}}\mathbf{x} \\ \vdots \\ \mathbf{x}_N^{\mathrm{T}}\mathbf{x} \end{bmatrix} = \mathbf{X}^{\mathrm{T}}\mathbf{x}.$$

• *The decision rule is*

$$\mathbf{x} \in \begin{cases} C_+ & \text{if } f(\mathbf{x}) \geq 0 \\ C_- & \text{if } f(\mathbf{x}) < 0 . \end{cases} \tag{8.74}$$

□

When $\rho \to 0$, Eq. (8.71) converges to Eq. (8.65), i.e. the FDA formulation. Assuming further that $\mathbf{K}$ is invertible, the RR solution in Eq. (8.72) converges to Eq. (8.66).

According to Theorem 8.2, this kernel-domain solution for linear ridge regression (RR) classification is basically equivalent to the PDA solution in Eq. (8.56). Since all three solutions are equivalent, the term *kernel ridge regressor* (KRR) will be used generically to represent all three classifiers in our subsequent discussion. For convenience, the term KRR will be used to represent classifiers that are based on linear and nonlinear kernels. In fact, for both cases, the KRR algorithm can be based on the same formulation as that prescribed in Eq. (8.72).

The empirical-space KRR algorithm is illustrated by the following example.

Example 8.11 (KRR solution for classification of four two-dimensional vectors) *Let us revisit the same dataset as in Example 8.1. Recall that the linear kernel matrix is given in Eq. (8.69). Suppose that the regularization parameter* $\rho = 0.01$. *Then we just have to apply Eq. (8.72) and obtain*

$$b = \frac{\mathbf{y}^{\mathrm{T}}[\mathbf{K} + \rho\mathbf{I}]^{-1}\mathbf{e}}{\mathbf{e}^{\mathrm{T}}[\mathbf{K} + \rho\mathbf{I}]^{-1}\mathbf{e}} = -0.793$$

and

$$\mathbf{a} = [\mathbf{K} + \rho\mathbf{I}]^{-1}[\mathbf{y} - b\mathbf{e}] = [+1.776 \quad +4.604 \quad +14.283 \quad -20.663]^{\mathrm{T}}.$$

Note that

$$\vec{\mathbf{k}}(\mathbf{x}) = \begin{bmatrix} K(\mathbf{x}_1, \mathbf{x}) \\ K(\mathbf{x}_2, \mathbf{x}) \\ \vdots \\ K(\mathbf{x}_N, \mathbf{x}) \end{bmatrix} = \begin{bmatrix} \mathbf{x}_1^{\mathrm{T}}\mathbf{x} \\ \mathbf{x}_2^{\mathrm{T}}\mathbf{x} \\ \vdots \\ \mathbf{x}_N^{\mathrm{T}}\mathbf{x} \end{bmatrix} = \mathbf{X}^{\mathrm{T}}\,\mathbf{x} = \begin{bmatrix} x^{(2)} \\ x^{(1)} \\ -0.2x^{(1)} \\ 0 \end{bmatrix}.$$

From the vector **a** *just obtained, it follows that the discriminant function is*

$$f(\mathbf{x}) = \vec{\mathbf{k}}(\mathbf{x})^{\mathrm{T}}\mathbf{a} + b = 1.747\mathbf{x}^{(1)} + 1.7756\mathbf{x}^{(2)} - 0.793, \tag{8.75}$$

which is the same as the solution obtained via the scatter-matrix formulation in Example 8.4.

8.6.3 Comparison of formulations in original versus empirical spaces

While both the original space and empirical space are working vector spaces for most learning formulations, they have very distinct computational requirements.

- In Eq. (8.54), the computational complexity is dictated by the inversion of the $M \times M$ scatter matrix $\mathbf{S}$ – amounting to an order of $O(M^3)$.
- In Eq. (8.71), the computational complexity is dictated by the inversion of the $N \times N$ kernel matrix – amounting to an order of $O(N^3)$.

In conclusion, in practical implementations of the learning methods, the equivalence between the two formulations (Eq. (8.54) and Eq. (8.71)) may be properly exploited for optimal computational efficiency. Obviously, Eq. (8.54) will be computationally preferable for the over-determined case that $M \leq N$, while Eq. (8.71) will enjoy an advantage for the under-determined case that $M > N$.

8.7 Summary

This chapter covers a broad spectrum of conventional linear classification techniques. Starting from linear regression and discriminant analysis, the well-known least-squares-error (LSE) classifiers and Fisher's linear discriminant analysis (FDA) can be developed. Theorem 8.1 further establishes the equivalence between the LSE and FDA classifiers. Hence the same solution will be obtained via any of the following three algorithms: (1) learning algorithm for LSE classifier (Algorithm 8.1), (2) conventional learning algorithm for Fisher's discriminant analysis (Algorithm 8.2), and (3) modified learning algorithm for Fisher's discriminant analysis (Algorithm 8.3).

To enhance the robustness, ridge regression or errors-in-variables models may be incorporated into the conventional linear classifiers. This leads to two seemingly different supervised learning classifiers: the ridge regressor and PDA, whose equivalence is established in Theorem 8.2.

Finally, the learning subspace property (LSP) can be established for all the linear learning models introduced in this chapter. (See Theorem 1.1 in Chapter 1.) The LSP effectively bridges the formulations in the original and empirical spaces. Algorithms 8.4 and 8.5 respectively describe a scatter-matrix-based and a kernel-matrix-based learning algorithm for linear ridge classifiers.

8.8 Problems

Problem 8.1 (Margin of separation) *Suppose that two training data points, say* $\mathbf{x}_1$ *and* $\mathbf{x}_2$, *are known to fall exactly on the two parallel marginal hyperplanes, i.e.*

$$\mathbf{w}^{\mathrm{T}}\mathbf{x}_1 + b = +1 \quad \textit{and} \quad \mathbf{w}^{\mathrm{T}}\mathbf{x}_2 + b = -1,$$

respectively. Show that the margin of separation after the projection along $\mathbf{w}$ *is*

$$\left(\frac{\mathbf{w}^{\mathrm{T}}}{\|\mathbf{w}\|}\right)(\mathbf{x}_1 - \mathbf{x}_2) = \frac{2}{\|\mathbf{w}\|}.$$

Problem 8.2 (LSE versus RR solutions)
Consider the following supervised training dataset.

$$\mathbf{X} = \begin{bmatrix} 2 & 1 \\ 1 & 0 \end{bmatrix} \quad \textit{and} \quad \mathbf{y} = \begin{bmatrix} +1 \\ -1 \end{bmatrix}.$$

(a) *Show that the linear kernel matrix is*

$$\mathbf{K} = \mathbf{X}^{\mathrm{T}}\mathbf{X} = \begin{bmatrix} 5 & 2 \\ 2 & 5 \end{bmatrix}.$$

(b) *Derive* **a** *and* b *from Eq. (8.65).*

(c) *Show that* $\mathbf{w} = a_1\mathbf{x}_1 + a_2\mathbf{x}_2 = [1 \quad 1]^{\mathrm{T}}$, *and that the corresponding decision boundary is:*

$$f(\mathbf{x}) = \mathbf{w}^{\mathrm{T}}\,\mathbf{x} + b = [1 \quad 1]\mathbf{x} - 2 = x^{(1)} + x^{(2)} - 2 = 0.$$

(d) *Show that the same solution can be derived via Eq. (8.66).*

(e) *Show that the maximal margin of separation is indeed achieved.*

(f) *Find the ridge regressor (RR) with* $\rho = 1.0$.

(g) *Compare the LSE and RR solutions.*

Problem 8.3 *In order to demonstrate that Eq. (8.65) is more flexible than Eq. (8.66), let us consider the dataset*

$$\mathbf{X} = \begin{bmatrix} 0 & 1 \\ 0 & 0 \end{bmatrix} \textit{ and } \mathbf{y} = \begin{bmatrix} +1 \\ -1 \end{bmatrix}.$$

(a) *Show that* **K** *is singular, rendering Eq. (8.66) numerically invalid.*

(b) *Show that Eq. (8.65) remains numerically valid for the dataset.*

Problem 8.4 *Note that the two Fisher scores have different ranges.*

(a) *Show that the range for* $\tilde{J}(\mathbf{w})$ *is* $[0, \infty]$.

(b) *Show that the range for the modified Fisher score* $J(\mathbf{w})$ *is* $[0, 1]$.

Problem 8.5 *Show that the centered (i.e. center-adjusted) scatter matrix can be expressed as*

$$\bar{\mathbf{S}} = \bar{\mathbf{X}}\bar{\mathbf{X}}^{\mathrm{T}} = \mathbf{X}\left(I - \frac{\mathbf{e}\mathbf{e}^{\mathrm{T}}}{N}\right)\left(I - \frac{\mathbf{e}\mathbf{e}^{\mathrm{T}}}{N}\right)\mathbf{X}^{\mathrm{T}} = \mathbf{X}\left(I - \frac{\mathbf{e}\mathbf{e}^{\mathrm{T}}}{N}\right)\mathbf{X}^{\mathrm{T}}.$$

Problem 8.6 *Verify that*

$$\bar{\mathbf{S}} = \mathbf{S}_{\mathrm{W}} + \mathbf{S}_{\mathrm{B}}.$$

Problem 8.7 (Subspace projection: PCA and FDA) *The optimal subspace projection has different criteria for unsupervised and supervised learning. For the former, PCA offers* *a simple analysis for optimal feature extraction. For the latter, FDA may prove more effective.*

(a) *Explain why an optimal subspace solution for one-dimensional feature extraction may be obtained via the FDA solution given in Eq. (8.32) in Algorithm 8.3.*
(b) *Show how FDA may be extended to yield an optimal solution for m-dimensional subspace problems.*

Hint: *See also the discussion on DCA and SODA in Chapter 9.*

Problem 8.8 (LSE classifiers and FDA) *You are given a training dataset with three negative samples,* $\mathbf{x}_1 = (1, 2)$, $\mathbf{x}_2 = (2, 4)$, *and* $\mathbf{x}_3 = (5, 1)$, *and four positive samples,* $\mathbf{x}_4 = (6, 5)$, $\mathbf{x}_5 = (7, 9)$, $\mathbf{x}_6 = (4, 6)$, *and* $\mathbf{x}_7 = (3, 7)$.

(a) *Find the optimal LSE classifier.*
(b) *Find the optimal FDA classifier.*
(c) *Compare the two classifiers.*

Problem 8.9 (Margin of separation)
To study further the maximum margin formulation prescribed by Eq. (8.38), let us consider the dataset with $M = 4 > N = 3$ *and*

$$\mathbf{X} = \begin{bmatrix} 2 & 1 & 0 \\ 1 & 1 & 0 \\ 1 & 1 & 1 \\ 1 & 2 & 3 \end{bmatrix} \quad \textit{and} \quad \mathbf{y} = \begin{bmatrix} +1 \\ -1 \\ -1 \end{bmatrix}.$$

(a) *Compute the kernel matrix*

$$\mathbf{K} = \mathbf{X}^{\mathrm{T}}\mathbf{X}.$$

(b) *Derive the optimal margin solutions for* $\mathbf{a}$ *and* b *by Eq. (8.65).*
(c) *Show that the data hyperplane, prescribed by* $\mathbf{X}^{\mathrm{T}}\mathbf{p} = \mathbf{e}$, *is a two-dimensional plane. Verify that all training vectors lie right on the marginal hyperplanes.*
(d) *Verify that the optimal decision vector satisfies the OHP rule.*

Problem 8.10 (KRR solution meets the OHP condition)
Show that the KRR solution given in Eq. (8.72) satisfies the OHP condition prescribed by Eq. (8.42), i.e. $\mathbf{e}^{\mathrm{T}}\mathbf{a} = 0$.

Problem 8.11 *Note that KRR offers a unified solution for both scenarios,* $N > M$ *and* $M \geq N$.

(a) *Create a dataset with $N = 3$ and $M = 4$, and find the optimal KRR solution – assuming that $\rho = 1.0$.*

(b) *Create a dataset with $N = 4$ and $M = 3$, and find the optimal KRR solution – assuming that $\rho = 1.0$.*

Problem 8.12 (Equivalence between LSE and FDA and between RR and PDA) *Recall that $\mathbf{\Delta} \equiv \overrightarrow{\mu}_+ - \overrightarrow{\mu}_-$.*

(a) *Show that*

$$\overrightarrow{\mu}_+ - \overrightarrow{\mu} = \frac{N_-}{N_+}(\overrightarrow{\mu} - \overrightarrow{\mu}_-).$$

(b) *Assuming that the data are center-adjusted, show that, for this special case,*

$$\begin{bmatrix} \bar{\mathbf{S}} & 0 \\ 0 & N \end{bmatrix} \begin{bmatrix} \bar{\mathbf{S}}^{-1}\mathbf{\Delta} \\ (N_+ - N_-)/(2N_+N_-) \end{bmatrix} = \kappa \begin{bmatrix} \mathbf{Xy} \\ \mathbf{e}^{\mathrm{T}}\mathbf{y} \end{bmatrix}, \tag{8.76}$$

where $\kappa = N/(2N_+N_-)$.

(c) *To show the equivalence between LSE and FDA, verify that*

$$\begin{bmatrix} \mathbf{S} & \mathbf{Xe} \\ \mathbf{e}^{\mathrm{T}}\mathbf{X}^{\mathrm{T}} & N \end{bmatrix} \begin{bmatrix} \bar{\mathbf{S}}^{-1}\mathbf{\Delta} \\ -\overrightarrow{\mu}^{\mathrm{T}}\bar{\mathbf{S}}^{-1}\mathbf{\Delta} + (N_+ - N_-)/(2N_+N_-) \end{bmatrix}$$
$$= \kappa \begin{bmatrix} \mathbf{Xy} \\ \mathbf{e}^{\mathrm{T}}\mathbf{y} \end{bmatrix}. \tag{8.77}$$

(d) *To show the equivalence between RR and PDA, verify that*

$$\begin{bmatrix} \mathbf{S} + \rho\mathbf{I} & \mathbf{Xe} \\ \mathbf{e}^{\mathrm{T}}\mathbf{X}^{\mathrm{T}} & N \end{bmatrix} \begin{bmatrix} [\bar{\mathbf{S}} + \rho\mathbf{I}]^{-1}\mathbf{\Delta} \\ -\overrightarrow{\mu}^{\mathrm{T}}[\bar{\mathbf{S}} + \rho\mathbf{I}]^{-1}\mathbf{\Delta} + (N_+ - N_-)/(2N_+N_-) \end{bmatrix}$$
$$= \kappa \begin{bmatrix} \mathbf{Xy} \\ \mathbf{e}^{\mathrm{T}}\mathbf{y} \end{bmatrix}. \tag{8.78}$$

9 Kernel ridge regression for supervised classification

9.1 Introduction

In the previous chapter, several prominent supervised linear classifiers have been developed. According to Theorem 1.1, they all satisfy the learning subspace property (LSP) and therefore the optimal solution of $\mathbf{w}$ has the following form:

$$\mathbf{w} = \sum_{n=1}^{N} a_n \mathbf{x}_n, \tag{9.1}$$

for certain coefficients $\{a_n\}$. It follows that the original linear discriminant function

$$f(\mathbf{x}) = \mathbf{w}^{\mathrm{T}}\mathbf{x} + b = \mathbf{x}^{\mathrm{T}}\mathbf{w} + b$$

may now be re-expressed as

$$f(\mathbf{x}) = \sum_{n=1}^{N} (\mathbf{x}^{\mathrm{T}}\mathbf{x}_n) a_n + b, \tag{9.2}$$

which has the appearance of a kernel-based formulation. This chapter will further demonstrate that a nonlinear discriminant function may be obtained by simply replacing the Euclidean inner product $\mathbf{x}^{\mathrm{T}}\mathbf{x}_n$ by a nonlinear function $K(\mathbf{x}, \mathbf{x}_n)$, resulting in

$$f(\mathbf{x}) = \sum_{n=1}^{N} K(\mathbf{x}, \mathbf{x}_n) a_n + b. \tag{9.3}$$

By being allowed to choose a desirable nonlinear kernel function, we gain a great deal of design versatility to cope with various application scenarios.

This chapter will explore the following topics related to kernel-based regressors for supervised classification.

(i) In Section 9.2, the linear classifier FDA is extended to its nonlinear counterpart, named *kernel discriminant analysis* (KDA). Such a kernel-based classifier is formally derived by optimizing a safety margin measured by the distance metric defined in the kernel-induced intrinsic space. The same result may also be obtained by using the kernel trick, i.e. by simply substituting the linear kernel in FDA by a nonlinear kernel.

(ii) In Section 9.3, we shall develop kernel ridge regression (KRR) learning models. Ridge regression is one of the classic techniques used to enhance the robustness of classifiers. The principle lies in the incorporation of a penalty term, parameterized by the ridge factor ρ, into the loss function in order to control the regressor coefficients. KRR models may be developed via one of the following two kernel-induced vector spaces.

- *Intrinsic vector space.* In this approach, the classic ridge regression techniques, which were originally applied to the original vector space, will be reapplied to the training feature vectors in the intrinsic space, whose dimension equals to the intrinsic degree J.
- *Empirical vector space.* Using the LSP, we can convert the intrinsic-space optimizer into its empirical-space counterpart. This leads to a kernel-matrix-based learning model whose dimension equals the empirical degree N, i.e. the size of the training dataset.

This section also explores the intricate relationship and tradeoff between the intrinsic and empirical representations.

(iii) In Section 9.4, the perturbational discriminant analysis (PDA), which was originally applied to the original vector space, will be reapplied to the intrinsic space, leading to a kernel-based PDA. The section will also show that the three kernel-based classifiers (KRR, LS-SVM, and PDA) are basically equivalent; therefore, for convenience, the term KRR will be used to represent these three equivalent classifiers.

(iv) The focus of Section 9.5 is placed on numerical properties and robustness of the KRR learning models. The robustness analysis would be best conducted in the *spectral space* because the effect of errors in variables can be isolated componentwise. The regularization effect can be quantitatively expressed by a *regression ratio*. This offers a simple explanation of how oversubscription of sensitive components can be effectively avoided.

(v) In Section 9.6, simulation studies are conducted on several real-world datasets. The performance comparison between KDA and KRR demonstrates that the robustness and performance of the classifiers can be improved significantly by incorporating a proper ridge parameter ρ into the KRR learning models.

(vi) Section 9.7 presents a new way of exploiting the WEC analysis to improve the learned model. The most alarming aspect of KRR's WEC is that error ϵ_i is linearly proportional to a_i, implying that erroneous and untrustworthy training vectors unduly receive high empirical weights. Intuitively, the performance should improve if the learned model can be freed from the undue influence of the removed subset. This leads to a new pruned-KRR technique (PPDA). The basic principle behind PPDA lies in the removal of a small fraction of potentially harmful "anti-support" vectors from the training dataset in each iteration. In short, PPDA is an iterative algorithm aiming to trim the training dataset to a selective subset. Experimental studies on an ECG dataset demonstrated that each iteration of PPDA can continue improving the prediction performance until the "surviving vectors" have been reduced to a small subset of the original training size.

(vii) Section 9.8 extends the binary classification formulation to multi-class, and, moreover, multi-label, classification formulations.

(viii) Unsupervised learning criteria designed for PCA are far from being effective for supervised application, whose objective is to discriminate among different classes. In this regard, the SNR criterion adopted by FDA is a much more relevant metric. In Section 9.9, a SODA subspace projection method offers a numerically efficient procedure to approximately maximize an SoSNR criterion. On the other hand, the PCA's trace-norm optimizer can be naturally modified to permit the teacher's information to be incorporated into the optimizer, thus enhancing the discriminant capability. It can be shown that all PCA, MD-FDA, PC-DCA, and DCA have the same form of trace-norm formulation and their optimal solutions may be obtained from the (principal or mixed) eigenvectors of their respective discriminant matrices.

9.2 Kernel-based discriminant analysis (KDA)

There is a standard process to extend linear classification to kernel-based nonlinear classification. First, an intrinsic space can be induced from any given kernel function that meets the Mercer condition. Then most (if not all) linear classifiers, such as LSE or LDA) can be readily applied to the kernel-induced space, resulting in kernel-based nonlinear classifiers. Learning models of this type have been explored by numerous researchers [10, 63, 76, 147, 176, 177, 178, 179, 187, 224, 239]. Moreover, they are commonly referred to as Fisher discriminant analysis with kernels. To highlight the contrast with respect to its linear variant, i.e. FDA or LDA, we shall name the kernel-based variant *kernel discriminant analysis* (KDA).

With reference to Figure 9.1, the learning of the decision vector $\mathbf{u}$ can be guided by the following desired equality:

$$f(\mathbf{x}_i) = \overrightarrow{\phi}(\mathbf{x}_i)^{\mathrm{T}}\mathbf{u} + b = \mathbf{y}_i, \quad i = 1, \ldots, N. \tag{9.4}$$

Recall that the dimension of the intrinsic space is called the intrinsic degree J. A useful kernel is expected to be one that is endowed with an adequate degree. Therefore, here we shall simply assume that $J > N$. In this case, the number of constraints prescribed by Eq. (9.4) is lower than that of the unknowns. Hence we can just make use of the algebraic formulation tailored to an under-determined system of equations, as discussed previously in Section 8.4.

For under-determined systems, the objective is to find a classifier with maximum margin of separation measured in the kernel-induced intrinsic space. More exactly, the separation margin is now characterized by the norm of the decision vector $\mathbf{u}$. As in Eq. (8.38), this leads to the following optimization formulation:

$$\min_{\mathbf{u},b} \left\{ \frac{1}{2}\|\mathbf{u}\|^2 \right\}$$
$$\text{subject to} \quad \epsilon_i = 0 \quad \forall i = 1, \ldots, N, \tag{9.5}$$

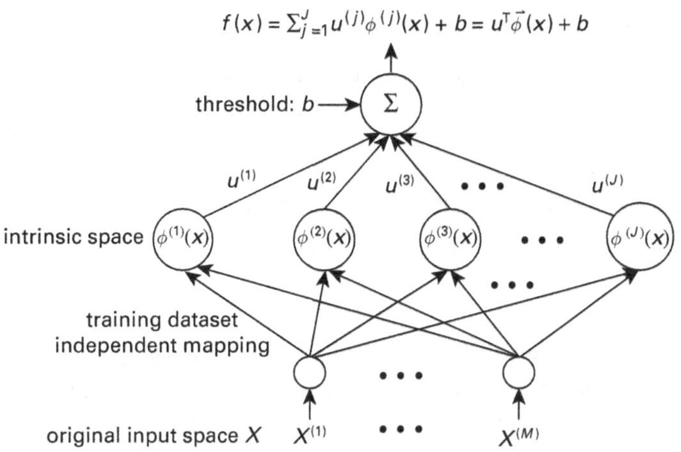

Fig. 9.1. The intrinsic space is structurally represented by the middle layer in a two-layer network. Here, a vector $\mathbf{x}$ in the original space is mapped to a new representative vector in its intrinsic space. The dimension of the intrinsic space is denoted by J, which may be finite or infinite.

where the errors are

$$\epsilon_i \equiv f(\mathbf{x}_i) - y_i = \mathbf{u}^{\mathrm{T}}\overrightarrow{\phi}(\mathbf{x}_i) + b - y_i.$$

On adopting $\{a_i,\ i = 1, \ldots, N\}$ as the Lagrange multipliers, the Lagrangian function becomes

$$\begin{aligned} L(\mathbf{u}, b, \mathbf{a}) &= \frac{1}{2}\|\mathbf{u}\|^2 - \sum_{i=1}^{N} a_i\,\epsilon_i \\ &= \frac{1}{2}\|\mathbf{u}\|^2 - \sum_{i=1}^{N} a_i(\mathbf{u}^{\mathrm{T}}\overrightarrow{\phi}(\mathbf{x}_i) + b - y_i). \\ &= \frac{1}{2}\|\mathbf{u}\|^2 - \mathbf{u}^{\mathrm{T}}\mathbf{\Phi}\mathbf{a} + \mathbf{a}^{\mathrm{T}}(\mathbf{y} - b\mathbf{e}). \end{aligned} \tag{9.6}$$

The zero gradient of $L(\mathbf{u}, b, \mathbf{a})$ with respect to $\mathbf{u}$ results in the LSP condition:

$$\mathbf{u} = \mathbf{\Phi}\mathbf{a}. \tag{9.7}$$

By substituting Eq. (9.7) back into Eq. (9.6), we obtain

$$L(\mathbf{a}, b) = -\frac{1}{2}\mathbf{a}^{\mathrm{T}}\mathbf{K}\mathbf{a} + \mathbf{a}^{\mathrm{T}}(\mathbf{y} - b\mathbf{e}), \tag{9.8}$$

where we denote the kernel matrix as $\mathbf{K} = \{K_{ij}\}$, whose (i,j)th element is $K_{ij} = K(\mathbf{x}_i, \mathbf{x}_j)$. The zero gradient of $L(\mathbf{a}, b)$ with respect to b and $\mathbf{a}$ yields respectively the OHP condition

$$\mathbf{e}^{\mathrm{T}}\mathbf{a} = 0$$

and

$$\mathbf{K}\mathbf{a} = \mathbf{y} - b\mathbf{e}.$$

Equivalently, in a more concise matrix form, we have

$$\begin{bmatrix} \mathbf{K} & \mathbf{e} \\ \mathbf{e}^{\mathrm{T}} & 0 \end{bmatrix} \begin{bmatrix} \mathbf{a} \\ b \end{bmatrix} = \begin{bmatrix} \mathbf{y} \\ 0 \end{bmatrix}, \tag{9.9}$$

which has exactly the same appearance as Eq. (8.65). Note that, when the kernel matrix $\mathbf{K}$ is nonsingular, it has again a closed-form solution:

$$\mathbf{a} = \mathbf{K}^{-1}[\mathbf{y} - b\mathbf{e}], \quad \text{where } b = \frac{\mathbf{y}^{\mathrm{T}}\mathbf{K}^{-1}\mathbf{e}}{\mathbf{e}^{\mathrm{T}}\mathbf{K}^{-1}\mathbf{e}}. \tag{9.10}$$

Generically speaking, $\mathbf{K}$ will be nonsingular if $J \geq N$.[1] Once $\mathbf{a}$ has been optimally solved, the discriminant function can be readily obtained as $f(\mathbf{x}) = \mathbf{a}^{\mathrm{T}} \vec{\mathbf{k}}(\mathbf{x}) + b$.

In the literature, such a closed-form solution is referred to as the *kernel discriminant analysis* (KDA) solution.

Example 9.1 (XOR datasets) *In the XOR dataset, the training vectors are*

$$\mathbf{x}_1 = \begin{bmatrix} +1 \\ +1 \end{bmatrix}, \quad \mathbf{x}_2 = \begin{bmatrix} -1 \\ -1 \end{bmatrix}, \quad \mathbf{x}_3 = \begin{bmatrix} +1 \\ -1 \end{bmatrix}, \quad \mathbf{x}_4 = \begin{bmatrix} -1 \\ +1 \end{bmatrix},$$

where $\mathbf{x}_1$ and $\mathbf{x}_2$ are positive while $\mathbf{x}_3$ and $\mathbf{x}_4$ are negative. If $K(\mathbf{x}, \mathbf{x}') = (1 + \mathbf{x}^{\mathrm{T}}\mathbf{x}')^2$, the kernel matrix for XOR is

$$\mathbf{K} = \begin{bmatrix} 9 & 1 & 1 & 1 \\ 1 & 9 & 1 & 1 \\ 1 & 1 & 9 & 1 \\ 1 & 1 & 1 & 9 \end{bmatrix}. \tag{9.11}$$

The closed-form solution

The optimal solution of $\mathbf{a}$ *and b can be obtained by solving Eq. (9.9), i.e.*

$$\begin{bmatrix} 9 & 1 & 1 & 1 & 1 \\ 1 & 9 & 1 & 1 & 1 \\ 1 & 1 & 9 & 1 & 1 \\ 1 & 1 & 1 & 9 & 1 \\ 1 & 1 & 1 & 1 & 0 \end{bmatrix} \begin{bmatrix} a_1 \\ a_2 \\ a_3 \\ a_4 \\ b \end{bmatrix} = \begin{bmatrix} +1 \\ +1 \\ -1 \\ -1 \\ 0 \end{bmatrix}, \tag{9.12}$$

and the solution of the linear equations can be obtained as

$$\mathbf{a} = \begin{bmatrix} a_1 \\ a_2 \\ a_3 \\ a_4 \end{bmatrix} = \begin{bmatrix} +\frac{1}{8} \\ +\frac{1}{8} \\ -\frac{1}{8} \\ -\frac{1}{8} \end{bmatrix} \quad \textit{and } b = 0.$$

[1] If $J < N$, $\mathbf{K}$ will become singular, as shown by Example 2.4.

Note that the empirical feature vector $\vec{\mathbf{k}}(\mathbf{x})$ *was derived previously in Eq. (3.50). This leads to the following (nonlinear) decision boundary:*

$$f(\mathbf{x}) = \mathbf{a}^{\mathrm{T}}\vec{\mathbf{k}}(\mathbf{x}) + b = uv = 0. \qquad \square$$

9.3 Kernel ridge regression (KRR) for supervised classification

This section extends the linear regression/regularization techniques introduced in Chapter 7 to kernel-based learning models, thus extending linear classification to nonlinear classification.

9.3.1 KRR and LS-SVM models: the intrinsic-space approach

The principle of ridge regression lies in the incorporation of a penalty term into the loss function to control the regressor coefficients. Being adjustable by the ridge parameter ρ, the penalty term can effectively mitigate the over-fitting or ill-posed problems and thus enhance the robustness of the learned classifier. Therefore, the KRR provides a unifying treatment of both over-determined and under-determined systems. The KRR is basically equivalent to the *least-squares SVM* (LS-SVM) proposed by Suykens and Vandewalle [260]. They share the same learning formulation rooted in the *ridge regression* (RR) in Eq. (8.49).

KRR (LS-SVM) learning models

The learning objective is to find the decision vector $\mathbf{u}$ and the threshold b such that

$$\min_{\mathbf{u},b} E(\mathbf{u}, b) = \min_{\mathbf{u},b}\left\{\sum_{i=1}^{N}\epsilon_i^2 + \rho\|\mathbf{u}\|^2\right\}, \tag{9.13}$$

where

$$\epsilon_i = \mathbf{u}^{\mathrm{T}}\vec{\phi}(\mathbf{x}_i) + b - y_i \quad \forall i = 1, \ldots, N.$$

$\square$

In matrix notation,

$$E(\mathbf{u}, b) = \|\mathbf{\Phi}^{\mathrm{T}}\mathbf{u} + \mathbf{e}b - \mathbf{y}\|^2 + \rho\|\mathbf{u}\|^2. \tag{9.14}$$

Solution in intrinsic space

The zero-gradient point of $E(\mathbf{u}, b)$ with respect to $\mathbf{u}$ can be obtained as

$$\frac{\partial E(\mathbf{u}, b)}{\partial u} = 2\mathbf{\Phi}(\mathbf{\Phi}^{\mathrm{T}}\mathbf{u} + \mathbf{e}b - \mathbf{y}) + 2\rho\mathbf{u} = 0. \tag{9.15}$$

This leads to the following optimal decision vector:

$$\mathbf{u} = [\mathbf{\Phi}\mathbf{\Phi}^{\mathrm{T}} + \rho\mathbf{I}]^{-1}\mathbf{\Phi}[\mathbf{y} - b\mathbf{e}] = [\mathbf{S} + \rho\,\mathbf{I}]^{-1}\mathbf{\Phi}[\mathbf{y} - b\mathbf{e}]. \tag{9.16}$$

Zeroing the first-order gradient of $E(\mathbf{u}, b)$ with respect to b leads to

$$\frac{\partial E(\mathbf{u}, b)}{\partial b} = \mathbf{e}^{\mathrm{T}}\mathbf{\Phi}^{\mathrm{T}}\mathbf{u} + b\mathbf{e}^{\mathrm{T}}\mathbf{e} - \mathbf{e}^{\mathrm{T}}\mathbf{y} = \mathbf{e}^{\mathrm{T}}\mathbf{\Phi}^{\mathrm{T}}\mathbf{u} + Nb - \mathbf{e}^{\mathrm{T}}\mathbf{y} = 0. \tag{9.17}$$

On combining Eqs. (9.15) and (9.17), the solution for KRR may be derived from the matrix system similar to Eq. (8.54), i.e.

$$\begin{bmatrix} \mathbf{S} + \rho\mathbf{I} & \mathbf{\Phi}\mathbf{e} \\ \mathbf{e}^{\mathrm{T}}\mathbf{\Phi}^{\mathrm{T}} & N \end{bmatrix} \begin{bmatrix} \mathbf{u} \\ b \end{bmatrix} = \begin{bmatrix} \mathbf{\Phi}\mathbf{y} \\ \mathbf{e}^{\mathrm{T}}\mathbf{y} \end{bmatrix}, \tag{9.18}$$

where $\mathbf{S} = \mathbf{\Phi}\mathbf{\Phi}^{\mathrm{T}}$ and the perturbational LSE classifiers are the same.

9.3.2 Kernelized learning models: the empirical-space approach

Learning subspace property

By Eq. (9.15), we have

$$\mathbf{u} = -\rho^{-1}\mathbf{\Phi}(\mathbf{\Phi}^{\mathrm{T}}\mathbf{u} + \mathbf{e}b - \mathbf{y}).$$

Thus, there exists an N-dimensional vector $\mathbf{a}$ (which at this moment is still an unknown) such that

$$\mathbf{u} = \mathbf{\Phi}\mathbf{a}. \tag{9.19}$$

This establishes the validity of LSP, i.e. $\mathbf{u} \in \mathtt{span}[\mathbf{\Phi}]$. The knowledge of the LSP is instrumental for the actual solution for $\mathbf{u}$. More exactly, on plugging the LSP, Eq. (9.19), into Eq. (9.14), we obtain

$$\begin{aligned} E'(\mathbf{a}, b) &= \|\mathbf{\Phi}^{\mathrm{T}}\mathbf{\Phi}\mathbf{a} + \mathbf{e}b - \mathbf{y}\|^2 + \rho\mathbf{a}^{\mathrm{T}}\mathbf{\Phi}^{\mathrm{T}}\mathbf{\Phi}\mathbf{a} \\ &= \|\mathbf{K}\mathbf{a} + \mathbf{e}b - \mathbf{y}\|^2 + \rho\mathbf{a}^{\mathrm{T}}\mathbf{K}\mathbf{a}. \end{aligned} \tag{9.20}$$

Roles of the Mercer condition

Assuming that the Mercer condition is not met and $\mathbf{K}$ is not positive semi-definite, the cost function in Eq. (9.20) has no lower bound. In other words, Eq. (9.20) does not constitute a meaningful minimization criterion. Assuming that the Mercer condition is met, $\mathbf{K}$ will be positive semi-definite, whereupon a legitimate optimal solution always exists.

Derivation of the optimal KRR solution

The zero-gradient point of $E'(\mathbf{a}, b)$ with respect to $\mathbf{a}$ leads to

$$[\mathbf{K} + \rho\mathbf{I}]\mathbf{a} = \mathbf{y} - b\mathbf{e}.$$

The zero-gradient point of $E'(\mathbf{a}, b)$ with respect to b is

$$\mathbf{e}^{\mathrm{T}}\mathbf{a} = 0.$$

On combining the two zero-gradient equations, we obtain a formulation just like Eq. (8.71) (except that now $\mathbf{K} = \mathbf{\Phi}^{\mathrm{T}}\mathbf{\Phi}$):

$$\begin{bmatrix} \mathbf{K} + \rho\mathbf{I} & \mathbf{e} \\ \mathbf{e}^{\mathrm{T}} & 0 \end{bmatrix} \begin{bmatrix} \mathbf{a} \\ b \end{bmatrix} = \begin{bmatrix} \mathbf{y} \\ 0 \end{bmatrix}. \tag{9.21}$$

Since $\mathbf{K} + \rho\mathbf{I}$ is always nonsingular if $\rho > 0$, the RR has a closed-form solution as follows:

$$\mathbf{a} = [\mathbf{K} + \rho\mathbf{I}]^{-1}[\mathbf{y} - b\mathbf{e}], \quad \text{where } b = \frac{\mathbf{y}^{\mathrm{T}}[\mathbf{K} + \rho\mathbf{I}]^{-1}\mathbf{e}}{\mathbf{e}^{\mathrm{T}}[\mathbf{K} + \rho\mathbf{I}]^{-1}\mathbf{e}}. \tag{9.22}$$

It follows that the discriminant function is

$$f(\mathbf{x}) = \mathbf{a}^{\mathrm{T}}\vec{\mathbf{k}}(\mathbf{x}) + b. \tag{9.23}$$

When $\rho \to 0$, Eq. (9.21) converges to the KDA formulation, see Eq. (9.9). Assuming further that $\mathbf{K}$ is invertible, the KRR solution in Eq. (9.22) converges to the KDA solution in Eq. (9.10).

The KRR learning model in empirical space is summarized as follows.

ALGORITHM 9.1 (KRR learning algorithm in empirical space) *Given a training dataset $[\mathcal{X}, \mathcal{Y}]$ and a specific kernel function $K(\mathbf{x}, \mathbf{y})$, the KRR regression algorithm contains the following steps.*

- *Compute the $N \times N$ symmetric kernel matrix:*

$$\mathbf{K} = \begin{bmatrix} K(\mathbf{x}_1, \mathbf{x}_1) & K(\mathbf{x}_1, \mathbf{x}_2) & \ldots & K(\mathbf{x}_1, \mathbf{x}_M) \\ K(\mathbf{x}_2, \mathbf{x}_1) & K(\mathbf{x}_2, \mathbf{x}_2) & \ldots & K(\mathbf{x}_2, \mathbf{x}_M) \\ \ldots & \ldots & \ldots & \ldots \\ K(\mathbf{x}_M, \mathbf{x}_1) & K(\mathbf{x}_M, \mathbf{x}_2) & \ldots & K(\mathbf{x}_M, \mathbf{x}_M) \end{bmatrix}. \tag{9.24}$$

- *Compute the empirical decision vector* **a** *and the threshold b via Eq. (9.21):*

$$\begin{bmatrix} \mathbf{K} + \rho\mathbf{I} & \mathbf{e} \\ \mathbf{e}^{\mathrm{T}} & 0 \end{bmatrix} \begin{bmatrix} \mathbf{a} \\ b \end{bmatrix} = \begin{bmatrix} \mathbf{y} \\ 0 \end{bmatrix}. \tag{9.25}$$

- *The discriminant function is*

$$f(\mathbf{x}) = \vec{\mathbf{k}}(\mathbf{x})^{\mathrm{T}}\mathbf{a} + b = \sum_{i=1}^{N} a_i K(\mathbf{x}_i, \mathbf{x}) + b. \tag{9.26}$$

- *The decision rule can be formed as follows:*

$$\mathbf{x} \in \begin{cases} C_+ & iff(\mathbf{x}) \geq 0 \\ C_- & iff(\mathbf{x}) < 0. \end{cases} \tag{9.27}$$

□

9.3.3 A proof of equivalence of two formulations

We have so far independently derived the optimal KRR solutions both for the intrinsic-space and for the empirical-space formulation. Logically, both approaches should lead to the same solutions. However, as an alternative verification, we shall now provide an algebraic method to directly connect the two solutions.

For the kernel-matrix-based approach, via pre-multiplying Eq. (9.25) by $[\mathbf{e}^{\mathrm{T}} \ -\rho]$ and noting that $\mathbf{K} = \mathbf{\Phi}^{\mathrm{T}}\mathbf{\Phi}$, we obtain

$$
\begin{aligned}
0 &= \mathbf{e}^{\mathrm{T}}\mathbf{K}\mathbf{a} + \mathbf{e}^{\mathrm{T}}\mathbf{e}b - \mathbf{e}^{\mathrm{T}}\mathbf{y} \\
&= \mathbf{e}^{\mathrm{T}}\mathbf{\Phi}^{\mathrm{T}}\mathbf{\Phi}\mathbf{a} + Nb - \mathbf{e}^{\mathrm{T}}\mathbf{y} \\
&\overset{\text{Eq. (9.19)}}{=} \mathbf{e}^{\mathrm{T}}\mathbf{\Phi}^{\mathrm{T}}\mathbf{u} + Nb - \mathbf{e}^{\mathrm{T}}\mathbf{y}.
\end{aligned} \tag{9.28}
$$

By Woodbury's matrix identity [301], we have

$$
[\mathbf{K} + \rho\mathbf{I}]^{-1} = \rho^{-1}\mathbf{I} - \rho^{-1}\mathbf{\Phi}^{\mathrm{T}}[\rho\mathbf{I} + \mathbf{S}]^{-1}\mathbf{\Phi},
$$

and it follows that

$$
\mathbf{\Phi}[\mathbf{K} + \rho\mathbf{I}]^{-1} = \rho^{-1}\mathbf{\Phi} - \rho^{-1}\mathbf{S}[\rho\mathbf{I} + \mathbf{S}]^{-1}\mathbf{\Phi} = [\rho\mathbf{I} + \mathbf{S}]^{-1}\mathbf{\Phi}. \tag{9.29}
$$

From Eqs. (9.19) and (9.22), we obtain

$$
\mathbf{u} = \mathbf{\Phi}\mathbf{a} = \mathbf{\Phi}[\mathbf{K} + \rho\mathbf{I}]^{-1}[\mathbf{y} - b\mathbf{e}] = [\rho\mathbf{I} + \mathbf{S}]^{-1}\mathbf{\Phi}[\mathbf{y} - b\mathbf{e}].
$$

On pre-multiplying the above by $[\rho\mathbf{I} + \mathbf{S}]$, we arrive at

$$
[\rho\mathbf{I} + \mathbf{S}]\,\mathbf{u} = \mathbf{\Phi}\mathbf{y} - \mathbf{\Phi}\mathbf{e}b. \tag{9.30}
$$

By combining Eqs. (9.28) and (9.30), we obtain the following matrix system:

$$
\begin{bmatrix} \mathbf{S} + \rho\mathbf{I} & \mathbf{\Phi}\mathbf{e} \\ \mathbf{e}^{\mathrm{T}}\mathbf{\Phi}^{\mathrm{T}} & N \end{bmatrix} \begin{bmatrix} \mathbf{u} \\ b \end{bmatrix} = \begin{bmatrix} \mathbf{\Phi}\mathbf{y} \\ \mathbf{e}^{\mathrm{T}}\mathbf{y} \end{bmatrix}, \tag{9.31}
$$

which is equivalent to the formulation given in Eq. (8.54) derived for the original space.

9.3.4 Complexities of intrinsic and empirical models

Both for the learning phase and for the prediction phase, the computational complexities of the intrinsic and empirical learning models are dictated by the intrinsic and empirical degrees, J and N, respectively.

- For the scenario that $J \leq N$, it will be more cost-effective to adopt Eq. (9.31), where the computational complexity is dictated by the inversion of the $(J+1) \times (J+1)$ matrix system – amounting to a complexity of $O(J^3)$.
- For the scenario that $J > N$, it will be more cost-effective to adopt Eq. (9.25), where the computational complexity is dictated by the inversion of the $(N+1) \times (N+1)$ matrix system – amounting to a complexity of $O(N^3)$.

Since they produce equivalent results, Eq. (9.31) versus Eq. (9.25), the learning model with lesser complexity should obviously be chosen for practical implementation. Indeed, there exist applications for which the intrinsic approach could be hugely more efficient than the empirical approach – and vice versa. (See Chapter 13.)

9.4 Perturbational discriminant analysis (PDA)

This section aims to prove that the following kernel-based learning models are equivalent:

(i) *kernel-based ridge regression (KRR) and LS-SVM classifier, and*
(ii) *kernel-based perturbational discriminant analysis (PDA).*

Recall that $\bar{\mathbf{\Phi}}$ denotes the center-adjusted data matrix in the intrinsic space. Now suppose that the data matrix is perturbed by an (additive and white) noise matrix:

$$\bar{\mathbf{\Phi}} \rightarrow \bar{\mathbf{\Phi}} + \mathbf{N}, \tag{9.32}$$

where the "noise matrix" $\mathbf{N}$ represents random and additive noise terms, which are uncorrelated with $\bar{\mathbf{\Phi}}$: $E[\mathbf{\Phi}^{\mathrm{T}}\mathbf{N}] = 0$. Assume further that (1) $E[\mathbf{N}] = 0$ and (2) $E[\mathbf{N}^{\mathrm{T}}\mathbf{N}] \propto \mathbf{I}$. This leads to the following center-adjusted perturbational scatter matrix:

$$(\bar{\mathbf{\Phi}} + \mathbf{N})(\bar{\mathbf{\Phi}} + \mathbf{N})^{\mathrm{T}} \approx \bar{\mathbf{\Phi}}\bar{\mathbf{\Phi}}^{\mathrm{T}} + \rho\mathbf{I} = \bar{\mathbf{S}} + \rho\mathbf{I}, \tag{9.33}$$

where the parameter ρ denotes the power of the additive noise in the errors in variables. Consequently, the modified Fisher score is

$$J_{\mathrm{PDA}} = \frac{\mathbf{u}^{\mathrm{T}}[\vec{\mu}_+ - \vec{\mu}_-][\vec{\mu}_+ - \vec{\mu}_-]^{\mathrm{T}}\mathbf{u}}{\mathbf{u}^{\mathrm{T}}[\bar{\mathbf{\Phi}}\bar{\mathbf{\Phi}}^{\mathrm{T}} + \rho\mathbf{I}]\mathbf{u}}, \tag{9.34}$$

where $\vec{\mu}_+$ and $\vec{\mu}_-$ denote the positive and negative centroids in the intrinsic space. Maximizing Eq. (9.34) leads to the following PDA solution (see Eq. (8.26)):

$$\mathbf{u}_{\mathrm{PDA}} = [\bar{\mathbf{S}} + \rho\mathbf{I}]^{-1}\mathbf{\Delta}, \tag{9.35}$$

where $\bar{\mathbf{S}} = \bar{\mathbf{\Phi}}\bar{\mathbf{\Phi}}^{\mathrm{T}}$ and $\mathbf{\Delta} = [\vec{\mu}_+ - \vec{\mu}_-]$. Likewise, the threshold can be obtained as

$$b = -\vec{\mu}^{\mathrm{T}}[\bar{\mathbf{S}} + \rho\mathbf{I}]^{-1}\mathbf{\Delta} + \frac{N_+ - N_-}{2N_+N_-}. \tag{9.36}$$

Equivalence of KRR, LS-SVM, and PDA

The equivalence between KRR and PDA (Eq. (8.56)) can be easily verified by substituting the PDA solutions in Eqs. (9.35) and (9.36) into the KRR solver given by Eq. (9.18) and verifying their mathematical equality. More precisely, it is easy to verify that, cf. Eq. (8.78),

$$\begin{aligned}
&\begin{bmatrix} \mathbf{S} + \rho\mathbf{I} & \mathbf{\Phi}\mathbf{e} \\ \mathbf{e}^{\mathrm{T}}\mathbf{\Phi}^{\mathrm{T}} & N \end{bmatrix} \begin{bmatrix} \mathbf{u}_{\mathrm{PDA}} \\ b \end{bmatrix} \\
&= \begin{bmatrix} \mathbf{S} + \rho\mathbf{I} & \mathbf{\Phi}\mathbf{e} \\ \mathbf{e}^{\mathrm{T}}\mathbf{\Phi}^{\mathrm{T}} & N \end{bmatrix} \begin{bmatrix} [\bar{\mathbf{S}} + \rho\mathbf{I}]^{-1}\mathbf{\Delta} \\ -\vec{\mu}^{\mathrm{T}}[\bar{\mathbf{S}} + \rho\mathbf{I}]^{-1}\mathbf{\Delta} + (N_+ - N_-)/(2N_+N_-) \end{bmatrix} \\
&= \kappa \begin{bmatrix} \mathbf{\Phi}\mathbf{y} \\ \mathbf{e}^{\mathrm{T}}\mathbf{y} \end{bmatrix}.
\end{aligned}$$

In conclusion, when $\rho > 0$, the three kernel-based classifiers (KRR, LS-SVM, and PDA) share the same optimal solution. Given their equivalence, for convenience, the term KRR will be used to generically represent all the three kernel-based classifiers.

It is worth noting that the equivalence between KRR and PDA (see Section 9.4) has an important meaning in understanding KRR's robustness. Recall that the parameter ρ used in PDA denotes the power of the additive input noise. The equivalence between KRR and PDA suggests that the ridge factor ρ used in KRR should be chosen to be consistent with the estimated power of the input noise so as to best alleviate the sensitivity of the learned classifier. Section 9.5 will further provide a quantitative assessment of the role of the ridge factor ρ in determining the robustness of the learned classifiers.

As demonstrated by several real-world application datasets (see Section 9.6), regulated KRRs exhibit greater robustness than do unregulated KDAs. The results are reflected by the significantly improved performance for all the application datasets with which experiments have been done.

Other variants of KRR learning models

It is common to assume that the input perturbation $\Delta\vec{\phi}(\mathbf{x})$ and the input vector $\vec{\phi}(\mathbf{x})$ are statistically independent. By assuming that $\Delta\vec{\phi}(\mathbf{x})$ is white and isotropic, we can obtain Eq. (9.33). However, when $\Delta\vec{\phi}(\mathbf{x})$ is non-white, Eq. (9.33) has to be modified as follows:

$$(\bar{\mathbf{\Phi}} + \mathbf{N})(\bar{\mathbf{\Phi}} + \mathbf{N})^{\mathrm{T}} \approx \bar{\mathbf{\Phi}}\bar{\mathbf{\Phi}}^{\mathrm{T}} + \mathbf{S}_0,$$

where $\mathbf{S}_0$ represents the noise covariance matrix. Accordingly, the KRR learning model prescribed by Eq. (9.18) can be generalized as follows:

$$\begin{bmatrix} \mathbf{S} + \mathbf{S}_0 & \mathbf{\Phi}\mathbf{e} \\ \mathbf{e}^{\mathrm{T}}\mathbf{\Phi}^{\mathrm{T}} & N \end{bmatrix} \begin{bmatrix} \mathbf{u} \\ b \end{bmatrix} = \begin{bmatrix} \mathbf{\Phi}\mathbf{y} \\ \mathbf{e}^{\mathrm{T}}\mathbf{y} \end{bmatrix}. \tag{9.37}$$

Note that the generalized KRR model given in Eq. (9.37) requires $\Delta\vec{\phi}(\mathbf{x})$ and $\vec{\phi}(\mathbf{x})$ to be statistically independent. While such an independence assumption is valid for linear kernels, it generally does not hold for nonlinear kernels. Convincing evidence is given in Example 14.2, where $\Delta\vec{\phi}(\mathbf{x})$ is demonstrated to be dependent on $\vec{\phi}(\mathbf{x})$. The learning algorithm for the general errors-in-variables model is much more involved, and its full treatment is deferred to Chapter 15.

9.5 Robustness and the regression ratio in spectral space

The robustness analysis would be best conducted in the *spectral space* because the spectral components are mutually orthogonal and, consequently, the perturbation effect on each of the components can be isolated componentwise to facilitate individual sensitivity analysis.

9.5.1 The decision vector of KDA in spectral space

As discussed in Section 3.5.5, a kernel matrix $\mathbf{K}$ can be spectrally decomposed as

$$\mathbf{K} = \mathbf{U}^{\mathrm{T}}\mathbf{\Lambda}\mathbf{U} = \mathbf{E}^{\mathrm{T}}\mathbf{E}, \quad \text{where } \mathbf{E} = \mathbf{\Lambda}^{\frac{1}{2}}\mathbf{U}, \tag{9.38}$$

which leads to the notion of a *spectral feature vector* defined as follows:

$$\vec{\mathbf{s}}(\mathbf{x}) \equiv \mathbf{E}^{-\mathrm{T}}\vec{\mathbf{k}}(\mathbf{x}) = \mathbf{\Lambda}^{-\frac{1}{2}}\mathbf{U}\vec{\mathbf{k}}(\mathbf{x}). \tag{9.39}$$

Equivalently,

$$\vec{\mathbf{k}}(\mathbf{x}) = \mathbf{U}^{\mathrm{T}}\mathbf{\Lambda}^{\frac{1}{2}}\vec{\mathbf{s}}(\mathbf{x}) = \mathbf{E}^{\mathrm{T}}\vec{\mathbf{s}}(\mathbf{x}). \tag{9.40}$$

After pre-multiplying it by $\mathbf{a}^{\mathrm{T}}$, we have

$$\mathbf{a}^{\mathrm{T}}\vec{\mathbf{k}}(\mathbf{x}) = \mathbf{a}^{\mathrm{T}}\mathbf{E}^{\mathrm{T}}\vec{\mathbf{s}}(\mathbf{x}) = \mathbf{v}^{\mathrm{T}}\vec{\mathbf{s}}(\mathbf{x}). \tag{9.41}$$

Therefore, the decision vector in the spectral space is

$$\mathbf{v} = \mathbf{E}\mathbf{a}. \tag{9.42}$$

From Eqs. (9.10) and (9.42) for $\mathbf{v}$, we arrive at

$$\mathbf{v} = \mathbf{E}\mathbf{K}^{-1}[\mathbf{y} - b\mathbf{e}] \overset{\text{Eq. (9.38)}}{=} \mathbf{\Lambda}^{-1}\mathbf{E}[\mathbf{y} - b\mathbf{e}], \quad \text{where } b = \frac{\mathbf{y}^{\mathrm{T}}\mathbf{K}^{-1}\mathbf{e}}{\mathbf{e}^{\mathrm{T}}\mathbf{K}^{-1}\mathbf{e}}. \tag{9.43}$$

It follows that the decision boundary is

$$f(\mathbf{x}) = \mathbf{v}^{\mathrm{T}}\vec{\mathbf{s}}(\mathbf{x}) + b = 0.$$

In summary, the discriminant function can be expressed in any of the three spaces ($\mathcal{H}$, $\mathcal{K}$, or $\mathcal{S}$), in the following forms:

$$\begin{aligned} f(\mathbf{x}) &= \mathbf{u}^{\mathrm{T}}\vec{\phi}(\mathbf{x}) + b \\ &= \mathbf{a}^{\mathrm{T}}\vec{\mathbf{k}}(\mathbf{x}) + b \\ &= \mathbf{v}^{\mathrm{T}}\vec{\mathbf{s}}(\mathbf{x}) + b, \end{aligned} \tag{9.44}$$

where the decision vectors corresponding to the three kernel spaces are denoted by $\mathbf{u}$, $\mathbf{a}$, and $\mathbf{v}$. See Eq. (9.41)

9.5.2 Resilience of the decision components of KDA classifiers

In the spectral space, the spectral feature vector is

$$\vec{\mathbf{s}}(\mathbf{x}) = [s^{(1)}(\mathbf{x}), s^{(2)}(\mathbf{x}), \ldots, s^{(N)}(\mathbf{x})],$$

and the discriminant function is

$$f(\mathbf{x}) = \mathbf{v}^{\mathrm{T}}\vec{\mathbf{s}}(\mathbf{x}) + b = \sum_{i=1}^{N} v^{(i)}s^{(i)} + b. \tag{9.45}$$

In short, the discriminant function can be expressed as a linear combination of N *decision component(s)*:

$$v^{(i)}s^{(i)}, \quad i = 1, 2, \ldots, N.$$

The *component magnitudes* are defined as the magnitudes of the elements of the *spectral decision vector* $\mathbf{v} = [v^{(1)}, v^{(2)}, \ldots, v^{(N)}]$.

The major decision component(s), i.e. those associated with the largest component magnitudes are the ones primarily responsible for the classification performance. Under the perfect (but rarely valid) assumption that there exists little or no perturbation, such a classifier could indeed lead to very high training accuracy.

Let us first study such an ideal case and then extend it to the more complex sensitivity analysis. As an example, the *spectral feature vector* for the XOR dataset is shown pictorially in Figure 9.2. Moreover, as derived in Example 9.2, the *decision component* will be the second spectral component $s^{(2)}(\mathbf{x})$.

Example 9.2 (XOR case study: decision component) *With* $K(\mathbf{x}, \mathbf{y}) = (1 + \mathbf{x}^{\mathrm{T}}\mathbf{y})^2$, *the kernel matrix* $\mathbf{K}$ *has already been derived in Eq. (9.11). The spectral decomposition of* $\mathbf{K}$ *is*

$$\mathbf{K} = \mathbf{U}^{\mathrm{T}}\mathbf{\Lambda}\mathbf{U}$$
$$= \begin{bmatrix} \frac{1}{2} & \frac{1}{2} & \frac{1}{2} & \frac{1}{2} \\ \frac{1}{2} & \frac{1}{2} & -\frac{1}{2} & -\frac{1}{2} \\ \frac{1}{2} & -\frac{1}{2} & \frac{1}{2} & -\frac{1}{2} \\ \frac{1}{2} & -\frac{1}{2} & -\frac{1}{2} & \frac{1}{2} \end{bmatrix} \begin{bmatrix} 12 & 0 & 0 & 0 \\ 0 & 8 & 0 & 0 \\ 0 & 0 & 8 & 0 \\ 0 & 0 & 0 & 8 \end{bmatrix} \begin{bmatrix} \frac{1}{2} & \frac{1}{2} & \frac{1}{2} & \frac{1}{2} \\ \frac{1}{2} & \frac{1}{2} & -\frac{1}{2} & -\frac{1}{2} \\ \frac{1}{2} & -\frac{1}{2} & \frac{1}{2} & -\frac{1}{2} \\ \frac{1}{2} & -\frac{1}{2} & -\frac{1}{2} & \frac{1}{2} \end{bmatrix}. \tag{9.46}$$

In a slightly different expression:

$$\mathbf{K} = [\mathbf{U}^{\mathrm{T}}\mathbf{\Lambda}^{\frac{1}{2}}][\mathbf{\Lambda}^{\frac{1}{2}}\mathbf{U}] = [\mathbf{E}^{\mathrm{T}}][\mathbf{E}]$$
$$= \begin{bmatrix} \sqrt{3} & \sqrt{2} & \sqrt{2} & \sqrt{2} \\ \sqrt{3} & \sqrt{2} & -\sqrt{2} & -\sqrt{2} \\ \sqrt{3} & -\sqrt{2} & \sqrt{2} & -\sqrt{2} \\ \sqrt{3} & -\sqrt{2} & -\sqrt{2} & \sqrt{2} \end{bmatrix} \begin{bmatrix} \sqrt{3} & \sqrt{3} & \sqrt{3} & \sqrt{3} \\ \sqrt{2} & \sqrt{2} & -\sqrt{2} & -\sqrt{2} \\ \sqrt{2} & -\sqrt{2} & \sqrt{2} & -\sqrt{2} \\ \sqrt{2} & -\sqrt{2} & -\sqrt{2} & \sqrt{2} \end{bmatrix}, \tag{9.47}$$

where

$$\mathbf{E} = \begin{bmatrix} \sqrt{3} & \sqrt{3} & \sqrt{3} & \sqrt{3} \\ \sqrt{2} & \sqrt{2} & -\sqrt{2} & -\sqrt{2} \\ \sqrt{2} & -\sqrt{2} & \sqrt{2} & -\sqrt{2} \\ \sqrt{2} & -\sqrt{2} & -\sqrt{2} & \sqrt{2} \end{bmatrix}.$$

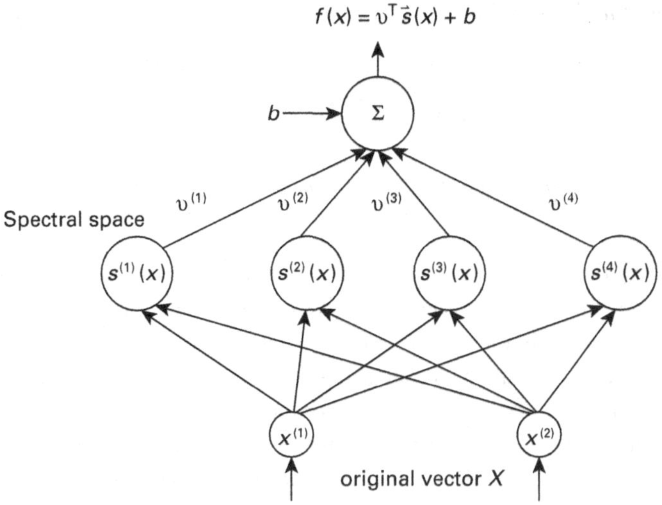

Fig. 9.2. The spectral space $\mathcal{S}$ is an N-dimensional vector space. The basis function of $\mathcal{S}$ is highly dependent on the training dataset. The two-layer network shown here depicts the four bases for the spectral-space representation for both datasets in Examples 9.2 and 9.3. For the XOR dataset, see Example 9.2, the decision component is $s^{(2)}(\mathbf{x})$. For the two modified XOR datasets, see Example 9.3, (1) the decision component will be $s^{(2)}(\mathbf{x})$ for the easy dataset; and (2) the decision component will be $s^{(3)}(\mathbf{x})$ for the hard dataset.

Basis functions for spectral space

The basis for the spectral space is

$$\vec{\mathbf{s}}(\mathbf{x}) = \mathbf{E}^{-\mathrm{T}} \begin{bmatrix} K(\mathbf{x}_1, \mathbf{x}) \\ K(\mathbf{x}_2, \mathbf{x}) \\ K(\mathbf{x}_3, \mathbf{x}) \\ K(\mathbf{x}_4, \mathbf{x}) \end{bmatrix} = \begin{bmatrix} (1/\sqrt{3})(1 + u^2 + v^2) \\ \sqrt{2}uv \\ \sqrt{2}(u + v) \\ \sqrt{2}(u - v) \end{bmatrix}. \tag{9.48}$$

Note that

$$\mathbf{y} = \begin{bmatrix} 1 \\ 1 \\ -1 \\ -1 \end{bmatrix} \quad \text{and} \quad \mathbf{e} = \begin{bmatrix} 1 \\ 1 \\ 1 \\ 1 \end{bmatrix}.$$

From Eq. (9.43), the decision vector in the spectral space can be obtained as

$$\mathbf{v} = \mathbf{E}\mathbf{K}^{-1}\mathbf{y} = \mathbf{E}^{-\mathrm{T}}\mathbf{y} = \begin{bmatrix} 0 \\ 1/\sqrt{2} \\ 0 \\ 0 \end{bmatrix} \quad \text{and } b = 0.$$

It follows that the decision boundary can be expressed by the second component $s^{(2)}(\mathbf{x})$ alone:

$$f(\mathbf{x}) = \mathbf{v}^{\mathrm{T}}\vec{\mathbf{s}}(\mathbf{x}) = uv = 0.$$

In this case, the (major) decision component is obviously $s^{(2)}(\mathbf{x})$. □

For the XOR dataset, all the eigenvalues are approximately the same; thus all spectral components are equally resilient/sensitive to random perturbation. In this case, the component magnitude is the only criterion dictating the role played by each component in classification. For the XOR dataset, the second component $s^{(2)}(\mathbf{x})$ is the one best separating $(\mathbf{x}_1, \mathbf{x}_2)$ from $(\mathbf{x}_3, \mathbf{x}_4)$. On the other hand, if the class labels are shuffled, the major decision component(s) change accordingly. For example, for optimally separating $(\mathbf{x}_1, \mathbf{x}_3)$ and $(\mathbf{x}_2, \mathbf{x}_4)$, $s^{(3)}(\mathbf{x})$ will be the major decision component. By the same token, $s^{(4)}(\mathbf{x})$ will become the choice for separating $(\mathbf{x}_2, \mathbf{x}_3)$ and $(\mathbf{x}_1, \mathbf{x}_4)$.

In practice, the kernel matrices may sometimes become ill-conditioned and there will be a great variation of resiliency among different components. In this case, the component magnitude alone will no longer suffice to judge the importance of the components. To strive for the best possible prediction accuracy, one must consider the components' magnitudes as well as their sensitivity/resilience against perturbation.

To better appreciate the role of the sensitivity/resilience of the decision components, let us study the two other datasets depicted in Figure 9.3. The *spectral feature vector* for the two modified XOR datasets can again be represented by the two-layer network shown in Figure 9.2.

Example 9.3 (Modified XOR datasets) *With reference to Figure 9.3, the modified XOR-type dataset is represented by the following data matrix:*

$$\mathbf{X} = \begin{bmatrix} +1 & +1.1 & -1 & -1.1 \\ +1 & +0.8 & -1 & -0.8 \end{bmatrix}.$$

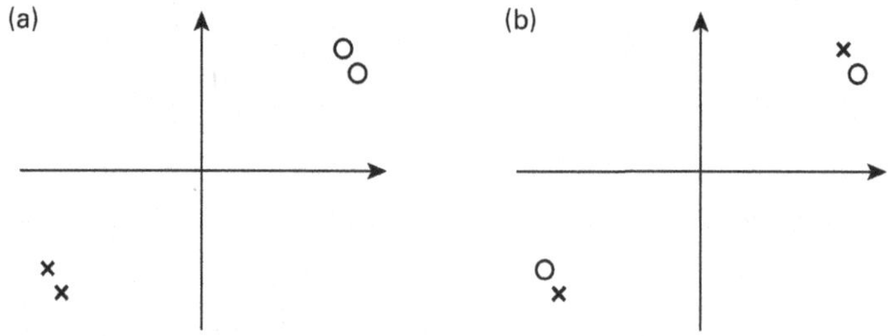

Fig. 9.3. Modified XOR datasets. With a proper kernel, the data become linearly separable in the kernel space. (a) An easy case: partition separable by a major component. (b) A hard case: partition separable by a minor component in the spectral space.

- *For the "easy" XOR-type dataset depicted in Figure 9.3(a), the task is to separate* $(\mathbf{x}_1, \mathbf{x}_2)$ *and* $(\mathbf{x}_3, \mathbf{x}_4)$. *It will be shown that the decision component* $s^{(2)}(\mathbf{x})$ *is already very robust.*
- *For the "hard" XOR-type dataset depicted in Figure 9.3(b), the task is to separate* $(\mathbf{x}_1, \mathbf{x}_3)$ *and* $(\mathbf{x}_2, \mathbf{x}_4)$. *It will be shown that the decision component is now* $s^{(3)}(\mathbf{x})$, *which is relatively more sensitive, making regularization worthy of consideration.*

With $K(\mathbf{x}, \mathbf{y}) = (1 + \mathbf{x}^{\mathrm{T}}\mathbf{y})^2$, *we have*

$$\mathbf{K} = \begin{bmatrix} 9.000 & 8.410 & 1.000 & 0.810 \\ 8.410 & 8.122 & 0.810 & 0.722 \\ 1.000 & 0.810 & 9.000 & 8.410 \\ 0.810 & 0.722 & 8.410 & 8.122 \end{bmatrix},$$

whose spectral decomposition leads to four eigenvalues,

$$\{\lambda_i\} = \{18.6607, 15.3061, 0.1844, 0.0941\},$$

and $\mathbf{K} = \mathbf{E}^{\mathrm{T}}\mathbf{E}$, *where*

$$\mathbf{E} = \begin{bmatrix} 2.226 & 2.091 & 2.226 & 2.091 \\ -1.994 & -1.917 & 1.994 & 1.917 \\ -0.208 & 0.221 & -0.208 & 0.221 \\ 0.150 & -0.156 & -0.150 & 0.156 \end{bmatrix}.$$

After center-adjustment, we have

$$\bar{\mathbf{E}} = \begin{bmatrix} 0.067 & -0.067 & 0.067 & -0.067 \\ -1.956 & -1.956 & 1.956 & 1.956 \\ -0.215 & 0.215 & -0.215 & 0.215 \\ 0.153 & -0.153 & -0.153 & 0.153 \end{bmatrix}.$$

Note that the first component corresponds to the first row with very small values. The first row is reduced to a minor component due to center-adjustment. In fact, only the second component has a relatively higher power, with $\sqrt{\lambda_2} = 3.91$. *The other two are also relatively minor, with* $\sqrt{\lambda_3} = 0.43$ *and* $\sqrt{\lambda_4} = 0.31$. *Intuitively, a major decision component would better assure an error-resilient classifier. On the other hand, a minor decision component will lead to a less robust classifier.*

- *As depicted in Figure 9.3(a),* $(\mathbf{x}_1, \mathbf{x}_2)$ *and* $(\mathbf{x}_3, \mathbf{x}_4)$ *are linearly separable in the original vector space. Hence this is deemed an "easy" XOR-type dataset. The KDA solution (Eq. (9.43)) yields a decision vector* $\mathbf{v} = [0.00\ -0.51\ 0.00\ -0.13]^{\mathrm{T}}$. *This implies that* $s^{(2)}(\mathbf{x})$ *is the major decision component. Owing to the (relatively) large eigenvalue,* $\sqrt{\lambda_2} = 3.912$, *the second component alone would map positive/negative patterns to* $+1.956$ *and* -1.956, *respectively. Thus, one can say that the resilience margin is effectively* 1.956. *Namely, a perturbation has to be greater than* 1.956 *to have a chance of flipping the decision. This makes the KDA solution a robust classifier and renders any further regularization unnecessary.*

- *As depicted in Figure 9.3(b),* $(\mathbf{x}_1, \mathbf{x}_3)$ *and* $(\mathbf{x}_2, \mathbf{x}_4)$ *are not linearly separable. Hence these training data are considered to constitute a "hard" XOR-type dataset. The KDA solution yields a decision vector* $\mathbf{v} = [1.33\ 0.00\ -4.24\ 0.00]^{\mathrm{T}}$. *In this case, the major decision component becomes* $s^{(3)}(\mathbf{x})$, *which is primarily responsible for the classification of* $(\mathbf{x}_1, \mathbf{x}_3)$ *and* $(\mathbf{x}_2, \mathbf{x}_4)$. *Note that the third component would map positive/negative patterns to* $+0.215$ *and* -0.215, *respectively. Namely, the resilience margin is now reduced to* 0.215. *The degraded resilience is due to the much smaller eigenvalue:* $\sqrt{\lambda_3} = 0.43$. *As a result, any deviation exceeding* 0.215 *could flip the classification result.*
- *As another example, the major decision component for the classification of* $(\mathbf{x}_2, \mathbf{x}_3)$ *versus* $(\mathbf{x}_1, \mathbf{x}_4)$ *would be the fourth spectral component* $s^{(4)}(\mathbf{x})$. *In this case, the use of the kernel only helps widen the separation margin a little since the two classes are already linearly separable in the original space.* □

9.5.3 Component magnitude and component resilience

It can be shown that a kernel matrix $\mathbf{K}$ will be generically nonsingular, assuming that a sufficiently high-order polynomial kernel is adopted. (See Problems 9.4 and 9.5.) This in turn assures the existence of a KDA solution that can perfectly separate the training dataset theoretically speaking. However, no supervised learning objective would place its focus on the training accuracy alone. To strive for the best prediction accuracy, a designer must aim at the generalization capability of the learned classifier by taking into account the inevitable variations in different data-acquisition environments. In fact, the environments could be very different for training and predicting datasets. To this end, the robustness analysis must address two important aspects of the decision components, i.e.

- **component magnitude**, defined as the magnitudes of the elements of the *spectral decision vector*: $|v^{(i)}|$; and
- **component resilience**, characterized by the eigenvalue (i.e. power) associated with each of the spectral components defined in the spectral space.

(i) If $\lambda^{(i)}$ is large, then the ith component is considered to be a strong (or resilient) component.
(ii) If $\lambda^{(i)}$ is small, then it is viewed as a weak (or vulnerable) component.

Robustness of a classifier

A decision component is said to be dominant if its corresponding magnitude in the (spectral) decision vector is higher than the other competing components. A classifier is considered to be robust only when the dominant component(s) is (are) resilient. On the other hand, the classifier will be viewed as sensitive if the dominant component(s) is (are) weak and vulnerable.

In fact, how much a component is regulated by KRR is proportional to the so-called regression ratio, which is a simple function of the relative ratio $\lambda^{(i)}/\rho$. The detail will be elaborated on next.

9.5.4 Regression ratio: KDA versus KRR

The presence of sensitive (or vulnerable) decision component(s) emphasizes the importance of robust classifiers. In particular, when the kernel matrix $\mathbf{K}$ is not well-conditioned, the numerical property of the KDA classifier will be of major concern. This motivates the adoption of regularization for deriving numerically stable variants of KDA, i.e. KRR. The regularization effect can be quantitatively studied by means of the so-called *regression ratios*. This approach offers a simple explanation for why the ridge parameter ρ is effective in controlling oversubscription of sensitive components. The analysis provides a theoretical footing for a ridge-based regularization technique that is widely considered to be one of the most effective for many numerical problems.

In the spectral space $\mathcal{S}$, the data matrix is $\mathbf{E}$, and it follows that the corresponding scatter matrix is

$$\mathbf{S} = \mathbf{E}\mathbf{E}^{\mathrm{T}} = [\mathbf{\Lambda}^{\frac{1}{2}}\mathbf{U}][\mathbf{U}^{\mathrm{T}}\mathbf{\Lambda}^{\frac{1}{2}}] = [\mathbf{\Lambda}].$$

By plugging the above into Eq. (9.43), the decision vector in the spectral space $\mathcal{S}$ can be obtained as

$$\begin{aligned} \mathbf{v}_{\mathrm{KRR}} &= [\mathbf{\Lambda} + \rho\mathbf{I}]^{-1}\mathbf{E}[\mathbf{y} - b\mathbf{e}] \\ &= \mathrm{Diag}\left[\frac{1}{\lambda_i + \rho}\right]\mathbf{E}[\mathbf{y} - b\mathbf{e}], \quad \text{where } b = \frac{\mathbf{y}^{\mathrm{T}}[\mathbf{K} + \rho\mathbf{I}]^{-1}\mathbf{e}}{\mathbf{e}^{\mathrm{T}}[\mathbf{K} + \rho\mathbf{I}]^{-1}\mathbf{e}}. \end{aligned} \tag{9.49}$$

Likewise, the decision vector in the spectral space for KDA is

$$\mathbf{v}_{\mathrm{KDA}} = \mathrm{Diag}\left[\frac{1}{\lambda_i}\right]\mathbf{E}[\mathbf{y} - b\mathbf{e}], \quad \text{where } b = \frac{\mathbf{y}^{\mathrm{T}}\mathbf{K}^{-1}\mathbf{e}}{\mathbf{e}^{\mathrm{T}}\mathbf{K}^{-1}\mathbf{e}}. \tag{9.50}$$

Ignoring the variation in b due to ρ (which is presumably small), we can obtain a simple *regression ratio* on the amounts of the ith component before versus after regularization:

$$\frac{\lambda_i}{\lambda_i + \rho}. \tag{9.51}$$

The notion of decision resilience plays a vital role in the regularization of KRR. For the sake of argument, let us assume that two components (say the ith and jth components) are primarily responsible for a KDA classifier. One of them is stronger and one weaker, say $\lambda_i > \lambda_j$. (Consider, for example, the KDA classifier for the easy XOR-type dataset. Here the strong component is the second one ($\lambda_2 = 3.91$) and the weak component is the fourth one ($\lambda_4 = 0.31$).) Intuitively, for robustness, more emphasis should be placed on the resilient component and less on the sensitive component. The KRR solution basically complies with this intuitive principle. Note that the component magnitudes before and after regularization are respectively

$$v^{(i)} \to \frac{\lambda_i}{\lambda_i + \rho}v^{(i)} \quad \text{and} \quad v^{(j)} \to \frac{\lambda_j}{\lambda_j + \rho}v^{(j)},$$

Note that the magnitude of the weak component ($v^{(4)}$) is suppressed more than the strong components ($v^{(2)}$). More exactly, for the easy XOR-type dataset,

- for KDA, with $\rho = 0$, $v^{(i)} = v^{(2)} = -0.51$ and $v^{(j)} = v^{(4)} = -0.13$; and
- for KRR, with $\rho = 1$, the new coefficient $v'^{(2)} = -(0.51 \times 3.91)/(3.91 + 1) = -0.41$ and $v^{(j)} = v'^{(4)} = -(0.13 \times 0.31)/(0.31 + 1) = -0.031$. (Note that, while the weaker component is suppressed by a factor of 4, the stronger component drops only by 20%.)

This example explains how the ridge parameter ρ effectively copes with oversubscription of sensitive components in KRR.

Evaluation criterion of robust classifiers

Almost any dataset can be perfectly separated by a learned KDA classifier, assuming a sufficiently high-order polynomial kernel is adopted. This suggests that training accuracy alone is not a meaningful metric for the selection of a good kernel function for KRRs. Some sensitivity/robustness aspects must be taken into consideration. Unfortunately, this is a very complex topic. Here we experimented with two kernel functions, and (1) for both kernels the ith component happens to be the only (major) decision component, i.e. $|v^{(i)}| > |v^{(j)}|, \forall j \neq i$; and (2) their sensitivity pictures are completely different. More exactly, for one of the kernels one has the best possible circumstance, namely the highest power component being the most resilient, i.e. $\lambda_i > \lambda_j, \forall j \neq i$. For the other kernel it is just the opposite, i.e. $\lambda_i < \lambda_j, \forall j \neq i$. In this case, it is obvious that the former would be the preferred choice. In summary, a general guideline is that an ideal KRR classifier, if one exists, should have major components having large magnitude and high resilience simultaneously.

A more practical approach to the selection of an optimal kernel function usually involves extensive simulation study on the prediction accuracies tested on an independent testing dataset. Ideally, similar environments of data acquisition are usually assumed for the testing and predicting datasets. Hence it is a common practice to choose, among all the values of ρ experimented with, the one which yields the highest accuracy. However, in preparing for circumstances in which the acquisition environment during the live prediction phase is more hostile or uncontrollable than what is presumed in the evaluation phase, an evaluator might want to consider the use of the average performance, instead of the peak performance, over the range of expected perturbation power, say $\rho \in [0, \rho_0]$.

9.6 Application studies: KDA versus KRR

To assess the performances of KDA and KRR, simulation studies have been conducted on several datasets, including those from the UCI machine learning repository, microarray cancer diagnosis, and subcellular protein sequence analyses.

9.6.1 Experiments on UCI data

Data and procedures

In the simulation conducted by Kung and Mak [139], the performances of the KDA and KRR classifiers were evaluated for six UCI datasets (Iris, Wine, Liver, Glass, Yeast, and Red Wine Quality) from http://archive.ics.uci.edu/ml/.

Table 9.1. Performance of KDA, kernel ridge regressor (KRR), support vector machines (SVM) on UCI datasets. In all cases, $C = 10$, and ρ, C_{min}, and σ were set to values specified in Table 12.3.

	UCI dataset					
Method	Iris	Wine	Liver	Glass	Yeast	Red wine
KDA*	84.00%	92.70%	53.33%	38.32%	36.22 %	35.08%
KRR	95.33%	91.57%	72.17%	56.07%	**59.77%**	57.10%
SVM	96.00%	98.31%	73.04%	64.02%	54.94%	62.66%

*The accuracies for KDA shown here were based on a trimmed training set such that only one copy of the repeated samples was kept.

For KDA, it is important to ensure that the training set does not contain any repeated samples. The accuracies for KDA shown here were obtained for a trimmed training set such that only one copy of the repeated samples was kept. For more details, see Section 12.6.

A one-versus-all classification technique was used to solve the multi-class problems. Specifically, for a problem of K classes, we trained K classifiers, with the kth classifier being trained to classify the kth class against the rest. Given a test vector, its predicted class label is obtained by picking the classifier with the highest score among the K classifiers. (See Section 9.8.)

Results and discussion

For the yeast dataset, the accuracies of 20 runs of five-fold cross-validation were averaged, with each run starting with a random partitioning of the data. For all the other datasets, leave-one-out cross-validation was applied to obtain the classification accuracies.

The best values of σ (the RBF kernel parameter) for the six different datasets are 1.0, 2.0, 5.0, 3.0, 1.0, and 1.0, respectively. The classification accuracies of KDA, KRR, and SVM can be found in Table 9.1. Since KDA is merely a special case of KRR for which the ridge factor is set to $\rho = 0$, it is not at all surprising that KRR consistently outperforms KDA for all six cancer datasets. However, KRR appears to be somewhat inferior compared with the prominent SVM classifiers. KRR leads for just one of the six datasets. More precisely, for the yeast dataset, KRR's 59.77% outperforms SVM's 54.94%.

9.6.2 Experiments on microarray cancer diagnosis

Data and procedures

Six cancer datasets were considered [206]: carcinoma [107], colon [5], glioma [195], leukemia [82], prostate [247], and breast [277]. These datasets contain gene expression profiles of healthy and cancerous samples.

Results and discussion

The five-fold cross-validation method was used to assess the performance of a KDA classifier with an RBF kernel. The cross-validations were carried out 20 times, each

Table 9.2. Performance of KDA, KRR with $\rho = 1$, and SVM with $C = 4$ on cancer data. In all cases, an RBF kernel with radius = 10 was used and $C = 4$.

	Cancer dataset					
Method	Carcinoma	Colon	Glioma	Leukemia	Prostate	Breast
KDA	63.42%	84.35%	73.00%	95.07%	91.58%	77.95%
KRR	64.92%	84.27%	72.50%	95.62%	92.43%	75.45%
SVM	63.75%	83.79%	72.10%	96.25%	92.32%	77.73%

Table 9.3. Performance of KDA, KRR with $\rho = 1$, and SVM with $C = 1$ on protein data

	Subcellular localization dataset		
Method	Huang and Li [104]	Mak, Guo, and Kung [166]	Reinhardt and Hubbard [216]
KDA	51.54%	96.96%	69.74%
KRR	75.34%	98.00%	75.34%
SVM	75.89%	98.67%	79.49%

starting with a random partitioning of the data. The classification accuracies of KDA, KRR, and SVM can be found in Table 9.2. Since KDA is only a special case of KRR when the ridge factor is set to $\rho = 0$, it is not at all surprising that KRR consistently outperforms KDA for all six cancer datasets. It is interesting to note that the performance of KRR is comparable to that of SVM for the cancer datasets. (Because of the closed-form solution of KRR, however, its training time is only 25% that of SVM.)

9.6.3 Experiments on subcellular localization

Data and procedures

To illustrate the application of the KDA classifier, simulation studies were conducted on three different protein sequence datasets by Huang and Li [104], Mak, Guo and Kung [166], and Reinhardt and Hubbard [216]. Each of the datasets contains eukaryotic protein sequences with annotated subcellular locations. A one-versus-rest classification technique was used to solve the multi-class problems. We used five-fold cross-validation for performance evaluation so that every sequence in the datasets was tested. For more details, see Section 10.6.4.3 and Kung and Mak [140].

Results and discussion

Table 9.3 shows that KRR's performance is, while much better than that of KDA, slightly inferior to that of SVM.

9.7 Trimming detrimental (anti-support) vectors in KRR learning models

KRR is an LSP-based learning model in the intrinsic space, i.e.

$$\mathbf{u} = \sum_{n=1}^{N} a_n \overrightarrow{\phi}(\mathbf{x}_n). \tag{9.52}$$

In this case, the discriminant function can be expressed as

$$f(\mathbf{x}) = \sum_{n=1}^{N} a_n K(\mathbf{x}, \mathbf{x}_n) + b = \mathbf{a}^{\mathrm{T}} \overrightarrow{\mathbf{k}}(\mathbf{x}) + b, \tag{9.53}$$

and the errors $\{\epsilon_i\}$ can be expressed as functions of the empirical weights $\{a_i\}$ which are the coefficients of the vector $\mathbf{a}$. More exactly,

$$\epsilon_i = f(\mathbf{x}_i) - y_i = \mathbf{a}^{\mathrm{T}} \overrightarrow{\mathbf{k}}(\mathbf{x}_i) + b - y_i. \tag{9.54}$$

We note that, to each of the N training vectors, say $\mathbf{x}_i$, there are two kinds of parameters assigned: (1) one weight coefficient a_i and (2) one error value ϵ_i. The two parameters are related by the so-called weight–error curve (WEC), which will be described presently. The performance of any LSP-based supervised classifier can be effectively characterized by the WEC associated with the classifier. For examples, WECs associated with KRR (or PDA) provide good guidance on possible improvements of the classification accuracy by weeding out those training vectors which are detrimental according to the WEC. This ultimately leads to a pruned-KRR learning model named pruned PDA (PPDA).

WEC for KRR

For KRR's WEC, there is a one-to-one mapping between ϵ_i and a_i. For any classifier, there is an error value $\epsilon_i = f(\mathbf{x}_i) - y_i$ associated with each training vector $\mathbf{x}_i$:

$$\epsilon_i = f(\mathbf{x}_i) - y_i = \left[\mathbf{a}^{\mathrm{T}} \overrightarrow{\mathbf{k}}(\mathbf{x}_i) + b\right] - y_i.$$

On cascading the errors ϵ_i, $i = 1, \ldots, N$, into an N-dimensional *error vector*, $\overrightarrow{\epsilon}$, we obtain

$$\overrightarrow{\epsilon} \equiv [\mathbf{K}\mathbf{a} + b\mathbf{e}] - \mathbf{y}.$$

It follows that

$$\begin{aligned}
\overrightarrow{\epsilon} &= [\mathbf{K}\mathbf{a} + b\mathbf{e}] - \mathbf{y} \\
&= \mathbf{K}\mathbf{a} - [\mathbf{y} - b\mathbf{e}] \\
&\overset{\text{Eq. (9.22)}}{=} \mathbf{K}[\mathbf{K} + \rho\mathbf{I}]^{-1}[\mathbf{y} - b\mathbf{e}] - [\mathbf{K} + \rho\mathbf{I}][\mathbf{K} + \rho\mathbf{I}]^{-1}[\mathbf{y} - b\mathbf{e}] \\
&= (\mathbf{K} - [\mathbf{K} + \rho\mathbf{I}])\,[\mathbf{K} + \rho\mathbf{I}]^{-1}[\mathbf{y} - b\mathbf{e}] \\
&= -\rho[\mathbf{K} + \rho\mathbf{I}]^{-1}[\mathbf{y} - b\mathbf{e}] = -\rho\mathbf{a}.
\end{aligned} \tag{9.55}$$

Accordingly, the error ϵ_i is linearly proportional to a_i:

$$\text{error}_i = \epsilon_i = -\rho a_i, \quad \text{for} \quad i = 1, \ldots, N. \tag{9.56}$$

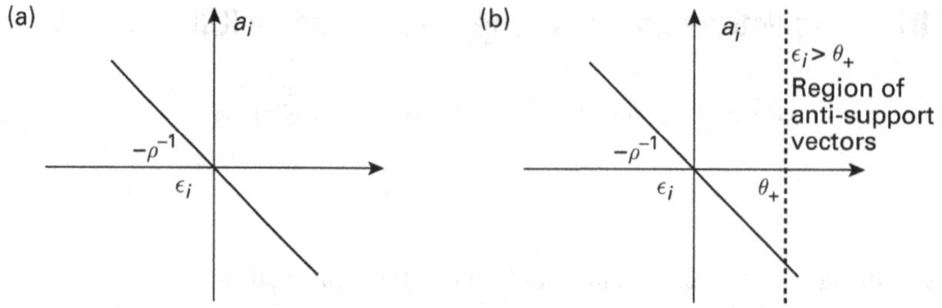

Fig. 9.4. (a) A WEC for KRR is a straight line, governed by a negative slope equal to $-\rho^{-1}$. All the training vectors will receive nonzero (positive or negative) weights. (b) Pruning of positive training vectors: depending on the WEC (of the positive dataset), the positive training vectors are divided into two subgroups, namely those deemed anti-support vectors (the area on the right-hand side) and those to be retained as surviving vectors (the area on the left-hand side).

This leads to a linear WEC for KRR as depicted in Figure 9.4(a). Moreover, according to Eq. (9.3), $|a_i| = \rho^{-1}|\epsilon_i|$ reflects the voting weight assigned to the ith vector.

This means that those training vectors which are remote from the decision boundary are assigned higher weights. It is counterintuitive that such detrimental training vectors are assigned higher weights in their influence on the decision rule. To rectify this problem, the pruned KRR weeds out those detrimental training vectors for the purpose of improving the classification results.

9.7.1 A pruned-KRR learning model: pruned PDA (PPDA)

The pruned-KRR (PPDA) approach is based on identifying a small fraction of potentially harmful "anti-support" vectors and then removing them from the pool of training vectors to be reused in the future learning process.

The development of PPDA stems from the concern regarding the linear relationship between ϵ_i and a_i, i.e. $\text{error}_i = \epsilon_i = -\rho a_i$ (Eq. (9.56)), shown in Figure 9.4(a). Note that those training vectors which are far away from the decision boundary clearly have error values of very large magnitude, i.e. $|\epsilon_i|$. This is why they will be termed *anti-support vectors.* In KRR, training vectors are assigned weights according to a linear relationship with respect to their corresponding errors. Consequently, potentially detrimental training vectors (as judged by their large errors) are assigned higher weights and thus are allowed to exercise greater influence on the learned model. This is completely counterintuitive.

In order to pinpoint such detrimental training vectors, one must first of all divide the positive (negative) training vectors into two regions according to the values of their errors ϵ_i. As shown in Figure 9.4(b), the positive training vectors are divided into two subsets as follows.

(i) **"Anti-support" training vectors.** The anti-support vectors $\mathbf{x}_i$ are those with error ϵ_i exceeding a pre-specified threshold.[2]

[2] In the following simulation study, a pre-specified fraction of training vectors (e.g. 4%) associated with the highest ϵ_i will be labeled "anti-support." Here setting a fraction serves the same purpose as setting a threshold.

(ii) **"Surviving" training vectors.** The remaining positive training vectors will be labeled *surviving vectors*. They include all those training vectors with ϵ_i less than the given threshold, including all the negative-valued ones.

(A similar division is applied to the negative training vectors.) The *anti-support vectors* (anti-SVs) are detrimental to learning because they have large errors and yet are assigned proportionally high weights, making them most counterproductive in our pursuit of a good decision boundary. Intuitively, it makes sense to exclude potentially detrimental anti-SVs from participating in any future learning process. As a result, only the *surviving vectors* will be retained in the next iteration of the learning process. In each iteration, only a small fraction of the remaining training vectors should be labeled anti-SVs, because once they have been removed they will not be reused again. With such a conservative reduction of training vectors, such a pruning process must be repeated for a good number of iterations so that the number of the ultimate "surviving vectors" can reach a desirable level. Of course, the number of iterations must also be properly controlled to assure that the surviving vectors can "support" the final decision-making endeavor.

Note that the anti-SVs for positive and negative training vectors are defined differently.

- For positive training vectors, those with errors $\epsilon_i > +\theta_+$ are anti-SVs. The region of anti-SVs is shown in Figure 9.4(b)).
- For negative training vectors (figure not shown), those errors $\epsilon_i < -\theta_-$ are considered anti-SVs.

The thresholds $\theta_+ > 0$ and $\theta_- < 0$ dictate the desired pruning ratios of the positive and negative training vectors, respectively.

The iterative PPDA algorithm is formally stated as follows.

ALGORITHM 9.2 (PPDA iterative learning model) *Denote the initial training dataset as $\mathcal{X}_0 = \mathcal{X}$. Repeat the iterative procedure until it terminates. In each iteration, say the kth one, a fraction of the unwanted training vectors from $\mathcal{X}_k$ will be removed, and the surviving vectors form a new training dataset $\mathcal{X}_{k+1}$.*

Formally, starting with iteration $k = 0$, the algorithm recursively executes the following procedures.

(i) **Compute the error values $\{\epsilon_n\}$.** *Apply KRR (i.e. PDA) to the current training dataset $\mathcal{X}_k$ to learn the discriminant function $f_k(\mathbf{x})$. Compute the error values:*

$$\epsilon_n = f_k(\mathbf{x}_n) - y_n, \ \forall n \in \mathcal{X}_k.$$

(ii) **Identify anti-support vectors.** *The anti-support vectors are defined as*[3]

[3] The anti-support vectors may also be selected according to a pre-set rejection ratio instead of the thresholds on the error values. Also, it is common to use the same rejection ratio both for the positive and for the negative training vectors.

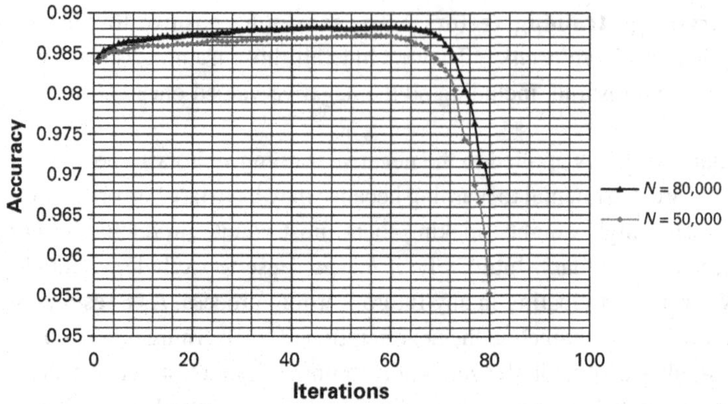

Fig. 9.5. The TRBF3-PPDA simulation shows that the performance monotonically improves as the number of iterations increases. Here we start with $N = N_0 = 80,000$ (the upper curve) and $N = N_0 = 50,000$ (the lower curve). The improvement lasts for more than 60 iterations. From that point on, the performance deteriorates gracefully until $N = N_{70}$. Note also that, when $N = N_{80} \approx 3000$, the performance drops drastically.

- *those positive vectors in $\mathcal{X}_k$ with errors $\epsilon_i > +\theta_+$ and*
- *those negative vectors in $\mathcal{X}_k$ with errors $\epsilon_i < -\theta_-$.*

(iii) **Discard the anti-support vectors.** *Discard the identified anti-support vectors from $\mathcal{X}_k$ to create a trimmed subset $\mathcal{X}_{k+1}$ to be used as the training dataset for the next iteration.*

(vi) **Termination condition.** *Let $N_0 = N$ and N_{k+1} denote the size of $\mathcal{X}_{k+1}$. If N_{k+1} becomes lower than a pre-specified minimum level, the learning process will terminate and the discriminant function $f_k(\mathbf{x})$ last learned will become the final output of the PPDA learning model.* □

In PPDA, or pruned KRR, the remaining vectors in the final training dataset essentially play the role of the "support vectors" associated with PPDA since they alone exclusively determine the decision rule of the learned classifier.

Figure 9.5 clearly shows that there is a significant and consistent improvement during the early iterations of the pruning process. Moreover, the accuracy remains high for a good range of iterations until the training size, N_k, reaches a level that is inadequate for finding an effective decision boundary.

9.7.2 Case study: ECG arrhythmia detection

Simulation studies were conducted with the MIT/BIH dataset [203] by Kung and Wu [144] on applications of PPDA to ECG data analysis for detection of arrhythmia. For classification of all kinds of abnormal heart beats [46], waveform morphology features are considered to be most generic and effective. In the study, the total data size exceeds 100,000 heart beats, with each beat represented by a feature vector formed by $M = 21$ morphology features.

Prediction performance of TRBF3-PPDA

In this simulation study, the PPDA algorithm with a truncated-RBF kernel function of order 3, namely TRBF3 (Eq. (13.5)) is adopted. The prediction performances of PPDA throughout the iterations (1–80) are depicted in Figure 9.5. It shows that the PPDA's performance monotonically improves as the number of iterations increases. The first iteration corresponds to the ordinary KRR classification, in which all $N = 80,000$ training vectors are involved in the learning phase. The accuracy is already as high as 98.43%, as shown at the left-most end of the performance curve.

Still, the PPDA iterative learning appears to continuously and consistently raise the performance curve for as many as $q = 60$ iterations. The accuracy is improved to 98.82% when $q = 60$. Note that the same peak performance is obtained over a very wide range: $q \in [50, 70]$.

Number of surviving vectors: S'

Note that the performance of PPDA is also related to S', the number of surviving vectors. For example, at 4% trimming ratio per iteration, for which the best accuracy (98.82%) is achieved with $q = 60$, the number of surviving vectors is $S' \approx 7000$, half of the number of support vectors retained by the RBF-SVM ($S \approx 15,000$). As a reference, when $q = 80$, the number of surviving vectors drops to merely $S' \approx 3000$. Figure 9.5 shows that there is a very poor performance when $q = 80$, indicating that such a small training size provides an inadequate subspace to define a good decision boundary.

9.8 Multi-class and multi-label supervised classification

In most applications, the datasets are classified into more than two classes. This section extends the binary-class kernel-based learning models to multi-class applications and, furthermore, to multi-label classification.

9.8.1 Multi-class supervised classification

Most binary classification algorithms are naturally extendable to multi-classification applications. Typically, a multi-class classifier can be constructed from binary classifiers via one of the following two approaches: (1) a one-versus-one scheme and (2) a one-versus-all (OVA) scheme.

- **One on one for all pairs (AP).** In one-on-one classification, one binary classifier is trained for each possible pair of the K classes. This results in $K(K-1)/2$ binary classifiers. In the testing phase, for a specific test sample, each class will receive a score from the binary classifier it participates in. The class which has the highest total score will be identified as the most likely class for the test sample.

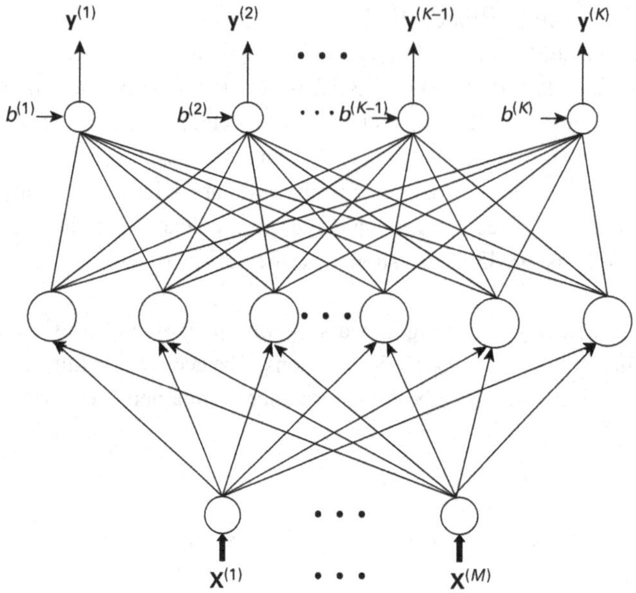

Fig. 9.6. A schematic diagram of the OVA approach. Note that the mapping lower layer may be the same as in Figure 9.1. Namely, a vector $\mathbf{x}$ in the original space can be mapped to a new representative vector, which may very well be in its intrinsic or empirical space. (Note that the nodes in the middle layer are deliberately left unspecified.) The dimension of the output space is now K, which represents the number of pure classes. The output is coded as (1) multi-class, with pure labels using a one-of-K encoding scheme; or (2) multi-class, with some multi-label training vectors adopting a modified one-of-K encoding scheme.

- **One versus all (OVA).** Given a K-class problem, a one-versus-all (OVA) classifier contains K binary classifiers, each of which is trained to separate one of the K classes from the rest. In other words, for the kth binary classifier, patterns belonging to the kth class are considered to be positive and the rest are considered to be negative. It is worth mentioning that the OVA approach requires much fewer binary classifiers than does its AP counterpart.

Let us elaborate more on the OVA approach, which has shown a lot of promising potential for various applications. Depicted in Figure 9.6 is a two-layer network architecture with a one-of-K encoded output layer.

The one-of-K encoding scheme

Suppose that there are K classes, $\{\mathcal{C}_k,\ k = 1, \ldots, K\}$, and each of the N training vectors, say $\{\mathbf{x}_i,\ i = 1, \ldots, N\}$, belong to one and only one of the K classes. The teacher values may be viewed from two perspectives.

- Consider a specific $\mathbf{x}_i$. It is assigned a K-dimensional teacher (row) vector:

$$\overrightarrow{y_i} = [y_i^{(1)}, y_i^{(2)}, \ldots, y_i^{(K)}],$$

where

$$y_i^{(k)} = \begin{cases} 1 & \text{if } \mathbf{x}_i \in \mathcal{C}_k \\ 0 & \text{otherwise.} \end{cases} \tag{9.57}$$

- In contrast, let us now consider the kth encoded teacher values for all the N training vectors. In vector form, one can represent this by an N-dimensional teacher (column) vector:

$$\mathbf{y}^{(k)} = [y_1^{(k)}, y_2^{(k)}, \ldots, y_N^{(k)}]^{\mathrm{T}},$$

  where $y_i^{(k)}$ is defined in Eq. (9.57).

Two-layer network structures

For kernel-based learning models, a vector $\mathbf{x}$ in the original space can be mapped to a new representation in either the intrinsic space or empirical space.

(i) For the intrinsic-space approach, the lower layer of the network maps a vector $\mathbf{x}$ in the original vector space to its kernel-induced intrinsic representation:

$$\mathbf{x} \to \vec{\phi}(\mathbf{x}).$$

In the upper layer, there are K linear mappings from $\vec{\phi}(\mathbf{x})$ to the K output nodes:

$$f^{(k)}(\mathbf{x}) = [\mathbf{u}^{(k)}]^{\mathrm{T}} \vec{\phi}(\mathbf{x}) + b^{(k)}, \quad \text{for } k = 1, \ldots, K.$$

(ii) For the empirical-space approach, the lower layer maps $\mathbf{x}$ to its kernel-induced empirical representation:

$$\mathbf{x} \to \vec{\mathbf{k}}(\mathbf{x}),$$

while the upper layer maps $\vec{\mathbf{k}}(\mathbf{x})$ to each of the K output nodes:

$$f^{(k)}(\mathbf{x}) = [\mathbf{a}^{(k)}]^{\mathrm{T}} \vec{\mathbf{k}}(\mathbf{x}) + b^{(k)}, \quad \text{for } k = 1, \ldots, K.$$

The learning phase

- **Lower layer.** Once the kernel has been fixed, the mapping in the lower layer of a KRR model is fully pre-specified, and no learning needs to take place. This constitutes an important advantage, especially when compared with the neural network model, whose lower layer must be trained by the back-propagation algorithm.
- **Upper layer.** The objective of the KRR learning model is minimization of the total LSE at the output layer. This amounts to minimization of the individual LSE at each of the K output nodes. Consequently, the individual decision vector pertaining to each output node can be independently trained by the KRR learning algorithm given by, say, Eq. (9.22). More exactly, the optimal decision vector, in the empirical-space approach, corresponding to the kth output is

$$\mathbf{a}^{(k)} = [\mathbf{K} + \rho\mathbf{I}]^{-1}[\mathbf{y}^{(k)} - b^{(k)}\mathbf{e}], \quad \text{where } b^{(k)} = \frac{[\mathbf{y}^{(k)}]^{\mathrm{T}}[\mathbf{K} + \rho\mathbf{I}]^{-1}\mathbf{e}}{\mathbf{e}^{\mathrm{T}}[\mathbf{K} + \rho\mathbf{I}]^{-1}\mathbf{e}}, \quad \text{for } k = 1, \ldots, K. \tag{9.58}$$

The classification phase

Given a new test sample $\mathbf{x}$, the score associated with the kth output node is

$$f^{(k)}(\mathbf{x}) = [\mathbf{a}^{(k)}]^{\mathrm{T}} \overrightarrow{\mathbf{k}}(\mathbf{x}) + b^{(k)} = \sum_{i=1}^{N} a_i^{(k)} K(\mathbf{x}_i, \mathbf{x}) + b^{(k)}, \quad \text{for } k = 1, \ldots, K. \tag{9.59}$$

The identified class of $\mathbf{x}$ should be the one with the highest score, i.e.

$$k* = \arg \max_{k=1,\ldots,K} f^{(k)}(\mathbf{x}). \tag{9.60}$$

9.8.2 Multi-label classification

In supervised learning, the problem of assigning more than one label to each data instance is known as multi-label classification. It has recently received a great deal of attention in a wide range of problem domains, such as text classification [231], semantic annotation of images [26], and music categorization [154].

The existing methods for multi-label classification can be grouped into two main categories: (1) algorithm adaptation and (2) problem transformation. Algorithm adaptation methods extend single-label algorithms to solve multi-label classification problems. Typical methods include multi-label C4.5 [40], multi-label decision trees [282], and AdaBoost.MH [231]. Problem transformation methods transform a multi-label learning problem into one or more single-label classification problems [26] so that traditional single-label classifiers can be applied without modification. Typical methods include label powerset (LP) [274], binary relevance (BR) [273], ensembles of classifier chains (ECC) [214], and compressive sensing [102]. The LP method reduces a multi-label task to a single-label task by treating each possible multi-label subset as a new class in the single-label classification task. This method is simple, but is likely to generate a large number of classes, many of which are associated with very few examples. BR is a popular problem-transformation method. It transforms a multi-label task into many binary classification tasks, one for each label. Given a query instance, its predicted label(s) are the union of the positive-class labels output by these binary classifiers. BR is effective, but it neglects the correlation between labels, which may carry useful information for multi-label classification. The classifier chain method is a variant of BR but it can take the correlation between labels into account. Similarly to BR, a set of one-vs.-rest binary classifiers is trained. But, unlike in BR, the classifiers are linked in a chain and the feature vectors presented to the ith classifier in the chain are augmented with the binary values representing the label(s) of the feature vectors up to the $(i-1)$th class. Therefore, label dependence is preserved through the feature space. The classification performance, however, depends on the chain order. This order-dependence can be overcome by ensembles of classifier chains [214]. The compressive sensing approach is motivated by the fact that when the number of classes is large, the actual labels are often sparse. In other words, a typical query instance will belong to a few classes only, even though the total number of classes is large. This approach exploits the sparsity of the output (label) space by means of compressive sensing to obtain a more efficient output coding scheme for large-scale multi-label learning problems. Compared with algorithm adaptation methods, one advantage of problem transformation methods is that any algorithm that is not capable of dealing with multi-label classification problems can be easily extended to deal with multi-label classification via transformation.

Various multi-label classification methods have successfully been applied in bioinformatics, especially in protein subcellular localization. Protein subcellular localization is the problem of predicting in which part(s) in a cell a protein resides. This information is vitally important for understanding the functions of proteins and for identifying drug targets [161]. Recently, several multi-label predictors have been proposed to deal with the prediction of multi-label proteins, such as Virus-mPLoc [245], iLoc-Virus [304], KNN-SVM ensemble classifier [153], and mGOASVM [285]. In particular, Virus-mPLoc and iLoc-Virus use algorithm adaptation methods, while KNN-SVM and mGOASVM use problem transformation methods. They all use gene ontology (GO) information as the features; see the website http://www.geneontology.org.

The modified one-of-N coding scheme for multi-label classification

This section will demonstrate that the KRR solution proposed for multi-class classification may be naturally extended to multi-label classification. In fact, the very same architecture as that of the kernel-based learning model, depicted in Figure 9.6, can again be adopted unaltered. The only modification lies in the new definition needed for multi-label classes.

Suppose that there are K pure-label classes and K' multi-label classes. For the K pure classes, we shall introduce K distinctive teacher (row) vectors as follows:

$$\vec{t}_k, \quad k = 1, 2, \ldots, K,$$

where

$$\begin{bmatrix} \vec{t}_1 \\ \vec{t}_2 \\ \vdots \\ \vec{t}_K \end{bmatrix} = \mathbf{I}_{K\times K}. \tag{9.61}$$

If the ith training vector is known to belong to the kth pure class, then its teacher (row) vector will be set to be

$$\begin{aligned} \mathbf{y}^{(k)} &= [y_1^{(k)}, y_2^{(k)}, \ldots, y_N^{(k)}]^{\mathrm{T}} \\ &= \vec{t}_k = [0\,0 \ldots 0\,1\,0 \ldots 0\,0], \end{aligned} \tag{9.62}$$

in which only the kth element is nonzero.

Suppose also that the $K + K'$ distinct teacher vectors are denoted by

$$\{\vec{t}_k, k = 1, \ldots, K + K'\}.$$

As elaborated on below, these teacher vectors can be further divided into two categories.

(i) **Teacher vector for pure-label classes.** The first subset, $\{\vec{t}_k, k = 1, \ldots K\}$, is reserved for pure-label classes. If a training sample, say $\mathbf{x}_i$, is from a pure class C_k, it will be assigned the following teacher vector:

$$y_i = \vec{t}_k = [0\,0 \ldots 0\,1\,0 \ldots 0\,0],$$

in which only the kth element is nonzero.

(ii) **Teacher vector for multi-label classes.** The second subset, $\{\vec{t}_{K+k'}, k' = 1, \ldots K'\}$, is reserved for *multi-label* classes. If a training sample, say $\mathbf{x}_j$, is from a multi-label class $C_{K+k'}$, then it will be assigned a "*multi-label*" teacher vector:

$$y_j = \vec{t}_{K+k'} = [0 \ldots 0\; 1/L \ldots 0\; 1/L \ldots 0\; 1/L\; 0\; 0], \tag{9.63}$$

in which only L of the K elements are nonzero, where L denotes the number of co-labeled classes associated with $\mathbf{x}_j$.

The multi-label learning formulation

Now that the encoded teacher values are no longer binary, real-valued kernel ridge regression (KRR), see Section 7.3, may be adopted to obtain the learned discriminant vectors for each of the (pure or multi-label) classes:

$$\mathbf{a}^{(k)} = [\mathbf{K} + \rho\mathbf{I}]^{-1}[\mathbf{y}^{(k)} - b^{(k)}\mathbf{e}], \quad \text{where } b^{(k)} = \frac{[\mathbf{y}^{(k)}]^{\mathrm{T}}[\mathbf{K} + \rho\mathbf{I}]^{-1}\mathbf{e}}{\mathbf{e}^{\mathrm{T}}[\mathbf{K} + \rho\mathbf{I}]^{-1}\mathbf{e}}, \quad \text{for } k = 1, \ldots, K + K'. \tag{9.64}$$

In the prediction phase, subsequently, given a new test sample $\mathbf{x}$, the score for the kth class is

$$\begin{aligned} f^{(k)}(\mathbf{x}) &= [\mathbf{a}^{(k)}]^{\mathrm{T}} \vec{\mathbf{k}}(\mathbf{x}) + b^{(k)} \\ &= \sum_{i=1}^{N} a_i^{(k)} K(\mathbf{x}_i, \mathbf{x}) + b^{(k)}, \quad \text{for} \quad k = 1, \ldots, K + K', \end{aligned} \tag{9.65}$$

which forms the following *score vector*:

$$\vec{f}(\mathbf{x}) = [f^{(1)}(\mathbf{x})\; f^{(2)}(\mathbf{x}) \ldots f^{(K)}(\mathbf{x})]^T.$$

The predicted class of $\mathbf{x}$ should be

$$k^* = \mathop{\arg\max}_{\{k=1,\ldots,K+K'\}} \cos\left(\vec{f}(\mathbf{x}), \vec{t}_k\right). \tag{9.66}$$

Namely, the teacher vector which is most parallel to the score vector will be identified.

In addition to Eq. (9.63), there are some alternative encoding schemes for multi-label classes, including one with equalized 2-norms and, more progressively, another scheme with adaptively trained teacher values. As an example, simulation results suggest that, a multi-class predictor can deliver substantial performance improvement on adopting adaptive thresholds [285, 286].

9.9 Supervised subspace projection methods

Given a supervised training dataset $[\mathcal{X}, \mathcal{Y}]$, we wish to find an optimal $M \times m$ matrix matrix: $\mathbf{W} = [\mathbf{w}_1 \ldots \mathbf{w}_m]$ such that the subspace vector $\mathbf{x} \rightarrow \mathbf{W}^{\mathrm{T}}\mathbf{x}$ offers a lower m-dimensional representation of the original M-dimensional vector $\mathbf{x}$ for best classification performance.

Supposing that there are L classes, the (multi-class) between-class scatter matrix $\mathbf{S}_{\mathrm{B}}$ can be defined as

$$\mathbf{S}_{\mathrm{B}} = \sum_{\ell=1}^{L} N_\ell[\overrightarrow{\mu}^{(\ell)} - \overrightarrow{\mu}][\overrightarrow{\mu}^{(\ell)} - \overrightarrow{\mu}]^{\mathrm{T}}$$

and the (multi-class) within-class scatter matrix $\mathbf{S}_{\mathrm{W}}$ can be defined as

$$\mathbf{S}_{\mathrm{W}} = \sum_{\ell=1}^{L} \sum_{j=1}^{N_\ell} [\mathbf{x}_j^{(\ell)} - \overrightarrow{\mu}^{(\ell)}][\mathbf{x}_j^{(\ell)} - \overrightarrow{\mu}^{(\ell)}]^{\mathrm{T}}, \tag{9.67}$$

where N_ℓ is the number of samples in class ℓ.

Note the "center-adjusted" *scatter matrix* (Eq. (8.7)) is defined as

$$\bar{\mathbf{S}} \equiv \bar{\mathbf{X}}\bar{\mathbf{X}}^{\mathrm{T}} = \sum_{i=1}^{N} [\mathbf{x}_i - \overrightarrow{\mu}][\mathbf{x}_i - \overrightarrow{\mu}]^{\mathrm{T}}. \tag{9.68}$$

The criteria designed for unsupervised learning (such as PCA) may not be effective for the purpose of discriminating different classes in supervised learning scenarios. In this regard, the SNR criterion (used by e.g. FDA) offers a much more relevant and appealing alternative. As such, SNR will play a major role in our subsequent optimality analysis.

9.9.1 Successively optimized discriminant analysis (SODA)

Suppose that there are m components to be extracted, let us define the SNR pertaining to the ith component as

$$SNR_i = \frac{\mathbf{w}_i^{\mathrm{T}}\mathbf{S}_{\mathrm{B}}\mathbf{w}_i}{\mathbf{w}_i^{\mathrm{T}}\mathbf{S}_{\mathrm{W}}\mathbf{w}_i}, \quad i = 1, \ldots, m. \tag{9.69}$$

Ideally, we would like to maximize the Sum-of-SNRs (SoSNR) of all the components. More exactly, such an optimizer aims at finding a solution $\mathbf{W}_{SoSNR}$ such that

$$\mathbf{W}_{SoSNR} = \underset{\mathbf{W}=[\mathbf{w}_1 \ldots \mathbf{w}_m]:\mathbf{W}^{\mathrm{T}}\mathbf{W}=I}{\arg\max} \left(\sum_{i=1}^{m} \frac{\mathbf{w}_i^{\mathrm{T}}\mathbf{S}_{\mathrm{B}}\mathbf{w}_i}{\mathbf{w}_i^{\mathrm{T}}\mathbf{S}_{\mathrm{W}}\mathbf{w}_i} \right). \tag{9.70}$$

Unfortunately, the complexity for computing the SoSNR-optimal solution is NP-complete [311b]. For numerical efficiency, an approximated variant, i.e. "Successively Orthogonal Discriminant Analysis" (SODA) was proposed by Yu, McKelvey and

Kung. [311] The optimality criterion of SODA optimizer aims at sequentially finding $\mathbf{w}_1, \mathbf{w}_2, \ldots, \mathbf{w}_m$ such that

$$\begin{aligned} \underset{\mathbf{w}_i}{\text{maximize}} \quad & \frac{\mathbf{w}_i^{\mathrm{T}} \mathbf{S}_{\mathrm{B}} \mathbf{w}_i}{\mathbf{w}_i^{\mathrm{T}} \mathbf{S}_{\mathrm{W}} \mathbf{w}_i} \\ \text{subject to} \quad & \mathbf{w}_i \perp \mathbf{w}_{1,\ldots,i-1} \\ & \mathbf{w}_i^{\mathrm{T}} \mathbf{w}_i = 1 \\ & \mathbf{w}_i \in \text{range}(\mathbf{X}). \end{aligned} \tag{9.71}$$

SODA Algorithm. The SODA algorithm may be applied to either binary or multi-class classification. [311] Let us now focus on the SODA procedure for binary classification, i.e. $L = 2$. In this case, the SODA optimizer in Eq. 9.71 can be efficiently solved by the following procedure.

ALGORITHM 9.3 (Successively orthogonal discriminant analysis (SODA)) *Denote* $\boldsymbol{\Delta} \equiv \vec{\mu}_+ - \vec{\mu}_-$, *i.e. the difference between the positive and negative centroids in the original space.*

Set the initial pseudo-inverse as $\mathbf{Q}^{(1)} \equiv (\mathbf{S}_{\mathrm{W}})^+$.

For $i = 1 : m$, *recursively do the following:*

(i) Compute

$$\mathbf{w}_i = \mathbf{v}_i / ||\mathbf{v}_i||, \quad \textit{where } \mathbf{v}_i = \mathbf{Q}^{(i)} \boldsymbol{\Delta}.$$

(ii) Compute

$$\mathbf{Q}^{(i+1)} = \mathbf{D}^{(i)} \mathbf{Q}^{(i)} \mathbf{D}^{(i)}, \tag{9.72}$$

where $\mathbf{D}^{(i)}$ *is the deflation matrix:*

$$\mathbf{D}^{(i)} = \mathbf{I} - \mathbf{w}_i \mathbf{w}_i^{\mathrm{T}}. \tag{9.73}$$

□

Note that this procedure enjoys an important merit that no eigenvalue decomposition is required, making it computationally simpler than PCA and many others. Let us verify that the procedure indeed yields an optimal solution for the SODA criterion given in Eq. (9.71).

- When $i = 1$, the first principle vector for SODA $\mathbf{w}_1$ can be computed via Eq. (9.72). Then the deflation operator (Eq. (9.73)) removes $\mathbf{w}_1$ component from $\mathbf{Q}^{(1)}$, forcing $\text{Range}\left(\mathbf{Q}^{(2)}\right)$ to become orthogonal to $\mathbf{w}_1$.
- At the iteration $i = 2$, note that $\mathbf{w}_2$ is orthogonal to $\mathbf{w}_1$ because $\mathbf{w}_2 \in \text{Range}\left(\mathbf{Q}^{(2)}\right)$. Now, in this iteration, a new deflation operator (Eq. (9.73)) will further remove $\mathbf{w}_2$ component from $\mathbf{Q}^{(2)}$, forcing $\text{Range}\left(\mathbf{Q}^{(3)}\right)$ to become orthogonal to both $\mathbf{w}_1$ and $\mathbf{w}_2$.
- By induction, it can be shown that $\mathbf{w}_1 \perp \mathbf{w}_2 \perp \cdots \perp \mathbf{w}_m$ and thus the proof.

REMARK *When* $\mathbf{S}_{\mathrm{W}}$ *is nonsingular, then*

$$\mathbf{w}_1 \propto \mathbf{v}_1 = (\mathbf{S}_{\mathrm{W}}^{(1)})^+ \boldsymbol{\Delta} = \mathbf{S}_{\mathrm{W}}^{-1} \boldsymbol{\Delta}, \tag{9.74}$$

i.e. FDA is the same as SODA's first vector.

To help illustrate the differences between PCA, FDA, PDA, and SODA, it is useful to look into several numerical examples. First, we start with a simple example with $M = 2$ and $m = 1$.

Example 9.4 (Comparison of PCA, FDA, PDA, and SODA) *Consider the same dataset as in Example 8.6. There are four training vectors:*

$$\mathbf{x}_1 = \begin{bmatrix} 1.0 \\ 0.1 \end{bmatrix}, \quad \mathbf{x}_2 = \begin{bmatrix} 0.8 \\ 0.1 \end{bmatrix}, \quad \mathbf{x}_3 = \begin{bmatrix} -0.8 \\ -0.1 \end{bmatrix}, \quad \mathbf{x}_4 = \begin{bmatrix} -1.0 \\ -0.1 \end{bmatrix},$$

with teacher values $y_1 = -1$, $y_2 = -1$, $y_3 = +1$, and $y_4 = +1$. It can be shown that the principal vectors for PCA, FDA, PDA($\rho = 0.0001$), and SODA are respectively

$$\mathbf{w}_{\text{PCA}} = \begin{bmatrix} 0.9940 \\ 0.1091 \end{bmatrix}, \quad \mathbf{w}_{\text{FDA}} = \begin{bmatrix} 0 \\ 1.0 \end{bmatrix},$$

$$\mathbf{w}_{\text{PDA}} = \begin{bmatrix} 0.0226 \\ 0.9997 \end{bmatrix}, \quad \mathbf{w}_{\text{SODA}} = \begin{bmatrix} 1.0 \\ 0 \end{bmatrix}.$$

The ridge parameter ρ has a major influence on the PDA solution:

- *If we set $\rho = 0.0001$, then PDA is $[0.0226\ 0.9997]^{\text{T}}$, which is basically equivalent to FDA.*
- *If we set $\rho = 0.01$, then PDA is $[0.8833\ 0.4688]^{\text{T}}$, which is much closer to PCA than FDA.*

When $N_+ = N_-$, PCA approaches $\boldsymbol{\Delta}$. Likewise, PDA also approaches $\boldsymbol{\Delta}$ when ρ is very large. For example, if we set $\rho = 100$, then PDA ($= [0.9940\ 0.1092]^{\text{T}}$) is very close to PCA ($= [0.9940\ 0.1091]^{\text{T}}$).

For this dataset, the SODA and FDA solutions are different due to the pseudoinverse adopted by SODA. However, when $\mathbf{S}_W$ is nonsingular, FDA and SODA will be the same. This may be demonstrated by a slightly modified dataset:

$$\mathbf{x}_1 = \begin{bmatrix} 1.0 \\ 0.1 \end{bmatrix}, \quad \mathbf{x}_2 = \begin{bmatrix} 0.8 \\ 0.1 \end{bmatrix}, \quad \mathbf{x}_3 = \begin{bmatrix} -0.8 \\ -0.11 \end{bmatrix}, \quad \mathbf{x}_4 = \begin{bmatrix} -1.0 \\ -0.1 \end{bmatrix}.$$

In this case, the four solutions ($\rho = 0.0001$) become

$$\mathbf{w}_{\text{PCA}} = \begin{bmatrix} 0.9942 \\ 0.1080 \end{bmatrix}, \quad \mathbf{w}_{\text{FDA}} = \begin{bmatrix} .0110 \\ .9999 \end{bmatrix},$$

$$\mathbf{w}_{\text{PDA}} = \begin{bmatrix} .0331 \\ .9995 \end{bmatrix}, \quad \mathbf{w}_{\text{SODA}} = \begin{bmatrix} .0110 \\ .9999 \end{bmatrix}.$$

Note that, as theorized by Eq. (9.74), $\mathbf{w}_{\text{FDA}} = \mathbf{w}_{\text{SODA}}$ for the new dataset. Moreover, PDA shows the least change between the two datasets, once again demonstrating its robustness. □

Let us further compare the PCA, FDA, and SODA solutions via a higher-dimensional numeric example with $M = 3$ and $m = 2$.

Example 9.5 (Comparison of PCA, FDA, and SODA) *Consider a dataset with* $L = 2$, $N_+ = N_- = 5$, $\boldsymbol{\Delta} = [2\ 2\ 2]^{\mathrm{T}}$, *and the between-class and within-class scatter matrices*

$$\mathbf{S}_{\mathrm{B}} = \begin{bmatrix} 10 & 10 & 10 \\ 10 & 10 & 10 \\ 10 & 10 & 10 \end{bmatrix} \quad \text{and} \quad \mathbf{S}_{\mathrm{W}} = \begin{bmatrix} 2 & 2 & 3 \\ 2 & 5 & 4 \\ 3 & 4 & 6 \end{bmatrix}.$$

The centered scatter matrix is

$$\bar{\mathbf{S}} = \mathbf{S}_{\mathrm{B}} + \mathbf{S}_{\mathrm{W}} = \begin{bmatrix} 12 & 12 & 13 \\ 12 & 15 & 14 \\ 13 & 14 & 16 \end{bmatrix}.$$

PCA solution

The projection matrix for PCA can be a submatrix of a full matrix formed from all the three eigenvectors of $\bar{\mathbf{S}}$, *i.e.*

$$\mathbf{W}_{\mathrm{PCA}} = \begin{bmatrix} 0.5275 & -0.3878 & -0.7559 \\ 0.5861 & 0.8102 & -0.0067 \\ 0.6150 & -0.4395 & 0.6547 \end{bmatrix}.$$

FDA solution

The FDA solution is

$$\mathbf{w}_{\mathrm{FDA}} = \mathbf{S}_{\mathrm{W}}^{-1}\boldsymbol{\Delta} = [2\ \ 0.2857\ \ -0.8571]^{\mathrm{T}}.$$

SODA solution

For the first vector of SODA,

$$\mathbf{Q}^{(1)} = \mathbf{S}_{\mathrm{W}}^{+} = \begin{bmatrix} 2 & 0 & -1 \\ 0 & 0.4286 & -0.2857 \\ -1 & -0.2857 & 0.8571 \end{bmatrix},$$

and it follows that

$$\mathbf{v}_1 = \mathbf{Q}^{(1)}\boldsymbol{\Delta} = [2\ \ 0.2857\ \ -0.8571]^{\mathrm{T}}.$$

After normalization, we have

$$\mathbf{w}_1 = \mathbf{v}_1/||\mathbf{v}_1|| = \begin{bmatrix} 0.9113 \\ 0.1302 \\ -0.3906 \end{bmatrix}.$$

According to Eq. (9.72), the pseudoinverse can be updated as

$$\begin{aligned}\mathbf{Q}^{(2)} &= \mathbf{D}^{(1)}\mathbf{Q}^{(1)}\mathbf{D}^{(1)} \\ &= \begin{bmatrix} 0.1695 & -0.1186 & 0.3559 \\ -0.1186 & 0.9831 & 0.0508 \\ 0.3559 & 0.0508 & 0.8475 \end{bmatrix} \begin{bmatrix} 2 & 0 & -1 \\ 0 & 0.4286 & -0.2857 \\ -1 & -0.2857 & 0.8571 \end{bmatrix} \\ &\times \begin{bmatrix} 0.1695 & -0.1186 & 0.3559 \\ -0.1186 & 0.9831 & 0.0508 \\ 0.3559 & 0.0508 & 0.8475 \end{bmatrix} \\ &= \begin{bmatrix} 0.0756 & -0.1393 & 0.1298 \\ -0.1393 & 0.4280 & -0.1824 \\ 0.1298 & -0.1824 & 0.2422 \end{bmatrix}\end{aligned}$$

As to the second vector of SODA, we first compute

$$\mathbf{v}^{(2)} = \mathbf{Q}^{(2)}\boldsymbol{\Delta} = \begin{bmatrix} 0.1321 \\ 0.6126 \\ 0.3792 \end{bmatrix},$$

then, after normalization, we obtain

$$\mathbf{w}_2 = \mathbf{v}_2/||\mathbf{v}_2|| = \begin{bmatrix} 0.2908 \\ 0.4679 \\ 0.8346 \end{bmatrix}.$$

Likewise, the third vector can be obtained as:

$$\mathbf{w}_3 = \begin{bmatrix} -0.2914 \\ 0.8742 \\ -0.3885 \end{bmatrix}.$$

Just as theoretically predicted, the following can now be verified:

- The principal vector of PCA, largely ignoring the influence of $\mathbf{S}_W$, is approximately parallel to $\boldsymbol{\Delta}$.
- After normalization, the first vector of SODA is the same as FDA when $\mathbf{S}_W$ is nonsingular.

Experiments on the ischemic stroke dataset

Some subspace methods were tested on high-dimensional medical data for detecting brain strokes and compared with existing techniques. In the ischemic stroke study, the main interest is to discriminate patients suffering from ischemic strokes from healthy subjects. The measured signals are the (complex) scattering parameters [211] of microwave signals with a frequency range of 0.1–3.0 GHz. Each signal contains 401 frequency points, and 78 different channels are involved. On considering the real and imaginary parts of the complex signal, the feature vector has an extremely high dimension of 62, 556. This motivates the adoption of SODA, which efficiently extracts the discriminant information with a dramatically reduced dimensionality.

The experiment involves 27 samples from ischemic stroke patients (class +) and 45 healthy cases (class −). A leave-one-out test is applied. Figure 12.9 illustrates how the

Table 9.4. Comparison of rate of detection of class 1 with a constant false alarm rate of 20% for the different scenarios tested, where for Ridge-SVM $C_{min} = -1$, $C_{max} = 1$ and $\rho = 0.4$. For SVM, $C_{min} = 0$, $C_{max} = 1$, and $\rho = 0$. Both for SVM and for Ridge-SVM, see Chapters 10 and 12, respectively, learning parameters may be further tuned to improve the rates. For more information, see Table 12.7.

Feature selection	Feature transform	Number of features	Type of classifier	Detection rate (%)
LASSO (40 features)	–	40	Ridge-SVM (RBF kernel)	73
LASSO (40 features)	Linear scaling	40	Ridge-SVM (RBF kernel)	88
LASSO (40 features)	SODA	10	Ridge-SVM (RBF kernel)	78
LASSO (40 features)	SODA	10	SVM (RBF kernel)	72
Fisher Scores (400)	–	400	LDA	74
Fisher Scores (400)	PCA	10	Ridge-SVM (RBF kernel)	68
Fisher Scores (400)	SODA	10	Ridge-SVM (RBF kernel)	92
–	–	44,110	SVM (RBF kernel)	75

detection rate depends on the number of Fisher-score-based features. Note that the rates saturate when the feature number reaches 400 and beyond.

Table 9.4 illustrates experimental results with various feature types, feature numbers, feature transformations, and classifiers. The numbers in the last column reflect the detection rates of class + at a constant false-alarm rate of 20% estimated as the empirical probabilities derived from the leave-one-out validation. Note that the combination of the Fisher-score-based method and SODA yields very high detection rates even after SODA's dimension reduction. Using 400 Fisher-score-based features as input to SODA and again using 10 as the SODA's output dimension, the performance can be increased to 92%, which is far higher than with the conventional PCA and LASSO approaches (68% and 88%, respectively). In summary, when combined with Fisher-score-based feature selection, SODA can effectively reduce the dimensionality needed for classifiers while still retaining very high performance.

9.9.2 Trace-norm optimization for subspace projection

This section will present trace-norm optimizers applicable to PCA and FDA and then extend the formulation for the purpose of extracting optimal discriminant components.

9.9.2.1 Trace-norm optimizers for PCA and FDA

Trace-norm optimizer for PCA

The PCA formulation can be expressed as a trace-norm optimizer targeting the $M \times m$ projection matrix

$$\mathbf{W}_{\text{PCA}} = [\mathbf{w}_1 \mathbf{w}_2 \ldots \mathbf{w}_m]$$

such that

$$\mathbf{W}_{\text{PCA}} = \underset{\{\mathbf{W}\in\mathbb{R}^{M\times m}:\mathbf{W}^{\mathrm{T}}\mathbf{W}=\mathbf{I}\}}{\arg\max} \; \mathtt{tr}\left(\mathbf{W}^{\mathrm{T}}\bar{\mathbf{S}}\mathbf{W}\right), \tag{9.75}$$

where $\mathtt{tr}\,(\cdot)$ denotes the trace norm of the matrix inside the parentheses.

Trace-norm optimizer for FDA

Note that PCA's optimizer fails to use any of the teacher's information. To rectify this problem, renders it less appealing for classification or prediction applications. Fortunately, the PCA optimizer is extended to a more general formulation:

$$\underset{\{\mathbf{W}:\mathbf{W}\mathbf{M}\mathbf{W}^{\mathrm{T}}=\mathbf{I}\}}{\arg\max} \; \mathtt{tr}\left(\mathbf{W}^{\mathrm{T}}\bar{\mathbf{S}}\mathbf{W}\right), \tag{9.76}$$

so that the teacher's information may be naturally embedded in the Mahalanobis matrix $\mathbf{M}$ in the orthogonality constraint. This may serve the purpose of enhancing the discriminant capability of the learning model. One prominent example is the FDA model, which corresponds to the trace-norm optimizer in Eq. (9.76) with $\mathbf{M} = \mathbf{S}_{\mathrm{W}}$.

9.9.2.2 Maximize SNR for extraction of signal-subspace components

Traditionally, the objective of FDA is to find the optimal projection vector which maximizes the Fisher score, i.e.

$$\mathbf{w}_{\text{FDA}} = \underset{\mathbf{w}}{\arg\max} \left\{ \frac{\mathbf{w}^{\mathrm{T}}\mathbf{S}_{\mathrm{B}}\mathbf{w}}{\mathbf{w}^{\mathrm{T}}\mathbf{S}_{\mathrm{W}}\mathbf{w}} \right\}. \tag{9.77}$$

The traditional FDA is originally designed for one-dimensional subspace optimization which is all that is required for the purpose of linear classification. (This is because the decision score of a linear classifier is a function of a one-dimensional projection.) In order to foster a multi-dimensional FDA (MD-FDA), with $m = L - 1$. The traditional FDA is first re-formulated as a trace-norm optimizer:

$$\mathbf{w}_{\text{FDA}} = \underset{\{\mathbf{w}:\mathbf{w}^{\mathrm{T}}\mathbf{S}_{\mathrm{W}}\mathbf{w}=1\}}{\arg\max} \; \{\mathbf{w}^{\mathrm{T}}\mathbf{S}_{\mathrm{B}}\mathbf{w}\} = \underset{\{\mathbf{w}:\mathbf{w}^{\mathrm{T}}\mathbf{S}_{\mathrm{W}}\mathbf{w}=1\}}{\arg\max} \; \mathtt{tr}\left(\mathbf{w}^{\mathrm{T}}\mathbf{S}_{\mathrm{B}}\mathbf{w}\right),$$

and the projection vector $\mathbf{w}$ is then substituted by an $M \times (L-1)$ projection matrix $\mathbf{W}$. This leads to a trace-norm optimizer which aims at finding

$$\begin{aligned}
\mathbf{W}_{\text{MD-FDA}} &= \underset{\{\mathbf{W}:\mathbf{W}\mathbf{S}_{\mathrm{W}}\mathbf{W}^{\mathrm{T}}=\mathbf{I}\}}{\arg\max} \; \mathtt{tr}\left(\mathbf{W}^{\mathrm{T}}\mathbf{S}_{\mathrm{B}}\mathbf{W}\right) \\
&= \underset{\{\mathbf{W}:\mathbf{W}^{\mathrm{T}}\mathbf{S}_{\mathrm{W}}\mathbf{W}=\mathbf{I}\}}{\arg\max} \; \mathtt{tr}\left(\mathbf{W}^{\mathrm{T}}\mathbf{S}_{\mathrm{B}}\mathbf{W} + \mathbf{I}\right) \\
&= \underset{\{\mathbf{W}:\mathbf{W}^{\mathrm{T}}\mathbf{S}_{\mathrm{W}}\mathbf{W}=\mathbf{I}\}}{\arg\max} \; \mathtt{tr}\left(\mathbf{W}^{\mathrm{T}}[\mathbf{S}_{\mathrm{B}} + \mathbf{S}_{\mathrm{W}}]\mathbf{W}\right) \\
&= \underset{\{\mathbf{W}:\mathbf{W}^{\mathrm{T}}\mathbf{S}_{\mathrm{W}}\mathbf{W}=\mathbf{I}\}}{\arg\max} \; \mathtt{tr}\left(\mathbf{W}^{\mathrm{T}}\bar{\mathbf{S}}\mathbf{W}\right).
\end{aligned} \tag{9.78}$$

For simplicity, we shall assume that $\mathbf{S}_{\mathrm{W}}$ is nonsingular. Then the optimal solution can be obtained from its *discriminant matrix*, defined as

$$\mathbf{D}_{\text{MD-FDA}} \equiv \mathbf{S}_{\mathrm{W}}^{-1}\bar{\mathbf{S}}. \tag{9.79}$$

More exactly, the solution can be extracted from the real-valued principal $(L-1)$ eigenvectors of $\mathbf{D}_{\text{MD}-\text{FDA}}$:

$$\mathbf{S}_{\text{W}}^{-1}\bar{\mathbf{S}}\mathbf{v}_i = \lambda_i \mathbf{v}_i, \quad i = 1, \ldots, L-1, \tag{9.80}$$

with descending eigenvalues:

$$\lambda_1 \geq \lambda_2 \geq \ldots \geq \lambda_{L-1} > 1.0.$$

Because the rank of the *between-class* scatter matrix $\mathbf{S}_{\text{B}}$ is $L-1$, MD-FDA is applicable only to the $(L-1)$-dimensional *signal subspace*. If it happens that $m < L$, then the trace-norm-optimal discriminant components can be simply obtained from the m principal eigenvectors of $\mathbf{D}_{\text{MD-FDA}}$, i.e.

$$\mathbf{W}_{\text{MD-FDA}} = [\mathbf{v}_1 \ldots \mathbf{v}_m]. \tag{9.81}$$

MD-FDA offers only a partial answer for the m ≥ L case

In practical application, it frequently happens that $m \geq L$. In this case, the optimal solution for the $M \times m$ projection matrix $\mathbf{W}$ may be partitioned into two parts:

$$\begin{aligned}\mathbf{W} &= [\mathbf{W}_{\text{signal}} | \mathbf{W}_{\text{noise}}] \\ &= [\mathbf{w}_1 \ldots \mathbf{w}_{L-1} | \mathbf{w}_L \mathbf{w}_{L+1} \ldots \mathbf{w}_m],\end{aligned} \tag{9.82}$$

where $\mathbf{W}_{\text{signal}} \in \mathbb{R}^{(L-1)\times M}$ and $\mathbf{W}_{\text{noise}} \in \mathbb{R}^{(m-L+1)\times M}$.

- **Projection matrix $\mathbf{W}_{\text{signal}}$ for the signal subspace.** According to Eq. (9.81), the optimal solution for $\mathbf{W}_{\text{signal}}$ is

$$\mathbf{W}_{\text{signal}} = [\mathbf{v}_1 \ldots \mathbf{v}_{L-1}], \tag{9.83}$$

  i.e. the *signal subspace* is spanned by the $(L-1)$ principal vectors of the discriminant matrix $\mathbf{W}_{\text{MD-FDA}}$.
- **Projection matrix $\mathbf{W}_{\text{noise}}$ for the noise subspace.** The *noise subspace* is defined as the subspace orthogonal to the signal subspace in a Mahalanobis sense. Note that all the remaining eigenvalues of the discriminant matrix $\mathbf{W}_{\text{MD-FDA}}$ have the same value:

$$\lambda_L = \ldots = \lambda_M = 1.0 \tag{9.84}$$

  It is well known, but somewhat unfortunate, that the eigenvectors corresponding to identical eigenvalues are randomly generated from their shared subspace. Such a randomness disqualifies the direct use of any of the remaining $M - L + 1$ eigenvectors to effectively complement the $L-1$ principal eigenvectors associated with the signal subspace. We will need to seek an alternative approach so as to avoid such randomness and produce a set of systematically ranked eigenvectors. This is the topic of the subsequent discussion.

9.9.2.3 Minimize noise power for extraction of noise-subspace components

Note that, in the SoSNR criterion, a SNR-type evaluation criterion is being uniformly applied to all of the m components. Such a uniform assessment is not applicable to trace-norm based learning models. Since the noise space contains no signal component, SNR becomes meaningless for the noise-subspace components. This prompts the use of a two-tier standard which may be used to separately assess *signal-subspace* and *noise-subspace* components.

- The SNR criterion is reserved exclusively for the signal-subspace components.
- The noise power of the *noise-subspace* components serves as an effective criterion to take into account the influence of those components.

Some useful insight may be gained by exploring a case study exemplified by Figure 9.7, in which the distributions of two classes of data (positive and negative) are shown as solid and dashed ellipses, respectively. Figures 9.7(a) and (b) show two competing 2D displays using two of the three eigenvectors, $\mathbf{v}_1$, $\mathbf{v}_2$, and $\mathbf{v}_3$, prescribed by Eq. (9.80). More exactly, the two eigenvectors comprise the following.

- **One signal-subspace component.** Since $L=2$, the signal subspace will be one-dimensional ($L-1=1$), which is in this case represented by the eigenvector $\mathbf{v}_1$.
- **One noise-subspace component.** Note that both $\mathbf{v}_2$ and $\mathbf{v}_3$ are from the noise subspace since they have zero SNR. The question is which of the two should be preferred.

The combined $\mathbf{v}_1$–$\mathbf{v}_2$ display is shown in Figure 9.7(a), while the $\mathbf{v}_1$–$\mathbf{v}_3$ display is shown in Figure 9.7(b). Taking the viewpoint from the right-hand-side observer, $\mathbf{v}_3$ incurs less noise perturbation than does $\mathbf{v}_2$. Consequently, the two classes of data will appear to be more separated from the $\mathbf{v}_1$–$\mathbf{v}_3$ display than they do from the $\mathbf{v}_1$–$\mathbf{v}_2$ display. This example highlights the essential role of the noise variances.

9.9.2.4 Optimality criteria for discriminant components

In order to obtain a more comprehensive criterion taking into account both the SNR and noise power, let us introduce a new criterion named Overall-SNR or Omnidirectional-SNR (OSNR),

$$\mathrm{OSNR} \equiv \frac{\sum \mathrm{signal}_i}{\sum \mathrm{noise}_i} \tag{9.85}$$

The fact that the OSNR criterion may effectively compliment the SNR criterion may be justified from two aspects:

- From the classification perspective, the SNR criterion by itself is an effective performance indicator only for a linear classifier, but no longer so for a nonlinear classifier. With reference to Figure 9.7, the discriminating capability of a linear classifier only depends on what the top observer sees. However, the discriminating capability of nonlinear classifier will depend on more than one viewing angle.

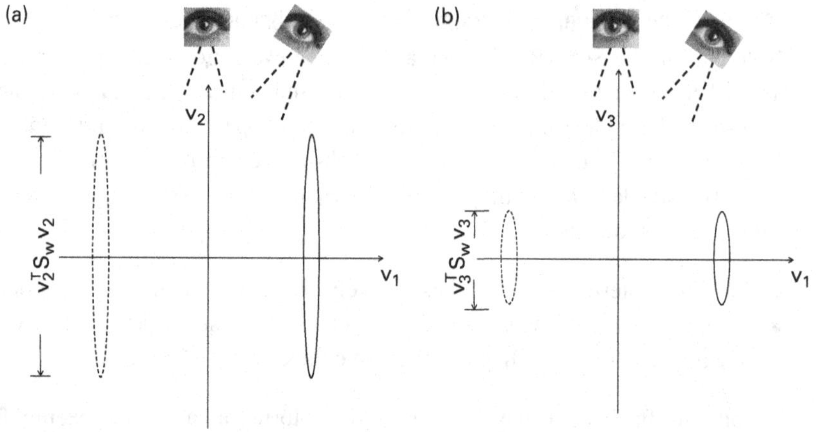

Fig. 9.7. A 2D visualization based on two of the three eigenvectors, $\mathbf{v}_1$, $\mathbf{v}_2$, and $\mathbf{v}_3$, obtained via Eq. (9.80). Two 2D displays are shown here: (a) the combined $\mathbf{v}_1$–$\mathbf{v}_2$ display and (b) the combined $\mathbf{v}_1$–$\mathbf{v}_3$ display. The question is which of the two displays offers a more discriminating visualization. From the viewpoint of the top observer, it probably makes no difference, because in this case one views the distribution purely from the signal-subspace angle (i.e. $\mathbf{v}_1$). However, a very different conclusion could be drawn from the viewpoint of the right-hand-side observer. For the side observer, display (b) would be better than (a) because the two classes would appear more separated. Note that $\mathbf{v}_3$, having a smaller variance, creates less perturbation than does $\mathbf{v}_2$. This motivates the choice of a criterion that is based on the projected noise variance, cf. Eq. (9.86). It turns out that minimizing the noise power of such side components may optimize a useful visualization criterion called OSNR, cf. Eq. (9.85).

- From the visualization perspective, a good visualizer should provides a high discriminating capability from a widest possible viewing angle. This necessitates the use of the OSNR criterion given in Eq. (9.85).

The OSNR criterion includes the noise power of the noise-subspace components as an integral part of evaluation metric. For the best performance for a (normalized) projection vector $\mathbf{w}$ in the noise subspace, one would want to have a minimal projected variance, defined as

$$\texttt{noise-power} = \mathbf{w}^{\mathrm{T}}\mathbf{S}_{\mathrm{W}}\mathbf{w}, \tag{9.86}$$

under the noise-subspace constraint that

$$\mathbf{w}^{\mathrm{T}}\mathbf{S}_{\mathrm{B}}\mathbf{w} = 0.$$

This leads to a constrained optimizer which aims at finding a vector $\mathbf{w}$ such that

$$\arg\min_{\mathbf{w}:\mathbf{w}^{\mathrm{T}}\mathbf{S}_{\mathrm{B}}\mathbf{w}=0} \frac{\mathbf{w}^{\mathrm{T}}\mathbf{S}_{\mathrm{W}}\mathbf{w}}{\mathbf{w}^{\mathrm{T}}\mathbf{w}}, \text{ where } \mathbf{w} \in \texttt{span}[\bar{\mathbf{X}}].$$

Equivalently,

$$\arg\max_{\mathbf{w}:\mathbf{w}^{\mathrm{T}}\mathbf{S}_{\mathrm{B}}\mathbf{w}=0} \frac{\mathbf{w}^{\mathrm{T}}\mathbf{w}}{\mathbf{w}^{\mathrm{T}}\mathbf{S}_{\mathrm{W}}\mathbf{w}}, \text{ where } \mathbf{w} \in \texttt{span}[\bar{\mathbf{X}}].$$

This leads to a mathematically equivalent optimizer,

$$\arg\max_{\mathbf{w}:\mathbf{w}^{\mathrm{T}}\mathbf{S}_{\mathrm{B}}\mathbf{w}=0,\mathbf{w}^{\mathrm{T}}\mathbf{S}_{\mathrm{W}}\mathbf{w}=1} \mathbf{w}^{\mathrm{T}}\mathbf{w}, \text{ where } \mathbf{w} \in \mathtt{span}[\bar{\mathbf{X}}],$$

which can be naturally extended to the following multi-dimensional "trace-norm" optimizer:

$$\arg\max_{\mathbf{W}:\mathbf{W}^{\mathrm{T}}\mathbf{S}_{\mathrm{B}}\mathbf{W}=0,\mathbf{W}^{\mathrm{T}}\mathbf{S}_{\mathrm{W}}\mathbf{W}=\mathbf{I}} \mathtt{tr}\left(\mathbf{W}^{\mathrm{T}}\mathbf{W}\right), \text{ where } \mathbf{W} \in \mathtt{span}[\bar{\mathbf{X}}]. \tag{9.87}$$

Note that the LSP constraint imposed here plays an important role for the kernelization of DCA learning models, cf. Section 9.9.5.

Now we have a formal formulation for the extraction of discriminant components in the noise subspace. However, solving for Eq. (9.87) requires an efficient numerical method which simultaneously meets both constraints, (1) $\mathbf{W}^{\mathrm{T}}\mathbf{S}_{\mathrm{B}}\mathbf{W} = 0$, and (2) $\mathbf{W}^{\mathrm{T}}\mathbf{S}_{\mathrm{W}}\mathbf{W} = \mathbf{I}$. Even more formidable will be the task to find a trace-norm formulation which can simultaneously seek optimal solutions for signal- and noise-subspace components. This challenge will be addressed subsequently.

9.9.2.5 Principal-component discriminant component analysis (PC-DCA)

A desirable solution must be able to assure that the eigenvalues/eigenvectors are ranked according to their usefulness. In other words, it must obviate the randomness of eigenvectors caused by the equal eigenvalues associated with $\mathbf{D}_{\text{MD-FDA}}$. This motivates the introduction of the so-called principal-component DCA (PC-DCA).

Suppose that $\mathbf{S}_{\mathrm{W}}$ is nonsingular and numerically well-conditioned, then we can adopt a trace-norm maximizer which aims at finding an $M \times (L-1)$ matrix $\mathbf{W}_{\text{signal}}$ such that

$$\mathbf{W}_{\text{signal}} = \arg\max_{\mathbf{W}:\mathbf{W}^{\mathrm{T}}\mathbf{S}_{\mathrm{W}}\mathbf{W}=\mathbf{I}} \mathtt{tr}\left(\mathbf{W}^{\mathrm{T}}[\bar{\mathbf{S}} + \rho\mathbf{I}]\mathbf{W}\right). \tag{9.88}$$

There exists a twin-maximizer which aims instead at finding an $M \times (m-L+1)$ matrix $\mathbf{W}_{\text{noise}}$ such that

$$\begin{aligned}\mathbf{W}_{\text{noise}} &= \arg\max_{\mathbf{W}:\mathbf{W}^{\mathrm{T}}\mathbf{S}_{\mathrm{B}}\mathbf{W}=0,\ \mathbf{W}^{\mathrm{T}}\mathbf{S}_{\mathrm{W}}\mathbf{W}=\mathbf{I}} \mathtt{tr}\left(\mathbf{W}^{\mathrm{T}}[\bar{\mathbf{S}} + \rho\mathbf{I}]\mathbf{W}\right)\\ &= \arg\max_{\mathbf{W}:\mathbf{W}^{\mathrm{T}}\mathbf{S}_{\mathrm{B}}\mathbf{W}=0,\ \mathbf{W}^{\mathrm{T}}\mathbf{S}_{\mathrm{W}}\mathbf{W}=\mathbf{I}} \mathtt{tr}\left(\mathbf{W}^{\mathrm{T}}\,[\mathbf{S}_{\mathrm{B}} + \mathbf{S}_{\mathrm{W}} + \rho\mathbf{I}]\mathbf{W}\right)\\ &= \arg\max_{\mathbf{W}:\mathbf{W}^{\mathrm{T}}\mathbf{S}_{\mathrm{B}}\mathbf{W}=0,\ \mathbf{W}^{\mathrm{T}}\mathbf{S}_{\mathrm{W}}\mathbf{W}=\mathbf{I}} m + \mathtt{tr}\left(\rho\mathbf{W}^{\mathrm{T}}\mathbf{W}\right).\end{aligned} \tag{9.89}$$

This formulation is consistent with formulation established in Eq. (9.87). Heuristically speaking, the incorporation of the regularization term (parameterized by ρ) into PC-DCA effectively introduces a tiny signal-power in all directions, including those along the noise-subspace. Mathematically, it replaces the original rank-deficient matrix $\mathbf{S}_{\mathrm{B}}$ by $\mathbf{S}_{\mathrm{B}} + \rho\mathbf{I}$, i.e. a regularized matrix with the full rank. As such, it artificially creates a pseudo-SNR for the noise-subspace components, which originally bears no signal power. Moreover, the largest pseudo-SNR will correspond to the component with the least noise power since the power of the pseudo-signal is uniformly distributed in all directions.

This justifies the selection of the eigenvector(s) associated with the largest eigenvalue(s) – not counting those associated with the signal-subspace. Ironically, a similar heuristic, when applied to DCA (to be introduced momentarily) would justify the selection of the minor eigenvectors.

The twin maximizers, Eqs. (9.88) and (9.89), may be merged into a single trace-norm maximizer aiming at finding an $M \times m$ matrix $\mathbf{W}_{\text{PC-DCA}}$ such that

$$\mathbf{W}_{\text{PC-DCA}} = \underset{\mathbf{W}:\mathbf{W}^{\mathrm{T}}\mathbf{S}_{\mathrm{W}}\mathbf{W}=\mathbf{I}}{\arg\max} \ \mathtt{tr}\left(\mathbf{W}^{\mathrm{T}}[\bar{\mathbf{S}} + \rho\mathbf{I}]\mathbf{W}\right), \tag{9.90}$$

whose solution can be obtained from the principal eigenvectors of its corresponding *discriminant matrix* (assuming nonsingular $\mathbf{S}_{\mathrm{W}}$):[4]

$$\mathbf{D}_{\text{PC-DCA}} \equiv \mathbf{S}_{\mathrm{W}}^{-1}[\bar{\mathbf{S}} + \rho\mathbf{I}]. \tag{9.91}$$

This leads to the following PC-DCA learning model.

ALGORITHM 9.4 (PC-DCA learning model) *Given a supervised training dataset with L classes, the optimal solution for the trace-norm optimizer prescribed by Eq. (9.90) can be derived as follows: Let ρ be an infinitesimal positive value, i.e. $\rho > 0$ and $\rho \to 0$. Compute the m principal eigenvectors (with descending eigenvalues) of the discriminating matrix $\mathbf{D}_{\text{PC-DCA}}$, i.e.*

$$\mathbf{S}_{\mathrm{W}}^{-1}[\bar{\mathbf{S}} + \rho\mathbf{I}]\mathbf{v}_i = \lambda_i \mathbf{v}_i, \quad i = 1, \ldots, m,$$

and the optimal projection matrix can be formed as

$$\begin{aligned} \mathbf{W}_{\text{PC-DCA}} &= [\mathbf{W}_{\text{signal}} | \mathbf{W}_{\text{noise}}] \\ &= [\mathbf{v}_1 \ldots \mathbf{v}_{L-1} | \mathbf{v}_L \mathbf{v}_{L+1} \ldots \mathbf{v}_m] \\ &= [\mathbf{v}_1 \ldots \mathbf{v}_m]. \end{aligned} \tag{9.92}$$

□

Infinitesimal positive value of ρ for PC-DCA

Note that, when $\rho \to 0$, the discriminating matrix $\mathbf{D}_{\text{PC-DCA}}$ in Eq. (9.91) approaches $\mathbf{D}_{\text{MD-FDA}}$ in Eq. (9.79), thus the optimality of the signal-subspace solution can be established. It can be theoretically shown that the minimum power of the noise-subspace components is reached with $\rho \to 0$. This assertion may also be verified by applying PC-DCA to the same dataset in Example 9.5. Various performance metrics of PC-DCA with respect to different values of ρ are listed in Table 9.5. Briefly speaking, the experiment verifies that the SNR and OSNR are highest when the smallest value of $\rho = 0.00001$ is adopted. The results confirm the postulate that the larger the magnitude of ρ, the greater the noise power and smaller the SNR and OSNR. Consequently, the optimal PC-DCA solution can be reached only by using an infinitesimal positive ρ.

[4] When $M \geq N$ or $J \geq N$ (i.e. $\mathbf{S}_{\mathrm{W}}$ is singular), use $\mathbf{S}_{\mathrm{W}}^{+}[\mathbf{S} + \rho\mathbf{I}]$ or kernel PC-DCA, cf. Section 9.9.5.

Table 9.5. Various performance metrics of the PC-DCA learning model with respect to different values of ρ. This confirms the theoretical prediction that the best result is obtained when an infinitesimal positive ρ is adopted.

Method	Principal components DCA (PC-DCA)							
ρ	0.00001	0.0001	0.001	0.01	0.1	1.0	10	100
SNR_1	7.1429	7.1429	7.1429	7.1428	7.1409	6.9861	5.3733	4.6487
Noise_2	1.0	1.0	1.0004	1.004	1.041	1.4933	1.6559	1.6542
λ_2	1.00001	1.0001	1.001	1.0004	1.004	1.041	7.0623	61.4644
OSNR	2.6596	2.6595	2.6585	2.6489	2.5538	1.7379	1.0284	0.8798

9.9.3 Discriminant component analysis (DCA)

Note that PC-DCA does not admit a useful and adjustable parameter. In addition, $\mathbf{S}_W$ may sometimes be ill-conditioned. To combat these problems. a powerful model named discriminant component analysis (DCA) is proposed. The trace-norm maximizer/minimizer and the corresponding discriminant matrix for DCA will be formulated and verified. It can be shown that DCA embraces PC-DCA as a special case. Moreover, DCA is numerically more stable than PC-DCA. Most importantly, the parameter of DCA may be optimally adjusted to enhance the robustness and OSNR of the discriminant components.

9.9.3.1 Trace-norm maximizer/minimizer for DCA

Since $\mathbf{S}_W$ may occasionally be ill-conditioned, e.g. when $M \geq N$ or $J \geq N$, a numerically more stable approach would be preferred. To this end, it is a common practice to incorporate a small positive parameter ρ into the orthogonality constraint of the trace-norm optimizer in Eq. (9.78). This results in a new trace-norm optimizer targeting an $M \times (L-1)$ matrix $\mathbf{W}_{\text{signal}}$ such that

$$\mathbf{W}_{\text{signal}} = \underset{\mathbf{W}:\mathbf{W}^{\mathrm{T}}[\mathbf{S}_W+\rho\mathbf{I}]\mathbf{W}=\mathbf{I}}{\arg\max} \; \texttt{tr}\left(\mathbf{W}^{\mathrm{T}}\bar{\mathbf{S}}\mathbf{W}\right). \tag{9.93}$$

This optimizer has a twin formulation which aims at finding an $M \times (m-L+1)$ matrix $\mathbf{W}_{\text{noise}}$ such that (cf. Eq. (9.87))

$$\mathbf{W}_{\text{noise}} = \underset{\mathbf{W}:\mathbf{W}^{\mathrm{T}}\mathbf{S}_B\mathbf{W}=0,\ \mathbf{W}^{\mathrm{T}}[\mathbf{S}_W+\rho\mathbf{I}]\mathbf{W}=\mathbf{I}}{\arg\max} \; \texttt{tr}\left(\mathbf{W}^{\mathrm{T}}\mathbf{W}\right).$$

Equivalently,

$$\begin{aligned}
\mathbf{W}_{\text{noise}} &= \underset{\mathbf{W}:\mathbf{W}^{\mathrm{T}}\mathbf{S}_B\mathbf{W}=0,\ \mathbf{W}^{\mathrm{T}}[\mathbf{S}_W+\rho\mathbf{I}]\mathbf{W}=\mathbf{I}}{\arg\min} \; \texttt{tr}\left(\mathbf{W}^{\mathrm{T}}\left[-\rho\mathbf{I}\right]\mathbf{W}\right) \\
&= \underset{\mathbf{W}:\mathbf{W}^{\mathrm{T}}\mathbf{S}_B\mathbf{W}=0,\ \mathbf{W}^{\mathrm{T}}[\mathbf{S}_W+\rho\mathbf{I}]\mathbf{W}=\mathbf{I}}{\arg\min} \; \texttt{tr}\left(\mathbf{W}^{\mathrm{T}}\left[\mathbf{S}_B-\rho\mathbf{I}\right]\mathbf{W}\right) \\
&= \underset{\mathbf{W}:\mathbf{W}^{\mathrm{T}}\mathbf{S}_B\mathbf{W}=0,\ \mathbf{W}^{\mathrm{T}}[\mathbf{S}_W+\rho\mathbf{I}]\mathbf{W}=\mathbf{I}}{\arg\min} \; \texttt{tr}\left(\mathbf{W}^{\mathrm{T}}\bar{\mathbf{S}}\mathbf{W}\right).
\end{aligned} \tag{9.94}$$

The trace-norm maximizer in Eq. (9.93) and minimizer in Eq. (9.94) share the same cost function and almost the same orthogonality constraints. Consequently, they also share the same *discriminant matrix*:

$$\mathbf{D}_{\mathrm{DCA}} \equiv [\mathbf{S}_{\mathrm{W}} + \rho\mathbf{I}]^{-1}\,\bar{\mathbf{S}}. \tag{9.95}$$

Let $\{\mathbf{v}_1\mathbf{v}_2\ldots\mathbf{v}_{L-1}\ \ \mathbf{v}_L\ldots\mathbf{v}_M\}$ denote the M eigenvectors of the *discriminating matrix*, i.e.

$$[\mathbf{S}_{\mathrm{W}} + \rho\mathbf{I}]^{-1}\,\bar{\mathbf{S}}\mathbf{v}_i = \lambda_i\mathbf{v}_i, \text{ for a small and positive } \rho, \tag{9.96}$$

with descending eigenvalues (denoting $r \equiv \mathrm{rank}(\bar{\mathbf{S}})$):

$$\lambda_1 \geq \ldots \lambda_{L-1} > 1 > \lambda_L \geq \ldots \geq \lambda_r > 0 = \lambda_{r+1} = \ldots = \lambda_M.$$

Then

- the signal-subspace components or $\mathbf{W}_{\mathrm{signal}}$ can be formed from the $L-1$ principal eigenvectors: $[\mathbf{v}_1\ldots\mathbf{v}_{L-1}]$; and
- the noise-subspace components or $\mathbf{W}_{\mathrm{noise}}$ can be formed from the $m-L+1$ minor eigenvectors: $[\mathbf{v}_r\ \mathbf{v}_{r-1}\ldots\mathbf{v}_{r+L-m}]$.

This is why DCA may also be more precisely named as the (mixed-component) "discriminant component analysis" (MC-DCA).

ALGORITHM 9.5 (DCA learning model) *Given a supervised training dataset with L classes, the optimal solution for the twin optimizers given in Eqs. (9.93) and (9.94) can be derived as follows:*

- *Compute the M eigenvectors (with descending eigenvalues) of the "discriminating matrix"* $\mathbf{D}_{\mathrm{DCA}}$ *in Eq. (9.95), i.e.*

$$[\mathbf{S}_{\mathrm{W}} + \rho\mathbf{I}]^{-1}\,\bar{\mathbf{S}}\mathbf{v}_i = \lambda_i\mathbf{v}_i, \quad i = 1,\ldots,M.$$

- *The optimal projection matrix is*

$$\begin{aligned}\mathbf{W}_{\mathrm{DCA}} &= [\mathbf{W}_{\mathrm{signal}}|\mathbf{W}_{\mathrm{noise}}]\\ &= [\mathbf{v}_1\ldots\mathbf{v}_{L-1}|\mathbf{v}_r\ \mathbf{v}_{r-1}\ldots\mathbf{v}_{r+L-m}].\end{aligned} \tag{9.97}$$

The SNR of each signal component is (cf. Eq. (9.101))

$$\mathrm{SNR}_i \equiv \frac{\mathbf{v}_i^{\mathrm{T}}\mathbf{S}_{\mathrm{B}}\mathbf{v}_i}{\mathbf{v}_i^{\mathrm{T}}\mathbf{S}_{\mathrm{W}}\mathbf{v}_i} \approx \lambda_i - 1, \quad \textit{for } i = 1,\ldots,L-1. \tag{9.98}$$

The variance of each noise component is (cf. Eq. (9.103))

$$\mathtt{noise}_i = \mathbf{v}_i^{\mathrm{T}}\mathbf{S}_{\mathrm{W}}\mathbf{v}_i = \frac{\lambda_i\rho}{1-\lambda_i}, \quad \textit{for } i = r+L-m,\ldots,r. \tag{9.99}$$

□

Proof of DCA algorithm. Let us now prove that the above (principal and minor) eigenvectors are indeed optimal solutions pursuant to their own respective criteria.

- **Optimality and ranking of the signal-subspace components.** Note that, when $\rho \rightarrow 0$, the discriminating matrix $\mathbf{D}_{\text{DCA}}$ in Eq. (9.95) approaches $\mathbf{D}_{\text{MD-FDA}}$ in Eq. (9.79). Thus the optimality of the signal-subspace solution is established. The SNR of each signal-subspace component is

$$\begin{aligned}\text{SNR}_i &\equiv \frac{\mathbf{v}_i^{\text{T}}\mathbf{S}_{\text{B}}\mathbf{v}_i}{\mathbf{v}_i^{\text{T}}\mathbf{S}_{\text{W}}\mathbf{v}_i} \\ &= \frac{\mathbf{v}_i^{\text{T}}\bar{\mathbf{S}}\mathbf{v}_i}{\mathbf{v}_i^{\text{T}}\mathbf{S}_{\text{W}}\mathbf{v}_i} - 1 \\ &\approx \frac{\mathbf{v}_i^{\text{T}}\bar{\mathbf{S}}\mathbf{v}_i}{\mathbf{v}_i^{\text{T}}[\mathbf{S}_{\text{W}} + \rho\mathbf{I}]\mathbf{v}_i} - 1 \\ &= \lambda_i - 1, \text{ for } i = 1, \ldots, L-1. \end{aligned} \tag{9.100}$$

  The descending eigenvalues implies the following rank order:

$$\text{SNR}_1 \geq \text{SNR}_2 \geq \ldots \geq \text{SNR}_{L-1}.$$

- **Optimality and ranking of the noise-subspace components.** The projection matrix formed from the noise-subspace eigenvectors

$$\mathbf{W}_{\text{noise}} = \left[\mathbf{w}_L\mathbf{w}_{L+1}\ldots\mathbf{w}_m\right] = \left[\mathbf{v}_r\mathbf{v}_{r-1}\ldots\mathbf{v}_{r+L-m}\right]$$

  provides the optimal solution for the trace-norm optimizer in Eq. (9.94). Note that Eq. (9.94) approaches Eq. (9.87) when $\rho \rightarrow 0$. Thus the optimality of the noise-subspace solution is established.

Verify the zero-signal constraint of noise-subspace eigenvectors

Note that

$$\frac{\mathbf{v}_i^{\text{T}}\mathbf{S}_{\text{B}}\mathbf{v}_i}{\mathbf{v}_i^{\text{T}}[\mathbf{S}_{\text{W}} + \rho\mathbf{I}]\mathbf{v}_i} = \frac{\mathbf{v}_i^{\text{T}}\bar{\mathbf{S}}\mathbf{v}_i}{\mathbf{v}_i^{\text{T}}[\mathbf{S}_{\text{W}} + \rho\mathbf{I}]\mathbf{v}_i} - 1 = \lambda_i - 1,\ i = r+L-m, \ldots, r. \tag{9.101}$$

By Eq. (9.84), when ρ is very small,

$$\lambda_i \approx 1, \text{ for } i = L, \ldots, r. \tag{9.102}$$

On combining Eqs. (9.101) and (9.102), we can verify that $\mathbf{v}_i^{\text{T}}\mathbf{S}_{\text{B}}\mathbf{v}_i^{\text{T}} \approx 0$ and thus confirm that $\mathbf{v}_i$ falls in the noise subspace.

For the noise power of the ith component (denoted as $\texttt{noise}_i$), we have

$$\begin{aligned}\texttt{noise}_i &= \mathbf{v}_i^{\text{T}}\mathbf{S}_{\text{W}}\mathbf{v}_i \\ &= \mathbf{v}_i^{\text{T}}\left[\mathbf{S}_{\text{B}} + \mathbf{S}_{\text{W}}\right]\mathbf{v}_i \\ &= \mathbf{v}_i^{\text{T}}\bar{\mathbf{S}}\mathbf{v}_i \\ &\overset{\text{Eq. (9.96)}}{=} \lambda_i\mathbf{v}_i^{\text{T}}\left[\mathbf{S}_{\text{W}} + \rho\mathbf{I}\right]\mathbf{v}_i \\ &= \lambda_i\mathbf{v}_i^{\text{T}}\mathbf{S}_{\text{W}}\mathbf{v}_i + \lambda_i\rho, \\ &= \lambda_i\,\texttt{noise}_i + \lambda_i\rho, \end{aligned}$$

which in turn implies

$$\mathtt{noise}_i = \frac{\lambda_i \rho}{1 - \lambda_i}. \tag{9.103}$$

The descending eigenvalues implies the following rank order:

$$\mathtt{noise}_r \le \mathtt{noise}_{r-1} \cdots \le \mathtt{noise}_{r+L-m}.$$

Combining Eqs. (9.102) and (9.103), we have

$$1 - \frac{\rho}{\mathtt{noise}_i} \approx \lambda_i, \quad i = L, \ldots, r. \tag{9.104}$$

As exemplified by a case study, the value of λ_r/θ, where $\theta = 1 - \rho/\mathtt{noise}_r$, remains pretty much a constant for a wide dynamic range of ρ: $0.00001 \le \rho \le 0.1$, cf. Table 9.7.

9.9.3.2 Commonality among PCA, MD-FDA, PC-DCA, and DCA

We have demonstrated that the teacher's information can be incorporated into various trace-norm optimizers for the purpose of enhancing the discriminant capability.

As shown in Table 9.6, all PCA, MD-FDA, PC-DCA, and DCA have the same type of trace-norm formulation, the only difference being their respective trace-norm matrices and orthogonality constraints. They share the commonality that all their optimal solutions can be derived from the (principal or mixed) eigenvectors of their respective discriminant matrices.

The difference between PCA and MD-FDA lies in the fact that the latter incorporates a "pre-whitening" operation (in form of a Mahalanobis matrix) to enhance the discriminant capability. While both MD-FDA and PC-DCA employ the same "pre-whitening" operation, a regularization term (parameterized by ρ) is added to PC-DCA's cost function in Eq. (9.90), which is absent in Eq. (9.78). Finally, for robustness and better OSNR, a regularization term is incorporated into the denominator of DCA's discriminant matrix, a unique and important feature absent in the other models.

Table 9.6. A comparison of PCA, MD-FDA, PC-DCA, and DCA may be summarized in terms of their trace-norm cost functions, optimization constraints, discriminant matrices, and principal-versus-mixed eigenvectors used for the optimal solution.

Learning model	PCA	MD-FDA	PC-DCA	DCA
Trace-norm matrix	$\bar{\mathbf{S}}$	$\bar{\mathbf{S}}$	$\bar{\mathbf{S}} + \rho\mathbf{I}$	$\bar{\mathbf{S}}$
Orthogonality constraint	$\mathbf{W}^{\mathrm{T}}\mathbf{W} = \mathbf{I}$	$\mathbf{W}^{\mathrm{T}}\mathbf{S}_{\mathrm{W}}\mathbf{W} = \mathbf{I}$	$\mathbf{W}^{\mathrm{T}}\mathbf{S}_{\mathrm{W}}\mathbf{W} = \mathbf{I}$	$\mathbf{W}^{\mathrm{T}}[\mathbf{S}_{\mathrm{W}} + \rho\mathbf{I}]\mathbf{W} = \mathbf{I}$
Discriminant matrix	$\bar{\mathbf{S}}$	$\mathbf{S}_{\mathrm{W}}^{-1}\bar{\mathbf{S}}$	$\mathbf{S}_{\mathrm{W}}^{-1}[\bar{\mathbf{S}} + \rho\mathbf{I}]$	$[\mathbf{S}_{\mathrm{W}} + \rho\mathbf{I}]^{-1}\,\bar{\mathbf{S}}$
Eigenvectors selected	Principal	Principal	Principal	Mixed

9.9.3.3 Choice of ρ for DCA

Let us first provide a brief analysis on the choice of ρ for DCA's signal- and noise-subspace components, respectively.

- **Impact of ρ on DCA's SNR of signal-subspace components.** In a nutshell, the highest SNR can be reached only with an infinitesimal positive ρ. The SNR associated with a signal-subspace component is equal to its corresponding eigenvalue λ of the *discriminating matrix* $[\mathbf{S}_W + \rho\mathbf{I}]^{-1}\bar{\mathbf{S}}$. More exactly, let $\mathbf{w}$ denote the (normalized) eigenvector corresponding to λ, then the SNR and the eigenvalue λ are both equal to

$$\mathbf{w}[\mathbf{S}_W + \rho\mathbf{I}]^{-1}\bar{\mathbf{S}}\mathbf{w}. \tag{9.105}$$

  Treating $\mathbf{w}$ as a constant vector and taking the directive of the above function with respect to ρ, we have

$$-\rho\mathbf{w}[\mathbf{S}_W + \rho\mathbf{I}]^{-2}\bar{\mathbf{S}}\mathbf{w}, \tag{9.106}$$

  which is always negative for a positive ρ. It implies that the SNR (and the corresponding eigenvalue) reaches an maximum when $\rho \to 0$ and then monotonically decreases when ρ increases. However, increasing ρ usually brings about enhanced robustness; therefore, it may be worthwhile even if the SNR is somewhat compromised.
- **Impact of ρ on DCA's noise power of noise-subspace components.** As shown in Table 9.7, both the eigenvalue and the power associated with the noise-subspace components decrease with increasing ρ. The result confirms the postulate that, in contrast to PC-DCA, the noise power of DCA monotonically decrease with ρ.

Choice of ρ for DCA based on weighted OSNR

The OSNR-optimal ρ-value depends on the tradeoff between the following two factors: (i) In order to obtain a high SNR of the signal-subspace components, we want ρ to be as small as possible. (ii) On the other hand, in order to reduce the noise power of the noise-subspace components, we want ρ to be not too small. Such a tradeoff motivates the introduction of a new criterion named Weighted-Overall-SNR (WOSNR):

$$\text{WOSNR} \equiv \frac{\alpha \sum_{i \in \text{signal subspace}} \text{signal}_i}{\alpha \sum_{i \in \text{signal subspace}} \text{noise}_i + \sum_{j \in \text{noise subspace}} \text{noise}_j}, \tag{9.107}$$

where we usually set $\alpha \gg 1$ to stress the vital role of the signal-subspace components.

From the perspective of (weighted) OSNR, the best ρ may be experimentally obtained by exhaustive search. It is worth noting that there is a simple selection rule on ρ to expedite the experimentation. It is found that, with both simulation and theoretically supports, the SNR decreases slowly as long as a proper upper bound is imposed on the largest Pseudo-SNR: $\rho/\texttt{noise}_r$. (The bound serves to prevent an excessive value of pseudo-SNR from being artificially created.) Mathematically, imposing an upper bound on ρ is equivalent to imposing a lower bound on $\theta \equiv 1 - \rho/\texttt{noise}_r$. In Eq. (9.104),

Table 9.7. Various performance metrics of the DCA learning model with respect to different values of ρ. Here the weighting factor is set to be $\alpha = 10$ for WOSNR. For this dataset, considering the overall performance including SNR, OSNR, and WOSNR, the best result is reached by setting $\rho = 0.1$. (Here $r = \text{rank}(\bar{\mathbf{S}}) = 3$.)

Method	Discriminant component analysis (DCA)							
ρ	0.00001	0.0001	0.001	0.01	0.1	1.0	10	100
SNR_1	7.1429	7.1429	7.1428	7.1415	7.0325	4.8859	3.0749	2.8424
Noise_3	1.0	1.0	0.9996	0.9960	0.9645	0.8319	0.7449	0.7320
λ_3	0.99999	0.9999	0.9990	0.9901	0.9076	0.4763	0.0789	0.0084
λ_3/θ	1.0	1.0	1.0	1.0001	1.0126	−0.23573	−0.0063	−0.000062
OSNR	2.65996	2.6600	2.6635	2.6985	3.0180	3.7793	2.8540	2.6577
WOSNR	6.1125	6.1127	6.1145	6.1319	6.6029	4.7469	3.0513	2.8227

it is theoretically derived that $\theta \approx \lambda_r$. Suppose further that the lower bound is pre-set to be θ_0, where $\theta_0 < 1$, then we can derive a simple selection rule based on the value of λ_r:

$$\theta_0 \leq \theta \approx \lambda_r < 1.0. \tag{9.108}$$

This lower bound may be lowered to accommodate noisy experimental environment.

Let us now use a numerical example to illustrate the DCA algorithm and then compare DCA with PCA, FDA, and SODA.

Example 9.6 (DCA: numerical example) *Let us consider the previous dataset used in Example 9.6. Recall that* $\mathbf{\Delta} = [2 \quad 2 \quad 2]^{\mathrm{T}}$ *and*

$$\mathbf{S}_{\mathrm{B}} = \begin{bmatrix} 10 & 10 & 10 \\ 10 & 10 & 10 \\ 10 & 10 & 10 \end{bmatrix} \text{ and } \mathbf{S}_{\mathrm{W}} = \begin{bmatrix} 2 & 2 & 3 \\ 2 & 5 & 4 \\ 3 & 4 & 6 \end{bmatrix}.$$

DCA projection matrix

When $\rho = 0.1$, *the three eigenvectors of* $[\mathbf{S}_{\mathrm{W}} + \rho\mathbf{I}]^{-1}\bar{\mathbf{S}}$ *are*

$$\mathbf{v}_1 = \begin{bmatrix} 0.9221 \\ 0.1490 \\ -0.3571 \end{bmatrix} \quad \mathbf{v}_2 = \begin{bmatrix} -0.4065 \\ 0.8160 \\ -0.4110 \end{bmatrix}, \quad \mathbf{v}_3 = \begin{bmatrix} 0.7134 \\ 0.0001 \\ -0.7008 \end{bmatrix},$$

and the three descending eigenvalues are $\lambda_1 = 141.3193$, $\lambda_2 = 0.9998$, *and* $\lambda_3 = 0.9992$. *(Here* $r = \text{rank}(\bar{\mathbf{S}}) = 3$.*)*

Based on Eq. (9.97),

$$\mathbf{W}_{\mathrm{DCA}} = \begin{bmatrix} \mathbf{v}_1 & \mathbf{v}_3 \end{bmatrix} = \begin{bmatrix} 0.9221 & 0.7134 \\ 0.1490 & 0.0001 \\ -0.3571 & -0.7008 \end{bmatrix}. \tag{9.109}$$

The simulation study confirms that

$$0.9645 = \frac{\mathbf{v}_3^{\mathrm{T}}\mathbf{S}_{\mathrm{W}}\mathbf{v}_3}{\mathbf{v}_3^{\mathrm{T}}\mathbf{v}_3} \leq \frac{\mathbf{w}^{\mathrm{T}}\mathbf{S}_{\mathrm{W}}\mathbf{w}}{\mathbf{w}^{\mathrm{T}}\mathbf{w}} \leq \frac{\mathbf{v}_2^{\mathrm{T}}\mathbf{S}_{\mathrm{W}}\mathbf{v}_2}{\mathbf{v}_2^{\mathrm{T}}\mathbf{v}_2} = 1.6659,$$

for any normalized projection vector $\mathbf{w}$ *in the noise space. This means that*

(i) the third eigenvector is the best projection vector in the noise space,
(ii) while the second eigenvector is the worst choice among all the possible projection vectors. Namely, any other projection vector in the noise space would do better.

Wide dynamic range of ρ

For example, if $\rho' = 0.00001$ *then*

$$\mathbf{W}_{\mathrm{DCA}} = \begin{bmatrix} 0.9113 & 0.7071 \\ 0.1302 & 0.0000 \\ -0.3906 & -0.7071 \end{bmatrix}$$

which is almost identical to the solution for $\rho = 0.1$. *Note that* $\rho = 1000 \times \rho'$, *a difference of three orders of magnitude. The results suggest that the solutions are insensitive to a wide dynamic range of* ρ. *This is a good news as it means that the SNR can continue to remain high for a good dynamic range of* ρ. *In fact*

$$SNR' = \frac{signal'_1}{noise'_1} = \frac{4.2373}{0.5932} = 7.1429$$

and

$$SNR = \frac{signal_1}{noise_1} = \frac{5.0994}{0.7251} = 7.0325. \tag{9.110}$$

The choice of ρ*-value depends on the tradeoff between SNR and OSNR. For example, let us use DCA(*$\rho = 0.00001$*) as the baseline for comparison, which has an SNR (*$= 7.1429$*) and OSNR (=2.6596). If we set* $\rho = 0.1$, *its SNR drops only by 1.5%. Moreover, there is another silver lining very worth mentioning. Note that the SNR, albeit a bit lower, is in exchange with a higher signal power, which in turn improves the robustness and, in this case, helps raise the OSNR which gains an improvement of 13.5%. Therefore, for this dataset, it is nearly optimal to set* $\rho = 0.1$ *in both SNR and OSNR sense.*

When $\rho = 1.0$, *the OSNR gains substantially but the SNR drops by 32%, causing WOSNR to drop by 22%. Therefore,* $\rho = 1.0$ *is deemed to be too high to be useful.*

9.9.4 Comparisons between PCA, DCA, PC-DCA, and SODA

9.9.4.1 Relationship between DCA and PC-DCA

PC-DCA can be shown to be effectively a special case of DCA. More exactly, that PC-DCA with infinitesimal negative ρ is equivalent to DCA with an infinitesimal negative $\rho' = -\rho$.

As far as signal-subspace components are concerned, PC-DCA and DCA are both equivalent to MD-FDA, when ρ and ρ' are infinitesimal. So what remains to be shown is that they share the same solution in the noise-subspace. Note that, for DCA with an infinitesimal negative $\rho' = -\rho$, the *discriminating matrix* (cf. Eq. (9.95)) can be re-expressed as follows:

$$\mathbf{D}_{\text{DCA}} \equiv \left[\mathbf{S}_{\text{W}} + \rho'\mathbf{I}\right]^{-1} \bar{\mathbf{S}} = [\mathbf{S}_{\text{W}} - \rho\mathbf{I}]^{-1} \bar{\mathbf{S}} \approx \mathbf{S}_{\text{W}}^{-1}\bar{\mathbf{S}} + \rho\mathbf{S}_{\text{W}}^{-2}\bar{\mathbf{S}} \tag{9.111}$$

Suppose that $\mathbf{w}$ is an eigenvector in the noise-space of $\mathbf{D}_{\text{DCA}}$, then $\mathbf{S}_{\text{B}}\mathbf{w} = 0$ and it follows that

$$\mathbf{S}_{\text{W}}^{-2}\bar{\mathbf{S}}\,\mathbf{w} = \mathbf{S}_{\text{W}}^{-2}[\mathbf{S}_{\text{B}} + \mathbf{S}_{\text{W}}]\mathbf{w} = \mathbf{S}_{\text{W}}^{-2}[\mathbf{S}_{\text{W}}]\mathbf{w} = \mathbf{S}_{\text{W}}^{-1}\mathbf{w}. \tag{9.112}$$

The eigenvalue corresponding to the eigenvector $\mathbf{w}$ is

$$\begin{aligned}
\mathbf{w}^{\text{T}}\mathbf{D}_{\text{DCA}}\mathbf{w} &\equiv \mathbf{w}^{\text{T}}\left[\mathbf{S}_{\text{W}} - \rho\mathbf{I}\right]^{-1}\bar{\mathbf{S}}\mathbf{w} \\
&\approx \mathbf{w}^{\text{T}}\mathbf{S}_{\text{W}}^{-1}\bar{\mathbf{S}}\mathbf{w} + \rho\mathbf{w}^{\text{T}}\mathbf{S}_{\text{W}}^{-2}\bar{\mathbf{S}}\mathbf{w} \\
&\overset{\text{Eq. (9.112)}}{=} \mathbf{w}^{\text{T}}\mathbf{S}_{\text{W}}^{-1}\bar{\mathbf{S}}\mathbf{w} + \rho\mathbf{w}^{\text{T}}\mathbf{S}_{\text{W}}^{-1}\mathbf{w} \\
&= \mathbf{w}^{\text{T}}\mathbf{S}_{\text{W}}^{-1}[\bar{\mathbf{S}} + \rho\mathbf{I}]\mathbf{w} \\
&= \mathbf{w}^{\text{T}}\mathbf{D}_{\text{PC-DCA}}\mathbf{w}.
\end{aligned} \tag{9.113}$$

Thus the equivalence can be established between PC-DCA and DCA for infinitesimal ρ and ρ'. This equivalence can be further confirmed by Example 9.7.

Example 9.7 (PC-DCA is equivalent to DCA with an infinitesimal negative ρ) *Consider the previous dataset used in Example 9.6, the eigenvectors (in descending order) associated with the discriminant matrix* $\mathbf{D}_{\text{PC-DCA}}$ *(with* $\rho = 0.001$*) are*

$$\begin{bmatrix} \mathbf{v}_1 & \mathbf{v}_2 & \mathbf{v}_3 \end{bmatrix} = \begin{bmatrix} 0.9113 & -0.4083 & 0.7070 \\ 0.1302 & 0.8165 & 0.0000 \\ -0.3906 & -0.4082 & -0.7070 \end{bmatrix}.$$

Likewise, the eigenvectors associated with $\mathbf{D}_{DCA}$ *(with* $\rho' = -0.001$*) are*

$$\begin{bmatrix} \mathbf{v}'_1 & \mathbf{v}'_2 & \mathbf{v}'_3 \end{bmatrix} = \begin{bmatrix} 0.9112 & 0.7070 & -0.4083 \\ 0.1300 & 0.0000 & 0.8165 \\ -0.3909 & -0.7072 & -0.4082 \end{bmatrix}.$$

By noting that $\mathbf{v}_1 \approx \mathbf{v}'_1$ *and* $\mathbf{v}_2 = \mathbf{v}'_3$*, we can verify the equivalence between the two learning models in terms of both signal and noise subspaces.*

Putting Tables 9.5 and 9.7 side by side exhibits an obvious continuity of performance trends from DCA to PC-DCA. Therefore, DCA embraces PC-DCA as a special case, More importantly, DCA offers more flexility and is numerically more reliable.

9.9.4.2 Comparison between PCA, DCA, and SODA

Recall that the same dataset was used in Example 9.5 as well as Example 9.6. The SODA and DCA solutions are respectively

$$\mathbf{W}_{SODA} = \begin{bmatrix} 0.9113 & 0.2908 \\ 0.1302 & 0.4679 \\ -0.3906 & 0.8346 \end{bmatrix} \text{ and } \mathbf{W}_{DCA} = \begin{bmatrix} 0.9221 & 0.7134 \\ 0.1490 & 0.0001 \\ -0.3571 & -0.7008 \end{bmatrix}.$$

The SODA and DCA($\rho = 0.1$) solutions can be briefly compared as follows.

- **SNR.** The SNR for SODA is 7.1429, while the SNR for DCA($\rho = 0.1$) is 7.0325, cf. Table 9.7. As mentioned earlier, the lower SNR of DCA is a consequence of trade-off for higher OSNR and enhanced robustness. To have the best of the two worlds, i.e. both high SNR and enhanced robustness, SODA and DCA may be properly combined to produce an optimal hybrid representation.
- **OSNR and WOSNR.** The SODA's OSNR and WOSNR ($\alpha = 10$) are 1.3265 and 3.2086, substantially lower than DCA's OSNR (=3.0180) and WOSNR (=6.6029), cf. Table 9.7. However, not surprisingly, SODA outperforms DCA in terms of SoSNR: 9.5451 to 7.0325.
- For comparison, let us provide here the performance associated with the two principal vectors of the PCA solution (cf. Example 9.5): $OSNR = 0.9475$, $WOSNR = 0.9945$, and $SoSNR = 1.0018$. Not surprisingly, they are substantially inferior to SODA or DCA.

9.9.4.3 Extended applications of DCA

The mixed minimization/maximization modes of DCA make it potentially appealing to several other applications. For example, in radar/sonar applications, a moving object is often viewed as the targeted signal (to be enhanced) while the interference is treated as unwanted noise (to be suppressed). It is plausible that some applications would call for the extraction of components which accentuate the signal subspace (represented by a correlation matrix $\mathbf{S}_{\text{signal}}$) while suppressing the interference subspace (represented by $\mathbf{S}_{\text{noise}}$). The matrices $\mathbf{S}_{\text{signal}}$ and/or $\mathbf{S}_{\text{noise}}$ may be rank-deficient or with full-rank. By denoting $\bar{\mathbf{S}} \equiv \mathbf{S}_{\text{signal}} + \mathbf{S}_{\text{noise}}$ and substituting $\mathbf{S}_W$ by $\mathbf{S}_{\text{noise}}$, the DCA formulation may become applicable.

9.9.5 Kernelized DCA and SODA learning models

By embedding the LSP constraints into the solution search space, e.g. Eq. (9.87), it guarantees the kernelizability of DCA and SODA learning models. Moreover, they share a very similar kernelization procedure. In this section, we shall elaborate the kernelization of the PC-DCA and DCA. The derivation of the kernelized SODA (KSODA) learning model basically just follows suit as to be further elaborated in Problem 9.13. For the full treatment on KSODA models, see [311b].

Intrinsic-space formulation

Given a training dataset $[\mathcal{X}, \mathcal{Y}]$, a learning model in intrinsic space may be formulated as follows: (1) map the training vectors in the original space to the intrinsic space, and (2) apply the DCA formulation the new feature vectors.

Let us first focus on the center-adjusted data matrix $\bar{\Phi}$:

$$\bar{\Phi} = \left[I - \frac{1}{N}\mathbf{e}^{\mathrm{T}}\mathbf{e} \right] \Phi, \tag{9.114}$$

where $\mathbf{e} \equiv \begin{bmatrix} 1 & 1 & \ldots & 1 \end{bmatrix}^{\mathrm{T}}$. Now the "center-adjusted" *scatter matrix* is defined as

$$\bar{\mathbf{S}} \equiv \bar{\Phi}\bar{\Phi}^{\mathrm{T}}. \tag{9.115}$$

The (multi-class) between-class scatter matrix $\mathbf{S}_{\mathrm{W}}$ can be defined as

$$\mathbf{S}_{\mathrm{W}} = \sum_{\ell=1}^{L}\sum_{j=1}^{N_\ell} [\vec{\phi}\,(\mathbf{x})_j^{(\ell)} - \vec{\mu}_{\vec{\phi}}^{(\ell)}][\vec{\phi}\,(\mathbf{x})_j^{(\ell)} - \vec{\mu}_{\vec{\phi}}^{(\ell)}]^{\mathrm{T}}, \tag{9.116}$$

where N_ℓ is the number of samples in class ℓ and the centroids are defined in the intrinsic space.

The PC-DCA formulation in the intrinsic space can be expressed as a trace-norm optimizer targeting (assuming $m \le \mathrm{rank}(\mathbf{S}_{\mathrm{W}})$):

$$\underset{\{\mathbf{U}\in\mathbb{R}^{J\times m}:\mathbf{U}^{\mathrm{T}}[\mathbf{S}_{\mathrm{W}}]\mathbf{U}=\mathbf{I}\}}{\arg\max} \quad \mathtt{tr}\left(\mathbf{U}^{\mathrm{T}}[\bar{\mathbf{S}} + \rho\mathbf{I}]\mathbf{U}\right). \tag{9.117}$$

Kernelization of PC-DCA

Thanks to the learning subspace property (LSP), there exists an $N \times m$ matrix $\mathbf{A}$ such that

$$\mathbf{U} = \bar{\Phi}\mathbf{A}.$$

Following basically the same conversion procedure leading to the kernelized model given in Eq. (3.45), the optimizer in Eq. (9.117) may be kernelized into the following trace-norm optimizer in the empirical space:

$$\underset{\{\mathbf{A}\in\mathbb{R}^{N\times m}:\mathbf{A}^{\mathrm{T}}\mathbf{K}_{\mathrm{W}}\mathbf{A}=\mathbf{I}_{m\times m}\}}{\arg\max} \quad \mathtt{tr}\left(\mathbf{A}^{\mathrm{T}}\left[\bar{\mathbf{K}}^2 + \rho\bar{\mathbf{K}}\right]\mathbf{A}\right), \tag{9.118}$$

where the "center-adjusted" *kernel matrix* $\bar{\mathbf{K}}$ is defined as, cf. Eq. (9.115),

$$\bar{\mathbf{K}} \equiv \bar{\Phi}^{\mathrm{T}}\bar{\Phi}, \tag{9.119}$$

and the between-class kernel matrix $\mathbf{K}_{\mathrm{W}}$ defined as, cf. Eq. (9.116),

$$\mathbf{K}_{\mathrm{W}} = \sum_{\ell=1}^{L}\sum_{j=1}^{N_\ell} [\vec{\mathbf{k}}\,(\mathbf{x})_j^{(\ell)} - \vec{\mu}_{\vec{\mathbf{k}}}^{(\ell)}][\vec{\mathbf{k}}\,(\mathbf{x})_j^{(\ell)} - \vec{\mu}_{\vec{\mathbf{k}}}^{(\ell)}]^{\mathrm{T}}, \tag{9.120}$$

with the centroids defined in the empirical space. This leads to the following *discriminant matrix* in the empirical space (assuming nonsingular $\mathbf{K}_{\mathrm{W}}$):

$$\mathbf{D}_{\mathrm{KPC\text{-}DCA}} \equiv [\mathbf{K}_{\mathrm{W}}]^{-1}\left[\bar{\mathbf{K}}^2 + \rho\bar{\mathbf{K}}\right].$$

The PC-DCA solution in the empirical space can be formed from the m principal eigenvectors of $\mathbf{D}_{\mathrm{KPC\text{-}DCA}}$.

Kernel-DCA (KDCA) formulations

Likewise, for DCA, the cost function and orthogonality constraint shared by the twin optimizers (cf. Eqs. (9.93) and (9.94)) have their respective kernelied formulations. More exactly, after kernelization, the cost function becomes $\mathbf{A}^T\bar{\mathbf{K}}^2\mathbf{A}$, and the orthogonality constraint becomes $\mathbf{A}^T[\mathbf{K}_W + \rho\bar{\mathbf{K}}]\mathbf{A} = \mathbf{I}_{m\times m}$. This leads to a *discriminant matrix* defined as[5]

$$\mathbf{D}_{\text{KDCA}} \equiv \left[\mathbf{K}_W + \rho\bar{\mathbf{K}}\right]^{-1}\left[\bar{\mathbf{K}}^2\right] \tag{9.121}$$

where $\bar{\mathbf{K}}$ and $\mathbf{K}_W$ are defined in Eqs. (9.119) and (9.120), respectively.

The kernel-DCA (KDCA) learning model is summarized as follows.

ALGORITHM 9.6 (Kernelized discriminant component analysis (KDCA)) *The optimal DCA solution in the empirical space, represented by an $N \times m$ matrix $\mathbf{A}_{\text{KDCA}}$, can be are formed from the $(L-1)$ principal eigenvectors and $(m-L+1)$ minor eigenvectors (excluding those associated with the zero eigenvalues) of the kernel-domain discriminating matrix:* $\mathbf{D}_{\text{KDCA}} \equiv \left[\mathbf{K}_W + \rho\bar{\mathbf{K}}\right]^{-1}\left[\bar{\mathbf{K}}^2\right]$. □

9.10 Summary

The chapter extends the conventional methods for linear classification to kernel methods for nonlinear classification. Without involving regularization, least-squares-error (LSE) classifiers and Fisher's linear discriminant analysis (FDA) can be applied to the kernel-induced intrinsic space. This is a direct formulation of the kernel-based LSE and kernel discriminant analysis (KDA) classifiers. By taking regularization into account, the two classifiers can be further extended to *kernel ridge regression* (KRR) and *perturbational discriminant analysis* (PDA), respectively. This chapter also formally establishes the equivalence of KRR, LS-SVM, and PDA. For simplicity, we shall use the term KRR to represent these three equivalent learning models. The robustness analysis would be best conducted in the *spectral space* because the spectral components are mutually orthogonal and, consequently, the perturbation effect on each of the components can be isolated componentwise to facilitate individual sensitivity analysis.

This chapter examines the characteristics of KRR's WEC, which suggests that detrimental training vectors should be pruned so as to avoid unwanted influence from those training vectors. This leads to a pruned-KRR learning model, called PPDA. The chapter addressed how binary classification models may be naturally extended to multi-classification and, more advanced, to multi-label classification problems. Finally, this chapter also proposed several trace-norm optimization formulations for subspace projection designed for class discrimination. DCA and SODA are presented; both of them may be viewed as hybrid learning models of PCA and FDA.

[5] When $[\mathbf{K}_W + \rho\bar{\mathbf{K}}]$ is singular, then $\mathbf{D}_{\text{KDCA}} \equiv \left[\mathbf{K}_W + \rho\bar{\mathbf{K}}\right]^{+}\left[\bar{\mathbf{K}}^2\right]$.

9.11 Problems

Problem 9.1 *Show that the XOR dataset is separable*

(i) *by a hyperbolic decision boundary,*

$$f(\mathbf{x}) = 4x^{(1)}x^{(2)} - 2x^{(1)} - 2x^{(2)} + 1.5 = 0;$$

(ii) *by an elliptic decision boundary,*

$$f(\mathbf{x}) = 6(x^{(1)})^2 + 6(x^{(2)})^2 + 8x^{(1)}x^{(2)} - 10x^{(1)} - 10x^{(2)} + 3 = 0;$$

(iii) *or by a Gaussian function,*

$$f(\mathbf{x}) = \left(e^{2x^{(1)}} - e^{-2x^{(1)}}\right)\left(e^{2x^{(2)}} - e^{-2x^{(2)}}\right) = 0.$$

Problem 9.2 *Consider a dataset with two positive training vectors ($[0\ 0]^{\mathrm{T}}$ and $[0\ 2]^{\mathrm{T}}$) and three negative training vectors ($[0\ -1]^{\mathrm{T}}$, $[0\ 1]^{\mathrm{T}}$, and $[0.5\ 0.5]^{\mathrm{T}}$). Can the training dataset be made perfectly separable by adopting a second-order polynomial kernel function?*

Problem 9.3 (Linear system solver (LSS) versus kernel perceptron) *Suppose that an RBF kernel is used and that the training set does not contain any repeated samples.*

(a) *Show that, in this case, the data will always be linearly separable in the intrinsic space, making it feasible to apply a kernel perceptron algorithm to separate the two classes of training vectors [72].*
(b) *Moreover, the kernel matrix* $\mathbf{K}$ *will be generically invertible, rendering it amenable to application of the linear system solver (LSS), i.e.* $\mathbf{a} = \mathbf{K}^{-1}\mathbf{y}$. *Show that such a solution can perfectly separate the two classes of training vectors.*
(c) *Compare the numerical efficiencies of the two approaches.*

Problem 9.4 *Note that the generic rank of the kernel matrix is* $\min\{J, N\}$. *Show that the condition* $J \geq N$ *is necessary (and generically sufficient) so as to assure that* $\mathbf{K} = \mathbf{\Phi}^{\mathrm{T}}\mathbf{\Phi}$ *is nonsingular and invertible. This implies that the order p must satisfy the condition that* $J = (M+p)!/(M!\,p!) \geq N$ *for the KDA learning algorithm to have a valid solution.*

Problem 9.5 *Consider a generically distributed training dataset, with no overlapping or otherwise pathologically distributed training patterns.*

(a) *Show that, theoretically speaking, the dataset can be perfectly separated by a Gaussian-based KDA.*
(b) *Show that the dataset can be perfectly separated by a polynomial-based KDA, assuming that a sufficiently high polynomial order is adopted.*

Hint: *Show that, generically speaking, the kernel matrix* $\mathbf{K}$ *will be nonsingular, which in turn implies the existence of a numerical solution for KDA.*

Problem 9.6 (Decision components in spectral space) *Consider a second-order polynomial supervised learning model for the following dataset:*

$$\mathbf{x}_1 = \begin{bmatrix} +1 \\ +0.5 \end{bmatrix}, \quad \mathbf{x}_2 = \begin{bmatrix} -0.5 \\ -1 \end{bmatrix},$$
$$\mathbf{x}_3 = \begin{bmatrix} +1 \\ -0.5 \end{bmatrix}, \quad \mathbf{x}_4 = \begin{bmatrix} -0.5 \\ +1 \end{bmatrix}.$$

(a) *Find the spectral-space representation for the data set.*

(b) *Which spectral component is most effective for discriminating* $(\mathbf{x}_1, \mathbf{x}_3)$ *from* $(\mathbf{x}_2, \mathbf{x}_4)$*? Find its optimal KDA solution.*

(c) *Which spectral component is most effective for discriminating* $(\mathbf{x}_1, \mathbf{x}_4)$ *from* $(\mathbf{x}_2, \mathbf{x}_3)$*. Find its optimal KDA solution.*

Problem 9.7 *Consider the modified XOR datasets in Problem 9.6. Show that the same optimal solution can be obtained via either the intrinsic space* $\mathcal{H}$ *or the spectral space* $\mathcal{S}$*. Find the solution which yields a maximum margin of separation of the two different classes.*

Problem 9.8 (Maximal separation margin in empirical space) *In order to maximize the separation margin in the empirical space, an optimizer is designed to find*

$$\min_{\mathbf{a}} \left\{ \frac{1}{2} \|\mathbf{a}\|^2 \right\}$$
$$\text{subject to} \quad \epsilon_i = 0 \ \forall i = 1, \ldots, N. \tag{9.122}$$

(a) *Show that its optimal solution can be obtained from the following matrix equation:*

$$\begin{bmatrix} \mathbf{K}^2 & \mathbf{e} \\ \mathbf{e}^{\mathrm{T}} & 0 \end{bmatrix} \begin{bmatrix} \mathbf{a} \\ b \end{bmatrix} = \begin{bmatrix} \mathbf{y} \\ 0 \end{bmatrix}. \tag{9.123}$$

(b) *Show that it has the following closed-form solution:*

$$\mathbf{a} = [\mathbf{K}^2 + \rho \mathbf{I}]^{-1}[\mathbf{y} - b\mathbf{e}], \quad \text{where } b = \frac{\mathbf{y}^{\mathrm{T}}[\mathbf{K}^2 + \rho \mathbf{I}]^{-1}\mathbf{e}}{\mathbf{e}^{\mathrm{T}}[\mathbf{K}^2 + \rho \mathbf{I}]^{-1}\mathbf{e}}. \tag{9.124}$$

(c) *Show that, by ignoring the variation in* b *due to* ρ*, we can obtain the following regression ratio for the ith component:*

$$\frac{\lambda_i^2}{\lambda_i^2 + \rho}.$$

Compare the regression ratios associated with the intrinsic-space PDA and the empirical-space PDA. Which classifier tends to suppress more the weaker decision components.

Problem 9.9 (PCA and FDA: isotropic case) *Show that the principal vector of PCA is equivalent to the FDA projection vector if and only if* $\mathbf{S}_{\mathrm{W}}$ *is isotropic.*

Problem 9.10 *Verify Eq. (9.94).*

Problem 9.11 (Case study: compare PCA, FDA, DCA, and SODA) *Consider the dataset in Example 8.6. Show that PCA, FDA, DCA($\rho = 0.01$), and SODA are respectively*

$$\mathbf{w}_{\text{PCA}} = \begin{bmatrix} 0.8761 \\ 0.4822 \end{bmatrix}, \qquad \mathbf{w}_{\text{FDA}} = \begin{bmatrix} 0 \\ 1.0 \end{bmatrix},$$
$$\mathbf{w}_{\text{DCA}} = \begin{bmatrix} 0.3402 \\ 0.9404 \end{bmatrix}, \qquad \mathbf{w}_{\text{SODA}} = \begin{bmatrix} 1.0 \\ 0 \end{bmatrix},$$

Which component is dominant in each of PCA, FDA, DCA, and SODA?

Problem 9.12 (Two types of SODA optimization criteria) *Consider four training vectors:*

$$\mathbf{x}_1 = \begin{bmatrix} 1.0 \\ 0.1 \end{bmatrix}, \quad \mathbf{x}_2 = \begin{bmatrix} 0.8 \\ 0.2 \end{bmatrix}, \quad \mathbf{x}_3 = \begin{bmatrix} -0.8 \\ -0.1 \end{bmatrix}, \quad \mathbf{x}_4 = \begin{bmatrix} -1.0 \\ -0.2 \end{bmatrix},$$

with teacher values $y_1 = -1$, $y_2 = -1$, $y_3 = +1$, and $y_4 = +1$.

(a) *Compute the in-between and within scatter matrices, $\mathbf{S}_B$ and $\mathbf{S}_W$ respectively.*

(b) *Use the SODA algorithm (Algorithm 9.3) to obtain the optimal solution for the sequential optimizer (Eq. (9.71)).*

(c) *Derive the optimal solution for the global optimizer (Eq. (9.70)) and compare it with the SODA solution.*

Problem 9.13 (Kernelized SODA (KSODA) and deflation method)

(a) *Show that the kernelized SODA (KSODA) optimizer has the following formulation to sequentially find $\mathbf{a}_1, \ldots, \mathbf{a}_k$:*

$$\begin{aligned} \underset{\mathbf{a}_i}{\text{maximize}} \quad & \frac{\mathbf{a}_i^{\mathrm{T}}\mathbf{M}\mathbf{a}_i}{\mathbf{a}_i^{\mathrm{T}}\mathbf{N}\mathbf{a}_i} \\ \textit{subject to} \quad & \mathbf{a}_i^{\mathrm{T}}\mathbf{K}\mathbf{a}_j = 0, \ \forall i \neq j \\ & \mathbf{a}_i^{\mathrm{T}}\mathbf{K}\mathbf{a}_i = 1 \\ & \mathbf{a}_i \in \text{Span}(\mathbf{N}). \end{aligned} \tag{9.125}$$

Determine the matrices $\mathbf{N}$ *and* $\mathbf{M}$.

(b) *Verify and complete the following KSODA algorithm. In particular, provide a proper definition for $\boldsymbol{\Delta}_{\text{empirical}}$.*
Initially, set $\mathbf{D}^{(1)} = \mathbf{K}^{-1}$ and, $\mathbf{Q}^{(1)} = \mathbf{N}^{+}$, then perform the following procedure recursively for $i = 1, \ldots, m$.

(i) *Compute $\mathbf{a}_i = \frac{\mathbf{F}^{(i)}}{\sqrt{(\mathbf{F}^{(i)})^{\mathrm{T}}\mathbf{K}\mathbf{F}^{(i)}}}$, where $\mathbf{F}^{(i)} = \mathbf{Q}^{(i)}\boldsymbol{\Delta}_{\theta}$*

(ii) *Apply the deflation operation:*

$$\mathbf{Q}^{(i+1)} = \mathbf{D}^{(i+1)}\mathbf{N}^{+}\mathbf{D}^{(i+1)}, \quad \textit{where } \mathbf{D}^{(i+1)} = \mathbf{D}^{(i)} - \mathbf{a}_i\mathbf{a}_i^{\mathrm{T}}.$$

Hint: *See [311b].*

Problem 9.14 *In Section 9.5 the robustness of the KRR classifier is analyzed with respect to spectral-space components, i.e. PCA or KPCA. Conduct a robustness analysis with respect to DCA or KDCA components.*

Problem 9.15 *A possible hybrid of DCA and SODA learning models is to replace the SODA's optimizing cost function by a PC-DCA-like function:*

$$\frac{\mathbf{w}_i^{\mathrm{T}}[\bar{\mathbf{S}} + \rho\mathbf{I}]\mathbf{w}_i}{\mathbf{w}_i^{\mathrm{T}}\mathbf{S}_{\mathrm{W}}\mathbf{w}_i}$$

subject to the same orthogonality constraint: $\mathbf{w}_i \perp \mathbf{w}_{1,\ldots,i-1}$.

(a) *Compare this (pure) maximizing learning model with the PC-DCA model.*

(b) *As another possible alternative, the cost function may be modified into a DCA-like function:*

$$\frac{\mathbf{w}_i^{\mathrm{T}}\bar{\mathbf{S}}\mathbf{w}_i}{\mathbf{w}_i^{\mathrm{T}}[\mathbf{S}_{\mathrm{W}} + \rho\mathbf{I}]\mathbf{w}_i}.$$

Let L denote the number of classes. At which stage of the sequentially optimizing procedure should the minimizing formulation be switched to a minimizer? Please explain.

(c) *Conduct a simulation study and compare the performances of the two hybrid models with PCA, PC-DCA, DCA, and SODA. Please use the UCI datasets (Iris, Wine, Liver, Glass, Yeast, and Red Wine Quality), cf. Section 9.6.*

Problem 9.16 (MATLAB simulation) *Given two classes of patterns with distributions* $p_1(x, y)$ *and* $p_2(x, y)$*, where for* p_1 *the mean and variance are, respectively,*

$$\vec{\mu}_1 = [1.0 \quad 1.0]^{\mathrm{T}} \text{ and } \Sigma_1 = \begin{bmatrix} 2.0 & 0.5 \\ 0.5 & 1.0 \end{bmatrix},$$

and for p_2 *the mean and variance are*

$$\vec{\mu}_1 = [-1.0 \quad -1.0]^{\mathrm{T}} \text{ and } \Sigma_1 = \begin{bmatrix} 1.0 & -1.0 \\ -1.0 & 2.0 \end{bmatrix},$$

write MATLAB code to generate 1000 patterns for each distribution.

Create a second-order polynomial kernel-based classifier to classify the data in these two classes. Find the classification accuracy and plot the decision boundary.

Problem 9.17 (MATLAB simulation) *Consider the following Gaussian kernel function:*

$$K(\mathbf{x}, \mathbf{x}_i) = \exp\left\{-\frac{\|\mathbf{x} - \mathbf{x}_i\|}{2\sigma^2}\right\}.$$

Conduct a simulation to study how the Gaussian KRR changes with σ*. In particular, study the case in which* σ *becomes extremely large, and compare the result of the extreme case with that for the case when a linear kernel is adopted for KRR.*

Part V

Support vector machines and variants

This part contains three chapters with the focus placed on support vector machines (SVM). The SVM learning model lies right at the heart of kernel methods. It has been a major driving force of modern machine learning technologies.

Chapter 10 is focused on the basic SVM learning theory, which relies on the identification of a set of "support vectors" via the well-known Karush–Kuhn–Tucker (KKT) condition. The "support vectors" are solely responsible for the formation of the decision boundary. The LSP is obviously valid for SVM learning models and the kernelized SVM learning models have exactly the same form for linear and nonlinear problems. This is evidenced by Algorithm 10.1.

Chapter 11 covers support-vector-based learning models aiming at outlier detection. The support vector regression (SVR), see Algorithm 11.1, aims at finding an approximating function to fit the training data under the guidance of teacher values. The chapter explores, in addition, several SVM-based learning models for outlier detection, including hyperplane OCSVM (Algorithm 11.2), hypersphere OCSVM (Algorithm 11.3), and SVC. For all these learning models, the fraction of outliers can be analytically estimated – a sharp contrast to the other SVM learning models. In fact, for Gaussian kernels, it can be shown that all three algorithms coincide with each other. However, when polynomial kernels are adopted, the translation-invariance property is a legitimate concern for the hyperplane-OCSVM learning models.

Chapter 12 introduces the notion of a weight–error curve (WEC) for characterization of kernelized supervised learning models, including KDA, KRR, SVM, and Ridge-SVM. Under the LSP condition, the decision vector can be "voted" as a weighted sum of training vectors in the intrinsic space – each vector is assigned a weight in voting. The weights can be obtained by solving the corresponding kernelized optimizer. In addition, each vector is also associated with an error, equal to its distance to the decision boundary in the intrinsic space. In short, given a learned classifier, each training vector has two characterizing parameters, weight and error, which together form a WEC. A particular concern with an SVM-type WEC lies in the steep transition for the weight to drop from its maximum value C to the minimum value 0. This might not bode well for the nearby training vectors since they are so close to the supporting zone and yet have no weight at all. A fairer scheme would be one allowing the voting weights to be gracefully reduced. This can be accomplished by employing a smooth transition ramp to gradually lower the weight from its maximal level to the minimal level. In this way, the nearby training vectors will be able to (rightfully) receive a pro-rata weight to vote on the decision boundary.

This leads to a hybrid classifier, named Ridge-SVM, see Algorithm 12.1. It can effectively rectify the concerns regarding KRR and SVM. More precisely, the weights of the two extreme ends of the WEC will be curbed by $C_{\max} = C$ and $C_{\min}$ respectively (i.e. following the SVM model), and the slope of the transition zone will be controlled by the ridge parameter ρ (i.e. following the KRR model). Ridge-SVM is endowed with a sufficient set of design parameters so as to embrace existing classifiers as its special cases, including KDA, KRR, and SVM. With properly adjusted parameters, Ridge-SVM is promising with regard to producing robust classifiers with improved generalization capability. This is evidenced by numerous experimental studies.

10 Support vector machines

10.1 Introduction

In Chapter 8, it is shown that the kernel ridge regressor (KRR) offers a unified treatment for over-determined and under-determined systems. Another way of achieving unification of these two linear systems approaches is by means of the support vector machine (SVM) learning model proposed by Vapnik [41, 280, 281].

- Just like FDA, the objective of SVM aims at the separation of two classes. FDA is focused on the separation of the positive and negative centroids with the total data distribution taken into account. In contrast, SVM aims at the separation of only the so-called support vectors, i.e. only those which are deemed critical for class separation.
- Just like ridge regression, the objective of the SVM classifier also involves minimization of the two-norm of the decision vector.

The key component in SVM learning is to identify a set of representative training vectors deemed to be most useful for shaping the (linear or nonlinear) decision boundary. These training vectors are called "support vectors." The rest of the training vectors are called non-support vectors. Note that only support vectors can directly take part in the characterization of the decision boundary of the SVM.

SVM has successfully been applied to an enormously broad spectrum of application domains, including signal processing and classification, image retrieval, multimedia, fault detection, communication, computer vision, security/authentication, time-series prediction, biomedical prediction, and bioinformatics. For a few examples, see [29, 33b, 35, 74, 89, 97, 99b, 103, 109, 113, 173, 182, 186, 209, 243, 254, 270, 271, 316].

This chapter will address the following topics.

(i) Section 10.2 derives linear support vector machines (SVM) for binary classification. The main objective is again to create a maximum margin to separate the two opposite classes – just like in the previous formulation used for the under-determined systems. The key component in SVM learning is to identify a set of representative training vectors deemed to be most useful for shaping the (linear or nonlinear) decision boundary. These training vectors are called "support vectors," and, for SVM, only support vectors need to lie right on the marginal hyperplanes.

(ii) Section 10.3 extends the basic SVM algorithm to the classification of dataset with fuzzy separation.

(iii) Section 10.4 extends the linear SVM to its nonlinear variant. By imposing additional constraints on the Lagrangian multipliers, parameterized by a penalty factor C, a robust nonlinear SVM can be obtained from the same optimization formulation.

(iv) In Section 10.5, some application studies for multi-class SVMs are presented. Training and prediction accuracies are compared. In addition, the relationship between prediction accuracy and the size of the training dataset is explored.

(v) Section 10.6 examines the possibility of reducing the dimension of the empirical space by trimming the support vectors. The objective of the proposed trimming algorithm, VIA-SVM, is to ultimately retain only a small subset of the training vectors and yet produce a high-performance decision rule. This may further lower the classification complexity.

10.2 Linear support vector machines

Given a two-class training dataset $\mathcal{T} \equiv [\mathcal{X}, \mathcal{Y}] = \{[\mathbf{x}_1, y_1], [\mathbf{x}_2, y_2], \ldots, [\mathbf{x}_N, y_N]\}$, a basic SVM learning model is to find two parallel marginal hyperplanes to separate the positive and negative training vectors. Ideally, the two parallel hyperplanes should cleanly separate the two classes, with the positive vectors falling on one side of the first hyperplane, while the negative vectors fall on the other side of the second hyperplane. The marginal hyperplanes are exemplified by the two dashed lines in Figure 10.1, wherein the decision boundary of the linear classifier is highlighted as the solid line. The region between the two hyperplanes serves as the safety zone. The *safety margin* created by the zone can be measured by the distance d between a marginal hyperplane (i.e. one of the two dashed lines) and the decision boundary (i.e. the solid line).

SVM with perfect linear separability

Recall that the objective of a linear learning model introduced earlier is to find a decision vector $\mathbf{w}$ to yield an error-free solution so as to satisfy the strict equalities prescribed by

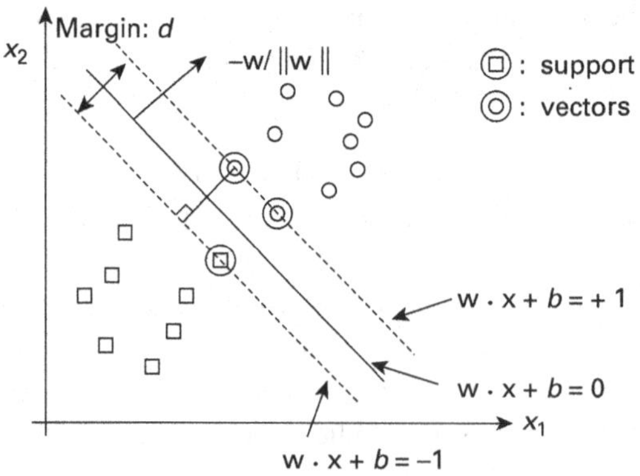

Fig. 10.1. An illustration of support vectors and the corresponding marginal hyperplanes in SVM. (b) The *marginal hyperplanes* are shown as the two dashed lines, prescribed by Eqs. (10.12) and (10.13). The decision hyperplane is shown as the solid line.

Eq. (8.37). In this respect, the SVM formulation has a different objective in that the strict equalities are now relaxed into inequalities:

$$\mathbf{w}^{\mathrm{T}}\mathbf{x}_i + b \geq +1 \text{ for all positive training vectors} \tag{10.1}$$

and

$$\mathbf{w}^{\mathrm{T}}\mathbf{x}_i + b \leq -1 \text{ for all negative training vectors.} \tag{10.2}$$

The two inequalities may be more concisely expressed by a single constraint:

$$y_i(\mathbf{w}^{\mathrm{T}}\mathbf{x}_i + b - y_i) \geq 0 \quad \forall i = 1, \ldots, N. \tag{10.3}$$

With the relaxed condition, SVM offers a unifying learning paradigm that is applicable both to under-determined ($M \geq N$) and to over-determined ($N > M$) scenarios.

10.2.1 The optimization formulation in original vector space

Just like in the previous learning models, the error term ϵ_i corresponding to a training vector, say $\mathbf{x}_i$, is denoted as

$$\epsilon_i \equiv \mathbf{w}^{\mathrm{T}}\mathbf{x}_i + b - y_i.$$

The constraint prescribed by Eq. (10.3) becomes

$$y_i\epsilon_i = y_i(\mathbf{w}^{\mathrm{T}}\mathbf{x}_i + b - y_i) \geq 0 \quad \forall i = 1, \ldots, N.$$

The training objective is to maximize the separation margin $2/\|\mathbf{w}\|$ by minimizing $\|\mathbf{w}\|$ under the constraints. This leads to the following optimization formulation [24, 280, 281]:

$$\begin{aligned} &\min_{\mathbf{w}}\{\tfrac{1}{2}\|\mathbf{w}\|^2\} \\ &\text{subject to the constraint } y_i\epsilon_i \geq 0 \; \forall i = 1, \ldots, N. \end{aligned} \tag{10.4}$$

10.2.2 The Wolfe dual optimizer in empirical space

The formulation in Eq. (10.4) is a *quadratic programming* optimization problem solvable by using standard convex optimization techniques [280, 281]. More specifically, a Lagrangian function can be derived as

$$L'(\mathbf{w}, b, \boldsymbol{\alpha}) = \frac{1}{2}\|\mathbf{w}\|^2 - \sum_{i=1}^{N} \alpha_i y_i \epsilon_i, \tag{10.5}$$

where the Lagrange multipliers α_i must be non-negative, i.e.

$$\alpha_i \geq 0, \tag{10.6}$$

so as to ensure that $y_i\epsilon_i = y_i(\mathbf{w}^{\mathrm{T}}\mathbf{x}_i + b) - 1 \geq 0$.

By zeroing the first-order gradients of $L'(\mathbf{w}, b, \boldsymbol{\alpha})$ with respect to $\mathbf{w}$, we can establish the LSP:

$$\mathbf{w} = \sum_{i=1}^{N} \alpha_i y_i \mathbf{x}_i. \tag{10.7}$$

For SVM, this has been the standard approach to verification of the LSP. It should be obvious that the optimization formulation in Eq. (10.4) meets the conditions prescribed by Theorem 1.1, thus providing an independent verification of the LSP.

In addition, by zeroing the first-order directive of $L'(\mathbf{w}, b, \boldsymbol{\alpha})$ with respect to b, we obtain the following orthogonal-hyperplane property (OHP) condition:

$$\sum_{i=1}^{N} \alpha_i y_i = 0. \tag{10.8}$$

Substituting Eqs. (10.7) and (10.8) into Eq. (10.5) results in a simplified expression:

$$L'(\boldsymbol{\alpha}) = \sum_{i=1}^{N} \alpha_i - \frac{1}{2} \sum_{i=1}^{N} \sum_{j=1}^{N} \alpha_i \alpha_j y_i y_j (\mathbf{x}_i^{\mathrm{T}} \mathbf{x}_j). \tag{10.9}$$

Wolfe dual optimization

Let us denote $a_i \equiv \alpha_i y_i$, for $i = 1, \ldots, N$. Then the SVM's objective function may be rewritten as follows:

$$L'(\boldsymbol{\alpha}) = \sum_{i=1}^{N} a_i y_i - \frac{1}{2} \sum_{i=1}^{N} \sum_{j=1}^{N} a_i a_j K_{ij} = \mathbf{a}^{\mathrm{T}} \mathbf{y} - \frac{1}{2} \mathbf{a}^{\mathrm{T}} \mathbf{K} \mathbf{a} = L(\mathbf{a}),$$

where $\mathbf{K}$ is the kernel matrix and $\mathbf{a} = [a_1\ a_2\ \ldots\ a_N]^{\mathrm{T}}$ is the decision vector in the empirical space. Note that the OHP constraint in Eq. (10.8) can be substituted by a new OHP condition, i.e.

$$\sum_{i=1}^{N} \alpha_i y_i = \sum_{i=1}^{N} a_i = \mathbf{e}^{\mathrm{T}} \mathbf{a} = 0.$$

This leads to the following Wolfe dual-optimization formulation in terms of the empirical decision vector $\mathbf{a}$:

$$\begin{aligned} &\max_{\mathbf{a}} L(\mathbf{a}) = \max_{\mathbf{a}} \{\mathbf{a}^{\mathrm{T}} \mathbf{y} - \frac{1}{2} \mathbf{a}^{\mathrm{T}} \mathbf{K} \mathbf{a}\}, \\ &\text{subject to the OHP condition } \mathbf{e}^{\mathrm{T}} \mathbf{a} = 0 \\ &\text{and the sign constraint } a_i y_i \geq 0\ i = 1, \ldots, N. \end{aligned} \tag{10.10}$$

Note that the sign constraint that $a_i y_i \geq 0$ is necessary due to Eq. (10.6). However, if we momentarily turn a blind eye on the sign constraint, then we simply need to account for the OHP constraint $\mathbf{e}^{\mathrm{T}} \mathbf{a} = 0$. By adopting a Lagrange multiplier, say b, for the OHP constraint, we arrive at a new Lagrangian function:

$$F(\mathbf{a}, b) = L(\mathbf{a}) - b\mathbf{e}^{\mathrm{T}} \mathbf{a} = -\frac{1}{2} \mathbf{a}^{\mathrm{T}} \mathbf{K} \mathbf{a} + \mathbf{a}^{\mathrm{T}} (\mathbf{y} - b\mathbf{e}).$$

On taking the first-order gradients of $F(\mathbf{a}, b)$ with respect to $\{a_i\}$ and b and equalizing them to zero, we obtain

$$\begin{cases} \sum_{j=1}^{N} K_{ij} a_j + b - y_i = 0, & \text{for } i \in \{1, 2, \ldots, N\}; \\ \sum_{j=1}^{N} a_j = 0. \end{cases}$$

This demonstrates the fact that an analytical solution would have been feasible if it were not bogged down by the sign constraint $a_i y_i \geq 0$.

Let us use a numerical example to show that the problem can be greatly simplified if only the sign constraint could be ignored.

Example 10.1 (SVM classifier of three three-dimensional (2D) training vectors) *Shown in Figure 10.2(a) are three training vectors:*

$$\mathbf{x}_1 = [0.0\ 0.0]^{\mathrm{T}}, \quad y_1 = -1,$$
$$\mathbf{x}_2 = [1.0\ 0.0]^{\mathrm{T}}, \quad y_2 = +1,$$
$$\mathbf{x}_3 = [0.0\ 1.0]^{\mathrm{T}}, \quad y_3 = +1.$$

According to Eq. (10.9), the objective function is now

$$L(\boldsymbol{\alpha}) = \sum_{i=1}^{3} \alpha_i - \frac{1}{2} \sum_{i=1}^{3} \sum_{j=1}^{3} \alpha_i \alpha_j y_i y_j (\mathbf{x}_i^{\mathrm{T}} \mathbf{x}_j) \tag{10.11}$$

subject to $\alpha_i \geq 0$ and $\sum_{i=1}^{3} \alpha_i y_i = 0$. For the equality constraint $\sum_{i=1}^{3} \alpha_i y_i = 0$, a Lagrange multiplier, say b, can be introduced to result in a new Lagrangian function:

$$F(\boldsymbol{\alpha}, b) = L(\boldsymbol{\alpha}) - b \sum_{i=1}^{3} \alpha_i y_i$$
$$= \alpha_1 + \alpha_2 + \alpha_3 - \frac{1}{2}\alpha_2^2 - \frac{1}{2}\alpha_3^2 - b(-\alpha_1 + \alpha_2 + \alpha_3).$$

On taking the first-order gradients of $F(\alpha, b)$ with respect to α_i and b and equalizing them to zero, we obtain

$$1 + b = 0,$$
$$1 - \alpha_2 - b = 0,$$
$$1 - \alpha_3 - b = 0,$$
$$-\alpha_1 + \alpha_2 + \alpha_3 = 0.$$

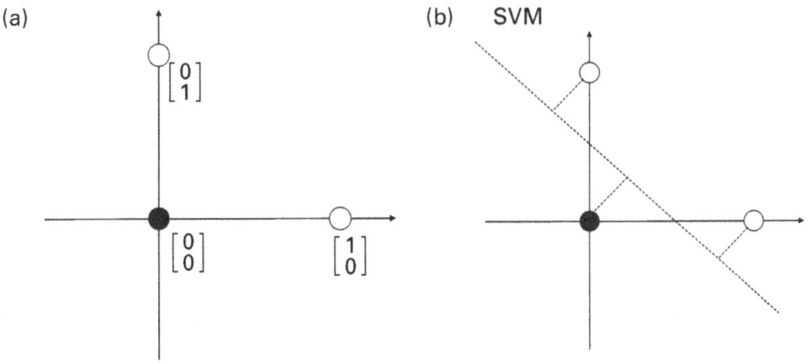

Fig. 10.2. A simple SVM classification. (a) The dataset. (b) The decision boundary of the SVM classification. In this case, all three training data are support vectors.

This yields $\alpha_1 = 4$, *and* $\alpha_2 = 2$, $\alpha_3 = 2$, *and the threshold* $b = -1$. *As shown by the dashed line in Figure 10.2(b), the decision boundary is*

$$\mathbf{w}^{\mathrm{T}}\mathbf{x} + b = 0 \Rightarrow \begin{bmatrix} 2 & 2 \end{bmatrix} \begin{bmatrix} x^{(1)} \\ x^{(2)} \end{bmatrix} - 1 = 0.$$

In general, the SVM solution cannot be directly obtained by solving Eq. (10.11). According to the KKT condition, Eq. (10.11) is only partially valid. More precisely, it holds for rows associated with the support vectors, but is invalid for rows associated with non-support vectors.

For the above numerical example, all three training vectors happen to be support vectors; thus the sign constraint $a_i y_i \geq 0, i = 1, 2, 3$, is automatically satisfied, making available an analytical solution by simply solving a set of linear equations. In general, enforcement of the sign constraint often incurs a tedious numerical procedure that has no closed-form solution. Such a procedure is necessary for identification of the support vectors and non-support vectors in SVM.

10.2.3 The Karush–Kuhn–Tucker (KKT) condition

In the SVM learning model, the equality prescribed by Eq. (10.11) is good only for a selective subset of the training vectors. The training vectors associated with this subset will be named *support vectors*, while the remaining training vectors will be termed *non-support vectors*.

More precisely, the positive training vectors can be subdivided as follows: (1) the support vectors which must satisfy the exact error-free equality

$$\mathbf{w}^{\mathrm{T}}\mathbf{x}_i + b = +1; \tag{10.12}$$

and (2) the non-supporting vectors satisfying the inequality

$$\mathbf{w}^{\mathrm{T}}\mathbf{x}_i + b > +1.$$

Likewise, the negative training vectors can be similarly subdivided: (1) the support vectors which satisfy the equality

$$\mathbf{w}^{\mathrm{T}}\mathbf{x}_i + b = -1; \tag{10.13}$$

and (2) the non-supporting ones satisfying the inequality

$$\mathbf{w}^{\mathrm{T}}\mathbf{x}_i + b < -1.$$

As will become clear presently, the support vectors are those associated with $\alpha_i > 0$, while the non-support vectors are those associated with $\alpha_i = 0$. Therefore, only the support vectors have an active role in defining the discriminant function, see Eq. (10.19).

For notational convenience, the indices of support vectors are denoted by $i \in \{i_1, \ldots, i_S\}$, where S denotes the number of support vectors. The identification of the optimal subset of support vectors plays a key role in the SVM learning model. In other words, if such subset were known, the solution would have been obtainable by simply solving the following set of equalities:

$$\begin{cases} \sum_{j=1}^{N} K_{ij} a_j + b - y_i = 0, \quad \text{for} \quad i \in \{i_1, \ldots, i_S\}; \\ \sum_{j=1}^{N} a_j = 0. \end{cases}$$

10.2.4 Support vectors

According to the well-known Karush–Kuhn–Tucker (KKT) condition in optimization theory [17, 69], an optimal solution must satisfy the following equality:

$$\alpha_i \epsilon_i = \alpha_i \left((\mathbf{w}^{\mathrm{T}} \mathbf{x}_i + b) - y_i \right) = 0, \quad \text{for } i = 1, 2, \ldots, N, \tag{10.14}$$

for all of the training vectors. This effectively divides the constraints into two categories.

- *Support vectors.* Vectors with $a_k \neq 0$ (i.e. $\alpha_k > 0$) are called *support vectors*. When $\alpha_k > 0$, the corresponding training vectors must satisfy

$$\epsilon_k = \mathbf{w}^{\mathrm{T}} \mathbf{x}_k + b - y_k = 0. \tag{10.15}$$

  Therefore, the support vector $\mathbf{x}_k$ lies right on the error-free *marginal hyperplanes*: $\mathbf{w}^{\mathrm{T}} \mathbf{x}_k + b = y_k$. These are also known as the *supporting hyperplanes* [239]. Equivalently, by making use of the LSP in Eq. (10.7), we obtain

$$\sum_j a_j \mathbf{x}_j^{\mathrm{T}} \mathbf{x}_k + b - y_k = \sum_j K_{jk} a_j + b - y_k = 0. \tag{10.16}$$

  In short, the kth training vector $\mathbf{x}_k$ qualifies as a support vector *only if* $\epsilon_k = 0$.
- *Non-support vectors.* If $a_k = 0$, then the KKT condition (Eq. (10.14)) will always be met regardless whether $\epsilon_k = 0$ or $\epsilon_k \neq 0$. This further implies that the kth training vector will not be directly involved in shaping the decision boundary. For this very reason, the kth training vector $\mathbf{x}_k$ shall be labeled as a *non-support vector*.

The difficulty in solving the Wolfe dual optimization, given in Eq. (10.10), lies in correctly identifying a proper set of the support vectors.

The decision boundary

Once the multipliers $\{\alpha_i\}$ have been determined, the decision vector $\mathbf{w}$ can be obtained from Eq. (10.7):

$$\mathbf{w} = \sum_{i=1}^{N} \alpha_i y_i \mathbf{x}_i. \tag{10.17}$$

The threshold b can be derived as

$$b = 1 - \mathbf{w}^{\mathrm{T}} \mathbf{x}_k, \tag{10.18}$$

where $\mathbf{x}_k$ is any support vector that lies exactly on the positive error-free plane $\mathbf{w}^{\mathrm{T}} \mathbf{x} + b = 1$.

It follows that the discriminant function can be expressed as

$$f(\mathbf{x}) = \mathbf{w}^{\mathrm{T}}\mathbf{x} + b = \sum_{i=1}^{N} y_i \alpha_i (\mathbf{x}^{\mathrm{T}}\mathbf{x}_i) + b, \tag{10.19}$$

and the decision boundary is characterized by $f(\mathbf{x}) = 0$.

Let us now explore a numerical example to help illustrate the critical roles played by the KKT condition.

Example 10.2 (SVM classifier of four 2D training vectors) *For the dataset shown in Figure 10.3, there are four training vectors*

$$\begin{aligned} \mathbf{x}_1 &= [-0.2 \quad 0.0]^{\mathrm{T}} & y_1 &= -1, \\ \mathbf{x}_2 &= [0.0 \quad 0.0]^{\mathrm{T}} & y_2 &= -1, \\ \mathbf{x}_3 &= [0.0 \quad 1.0]^{\mathrm{T}} & y_3 &= +1, \\ \mathbf{x}_4 &= [1.0 \quad 0.0]^{\mathrm{T}} & y_4 &= +1. \end{aligned}$$

The data matrix is

$$\mathbf{X} = \begin{bmatrix} -0.2 & 0 & 0 & 1 \\ 0 & 0 & 1 & 0 \end{bmatrix}.$$

The corresponding linear kernel matrix is

$$\mathbf{K} = \mathbf{X}^{\mathrm{T}}\mathbf{X} = \begin{bmatrix} 0.04 & 0 & 0 & -0.2 \\ 0 & 0 & 0 & 0 \\ 0 & 0 & 1 & 0 \\ -0.2 & 0 & 0 & 1 \end{bmatrix}.$$

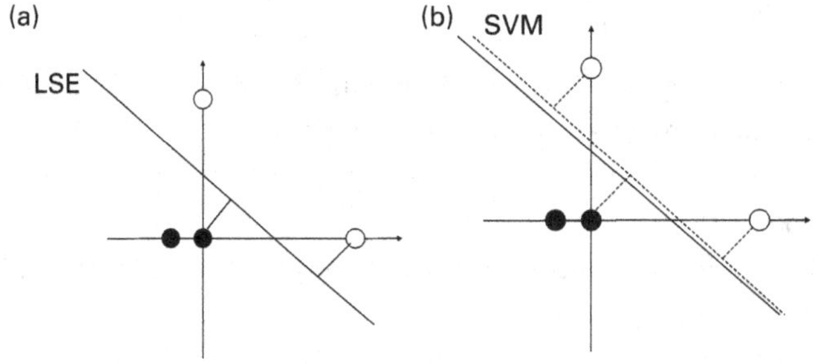

Fig. 10.3. Comparison of two separation margins shows that the SVM classifier yields a wider margin than the LSE classifier. (a) For the LSE classifier, the positive and negative margins are shown as solid lines. While the decision boundary is jointly determined by all four training vectors, the positive (or negative) safety margin is dictated by the positive (or negative) training pattern which is closest to the decision boundary. (b) The decision boundary of the SVM classifier is dictated by the three support vectors. For SVM, the positive and negative margins (shown as dashed lines) are always identical.

This leads to the following Lagrangian:

$$F(\alpha, b) = \alpha_1 + \alpha_2 + \alpha_3 + \alpha_4 - 0.02\alpha_1^2 - \frac{1}{2}\alpha_3^2 - \frac{1}{2}\alpha_4^2 - 0.2\alpha_1\alpha_4$$
$$-b(-\alpha_1 - \alpha_2 + \alpha_3 + \alpha_4). \quad (10.20)$$

By zeroing the first-order derivatives of the Lagrangian with respect to α_i *and* b*, we obtain*

$$\begin{aligned} 1 - 0.04\alpha_1 - 0.2\alpha_4 + b &= 0, \\ 1 + b &= 0, \\ 1 - \alpha_3 - b &= 0, \\ 1 - 0.2\alpha_1 - \alpha_4 - b &= 0, \\ -\alpha_1 - \alpha_2 + \alpha_3 + \alpha_4 &= 0. \end{aligned}$$

The linear system of equations admits no feasible solution. However, with the assistance of the additional knowledge that one of the training vectors, say $\mathbf{x}_1$*, may be a non-support vector, then, by virtue of the KKT condition, its corresponding multiplier has to be zero, i.e.* $\alpha_1 = 0$*. More importantly, according to the KKT condition, the derivative of* $F(\alpha, b)$ *with respect to* α_1 *is not required to be zero, and thus the constraint imposed by the first equation above can now be ignored. By solving for the remaining four equations, we can obtain a feasible solution:*

$$\alpha_2 = 4, \alpha_3 = 2, \alpha_4 = 2, \text{ and } b = -1.$$

It follows that the decision vector $\mathbf{w}$ *is*

$$\mathbf{w} = \sum_{i=2}^{4} \alpha_i y_i \mathbf{x}_i = -4\begin{bmatrix} 0 \\ 0 \end{bmatrix} + 2\begin{bmatrix} 1 \\ 0 \end{bmatrix} + 2\begin{bmatrix} 0 \\ 1 \end{bmatrix} = \begin{bmatrix} 2 \\ 2 \end{bmatrix}.$$

Finally, as depicted in Figure 10.3(b), the decision boundary is

$$2x^{(1)} + 2x^{(2)} - 1 = 0.$$

10.2.5 Comparison between separation margins of LSE and SVM

As theoretically intended, SVM yields an optimal separation margin between the two classes. In particular, it should have a better margin than its LSE counterpart. This result can be verified by comparing the classifiers obtained via LSE (Example 8.1) versus SVM (Example 10.2). For the dataset (with four 2D training vectors), SVM holds a slight advantage over LSE. The decision boundaries and the separation margins for both classifiers are displayed in Figure 10.3. The following example provides a more detailed comparison.

Example 10.3 (Comparison between LSE and SVM classifiers) *For the dataset (with four 2D training vectors) given in Example 10.2, we have the following observations.*

- *For the LSE classifier (Example 8.1), the decision boundary is prescribed by*

$$1.774x^{(1)} + 1.806x^{(2)} - 0.806 = 0.$$

The positive and negative safety margins are shown as the two short solid lines in Figure 10.3(a). The safety margin of the positive class is dictated by the closest positive training pattern to the decision boundary. The margin of the negative class is defined in a similar fashion. For this example, the two margins can be computed as 0.382 *and* 0.318, *respectively. The average is equal to* 0.35.

- *For the SVM classifier, the decision boundary is prescribed by*

$$2x^{(1)} + 2x^{(2)} - 1 = 0.$$

The positive and negative margins are shown as the dashed lines in Figure 10.3(b). Both margins have the same value: $1/2\sqrt{2} = 0.354$. *Note that* $0.354 > 0.35$, *so SVM holds a slight advantage over LSE in terms of the average margin.*

Let us present another example to illustrate the numerical comparison of FDA, RR, and SVM.

Example 10.4 (Case study: compare FDA, RR, and SVM) *Consider the same dataset as in Example 8.6. There are four training vectors:*

$$\mathbf{x}_1 = \begin{bmatrix} 1.0 \\ 0.1 \end{bmatrix}, \quad \mathbf{x}_2 = \begin{bmatrix} 0.8 \\ 0.1 \end{bmatrix}, \quad \mathbf{x}_3 = \begin{bmatrix} -0.8 \\ -0.1 \end{bmatrix}, \quad \mathbf{x}_4 = \begin{bmatrix} -1.0 \\ -0.1 \end{bmatrix}.$$

with teacher values $y_1 = -1$, $y_2 = -1$, $y_3 = +1$, *and* $y_4 = +1$.

The decision boundary of SVM is $8\mathbf{x}^{(1)} + \mathbf{x}^{(2)} = 0$, *with the first feature* $\mathbf{x}^{(1)}$ *dominating the decision rule. On the other hand, the decision boundary of LSE or FDA is* $\mathbf{x}^{(2)} = 0$, *with* $\mathbf{x}^{(2)}$ *as the only decision-making feature.*

For RR, the balance between the two features depends on the chosen value of ρ.

- *When* $0 \leq \rho < 32$, *the RR places more emphasis on the second feature* $\mathbf{x}^{(2)}$ *in comparison with SVM.*
- *When* $\rho = 32$, *the RR and SVM have exactly the same solution.*
- *When* $32 < \rho$, *the RR solution places a greater emphasis on the first feature* $\mathbf{x}^{(1)}$ *in comparison with SVM.*

By definition, SVM offers the widest separation margin between (any of) the positive and (any of) negative patterns after the training vectors have been projected along the decision vector. In this case, the SVM's separation margin is

$$\left(\frac{\mathbf{w}^{\mathrm{T}}}{\|\mathbf{w}\|}\right)(\mathbf{x}_2 - \mathbf{x}_3) = \frac{2}{\|\mathbf{w}\|} = 1.6125,$$

and no other classifiers can produce a wider post-projection separation between the positive and negative patterns. Recall that, when $\rho \to \infty$, the RR solution yields the widest post-projection separation width between the positive and negative centroids: $d_{\text{centroids}} = 1.8110$; see Eq. (8.61).

10.3 SVM with fuzzy separation: roles of slack variables

In real-world applications, the training vectors are unlikely to be clearly separable. Nevertheless, the same formulation based on maximum separability remains feasible as long as some selective training vectors are exempted, i.e. they are allowed to violate the minimum-margin rule. Obviously, the greater the number of exempted vectors the wider the separation margin. This is illustrated by Figure 10.4. First, we note that there was a clear margin (between the thin solid lines) characterized by three original support vectors. However, a considerably wider separation zone (between the dashed lines) can be created by artificially exempting the six violating training vectors. Nevertheless, a good majority of the training vectors is still clearly separable, and these vectors are kept outside the forbidden zone. These vectors will be viewed as non-support vectors for the fuzzy SVM classifier.

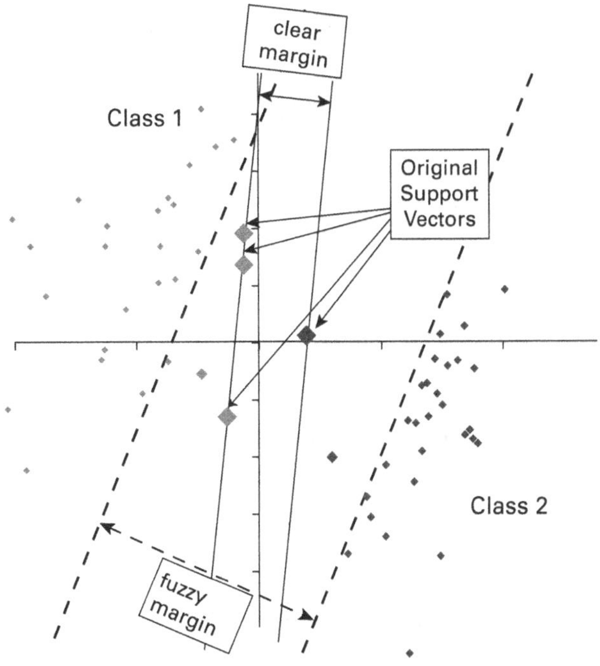

Fig. 10.4. This figure illustrates how a wider separation margin may be created by allowing some violations.

10.3.1 Optimization in original space

In the fuzzy SVM, a set of positive *slack variables* $\{\xi_i\}_{i=1}^N$ is used to relax the hard constraint $y_i\epsilon_i \geq 0$ prescribed by Eq. (10.4). With the slack variables, we obtain the following soft constraints:

$$y_i\epsilon_i + \xi_i \geq 0 \quad \forall i = 1, \ldots, N, \tag{10.21}$$

where $\epsilon_i = \mathbf{w}^{\mathrm{T}}\mathbf{x}_i + b - y_i$.

To discourage excessive relaxation, a penalty term $C\sum_i \xi_i$, where C is a pre-selected *penalty factor*, will be added to the original loss function (Eq. (10.4)), resulting in

$$\begin{gathered}\min_{\mathbf{w}} \left\{ \frac{1}{2}\|\mathbf{w}\|^2 + C\sum_{i=1}^{N} \xi_i \right\} \\ \text{subject to a set of soft constraints} \\ y_i\epsilon_i + \xi_i \geq 0, \text{ where } \epsilon_i = \mathbf{w}^{\mathrm{T}}\mathbf{x}_i + b - y_i \\ \text{and } \xi_i \geq 0, \ \forall i = 1, \ldots, N.\end{gathered} \tag{10.22}$$

Note again that Eq. (10.22) satisfies the condition prescribed by Theorem 1.1, which further assures the learning subspace property (LSP). The LSP may be reconfirmed via a standard optimization analysis elaborated below.

10.3.2 The learning subspace property and optimization in empirical space

The Lagrangian function corresponding to Eq. (10.22) becomes

$$L(\mathbf{w}, b, \boldsymbol{\alpha}, \boldsymbol{\beta}, \xi) = \frac{1}{2}\|\mathbf{w}\|^2 + C\sum_{i=1}^{N} \xi_i - \sum_{i=1}^{N} \alpha_i(y_i(\mathbf{x}_i^{\mathrm{T}}\mathbf{w} + b) - 1 + \xi_i) - \sum_{i=1}^{N} \beta_i\xi_i, \tag{10.23}$$

where two sets of Lagrange multipliers are being applied: (1) $\alpha_i \geq 0$ ensure that $y_i\epsilon_i + \xi_i \geq 0$ while (2) $\beta_i \geq 0$ ensure that $\xi_i \geq 0$.

The dual-optimization problem can be expressed as the following min–max formulation:

$$\underset{\{\boldsymbol{\alpha}, \boldsymbol{\beta}\} \in \mathbb{R}^N}{\text{maximize}} \left(\underset{\mathbf{w}, b, \xi \in \mathbb{R}^N}{\text{minimize}} \, L(\mathbf{w}, b, \boldsymbol{\alpha}, \boldsymbol{\beta}, \xi) \right),$$

where $\alpha_i \geq 0$, $\beta_i \geq 0$, and $\xi_i \geq 0$ for $i = 1, \ldots, N$.

By zeroing the first-order gradients of $L(\mathbf{w}, b, \boldsymbol{\alpha}, \boldsymbol{\beta}, \xi)$ with respect to $\mathbf{w}$, we obtain the LSP condition that

$$\mathbf{w} = \sum_{i=1}^{N} \alpha_i y_i \mathbf{x}_i. \tag{10.24}$$

By zeroing the first-order directive of $L(\mathbf{w}, b, \boldsymbol{\alpha}, \boldsymbol{\beta}, \xi)$ with respect to b, we obtain

$$\sum_{i=1}^{N} \alpha_i y_i = 0. \tag{10.25}$$

By zeroing the first-order directive of $L(\mathbf{w}, b, \boldsymbol{\alpha}, \boldsymbol{\beta}, \xi)$ with respect to ξ, we obtain

$$C - \alpha_i - \beta_i = 0. \tag{10.26}$$

Substituting Eqs. (10.24)–(10.26) into Eq. (10.23) results in a modified Wolfe dual-optimization formulation:

$$\max_{\boldsymbol{\alpha}} \sum_{i=1}^{N} \alpha_i - \frac{1}{2} \sum_{i=1}^{N} \sum_{j=1}^{N} \alpha_i \alpha_j y_i y_j (\mathbf{x}_i^{\mathrm{T}} \mathbf{x}_j) \tag{10.27}$$

subject to the constraints $\sum_{i=1}^{N} \alpha_i y_i = 0$ and $0 \leq \alpha_i \leq C$, $i = 1, \ldots, N$. (Note that the constraints are due to Eqs. (10.25) and (10.26), respectively.)

- Once α_i have been derived from Eq. (10.27), the vector $\mathbf{w}$ can be obtained from Eq. (10.24).
- The threshold b can be obtained from

$$b = y_k - \mathbf{w}^{\mathrm{T}} \mathbf{x}_k, \tag{10.28}$$

for any integer k such that $0 < \alpha_k < C$. (In this case, $\mathbf{x}_k$ is a support vector that lies exactly on the (positive or negative) error-free plane $\mathbf{w}^{\mathrm{T}} \mathbf{x} + b = y_i$.)

Thereafter, the decision boundary can be derived as follows:

$$f(\mathbf{x}) = \mathbf{w}^{\mathrm{T}} \mathbf{x} + b = \sum_{i=1}^{N} y_i \alpha_i (\mathbf{x}^{\mathrm{T}} \mathbf{x}_i) + b = \sum_{i=1}^{N} a_i (\mathbf{x}^{\mathrm{T}} \mathbf{x}_i) + b = 0. \tag{10.29}$$

Let the empirical decision vector $\mathbf{a}$ be the vector formed from $a_i = \alpha_i y_i$. Then the cost function in Eq. (10.27) may be expressed in terms of $\mathbf{a}$ and $\mathbf{K} = \{K_{ij}\}$ ($K_{ij} = \mathbf{x}_i^{\mathrm{T}} \mathbf{x}_j$):

$$\max_{\mathbf{a}} \mathbf{a}^{\mathrm{T}} \mathbf{y} - \frac{1}{2} \mathbf{a}^{\mathrm{T}} \mathbf{K} \mathbf{a} \tag{10.30}$$

subject to $\mathbf{e}^{\mathrm{T}} \mathbf{a} = 0$ and $0 \leq a_i y_i \leq C$, $i = 1, \ldots, N$.

Margin of separation versus C

The *margin of separation*, i.e. $d = 2/\|\mathbf{w}\|$, may be adjusted by changing the *penalty factor* C, whose effect on the margin of (fuzzy) separation is exemplified by Figure 10.5. Note that a larger value of C yields a narrower fuzzy separation zone, containing fewer SVs within the zone. In contrast, a smaller C yields a wider zone within which more SVs can be found. The optimal C depends very much on the data distribution and is often obtained by trial and error.

The penalty factor C also plays a major role in determining the robustness of the learned SVM model. When C is sufficiently small, it will create a respectably large pool of support vectors, with all of them participating in the decision making. This means that the resultant decision boundary becomes a consensus of a greater subset of training vectors. It is commonly believed that including more support vectors means that the

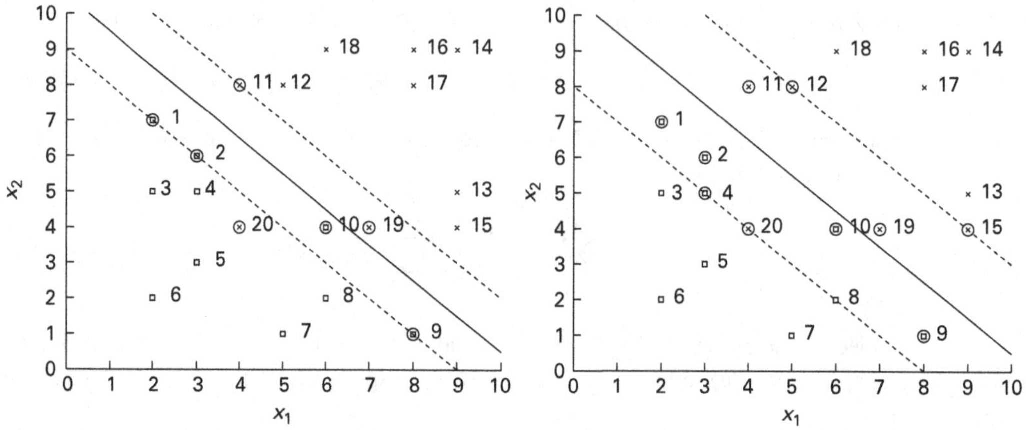

(a) Linear SVM: $C = 10$ (b) Linear SVM: $C = 0.1$

Fig. 10.5. Decision boundaries (solid lines) and marginal boundaries (dashed lines) created by linear SVMs for 20-point data. (a) A linear SVM with $C = 10$. (b) A linear SVM with $C = 0.1$. The decision boundaries are almost the same for the two cases. The region between the two dashed lines is considered the "fuzzy region." A small C creates a larger fuzzy region. The data set is from A. Schwaighofer [45].

classifier tends to be more robust in generalization capability. See Figure 10.11 for a demonstration of the role of C in practical applications.

Example 10.5 (Fuzzily separable dataset.) *In this example, a linear SVM is applied to classify 20 data points that are not linearly separable. Figure 10.5 depicts the two (slightly different) decision boundaries (shown as solid lines) and the two (very different) separation margins (bounded by two dashed lines) for* $C = 10$ *and* $C = 0.1$. *Note that most (but not all) support vectors lie on or between the marginal hyperplanes. It is evident that, when C is small, the separation margin is wider, allowing more support vectors.*

10.3.3 Characterization of support vectors and WEC analysis

For the clearly separable case, there is a very simple characterization of the support vectors. It is known that the kth training vector $\mathbf{x}_k$ qualifies as a support vector only if $\epsilon_k = 0$, where $\epsilon_k \equiv \mathbf{w}^{\mathrm{T}}\mathbf{x}_k + b - y_k$.

The KKT condition and support vectors

Both for the clearly separable and for the fuzzily separable cases, support vectors can be characterized by the simple fact that the ith training vector $\mathbf{x}_i$ is a support vector if and only if $\alpha_i = a_i y_i \neq 0$. Note that the KKT condition stated in Eq. (10.14), namely

$$\alpha_i \epsilon_i = \alpha_i \left((\mathbf{w}^{\mathrm{T}}\mathbf{x}_i + b) - y_i \right) = 0, \quad \text{for } i = 1, 2, \ldots, N, \tag{10.31}$$

or, equivalently,

$$\alpha_i y_i \epsilon_i = \alpha_i \left(y_i(\mathbf{w}^{\mathrm{T}}\mathbf{x}_i + b) - 1 \right) = 0, \quad \text{for } i = 1, 2, \ldots, N, \tag{10.32}$$

was valid only for clearly separable cases. For the fuzzily separable case, the KKT condition needs to be modified to

$$\alpha_i \{ y_i \epsilon_i + \xi_i \} = \alpha_i \left\{ y_i(\mathbf{w}^{\mathrm{T}}\mathbf{x}_i + b) - 1 + \xi_i \right\} = 0 \quad \forall i = 1, \ldots, N. \tag{10.33}$$

This results in a somewhat more complex characterization of the support and non-support vectors.

Characterization of support vectors

If the multiplier $\alpha_i \neq 0$, then the training vector $\mathbf{x}_i$ will be a support vector and it must strictly obey the equality

$$y_i(\mathbf{w}^{\mathrm{T}}\mathbf{x}_i + b) = 1 - \xi_i,$$

as opposed to the inequality given in Eq. (10.21). In Figure 10.5(b), points 1, 2, 4, 9, and 10 are SVs from the negative dataset, while points 11, 12, 15, 19, and 20 are SVs from the positive dataset.

- Strictly speaking, the condition $\epsilon_i y_i \leq 0$ is only a necessary condition (but not a sufficient one) for $\mathbf{x}_i$ to be a support vector.
- Generically and practically speaking, on the other hand, the condition $\epsilon_i y_i \leq 0$ may be considered to be both necessary and sufficient for $\mathbf{x}_i$ to be a support vector.[1]

Characterization of non-support vectors

If the multiplier $\alpha_i = 0$, this implies that $y_i f(\mathbf{x}_i) \geq 1$. In this case, the corresponding training vector $\mathbf{x}_i$ will be a non-support vector and will be kept outside the forbidden zone. In Figure 10.5(b), points 3, 5, 6, 7, and 8 are non-SVs from the negative dataset, while points 13, 14, 16, 17, and 18 are non-SVs from the positive dataset.

- Strictly speaking, the condition $\epsilon_i y_i > 0$ is only a sufficient condition (but not a necessary one) for $\mathbf{x}_i$ to be a non-support vector.
- Generically speaking, the condition $\alpha_i = 0$ is both necessary and sufficient for $\mathbf{x}_i$ to be a non-support vector.

In summary, as depicted in Figure 10.5, all the support vectors are characterized by two marginal hyperplanes, one defined by $f(\mathbf{x}) = 1$ (equivalently, $\epsilon = f(\mathbf{x}) - 1 = 0$) for positive training samples and one by $f(\mathbf{x}) = -1$ (equivalently, $\epsilon = f(\mathbf{x}) + 1 = 0$) for negative training samples. This leads to the WEC of SVM shown in Figure 10.6.

[1] For a positive training dataset, according to the KKT condition $\mathbf{x}_i$ is a support vector (SV) only if $\epsilon_i + \xi_i = 0$, which further implies that $\epsilon_i \leq 0$. However, $\epsilon_i \leq 0$ is almost a sufficient condition for $\mathbf{x}_i$ being an SV, since it is exempted for only (rare) pathological data distributions such as repeated or coplanar training vectors. Therefore, it is also generically a sufficient condition. (The argument for the negative dataset is similar.)

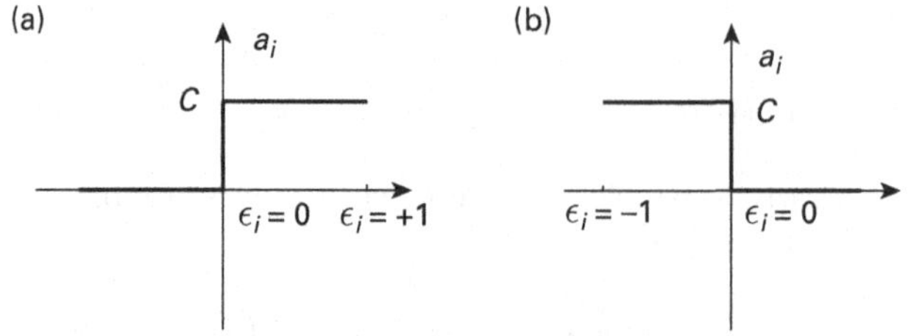

Fig. 10.6. The necessary (and generically sufficient) condition for $\mathbf{x}_i$ being a support vector is $\epsilon_i y_i < 0$. This is supported by the WECs pertaining to SVM. (a) WEC for negative training vectors. Since $y_i = -1$, the decision boundary is where $f(\mathbf{x}) = 0$, which corresponds to the point $\epsilon_i = f(\mathbf{x}_i) - y_i = f(\mathbf{x}) + 1 = +1$. (b) WEC for positive training vectors. Now that $y_i = +1$, the decision point corresponds to $\epsilon_i = f(\mathbf{x}_i) - y_i = f(\mathbf{x}_i) - 1 = -1$. When C is small, a good many support vectors have constant values $\alpha_i = C$. The only exception is for those corresponding to $\epsilon_i = 0$. The (open) separation zone may also be called the constant-α zone.

The WEC, KKT condition, and Lagrange Multipliers

The WEC shown in Figure 6 can be divided into three different regions: (a) the lower-flat region; (b) the vertical-line region; and (c) the upper-flat region. This division is closely related to the KKT condition and its associated Lagrange multipliers. It provides a simple characterization of the training vectors.

1. The division between non-support vectors and support vectors hinges upon the value of the Lagrange multipliers $\{ \alpha_i \}$. More precisely, the *ith* training vector is a support vector if and only if $\alpha_i > 0$.
2. Dependent upon the value of the Lagrange multipliers $\{ \beta_i \}$, the support vectors may be further divided into *marginal support vector* (MSVs) and *bounded support vectors* (BSVs). [16, 299b] More precisely:
   - **MSV**: A support vector, say the *ith* training vector, is an MSV if $\beta_i > 0$ In this case, according to Eq. (10.26), $0 < \alpha_i < C$. In terms of WEC, this vector falls on the vertical-line region, cf. Figure 10.6.
   - **BSV**: A support vector, say the *ith* training vector, is a BSV if $\beta_i = 0$ In this case, according to Eq. (10.26), $\alpha_i = C$. In terms of WEC, this vector falls on the upper-flat region (also known the constant-α zone), cf. Figure 10.6.

10.4 Kernel-induced support vector machines

To arrive at flexible decision boundaries, it is advisable to resort to a nonlinear kernel function in the SVM formulation [36, 281]. An informal derivation can be obtained simply via substituting the linear inner product by a nonlinear kernel function, i.e. $\mathbf{x}^{\mathrm{T}}\mathbf{x}' \to K(\mathbf{x}, \mathbf{x}')$. According to Eq. (10.27), this directly yields the following optimization formulation for a nonlinear fuzzy SVM:

$$\max_{\alpha} \sum_{i=1}^{N} \alpha_i - \frac{1}{2} \sum_{i=1}^{N} \sum_{j=1}^{N} \alpha_i \alpha_j y_i y_j K(\mathbf{x}_i, \mathbf{x}_j)$$

subject to $\sum_{i=1}^{N} \alpha_i y_i = 0$ and $0 \leq \alpha_i \leq C, i = 1, \ldots, N$.

10.4.1 Primal optimizer in intrinsic space

For a formal derivation, first let us denote the discriminant function in the intrinsic space as

$$f(\mathbf{x}) = \mathbf{u}^{\mathrm{T}}\overrightarrow{\boldsymbol{\phi}}(\mathbf{x}) + b,$$

and the error as

$$\epsilon_i = \mathbf{u}^{\mathrm{T}}\overrightarrow{\boldsymbol{\phi}}(\mathbf{x}_i) + b - y_i.$$

Following the same idea as that behind Eq. (10.4), a rigid constraint $y_i\epsilon_i \geq 0$ must be imposed in order to derive a clearly separable SVM. In the fuzzy SVM, on the other hand, a set of *slack variables* $\{\xi_i\}_{i=1}^N \geq 0$ is introduced in order to relax such a rigid constraint. More exactly, the relaxed constraint becomes

$$y_i\epsilon_i + \xi_i \geq 0 \quad \forall i = 1, \ldots, N. \tag{10.34}$$

In order to prevent excessive violation, a penalty term $C\sum_i \xi_i$ is again incorporated into the objective function. Now the fuzzy SVM learning model has the following optimization formulation in the intrinsic space:

$$\begin{aligned} \underset{\mathbf{u},b,\boldsymbol{\xi}\in\mathbb{R}^N}{\text{minimize}} \left\{\frac{1}{2}\|\mathbf{u}\|^2 + C\sum_{i=1}^N \xi_i\right\} \\ \text{subject to the constraints} \\ y_i\epsilon_i + \xi_i \geq 0, \text{ where } \epsilon_i \equiv \mathbf{u}^{\mathrm{T}}\overrightarrow{\boldsymbol{\phi}}(\mathbf{x}_i) + b - y_i \\ \text{and } \xi_i \geq 0,\ \forall i = 1, \ldots, N. \end{aligned} \tag{10.35}$$

Note also that this formulation satisfies the condition set forth in Theorem 1.1, which further assures the learning subspace property (LSP) in the intrinsic space. Again, in the subsequent discussion, the LSP will be independently reconfirmed via the standard optimization analysis.

10.4.2 Dual optimizer in empirical space

The Lagrangian function corresponding to Eq. (10.35) is

$$\begin{aligned} L(\mathbf{u}, b, \boldsymbol{\alpha}, \boldsymbol{\beta}, \xi) = \frac{1}{2}\|\mathbf{u}\|^2 + C\sum_{i=1}^N \xi_i - \sum_{i=1}^N \alpha_i(y_i(\mathbf{u}^{\mathrm{T}}\overrightarrow{\boldsymbol{\phi}}(\mathbf{x}_i) + b) - 1 + \xi_i) \\ - \sum_{i=1}^N \beta_i\xi_i, \end{aligned} \tag{10.36}$$

where the Lagrange multipliers $\alpha_i \geq 0$ so as to ensure that $y_i\epsilon_i + \xi_i \geq 0$, while $\beta_i \geq 0$ serves a similar purpose to ensure that $\xi_i \geq 0$. The dual-optimization problem can be expressed as the following min–max formulation:

$$\underset{\{\boldsymbol{\alpha},\boldsymbol{\beta}\}\in\mathbb{R}^N}{\text{maximize}}\ \underset{\mathbf{u},b,\boldsymbol{\xi}\in\mathbb{R}^N}{\text{minimize}}\ L(\mathbf{u}, b, \boldsymbol{\alpha}, \boldsymbol{\beta}, \xi).$$

where $\alpha_i \geq 0$, $\beta_i \geq 0$, and $\xi_i \geq 0$ for $i = 1, \ldots, N$.

Following the very same mathematical manipulation as was used for the derivation of Eq. (10.27) for the linear case, we shall arrive at the following Wolfe dual formulation:

$$\max_{\alpha} \sum_{i=1}^{N} \alpha_i - \frac{1}{2} \sum_{i=1}^{N} \sum_{j=1}^{N} \alpha_i \alpha_j y_i y_j K(\mathbf{x}_i, \mathbf{x}_j) \tag{10.37}$$

subject to $\sum_{i=1}^{N} \alpha_i y_i = 0$ and $0 \le \alpha_i \le C, i = 1, \ldots, N$.

On substituting α_i by $a_i y_i$, we have an equivalent optimization formulation for the learning of $\mathbf{a}$:

$$\max_{\mathbf{a}} \sum_{i=1}^{N} a_i y_i - \frac{1}{2} \sum_{i=1}^{N} \sum_{j=1}^{N} a_i a_j K(\mathbf{x}_i, \mathbf{x}_j). \tag{10.38}$$

Just like in Eq. (10.28), the threshold b can again be obtained from

$$b = 1 - \mathbf{u}^{\mathrm{T}} \vec{\boldsymbol{\phi}}(\mathbf{x}_k), \tag{10.39}$$

for any integer k such that $0 < \alpha_k < C$.

This leads us to the following SVM learning algorithm.

ALGORITHM 10.1 (SVM learning model) *Given the kernel matrix* $\mathbf{K}$ *and the teacher vector* $\mathbf{y}$*, the SVM learning amounts to*

- *solving for the multiplier coefficients* $\{\alpha_i\}$ *via*

$$\begin{aligned} &\max_{\alpha} \quad \sum_{i=1}^{N} \alpha_i - \frac{1}{2} \sum_{i=1}^{N} \sum_{j=1}^{N} \alpha_i \alpha_j y_i y_j K(\mathbf{x}_i, \mathbf{x}_j), \\ &\textit{subject to } \sum_{i=1}^{N} \alpha_i y_i = 0 \textit{ and } 0 \le \alpha_i \le C, i = 1, \ldots, N. \end{aligned} \tag{10.40}$$

- *or, equivalently, solving for the empirical decision vector* $\mathbf{a}$ *via*

$$\begin{aligned} &\max_{\mathbf{a}} L(\mathbf{a}) = \mathbf{a}^{\mathrm{T}} \mathbf{y} - \frac{1}{2} \mathbf{a}^{\mathrm{T}} \mathbf{K} \mathbf{a}, \\ &\textit{subject to} \sum_{i=1}^{N} a_i = 0 \quad \textit{and} \quad 0 \le a_i y_i \le C, \ i = 1, \ldots, N. \end{aligned} \tag{10.41}$$

The LSP clearly holds for SVM, and we have

$$\mathbf{u} = \sum_{i=1}^{N} a_i \vec{\boldsymbol{\phi}}(\mathbf{x}_i).$$

Hence the discriminant function is

$$\begin{aligned} f(\mathbf{x}) &= \mathbf{u}^{\mathrm{T}} \vec{\boldsymbol{\phi}}(\mathbf{x}) + b \\ &= \sum_{i=1}^{N} \left(a_i \vec{\boldsymbol{\phi}}(\mathbf{x}_i)^{\mathrm{T}} \vec{\boldsymbol{\phi}}(\mathbf{x}) \right) + b \end{aligned}$$

$$= \sum_{i=1}^{N} a_i K(\mathbf{x}_i, \mathbf{x}) + b, \tag{10.42}$$

where **a** *can be obtained from Eq. (10.41) and b from Eq. (10.39). Finally,* sgn$[f(\mathbf{x})]$ *can be used to make the decision.* □

Once again, let us use the XOR dataset as a numerical example for the optimization formulation.

Example 10.6 (Nonlinear SVM for the XOR dataset) *The XOR dataset is not linearly separable; it is necessary to adopt a nonlinear kernel function $K(\mathbf{x}, \mathbf{x}') = (1 + \mathbf{x}^{\mathrm{T}}\mathbf{x}')^2$. The nonlinear SVM classifier can be obtained by maximizing*

$$L(\boldsymbol{\alpha}) = \sum_{i=1}^{4} \alpha_i - \frac{1}{2}\sum_{i=1}^{4}\sum_{j=1}^{4} \alpha_i \alpha_j y_i y_j K(\mathbf{x}_i, \mathbf{x}_j)$$

$$= \sum_{i=1}^{4} \alpha_i - \frac{1}{2}\begin{bmatrix}\alpha_1 & \alpha_2 & \alpha_3 & \alpha_4\end{bmatrix}\begin{bmatrix} 9 & 1 & -1 & -1 \\ 1 & 9 & -1 & -1 \\ -1 & -1 & 9 & 1 \\ -1 & -1 & 1 & 9 \end{bmatrix}\begin{bmatrix}\alpha_1 \\ \alpha_2 \\ \alpha_3 \\ \alpha_4\end{bmatrix}$$

under the constraints that

$$\alpha_1 + \alpha_2 - \alpha_3 - \alpha_4 = 0 \quad \text{and} \quad 0 \le \alpha_i \le C = 1,\ i = 1, \ldots, 4,$$

where the penalty factor is set to be $C = 1$. The optimization solution is

$$\alpha_1 = \alpha_2 = \alpha_3 = \alpha_4 = \frac{1}{8},$$

and, in addition, $b = 0$. This leads to the following discriminant function:

$$\begin{aligned} f(\mathbf{x}) &= \sum_{i=1}^{4} y_i \alpha_i K(\mathbf{x}, \mathbf{x}_i) + b \\ &= \frac{1}{8}\{K(\mathbf{x}, \mathbf{x}_1) + K(\mathbf{x}, \mathbf{x}_2) - K(\mathbf{x}, \mathbf{x}_3) - K(\mathbf{x}, \mathbf{x}_4)\} \\ &= \frac{1}{8}\{(1 + u + v)^2 + (1 - u - v)^2 - (1 + u - v)^2 - (1 - u + v)^2\} \\ &= uv. \end{aligned}$$

10.4.3 Multi-class SVM learning models

In many practical applications, there are more than two classes to be identified. Fortunately, the binary SVM learning models may be naturally extended to multi-classification applications [297]. In this section, some exemplifying experimental results are reported, and the training and prediction accuracies are compared.

Suppose that the (one-versus-all) OVA-SVM learning model is adopted. Then K independent SVM classifiers will be trained during the learning phase, as depicted in Figure 9.6.

If the ith training vector is known to belong to the kth class, then its teacher vector will be set to be

$$\mathbf{y}_i = \vec{t}^{(k)} = [-1 -1 \quad \ldots \quad -1 +1 -1 \quad \cdots \quad -1 -1],$$

in which only the kth element is set to be $+1$. This means that K binary-valued SVM classifiers will be independently trained.

During the classification phase, given any new sample $\mathbf{x}$, its empirical-space-based score associated with the kth SVM classifier can be obtained as

$$f_k(\mathbf{x}) = f^{(k)}(\mathbf{x}) = [\mathbf{a}^{(k)}]^{\mathrm{T}} \vec{\mathbf{k}}(\mathbf{x}) + b^{(k)} = \sum_{i=1}^{N} a_i^{(k)} K(\mathbf{x}_i, \mathbf{x}) + b^{(k)}. \tag{10.43}$$

The predicted class of $\mathbf{x}$ is the one with the highest score, i.e.

$$k^* = \arg\max_k f^{(k)}(\mathbf{x}), \; k = 1, \ldots, K. \tag{10.44}$$

10.4.4 SVM learning softwares

A comprehensive set of software tools for SVM learning models has been developed. Some basic Matlab codes of the main SVM routines can be found in [87]. For practical applications, however, numerical solutions to SVM learning models can become a serious computational challenge when the size of the dataset grows due to the optimizer's inherent curse of dimensionality [12]. There are plenty of application problems with an extremely large size of training dataset. Numerical methods that decompose the problem into smaller ones, including both approximate and exact methods, have been proposed in order to expedite learning [197, 258]. In particular, one of the fastest algorithms implemented for SVM is the sequential minimal optimization (SMO) introduced by Platt [204]. (See Section 5.5.) For suggestions on further improving Platt's SMO algorithm, see [122]. More generally, for some recent advances of large-scale linear classification, see [101, 312]. The website kernel-machines.org provides a comprehensive list of SVM softwares, including some popular ones, e.g. [34, 172, 241, 261, 295].

10.5 Application case studies

As reported in the literature, many simulation studies have been conducted on SVM, as well as comparative studies on SVM and other classifiers. See e.g. [30, 37, 185, 234]. Some application studies will be highlighted in this section.

10.5.1 SVM for cancer data analysis

Ramaswamy *et al.* [213] adopted SVM-OVA to effectively classify a tumor into currently known categories in terms of the gene expression of the tissue of origin of the tumor. The expression levels of 16,063 genes and expressed sequence tags were used to evaluate the effectiveness of the SVM-OVA classifier for the diagnosis of multiple common adult malignancies. In the study, oligonucleotide microarray gene expression analysis was conducted on 90 tissue samples of healthy and 218 tumor samples, spanning 14 common tumor types,[2] including prostate-specific antigen (PSA), carcinoembryonic antigen (CEA), and estrogen receptor (ER), were identified.

Gene selections

First of all, a variation filter is used to eliminate 2741 genes whose scores are below a certain threshold. Ultimately, only 11,322 passed the filtering process.

Then the SVM-RFE method was adopted to recursively remove features [89]. More precisely, for each OVA SVM classifier, the class label is determined by sign[$f(x)$], where $f(x) = \sum_i w^{(i)}x^{(i)} + b$, thus the absolute magnitude of $w^{(i)}$ will be used to rank the importance the ith gene in classifying a sample. It was proposed by Ramaswamy *et al.* [213] that "each OVA SVM classifier is first trained with all genes, then genes corresponding to $|w^{(i)}|$ in the bottom 10% are removed, and each classifier is retrained with the smaller gene set. This procedure is repeated iteratively to study prediction accuracy as a function of gene number."

Performance of SVM-OVA

The OVA multi-class classification approach is depicted in Figure 9.6. During the training phase, each classifier uses the linear SVM algorithm to train a hyperplane that best separates training samples into two classes. In the testing phase, a test sample is presented to each of 14 OVA classifiers sequentially, where the prediction strength of each SVM prediction is determined as $f(x) = \sum_i w^{(i)}x^{(i)} + b$. According to Eq. (10.44), the class with maximally positive strength will be identified.

As reported by Ramaswamy *et al.* [213], with over 1000 genes used per OVA classifier, SVM-OVA had an accuracy around 75%, clearly outperforming kNN-SVM's 65% (kNN denoting k-nearest neighbors) as well as SVM-AP's 65%.

Training and testing accuracies

A comprehensive comparison between training and testing accuracies for classification of the tumor types was reported by Ramaswamy *et al.* [213]. The multi-classification accuracies on the training and test datasets were noticeably different. For example, for the colorectal adenocarcinoma (CO) tumor type, although the identification accuracy reached 100% for the CO test dataset, only 75% of the CO training dataset could be correctly identified. On the other hand, for the leukemia (LE) tumor type, while the accuracy reached 100% for the LE training dataset, only 83% of the LE test dataset could be correctly identified. It is common practice to use the testing accuracy (as opposed to the training accuracy) to evaluate the goodness of a trained classifier.

[2] Labeled BR (breast adenocarcinoma), PR (prostate adenocarcinoma), LU (lung adenocarcinoma), CO (colorectal adenocarcinoma), LY (lymphoma), BL (bladder transitional cell carcinoma), ML (melanoma), UT (uterine adenocarcinoma), LE (leukemia), RE (renal cell carcinoma), PA (pancreatic adenocarcinoma), OV (ovarian adenocarcinoma), ME (pleural mesothelioma), and CNS (central nervous system).

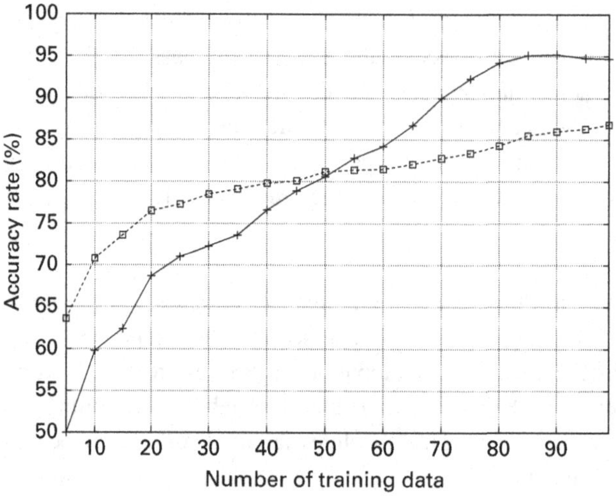

Fig. 10.7. The performance of SVM classification on the image database: http://wang.ist.psu.edu/docs/related/. It is interesting to note that OVA (one versus all), labeled by "+," is better than AP (one versus one), labeled by "□," when the size of the training dataset increases. Conversely, the opposite result is found when the size of the training dataset decreases.

10.5.2 Prediction performances w.r.t. size of training datasets

Intuitively, a larger training dataset has a greater chance of yielding statistically trustworthy learning results. In real-world experiments, it was reported that the prediction performance usually improves with increasing training dataset size [144, 319]. In the simulation for a popular image database, whose results are depicted in Figure 10.7, it is found that SVM-OVA (one versus all) is better than SVM-AP (one versus one) when the size of the training dataset is increased. Conversely, the result deteriorates when the size of the training dataset is decreased [319].

10.5.3 KRR versus SVM: application studies

To assess the performance of SVM, in comparison with KDA and KRR, simulation studies have been conducted on several datasets, including those from the UCI machine learning repository, a microarray cancer diagnosis, and subcellular protein sequence analyses.

- **Performance of SVM on UCI data.** The performance of SVM was evaluated on six UCI datasets: Iris, Wine, Liver, Glass, Yeast, and Red Wine Quality [139]. For SVM, the upper bound on α_i was set to 10, i.e. $C = 10$. A one-versus-rest classification technique was used to solve the multi-class problems. The classification accuracies of SVM, in comparison with KDA and KRR, are shown in Table 9.1. Note that SVM clearly achieves the highest accuracy for five out of six datasets: Iris, Wine, Liver, Glass, and Red Wine Quality.
- **Performance of SVM on microarray cancer diagnosis.** Six cancer datasets were considered [206]: carcinoma [107], colon [5], glioma [195], leukemia [82], prostate

[247], and breast [277]. Table 9.2 shows that SVM's performance on the cancer datasets is roughly on a par with that of KRR.

- **Performance of SVM on subcellular protein sequence classification.** Simulation studies were conducted on three different protein sequence datasets by Huang and Li [104], Mak, Guo, and Kung [166], and Reinhart [216]. Each of the datasets contains eukaryotic protein sequences with annotated subcellular locations. A one-versus-rest classification technique was used to solve the multi-class problems. Table 9.3 shows SVM's performance on the subcellular protein sequence datasets. Note that, while SVM clearly outperforms KRR in Reinhart's dataset, it only has a slight edge over KRR for the other two datasets.

10.6 Empirical-space SVM for trimming of support vectors

Starting with the set of support vectors trained by SVM, it is sometimes advisable to cherry-pick from the existing support vectors those which are the most relevant ones so as to further trim the set of selected vectors.

10.6.1 ℓ_1-Norm SVM in empirical space

It is natural to adopt an empirical-space-based SVM formulation for the purpose of trimming of support vectors. In fact, in this context, it is possible to use some feature-reduction tools originally proposed for dimension reduction in the original feature space. Following a LASSO-type formulation, an SVM learning model in the empirical space can be obtained as follows:

$$\min_{\mathbf{a}}\{|\mathbf{a}|_1 + C\textstyle\sum_i \xi_i\}$$

$$\text{subject to the constraints } y_i\epsilon_i + \xi_i \geq 0, \text{ where}$$

$$\epsilon_i \equiv f(\mathbf{x}) - y_i = \mathbf{a}^{\mathrm{T}}\overrightarrow{\mathbf{k}}(\mathbf{x}_i) + b - y_i \text{ and } \xi_i \geq 0,\ \forall i = 1, \ldots, N, \tag{10.45}$$

where $|\mathbf{a}|_1$ denotes the ℓ_1-norm of the vector $\mathbf{a}$. The ℓ_1-norm nature of the LASSO-type learning model can effectively suppress the irrelevant or redundant training vectors and thus allows us to selectively retain only the most informative ones.

10.6.2 ℓ_2-Norm SVM in empirical space

It is natural to extend the optimization criteria given in Eqs. (10.22) and (10.35) to the empirical space, resulting in three contrasting criteria:

- SVM on the original space: $\min_{\mathbf{w}}\{\frac{1}{2}\|\mathbf{w}\|^2 + C\sum_i \xi_i\}$, Eq. (10.22);
- SVM on the intrinsic space: $\min_{\mathbf{u}}\{\frac{1}{2}\|\mathbf{u}\|^2 + C\sum_i \xi_i\}$, Eq. (10.35); and
- SVM on the empirical space: $\min_{\mathbf{a}}\{\frac{1}{2}\|\mathbf{a}\|^2 + C\sum_i \xi_i\}$.

Their corresponding kernel functions are respectively

- SVM on the original space adopts the linear kernel, $\mathbf{x}^{\mathrm{T}}\mathbf{y}$;
- SVM on the intrinsic space adopts a nonlinear kernel, $K(\mathbf{x}, \mathbf{y}) = \overrightarrow{\boldsymbol{\phi}}(\mathbf{x})^{\mathrm{T}}\overrightarrow{\boldsymbol{\phi}}(\mathbf{y})$; and

- the kernel corresponding to SVM on the empirical space is

$$K'(\mathbf{x},\mathbf{y}) = \vec{\boldsymbol{\phi}}(\mathbf{x})^{\mathrm{T}}\boldsymbol{\Phi}\boldsymbol{\Phi}^{\mathrm{T}}\vec{\boldsymbol{\phi}}(\mathbf{y}) = \vec{\mathbf{k}}(\mathbf{x})^{\mathrm{T}}\vec{\mathbf{k}}(\mathbf{y}),$$

  where

$$\vec{\mathbf{k}}(\mathbf{x}) \equiv \boldsymbol{\Phi}\vec{\boldsymbol{\phi}}(\mathbf{x}) = \begin{bmatrix} K(\mathbf{x}_1,\mathbf{x}) \\ K(\mathbf{x}_2,\mathbf{x}) \\ \vdots \\ K(\mathbf{x}_N,\mathbf{x}) \end{bmatrix}. \tag{10.46}$$

We have already covered the first and second types of SVMs. Let us now elaborate upon the third type of SVM.

Given a training dataset $\{\mathbf{x}_1,\mathbf{x}_2,\ldots,\mathbf{x}_N\}$ and a known kernel function $K(\mathbf{x},\mathbf{y})$, the mapping $\mathbf{x} \rightarrow \vec{\mathbf{k}}(\mathbf{x})$ maps the original space onto the *empirical space*. By applying the SVM learning algorithm to the N empirical feature vectors $\{\vec{\mathbf{k}}(\mathbf{x}_i), i = 1,\ldots,N\}$ as the training vectors, we can derive another variant of the SVM learning model in the empirical space.

With the empirical feature vectors $\vec{\mathbf{k}}(\mathbf{x}_1),\ldots,\vec{\mathbf{k}}(\mathbf{x}_N)$ being used as the training vectors, the learning formulation can be correspondingly modified as follows:

$$\min_{\mathbf{a}} \left\{ \frac{1}{2}\|\mathbf{a}\|^2 + C\sum_i \xi_i \right\}$$

subject to the constraints $y_i\epsilon_i + \xi_i \geq 0$,

where $\xi_i \geq 0$ and $\epsilon_i = \mathbf{a}^{\mathrm{T}}\vec{\mathbf{k}}(\mathbf{x}_i) + b - y_i \quad \forall i = 1,\ldots,N.$

The new Lagrangian function becomes

$$L(\mathbf{u},b,\boldsymbol{\alpha},\beta,\xi) = \frac{1}{2}\|\mathbf{a}\|^2 + C\sum_i \xi_i - \sum_{i=1}^{N}\alpha_i(y_i(\mathbf{a}^{\mathrm{T}}\vec{\mathbf{k}}(\mathbf{x}_i) + b) - 1 + \xi_i) - \sum_{i=1}^{N}\beta_i\xi_i. \tag{10.47}$$

Its zero gradient with respect to $\mathbf{a}$ and b leads to

$$\mathbf{a} = \sum_{i=1}^{N}\alpha_i y_i \vec{\mathbf{k}}(\mathbf{x}_i) \quad \text{and} \quad \sum_{i=1}^{N}\alpha_i y_i = 0, \tag{10.48}$$

which in turn leads to the following optimization formulation in the dual domain:

$$\max_{\alpha} \quad \sum_{i=1}^{N}\alpha_i - \frac{1}{2}\sum_{i=1}^{N}\sum_{j=1}^{N}\alpha_i\alpha_j y_i y_j K'(\mathbf{x}_i,\mathbf{x}_j),$$

$$\text{subject to: } \sum_{i=1}^{N}\alpha_i y_i = 0 \quad \text{and} \quad 0 \leq \alpha_i \leq C, i = 1,\ldots,N. \tag{10.49}$$

Here

$$K'(\mathbf{x}_i,\mathbf{x}_j) = \vec{\boldsymbol{\phi}}(\mathbf{x}_i)^{\mathrm{T}}\boldsymbol{\Phi}\boldsymbol{\Phi}^{\mathrm{T}}\vec{\boldsymbol{\phi}}(\mathbf{x}_j) = \vec{\mathbf{k}}(\mathbf{x}_i)^{\mathrm{T}}\vec{\mathbf{k}}(\mathbf{x}_j).$$

Once the empirical decision vector $\mathbf{a}$ has been learned, the discriminant function can be obtained as

$$f(\mathbf{x}) = \mathbf{a}^{\mathrm{T}} \vec{\mathbf{k}}(\mathbf{x}) + b = \sum_{i=1}^{N} a_i K(\mathbf{x}_i, \mathbf{x}) + b. \tag{10.50}$$

The optimization formulation in Eq. (10.49) has a striking resemblance to Eq. (10.40) except that $K(\mathbf{x}_i, \mathbf{x}_j)$ has been replaced by $K'(\mathbf{x}_i, \mathbf{x}_j)$, or, equivalently, the conventional kernel matrix $\mathbf{K}$ has been replaced by a newly induced $N \times N$ kernel matrix:

$$\mathbf{K}' = \mathbf{K}^2. \tag{10.51}$$

10.6.3 Empirical learning models for vectorial and nonvectorial data analysis

Let us compare the kernel matrices corresponding to the SVM learning formulations in two different induced spaces.

- The kernel matrix for SVM on the intrinsic space is $\mathbf{K} = \mathbf{\Phi}^{\mathrm{T}}\mathbf{\Phi}$.
- Note that

$$[\, \vec{\mathbf{k}}(\mathbf{x}_1) \;\ldots\; \vec{\mathbf{k}}(\mathbf{x}_N)] = [\mathbf{\Phi}^{\mathrm{T}} \vec{\phi}(\mathbf{x}_1) \;\ldots\; \mathbf{\Phi}^{\mathrm{T}} \vec{\phi}(\mathbf{x}_N)] = \mathbf{\Phi}^{\mathrm{T}}\mathbf{\Phi} = \mathbf{K};$$

therefore, the kernel matrix for SVM on the empirical space is

$$\mathbf{K}' = [\, \vec{\mathbf{k}}(\mathbf{x}_1) \;\ldots\; \vec{\mathbf{k}}(\mathbf{x}_N)]^{\mathrm{T}} [\, \vec{\mathbf{k}}(\mathbf{x}_1) \;\ldots\; \vec{\mathbf{k}}(\mathbf{x}_N)] = \mathbf{K}^{\mathrm{T}}\mathbf{K} = \mathbf{K}^2. \tag{10.52}$$

The *induced data matrix* in the empirical space is an $N \times N$ symmetric matrix:

$$\begin{bmatrix} K(\mathbf{x}_1, \mathbf{x}_1) & K(\mathbf{x}_1, \mathbf{x}_2) & \ldots & K(\mathbf{x}_1, \mathbf{x}_N) \\ K(\mathbf{x}_2, \mathbf{x}_1) & K(\mathbf{x}_2, \mathbf{x}_2) & \ldots & K(\mathbf{x}_2, \mathbf{x}_N) \\ \ldots & \ldots & \ldots & \ldots \\ K(\mathbf{x}_N, \mathbf{x}_1) & K(\mathbf{x}_N, \mathbf{x}_2) & \ldots & K(\mathbf{x}_N, \mathbf{x}_N) \end{bmatrix}, \tag{10.53}$$

where $K(\mathbf{x}_i, \mathbf{x}_j)$ represents the similarity score (e.g. the alignment score) between patterns $\mathbf{x}_i$ and $\mathbf{x}_j$.

The doubly supervised learning model for vectorial data analysis

In a typical wrapper approach (see Section 4.3.1), the class labels are usually indexed column-wise, whereas the features are indexed row-wise in a conventional data matrix. This is illustrated by Figure 10.8(a).

A vital characteristic of the new formulation hinges upon the symmetry of the newly *induced data matrix* $\mathbf{K}$ given by Eq. (10.53). Note that the new data matrix $\mathbf{K}$ is symmetric, which means that the class labels are both column-wise and row-wise indexed. This is illustrated by Figure 10.8(b). Therefore, the learning formulation in Eq. (10.49) can be called *a doubly supervised* (DS) SVM learning model.

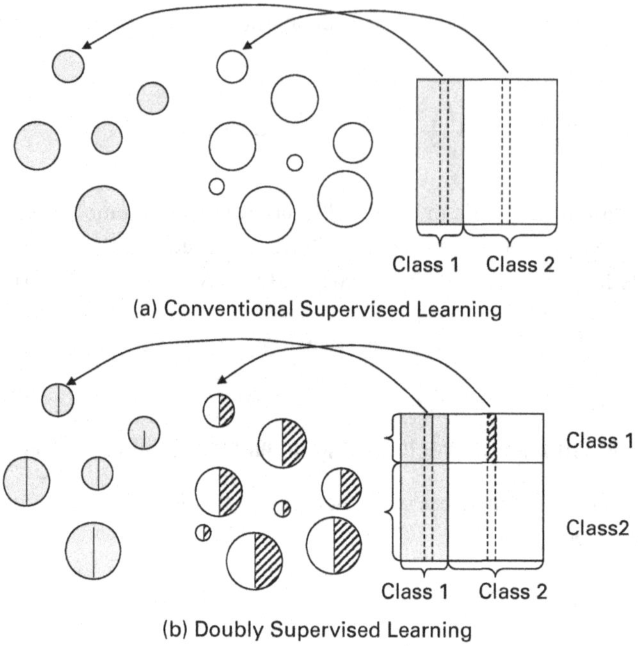

Fig. 10.8. A comparison of different teacher's information content for conventional supervised learning versus doubly supervised learning. (a) Conventional supervised learning. Here, each (circle) node represents one training vector. The uniform gray-level nodes indicate that there is no row-wise indexed information that may be used to facilitate the selection process. More exactly, the importance of an individual training vector hinges upon the role it has in shaping the decision rule. For example, in an SV-based selection rule, support vectors have a higher priority to be selected because they tend to be more critical to decision making than are non-support vectors. However, in such an assessment criterion, the selection of a training vector will depend closely on whether it is strategically located relative to the overall training dataset. In other words, there exists no mechanism to independently assess a single training vector by itself. (b) Doubly supervised supervised learning. Note that the *induced data matrix* $\mathbf{K}$ is symmetric, which means that the class labels are both column-wise and row-wise indexed. As a result, the training vectors are represented by non-uniform nodes to indicate that in each individual vector there is embedded inter-class information that may be effectively utilized for the selection process. Such information is often manifested by an SNR-type metric. In the schematic diagram, the higher the SNR the larger the node. This means that some vectors are more informative due to their higher SNRs and they deserve a higher priority to be selected. This rule is effectively the same as that adopted in the so-called filtering approach, see Chapter 4. In summary, in the DS learning formulation, the importance of an individual training vector may now be independently assessed. This permits a filtering-type selection rule, which complements very well the SV-based selection rule.

The doubly supervised learning model for nonvectorial data analysis

The doubly supervised learning model naturally applies to analysis of nonvectorial objects. From the N nonvectorial training objects, we first process all the pairwise similarity values:

$$\{S(\mathbf{x}_i, \mathbf{x}_j), i = 1, \ldots, N; j = 1, \ldots, N\}$$

so as to derive an $N \times N$ similarity matrix $\mathbf{S} = \{S_{i,j}\}$. Note that it will be just fine that the similarity matrix is not positive semi-definite. This is because the DS learning formulation is based on the induced kernel matrix, $\mathbf{K}' = \mathbf{S}^2$, which will always be positive semi-definite.

Example 10.7 (DS-SVMs for subcelluar localization) *The doubly supervised learning formulation is naturally applicable to the classification of nonvectorial objects. Taking protein sequence analysis, as an example, we need to process all the similarity functions* $S(\mathbf{x}_i, \mathbf{x}_j)$, $i = 1, \ldots, N$ *and* $j = 1, \ldots, N$, *represented by the pair's sequence alignment score (e.g. the Smith–Waterman score [249]). Computationally, this is an extremely time-consuming process. (It took about one month to compile the entire* $N \times N$ *similarity matrix for* $N \approx 2400$ *training sequences [140].)*

In Example 2.6, we reported different subcellular prediction accuracies obtained by SVM using various kernel matrices derived from a eukaryotic protein dataset [216]. In the example, the first kernel matrix $\mathbf{K}_1$ *coincides with the* $N \times N$ *similarity matrix* $\mathbf{S}$ *obtained by pairwise sequence alignments. This basic matrix eventually leads to a Mercer kernel matrix,* $\mathbf{K}_5 = \mathbf{K}_1^2 = \mathbf{S}^2$, *which is obviously positive semi-definite.*

Now let us compare the performances of SVM using $\mathbf{K}_1$ *versus* $\mathbf{K}_5$. *Not surprisingly, not being a Mercer kernel matrix, the former yields an extremely poor prediction accuracy of 45.9%. In contrast, the latter delivers a drastically improved accuracy of 99.1%. The improved accuracy is evidently due to the fact that* $\mathbf{S}^2$ *is always assured to be a Mercer kernel matrix.*

It is worth noting that the kernel matrix $\mathbf{K}_5$ *is what is adopted by doubly supervised support vector machines (DS-SVMs). In conclusion, the doubly supervised learning formulation is especially effective for the classification of nonvectorial objects.*

10.6.4 Wrapper methods for empirical learning models

The doubly supervised (DS) learning model allows the adoption of two different types of wrapper method, recursive feature elimination (RFE) and vector-indicator-adaptive (VIA) selection, for the selection of the training vectors. They adopt very different kinds of indicators, which will be elaborated on below.

10.6.4.1 Wrapper methods for trimming of training vectors

The training vectors may be eliminated/retained by applying either of the following selection schemes.

(i) **Selection via a_i.** Guyon *et al.* [89] proposed a wrapper approach combining the SVM with RFE, see Figure 4.8. RFE eliminates unimportant features (which happen to correspond to the training vectors) recursively according to the magnitude of coefficients in the decision vector. In this application, the decision vector $\mathbf{a}$ is defined over the empirical space. According to Eq. (10.50), $f(\mathbf{x}) = \sum_i^N a_i K(\mathbf{x}_i, \mathbf{x}) + b$, this means that the greater the magnitude of a_i, the greater the role its corresponding kernel value $K(\mathbf{x}_i, \mathbf{x})$ plays in the discriminant function. In compliance with the RFE rule, a training vector $\mathbf{x}_i$ should be eliminated if $|a_i| < \theta_a$ for a pre-set threshold θ_a.

(ii) **Selection via ϵ_i.** An alternative selection criterion is based on ϵ_i, i.e. the error associated with the training vector $\mathbf{x}_i$. More exactly, a training vector $\mathbf{x}_i$ will be a preferred choice if $0 \leq |\epsilon_i| \leq \theta_\epsilon$ for a pre-set threshold θ_ϵ. This motivates a so-called *vector-indicator-adaptive* (VIA) selection scheme proposed by Kung and Mak [140]. See Figure 10.9.

10.6.4.2 A selection scheme that is based on ϵ_i

With reference to the WEC functions in Figure 10.6, for the flat region where $\alpha_i = C$, knowing ϵ_i means knowing α_i, but not vice versa. This means that ϵ_i offers more information in that region. Conversely, for the vertical region corresponding to the constant-valued $\epsilon_i = 0$, α_i may vary between $0 \leq \alpha_i \leq C$, i.e. knowing α_i means knowing ϵ_i, but not vice versa. In other words, α_i offers more information in that region.

For the purpose of vector selection, it is worth stressing that ϵ_i is a much more effective indicator than α_i. Two major reasons are as follows.

- Usually, the support vectors in the flat region outnumber those in the vertical region.
- Moreover, in practical applications, the critical selection cutoff threshold θ_ϵ is likely to be $0 < \theta_\epsilon \leq 2$, which falls within the flat region. (See Figures 10.10 and 10.11.)

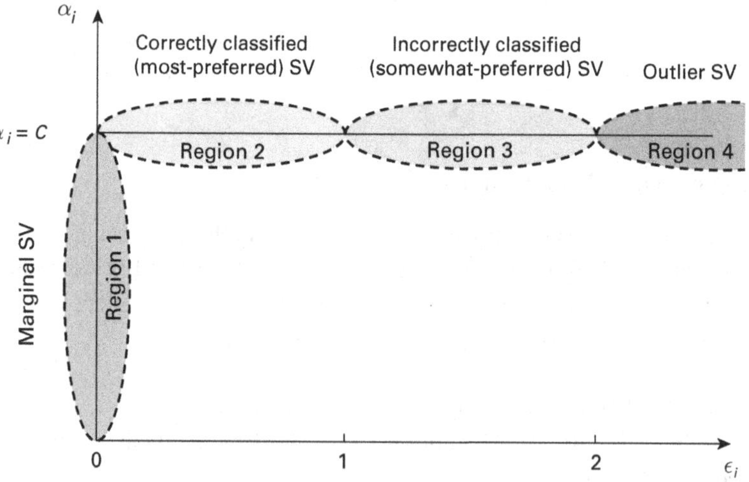

Fig. 10.9. In the VIA-SVM trimming scheme, all the support vectors are considered as possible candidates for the final selection. Depending on the error values associated with the training vectors, four different regions are defined to facilitate the selection process. In strategy 1, only the support vectors in region 1 are considered. In strategy 2, region 1 and region 2 are considered. In strategy 3, regions 1, 2, and 3 are considered. Finally, in strategy 4, all of the support vectors are retained.

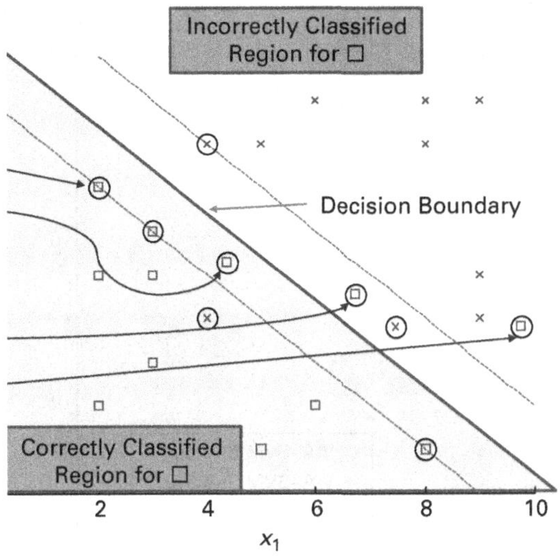

Fig. 10.10. In strategy 2, support vectors are divided into two types: correctly classified ($0 \leq \epsilon_i < 1$) and incorrectly classified ($\epsilon_i > 1$). Those which correspond to the former type are shown within the shaded zone.

More exactly, four possible threshold values for the positive training vectors may be considered.[3]

- Strategy 1. $\theta_\epsilon = 0$, i.e. the range of selection is $\epsilon_i = 0$. In this approach one selects support vectors that fall right on the positive-margin hyperplane only. In Figure 10.9, only the support vectors in region 1 are considered. This threshold is indicated by the bottom anti-diagonal line in the gray zone in Figure 10.10.
- Strategy 2. $\theta_\epsilon = 1.0$, i.e. the range of selection is $0 \leq \epsilon_i \leq 1.0$. Select all (and only the) SVs that are correctly classified. With reference to Figure 10.9, the support vectors in regions 1 and 2 are retained. In Figure 10.9, this threshold is indicated by the middle anti-diagonal line which separates the gray and white zones.
- Strategy 3. $\theta_\epsilon = 2.0$, i.e. the range of selection is $0 \leq \epsilon_i \leq 2.0$. Select all the SVs that are correctly classified and those SVs which are within the separation zone, even though they have been incorrectly classified. Namely, only the outlier SVs that are not only incorrectly classified but also have exceedingly large errors are excluded. With reference to Figure 10.9, the support vectors in regions 1, 2, and 3 are retained. This threshold is indicated by the top anti-diagonal line in the white zone in Figure 10.10.
- Strategy 4. $\theta_\epsilon = \infty$. In Figure 10.9, the support vectors in all four regions are included. In short, all the support vectors are retained.

Our simulation studies, displayed in Figure 10.11, suggest that strategies 2 and 3 can deliver the best compromise in terms of cost–performance tradeoff.

[3] The threshold values for the negative training vectors involve a sign change.

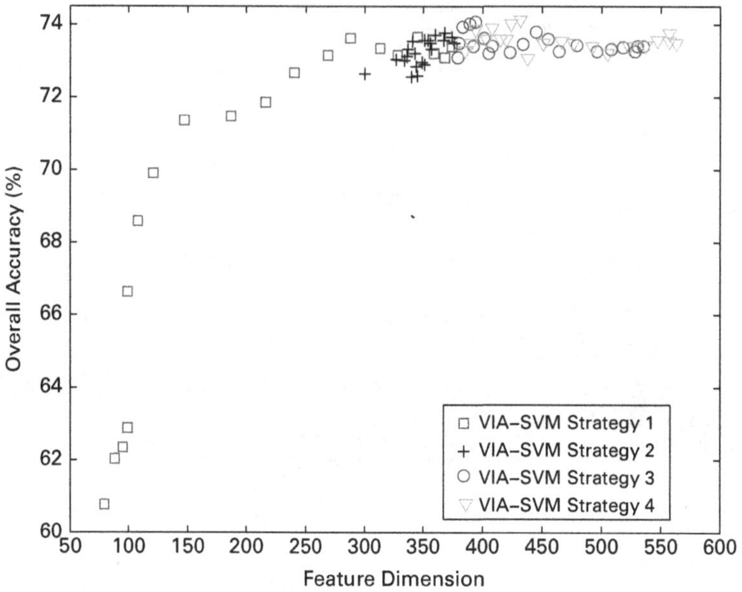

Fig. 10.11. The prediction performance of VIA-SVM on Huang and Li's dataset for different levels of preferences on support vectors when the penalty factor C varies from 0.004 to 4000. In this figure, it was observed that the points move from the right towards the left (i.e. decreasing the number of vectors retained) when C increases. Note that, for a given penalty factor C, the number of vectors retained is automatically determined by the SVMs. A smaller penalty factor C will generally lead to a larger number of features, and vice versa for a larger C. Therefore, markers from left to right generally correspond to a decreasing value of C. The results show that using all of the support vectors (regions 1–4) will lead to over-selection; on the other hand, retaining only the SVs in region 1 will lead to under-selection, especially when the penalty factor C becomes large. In short, strategies 2 and 3 appear to be the most appealing. For this dataset, strategy 2 uses a smaller dimension (than strategy 3), while strategy 3 has a slight edge in terms of the (average and peak) accuracy.

10.6.4.3 Application to subcellular sequence classification

To illustrate the application of the doubly supervised SVM, a simulation study was conducted on the protein sequence dataset provided by Huang and Li [104]. The dataset contains eukaryotic protein sequences with annotated subcellular locations. It was created by selecting all of the eukaryotic proteins with annotated subcellular locations from SWILSPROT 41.0 and setting the identity cutoff to 50%. The dataset comprises 3572 proteins (622 cytoplasm, 1188 nuclear, 424 mitochondria, 915 extracellular, 26 golgi apparatus, 225 chloroplast, 45 endoplasmic reticulum, 7 cytoskeleton, 29 vacuole, 47 peroxisome, and 44 lysosome). The five-fold cross-validation technique was used for performance evaluation so that every sequence in the datasets was tested. The simulation results are summarized as follows. For more details, see Kung and Mak [140].

- **The role of C in determining the number of support vectors retained.** As stated previously, the higher the mitigation factor C the smaller the number of support vectors. This is evidenced by Figure 10.11. Taking strategy 1 as an example, as C increases from 0.004 to 4000, the □s migrate leftwards, i.e. the number of vectors retained decreases. For strategies 2, 3, and 4, similar trends can be observed in Figure 10.11, i.e. the number of vectors retained decreases with increasing C (from 0.004 to 4000).

- **Comparison of different threshold strategies.** Figure 10.11 suggests that, considering the cost–performance tradeoff, strategies 2 and 3 are more appealing than strategies 1 and 4. Strategy 2 uses a smaller dimension (than strategy 3), while strategy 3 has a slight edge in terms of the (average and peak) accuracy. Note also that, for most cost-effective classifier designs, strategy 2 is seen to be attractive insofar as it is least sensitive to the penalty factor. Namely, it can keep the number of selected vectors within a small range and maintain the accuracy at a constant level for a wide range of C.
- **Comparison between SVM-RFE and VIA-SVM .** Comparisons were made for a subcellular localization benchmark. Figure 10.12 and Table 10.1 show the performance of SVM-RFE (□) and that of VIA-SVM (○). Evidently, VIA-SVM is superior to SVM-RFE in two aspects: (1) it outperforms SVM-RFE at almost all feature dimensions, particularly at low feature dimensions; and (2) it automatically bounds the number of selected features within a small range. A drawback of SVM-RFE is that it requires a cutoff point for stopping the selection. On the other hand, VIA-SVM is insensitive to the penalty factor in SVM training, and one can avoid the need to set a cutoff point for stopping the feature-selection process.

10.6.5 Fusion of filtering and wrapper methods

The doubly supervised (DS) data matrix paves the way for fusion of diversified information critical to the selection of training vectors. More exactly, each newly induced training vector contains N entries, with N_+ of them associated with the positive class and N_- of them with the negative class. The differential gap between these two subsets of entries of any induced training vector provides an SNR-type evaluation of the vector. This is shown in Figure 10.8(b). The higher the SNR, the richer the information embedded in the vector. The SNR-based criteria may be adopted to effectively rank all the training vectors.

Note that the SNR fails to consider the effect of inter-feature redundancy, while the wrapper approach considers the inter-feature redundancy. So the two types of information are fundamentally different and can potentially be complementary to each other. Therefore, a fusion strategy combining both types of information should be promising for facilitating the best possible selection of the critical training vectors.

Fusion experiments on subcellular localization

For the simulation study on subcellular localization, the two complementary types of information embedded in the DS formulation can be combined via the following overselect-and-prune strategy.

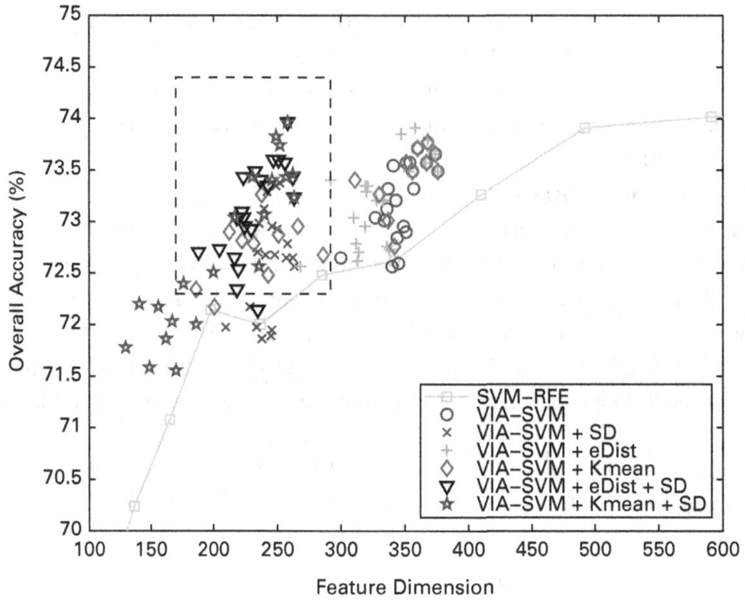

Fig. 10.12. Simulation results obtained by applying various re-selection schemes to Huang and Li's dataset. The prediction performances of SVM-RFE , VIA-SVM , and VIA-SVM cascaded with a filter method are shown. Compared with the baseline performance (represented by the well-known SVM-RFE method), all the proposed schemes yield noticeable improvements.

(i) **Over-selection phase.** This phase involves a quick and coarse (suboptimal) evaluation. This phase can be implemented by a filter method using SNR or wrapper methods.

(ii) **Pruning phase.** With DS, feature selection via SNR-based filtering is now feasible. This phase serves as a fine-tuning process. In the simulation study, a symmetric divergence (SD) criterion (see Eq. (4.3)) was used to sort the features found in the first stage and keep the most relevant $\beta\%$. (Here, β is set to 70.)

The performance of SVM-RFE, highlighted by the connected line in Figure 10.12, may be viewed as the standard bearer to show the relative performances of various selection schemes. For example, the fusion of SD and VIA-SVM delivers nearly the best performance with a relatively small number of retained training vectors. In this simulation study, those training vectors with $0 \leq \epsilon_i \leq 1$ (strategy 2) were selected. Figure 10.12 suggests that the combined information can indeed be used to reduce the feature dimension without causing a discernible compromise in prediction accuracy.

10.7 Summary

The chapter is focused on the learning models of support vector machines (SVMs). First, we introduce the basic SVM formulations for linear classification, where hard constraints are used to enforce a clear separation. Then, soft constraints are used to allow more support vectors to be included in the so-called fuzzy SVM formulations. The transition from linear classification to nonlinear classification involves the use of a nonlinear

Table 10.1. The means and standard deviations (in parentheses) of the classification accuracies and feature dimensions for 21 penalty factors ranging from 0.004 to 4000, see Figure 10.12

	Accuracy (%)	Feature dimension
VIA-SVM	73.23 (0.38)	348 (17.22)
VIA-SVM + SD	72.66 (0.51)	244 (12.07)
SVM-RFE	71.90 (1.45)	264 (129.10)

kernel function. More exactly, after the data in the original space have been mapped to kernel-induced intrinsic space, the same linear SVM formulations are applicable to the new feature space. This leads to the kernel-based SVM learning model presented in Algorithm 10.1, where the learning model is expressed in terms of a kernel matrix. It is worth noting that the linear and kernel-based SVMs share exactly the same formulation. Moreover, the mapping to intrinsic space is no longer explicitly involved.

Another promising application domain has to do with the identification of a subset of critical training vectors. Note that the support vectors are themselves the most desirable and relevant training vectors from the perspective of classification. (Note that, given only the SVs as the training dataset, we would learn the exactly the same classifier as the one trained from the full and original training dataset [278]). Hence, the reduction from a training dataset with N vectors to one with only S vectors already accomplishes an important initial step. In order to cherry-pick from the existing pool of support vectors to further reduce the training set, we propose a 2-norm-based and doubly supervised SVM learning model formulated in the empirical space, prompting rich information useful for the re-selection of support vectors.

Finally, iterative methods for Lagrangian SVM are explored in [239], leading to the conclusion that some sort of approximation must be performed in order to have efficient online adaptive methods. This is partially the reason why the development of online SVM learning models remains an active research topic.

10.8 Problems

Problem 10.1 *Consider the dataset in Example 10.1. It is known that all of the three training vectors ($\mathbf{x_1}$, $\mathbf{x_2}$, and $\mathbf{x_3}$) are support vectors.*

(a) *Show that the solution for the threshold value b may be obtained from any of the support vector as $b = y_i - \mathbf{w}^{\mathrm{T}}\mathbf{x_i}$, for $i = 1, 2, 3$.*

(b) *Verify that*

$$y_1 - \mathbf{w}^{\mathrm{T}}\mathbf{x_1} = y_2 - \mathbf{w}^{\mathrm{T}}\mathbf{x_2} = y_3 - \mathbf{w}^{\mathrm{T}}\mathbf{x_3}.$$

Problem 10.2 *Apply the linear SVM to two different datasets: (1) the XOR dataset and (2) the dataset in Example 10.1. Show that they have the same support vectors and decision boundary.*

Problem 10.3 *Consider a dataset in a two-dimensional vector space with two positive training vectors,* $(0.0, 1.0)$ *and* $(1.0, 0.0)$*, and two negative training vectors,* $(-0.2, -0.2)$ *and* $(0.0, 0.0)$*.*

(a) *Find the LSE, FDA, and linear SVM classifiers.*
(b) *Show that they share the same decision vectors,* $\mathbf{w}$*.*
(c) *Compare their respective thresholds.*
(d) *Compare their respective decision boundaries.*

Problem 10.4 (SVM for a small dataset) *Suppose that the training dataset has one negative pattern,* $\mathbf{x}_1 = (-1, 0)$*, and two positive patterns,* $\mathbf{x}_2 = (0, 0)$ *and* $\mathbf{x}_3 = (1, 1)$*.*

(a) *Find the optimal solution for the formulation prescribed by Eq. (8.38). Verify that all training vectors lie right on the marginal hyperplanes.*
(b) *Find the optimal SVM solution according to Eq. (10.4). Show that there are only two support vectors on the marginal hyperplanes.*
(c) *Verify that the SVM solution delivers a wider separation margin.*

Problem 10.5 *Suppose that an SVM, after the learning phase with the original N training dataset, yields S support vectors. Now we intend to train the SVM the second time, this time with a training dataset containing only the S support vectors.*

(a) *Show that all of the original S support vectors remain to be the support vectors for the second training process.*
(b) *Show that the second training process produces the very same discriminant function as the first training process. Explain why.*

Problem 10.6 *This problem studies the effect of scaling on linear SVMs, see Eq. (10.22). Let an original training vector, say* $\mathbf{x}_i$*, be scaled to become* $\mathbf{x}'_i = \beta\mathbf{x}$ *by a scaling factor* β*.*

(a) *Show that the output weight of the linear SVM in the scaled vector space is* $\mathbf{w}' = \mathbf{w}/\beta$ *and that the bias term is* $b' = 1 - \mathbf{w}' \cdot \mathbf{x}'_i = b$*.*
(b) *Show that the distance from the origin to the decision plane in the scaled vector space is* $b'/\|\mathbf{w}'\| = \beta b/\|\mathbf{w}\|$*.*

Problem 10.7 *Assume that the original SVM adopts a polynomial kernel:* $K(\mathbf{x}, \mathbf{x}_i) = (1 + \mathbf{x} \cdot \mathbf{x}_i)^2$*. When the training data is scaled by a factor* β*, however, the kernel function is also accordingly adapted to* $K'(\mathbf{x}', \mathbf{x}'_i) = (\beta^2 + \mathbf{x}' \cdot \mathbf{x}'_i)^2$*, where* $\mathbf{x}'_i = \beta\mathbf{x}_i\ \forall i$*.*

Denote the Lagrange multipliers and the Lagrangian corresponding to the new SVM in the scaled space as α'_i *and* $L(\alpha'_i)$*, respectively.*

(a) *Show that the Lagrangian corresponding to the scaled data is given by* $L(\alpha') = L(\alpha)/\beta^4$*, where* $L(\cdot)$ *is the Lagrangian corresponding to the unscaled data.*
(b) *Show that the decision boundary of an SVM that uses* $(\beta^2 + \mathbf{x}' \cdot \mathbf{x}'_i)^2$ *as the kernel function will produce a scaled version of the decision boundary given by the SVM that uses* $(1 + \mathbf{x} \cdot \mathbf{x}_i)^2$ *as the kernel function.*

Problem 10.8 *Consider a dataset with two positive training vectors* ($[0\ 0]^{\mathrm{T}}$ *and* $[0\ 2]^{\mathrm{T}}$) *and three negative training vectors* ($[0\ \ -1]^{\mathrm{T}}$, $[0\ 1]^{\mathrm{T}}$, *and* $[0.5\ 0.5]^{\mathrm{T}}$). *Can the training dataset be completely separated by adopting a second-order polynomial kernel function?*

Problem 10.9 *Consider a dataset with two positive training vectors* ($[0\ 0]^{\mathrm{T}}$ *and* $[0.45\ 0.45]^{\mathrm{T}}$) *and three negative training vectors* ($[1\ 0]^{\mathrm{T}}$, $[0\ 1]^{\mathrm{T}}$, *and* $[1\ 1]^{\mathrm{T}}$). *Derive the SVM learning models based on the following kernels:*

(a) *a linear kernel;*
(b) *a second-order polynomial kernel; and*
(c) *an RBF kernel.*

Problem 10.10 *Consider a shifted version of the dataset in Problem 10.9. Now the dataset has two positive training vectors* ($[-0.5\ \ -0.5]^{\mathrm{T}}$ *and* $[-0.05\ \ -0.05]^{\mathrm{T}}$) *and three negative training vectors* ($[0.5\ \ -0.5]^{\mathrm{T}}$, $[-0.5\ 0.5]^{\mathrm{T}}$, *and* $[0.5\ 0.5]^{\mathrm{T}}$). *Derive the SVM learning models for the following kernels and compare your results with the results obtained in Problem 10.9:*

(a) *a linear kernel;*
(b) *a second-order polynomial kernel; and*
(c) *an RBF kernel.*

Problem 10.11 (Support vectors for fuzzily separable SVM) *Consider a fuzzily separable SVM classifier. Let* $\mathbf{S}_{\mathrm{A}}$ *denote the set of training vectors with* $\alpha_i > 0$ *and let* $\mathbf{S}_{\mathrm{B}}$ *denote the set of training vectors for which* $\xi_i = 1 - y_i(\mathbf{x}_i \cdot \mathbf{w} + b) > 0$. *Show that* $\mathbf{S}_{\mathrm{A}} \supseteq \mathbf{S}_{\mathrm{B}}$.

Problem 10.12 *For SVM, several methods to determine the threshold b from the decision vector* $\mathbf{w}$ *have been proposed.*

(a) *Use* $b = 1 - \mathbf{w}^{\mathrm{T}}\mathbf{x}_i$, *where* $\mathbf{x}_i$ *is any of the support vectors with* $y_i = 1$.
(b) *Determine b from the mean value of*

$$1 - \mathbf{w}^{\mathrm{T}}\mathbf{x}_i, \ \mathbf{x}_i \in \mathcal{S}^+,$$

and

$$-1 - \mathbf{w}^{\mathrm{T}}\mathbf{x}_j, \ \mathbf{x}_j \in \mathcal{S}^-,$$

where $\mathcal{S}^+$ *and* $\mathcal{S}^-$ *contain support vectors for which the corresponding target values* (y_i *and* y_j) *are equal to* $+1$ *and* -1, *respectively.*
(c) *Compare the results of (a) and (b). Are they theoretically equivalent?*

Problem 10.13 *For two-dimensional training data, suppose that training data points are generically random and that no more than two data points are collinear. What is the maximum number of marginal support vectors (MSVs) for a linear SVM?*

Problem 10.14 *Show that, generically speaking, the number of support vectors right on the marginal planes is upper bounded by the intrinsic degree J.*

Problem 10.15 (Slack minimization) *Consider the linear classification problem Eq. (9.3) and let* $\xi_i = \max\{-y_i\epsilon_i, 0\}$. *Clearly,* ξ_i *satisfies the inequality (9.21) and* $\xi_i \geq 0$ *with equality iff* $y_i\epsilon_i \geq 0$. *The so-called* minimum squared slack *cost function is defined as follows:*

$$\mathcal{E}_{\text{MSS}} = \sum_{i=1}^{N} \xi_i^2 = \sum_{y_i\epsilon_i<0} \epsilon_i^2.$$

Prove the following statements.

(a) *If the problem is linearly separable, then the minimum* $\mathcal{E}_{\text{MSS}} = 0$ *is attained by* $[\mathbf{w}^{\text{T}}, b]^{\text{T}}$ *iff* $[\mathbf{w}^{\text{T}}, b]^{\text{T}}$ *is a separating vector.*

(b) *If the problem is not linearly separable then the cost function* $\mathcal{E}_{\text{MSS}}$ *attains its minimum for some* $[\mathbf{w}^{\text{T}}, b]^{\text{T}}$ *with* $0 < \|[\mathbf{w}^{\text{T}}, b]\| < \infty$.

Hint: *See [49, 310].*

Problem 10.16 (OVA versus AP) *Given* $K = 10$ *classes, each with* $10,000$ *training data, the total training data size is* $N = 100,000$.

(a) *Compare OVA versus AP in terms of learning and prediction computational complexities for (i) KRR and (ii) SVM learning models.*

(b) *A scheme published by Dietterich and Bakiri [51] encodes the labels of the K classes by K M-dimensional vectors whose elements are either* $+1$ *or* -1. *Then, M binary classifiers are trained so that, during retrieval, an M-dimensional vector in* $\{\pm 1\}^M$ *space is produced for each test pattern. The test pattern is classified according to the class whose corresponding encoded vector in* $\{\pm 1\}^M$ *space is closest (in terms of Hamming distance) to the vector produced by the binary classifiers. Provide an assessment of the computational complexities associated with the proposed multi-classification approach.*

Problem 10.17 *Compare the WEC of KDA and that of SVM with* $C \to \infty$.

Problem 10.18 *Show that the following two optimizers (one without constraints and one with) lead to the same optimal solution for SVM.*

- **Optimizer I:**

$$\min_{\alpha} \frac{1}{2} \sum_{i=1}^{N} \sum_{j=1}^{N} \alpha_i \alpha_j y_i y_j K(\mathbf{x}_i, \mathbf{x}_j) + C \sum_{i=1}^{N} \left(1 - y_i(\mathbf{a}^T \vec{\mathbf{k}}(\mathbf{x}_i) + b)\right)_+,$$

subject to $0 \leq \alpha_i \leq C$, $i = 1, \ldots, N$.

- **Optimizer II:**

$$\min_{\alpha} \frac{1}{2} \sum_{i=1}^{N} \sum_{j=1}^{N} \alpha_i \alpha_j y_i y_j K(\mathbf{x}_i, \mathbf{x}_j) + C \sum_{i=1}^{N} \left(1 - y_i(\mathbf{a}^T \overrightarrow{\mathbf{k}}(\mathbf{x}_i) + b)\right)_+ ,$$

Problem 10.19 (MATLAB simulation on image database) *An image database containing ten categories each with 100 JPG images can be found at http://wang.ist.psu.edu/docs/related/. Apply linear supervised classifiers, LDA, and linear SVM (see Chapter 8) to the dataset and compare their performances.*

11 Support vector learning models for outlier detection

11.1 Introduction

Outlier detection is an important subject in machine learning and data analysis. The term outlier refers to abnormal observations that are inconsistent with the bulk of the data distribution [16, 32, 98, 240, 265, 266, 287]. Some sample applications are as follows.

- Detection of imposters or rejection of unauthorized access to computer networks.
- Genomic research – identifying abnormal gene or protein sequences.
- Biomedical, e.g. ECG arrythmia monitoring.
- Environmental safety detection, where outliers indicate abnormality.
- Personal safety, with security aids embedded in mobile devices.

For some real-world application examples, see e.g Hodge and Austin [98].

The standard approach to outlier detection is density-based, whereby the detection depends on the outlier's relationship with the bulk of the data. Many algorithms use concepts of proximity and/or density estimation in order to find outliers. However, in high-dimensional spaces the data become increasingly sparse and the notion of proximity/density has become less meaningful, and consequently model-based methods have become more appealing [1, 39]. It is also a typical assumption that a model is to be trained from only one type of (say, positive) training patterns, making it a fundamentally different problem, and thereby creating a new learning paradigm leading to one-class-based learning models.

SVM-type learning models are naturally amenable to outlier detection since certain support vectors can be identified as outliers. This chapter will address the following topics.

(i) Section 11.2 explores an important variant of SVM, i.e. support vector regression (SVR), which is intended for regression analysis whose aim is to find an approximating function to fit a set of training data.

(ii) Sections 11.3, 11.4, and 11.5 respectively explore three other SVM-based learning models (hyperplane OCSVM, hypersphere OCSVM, and SVC), which are useful for for outlier-detection applications. It will be shown that, for Gaussian kernels, all three algorithms coincide with each other. In addition, we shall also probe into critical issues such as the fraction of outliers and translation-invariance properties.

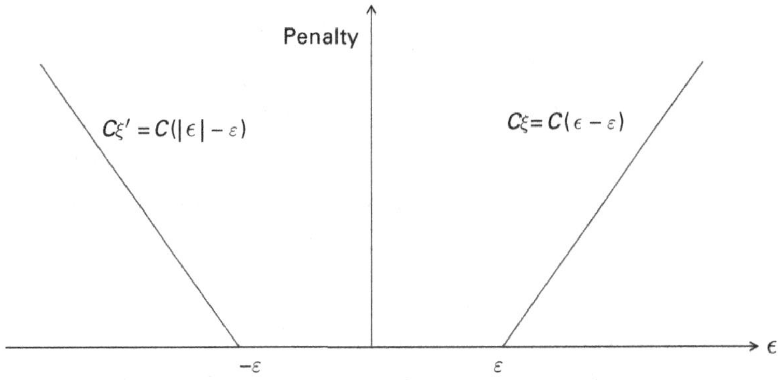

Fig. 11.1. An ε-insensitive penalty function with "grace interval" ε.

11.2 Support vector regression (SVR)

Support vector regression (SVR), which was proposed by Vapnik *et al.* [52, 279], is an important variant of SVM. It is meant for regression analysis whose aim is to find an approximating function to fit a set of training data. Its formulation is largely similar to that of SVM for classification, except for the introduction of the new notion of an ε-insensitive loss function, which will be explained below.

Given the training dataset $\{\mathbf{x}_i, y_i\}_{i=1}^N$, the kernel-induced training dataset is denoted as $\{(\vec{\phi}_i, y_i\}_{i=1}^N$, where for simplicity we shall denote

$$\vec{\phi}_i \equiv \vec{\phi}(\mathbf{x}_i).$$

The estimation error corresponding to each training vector $\vec{\phi}_i$, denoted by

$$\epsilon_i = \mathbf{u}^{\mathrm{T}}\vec{\phi}_i + b - y_i \quad \forall i = 1, \ldots, N,$$

will dictate the penalty function.

The ε-insensitive penalty

As shown in Figure 11.1, there will be no penalty if the violation $|\epsilon_i|$ is within a given grace margin ε. If $|\epsilon_i|$ does exceed ε, the penalty imposed will be linearly proportional to the exceeding amount only, i.e. $|\epsilon_i| - \varepsilon$. More exactly, the penalty function is

$$\text{penalty} = \begin{cases} C\xi_i = C(\epsilon_i - \varepsilon), & \text{if } \epsilon_i > \varepsilon \\ 0, & \text{if } -\varepsilon \le \epsilon_i \le \varepsilon \\ C\xi_i' = C(|\epsilon_i| - \varepsilon), & \text{if } \epsilon_i < -\varepsilon, \end{cases} \tag{11.1}$$

where $\varepsilon > 0$ denotes a pre-specified and positive "grace interval." Taking into account the grace interval ε, the primal optimization formulation in the intrinsic space becomes

$$\underset{\mathbf{u},b,\{\xi,\xi'\}\in\mathbb{R}^N}{\text{minimize}} \frac{1}{2}\|\mathbf{u}\|^2 + C\left(\sum_{i=1}^{N}(\xi_i + \xi'_i)\right)$$

subject to the adjusted soft-constraints

$$\begin{aligned} \epsilon_i &\leq \varepsilon + \xi_i, \text{ with } \xi_i \geq 0 \quad \forall i = 1,\ldots,N, \\ -\epsilon_i &\leq \varepsilon + \xi'_i, \text{ with } \xi'_i \geq 0 \quad \forall i = 1,\ldots,N, \\ \text{where } \epsilon_i &= \mathbf{u}^{\mathrm{T}}\vec{\boldsymbol{\phi}}_i + b - y_i \quad \forall i = 1,\ldots,N, \end{aligned} \tag{11.2}$$

where C is a user-specified constant.

The optimizer satisfies the LSP condition in Theorem 1.1; therefore, the learning model has a kernelized formulation. For the two sets of non-negative slack variables $\{\xi_i,\ i = 1,\ldots,N\}$ and $\{\xi'_i,\ i = 1,\ldots,N\}$ used to characterize the ε-insensitive loss function, two corresponding sets of Lagrange multipliers $\{\alpha_i\}_{i=1}^N$ and $\{\alpha'_i\}_{i=1}^N$ need to be incorporated into the optimizer in the dual domain. This leads to the following learning model in the empirical space.

ALGORITHM 11.1 (SVR learning model) *Given the kernel matrix* **K** *and the teacher vector* **y**, *the SVR learning model aims at finding the coefficients* $\{\alpha_i\}$ *and* $\{\alpha'_i\}$ *such that*

$$\begin{aligned} \underset{\boldsymbol{\alpha},\alpha'\in\mathbb{R}^N}{\text{maximize}}\ L(\boldsymbol{\alpha},\boldsymbol{\alpha}') = &-\left(\sum_{i=1}^{N} y_i(\alpha_i - \alpha'_i) + \varepsilon\sum_{i=1}^{N}(\alpha_i + \alpha'_i)\right. \\ &\left. + \frac{1}{2}\sum_{i,j=1}^{N}(\alpha_i - \alpha'_i)(\alpha_j - \alpha'_j)K(\mathbf{x}_i,\mathbf{x}_j)\right) \end{aligned}$$

subject to

$$\begin{aligned} \sum_{i=1}^{N}(\alpha_i - \alpha'_i) = 0 \quad \textit{with} \quad & 0 \leq \alpha_i \leq C, \\ & 0 \leq \alpha'_i \leq C, \\ & i = 1,2,\ldots,N. \end{aligned} \tag{11.3}$$

By application of the LSP,

$$\mathbf{u} = \sum_{i=1}^{N} a_i\vec{\boldsymbol{\phi}}(\mathbf{x}_i),$$

where $a_i = \alpha'_i - \alpha_i$. *Hence the discriminant function is*

$$\begin{aligned} f(\mathbf{x}) &= \mathbf{u}^{\mathrm{T}}\vec{\boldsymbol{\phi}}(\mathbf{x}) + b \\ &= \sum_{i=1}^{N}\left(a_i\vec{\boldsymbol{\phi}}(\mathbf{x}_i)^{\mathrm{T}}\vec{\boldsymbol{\phi}}(\mathbf{x})\right) + b \\ &= \sum_{i=1}^{N} a_i K(\mathbf{x}_i,\mathbf{x}) + b, \end{aligned} \tag{11.4}$$

where the threshold value b may be derived from Eq. (11.2), pursuant to the KKT conditions. □

Note that SVR is more intricate than SVM, since one needs to simultaneously pre-select two design parameters, namely the penalty factor C and the tolerance ε.

SVR has successfully been applied to the detection of outliers in industrial use [116] and financial prediction [309]. In addition, there are other varieties of applications, for example, time-series prediction and modeling problems [184, 186].

11.3 Hyperplane-based one-class SVM learning models

Outlier detection is an important subject in machine learning and data analysis. Various outlier-detecting learning models have been proposed by Tax and Duin [265, 266], Schölkopf *et al.* [237, 240], and Campbell and Bennett [32], all being inspired by the prior works by Vapnik [280, 281] and Ben-David and Lindenbaum [14].

11.3.1 Hyperplane-based ν-SV classifiers

In this section, we shall first derive an SV-based learning model for two-class classification, named the ν-SVM [238b], classifier, in which the support vectors are characterized by the decision hyperplane in the kernel-induced intrinsic space. The two-class ν-SV classifier can then be converted into a one-class variant, which is then applicable to outlier detection and related applications.

A ν-SV classifier is motivated by the notion of a *tunable* or *adjustable* teacher value:

$$y_i' = y_i\eta = \begin{cases} +\eta & \text{if} \quad \mathbf{x}_i \in \mathcal{C}_+ \\ -\,\eta & \text{if} \quad \mathbf{x}_i \in \mathcal{C}_- . \end{cases} \tag{11.5}$$

It is known that the separation margin between the positive and negative hyperplanes (characterized by their respective support vectors) is [251]

$$\text{margin separation} = \frac{2\eta}{\|\mathbf{u}\|}.$$

In order to best optimize the separation margin, we aim at achieving two objectives in parallel: (1) one is to minimize $\|\mathbf{u}\|$, while (2) the other is to maximize η. Since the two objectives are inherently contradictory, they can be balanced by means of a positive weighting factor ν. This leads to the following primal optimizer in intrinsic space:

$$\begin{gathered} \underset{\mathbf{u},b,\eta}{\text{minimize}}\ \tau(\mathbf{u}, b, \eta) = \tfrac{1}{2}\|\mathbf{u}\|^2 - \nu\eta \\ \text{subject to the hard constraints} \\ y_i\epsilon_i \geq 0, \quad \text{where} \quad \epsilon_i \equiv \mathbf{u}^{\mathrm{T}}\vec{\boldsymbol{\phi}}_i + b - y_i' = \mathbf{u}^{\mathrm{T}}\vec{\boldsymbol{\phi}}_i + b - y_i\eta \\ \text{and } \eta \geq 0,\ \forall\, i = 1, \ldots, N. \end{gathered} \tag{11.6}$$

Note that this formulation resembles Eq. (10.4), which was used for the clearly separable SVM. It follows that the corresponding dual optimizer is

$$\underset{\boldsymbol{\alpha}\in\mathbb{R}^N}{\text{maximize}}\ L(\boldsymbol{\alpha}) = -\frac{1}{2}\sum_{i,j=1}^{N}\alpha_i\alpha_j y_i y_j K(\mathbf{x}_i,\mathbf{x}_j)$$

$$\text{subject to } 0 \le \alpha_i,\ \sum_{i=1}^{N}\alpha_i y_i = 0 \text{ and } \sum_{i=1}^{N}\alpha_i \ge \nu. \tag{11.7}$$

Primal optimizer in intrinsic space

The assumption of clear separability between the two classes is not practical for real-world applications. Borrowing the same idea as for fuzzy SVMs, the hard constraints are often replaced by soft constraints. More precisely, the hard constraint $y_i\epsilon_i \ge 0$ can be relaxed into softer constraints $y_i\epsilon_i + \xi_i \ge 0$, by invoking a positive *slack variable* ξ_i, for all $i = 1, \ldots, N$. To prevent excessive relaxation from taking place, a penalty term $C\sum_i \xi_i$, $C > 0$, must be incorporated into the cost function, resulting in

$$\tau(\mathbf{u}, \boldsymbol{\xi}, \eta) = \frac{1}{2}\|\mathbf{u}\|^2 - \nu\eta + C\sum_{i=1}^{N}\xi_i.$$

Moreover, without loss of generality, we can simply set $\nu = 1$.[1] This leads to the following primal optimizer:

$$\underset{\mathbf{u},b,\eta,\boldsymbol{\xi}}{\text{minimize}}\ \tau(\mathbf{u}, \boldsymbol{\xi}, \eta) = \frac{1}{2}\|\mathbf{u}\|^2 - \eta + C\sum_{i=1}^{N}\xi_i$$

subject to the soft constraints

$$y_i\epsilon_i + \xi_i \ge 0, \quad \text{where} \quad \epsilon_i \equiv \mathbf{u}^{\mathrm{T}}\overrightarrow{\boldsymbol{\phi}}_i + b - y_i\eta$$

$$\text{and } \xi_i \ge 0,\ \eta \ge 0,\ \forall i = 1, \ldots, N. \tag{11.8}$$

Equivalence/Difference between ν-SVM and SVM

Note that when the teacher value is fixed to $\eta = 1$, Eq. (11.8) reduces to Eq. (10.35) which is the formulation for the conventional SVM. (See Problem 11.3.) It should be obvious that the teacher value η should be strictly positive to create a meaningful separation between the two classes. In this case, it can be shown that the ν-SVM and SVM are basically equivalent. The justification is briefly explained as follows [238b]. Suppose that the optimizer in Eq. (11.8) returns a positive optimal teacher value, say $\eta^* > 0$. If we fix η to η^* and then solve for the very same optimizer in Eq. (11.8) with respect to the remaining variables, then it becomes basically the same mathematical problem as that

[1] The role of ν may be substituted by a transformation $\overrightarrow{\boldsymbol{\phi}}' = r\overrightarrow{\boldsymbol{\phi}}$ with a scaling factor r, $r = \nu^{\frac{1}{2}}$. In this case, $\mathbf{u} = r\mathbf{u}'$ and the cost function can be re-expressed as

$$\tau(\mathbf{u}, \boldsymbol{\xi}, \eta) = \frac{1}{2}\|\mathbf{u}\|^2 - \nu\eta + C\sum_{i=1}^{N}\xi_i = \nu\left(\frac{1}{2}\|\mathbf{u}'\|^2 - \eta + C'\sum_{i=1}^{N}\xi_i\right),$$

where $C' = \nu^{-1}C$.

solve for the conventional SVM in Eq. (10.35), except for an inconsequential scaling factor of η^{*-1} on the adaptable variables $\mathbf{u}$, b, ξ, as well as the penalty factor C.

At first glance, by allowing the teacher value η to be adaptable, the ν-SVM formulation appears to expand the design scope beyond that of SVM. Ironically, under the positive teacher-value requirement, the ν-SVM's scope becomes narrower than SVM. (This is evidenced by the fact that Eq. (10.40) remains solvable, but not Eq. (11.10), when $C < N^{-1}$.)

More explicitly, the primal formulation for the two-class ν-SV classifier can be expressed as follows [239]:

$$\begin{aligned}&\underset{\mathbf{u},b,\eta,\boldsymbol{\xi}}{\text{minimize}}\ \tau(\mathbf{u},\boldsymbol{\xi},\eta) = \frac{1}{2}\|\mathbf{u}\|^2 - \eta + C\sum_{i=1}^{N}\xi_i\\ &\text{subject to the soft-constraints } y_i(\mathbf{u}^{\mathrm{T}}\vec{\boldsymbol{\phi}}_i + b) \geq \eta - \xi_i\\ &\text{and } \xi_i \geq 0,\ \eta \geq 0\ \forall\, i = 1,\ldots,N.\end{aligned} \tag{11.9}$$

The dual optimizer in empirical space

For the non-negative slack variables $\{\xi_i, i = 1,\ldots,N\}$, a set of Lagrange multipliers $\{\alpha_i\}_{i=1}^N$ can be used to lead to the following dual-optimization formulation:

$$\begin{aligned}&\underset{\boldsymbol{\alpha}\in\mathbb{R}^N}{\text{maximize}}\ L(\boldsymbol{\alpha}) = -\frac{1}{2}\sum_{i,j=1}^{N}\alpha_i\alpha_j y_i y_j K(\mathbf{x}_i,\mathbf{x}_j)\\ &\text{subject to } 0 \leq \alpha_i \leq C,\ \sum_{i=1}^{N}\alpha_i y_i = 0, \text{ and } \sum_{i=1}^{N}\alpha_i \geq 1.\end{aligned} \tag{11.10}$$

The LSP clearly holds for the two-class ν-SV classifier, and in fact

$$\mathbf{u} = \sum_{i=1}^{N}\alpha_i y_i \vec{\boldsymbol{\phi}}(\mathbf{x}_i).$$

Hence the discriminant function is

$$\begin{aligned}f(\mathbf{x}) &= \mathbf{u}^{\mathrm{T}}\vec{\boldsymbol{\phi}}(\mathbf{x}) + b\\ &= \sum_{i=1}^{N}\left(\alpha_i y_i \vec{\boldsymbol{\phi}}(\mathbf{x}_i)^{\mathrm{T}}\vec{\boldsymbol{\phi}}(\mathbf{x})\right) + b\\ &= \sum_{i=1}^{N}\alpha_i y_i K(\mathbf{x}_i,\mathbf{x}) + b\end{aligned} \tag{11.11}$$

where b can be derived via the KKT condition. Finally, the decision boundary is given as $f(\mathbf{x}) = 0$.

11.3.2 Hyperplane-based one-class SVM

The basic principle behind the two-class SVM is based on separating the positive and negative training vectors. For outlier detection, however, we have access to only one

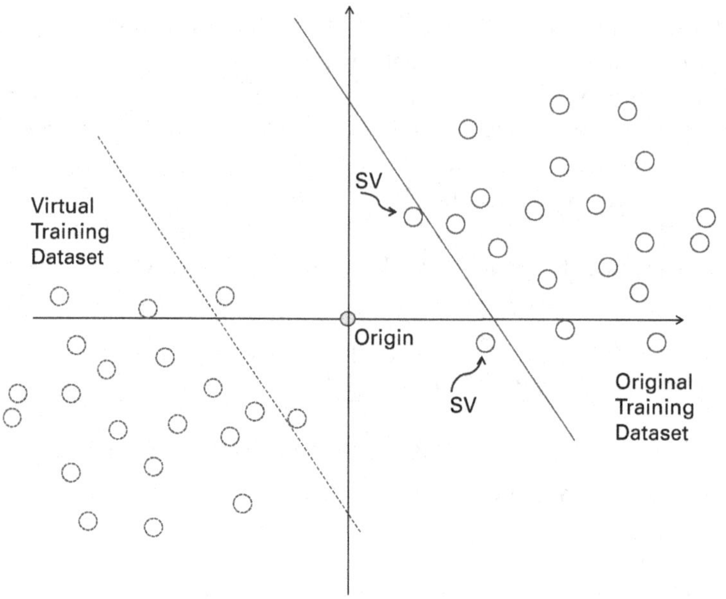

Fig. 11.2. The formation of virtual training vectors may lead to hyperplane-based OCSVM learning models as proposed by Schölkopf *et al.* [237, 240].

class of training vectors, which, without loss of generality, will be labeled as the positive training dataset. Since no information about the negative class is given, the first item of business is to characterize or identify a plausible representation of the negative training vectors. There are several possible approaches. One possibility is to assume a totally random distribution of the negative patterns. Another popular model is that the known patterns are presumably encircled by a spherical circumference, thus the potential negative patterns are expected to be found outside the perimeter of the spherical ball. This assumption leads to the hypersphere-based one-class SVM model proposed by Tax and Duin [265, 266].

Another model adopts a mirror-image approach to the creation of the negative training dataset. As shown in Figure 11.2, the real and virtual datasets form mirror images of each other. More exactly, the given training vectors form the positive training dataset,

$$\{+\vec{\phi}_i, +y_i\eta\}, \quad i = 1, \ldots, N,$$

and the virtual training vectors form the negative training dataset,

$$\{\vec{\phi}_{N+i}, \ y_{N+i}\eta\} \equiv \{-\vec{\phi}_i, \ -y_i\eta\}, i = 1, \ldots, N.$$

All combined, there are $2N$ training vectors, N positive and N negative, and the two-class ν-SV classifier is ready to be applied. This leads to the formulation for the hyperplane-based one-class SVM (OCSVM) derived below.

The primal optimizer in intrinsic space

On applying Eq. (11.8) to the newly created positive and negative datasets, we have the following primal optimization program:

$$\underset{\mathbf{u},b,\eta,\boldsymbol{\xi}}{\text{minimize}}\ \tau(\mathbf{u},\boldsymbol{\xi},\eta) = \frac{1}{2}\|\mathbf{u}\|^2 - \eta + C\sum_{i=1}^{N}\xi_i$$

subject to the positive constraints

$$y_i\epsilon_i + \xi_i \geq 0, \text{ where } \epsilon_i = +\mathbf{u}^{\mathrm{T}}\overrightarrow{\boldsymbol{\phi}}_i + b - \eta \quad \forall i = 1,\ldots,N,$$

and to the negative constraints

$$y_{N+i}\epsilon_{N+i} + \xi_{N+i} \geq 0, \text{ where } \epsilon_{N+i} \equiv -\mathbf{u}^{\mathrm{T}}\overrightarrow{\boldsymbol{\phi}}_i + b + \eta \quad \forall i = 1,\ldots,N,$$

$$\text{and } \xi_i = \xi_{N+i} \geq 0, \quad \eta \geq 0, \quad \forall i = 1,\ldots,N. \tag{11.12}$$

Let us probe into the positive constraint Eq. (11.12). We have

$$y_i\epsilon_i + \xi_i = +\left(+\mathbf{u}^{\mathrm{T}}\overrightarrow{\boldsymbol{\phi}}_i + b - \eta\right) + \xi_i \geq 0,$$

i.e.

$$\eta \leq b + \xi_i + \mathbf{u}^{\mathrm{T}}\overrightarrow{\boldsymbol{\phi}}(\mathbf{x}_i).$$

Likewise, from the negative constraint Eq. (11.12), we have

$$y_{N+i}\epsilon_{N+i} + \xi_{N+i} = -\left(-\mathbf{u}^{\mathrm{T}}\overrightarrow{\boldsymbol{\phi}}_i + b + \eta\right) + \xi_i \geq 0,$$

i.e.

$$\eta \leq -b + \xi_i + \mathbf{u}^{\mathrm{T}}\overrightarrow{\boldsymbol{\phi}}(\mathbf{x}_i).$$

On combining the above, we arrive at

$$\eta \leq -|b| + \xi_i + \mathbf{u}^{\mathrm{T}}\overrightarrow{\boldsymbol{\phi}}(\mathbf{x}_i).$$

It is evident that any nonzero b (positive or negative) can only decrease the magnitude of η, which would work against the goal of optimization. Therefore, in order to attain optimality, it is necessary to set $b = 0$.

By using the fact that $b = 0$, the positive constraints in Eq. (11.12) can be simplified to

$$y_i\epsilon_i + \xi_i = +\left(+\mathbf{u}^{\mathrm{T}}\overrightarrow{\boldsymbol{\phi}}_i - \eta\right) + \xi_i = \mathbf{u}^{\mathrm{T}}\overrightarrow{\boldsymbol{\phi}}_i - \eta + \xi_i \geq 0.$$

Likewise, the negative constraints in Eq. (11.12) can be simplified to

$$y_{N+i}\epsilon_{N+i} + \xi_{N+i} = -\left(-\mathbf{u}^{\mathrm{T}}\overrightarrow{\boldsymbol{\phi}}_i + \eta\right) + \xi_i = \mathbf{u}^{\mathrm{T}}\overrightarrow{\boldsymbol{\phi}}_i - \eta + \xi_i \geq 0.$$

The two sets of constraints are apparently identical, so they can merge into just one set. This leads to the following primal optimization formulation for the hyperplane OCSVM:

$$\underset{\mathbf{u},\eta,\boldsymbol{\xi}}{\text{minimize}}\ \tau(\mathbf{u},\boldsymbol{\xi},\eta) = \frac{1}{2}\|\mathbf{u}\|^2 - \eta + C\sum_{i=1}^{N}\xi_i$$

$$\text{subject to } \mathbf{u}^{\mathrm{T}}\overrightarrow{\boldsymbol{\phi}}_i - \eta + \xi_i \geq 0,$$

$$\text{where } \xi_i \geq 0 \quad \text{and} \quad \eta \geq 0. \tag{11.13}$$

The dual optimizer in empirical space

Via the typical procedure used before, the dual optimization formulation can be derived as

$$\underset{\boldsymbol{\alpha}\in\mathbb{R}^N}{\text{maximize}}\ L(\boldsymbol{\alpha}) = -\frac{1}{2}\sum_{i,j=1}^{N}\alpha_i\alpha_j K(\mathbf{x}_i,\mathbf{x}_j)$$

$$\text{subject to } 0 \le \alpha_i \le C \textit{ and } \sum_{i=1}^{N}\alpha_i = 1. \tag{11.14}$$

Note that there exists a subtle difference between the constraints in Eq. (11.10) (i.e. $\sum_{i=1}^{N}\alpha_i \ge 1$) for the two-class ν-SV classifier and those in Eq. (11.14) (i.e. $\sum_{i=1}^{N}\alpha_i = 1$) for OCSVM. For a Mercer kernel, the change is inconsequential because, for OCSVM, the smaller the magnitude of $\{\alpha_i\}$ the better the solution. Therefore, only when the equality $\sum_{i=1}^{N}\alpha_i = 1$ is exactly met (instead of $\sum_{i=1}^{N}\alpha_i > 1$) can the optimum be attained.

Analogously to the two-class case, the resultant discriminant function is

$$f(\mathbf{x}) = \sum_{i=1}^{N}\alpha_i\Big(K(\mathbf{x}_i,\mathbf{x}) - K(\mathbf{x}_i,\mathbf{x}_k)\Big), \tag{11.15}$$

for any integer k such that $0 < \alpha_k < C$. Finally, the class (or cluster boundary) will be characterized by $f(\mathbf{x}) = 0$ and a test vector $\mathbf{x}$ will be identified as an outlier if and only if $f(\mathbf{x}) < 0$. With reference to Figure 11.2, it means that $\mathbf{x}$ will be viewed as an outlier if it falls on the "virtual" territory.

ALGORITHM 11.2 (Hyperplane one-class SVM learning model) *Given the kernel matrix* $\mathbf{K}$ *formed by one class of training vectors, the hypersphere OCSVM learning model aims at finding the coefficients* $\{\alpha_i\}$ *such that*

$$\underset{\boldsymbol{\alpha}\in\mathbb{R}^N}{\text{maximize}}\ L(\boldsymbol{\alpha}) = -\frac{1}{2}\sum_{i,j=1}^{N}\alpha_i\alpha_j K(\mathbf{x}_i,\mathbf{x}_j) \tag{11.16}$$

$$\textit{subject to } 0 \le \alpha_i \le C \textit{ and } \sum_{i=1}^{N}\alpha_i = 1. \tag{11.17}$$

The discriminant function is

$$f(\mathbf{x}) = \sum_{i=1}^{N}\alpha_i\Big(K(\mathbf{x}_i,\mathbf{x}) - K(\mathbf{x}_i,\mathbf{x}_k)\Big), \tag{11.18}$$

for any integer k such that $0 < \alpha_k < C$. *In this case,* $\mathbf{x}_k$ *can be called a marginal support vector. Finally, a test vector* $\mathbf{x}$ *will be identified as an outlier if and only if* $f(\mathbf{x}) < 0$. □

An important merit of OCSVM lies in the fact that the number of outliers (or outlier support vectors) can be controlled by properly adjusting the parameter C, see Eq. (11.25) [237, 240]. There is concern regarding its translation invariance, which will be treated in Section 11.5.

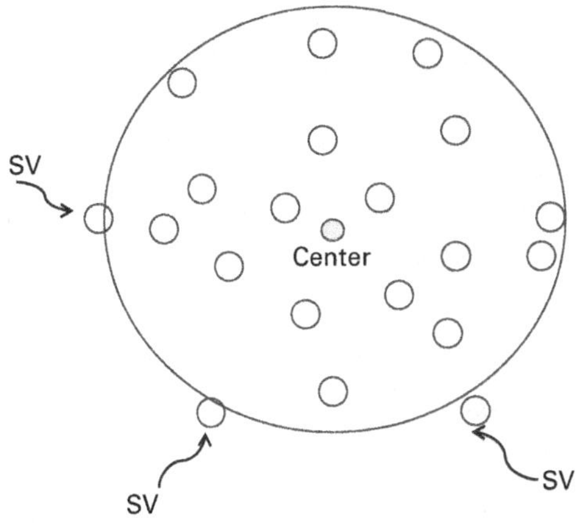

Fig. 11.3. The hypersphere one-class SVM proposed by Tax and Duin [265, 266].

11.4 Hypersphere-based one-class SVM

The principle behind the hypersphere one-class SVM (hypersphere OCSVM) proposed by Tax and Duin [265, 266] is illustrated by Figure 11.3. It aims at finding a minimum radius sphere (or hypersphere) to surround the majority of the data, allowing a small fraction of "outliers" to fall outside. In order to control the number of "outliers," a penalty for outliers must be incorporated into the objective function of the hypersphere-OCSVM learning model.

The primal optimizer in intrinsic space

Given the training dataset $\{\mathbf{x}_i)\}_{i=1}^N$, the kernel-induced training dataset is denoted as $\{(\overrightarrow{\boldsymbol{\phi}}_i)\}_{i=1}^N$, where for simplicity we shall denote

$$\overrightarrow{\boldsymbol{\phi}}_i \equiv \overrightarrow{\boldsymbol{\phi}}(\mathbf{x}_i). \tag{11.19}$$

In the kernel-induced intrinsic space, we look for the smallest enclosing sphere of radius R surrounding the sphere's center, denoted by $\mathbf{u}$. This is illustrated by Figure 11.3. Using soft constraints, we arrive at the following primal optimizer:

$$\begin{aligned} &\underset{\mathbf{u},R,\boldsymbol{\xi}}{\text{minimize}} \left\{R^2 + C\sum_{i=1}^N \xi_i\right\} \\ &\text{subject to } ||\overrightarrow{\boldsymbol{\phi}}_i - \mathbf{u}||^2 \leq R^2 + \xi_i \text{ and } \xi_i \geq 0, \end{aligned} \tag{11.20}$$

which can be slightly modified into

$$\begin{aligned} &\underset{\mathbf{u},R,\boldsymbol{\xi}}{\text{minimize}} \left\{R^2 + C\sum_{i=1}^N \xi_i\right\} \\ &\text{subject to } ||\mathbf{u}||^2 + ||\overrightarrow{\boldsymbol{\phi}}_i||^2 - 2\mathbf{u}^{\mathrm{T}}\overrightarrow{\boldsymbol{\phi}}_i - R^2 - \xi_i \leq 0 \text{ and } \xi_i \geq 0. \end{aligned} \tag{11.21}$$

Now, the inequality term monotonically increases with $\|\vec{\phi}_i\|^2$; therefore, the LSP holds according to Theorem 1.1.

The dual optimizer in empirical space

The above intrinsic-space optimizer satisfies the LSP condition in Theorem 1.1; therefore, the learning model has a kernelized formulation. This leads to the following learning model in the empirical space.

ALGORITHM 11.3 (Hypersphere one-class SVM learning model) *Given the kernel matrix* $\mathbf{K}$ *formed by one class of training vectors, the hypersphere-OCSVM learning model aims at finding the coefficients* $\{\alpha_i\}$ *such that*

$$\underset{\boldsymbol{\alpha}\in\mathbb{R}^N}{\text{maximize}}\ L(\boldsymbol{\alpha}) = \sum_{i}^{N} \alpha_i K(\mathbf{x}_i, \mathbf{x}_i) - \sum_{i,j=1}^{N} \alpha_i\alpha_j K(\mathbf{x}_i, \mathbf{x}_j)$$

$$\textit{subject to } 0 \le \alpha_i \le C, \sum_{i=1}^{N} \alpha_i = 1. \tag{11.22}$$

By application of the LSP, we have

$$\mathbf{u} = \sum_{i=1}^{N} \vec{\phi}(\mathbf{x}_i)\alpha_i, \tag{11.23}$$

and the discriminant function is

$$\begin{aligned} f(\mathbf{x}) &= R^2 - ||\vec{\phi}(\mathbf{x}) - \mathbf{u}||^2 \\ &= R^2 - \sum_{i,j=1}^{N} \alpha_i\alpha_j K(\mathbf{x}_i, \mathbf{x}_j) \\ &\quad + 2\sum_{i}^{N} \alpha_i K(\mathbf{x}_i, \mathbf{x}) - K(\mathbf{x}, \mathbf{x}), \end{aligned} \tag{11.24}$$

where $R^2 = ||\vec{\phi}(\mathbf{x}_k) - \mathbf{u}||^2$ *for any MSV* $\mathbf{x}_k$*, i.e.* $0 < \alpha_k < C$*. Finally, a test vector* $\mathbf{x}$ *will be identified as an outlier if and only if* $f(\mathbf{x}) < 0$. □

The number of outlier support vectors (OSVs)

According to the value of the discriminant function, $\epsilon_i = f(\mathbf{x}_i)$, associated with the training vector $\mathbf{x}_i$, the training vectors can be divided into (1) in-class vectors and (2) support vectors. The in-class vectors are those vectors corresponding to $f(\mathbf{x}_i) > 0$. These vectors fall within the circumference of the circle, and they are considered to be non-support vectors since they do not directly participate in defining $\mathbf{u}$ in Eq. (11.23), which represents the "center" of the circle.

In contrast, as shown in Eq. (11.23), the center $\mathbf{u}$ is a linear combination of the support vectors. In fact, the support vectors of OCSVM can be divided into two categories.

- **Marginal support vectors (MSVs):** $\epsilon_i = f(\mathbf{x}_i) = 0$. Relatively few support vectors happen to fall on the vertical-edge region shown in Figure 10.6(a), i.e. $\epsilon_i = 0$. In this sense, the *marginal support vectors* (MSVs) serve to characterize the class boundary of the OCSVM.
- **Outlier support vectors (OSVs):** $\epsilon_i = f(\mathbf{x}_i) < 0$. As shown in Figure 10.6(a), most support vectors fall within the so-called constant-α zone, i.e. $\epsilon_i < 0$ and $\alpha_i = C$. The OSVs are also known as *bounded support vectors* (BSVs). These types of support vectors lie strictly outside the class boundary and will be viewed as *outliers*.

To facilitate estimating the number of outliers or support vectors, let us note that, by virtue of the condition in Eq. (11.22), $\alpha_i = C$ for those outlier SVs. We use $N_{\rm O}$ to denote the total number of those outlier SVs. Then, according to Eq. (11.22), we have

$$N_{\rm O} \times C \leq \sum_{i=1}^{N} \alpha_i = 1.$$

This means that the ratio between the number of outlier SVs and that of all training vectors is

$$\frac{N_{\rm O}}{N} \leq \frac{1}{NC}. \tag{11.25}$$

Hence $1/(NC)$ constitutes an upper bound on the fraction of SVs or outliers. It was shown by Schölkopf *et al.* [237, 240] that the fraction of outliers tends to $1/(NC)$, asymptotically when N grows extremely large.

The Gaussian kernel case: equivalence between hyperplane and hypersphere OCSVMs

In fact, both hyperplane and hypersphere OCSVMs can find useful applications in several anomaly-detection problems. In addition, the presence of support vectors facilitates clustering, see Section 11.5. Hence they may also be applicable to clustering. It can be shown that polynomial kernels do not yield tight contour representations of a cluster [265, 266], thus necessitating the use of Gaussian kernels for clustering applications.

In this case, we can establish the equivalence between hyperplane and hypersphere OCSVMs [239]. Since Gaussian kernels are shift-invariant, i.e. the kernel $K(\mathbf{x}, \mathbf{x}')$ is a function of $\mathbf{x} - \mathbf{x}'$, and, in particular, $K(\mathbf{x}_i, \mathbf{x}_i) = K(0, 0)$ for all $i = 1, \ldots, N$, it follows that the equality constraint in Eq. (11.22), $\sum_{i=1}^{N} \alpha_i = 1$, implies that the linear term in the corresponding cost function is a constant:

$$\sum_{i}^{N} \alpha_i K(\mathbf{x}_i, \mathbf{x}_i) = \sum_{i}^{N} \alpha_i K(0, 0) = K(0, 0).$$

This implies that the optimization problem prescribed in Eqs. (11.22) is equivalent to that in Eq. (11.17). Consequently, the solutions given in Eq. (11.18) and Eq. (11.24) are equivalent.

11.5 Support vector clustering

Since a sphere in the original vector space might not be the most effective geometry to describe the distribution of data, a sphere in the kernel-induced vector space offers a more flexible substitute. This becomes a hypersphere when mapped back to the original space. As pointed out by Tax and Duin [265, 266], polynomial kernels do not yield tight contour representations of a cluster. Therefore, the use of Gaussian kernels is specifically required for clustering applications. For Gaussian RBF kernels, the hyperplane and hypersphere OCSVMs are equivalent. Moreover, either of these two models suffices to provide an adequate theoretical footing for the support vector clustering (SVC) model proposed by Ben-Hur, Horn, Siegelmann, and Vapnik [16]. Conceptually, the development of SVC is reminiscent of that for hypersphere OCSVM. In fact, both models aim at finding the smallest sphere that encloses the training vectors in the kernel-induced feature space, leading to the optimizer given in Eq. (11.20).

In short, for Gaussian RBF kernels, all three learning models (hyperplane OCSVM, hypersphere OCSVM, and SVC) coincide with each other.

Split into subclusters when mapped back to original space

An important clustering property of OCSVM and SVC highlighted in [16] is that a sphere in the intrinsic space can split into several subclusters when mapped back to the original space, with the boundaries of the subclusters characterized by their respective outlier support vectors (OSVs). With a Gaussian kernel,

$$K(\mathbf{x}, \mathbf{x}') = \exp\left\{-q\|\mathbf{x} - \mathbf{x}'\|^2\right\},$$

experiments were conducted on a dataset of 183 points with $C = 1$ and $q = 1, 20, 24, \text{and } 48$ [16]. The "width" parameter q of the Gaussian kernel determines the scale or granularity at which the data structure is analyzed. It was reported that the parameter has a major effect on the cluster solutions. When $q = 1$, the single cluster shows the smoothest cluster boundary, characterized by merely six SVs. When $q = 20, 24, \text{and } 25$ the cluster(s) splits, resulting in an increasing number of subclusters, each having its own enclosed boundary. With increasing q, the number of support vectors S increases and, furthermore, the boundaries (of subclusters) fit the data more tightly.

Moreover, the number of OSVs can be controlled by the penalty factor C, which should be carefully chosen so as to reach a delicate tradeoff between two contradictory objectives as follows.

- *Smooth cluster boundaries.* For this, one should aim at a minimal number of support vectors so as to assure smooth subcluster boundaries.
- *Clear separation between subclusters.* For this, one should aim at a higher number of SVs so as to help create greater separation between subclusters.

Choice of kernels and translation invariance

Let us look into some issues related to translation invariance. If a Gaussian RBF kernel is adopted, it will be shift-invariant in the original vector space. Moreover, in this case, there is basically no difference between hyperplane and hypersphere OCSVMs.

When a polynomial kernel is adopted, the hypersphere OCSVM remains translation-invariant since the sphere's center **u** is adjustable during the learning phase, thus preempting any translation-variance problem.

In contrast, a hyperplane OCSVM is in general translation dependent. Note that the ν-SV classifier implicitly targets the virtual training vectors as the negative training vectors. However, the formation of virtual training vectors depends on the location of the origin, which in turn depends on the translation. To show this, note that, if we translate the whole dataset by **v**, i.e.

$$\vec{\phi}_i \to \vec{\phi}(\mathbf{x}_i) + \mathbf{v},$$

then, relatively speaking, the origin is also shifted by **v**, resulting in a different set of virtual training vectors. The change should in turn affect the learned classifier and its associated SVs. Thus, we conclude that the detection performance may depend on the choice of coordinate system in the kernel-induced feature space. (See also Problems 11.5 and 11.6.)

For some big-data learning scenarios, one needs to resort to polynomial kernels, TRBF kernels, or other shift-variant kernels, for computational consideration; see Chapter 13. In this case, it is important to pay attention to the following precautions.

- A hypersphere OCSVM is favored since it is free from any variation that might possibly be incurred by coordinate translation.
- For a hyperplane OCSVM, the choice of coordinate in the kernel-induced feature space may actually affect the outliers identified. Hence its coordinate system must be properly selected.

11.6 Summary

This chapter presents several support-vector-based learning models for outlier detection. The term SVM refers to classification, support vector regression (SVR) for regression, and support vector clustering (SVC) for clustering, the last being equivalent to one-class SVMs (OCSVM). While SVM is designed for classification, SVR is meant for regression analysis whose aim is to find an approximating function to fit a set of training data. For applications related to outlier detection, three learning models (hyperplane OCSVM, hypersphere OCSVM, and SVC) are explored, and it is shown that all three models coincide when a shift-invariant kernel function is adopted, e.g. a Gaussian RBF kernel.

11.7 Problems

Problem 11.1 *Consider the following one-class training dataset:*

$$\mathbf{x}_1 = \begin{bmatrix} 0 \\ 0 \end{bmatrix}, \quad \mathbf{x}_2 = \begin{bmatrix} +1 \\ 0 \end{bmatrix}, \quad \mathbf{x}_3 = \begin{bmatrix} -1 \\ 0 \end{bmatrix},$$

$$\mathbf{x}_4 = \begin{bmatrix} 0 \\ +1 \end{bmatrix}, \quad \mathbf{x}_5 = \begin{bmatrix} 0 \\ -1 \end{bmatrix}, \quad \mathbf{x}_6 = \begin{bmatrix} +1 \\ +1 \end{bmatrix}.$$

Suppose that a linear kernel is adopted.

(a) *Derive the hyperplane-OCSVM learning model.*
(b) *Derive the hypersphere-OCSVM learning model.*
(c) *Compare the two learning models.*

Problem 11.2 *Consider the same one-class training dataset as that given in Problem 11.1. Now suppose that a Gaussian RBF kernel is adopted.*

(a) *Derive the hyperplane-OCSVM learning model.*
(b) *Derive the hypersphere-OCSVM learning model.*
(c) *Compare the two learning models.*

Problem 11.3 *This problem explores two special cases of the ν-SVM learning models.*

(a) *Show that, if the linear kernel is adopted and the magnitude of the teacher value is fixed to $\eta = 1$, Eq. (11.6) degenerates into Eq. (10.4).*
(b) *Show that Eq. (11.8) degenerates into Eq. (10.35) when it is fixed that $\eta = 1$.*

Problem 11.4 *For the ν-SVM, derive the optimal threshold value b and the optimal teacher value η in terms of kernels.*

Hint: *The KKT conditions imply that, if $\alpha_i > 0$ and $\beta_i > 0$, then the primal inequality constraints become equality constraints [239].*

Problem 11.5 (Translation invariance/dependence of OCSVMs: linear kernels) *Consider two linear kernels: $K_1(\mathbf{x}, \mathbf{x}') = \mathbf{x}^{\mathrm{T}}\mathbf{x}'$ and $K_2(\mathbf{x}, \mathbf{x}') = 1 + \mathbf{x}^{\mathrm{T}}\mathbf{x}'$.*

(a) *Given a five-pattern (one-dimensional) set of training data, $\{x_1 = 1.0,\ x_2 = 1.2,\ x_3 = 1.5,\ x_4 = 3.0,\ x_5 = 5.0\}$, find the five mapped feature vectors in the intrinsic space for kernels $K_1(\mathbf{x}, \mathbf{x}')$ and $K_2(\mathbf{x}, \mathbf{x}')$, respectively.*
(b) *Show that the support vectors identified by the hypersphere OCSVM are the same for $K_1(\mathbf{x}, \mathbf{x}')$ and $K_2(\mathbf{x}, \mathbf{x}')$, due to the shift-invariance property of the learning model.*
(c) *Will the support vectors identified by the hyperplane OCSVM for $K_1(\mathbf{x}, \mathbf{x}')$ and $K_2(\mathbf{x}, \mathbf{x}')$ remain the same, just like for its hypersphere counterpart?*

Problem 11.6 (Translation invariance/dependence of OCSVMs: polynomial kernels) *Repeat Problem 11.5, but now considering two second-order polynomial kernels: $K_1(\mathbf{x}, \mathbf{x}') = (1 + \mathbf{x}^{\mathrm{T}}\mathbf{x}')^2$ and $K_2(\mathbf{x}, \mathbf{x}') = 1 + (1 + \mathbf{x}^{\mathrm{T}}\mathbf{x}')^2$.*

12 Ridge-SVM learning models

12.1 Introduction

It is well known that a classifier's effectiveness depends strongly on the distribution of the (training and testing) datasets. Consequently, we will not know in advance the best possible classifiers for data analysis. This prompts the need to develop a versatile classifier endowed with an adequate set of adjustable parameters to cope with various real-world application scenarios. Two common ways to enhance the robustness of the classifiers are by means of (1) using a proper ridge factor to mitigate over-fitting problems (as adopted by KRR) and/or (2) selecting an appropriate number of support vectors to participate in the decision making (as adopted by SVM). Both regularization mechanisms are meant to enhance the robustness of the learned models and, ultimately, improve the generalization performance.

This chapter introduces the notion of a weight–error curve (WEC) for characterization of kernelized supervised learning models, including KDA, KRR, SVM, and Ridge-SVM. Under the LSP condition, the decision vector can be "voted" as a weighted sum of training vectors in the intrinsic space – each vector is assigned a weight in voting. The weights can be obtained by solving the kernelized learning model. In addition, each vector is also associated with an error, which is dictated by its distance from the decision boundary. In short, given a learned model, each training vector is endowed with two parameters: weight and error. These parameters collectively form the so-called WEC. The analysis of the WEC leads us to a new type of classifier named Ridge-SVM.

(i) Section 12.2 compares two major design parameters that are useful for enhancing the robustness of learned classifiers. In KRR, the ridge parameter ρ is used to regulate the robustness of the classifiers. (The detailed numerical analysis can be found in Section 9.5.) In the SVM approach, the robustness may be enhanced by allowing a fuzzy separation margin regulated by a penalty factor C. It is not only the case that the two controlling parameters, C and ρ, are instrumental for the robustness of the learned models, but also, and more importantly, that the distinctive roles played by C and ρ are complementary to each other. The section analyzes the inadequacy of the WECs of KDA, KRR, and SVM.

(ii) Section 12.3 extends the previous learning models to the Ridge-SVM classifier, which unifies KRR and SVM and effectively alleviates some of the design concerns relating to KRR and SVM. More precisely, the weights of the two extreme ends of the WEC can now be curbed by $C_{\rm max} = C$ and $C_{\rm min}$, respectively (i.e. following the SVM model), and the slope of the transition zone can be made adjustable by the ridge parameter ρ (i.e. following the KRR model). Ridge-SVM is endowed with a sufficient set of design parameters to embrace existing classifiers, including KDA, KRR, and SVM, as its special cases.

(iii) Section 12.4 explores how the characteristics of the WEC depend on the three Ridge-SVM parameters ρ, C, and $C_{\rm min}$.

(iv) Section 12.5 shows that two Ridge-SVM parameters, namely ρ and $C_{\rm min}$, may affect not only the prediction accuracy but also the training time.

(v) Section 12.6 reports numerous experimental studies. With properly adjusted parameters, Ridge-SVM is promising for producing robust classifiers with improved generalization capability. This is evidenced by numerous experimental studies reported in Section 12.6.

12.2 Roles of ρ and C on WECs of KRR and SVM

12.2.1 Roles of ρ and C

In order to develop a unified classifier, it is vital to have a deep understanding of the similarity/difference between the KRR and SVM optimizers, and more importantly, the distinctive roles played by the two controlling parameters, C and ρ, in determining the robustness of the learned models.

- **Role of ρ in KRR.** The KRR learning model has the following optimization formulation:

$$\max_{\mathbf{a}} \left\{ \mathbf{a}^{\rm T}\mathbf{y} - \frac{1}{2}\mathbf{a}^{\rm T}[\mathbf{K} + \rho\mathbf{I}]\mathbf{a} \right\} \quad \text{subject to} \quad \mathbf{a}^{\rm T}\mathbf{e} = 0.$$

Note that there are no constraints attached to a_i.

In KRR, the ridge parameter ρ is used to regulate the robustness of the classifiers. The principle of ridge regression lies in the incorporation of a penalty term, parameterized by the ridge factor ρ, into the loss function to control the regressor coefficients. The equivalence between KRR and PDA suggests that the ridge factor ρ used in KRR is meant to alleviate the effect of errors in variables, when its noise level is ρ. In addition, the notion of the *regression ratio* (introduced in Section 9.5) provides an analysis showing how the ridge parameter ρ may be used to quantitatively redistribute the weight so as to suppress more aggressively the weaker (i.e. more sensitive) components, thus, relatively speaking, enhancing the stronger (i.e. more resilient) components. Consequently, the regularization can effectively alleviate over-fitting problems, preempting oversubscription of sensitive components, and ultimately improving the generalization capability of the learned models. Indeed, regulated KRRs exhibit superior performance to unregulated KDAs across the board in the application studies covered in Section 9.6.

- **Role of C in SVM.** The SVM solution can be obtained from the following optimization problem:

$$\max_{\mathbf{a}} \mathcal{L} \equiv \max_{\mathbf{a}} \left\{ \mathbf{a}^{\mathrm{T}}\mathbf{y} - \frac{1}{2}\mathbf{a}^{\mathrm{T}}\mathbf{K}\mathbf{a} \right\} \tag{12.1}$$

subject to the OHP $\mathbf{a}^{\mathrm{T}}\mathbf{e} = 0$ and $0 \leq \alpha_i \leq C$, where $\alpha_i = a_i y_i$.

In the SVM approach, the robustness may be enhanced by allowing a fuzzy or soft separation margin regulated by a penalty factor C. When C is sufficiently small, it will create a relatively larger pool of support vectors, all of them participating in the final decision making. The resultant decision boundary can thus be viewed as a consensus reached by a greater number of support vectors, hence making the learned classifier more robust.

Complementary roles of ρ and C

Note that the two controlling parameters, C and ρ, play critical roles in enhancing the robustness of the learned models. While KRR can take into account the effect of errors in variables (i.e. perturbation in input) very well, it fails to be more selective in training vectors. On the other hand, while SVM places emphasis on the selection of support vectors, it does not directly address the issue of errors in variables.

- In KRR, the ridge parameter ρ regulates the robustness of the classifiers. More specifically, it mitigates oversubscription of minor (and weaker) components and, relatively speaking, reinforces the major (and stronger) components in the spectral space. (See Eq. (9.51) in Section 9.5.)
- In SVM, the robustness may be enhanced by allowing a fuzzy separation margin regulated by a mitigating factor C. A small C tends to enlarge the pool of support vectors. See Section 10.4.

This suggests that C and ρ may be used to complement each other, to derive a more versatile learning model.

12.2.2 WECs of KDA, KRR, and SVM

KDA's WEC

Note that KDA is a special case of KRR. In a relaxed interpretation, KDA is closely related to SVM. (Note that, by substituting the inequality in Eq. (10.4) with an equality, the SVM is reduced to KDA.) Therefore, it should not be surprising that KDA's WEC shares some commonality with both KRR and SVM. As shown in Figure 12.1(a), KDA's WEC shows a steep slope just like SVM's WEC. On the other hand, KDA's WEC is represented by a straight line just like KRR's WEC.

KRR's WEC

KRR's WEC is much simpler because there is a one-to-one and linear functional mapping between ϵ_i and a_i:

$$\epsilon_i = -\rho a_i, \; i = 1, \ldots, N.$$

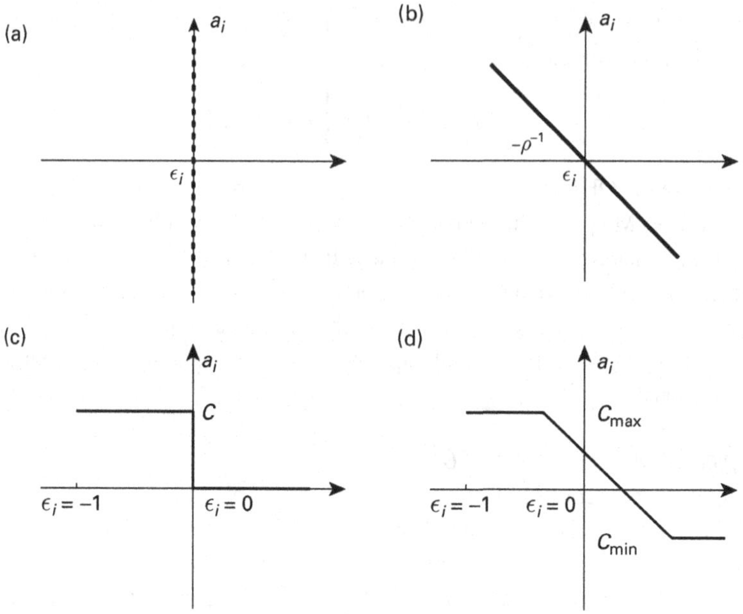

Fig. 12.1. Shown here are the weight–error curves (WECs) for four different learning models. For positive training vectors, the WEC describes the relationship between the errors $\{\epsilon_i\}$ and the weights $\{a_i\}$ for all $i \in$ positive training set. Likewise, the negative WEC display such a relationship for all $i \in$ negative training set. (The negative WECs are not displayed here.) (a) KDA's WEC shown as a dashed line: KDA produces a maximum margin under the error-free constraint, i.e. $\epsilon_i = 0$ for all the training vectors. (Therefore, strictly speaking the WEC is not a function.) (b) KRR's WEC: KRR's WEC (for positive training vectors) exhibits a simple linear relationship. The main concern regarding the KRR's WEC hinges upon its two ends, where the potentially detrimental anti-support vectors are assigned excessive weights. (c) SVM's WEC: according to the KKT condition in SVM, the non-support vectors (i.e. those with positive error, $\epsilon_i > 0$) receive zero weights. Moreover, there is a steep transition taking place at the origin, i.e. $\epsilon_i = 0$. Finally, the maximum weight for the support vectors is C, which is adjustable for improving the performance and robustness of the learned model. (d) Ridge-SVM's WEC: an idealistic WEC combines meritable advantages in both WECs while avoiding their undesirable properties. Such a type of WEC can be realized by Ridge-SVM, a hybrid of the KRR and SVM classifiers. In Ridge-SVM, for maximal flexibility several design parameters may be adjusted, including the transition slope as well as the maximum and minimum levels of the weights, i.e. C_{max} and C_{min}, respectively.

As shown in Figure 12.1(b), KRR's WEC (for positive training vectors) exhibits a simple linear relationship with a negative slope.

SVM's WEC

Note that, for SVM learning models, the mapping from weight values a_i to the corresponding errors ϵ_i is not one-to-one. Neither is the reverse mapping from ϵ_i back to a_i. Mathematically, the relationship between ϵ_i and a_i is not a functional mapping, so their relationship can only be characterized by a curve. This curve is named the WEC. The SVM's WEC is shown in Figure 12.1(c).

The mathematical theory behind the WEC for the SVM model is the well-known KKT condition. More exactly, for positive training vectors, we have the following.

- If $\epsilon_i > 0$, then the corresponding weight value $a_i = 0$.
- If $\epsilon_i < 0$, then the corresponding weight value $a_i = C$.
- If $\epsilon_i = 0$, then the corresponding weight value a_i cannot be determined exactly, but it will fall within the range $0 \leq a_i \leq C$.

The property for the negative training patterns is very similar, so the details are omitted.

Let us now explore some concerns regarding the WECs for SVM and KRR with the intention of gaining some insight that can provide guidance for future classifier designs.

- **Concern regarding SVM's WEC.** There is legitimate concern that SVM's WEC has a steep transition for the weight to drop from its maximum value C to the minimum value 0. This might not bode well for the nearby training vectors, since they are very close to the supporting zone and yet receive no weight at all in making the decision rule. A fairer scheme is to have a smooth transition ramp to gradually lower the weight from its maximal level to the minimal level. This allows the nearby training vectors to be assigned a pro-rata weight. In Ridge-SVM, this problem can be easily rectified by incorporating a nonzero controlling parameter, ρ, into the cost function.
- **Concern regarding KRR's WEC.** The main concern regarding the KRR's WEC's hinges upon its two ends, where the potentially detrimental anti-support vectors are assigned excessive weights. This problem is rectified by an *ad hoc* method in PPDA, where the anti-support vectors are bluntly removed, see Figure 9.4(b). The method used by the Ridge-SVM is more elegant; the values of the two ends are quantitatively curbed by $C_{\max} = C$ and $C_{\min}$, see Figure 12.1(d).

The study on WEC analysis helps us find a way to design a more desirable learning model via some suitable adjustments to the WEC. For example, the concerns regarding the WECs of SVM and KRR can be effectively tackled by the proposed Ridge-SVM. As shown in Figure 12.1(d), the Ridge-SVM's WEC enjoys the merits of both KRR's and SVM's WECs, while avoiding some of their undesirable attributes.

12.3 Ridge-SVM learning models

According to various simulation results and practical applications reported to date, neither KRR (equivalently PDA) nor SVM alone can be considered as a universal solution for all likely applications. This motivates us to develop a versatile hybrid classifier, called Ridge-SVM (which was previously named PDA-SVM [136, 139]), which is endowed with an adequate set of adjustable parameters to cope with various real-world application scenarios. As shown in Figure 12.2, Ridge-SVM covers many existing classifiers, including KDA, KRR, and SVM, as special cases.

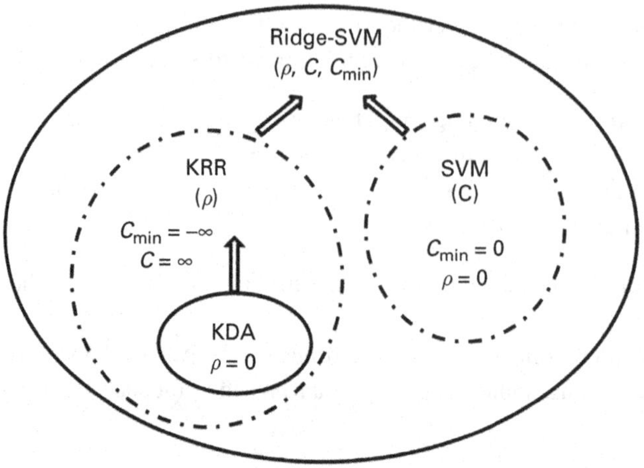

Fig. 12.2. By allowing more flexible mitigating factors (adopted by SVM) and incorporation of the ridge parameter (adopted by KRR), a hybrid Ridge-SVM (also known as PDA-SVM) classifier can be developed. Many existing classifiers such as KDA, KRR (or LS-SVM or PDA), and SVM can be viewed as special cases of Ridge-SVM.

Design parameters of Ridge-SVM

In order to achieve the aforementioned objective, the Ridge-SVM learning model is endowed with an array of design parameters imposed on its optimizer in the empirical space.[1] The objective of Ridge-SVM is to realize WEC with the following attributes.

(i) It curbs weights on potentially detrimental training vectors at both ends of the WEC. The curbing magnitudes are controlled by the design parameters $C_{\max}$ to $C_{\min}$.
(ii) It allows a smooth transition of weights from $C_{\max}$ to $C_{\min}$, with a slope controlled by the design parameter ρ.

As shown in Figure 12.1(d), the weights of the two ends of the curve are curbed by $C_{\max} = C$ and $C_{\min}$, respectively. In addition, the slope of the transition zone can be precisely controlled by its design parameter ρ. (In fact, the slope for the positive WEC is $-\rho^{-1}$, while the slope of the negative WEC is $+\rho^{-1}$.) This point is further elaborated on as follows.

- **Curbing weights by imposing both $C_{\min}$ and $C_{\max}$.** Again, in the empirical space, KRR and SVM optimizers can naturally impose both the upper and lower bounds of the weights α_i, i.e. $C_{\min} \leq \alpha_i \leq C_{\max}$. This serves the intended purpose of moderating the magnitudes of the weights and thus preventing excessive influence by any individual training vectors, especially those located at the two ends of the WEC.

[1] Unfortunately, while the design parameter ρ is amenable to optimizers in the intrinsic space, two other key design parameters $C_{\max}$ and $C_{\min}$, are not easy to work with for optimizing formulation in the intrinsic space. This is why Ridge-SVM is defined only in empirical space, not in intrinsic space. Nevertheless, the adoption of an empirical optimizer implies that the LSP is by definition valid. Namely, the intrinsic decision vector $\mathbf{u}$ can be derived as $\mathbf{u} = \mathbf{\Phi a}$, once $\mathbf{a}$ has been solved.

- **Graceful transition by ridge regularization.** Note that, in the empirical space, the only difference between the cost functions of the KRR and SVM optimizers lies in the ridge factor ρ, which happens to be the controlling parameter for adjusting the slope in transition – the greater the magnitude of ρ the smoother the transition.

As depicted in Figure 12.1(d), the WEC of the learned Ridge-SVM model can be divided into three zones, the $C_{\max}$ zone, transition zone, and $C_{\min}$ zone. A proper zoning of the training vectors will dictate the performance of the learned models. Moreover, the exact zoning of the training vectors is mathematically governed by the well-known KKT theory. Unfortunately, the best zoning strategy is closely dependent on the specific application domains and is usually determined by cross-validation and trial and error.

12.3.1 Ridge-SVM: a unifying supervised learning model

The Ridge-SVM model, a hybrid of KRR and SVM, is formally described as follows.

ALGORITHM 12.1 (Ridge-SVM learning model) *Given the kernel matrix* **K** *and the teacher vector* **y**, *find the optimal vector* **a** *such that*

$$\max_{\mathbf{a}} \mathcal{L} \equiv \max_{\mathbf{a}} \left\{ \mathbf{a}^{\mathrm{T}}\mathbf{y} - \tfrac{1}{2}\mathbf{a}^{\mathrm{T}}[\mathbf{K} + \rho\mathbf{I}]\mathbf{a} \right\}$$

$$\text{subject to } \mathbf{a}^{\mathrm{T}}\mathbf{e} = 0$$

$$\text{and } C_{\min} \leq \alpha_i \leq C_{\max} \equiv C, \text{ where } \alpha_i = a_i y_i. \tag{12.2}$$

The discriminant function is

$$f(\mathbf{x}) = \sum_{i=1}^{N} a_i K(\mathbf{x}_i, \mathbf{x}) + b, \tag{12.3}$$

where **a** *is obtained from Eq. (12.2) and b can be derived according to the KKT conditions, see Eq. (12.4). Finally, the decision function is characterized by* $f(\mathbf{x}) = 0$. □

For the best possible performance, the four key parameters σ (the variance defining the kernel function), ρ (the ridge factor), $C_{\min}$, and $C_{\max} \equiv C$ have to be learned via an exhaustive trial-and-error process. Computationally, this is obviously a very costly process. One solution is to adopt parallel processors. Another is to subscribe to services offered by cloud computing. At any rate, it becomes critical to look into fast algorithms such as SMO, see Section 12.3.3, or some other parallel processing platforms.

12.3.2 Important special cases of Ridge-SVM models

Many existing classifiers (KDA [68], KRR (or LS-SVM or PDA) [136, 139, 260], and SVM [280]) can be viewed as special cases of Ridge-SVM. They are listed in Table 12.1. The new learning model may viewed from two different perspectives.

- **Compare KRR and Ridge-SVM.** From KRR's perspective, positive and negative errors are penalized equally, i.e. the penalty depends only on the magnitude of the

Table 12.1. A unifying comparison of three types of classifiers. Another special case is the perturbational SVM, a variant of SVM except that $\mathbf{K}$ is substituted by $\mathbf{K}+\rho\mathbf{I}$. Here LSS denotes linear system solver.

	No constraint	OHP constraint	Full constraint
$\rho = 0$	LSS $\mathbf{K}^{-1}\mathbf{y}$	KDA $\mathbf{K}^{-1}[\mathbf{y} - b\mathbf{e}]$	SVM $(C_{\min} = 0)$
$\rho > 0$	Regularized LSS $[\mathbf{K}+\rho\mathbf{I}]^{-1}\mathbf{y}$	KRR $[\mathbf{K}+\rho\mathbf{I}]^{-1}[\mathbf{y} - b\mathbf{e}]$	Ridge-SVM Hybrid

error, not on its sign. This motivates the usage of a symmetric constraint in the optimization formulation:

$$\max_{\mathbf{a}} \mathcal{L} \text{ subject to } \mathbf{a}^{\mathrm{T}}\mathbf{e} = 0 \quad \text{and} \quad -C \le \alpha_i \le C, \forall i.$$

KRR is a special case when we set $C = \infty$. (KRR appears in the left-hand circle in Figure 12.2.) Note that KDA is an even more special case of KRR when $\rho = 0$. (KDA is shown in the innermost circle in Figure 12.2.)

- **Compare SVM and Ridge-SVM.** In SVM, positive and negative errors receive completely different penalties, i.e. the penalty depends not only on the magnitude of the error but also on its sign. This motivates the usage of an asymmetric constraint in the optimization formulation:

$$\max_{\mathbf{a}} \mathcal{L}, \quad \text{subject to } \mathbf{a}^{\mathrm{T}}\mathbf{e} = 0 \quad \text{and} \quad 0 \le \alpha_i \le C, \forall i.$$

The conventional SVM is a special case of this type when $\rho = 0$, $C_{\min} = 0$, and $C > 0$. Such a constraint leads to a WEC with a *steep slope* (caused by the KKT condition) as shown in Figure 12.1(b). (SVM appears in the right-hand circle in Figure 12.2.)

12.3.3 Subset selection: KKT and the termination condition

There are two different motivations for subset selections: (1) one emphasizes performance with little concern for the implementation efficiency; and (2) the other is exclusively driven by the computational efficiency.

- The former is exemplified by PKRR or PPDA, which is largely based on the idea of trading computational efficiency for improved performance. More exactly, it starts with all of the N given training vectors, finds an optimal classifier, then eliminates only a very small fraction of non-qualifying vectors, and then retrains a new classifier with the surviving vectors. Such a process will be referred to as an elimination-based scheme for subset selection. It is feasible only when it is affordable to support the hugely extensive computations for repeated model learning processes, each time handling a large size of training dataset. It is made possible, fortunately, due to the fact that KRR has an $O(N)$ learning complexity and the (possibly wishful) assumption that the intrinsic degree J is finite and manageable.

- The latter is exemplified by the chunking approach originally proposed by Vapnik [278]. The basic idea is to always keep the sizes of coefficients to be learned within a manageable level throughout all the iterations. It starts with a small working set, finding its support vectors, and then iteratively updating the SV set by gradually admitting new support vectors.

The chunking approach involves decomposing the original optimization problem into subproblems of manageable size and then solving the subproblems iteratively [132]. The basic chucking idea makes use of the fact that only the SVs play a role in the final discriminant function. It should be evident that, given only the SVs as the training dataset, we would obtain exactly the same classifier as the one trained from the full and original training dataset. Obviously, having obtained knowledge of the SVs makes the learning task much more manageable in terms of the memory requirement and processing time. However, we must face the reality that we will not be able to know the SVs unless we can actually solve the optimization problem first. To get around this dilemma, an intuitive approach is proposed as follows.

(i) Start with an arbitrary subset and use it to train a preliminary classifier.
(ii) Then we keep only the SVs, discarding the non-SV data and replacing them with other training data.
(iii) The classifier is then to be retrained on the modified dataset.

This data-updating and retraining procedure will be repeated until all the samples under training satisfy the KKT conditions.

Working set for Ridge-SVM

When training a conventional SVM, it is common practice to select a subset (called the *working set*) from the training dataset [114]. The working set is then used to compute a subset of SVM weights by solving a quadratic programming problem, with the remaining weights typically set to a default value of zero. Then, the training program checks whether all of the training data satisfy the KKT condition. If they do, we have an optimal solution and the program stops. Otherwise, another working set (which may contain some data in the earlier working sets) is selected, and the process is repeated.

Note that, when $\rho > 0$, the KKT condition for Ridge-SVM should be modified to

$$\alpha_i \left(\sum_{j=1}^{N} a_j K(\mathbf{x}_i, \mathbf{x}_j) + \rho a_i + b - 1 + \xi_i \right) = 0. \tag{12.4}$$

Note also that, when $C_{\min} \neq 0$, some of the training vectors can satisfy neither the original KKT condition nor this modified KKT condition. Some training algorithms will terminate the learning process when there is no change in the *working set* for several iterations. This is the case with the algorithm in Ref. [241], which was adopted for our simulation.

It is important to note that, because of the parameters ρ and $C_{\min}$, a Ridge-SVM may have all the values of α_i nonzero. In particular, when $C_{\min} \geq 0$, then $\alpha_i \geq 0$ $\forall i$. Therefore, the initial values of α_i should be set to $\max\{C_{\min}, 0\}$ instead of 0. By using this initial condition for the quadratic-programming solver, we can ensure that $\alpha_i \geq C_{\min}$.

Fast learning via sequential minimal optimization (SMO)

Sequential minimal optimization (SMO), which was introduced by Platt [204], is one of the fastest algorithms to have been implemented for SVM. The basic idea involves extreme chunking by iteratively selecting subsets of size 2, which happens to be the smallest still meaningful size for the SVM, and then maximizing the cost function with respect to these two coefficients only. The key is that, for a working subset of 2, the optimization subproblem is endowed with an analytical and closed-form solution. This implies a substantial saving, compared with the iterative computation which is usually used for a quadratic optimizer. For some applications, SMO is reportedly faster by several orders of magnitude (up to a factor of 1000) than classical chunking. Just like SVM, the constraints in the Ridge-SVM optimization also involve only one equality, making us hopeful that it will admit an SMO-like algorithm.

12.4 Impacts of design parameters on the WEC of Ridge-SVM

This section will explore how the WEC depends on the three Ridge-SVM parameters (ρ, C, and $C_{\min}$). Assuming that $\rho > 0$, ϵ_i may be mapped to a_i by a functional mapping:

$$a = a_{\rho, C_{\min}, C}(\epsilon).$$

The function is characterized by the following parameters:

(i) the upper and lower bounds of weights (denoted by C and $C_{\min}$, respectively);
(ii) the slope of the transitional ramp (given by $-\rho^{-1}$ and ρ^{-1} for positive and negative WECs, respectively); and
(iii) the transition zone, i.e. the locations of the front and back ends of the transition.

The WEC for the negative training vectors is basically a mirror image of the WEC for the positive training vectors. Therefore, in the subsequent discussion, we shall treat only the WECs associated with the positive training vectors. (See Problem 12.1.)

12.4.1 Transition ramps and the number of support vectors

Relative to SVM, the two parameters ρ and $C_{\min}$ are newly introduced. The effect of ρ is on the slope of the WEC's transition, while the effect of $C_{\min}$ is on the location of the transition ramp and the number of support vectors. These effects will be further explored in the subsequent discussion.

12.4.2 Effects of ρ and $C_{\min}$ on the transition ramp

The effect of ρ is on the slope of the WEC's transition, while the effect of $C_{\min}$ is on the location of the transition zone.

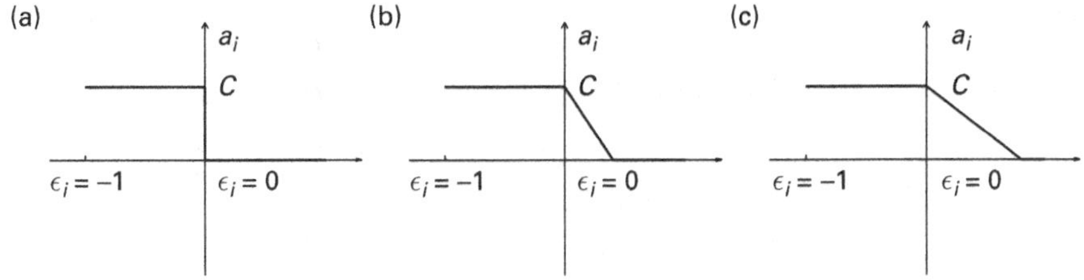

Fig. 12.3. A special case of Ridge-SVM is when we fix the lower bound of the weight to $C_{\min} = 0$. In this case, the WEC for the (positive) training vectors is governed by the ridge factor ρ. Shown here are the WECs for three different values of ρ: (a) $\rho = 0$, (b) $\rho = \rho_1 > 0$, and (c) $\rho = \rho_2 > \rho_1$.

- **The effect of ρ on the transition ramp.** To study how the slope changes with respect to ρ, we shall first focus on the case of $C_{\min} = 0$ (see Figure 12.3). When $C_{\min} = 0$ and $\rho = 0$, Ridge-SVM reduces to SVM, whose WEC (for positive training vectors) is depicted in Figure 12.3(a), which has a steep fall at the origin, i.e. $\epsilon = 0$.

  When $C_{\min} = 0$ and $\rho > 0$, the original steep transition will be replaced by a smooth ramp. Note that the ramp starts approximately at the origin with a negative slope, $-\rho^{-1}$. The higher the magnitude of ρ the smoother the transition, regulating in a greater ridge-type regularization effect. As illustrated by Figures 12.3(b) and (c), because $\rho_2 > \rho_1$, the ramp associated with ρ_2 is smoother than that associated with ρ_1. This provides a basis for the derivation of an empirical formula for the evaluation of the values of a_i in the transitional region:

$$a_i \approx C - \rho^{-1}\epsilon_i, \tag{12.5}$$

  for the transition zone, with $\epsilon_i \in [0, \rho C]$. Equivalently,

$$\epsilon_i \approx \rho C - \rho a_i.$$

  Such a slope is confirmed by Figure 12.4(a) showing the simulation results based on the prostate-cancer dataset [247]. The predictable slope prompts us to introduce a slope-adjusted error term:

$$\epsilon_i' \equiv \epsilon_i + \rho a_i,$$

  which in turn leads to the WEC depicted in Figure 12.4(b). Note that, when $C_{\min} = 0$, there is a steep fall near $\epsilon' = 0$, just like for the conventional SVM with $\rho = 0$.
- **The effect of $C_{\min}$ on the location of the ramp.** Three possible locations of the transition ramps are depicted in Figure 12.5 for three different values of $C_{\min}$: (a) $C_{\min} < 0$, (b) $C_{\min} = 0$, and (c) $C_{\min} > 0$.

  (i) If $C_{\min} < 0$, there exists a number C^-, with $C^- < C$, such that the range of the transition zone is as follows:

$$\epsilon_i \in [\rho(C^- - C), \rho(C^- - C_{\min})]. \tag{12.6}$$

  The weights in that zone fall on a linear line:

$$a_i \approx C^- - \rho^{-1}\epsilon_i. \tag{12.7}$$

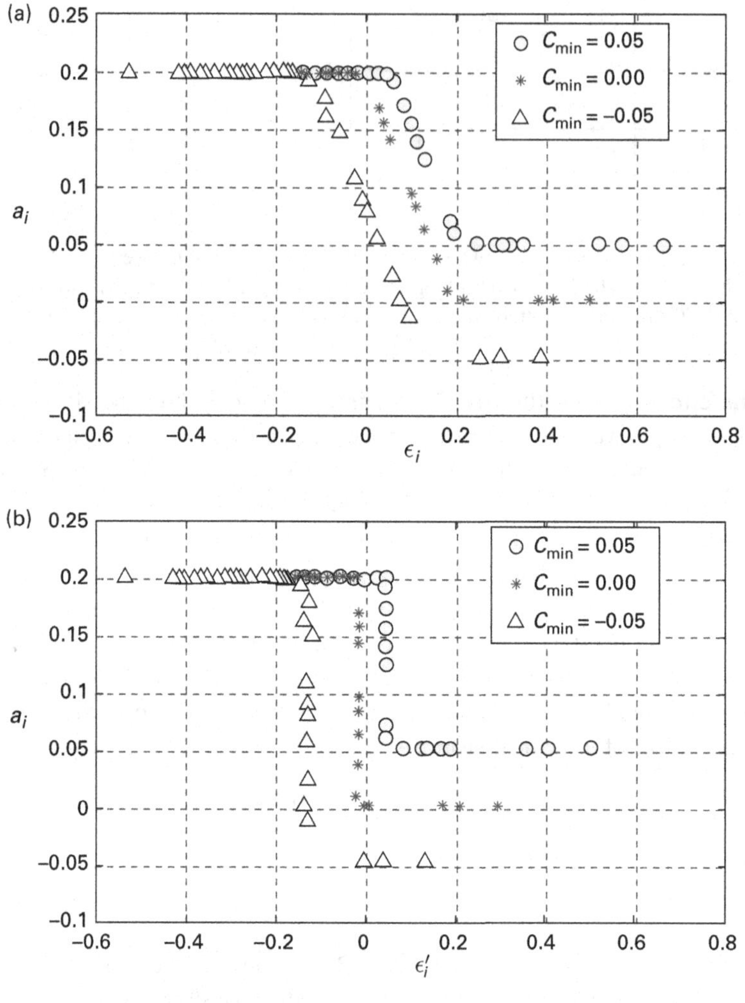

Fig. 12.4. Weights a_i versus the training error in Ridge-SVM for positive training vectors, for negative, zero, and positive $C_{\min}$. For (a), the training error is defined as $\epsilon_i = f(\mathbf{x}_i) - y_i$. For (b), the "adjusted" training error is defined as $\epsilon_i' = \epsilon_i + \rho a_i$. In all cases, $C = 0.2$ and $\rho = 1$, and prostate data were used to train the Ridge-SVM. (The WECs labeled by "o", "*", and "Δ" correspond to $C_{\min} = 0.05, 0,$ and -0.05, respectively.)

According to Eq. (12.7), it is known that (1) the transition width is expanded from ρC to $\rho(C - C_{\min}) = \rho(C + |C_{\min}|)$ and (2) the transition region is left-shifted by a (negative) amount, $\rho(C^- - C)$. As shown in Figure 12.4(a), when $C_{\min} = -0.05$ (i.e. $C_{\min} < 0$), we obtain the lower WEC with a broader and left-shifted transition zone.

(ii) If $C_{\min} = 0$, then the transition zone is as follows:

$$\epsilon_i \in [0, \rho C], \tag{12.8}$$

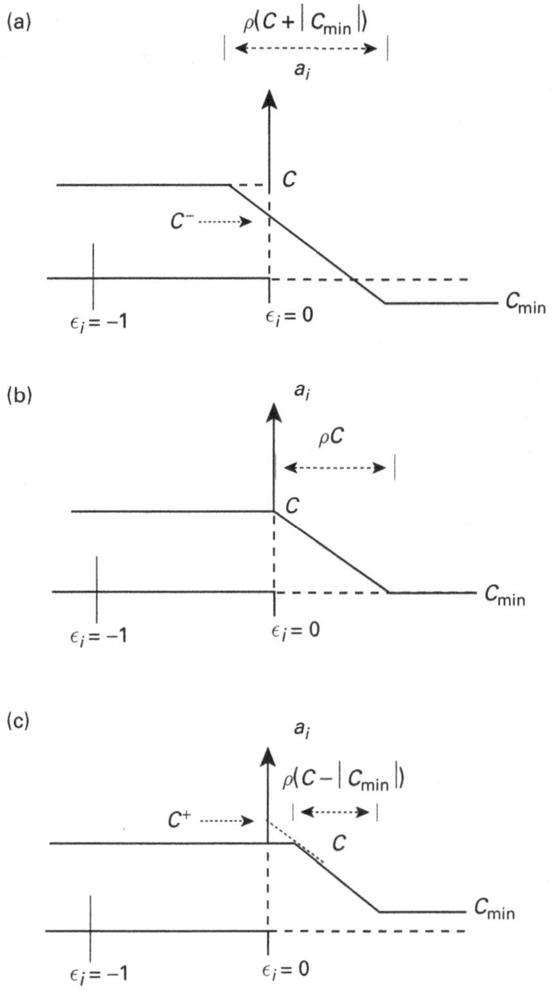

Fig. 12.5. Ridge-SVM's WECs for positive training vectors (assuming a fixed $\rho > 0$) for three different values of $C_{\min}$: (a) $C_{\min} < 0$, (b) $C_{\min} = 0$, and (c) $C_{\min} > 0$.

and the weights in that zone are linearly mapped:

$$a_i \approx C - \rho^{-1}\epsilon_i. \tag{12.9}$$

Setting $C_{\min} = 0$ leads to the middle WEC in Figure 12.4(b). After the adjustment, a steep transition takes place at the origin, just like for the WEC of SVM.

(iii) If $C_{\min} > 0$, there exists a number C^+, with $C^+ > C$, such that the transition zone is as follows:

$$\epsilon_i \in [\rho(C^+ - C), \rho(C^+ - C_{\min})], \tag{12.10}$$

with linearly mapped weights:

$$a_i \approx C^+ - \rho^{-1}\epsilon_i. \tag{12.11}$$

According to Eq. (12.11), it is known that (1) the transition width is shrunk from ρC to $\rho(C - C_{\min}) = \rho(C - |C_{\min}|)$ and (2) the transition region is right-shifted by a (positive) amount, $\rho(C^+ - C)$. As shown in Figure 12.4(a), when $C_{\min} = +0.05$ (i.e. $C_{\min} > 0$), we obtain the higher WEC with a narrower and right-shifted transition zone.

12.4.3 The number of support vectors w.r.t. $C_{\min}$

It is important to acknowledge that knowing the WEC is only a prelude to understanding its full effect on classification. The actual mapping of training vectors onto the WEC depends closely on the distribution of the training dataset as well as on the kernel function and its defining parameter(s), e.g. the value of σ for a Gaussian kernel. Note also that the distribution of positive training vectors on the positive WEC can be quite different from that of negative training vectors on the negative WEC.

In the conventional SVM, a positive training vector $\mathbf{x}_i$ is a non-support vector if and only if its associated weight a_i reaches its minimum level, i.e. $a_i = 0$. Likewise, for Ridge-SVM, a positive training vector $\mathbf{x}_i$ is a non-support vector (non-SV) if and only if its associated weight a_i reaches its minimum level, i.e. $a_i = C_{\min}$.

With reference to Figure 12.4, when $C_{\min} = 0$, five training vectors receive zero weights. Namely, there are five non-SVs and the rest are all support vectors (SVs). Now let us examine the effects of $C_{\min} \neq 0$.

- $C_{\min} < 0$. When $C_{\min} = -0.05$ ($C_{\min} < 0$), we obtain the lower WEC with a broader and left-shifted transition zone. Now three training vectors receive the minimum weights -0.05. Namely, there are three non-SVs (their number has gone from five down to three) and the rest are all SVs. It may be heuristically argued that having a small number of negatively weighted non-SVs could offset the effect due to the increasing number of positively weighted SVs.
- $C_{\min} > 0$. When $C_{\min} = +0.05$ ($C_{\min} > 0$), we obtain the upper WEC with a narrower and right-shifted transition zone. There are now eight training vectors that receive minimum weight $+0.05$. Namely, there are eight non-SVs (their number has gone from five up to eight) and, consequently, the number of SVs decreases. The effect caused by the reduced number of positively weighted SVs can be compensated for by the contribution made by positively weighted (albeit small) non-SVs.

12.5 Prediction accuracy versus training time

It is well known that the performance of any learning model depends on the dimension and distribution of the dataset, Ridge-SVM being no exception. This is verified again by the experimental study by Rothe, Yu, and Kung [225], with extensive tests on four UCI datasets (Iris, Wine, Liver, Glass) from http://archive.ics.uci.edu/ml/. Somewhat surprisingly, according to the study, the choice of the parameters significantly affects

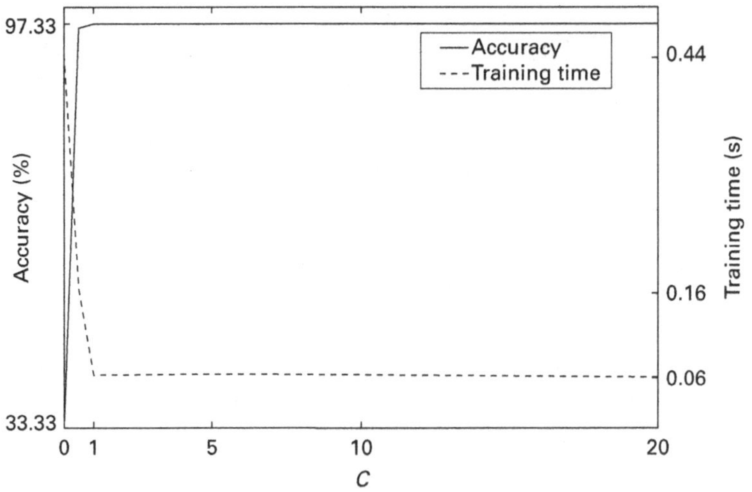

Fig. 12.6. Simulation results with varying values of C for Ridge-SVM for the Iris dataset ($C_{\min} = -0.5, \rho = 1.5$, and $\sigma = 1$).

not only the prediction accuracy but also the training time, a phenomenon to be further explored subsequently.

12.5.1 The tuning of the parameter C

A consistent observation across all four datasets is that the training time increases while the prediction accuracy decreases when C approaches 0. This is exemplified by Figure 12.6. Some intuitive explanations are provided as follows.

- Regarding the learning time, an extremely small value of C limits the choices for the α_is (given by $C_{\min} \le \alpha_i \le C$), which will in turn make the optimization process more difficult.
- Regarding the prediction performance, a direct consequence of using a small C is that only the most selective subset of training vectors can be retained, which will in turn adversely affect the prediction capability.

The good news is that, throughout the study, the parameter can be safely fixed to $C = 10$ for all the datasets, yielding a satisfactory training time and prediction accuracy. Moreover, as evidenced by Figure 12.6, the choice of C seems to be insensitive for a fairly wide range – making C the safest to deal with among all the parameters. In contrast, the tuning of $C_{\min}$ and ρ is far from being so straightforward.

12.5.2 The tuning of the parameter $C_{\min}$

Shown in Figure 12.7 are the learning speed and prediction performance for different values of $C_{\min}$ for all the datasets, with all other parameters fixed to their nearly best values.

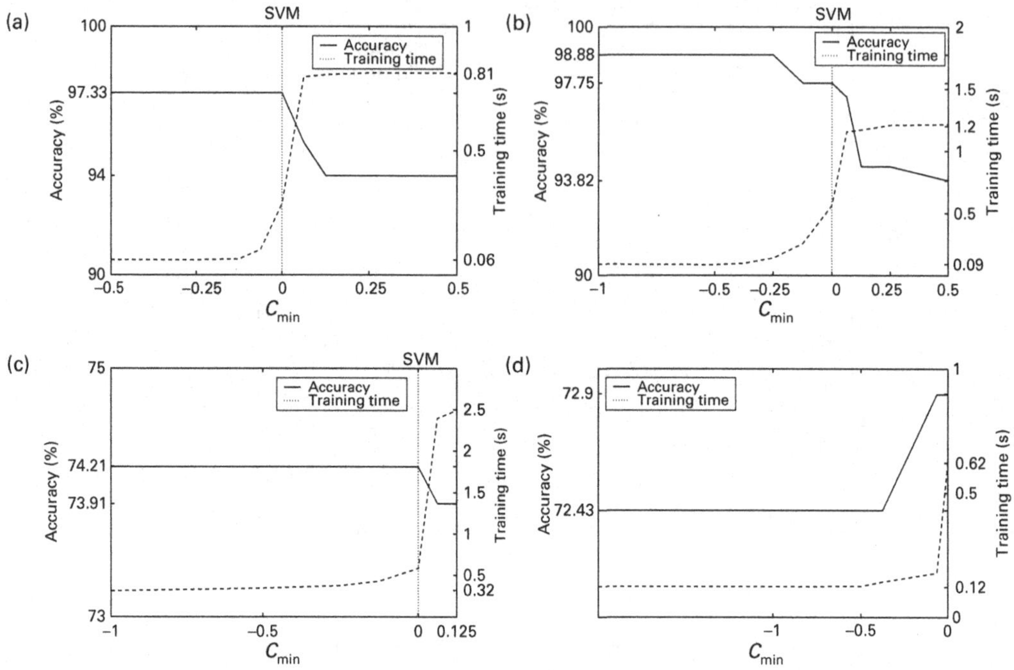

Fig. 12.7. Simulation results with varying values of C_{min} for Ridge-SVM. As C_{min} approaches 0, the training time significantly increases. Except for the glass dataset, a lower C_{min} value yields a better accuracy. Thus, only in the case of the glass dataset does the user face a tradeoff between accuracy and training time.

- For the four datasets, the learning speed slows down noticeably when C_{min} approaches 0,[2] whereas it increases by about a factor of 10 when C_{min} is tuned to be sufficiently negative.
- From the perspective of the prediction accuracy, a negatively valued C_{min} appears to be advantageous for three UCI datasets, see Figures 12.7 (a)–(c), with the sole exception being the glass dataset, see Figure 12.7(d). Therefore, a negative-valued C_{min} will be good for the Iris/Wine/Liver datasets, in terms of both accuracy and efficiency.

For the glass dataset, however, we must face a tradeoff between prediction accuracy and training time. If we want a higher performance at the expense of learning time, then a positive-valued C_{min} can be used. According to the simulation study, on setting $C_{min} = +0.125, C = 10, \rho = 0.4,$ and $\sigma = 0.6$, Ridge-SVM reaches its peak performance and delivers an accuracy improvement over SVM by nearly 10%.

[2] It was observed that, when C_{min} approaches 0, the training takes much longer. A possible explanation for this is that, for a fixed C, increasing C_{min} tightens the constraints for α_i (which are given by $C_{min} \leq \alpha_i \leq C$) and thus limits the choices for the α_is, making the optimization process more difficult.

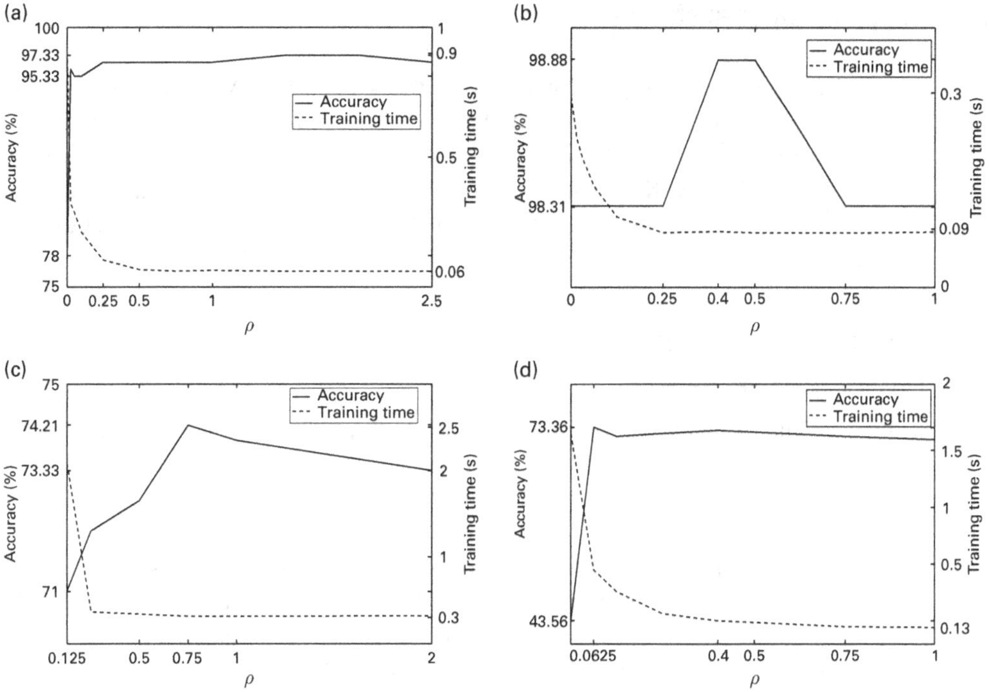

Fig. 12.8. Simulation results with varying values of ρ for Ridge-SVM. For each dataset a distinct peak value for ρ yields the highest accuracy. The training time increases significantly when ρ approaches 0. For the glass dataset there is a tradeoff between training time and accuracy.

12.5.3 The tuning of the parameter ρ

Another interesting design parameter is ρ. Figure 12.8 shows the learning time and prediction accuracy for different values of ρ for all the datasets. A consistent observation across all the datasets is the fact that the training time increases exponentially as ρ approaches 0. On the other hand, the training generally gains speed with increasing ρ. (Note that, as ρ increases, $\mathbf{K} + \rho\mathbf{I}$ becomes dominated by the identity matrix and thus the inverse can be calculated faster when solving the quadratic optimization problem.)

From the prediction's perspective, if ρ is set to 0, this can lead to over-fitting so that the accuracy drops. Obviously, from the perspective both of accuracy and of efficiency, it is advisable to keep ρ above a certain minimum threshold. However, the performance may improve with increasing ρ only up to a certain range. If ρ is chosen too large, the accuracy will drop due to the fact that the updated kernel matrix $\mathbf{K} + \rho\mathbf{I}$ is then dominated by ρ, which results in under-fitting. Usually, the best ρ value for prediction is heavily data-dependent. This was confirmed by the experimental study. More specifically, for two (Wine and Liver) of the four datasets, the performance deteriorates noticeably when ρ exceeds the preferred range. For such datasets, the tuning of ρ must be treated prudently.

12.6 Application case studies

The advantages of the proposed unified framework of Ridge-SVM are confirmed by simulation studies reported by Kung and Mak [139]. For coding of an effective algorithm for Ridge-SVM, it is useful to consider a working set from the training set and verify whether it satisfies the KKT condition [114]. This section will discuss the results of experiments on datasets from the UCI machine learning repository and on datasets for microarray cancer diagnosis.

12.6.1 Experiments on UCI data

Data and procedures

In the simulation conducted by Kung and Mak [139], the performance of Ridge-SVM hybrid classifiers was evaluated for six UCI datasets: Iris, Wine, Liver, Glass, Yeast, and Red Wine Quality. The characteristics of these datasets are summarized in Table 12.2.

For each dataset, the RBF kernel parameter (σ) was optimized for the conventional SVM and applied the best value to all other classifiers. The best values of σ for different datasets are shown in Table 12.3. Both for SVM and for Ridge-SVM, the upper bound on α_i was set to 10, i.e. $C = 10$. For each dataset, a grid search ($\rho \in \{0, 1, 2\}$ and $C_{\min} \in \{\pm 0.1, \pm 0.5, \pm 1.0\}$) was performed to find the best combination of regularization parameters and the lower bound on α_i. These values are shown in Table 12.3.

For the yeast dataset, the accuracies of 20 runs of five-fold cross-validations were averaged, with each run starting with a random partitioning of the data. For all the other datasets, leave-one-out cross-validation was applied to obtain the classification accuracies.

Table 12.2. Characteristics of the UCI datasets used in this study. All of these datasets contain real-valued samples without any missing values.

Characteristic	Iris	Wine	Liver	Glass	Yeast	Red Wine
No. of samples (N)	150	178	345	214	1484	1599
No. of features (M)	4	13	6	9	8	11
No. of classes	3	3	2	6	10	6

Table 12.3. The best combination of $C_{\min}$, ρ, and σ (RBF kernel parameter) for Ridge-SVM for different UCI datasets. The upper bound C of α_i was set to 10.

Parameter	Iris	Wine	Liver	Glass	Yeast	Red Wine
$C_{\min}$	0.5	−0.1	0.1	0.1	−0.1	0.5
ρ	1	0	1	0	1	1
σ	1	2	5	3	1	1

Table 12.4. Performance of linear system solver (LSS: $\mathbf{a} = \mathbf{K}^{-1}\mathbf{y}$ with $b = 0$), KDA, KRR, SVM, and Ridge-SVM on UCI datasets. In all cases, $C = 10$, and ρ, $C_{\min}$, and σ were set to values specified in Table 12.3.

	UCI dataset					
Method	Iris	Wine	Liver	Glass	Yeast	Red Wine
LSS*	84.00%	96.63%	53.33%	38.32%	36.26%	36.27%
KDA*	84.00%	92.70%	53.33%	38.32%	36.22 %	35.08%
KRR	95.33%	91.57%	72.17%	56.07%	**59.77%**	57.10%
SVM	96.00%	98.31%	73.04%	64.02%	54.94%	62.66%
Ridge-SVM	**96.67%**	**98.88%**	**73.33%**	**64.95%**	59.48%	**62.91%**

* Note that there are several repeated entries in the Iris dataset, causing very poor performance if we compute the kernel inverse directly – 34.67% and 30.67%, respectively, for LSS and KDA. The accuracies for LSS and KDA shown here were based on a trimmed training set such that only one copy of the repeated samples was kept.

A one-versus-rest classification technique was used to solve the multi-class problems. Specifically, for a problem of K classes, we trained K classifiers, with the kth classifier being trained to classify the kth class against the rest. Given a test vector, its predicted class label is obtained by picking the classifier with the highest score among the K classifiers.

Results and discussion

The classification accuracies of different classifiers are shown in Table 12.4. Evidently, Ridge-SVM achieves the highest accuracy in five out of six datasets, primarily because it offers high flexibility. SVM is the runner-up, ranking second in five out of six datasets.

12.6.2 Experiments on microarray cancer diagnosis

Data and procedures

Six cancer datasets were considered [206]: carcinoma [107], colon [5], glioma [195], leukemia [82], prostate [247], and breast [277]. These datasets contain gene expression profiles of healthy and cancerous samples. The five-fold cross-validation method was used to assess the performance of KRR, SVM, and Ridge-SVM, all with an RBF kernel. The cross-validations were performed 20 times, each starting with a random partitioning of the data. To ensure that meaningful comparisons across different classifiers were obtained, in each of the 20 cross-validation runs the same random partitioning was applied to all classifiers. For each fold in the cross-validation, first the z-norm was used to normalize the gene expression profiles, followed by using RFE-SVM [89] to select the top 50 features (genes) for classification.

Results and discussion

Table 12.5 shows the performance on the cancer datasets. The results show that the performance of KRR is comparable to that of SVM. Because of the closed-form solution of KRR, its training time is only 25% of that of SVM and Ridge-SVM. The performance of

Table 12.5. Performance of linear system solver (LSS: $\mathbf{a} = \mathbf{K}^{-1}\mathbf{y}$), KDA, KRR with $\rho = 1$, SVM with $C = 4$, and Ridge-SVM with $C = 4$, $C_{\text{min}} = 0.2C$, and $\rho = 1$ on cancer data. In all cases, an RBF kernel with radius10 was used with $C = 4$. The values inside parentheses in the last row are the p values of two-sample t-tests between the accuracies of Ridge-SVM and SVM; $p < 0.05$ means that the difference in accuracies is considered to be statistically significant.

	Cancer dataset					
Method	Carcinoma	Colon	Glioma	Leukemia	Prostate	Breast
LSS	63.42%	84.68%	73.30%	95.21%	91.62%	79.32%
KDA	63.42%	84.35%	73.00%	95.07%	91.58%	77.95%
KRR	64.92%	84.27%	72.50%	95.62%	92.43%	75.45%
SVM	63.75%	83.79%	72.10%	96.25%	92.32%	77.73%
Ridge-SVM	**65.50%***	**85.65%**	**73.90%**	**96.60%**	**93.09%**	**88.41%**
	(0.022)	(0.025)	(0.049)	(0.123)	(0.037)	(0.000)

* This accuracy was achieved by setting $C_{\text{min}} \in [-C, 0]$. When $C_{\text{min}} = 0.2C$ (as in other datasets), the accuracy is 59.67%.

LSS and KDA is almost the same as that of SVM. The results also show that Ridge-SVM achieves the highest accuracy. These preliminary results confirm that the additional design parameters used by Ridge-SVM can be adjusted to improve the prediction performance. Note first that, for all six datasets, the simulation study shows that Ridge-SVM with the default choice of $C_{\text{min}} = 0$ fails to produce the best accuracy. In other words, some other choices with $C_{\text{min}} \neq 0$ yield superior results; see Table 12.5.

- For one of the six datasets, i.e. prediction of the carcinoma cancer, the best accuracy is achieved by setting $C_{\text{min}} < 0$.
- For the other five datasets (colon, glioma, leukemia, prostate, and breast cancer), the best accuracy is achieved by setting $C_{\text{min}} > 0$.

Even though Ridge-SVM can achieve better performance than either KRR or SVM, as exemplified by the microarray datasets, the hybrid classifier needs to adjust more design parameters, making its learning computationally costly.

12.6.3 Experiments on subcellular ocalization

Data and procedures

To illustrate the application of Ridge-SVM, simulation studies were conducted on three different protein sequence datasets by Huang and Li [104], Mak and Kung [168], and Reinhardt and Hubbard [216]. Each of the datasets contains eukaryotic protein sequences with annotated subcellular locations. A one-versus-rest classification technique was used to solve the multi-class problems. We used five-fold cross-validation for performance evaluation so that every sequence in the datasets was tested [140].

Results and discussion

The results also show that Ridge-SVM achieves the highest accuracy due to the fact that the additional design parameters used by Ridge-SVM are helpful in improving the prediction performance. See Table 12.6.

Table 12.6. Performance of linear system solver (LSS: $\mathbf{a} = \mathbf{K}^{-1}\mathbf{y}$), KDA, KRR with $\rho = 1$, SVM with $C = 1$, and Ridge-SVM with $C_{min} = 0$, $C = 1$, and $\rho = 1$ on protein data

	Subcellular localization dataset		
Method	Huang and Li [104]	Mak, Guo, and Kung [166]	Reinhardt and Hubbard [216]
LSS	51.46%	96.80%	69.04%
KDA	51.54%	96.96%	69.74%
KRR	75.34%	98.00%	75.34%
SVM	75.89%	98.67%	79.49%
Ridge-SVM	76.12%	98.67%	80.56%

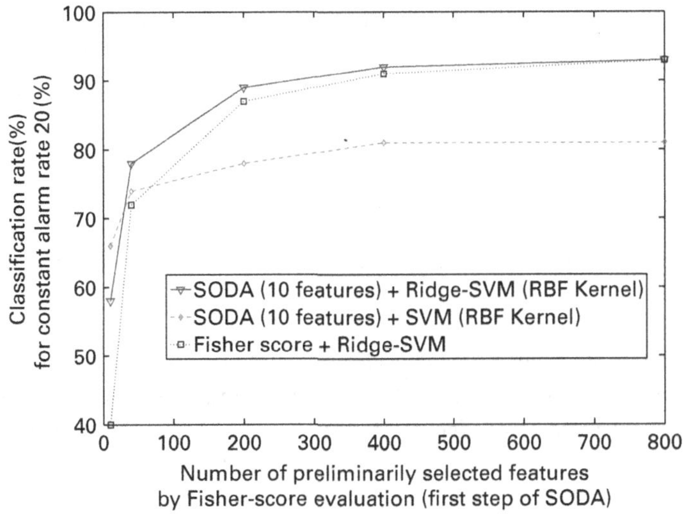

Fig. 12.9. SODA comparison: different SODA output dimensions (i.e. the numbers of features used in Ridge-SVM) versus detection rate, with the false-alarm rate fixed at 20%.

12.6.4 Experiments on the ischemic stroke dataset

The proposed methods were tested on high-dimensional medical data for the application of brain stroke detection and compared with existing techniques [211]; see Section 9.9.3.

By considering the real and imaginary parts of the complex signal, the feature vector is found to have an extremely high dimension of 62,556. This motivates the adoption of SODA, which efficiently extracts the discriminant information with a dramatically reduced dimensionality. After the dimension-reduction via SODA (see Algorithm 9.3), Ridge-SVM can then be applied and attain a high detection accuracy [311].

The experiment involves 27 samples from ischemic stroke patients (class +) and 45 healthy cases (class −). A leave-one-out test is applied. Figure 12.9 illustrates how the detection rate depends on the number of Fisher-score-based features. Note that the rates saturate when the number of features reaches 400 and beyond.

Table 12.7. In this experiment, the input vector of SVM or Ridge-SVM classifiers comprises ten SODA outputs reduced from 200 Fisher-score-based features. Shown here are detection rates for class 1 for different values of C, $C_{\min}$, and $C_{\max}$, again with the false-alarm rate fixed at 20%. In our study, setting $C = 10$ appears to lead to the best SVM result. For Ridge-SVM, on the other hand, setting $(C_{\min}, C_{\max}) = (-10, 10)$ produces a much higher rate than do the settings $(-1, 1)$ and $(-100, 100)$.

	$C_{\min}$	$C_{\max}$	Detection rate
SVM	0	1	74.6%
$\rho = 0$	0	10	86.8%
	0	100	67.9%
SVM	0	1	81.2%
$\rho = 0.4$	0	10	89.4%
Ridge-SVM	−0.1	0.1	91.2%
$\rho = 0.4$	0.1	1	87.3%
	−1	1	92.9%
	−1	10	87.6%
	1	10	91.4%
	−10	10	95.2%
	−10	100	85.6%
	10	100	89.0 %
	−100	100	94.2 %

Our simulation study suggests that Ridge-SVM is promising in terms of providing an enhanced generalization ability for datasets with unknown distributions [136, 139]. The detection rates of SVM and Ridge-SVM, with various learning parameters $C_{\min}$, $C_{\max}$, and ρ, are summarized in Table 12.7. According to the detection rates in our study, Ridge-SVM's 95.2% clearly outperforms SVM's 86.8% and 92.1% (with $\rho = 0.4$ and $\rho = 0.4$, respectively).

12.7 Summary

A frequently asked question is what kernel functions and learning models should be chosen. Naturally, the performance of a learned classifier often dictates such choices. The performance, however, depends closely on the distribution of the (training and testing) datasets, which is often not known a priori. Consequently, the most suitable kernel or learning models for a particular application are rarely identifiable in advance. Trial and error is a common approach employed in order to achieve the best performance. Methods such as bootstrapping and cross-validation will remain the most convincing approach [87].

This prompts us to look into a versatile classifier that uses a broad array of design parameters to best cope with unknown data distributions encountered in various application scenarios. We adopt the notion of the weight–error curve (WEC) to effectively characterize the supervised learning models. We analyze the advantages and pitfalls of both KRR's and SVM's WECs. Our design objective is to come up with a learning model whose WEC can enjoy the advantages while avoiding the undesirable attributes of KRR and SVM. This leads us to a unified hybrid classifier, named Ridge-SVM, described in Algorithm 12.1. The classifier is versatile, embracing most of the existing kernelized learning models such as KDA, KRR, and SVM.

12.8 Problems

Problem 12.1 (WEC for negative training vectors) *Note that Figures 12.3 and 12.4 show only the WECs for the positive training vectors of Ridge-SVM. Sketch the WECs for the corresponding negative training vectors, i.e. the negative counterparts to Figures 12.3 and 12.4.*

Problem 12.2 *As a special case of Ridge-SVM, the learning objective is to find* $\mathbf{a}$ *for*

$$\max_{\mathbf{a}} \left\{ \mathbf{a}^{\mathrm{T}}\mathbf{y} - \frac{1}{2}\mathbf{a}^{\mathrm{T}}[\mathbf{K} + \rho\mathbf{I}]\mathbf{a} \right\} \tag{12.12}$$

subject to the OHP constraint $\mathbf{e}^{\mathrm{T}}\mathbf{a} = 0$ *and* $0 \leq \alpha_i \leq C$. *Show that the ridge parameter* ρ *and the penalty factor* C *play complementary roles. More specifically, the trained classifiers tend to be more robust (not necessarily more accurate) when we increase* ρ*, decrease* C*, or do both of the above.*

Problem 12.3 (SVM with weighted penalty factor) *There exist application scenarios in which, by some prior knowledge, not all the training patterns will carry the same importance or confidence. For example, in transductive learning, the importance of a training vector* $\mathbf{x}_i$ *can be determined by its proximity to the test vector. On the other hand, if a training vector* $\mathbf{x}_i$ *has a high probability of being an outlier, then there will be less confidence to let the training vector carry an equal influence on the learning result. This motivates the adjustment of the penalty factor* $\{C\}$ *for each individual training vector [73b, 319b]. This leads to the following primal-domain learning model in the intrinsic space:*

$$\begin{aligned} &\underset{\mathbf{u},b,\xi\in\mathbf{R}^N}{\text{minimize}} \left\{ \frac{1}{2}|||\mathbf{u}|||^2 + \sum_i C_i\xi_i \right\} \\ &\qquad \textit{subject to the constraints} \\ &y_i\epsilon_i + \xi_i \geq 0, \ \textit{where } \epsilon_i \equiv \mathbf{u}^{\mathrm{T}}\vec{\boldsymbol{\phi}}(\mathbf{x}_i) + b - y_i \\ &\qquad \textit{and } \xi_i \geq 0, \ \forall i = 1, \ldots, N. \end{aligned} \tag{12.13}$$

Show that the typical Lagrangian approach will lead to the following dual-domain optimizer in the empirical space:

$$\sum_{i=1}^{N} \alpha_i - \frac{1}{2}\sum_{i=1}^{N}\sum_{j=1}^{N} \alpha_i\alpha_j y_i y_j K(\mathbf{x}_i, \mathbf{x}_j),$$

under the constraints that

$$\sum_{i=1}^{N} \alpha_i y_i = 0 \textit{ and } 0 \leq \alpha_i \leq C_i,\ i = 1, \ldots, N.$$

In this case, if a particular training vector, say $\mathbf{x}_i$*, is deemed a priori to be accorded less importance/confidence, then its corresponding coefficient* α_i *can be suppressed by applying a smaller* C_i*. For some application examples, see Problems 12.4 and 12.5.*

Problem 12.4 (Post-processing with weight adjustment) *This problem studies how the weights on* $\{C_i\}$ *may be used to mitigate the impact of possible outliers identified by the KRR, SVM, and Ridge-SVM learning models. It adopts a two-stage training process. (1) First, apply KRR with regularization factor* ρ*, a SVM with a penalty factor C, or even a Ridge-SVM. (2) Then adjust the penalty factor as follows:*

$$C_i = \begin{cases} 0 & \textit{if } \xi'_i \leq -\Delta \\ C & \textit{if } -\Delta \leq \xi'_i \leq +\Delta \\ C \times e^{\xi'_i - \Delta} & \textit{if } \Delta \leq \xi'_i, \end{cases} \qquad (12.14)$$

where $\xi'_i = 1 - y_i(\mathbf{x}_i \cdot \mathbf{w} + b - \rho C$ *and* $\Delta > 0$*. Conduct a simulation study to analyze the effect of the weight adjustment.*

Problem 12.5 (Online learning with weight adjustment) *This problem studies how the weighted learning model may be applied to transductive online learning models. In this case, the location or the distribution of testing pattern(s), say* $\mathbf{x}_t$*, is assumed to be known prior to the learning phase. Consequently, the importance of a training vector* $\mathbf{x}_i$ *can be modeled as a function of its proximity to the test vector* $\mathbf{x}_t$*:*

$$C_i = C \exp\left\{-\frac{\|\mathbf{x}_t - \mathbf{x}_i\|^2}{2\sigma^2}\right\}.$$

Conduct a simulation study to analyze the effect of the weight adjustment.

Problem 12.6 (MATLAB simulation on image database) *An image database containing ten categories, each with 100 JPG images, can be found at http://wang.ist.psu.edu/docs/related/. Try nonlinear supervised classifiers, BP-MLP (see Chapter 9), KRR, SVM, and Ridge-SVM, and compare their performance.*

Problem 12.7 (MATLAB simulation on UCI datasets using Ridge-SVM) *Download the UCI datasets from http://archive.ics.uci.edu/ml/ and apply Ridge-SVM with various design parameters.*

(a) *Fix* $C_{\max}$ *and* ρ *to certain properly chosen constants, vary the parameter* $C_{\min}$*, and compare the learning speeds and prediction performance. (A case of special interest is when* $\rho = 0$*.)*

(b) *Fix* $C_{\max}$ *and* $C_{\min}$ *to certain properly chosen constants, vary the parameter* ρ*, and compare the learning speeds and prediction performance.*

Part VI

Kernel methods for green machine learning technologies

The traditional curse of dimensionality is often focused on the extreme dimensionality of the feature space, i.e. M. However, for kernelized learning models for big data analysis, the concern is naturally shifted to the extreme dimensionality of the kernel matrix, N, which is dictated by the size of the training dataset. For example, in some biomedical applications, the sizes may be hundreds of thousands. In social media applications, the sizes could be easily of the order of millions. This creates a new large-scale learning paradigm, which calls for a new level of computational tools, both in hardware and in software.

Given the kernelizability, we have at our disposal two learning models, respectively represented by two different kernel-induced vector spaces. Now our focus of attention should be shifted to the interplay between two kernel-induced representations. Even though the two models are theoretically equivalent, they could incur very different implementation costs for learning and prediction. For cost-effective system implementation, one should choose the lower-cost representation, whether intrinsic or empirical. For example, if the dimension of the empirical space is small and manageable, an empirical-space learning models will be more appealing. However, this will just be the opposite if the number of training vectors is extremely large, which is the case for the "big data" learning scenario. In this case, one must give a serious consideration to the intrinsic model whose cost can be controlled by properly adjusting the order of the kernel function.

Chapter 13 explores cost-effective design for kernel-based machine learning and classification. Algorithm 13.1 summarizes cost-effective kernel-based learning algorithms for situations in which a large training dataset of size N is made available for training classifiers. Algorithm 13.2 describes a recursive tensor-based classification algorithm that allows a further reduction of the classification complexity.

The chapter also develops time-adaptive KRR learning models that are critical for applications to time-series analysis. The recursive algorithms for time-adaptive KRR learning models may be derived from either deterministic or statistical formulations. The recursive (or time-adaptive) KRR algorithm in the intrinsic space requires only $O(J^2)$ operations per sample update.

13 Efficient kernel methods for learning and classification

13.1 Introduction

Since the invention of integrated circuits in the 1950s, processing gates and memory storages on a chip have grown at an exponential rate. Major breakthroughs in wireless and internet technologies have further promoted novel information technologies (IT). New applications, such as cloud computing and green computing, will undoubtedly have profound impacts on everyone's daily life.

Machine learning will play a vital part in modern information technology, especially in the era of big data analysis. For the design of kernel-based machine learning systems, it is important to find suitable kernel functions that lead to an optimal tradeoff between design freedom and computational complexity, which involves very often a choice between the intrinsic-space and empirical-space learning models.

A successful deployment of a machine learning system hinges upon a well-coordinated co-design of algorithm and hardware. This chapter addresses practical design issues related to cost-effective learning or low-power prediction that are vital for green IT applications.

This chapter addresses the following topics concerning cost-effective system implementations both in the learning phase and in the prediction phase.

(i) In the internet-based IT era, a system designer must first decide where to process the bulk of the information: a local/private client (e.g. a mobile device) or a data center (e.g. "the cloud"). Section 13.2 addresses the pros and cons of both options. The choice of strategy depends on a delicate tradeoff between the computation and communication costs, among many other system design factors. Local processing (e.g. using an implanted pacemaker or a mobile device) offers some unique advantages, including reliable and locally controllable performance and personal privacy and security. This motivates the investigation into green IT system design for local clients. A practical system designer must consider the tradeoff between cloud computing and client computing, which can be viewed as a new kind of "C-&-C" tradeoff in machine learning applications.

(ii) For a kernel-based machine learning system, the design freedom and computational complexity are dictated by one or both of the following parameters:

- the empirical degree N associated with the size of the training dataset; and
- the intrinsic degree J associated with the kernel function used.

In Section 13.3, we shall look into kernels with a finite intrinsic degree. A truncated-RBF (TRBF) kernel will be proposed as a reasonable compromise between two desirable properties, namely a finite intrinsic degree and shift-invariance.

(iii) Section 13.4 addresses issues concerning the classification complexities. The classification and learning complexities depend on the feature size M, the intrinsic degree J, and the empirical degree N. Simulation suggests that there is a clear trend that the performance of classifiers improves with increasing N. The complexity for computing the discriminant function represented by the empirical space will also increase with N. This may severely jeopardize the low power budget desired by many mobile-based applications. A simple solution to such a curse of the dimension regarding the empirical degree is by opting for kernels with finite intrinsic degree J. In this case, the complexity for computing the discriminant function represented by the intrinsic space will be a function of J and will not increase with N. Moreover, as elaborated on in the section, further saving of classification complexity may be attained by having the discriminant function processed by a tensor form.

(iv) Section 13.5 addresses issues concerning the learning complexity, which again depends on the feature size M, the intrinsic degree J, and the empirical degree N. More importantly, it also depends closely on the learning methods adopted. We will compare the learning complexities associated with SVM and KRR (or, equivalently, PDA). Briefly, with respect to the empirical degree N, the traditional KRR has a learning complexity of $O(N^3)$. The learning complexity associated with SVM is only $O(N^2)$. In this sense, SVM holds a clear advantage over KRR or PDA when N grows large. However, such an advantage is completely reversed with kernel that has a finite intrinsic degree. In this case, one may adopt a scatter-matrix-based KRR with a learning complexity that is linearly dependent on N, i.e. $O(N)$, which is much more efficient than its SVM counterpart when N is large.

(v) Section 13.6 examines the tradeoff between the prediction accuracy and the computational efficiency of the trained classifiers. This section will focus on finding kernels with finite-degree kernels such that both the classification complexity and the prediction performance may be deemed acceptable. In the case of an extra huge empirical degree N, the processing efficiency of the scatter-matrix-based KRR and prediction improvement offered by PPDA may be combined to deliver a promising machine learning solution.

(vi) Section 13.7 develops a time-adaptive learning formulation for a KRR algorithm, which requires only $O(J^2)$ operations per sample update. The time-adaptive KRR algorithm formulation has a natural empirical-space approach. Moreover, its derivation is somewhat simpler than that of its intrinsic-space counterpart. The flip side is that its complexity amounts to $O(n^2)$ per sample, which may grow infinitely with n, i.e. $n = 1, 2, \ldots$, without a foreseeable termination point.

13.2 System design considerations

For machine learning techniques to be applicable to real-world application systems, several practical computational aspects need consideration. In particular, from a system designer's perspective, it is vital to determine whether the bulk of information processing should be executed by a centralized data platform (e.g. cloud computing) or by local or client processing units.

13.2.1 Green processing technologies for local or client computing

Local processing (e.g. using an implanted pacemaker or a mobile device) offers some unique advantages, including reliable and locally controllable performance and personal privacy and security, especially for e.g. medical or financial data. However, mobile devices often have to operate under a stringent power budget. This motivates the study of effective designs for green IT computing systems.

Green and low-power processing applications have recently become one of the main focuses of modern IT technologies. This has crucial implications for health-care monitoring devices, pacemakers, therapeutics, prosthesis, and brain–computer interface. For biomedical devices to be clinically viable, there are several system requirements.

- The system should enable constant and simultaneous recording from an array of electrode channels to actuate neuroprosthetic devices.
- The system should support signal processing for early extraction of critical features (e.g. detection of spikes) and to reduce system latency.
- The system may be miniaturized to meet implantability constraints.
- The system must consume little power (less than $65\text{mW}/\text{cm}^2$) in order to prevent excessive heating of surrounding tissue and maintain long battery usage.

In addition, for certain applications such as personal security/finance data processing, it will be imperative to have data processed and stored locally. In this case, the required computation for classification/prediction must be supported by local or on-site processing devices. For more application examples, see e.g. [144, 150, 169].

13.2.2 Cloud computing platforms

Cloud computing is a data processing platform supplying remotely hosted application logic units, data stores, and a diversity of application resources. Cloud computing is quickly gaining popularity due to the mature wireless, internet, and parallel processing technologies. There are several distinct advantages of cloud computing.

- It offers data processing services ubiquitously, i.e. at any time, anywhere, and for anyone.
- It manages the server farm, supports extensive database and vast storage space, and is ready to lease out, on demand from clients, a variable number of machines.

- More importantly, it has the premise of elastic hosting, e.g. Microsoft's Windows Azure, which bears an important design implication in offering application domains for lease to clients.

For some applications, it may be appealing to have raw data transmitted to the cloud so as to leverage its rich computing resources. From the perspective of machine learning, thanks to the increasing demand for data mining, intelligent search software will undoubtedly become a vital and integral part of the cloud computing paradigm.

13.2.3 Local versus centralized processing

From the perspective of power saving, it is vital to decide whether it is more cost-effective to have the data processed using cloud computing or by the client's processing units. This decision depends on a delicate tradeoff between the computation and communication costs. This is explained as follows.

The main problem of cloud computing lies in the relatively high communication cost of transmitting the raw input data to the center unit. If the computation cost is much greater than the communication cost, then it is advisable to have data transmitted to a data processing center to effectively leverage its computing capability and application support. Otherwise, it may be more cost-effective to first process data locally and transmit only the compressed information or the final analysis to the centralized information system.

For tradeoff analysis of communication versus computation costs, we shall assume a somewhat controlled environment for transmission and, consequently, the unit energy cost of communication per bit is estimated to be around the order of 1 nJ. Moreover, we shall also assume that the energy consumption per 16-bit-ALU operation can be estimated to be around 10 pJ.[1] Given these preliminary figures, the following observations may be made.

(i) When M is small, the (online) classification power becomes relatively more affordable than that required for raw data transmission. In this case, local processing (i.e. on-site classification) will be preferred.

(ii) On the other hand, as depicted in Figure 13.1(a), the computation power grows nonlinearly with respect to the number of features M. Consequently, the economy tends to favor centralized processing when M becomes large.

13.3 Selection of cost-effective kernel functions

Note also that the computational costs for off-line versus online processing are often in completely different scales. Note also that the computation required for the off-line learning will not be counted against the online power budget. In particular, from the perspective of kernel-based machine learning, the kernel function chosen could

[1] According to an Intel report, a 32-bit multiplication consumes 496 GOPS/watt. It needs four-way 16-bit SIMD, each with 124 GOPS/watt. This leads to around 10 pJ for a 16-bit operation.

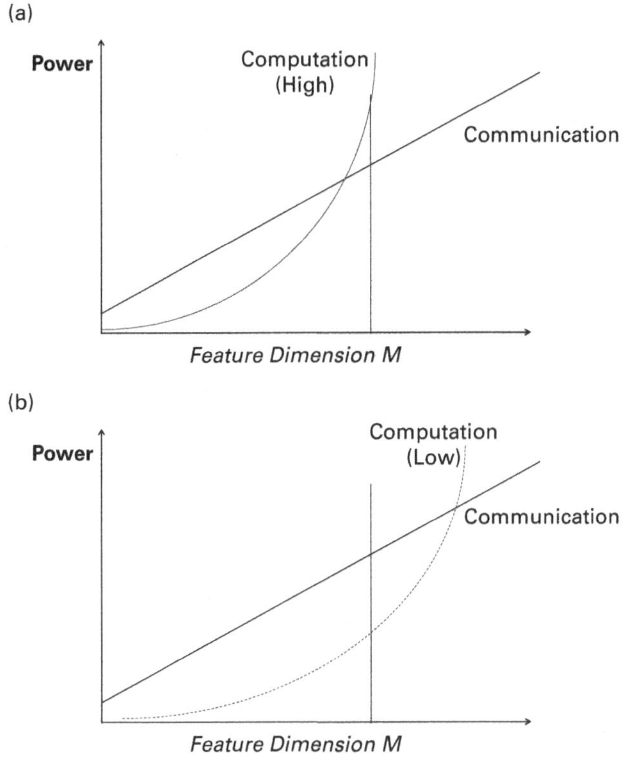

Fig. 13.1. Quantifiable applications: power consumption for computation versus communication. While the communication cost usually grows linearly with the feature size M, the computational complexity grows nonlinearly with it. (a) For the targeted M (indicated by the vertical dotted line), a highly nonlinear classification complexity would consume more power if the computation is locally processed. (Note that the computation consumes more power than the communication.) (b) On the other hand, e.g. via a new kernel method, local processing may become feasible and/or appealing if its computation may be performed with less complexity.

significantly impact the performance/power both of the (off-line) learning phase and of the (online) prediction phase. The latter will be especially critical to green IT, since the power budget is often very stringent.

From the perspective of prediction accuracy, the Gaussian kernel function offers one a greater discriminating power than do other kernels. This is highlighted by the RBF-kernel-induced patterns of the ECG dataset displayed in Figure 13.2. Hence, the RBF kernel is generally expected to deliver a higher prediction performance than those of other kernels, an expectation that has been confirmed by numerous experimental studies. Consequently, the RBF kernel has naturally become the default choice in the kernel approach to machine learning, be it supervised or unsupervised.

However, as will be explained later, the RBF kernel may incur an enormous classification complexity when the training size N is extremely large, which is a scenario that frequently arises in biomedical and genomic applications. In this case, the RBF kernels may become computationally unsupportable, and thus it is necessary to opt for kernel

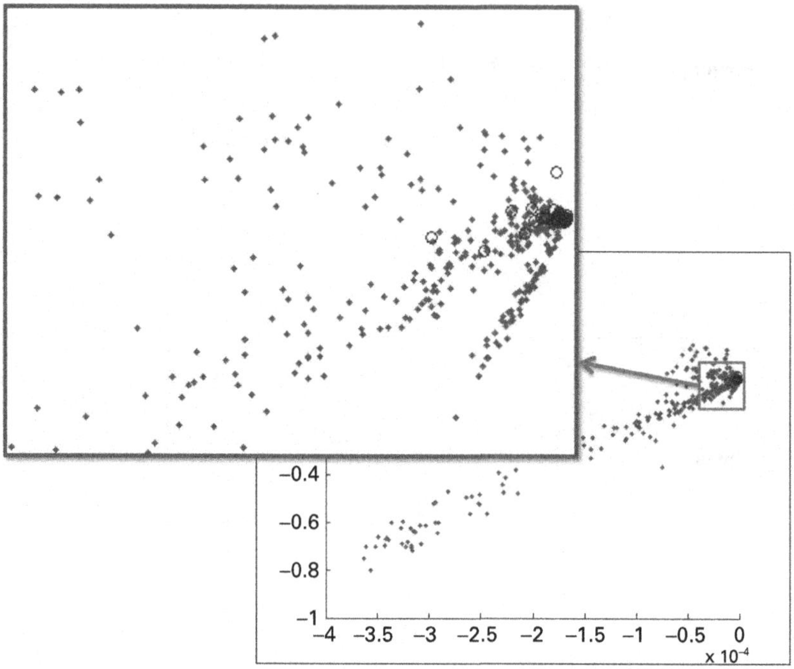

Fig. 13.2. This figure highlights the discriminating power of adoption of Gaussian kernel in SVM classifier. The two axes correspond to the two largest decision components. The simulation study was based on the MIT/BIH ECG database [203].

functions with a finite and reasonable intrinsic degree J. This is due to the fact that, when J is relatively small, the intrinsic degree J dictates the computational complexity both for the learning phase and for the prediction phase.

13.3.1 The intrinsic degree J

Assuming a finite intrinsic degree J, the intrinsic feature vector associated with a kernel function can be written as

$$\vec{\phi}(\mathbf{x}) = \begin{bmatrix} \phi^{(1)}(\mathbf{x}) \\ \phi^{(2)}(\mathbf{x}) \\ \vdots \\ \phi^{(J)}(\mathbf{x}) \end{bmatrix},$$

where the last element of the intrinsic feature vector is usually reserved for the constant term, i.e. we usually set $\phi^{(J)}(\mathbf{x}) = 1$. Hence a kernel function can be written as

$$K(\mathbf{x}, \mathbf{x}') = \sum_{j=1}^{J} \phi^{(j)}(\mathbf{x})\phi^{(j)}(\mathbf{x}'),$$

where the intrinsic degree J represents the number of independent basis functions in the associated intrinsic space.

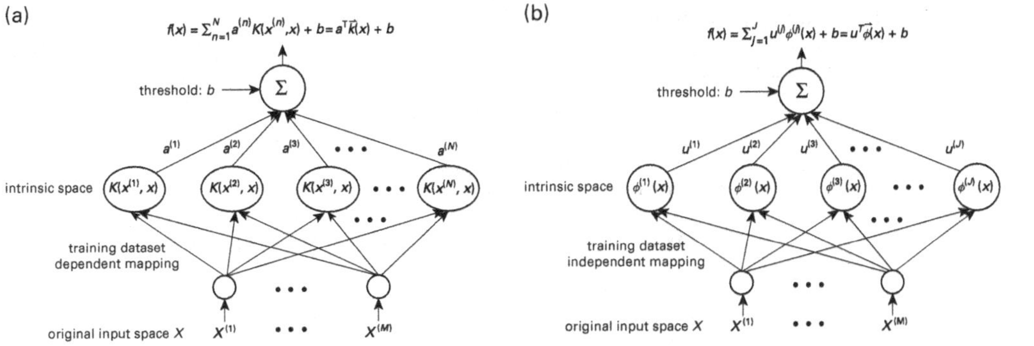

Fig. 13.3. For the purpose of finding the lowest computational complexity to process a kernel-based discriminant function, the best representation of the vector $\mathbf{x}$ in the original space must be identified. Two major contending kernel-induced representations are shown here. Naturally, the representation with lower complexity will be preferred. (a) The empirical space $\mathcal{K}$ is an N-dimensional vector space. (b) The intrinsic space is of dimension J, which may be finite or infinite.

All kernel-based classifiers work with a kernel matrix that is tightly linked to the intrinsic data matrix $\mathbf{\Phi}$:

$$\mathbf{K} = \mathbf{\Phi}^{\mathrm{T}}\mathbf{\Phi}, \text{ where } \mathbf{\Phi} = \left[\begin{array}{cccc} \vec{\phi}(\mathbf{x}_1) & \vec{\phi}(\mathbf{x}_2) & \ldots & \vec{\phi}(\mathbf{x}_N) \end{array} \right].$$

The intrinsic feature vector offers a new representation layer exemplified by Figure 13.3(b). For example, a pth-order polynomial kernel (abbreviated as POLY_p) is $K(\mathbf{x}, \mathbf{x}') = \left(1 + (\mathbf{x} \cdot \mathbf{x}')/\sigma^2\right)^p$. Denote $x^{(M+1)} = 1$. Then each basis function has an appearance as follows:

$$\left(x^{(1)}\right)^{d_1} \ldots \left(x^{(M)}\right)^{d_M} \left(x^{(M+1)}\right)^{d_{M+1}}, \tag{13.1}$$

where the d_is are non-negative integers such that

$$\sum_{m=1}^{M+1} d_m = p, \tag{13.2}$$

where $x^{(m)}$ denotes the mth element of $\mathbf{x}$. Thus the intrinsic degree is

$$J = J^{(p)} = \left(\begin{array}{c} M+p \\ p \end{array} \right) = \frac{(M+p)!}{M!\,p!}, \tag{13.3}$$

since this is exactly the number of different combinations satisfying Eq. (13.1).

For linear kernels, the discriminant function is $f(\mathbf{x}) = \mathbf{w}^{\mathrm{T}}\mathbf{x} + b$, and there are $M + 1$ free parameters: $\{w^{(j)}, j = 1, \ldots, M.\} \bigcup \{b\}$.

Fore example, let us assume $M = 21$, then we have[2]

- for POLY2 (or TRBF2) kernels

$$J = J^{(2)} = \frac{M^2 + 3M + 2}{2} = 253,$$

- for POLY3 (or TRBF3) kernels

$$J = J^{(3)} = \frac{(M+1)(M+2)(M+3)}{6} = \frac{M^3 + 6M^2 + 11M + 6}{6} = 2024,$$

- and for POLY4 (or TRBF4) kernels

$$J = J^{(4)} = \frac{(M+1)(M+2)(M+3)(M+4)}{24}$$
$$= \frac{M^4 + 10M^3 + 35M^2 + 50M + 24}{6} = 12{,}650.$$

In summary, a kernel is quantitatively characterized by its intrinsic degree J, which in turn dictates the learning/classification complexities and prediction performance. This inevitably leads to tradeoff analysis.

- A high degree of design freedom is critical to a high prediction performance insofar as it provides a greater flexibility to cope with a complex data structure or distribution.
- On the other hand, a low model complexity has the advantage of requiring a shorter training time in the learning phase as well as a smaller power budget during the online prediction phase.

13.3.2 Truncated-RBF (TRBF) kernels

Another interesting aspect in kernel selection is the shift-invariance property. An RBF kernel has the form $f(\mathbf{x} - \mathbf{y})$ and is thus obviously shift-invariant. In contrast, any finite-order polynomial kernels cannot be shift-invariant. In other words, they may be affected by the translation of the coordinate.

Now we are faced with only two options: (1) shift-invariant but without a finite intrinsic degree J; or (2) with finite intrinsic degree J, but not shift-invariant. This section introduces a truncated-RBF (TRBF) kernel, which has a finite intrinsic degree but is not shift-invariant [33, 144].

Let us consider a Gaussian kernel

$$K(\mathbf{x}, \mathbf{y}) = \exp\left\{-\frac{\|\mathbf{x} - \mathbf{y}\|^2}{2\sigma^2}\right\},$$

which can be expanded into a special Taylor series:

$$K(\mathbf{x}, \mathbf{y}) = \exp\left\{-\frac{\|\mathbf{x}\|^2}{2\sigma^2}\right\}\left[\sum_{k=1}^{\infty} \frac{1}{k!}\left(\frac{\mathbf{x} \cdot \mathbf{y}}{\sigma^2}\right)^k\right] \exp\left\{-\frac{\|\mathbf{y}\|^2}{2\sigma^2}\right\}. \tag{13.4}$$

[2] In our subsequent simulation study on arrhythmia detection using an ECG dataset, 21 morphology features of each heart beat form a feature vector [46].

Such an expansion suggests that the number of basis functions is infinite, i.e. $J = J^{(\mathrm{RBF})} \to \infty$.

We now face the dilemma that, on the one hand, the RBF kernel can deliver the best performance, but it has an infinite intrinsic degree; while, on the other hand, polynomial kernels may compromise the performance, but offer cost-effective implementation due to their finite intrinsic degree.

Fortunately, polynomial kernels are not the only kernels that have a finite intrinsic degree. A simple and intuitive way to combine the best of (the performance of) RBF and (the finite degree of) POLY kernels is by using the following truncated-RBF (TRBF_*p*) kernel of order *p*:

$$K(\mathbf{x},\mathbf{y}) = \exp\left\{-\frac{\|\mathbf{x}\|^2}{2\sigma^2}\right\}\left[\sum_{k=1}^{p}\frac{1}{k!}\left(\frac{\mathbf{x}\cdot\mathbf{y}}{\sigma^2}\right)^k\right]\exp\left\{-\frac{\|\mathbf{y}\|^2}{2\sigma^2}\right\}, \tag{13.5}$$

with each basis function, barring a factor, having the form

$$\exp\left\{-\frac{\|\mathbf{x}\|^2}{2\sigma^2}\right\}\left(x^{(1)}\right)^{d_1}\cdots\left(x^{(M)}\right)^{d_M}\left(x^{(M+1)}\right)^{d_{M+1}},$$

which, strictly speaking, is non-polynomial. Nevertheless, the intrinsic degree of TRBF_*p* remains

$$J = J^{(p)} = \begin{pmatrix} M+p \\ p \end{pmatrix} = \frac{(M+p)!}{M!p!}. \tag{13.6}$$

Moreover, since the intrinsic degree for TRBF_*p* is $J' \approx J = J^{(p)}$, which is exactly the same as for the POLY_*p* kernel, the classification complexity will remain similar.

The TRBF kernel provides a good approximation to the RBF kernel and yet it has a finite intrinsic degree. This allows us to harness the full power of a degree-J kernel and gain a deeper insight into a reduced-degree RBF kernel.

For example, it can be shown that, with $\mathbf{x} = [u\ v]^{\mathrm{T}}$ and $\sigma = 1$, the TRBF2 kernel $K(\mathbf{x},\mathbf{y})$,

$$\exp\left\{-\frac{\|\mathbf{x}\|^2}{2\sigma^2}\right\}\left[1+\frac{\mathbf{x}\cdot\mathbf{y}}{\sigma^2}+\frac{1}{2}\left(\frac{\mathbf{x}\cdot\mathbf{y}}{\sigma^2}\right)^2\right]\exp\left\{-\frac{\|\mathbf{y}\|^2}{2\sigma^2}\right\},$$

induces the following intrinsic feature vector $\vec{\phi}(\mathbf{x})$:

$$[e^{-(u^2+v^2)}\ ue^{-(u^2+v^2)}\ ve^{-(u^2+v^2)}\ uve^{-(u^2+v^2)}\ \sqrt{0.5}u^2e^{-(u^2+v^2)}\ \sqrt{0.5}v^2e^{-(u^2+v^2)}]^{\mathrm{T}},$$

with $J = J^{(2)} = 6$ independent basis functions.

Modified polynomial kernels

Note further that pre-scaling of $\exp\{-\|\mathbf{x}\|^2/(2\sigma^2)\}$ and post-scaling of $\exp\{-\|\mathbf{y}\|^2/(2\sigma^2)\}$ would cost substantial computations. Since the effect (of inclusion or exclusion) of the scaling factors will be canceled out if auto-normalization is used, it is worthwhile to consider a simpler POLY-TRBF kernel function:

$$K(\mathbf{x},\mathbf{y}) = \sum_{k=1}^{p}\frac{1}{k!}\left(\frac{\mathbf{x}\cdot\mathbf{y}}{\sigma^2}\right)^k.$$

For example, the basis function for the POLY-TRBF2 kernel is

$$\mathbf{z} = [1 \quad u \quad v \quad uv \quad \sqrt{0.5}u^2 \quad \sqrt{0.5}v^2]^{\mathrm{T}},$$

which bears a strong resemblance to the POLY2 kernel – but is not exactly the same.

As another example, the POLY-TRBF3 kernel will simply be

$$K(\mathbf{x}, \mathbf{y}) = 1 + \frac{\mathbf{x} \cdot \mathbf{y}}{\sigma^2} + \frac{1}{2}\left(\frac{\mathbf{x} \cdot \mathbf{y}}{\sigma^2}\right)^2 + \frac{1}{6}\left(\frac{\mathbf{x} \cdot \mathbf{y}}{\sigma^2}\right)^3.$$

This provides an interesting variant of the original version of a pth-order polynomial kernel function (i.e. $K(\mathbf{x}, \mathbf{y}) = \left(1 + (\mathbf{x} \cdot \mathbf{y})/\sigma^2\right)^p$).

13.4 Classification complexities: empirical and intrinsic degrees

As exemplified by the ECG arrhythmia detection system depicted in Figure 13.4, an overall machine learning system includes two phases: a learning phase and a prediction phase. Accordingly, we shall explore two types of computational complexity: *prediction complexity* (in this section) and *learning complexity* (in Section 13.5).

The prediction complexity reflects the power consumption required for online and local processing. As shown in Figure 13.5, the power budget for the prediction phase comprises two major components: feature extraction and classification.

The low-power condition is satisfied only if the sum of powers for both feature extraction and classification remains within a prescribed budget. The power/energy required for feature extraction depends on the types of the features and the number of features required for data analysis. Usually, the power of feature extraction is given and fixed,

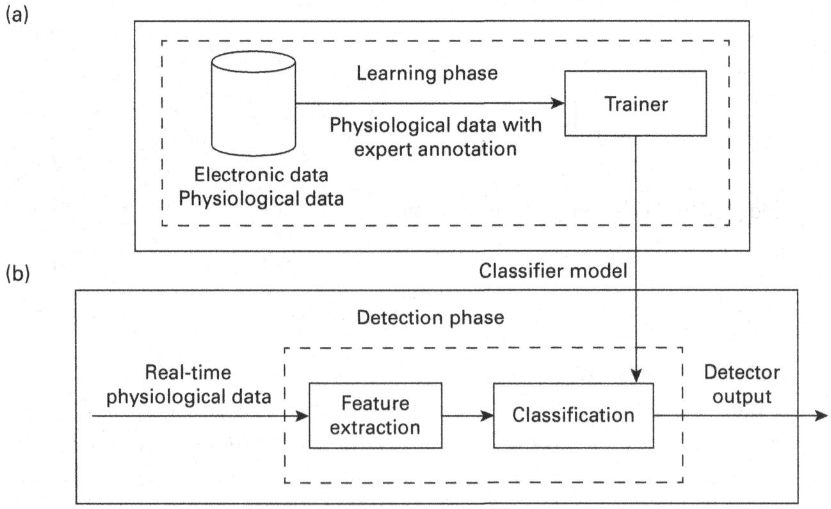

Fig. 13.4. The learning and detection (prediction) subsystems for the ECG application. (a) In the learning phase, the training data (with known class labels) are used to train a desired classifier. (b) In the prediction/detection phase, the class of a test signal is predicted by the trained classifier.

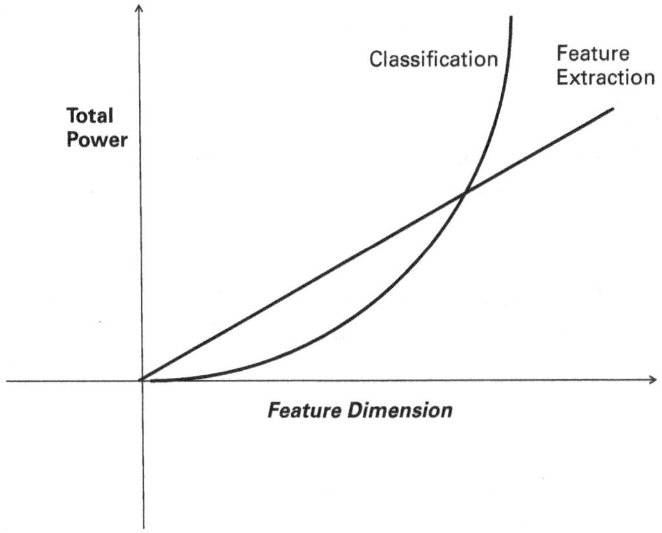

Fig. 13.5. In the prediction phase, the total local processing power consists of two components: (1) feature extraction and (2) classification. The two costs grow at different rates with respect to the feature dimension.

which means that the total power is acceptable if and only if the classification power remains under a certain threshold.

Example 13.1 (Kernel methods for ECG arrhythmia detection) *Kernel methods were applied to cardiac monitoring systems [144, 149, 150]. The simulation study presented below is based on the MIT/BIH ECG database [203].*

Morphology features

For arrhythmia detection, waveform morphology features are considered to be most generic and effective for classification of all kinds of abnormal heart beats [46]. Here, 21 morphology features of each heart beat form a feature vector.

Training vectors

The full database contains ECG recordings obtained over 24 hours from 47 subjects – each individual record being divided into 48 half-hour excerpts. Of those, 40 records (for a total of 112,803 beats) were used. The SVM classifier is learned from a generic dataset derived from more than 40 patients, leading to over 15,000 *support vectors.*

Low power budget

According to Lee, Kung, and Verma [149, 150], the power budgeted for ECG applications is typically limited to 1–10 mW for wearable devices. For the sake of argument, let us suppose that the total power budget is set at 5 *mW, in which the power reserved for feature extraction was estimated to be around* 1.56 *mW [149, 150]. This leaves a very low budget of 3.44 mW for classification, and a careful selection of kernels becomes imperative.*

RBF-SVM classifiers

Owing to the high discriminating power pertaining to RBF-SVM classifiers, they have been a popular choice for handling complex data analysis including arrhythmia detection. However, the good performance is often at the expense of a high classification power cost.

The large number of support vectors implies that the power required for the RBF classifier will be unreasonably high. Indeed, it was estimated to be around 49.52 mW,[3] *which clearly fails to meet the low-power budget. In order to meet the set budget, it is necessary to cut the classification power by one order of magnitude or more.*

The green-computing (i.e. low-power) problem may be solved by adopting kernels with a finite and reasonable intrinsic degree. The rest of this section will demonstrate how such kernels may lead to substantial savings in classification power.

13.4.1 The discriminant function in the empirical representation

Heuristically, use of the full training dataset would be more likely to learn a statistically more reliable classifier [144, 319]. This is supported by the numerical evidence depicted in Figures 9.5 and 13.6, where the prediction performance indeed improves with increasing empirical degree N.

The price of the high performance of the RBF classifier is that the learning and classification complexities will also increase with N. Such a curse of empirical degree will almost surely jeopardize the green computing or low-power requirements for many local and mobile processing devices.

Under the LSP discussed in Section 1.3, the discriminant function has a representation in the empirical space:

$$f(\mathbf{x}) = \sum_{n=1}^{N} a_n K(\mathbf{x}, \mathbf{x}_n) + b = \mathbf{a}^{\mathrm{T}} \overrightarrow{\mathbf{k}}(\mathbf{x}) + b, \tag{13.7}$$

where $\overrightarrow{\mathbf{k}}(\mathbf{x})$ and $\mathbf{a}$ are respectively the representative vector and decision vector in the *empirical space* $\mathcal{K}$. In this representation, the design freedom is equal to the empirical degree N.

The computational process is illustrated by a two-layer network depicted in Figure 13.3(a).

(i) **Lower layer.** Given a test pattern $\mathbf{x}$, for each of the N training data we need to compute the squared distance $||\mathbf{x}||^2 + ||\mathbf{x}_i||^2 - 2\mathbf{x}^{\mathrm{T}}\mathbf{x}_i$ in the exponent of the RBF

[3] This estimate is based on a simulation conducted on a real processor model, MSPsim, reported by Lee, Kung, and Verma [150], a cycle-accurate MSP430 instruction set simulator [183]. The results suggest that the energy cost per multiply-and-add operation can be estimated to be around 0.03 μJ.

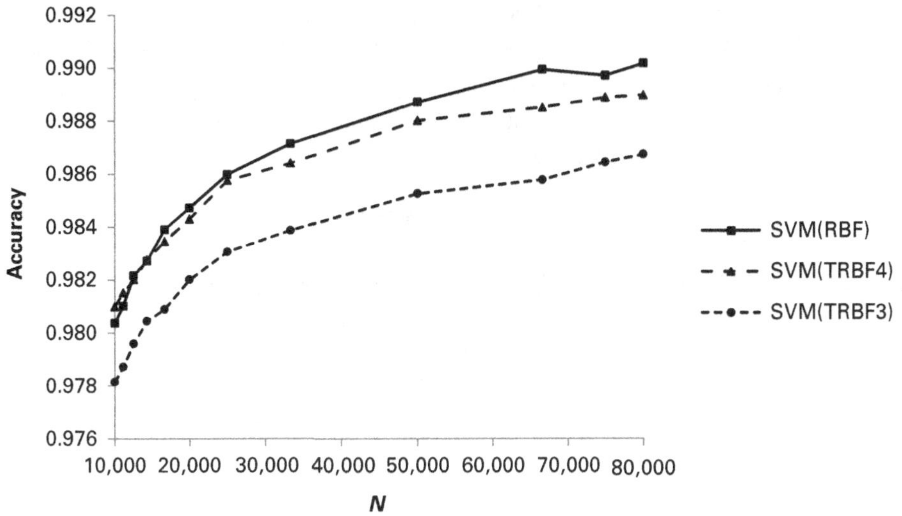

Fig. 13.6. Experimental results of arrhythmia detection. The accuracies of the SVM classifier are plotted for different kernels: RBF, TRBF3, and TRBF4 kernels. The following parameters were adopted: $\sigma = 2.5$ for RBF and TRBF3 kernels, $C = 10$ for SVM, and $\rho = 0.1$ for KRR and PPDA.

function $K(\mathbf{x}, \mathbf{x}_i)$. This requires roughly M operations, and each operation involves one multiplication-and-addition (MAC) step. It amounts to NM operations for this layer.

(ii) **Upper layer.** It costs N operations to process the inner product in the upper layer.

This amounts to a total of approximately NM operations, i.e. the number of operations grows linearly with the empirical degree N.

13.4.2 The discriminant function in the intrinsic representation

For polynomial or TRBF kernels, but not Gaussian kernels, the discriminant function has enjoys an alternative representation in the intrinsic space:

$$f(\mathbf{x}) = \sum_{i=1}^{N} a_i \overrightarrow{\boldsymbol{\phi}}(\mathbf{x}_i)^{\mathrm{T}} \overrightarrow{\boldsymbol{\phi}}(\mathbf{x}) + b = \mathbf{u}^{\mathrm{T}} \overrightarrow{\boldsymbol{\phi}}(\mathbf{x}) + b.$$

In this representation, the degree of design freedom is equal to the intrinsic degree J.

The computational process is illustrated by the two-layer network depicted in Figure 13.3(b).

(i) **Lower layer.** Given a test pattern $\mathbf{x}$, it costs $(p-1)$ operations (or less) to compute each intrinsic basis function of a POLY_p kernel. Consequently, the complexity for producing all elements of $\overrightarrow{\boldsymbol{\phi}}(\mathbf{x})$ is upper bounded by $(p-1)J^{(p)}$.

(ii) **Upper layer.** It costs $J^{(p)}$ operations to compute the inner product $\mathbf{u}^{\mathrm{T}} \overrightarrow{\boldsymbol{\phi}}(\mathbf{x})$.

The total classification complexity is bounded by $pJ^{(p)}$. It is worth noting that the complexity is independent of N, freeing us from the previous curse of empirical degree.

Derivation of the POLY2 kernel-based discriminant function

However, the two-layer structure in Figure 13.3(b) fails to show the best way to compute the discriminant function pertaining to polynomial kernels. To justify this point, let us now look into the discriminant function for POLY2 kernel. Denote the $(M+1)$-dimensional vector

$$\tilde{\mathbf{x}} \equiv \begin{bmatrix} \mathbf{x}\sigma^{-1} \\ 1 \end{bmatrix}.$$

The discriminant function for POLY2 kernels can be derived as

$$f(\mathbf{x}) = \sum_{n=1}^{N} a_n K(\mathbf{x}, \mathbf{x}_n) + b \tag{13.8}$$

$$= \sum_{n=1}^{N} a_n \left(1 + \frac{\mathbf{x}\cdot\mathbf{x}_n}{\sigma^2}\right)^2 + b \tag{13.9}$$

$$= \sum_{n=1}^{N} a_n \left(\tilde{\mathbf{x}}^{\mathrm{T}}\tilde{\mathbf{x}}_n\right)^2 + b \tag{13.10}$$

$$= \tilde{\mathbf{x}}^{\mathrm{T}} \left(\sum_{n=1}^{N} a_n \tilde{\mathbf{x}}_n \tilde{\mathbf{x}}_N^{\mathrm{T}}\right) \tilde{\mathbf{x}} + b. \tag{13.11}$$

This leads to the representation

$$f(\mathbf{x}) = \tilde{\mathbf{x}}^{\mathrm{T}}\tilde{\mathbf{W}}\tilde{\mathbf{x}} + b, \tag{13.12}$$

where $\tilde{\mathbf{W}}$ is defined as an $(M+1) \times (M+1)$ symmetric weight matrix:

$$\tilde{\mathbf{W}} \equiv \sum_{n=1}^{N} a_n \tilde{\mathbf{x}}_n \tilde{\mathbf{x}}_N^{\mathrm{T}}.$$

This is illustrated in Figure 13.7(a).

Denote $\tilde{x}_n^{(i)}, i = 1, \ldots, M+1$ as the variables in the expanded vector $\tilde{\mathbf{x}} \equiv \left[\sigma^{-1}\mathbf{x}^{\mathrm{T}}\ 1\right]^{\mathrm{T}}$. The (i,j)th element of the *decision matrix* $\tilde{\mathbf{W}}$ can be derived (off-line) as

$$\tilde{w}_{ij} \equiv \sum_{n=1}^{N} a_n \tilde{x}_n^{(i)} \tilde{x}_n^{(j)}.$$

The online classification complexity amounts to $(1+M)^2$ operations, which accounts for the majority of the operations. Furthermore, by exploiting the symmetry of $\tilde{\mathbf{W}}$, the number of operations can be further reduced approximately to $J^{(2)} = (M+1)(M+2)/2$. This represents a 50% saving from the direct method based on the two-layer intrinsic representation.

Example 13.2 (Power saving by second-order polynomial kernel) *Various kernel solutions have been applied to cardiac or neurological monitoring systems [150]. In particular, Gaussian and second-order polynomial kernels are compared. The kernel–power tradeoff analysis shows that the second-order polynomial kernel could result in a*

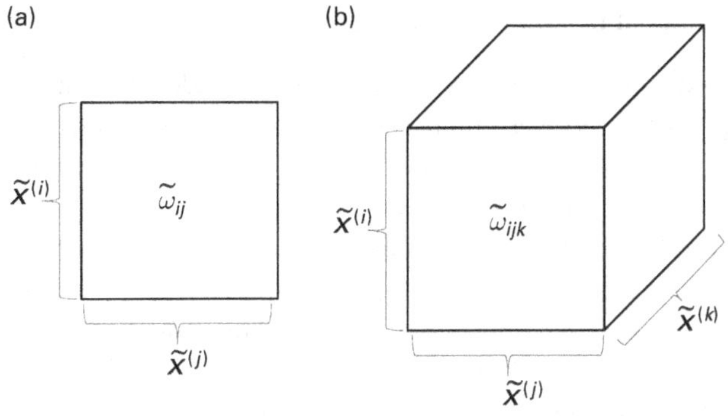

Fig. 13.7. Tensor representations for discriminant functions pertaining to polynomial kernels. (a) A two-dimensional "decision matrix" used in the discriminant function associated with a second-order polynomial kernel. (b) A three-dimensional "decision tensor," the discriminant function associated with a third-order polynomial kernel.

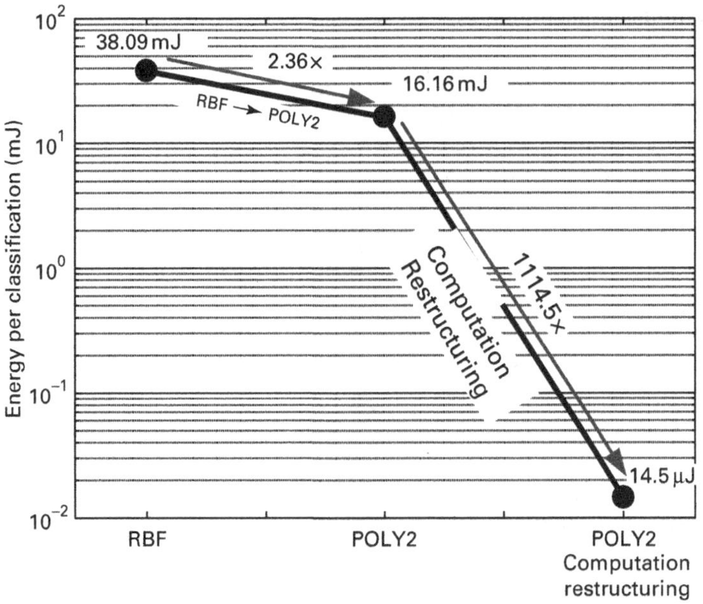

Fig. 13.8. Power savings for arrhythmia detection. A comparison between RBF and second-order polynomial kernels. The computational complexity based on intrinsic space is 1000-fold lower than that based on empirical space. (Adapted from [149].)

drastic saving in classification power requirements. The level of savings is displayed in Figure 13.8, where several order of magnitude of savings may be achieved by adopting the computational procedure via the intrinsic representation as opposed to the empirical representation. More importantly, it indirectly verifies that Eq. (13.14) provides a good approximation of the power estimate.

13.4.3 Tensor representation of discriminant functions

Using a second-order polynomial kernel provides an inadequate amount of design freedom, causing unnecessary performance degradation. Since accuracy is usually the primary concern, it is vital to have high flexibility (as measured by the degree of design freedom) so as to achieve a high discrimination capability.

Note that Eq. (13.12) is a special formulation tailored to second-order polynomial kernels. Via a tensor representation, see Figure 13.7(b), it may be naturally extended to higher-order polynomial functions. As a result, a similar saving is possible also for higher-order polynomial functions. In order to provide a simpler illustration, we shall only derive the tensor representation for POLY3 kernels and leave the general higher-order analysis as an exercise.

Figure 13.7 highlights the similarity/difference between the tensor representations of POLY2 and POLY3 kernels.

Derivation of the POLY3 kernel-based discriminant function

The discriminant function of POLY3 kernels can be written as

$$
\begin{aligned}
f(\mathbf{x}) &= \sum_{n=1}^{N} a_n K(\mathbf{x}_n, \mathbf{x}) + b \\
&= \sum_{n=1}^{N} a_n \left(\tilde{\mathbf{x}}_N^{\mathrm{T}}\tilde{\mathbf{x}}\right)^3 + b \\
&= \sum_{i=1}^{M+1}\sum_{j=1}^{M+1}\sum_{k=1}^{M+1} \tilde{w}_{ijk}\tilde{x}^{(i)}\tilde{x}^{(j)}\tilde{x}^{(k)} + b,
\end{aligned}
$$

where

$$
\tilde{w}_{ijk} \equiv \sum_{n=1}^{N} a_n \tilde{x}_n^{(i)}\tilde{x}_n^{(j)}\tilde{x}_n^{(k)}.
$$

Consecutive tensor operations

For the best possible computational efficiency, the order of computations can better be rearranged as follows:

$$
f(\mathbf{x}) = \sum_{i=1}^{M+1} \tilde{x}^{(i)} \left[\sum_{j=1}^{M+1} \tilde{x}^{(j)} \left(\sum_{k=1}^{M+1} \tilde{w}_{ijk}\tilde{x}^{(k)}\right)\right] + b.
$$

By exploiting the (three-way) symmetry of the tensor represented by $\tilde{w}_{ijk}$, we have

$$
f(\mathbf{x}) = \sum_{i=1}^{M+1} \tilde{x}^{(i)} \left[\sum_{j=1}^{i} \tilde{x}^{(j)} \left(\sum_{k=1}^{j} u_{ijk}\tilde{x}^{(k)}\right)\right] + b,
$$

where $u_{ijk} = \gamma_{ijk}\tilde{w}_{ijk}$ and $\{\gamma_{ijk}\}$ denote the multinomial coefficients. Note that the u_{ijk}s correspond exactly to the coefficients of the intrinsic decision vector $\mathbf{u}$.

Therefore, the classification complexity amounts to

$$J' = J^{(3)} + J^{(2)} + J^{(1)} + 1.$$

Classification complexity for POLY_p kernels

The derivation for the POLY3 kernel case may be naturally extended to the POLY_p kernels. By induction, the classification complexity for a POLY_p kernel is

$$J' = \sum_{q=1}^{p} J^{(q)} + 1 = \sum_{q=1}^{p} \begin{pmatrix} M+q \\ q \end{pmatrix} + 1 = \begin{pmatrix} M+p+1 \\ p \end{pmatrix}.$$

(See Problem 13.2.) When the training size N is huge, its complexity amounts to $J' \approx J$. It should be apparent that this is far more cost-effective than other alternative kernel-based computational methods in the prediction phase.

For example, let us assume $M = 21$. Then we have

- for POLY2 (or TRBF2) kernels, $J' = 1 + J^{(1)} + J^{(2)} = 1 + 22 + 253 = 276$;
- for POLY3 (or TRBF3) kernels, $J' = 1 + J^{(1)} + J^{(2)} + J^{(3)} = 1 + 22 + 253 + 2024 = 2300$; and
- for POLY4 (or TRBF4) kernels, $J' = 1 + J^{(1)} + J^{(2)} + J^{(3)} + J^{(4)} = 1 + 22 + 253 + 2024 + 12{,}650 = 14{,}950$.

In addition to the reduced complexity, by effectively employing the structural regularity which is inherently embedded in tensor processing, systolic parallel processing architectures may be designed to achieve extra power savings [133, 134].

Tensor representation of TRBF-based discriminant functions

For example, the discriminant function of TRBF3 kernels can be written as

$$\begin{aligned} f(\mathbf{x}) &= \sum_{n=1}^{N} a_n K(\mathbf{x}_n, \mathbf{x}) + b \\ &= \sum_{n=1}^{N} a_n \exp\left\{-\frac{\|\mathbf{x}_n\|^2}{2\sigma^2}\right\} \left[1 + \frac{\mathbf{x}_n \cdot \mathbf{x}}{\sigma^2} + \frac{1}{2}\left(\frac{\mathbf{x}_n \cdot \mathbf{x}}{\sigma^2}\right)^2 + \frac{1}{6}\left(\frac{\mathbf{x}_n \cdot \mathbf{x}}{}\sigma^2\right)^3\right] \\ &\quad \times \exp\left\{-\frac{\|\mathbf{x}\|^2}{2\sigma^2}\right\} + b \\ &= \sum_{i=1}^{M+1} \sum_{j=1}^{M+1} \sum_{k=1}^{M+1} \tilde{w}_{ijk} \tilde{x}^{(i)} \tilde{x}^{(j)} \tilde{x}^{(k)} \exp\left\{-\frac{\|\mathbf{x}\|^2}{2\sigma^2}\right\} + b, \end{aligned} \tag{13.13}$$

where

$$\tilde{w}_{ijk} \equiv \sum_{n=1}^{N} a_n \tilde{x}_n^{(i)} \tilde{x}_n^{(j)} \tilde{x}_n^{(k)} \exp\left\{-\frac{\|\mathbf{x}_n\|^2}{2\sigma^2}\right\}.$$

Again the u_{ijk}s are directly obtainable as the coefficients of the intrinsic decision vector $\mathbf{u}$.

13.4.4 Complexity comparison of RBF and TRBF classifiers

Let us explore the savings in classification complexity due to the different choices of (RBF versus TRBF) kernel.

- In the case of KRR classifiers, all the N training vectors directly participate in the formation of discriminant function. The classification complexity will be determined either by the empirical degree (with the complexity being NM) or the intrinsic degree (with the complexity J').
  - For RBF kernels, $J \to \infty$, the classification complexity will be NM.
  - For polynomial or TRBF kernels, we can always choose the lower of NM and J'. It follows that

$$\text{classification complexity} = \min\left(NM, J'\right).$$

Therefore, we can potentially reduce the classification complexity by a factor of $J'/(NM)$.

- In the case of SVMs, the complexity has a slight difference.
  - For RBF kernels, $J \to \infty$, the classification complexity will be SM, where S denotes the number of support vectors.
  - For polynomial or TRBF kernels, we can always choose the lower of SM and J'. It follows that

$$\text{classification complexity} = \min\left(SM, J'\right).$$

Therefore, we can potentially reduce the classification complexity by a factor of

$$\frac{J'}{SM}. \tag{13.14}$$

13.4.5 Case study: ECG arrhythmia detection

Supposing that the ECG dataset of all patients (more than 40 of them in Example 13.1) is used to train the RBF-SVM classifier, a large number of support vectors ($S = 15{,}000$) will be identified. Recall that, in this case, the RBF classifier (costing 49.52 mW) will fail to meet the low-power green-computing condition. The classification power must be reduced by at least one order of magnitude to meet the low-power condition. According to Eq. (13.14), this gap can be bridged by opting for polynomial or TRBF kernels with a respectable intrinsic degree. Two acceptable kernels are as follows.

- For TRBF3, the saving ratio is $J'/(MS) \approx J^{(3)}/(MS) = 2024/(21 \times 15{,}000) \approx 1/155$, leading to a classification power requirement of $50\,\text{mW}/155 = 0.32$ mW. The total power requirement would become $1.56\,\text{mW} + 0.32\,\text{mW} = 1.88$ mW.
- For TRBF4, the saving ratio is $J'/(MS) \approx J^{(4)}/(MS) = 12{,}650/(21 \times 15{,}000) \approx 0.04$, leading to a classification power requirement of $.04 \times 50\,\text{mW} = 2$ mW. The total power requirement would become $1.56\,\text{mW} + 2\,\text{mW} = 3.56$ mW.

Therefore, TRBF3 and TRBF4 can operate within 5 mW, which is the previously allocated power budget. In Section 13.6, we will further show that TRBF3 or TRBF4 PPDAs can deliver very respectable accuracies (98.66% and 98.91%, respectively) – very close to that of RBF-SVM (99%).

13.5 Learning complexities: empirical and intrinsic degrees

The learning complexity depends on the feature size M, the empirical degree N, and (if applicable) the intrinsic degree J. It also depends closely on the learning methods adopted. Let us show two contrasting types of kernels.

- For Gaussian kernels, the learning has to be via the empirical space. For the two major kernel-based methods (SVM and KRR), it is known that KRR's complexity is $O(N^3)$, while SVM's is only $O(N^2)$. Thus SVM holds a clear advantage over KRR for large N.
- For TRBF kernels, or other finite-degree kernels, for the KRR learning one may choose either the empirical or the intrinsic space. When the empirical degree N is huge, the scatter-matrix-based KRR algorithm has a learning complexity that grows only linearly with N, i.e. $O(N)$. This means that the KRR learning is more efficient than SVM when N is enormous.

13.5.1 Learning complexities for KRR and SVM

For KRR and SVM classifiers, the learning complexities grow with N at very different rates.

- **Learning complexity of KRR.** The KRR discriminant function is $f(\mathbf{x}) = \mathbf{a}^{\mathrm{T}}\vec{\mathbf{k}}(\mathbf{x}) + b$, with

$$\mathbf{a} = [\mathbf{K} + \rho\mathbf{I}]^{-1}[\mathbf{y} - b\mathbf{e}],$$

  where $\mathbf{y} \equiv \left[y_1 \ \ldots \ y_N\right]^{\mathrm{T}}$, $\mathbf{e} \equiv [1 \ \ldots \ 1]^{\mathrm{T}}$, and ρ denotes the perturbation variance. The direct KRR solution involves the inversion of the $N \times N$ matrix $(\mathbf{K} + \rho\mathbf{I})$ and therefore incurs a high complexity, of $O(N^3)$.
- **Learning complexity of SVM.** The SVM learning involves a quadratic programming problem. Invoking the SMO scheme, the SVM learning cost reportedly grows quadratically w.r.t. N, at a rate of N^2 [205]. In fact, the SVM learning complexity is at least $O(N^2M)$.[4]

If N is extremely large, then neither KRR's $O(N^3)$ nor SVM's $O(N^2)$ will be affordable. Fortunately, when the intrinsic degree is of a reasonable finite size, it is possible to come up with a numerically more efficient method, with complexity growing only linearly with N.

[4] Obviously, the formulation of the kernel matrix per se will be rather costly. Note that, without considering the symmetry, there are N^2 elements in the kernel matrix, each requiring $O(M)$ operations.

13.5.2 A scatter-matrix-based KRR algorithm

Note that, in the intrinsic space, the scatter matrix is $\mathbf{S} = \mathbf{\Phi}\mathbf{\Phi}^{\mathrm{T}}$ and, with reference to Eq. (9.16), the decision vector $\mathbf{u}$ may be derived from the scatter matrix as

$$\mathbf{u} = [\mathbf{S} + \rho\mathbf{I}]^{-1}\ \mathbf{\Phi}[\mathbf{y} - b\mathbf{e}]. \tag{13.15}$$

Then the discriminant function can be obtained as

$$f(\mathbf{x}) = \mathbf{u}^{\mathrm{T}}\vec{\boldsymbol{\phi}}(\mathbf{x}) + b. \tag{13.16}$$

Computationally, this KRR algorithm incurs three main costs.

(i) The computation of the $J \times J$ scatter matrix $\mathbf{S}$ requires J^2N operations.
(ii) The inversion of the $J \times J$ matrix $\mathbf{S} + \rho\mathbf{I}$ requires roughly J^3 operations.[5]
(iii) The matrix–vector multiplication will require NJ operations, which can be ignored.

13.5.3 KRR learning complexity: RBF versus TRBF kernels

The KRR learning complexity depends very much on the type of kernels adopted.

- For RBF kernels, $J \to \infty$, the solution has to be derived via the kernel matrix, leading to a complexity of N^3.
- For polynomial or TRBF kernels, the solution may be derived via either the kernel matrix or the scatter matrix. Thus the learning complexity is

  $$\min\left(N^3, J^3 + J^2N\right).$$

  When $N \gg J$, the cost of J^3 operations is negligible when compared with that of J^2N operations. So the complexity will be dictated by J^2N.

Therefore, on comparing the best learning strategies applicable to RBF versus TRBF kernels, we find that the latter has a potential saving by a factor of $N^3/(J^2N) = N^2/J^2$, via an effective use of the intrinsic space.

It should by now be obvious that the scatter-matrix-based KRR can result in substantial computational savings relative to KRR and SVM. As an example, for $N = 80{,}000$, RBF-KRR may take days and SVM more than 10 min, whereas TRBF3-KRR takes only 1 min, permitting 60 iterations of TRBF3 PPDA within one hour.

13.5.4 A learning and classification algorithms for big data size N

The scatter-matrix-based KRR learning and classification algorithm will be summarized below:

[5] For simplicity, the exact scaling factor is omitted here.

ALGORITHM 13.1 (Scatter-matrix-based KRR learning and classification algorithm) *Given a kernel function with a finite intrinsic degree, the intrinsic feature vector associated with a kernel function can be written as*

$$\vec{\phi}(\mathbf{x}) = \begin{bmatrix} \phi^{(1)}(\mathbf{x}) \\ \phi^{(2)}(\mathbf{x}) \\ \vdots \\ \phi^{(J)}(\mathbf{x}) \end{bmatrix}.$$

Recall also that the intrinsic data matrix $\mathbf{\Phi}$ *is defined as*

$$\mathbf{\Phi} = \begin{bmatrix} \vec{\phi}(\mathbf{x}_1) & \vec{\phi}(\mathbf{x}_2) & \ldots & \vec{\phi}(\mathbf{x}_N) \end{bmatrix}.$$

The scatter-matrix-based KRR algorithm contains the following steps:

(i) We have

$$\mathbf{S} = \mathbf{\Phi}\mathbf{\Phi}^{\mathrm{T}}.$$

The computation of the $J \times J$ *scatter matrix* $\mathbf{S}$ *requires* J^2N *operations.*

(ii) Using Eq. (9.18), the KRR solution may be derived from the following matrix system:

$$\begin{bmatrix} \mathbf{S}+\rho\mathbf{I} & \mathbf{\Phi}\mathbf{e} \\ \mathbf{e}^{\mathrm{T}}\mathbf{\Phi}^{\mathrm{T}} & N \end{bmatrix} \begin{bmatrix} \mathbf{u} \\ b \end{bmatrix} = \begin{bmatrix} \mathbf{\Phi}\mathbf{y} \\ \mathbf{e}^{\mathrm{T}}\mathbf{y} \end{bmatrix}. \tag{13.17}$$

The inversion of the $(J+1)\times(J+1)$ *matrix requires roughly* J^3 *operations. (For simplicity, the exact scaling factor is omitted here.)*

After $\mathbf{u}$ *has been learned, the decision boundary is characterized by* $f(\mathbf{x}) = 0$*, where* $f(\mathbf{x})$ *is the discriminant function*

$$f(\mathbf{x}) = \mathbf{u}^{\mathrm{T}}\vec{\phi}(\mathbf{x}) + b. \tag{13.18}$$

□

Learning complexity

The total learning complexity amounts to J^2N operations, which grows linearly with the empirical degree N [144, 302b].

Classification complexity

In the intrinsic-space representation, the discriminant function can be obtained as $f(\mathbf{x}) = \mathbf{u}^{\mathrm{T}}\vec{\phi}(\mathbf{x}) + b$, whose direct computation leads to a complexity that is upper bounded by $pJ^{(p)}$. As elaborated on below, classification via consecutive tensor operations may result in a lower complexity.

ALGORITHM 13.2 (Fast KRR classification algorithm) *For the best possible computational efficiency, it is critical that we fully exploit the symmetry inherently embedded in the tensor coefficients* $\tilde{w}_{ijk}$*. Consequently, the role of* $\tilde{w}_{ijk}$ *would be better substituted by* u_{ijk}*. We shall describe two important application scenarios.*

(i) *Denote $x^{(M+1)} = 1$, for POLY_p kernels, each basis function has an appearance as follows:*

$$\left(x^{(1)}\right)^{d_1} \ldots \left(x^{(M)}\right)^{d_M} \left(x^{(M+1)}\right)^{d_{M+1}}, \quad \text{with} \sum_{m=1}^{M+1} d_m = p. \tag{13.19}$$

Now we can obtain the u_{ijk}s directly as the coefficients of the intrinsic decision vector **u**, *and it follows that the discriminant function is*

$$f(\mathbf{x}) = \sum_{i_1=1}^{M+1} x^{(i_1)} \left[\sum_{i_2=1}^{i_1} x^{(i_2)} \ldots \left(\sum_{i_p=1}^{i_{p-1}} u_{i_1 i_2 \cdots i_p} x^{(i_p)} \right) \right] + b.$$

(ii) *For TRBF_p without normalization,*

$$\exp\left\{-\frac{\|\mathbf{x}\|^2}{2\sigma^2}\right\} \left(x^{(1)}\right)^{d_1} \ldots \left(x^{(M)}\right)^{d_M} \left(x^{(M+1)}\right)^{d_{M+1}},$$

$$\text{with} \sum_{m=1}^{M+1} d_m = p.$$

Using Eq. (13.13), the discriminant function of TRBF3 kernels is

$$f(\mathbf{x}) = \exp\left\{-\frac{\|\mathbf{x}\|^2}{2\sigma^2}\right\} \sum_{i_1=1}^{M+1} x^{(i_1)} \left[\sum_{i_2=1}^{i_1} x^{(i_2)} \ldots \left(\sum_{i_p=1}^{i_{p-1}} u_{i_1 i_2 \cdots i_p} x^{(i_p)} \right) \right] + b,$$

where the u_{ijk}s are again directly computable as the coefficients of the intrinsic decision vector **u**. □

Classification complexity

The classification complexity for a POLY_p or TRBF_p kernel is

$$J' = \sum_{q=1}^{p} J^{(q)} + 1 = \sum_{q=1}^{p} \binom{M+q}{q} + 1 = \binom{M+p+1}{p}.$$

With a complexity $J' \approx J$, it is the most cost-effective when the training size N is large.

13.5.5 Case study: ECG arrhythmia detection

To verify the learning efficiency of the scatter-matrix-based KRR, a simulation study on the MIT/BIH ECG dataset for arrhythmia detection was conducted [203]. The accuracies and computer cycles recorded in the simulation provide important and empirical support for our theoretical comparative analysis.

If a TRBF3 kernel is adopted, then the intrinsic degree is $J = (22 \times 23 \times 24)/6 \approx 2000$. The computer run-time for SVM, KRR, and scatter-matrix-based KRR, for various values of N, is depicted in Figure 13.9. The simulation results convincingly demonstrate that scatter-matrix-based KRR has an overwhelming speed advantage over

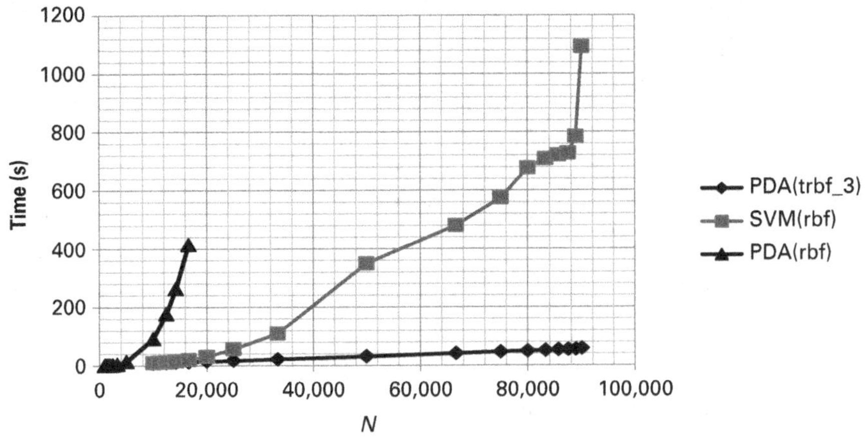

Fig. 13.9. The computer cycles recorded with the MATLAB classification codes on an Intel-Core-I5-2410M microprocessor (2.3 GHz), when training the ECG dataset. This shows that kernel-matrix-based KRR (with RBF kernel) $O(N^3)$ and SVM requires $O(N^2)$ operations, while the curve of the scatter-matrix-based KRR (with TRBF3 kernel) grows linearly with N, or, more exactly, J^2N. (Recall that KRR is equivalent to PDA.)

SVM, when the training size reaches $N = 25{,}000$ or beyond. Let us take a closer look at two examples.

- For a modest empirical degree, say $N = 25{,}000$, the saving by the scatter-matrix-based KRR is already very significant. As empirical evidence, the computer run-times for KRR, SVM, and scatter-matrix-based KRR (with TRBF3 kernel) are respectively 1 h, 1 min, and 20 s.
- For an extra-huge empirical degree, say $N = 80{,}000 = 8 \times 10^4$, we have the following observations.
  - *SVM versus scatter-matrix-based KRR.* We note that the training time for TRBF3-SVM (not shown) is almost the same as that for RBF-SVM. According to the computer run-times depicted in Figure 13.9, the scatter-matrix-based KRR is much faster than SVM and the speed-up is around 15-fold.
  - *KRR versus scatter-matrix-based KRR.* We have to rely on the theoretical formula to show the comparative analysis between KRR and scatter-matrix-based KRR. While the conventional KRR's complexity is $N^3 = 5.12 \times 10^{14}$, the complexity of the scatter-matrix-based KRR is $\max\{J^3, NJ^2\} = \max\{2000^3, 8 \times 10^4 \times 2000^2\} = 3.2 \times 10^{11}$. This represents a major saving (more than 1000-fold) in computational time.

This shows that when N is huge, say $N \geq 80{,}000$, the learning complexity becomes very costly both for direct KRR and for SVM. In contrast, the scatter-matrix based KRR has a complexity with a growth rate proportional to N. It allows a super-saving when N becomes enormously large. It effectively overcomes the curse of empirical degree. Moreover, it offers an economic and affordable type of software that is applicable to iterative algorithms such as PPDA. This is the subject of discussion in Section 13.6.2.2.

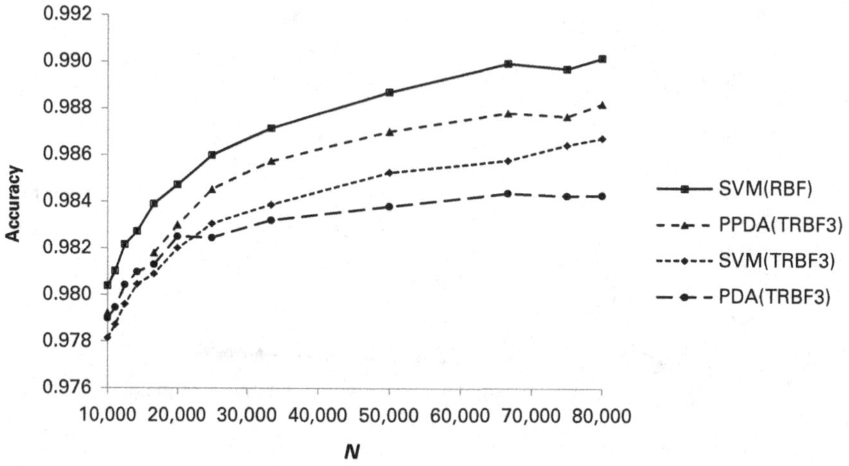

Fig. 13.10. Experimental results of arrhythmia detection. Accuracies for different classifiers but with the RBF and TRBF3 kernels,. The following parameters were adopted: $\sigma = 2.5$ for RBF and TRBF3 kernels, $C = 10$ for SVM, and $\rho = 0.1$ for KRR and PPDA.

13.6 The tradeoff between complexity and prediction performance

Our study will be focused on ECG data analysis for arrhythmia detection, with the MIT/BIH ECG dataset [203]. The prediction accuracies and running times reported here were obtained by executing MATLAB classification codes on an Intel-Core-I5-2410M microprocessor (2.3 GHz). The power estimates reported are for simulations conducted on a real processor model, MSPsim, a cycle-accurate MSP430 instruction-set simulator [183].

- Section 13.6.1 studies the prediction accuracies with respect to various empirical degrees N, kernel functions, and classifiers.
- Section 13.6.2 studies learning and classification complexities and, more importantly, their tradeoff with respect to the prediction accuracies.

13.6.1 Comparison of prediction accuracies

In order to perform a comprehensive comparison study, various combinations of data size N, kernel types, and classifier types have been tested. The results on their prediction accuracies are reported below.

13.6.1.1 Performances w.r.t. empirical degree N

As confirmed by Figures 13.6, 13.10, and 13.11, the accuracies monotonically increase with data size N, for all the kernel/classifier combinations.

13.6.1.2 Performances of SVM classifier w.r.t. different kernels

After a substantial effort in fine-tuning for the optimal parameters, the following sets of parameters were finally chosen for the simulation study.

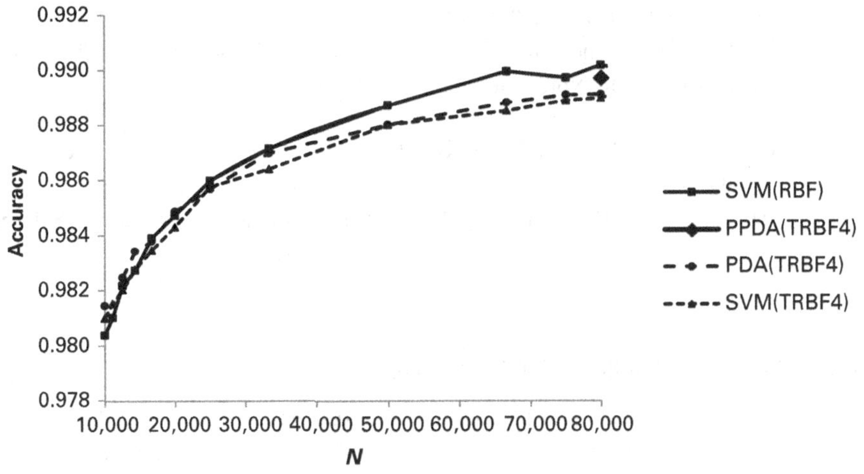

Fig. 13.11. Experimental results of arrhythmia detection. Accuracies for different classifiers but with the RBF and TRBF4 kernels,. The following parameters were adopted $\sigma = 2.5$ for RBF and TRBF3 kernels, $C = 10$ for SVM, and $\rho = 0.1$ for KRR and PPDA.

- In terms of *kernel parameters*, we use $\sigma = 2.5$ for RBF and TRBF3 kernels.
- In terms of *classifier parameters*, $C = 10$ for SVM and $\rho = 0.1$ for KRR and PPDA.

As shown in Figure 13.6, RBF-SVM delivers the very best performance. There is no surprise that, with TRBF4 being a better approximation of RBF than TRBF3, TRBF4-SVM and TRBF4-KRR outperform TRBF3-SVM and TRBF3-KRR, respectively.

Throughout the experiments, the highest-accuracy benchmark 99% is set by RBF-SVM with $N = 80{,}000$. It is worth noting that, for $N = 80{,}000$, TRBF3-SVM and TRBF4-SVM also deliver very respectable accuracies, of 98.66% and 98.91%, respectively. From the perspective of green computing, it is worth noting that TRBF3-SVM and TRBF4-SVM have an advantage over RBF-SVM in terms of power saving. More precisely, the required classification powers for TRBF3-SVM, TRBF4-SVM, and RBF-SVM are estimated to be 0.46, 2.5, and 50 mW, respectively. The power savings over RBF-SVM are 20-fold and 130-fold for TRBF3-SVM and TRBF4-SVM, respectively.

13.6.1.3 Accuracies of various classifiers using TRBF kernels

Performance of classifiers using TRBF3 kernels

For the TRBF3 kernel, the three performance curves (dashed), from top down, shown in Figure 13.10 are respectively for PPDA(TRBF3), SVM(TRBF3), and PDA(TRBF3). SVM generally outperforms KRR. However, after pruning a good number of anti-support training vectors, PPDA holds a slight performance advantage over SVM. For $N = 80{,}000$, the accuracies for the different classifiers are rank ordered (from best to worst) as follows:

(i) the accuracy of KRR (TRBF3) is the lowest at 98.33%;
(ii) the accuracy of SVM (TRBF3) is 98.66%; and
(iii) the accuracy of PPDA (TRBF3) is the lowest, 98.82%.

Performance of classifiers using TRBF4 kernels

The two performance curves shown in Figure 13.11 are respectively for TRBF4-SVM and TRBF4-KRR. Note that, when $N = 80{,}000$,

(i) TRBF4-SVM and TRBF4-KRR have almost the same performance around 98.91%; and
(ii) TRBF4-PPDA reaches 98.97%, which is statistically the same as RBF-SVM's 99% accuracy.

13.6.2 Prediction–complexity tradeoff analysis

Various combinations of classifiers and kernels are tested and their prediction accuracies, training times, and power budgets are evaluated. The simulation results are summarized below.

13.6.2.1 RBF-SVM versus RBF-KRR: complexity and performance

It is curious to compare RBF-SVM and RBF-KRR and help assess the performance–complexity tradeoff. Unfortunately, learning of RBF-KRR for $N \geq 80{,}000$ is computationally infeasible. As a consolation, various TRBF-KRRs were tested and the results are used to serve as an approximate comparison. According to the simulation, the accuracy of TRBF-KRR is already as high as 98.8%. The 0.2% gap may be attributed to truncation approximation incurred by TRBF. It may also be caused by the fact that SVM uses a more selective subset of (supporting) training vectors. To explore this possibility, we decided to train a TRBF4-PPDA, with almost one day's computing time, and obtained again a 99% accuracy – more exactly 98.97% – shown as the big diamond "♦" on the rightmost side of Figure 13.7. From the perspective of green computing, TRBF4-PPDA's classification power is estimated to be 2 mW which is a much more agreeable than RBF-SVM's 50 mW.

13.6.2.2 PPDA versus SVM: complexity and performance

The fast learning speed offered by the scatter-matrix-based KRR (see Algorithm 13.1) makes it feasible to consider the option of using PPDA, where tens of learning iterations need to be executed in order to trim down the training vectors and, ultimately, improve the prediction performance. This is evidenced by Figure 9.5, where it is shown that the prediction accuracy monotonically improves with increasing iteration number, until it goes beyond 60 iterations.

Our discussion below focuses on how the learning complexities of TRBF-SVM and TRBF-PPDA compare with each other.

- *SVM.* SVM learning involves an iterative algorithm. Therefore, the actual computing time of SMO-based SVM depends on its initial condition and convergence criterion. As a result, its total complexity must be pre-fixed with a constant c to reflect the number of iterations involved, i.e. the total complexity of SMO-based SVM is cN^2. It can be roughly estimated that $c \approx 1000$ in our simulation study.[6]

- *PPDA.* On the other hand, the scatter-matrix-based KRR learning involves a finite algorithm, so its complexity can be exactly estimated to be J^2N. (Here we have ignored the potential saving by exploiting the symmetry property of the scatter matrix $S = \mathbf{\Phi}\mathbf{\Phi}^{\mathrm{T}}$.)

  Thus the complexity pertaining to PPDA should be qJ^2N. For example, if a *TRBF*3 kernel is adopted, we have the following comparison:
  - *Prediction performance.* With $q = 60$ iterations, the number of surviving vectors is around $S' = 7000$, almost half of the number of support vectors for TRBF3-SVM ($S \approx 15,000$). In terms of error rate, TRBF3-PPDA's 1.18% has a slight edge over TRBF3-SVM's 1.33%.
  - *Learning complexity.* If $q = 60$, then TRBF3-PPDA will more than triple the time used by SMO-based TRBF3-SVM.
  - *Classification complexity.* With a somewhat longer learning time, take over TRBF3-PPDA (98.82%) and TRBF4-PPDA (98.97%) can outperform TRBF3-SVM (98.66%) and TRBF4-SVM (98.91%), respectively. From the perspective of green computing, we note that TRBF3-PPDA requires the same classification power as TRBF3-SVM. Likewise, TRBF4-PPDA requires the same classification power as TRBF4-SVM.

In summary, this section focuses on finding a finite-degree kernel to best balance the tradeoff among all of the three major system considerations:

- acceptable *classification complexity*;
- acceptable *learning complexity*; and
- acceptable *prediction performance*.

In conclusion, under low-power processing requirement, the role of the traditionally prevailing and popular RBF may better be substituted by TRBFs, which could result in lower powers and yet deliver highly competitive prediction accuracies.

13.7 Time-adaptive updating algorithms for KRR learning models

When N is extremely large, the usefulness of learning models hinges upon their algorithmic effectiveness. In the previous chapter, it was shown that, when one is training a KRR model, in a batch learning mode, its complexity grows linearly with N, assuming that the intrinsic degree is of a reasonable finite size. A totally different category of machine learning applications concerns the adaptation of a learning model to problems involving time-series analysis, especially for those in a changing environment [23, 188, 229, 299].

[6] Note that, in Figure 13.9, SMO-based SVM takes a computational time roughly 20 times that of the scatter-matrix-based KRR, when $N = 80{,}000$ and $J = 2000$, implying that $c(80000)^2 \approx 20(2000)^2 80{,}000$. Thus the estimation $c \approx 1000$.

This has been one of the major research topics in the fields of adaptive control, filtering, and signal processing [83, 94, 228, 248, 298].

Instead of the batch learning model, it is vital to develop time-adaptive learning algorithms so as to reduce the computational complexity. This section addresses this problem from two perspectives, one in intrinsic space and the other in empirical space.

13.7.1 Time-adaptive recursive KRR algorithms

This section will tackle the algorithmic efficiency using a deterministic formulation. In this case, it will be computationally prohibitive to learn the estimator from scratch, upon the arrival of every new item of data. (It would take $O(J^3)$ operations to invert the $J \times J$ matrix in Eq. (13.15) per new sample.) Therefore, it becomes imperative to develop a time-adaptive algorithm to effectively update the estimator for a new sample, or a small subset of new samples. This section will demonstrate that recursive algorithms tailor-designed for time-adaptive KRR learning models will require only $O(J^2)$ operations per sample, instead of $O(J^3)$.

For notational simplicity, we shall assume that the threshold b is absorbed by a constant basis function, which is adopted as one of the basis functions.[7] Consequently, in our subsequent analysis, the threshold parameter b will no longer be used.

For notational convenience, we shall denote the input at the time t as

$$\overrightarrow{\phi}(\mathbf{x}_t) = \overrightarrow{\phi}_t.$$

Let us assume that its true response y_t will be made available with some waiting period after $\overrightarrow{\phi}_t$ is known but before $\overrightarrow{\phi}_{t+1}$ arrives.

Given the input/output observations from time $=$ 1 through time $= t$, we can construct the induced data matrix

$$\mathbf{\Phi}_t = [\overrightarrow{\phi}_1, \overrightarrow{\phi}_2, \ldots, \overrightarrow{\phi}_t]$$

and teacher vector

$$\overrightarrow{\mathbf{y}}_t = [y_1, y_2, \ldots, y_t]^{\mathrm{T}}.$$

According to the KRR formulation in Eq. (7.16), given all the data from $n = 1$ to $n = t$, the objective is to find a solution for the following KRR cost function:

$$\min_{\hat{\mathbf{u}}} E_{\mathrm{KRR}} = ||\mathbf{\Phi}_t^{\mathrm{T}}\hat{\mathbf{u}} - \overrightarrow{\mathbf{y}}_t||^2 + \rho_0\|\mathbf{u}\|^2. \tag{13.20}$$

This leads to the following optimal KRR regressor at time $t = n$:

$$\hat{\mathbf{u}}_t = P_t^{-1}\mathbf{\Phi}_t\overrightarrow{\mathbf{y}}_t = \mathbf{\Sigma}_t\mathbf{\Phi}_t\overrightarrow{\mathbf{y}}_t, \tag{13.21}$$

where we denote

$$P_t \equiv \mathbf{\Phi}_t\mathbf{\Phi}_t^{\mathrm{T}} + \rho_0\mathbf{I} = \sum_{t=1}^{n} \overrightarrow{\phi}_t^{\mathrm{T}}\overrightarrow{\phi}_t + \rho_0\mathbf{I},\ t = 1, 2, \ldots.$$

[7] Even if the constant basis function is not naturally induced by the kernel function, it can always be artificially added to the original set of intrinsic basis functions.

13.7.2 The intrinsic-space recursive KRR algorithm

Denote also that

$$\mathbf{\Sigma}_t \equiv [P_t]^{-1},$$

where P_i is known as the "*precision matrix*" in linear estimation [151]. It follows that

$$\mathbf{\Sigma}_{t+1} = [P_t + \vec{\phi}_{t+1}\vec{\phi}_{t+1}^{\mathrm{T}}]^{-1}.$$

Given the observations up to this point, i.e. $\mathbf{\Phi}_t$, $\mathbf{y}_t$, and $\vec{\phi}_{t+1}$, the prediction of the response to a new input, $\mathbf{x}_{t+1}$ at time $t+1$, will be

$$\hat{y}_{t+1} = \hat{\mathbf{u}}_t^{\mathrm{T}}\vec{\phi}_{t+1}. \tag{13.22}$$

Once the true response at time $t+1$, i.e. y_{t+1}, is known, the estimator may be further updated to

$$\begin{aligned}\hat{\mathbf{u}}' = \hat{\mathbf{u}}_{t+1} &= \mathbf{\Sigma}_{t+1}\mathbf{\Phi}'\mathbf{y}' \\ &= \mathbf{\Sigma}_{t+1}\left(\mathbf{\Phi}\mathbf{y} + y_{t+1}\vec{\phi}_{t+1}\right).\end{aligned} \tag{13.23}$$

The zero-innovation property (ZIP)

Intuitively, the updated coefficients should remains the same as before if the newly observed response happens to be exactly identical to the predicted value. Namely, when $y_{t+1} = \hat{y}_{t+1}$, there will be no net update of the estimator:

$$\hat{\mathbf{u}}_t = \hat{\mathbf{u}}'|_{y_{t+1}=\hat{y}_{t+1}},$$

which means that

$$\hat{\mathbf{u}}_t = \mathbf{\Sigma}_{t+1}\left(\mathbf{\Phi}\mathbf{y} + \hat{y}_{n+1}\vec{\phi}_{t+1}\right). \tag{13.24}$$

On subtracting Eq. (13.23) from Eq. (13.24), we know by how much the regressor vector changes for the one-step update, cf. Eq. (13.29),

$$\hat{\mathbf{u}}_{t+1} - \hat{\mathbf{u}}_t = -e_{n+1}\mathbf{\Sigma}_{t+1}\vec{\phi}_{t+1},$$

where e_{t+1} denotes the prediction error at time $t+1$:

$$e_{t+1} \equiv \hat{y}_{t+1} - y_{t+1} = \hat{\mathbf{u}}_t^{\mathrm{T}}\vec{\phi}_{t+1} - y_{t+1}. \tag{13.25}$$

By Woodbury's matrix identity [301],

$$\mathbf{\Sigma}_{t+1} = \mathbf{\Sigma}_t - \gamma_{t+1}\mathbf{\Sigma}_t\vec{\phi}_{t+1}\vec{\phi}_{t+1}^{\mathrm{T}}\mathbf{\Sigma}_t, \quad \gamma_{t+1} \equiv (1 + \vec{\phi}_{t+1}^{\mathrm{T}}\mathbf{\Sigma}_t\vec{\phi}_{t+1})^{-1}. \tag{13.26}$$

In summary, the time-adaptive KRR algorithm is as specified below.

- **Prediction phase.** Assume that $\hat{\mathbf{u}}_t$ is just obtained by the due learning process based on the dataset $\{\mathbf{x}_1, \mathbf{x}_2, \ldots, \mathbf{x}_t\}$. Now a sample $\vec{\phi}_{t+1}$ is newly observed at $t = t+1$, whose correct response y_{t+1} is not known yet. The objective of the prediction phase is to predict the response. Using $\vec{\phi}_{t+1}$ as the input of the regressor, the predicted response can be obtained as

$$\hat{y}_{t+1} = \hat{\mathbf{u}}_t^{\mathrm{T}} \vec{\phi}_{t+1}.$$

- **Estimator updating.** It is assumed that, at a somewhat later stage, the correct response y_{t+1} is made available. Now the training dataset is expanded to $\{\mathbf{x}_1, \mathbf{x}_2, \ldots, \mathbf{x}_t, \mathbf{x}_{t+1}\}$, all with their corresponding teachers. By harnessing the newly available input/ouput pair $\{\mathbf{x}_{t+1}, y_{t+1}\}$, the optimal regressor parameters can be updated as follows.
  (i) First, we update

$$e_{t+1} = \hat{\mathbf{u}}_t^{\mathrm{T}} \vec{\phi}_{t+1} - y_{t+1} \quad \text{and} \quad \gamma_{t+1} \equiv (1 + \vec{\phi}_{t+1}^{\mathrm{T}} \boldsymbol{\Sigma}_t \vec{\phi}_{t+1})^{-1}, \tag{13.27}$$

  and

$$\boldsymbol{\Sigma}_{t+1} = \boldsymbol{\Sigma}_t - \gamma_{t+1} \boldsymbol{\Sigma}_t \vec{\phi}_{t+1} \vec{\phi}_{t+1}^{\mathrm{T}} \boldsymbol{\Sigma}_t. \tag{13.28}$$

  Initially, $\boldsymbol{\Sigma}_0 \equiv \rho_0^{-1} \mathbf{I}$.
  (ii) The optimal estimator can be updated as follows:

$$\hat{\mathbf{u}}_{t+1} = \hat{\mathbf{u}}_t - \boldsymbol{\Sigma}_{t+1} \vec{\phi}_{t+1} e_{t+1}. \tag{13.29}$$

We shall illustrate the recursive procedure by means of a simple numerical example.

Example 13.3 (Recursive KRR procedure) *Consider four training vectors:*

$$\begin{aligned}
&\text{at } t = 1 \colon \mathbf{x}_1 = [1.0 \quad 0.1]^{\mathrm{T}}, && y_1 = +1, \\
&\text{at } t = 2 \colon \mathbf{x}_2 = [0.8 \quad 0.1]^{\mathrm{T}}, && y_2 = +1, \\
&\text{at } t = 3 \colon \mathbf{x}_3 = [-0.8 \quad -0.1]^{\mathrm{T}}, && y_3 = -1, \\
&\text{at } t = 4 \colon \mathbf{x}_4 = [-1.0 \quad -0.1]^{\mathrm{T}}, && y_4 = -1.
\end{aligned}$$

Assume we have initially that $\hat{\mathbf{w}}_0 = [1 \quad 1]^{\mathrm{T}}$ *and also that* $\rho_0 = 0.01$, *so*

$$\boldsymbol{\Sigma}_0 = \rho_0^{-1} \begin{bmatrix} 1 & 0 \\ 0 & 1 \end{bmatrix} = \begin{bmatrix} 100 & 0 \\ 0 & 100 \end{bmatrix}.$$

Training order: $\mathbf{x}_1$, $\mathbf{x}_2$, $\mathbf{x}_3$, *and* $\mathbf{x}_4$

It follows that the solution for different iterations is as given below.

(i) Given the first training vector, according to Eq. (13.27),

$$e_1 = \hat{\mathbf{w}}_0^{\mathrm{T}} \mathbf{x}_1 - y_1 = 0.1, \quad \gamma_1 = (1 + \mathbf{x}_1^{\mathrm{T}} \boldsymbol{\Sigma}_0 \mathbf{x}_1)^{-1} = 0.0098.$$

According to Eq. (13.28), we update

$$\begin{aligned}
\boldsymbol{\Sigma}_1 &= \boldsymbol{\Sigma}_0 - \gamma_1 \boldsymbol{\Sigma}_0 \mathbf{x}_1 \mathbf{x}_1^{\mathrm{T}} \boldsymbol{\Sigma}_0 \\
&= \begin{bmatrix} 100 & 0 \\ 0 & 100 \end{bmatrix} - 0.0098 \begin{bmatrix} 100 & 0 \\ 0 & 100 \end{bmatrix} \\
&\quad \times \begin{bmatrix} 1.0 \\ 0.1 \end{bmatrix} [1.0 \quad 0.1] \begin{bmatrix} 100 & 0 \\ 0 & 100 \end{bmatrix} \\
&= \begin{bmatrix} 1.9608 & -9.8039 \\ -9.8039 & 99.0196 \end{bmatrix},
\end{aligned}$$

and then, by Eq. (13.29), the optimal estimator can be updated as

$$\hat{\mathbf{w}}_1 = \hat{\mathbf{w}}_0 - e_1 \mathbf{\Sigma}_1 \mathbf{x}_1$$
$$= \begin{bmatrix} 1.0 \\ 1.0 \end{bmatrix} - 0.1 \times \begin{bmatrix} 1.9608 & -9.8039 \\ -9.8039 & 99.0196 \end{bmatrix} \begin{bmatrix} 1.0 \\ 0.1 \end{bmatrix} = \begin{bmatrix} 0.9020 \\ 0.9902 \end{bmatrix}.$$

(ii) After two training vectors, according to Eq. (13.27),

$$e_2 = \hat{\mathbf{w}}_1^{\mathrm{T}} \mathbf{x}_2 - y_2 = -0.1794, \quad \gamma_2 = (1 + \mathbf{x}_2^{\mathrm{T}} \mathbf{\Sigma}_1 \mathbf{x}_2)^{-1} = 0.5965,$$

and, by Eq. (13.29), the optimal estimator can then be updated as

$$\hat{\mathbf{w}}_2 = \hat{\mathbf{w}}_1 - e_2 \mathbf{\Sigma}_2 \mathbf{x}_2 = [0.9649 \quad 1.2105]^{\mathrm{T}}.$$

(iii) After three training vectors, we have

$$\hat{\mathbf{w}}_3 = \hat{\mathbf{w}}_2 - e_3 \mathbf{\Sigma}_3 \mathbf{x}_3 = [0.9917 \quad 1.3042]^{\mathrm{T}}.$$

(iv) After four training vectors, we have

$$\hat{\mathbf{w}}_4 = \hat{\mathbf{w}}_4 - e_4 \mathbf{\Sigma}_4 \mathbf{x}_4 = [0.9427 \quad 1.4126]^{\mathrm{T}}.$$

The progressive change of decision vectors for different iterations is pictorially shown in Figure 13.12.

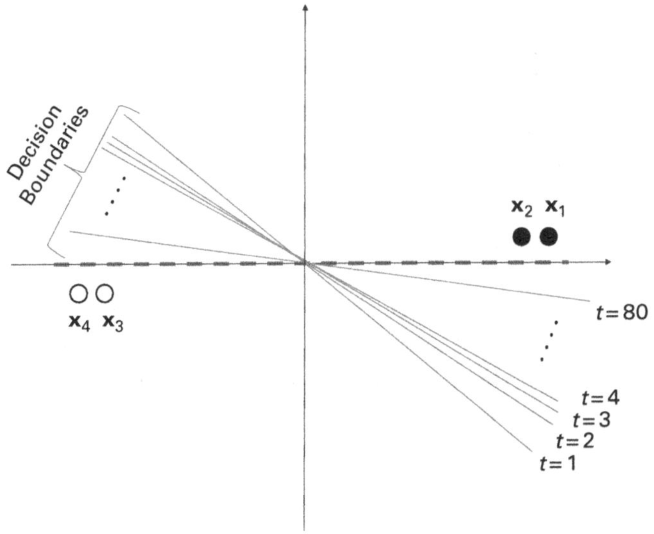

Fig. 13.12. A time-adaptive ridge regressor for a four-sample dataset. Initially, the ridge factor $\rho = 0.01$ is adopted, which leads to a decision boundary with a somewhat balanced role between $\mathbf{x}^{(1)}$ and $\mathbf{x}^{(2)}$. As more training data are being learned, the second decision component, $\mathbf{x}^{(2)}$, is gradually gaining dominance as the solution is converging towards the optimal LSE solution, whose decision vector is shown as the dashed horizontal line.

Different training order: $\mathbf{x}_1$, $\mathbf{x}_4$, $\mathbf{x}_2$, *and* $\mathbf{x}_3$

For comparison purposes, a different training order is adopted and we obtain the following decision vectors.

(i) *After the first training vector,* $\mathbf{x}_1$, *we again obtain* $\hat{\mathbf{w}}_1 = [0.9020 \quad 0.9902]^{\mathrm{T}}$.
(ii) *After two training vectors,* $\mathbf{x}_1$ *and* $\mathbf{x}_4$, *we obtain* $\hat{\mathbf{w}}_2 = [0.9015 \quad 0.9901]^{\mathrm{T}}$.
(iii) *After three training vectors (*$\mathbf{x}_1$, $\mathbf{x}_4$, *and* $\mathbf{x}_2$*), we obtain* $\hat{\mathbf{w}}_3 = [0.9275 \quad 1.2572]^{\mathrm{T}}$.
(vi) *After all four training vectors, we again obtain* $\hat{\mathbf{w}}_4 = [0.9427 \quad 1.4126]^{\mathrm{T}}$.

Note that, after all four training vectors have been learned, the final result converges to the same solution as the one trained by the original order. This demonstrates that the order of training will have no effect on the final optimal estimator.

Multiple epochs

In this example, four training vectors are learned in each epoch. In what follows, the same four training vectors will be used for learning. After 20 *epochs, i.e.* $t = 4 \times 20 = 80$, *the optimal estimator is derived as* $\hat{\mathbf{w}}_{80} = [0.5031 \quad 5.4168]^{\mathrm{T}}$. *Note that the second component is dominant in the decision boundary. This phenomenon can be explained as follows. Note that the effect of the original ridge factor* ρ_0 *tends to diminish when the decision vector becomes more and more influenced by the increasing number of training vectors used for learning. As such, the final solution tends to converge towards the optimal LSE solution:* $\hat{\mathbf{w}}_{\mathrm{LSE}} = [0 \quad 10]^{\mathrm{T}}$, *which corresponds to the case with* $\rho = 0$. *(See Example 8.6.)* □

13.7.3 A time-adaptive KRR algorithm with a forgetting factor

For applications to semi-stationary time series, it is customary to incorporate into the updating procedure a built-in forgetting factor α, resulting in

$$E_{\mathrm{KRR},\alpha} = \sum_{i=1}^{t} \alpha^{-i} |y_i - \mathbf{u}^{\mathrm{T}} \overrightarrow{\boldsymbol{\phi}}_i|^2 + \rho_0 ||\mathbf{u}||^2, \tag{13.30}$$

where α is often chosen to be a positive scalar slightly less than 1.0. Note that the time-adjusted weights reflect the diminishing influence of the (long-past) training data. This cost function leads to the following time-adaptive KRR algorithm with a forgetting factor. For the $(t+1)$th iteration, with the newly available information on $\{\mathbf{x}_{t+1}, y_{t+1}\}$, we first update

$$e_{t+1} = \hat{\mathbf{u}}_t^{\mathrm{T}} \overrightarrow{\boldsymbol{\phi}}_{t+1} - y_{t+1},$$

and

$$\gamma_{t+1} = \frac{1}{\alpha^{t+1} + \overrightarrow{\boldsymbol{\phi}}_{t+1}^{\mathrm{T}} \boldsymbol{\Sigma}_t \overrightarrow{\boldsymbol{\phi}}(\mathbf{x}_{t+1})},$$

Then we can update

$$\hat{\mathbf{u}}_{t+1} = \hat{\mathbf{u}}_t - \gamma_{t+1}\boldsymbol{\Sigma}_t \overrightarrow{\boldsymbol{\phi}}_{t+1} e_{t+1} \tag{13.31}$$

and

$$\boldsymbol{\Sigma}_{t+1} = \boldsymbol{\Sigma}_t - \gamma_{t+1}\boldsymbol{\Sigma}_t \overrightarrow{\boldsymbol{\phi}}_{t+1} \overrightarrow{\boldsymbol{\phi}}^{\mathrm{T}}_{t+1} \boldsymbol{\Sigma}_t. \tag{13.32}$$

Initially, $\boldsymbol{\Sigma}_0 \equiv \rho_0^{-1}\mathbf{I}$.

13.8 Summary

The chapter explores cost-effective design for kernel-based machine learning and classification. Algorithm 13.1 summarizes cost-effective kernel-based learning algorithms for situations when a training dataset of large size N is made available for training classifiers. Algorithm 13.2 describes a recursive tensor-based classification algorithm that allows a further reduction of the classification complexity. In addition, time-adaptive recursive KRR algorithms that promise one order of magnitude of computational saving for active learning applications are introduced.

13.9 Problems

Problem 13.1 *Let us assume that $M = 2$, i.e. $\mathbf{x} = [u\ v\ ]^{\mathrm{T}}$. In this case the bilinear kernel function with $\sigma = 1$ is $K(\mathbf{x}, \mathbf{x}') = \left([1\ u\ v][1\ u'\ v']^{\mathrm{T}}\right)^2$. Show that the nonlinear decision boundary can be expressed as*

$$\begin{aligned} f(\mathbf{x}) &= \sum_{i=1}^{N} y_i\alpha_i K(\mathbf{x}, \mathbf{x}_i) + b \\ &= \sum_{i=1}^{N} y_i\alpha_i \left([1\ u\ v][1\ u_i\ v_i]^{\mathrm{T}}\right)^2 + b \\ &= [1\ u\ v]\left(\sum_{i=1}^{N} y_i\alpha_i [1\ u_i\ v_i]^{\mathrm{T}}[1\ u_i\ v_i]\right)[1\ u\ v]^{\mathrm{T}} + b \\ &= [1\ u\ v]\mathbf{W}[1\ u\ v]^{\mathrm{T}} + b, \end{aligned}$$

where $\mathbf{W}$ is a symmetric weight matrix defined as

$$\mathbf{W} \equiv \sum_{i=1}^{N} y_i\alpha_i \begin{bmatrix} 1 \\ u_i \\ v_i \end{bmatrix} \begin{bmatrix} 1 & u_i & v_i \end{bmatrix},$$

for the two-dimensional case.

Problem 13.2 *For the classification complexity for a POLY_p kernel, prove the following equality:*

$$J' = J^{(p)} + \cdots + J^{(2)} + J^{(1)} + 1 = \sum_{q=1}^{p} \binom{M+q}{q} + 1 = \binom{M+p+1}{p}.$$

Hint: *Note the following power-series expansion of x:*

$$(1+x)^{M+p} = 1 + c_1 x + \cdots + c_q x^q + \cdots + x^{M+p},$$

where

$$c_q = \binom{M+p}{q}.$$

Note that

$$\sum_{m=1}^{p}(1+x)^{M+m} = \sum_{m=1}^{p}\left(1 + c_1 x + \cdots + c_q x^q + \cdots + x^{M+m}\right)$$
$$= 1 + d_1 x + \cdots + d_q x^q + \cdots + x^{M+p},$$

which shows that

$$d_q = \sum_{m=1}^{p} c_m = \sum_{q=1}^{p} \binom{M+q}{q}. \quad (13.33)$$

On the other hand, the expansion

$$\sum_{q=1}^{p}(1+x)^{M+q} = \frac{(1+x)^{M+p+1} - (1+x)^M}{x}$$

shows that

$$d_q = \binom{M+p+1}{q} - 1. \quad (13.34)$$

It follows that

$$J' = 1 + \sum_{q=1}^{p} J^{(q)} \overset{\text{Eq. (13.3)}}{=} 1 + \sum_{q=1}^{p} \binom{M+q}{q} \overset{\text{Eq. (13.33)}}{=} 1 + d_q \overset{\text{Eq. (13.34)}}{=} \binom{M+p+1}{q}.$$

Problem 13.3 *The discriminant function has the following intrinsic representation:*

$$f(\mathbf{x}) = \mathbf{u}^{\mathrm{T}} \overrightarrow{\boldsymbol{\phi}}(\mathbf{x}) + b = \sum_{\ell=1}^{J} u_\ell \phi^{(\ell)}(\mathbf{x}) + b.$$

(a) *For a third-order polynomial kernel function, show that the discriminant function has the following tensor representation:*

$$f(\mathbf{x}) = \sum_{i=1}^{M+1} \tilde{x}^{(i)} \left[\sum_{j=1}^{i} \tilde{x}^{(j)} \left(\sum_{k=1}^{j} \gamma_{ijk} \tilde{w}_{ijk} \tilde{x}^{(k)} \right) \right] + b,$$

where the multinomial coefficients $\gamma_{ijk} = 3!/(a!b!c!)$, *where a, b, and c, are the occurrences of i, j, and k, respectively. Note that the multiplication of* $\gamma_{ijk}\tilde{w}_{ijk}$ *can be performed in the training phase, thus the number of online operations becomes*

$$\binom{M+4}{3}.$$

(b) *Show that there is a one-to-one correspondence between the parameters* $\{u_\ell, \ell = 1, 2, \ldots, J\}$ *and* $\{\gamma_{ijk}\tilde{w}_{ijk}, i = 1, \ldots, M, j = 1, \ldots, M, k = 1, \ldots, M, \}$. *This implies that the tensor coefficients can be directly obtained from the intrinsic-space learning model and no further computations will be required.*

Problem 13.4 (Parallel processing for tensor-based classification) *When the prediction speed is important, parallel-processing hardware may have to be considered. Show that systolic arrays are amenable to tensor-based algorithms for classification [133, 134].*

Problem 13.5 (Storage requirement) *This problem explores some storage-related issues. Verify the following.*

(a) *It should by now have become obvious that the storage requirement the for POLY3 kernel is* $(M+1)(M+2)(M+3)/6$, *which represents the number of distinct parameters of* $\tilde{w}_{ijk}$. *For the POLY_p kernel, the storage need is*

$$\binom{M+p}{p},$$

which is exactly the same as the intrinsic degree.

(b) *Note that, for RBF kernels, not only the S nonzero empirical coefficients but also their associated support vectors need to be stored – the former requires* ηN *and latter* ηMN *in storage. In other words, the storage need is approximately the same as the degree of design freedom, a factor to be taken into account for cost-effective design.*

Problem 13.6 *Verify the following equality:*

$$\boldsymbol{\Sigma}_{t+1}\overrightarrow{\phi}_{t+1} = \gamma_{t+1}\boldsymbol{\Sigma}_t\overrightarrow{\phi}_{t+1}. \qquad (13.35)$$

Hint: *On post-multiplying Eq. (13.26) by* $\overrightarrow{\phi}_{t+1}$, *we obtain*

$$\boldsymbol{\Sigma}_{t+1}\overrightarrow{\phi}_{t+1} = \boldsymbol{\Sigma}_t\overrightarrow{\phi}_{t+1} - \gamma_{t+1}\boldsymbol{\Sigma}_t\overrightarrow{\phi}_{t+1}\beta = (1-\gamma_{t+1}\beta)\boldsymbol{\Sigma}_t\overrightarrow{\phi}_{t+1},$$

where $\beta \equiv \overrightarrow{\phi}_{t+1}^{\mathrm{T}}\boldsymbol{\Sigma}_t\overrightarrow{\phi}_{t+1}$. *The proof can be completed by showing that* $\gamma_{t+1} = 1-\gamma_{t+1}\beta$.

Problem 13.7 *Verify the following updating procedure which leads to an updating rule identical to that derived via the zero-input property (ZIP). Upon the arrival of a new training sample* $\mathbf{x}_{t+1}$, *the estimated regressor can be updated as follows:*

$$
\begin{aligned}
\hat{\mathbf{u}}_{t+1} &= [\boldsymbol{\Phi}_{t+1}\boldsymbol{\Phi}_{t+1}^{\mathrm{T}} + \rho\mathbf{I}]^{-1}\left(\boldsymbol{\Phi}_{t+1}\overrightarrow{\mathbf{y}}_{t+1}\right)\\
&= \boldsymbol{\Sigma}_{t+1}\left(\boldsymbol{\Phi}_t\overrightarrow{\mathbf{y}}_t + \overrightarrow{\phi}_{t+1}y_{t+1}\right)\\
&\overset{\text{Eq. (13.26)}}{=} \boldsymbol{\Sigma}_t\boldsymbol{\Phi}_t\overrightarrow{\mathbf{y}}_t - \gamma_{t+1}\boldsymbol{\Sigma}_t\overrightarrow{\phi}_{t+1}\overrightarrow{\phi}_{t+1}^{\mathrm{T}}\boldsymbol{\Sigma}_t\boldsymbol{\Phi}_t\overrightarrow{\mathbf{y}}_t + \boldsymbol{\Sigma}_{t+1}\overrightarrow{\phi}_{t+1}y_{t+1}\\
&\overset{\text{Eqs. (13.21) \& (13.22)}}{=} \hat{\mathbf{u}}_t - \gamma_{t+1}\boldsymbol{\Sigma}_t\overrightarrow{\phi}_{t+1}\hat{y}_{t+1} + \boldsymbol{\Sigma}_{t+1}\overrightarrow{\phi}_{t+1}y_{t+1}.\\
&\overset{\text{Eq. (13.35)}}{=} \hat{\mathbf{u}}_t - \boldsymbol{\Sigma}_{t+1}\overrightarrow{\phi}_{t+1}\hat{y}_{t+1} + \boldsymbol{\Sigma}_{t+1}\overrightarrow{\phi}_{t+1}y_{t+1}\\
&= \hat{\mathbf{u}}_t - \boldsymbol{\Sigma}_{t+1}\overrightarrow{\phi}_{t+1}e_{t+1}.
\end{aligned}
$$

Show that this result is consistent with Eq. (13.29).

Problem 13.8 (Adaptively learning PCA algorithm) *Kung and Diamantaras [50, 137] proposed an APEX learning rule for adaptively extracting principal components. Derive a kernel-APEX extension for the second-order polynomial kernel:* $K(\mathbf{x},\mathbf{y}) = 1 + (\mathbf{x}\cdot\mathbf{y})^2$.

Problem 13.9 (Simulation on the ECG dataset) *Conduct a simulation study on the ECG dataset and compare the performance of KRRs using RBF and TRBF kernels [145].*

Part VII

Kernel methods and statistical estimation theory

Linear prediction and system identification has become a well-established field in information sciences. On the other hand, kernel methods have acquired their popularity only during the past two decades, so they have a relatively short history. It is vital to establish a theoretical foundation linking kernel methods and the rich theory in estimation, prediction, and system identification. This part contains two chapters addressing this important issue. Chapter 14 focuses on statistical analysis employing knowledge of the (joint) density functions of all the input and output variables and their respective noises. Chapter 15 focuses on estimation, prediction, and system identification using observed samples and prior knowledge of the first- and second-order statistics of the system parameters.

In Chapter 14, the classical formulation for (linear) ridge regression will be extended to (nonlinear) kernel ridge regression (KRR). Using the notion of orthogonal polynomials (Theorem 14.1), closed-form results for the error analysis can be derived for KRR, see Theorem 14.2. The regression analysis can be further generalized to the errors-in-variables models, where the measurements of the input variable are no longer perfect. This leads to the development of *perturbation-regulated regressors* (PRRs), regarding which two major theoretical fronts will be explored:

- Under the Gaussian distribution assumption, the analysis on PRR benefits greatly from the exact knowledge of the joint statistical property of the ideal and perturbed input variables. The property of conventional orthogonal polynomials (Theorem 14.1) is extended to harness the cross-orthogonality between the original and perturbed input variables. Theorems 14.3 and 14.5 cover the theory of cross-orthogonality, respectively for single-variate and multivariate cases. The theorems facilitate the derivation of optimal PRRs and an analytical assessment of the error–order tradeoff (Theorems 14.4 and 14.6).
- For any arbitrary distribution, be it Gaussian or not, the procedure of estimating the system parameters can be subdivided into two stages. (1) In the first stage, we shall perform estimation by taking projection onto a perturbation-free kernel space. (2) In the second stage, the result will be further projected onto a perturbation-prone kernel space. For many situations, a notion termed the "two-projection property" will be useful both theoretically and computationally. The property means that performing two consecutive simple projections yields the same result as performing the

direct projection to the perturbed space. For safe employment of the two-projection procedure, it is vital to establish the necessary and sufficient conditions for the two-projection property to be valid. Theorems 14.7 and 14.8 state formally such a condition for the general case and for the polynomial kernel case, respectively.

Chapter 15 provides a mathematical formulation for the optimal estimator, regressor, and/or predictor. In this chapter, we shall assume only prior knowledge of the first- and second-order statistics of $\mathbf{u}$ and $\mathbf{y}$, which are generally much easier to obtain than the densities $p_{\mathbf{u}|\mathbf{y}}(\mathbf{u}|\mathbf{y})$ and $p_{\mathbf{u}}(\mathbf{u})$ required in general Bayesian estimation problems. Nevertheless, estimators can be recognized as employing a Bayesian method when the system vector $\mathbf{u}$ is modeled by a random vector with its first- and second-order statistics [151].

The chapter substantially extends the well-known Gauss–Markov theorem. Three different scenarios will be considered.

- The Gauss–Markov theorem, which was established for linear models with deterministic system parameters defined over the original space, can be extended to the kernel-induced vector space. It will be shown that the best unbiased linear estimator, the predictor, and the LSE regressor are all identical to each other, see Theorem 15.1.
- The Gauss–Markov theorem can be further extended to statistical learning models. Again, in this case, the best linear estimator, the predictor, and the optimal KRR regressor are all identical to each other, see Theorem 15.2.
- The Gauss–Markov theorem may be further extended to the errors-in-variables learning models. It will be shown that the best linear prediction, the best linear estimator, the predictor, and the optimal EiV regressor are all identical to each other, see Theorem 15.3.

In time-series prediction, the prior knowledge may be interpreted as the state which summarizes the useful information embedded in the past observations. Moreover, it should be constantly updated when new data are made available. This section develops recursive incremental learning models to effectively update the estimators in time-adaptive fashion, both for perturbation-free and for perturbational models. Finally, the notion of a weighted kernel function is introduced, naturally leading to the dual-optimization formulation in the empirical space. Recursive and time-adaptive algorithms in the empirical space can also be developed.

14 Statistical regression analysis and errors-in-variables models

14.1 Introduction

Regression analysis has been a major theoretical pillar for supervised machine learning since it is applicable to a broad range of identification, prediction and classification problems. There are two major approaches to the design of robust regressors. The first category involves a variety of regularization techniques whose principle lies in incorporating both the error and the penalty terms into the cost function. It is represented by the ridge regressor. The second category is based on the premise that the robustness of the regressor could be enhanced by accounting for potential measurement errors in the learning phase. These techniques are known as errors-in-variables models in statistics and are relatively new to the machine learning community. In our discussion, such errors in variables are viewed as additive input perturbation.

This chapter aims at enhancing the robustness of estimators by incorporating input perturbation into the conventional regression analysis. It develops a kernel perturbation-regulated regressor (PRR) that is based on the errors-in-variables models. The PRR offers a strong smoothing capability that is critical to the robustness of regression or classification results. For Gaussian cases, the notion of orthogonal polynomials is instrumental to optimal estimation and its error analysis. More exactly, the regressor may be expressed as a linear combination of many simple Hermite regressors, each focusing on one (and only one) orthogonal polynomial.

This chapter will cover the fundamental theory of linear regression and regularization analysis. The analysis leads to a closed-form error formula that is critical for order–error tradeoff. The simulation results not only confirm the theoretical prediction but also demonstrate the superiority of PRR over the conventional ridge regression method in MSE reduction.

This chapter explores several relatively theoretical topics summarized as follows.

- Section 14.2 discusses two major models used for regularization, namely ridge regression (RR) and the errors-in-variables model. For the RR model, we discuss the derivation of the basic MMSE and linear-least-MSE estimators. In the errors-in-variables model, the effect of (practically inevitable) input measurement error is taken into account. For this model, both MMSE and linear-least-MSE estimators will be derived and compared.
- Section 14.3 explores the theory of orthogonal polynomials. Assuming a Gaussian distribution, Theorem 14.1 describes the well-known orthogonality property

of Hermite orthogonal polynomials. Hermite polynomials are instrumental for the derivation of optimal KRR solutions as well as their closed-form error analysis. The latter is useful for proper selection of the kernel order.

- Section 14.4 explores the potential use of the errors-in-variables model for regression analysis. In standard regression analysis, the input is assumed to be perfectly measurable. For practical applications, however, input measurement error is essentially inevitable for most real-life applications. In order to arrive at a robust solution, it is imperative to take into account such input perturbation. As a new approach to regression analysis [145], the errors-in-variables model leads to a perturbation-regulated regressor (PRR).
- Section 14.5 discusses single-variate kernel PRR estimators for the Gaussian cases. For PRR, different regression ratios apply for low-order and high-order components. This represents a major departure from KRR. This highlights the regularization and smoothing capability existing exclusively in PRR but not in KRR. Section 14.5.5 extends the previous results to multivariate kernel PRR estimators for the Gaussian cases.
- Section 14.6 shows that the two-projection theorem is not limited to either polynomial kernel-induced basis functions or Gaussian distributions. For Gaussian or non-Gaussian cases, this section formally establishes a "two-projection theorem" allowing the estimation task to be divided into two projection stages: the first projection reveals the effect of model-induced error (caused by under-represented regressor models), while the second projection reveals the extra estimation error due to the (inevitable) input measuring error. The two-projection theorem is useful for finding the optimal estimator and its associated error analysis. First, in the first projection, the error due to under-represented regressors is identified. Then, in the second projection, a new notion of Hermite estimators will be introduced.

14.2 Statistical regression analysis

Regression analysis can be viewed as a system identification problem, where an unknown system is viewed as a black box characterized by its input $\mathbf{x}$ and the corresponding response y. As depicted in Figure 14.1(a), a regression system is characterized by a deterministic but unknown function $h(\mathbf{x})$, where the output is commonly expressed as

$$y = h(\mathbf{x}) + \varepsilon.$$

Here $\mathbf{x} = [x_1, x_2, \ldots, x_M]^{\mathrm{T}}$ denotes the input vector, and ε is an independent zero-mean random noise term.

In a basic regression learning model, see Figure 14.1(a), the observed output response is often assumed to be corrupted by a statistically independent noise. Regression analysis involves the determination of a nonlinear regressor function $\hat{h}(\mathbf{x})$ to best estimate the original model $h(\mathbf{x})$ from the given statistical information on the *independent* variable $\mathbf{x}$ and *dependent* variable y.

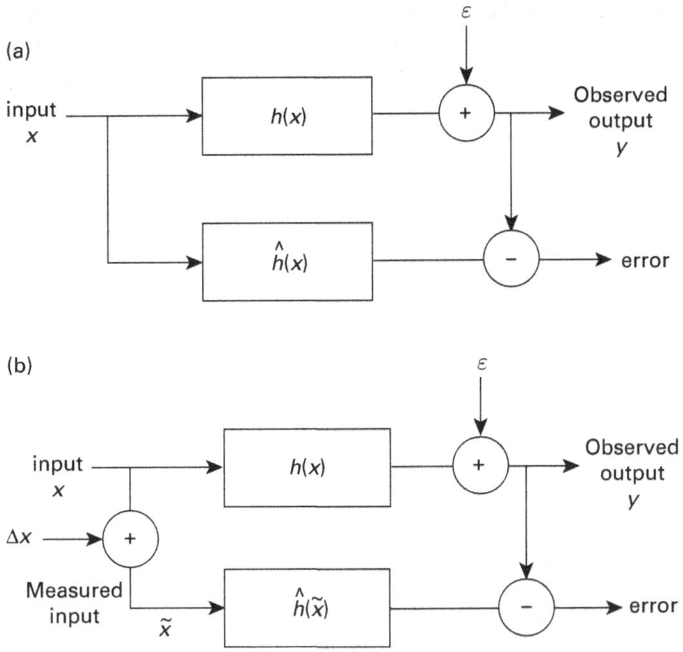

Fig. 14.1. (a) In a basic regression model, it is often assumed that the observed output response is corrupted by an additive noise term. (b) The perturbation-regulated regression (PRR) analysis is based on the errors-in-variables model, where both the input and the output are corrupted by measurement errors.

14.2.1 The minimum mean-square-error (MMSE) estimator/regressor

The MMSE regressor is a non-parametric method aiming at minimizing the so-called mean-squared error (MSE) [120, 151, 230]:

$$L = E[||\epsilon||^2] = E[||y - \hat{h}(\mathbf{x})||^2],$$

which leads to the following optimal regressor:

$$\hat{h}(\mathbf{x}) = E[y|\mathbf{x}] = \int y p_{y|\mathbf{x}}(y|\mathbf{x})dy = h(\mathbf{x}).$$

The MMSE estimator, being a non-parametric method, can deliver an optimal estimation result. From computational considerations, some parametric methods are appealing even though they are likely to result in suboptimal estimation. Two prominent examples are the following.

- **Linear estimation.** A linear estimator has the simplest formulation:

  $$\hat{y} = \hat{h}_{\mathbf{x}}(\mathbf{x}) = \mathbf{x}^{\mathrm{T}}\mathbf{w}.$$

  The objective is to find the best vector $\mathbf{w}$ to minimize the following MSE:

  $$E[||y - \mathbf{x}^{\mathrm{T}}\mathbf{w}||^2].$$

- **Kernel-based estimation.** Let $\{z_j(x), j = 1, \ldots, J\}$ denote a set of kernel-induced basis functions up to a pre-specified order. A kernel-based estimator can be expressed in terms of a linear combination of the set of kernel-induced basis functions:

$$\hat{y} = \sum_{j=1}^{J} u_i z_j(\mathbf{x}).$$

The corresponding kernel-induced basis vector is defined as

$$\mathbf{z} \equiv [z_1(x)\ z_2(x) \ldots\ z_J(x)]^{\mathrm{T}} \tag{14.1}$$

then

$$\hat{y} = \hat{h}_{\mathbf{z}}(\mathbf{x}) = \mathbf{z}^{\mathrm{T}}\mathbf{u}.$$

The objective now is to find the best vector **u** to minimize the following MSE:

$$E[||y - \mathbf{z}^{\mathrm{T}}\mathbf{u}||^2].$$

14.2.2 Linear regression analysis

The linear-least-MSE regressor

Let us for simplicity assume that the input and output variables **x** and **y** both have zero mean. The *linear-least-MSE* estimator aims at finding a linear solution $\mathbf{x}^{\mathrm{T}}\mathbf{w}$ that minimizes the MSE:

$$E[||y - \mathbf{x}^{\mathrm{T}}\mathbf{w}||^2] = E[y^2] + \mathbf{w}^{\mathrm{T}}E[\mathbf{x}\mathbf{x}^{\mathrm{T}}]\mathbf{w} - 2\mathbf{w}^{\mathrm{T}}E[\mathbf{x}y],$$

whose zero-gradient point with respect to **w** leads to the following formulation for the optimal *linear-least-MSE* estimator:

$$\hat{h}_{\mathbf{x}}(\mathbf{x}) = \mathbf{x}^{\mathrm{T}}\mathbf{w}, \quad \text{with} \quad \mathbf{w} = R_{\mathbf{x}}^{-1}R_{\mathbf{x}y}, \tag{14.2}$$

where we denote $R_{\mathbf{x}} = E[\mathbf{x}\mathbf{x}^{\mathrm{T}}]$ and $R_{\mathbf{x}y} = E[\mathbf{x}y]$. This is the typical derivation used in linear estimation theory [120].

Alternatively, the linear-least-MSE estimator may also be derived as the optimal (i.e. shortest-distance) projection of y onto the *original input subspace*:

$$\text{span}\{\mathbf{x}\} \equiv \{\mathbf{x}^{\mathrm{T}}\mathbf{w} : \mathbf{w} \in \mathbb{R}^M\}.$$

In a projection language, the optimal estimation can be expressed as

$$\hat{y} = \hat{h}_{\mathbf{x}}(\mathbf{x}) \equiv h(\mathbf{x})/\{\mathbf{x}\} = \mathbf{x}^{\mathrm{T}}R_{\mathbf{x}}^{-1}R_{\mathbf{x}y}, \tag{14.3}$$

where, for notational convenience, we denote $\{\mathbf{x}\} \equiv \text{span}\{\mathbf{x}\}$ and the projection operator is denoted by the solidus /. The inner product adopted by the projection here is defined as

$$\langle f(\mathbf{x}), g(\mathbf{x})\rangle = E[f(\mathbf{x})g(\mathbf{x})],$$

for all functions $f(\mathbf{x}) \in \mathcal{L}^2(\mathbf{x})$ and $g(\mathbf{x}) \in \mathcal{L}^2(\mathbf{x})$. Here $\mathcal{L}^2(\mathbf{x})$ covers all the functions which have a finite two-norm, i.e.

$$\langle f(\mathbf{x}), f(\mathbf{x})\rangle = E[f(\mathbf{x})^2] < \infty.$$

The ridge regressor (RR)

Ridge regression, also known as Tikhonov regularization [99, 275], is the most common approach to regularization of over-fitting or ill-posed problems. Its principle relies on the notion of a penalty-augmented loss function to keep the regressor coefficients under control. It aims to minimize a penalty-augmented loss function, $L_{\text{RR}} = E[|y - \mathbf{x}^{\text{T}}\mathbf{w}|^2] + \rho||\mathbf{w}||^2$, which leads to the following optimal solution:

$$\mathbf{w} = [R_{\mathbf{x}} + \rho\mathbf{I}]^{-1}R_{xy}. \tag{14.4}$$

14.3 Kernel ridge regression (KRR)

Recall that, in Eq. (14.1), a kernel-induced basis vector has the following representation:

$$\mathbf{z} \equiv [z_1(x)\ z_2(x) \ldots\ z_J(x)]^{\text{T}}.$$

The vector $\mathbf{z}$ may take various definitions, a basic kind for single-variate polynomial kernels being the elementary set

$$\{z_n(x) = x^n,\ n = 0, 1, \ldots, p\}. \tag{14.5}$$

However, a non-elementary set (obtained as a linearly independent combination of the elementary set) will prove more versatile for kernel regression analysis.

A *kernel ridge regressor* (KRR) aims to minimize the loss function

$$L_{\text{KRR}(p)} = E[|y - \mathbf{z}^{\text{T}}\mathbf{u}|^2] + \rho||\mathbf{u}||^2 \tag{14.6}$$

in order to control the regressor coefficients $\{u_i\}$. This leads to the following KRR solution:

$$\hat{y}_{\text{KRR}(p)} = \hat{h}_{\mathbf{z}}(\mathbf{x}) = \mathbf{z}^{\text{T}}[R_{\mathbf{z}} + \rho\mathbf{I}]^{-1}R_{\mathbf{z}y}. \tag{14.7}$$

Definition: orthogonal polynomials

With the distribution of the variable x known in advance, a set of polynomials $\{\phi_n(x)\}$ consists of orthogonal polynomials if

$$E[\phi_m(x)\phi_n(x)] = 0, \quad \text{if } m \neq n.$$

The notion of orthogonal polynomials can effectively facilitate kernel regression analysis.

14.3.1 Orthonormal basis functions: single-variate cases

In our present analysis, we shall assume that the input variable has zero mean and a Gaussian distribution. The following theorem formally states the conventional orthogonality property pertaining to the single-variate Hermite orthogonal polynomials.

THEOREM 14.1 (Orthogonality property of Hermite polynomials) *The orthogonal polynomials corresponding to a Gaussian distribution, $x \sim \mathcal{N}(0, \sigma_x^2)$, are as follows:*

$$\text{He}_n(x) = (-1)^n e^{\frac{x^2}{2}} \frac{d^n}{dx^n} e^{-\frac{x^2}{2}}, \quad n = 0, 1, 2, \ldots,$$

which are called Hermite polynomials. Denote their corresponding orthonormal basis functions as

$$\psi_n(x) = \frac{1}{\sqrt{n!}} \text{He}_n\left(\frac{x}{\sigma_x}\right). \tag{14.8}$$

Then we can establish the following orthonormal property:

$$E[\psi_i(x)\psi_j(x)] = \delta(i - j). \tag{14.9}$$

□

Proof. Note that $\text{He}_0(x) = 1$, $\text{He}_1(x) = x$, and the rest are derivable recursively via $\text{He}_{n+1}(x) = x\,\text{He}_n(x) - n\,\text{He}_{n-1}(x)$. Then Eq. (14.9) can be proved by induction via repeatedly applying integration by parts.

Suppose that the regression model $h(x)$ is of qth order, and q may be finite or infinite. Then $h(x)$ may be decomposed into a linear combination of the orthonormal basis functions,

$$h(x) = \sum_{n=0}^{q} \gamma_n \psi_n(x), \tag{14.10}$$

for some real coefficients $\{\gamma_n\}$. Suppose further that the estimator is of pth order, $p \le q$. Then

$$\hat{h}(x) = \sum_{m=0}^{p} u_m \psi_m(x)$$

for some real coefficients $\{u_n\}$.

Denote $\mathbf{z}$ as the $(p+1)$-dimensional intrinsic feature vector formed from the first $p+1$ orthonormal basis functions:

$$\{z_n(x) = \psi_n(x),\ 0 \le n \le p\}, \tag{14.11}$$

and, in a vector form,

$$\mathbf{z} \equiv [\psi_0(x)\ \psi_1(x) \ldots \psi_p(x)]^{\mathrm{T}}.$$

Denote further that

$$\mathbf{v} = [\gamma_0\ \gamma_1\ \ldots\ \gamma_p]^{\mathrm{T}},$$

and denote the *model-induced error* as

$$\Delta_h(x) \equiv \sum_{i=p+1}^{q} \gamma_n \psi_n(x). \tag{14.12}$$

Then the regression function can be expressed as

$$h(x) = \sum_{n=0}^{p} \gamma_n \psi_n(x) + \sum_{n=p+1}^{q} \gamma_n \psi_n(x) = \mathbf{z}^{\mathrm{T}}\mathbf{v} + \Delta_h(x),$$

where $\Delta_h(x) \equiv \sum_{i=p+1}^{q} \gamma_n \psi_n(x)$.

Using Eq. (14.6), and ignoring the output noise ε, we would like to minimize the following augmented MSE criterion:

$$\begin{aligned} L_{\mathrm{KRR}(p)} &= E[||h(x) - \hat{h}(x)||^2] + \rho||\mathbf{u}||^2 \\ &= E\left[\left\|\sum_{m=0}^{p}(\gamma_m - u_m)\psi_m(x) + \sum_{m=p+1}^{q} \gamma_m \psi_m(x)\right\|^2\right] + \rho \sum_{m=0}^{p} u_m^2 \\ &= \left(\sum_{m=0}^{p}[(\gamma_m - u_m)^2 + \rho u_m^2]\right) + \left(\sum_{m=p+1}^{q} \gamma_m^2\right), \end{aligned}$$

which has its minimum when

$$u_m = \frac{1}{1+\rho}\gamma_m, \quad m = 0, 1, \ldots, p. \tag{14.13}$$

According to Eq. (14.6), the formula for the optimal KRR estimation is

$$\hat{y}_{\mathrm{KRR}(p)} = \mathbf{z}^{\mathrm{T}}\frac{\mathbf{v}}{1+\rho} = \mathbf{z}^{\mathrm{T}}\mathbf{u}, \tag{14.14}$$

where we denote

$$\mathbf{u} = \frac{\mathbf{v}}{1+\rho}.$$

Equation (14.14) may be alternatively (and somewhat more directly) derived from Eq. (14.7). More exactly, as supported by Eqs. (14.16) and (14.17) below, the optimal KRR solution can be shown to be

$$\hat{y}_{\mathrm{KRR}(p)} = \mathbf{z}^{\mathrm{T}}[R_{\mathbf{z}} + \rho\mathbf{I}]^{-1}R_{\mathbf{z}y} = \mathbf{z}^{\mathrm{T}}\frac{\mathbf{v}}{1+\rho} = \mathbf{z}^{\mathrm{T}}\mathbf{u}. \tag{14.15}$$

On recalling that $h(x) = \mathbf{z}^{\mathrm{T}}\mathbf{v} + \Delta_h(x)$, it follows that

$$R_{\mathbf{z}y} = E[\mathbf{z}y] = E[\mathbf{z}h(x)] = E[\mathbf{z}\mathbf{z}^{\mathrm{T}}\mathbf{v}] + E[\mathbf{z}\Delta_h(x)] = E[\mathbf{z}\mathbf{z}^{\mathrm{T}}]\mathbf{v} = \mathbf{v}. \tag{14.16}$$

Note also that the auto-orthogonality property prescribed by Eq. (14.9)) implies that

$$R_{\mathbf{z}} = \mathbf{I}. \tag{14.17}$$

The following theorem summarizes the single-variate KRR formulation and its associated error analysis.

THEOREM 14.2 (Kernel ridge regression and error analysis) *Assuming that the regression model is of qth order, say $h(x) = \sum_{n=0}^{q} \gamma_n \psi_n(x)$, where $h(x) \in \mathcal{L}^2(\mathbf{x})$ and q may be finite or infinite, the optimal KRR of finite order p is*

$$\hat{y}_{\mathrm{KRR}(p)} = \mathbf{z}^{\mathrm{T}}\mathbf{u} = \sum_{n=0}^{p}\left(\frac{\gamma_n}{1+\rho}\right)\psi_n(x). \tag{14.18}$$

The minimal estimation error achievable by KRR is

$$L_{\mathrm{KRR}(p)} = \left(\frac{\rho}{1+\rho}\sum_{m=0}^{p} u_m^2\right) + \left(\sum_{m=p+1}^{q} \gamma_m^2\right). \qquad \square$$

14.3.2 Orthonormal basis functions: multivariate cases

For example, the polynomial kernel $K(\mathbf{x}, \mathbf{x}') = (1 + \mathbf{x}^{\mathrm{T}}\mathbf{x}')^p$ for an M-dimensional vector $\mathbf{x}$ has basis functions in the following form:

$$\left\{ z_{\mathbf{n}}(\mathbf{x}) = x_1^{n_1} x_2^{n_2} \ldots x_M^{n_M}, \quad 0 \leq \sum_{i=1}^{M} n_i \leq p \right\}. \tag{14.19}$$

In this case, there are $J = (M + p)!/(M!\, p!)$ basis functions in the intrinsic space [144]. Orthonormal polynomials are expressed as linear combinations of such basis functions, depending on the distribution of $\mathbf{x}$.

For a Gaussian distributed input $\mathbf{x} \sim \mathcal{N}(0, R_{\mathbf{x}})$, we first apply a linear transformation $\mathbf{x}' = R_{\mathbf{x}}^{-1/2}\mathbf{x}$, resulting in a normal distribution $\mathbf{x}' \sim \mathcal{N}(\mathbf{0}, \mathbf{I})$. Thanks to the statistical independence of the M variables, $\{x_i', i = 1, 2, \ldots, M\}$, we can obtain the following orthonormal basis functions:

$$\left\{ z_{\mathbf{n}}(\mathbf{x}) = \psi_{\mathbf{n}}(\mathbf{x}) = \prod_{i=1}^{M} \frac{1}{\sqrt{n_i!}} \mathrm{He}_{n_i}(x_i'), \quad 0 \leq \sum_{i=1}^{M} n_i \leq p \right\}. \tag{14.20}$$

Under such a basis function, Eq. (14.14) can be carried to multivariate cases. Now we denote $\mathbf{z}$ as the J-dimensional intrinsic feature vector formed from all the normalized orthogonal multivariate basis functions of up to pth order, i.e.

$$\mathbf{z} \equiv [\psi_{\mathbf{0}}(\mathbf{x}) \ \ldots \ \psi_{\mathbf{p}}(\mathbf{x})]^{\mathrm{T}}.$$

The transformation procedure for the two-variable case is illustrated by the following numerical example.

Example 14.1 *Consider a two-variate variable $\mathbf{x} \sim \mathcal{N}(\mathbf{0}, \mathbf{\Sigma}_{\mathbf{x}})$, where*

$$\mathbf{\Sigma}_{\mathbf{x}} = \begin{pmatrix} 2.5 & 1.5 \\ 1.5 & 2.5 \end{pmatrix}.$$

The orthonormal basis function for the variable $\mathbf{x}$ has the following form:

$$\begin{aligned}
\psi_{m,n}(\mathbf{x}) &= \frac{1}{\sqrt{m!}}\frac{1}{\sqrt{n!}} \mathrm{He}_{m,n}(\mathrm{P}^{\mathrm{T}}\mathbf{\Sigma}_{\mathbf{x}}^{-1/2}\mathbf{x}) \\
&= \frac{1}{\sqrt{m!}}\frac{1}{\sqrt{n!}} \mathrm{He}_{m,n}\left(\begin{pmatrix} 0.45 & 0.25 \\ -0.65 & 0.75 \end{pmatrix}\mathbf{x}\right) \\
&= \frac{1}{\sqrt{m!}}\frac{1}{\sqrt{n!}} \mathrm{He}_m(0.45x_1 + 0.25x_2)\mathrm{He}_n(-0.65x_1 + 0.75x_2).
\end{aligned} \tag{14.21}$$

The multivariate KRR formula

Let the output response to a regression model $h(\mathbf{x})$ be $y = h(\mathbf{x}) + \varepsilon$, where ε is the independent additive noise. We assume that $h(\mathbf{x})$ is of qth order, say

$$h(\mathbf{x}) = \sum_{\mathbf{n}\in\mathcal{S}_q} \gamma_{\mathbf{n}}\psi_{\mathbf{n}}(\mathbf{x}),$$

where q may be finite or infinite, $h(\mathbf{x}) \in \mathcal{L}^2(\mathbf{x})$ and $\mathbf{n} = [n_1 \; \ldots \; n_M]^{\mathrm{T}}$ denotes the vector of non-negative integer indices with

$$\mathcal{S}_q = \left\{ \mathbf{n} \in \mathbb{N}^M, 0 \le \sum_{i=1}^{M} n_d \le q \right\}.$$

Assuming again that the estimator is of pth order, $p \le q$, the regression function can be re-expressed as

$$h(x) = \sum_{\mathbf{n}\in\mathcal{S}_q} \gamma_{\mathbf{n}}\psi_{\mathbf{n}}(\mathbf{x}) = \mathbf{z}^{\mathrm{T}}\mathbf{v} + \text{higher-order terms},$$

where

$$\mathbf{v} \equiv [v_1 \; v_1 \; \ldots v_J]^{\mathrm{T}},$$

with the coefficients $\{v_i\}$ properly matched to their corresponding values in $\{\gamma_{\mathbf{n}}\}$. Then the optimal KRR regressor of finite order p is a simple extension of the single-variate estimator given in Eq. (14.14). More precisely, the formula for the optimal multivariate KRR estimator is

$$\hat{y}_{\mathrm{KRR}(p)} = \mathbf{z}^{\mathrm{T}}\frac{\mathbf{v}}{1+\rho} = \mathbf{z}^{\mathrm{T}}\mathbf{u}, \tag{14.22}$$

where $\mathbf{u} = \mathbf{v}/(1+\rho)$.

14.4 The perturbation-regulated regressor (PRR) for errors-in-variables models

In standard regression analysis, the input is assumed to be perfectly measurable. For most real-life applications, however, some input measurement errors are inevitable. In order to arrive at a robust solution that is resilient with respect to such (input) measurement perturbation, we explore the adoption of the errors-in-variables model [86, 233], which has found broad applications, e.g. regression analysis, adaptive filtering, channel estimation, system identification, and supervised classification. For example, from the perspective of machine learning, in [18], the presence of input error is incorporated into the constraints of an SVM-type optimization formulation for improving the robustness of supervised classification.

As a new approach to regression analysis [145], the errors-in-variables model leads to a perturbation-regulated regressor (PRR) as illustrated by Figure 14.1(b). Given the perturbed input $\tilde{\mathbf{x}}$, the objective of the PRR is to find an optimal regressor $\hat{h}(\tilde{\mathbf{x}})$ to best estimate the output y.

14.4.1 MMSE solution for errors-in-variables models

This approach is based on the premise that the regressor's robustness could be enhanced by explicitly accounting for measurement errors in the independent variables. Given the complete statistics of $\tilde{\mathbf{x}}$ and y, the MMSE regressor aims to minimizes the following MSE:

$$L = E[||y - \hat{h}(\tilde{\mathbf{x}})||^2]. \tag{14.23}$$

The optimal regressor is represented by

$$\hat{h}(\tilde{\mathbf{x}}) = E[y|\tilde{\mathbf{x}}] = \int y p_{y|\tilde{\mathbf{x}}}(y|\tilde{\mathbf{x}}) dy. \tag{14.24}$$

From a projection perspective, see Figure 14.2(a), the MMSE regressor can be viewed as the projection of y onto the $\mathcal{L}^2(\tilde{\mathbf{x}})$ Hilbert space spanned by all (square-integrable) functions of $\tilde{\mathbf{x}}$. In this case, the Hilbert space is endowed with an inner product on $\mathcal{L}^2(\mathbf{x})$ defined as follows:

$$\langle f(\mathbf{x}, \tilde{\mathbf{x}}), g(\mathbf{x}, \tilde{\mathbf{x}}) \rangle = E[f(\mathbf{x}, \tilde{\mathbf{x}}) g(\mathbf{x}, \tilde{\mathbf{x}})].$$

From a computational perspective, the following parametric methods are worth considering.

- **Linear estimation.** An linear estimator has the simplest formulation

$$\hat{y} = \hat{h}_{\tilde{\mathbf{x}}}(\tilde{\mathbf{x}}) = \tilde{\mathbf{x}}^{\mathrm{T}} \mathbf{w}.$$

- **Kernel-based estimation.** Let $\{\tilde{z}_j(x), j = 1, \ldots, J\}$ denote a set of kernel-induced basis functions up to a pre-specified order. A kernel-based estimator can be expressed in terms of a linear combination of the set of kernel-induced basis functions:

$$\hat{y} = \sum_{j=1}^{J} u_j \tilde{z}_j(\mathbf{x}).$$

The corresponding kernel-induced basis vector is defined as

$$\tilde{\mathbf{z}} \equiv [\tilde{z}_1(x)\ \tilde{z}_2(x) \ldots \tilde{z}_J(x)]^{\mathrm{T}}. \tag{14.25}$$

Then

$$\hat{y} = \hat{h}_{\tilde{\mathbf{z}}}(\tilde{\mathbf{x}}) = \tilde{\mathbf{z}}^{\mathrm{T}} \mathbf{u}.$$

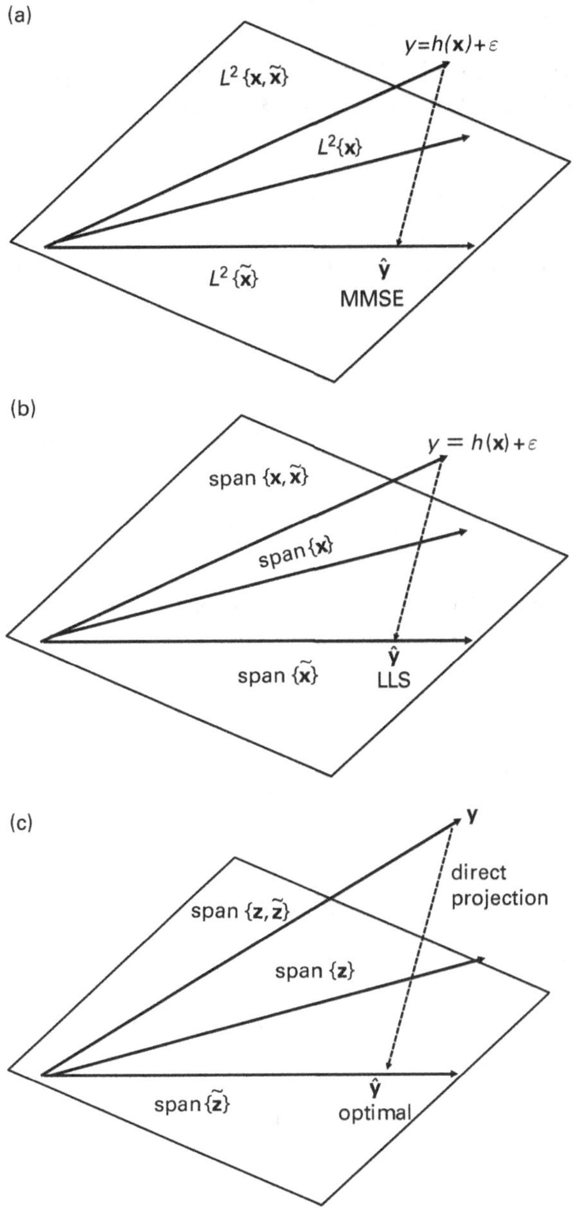

Fig. 14.2. (a) For the MMSE estimator, the optimal estimation is a projection to the Hilbert space $\mathcal{L}^2(\tilde{\mathbf{x}})$. (b) For the linear-least-MSE estimator, the optimal estimation is a projection to the linear span of $\tilde{\mathbf{x}}$, i.e. the estimation is now limited to a linear function of the variables of $\tilde{\mathbf{x}}$. (c) The PRR is the projection of the response y onto span$\{\tilde{\mathbf{z}}\}$. It represents a compromise between the non-parametric MMSE regressor and the linear-least-MSE regressor.

14.4.2 Linear perturbation-regulated regressors

Assume still that $E[\tilde{\mathbf{x}}] = 0$ and $E[y] = 0$. Given that only the second-order statistics on the independent and dependent variables (i.e. $\tilde{\mathbf{x}}$ and y) are available, the best linear PRR is

$$\hat{h}_{\tilde{\mathbf{x}}}(\tilde{\mathbf{x}}) = \tilde{\mathbf{x}}^{\mathrm{T}}\mathbf{w}, \quad \text{where} \quad \tilde{\mathbf{x}} = \mathbf{x} + \Delta_{\mathbf{x}}.$$

Following the same derivation as was used for Eq. (14.2), the optimal solution minimizing the MSE $E[||y - \tilde{\mathbf{x}}^{\mathrm{T}}\mathbf{w}||^2]$ can be derived as

$$\mathbf{w} = R_{\tilde{\mathbf{x}}}^{-1} R_{\tilde{\mathbf{x}}y}. \tag{14.26}$$

By employing a projection denotation, see Figure 14.2(b), the optimal regressor can be expressed as

$$\hat{y} = \hat{h}_{\tilde{\mathbf{x}}}(\tilde{\mathbf{x}}) = h(\mathbf{x})/\{\tilde{\mathbf{x}}\} = \tilde{\mathbf{x}}^{\mathrm{T}} R_{\tilde{\mathbf{x}}}^{-1} R_{\tilde{\mathbf{x}}y}, \tag{14.27}$$

where for notational convenience we denote $\{\tilde{\mathbf{x}}\} \equiv \mathrm{span}\{\tilde{\mathbf{x}}\}$ and the inner product adopted by the projection here is defined as

$$\langle f(\mathbf{x}, \tilde{\mathbf{x}}), g(\mathbf{x}, \tilde{\mathbf{x}}) \rangle = E[f(\mathbf{x}, \tilde{\mathbf{x}}) g(\mathbf{x}, \tilde{\mathbf{x}})].$$

Assuming that the input noise has zero mean and covariance matrix ρI and is statistically independent of the input (and thus of the output), $E[\mathbf{x}\Delta_{\mathbf{x}}] = 0$. It follows that

$$\begin{aligned} R_{\tilde{\mathbf{x}}} &= E[(\mathbf{x} + \Delta_{\mathbf{x}})(\mathbf{x} + \Delta_{\mathbf{x}})^{\mathrm{T}}] = E[\mathbf{x}\mathbf{x}^{\mathrm{T}}] + 2E[\mathbf{x}\Delta_{\mathbf{x}}^{\mathrm{T}}] + E[\Delta_{\mathbf{x}}\Delta_{\mathbf{x}}^{\mathrm{T}}] \\ &= R_{\mathbf{x}} + \rho\mathbf{I}. \end{aligned} \tag{14.28}$$

Moreover, because $\Delta_{\mathbf{x}}$ is independent of the input $\mathbf{x}$, it is also independent of the output y. It then follows that

$$R_{\tilde{\mathbf{x}}y} = E[\tilde{\mathbf{x}}y] = E[\mathbf{x}y + \Delta_{\mathbf{x}}y] = E[\mathbf{x}y] = R_{\mathbf{x}y}.$$

Thus we have

$$\mathbf{w} = R_{\tilde{\mathbf{x}}}^{-1} R_{\tilde{\mathbf{x}}y} = [R_{\mathbf{x}} + \rho\mathbf{I}]^{-1} R_{xy}, \tag{14.29}$$

i.e. it is identical to Eq. (14.4). Thus, the linear RR and PRR have exactly the same form.

From the perspective of practical applications, Eq. (14.4) for RR and Eq. (14.29) for PRR, while having the same form, have slightly different motivations. The former is meant to control the magnitude of the coefficients in the RR, whereas the latter considers the possible variation of the system environments between the training phase and the prediction phase. More exactly, in a somewhat controlled environment, it is plausible that perturbation-free input variables $\mathbf{x}$ may be acquired, leading to an estimation of a perturbation-free covariance matrix $R_{\mathbf{x}}$. However, in anticipating errors in variables during the testing phase, by modeling them as white noise with variance ρ, the PRRs opt to replace $R_{\mathbf{x}}$ by $R_{\mathbf{x}} + \mathbf{I}$ for the purpose of mitigating the effect of errors in variables and thus creating a more robust regressor.

14.4.3 Kernel-based perturbation-regulated regressors

Denote $\tilde{\mathbf{z}}$ as the kernel-induced basis vector of the perturbed input $\tilde{\mathbf{x}}$. A kernel-based regressor can be expressed in a "linearized" form:

$$\hat{y} = \hat{h}_{\tilde{\mathbf{z}}}(\tilde{\mathbf{x}}) = \tilde{\mathbf{z}}^{\mathrm{T}}\mathbf{u},$$

where $\mathbf{u} = [u_1, u_2, \ldots, u_J]^{\mathrm{T}}$. Following Eq. (14.27) and with reference to Figure 14.2(c), the PRR estimator is the projection of y onto span$\{\tilde{\mathbf{z}}\}$:

$$\hat{y}_{\mathrm{PRR}(p)} = y/\{\,\tilde{\mathbf{z}}\,\} = \tilde{\mathbf{z}}^{\mathrm{T}} R_{\tilde{\mathbf{z}}}^{-1} R_{\tilde{\mathbf{z}}y}. \tag{14.30}$$

Distinction between KRR and PRR

Note that PRR has a very distinctive formulation from KRR. This point is elaborated on here.

Under the assumption that $\mathbf{x}$ and $\Delta_{\mathbf{x}}$ are statistically independent, we have $E[\mathbf{x}\Delta_{\mathbf{x}}^{\mathrm{T}}] = 0$. It is also common to assume that the distribution of the noise $\Delta_{\mathbf{x}}$ is isotropic, i.e. its components along different feature coordinates (in the original Euclidean vector space) are of the same variance and mutually uncorrelated. From this it then follows that $R_{\tilde{\mathbf{x}}} = R_{\mathbf{x}} + \rho\mathbf{I}$. Consequently, we can conclude that the linear RR and PRR are identical.

However, the counterparts of RR and PRR in kernel space are no longer identical to each other even with the assumption that $\mathbf{x}$ and $\Delta_{\mathbf{x}}$ are independent and that $\Delta_{\mathbf{x}}$ is isotropic. Namely, $R_{\tilde{\mathbf{z}}} \neq R_{\mathbf{z}} + \rho\mathbf{I}$. Indeed, generally speaking, $\mathbf{z}$ and $\Delta_{\mathbf{z}}$ are correlated, as demonstrated by the example given below.

Example 14.2 (Correlation between $\mathbf{z}$ and $\Delta_{\mathbf{z}}$) *For notational simplicity, and without loss of generality, our discussion will be focused on one-dimensional input space, i.e.* $\mathbf{x} = x$. *In this case,* $\mathbf{z} = [1\ x\ x^2\ \ldots\ x^J]^{\mathrm{T}}$ *and* $\tilde{\mathbf{z}} = [1\ \tilde{x}\ \tilde{x}^2\ \ldots\ \tilde{x}^J]^{\mathrm{T}}$.

Assume that the original input and the perturbed input are respectively x *and* $\tilde{x} = x + \Delta x$. *Moreover, assume that* $x \in \mathcal{U}(-a, a)$ *and* $\Delta x \in \mathcal{U}(-\Delta a, \Delta a)$, *with both having a uniform distribution.*

Let $p = 3$. *Then* $J = p + 1 = 4$, *and*

$$\mathbf{z} = \begin{bmatrix} 1 \\ x \\ x^2 \\ x^3 \end{bmatrix} \quad \textit{and} \quad \tilde{\mathbf{z}} = \begin{bmatrix} 1 \\ x + \Delta x \\ (x + \Delta x)^2 \\ (x + \Delta x)^3 \end{bmatrix}$$

It follows that

$$\Delta_{\mathbf{z}} = \begin{bmatrix} 0 \\ \Delta x \\ 2x\Delta x + (\Delta x)^2 \\ 3x^2\Delta x + 3x(\Delta x)^2 + (\Delta x)^3 \end{bmatrix}$$

and

$$E\left[\Delta_{\mathbf{z}}\mathbf{z}^{\mathrm{T}}\right] = \begin{bmatrix} 0 & 0 & 0 & 0 \\ 0 & 0 & 0 & 0 \\ \rho & 0 & \rho E[x^2] & 0 \\ 0 & 3\rho E[x^2] & 0 & 3\rho E[x^4] \end{bmatrix}.$$

In conclusion, even though $\mathbf{x}$ and $\Delta_{\mathbf{x}}$ are statistically independent, their kernel-space counterparts $\mathbf{z}$ and $\Delta_{\mathbf{z}}$ will in general be correlated. This means that the simple formula in Eq. (14.28) will no longer apply to the kernel case. Consequently, PRR $\neq$ KRR in general. In fact, they play somewhat different roles in regularization.

14.5 The kernel-based perturbation-regulated regressor (PRR): Gaussian cases

In order to arrive at a simple derivation of the PRR solution, we need to make use of the orthogonal basis functions associated with the distribution of $\tilde{\mathbf{x}}$. We shall first focus our analysis on single-variate Gaussian-distributed data before extending the results to multivariate cases.

14.5.1 Orthonormal basis functions: single-variate cases

Assume that $x \sim \mathcal{N}(0, \sigma_x^2)$, $\Delta_x \sim \mathcal{N}(0, \sigma_{\Delta_x})$, and $\eta \equiv \sigma_{\Delta_x}/\sigma_x$. Two useful relationships of Hermite orthogonal polynomials are as follows:

- $\partial \mathrm{He}_n(x)/\partial x = n\,\mathrm{He}_{n-1}(x)$ and

$$\mathrm{He}_{n+1}(x) = x\,\mathrm{He}_n(x) - n\,\mathrm{He}_{n-1}(x). \tag{14.31}$$

The auto-orthogonality property: single-variate cases

It can be verified that also the perturbed input variable has a Gaussian distribution:

$$\tilde{x} \sim \mathcal{N}\big(\,0, (1+\eta)\sigma_x^2\,\big).$$

Moreover, the orthogonal polynomials associated with $\tilde{x}$ are the following (modified) Hermite polynomials:

$$\left\{ \tilde{z}_n(\tilde{x}) = \tilde{\psi}_n(\tilde{x}) = \frac{1}{\sqrt{n!}}\,\mathrm{He}_n\left(\frac{\tilde{x}}{\sigma_x\sqrt{1+\eta}}\right), 0 \le n \le p \right\}. \tag{14.32}$$

The following auto-orthogonality always holds:

$$E[\tilde{\psi}_m(\tilde{x})\tilde{\psi}_n(\tilde{x})] = \delta(m-n), \tag{14.33}$$

which effectively whitens the covariance matrix of $\tilde{\mathbf{z}}$, i.e.

$$R_{\tilde{\mathbf{z}}} = \mathbf{I}. \tag{14.34}$$

The cross-orthogonality property: single-variate cases

It can be shown that the two sets of orthonormal basis functions, one for x and the other for $\tilde{x}$, have a vital cross-orthogonality property as stated in the following theorem [145].

THEOREM 14.3 (Cross-orthogonality theorem: single-variate cases) *Under the assumption of Gaussian distributions, the following cross-orthogonality always holds true for two normalized orthogonal polynomials, one for x and the other for $\tilde{x}$:*

$$E[\tilde{\psi}_m(\tilde{x})\psi_n(x)] = \lambda_n\delta(m-n), \tag{14.35}$$

where

$$\lambda_n = \left(\frac{1}{\sqrt{1+\eta}}\right)^n. \qquad \square$$

Proof. First, note that the equality obviously holds if either $m = 0$ or $n = 0$. Moreover, note that $E[\tilde{\psi}_0(\tilde{x})\psi_0(x)] = 1$. Then we shall establish below the following equality:

$$E[\psi_{m+1}(x)\tilde{\psi}_{n+1}(\tilde{x})] = \frac{\sqrt{n+1}}{\sqrt{m+1}\sqrt{1+\eta}}E[\psi_m(x)\tilde{\psi}_n(\tilde{x})],$$
$$m = 0, 1, \ldots, n = 0, 1, \ldots. \tag{14.36}$$

The cross-orthogonality in Eq. (14.35) can be established by applying induction using Eq. (14.36). (The proof of Eq. (14.36) will be detailed in Problem 14.9.)

14.5.2 Single-variate Hermite estimators

A direct consequence of the cross-orthogonality property arises if the regression function happens to be an orthogonal polynomial associated with x, say, $h(x) = \psi_n(x)$. In this case, according to the MSE criterion in Eq. (14.23), we aim at minimizing

$$L = E[||\psi_n(x) - \hat{h}(\tilde{x})||^2]. \tag{14.37}$$

Let $\hat{h}(\tilde{x}) = \sum_{m=0}^{\infty}\hat{h}_m\tilde{\psi}_m(\tilde{x})$ and substitute it into Eq. (14.37). Then we arrive at (see Eq. (14.35))

$$\begin{aligned}
L &= E[||\psi_n(x) - \hat{h}(\tilde{x})||^2] \\
&= E[\psi_n(x)^2] + \sum_{m=0}^{\infty}\hat{h}_m^2E[\tilde{\psi}_m(\tilde{x})^2 - 2\sum_{m=0}^{\infty}\hat{h}_mE[\psi_n(x)\tilde{\psi}_m(\tilde{x})] \\
&= 1 + \sum_{m=0}^{\infty}\hat{h}_m^2 - 2\left(\frac{1}{\sqrt{1+\eta}}\right)^n\hat{h}_n,
\end{aligned}$$

which has a minimum when

$$\hat{h}_m = \left(\frac{1}{\sqrt{1+\eta}}\right)^n \delta(m-n).$$

This, combined with Eq. (14.35), leads to a closed-form MMSE estimation given $\tilde{x}$:

$$E[\psi_n(x)|\tilde{x}] = \left(\frac{1}{\sqrt{1+\eta}}\right)^n \tilde{\psi}_n(\tilde{x}). \tag{14.38}$$

Equivalently, we have

$$E\left[\mathrm{He}_n\left(\frac{x}{\sigma_x}\right)|\tilde{x}\right] = \left(\frac{1}{\sqrt{1+\eta}}\right)^n \mathrm{He}_n\left(\frac{\tilde{x}}{\sigma_x\sqrt{1+\eta}}\right). \tag{14.39}$$

In our subsequent discussion, this result will be referred to as the *Hermite estimator.*

Hermite estimator for a high-order Gaussian distribution

For any regression function $h(x)$ represented by Eq. (14.10), one can apply the linear superposition principle to arrive at Eq. (14.40), i.e.

$$\hat{y}_{\mathrm{MMSE}} = E[y|\tilde{x}] = E[h(\mathbf{x})+\varepsilon|\tilde{x}] = E[h(\mathbf{x})|\tilde{x}] \overset{\text{Eq. (14.39)}}{=} \sum_{n=0}^{\infty}\left(\frac{1}{\sqrt{1+\eta}}\right)^n \gamma_n\tilde{\psi}_n(\tilde{x}). \tag{14.40}$$

A PRR of finite order p is restricted to a linear combination of $p+1$ basis functions $\{\tilde{\psi}_n(\tilde{x}), n = 0, 1, \ldots, p.\}$

The single-variate Hermite estimator and error analysis

The following theorem states the formulation of the single-variate Hermite estimation and the associated error analysis in closed form.

THEOREM 14.4 (Single-variate Hermite estimator and error analysis) *Let the output response to a regression model $h(\mathbf{x})$ be $y = h(\mathbf{x})+\varepsilon$, where ε is the independent additive noise. Let us denote*

$$\mathbf{z}' \equiv [\psi_0(x)\ \psi_1(x)\ \ldots\ \psi_p(x)],$$

and

$$\tilde{\mathbf{z}}' \equiv [\tilde{\psi}_0(x)\ \tilde{\psi}_1(x)\ \ldots\ \tilde{\psi}_p(x)],$$

where $\{\psi_n(x), n = 0, 1, \ldots, p\}$ and $\{\tilde{\psi}_n(x), n = 0, 1, \ldots, p\}$ are the Hermite polynomials associated with x and $\tilde{x}$, respectively.

Assume that $h(\mathbf{x})$ is of qth order, say

$$h(\mathbf{x}) = \sum_{n=0}^{q}\gamma_n\psi_n(\mathbf{x}),$$

where q may be finite or indefinite. In vector form,

$$h(x) = \sum_{n=0}^{p} \gamma_n \psi_n(\mathbf{x}) + \sum_{n=p+1}^{q} \gamma_n \psi_n(\mathbf{x}) \equiv \mathbf{z}'^{\mathrm{T}}\mathbf{v} + \Delta_h(x),$$

where $\mathbf{v} \equiv [\gamma_0 \gamma_1 \ldots \gamma_p]^{\mathrm{T}}$.

(i) *The single-variate PRR estimator of finite order p is*

$$\hat{y}_{\mathrm{PRR}(p)} = \tilde{\mathbf{z}}'^{\mathrm{T}}\mathbf{u}'_{\mathrm{PRR}} \quad \textit{with} \quad \mathbf{u}'_{\mathrm{PRR}} = \Lambda\mathbf{v}'. \tag{14.41}$$

More explicitly, Λ *is a diagonal matrix such that*

$$\hat{y}_{\mathrm{PRR}(p)} = \sum_{n=0}^{p} \left(\frac{1}{\sqrt{1+\eta}}\right)^{n} \gamma_n \tilde{\psi}_n(\tilde{x}). \tag{14.42}$$

(ii) *The total MSE associated with the regressor* $\hat{y}_{\mathrm{PRR}(p)}$ *is*

$$MSE_{\mathrm{PRR}(p)} = E[||\epsilon||^2] = \sigma_\varepsilon^2 + \sum_{n=p+1}^{q} \gamma_n^2 + \sum_{n=0}^{p}\left(1 - \left(\frac{1}{1+\eta}\right)^{n}\right)\gamma_n^2. \tag{14.43}$$

□

Proof. Equation (14.42) is a direct consequence of the Hermite Estimator given in Eq. (14.39). (This result may alternatively be established by following the procedure detailed in Problem 14.8.)

The total estimation error associated with the regressor $\hat{y}_{\mathrm{PRR}(p)}$ can be decomposed into three orthogonal components:

$$\epsilon = \varepsilon + \Delta_h(\mathbf{x}) + \left(\hat{h}_{\mathbf{z}}(\mathbf{x}) - \hat{h}_{\tilde{\mathbf{z}}}(\tilde{\mathbf{x}})\right).$$

Under the Gaussian assumption, the last of the three terms (which is induced exclusively by the input perturbation) is merely the sum of MSEs incurred by individual Hermite estimators:

$$\sum_{n=0}^{p}\left(1 - \left(\frac{1}{1+\eta}\right)^{n}\right)\gamma_n^2, \tag{14.44}$$

where γ_n^2 is the signal power of the nth component. It follows that

$$\mathrm{MSE}_{\mathrm{PRR}(p)} = E[||\epsilon\ ||^2] = \sigma_\varepsilon^2 + \sum_{n=p+1}^{q} \gamma_n^2 + \sum_{n=0}^{p}\left(1 - \left(\frac{1}{1+\eta}\right)^{n}\right)\gamma_n^2. \tag{14.45}$$

14.5.3 Error–order tradeoff

Since $h(x)$ has an infinite order,

$$\mathrm{MSE}_{\mathrm{MMSE}} = \sigma_\varepsilon^2 + \sum_{n=0}^{\infty}\left(1 - \left(\frac{1}{1+\eta}\right)^{n}\right)\gamma_n^2.$$

According to Eq. (14.43), a pth order PRR will suffer from some extra loss in MSE:

$$L_{\text{extra}} = \text{MSE}_{\text{PRR(p)}} - \text{MSE}_{\text{MMSE}} = \sum_{n=p+1}^{\infty} \left(\frac{1}{1+\eta}\right)^n \gamma_n^2. \quad (14.46)$$

Necessary and sufficient regressor order for optimal estimation

Suppose that a *dependent* variable y is a nonlinear regressor function of an *independent* variable $\mathbf{x}$ corrupted by a statistically independent noise term, i.e.

$$y = h(\mathbf{x}) + \varepsilon.$$

In this section, we shall assume that, although $\mathbf{x}$ is unknown, $\tilde{\mathbf{x}} = \mathbf{x} + \Delta_{\mathbf{x}}$ is measurable. We shall also assume that, although $h(\mathbf{x})$ is unknown, its order q can be assumed to be known.

Both MMSE and PRR estimators involve the optimal estimation of a *dependent* variable y that is based on $\tilde{\mathbf{x}}$. The non-parametric MMSE estimator

$$\hat{h}(\tilde{\mathbf{x}}) = E[y|\tilde{\mathbf{x}}] = \int y p_{y|\tilde{\mathbf{x}}}(y|\tilde{\mathbf{x}}) dy$$

provides an optimal solution that minimizes the MSE

$$E[||y - \hat{h}(\tilde{\mathbf{x}})||^2].$$

When the regressor order $p \to \infty$, it is known that

$$\lim_{p\to\infty} \hat{y}_{\text{PRR}(p)} = \hat{y}_{\text{MMSE}}. \quad (14.47)$$

Now let us propose a slightly different question, namely, given a finite regression order q, what is the necessary and sufficient regressor order of PRR, say p, that may result in a globally optimal MSE? Assuming that $\mathbf{x}$ and $\Delta_{\mathbf{x}}$ are both Gaussian distributed, it can be shown that $\hat{y}_{\text{PRR}(q)}$ will already be sufficient to yield an optimal estimation. Namely, the qth-order PRR estimator is equivalent to the MMSE estimator, i.e.

$$\hat{y}_{\text{PRR}(q)} = \hat{y}_{\text{MMSE}}. \quad (14.48)$$

The proof is very brief. When the regression model is of qth order, $\gamma_n = 0$ for any integer $n > q$, which further implies that Eq. (14.40) is equivalent to Eq. (14.42) if the full order is used, i.e. with $p = q$. Although the general claim as given in Eq. (14.48) is relatively novel, two special cases (for $q = 1$ and $q = 2$) have long been quite well known.

- **When $q = 1$.** Since the independent variable $\mathbf{x}$ and the additive output noise ε are both Gaussian distributed and the regression model itself is linear, the dependent variable y must also be Gaussian distributed. This amounts to the classical knowledge, in linear estimation theory [120], that the optimal linear estimator $\hat{y} = \mathbf{w}^{\mathrm{T}}\tilde{\mathbf{x}}$ is itself an optimal estimator.

- **When** $q = 2$. Note that the independent variable $\mathbf{x}$ and the additive output noise ε are both Gaussian distributed. Because the regression model is now of second order, its response y can be said to be second-order Gaussian-distributed. (By the same token, if the regression model is of qth order, the corresponding response y will be considered to be qth-order Gaussian-distributed.) As shown by Griliches and Ringstad [86], the optimal second-order PRR estimator $\hat{y} = \mathbf{u}^{\mathrm{T}}\tilde{\mathbf{z}}$, with $\tilde{\mathbf{z}}$ being formed by all the first- and second-order polynomial basis functions of $\tilde{\mathbf{x}}$, is already sufficient to yield the same minimum MSE as that achieved by the MMSE estimator. Namely, $\hat{y}_{\mathrm{PRR}(2)} = \hat{y}_{\mathrm{MMSE}}$.

Note that, if either $\mathbf{x}$ or $\Delta_{\mathbf{x}}$ has a non-Gaussian distribution, then the response y will no longer be qth-order Gaussian-distributed. In this case, the equality in Eq. (14.48) will no longer hold. The following is a simple example to demonstrate such a discrepancy between a Gaussian and a non-Gaussian distribution.

Example 14.3 *Assume that the input is a scalar, i.e.* $\mathbf{x} = x$, *the output is* $y = h(x) = \alpha x$, *and the perturbed input is* $\tilde{x} = x + \Delta x$.

(a) **Gaussian distribution.** *It is well known that, if both* x *and* Δx *have Gaussian distributions, then the optimal MMSE estimator,* $E[y|\tilde{x}]$, *is linear. (This can be viewed as a special case of Eq. (14.48).)*

(b) **Non-Gaussian distribution.** *Let us now assume unform distributions,* $x \in \mathcal{U}(-1, 1)$ *and* $\Delta x \in \mathcal{U}(-\delta, \delta)$, $\delta \leq 1$. *On substituting* $y = x$ *into Eq. (14.24), we obtain*

$$E[x|\tilde{x}] = \begin{cases} \frac{1}{2}(\tilde{x} - 1 + \delta), & \text{if } \tilde{x} < -1 + \delta \\ \tilde{x}, & \text{if } -1 + \delta \leq \tilde{x} \leq 1 - \delta \\ \frac{1}{2}(\tilde{x} + 1 - \delta), & \text{if } \tilde{x} > 1 - \delta. \end{cases} \tag{14.49}$$

Hence the optimal MMSE estimator is $E[y|\tilde{x}] = \alpha E[x|\tilde{x}]$, *which is obviously a nonlinear function of* x. *Hence, Eq. (14.48) has been proven invalid.*

14.5.4 Simulation results

For quantitative comparison, the regression ratios with respect to different values of the polynomial order p and regularization factor ρ are shown in Figure 14.3.

- Note that KRR fails to treat low-order and high-order models differentially since it imposes identical regression ratios, $1/(1 + \rho)$, on all the terms across the board, be they of low order or high. In other words, for KRR, orthogonal polynomials of any order will have exactly the same regression ratio as the first-order polynomial.
- In contrast, the higher-order terms will have relatively lower regression ratios, i.e. $(1/\sqrt{1 + \eta})^n$ in Eq. (14.39), implying that lower-order terms are suppressed less while higher-order terms are suppressed more.

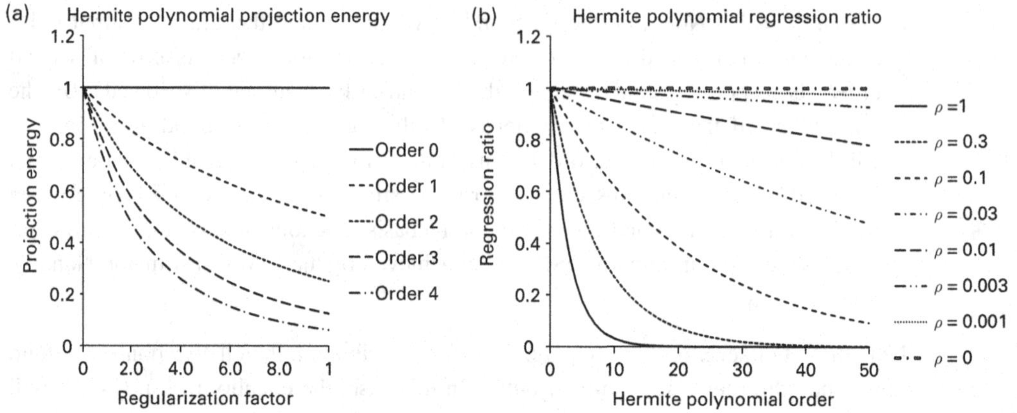

Fig. 14.3. This figure shows that higher-order polynomial functions will have higher regression ratios. (a) Plots of regression ratios with respect to the regularization factor ρ; here curves for different orders p are plotted separately. (b) Plots of regression ratios with respect to the polynomial order p, here curves for different values of the regularization factor ρ are plotted separately.

There is a greater need to smoothe the higher-order terms since they are more likely to be associated with noise. PRR can effectively rectify this problem and provide greater smoothing capability. PRR can effectively achieve the wanted regularization effect insofar as it suppresses more the high-order terms which tend to reflect the noise-like fluctuation of the observed signals. It is advantageous for enhancing the robustness of regressors or classifiers in applications with noisy environments.

To better illustrate how the PR analysis (and the two-projection theorem) may be applied, let us now look at a regression model: $y = h(x) + \epsilon = 1/(1 - x + x^2) + \varepsilon$, where ε has zero mean and the variance is $\sigma_\varepsilon^2 = 0.0073$. Moreover, $\mathbf{x}$ and Δ_{x} are Gaussian distributed with zero mean and variances 1 and η, respectively. All the following simulation studies are based on a total of $N = 10{,}000$ samples.

Let us now explore numerically how much extra loss there is for a finite-order PRR regressor. Figure 14.4(a) summarizes the order–error tradeoff in terms of Eq. (14.44). First, we assume that 1% of extra loss is deemed tolerable. More exactly, $\mathrm{MSE}_{\mathrm{PRR}(p)} = 1.01 \times \mathrm{MSE}_{\mathrm{MMSE}}$, which means $L_{\mathrm{extra}} = 1.21 \times 10^{-3}, 4.16 \times 10^{-4}, 1.17 \times 10^{-4}$, and 7.78×10^{-5} for $\eta = 1, 0.1, 0.01$, and 0.001, respectively. Exactly as predicted previously in Eq. (14.46), the minimum required orders are 3, 13, 26, and 30, respectively. (See the "×"s in Figure 14.4.) However, if 5% extra loss is deemed acceptable, then $L_{\mathrm{extra}} = 6.04 \times 10^{-3}, 2.08 \times 10^{-3}, 5.85 \times 10^{-4}$, and 3.89×10^{-4}, and the orders may be further reduced to 2, 9, 17, and 21, respectively. (See the "•"s in Figure 14.4.)

Performance comparison of KRR and PRR

Figure 14.4(b) compares $\mathrm{MSE}_{\mathrm{MMSE}}$ (Eq. (14.24)), $\mathrm{MSE}_{\mathrm{KRR}(p)}$ (Eq. (14.7)), and $\mathrm{MSE}_{\mathrm{PRR}(p)}$ (Eq. (14.42)). Note that $\mathrm{MSE}_{\mathrm{PRR(p)}}$ obtained in simulation matches very closely the theoretical prediction; consequently, the two curves almost overlap. The two dashed horizontal lines are explained as follows.

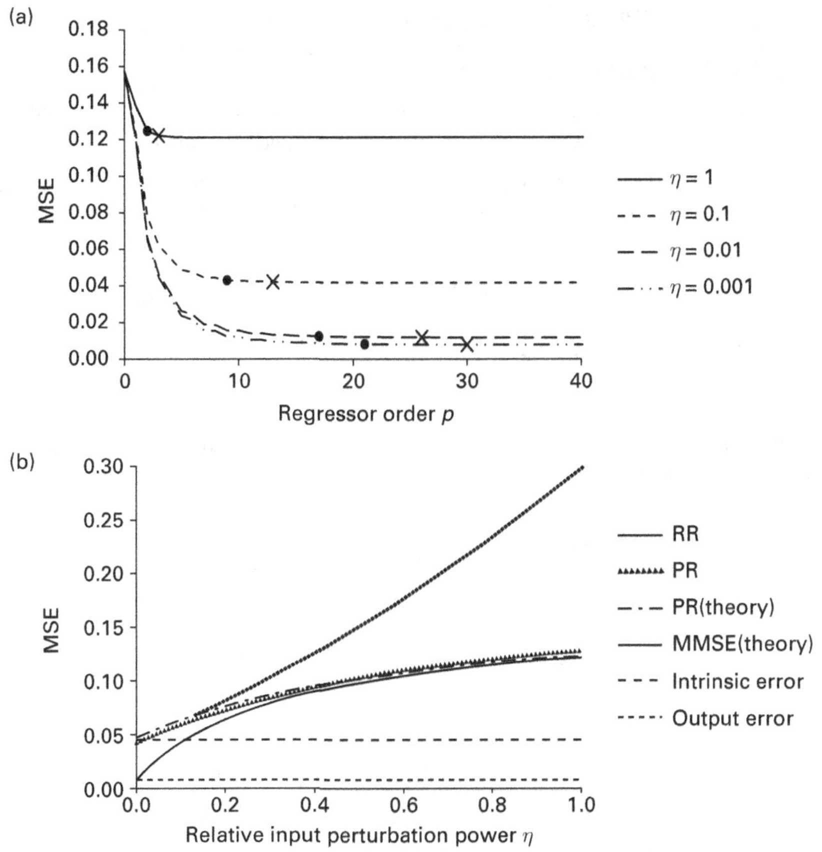

Fig. 14.4. (a) An illustration of order–error tradeoffs. The minimum required orders are labeled as "×" and "•" respectively for 1% and 5% error tolerance. (b) A performance comparison of MMSE, third-order PR, and third-order RR regressors. At the rightmost end in (b), the gap between PR and MMSE is within 1% when $\eta = 1$. This is confirmed in (a), where the leftmost "×" for $\eta = 1$ also suggests that the order $p = 3$ is sufficient for 1% tolerance.

- The lower dashed line reflects the power level of the output noise.
- The upper dashed line reflects (the power level of) the sum of the output noise and model-induced error.

Obviously, they are unaffected by the change of η. Most importantly, the following apply.

- $\text{MSE}_{\text{KRR}(p)}$ is greater than $\text{MSE}_{\text{PRR}(p)}$ which, in turn, is greater than the MSE_{MMSE}. As predicted by Eq. (14.46), $L_{\text{extra}} = \text{MSE}_{\text{PRR}(p)} - \text{MSE}_{\text{MMSE}}$ decreases rather rapidly w.r.t. η. In fact, when η increases the simulation suggests that $\text{MSE}_{\text{PRR}(p)}$ approaches MSE_{MMSE} (even with the regressor's order being as low as $p = 3$), while $\text{MSE}_{\text{KRR}}(p)$ suffers an increasing loss.
- The difference between $\text{MSE}_{\text{KRR}}(p)$ and $\text{MSE}_{\text{PRR}(p)}$ increases drastically w.r.t. η. This highlights the fact that PRR has a greater smoothing capability than KRR, especially when η is relatively large.

14.5.5 Multivariate PRR estimators: Gaussian distribution

14.5.5.1 Multivariate orthonormal basis functions

Assume a multivariate Gaussian-distributed input $\mathbf{x} \sim \mathcal{N}(0, R_{\mathbf{x}})$ and perturbation $\Delta_{\mathbf{x}} \sim \mathcal{N}(0, R_{\Delta_{\mathbf{x}}})$, with $\mathbf{x}$ and $\Delta_{\mathbf{x}}$ being independent, and let $R_{\mathbf{x}} = R_{\mathbf{x}}^{1/2} R_{\mathbf{x}}^{\mathrm{T}/2}$. Now we apply SVD to obtain $R_{\mathbf{x}}^{-1/2} R_{\Delta_{\mathbf{x}}} R_{\mathbf{x}}^{-\mathrm{T}/2} = \mathbf{PDP}^{\mathrm{T}}$, where $\mathbf{D} = \mathrm{Diag}\{\eta_1, \eta_2, \ldots, \eta_M\}$. To simultaneously whiten both the input $\mathbf{x}$ and the perturbation $\Delta_{\mathbf{x}}$, let us apply the transformation

$$\mathbf{x}' = \mathbf{P}^{\mathrm{T}} R_{\mathbf{x}}^{-1/2} \mathbf{x}, \qquad \Delta_{\mathbf{x}'} = \mathbf{P}^{\mathrm{T}} R_{\mathbf{x}}^{-1/2} \Delta_{\mathbf{x}},$$

resulting in $\mathbf{x}' \sim \mathcal{N}(\mathbf{0}, I)$, $\Delta_{\mathbf{x}'} \sim \mathcal{N}(\mathbf{0}, \mathbf{D})$, and $\tilde{\mathbf{x}}' \sim \mathcal{N}(\mathbf{0}, \mathbf{I} + \mathbf{D})$.

Example 14.4 *Consider the variable* $\mathbf{x}$ *with the same distribution as in Example 14.1, i.e.* $\mathbf{x} \sim \mathcal{N}(\mathbf{0}, \Sigma_{\mathbf{x}})$, *and* $\Delta\mathbf{x} \sim \mathcal{N}(\mathbf{0}, \Sigma_{\Delta\mathbf{x}})$, *where*

$$\boldsymbol{\Sigma}_{\mathbf{x}} = \begin{pmatrix} 2.5 & 1.5 \\ 1.5 & 2.5 \end{pmatrix}, \qquad \Sigma_{\Delta_{\mathbf{x}}} = \begin{pmatrix} 0.475 & 0.345 \\ 0.345 & 0.419 \end{pmatrix}.$$

We have

$$H = \boldsymbol{\Sigma}_{\mathbf{x}}^{-1/2} \boldsymbol{\Sigma}_{\Delta_{\mathbf{x}}} \Sigma_{\mathbf{x}}^{-1/2} = \begin{pmatrix} 0.164 & 0.048 \\ 0.048 & 0.136 \end{pmatrix} = \mathrm{PDP}^{\mathrm{T}},$$

where

$$\mathbf{P} = \begin{pmatrix} 0.8 & -0.6 \\ 0.6 & 0.8 \end{pmatrix}, \qquad \mathbf{D} = \begin{pmatrix} 0.2 & 0 \\ 0 & 0.1 \end{pmatrix}.$$

In this case, the orthonormal basis on $\tilde{\mathbf{x}}$ *is*

$$\begin{aligned}
\tilde{\psi}_{m,n}(\tilde{\mathbf{x}}) &= \frac{1}{\sqrt{m!}} \frac{1}{\sqrt{n!}} \mathrm{He}_{m,n}\left((\mathrm{I} + \mathrm{D})^{-1/2} \mathbf{P}^{\mathrm{T}} \Sigma_{\tilde{\mathbf{x}}}^{-1/2} \tilde{\mathbf{x}} \right) \\
&= \frac{1}{\sqrt{m!}} \frac{1}{\sqrt{n!}} \mathrm{He}_{m,n}\left(\begin{pmatrix} 0.45/\sqrt{1+0.2} & 0.25/\sqrt{1+0.2} \\ -0.65/\sqrt{1+0.1} & 0.75/\sqrt{1+0.1} \end{pmatrix} \tilde{\mathbf{x}} \right) \\
&= \frac{1}{\sqrt{m!}} \frac{1}{\sqrt{n!}} \mathrm{He}_{m}\left(\frac{0.45\tilde{x}_1 + 0.25\tilde{x}_2}{\sqrt{1.2}} \right) \mathrm{He}_{n}\left(\frac{-0.65\tilde{x}_1 + 0.75\tilde{x}_2}{\sqrt{1.1}} \right).
\end{aligned}$$

They are related by

$$E[\psi_{m,n}(\mathbf{x})|\tilde{\mathbf{x}}] = \left(\frac{1}{\sqrt{1.2}} \right)^m \left(\frac{1}{\sqrt{1.1}} \right)^n \tilde{\psi}_{m,n}(\tilde{\mathbf{x}}). \tag{14.50}$$

14.5.5.2 Multivariate Hermite estimators

Let $\mathrm{He}_{\mathbf{n}}(\mathbf{x}') = \prod_{i=1}^{M} \mathrm{He}_{n_i}(x_i')$ be the multivariate Hermite polynomial functions. It can be shown that

$$E[\mathrm{He}_{\mathbf{n}}(\mathbf{x}')|\tilde{\mathbf{x}}'] = \left(\prod_{i=1}^{M} \left(\frac{1}{\sqrt{1+\eta_i}} \right)^{n_i} \right) \mathrm{He}_{\mathbf{n}}((\mathbf{I} + \mathbf{D})^{-1/2} \tilde{\mathbf{x}}'). \tag{14.51}$$

This leads to a new set of orthonormal basis functions:

$$\left\{ \tilde{\psi}_{\mathbf{n}}(\tilde{\mathbf{x}}) = \prod_{i=1}^{M} \frac{1}{\sqrt{n_i!}} \mathrm{He}_{n_i}\left(\frac{\tilde{x}'_i}{\sqrt{1+\eta_i}}\right), \ 0 \le \sum_{i=1}^{M} n_i \le p \right\}. \tag{14.52}$$

Just like its single-variate counterpart, the multivariate Hermite polynomial again possesses the vital orthogonality and cross-orthogonality properties. Namely,

$$E[|\hat{h}_{\mathbf{z}}(\mathbf{x})|^2] = \sum_{\mathbf{n}\in\mathbb{N}^M} \gamma_{\mathbf{n}}^2$$

and

$$E[|\hat{h}_{\tilde{\mathbf{z}}}(\tilde{\mathbf{x}})|^2] = \sum_{\mathbf{n}\in\mathbb{N}^M} \tilde{\gamma}_{\mathbf{n}}^2,$$

where

$$\tilde{\gamma}_{\mathbf{n}} \equiv \prod_{i=1}^{M} \left(\frac{1}{\sqrt{1+\eta_i}}\right)^{n_i} \gamma_{\mathbf{n}}.$$

This will be instrumental for order–error tradeoff in multivariate applications.

The cross-orthogonality property: multivariate cases

It can be shown that the cross-orthogonality for single-variate cases may be easily extended to multivariate cases. (The detailed proof is omitted.)

THEOREM 14.5 (Cross-orthogonality theorem: multivariate cases) *Under the assumption of Gaussian distributions, the following cross-orthogonality always holds for two normalized orthogonal polynomials, one for the vector variable* $\mathbf{x}$ *and the other for its disturbed variant* $\tilde{\mathbf{x}}$*:*

$$E[\tilde{\psi}_{\mathbf{m}}(\tilde{\mathbf{x}})\psi_{\mathbf{n}}(\mathbf{x})] = \lambda_{\mathbf{n}}\delta(\mathbf{m}-\mathbf{n}), \tag{14.53}$$

where

$$\lambda_{\mathbf{n}} = \prod_{i=1}^{M} \left(\frac{1}{\sqrt{1+\eta_i}}\right)^{n_i}.$$

□

14.5.5.3 The Hermite estimator and error–order tradeoff analysis

The following theorem states the formulation of the multivariate Hermite estimation and the associated error analysis in closed form.

THEOREM 14.6 (Multivariate Hermite estimator and error analysis) *Let the output response to a regression model* $h(\mathbf{x})$ *be* $y = h(\mathbf{x}) + \varepsilon$*, where* ε *is the independent additive noise. Assume that* $h(\mathbf{x})$ *is of qth order, say*

$$h(\mathbf{x}) = \sum_{\mathbf{n}\in\mathcal{S}_q} \gamma_{\mathbf{n}}\psi_{\mathbf{n}}(\mathbf{x}),$$

where q may be finite or infinite, $h(\mathbf{x}) \in \mathcal{L}^2(\mathbf{x})$*, and* $\mathbf{n} = [n_1 \ \ldots \ n_M]^{\mathrm{T}}$ *denotes the vector of non-negative integer indices with*

$$\mathcal{S}_q = \left\{ \mathbf{n} \in \mathbb{N}^M, 0 \leq \sum_{i=1}^{M} n_d \leq q \right\}.$$

Then the optimal PRR regressor of finite order p is just a simple extension of the single-variate estimator given in Eq. (14.42):

$$\hat{y}_{\mathrm{PRR}(p)} = \sum_{\mathbf{n} \in \mathcal{S}_p} \prod_{d=1}^{M} \left(\frac{1}{\sqrt{1+\eta_d}} \right)^{n_d} \gamma_{\mathbf{n}} \tilde{\psi}_{\mathbf{n}}(\tilde{\mathbf{x}}),$$

where

$$\mathcal{S}_p = \left\{ \mathbf{n} \in \mathbb{N}^M, 0 \leq \sum_{i=1}^{M} n_d \leq p \right\}.$$

The total MSE of PRR is a simple extension of the single-variate error analysis given in Eq. (14.43). Let $\mathcal{S}_q/\mathcal{S}_p$ *denote the remaining subset of* $\mathcal{S}_q$ *after the removal of* $\mathcal{S}_p$*, then*

$$\mathrm{MSE}_{\mathrm{PRR}(p)} = \sigma_\varepsilon^2 + \sum_{\mathbf{n} \in \mathcal{S}_q/\mathcal{S}_p} \gamma_{\mathbf{n}}^2 + \sum_{\mathbf{n} \in \mathcal{S}_p} \left(1 - \prod_{d=1}^{M} \left(\frac{1}{1+\eta_d} \right)^{n_d} \right) \gamma_{\mathbf{n}}^2. \qquad \square$$

Proof. The derivation of the formula for the multivariate PRR estimator and the MSE error will be omitted. Regarding the order–error tradeoff, we note that

$$\mathrm{MSE}_{\mathrm{MMSE}} = \sigma_\varepsilon^2 + \sum_{\mathbf{n} \in \mathcal{S}_q} \left(1 - \prod_{d=1}^{M} \left(\frac{1}{1+\eta_d} \right)^{n_d} \right) \gamma_{\mathbf{n}}^2,$$

Therefore, the extra MSE due to the input perturbation is merely the sum of MSEs incurred by individual Hermite estimators:

$$L_{\mathrm{extra}} = \mathrm{MSE}_{\mathrm{PRR}(p)} - \mathrm{MSE}_{\mathrm{MMSE}} = \sum_{\mathbf{n} \in \mathcal{S}_q/\mathcal{S}_p} \left(\prod_{d=1}^{M} \left(\frac{1}{1+\eta_d} \right)^{n_d} \right) \gamma_{\mathbf{n}}.$$

14.6 Two-projection theorems

The development of a *two-projection theorem* for PRR estimation is motivated by the potential benefit to be gained by dividing the estimation into two stages: (1) in the first stage, we shall perform estimation (i.e. projection) assuming the absence of any input perturbation; and (2) in the second stage, the effect of input perturbation will be taken into account. For the first stage, the conventional linear estimation theory proves to be adequate. For the second stage, some new theory will be needed in order to take into account the joint statistical property of the unperturbed and perturbed input variables.

For the estimation to be cleanly divisible into two stages, there are necessary and sufficient conditions. Note that the two-projection property may hold both for

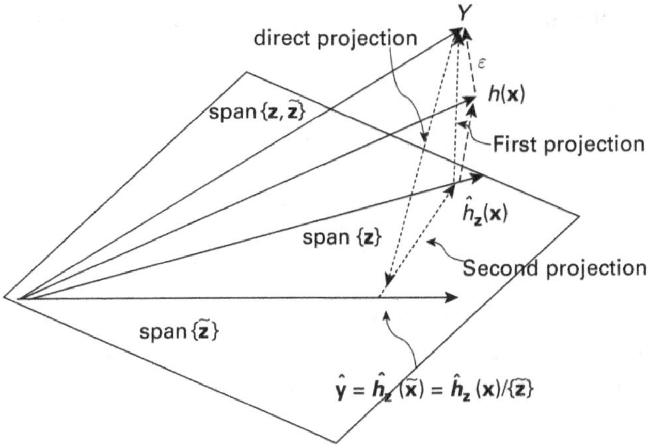

Fig. 14.5. Two equivalent ways to obtain the kernel-based PRR. (1) By indirect projection (i.e. two-projection): the response y is first projected to span$\{\mathbf{z}\}$, resulting in $\hat{h}_{\mathbf{z}}(\mathbf{x})$, which will subsequently be projected onto span$\{\tilde{\mathbf{z}}\}$, i.e. $(h(\mathbf{x})/\{\mathbf{z}\})\,/\{\tilde{\mathbf{z}}\}$. (2) An identical result may be obtained by directly projecting the response y onto span$\{\tilde{\mathbf{z}}\}$, i.e. $\hat{h}_{\tilde{\mathbf{z}}}(\tilde{\mathbf{x}})$.

Gaussian- and for non-Gaussian-distributed variables. Moreover, it need not be limited strictly to polynomial kernels. Sometimes, it may even be possible to relax the popular assumption on the statistical independence of $\mathbf{x}$ and $\Delta_{\mathbf{x}}$.

Section 14.6.1 provides a general theory on the necessary and sufficient condition of the validity of the *two-projection* property. A formal statement is summarized in Theorem 14.7. For polynomial kernels, Section 14.6.2 focuses on the *two-projection* property from the perspective of finite-order polynomial kernels, which is more relevant to most kernel-based regression, estimation, and machine learning problems. The theoretical result is summarized in Theorem 14.8. It provides the theoretical foundation for the PRR analysis to fully benefit from the theorem (Section 14.6.3).

14.6.1 The two-projection theorem: general case

It is vital to establish theoretically a necessary and sufficient condition for the validity of the two-projection theorem.

THEOREM 14.7 (Two-projection theorem) *Consider a regression model:* $\mathbf{y} = h(\mathbf{x}) + \varepsilon$. *Let* $\mathbf{z}$ *and* $\tilde{\mathbf{z}}$ *be the kernel-induced vectors of* $\mathbf{x}$ *and* $\tilde{\mathbf{x}}$, *respectively, with finite 2-norm. Then (see Figure 14.5)*

$$y/\{\tilde{\mathbf{z}}\} = \left(y/\{\mathbf{z},\tilde{\mathbf{z}}\}\right)/\{\tilde{\mathbf{z}}\} = \left(y/\{\mathbf{z}\}\right)/\{\tilde{\mathbf{z}}\}$$

for arbitrary $h(\mathbf{x}) \in \mathcal{L}^2(\mathbf{x})$, **if and only if**

$$E[\tilde{\mathbf{z}}|\mathbf{x}] = \tilde{\mathbf{z}}/\{\mathbf{z}\}, \tag{14.54}$$

where for notational convenience we denote

$$\{\mathbf{z}\} \equiv \text{span}\{\mathbf{z}\} \quad \textit{and} \quad \{\tilde{\mathbf{z}}\} \equiv \text{span}\{\tilde{\mathbf{z}}\}.$$

□

Proof. We shall ignore the presence of ε since $\varepsilon/\{\mathbf{z}\} = \varepsilon/\{\tilde{\mathbf{z}}\} = 0$. Denote

$$\mathbf{z}^{\perp} \equiv \tilde{\mathbf{z}} - \tilde{\mathbf{z}}/\{\mathbf{z}\},$$

namely $z_k^{\perp} \equiv \tilde{z}_k - \tilde{z}_k/\{\mathbf{z}\}$. By application of the orthogonality principle in estimation theory, $E[h(\mathbf{x})\left(\mathbf{z}^{\perp} - E[\mathbf{z}^{\perp}|\mathbf{x}]\right)] = 0$, i.e.

$$E[h(\mathbf{x})\mathbf{z}^{\perp}] = E\left[h(\mathbf{x})E[\mathbf{z}^{\perp}|\mathbf{x}]\right]. \tag{14.55}$$

Note that $E[\mathbf{z}^{\perp}|\mathbf{x}] = 0$ if and only if $E[h(\mathbf{x})E[\mathbf{z}^{\perp}|\mathbf{x}]] = 0$ for arbitrary $h(\mathbf{x})$. Equivalently, by Eq. (14.55), $E[\mathbf{z}^{\perp}|\mathbf{x}] = E[\tilde{\mathbf{z}}|\mathbf{x}] - \tilde{\mathbf{z}}/\{\mathbf{z}\} = 0$ if and only if $E[h(\mathbf{x})\mathbf{z}^{\perp}] = 0$.

The optimal projection to $\{\mathbf{z}\}$ can be expressed as $h(\mathbf{x})/\{\mathbf{z}\} = \mathbf{a}^{\mathrm{T}}\mathbf{z}$, where $\mathbf{a}$ is the vector minimizing

$$L_1 = E[|h(\mathbf{x}) - \mathbf{a}^{\mathrm{T}}\mathbf{z}|^2]. \tag{14.56}$$

On the other hand, the projection to $\{\mathbf{z}, \tilde{\mathbf{z}}\}$ can be expressed as $h(\mathbf{x})/\{\mathbf{z}, \tilde{\mathbf{z}}\} = \mathbf{a}^{\mathrm{T}}\mathbf{z} + \mathbf{b}^{\mathrm{T}}\mathbf{z}^{\perp}$, because $\mathrm{span}\{\mathbf{z}, \tilde{\mathbf{z}}\} = \mathrm{span}\{\mathbf{z}, \mathbf{z}^{\perp}\}$.

The projection objective is to find $\mathbf{a}$ and $\mathbf{b}$ to minimize

$$\begin{aligned} L_2 &= E[|h(\mathbf{x}) - (\mathbf{a}^{\mathrm{T}}\mathbf{z} + \mathbf{b}^{\mathrm{T}}\mathbf{z}^{\perp})|^2] \\ &= E[|h(\mathbf{x}) - \mathbf{a}^{\mathrm{T}}\mathbf{z}|^2] + 2\mathbf{b}^{\mathrm{T}}E[\mathbf{z}^{\perp}\left(h(\mathbf{x}) - \mathbf{z}^{\mathrm{T}}\mathbf{a}\right)] + E[|\mathbf{b}^{\mathrm{T}}\mathbf{z}^{\perp}|^2] \\ &= E[|h(\mathbf{x}) - \mathbf{a}^{\mathrm{T}}\mathbf{z}|^2] + 2\mathbf{b}^{\mathrm{T}}E[\mathbf{z}^{\perp}h(\mathbf{x})] + E[|\mathbf{b}^{\mathrm{T}}\mathbf{z}^{\perp}|^2]. \end{aligned} \tag{14.57}$$

Sufficiency

If $E[\mathbf{z}^{\perp}h(\mathbf{x})] = 0$, then $L_2 = E[|h(\mathbf{x}) - \mathbf{a}^{\mathrm{T}}\mathbf{z}|^2] + E[|\mathbf{b}^{\mathrm{T}}\mathbf{z}^{\perp}|^2]$, implying that $\mathbf{b} = 0$ for any optimal estimation. This implies that

$$h(\mathbf{x})/\{\mathbf{z}, \tilde{\mathbf{z}}\} = \mathbf{a}^{\mathrm{T}}\mathbf{z} = h(\mathbf{x})/\{\mathbf{z}\}, \tag{14.58}$$

which further implies that

$$h(\mathbf{x})/\{\tilde{\mathbf{z}}\} = \left(h(\mathbf{x})/\{\mathbf{z}, \tilde{\mathbf{z}}\}\right)/\{\tilde{\mathbf{z}}\} = \left(h(\mathbf{x})/\{\mathbf{z}\}\right)/\{\tilde{\mathbf{z}}\}. \tag{14.59}$$

Necessity

If $E[\mathbf{z}^{\perp}h(\mathbf{x})] \neq 0$, there exists a nonzero vector $\mathbf{b}$ such that $L_1 > L_2$. (For example, $\mathbf{b} = -\delta E[\mathbf{z}^{\perp}h(\mathbf{x})]$ for a very small positive δ.) Denote $\Delta = h(\mathbf{x})/\{\mathbf{z}, \tilde{\mathbf{z}}\} - h(\mathbf{x})/\{\mathbf{z}\}$, then $\Delta = \mathbf{b}^{\mathrm{T}}\mathbf{z}^{\perp} \neq 0$ (because $L_1 \neq L_2$), which further implies that $\Delta/\{\tilde{\mathbf{z}}\} \neq 0$.[1] Thus,

$$h(\mathbf{x})/\{\tilde{\mathbf{z}}\} = \left(h(\mathbf{x})/\{\mathbf{z}, \tilde{\mathbf{z}}\}\right)/\{\tilde{\mathbf{z}}\} = \left(h(\mathbf{x})/\{\mathbf{z}\}\right)/\{\tilde{\mathbf{z}}\} + \Delta/\{\tilde{\mathbf{z}}\},$$

invalidating the two-projection condition. □

[1] Note first that $E[\tilde{\mathbf{z}}\Delta] = E[\mathbf{z}^{\perp}\Delta] + E[\left(\tilde{\mathbf{z}}/\{\mathbf{z}\}\right)\Delta] = E[\mathbf{z}^{\perp}\Delta]$, because Δ is by definition orthogonal to $\mathbf{z}$. If $\Delta/\{\tilde{\mathbf{z}}\} = 0$, then $E[\tilde{\mathbf{z}}\Delta] = E[\mathbf{z}^{\perp}\Delta] = 0$. On pre-multiplying it by $\mathbf{b}^{\mathrm{T}}$, we obtain $E[\mathbf{b}^{\mathrm{T}}\mathbf{z}^{\perp}\Delta] = E[\Delta^2] = 0$, i.e. $\Delta = 0$. This produces a contradiction.

14.6.2 The two-projection theorem: polynomial case

Elementary set

A set is called elementary if each element is an elementary polynomial, e.g. $u^i v^j$ when $\mathbf{x} = [u, v]$. On the other hand, $u^i + v^j$ is not an elementary polynomial because it is a combination of products.

Packed elementary set

For a single-variate case, a *packed* elementary set has a simple form $\mathbf{z} = [1\ x\ x^2 \ldots\ x^p]^{\mathrm{T}}$, where all consecutive polynomial orders are present, i.e. every element is legitimate. (An element is illegitimate if any of its factors is missing from the set.) Likewise, a multivariate elementary set is packed if and only if each of its elements is legitimate. For example, if $\mathbf{x} = [u, v]$, then both $\{1, u, u^2\}$ and $\{1, u, v, u^2\}$ are packed. On the other hand, $\{1, u, uv\}$ is **not** packed because uv is illegitimate since one of its factors (v) is not in the set.

Any set of polynomial basis functions can always be equivalently **represented** by an elementary set. (For example, $[1\ \ 1 + x^2\ \ x^2 + x^3]$ has an elementary representation $[1\ x^2\ x^3]$ because the elements are related by a nonsingular matrix.)

THEOREM 14.8 (Two-projection theorem: polynomial kernels) *Consider only polynomial basis functions and assume that* $\mathbf{x}$ *and* $\Delta_{\mathbf{x}}$ *are statistically independent. The two-projection theorem holds for an arbitrary regression model* $h(\mathbf{x}) \in \mathcal{L}^2(\mathbf{x})$ *and arbitrary distributions of* $\mathbf{x}$ *and* $\Delta_{\mathbf{x}}$ **if and only if** *the basis functions can be* "**represented**" *by a* **packed** *elementary set.*[2] □

Proof of sufficiency

We shall prove just the single-variate case here, and it has an obvious extension to the multivariate case. First, let $\tilde{x}^k = (x + \Delta_x)^k \equiv \sum_{i=0}^{k} \beta_i \mathbf{x}^i \Delta_x^{k-i}$. It can be shown that $\tilde{x}^k/\{\mathbf{z}\} = \sum_{i=0}^{k} \beta_i E[\Delta_x^{k-i}] x^i$. Thus the *kth* element of the vector $\mathbf{z}^\perp$ is

$$z_k^\perp \equiv \tilde{x}^k - \tilde{x}^k/\{\mathbf{z}\} = \sum_{i=0}^{k} \beta_i x^i (\Delta_x^{k-i} - E[\Delta_x^{k-i}]).$$

It follows that

$$E[z_k^\perp h(\mathbf{x})] = \sum_{i=0}^{k} \beta_i E\left[\Delta_x^{k-i} - E[\Delta_x^{k-i}]\right] E[x^i h(\mathbf{x})] = 0$$

for an arbitrary function $h(\mathbf{x})$. So $E[\mathbf{z}^\perp h(\mathbf{x})] = 0$ for any function $h(\mathbf{x})$, thus justifying the sufficiency condition.

[2] Here we have implicitly assumed that the subspaces covered by $\mathbf{z}$ and $\tilde{\mathbf{z}}$ have exactly the same dimension. In general, the two-projection condition holds **iff** all the basis functions for $\tilde{\mathbf{z}}$ can be "**represented**" by the (unique) maximal **packed** elementary set which, in combination of other augmenting basis functions, "**represents**" $\mathbf{z}$. For single-variate cases, the condition holds **iff** the order of the basis functions used for $\tilde{\mathbf{z}}$ is no higher than d, the degree of the maximum elementary subset contained by the set of basis functions for $\mathbf{z}$.

Proof of necessity

If the set of basis functions is *non-packed*, there will exist a function $h(x)$ such that $E[\mathbf{z}^{\perp}h(\mathbf{x})] \neq 0$, thus causing $h(\mathbf{x})/\{\mathbf{z}, \tilde{\mathbf{z}}\} \neq h(\mathbf{x})/\{\mathbf{z}\}$, see Eq. (14.57). As an example, suppose that $\mathbf{z} = [1\ x^2]^{\mathrm{T}}$ (and $\tilde{\mathbf{z}} = [1\ \tilde{x}^2]^{\mathrm{T}}$). Set $h(x) = x$, then $E[\mathbf{z}^{\perp}h(x)] = E[\mathbf{z}^{\perp}x] \neq 0$ due to the fact that the first-order term x plays a role in $\mathbf{z}^{\perp}$ since x is absent from $\mathbf{z} = [1\ x^2\ x^3]^{\mathrm{T}}$.

14.6.3 Two-projection for the PRR

COROLLARY 14.1 *Given that* $\mathbf{x}$ *and* $\Delta_{\mathbf{x}}$ *are statistically independent, the two projection procedure will always be valid for either (1) the set of polynomial kernel-induced basis functions, (Eq. (14.19)) or (2) the set of orthogonal polynomial basis functions (Eq. (14.20)).*

The two-projection theorem is valid for all polynomial PRR regressors because the kernel-induced sets are always *packed*, including those prescribed in Eqs. (14.5), (14.11), (14.19), (14.52), and (14.52).

14.6.4 Error analysis

We denote

$$\hat{h}_{\mathbf{z}} \equiv h(\mathbf{x})/\mathbf{z}$$

and

$$\hat{y} = \hat{h}_{\tilde{\mathbf{z}}} \equiv h(\mathbf{x})/\tilde{\mathbf{z}}.$$

It can be shown that the estimation error $\epsilon = y - \hat{y}$ may be decomposed into three components:

$$\begin{aligned}\epsilon &= y - \hat{y} \\ &= \varepsilon + \{h(\mathbf{x}) - \hat{h}_{\mathbf{z}}\} + \{\hat{h}_{\mathbf{z}} - \hat{h}_{\tilde{\mathbf{z}}}\}.\end{aligned}$$

When the two-projection condition holds, then $\hat{h}_{\tilde{\mathbf{z}}} = \hat{h}_{\mathbf{z}}/\tilde{\mathbf{z}}$. It then follows that the three components become orthogonal to each other. The orthogonality property facilitates the error analysis on PRRs. More exactly, all three error components are mutually statistically uncorrelated, so the MSE is simply (cf. Figure 14.5)

$$E[||\epsilon||^2] = E[||\varepsilon||^2] + E[||\{h(\mathbf{x}) - E[\hat{h}(\tilde{\mathbf{x}})|\mathbf{x})\}||^2] + E[||\{E[\hat{h}(\tilde{\mathbf{x}})|\mathbf{x}) - \hat{h}(\tilde{\mathbf{x}})\}||^2].$$

Linear-least-MSE estimation

Now let us now place the focus on the linear-least-MSE estimation. Supposing that (1) the regression model $h(\mathbf{x})$ may be either linear or nonlinear, (2) the regressor $\hat{h}(\tilde{\mathbf{x}})$ is linear, and (3) the input and the input noise are statistically independent, then the optimal linear-least-MSE solution is as given in Eq. (14.29):

$$\hat{\mathbf{w}} = R_{\tilde{\mathbf{x}}}^{-1}R_{\tilde{\mathbf{x}}y} = [R_{\mathbf{x}} + \rho\mathbf{I}]^{-1}R_{\mathbf{x}y}. \tag{14.60}$$

For the linear case, the error decomposition has a simplified expression:

$$\epsilon = \varepsilon + (\mathbf{w}^{\mathrm{T}} - \hat{\mathbf{w}}^{\mathrm{T}})\mathbf{x} + \hat{\mathbf{w}}^{\mathrm{T}}\Delta_{\mathbf{x}}. \tag{14.61}$$

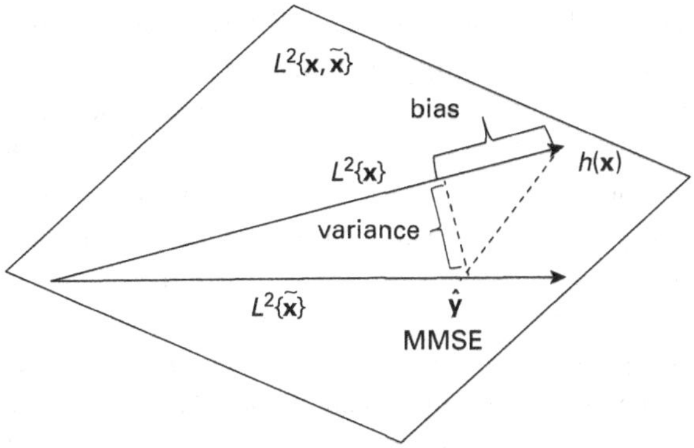

Fig. 14.6. Bias-variance error decomposition. The two kinds of errors are uncorrelated. In mathematical notation, let η denote the error associated with the variance, then bias$\perp\eta$.

Since the three errors are statistically uncorrelated,

$$E[||\epsilon||^2] = E[||\varepsilon||^2] + E[\text{bias}^2] + \rho||\hat{\mathbf{w}}||^2.$$

The MSE can be rewritten as

$$E[||\epsilon||^2] = \sigma_\varepsilon^2 + (\mathbf{w} - \hat{\mathbf{w}})^{\mathrm{T}} R_{\mathbf{x}} (\mathbf{w} - \hat{\mathbf{w}}) + \rho||\hat{\mathbf{w}}^{\mathrm{T}}||^2. \qquad (14.62)$$

Note that the linear-least-MSE estimator, $\hat{y} = R_{\tilde{\mathbf{x}}y}^{\mathrm{T}}[R_{\mathbf{x}} + \rho\mathbf{I}]^{-1}\mathbf{x}$, falls on the linear span: span$\{\tilde{\mathbf{x}}\}$. As depicted in Figure 14.6, for the output-error-free case, the power of the total error is the sum of that of the bias-type and variance-type errors. For a tradeoff analysis between bias and variance, see Problem 14.14.

14.7 Summary

This chapter discusses a fundamental statistical analysis for kernel regression and regularization methods that has been a major theoretical pillar for supervised machine learning. We have extended the problem formulation for classical (linear) ridge regression to (nonlinear) kernel ridge regression (KRR). Given the property of orthogonal polynomials (Theorem 14.1), closed-form results for the error analysis can be derived for KRR (Theorem 14.2).

A major novelty in the chapter lies in its extending the classical regression analysis to the errors-in-variables models, where the measurement of the input variable is assumed to suffer from some input noise. This leads to the development of kernel-based PRR. Two major theoretical fronts have been explored.

- The analysis on kernel-based PRR benefits greatly from the prior knowledge on the joint statistical property of the ideal and perturbed input variables. In this chapter, under the assumption of a Gaussian distribution, the property of conventional orthogonal polynomials (cf. Theorem 14.1) is extended to harness the cross-orthogonality between the original and perturbed input variables. Theorems 14.3 and 14.5 cover the theory of cross-orthogonality, for single-variate and multivariate cases, respectively.

The theorems facilitate the derivation of optimal PRR estimators and the assessment of the error–order tradeoff (Theorems 14.4 and 14.6).

- The chapter also explores PRR regressors via a two-projection procedure. The overall estimation may be divided into two stages. (1) In the first stage, we shall perform estimation (i.e. projection) pretending that there is no input perturbation. (2) In the second stage, the effect of input perturbation has to be taken into account, for which the joint statistical property of the unperturbed and perturbed input variables will play a vital role. Theoretically, this chapter establishes the necessary and sufficient conditions for the two-projection property to hold valid. Theorem 14.7 presents a general theory on the necessary and sufficient condition. Theorem 14.8 focuses on the *two-projection* condition for polynomial kernel cases. The latter is good for kernel-based regression or classification applications.

Connection between PRR and LASSO.

It is worth mentioning that an alternative linear PRR formulated under a worst-case consideration reduces to a LASSO-type problem [306].

14.8 Problems

Problem 14.1 *Assume that the variable x has a uniform distribution function from −1 to +1.*

(a) *Find the parameters a and b which minimize*

$$\int_{-1}^{1} |x^2 - (a+bx)|^2 \, dx.$$

(b) *Find the parameters a and b which minimize*

$$\int_{-1}^{1} |x^3 - (a+bx)|^2 \, dx.$$

Hint: *Note the useful projection formulas* $\langle f(x), 1\rangle = \int_{-1}^{1} f(x)dx$ *and* $\langle f(x), x\rangle = \int_{-1}^{1} f(x)x \, dx$.

Problem 14.2 (MMSE and MAP) *The MAP estimation problem has the following optimization formulation:*

$$y_{\mathrm{MAP}}(x) = \arg\max_{y} \, p_{y|x}(y|x).$$

Show that, for Gaussian-distributed variables, the MMSE and MAP estimators are identical.

Problem 14.3 (Optimality of linear-least-MSE estimator under Gaussian distribution) *If all the variables (input, output, input noise, and output noise) are known to have jointly Gaussian distributions, show that the optimal MSSE and linear-least-MSE estimators have an identical solution.*

Problem 14.4 *Let* $x \sim \mathcal{N}(\mu, \Sigma_x)$, $\Delta x | x \sim \mathcal{N}(0, \Sigma_{\Delta x})$, and $\tilde{x} = x + \Delta x$.

(a) *Show that* $x|\tilde{x} \sim \mathcal{N}(\mu_{x|\tilde{x}}, \Sigma_{x|\tilde{x}})$, *where*

$$\Sigma_{x|\tilde{x}}^{-1} = \Sigma_x^{-1} + \Sigma_{\Delta x}^{-1}$$

and

$$\begin{aligned}\mu_{x|\tilde{x}} &= (\Sigma_x^{-1} + \Sigma_{\Delta x}^{-1})^{-1}(\Sigma_x^{-1}\mu + \Sigma_{\Delta x}^{-1}\tilde{x}) \\ &= \Sigma_{\Delta x}(\Sigma_x + \Sigma_{\Delta x})^{-1}\mu + \Sigma_x(\Sigma_x + \Sigma_{\Delta x})^{-1}\tilde{x}.\end{aligned}$$

(b) Show that, if $\mu = 0$, *the optimal estimator is given by*

$$E[w^{\mathrm{T}}x|\tilde{x}] = w^{\mathrm{T}}\mu_{x|\tilde{x}} = ((\Sigma_x + \Sigma_{\Delta x})^{-1}\Sigma_x w)^{\mathrm{T}}\tilde{x}. \tag{14.63}$$

Hint:

$$\begin{aligned}\Pr[x|\tilde{x}] \propto \Pr[x, \tilde{x}] &= \exp\left(-\frac{1}{2}\left((x-\mu)^{\mathrm{T}}\Sigma_x^{-1}(x-\mu) + (\tilde{x}-x)^{\mathrm{T}}\Sigma_{\Delta x}^{-1}(\tilde{x}-x)\right)\right) \\ &\propto \exp\left(-\frac{1}{2}\left(x^{\mathrm{T}}(\Sigma_x^{-1} + \Sigma_{\Delta x}^{-1})x - 2(\Sigma_x^{-1}\mu + \Sigma_{\Delta x}^{-1}\tilde{x})^{\mathrm{T}}x\right)\right).\end{aligned}$$

Problem 14.5 *If* $h(x) = x^3$, *is it true or false that the two projection angles* θ' *and* θ *depicted below are always identical?*

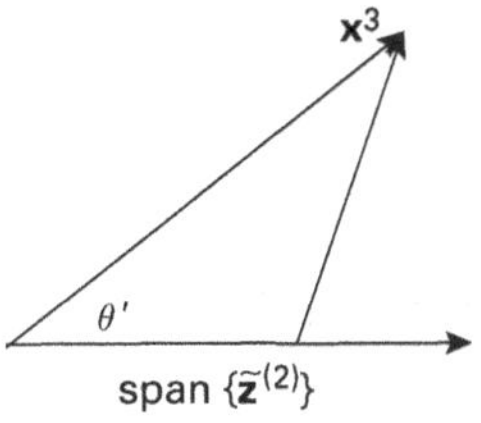

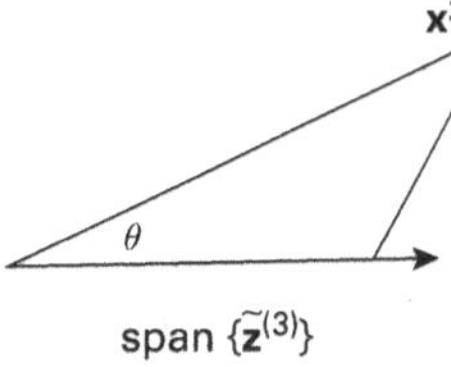

What if the regression model in the figures is replaced by $h(x) = x^2$?

Problem 14.6 *Given the statistical distribution of the input, there is a corresponding set of orthogonal polynomials* $\{L_i(x)\}$, *with* $L_i(x)$ *being a polynomial of order i.*

(a) *For a uniformly distributed variable,* $x \in [-1\ 1]$, *show that the orthogonal basis functions are the Legendre polynomials characterized as follows:*

$$z_n = L_n(x) = \frac{1}{2^n n!}\frac{d^n}{dx^n}\left[(x^2-1)^n\right]. \tag{14.64}$$

(b) *Show that the first three Legendre polynomials are* $z_0 = L_0(x) = 1.0000$, $z_1 = L_1(x) = 1.7303x$, *and* $z_2 = L_2(x) = 3.3474(x^2 - 1/3)$.

Problem 14.7 *Consider a variable x with a zero-mean Gaussian-distribution function with variance* ρ.

(a) *Let a kernel-induced vector* $\mathbf{z}$ *be* $\mathbf{z} = [1\ x\ x^2]^{\mathrm{T}}$. *Show that* $\mathbf{R_z}$ *is a non-diagonal matrix:*

$$\mathbf{R_z} = \begin{bmatrix} 1 & 0 & \frac{1}{3}+\rho \\ 0 & \frac{1}{3}+\rho & 0 \\ \frac{1}{3}+\rho & 0 & \frac{1}{5}+2\rho \end{bmatrix}.$$

This suggests that the three basis functions $\{1, x, x^2\}$ *do not form a set of orthogonal polynomials.*

(b) *Apply the Cholesky decomposition to* $\mathbf{R_z}$, *to obtain an orthogonal set of basis functions:*

$$\mathbf{R_z} = \mathbf{L\Lambda L} = \begin{bmatrix} 1 & 0 & 0 \\ 0 & 1 & 0 \\ \frac{1}{3}+\rho & 0 & 1 \end{bmatrix} \begin{bmatrix} 1 & 0 & \\ 0 & \frac{1}{3}+\rho & 0 \\ 0 & 0 & 4/45+\frac{1}{5}\rho-\rho^2 \end{bmatrix} \begin{bmatrix} 1 & 0 & \frac{1}{3}+\rho \\ 0 & 1 & 0 \\ 0 & 0 & 1 \end{bmatrix}.$$

Show that

$$\tilde{\mathbf{z}} = \mathbf{L}^{-1}\mathbf{z} = \begin{bmatrix} 1 \\ x \\ x^2 - (\frac{1}{3}+\rho) \end{bmatrix}$$

and that

$$\mathbf{R}_{\tilde{\mathbf{z}}} = \begin{bmatrix} 1 & 0 & \\ 0 & \frac{1}{3}+\rho & 0 \\ 0 & 0 & 4/45+\frac{1}{5}\rho-\rho^2 \end{bmatrix}.$$

This suggests that the three new basis functions $\{1, x, x^2 - \frac{1}{3} - \rho\}$ *do form a set of orthogonal polynomials.*

Problem 14.8 *Verify that the single-variate PRR estimator given in Eq. (14.42) may also be alternatively proved as follows.*

- $E[\tilde{z}_i z_j] = \lambda_i \delta(i-j)$, *i.e.*

$$R_{\tilde{\mathbf{z}}\mathbf{z}} = \mathbf{\Lambda} \equiv \mathrm{Diag}\{\lambda_0, \lambda_1, \ldots, \lambda_p\}, \tag{14.65}$$

  where $\lambda_n = (1/\sqrt{1+\eta})^n, n = 1, \ldots, p$.
- *Note that, since* $E[\tilde{z}_i z_j] = \lambda_i \delta(i-j)$, *we have*

$$E[\tilde{\mathbf{z}}h(x)] = \Lambda\mathbf{u},$$

  where, according to the previous denotation, $\mathbf{u} = [\gamma_0 \gamma_1 \ldots \gamma_p]^T$.
  It follows that the PRR solution given by Eq. (14.27) is

$$\begin{aligned} \hat{y}_{\mathrm{PRR}(p)} &= \tilde{\mathbf{z}}^{\mathrm{T}} R_{\tilde{\mathbf{z}}}^{-1} R_{\tilde{\mathbf{z}}y} \\ &= \tilde{\mathbf{z}}^{\mathrm{T}} R_{\tilde{\mathbf{z}}}^{-1} E[\tilde{\mathbf{z}}h(x)] \\ &= \tilde{\mathbf{z}}^{\mathrm{T}} R_{\tilde{\mathbf{z}}}^{-1} R_{\tilde{\mathbf{z}}\mathbf{z}}\mathbf{u} \\ &= \tilde{\mathbf{z}}^{\mathrm{T}} \Lambda \mathbf{u}, \end{aligned} \tag{14.66}$$

where we note that $R_{\tilde{\mathbf{z}}} = \mathbf{I}$ (see Eq. (14.34)). This can be viewed as the matrix formulation of Eq. (14.42).

Problem 14.9 (Induction equation for proving cross-orthogonality) *This problem provides the detailed procedure leading to the proof of Eq. (14.36). Assume that $\sigma_x = 1$. Note that $\partial \mathrm{He}_n(x)/\partial x = n\,\mathrm{He}_{n-1}(x)$, thus $\partial \psi_n(x)/\partial x = \sqrt{n}\psi_{n-1}(x)$. Denote*

$$f_{m,n} \equiv \frac{1}{2\pi} e^{-\frac{x^2}{2}} e^{-\frac{(\tilde{x}-x)^2}{2\eta}} \psi_m(x)\tilde{\psi}_n(\tilde{x}).$$

Then, by simple integration, we arrive at $\int_x \int_{\tilde{x}} (A+B)dx\,d\tilde{x} = 0$, where

$$A = \frac{\partial f_{m,n+1}}{\partial x} = \sqrt{m} f_{m-1,n+1} - (x + \left(\frac{x-\tilde{x}}{\eta}\right) f_{m,n+1}$$

and

$$B = \frac{\partial f_{m,n+1}}{\partial \tilde{x}} = \frac{\sqrt{n+1}}{\sqrt{1+\eta}} f_{m,n} + \frac{x-\tilde{x}}{\eta} f_{m,n+1}.$$

It then follows that

$$\begin{aligned}
0 &= \int_x \int_{\tilde{x}} (A+B)dx\,d\tilde{x} \\
&= \int_x \int_{\tilde{x}} \left(\sqrt{m} f_{m-1,n+1} + \frac{\sqrt{n+1}}{\sqrt{1+\eta}} f_{m,n} - x f_{m,n+1} \right) dx\,d\tilde{x} \\
&\overset{\text{Eq. (14.31)}}{=} \int_x \int_{\tilde{x}} \left(\sqrt{m} f_{m-1,n+1} + \frac{\sqrt{n+1}}{\sqrt{1+\eta}} f_{m,n} - \sqrt{m+1} f_{m+1,n+1} - \sqrt{m} f_{m-1,n+1} \right) dx\,d\tilde{x} \\
&= \int_x \int_{\tilde{x}} \left(\frac{\sqrt{n+1}}{\sqrt{1+\eta}} f_{m,n} - \sqrt{m+1} f_{m+1,n+1} \right) dx\,d\tilde{x} \\
&= \frac{\sqrt{n+1}}{\sqrt{1+\eta}} E[\psi_m(x)\tilde{\psi}_n(\tilde{x})] - \sqrt{m+1} E[\psi_{m+1}(x)\tilde{\psi}_{n+1}(\tilde{x})].
\end{aligned}$$

This proves Eq. (14.36).

Problem 14.10 *Prove that Eq. (14.36) is valid for any positive value of σ_x.*

Hint: *Show that, for a general value of σ_x,*

$$A = \frac{\partial f_{m,n+1}}{\partial x} = \frac{\sqrt{m}}{\sigma_x} f_{m-1,n+1} - \frac{1}{\sigma_x^2} \left(x + \frac{x-\tilde{x}}{\eta} \right) f_{m,n+1}$$

and

$$B = \frac{\partial f_{m,n+1}}{\partial \tilde{x}} = \frac{\sqrt{n+1}}{\sigma_x \sqrt{1+\eta}} f_{m,n} + \frac{1}{\sigma_x^2} \left(\frac{x-\tilde{x}}{\eta} \right) f_{m,n+1}.$$

Problem 14.11 *Show that, if the two-projection condition holds, then any function that is orthogonal to $\{\mathbf{z}\}$ must be orthogonal to $\{\tilde{\mathbf{z}}\}$.*

Problem 14.12 *Under the assumption of a zero-mean Gaussian distribution, which of the following basis vectors satisfies the two-projection condition:*

(i) $\mathbf{z} = [1\ x^2]^{\mathrm{T}}$ *(and* $\tilde{\mathbf{z}} = [1\ \tilde{x}^2]^{\mathrm{T}}$*).*
(ii) $\mathbf{z} = [1\ x^2\ x^3]^{\mathrm{T}}$ *(and* $\tilde{\mathbf{z}} = [1\ \tilde{x}^2\ \tilde{x}^3]^{\mathrm{T}}$*).*

Problem 14.13 (Transitiveness of orthogonality) *The two-projection condition implies that (Eq. (14.58))* $h(\mathbf{x})/\{\mathbf{z}, \tilde{\mathbf{z}}\} = h(\mathbf{x})/\{\mathbf{z}\}$. *Show that it further implies that the model-induced error is orthogonal to both* $\{\mathbf{z}\}$ *and* $\{\tilde{\mathbf{z}}\}$*, i.e.*

$$E[\Delta_h(\mathbf{x})\mathbf{z}] = 0 \quad \text{and} \quad E[\Delta_h(\mathbf{x})\tilde{\mathbf{z}}] = 0. \tag{14.67}$$

This is illustrated in Figure 14.5.

Problem 14.14 (Tradeoff between bias and variance) *Suppose that a different ridge factor* $\rho' \neq \rho$ *is adopted, instead of the original variance of the input noise* ρ. *This leads to a new and non-optimal linear regressor:*

$$\hat{\mathbf{w}} = [R_x + \rho'\mathbf{I}]^{-1}R_{xy}. \tag{14.68}$$

It follows that the new estimate becomes $\hat{y} = R_{\tilde{\mathbf{x}}y}^{\mathrm{T}}[R_{\mathbf{x}} + \rho'\mathbf{I}]^{-1}\mathbf{x}$. *Obviously, the new estimate again falls on the linear span,* span$\{\tilde{\mathbf{x}}\}$*, as depicted in Figure 14.7.*

In the linear estimation theory, the choice of ρ' *plays a direct role on the tradeoff between the variance and bias of the estimation error. Verify the following two extreme cases.*

- **Zero-variance linear-least-MSE estimation.** *On setting* $\rho' \to \infty$*, we have*

$$\hat{\mathbf{w}} = \lim_{\rho' \to \infty} [R_x + \rho'\mathbf{I}]^{-1}R_{xy} \to 0.$$

This leads to a zero-variance linear estimator with a non-optimal MSE.

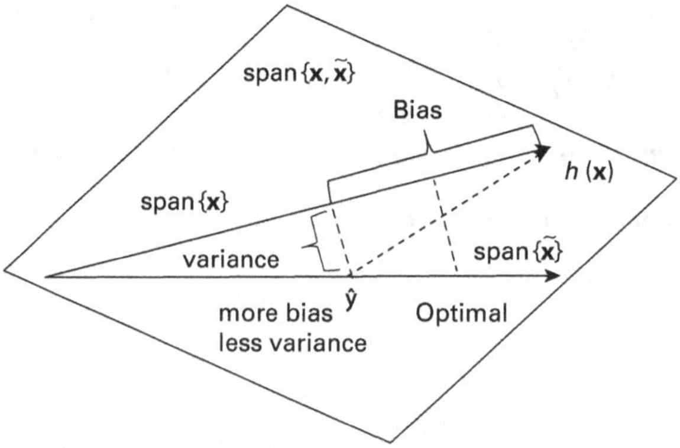

Fig. 14.7. Tradeoff with less variance for a linear regression model, i.e. $h(\mathbf{x}) = \mathbf{w}^{\mathrm{T}}\mathbf{x}$. The variance may be reduced by using a larger ρ' thus forcing $||\hat{\mathbf{w}}||$ to become smaller. The extreme case is when $||\hat{\mathbf{w}}|| = 0$, whereupon the non-intrinsic variance becomes zero. (The spans to $\mathbf{x}$ and to $\tilde{\mathbf{x}}$ have different definitions for MMSE and linear-least-MSE estimators.)

- **Unbiased (zero-bias) linear-least-MSE estimation.** *On setting $\rho' \to 0$, we have*

$$\hat{\mathbf{w}} = \lim_{\rho' \to 0} [R_x + \rho' \mathbf{I}]^{-1} R_{xy} \to \mathbf{w}.$$

This leads to a linear unbiased estimator with the following (non-optimal) MSE:

$$L_{\text{unbiased}} = \sigma_\varepsilon^2 + \rho R_{\mathbf{x}d}^{\mathrm{T}} R_{\mathbf{x}}^{-2} R_{\mathbf{x}d}. \tag{14.69}$$

Problem 14.15 (Order–error tradeoff) *Suppose that a scalar input variable x has a zero-mean Gaussian distribution and the response $y = h(x)$ is a tenth-order polynomial function of the input. Therefore, $h(x)$ may be expressed as a linear combination of a total of 11 orthogonal polynomial functions, including the constant term. Let us further assume that all 11 orthogonal components have approximately the same power.*

(i) *When the perturbation factor is $\eta = 0.01$, where η denotes the ratio of the SNR in the input, what is the minimum regressor order if the power of the estimation error is kept within 10%?*
(ii) *Repeat the same problem but with the perturbation factor changed to $\eta = 0.1$?*

Problem 14.16 (Optimal inverse problem) *Suppose that the input v and output x of a nonlinear system are related as follows:*

$$x = 2 + \frac{1}{5+v}.$$

Suppose that the observed response is $\tilde{x} = x + \Delta_x$, where x and Δ_x are assumed to have zero-mean Gaussian distributions with variances $\sigma_x^2 = 1.0$ and $\sigma_{\Delta_x}^2 = 0.1$, respectively. Find the optimal linear solution which can best estimate v from $\tilde{x}$ in the MSE sense.

15 Kernel methods for estimation, prediction, and system identification

15.1 Introduction

It is vital to explore the theoretical foundation linking the field of kernel methods and that of estimation and identification. This chapter provides a mathematical formulation for the optimal estimator, regressor, and/or predictor, assuming prior knowledge on the first- and second-order statistics of the generation vector, which is generally much easier to obtain than the complete density function. Nevertheless, the methods proposed here may still be recognized as a Bayesian method since the generation vector is modeled by a random vector [151].

Conventionally, LSE and ridge regression have been popular techniques for non-regularized and regularized regression analysis for the original vector space, where the optimal regressor is learned from a training dataset given in the original space:

$$\{\mathcal{X}, \mathcal{Y}\} = \{(\mathbf{x}_1, y_1)\, (\mathbf{x}_2, y_2)\, \ldots\, (\mathbf{x}_N, y_N)\},$$

where $(\mathbf{x}_t, y_t)$ denotes the input and output teacher pair recorded at time t. The conventional Gauss–Markov model is described by

$$y = \mathbf{w}^{\mathrm{T}}\mathbf{x} + \varepsilon, \tag{15.1}$$

which leads to the celebrated Gauss–Markov theorem [2].

On the other hand, the mathematical models used in kernel methods assume that a set of training vectors in the intrinsic space and their associated teacher values can become accessible:

$$\{\Phi, \mathcal{Y}\} = \{(\vec{\boldsymbol{\phi}}(\mathbf{x}_1), y_1)\, (\vec{\boldsymbol{\phi}}(\mathbf{x}_2), y_2)\, \ldots\, (\vec{\boldsymbol{\phi}}(\mathbf{x}_N), y_N)\},$$

which conveniently leads to a kernel-based Gauss–Markov generation model:

$$y = \mathbf{u}^{\mathrm{T}}\vec{\boldsymbol{\phi}}(\mathbf{x}) + \varepsilon = \sum_{j=1}^{J} u^{(j)}\phi^{(j)}(\mathbf{x}) + \varepsilon, \tag{15.2}$$

where the system vector $\mathbf{u}$ is first assumed to be deterministic and fixed but unknown. In this case, the Gauss–Markov theorem remains applicable. The primary objective of this chapter is to extend the Gauss–Markov theorem to statistical learning models, assuming prior knowledge on the first- and second-order statistics of system parameters. The regression formulation has a natural statistical interpretation that is based on the following prior-driven statistical models. The prior knowledge may be inferred from the underlying physics pertaining to the system parameters responsible for the generation of the system responses, from previous observations on time-adaptive systems. Incorporating prior knowledge into the learning problem has been an active research area [170, 246].

The topics addressed in this chapter are as follows.

(i) Section 15.2 covers kernel methods for regression models with deterministic parameters. The Gauss–Markov theorem, which was established for linear models in the original space, can be naturally extended to linear models in the kernel-induced vector space. It will be shown that the best unbiased linear estimator, the best unbiased linear predictor, and the LSE regressor are all identical to each other.

(ii) Section 15.3 treats a KRR learning model for prior-driven statistical system parameters. The Gauss–Markov theorem, which was originally established for models with deterministic system vector $\mathbf{u}$, will be extended to statistical learning models. It will be shown that the best unbiased linear estimator, the best unbiased linear predictor, and the optimal KRR regressor are all identical to each other. The notion of a weighted kernel function is introduced, leading to the dual-optimization formulation in the empirical space. Subsequently, the KRR learning model in the empirical space can be naturally developed.

(iii) In Section 15.4, the Gauss–Markov theorem may be further extended to the errors-in-variables (EiV) learning models. It will be shown that the best unbiased linear estimator, the best unbiased linear predictor, and the optimal EiV regressor are all identical to each other. Again, the EiV learning model in the empirical space will be treated in terms of a weighted kernel function, leading to the dual. This section also addresses the design of optimal nth-order EiV regressors.

(iv) Section 15.5 discusses a recursive KRR algorithm in the intrinsic and empirical spaces. The prior knowledge may be inferred from the previous observations in time-series prediction. This interpretation leads to the development of a recursive algorithm for the KRR learning models, which require only $O(J^2)$ operations per sample update. Subsequently, a recursive KRR algorithm in the empirical space can also be naturally developed. However, the recursive algorithm in the empirical space requires a processing time which grows with time. To rectify this problem, the notion of a forgetting factor is introduced. More importantly, a fixed finite window is imposed on the kernel matrix, leading to a so-called doubly Woodbury updating algorithm.

(v) Section 15.6 covers recursive EiV learning algorithms both for the intrinsic space and for the empirical space.

15.2 Kernel regressors for deterministic generation models

In kernel methods, a Mercer kernel function $K(\cdot,\cdot)$ from $\mathcal{X} \times \mathcal{X}$ to $\mathbb{R}$ is specified first. According to Mercer's theorem [175], there exists a mapping

$$\boldsymbol{\phi} : \mathbf{x} \rightarrow \overrightarrow{\boldsymbol{\phi}}(\mathbf{x}) \in \mathcal{H}.$$

With reference to Figure 2.1, the associated *intrinsic feature vector*, or simply *intrinsic vector*, in the reproducing kernel Hilbert space $\mathcal{H}$ is represented by

$$\overrightarrow{\boldsymbol{\phi}}(\mathbf{x}) = [\phi^{(1)}(\mathbf{x}), \phi^{(2)}(\mathbf{x}), \ldots, \phi^{(J)}(\mathbf{x})]^{\mathrm{T}}. \tag{15.3}$$

In this sense, $K(\mathbf{x}, \mathbf{x}') = \boldsymbol{\phi}(\mathbf{x})^{\mathrm{T}}\boldsymbol{\phi}(\mathbf{x}')$ can be viewed as the inner product in the intrinsic space $\mathcal{H}$.

Consider an input–output relationship characterized by the following Gauss–Markov model (which can be viewed as a "linear" system in the intrinsic space):

$$y = \mathbf{u}^{\mathrm{T}}\overrightarrow{\boldsymbol{\phi}}(\mathbf{x}) + \varepsilon = \sum_{j=1}^{J} u^{(j)}\phi^{(j)}(\mathbf{x}) + \varepsilon, \tag{15.4}$$

where the system vector $\mathbf{u}$ is, in this section, assumed to be deterministic and fixed but unknown. In kernel processing, the training dataset is given in its intrinsic-space representation:

$$\{(\mathbf{x}_1, y_1)\ (\mathbf{x}_2, y_2)\ \ldots\ (\mathbf{x}_N, y_N)\},$$

where any input–output pair of vectors is related as follows:

$$y_i = \mathbf{u}^{\mathrm{T}}\overrightarrow{\boldsymbol{\phi}}(\mathbf{x}_i) + \varepsilon_i,\ i = 1, \ldots, N, \tag{15.5}$$

where the output noise terms $\{\varepsilon_i,\ i = 1, \ldots, N\}$ are assumed to have zero mean, and to be independently and identically distributed (i.i.d.) with variance $E[\varepsilon_i^2] \equiv \sigma_\varepsilon^2$. Define the output noise vector

$$\boldsymbol{\varepsilon} = [\varepsilon_1,\ \varepsilon_2,\ \ldots,\ \varepsilon_N]^{\mathrm{T}}.$$

Then its covariance matrix will have the following form:

$$\boldsymbol{\Sigma}_{\boldsymbol{\varepsilon}} = \sigma_\varepsilon^2\mathbf{I}.$$

Furthermore, let us define

$$\mathbf{D}_{\mathbf{x}} \equiv \{\mathbf{x}_1, \mathbf{x}_2, \ldots, \mathbf{x}_N\}.$$

Kernel-based least-squares-errors estimators

In general, the optimal estimation function has the following form:

$$f(\mathbf{x}) = \hat{\mathbf{u}}^{\mathrm{T}}\overrightarrow{\boldsymbol{\phi}}(\mathbf{x}) = \sum_{j=1}^{J} \hat{u}^{(j)}\phi^{(j)}(\mathbf{x}) + b. \tag{15.6}$$

In this section, we shall make a simplifying assumption that the threshold parameter b can be dropped either due to (1) the existence of an implicit bias term in $\overrightarrow{\boldsymbol{\phi}}(\mathbf{x})$ and/or (2) the pre-centered coordinate system, i.e. the input and output training vectors both have zero mean. (See Problem 7.5.) Consequently, the estimation function becomes

$$f(\mathbf{x}) = \hat{\mathbf{u}}^{\mathrm{T}}\overrightarrow{\boldsymbol{\phi}}(\mathbf{x}) = \sum_{j=1}^{J} \hat{u}^{(j)}\phi^{(j)}(\mathbf{x}). \tag{15.7}$$

We adopt a linear estimator of $\mathbf{u}$, which takes the form

$$\hat{\mathbf{u}} = \sum_{i=1}^{N} y_i\mathbf{v}_i = \mathbf{V}\mathbf{y},$$

where $\mathbf{V} = [\mathbf{v}_1 \ \ldots \ \mathbf{v}_N] \in \mathbb{R}^{J\times N}$ depends only on the N inputs $\mathbf{x}_1, \ldots, \mathbf{x}_N$, and, more specifically, it depends only on the training data matrix in the intrinsic space, which is denoted as

$$\mathbf{\Phi} = \left[\overrightarrow{\boldsymbol{\phi}}(\mathbf{x}_1)\ \overrightarrow{\boldsymbol{\phi}}(\mathbf{x}_2)\ \ldots\ \overrightarrow{\boldsymbol{\phi}}(\mathbf{x}_N)\right].$$

Most importantly, $\mathbf{V}$ cannot be dependent on the output vector $\mathbf{y}$, where $\mathbf{y} = [y_1 \ \ldots \ y_N]^{\mathrm{T}}$ and, according to Eq. (15.5),

$$\mathbf{y} = \mathbf{\Phi}^{\mathrm{T}}\mathbf{u} + \boldsymbol{\varepsilon},$$

where $\boldsymbol{\varepsilon} = [\varepsilon_1 \ \ldots \ \varepsilon_N]^{\mathrm{T}}$.

Terminologies for Theorem 15.1

Under the Gauss–Markov model, we adopt the following denotations.

(i) **Best linear unbiased estimator (BLUE).** The best (i.e. "minimum-variance") linear unbiased estimation of the system vector $\mathbf{u}$ is defined as

$$\hat{\mathbf{u}}_{\mathrm{BLUE}} = \underset{\hat{\mathbf{u}}=\mathbf{V}\mathbf{y}, E[\hat{\mathbf{u}}]=\mathbf{u}}{\arg\min} \ E[||\hat{\mathbf{u}} - \mathbf{u}||^2|\mathcal{D}_{\mathbf{x}}], \tag{15.8}$$

where $\mathbf{V} \in \mathbb{R}^{J\times N}$ is independent of $\mathbf{y}$.

(ii) **Best linear unbiased predictor (BLUP).** The best unbiased linear predictor is defined as the one which minimizes the following "conditional" MSE (between the prediction $\hat{y} = \hat{\mathbf{u}}^{\mathrm{T}}\overrightarrow{\boldsymbol{\phi}}(\mathbf{x})$ and the actual response y):

$$\hat{\mathbf{u}}_{\mathrm{BLUP}} = \underset{\hat{\mathbf{u}}=\mathbf{V}\mathbf{y}, E[\hat{\mathbf{u}}]=\mathbf{u}}{\arg\min} \ E[||\hat{\mathbf{u}}^{\mathrm{T}}\overrightarrow{\boldsymbol{\phi}}(\mathbf{x}) - y||^2|\mathcal{D}_{\mathbf{x}}], \tag{15.9}$$

where $\mathbf{V} \in \mathbb{R}^{J\times N}$ is independent of $\mathbf{y}$.

(iii) **Least-squares-error (LSE) regressor.** The objective of the *least-squares-error* regressor is to find a vector $\hat{\mathbf{u}}$ to minimize the following cost function:

$$E_{\mathrm{LSE}}(\hat{\mathbf{u}}) = \sum_{i=1}^{N}\left(\hat{\mathbf{u}}^{\mathrm{T}}\overrightarrow{\boldsymbol{\phi}}(\mathbf{x}_i) - y_i\right)^2, \tag{15.10}$$

or, equivalently, in matrix notation,

$$E_{\mathrm{LSE}}(\hat{\mathbf{u}}) = ||\mathbf{\Phi}^{\mathrm{T}}\hat{\mathbf{u}} - \mathbf{y}||^2. \tag{15.11}$$

The LSE solution is well known to be[1]

$$\hat{\mathbf{u}}_{\mathrm{LSE}} \equiv \underset{\hat{\mathbf{u}}\in\mathbb{R}^J}{\arg\min}||\hat{\mathbf{u}}^{\mathrm{T}}\tilde{\mathbf{\Phi}} - \mathbf{y}||^2 = \left[\mathbf{\Phi}\mathbf{\Phi}^{\mathrm{T}}\right]^{-1}\mathbf{\Phi}\mathbf{y}.$$

[1] In this chapter, we shall assume an over-determined systems, namely that $J \leq N$. Consequently, the scatter matrix in the intrinsic space, $\mathbf{S} \equiv \mathbf{\Phi}\mathbf{\Phi}^{\mathrm{T}}$, is generically nonsingular. Therefore, for notational convenience, $\mathbf{S}$ will be assumed to be invertible. However, a simple LSE formulation also exists even when $\mathbf{S} = \mathbf{\Phi}\mathbf{\Phi}^{\mathrm{T}}$ is not invertible. In that case, the LSE solution can be expressed as

$$\hat{\mathbf{u}}_{\mathrm{LSE}} = \left[\mathbf{\Phi}\mathbf{\Phi}^{\mathrm{T}}\right]^{\dagger}\mathbf{\Phi}\mathbf{y}.$$

THEOREM 15.1 (Gauss–Markov theorem for deterministic (Gauss–Markov) models) *We have a set of training vectors*

$$\{\Phi, \mathcal{Y}\} = \{(\vec{\phi}_1, y_1)\,(\vec{\phi}_2, y_2)\,\ldots\,(\vec{\phi}_N, y_N)\},$$

generated by the Gauss–Markov model prescribed by Eq. (15.4), with a deterministic but unknown system vector $\mathbf{u}$. *The best linear unbiased estimator (Eq. (15.8)) and the best linear unbiased predictor (Eq. (15.9)) are identical to each other and, moreover, match with the LSE solution (Eq. (15.12)). Mathematically,*

$$\hat{\mathbf{u}}_{\text{BLUE}} = \hat{\mathbf{u}}_{\text{BLUP}} = \hat{\mathbf{u}}_{\text{LSE}} = \left[\mathbf{\Phi}\mathbf{\Phi}^{\text{T}}\right]^{-1}\mathbf{\Phi}\mathbf{y}. \tag{15.12}$$

□

Proof of $\hat{\mathbf{u}}_{\text{BLUE}} = \hat{\mathbf{u}}_{\text{LSE}}$. Denote

$$\mathbf{U}_{\text{LSE}} \equiv \left[\mathbf{\Phi}\mathbf{\Phi}^{\text{T}}\right]^{-1}\mathbf{\Phi}.$$

Then $\hat{\mathbf{u}}_{\text{BLUE}} = \mathbf{U}_{\text{LSE}}\mathbf{y}$. Recall that $\hat{\mathbf{u}} = \mathbf{V}\mathbf{y}$ for a matrix $\mathbf{V} \in \mathbb{R}^{M\times N}$. The expectation of $\hat{\mathbf{u}}$ is

$$E[\hat{\mathbf{u}}] = E[\mathbf{V}\mathbf{y}] = E[\mathbf{V}(\mathbf{\Phi}^{\text{T}}\mathbf{u} + \boldsymbol{\varepsilon})] = \mathbf{V}\mathbf{\Phi}^{\text{T}}\mathbf{u}. \tag{15.13}$$

It is obvious that $\hat{\mathbf{u}}$ is unbiased if and only if $\mathbf{V}\mathbf{\Phi}^{\text{T}} = \mathbf{I}$.

Note further that the covariance matrix of $\hat{\mathbf{u}}$ is

$$\begin{aligned}
\text{MSE}_{\text{estimator}} &= E[||\mathbf{V}(\mathbf{\Phi}^{\text{T}}\mathbf{u} + \boldsymbol{\varepsilon}) - \mathbf{u}||^2] \\
&= E[\left(\mathbf{V}(\mathbf{\Phi}^{\text{T}}\mathbf{u} + \boldsymbol{\varepsilon}) - \mathbf{u}\right)^{\text{T}}\left(\mathbf{V}(\mathbf{\Phi}^{\text{T}}\mathbf{u} + \boldsymbol{\varepsilon}) - \mathbf{u}\right)] \\
&= \mathbf{u}^{\text{T}}E[(\mathbf{V}\mathbf{\Phi}^{\text{T}} - \mathbf{I})^{\text{T}}(\mathbf{V}\mathbf{\Phi} - \mathbf{I})]\mathbf{u} + E[(\mathbf{V}\boldsymbol{\varepsilon})^{\text{T}}(\mathbf{V}\boldsymbol{\varepsilon})].
\end{aligned}$$

For any unbiased estimator, it is necessary that $\mathbf{V}\mathbf{\Phi}^{\text{T}} = \mathbf{I}$, therefore

$$\begin{aligned}
\text{MSE}_{\text{estimator}} &= E[(\mathbf{V}\boldsymbol{\varepsilon})^{\text{T}}(\mathbf{V}\boldsymbol{\varepsilon})] \\
&= \mathtt{tr}\left(E[(\mathbf{V}\boldsymbol{\varepsilon})^{\text{T}}(\mathbf{V}\boldsymbol{\varepsilon})]\right) \\
&= \mathtt{tr}\left(\mathbf{V}E[\boldsymbol{\varepsilon}\boldsymbol{\varepsilon}^{\text{T}}]\mathbf{V}^{\text{T}}\right) \\
&= \mathtt{tr}\left(\mathbf{V}\mathbf{\Sigma}_{\varepsilon}\mathbf{V}^{\text{T}}\right) \\
&= \sigma_{\varepsilon}^2\,\mathtt{tr}\left(\mathbf{V}\mathbf{V}^{\text{T}}\right),
\end{aligned} \tag{15.14}$$

where $\mathtt{tr}(\cdot)$ denotes the trace operator. Recall that $\hat{\mathbf{u}} = \mathbf{V}\mathbf{y}$ and denote further that $\mathbf{Z} \equiv \mathbf{V} - \mathbf{U}_{\text{LSE}}$, i.e.

$$\mathbf{V} = \mathbf{U}_{\text{LSE}} + \mathbf{Z}. \tag{15.15}$$

The expectation of $\hat{\mathbf{u}}$ is

$$E[\hat{\mathbf{u}}] = E[\mathbf{V}\mathbf{y}] = E[\mathbf{V}(\mathbf{\Phi}^{\text{T}}\mathbf{u} + \boldsymbol{\varepsilon})] = \mathbf{V}\mathbf{\Phi}^{\text{T}}\mathbf{u} = (\mathbf{I} + \mathbf{Z}\mathbf{\Phi}^{\text{T}})\mathbf{u}. \tag{15.16}$$

Therefore, $\hat{\mathbf{u}}$ is unbiased if and only if $\mathbf{Z}\mathbf{\Phi}^{\mathrm{T}} = 0$, or, equivalently, $\mathbf{\Phi}\mathbf{Z}^{\mathrm{T}} = 0$. It follows that

$$\mathrm{U_{LSE}}\mathbf{Z}^{\mathrm{T}} = \left[\mathbf{\Phi}\mathbf{\Phi}^{\mathrm{T}}\right]^{-1}\mathbf{\Phi}\mathbf{Z}^{\mathrm{T}} = 0, \tag{15.17}$$

which in turn implies that

$$\begin{aligned}\mathbf{V}\mathbf{V}^{\mathrm{T}} &= \mathbf{U}_{\mathrm{LSE}}\mathbf{U}_{\mathrm{LSE}}^{\mathrm{T}} + \mathbf{Z}\mathbf{Z}^{\mathrm{T}} + \mathbf{\Phi}\mathbf{Z}^{\mathrm{T}} + \mathbf{Z}\mathbf{\Phi}^{\mathrm{T}} \\ &= \mathbf{U}_{\mathrm{LSE}}\mathbf{U}_{LSE}^{\mathrm{T}} + \mathbf{Z}\mathbf{Z}^{\mathrm{T}}.\end{aligned} \tag{15.18}$$

The MSE of an unbiased estimator given in Eq. (15.14) becomes

$$\begin{aligned}\mathrm{MSE_{estimator}} &= \sigma_\varepsilon^2\,\mathtt{tr}\left(\mathbf{V}\mathbf{V}^{\mathrm{T}}\right) \\ &= \sigma_\varepsilon^2\,\mathtt{tr}\left(\mathbf{U}_{\mathrm{LSE}}\mathbf{U}_{\mathrm{LSE}}^{\mathrm{T}}\right) + \sigma_\varepsilon^2\,\mathtt{tr}\left(\mathbf{Z}\mathbf{Z}^{\mathrm{T}}\right),\end{aligned} \tag{15.19}$$

which reaches the minimum when $\mathbf{Z} = 0$. Thus the proof has been established.

Proof that the LSE regressor is the best linear unbiased predictor. Now let us prove $\hat{\mathbf{u}}_{\mathrm{BLUP}} = \hat{\mathbf{u}}_{\mathrm{LSE}}$. According to Eq. (15.9) the variance of the prediction error is

$$\begin{aligned}\mathrm{MSE_{prediction}} &= E[||\hat{\mathbf{u}}^{\mathrm{T}}\vec{\boldsymbol{\phi}}(\mathbf{x}) - y||^2|\mathbf{D_x}] \\ &= E[||\vec{\boldsymbol{\phi}}(\mathbf{x})^{\mathrm{T}}(\hat{\mathbf{u}} - \mathbf{u}) - \varepsilon||^2|\mathbf{D_x}] \\ &= E[(\hat{\mathbf{u}} - \mathbf{u})^{\mathrm{T}}\vec{\boldsymbol{\phi}}(\mathbf{x})\vec{\boldsymbol{\phi}}(\mathbf{x})^{\mathrm{T}}(\hat{\mathbf{u}} - \mathbf{u})|\mathbf{D_x}] + \sigma_\varepsilon^2 \\ &= \mathtt{tr}\left(E[(\hat{\mathbf{u}} - \mathbf{u})^{\mathrm{T}}R_{\boldsymbol{\phi}}(\hat{\mathbf{u}} - \mathbf{u})|\mathbf{D_x}]\right) + \sigma_\varepsilon^2 \\ &= \mathtt{tr}\left(R_{\boldsymbol{\phi}}E[(\hat{\mathbf{u}} - \mathbf{u})(\hat{\mathbf{u}} - \mathbf{u})^{\mathrm{T}}|\mathbf{D_x}]\right) + \sigma_\varepsilon^2 \\ &\underset{\text{Eq. (15.18)}}{=} \mathtt{tr}\left(E\left[R_{\boldsymbol{\phi}}(\hat{\mathbf{u}} - \hat{\mathbf{u}}_{\mathrm{LSE}})(\hat{\mathbf{u}} - \hat{\mathbf{u}}_{\mathrm{LSE}})^{\mathrm{T}}\right.\right. \\ &\qquad \left.\left. + R_{\boldsymbol{\phi}}(\hat{\mathbf{u}}_{\mathrm{LSE}} - \mathbf{u})(\hat{\mathbf{u}}_{\mathrm{LSE}} - \mathbf{u})^{\mathrm{T}}|\mathbf{D_x}\right]\right) + \sigma_\varepsilon^2, \\ &\geq \mathtt{tr}\left(E[(\hat{\mathbf{u}}_{\mathrm{LSE}} - \mathbf{u})^{\mathrm{T}}R_{\boldsymbol{\phi}}(\hat{\mathbf{u}}_{\mathrm{LSE}} - \mathbf{u})|\mathbf{D_x}]\right) + \sigma_\varepsilon^2,\end{aligned}$$

where the inequality is due to the fact that

$$\mathtt{tr}\left(R_{\boldsymbol{\phi}}(\hat{\mathbf{u}}_{\mathrm{LSE}} - \hat{\mathbf{u}})(\hat{\mathbf{u}}_{\mathrm{LSE}} - \hat{\mathbf{u}})^{\mathrm{T}}|\mathbf{D_x}]\right) = \mathtt{tr}\left(E[(\hat{\mathbf{u}}_{\mathrm{LSE}} - \hat{\mathbf{u}})^{\mathrm{T}}R_{\boldsymbol{\phi}}(\hat{\mathbf{u}}_{\mathrm{LSE}} - \hat{\mathbf{u}})|\mathbf{D_x}\,]\right) \geq 0.$$

Clearly, it has its minimum when $\hat{\mathbf{u}} = \hat{\mathbf{u}}_{\mathrm{LSE}}$. Thus the proof has been established.

The minimum variance property

It is worth highlighting that, given observations $\mathbf{D_x} = \{\mathbf{x}_i\}_{i=1}^N$, the optimal linear estimator $\hat{\mathbf{u}} = \mathbf{V}\mathbf{y}$ which minimizes

$$E[\|\hat{\mathbf{u}} - \mathbf{u}\|_{R_{\boldsymbol{\phi}}}^2|\mathbf{D_x}] \tag{15.20}$$

is independent of the input distribution $R_{\boldsymbol{\phi}}$. Also, with reference to Eq. (15.21), it should be obvious that, by setting $R_{\boldsymbol{\phi}} = \mathrm{Diag}\{0,\ldots,0,1,0\ldots,0\}$ in Eq. (15.20), with all terms being zero except the jth diagonal entry, we can prove that $\hat{\mathbf{u}}_{\mathrm{LSE}}$ minimizes the following:

$$E[(\hat{\mathbf{u}}_i - \mathbf{u}_i)^2|\mathbf{D_x}], \tag{15.21}$$

for each individual coefficient $i = 1, \ldots, J$. In summary, $\hat{\mathbf{u}}_{\text{LSE}}$ also minimizes the conditional error variance for every individual regressor coefficient, i.e. $E[(\hat{\mathbf{u}}_i - \mathbf{u}_i)^2|\mathbf{D_x}]$, $i = 1, \ldots, J$.

Output noise with a dependent and non-identical distribution

The Gauss–Markov theorem can be extended to cases in which the noise sequence is not necessarily independently and identically distributed [2]. In this case, the covariance matrix $\mathbf{\Sigma}_\varepsilon$ is no longer necessarily diagonal. The optimal solution is expressed as the following weighted LSE (WLSE) formulation [2, 230]:

$$\hat{\mathbf{u}}_{\text{LSE}} = \left[\mathbf{\Phi}\mathbf{\Sigma}_\varepsilon^{-1}\mathbf{\Phi}^{\text{T}}\right]^{-1}\mathbf{\Phi}\mathbf{\Sigma}_\varepsilon^{-1}\mathbf{y}.$$

Moreover, the Gauss–Markov theorem remains intact, i.e. the weighted LSE (WLSE) solution is a BLUE.

15.3 Kernel regressors for statistical generation models

The Gauss–Markov theorem was originally established for models with a deterministic and fixed system parameter $\mathbf{u}$. However, this section will show that the KRR formulation has a natural statistical interpretation. Moreover, some key properties remain intact for models with a random system parameter $\mathbf{u}$, characterized by its prior statistics, namely the mean value denoted by $\boldsymbol{\mu}$ and the second-order variance denoted by $\mathbf{\Sigma}_u$.

15.3.1 The prior model and training data set

The modified Gauss–Markov generation model is illustrated by Figure 15.1(a), in which the input–output relationship is described by a "linear" equation in the intrinsic space:

$$y = \mathbf{u}_\theta^{\text{T}}\vec{\boldsymbol{\phi}}(\mathbf{x}) + \varepsilon = \sum_{j=1}^{J} u_\theta^{(j)}\phi^{(j)}(\mathbf{x}) + \varepsilon. \tag{15.22}$$

Unlike in the traditional Gauss–Markov model, here we shall assume that the regression model is drawn from a collection of hypotheses $\theta \in \Theta$, i.e. the system vector $\mathbf{u}$ will be treated as a random vector with known prior mean $\boldsymbol{\mu}$ and variance $\mathbf{\Sigma}_u$. Just like before, the additive output noise ε is assumed to be zero-mean and independent of $\mathbf{x}$. From now on, we shall simply denote $\mathbf{u} \equiv \mathbf{u}_\theta$, while bearing in mind that $\mathbf{u}$ is actually representing a random vector. (We shall initially make use of the simplifying assumption that $\mathbf{u}_\theta$ has zero mean, $\boldsymbol{\mu} = 0$, leaving the case with $\boldsymbol{\mu} \neq 0$ to be treated at the end of the section.)

In matrix notation, we have

$$\mathbf{y} = \mathbf{\Phi}^{\text{T}}\mathbf{u} + \boldsymbol{\varepsilon}. \tag{15.23}$$

Assume further that the generating model, Eq. (15.22), creates the following training dataset in the intrinsic space:

$$\{\Phi, \mathcal{Y}\} = \{(\vec{\boldsymbol{\phi}}_1, y_1)\,(\vec{\boldsymbol{\phi}}_2, y_2)\,\ldots\,(\vec{\boldsymbol{\phi}}_N, y_N)\}.$$

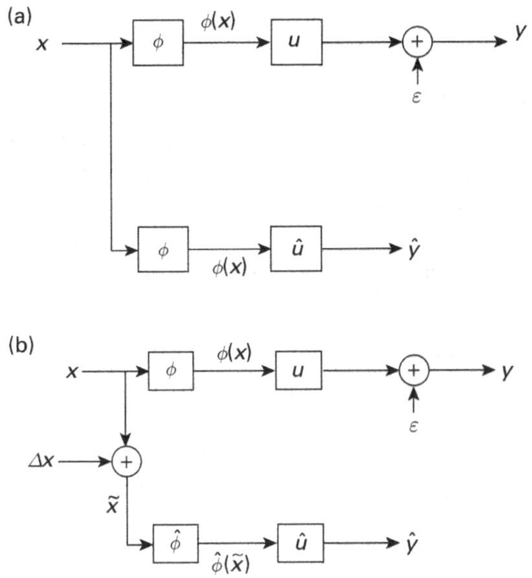

Fig. 15.1. A schematic diagram of the linear estimator for a statistical and kernel-based Gauss–Markov generation model. (a) The KRR learning model with perfect input measurement. (b) The KRR learning model with input corrupted by measurement noise $\Delta\mathbf{x}$.

Just like in Eq. (15.6), in this section, we shall also assume that the threshold value b may be inconsequentially dropped in the optimal solutions, which in turn have the following form:

$$\hat{y} = f(\mathbf{x}) = \sum_{j=1}^{J} \hat{u}_\theta^{(j)} \phi^{(j)}(\mathbf{x}) = \hat{\mathbf{u}}^{\mathrm{T}} \overrightarrow{\boldsymbol{\phi}}(\mathbf{x}).$$

15.3.2 The Gauss–Markov theorem for statistical models

For simplicity, let us denote $\overrightarrow{\boldsymbol{\phi}}_i \equiv \overrightarrow{\boldsymbol{\phi}}(\mathbf{x}_i)$. Suppose that a set of training vectors

$$\{\Phi, \mathcal{Y}\} = \{(\overrightarrow{\boldsymbol{\phi}}_1, y_1)\,(\overrightarrow{\boldsymbol{\phi}}_2, , y_2)\ \ldots\ (\overrightarrow{\boldsymbol{\phi}}_N, y_N)\}$$

is generated by the statistical model prescribed by Eq. (15.22), where the system vector $\mathbf{u}$ is assumed to have zero mean with prior covariance $\boldsymbol{\Sigma}_u$. Moreover, we denote $\mathbf{D_x} = \{\mathbf{x}_i\}_{i=1}^N$ and $R_{\boldsymbol{\phi}}$ as the correlation matrix of $\overrightarrow{\boldsymbol{\phi}}$. Furthermore, the output noise, concatenated in a vector form $\boldsymbol{\varepsilon} = [\varepsilon_1\ \ldots\ \varepsilon_N]^{\mathrm{T}}$, is assumed to have zero mean with covariance $\boldsymbol{\Sigma}_{\boldsymbol{\varepsilon}}$.

Terminologies for Theorem 15.2

Under the statistical Gauss–Markov model, we adopt the following denotations.

(i) **Best linear estimator (BLE).** The *best linear estimator* is defined as the estimator of the system vector $\mathbf{u}$ with the "minimum variance." It is formally defined as

$$\hat{\mathbf{u}}_{\mathrm{BLE}} = \arg\min_{\hat{\mathbf{u}}=\mathbf{V}\mathbf{y}} E[||\hat{\mathbf{u}} - \mathbf{u}||^2|\mathbf{D}_\mathbf{x}], \tag{15.24}$$

where $\mathbf{V} \in \mathbb{R}^{J\times N}$ is independent of $\mathbf{y}$.

(ii) **Best linear predictor (BLP).** The *best linear predictor* is defined as the one which minimizes the following conditional MSE (between the prediction $\hat{y} = \hat{\mathbf{u}}^{\mathrm{T}}\overrightarrow{\phi}(\mathbf{x})$ and the actual response y):

$$\hat{\mathbf{u}}_{\mathrm{BLP}} \equiv \arg\min_{\hat{\mathbf{u}}=\mathbf{V}\mathbf{y}} E[||\hat{\mathbf{u}}^{\mathrm{T}}\overrightarrow{\phi}(\mathbf{x}) - y||^2|\mathbf{D}_\mathbf{x}], \tag{15.25}$$

where $\mathbf{V} \in \mathbb{R}^{J\times N}$ is independent of $\mathbf{y}$.

(iii) **Kernel ridge regressor (KRR).** The (generalized) *kernel ridge regressor* is defined as

$$\hat{\mathbf{u}}_{\mathrm{KRR}} \equiv \arg\min_{\hat{\mathbf{u}}\in\mathbb{R}^J} \left(||\mathbf{\Phi}^{\mathrm{T}}\hat{\mathbf{u}} - \mathbf{y}||^2_{\mathbf{\Sigma}_\varepsilon^{-1}} + ||\hat{\mathbf{u}}||^2_{\mathbf{\Sigma}_u^{-1}}\right). \tag{15.26}$$

THEOREM 15.2 (Gauss–Markov theorem for models with random system parameters) *Given a set of training vectors $\{\Phi, \mathcal{Y}\}$, the best linear estimator (Eq. (15.24)) and best linear predictor (Eq. (15.25)) are identical to each other and, moreover, match with the optimal KRR regressor (Eq. (15.26)). Mathematically,*

$$\begin{aligned}
\hat{\mathbf{u}}_{\mathrm{BLE}} &= \hat{\mathbf{u}}_{\mathrm{BLP}} = \hat{\mathbf{u}}_{\mathrm{KRR}} \\
&= E\left[\mathbf{u}\mathbf{y}^{\mathrm{T}}|\mathbf{D}_\mathbf{x}\right] E\left[\mathbf{y}\mathbf{y}^{\mathrm{T}}|\mathbf{D}_\mathbf{x}\right]^{-1}\mathbf{y} \\
&= \left(E[\mathbf{u}\mathbf{u}^{\mathrm{T}}]\mathbf{\Phi}\right)\left(\mathbf{\Phi}^{\mathrm{T}}E[\mathbf{u}\mathbf{u}^{\mathrm{T}}]\mathbf{\Phi} + E[\boldsymbol{\varepsilon}\boldsymbol{\varepsilon}^{\mathrm{T}}]\right)^{-1}\mathbf{y} \\
&= \mathbf{\Sigma}_\mathbf{u}\mathbf{\Phi}\left(\mathbf{\Phi}^{\mathrm{T}}\mathbf{\Sigma}_u\mathbf{\Phi} + \mathbf{\Sigma}_\varepsilon\right)^{-1}\mathbf{y}. &(15.27) \\
&= \left(\mathbf{\Phi}\mathbf{\Sigma}_\varepsilon^{-1}\mathbf{\Phi}^{\mathrm{T}} + \mathbf{\Sigma}_u^{-1}\right)^{-1}\mathbf{\Phi}\mathbf{\Sigma}_\varepsilon^{-1}\mathbf{y}. &(15.28)
\end{aligned}$$

□

The proof is subdivided into two parts.

(i) Section 15.3.2.1 proves that the best linear estimator (Eq. (15.24)) is equivalent to the optimal KRR regressor (Eq. (15.26)), i.e. $\hat{\mathbf{u}}_{\mathrm{BLE}} = \hat{\mathbf{u}}_{\mathrm{KRR}}$.

(ii) Section 15.3.2.2 proves that the best linear estimator (Eq. (15.24)) and the best linear predictor (Eq. (15.25)) are equivalent, i.e. $\hat{\mathbf{u}}_{\mathrm{BLE}} = \hat{\mathbf{u}}_{\mathrm{BLP}}$.

15.3.2.1 Best linear estimator equals optimal KRR regressor

This section aims at showing that the best linear estimator (Eq. (15.24)) is equivalent to the optimal KRR regressor (Eq. (15.26)). The classic *orthogonality property* states that

$$E\left[(\hat{\mathbf{u}}_{\mathrm{BLE}} - \mathbf{u})\mathbf{y}^{\mathrm{T}}|\mathbf{D}_\mathbf{x}\right] = 0. \tag{15.29}$$

This in turn leads to the following (unique) solution [151]:

$$\hat{\mathbf{u}}_{\mathrm{BLE}} = E\left[\mathbf{u}\mathbf{y}^{\mathrm{T}}|\mathbf{D}_\mathbf{x}\right] E\left[\mathbf{y}\mathbf{y}^{\mathrm{T}}|\mathbf{D}_\mathbf{x}\right]^{-1}\mathbf{y}. \tag{15.30}$$

This is easily verifiable by plugging the solution into Eq. (15.29). By substituting $\mathbf{y} = \mathbf{\Phi}^{\mathrm{T}}\mathbf{u} + \boldsymbol{\varepsilon}$ (in Eq. (15.23)) into Eq. (15.30), we immediately arrive at

$$\begin{aligned}\hat{\mathbf{u}}_{\mathrm{BLE}} &= E\left[\mathbf{u}\mathbf{y}^{\mathrm{T}}|\mathbf{D_x}\right]E\left[\mathbf{y}\mathbf{y}^{\mathrm{T}}|\mathbf{D_x}\right]^{-1}\mathbf{y}\\ &= \left(E[\mathbf{u}\mathbf{u}^{\mathrm{T}}]\mathbf{\Phi}\right)\left(\mathbf{\Phi}^{\mathrm{T}}E[\mathbf{u}\mathbf{u}^{\mathrm{T}}]\,\mathbf{\Phi} + E[\boldsymbol{\varepsilon}\boldsymbol{\varepsilon}^{\mathrm{T}}]\right)^{-1}\mathbf{y}\\ &= \mathbf{\Sigma}_u\mathbf{\Phi}\left(\mathbf{\Phi}^{\mathrm{T}}\mathbf{\Sigma}_u\mathbf{\Phi} + \mathbf{\Sigma}_{\boldsymbol{\varepsilon}}\right)^{-1}\mathbf{y}.\end{aligned} \tag{15.31}$$

By some simple algebra, it can be shown that

$$\begin{aligned}\hat{\mathbf{u}}_{\mathrm{KRR}} &\equiv \arg\min_{\hat{\mathbf{u}}\in\mathbb{R}^J}\left(||\mathbf{\Phi}^{\mathrm{T}}\mathbf{u} - \mathbf{y}||^2_{\mathbf{\Sigma}_{\boldsymbol{\varepsilon}}^{-1}} + ||\hat{\mathbf{u}}||^2_{\mathbf{\Sigma}_u^{-1}}\right)\\ &= \left(\mathbf{\Phi}\mathbf{\Sigma}_{\boldsymbol{\varepsilon}}^{-1}\mathbf{\Phi}^{\mathrm{T}} + \mathbf{\Sigma}_u^{-1}\right)^{-1}\mathbf{\Phi}\mathbf{\Sigma}_{\boldsymbol{\varepsilon}}^{-1}\mathbf{y}\\ &= \mathbf{\Sigma}_u\mathbf{\Phi}\left(\mathbf{\Phi}^{\mathrm{T}}\mathbf{\Sigma}_u\mathbf{\Phi} + \mathbf{\Sigma}_{\boldsymbol{\varepsilon}}\right)^{-1}\mathbf{y}.\end{aligned} \tag{15.32}$$

Finally, the equivalence between Eq. (15.31) and Eq. (15.32) is based on Woodbury's matrix identity [301]. Thus, we have now formally established that $\hat{\mathbf{u}}_{\mathrm{BLE}} = \hat{\mathbf{u}}_{\mathrm{KRR}}$.

15.3.2.2 Best linear estimator equals best linear predictor

This section aims at showing that the best linear estimator (Eq. (15.24)) and the best linear predictor (Eq. (15.25)) are equivalent.

Generalized orthogonality property

Let us start with the classic linear MV estimation (Eq. (15.24)). By virtue of the well-known orthogonality property[151], it is known that $\hat{\mathbf{u}}_{\mathrm{BLE}} - \mathbf{u}$ must be orthogonal to any linear function of $\mathbf{y}$, i.e.

$$E[(\hat{\mathbf{u}}_{\mathrm{BLE}} - \mathbf{u})\mathbf{y}^{\mathrm{T}}\mathbf{A}|\mathbf{D_x}] = \mathbf{0}, \tag{15.33}$$

for any matrix $\mathbf{A} \in \mathbb{R}^{N\times J}$. Thus, we have

$$\begin{aligned}0 &= E[\mathtt{tr}\left((\hat{\mathbf{u}}_{\mathrm{BLE}} - \mathbf{u})\mathbf{y}^{\mathrm{T}}\mathbf{A}\right)|\mathbf{D_x}]\\ &= E[\mathtt{tr}\left(\mathbf{y}^{\mathrm{T}}\mathbf{A}(\hat{\mathbf{u}}_{\mathrm{BLE}} - \mathbf{u})\right)|\mathbf{D_x}]\\ &= E[\mathbf{y}^{\mathrm{T}}\mathbf{A}(\hat{\mathbf{u}}_{\mathrm{BLE}} - \mathbf{u})|\mathbf{D_x}],\end{aligned} \tag{15.34}$$

where $\mathtt{tr}(\cdot)$ denotes the trace operator. Equation (15.33) implies that $\hat{\mathbf{u}}_{\mathrm{BLE}} - \mathbf{u}$ will be uncorrelated with any linear mapping of $\mathbf{y}$, i.e. $\mathbf{A}^{\mathrm{T}}\mathbf{y}$. This will be referred to as a generalized orthogonality property.

Thanks to the generalized orthogonality property and to the fact that $R_{\phi}(\hat{\mathbf{u}} - \hat{\mathbf{u}}_{\mathrm{BLE}})$, for any R_{ϕ}, is obviously a linear mapping of $\mathbf{y}$, we arrive at

$$E[(\hat{\mathbf{u}}_{\mathrm{BLE}} - \mathbf{u})^{\mathrm{T}}R_{\phi}(\hat{\mathbf{u}} - \hat{\mathbf{u}}_{\mathrm{BLE}})|\mathbf{D_x}] = \mathbf{0}.$$

It follows that, for any alternative solution $\hat{\mathbf{u}}$,

$$\begin{aligned}E[(\hat{\mathbf{u}} - \mathbf{u})^{\mathrm{T}}R_{\phi}(\hat{\mathbf{u}} - \mathbf{u})|\mathbf{D_x}] &= E[(\hat{\mathbf{u}}_{\mathrm{BLE}} - \mathbf{u})^{\mathrm{T}}R_{\phi}(\hat{\mathbf{u}}_{\mathrm{BLE}} - \mathbf{u})|\mathbf{D_x}]\\ &\quad + E[(\hat{\mathbf{u}} - \hat{\mathbf{u}}_{\mathrm{BLE}})^{\mathrm{T}}R_{\phi}(\hat{\mathbf{u}} - \hat{\mathbf{u}}_{\mathrm{BLE}})|\mathbf{D_x}]\\ &\geq E[(\hat{\mathbf{u}}_{\mathrm{BLE}} - \mathbf{u})^{\mathrm{T}}R_{\phi}(\hat{\mathbf{u}}_{\mathrm{BLE}} - \mathbf{u})|\mathbf{D_x}].\end{aligned} \tag{15.35}$$

This implies that, for any R_{ϕ}, the solution $\hat{\mathbf{u}}_{\rm BLE}$ also minimizes the *weighted variance*

$$E[(\hat{\mathbf{u}} - \mathbf{u})^{\rm T} R_{\phi} (\hat{\mathbf{u}} - \mathbf{u})]|\mathbf{D}_{\mathbf{x}}], \quad \text{for any} \quad \mathbf{R}_{\phi}. \tag{15.36}$$

In summary, the optimal solution minimizing the unweighted variance (Eq. (15.24)) also minimizes any weighted variance (Eq. (15.36)). Conversely, on setting $R_{\phi} = \mathbf{I}$, it is obvious that the solution minimizing an arbitrarily weighted variance (Eq. (15.36)) should also, as a special case, minimize the unweighted variance (Eq. (15.24)). This establishes the equivalence of the two optimization problems, i.e.

$$\underset{\hat{\mathbf{u}}=\mathbf{V}\mathbf{y}}{\arg\min} \left(E[(\hat{\mathbf{u}} - \mathbf{u})^{\rm T} R_{\phi} (\hat{\mathbf{u}} - \mathbf{u}) | \mathbf{D}_{\mathbf{x}}] \right) = \underset{\hat{\mathbf{u}}=\mathbf{V}\mathbf{y}}{\arg\min} \left(E[||\hat{\mathbf{u}} - \mathbf{u}||^2 | \mathbf{D}_{\mathbf{x}}] \right). \tag{15.37}$$

Denote that

$$R_{\phi} \equiv \int \vec{\phi}(\mathbf{x}) \vec{\phi}(\mathbf{x})^{\rm T} \, d\kappa(\mathbf{x}).$$

By plugging $\hat{\mathbf{u}} = \mathbf{V}\mathbf{y}$ into Eq. (15.25), we can show that

$$E[||\hat{\mathbf{u}}^{\rm T} \vec{\phi}(\mathbf{x}) - \mathbf{y}||^2 | \mathbf{D}_{\mathbf{x}}] = E[(\hat{\mathbf{u}} - \mathbf{u})^{\rm T} R_{\phi} (\hat{\mathbf{u}} - \mathbf{u}) | \mathbf{D}_{\mathbf{x}}] + E[\boldsymbol{\varepsilon}\boldsymbol{\varepsilon}^{\rm T}].$$

Consequently,

$$\underset{\hat{\mathbf{u}}=\mathbf{V}\mathbf{y}}{\arg\min} \, E[||\hat{\mathbf{u}}^{\rm T} \vec{\phi}(\mathbf{x}) - y||^2 | \mathbf{D}_{\mathbf{x}}] = \underset{\hat{\mathbf{u}}=\mathbf{V}\mathbf{y}}{\arg\min} \left(E[(\hat{\mathbf{u}} - \mathbf{u})^{\rm T} R_{\phi} (\hat{\mathbf{u}} - \mathbf{u}) | \mathbf{D}_{\mathbf{x}}] \right), \tag{15.38}$$

which in turn implies that (see Eq. (15.37))

$$\underset{\hat{\mathbf{u}}=\mathbf{V}\mathbf{y}}{\arg\min} \, E[||\hat{\mathbf{u}}^{\rm T} \vec{\phi}(\mathbf{x}) - y||^2 | \mathbf{D}_{\mathbf{x}}] = \underset{\hat{\mathbf{u}}=\mathbf{V}\mathbf{y}}{\arg\min} \left(E[||\hat{\mathbf{u}} - \mathbf{u}||^2 | \mathbf{D}_{\mathbf{x}}] \right). \tag{15.39}$$

Namely, we have just established the mathematical equivalence between the optimization formulations for linear prediction (Eq. (15.25)) and linear MV estimation (Eq. (15.24)).

Let us use a numerical example to further illuminate this point.

Example 15.1 (Example of derivation of BLE and BLP solution and use of expectation) *With reference to Example 8.6, let us consider the four training vectors*

$$\vec{\phi}_1 = \mathbf{x}_1 = \begin{bmatrix} 1.0 \\ 0.1 \end{bmatrix}, \quad \vec{\phi}_2 = \mathbf{x}_2 = \begin{bmatrix} 0.8 \\ 0.1 \end{bmatrix},$$

$$\vec{\phi}_3 = \mathbf{x}_3 = \begin{bmatrix} -0.8 \\ -0.1 \end{bmatrix}, \quad \vec{\phi}_4 = \mathbf{x}_4 = \begin{bmatrix} -1.0 \\ -0.1 \end{bmatrix},$$

with teacher values $y_1 = -1$, $y_2 = -1$, $y_3 = +1$, *and* $y_4 = +1$. *The scatter matrix can be computed as*

$$\mathbf{S} = \mathbf{X}\mathbf{X}^{\rm T} = \begin{bmatrix} 1.0 & 0.8 & -0.8 & -1.0 \\ 0.1 & 0.1 & -0.1 & -0.1 \end{bmatrix} \begin{bmatrix} 1.0 & 0.1 \\ 0.8 & 0.1 \\ -0.8 & -0.1 \\ -1.0 & -0.1 \end{bmatrix} = \begin{bmatrix} 3.28 & 0.36 \\ 0.36 & 0.04 \end{bmatrix}.$$

Recall that

$$\hat{\mathbf{u}}_{\text{BLP}} \equiv \underset{\hat{\mathbf{u}}=\mathbf{V}\mathbf{y}}{\arg\min}\, E[||\hat{\mathbf{u}}^{\text{T}}\overrightarrow{\boldsymbol{\phi}}(\mathbf{x}) - y||^2|\mathbf{D_x}]. \tag{15.40}$$

Here, let us stress the fact that the expectation operator is taken over both of the random vectors, **u** *and* **x**. *More exactly,*

$$E[\text{MSE}] = E_{u,x}[\text{MSE}] = E_u\,[E_x[\text{MSE}]] = E_u\left[\|\hat{\mathbf{u}} - \mathbf{u}\|^2_{R_\phi}|\mathbf{D_x}\right]. \tag{15.41}$$

Note that, by the (generalized) Gauss–Markov theorem, the absence of knowledge of $R_{\boldsymbol{\phi}}$ does not prevent us from getting the final optimal solution. The theorem states that, see Eq. (15.39),

$$\underset{\hat{\mathbf{u}}=\mathbf{V}\mathbf{y}}{\arg\min}\, E[||\hat{\mathbf{u}}^{\text{T}}\overrightarrow{\boldsymbol{\phi}}(\mathbf{x}) - y||^2|\mathbf{D_x}] = \underset{\hat{\mathbf{u}}=\mathbf{V}\mathbf{y}}{\arg\min}\left(E[||\hat{\mathbf{u}} - \mathbf{u}||^2|\mathbf{D_x}]\right). \tag{15.42}$$

Best linear estimation

On plugging $\hat{\mathbf{u}} = \mathbf{V}\mathbf{y} = \mathbf{v}_i y_i$ into the cost function on the right-hand side of Eq. (15.41), we have

$$||\hat{\mathbf{u}} - \mathbf{u}||^2 = \left\|\left(\sum_{i=1}^{4}\mathbf{v}_i\mathbf{x}_i^{\text{T}} + \mathbf{I}\right)\mathbf{u}\right\|^2 + \sigma_\varepsilon^2\left(\sum_{i=1}^{4}||\mathbf{v}_i||^2\right), \tag{15.43}$$

whose minimizing solution can be derived as

$$\begin{aligned}\mathbf{V} &= \left(\mathbf{X}\boldsymbol{\Sigma}_\varepsilon^{-1}\mathbf{X}^{\text{T}} + \boldsymbol{\Sigma}_u^{-1}\right)^{-1}\mathbf{X}\boldsymbol{\Sigma}_\varepsilon^{-1} \\ &= \left(\mathbf{X}\mathbf{X}^{\text{T}} + \rho\mathbf{I}\right)^{-1}\mathbf{X}.\end{aligned} \tag{15.44}$$

Assume that

$$\boldsymbol{\Sigma}_u = \sigma_u^2\mathbf{I} = 0.1\mathbf{I} \quad \text{and} \quad \boldsymbol{\Sigma}_\varepsilon = \sigma_\varepsilon^2\mathbf{I} = 0.005\mathbf{I}.$$

Define $\rho \equiv \sigma_\varepsilon^2/\sigma_u^2$, and in this case

$$\rho \equiv \frac{0.005}{0.1} = 0.05.$$

Then we have

$$\begin{aligned}\mathbf{V} &= \left(\mathbf{X}\boldsymbol{\Sigma}_\varepsilon^{-1}\mathbf{X}^{\text{T}} + \boldsymbol{\Sigma}_u^{-1}\right)^{-1}\mathbf{X}\boldsymbol{\Sigma}_\varepsilon^{-1} \\ &= \left(\mathbf{X}\mathbf{X}^{\text{T}} + \rho\mathbf{I}\right)^{-1}\mathbf{X} \\ &= \left(\begin{bmatrix} 3.28 & 0.36 \\ 0.36 & 0.04 \end{bmatrix} + \begin{bmatrix} 0.05 & 0 \\ 0 & 0.05 \end{bmatrix}\right)^{-1}\begin{bmatrix} 1.0 & 0.8 & -0.8 & -1.0 \\ 0.1 & 0.1 & -0.1 & -0.1 \end{bmatrix}, \\ &= \begin{bmatrix} +0.3175 & +0.2116 & -0.2116 & -0.3175 \\ -0.1587 & +0.2646 & -0.2646 & +0.1587 \end{bmatrix}.\end{aligned} \tag{15.45}$$

It follows that the optimal linear estimator can be obtained as

$$\hat{\mathbf{u}}_{\text{KRR}} = \mathbf{V}\mathbf{y} = \sum_{i=1}^{4}\mathbf{v}_i y_i = [1.0582\ 0.2116]^{\text{T}}.$$

It is easy to verify that the solution is identical to the KRR solution directly from Eq. (15.32). Finally, the predicted response of the system given a test vector **x** *will be*

$$\hat{y}(\mathbf{x}) = \mathbf{u}_{\mathrm{KRR}}^{\mathrm{T}}\mathbf{x} = 1.0582x^{(1)} + 0.2116x^{(2)},$$

which is the same as the solution given in Example 8.6 when $\rho = 0.05$.

The case of extremely small ρ

Intuitively, an extremely large $\mathbf{\Sigma}_u$ *means that the prior statistics will bear little or no influence. Consequently, the solution has to largely depend only on the training dataset. Mathematically, when the prior uncertainty on* **u** *is much higher than the variance of the output noise, i.e.* $\rho \equiv \sigma_\varepsilon^2/\sigma_u^2 \to 0$, *then*

$$\hat{\mathbf{u}}_{\mathrm{KRR}(\rho\to 0)} \to \hat{\mathbf{u}}_{\mathrm{LSE}} = [0 \quad 10]^{\mathrm{T}}.$$

This implies that the KRR will be approximately a BLUE when ρ *is very small.*

Bias and variance of KRR estimator

The KRR estimator (or regressor) is generally biased with

$$\text{bias} = E[\hat{\mathbf{u}}_{\mathrm{KRR}}] - \mathbf{u} = -\left(\mathbf{\Phi}\mathbf{\Sigma}_\varepsilon^{-1}\mathbf{\Phi}^{\mathrm{T}} + \mathbf{\Sigma}_u^{-1}\right)^{-1}\mathbf{\Sigma}_u^{-1}\mathbf{u}, \tag{15.46}$$

i.e. there exists nonzero bias as long as the second-order prior statistics $\mathbf{\Sigma}_u$ is *finite*. On the other hand, the KRR estimator does approach an unbiased estimation when $\mathbf{\Sigma}_u^{-1} \to \mathbf{0}$. Note also that the variance of $\hat{\mathbf{u}}_{\mathrm{KRR}}$ is

$$\begin{aligned} &E\left[\left(\hat{\mathbf{u}}_{\mathrm{KRR}} - E[\hat{\mathbf{u}}_{\mathrm{KRR}}]\right)\left(\hat{\mathbf{u}}_{\mathrm{KRR}} - E[\hat{\mathbf{u}}_{\mathrm{KRR}}]\right)^{\mathrm{T}}\right] \\ &\quad = \left(\mathbf{\Phi}\mathbf{\Sigma}_\varepsilon^{-1}\mathbf{\Phi}^{\mathrm{T}} + \mathbf{\Sigma}_u^{-1}\right)^{-1}\mathbf{\Phi}\mathbf{\Sigma}_\varepsilon^{-1}\mathbf{\Phi}^{\mathrm{T}}\left(\mathbf{\Phi}\mathbf{\Sigma}_\varepsilon^{-1}\mathbf{\Phi}^{\mathrm{T}} + \mathbf{\Sigma}_u^{-1}\right)^{-1}. \end{aligned} \tag{15.47}$$

15.3.2.3 KRR learning models when **u** has nonzero mean

Now let us assume that there is another generation vector $\mathbf{u}'$ with the same second-order variance $\mathbf{\Sigma}_u$ but a nonzero mean $\boldsymbol{\mu} \neq 0$. Now consider the following training dataset (in the intrinsic space):

$$\{(\vec{\phi}_1, y'_1)\,(\vec{\phi}_2, y'_2)\,\ldots\,(\vec{\phi}_N, y'_N)\},$$

created by the model

$$y' = \mathbf{u}'^{\mathrm{T}}\vec{\phi}(\mathbf{x}) + \varepsilon. \tag{15.48}$$

We denote $\mathbf{u} \equiv \mathbf{u}' - \boldsymbol{\mu}$. Then it will be easier to work with a modified model,

$$y = \mathbf{u}^{\mathrm{T}}\vec{\phi}(\mathbf{x}) + \varepsilon, \tag{15.49}$$

with the corresponding training dataset,

$$\{(\vec{\phi}_1, y_1)\,(\vec{\phi}_2, y_2)\,\cdots\,(\vec{\phi}_N, y_N)\},$$

where

$$y_i \equiv y'_i - \boldsymbol{\mu}^{\mathrm{T}}\vec{\boldsymbol{\phi}}(\mathbf{x}_i).$$

Since $E[\mathbf{u}] = \mathbf{0}$ and $E[\mathbf{u}\mathbf{u}^{\mathrm{T}}] = \boldsymbol{\Sigma}_u$, Eq. (15.28) becomes applicable, leading to the following solution:

$$\hat{\mathbf{u}}_{\mathrm{KRR}} = \mathbf{V}_{\mathrm{KRR}}\,\mathbf{y}, \text{ where } \mathbf{V}_{\mathrm{KRR}} = \left(\boldsymbol{\Phi}\boldsymbol{\Sigma}_\varepsilon^{-1}\boldsymbol{\Phi}^{\mathrm{T}} + \boldsymbol{\Sigma}_u^{-1}\right)^{-1}\boldsymbol{\Phi}\boldsymbol{\Sigma}_\varepsilon^{-1}. \tag{15.50}$$

It means that the optimal estimator for the original generation model has to be

$$\begin{aligned}\hat{\mathbf{u}}'_{\mathrm{KRR}} &= \hat{\mathbf{u}}_{\mathrm{KRR}} + \boldsymbol{\mu} = \mathbf{V}_{\mathrm{KRR}}\mathbf{y} + \boldsymbol{\mu} \\ &= \mathbf{V}_{\mathrm{KRR}}(\mathbf{y}' - \boldsymbol{\Phi}^{\mathrm{T}}\boldsymbol{\mu}) + \boldsymbol{\mu} = \mathbf{V}_{\mathrm{KRR}}\mathbf{y}' + (\mathbf{I} - \mathbf{V}_{\mathrm{KRR}}\boldsymbol{\Phi}^{\mathrm{T}})\boldsymbol{\mu}.\end{aligned}$$

15.3.3 KRR regressors in empirical space

So far, we have treated only KRR algorithms in the intrinsic space, which is practically appealing when the intrinsic degree J is finite and of reasonable size. For Gaussian kernels, the intrinsic-space approach is highly impractical since its intrinsic degree J is infinite. Moreover, the intrinsic vector space is undefined for nonvectorial data analysis. This motivates kernelization of the learning models, i.e. converting the KRR optimizer given in the intrinsic space into an equivalent formulation defined in the empirical space.

In order to derive the empirical-space counterpart of the KRR algorithm, we shall first establish that a $\boldsymbol{\Sigma}_u$-modulated LSP condition holds for the current KRR formulation. Correspondingly, a $\boldsymbol{\Sigma}_u$-modulated kernel function can be defined, which will in turn lead to the dual-optimization formulation in the empirical space. Subsequently, a time-adaptive algorithm in the empirical space can be developed.

Without loss of generality, we shall make the simplifying assumption that $\mathbf{u}_\theta$ has zero mean, $\boldsymbol{\mu} = 0$.

According to Eq. (15.32), the KRR cost function in the intrinsic space is

$$\hat{\mathbf{u}}_{\mathrm{KRR}} \equiv \arg\min_{\hat{\mathbf{u}}\in\mathbb{R}^J}\left(||\boldsymbol{\Phi}^{\mathrm{T}}\hat{\mathbf{u}} - \mathbf{y}||^2_{\boldsymbol{\Sigma}_\varepsilon^{-1}} + ||\hat{\mathbf{u}}||^2_{\boldsymbol{\Sigma}_u^{-1}}\right). \tag{15.51}$$

Moreover, its optimal solution is

$$\hat{\mathbf{u}}_{\mathrm{KRR}} = \boldsymbol{\Sigma}_u\boldsymbol{\Phi}\left(\boldsymbol{\Phi}^{\mathrm{T}}\boldsymbol{\Sigma}_u\boldsymbol{\Phi} + \boldsymbol{\Sigma}_\varepsilon\right)^{-1}\mathbf{y}, \tag{15.52}$$

which can be expressed in the form

$$\hat{\mathbf{u}}_{\mathrm{KRR}} = \boldsymbol{\Sigma}_u\boldsymbol{\Phi}\mathbf{a}, \quad \mathbf{a} = \left(\boldsymbol{\Phi}^{\mathrm{T}}\boldsymbol{\Sigma}_u\boldsymbol{\Phi} + \boldsymbol{\Sigma}_\varepsilon\right)^{-1}\mathbf{y}. \tag{15.53}$$

This suggests that the solution observes a "$\boldsymbol{\Sigma}_u$-modulated" learning subspace property, i.e. the solution can always be expressed as a linear combination of the training vectors, i.e. $\boldsymbol{\Phi}\mathbf{a}$, post-transformed by $\boldsymbol{\Sigma}_u$. Accordingly, a $\boldsymbol{\Sigma}_u$-modulated kernel function can be defined as

$$K(\mathbf{x}, \mathbf{x}') = \vec{\boldsymbol{\phi}}(\mathbf{x})^{\mathrm{T}}\boldsymbol{\Sigma}_u\vec{\boldsymbol{\phi}}(\mathbf{x}'), \tag{15.54}$$

which in turn leads to the following $\mathbf{\Sigma}_u$-modulated kernel matrix:

$$\mathbf{K} = \mathbf{\Phi}^{\mathrm{T}}\mathbf{\Sigma}_u\mathbf{\Phi}, \tag{15.55}$$

whose (i,j)th entry is

$$K_{ij} = K(\mathbf{x}_i, \mathbf{x}_j) = \vec{\boldsymbol{\phi}}(\mathbf{x}_i)^{\mathrm{T}}\mathbf{\Sigma}_u\vec{\boldsymbol{\phi}}(\mathbf{x}_j), \quad i = 1, \ldots, N, j = 1, \ldots, N.$$

With the $\mathbf{\Sigma}_u$-modulated LSP, the cost function in $\hat{\mathbf{u}}$ (Eq. (15.51)) can be expressed as a function in $\mathbf{a}$:

$$\begin{aligned} ||\mathbf{\Phi}^{\mathrm{T}}\hat{\mathbf{u}} - \mathbf{y}||^2_{\mathbf{\Sigma}_\varepsilon^{-1}} + ||\hat{\mathbf{u}}||^2_{\mathbf{\Sigma}_u^{-1}} &= ||\mathbf{\Phi}^{\mathrm{T}}\mathbf{\Sigma}_u\mathbf{\Phi}\mathbf{a} - \mathbf{y}||^2_{\mathbf{\Sigma}_\varepsilon^{-1}} + \mathbf{a}^{\mathrm{T}}\mathbf{\Phi}^{\mathrm{T}}\mathbf{\Sigma}_u\mathbf{\Sigma}_u^{-1}\mathbf{\Sigma}_u\mathbf{\Phi}\mathbf{a} \\ &= ||\mathbf{K}\mathbf{a} - \mathbf{y}||^2_{\mathbf{\Sigma}_\varepsilon^{-1}} + \mathbf{a}^{\mathrm{T}}\mathbf{K}\mathbf{a}, \end{aligned} \tag{15.56}$$

which serves the objective function for the optimizer in the empirical space, whose optimal solution is

$$\mathbf{a} = [\mathbf{K} + \mathbf{\Sigma}_\varepsilon]^{-1}\mathbf{y}, \tag{15.57}$$

which by inspection is the same as Eq. (15.32). Once $\mathbf{a}$ has been found, the optimal estimation can be expressed as

$$\hat{y} = \mathbf{a}^{\mathrm{T}}\vec{\mathbf{k}}(\mathbf{x}), \tag{15.58}$$

where we denote $\vec{\mathbf{k}}(\mathbf{x}) = [K(\mathbf{x}_1, \mathbf{x}) \ \ldots \ K(\mathbf{x}_N, \mathbf{x})]^{\mathrm{T}}$, see Eq. (15.54).

An important advantage of the empirical-space approach lies in its versatility, ie. it is applicable to for any value of J, be it finite or infinite. This is exemplified by Example 15.2.

Example 15.2 *In this example, we adopt a Gaussian kernel function,* $k(x, x') = e^{-(x-x')^2/2}$. *Supposing that we are given* N *training samples* $\mathbf{D} = \{\mathbf{x}_i, \mathrm{y}_i\}_{i=1}^N$, *where the output noise covariance matrix is* $\mathbf{\Sigma}_\varepsilon$, *the KRR regressor in the empirical space is*

$$\mathbf{a}_{\mathrm{KRR}} = (\mathbf{K} + \mathbf{\Sigma}_\varepsilon)^{-1}\mathbf{y},$$

where $\mathbf{K} = \{\mathbf{K}_{ij}\} = \{e^{-(x_i - x_j)^2/2}\}$ *is the kernel matrix and* $\mathbf{\Sigma}_\varepsilon = \sigma_\varepsilon^2\mathbf{I}$. *Then the optimal prediction can be obtained as*

$$\hat{y}_{\mathrm{KRR}} = \mathbf{a}_{\mathrm{KRR}}^{\mathrm{T}}\vec{\mathbf{k}}(x).$$

In contrast, the intrinsic space will have an infinite intrinsic degree, with the following basis functions:

$$\phi^{(n)}(x) = \frac{x^n e^{-x^2/2}}{\sqrt{n!}}, \quad n = 0, 1, \ldots. \tag{15.59}$$

Consider a system whose input $x \in \mathbb{R}$ and output $y \in \mathbb{R}$ are described by a Gauss–Markov model

$$y = \sum_{n=0}^{\infty} u_n \phi^{(n)}(x) + \varepsilon, \tag{15.60}$$

where we have prior knowledge about the system parameters

$$E[u_n] = 0, \; E[u_m u_n] = \delta_{mn}. \tag{15.61}$$

It is easy to verify that its $\mathbf{\Sigma}_u$-modulated kernel function is

$$\begin{aligned} k(x, x') &= \sum_{m,n\geq 0} \delta_{mn} \left(\phi^{(m)}(x)\right)\left(\phi^{(n)}(x')\right) \\ &= \sum_{n\geq 0} \frac{1}{n!}(xx')^n e^{-x^2/2} e^{-x'^2/2} \\ &= e^{xx'} e^{-x^2/2} e^{-x'^2/2} = e^{-(x-x')^2/2}. \end{aligned} \tag{15.62}$$

15.3.4 KRR regressors with Gaussian distribution

To help illustrate the theoretical derivation, let us conclude this section by a simple example with scalar and Gaussian-distributed input.

Example 15.3 *Consider a single-variate linear Gauss–Markov model*

$$y = ux + \varepsilon,$$

where we assume prior mean $\mu_u = 0$ and covariance σ_u^2, and that the inputs are mutually independently generated according to a Gaussian distribution $x \sim \mathcal{N}(0, \sigma_x^2)$. We shall assume that $\sigma_x^2 = 1$ and $\sigma_{\varepsilon_i}^2 = \sigma_\varepsilon^2$.

Given N observations $\{(x_i, y_i)\}_{i=1}^N$, the KRR regressor is then given by (see Eq. (15.28))

$$\begin{aligned} \hat{u}_{\mathrm{KRR}} &= \left(\mathbf{\Phi}\mathbf{\Sigma}_\varepsilon^{-1}\mathbf{\Phi}^{\mathrm{T}} + \mathbf{\Sigma}_u^{-1}\right)^{-1} \mathbf{\Phi}\mathbf{\Sigma}_\varepsilon^{-1}\mathbf{y} \\ &= \frac{\sum_{i=1}^N x_i y_i}{\sum_{i=1}^N x_i^2 + \sigma_\varepsilon^2/\sigma_u^2}. \end{aligned} \tag{15.63}$$

It follows that

$$\begin{aligned} \hat{y} &= \hat{u}_{\mathrm{KRR}} \overrightarrow{\boldsymbol{\phi}}(\mathbf{x}) = \hat{u}_{\mathrm{KRR}} x \\ &= \frac{\sum_{i=1}^N x_i y_i}{\sum_{i=1}^N x_i^2 + \sigma_\varepsilon^2/\sigma_u^2} x. \end{aligned} \tag{15.64}$$

Kernelized formulation

Equation (15.63) has an alternative formula given in Eq. (15.27):

$$\hat{u}_{\text{KRR}} = \mathbf{\Sigma}_u \mathbf{\Phi} \left(\mathbf{\Phi}^{\text{T}} \mathbf{\Sigma}_u \mathbf{\Phi} + \mathbf{\Sigma}_{\boldsymbol{\varepsilon}} \right)^{-1} \mathbf{y},$$

which naturally leads to the following kernelized expression:

$$\hat{y} = \frac{\sum_{i=1}^{N} K(x_i, x) y_i}{\sum_{i=1}^{N} K(x_i, x_i) + \sigma_\varepsilon^2}, \tag{15.65}$$

where the kernel function for the KRR learning model is as defined in Eq. (15.54), i.e.

$$K(\mathbf{x}, \mathbf{x}') = \hat{\boldsymbol{\phi}}_{\mathbf{x}}(\mathbf{x})^{\text{T}} \mathbf{\Sigma}_u \hat{\boldsymbol{\phi}}_{\mathbf{x}}(\mathbf{x}').$$

15.4 Kernel regressors for errors-in-variables (EiV) models

Let us assume that the generation model is the same as before:

$$y = \mathbf{u}^{\text{T}} \overrightarrow{\boldsymbol{\phi}}(\mathbf{x}) + \varepsilon = \sum_{j=1}^{J} u^{(j)} \phi^{(j)}(\mathbf{x}) + \varepsilon, \tag{15.66}$$

in which the system vector $\mathbf{u}$ is assumed to have zero mean with prior covariance $\mathbf{\Sigma}_u$. (We shall for now assume that $\mathbf{u}$ has zero mean, $\boldsymbol{\mu} = 0$, deferring the case of $\boldsymbol{\mu} \neq 0$ to the end of this section.)

Let us also assume that $\mathbf{x}_1, \ldots, \mathbf{x}_N$ are mutually independent, being corrupted by additive observation noise. In addition, the output noise ε is assumed to be a zero-mean random noise term that is independent of $\mathbf{x}$. Furthermore, the output noise can be concatenated into a random vector $\boldsymbol{\varepsilon} = [\varepsilon_1 \ \ldots \ \varepsilon_N]^{\text{T}}$, which is assumed to have zero mean and covariance matrix $\mathbf{\Sigma}_{\boldsymbol{\varepsilon}}$.

Under the EiV model, see Figure 15.1(b), it is further assumed that the input measurements are corrupted by observation noise, i.e.

$$\tilde{\mathbf{x}} = \mathbf{x} + \Delta\mathbf{x}. \tag{15.67}$$

Finally, it is assumed that we are given a set of training vectors

$$\{(\tilde{\mathbf{x}}_1, y_1)\ (\tilde{\mathbf{x}}_2, y_2)\ \ldots\ (\tilde{\mathbf{x}}_N, y_N)\}$$

generated by the input-perturbed model prescribed by Eqs. (15.66) and (15.67).

Just like in Eq. (15.6), throughout this section, we shall again assume that the threshold value b may be inconsequentially dropped in the optimal predictor, which has the following form:

$$\hat{y} = f(\tilde{\mathbf{x}}) = \tilde{\mathbf{u}}^{\text{T}} \hat{\boldsymbol{\phi}}(\tilde{\mathbf{x}}) = \sum_{j=1}^{J} \tilde{u}^{(j)} \tilde{\phi}^{(j)}(\hat{\mathbf{x}}).$$

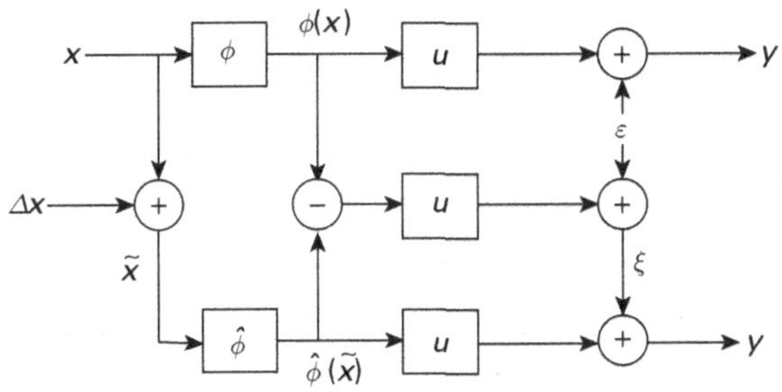

Fig. 15.2. A schematic diagram of the proposed new generation model. It is worth mentioning that ξ denotes the error combining both contributions from input and output noise, and ξ is uncorrelated with $\hat{\boldsymbol{\phi}}_{\tilde{\mathbf{x}}}(\tilde{\mathbf{x}})$.

15.4.1 The Gauss–Markov theorem for EiV learning models

In order to extend the Gauss–Markov theorem to the errors-in-variables learning models, we propose an alternative, but equivalent, generation model so that we can directly employ the same procedure as the one we used for the derivation of $\tilde{\mathbf{u}}_{\mathrm{KRR}}$ in Section 15.3

The proposed model is schematically illustrated by Figure 15.2, for which a conditionally expected value of an intrinsic feature vector is defined as

$$\hat{\boldsymbol{\phi}}_{\tilde{\mathbf{x}}}(\tilde{\mathbf{x}}) \equiv E[\overrightarrow{\boldsymbol{\phi}}(\mathbf{x})|\tilde{\mathbf{x}}].$$

In the subsequent discussion, we shall make use of the simplifying denotation that

$$\hat{\boldsymbol{\phi}}_i \equiv \hat{\boldsymbol{\phi}}_{\tilde{\mathbf{x}}}(\tilde{\mathbf{x}}_i) = E[\overrightarrow{\boldsymbol{\phi}}(\mathbf{x})|\tilde{\mathbf{x}}_i], \quad i = 1, \ldots, N. \tag{15.68}$$

With reference to the original model (Eq. (15.66)), we now propose an equivalent generation model:

$$y = \mathbf{u}^{\mathrm{T}}\hat{\boldsymbol{\phi}}_{\tilde{\mathbf{x}}}(\tilde{\mathbf{x}}) + \xi(\tilde{\mathbf{x}}), \tag{15.69}$$

where we define a "modified noise" as

$$\xi(\tilde{\mathbf{x}}) \equiv \mathbf{u}^{\mathrm{T}}\left(\overrightarrow{\boldsymbol{\phi}}(\mathbf{x}) - \hat{\boldsymbol{\phi}}_{\tilde{\mathbf{x}}}(\tilde{\mathbf{x}})\right) + \varepsilon, \tag{15.70}$$

which leads to a critical equality (see Problem 15.4):

$$E[\mathbf{u}\xi(\tilde{\mathbf{x}})|\tilde{\mathbf{x}}] = 0. \tag{15.71}$$

Note that, as is shown pictorially in Figure 15.3, the "modified noise" and $\hat{\boldsymbol{\phi}}_{\tilde{\mathbf{x}}}(\tilde{\mathbf{x}})$ are uncorrelated, i.e.

$$E[\hat{\boldsymbol{\phi}}_{\tilde{\mathbf{x}}}(\tilde{\mathbf{x}})\xi(\tilde{\mathbf{x}})] = 0. \tag{15.72}$$

In matrix notation, we have

$$\mathbf{y} = \hat{\boldsymbol{\Phi}}_{\tilde{\mathbf{x}}}^{\mathrm{T}}\mathbf{u} + \boldsymbol{\xi}, \tag{15.73}$$

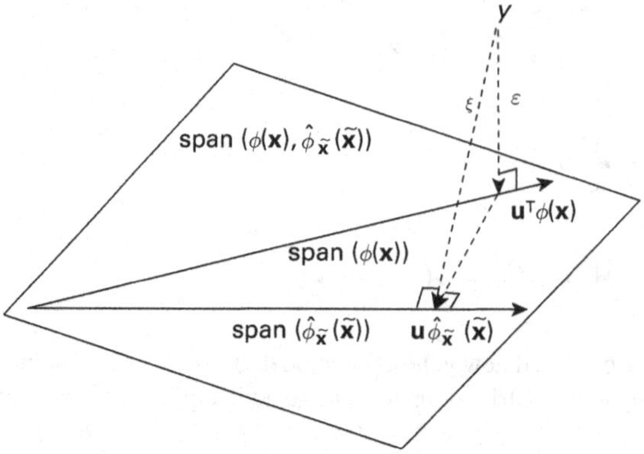

Fig. 15.3. The projection from y to span $(\hat{\boldsymbol{\phi}}_{\tilde{\mathbf{x}}}(\tilde{\mathbf{x}}))$. Here ξ denotes the error combining contributions from both input and output noise. Note that, as displayed here, ξ is uncorrelated with (or orthogonal to) $\hat{\boldsymbol{\phi}}_{\tilde{\mathbf{x}}}(\tilde{\mathbf{x}})$.

where the expected value of $\boldsymbol{\Phi}$ is denoted as

$$\begin{aligned}\hat{\boldsymbol{\Phi}}_{\tilde{\mathbf{x}}} &= E[\boldsymbol{\Phi}|\mathbf{D}_{\tilde{\mathbf{x}}}]\\ &= \left[E[\overrightarrow{\boldsymbol{\phi}}(\mathbf{x}_1)|\tilde{\mathbf{x}}_1]E[\overrightarrow{\boldsymbol{\phi}}(\mathbf{x}_2)|\tilde{\mathbf{x}}_2]\ \ldots\ E[\overrightarrow{\boldsymbol{\phi}}(\mathbf{x}_N)|\tilde{\mathbf{x}}_N]\right]\\ &= \left[\hat{\boldsymbol{\phi}}_1\hat{\boldsymbol{\phi}}_2\ \ldots\ \hat{\boldsymbol{\phi}}_N\right].\end{aligned} \tag{15.74}$$

Here we denote $\mathbf{D}_{\tilde{\mathbf{x}}} = \{\tilde{\mathbf{x}}_i\}_{i=1}^N$, where $\tilde{\mathbf{x}}_i = \mathbf{x}_i + \Delta\mathbf{x}_i$.

Note that the modified "output noise" $\boldsymbol{\xi}$ is now data-dependent. We denote its covariance matrix as

$$E[\boldsymbol{\xi}\boldsymbol{\xi}^{\mathrm{T}}|\mathbf{D}_{\tilde{\mathbf{x}}}] \equiv \boldsymbol{\Sigma}_{\xi} = \mathrm{Diag}(\sigma_{\xi_1}^2, \ldots, \sigma_{\xi_N}^2), \tag{15.75}$$

where

$$\begin{aligned}\sigma_{\xi_i}^2 &= E[\|(\overrightarrow{\boldsymbol{\phi}}(\mathbf{x}_i) - \hat{\boldsymbol{\phi}}_i)^{\mathrm{T}}\boldsymbol{\Sigma}_u(\overrightarrow{\boldsymbol{\phi}}(\mathbf{x}_i) - \hat{\boldsymbol{\phi}}_i)|\tilde{\mathbf{x}}_i] + E[\varepsilon_i^2|\tilde{\mathbf{x}}_i]\\ &= E[\overrightarrow{\boldsymbol{\phi}}(\mathbf{x}_i)^{\mathrm{T}}\boldsymbol{\Sigma}_u\overrightarrow{\boldsymbol{\phi}}(\mathbf{x}_i)|\tilde{\mathbf{x}}_i] - \hat{\boldsymbol{\phi}}_i^{\mathrm{T}}\boldsymbol{\Sigma}_u\hat{\boldsymbol{\phi}}_i + \sigma_\varepsilon^2.\end{aligned} \tag{15.76}$$

Terminologies for Theorem 15.3

Under the EiV learning model, we adopt the following denotations.

(i) **Best linear EiV estimator (EiVE).** Under the EiV learning model, the best linear estimator is defined as the one which delivers the "minimum variance" on the estimation of the system vector $\mathbf{u}$. It is formally defined as

$$\tilde{\mathbf{u}}_{\mathrm{EiV}E} = \underset{\tilde{\mathbf{u}}=\mathbf{V}\mathbf{y}}{\arg\min}\ E[||\tilde{\mathbf{u}} - \mathbf{u}||^2|\mathbf{D}_{\tilde{\mathbf{x}}}], \tag{15.77}$$

where $\mathbf{V} \in \mathbb{R}^{J\times N}$ is independent of $\mathbf{y}$.

(ii) **Best linear EiV predictor (EiVP).** Under the EiV learning model, the best linear predictor is defined as the one which minimizes the following conditional MSE between the prediction $\hat{y} = \tilde{\mathbf{u}}^{\mathrm{T}}\hat{\boldsymbol{\phi}}_{\tilde{\mathbf{x}}}(\tilde{\mathbf{x}})$ and the actual response y:

$$\tilde{\mathbf{u}}_{\mathrm{EiV}P} \equiv \arg\min_{\tilde{\mathbf{u}}=\mathbf{V}\mathbf{y}} E[||\tilde{\mathbf{u}}^{\mathrm{T}}\hat{\boldsymbol{\phi}}_{\tilde{\mathbf{x}}}(\tilde{\mathbf{x}}) - \mathbf{y}||^2|\mathbf{D}_{\tilde{\mathbf{x}}}], \tag{15.78}$$

for any $\tilde{\mathbf{x}}$ distribution, where $\mathbf{V} \in \mathbb{R}^{J\times N}$ is independent of $\mathbf{y}$.

(iii) **EiV regressor.** The EiV regressor is defined as

$$\tilde{\mathbf{u}}_{\mathrm{EiV}} \equiv \arg\min_{\tilde{\mathbf{u}}\in\mathbb{R}^J} \left(||\hat{\boldsymbol{\Phi}}_{\tilde{\mathbf{x}}}^{\mathrm{T}}\tilde{\mathbf{u}} - \mathbf{y}||^2_{\boldsymbol{\Sigma}_\xi^{-1}} + ||\tilde{\mathbf{u}}||^2_{\boldsymbol{\Sigma}_u^{-1}} \right). \tag{15.79}$$

THEOREM 15.3 (Generalized Gauss–Markov theorem for errors-in-variables models) *Given a set of training vectors $\{\tilde{\Phi}, \mathcal{Y}\}$ generated by the EiV learning model in Eqs. (15.66) and (15.67), the best linear estimator (Eq. (15.77)) and best linear predictor (Eq. (15.78)) are identical to each other and, moreover, match with the optimal EiV regressor (Eq. (15.79)). Mathematically,*

$$\begin{aligned}
\tilde{\mathbf{u}}_{\mathrm{EiV}E} = \tilde{\mathbf{u}}_{\mathrm{EiV}P} = \tilde{\mathbf{u}}_{\mathrm{EiV}}&\\
&= E\left[\mathbf{u}\mathbf{y}^{\mathrm{T}}|\mathbf{D}_{\tilde{\mathbf{x}}}\right] E\left[\mathbf{y}\mathbf{y}^{\mathrm{T}}|\mathbf{D}_{\tilde{\mathbf{x}}}\right]^{-1}\mathbf{y}\\
&= \left(E[\mathbf{u}\mathbf{u}^{\mathrm{T}}]\hat{\boldsymbol{\Phi}}_{\tilde{\mathbf{x}}}\right)\left(\hat{\boldsymbol{\Phi}}_{\tilde{\mathbf{x}}}^{\mathrm{T}}E[\mathbf{u}\mathbf{u}^{\mathrm{T}}]\hat{\boldsymbol{\Phi}}_{\tilde{\mathbf{x}}} + E[\boldsymbol{\xi}\boldsymbol{\xi}^{\mathrm{T}}]\right)^{-1}\mathbf{y}\\
&= \boldsymbol{\Sigma}_u\hat{\boldsymbol{\Phi}}_{\tilde{\mathbf{x}}}\left(\hat{\boldsymbol{\Phi}}_{\tilde{\mathbf{x}}}^{\mathrm{T}}\boldsymbol{\Sigma}_u\hat{\boldsymbol{\Phi}}_{\tilde{\mathbf{x}}} + \boldsymbol{\Sigma}_\xi\right)^{-1}\mathbf{y}. &(15.80)\\
&= \left(\hat{\boldsymbol{\Phi}}_{\tilde{\mathbf{x}}}\boldsymbol{\Sigma}_\xi^{-1}\hat{\boldsymbol{\Phi}}_{\tilde{\mathbf{x}}}^{\mathrm{T}} + \boldsymbol{\Sigma}_u^{-1}\right)^{-1}\hat{\boldsymbol{\Phi}}_{\tilde{\mathbf{x}}}\boldsymbol{\Sigma}_\xi^{-1}\mathbf{y}, &(15.81)
\end{aligned}$$

where $\boldsymbol{\Sigma}_\xi$ is defined in Eq. (15.75). □

Proof. The proof is similar to that for the KRR case. (For more detail, see Wu and Kung [302].) Briefly, note that the orthogonality property in this case becomes

$$E\left[(\tilde{\mathbf{u}} - \mathbf{u})\mathbf{y}^{\mathrm{T}}|\mathbf{D}_{\tilde{\mathbf{x}}}\right] = 0, \tag{15.82}$$

which immediately leads to the optimal solution for $\tilde{\mathbf{u}}_{\mathrm{EiV}}$:

$$\tilde{\mathbf{u}}_{\mathrm{EiV}} = E\left[\mathbf{u}\mathbf{y}^{\mathrm{T}}|\mathbf{D}_{\tilde{\mathbf{x}}}\right] E\left[\mathbf{y}\mathbf{y}^{\mathrm{T}}|\mathbf{D}_{\tilde{\mathbf{x}}}\right]^{-1}\mathbf{y}. \tag{15.83}$$

From Eq. (15.73), we have

$$E\left[\mathbf{u}\,\mathbf{y}^{\mathrm{T}}|\mathbf{D}_{\tilde{\mathbf{x}}}\right] = E[\mathbf{u}\mathbf{u}^{\mathrm{T}}]E[\boldsymbol{\Phi}|\mathbf{D}_{\tilde{\mathbf{x}}}] = \boldsymbol{\Sigma}_u\hat{\boldsymbol{\Phi}}_{\tilde{\mathbf{x}}}$$

and

$$\begin{aligned}
E\left[\mathbf{y}\mathbf{y}^{\mathrm{T}}|\mathbf{D}_{\tilde{\mathbf{x}}}\right] \underset{\text{Eq. (15.71)}}{=} & \; E[\boldsymbol{\Phi}^{\mathrm{T}}E[\mathbf{u}\mathbf{u}^{\mathrm{T}}]\boldsymbol{\Phi}|\mathbf{D}_{\tilde{\mathbf{x}}}] + E[\boldsymbol{\xi}\boldsymbol{\xi}^{\mathrm{T}}|\mathbf{D}_{\tilde{\mathbf{x}}}]\\
= & \; \hat{\boldsymbol{\Phi}}_{\tilde{\mathbf{x}}}^{\mathrm{T}}\boldsymbol{\Sigma}_u\hat{\boldsymbol{\Phi}}_{\tilde{\mathbf{x}}} + \boldsymbol{\Sigma}_\xi. &(15.84)
\end{aligned}$$

It follows that

$$\tilde{\mathbf{u}}_{\rm EiV} = \left(\boldsymbol{\Sigma}_u\hat{\boldsymbol{\Phi}}_{\tilde{\mathbf{x}}}\right)\left(\hat{\boldsymbol{\Phi}}_{\tilde{\mathbf{x}}}^{\rm T}\boldsymbol{\Sigma}_u\hat{\boldsymbol{\Phi}}_{\tilde{\mathbf{x}}} + \boldsymbol{\Sigma}_{\xi}\right)^{-1}\mathbf{y}$$
$$= \left(\hat{\boldsymbol{\Phi}}_{\tilde{\mathbf{x}}}\boldsymbol{\Sigma}_{\xi}^{-1}\hat{\boldsymbol{\Phi}}_{\tilde{\mathbf{x}}}^{\rm T} + \boldsymbol{\Sigma}_u^{-1}\right)^{-1}\boldsymbol{\Phi}\boldsymbol{\Sigma}_{\xi}^{-1}\mathbf{y}.$$

It is easy to verify that $\tilde{\mathbf{u}}_{\rm EiV}$ is also the optimal solution for the following optimizer:

$$\tilde{\mathbf{u}}_{\rm EiV} = \underset{\mathbf{u}}{\text{minimize}}||\hat{\boldsymbol{\Phi}}_{\tilde{\mathbf{x}}}^{\rm T}\mathbf{u} - \mathbf{y}||^2_{\boldsymbol{\Sigma}_{\xi}^{-1}} + ||\mathbf{u}||^2_{\boldsymbol{\Sigma}_u^{-1}}. \tag{15.85}$$

Bias and variance of the EiV estimator

The EiV estimator is biased by the following amount:

$$\text{bias} = E[\tilde{\mathbf{u}}_{\rm EiV}|\mathbf{D}_{\tilde{\mathbf{x}}}, \mathbf{u}] - \mathbf{u} = -\left(\hat{\boldsymbol{\Phi}}_{\tilde{\mathbf{x}}}\boldsymbol{\Sigma}_{\xi}^{-1}\hat{\boldsymbol{\Phi}}_{\tilde{\mathbf{x}}}^{\rm T} + \boldsymbol{\Sigma}_u^{-1}\right)^{-1}\boldsymbol{\Sigma}_u^{-1}\mathbf{u}. \tag{15.86}$$

Note also that the variance of $\tilde{\mathbf{u}}_{\rm EiV}$ is

$$E\left[\left(\tilde{\mathbf{u}}_{\rm EiV} - E[\tilde{\mathbf{u}}_{\rm EiV}|\mathbf{D}_{\tilde{\mathbf{x}}}, \mathbf{u}]\right)\left(\tilde{\mathbf{u}}_{\rm EiV} - E[\tilde{\mathbf{u}}_{\rm EiV}|\mathbf{D}_{\tilde{\mathbf{x}}}, \mathbf{u}]\right)^{\rm T}\right]$$
$$= \left(\hat{\boldsymbol{\Phi}}_{\tilde{\mathbf{x}}}\boldsymbol{\Sigma}_{\xi}^{-1}\hat{\boldsymbol{\Phi}}_{\tilde{\mathbf{x}}}^{\rm T} + \boldsymbol{\Sigma}_u^{-1}\right)^{-1}\boldsymbol{\Phi}\boldsymbol{\Sigma}_{\xi}^{-1}\boldsymbol{\Phi}^{\rm T}\left(\hat{\boldsymbol{\Phi}}_{\tilde{\mathbf{x}}}\boldsymbol{\Sigma}_{\xi}^{-1}\hat{\boldsymbol{\Phi}}_{\tilde{\mathbf{x}}}^{\rm T} + \boldsymbol{\Sigma}_u^{-1}\right)^{-1}. \tag{15.87}$$

EiV learning models when u has nonzero mean

Let us now treat the more general scenario in which there is another generation vector $\mathbf{u}'$ with the same variance $\boldsymbol{\Sigma}_u$ but a nonzero mean $\boldsymbol{\mu} \neq 0$. Consider the following expected training dataset (in the intrinsic space):

$$\{(\hat{\boldsymbol{\phi}}_1, y'_1)\,(\hat{\boldsymbol{\phi}}_2, y'_2)\,\ldots\,(\hat{\boldsymbol{\phi}}_N, y'_N)\},$$

corresponding to the modified generation model (see Eq. (15.69))

$$y = \mathbf{u}'^{\rm T}\hat{\boldsymbol{\phi}}_{\tilde{\mathbf{x}}}(\tilde{\mathbf{x}}) + \xi'(\tilde{\mathbf{x}}), \tag{15.88}$$

where

$$\xi'(\tilde{\mathbf{x}}) = \mathbf{u}'^{\rm T}E[\overrightarrow{\boldsymbol{\phi}}(\mathbf{x}) - \hat{\boldsymbol{\phi}}_{\tilde{\mathbf{x}}}(\tilde{\mathbf{x}})|\tilde{\mathbf{x}}] + \boldsymbol{\varepsilon}.$$

Moreover, the covariance matrix of $\boldsymbol{\xi}'$ is denoted as

$$\boldsymbol{\Sigma}_{\xi'} = \text{Diag}\{\sigma^2_{\xi'_1}, \ldots, \sigma^2_{\xi'_N}\}, \tag{15.89}$$

where

$$\sigma^2_{\xi'_i} = E[\|(\overrightarrow{\boldsymbol{\phi}}(\mathbf{x}_i) - \hat{\boldsymbol{\phi}}_i)^{\rm T}\boldsymbol{\Sigma}_{u'}(\overrightarrow{\boldsymbol{\phi}}(\mathbf{x}_i) - \hat{\boldsymbol{\phi}}_i)|\tilde{\mathbf{x}}_i] + E[\varepsilon^2|\tilde{\mathbf{x}}_i], \tag{15.90}$$

where $\boldsymbol{\Sigma}_{u'} = E[\mathbf{u}'\mathbf{u}'^{\rm T}] = \boldsymbol{\Sigma}_u + \mathbf{u}\mathbf{u}^{\rm T}$. On denoting $\mathbf{u} \equiv \mathbf{u}' - \boldsymbol{\mu}$, we have a modified generation model

$$y_\theta = \mathbf{u}^{\rm T}\hat{\boldsymbol{\phi}}_{\tilde{\mathbf{x}}}(\tilde{\mathbf{x}}) + \xi', \tag{15.91}$$

with the corresponding training dataset

$$\{(\hat{\boldsymbol{\phi}}_1, y_1)\,(\hat{\boldsymbol{\phi}}_2, y_2)\,\ldots\,(\hat{\boldsymbol{\phi}}_N, y_N)\},$$

where

$$y_i \equiv y_i' - \boldsymbol{\mu}^{\mathrm{T}}\hat{\boldsymbol{\phi}}_i.$$

Since $E[\mathbf{u}] = \mathbf{0}$ and $E[\mathbf{u}\mathbf{u}^{\mathrm{T}}] = \boldsymbol{\Sigma}_u$, Eq. (15.81) becomes applicable, leading to the following solution:

$$\tilde{\mathbf{u}}_{\mathrm{EiV}} = \mathbf{V}_{\mathrm{EiV}}\mathbf{y}, \text{ where } \mathbf{V}_{\mathrm{EiV}} = \left(\hat{\boldsymbol{\Phi}}_{\tilde{\mathbf{x}}}\boldsymbol{\Sigma}_{\xi'}^{-1}\hat{\boldsymbol{\Phi}}_{\tilde{\mathbf{x}}}^{\mathrm{T}} + \boldsymbol{\Sigma}_u^{-1}\right)^{-1}\hat{\boldsymbol{\Phi}}_{\tilde{\mathbf{x}}}\boldsymbol{\Sigma}_{\xi'}^{-1}.$$

This means that the optimal estimator for the original generation model has to be

$$\begin{aligned}\tilde{\mathbf{u}}_{\mathrm{EiV}}' &= \tilde{\mathbf{u}}_{\mathrm{EiV}} + \boldsymbol{\mu} = \mathbf{V}_{\mathrm{EiV}}\mathbf{y} + \boldsymbol{\mu} \\ &= \mathbf{V}_{\mathrm{EiV}}(\mathbf{y}' - \hat{\boldsymbol{\Phi}}_{\tilde{\mathbf{x}}}^{\mathrm{T}}\boldsymbol{\mu}) + \boldsymbol{\mu} = \mathbf{V}_{\mathrm{EiV}}\mathbf{y}' + (\mathbf{I} - \mathbf{V}_{\mathrm{EiV}}\hat{\boldsymbol{\Phi}}_{\tilde{\mathbf{x}}}^{\mathrm{T}})\boldsymbol{\mu}.\end{aligned}$$

15.4.2 EiV regressors in empirical space

Recall that, in the intrinsic space, the EiV cost function is

$$\tilde{\mathbf{u}}_{\mathrm{EiV}} \equiv \underset{\tilde{\mathbf{u}}\in\mathbb{R}^J}{\arg\min}\left(\sum_{i=1}^{N}||\hat{\boldsymbol{\Phi}}_{\tilde{\mathbf{x}}}^{\mathrm{T}}\mathbf{u} - \mathbf{y}||_{\boldsymbol{\Sigma}_{\xi}^{-1}}^2 + ||\tilde{\mathbf{u}}||_{\boldsymbol{\Sigma}_u^{-1}}^2\right). \tag{15.92}$$

This suggests that the solution observes a $\boldsymbol{\Sigma}_u$-modulated learning subspace property, and, accordingly, let us define a $\boldsymbol{\Sigma}_u$-modulated kernel function:

$$K(\tilde{\mathbf{x}}, \tilde{\mathbf{x}}') = \hat{\boldsymbol{\phi}}_{\tilde{\mathbf{x}}}(\tilde{\mathbf{x}})^{\mathrm{T}}\boldsymbol{\Sigma}_u\hat{\boldsymbol{\phi}}_{\tilde{\mathbf{x}}}(\tilde{\mathbf{x}}). \tag{15.93}$$

This leads to the following kernel matrix:

$$\hat{\mathbf{K}} = \{\hat{K}_{ij}\}, \quad \text{where } \hat{K}_{ij} = \hat{\boldsymbol{\phi}}_{\tilde{\mathbf{x}}}(\tilde{\mathbf{x}}_i)^{\mathrm{T}}\boldsymbol{\Sigma}_u\hat{\boldsymbol{\phi}}_{\tilde{\mathbf{x}}}(\tilde{\mathbf{x}}_j),\ i = 1,\ldots,N,\ j = 1,\ldots,N. \tag{15.94}$$

For the $\boldsymbol{\Sigma}_u$-modulated LSP, we can obtain a cost function in the empirical space:

$$\underset{\mathbf{a}}{\text{minimize}}||\hat{\mathbf{K}}^{\mathrm{T}}\mathbf{a} - \mathbf{y}||_{\boldsymbol{\Sigma}_{\xi}^{-1}}^2 + \mathbf{a}^{\mathrm{T}}\hat{\mathbf{K}}\mathbf{a}. \tag{15.95}$$

This leads us to a familiar and kernelized solution for the EiV regressor in empirical space:

$$\mathbf{a} = (\hat{\mathbf{K}} + \boldsymbol{\Sigma}_{\xi})^{-1}\mathbf{y}. \tag{15.96}$$

Once $\mathbf{a}$ has been found, the optimal estimation can be expressed as

$$\hat{y} = \mathbf{u}^{\mathrm{T}}\hat{\boldsymbol{\phi}}(\tilde{\mathbf{x}}) = \mathbf{a}^{\mathrm{T}}\hat{\mathbf{k}}(\tilde{\mathbf{x}}), \tag{15.97}$$

where we denote $\hat{\mathbf{k}}(\tilde{\mathbf{x}}) \equiv [\hat{K}(\tilde{\mathbf{x}}_1, \tilde{\mathbf{x}}), \hat{K}(\tilde{\mathbf{x}}_2, \tilde{\mathbf{x}}),\ \ldots,\ \hat{K}(\tilde{\mathbf{x}}_N, \tilde{\mathbf{x}})]^{\mathrm{T}}$, see Eq. (15.93).

For a numerical illustration, let us revisit Example 15.2, but now with errors in variables taken into account.

Example 15.4 *In an EiV model, suppose that all inputs are independently generated according to a Gaussian distribution $x \sim \mathcal{N}(0, 1)$, while the observed input $\tilde{x} = x + \Delta x$*

is contaminated with an independent input noise $\Delta x \sim \mathcal{N}(0, \eta)$. Then the conditional probabilities are given by

$$p(x|\tilde{x}) \sim \mathcal{N}(\tilde{x}/(1+\eta), \eta/(1+\eta)), \tag{15.98}$$

$$p(x_i|\mathbf{D}_{\tilde{x}}) = p(x_i|\tilde{x}_i) \sim \mathcal{N}(\tilde{x}_i/(1+\eta), \eta/(1+\eta)), \tag{15.99}$$

$$p(x_i, x_j|\mathbf{D}_{\tilde{x}}) = p(x_i|\tilde{x}_i)p(x_j|\tilde{x}_j). \tag{15.100}$$

Optimal EiV regressor

Given observed input–output pairs $\mathbf{D} = \{\tilde{x}_i, y_i\}_{i=1}^N$, the optimal EiV regressor is given by

$$\mathbf{a}_{\text{EiV}} = (\hat{\mathbf{K}} + \boldsymbol{\Sigma}_{\xi})^{-1}\mathbf{y} \equiv \tilde{\mathbf{K}}^{-1}\mathbf{y},$$

where the matrix $\tilde{\mathbf{K}}$ can be computed as follows.

Off-diagonal entries of $\tilde{K}$

The off-diagonal entries can be obtained from Eq. (15.93). More exactly,

$$\begin{aligned}
\tilde{\mathbf{K}}_{ij} = \hat{\mathbf{K}}_{ij} \overset{\text{Eq. (15.93)}}{=} & \hat{\boldsymbol{\phi}}_{\tilde{x}}(\tilde{x}_i)^{\mathrm{T}}\boldsymbol{\Sigma}_u\hat{\boldsymbol{\phi}}_{\tilde{x}}(\tilde{x}_j) \\
= & E[\overrightarrow{\boldsymbol{\phi}}(x_i)|\tilde{x}_i]^{\mathrm{T}}\boldsymbol{\Sigma}_u E[\overrightarrow{\boldsymbol{\phi}}(x_j)|\tilde{x}_j] \\
= & \left(\int \overrightarrow{\boldsymbol{\phi}}(x_i)p(x_i|\tilde{x}_i)dx_i\right)\boldsymbol{\Sigma}_u\left(\int \overrightarrow{\boldsymbol{\phi}}(x_j)p(x_j|\tilde{x}_j)dx_j\right) \\
= & \iint \boldsymbol{\phi}(x_i)^{\mathrm{T}}\boldsymbol{\Sigma}_u\boldsymbol{\phi}(x_j)p(x_i|\tilde{x}_i)p(x_j|\tilde{x}_j)dx_i\, dx_j \\
= & \iint K(x_i, x_j)p(x_i|\tilde{x}_i)p(x_j|\tilde{x}_j)dx_i\, dx_j \\
= & \sqrt{\frac{1+\eta}{1+3\eta}}\exp\left(-\frac{(\tilde{x}_i - \tilde{x}_j)^2}{2(1+\eta)(1+3\eta)}\right).
\end{aligned}$$

Diagonal entries of $\tilde{K}$

From Eq. (15.76), we have

$$\hat{\boldsymbol{\phi}}_i^{\mathrm{T}}\boldsymbol{\Sigma}_u\hat{\boldsymbol{\phi}}_i + \sigma_{\xi_i}^2 = E[\overrightarrow{\boldsymbol{\phi}}(x_i)^{\mathrm{T}}\boldsymbol{\Sigma}_u\overrightarrow{\boldsymbol{\phi}}(x_i)|\tilde{x}_i] + \sigma_\varepsilon^2.$$

Noting that by definition $\hat{\mathbf{K}}_{ii} = \hat{\boldsymbol{\phi}}_i^{\mathrm{T}}\boldsymbol{\Sigma}_u\hat{\boldsymbol{\phi}}_i$, we have

$$\tilde{\mathbf{K}}_{ii} = \hat{\mathbf{K}}_{ii} + \sigma_{\xi_i}^2 = E[\overrightarrow{\boldsymbol{\phi}}(x_i)^{\mathrm{T}}\boldsymbol{\Sigma}_u\overrightarrow{\boldsymbol{\phi}}(x_i)|\tilde{x}_i] + \sigma_\varepsilon^2.$$

It follows that

$$\begin{aligned}
\tilde{\mathbf{K}}_{ii} &= E[\overrightarrow{\boldsymbol{\phi}}(x_i)^{\mathrm{T}}\boldsymbol{\Sigma}_u\overrightarrow{\boldsymbol{\phi}}(x_i)|\tilde{x}_i] + \sigma_\varepsilon^2 \\
&= \int K(x_i, x_i)p(x_i|\tilde{x}_i)dx_i + \sigma_\varepsilon^2 \\
&= 1 + \sigma_\varepsilon^2.
\end{aligned}$$

Optimal EiV prediction

Once $\mathbf{a}_{\text{EiV}}$ has been computed, the optimal prediction can be obtained as

$$\hat{y}_{\text{EiV}} = \mathbf{a}_{\text{EiV}}^{\text{T}} \hat{\mathbf{k}}(\tilde{x}),$$

where $\hat{\mathbf{k}}(\tilde{\mathbf{x}}) \equiv [\hat{K}(\tilde{\mathbf{x}}_1, \tilde{\mathbf{x}}), \hat{K}(\tilde{\mathbf{x}}_2, \tilde{\mathbf{x}}) \ \ldots \ \hat{K}(\tilde{\mathbf{x}}_N, \tilde{\mathbf{x}})]^T$, whose ith element can be expressed as

$$\begin{aligned}\hat{K}(\tilde{\mathbf{x}}_i, \tilde{\mathbf{x}}) &= \iint K(x_i, x) p(x_i|\tilde{x}_i) p(x|\tilde{x}) dx_i \, dx \\ &= \sqrt{\frac{1+\eta}{1+3\eta}} \exp\left(-\frac{(\tilde{x}_i - \tilde{x})^2}{2(1+\eta)(1+3\eta)}\right).\end{aligned}$$

15.4.3 EiV regressors with Gaussian distribution

In this section, we shall show that analytical optimal solutions can be derived if the input variables and all of the kinds of noise terms are assumed to be Gaussian distributed. Let us first consider a single-variate linear Gauss–Markov model with errors in variables, under the assumption of a Gaussian distribution. The Gaussian input is modeled by $\mathbf{x} \sim \mathcal{N}(\mathbf{0}, \mathbf{\Sigma}_{\mathbf{x}})$, $\Delta\mathbf{x} \sim \mathcal{N}(\mathbf{0}, \mathbf{\Sigma}_{\Delta\mathbf{x}})$, where $\mathbf{x}$ and $\Delta\mathbf{x}$ are independent. Owing to the complexity of the analytical form of the optimal solution, we shall provide an illustrative example that is based on a single-variate linear-order estimator/predictior and defer the treatment of the polynomial regressors to Problem 15.10. (Further details are discussed by Wu and Kung [302].)

Example 15.5 *Consider a single-variate linear Gauss–Markov model with errors in variables*

$$y = ux + \varepsilon, \ \tilde{x} = x + \Delta x,$$

where we assume a prior mean $\mu_u = 0$ and a covariance σ_u^2, and that the inputs are mutually independently generated according to a Gaussian distribution $x \sim \mathcal{N}(0, \sigma_x^2)$, $\Delta x \sim \mathcal{N}(0, \sigma_{\Delta x}^2)$. For notational simplicity, we shall let $\sigma_x^2 = 1$ and denote $\sigma_{\Delta x}^2 = \eta$. The estimated (normalized) input in feature space is then given by

$$\hat{\boldsymbol{\phi}}_{\tilde{\mathbf{x}}}(\tilde{\mathbf{x}}) = \hat{x}_{\tilde{x}} = E[x|\tilde{x}] = \frac{\tilde{x}}{1+\eta}.$$

Suppose that the variance of the output noise is time-invariant, i.e. $\sigma_{\varepsilon_i}^2 = \sigma_\varepsilon^2$. Then the modified output noise will be independent of x_i, see Eq. (15.72). Moreover, according to Eq. (15.76),

$$\begin{aligned}\sigma_{\xi_i}^2 &= \sigma_u^2 E[|x_i - \hat{x}_i|^2 | \tilde{x}_i] + \sigma_{\varepsilon_i}^2 \\ &= \frac{\eta}{1+\eta}\sigma_u^2 + \sigma_\varepsilon^2 = \sigma_\xi^2.\end{aligned} \tag{15.101}$$

Given N observations $\{(\tilde{x}_i, y_i)\}_{i=1}^N$, the EiV regressor is then given by (see Eq. (15.81))

$$\hat{u}_{\text{EiV}} = \left(\hat{\boldsymbol{\Phi}}_{\tilde{\mathbf{x}}}\boldsymbol{\Sigma}_\xi^{-1}\hat{\boldsymbol{\Phi}}_{\tilde{\mathbf{x}}}^{\mathrm{T}} + \boldsymbol{\Sigma}_u^{-1}\right)^{-1}\hat{\boldsymbol{\Phi}}_{\tilde{\mathbf{x}}}\boldsymbol{\Sigma}_\xi^{-1}\mathbf{y}$$
$$= \frac{\sum_{i=1}^N (1/\sigma_\xi^2)\hat{x}_i y_i}{\sum_{i=1}^N (1/\sigma_\xi^2)\hat{x}_i^2 + 1/\sigma_u^2}$$
$$= \frac{\sum_{i=1}^N (\tilde{x}_i/1+\eta)\, y_i}{\sum_{i=1}^N (\tilde{x}_i/(1+\eta))^2 + \sigma_\xi^2/\sigma_u^2}. \quad (15.102)$$

It follows that

$$\hat{y} = \hat{u}_{\text{EiV}}\hat{\phi}_{\tilde{\mathbf{x}}}(\tilde{\mathbf{x}}) = \hat{u}_{\text{EiV}}\frac{\tilde{x}}{1+\eta}$$
$$= \frac{\sum_{i=1}^N \tilde{x}_i y_i}{\sum_{i=1}^N \tilde{x}_i^2 + \lambda}\tilde{x}, \quad \text{where } \lambda = (1+\eta)^2\left(\frac{\eta}{1+\eta} + \frac{\sigma_\varepsilon^2}{\sigma_u^2}\right). \quad (15.103)$$

Kernelized formulation

Equation (15.102) has an alternative formula given in Eq. (15.80):

$$\hat{u}_{\text{EiV}} = \boldsymbol{\Sigma}_u\hat{\boldsymbol{\Phi}}_{\tilde{\mathbf{x}}}\left(\hat{\boldsymbol{\Phi}}_{\tilde{\mathbf{x}}}^{\mathrm{T}}\,\boldsymbol{\Sigma}_u\hat{\boldsymbol{\Phi}}_{\tilde{\mathbf{x}}} + \boldsymbol{\Sigma}_\xi\right)^{-1}\mathbf{y},$$

which is more naturally tied to a kernelized formulation:

$$\hat{y} = \frac{\sum_{i=1}^N \hat{K}(\tilde{x}_i, \tilde{x})y_i}{\sum_{i=1}^N \hat{K}(\tilde{x}_i, \tilde{x}_i) + \sigma_\xi^2}, \quad (15.104)$$

where the kernel function for the EiV learning model is as defined in Eq. (15.93).

15.4.4 Finite-order EiV regressors

The previous section has demonstrated that, under the assumption of a Gaussian distribution, the optimal EiV regressors will be exactly the same as the order of the generation model. However, as evidenced below, this will no longer be the case for non-Gaussian distributions.

Example 15.6 (Non-Gaussian distribution and order of estimators) *It is assumed, in Example 14.3, that the input is a scalar random variable, i.e.* $\mathbf{x} = x$ *and the perturbed input is* $\tilde{x} = x + \Delta x$. *It is also assumed that* x *has a zero mean with a unform distribution,* $x \in \mathcal{U}(-1, 1)$. *Moreover,* $\Delta x \in \mathcal{U}(-\delta, \delta)$, $\delta \le 1$. *According to Eq. (14.49), we have*

$$\hat{\phi}_{\tilde{x}}(\tilde{x}) = \begin{cases} \frac{1}{2}(\tilde{x} - 1 + \delta), & \text{if } \tilde{x} < -1 + \delta \\ \tilde{x}, & \text{if } -1 + \delta \le \tilde{x} \le 1 - \delta \\ \frac{1}{2}(\tilde{x} + 1 - \delta), & \text{if } \tilde{x} > 1 - \delta, \end{cases}$$

which is obviously nonlinear w.r.t. $\tilde{x}$.

By Example 15.6, we have demonstrated that the optimal estimator $\hat{x}$ is a nonlinear function of $\tilde{x}$ of infinite order. Sometimes, however, it is more practical to restrict the estimator to a finite-order regressor w.r.t. $\tilde{x}$. In this section, we shall adopt a treatment inspired by the "two-projection property" (TPP) developed by Kung and Wu [145], see Chapter 14. More precisely, we propose an approach that is based on a generation model corresponding to the intrinsic space associated with an nth-order polynomial kernel of $\tilde{\mathbf{x}}$.

Suppose that our goal is to design an nth-order optimal regressor. To this end, let us define the nth-order projection of $\overrightarrow{\boldsymbol{\phi}}(\mathbf{x})$ onto the measured input $\tilde{\mathbf{x}}$ as follows:

$$\hat{\boldsymbol{\phi}}_{\tilde{\mathbf{x}}}^{[n]}(\tilde{\mathbf{x}}_i) \equiv \text{projection of } \overrightarrow{\boldsymbol{\phi}}(\mathbf{x}), \text{ the intrinsic space of an } n\text{th-order polynomial kernel function of } \tilde{\mathbf{x}}.$$

Let us denote the projection error as

$$\Delta^{[n]} \equiv \overrightarrow{\boldsymbol{\phi}}(\mathbf{x}) - \hat{\boldsymbol{\phi}}_{\tilde{\mathbf{x}}}^{[n]}(\tilde{\mathbf{x}}),$$

and we have

$$E[\Delta^{[n]}] = 0. \tag{15.105}$$

This results in the following error at the output:

$$\varepsilon^{[n]} \equiv \mathbf{u}^{\mathrm{T}}\Delta^{[n]} + \varepsilon.$$

By noting that

$$\varepsilon^{[n]} \equiv \mathbf{u}^{\mathrm{T}}\overrightarrow{\boldsymbol{\phi}}(\mathbf{x}) - \mathbf{u}^{\mathrm{T}}\hat{\boldsymbol{\phi}}_{\tilde{\mathbf{x}}}^{[n]}(\tilde{\mathbf{x}}) + \varepsilon,$$

we can derive an nth-order generation model as follows:

$$y = \mathbf{u}^{\mathrm{T}}\hat{\boldsymbol{\phi}}_{\tilde{\mathbf{x}}}^{[n]}(\tilde{\mathbf{x}}) + \varepsilon^{[n]}. \tag{15.106}$$

Note that the "modified output noise" $\varepsilon^{[n]}$ is of zero mean, i.e.

$$E[\varepsilon^{[n]}] = 0.$$

Moreover, its variance has a simple expression:

$$\sigma_{\boldsymbol{\varepsilon}^{[n]}}^2 = E[||\mathbf{u}^{\mathrm{T}}\Delta^{[n]}||^2 + \sigma_{\boldsymbol{\varepsilon}}^2] = E\left[K(\mathbf{x},\mathbf{x}') - K^{[n]}(\tilde{\mathbf{x}},\tilde{\mathbf{x}}')\right] + \sigma_{\boldsymbol{\varepsilon}}^2, \tag{15.107}$$

where

$$K(\mathbf{x},\mathbf{x}') = \overrightarrow{\boldsymbol{\phi}}(\mathbf{x})^{\mathrm{T}}\boldsymbol{\Sigma}_u\overrightarrow{\boldsymbol{\phi}}(\mathbf{x}') \tag{15.108}$$

and

$$K^{[n]}(\tilde{\mathbf{x}},\tilde{\mathbf{x}}') = \hat{\boldsymbol{\phi}}_{\tilde{\mathbf{x}}}^{[n]}(\tilde{\mathbf{x}})^{\mathrm{T}}\boldsymbol{\Sigma}_u\hat{\boldsymbol{\phi}}_{\tilde{\mathbf{x}}}^{[n]}(\tilde{\mathbf{x}}) \tag{15.109}$$

are termed $\boldsymbol{\Sigma}_u$-modulated kernel functions. In particular, if all the infinite number of basis functions associated with Gaussian kernels are used, Eq. (15.108) will simply become a conventional Gaussian kernel, see Example 15.2. Moreover, Eq. (15.109) will simply represent a truncated-RBF (TRBF) Gaussian kernel, see Chapter 13.

Proof of Eq. (15.107)
Note that

$$E[||\mathbf{u}^{\mathrm{T}}\Delta^{[n]}||^2] = \mathtt{tr}\left(E\left[\Delta^{[n]}[\Delta^{[n]}]^{\mathrm{T}}\mathbf{u}\mathbf{u}^{\mathrm{T}}\right]\right)$$
$$= \mathtt{tr}\left(E\left[\Delta^{[n]}[\Delta^{[n]}]^{\mathrm{T}}\right]E\left[\mathbf{u}\mathbf{u}^{\mathrm{T}}\right]\right)$$
$$= \mathtt{tr}\left(E\left[[\Delta^{[n]}]^{\mathrm{T}}\mathbf{\Sigma}_u\Delta^{[n]}\right]\right)$$
$$= E\left[K(\mathbf{x},\mathbf{x}') - K^{[n]}(\tilde{\mathbf{x}},\tilde{\mathbf{x}}')\right]. \tag{15.110}$$

Owing to the orthogonality between $\hat{\boldsymbol{\phi}}_{\tilde{\mathbf{x}}}^{[n]}(\tilde{\mathbf{x}})$ and $\Delta^{[n]}$, i.e. $E[\hat{\boldsymbol{\phi}}_{\tilde{\mathbf{x}}}^{[n]}(\tilde{\mathbf{x}})^{\mathrm{T}}\Delta^{[n]}] = 0$, we have

$$E[||\mathbf{u}^{\mathrm{T}}\Delta^{[n]}||^2] = E\left[\overrightarrow{\boldsymbol{\phi}}(\mathbf{x})^{\mathrm{T}}\mathbf{\Sigma}_u\overrightarrow{\boldsymbol{\phi}}(\mathbf{x})\right] - E\left[\hat{\boldsymbol{\phi}}_{\tilde{\mathbf{x}}}^{[n]}(\tilde{\mathbf{x}})^{\mathrm{T}}\mathbf{\Sigma}_u\Delta^{[n]}\hat{\boldsymbol{\phi}}_{\tilde{\mathbf{x}}}^{[n]}(\tilde{\mathbf{x}})\right]$$
$$= E\left[K(\mathbf{x},\mathbf{x}') - K^{[n]}(\tilde{\mathbf{x}},\tilde{\mathbf{x}}')\right]. \tag{15.111}$$

Thus Eq. (15.107) has been established.

Derivation of $\hat{\mathbf{u}}_{\mathrm{EiV}}^{[n]}$
The new generation model facilitates a simple derivation of finite-order regressors that may be directly linked to the KRRs introduced in the previous chapters, especially Chapter 7. For this model, the orthogonality property becomes

$$E\left[(\hat{\mathbf{u}} - \mathbf{u})\mathbf{y}^{\mathrm{T}}|\mathbf{D}_{\tilde{\mathbf{x}}}\right] = 0, \tag{15.112}$$

which immediately leads to the following optimal solution for $\hat{\mathbf{u}}_{\mathrm{EiV}}$:

$$\hat{\mathbf{u}}_{\mathrm{EiV}}^{[n]} = E\left[\mathbf{u}\mathbf{y}^{\mathrm{T}}|\mathbf{D}_{\tilde{\mathbf{x}}}\right]E\left[\mathbf{y}\mathbf{y}^{\mathrm{T}}|\mathbf{D}_{\tilde{\mathbf{x}}}\right]^{-1}\mathbf{y}. \tag{15.113}$$

By substituting the nth-order generation model prescribed in Eq. (15.106) into Eq. (15.113), we arrive at

$$\hat{\mathbf{u}}_{\mathrm{EiV}}^{[n]} \equiv \mathbf{\Sigma}_u\hat{\mathbf{\Phi}}^{[n]}\left((\hat{\mathbf{\Phi}}^{[n]})^{\mathrm{T}}\mathbf{\Sigma}_u\,\hat{\mathbf{\Phi}}^{[n]} + \mathbf{\Sigma}_{\varepsilon^{[n]}} + A + A^{\mathrm{T}}\right)^{-1}\mathbf{y}, \tag{15.114}$$

where

$$A = E[\mathbf{u}\mathbf{u}^{\mathrm{T}}]\sum_{i=1}^{N}E[\Delta^{[n]}|\tilde{\mathbf{x}}_i] \neq 0.$$

(See Problem 15.8.) In order to obtain a true optimal solution, it is necessary to undertake the tedious process of computing all the values.

Derivation of $\tilde{\mathbf{u}}_{\mathrm{EiV}}^{[n]}$
Alternatively, in favor of computational simplicity, a common compromise is to take advantage of the law of large numbers so that, according to Eq. (15.105), we can assume that, relatively speaking,

$$\sum_{i=1}^{N}E[\Delta^{[n]}|\tilde{\mathbf{x}}_i] \approx 0 \tag{15.115}$$

when the training size N is sufficiently large. For computational simplicity, we shall ignore the data-dependent nature of $\boldsymbol{\varepsilon}^{[n]}$ by assuming that $\boldsymbol{\Sigma}_{\boldsymbol{\varepsilon}^{[n]}} = \sigma^2_{\boldsymbol{\varepsilon}^{[n]}}\mathbf{I}$. [2] This leads us to the following KRR-type learning model:

$$\hat{\mathbf{u}}^{[n]}_{\text{EiV}} \approx \tilde{\mathbf{u}}^{[n]}_{\text{EiV}} \equiv \boldsymbol{\Sigma}_u\hat{\boldsymbol{\Phi}}^{[n]}\left((\hat{\boldsymbol{\Phi}}^{[n]})^{\text{T}}\boldsymbol{\Sigma}_u\hat{\boldsymbol{\Phi}}^{[n]} + \boldsymbol{\Sigma}_{\boldsymbol{\varepsilon}^{[n]}}\right)^{-1}\mathbf{y}. \tag{15.116}$$

Once $\tilde{\mathbf{u}}^{[n]}_{\text{EiV}}$ has been learned, the system response can be predicted as

$$y^{\text{T}} = \hat{\boldsymbol{\phi}}^{[n]}_{\tilde{\mathbf{x}}}(\tilde{\mathbf{x}}_i)^{\text{T}}\tilde{\mathbf{u}}^{[n]}_{\text{EiV}}.$$

For more treatment on optimal learning models with a finite order, see Wu and Kung [302].

A kernelized formulation for finite-order EiV regressors and its relationship with TRBF-based KRR

Just like all the previous cases, Eq. (15.116) immediately leads to a familiar kernelized formulation for the finite-order EiV regressors:

$$\mathbf{a}^{[n]} = \left(\hat{\mathbf{K}}^{[n]} + \boldsymbol{\Sigma}_{\boldsymbol{\varepsilon}^{[n]}}\right)^{-1}\mathbf{y},$$

where the entries of $\hat{\mathbf{K}}^{[n]}$ are defined in Eq. (15.109). Note that the formulation not only covers the traditional KRR algorithm, see Algorithm 7.1, but also offers a physically meaningful interpretation of the ridge factor. This attribute allows a full exploitation of any prior knowledge we may possess on the generation models and/or errors-in-variables models. Another useful application domain of the finite-order regressors lies in cost-effective or big-data kernel learning. Note that, when a finite subset of the infinite number of basis functions pertaining to a Gaussian kernel is allowed, the kernel function in Eq. (15.109) becomes the TRBF kernel advocated in Chapter 13, see e.g. Eq. (13.5).

15.5 Recursive KRR learning algorithms

This section develops recursive, time-adaptive, and incremental learning models. We adopt the interpretation that the prior knowledge may be inferred from the past observations. Therefore, it can be recursively updated when new data are made available. This interpretation leads to the derivation of both recursive KRR and EiV algorithms. In this section, the recursive KRR algorithms both in the intrinsic space and in the empirical space will be treated.

Given the observations from $n = 1$ through $n = t$, according to Eq. (15.32), the KRR's objective is to find the best regressor such that

$$\hat{\mathbf{u}}_t \equiv \arg\min_{\hat{\mathbf{u}}\in\mathbb{R}^J}\left(||\boldsymbol{\Phi}_t^{\text{T}}\hat{\mathbf{u}}_t - \mathbf{y}_t||^2_{\boldsymbol{\Sigma}^{-1}_{\varepsilon,t}} + ||\hat{\mathbf{u}}_t||^2_{\boldsymbol{\Sigma}^{-1}_u}\right), \tag{15.117}$$

[2] In general, $\boldsymbol{\varepsilon}^{[n]}$ will be $\tilde{\mathbf{x}}$-dependent for high-order kernels or non-Gaussian cases, except for the first-order Gaussian case, in which $\boldsymbol{\varepsilon}^{[1]}$ will be independent of $\tilde{\mathbf{x}}$.

where

$$\boldsymbol{\Phi}_t \equiv \left[\vec{\phi}(\mathbf{x}_1)\ \vec{\phi}(\mathbf{x}_2)\ \ldots\ \vec{\phi}(\mathbf{x}_t)\right], \quad \mathbf{y}_t \equiv \left[y_1\ y_2\ \cdots\ y_t\right]^{\mathrm{T}},$$

and

$$\boldsymbol{\Sigma}_{\varepsilon,t} \equiv \mathrm{Diag}[\sigma_{\varepsilon_i}^2,\ i = 1, \ldots, t].$$

Note that their dimensions all grow with increasing t.

In linear estimation theory [151], a "*precision matrix*" in an "information form" representation is denoted as

$$P_t \equiv \boldsymbol{\Phi}_t \boldsymbol{\Sigma}_{\varepsilon,t} \boldsymbol{\Phi}_t^{\mathrm{T}} + P_0 = \sum_{i=1}^{t} \sigma_{\varepsilon_i}^{-2} \vec{\phi}_i \vec{\phi}_i^{\mathrm{T}} + P_0.$$

Then

$$P_{t+1} = \sum_{i=1}^{t+1} \sigma_{\varepsilon_i}^{-2} \vec{\phi}_i \vec{\phi}_i^{\mathrm{T}} + P_0 = P_t + \sigma_{\varepsilon_{t+1}}^{-2} \vec{\phi}_{t+1} \vec{\phi}_{t+1}^{\mathrm{T}}. \tag{15.118}$$

With some deviation from Section 13.7, here the *covariance matrix* $\boldsymbol{\Sigma}_t$ is defined as the inverse of the precision matrix, i.e.

$$\boldsymbol{\Sigma}_t \equiv [P_t]^{-1} = \left[\sum_{i=1}^{t} \sigma_{\varepsilon_i}^{-2} \vec{\phi}_i \vec{\phi}_i^{\mathrm{T}} + P_0\right]^{-1},$$

and it follows that

$$\boldsymbol{\Sigma}_{t+1} = \left(\boldsymbol{\Phi} \boldsymbol{\Sigma}_{\varepsilon,t+1}^{-1} \boldsymbol{\Phi}^{\mathrm{T}} + \boldsymbol{\Sigma}_u^{-1}\right)^{-1} \tag{15.119}$$

and, by Woodbury's matrix identity [301],

$$\boldsymbol{\Sigma}_{t+1} = \boldsymbol{\Sigma}_t - \gamma_{t+1} \boldsymbol{\Sigma}_t \vec{\phi}_{t+1} \vec{\phi}_{t+1}^{\mathrm{T}} \boldsymbol{\Sigma}_t, \tag{15.120}$$

where

$$\gamma_{t+1} \equiv (\sigma_{\varepsilon_{t+1}}^2 + \vec{\phi}_{t+1}^{\mathrm{T}} \boldsymbol{\Sigma}_t \vec{\phi}_{t+1})^{-1}.$$

15.5.1 The recursive KRR algorithm in intrinsic space

For simplicity, in this section, let us assume that the output noises $\{\varepsilon_i,\ i = 1, \ldots, N\}$ have zero mean and be independently and identically distributed (i.i.d.) with variance $E[\varepsilon_i^2] \equiv \sigma_\varepsilon^2$. In this case, the cost function in Eq. (15.117) can be simplified to

$$\sum_{i=1}^{t} \sigma_\varepsilon^{-2} |y_i - \mathbf{u}^{\mathrm{T}} \vec{\phi}_i|^2 + \mathbf{u}^{\mathrm{T}} \boldsymbol{\Sigma}_u^{-1} \mathbf{u}. \tag{15.121}$$

Let us assume that, at some point shortly after the sample time t, but before time $t+1$, the input vector $\mathbf{x}_{t+1}$ becomes newly accessible, but **without** its corresponding teacher value y_{t+1}. In the time-adaptive learning paradigm, this is the opportune time to perform the *prediction* task, i.e. to predict the most likely system response to $\mathbf{x}_{t+1}$.

The zero-innovation property (ZIP)

If the optimal KRR is used, the best prediction would be

$$\hat{y}_{t+1} = \hat{\mathbf{u}}_t^{\mathrm{T}} \vec{\phi}_{t+1}. \tag{15.122}$$

When the true response y_{t+1} is also made available, at time $t+1$, then the estimator may be further updated by taking into account the new information.

Hypothetically speaking, if the newly observed response by coincidence exactly matches with the prediction, i.e. $y_{t+1} = \hat{y}_{t+1}$, then there will be no need to do any updating on the estimator. This will subsequently referred as the "zero-innovation property" (ZIP), meaning that the new estimator should remain just the same as before:

$$\hat{\mathbf{u}}_t \underset{ZIP}{=} \hat{\mathbf{u}}_{t+1}|_{y_{t+1}=\hat{y}_{t+1}} = \mathbf{\Sigma}_{t+1}\left(\mathbf{\Phi}_t \mathbf{\Sigma}_{\varepsilon,t}^{-1}\mathbf{y}_t + \hat{y}_{t+1}\sigma_\varepsilon^{-2}\vec{\phi}_{t+1}\right). \tag{15.123}$$

However, in general, the prediction error

$$e_{t+1} \equiv \hat{y}_{t+1} - y_{t+1} = \hat{\mathbf{u}}_t^{\mathrm{T}}\vec{\phi}_{t+1} - y_{t+1} \tag{15.124}$$

should be nonzero, in which case it is necessary to further update the estimator. Then, according to Eq. (15.31), we can arrive at the following updating formula:

$$\begin{aligned}\hat{\mathbf{u}}_{t+1} &= \mathbf{\Sigma}_{t+1}\mathbf{\Phi}_{t+1}\mathbf{\Sigma}_{\varepsilon,t+1}^{-1}\mathbf{y}_{t+1} \\ &= \mathbf{\Sigma}_{t+1}\left(\mathbf{\Phi}_t\mathbf{\Sigma}_{\varepsilon,t}^{-1}\mathbf{y}_t + y_{t+1}\sigma_\varepsilon^{-2}\vec{\phi}_{t+1}\right).\end{aligned} \tag{15.125}$$

The difference between the new and old estimators can be obtained by subtracting Eq. (15.125) from Eq. (15.123), which leads to

$$\hat{\mathbf{u}}_{t+1} - \hat{\mathbf{u}}_t = -\sigma_\varepsilon^{-2} e_{t+1}\mathbf{\Sigma}_{t+1}\vec{\phi}_{t+1}.$$

In conclusion, the time-adaptive KRR algorithm is summarized below.

ALGORITHM 15.1 (Recursive KRR learning model in intrinsic space)

Initialization

The iterations start with $\hat{\mathbf{u}}_0 = \boldsymbol{\mu}$ *and* $\mathbf{\Sigma}_0 = \mathbf{\Sigma}_u$.

Recursive procedure

For the recursive procedure, let us assume that, at the tth iteration, $\hat{\mathbf{u}}_t$ *is just learned from the dataset* $\{\mathbf{x}_1, \mathbf{x}_2, \ldots, \mathbf{x}_t\}$ *along with all their teacher values* $\{y_1, y_2, \ldots, y_t\}$. *There are two tasks during the tth iteration:*

- **Prediction phase.** *At some point shortly after time t, but before time* $t+1$, *the input vector* $\mathbf{x}_{t+1}$ *has just become accessible, but* **not** *its response* y_{t+1}. *Consequently, the most likely response given the current knowledge is predicted as follows:*

$$\hat{y}_{t+1} = \hat{\mathbf{u}}_t^{\mathrm{T}}\vec{\phi}_{t+1}.$$

- **Estimator updating.** *Suppose that, at time* $t+1$, *the actual output response* y_{t+1} *is known and can be harnessed in the following updates.*

(i) Compute the prediction error,

$$e_{t+1} = \hat{y}_{t+1} - y_{t+1} = \hat{\mathbf{u}}_t^{\mathrm{T}} \overrightarrow{\phi}_{t+1} - y_{t+1}, \tag{15.126}$$

and update the covariance matrix,

$$\boldsymbol{\Sigma}_{t+1} = \boldsymbol{\Sigma}_t - \gamma_{t+1} \boldsymbol{\Sigma}_t \overrightarrow{\phi}_{t+1} \overrightarrow{\phi}_{t+1}^{\mathrm{T}} \boldsymbol{\Sigma}_t,$$

where

$$\gamma_{t+1} \equiv (\sigma_\varepsilon^2 + \overrightarrow{\phi}_{t+1}^{\mathrm{T}} \boldsymbol{\Sigma}_t \overrightarrow{\phi}_{t+1})^{-1}.$$

(ii) The estimator itself can now be updated as follows:

$$\hat{\mathbf{u}}_{t+1} = \hat{\mathbf{u}}_t - \sigma_\varepsilon^{-2} e_{t+1} \boldsymbol{\Sigma}_{t+1} \overrightarrow{\phi}_{t+1}. \tag{15.127}$$

Now we are ready for the next iteration: $t+1$. □

15.5.2 The recursive KRR algorithm in empirical space

There have been some studies concerning recursive KRR algorithms in the empirical space. For example, see [62, 157].

The zero-innovation property (ZIP)

If the newly observed response happens to exactly match with the prediction, i.e. $y_{t+1} = \hat{y}_{t+1}$, then there will be no need to do any updating on the estimator. This is known as the "zero-innovation property" (ZIP), i.e.

$$\left[\mathbf{K}_{t+1} + \boldsymbol{\Sigma}_{\varepsilon,t+1}\right] \begin{bmatrix} \mathbf{a}_t \\ 0 \end{bmatrix} = \begin{bmatrix} \mathbf{y}_t \\ \hat{y}_{t+1} \end{bmatrix}, \tag{15.128}$$

where $\mathbf{K}_{t+1}$ denotes the kernel matrix formed from the first $t+1$ observed training data, see Eq. (15.55).

Proof

The upper part of Eq. (15.128) is directly verifiable by Eq. (15.57). Note also that

$$\left[\mathbf{K}_{t+1} + \boldsymbol{\Sigma}_{\varepsilon,t+1}\right] = \begin{bmatrix} \mathbf{K}_t + \boldsymbol{\Sigma}_{\varepsilon,t} & \overrightarrow{\mathbf{k}}(\mathbf{x}_{t+1}) \\ \overrightarrow{\mathbf{k}}(\mathbf{x}_{t+1})^{\mathrm{T}} & K_{t+1,t+1} + \sigma_\varepsilon^2 \end{bmatrix}. \tag{15.129}$$

Then the lower part of Eq. (15.128) yields that

$$\hat{y}_{t+1} = \mathbf{a}_t^{\mathrm{T}} \overrightarrow{\mathbf{k}}(\mathbf{x}_{t+1}),$$

which is consistent with the prediction formula given in Eq. (15.58).

On pre-multiplying Eq. (15.128) by $\left[\mathbf{K}_{t+1} + \boldsymbol{\Sigma}_{\varepsilon,t+1}\right]^{-1}$, we arrive at

$$\begin{bmatrix} \mathbf{a}_t \\ 0 \end{bmatrix} = \left[\mathbf{K}_{t+1} + \boldsymbol{\Sigma}_{\varepsilon,t+1}\right]^{-1} \begin{bmatrix} \mathbf{y}_t \\ y_{t+1} \end{bmatrix}. \tag{15.130}$$

Noting that $y_{t+1} = \hat{y}_{t+1} - e_{t+1}$, we have

$$\begin{aligned}
\mathbf{a}_{t+1} &= \left[\mathbf{K}_{t+1} + \boldsymbol{\Sigma}_{\varepsilon,t+1}\right]^{-1} \begin{bmatrix} \mathbf{y}_t \\ y_{t+1} \end{bmatrix} \\
&= \left[\mathbf{K}_{t+1} + \boldsymbol{\Sigma}_{\varepsilon,t+1}\right]^{-1} \begin{bmatrix} \mathbf{y}_t \\ \hat{y}_{t+1} \end{bmatrix} - \left[\mathbf{K}_{t+1} + \boldsymbol{\Sigma}_{\varepsilon,t+1}\right]^{-1} \begin{bmatrix} 0 \\ e_{t+1} \end{bmatrix} \\
&= \begin{bmatrix} \mathbf{a}_t \\ 0 \end{bmatrix} - \left[\mathbf{K}_{t+1} + \boldsymbol{\Sigma}_{\varepsilon,t+1}\right]^{-1} \begin{bmatrix} \mathbf{0} \\ e_{t+1} \end{bmatrix}.
\end{aligned} \tag{15.131}$$

By applying the Woodbury matrix identity, recursive KRR algorithms in the empirical space can be summarized as in Algorithm 15.2. (Here we denote $\mathbf{L}_t \equiv \left[\mathbf{K}_t + \boldsymbol{\Sigma}_{\varepsilon,t}\right]^{-1}$.)

ALGORITHM 15.2 (Recursive KRR algorithm (empirical space))

Initialization: $\mathbf{L}_0 \leftarrow []$, $\mathbf{a}_0 = []$
for $i \leftarrow 1$ *to* ∞ ***do***
    Given input $\mathbf{x}_i$
    for $j \leftarrow 1$ *to* $i-1$ ***do***
        Compute $[\mathbf{k}_i]_j \leftarrow k(\mathbf{x}_j, \mathbf{x}_i)$
    end for
    Predict $\hat{y}_i \leftarrow \mathbf{a}_{i-1}^{\mathrm{T}} \mathbf{k}_i$
    Given output y_i *with output noise variance* σ_ε^2
    Compute $\gamma_i \leftarrow 1/(\sigma_\varepsilon^2 + k(\mathbf{x}_i, \mathbf{x}_i) - \mathbf{k}_i^{\mathrm{T}} \mathbf{L}_{i-1} \mathbf{k}_i)$
    Compute $\boldsymbol{\zeta}_i \leftarrow \begin{bmatrix} \mathbf{L}_{i-1}\mathbf{k}_i \\ -1 \end{bmatrix}$
    Update $\mathbf{L}_i \leftarrow \begin{bmatrix} \mathbf{L}_{i-1} & 0 \\ 0 & 0 \end{bmatrix} + \gamma_i \boldsymbol{\zeta}_i \boldsymbol{\zeta}_i^{\mathrm{T}}$
    Compute prediction error $e_i \leftarrow \hat{y}_i - y_i$
    Update $\mathbf{a}_i \leftarrow \begin{bmatrix} \mathbf{a}_{i-1} \\ 0 \end{bmatrix} + \gamma_i e_i \boldsymbol{\zeta}_i$
end for

Concern regarding the growing complexity

The flip side of the KRR model in the empirical space is that its complexity amounts to $O(t^2)$ per update. This means that the complexity tends to grow with the iteration number t. This may appear to be less favorable when compared with the recursive KRR in the intrinsic space, which calls for a constant complexity of $O(J^2)$ operations per sample update.

15.5.3 The recursive KRR algorithm in intrinsic space with a forgetting factor

For analysis of semi-stationary time series, a *forgetting* factor is often used so as to gradually dilute the influence attributed to observations acquired in a distant past. The generation model with random parameters provides an effective means to incorporate the forgetting factor into the generation model. If we fix the present time to t and consider all the present and past observations in the time interval $\tau \in [1, 2, \ldots, t]$, the regression model is semi-stationary and the response is now expressed as follows:

$$y(\mathbf{x}, \tau) = h(\mathbf{x}, \tau) + \varepsilon(\tau). \tag{15.132}$$

The major focus of learning is naturally placed on estimation of the current model $h(\mathbf{x}, t)$. The prompts us to introduce a seemingly time-invariant generation model:

$$y(\mathbf{x}, \tau) = h(\mathbf{x}, t) + \varepsilon'(\tau), \tag{15.133}$$

where we denote the modified observation errors as

$$\varepsilon'(\tau) = \varepsilon(\tau) + (h(\mathbf{x}, \tau) - h(\mathbf{x}, t)). \tag{15.134}$$

In other words, all the temporal variations of the models over time are being treated as uncertain perturbations and can conveniently be incorporated into the modified observation errors. Furthermore, we shall make the simplifying assumption that $\varepsilon'(\tau)$ can be represented by white Gaussian noise with time-varying variance.

- Let us assume that, at the present time (i.e. t),

$$\varepsilon(t) \sim N\left(0, \sigma_\varepsilon^{-2}\right).$$

- Moreover, for all the past points of time,

$$\varepsilon'(\tau) = N\left(0, \sigma_{\varepsilon'(\tau)}^{-2}\right) \approx N\left(0,\ \sigma_\varepsilon^{-2}\alpha^{\tau-t}\right),$$

  where α is a positive forgetting factor slightly less than 1.0.

Note that, at a time point τ in the far past, $t - \tau$ will be very large and its variance $\lambda\alpha^{\tau-t}$ will grow exponentially with respect to $(t - \tau)$, further reducing any residual relevance of the observation made at time τ regarding the identification of the present generation model. Denoting $\lambda \equiv \sigma_\varepsilon^{-2}\alpha^{-t}$, we have

$$\varepsilon'(\tau) \approx N\left(0, \lambda\alpha^{\tau}\right), \quad \text{for } \tau = 1, 2, \ldots, t.$$

Accordingly, Eq. (15.121) may be modified into the following time-forgetting cost function:

$$\sum_{i=1}^{t} \lambda^{-1}\alpha^{-i}|y_i - \mathbf{u}^{\mathrm{T}}\vec{\boldsymbol{\phi}}_i|^2 + \mathbf{u}^{\mathrm{T}}\boldsymbol{\Sigma}_0^{-1}\mathbf{u}. \tag{15.135}$$

This leads to the following time-forgetting updating rules.

Initially, the iteration starts with $\hat{\mathbf{u}}_0 = \boldsymbol{\mu}$ and $\boldsymbol{\Sigma}_0 = \boldsymbol{\Sigma}_u$.

At the $(t+1)$th iteration, update the following three parameters:

$$e_{t+1} = \hat{\mathbf{u}}_t^{\mathrm{T}}\vec{\boldsymbol{\phi}}_{t+1} - y_{t+1},$$

$$\gamma_{t+1} = \left(\lambda\alpha^{t+1} + \vec{\boldsymbol{\phi}}_{t+1}^{\mathrm{T}}\boldsymbol{\Sigma}_t\vec{\boldsymbol{\phi}}_{t+1}\right)^{-1},$$

and

$$\boldsymbol{\Sigma}_{t+1} = \boldsymbol{\Sigma}_t - \gamma_{t+1}\boldsymbol{\Sigma}_t\vec{\boldsymbol{\phi}}_{t+1}\vec{\boldsymbol{\phi}}_{t+1}^{\mathrm{T}}\boldsymbol{\Sigma}_t.$$

Then the estimator itself can be updated as follows:

$$\hat{\mathbf{u}}_{t+1} = \hat{\mathbf{u}}_t - \sigma_\varepsilon^{-2} e_{t+1} \mathbf{\Sigma}_{t+1} \vec{\phi}_{t+1}. \tag{15.136}$$

15.5.4 The recursive KRR algorithm in empirical space with a forgetting factor and a finite window

Since α^N will become negligible when N is sufficiently large, we can approximate the cost function in Eq. (15.135) by a finite-window cost function:

$$\sum_{i=\max\{1,t-N\}}^{t} \lambda^{-1}\alpha^{-i}|y_i - \mathbf{u}^{\mathrm{T}}\vec{\boldsymbol{\phi}}_i|^2 + \mathbf{u}^{\mathrm{T}}\mathbf{\Sigma}_0^{-1}\mathbf{u}, \tag{15.137}$$

which immediately leads to a finite-window updating algorithm:

$$\mathbf{a}_t^{[N]} = \left[\mathbf{K}_t^{[N]} + \mathbf{\Sigma}_{\boldsymbol{\varepsilon}_t}^{[N]}\right]^{-1} \mathbf{y}_t^{[N]} \equiv \left[\tilde{\mathbf{K}}_t^{[N]}\right]^{-1} \mathbf{y}_t^{[N]}. \tag{15.138}$$

Since inverting an $N \times N$ matrix $\tilde{\mathbf{K}}_t^{[N]}$ consumes $O(N^3)$ operations, amounting to a computationally prohibitive cost for each updating when N is large, we propose a doubly Woodbury updating (DWU) algorithm to cut the cost by one order of magnitude, i.e. down to $O(N^2)$ operations per updating.

The doubly Woodbury updating (DWU) algorithm

For convenience, let us denote

$$\tilde{\mathbf{K}}_t^{[N]} = \begin{bmatrix} \tilde{\delta} & \tilde{\gamma}^{\mathrm{T}} \\ \tilde{\boldsymbol{\beta}} & \begin{bmatrix} \mathbf{A} \end{bmatrix} \end{bmatrix} \quad \text{and} \quad \tilde{\mathbf{K}}_{t+1}^{[N]} = \begin{bmatrix} \begin{bmatrix} \mathbf{A} \end{bmatrix} & \vec{\mathbf{b}} \\ \vec{\mathbf{c}}^{\mathrm{T}} & d \end{bmatrix}.$$

Note that the lower $(N-1) \times (N-1)$ principal minor of $\tilde{\mathbf{K}}_t^{[N]}$ happens to be exactly identical to the upper $(N-1) \times (N-1)$ principal minor of $\tilde{\mathbf{K}}_{t+1}^{[N]}$. This is the key observation behind the development of the DWU algorithm.

Assume that we have just completed the updating for $\mathbf{a}_t^{[N]} = \left[\tilde{\mathbf{K}}_t^{[N]}\right]^{-1} \mathbf{y}_t^{[N]}$ and, furthermore, that $\mathbf{A}^{-1}$ has been pre-computed and stored so that it can be used at no extra cost in the next iteration. The new iteration contains two steps.

1. **Increment Woodbury updating.** By applying Woodbury's matrix identity [301], we can compute

$$\left[\tilde{\mathbf{K}}_{t+1}^{[N]}\right]^{-1} =$$
$$\begin{bmatrix} \mathbf{A}^{-1} + \mathbf{A}^{-1}\vec{\mathbf{b}}(d - \vec{\mathbf{c}}^{\mathrm{T}}\mathbf{A}^{-1}\vec{\mathbf{b}})^{-1}\vec{\mathbf{c}}^{\mathrm{T}}\mathbf{A}^{-1} & \mathbf{A}^{-1}\vec{\mathbf{b}}(d - \vec{\mathbf{c}}^{\mathrm{T}}\mathbf{A}^{-1}\vec{\mathbf{b}})^{-1} \\ (d - \vec{\mathbf{c}}^{\mathrm{T}}\mathbf{A}^{-1}\vec{\mathbf{b}})^{-1}(d - \vec{\mathbf{c}}^{\mathrm{T}}\mathbf{A}^{-1}\vec{\mathbf{b}})^{-1}\vec{\mathbf{c}}^{\mathrm{T}}\mathbf{A}^{-1} & (d - \vec{\mathbf{c}}^{\mathrm{T}}\mathbf{A}^{-1}\vec{\mathbf{b}})^{-1} \end{bmatrix} \tag{15.139}$$

   using merely $O(N^2)$ operations.

2. **Decrement Woodbury updating.** Let us re-denote the newly computed inversion as

$$\left[\tilde{\mathbf{K}}_{t+1}^{[N]}\right]^{-1} = \begin{bmatrix} \delta & \vec{\gamma}^{\mathrm{T}} \\ \vec{\beta} & \begin{bmatrix} & \Gamma & \end{bmatrix} \end{bmatrix},$$

where Γ denotes the lower $(N-1)\times(N-1)$ principal minor of the big matrix. Then the inversion of $\left[\tilde{\mathbf{K}}_{t+2}^{[N-1]}\right]$ can be directly computed as

$$[\mathbf{A}']^{-1} = \left[\tilde{\mathbf{K}}_{t+2}^{[N-1]}\right]^{-1} = \Gamma - \vec{\beta}\,\delta^{-1}\vec{\gamma}^{\mathrm{T}}, \tag{15.140}$$

using again only $O(N^2)$ operations.

Now we can proceed with the next iteration by noting that $\tilde{\mathbf{K}}_{t+2}^{[N]}$ has a familiar form, i.e.

$$\tilde{\mathbf{K}}_{t+2}^{[N]} = \begin{bmatrix} \begin{bmatrix} & \mathbf{A}' & \end{bmatrix} & \vec{\mathbf{b}}' \\ \vec{\mathbf{c}}'^{\mathrm{T}} & d' \end{bmatrix},$$

and $\mathbf{A}'^{-1}$ has already been pre-computed in the previous iteration.

The ZIP-based updating algorithm

Apart for the above DWU scheme, the rest of the ZIP-based updating algorithm includes (1) computing the prediction error and (2) updating the regressor. The procedure in each iteration is now summarized as follows.

ALGORITHM 15.3 (Procedure in one update of finite-window EiV regressor) *It is assumed that, during the previous (i.e. tth) iteration, along with the tth finite-window EIV regressor* $\mathbf{a}_t^{\mathrm{T}}$, $\mathbf{A}^{-1} = \left[\tilde{\mathbf{K}}_{t+1}^{[N-1]}\right]^{-1}$ *has already been pre-computed and pre-stored. The process in the* $(t+1)$*th iteration contains the following two key steps.*

- **Step 1: Compute the prediction error.** *First, compute the prediction error*

$$e_{t+1} = \mathbf{a}_t^{\mathrm{T}}\vec{\mathbf{k}}(\mathbf{x}_{t+1}) - y_{t+1}. \tag{15.141}$$

- **Step 2: Update the regressor.** *Then, apply the ZIP updating rule to u and update the finite-window EiV regressor:*

$$\begin{aligned}
\mathbf{a}_{t+1}^{[N]} &= \begin{bmatrix} \mathbf{a}_t^{[N-1]} \\ 0 \end{bmatrix} - \left[\mathbf{K}_{t+1}^{[N]} + \boldsymbol{\Sigma}_{\varepsilon,t+1}^{[N]}\right]^{-1}\begin{bmatrix} \mathbf{0} \\ e_{t+1} \end{bmatrix} \\
&= \begin{bmatrix} \mathbf{a}_t^{[N-1]} \\ 0 \end{bmatrix} - \left[\tilde{\mathbf{K}}_{t+2}^{[N]}\right]^{-1}\begin{bmatrix} \mathbf{0} \\ e_{t+1} \end{bmatrix} \\
&= \begin{bmatrix} \mathbf{a}_t^{[N-1]} \\ 0 \end{bmatrix} - \begin{bmatrix} \mathbf{A}^{-1}\vec{\mathbf{b}}(d - \vec{\mathbf{c}}^{\mathrm{T}}\mathbf{A}^{-1}\vec{\mathbf{b}})^{-1}e_{t+1} \\ (d - \vec{\mathbf{c}}^{\mathrm{T}}\mathbf{A}^{-1}\vec{\mathbf{b}})^{-1}e_{t+1} \end{bmatrix}.
\end{aligned} \tag{15.142}$$

- **Step 3: Pre-compute $\left[\tilde{\mathbf{K}}_{t+2}^{[N-1]}\right]^{-1}$ via the DWU scheme.** *By the DWU scheme (see Eqs. (15.139) and (15.140)), we pre-compute the following:*

$$\left[\tilde{\mathbf{K}}_{t+1}^{[N-1]}\right]^{-1} \rightarrow \left[\tilde{\mathbf{K}}_{t+2}^{[N-1]}\right]^{-1}.$$

Now we are ready to proceed with the $(t+2)$th iteration. □

15.6 Recursive EiV learning algorithms

This section addresses recursive EiV learning algorithms in the intrinsic and empirical spaces.

15.6.1 Recursive EiV learning models in intrinsic space

With virtually the same derivation as that used for the recursive KRR, the formal algorithm for the recursive EiV regressor can be obtained as follows.

ALGORITHM 15.4 (Recursive EiV learning model in intrinsic space)

Initialization

The iterations start with $\hat{\mathbf{u}}_0 = \boldsymbol{\mu}$ and $\boldsymbol{\Sigma}_0 = \boldsymbol{\Sigma}_u$.

Recursive procedure

For the recursive procedure, let us assume that, at the tth iteration, $\hat{\mathbf{u}}_t$ is just learned from the dataset $\{\mathbf{x}_1, \mathbf{x}_2, \ldots, \mathbf{x}_t\}$ together with all their teacher values $\{y_1, y_2, \ldots, y_t\}$. There are two tasks during the tth iteration.

- **The prediction phase.** *Let us assume that, at some point shortly after the sample time t, but before $t+1$, the perturbed input vector $\tilde{\mathbf{x}}_{t+1}$ becomes newly accessible, but* **without** *its corresponding teacher value y_{t+1}. At this stage, the task is to predict the most likely system response. After computing the kernel-induced vector $\hat{\boldsymbol{\phi}}_{\tilde{\mathbf{x}}}(\tilde{\mathbf{x}}_{t+1})$, which is based on $\tilde{\mathbf{x}}_{t+1}$, the optimal prediction is*

$$\hat{y}_{t+1} = \hat{\mathbf{u}}_t^{\mathrm{T}} \hat{\boldsymbol{\phi}}_{\tilde{\mathbf{x}}}(\tilde{\mathbf{x}}_{t+1}).$$

- **Estimator updating.** *Suppose that, at time $t+1$, the actual output response y_{t+1} will become accessible, making available both the training dataset $\{\tilde{\mathbf{x}}_1, \tilde{\mathbf{x}}_2, \ldots, \tilde{\mathbf{x}}_t, \tilde{\mathbf{x}}_{t+1}\}$ and the corresponding teacher set $\{y_1, y_2, \ldots, y_{t+1}\}$. This allows the following updates to be executed.*

  (i) Compute the prediction error,

$$e_{t+1} = \hat{y}_{t+1} - y_{t+1} = \hat{\mathbf{u}}_t^{\mathrm{T}} \hat{\boldsymbol{\phi}}_{\tilde{\mathbf{x}}}(\tilde{\mathbf{x}}_{t+1}) - y_{t+1}, \tag{15.143}$$

  and update the covariance matrix,

$$\boldsymbol{\Sigma}_{t+1} = \boldsymbol{\Sigma}_t - \gamma_{t+1} \boldsymbol{\Sigma}_t \hat{\boldsymbol{\phi}}_{\tilde{\mathbf{x}}}(\tilde{\mathbf{x}}_{t+1}) \hat{\boldsymbol{\phi}}_{\tilde{\mathbf{x}}}(\tilde{\mathbf{x}}_{t+1})^{\mathrm{T}} \boldsymbol{\Sigma}_t, \tag{15.144}$$

where

$$\gamma_{t+1} \equiv \left(\sigma_\xi^2 + \hat{\boldsymbol{\phi}}_{\tilde{\mathbf{x}}}(\tilde{\mathbf{x}}_{t+1})^{\mathrm{T}} \boldsymbol{\Sigma}_t \hat{\boldsymbol{\phi}}_{\tilde{\mathbf{x}}}(\tilde{\mathbf{x}}_{t+1})\right)^{-1}.$$

(ii) The estimator itself can now be updated as follows:

$$\hat{\mathbf{u}}_{t+1} = \hat{\mathbf{u}}_t - \sigma_\xi^{-2} e_{t+1} \boldsymbol{\Sigma}_{t+1} \hat{\boldsymbol{\phi}}_{\tilde{\mathbf{x}}}(\tilde{\mathbf{x}}_{t+1}). \tag{15.145}$$

Now we are ready for the prediction phase for the new iteration at $n = t + 1$. □

15.6.2 The recursive EiV algorithm in empirical space

Denote $\boldsymbol{\Sigma}_{\xi,t} \equiv \mathrm{Diag}[\sigma_{\xi_i}^2,\ i = 1, \ldots, t]$, and denote $\hat{\mathbf{K}}_{t+1}$ as the weighted kernel matrix formed from the first $t + 1$ training data, see Eq. (15.94).

Following the same derivation as that used for Eq. (15.130), we can obtain an updating formulation in the empirical space:

$$\begin{aligned} \mathbf{a}_{t+1} &= \left[\hat{\mathbf{K}}_{t+1} + \boldsymbol{\Sigma}_{\xi,t+1}\right]^{-1} \begin{bmatrix} \mathbf{y}_t \\ y_{t+1} \end{bmatrix} \\ &= \begin{bmatrix} \mathbf{a}_t \\ 0 \end{bmatrix} - \left[\hat{\mathbf{K}}_{t+1} + \boldsymbol{\Sigma}_{\xi,t+1}\right]^{-1} \begin{bmatrix} \mathbf{0} \\ e_{t+1} \end{bmatrix}. \end{aligned} \tag{15.146}$$

By applying the Woodbury matrix identity, recursive EiV algorithms in the empirical space can be derived as summarized in Algorithm 15.5. (Here we denote $\mathbf{L}_t \equiv \left[\hat{\mathbf{K}}_t + \boldsymbol{\Sigma}_{\xi,t}\right]^{-1}$.)

ALGORITHM 15.5 (Recursive EiV algorithm (empirical space))

Initialization: $\mathbf{L}_0 \leftarrow [\,]$, $\mathbf{a}_0 = [\,]$
for *$i \leftarrow 1$ to ∞* ***do***
  Given input $\tilde{\mathbf{x}}_i$
  for *$j \leftarrow 1$ to $i - 1$* ***do***
    Compute $[\hat{\mathbf{k}}_i]_j \leftarrow \iint k(\mathbf{x}_j, \mathbf{x}_i) p(\mathbf{x}_j|\tilde{\mathbf{x}}_j) p(\mathbf{x}_i|\tilde{\mathbf{x}}_i) d\mathbf{x}_j\, d\mathbf{x}_i$
  end for
  Predict $\hat{y}_i \leftarrow \mathbf{a}_{i-1}^{\mathrm{T}} \hat{\mathbf{k}}_i$
  Given output y_i with output noise variance σ_ε^2
  Compute $\kappa_i \equiv \iint k(\mathbf{x}_i, \mathbf{x}_i) p(\mathbf{x}_i|\tilde{\mathbf{x}}_i) d\mathbf{x}_i$
  Compute $\gamma_i \leftarrow 1/(\sigma_\xi^2 + \kappa_i - \hat{\mathbf{k}}_i^{\mathrm{T}} \mathbf{L}_{i-1} \hat{\mathbf{k}}_i)$
  Compute $\boldsymbol{\zeta}_i \leftarrow \begin{bmatrix} \mathbf{L}_{i-1}\hat{\mathbf{k}}_i \\ -1 \end{bmatrix}$
  Update $\mathbf{L}_i \leftarrow \begin{bmatrix} \mathbf{L}_{i-1} & 0 \\ 0 & 0 \end{bmatrix} + \gamma_i \boldsymbol{\zeta}_i \boldsymbol{\zeta}_i^{\mathrm{T}}$
  Compute prediction error $e_i \leftarrow \hat{y}_i - y_i$
  Update $\mathbf{a}_i \leftarrow \begin{bmatrix} \mathbf{a}_{i-1} \\ 0 \end{bmatrix} + \gamma_i e_i \boldsymbol{\zeta}_i$
end for

The incorporation of a forgetting factor and a fixed window into EiV learning models can basically follow the procedure presented in Section 15.5.4, so the details are omitted here.

15.7 Summary

This chapter focuses on estimation, prediction, and system identification using the observed samples and prior knowledge of the first- and second-order statistics of the system parameters. For kernel-induced linear models with deterministic system parameters, it has been shown that the best unbiased linear estimator, the predictor, and the LSE regressor are all identical to each other. This is the well-known Gauss–Markov theorem, Theorem 15.1. In this chapter, the theorem has been extended to statistical learning models. The best linear estimator, the predictor, and the optimal KRR regressor can again be shown to be identical to each other, Theorem 15.2. Furthermore, the Gauss–Markov theorem may be extended to the errors-in-variables learning models, Theorem 15.3.

In time-series prediction, the prior knowledge may be interpreted as the state which summarizes the useful information embedded in the past observations. Therefore, it can be recursively updated when new data are made available. This chapter develops recursive incremental learning models to effectively update the estimators in time-adaptive fashion, both for perturbation-free (KRR) and for perturbational (EiV) learning models. The recursive algorithms both for time-adaptive KRR and for EiV learning models require only $O(J^2)$ operations per sample update.

In this chapter, the notion of a weighted kernel function is introduced, naturally leading to the dual-optimization formulation in the empirical space. Recursive KRR and EiV algorithms in the empirical space have also been developed. An important advantage of the empirical-space approach lies in its versatility, i.e. it is applicable for any value of J, be it finite or infinite, or possibly to nonvectorial data analysis. The flip side is that its complexity amounts to $O(t^2)$ per sample, i.e. it will grow with the number of iterations t. To rectify this problem, the notion of a forgetting factor is introduced. More specifically, a so-called doubly Woodbury updating (DWU) algorithm is proposed to effectively update KRR and EiV regressors (in the empirical space) using kernel matrices with a fixed window size.

15.8 Problems

Problem 15.1 (A BLUE might not be a BLE) *Prove that a BLUE might not deliver the minimum variance by showing that a zero estimator $\hat{\mathbf{u}} = \mathbf{0}$ yields a lower variance than a BLUE if and only if (see Eq. (15.14))*

$$||\mathbf{u}||^2 < \sigma_\varepsilon^2 \, \mathrm{tr}\left(\left[\mathbf{\Phi}\mathbf{\Phi}^{\mathrm{T}}\right]^{-1}\right),$$

assuming that $\mathbf{\Phi}\mathbf{\Phi}^{\mathrm{T}}$ is invertible.

Problem 15.2 (Tradeoff between bias and variance) *Consider the following Gauss–Markov model:*

$$y = ux + \varepsilon. \tag{15.147}$$

(a) *What is the estimation error for a BLUE with training inputs* $x_1 = 1$, $x_2 = 2$, $x_3 = 3$, *and* $x_4 = 4$, *with noise components* $\mathbf{\Sigma}_{\boldsymbol{\varepsilon}} = \text{Diag}(0.1, 0.2, 0.3, 0.4)$?

(b) *What is the estimation error for the estimator* $\hat{u} = 0$ *as a function of the unknown parameter* u?

(c) *Repeat (b) for the following cases: (i)* $u = 10$, *(ii)* $u = 1$ *(iii),* $u = 0.1$, *and (iv)* $u = 0.01$.

(d) *Does a BLUE always yield the minimum estimation error?*

Problem 15.3 (Estimation formula for linear kernels) *Assuming that both* $\mathbf{x}$ *and* $\Delta\mathbf{x}$ *are Gaussian distributed, show that*

$$\hat{\mathbf{x}}_{\tilde{\mathbf{x}}}(\tilde{\mathbf{x}}) \equiv E[\mathbf{x}|\tilde{\mathbf{x}}] = \frac{\sigma^2_{\Delta\mathbf{x}}}{\sigma^2_{\mathbf{x}} + \sigma^2_{\Delta\mathbf{x}}}\tilde{\mathbf{x}}.$$

Problem 15.4 *Show that* $E[\mathbf{u}\xi(\tilde{\mathbf{x}})|\tilde{\mathbf{x}}] = 0$.

Hint: $E\left[\mathbf{u}\xi(\tilde{\mathbf{x}})|\tilde{\mathbf{x}}\right] = E\left[\mathbf{u}\mathbf{u}^{\mathrm{T}}\right]\left(\hat{\boldsymbol{\phi}}_{\tilde{\mathbf{x}}}(\tilde{\mathbf{x}}) - \hat{\boldsymbol{\phi}}_{\tilde{\mathbf{x}}}(\tilde{\mathbf{x}})\right) + E[\mathbf{u}]E\left[\boldsymbol{\varepsilon}|\tilde{\mathbf{x}}\right] = 0.$

Problem 15.5 *Consider a single-variate Gauss–Markov model of a second-order polynomial system*

$$y = u'_0 + u'_1 x + u'_2 x^2 + \varepsilon,\ \tilde{x} = x + \Delta x, \tag{15.148}$$

where the parameters $\mathbf{u}' = [u'_0\ u'_1\ u'_2]^{\mathrm{T}}$ *have prior mean* $\boldsymbol{\mu}_{u'} = 0$ *and covariance matrix* $\mathbf{\Sigma}_{u'} = \mathbf{I}$, *and the output noise has variance* $E[\varepsilon^2|\tilde{x}] = 0.01$. *Assume that the input* $x \sim \mathcal{N}(0, 1)$ *and input noise* $\Delta x \sim \mathcal{N}(0, 0.1)$ *are Gaussian distributed and independent. You are given observed input–output pairs*

$$(\tilde{x}_1, y_1) = (0.3, 2.53), \qquad (\tilde{x}_2, y_2) = (1.2, 6.32), \qquad (\tilde{x}_3, y_3) = (-0.6, 1.71).$$

(a) *Express the Gauss–Markov model in terms of the Hermite polynomial basis*

$$y = u_0\phi_0(x) + u_1\phi_1(x) + u_2\phi_2(x) + \varepsilon,$$

where

$$\phi_0(x) = \frac{1}{0!}\,\mathrm{He}_0(x) = 1,$$
$$\phi_1(x) = \frac{1}{1!}\,\mathrm{He}_1(x) = x,$$
$$\phi_2(x) = \frac{1}{2!}\,\mathrm{He}_2(x) = \frac{x^2 - 1}{2}.$$

(b) *Compute the prior mean and covariance matrix for parameters* $\mathbf{u}$.

(c) *Compute* $\hat{\phi}_n(\tilde{x}) = E[\phi(x_n)|\tilde{x}]$, *for all* $n = 0, 1, 2$.

(d) *Compute* $\sigma^2_{\xi_i}$ *for each sample i.*
(e) *Derive the EiV regressor for optimal prediction.*

Problem 15.6 *Recall that* $\hat{\mathbf{u}}_{\text{KRR}}$ *and* $\hat{\mathbf{u}}_{\text{EiV}}$ *have been proven to be biased, see Eqs. (15.46) and (15.86).*

(a) *Show that*

$$E\left[\hat{\mathbf{u}}_{\text{KRR}}|\mathbf{D_x}\right] = E\left[\mathbf{u}|\mathbf{D_x}\right].$$

(b) *Show that*

$$E\left[\hat{\mathbf{u}}_{\text{EiV}}|\mathbf{D}_{\tilde{\mathbf{x}}}\right] = E\left[\mathbf{u}|\mathbf{D}_{\tilde{\mathbf{x}}}\right].$$

Problem 15.7 (Finite-order EiV regressors in the intrinsic space) *Write down the ZIP-type updating formula for a finite-order EiV regressor in the intrinsic space.*

Problem 15.8 *Show that, for each individual sample,*

$$E[\Delta^{[n]}|\tilde{\mathbf{x}}] = E[\overrightarrow{\boldsymbol{\phi}}(\mathbf{x})|\tilde{\mathbf{x}}] - \hat{\boldsymbol{\phi}}_{\tilde{\mathbf{x}}}^{[n]}(\tilde{\mathbf{x}}) \neq 0.$$

Problem 15.9 (Finite-order EIV regressors in the empirical space)

(a) *Derive the kernelized learning model for a finite-order EiV regressor in the empirical space.*
(b) *Write down the ZIP-type updating formula for a finite-order EiV regressor in the empirical space.*

Problem 15.10 (Polynomial EiV regressors: Gaussian cases) *In a single-variate case* $x \sim \mathcal{N}(0,1)$ *and* $\Delta x \sim \mathcal{N}(0, \sigma^2_{\Delta x})$. *Note that the conditional probability of x given* $\tilde{x}$ *is also Gaussian distributed:*

$$E[x|\tilde{x}] \sim \mathcal{N}\left(\frac{\tilde{x}}{1+\eta}, \frac{\eta}{1+\eta}\right). \tag{15.149}$$

The Hermite polynomial functions, as defined by probabilists, are

$$\text{He}_n(x) = (-1)^n e^{x^2/2} \frac{d^n}{dx^n} e^{-x^2/2}.$$

Define Hermite polynomials (up to order p) as basis functions

$$\phi_n(x) = \frac{1}{n!}\,\text{He}_n(x),\ 0 \le n \le p.$$

Then any Gauss–Markov model of a pth-order polynomial system can be expanded with Hermite polynomial basis

$$y = \sum_{n=0}^{p} u'_n x^n = \sum_{n=0}^{p} u_n \phi_n(x) = \mathbf{u}^{\text{T}}\boldsymbol{\phi}(x).$$

Given N observations $\{(\tilde{x}_i, y_i)\}_{i=1}^N$, *where each input is independently generated, denote the normalized (observed) input as*

$$\tilde{x}_i = \tilde{x}_i/\sigma_x = x_i + \Delta x_i.$$

(a) *To compute* $\hat{\boldsymbol{\phi}}(\tilde{x})$, *we refer to the following result in our previous work [144]:*

$$E[\mathrm{He}_n(x)|\tilde{x}] = \gamma^n \,\mathrm{He}_n(\gamma\tilde{x}), \tag{15.150}$$

where $\gamma = 1/\sqrt{1+\eta}$. *This gives a closed-form expression for elements in* $\hat{\boldsymbol{\phi}}(\tilde{x})$ *as*

$$\hat{\phi}_n(\tilde{x}) = E[\phi_n(x)|\tilde{x}] = \frac{\gamma^n}{n!}\,\mathrm{He}_n(\gamma\tilde{x}).$$

(b) *Show that*

$$E[\phi_m(x)\phi_n(x)|\tilde{x}] = \sum_{\ell=0}^{\min(m,n)} \frac{(\gamma^2\eta)^\ell}{\ell!}\hat{\phi}_{m-\ell}(\tilde{x})\hat{\phi}_{n-\ell}(\tilde{x}),$$

which in turn yields an explicit expression for the noise components $\sigma_{x_i}^2$:

$$\begin{aligned}\sigma_{x_i}^2 &= E[\|\boldsymbol{\phi}(x_i) - \hat{\boldsymbol{\phi}}(\tilde{x}_i)\|_{R_\mathbf{u}}^2|\tilde{x}_i] + \sigma_{\varepsilon_i}^2 \\ &= E[\|\boldsymbol{\phi}(x_i)\|_{R_\mathbf{u}}^2|\tilde{x}_i] + \|\hat{\boldsymbol{\phi}}(\tilde{x}_i)\|_{R_\mathbf{u}}^2 + \sigma_{\varepsilon_i}^2 \\ &= \sum_{0\le m,n\le p} (R_\mathbf{u})_{mn}\left(E[\phi_m(x_i)\phi_n(x_i)|\tilde{x}_i] - \hat{\phi}_m(\tilde{x}_i)\hat{\phi}_n(\tilde{x}_i)\right) + \sigma_\varepsilon^2 \qquad (15.151) \\ &= \sum_{0\le m,n\le p} (R_\mathbf{u})_{mn}\left(\sum_{\ell=1}^{\min(m,n)} \frac{(\gamma^2\eta)^\ell}{\ell!}\hat{\phi}_{m-\ell}(\tilde{x})\hat{\phi}_{n-\ell}(\tilde{x})\right) + \sigma_\varepsilon^2.\end{aligned}$$

(c) *Finally, the EiV regressor takes the following form:*

$$\hat{y} = \hat{\mathbf{u}}_{\mathrm{EiV}}^{\mathrm{T}}\hat{\boldsymbol{\phi}}(\tilde{x}), \tag{15.152a}$$

$$\begin{aligned}\hat{\mathbf{u}}_{\mathrm{EiV}} = &\left(\sum_{i=1}^N \frac{1}{\sigma_{x_i}^2}\hat{\boldsymbol{\phi}}(\tilde{x}_i)\hat{\boldsymbol{\phi}}(\tilde{x}_i)^{\mathrm{T}} + \boldsymbol{\Sigma}_u^{-1}\right)^{-1} \\ &\times \left(\sum_{i=1}^N \frac{1}{\sigma_{x_i}^2}\hat{\boldsymbol{\phi}}(\tilde{x}_i)y_i + \boldsymbol{\Sigma}_u^{-1}\boldsymbol{\mu}_u\right).\end{aligned} \tag{15.152b}$$

(d) *Show that the result may be extended to the multivariate case with arbitrary covariance matrices* $\boldsymbol{\Sigma}_\mathbf{x}$, *and* $\boldsymbol{\Sigma}_{\Delta\mathbf{x}}$ *[145].*

Problem 15.11 (Linkage between recursive algorithms in intrinsic space and empirical space) *Establish the relationship between the time-adaptive KRR updating rule in the intrinsic space and that in the empirical space, see Eq. (15.131).*

Hint: *Similarly to Eq. (7.29), show that*

$$\begin{aligned}\boldsymbol{\Sigma}_u\Phi_{t+1}\left[\mathbf{K}_{t+1}+\boldsymbol{\Sigma}_{\varepsilon,t+1}\right]^{-1} &= \left(\boldsymbol{\Phi}\boldsymbol{\Sigma}_{\varepsilon,t+1}^{-1}\boldsymbol{\Phi}^{\mathrm{T}}+\boldsymbol{\Sigma}_u^{-1}\right)^{-1}\Phi_{t+1}\boldsymbol{\Sigma}_{\varepsilon,t+1}^{-1} \\ &\underset{\text{Eq. (15.119)}}{=} \boldsymbol{\Sigma}_{t+1}\boldsymbol{\Phi}_{t+1}\boldsymbol{\Sigma}_{\varepsilon,t+1}^{-1}. \end{aligned} \tag{15.153}$$

By pre-multiplying Eq. (15.131) by $\boldsymbol{\Phi}_{t+1}$, and making use of the LSP, it can be shown that

$$\begin{aligned}\mathbf{u}_{t+1} &= \boldsymbol{\Sigma}_u\boldsymbol{\Phi}_{t+1}\mathbf{a}_{t+1} \\ &\underset{\text{Eq. (15.131)}}{=} \boldsymbol{\Sigma}_u\boldsymbol{\Phi}_{t+1}\begin{bmatrix}\mathbf{a}_t\\0\end{bmatrix} - \boldsymbol{\Sigma}_u\boldsymbol{\Phi}_{t+1}\left[\mathbf{K}_{t+1}+\boldsymbol{\Sigma}_{\varepsilon,t+1}\right]^{-1}\begin{bmatrix}\mathbf{0}\\e_{t+1}\end{bmatrix} \\ &\underset{\text{Eq. (15.153)}}{=} \boldsymbol{\Sigma}_u\boldsymbol{\Phi}_{t+1}\begin{bmatrix}\mathbf{a}_t\\0\end{bmatrix} - \boldsymbol{\Sigma}_{t+1}\boldsymbol{\Phi}_{t+1}\boldsymbol{\Sigma}_{\varepsilon,t+1}^{-1}\begin{bmatrix}\mathbf{0}\\e_{t+1}\end{bmatrix} \\ &= \mathbf{u}_t - \sigma_{\varepsilon_{t+1}}^{-2}\boldsymbol{\Sigma}_{t+1}\overrightarrow{\phi}_{t+1}e_{t+1}. \end{aligned} \tag{15.154}$$

Problem 15.12 (Time-adaptive KRR updating under Gaussian assumption) *Let us assume that the prior distribution of $\mathbf{u}_\theta$ is*

$$p[\mathbf{u}_\theta] \sim N(\mu_0, \boldsymbol{\Sigma}_0).$$

Upon observing t samples $\{\mathbf{x}_i, y_i\}_{i=1}^t$, assume that $\mathbf{u}_\theta$ has the following Gaussian distribution:

$$p[\mathbf{u}_\theta|\{\mathbf{x}_i, y_i\}_{i=1}^t] \sim N(\mu_t, \boldsymbol{\Sigma}_t).$$

Upon arrival of the new information $\{\overrightarrow{\phi}_{t+1}, y_{t+1}\}$, we seek an effective way to perform the following one-step update:

$$\{\boldsymbol{\mu}_t, \boldsymbol{\Sigma}_t\} \rightarrow \{\boldsymbol{\mu}_{t+1}, \boldsymbol{\Sigma}_{t+1}\}.$$

Under the Gaussian assumption, it hinges upon the one-step update of the conditional density function, i.e.

$$p[\mathbf{u}_\theta|\{\mathbf{x}_i, y_i\}_{i=1}^t] \rightarrow p[\mathbf{u}_\theta|\{\mathbf{x}_i, y_i\}_{i=1}^{t+1}].$$

Note that

$$p[\mathbf{u}_\theta|\{\mathbf{x}_i, y_i\}_{i=1}^{t+1}] = \frac{p[\mathbf{x}_{t+1}, y_{t+1}, \mathbf{u}_\theta|\{\mathbf{x}_i, y_i\}_{i=1}^t]}{\int p[\mathbf{x}_{t+1}, y_{t+1}, \mathbf{u}_\theta|\{\mathbf{x}_i, y_i\}_{i=1}^t]d\mathbf{u}_\theta}. \tag{15.155}$$

(a) *Derive the following updated Gaussian distribution:*

$$p[\mathbf{u}_\theta|\{\mathbf{x}_i, y_i\}_{i=1}^{t+1}] \sim N(\mu_{t+1}, \boldsymbol{\Sigma}_{t+1}),$$

with

- **covariance update:**

$$\boldsymbol{\Sigma}_{t+1}^{-1} = \boldsymbol{\Sigma}_t^{-1} + \lambda_0^{-1}\overrightarrow{\phi}_{t+1}\overrightarrow{\phi}_{t+1}^{\mathrm{T}}, \tag{15.156}$$

- **mean update:**

$$\boldsymbol{\mu}_{t+1} = \boldsymbol{\mu}_t - \boldsymbol{\Sigma}_{t+1}\overrightarrow{\phi}_{t+1}e_{t+1}. \tag{15.157}$$

(b) *By applying Woodbury's matrix identity[301] to Eq. (15.156), show that*

$$\boldsymbol{\Sigma}_{t+1} = \boldsymbol{\Sigma}_t - \gamma_{t+1}\left[\boldsymbol{\Sigma}_t \vec{\boldsymbol{\phi}}_{t+1} \vec{\boldsymbol{\phi}}_{t+1}^{\mathrm{T}} \boldsymbol{\Sigma}_t\right],$$

$$\text{with } \gamma_{t+1} = \left(\lambda_0 + \vec{\boldsymbol{\phi}}_{t+1}^{\mathrm{t}} \boldsymbol{\Sigma}_t \vec{\boldsymbol{\phi}}_{t+1}\right)^{-1}. \qquad (15.158)$$

Problem 15.13 (Time-adaptive EiV algorithm with a forgetting factor and a finite window) *With reference to Algorithm 15.5, develop a variant that takes into account a forgetting factor and uses a finite window. Can this variant make use of the doubly Woodbury updating (DWU) algorithm, as in Section 15.5.4?*

Part VIII

Appendices

Appendix A reviews useful validation techniques and test schemes for learning models. Appendix B covers supervised classifiers without an explicit learning process and the popular and fundamental Bayes classifiers.

Appendix A Validation and testing of learning models

Machine learning has successfully led to many promising tools for intelligent data filtering, processing, and interpretation. Naturally, proper metrics will be required in order to objectively evaluate the performance of machine learning tools. To this end, this chapter will address the following subjects.

- It is commonly agreed that the *testing accuracy* serves as a more reasonable metric for the performance evaluation of a learned classifier. Section A.1 discusses several *cross-validation* (CV) techniques for evaluating the classification performance of the learned models.
- Section A.2 explores two important test schemes: the *hypothesis test* and the *significance test*.

A.1 Cross-validation techniques

Suppose that the dataset under consideration has N samples to be used for training the classifier model and/or estimating the classification accuracy. Before the training phase starts, a subset of training dataset must be set aside as the testing dataset. The class labels of the test patterns are assumed to be unknown during the learning phase. These labels will be revealed only during the testing phase in order to provide the necessary guideline for the evaluation of the performance.

Some evaluation/validation methods are presented as follows.

(i) **Holdout validation.** N' ($N' < N$) samples are randomly selected from the dataset for training a classifier, and the remaining $N - N'$ samples are used for evaluating the accuracy of the classifier. Typically, N' is about two-thirds of N. Holdout validation solves the problem of which biased estimation occurs in re-substitution by completely separating the training data from the validation data. However, a smaller number of samples is used to train the classifier, which results in a less reliable classifier and a reduction in statistical significance. Moreover, the estimated accuracy will suffer from a large variance, because only one estimate is obtained. Therefore, holdout validation is impractical for problems with a small sample size – a situation that commonly occurs in bioinformatic applications.

(ii) ***K*-fold cross-validation.** The dataset is randomly partitioned into K (not necessarily equal) subsets. For each fold, $K - 1$ subsets are used for training a classifier and the remaining subset is used for evaluating the performance of the trained classifier. The process is repeated K times until all of the K subsets have been used for validation. The accuracies in all the K folds are then averaged to obtain the overall accuracy, i.e.

$$\text{overall accuracy} = \frac{1}{K}\sum_{k=1}^{K}\frac{\mathrm{TP}_k + \mathrm{TN}_k}{S_k}, \tag{A.1}$$

where TP_k, TN_k, and S_k are the number of true positives, true negatives, and total test samples in the kth fold, respectively. Alternatively, the overall accuracy can be computed as follows:

$$\text{overall accuracy} = \frac{1}{N}\sum_{k=1}^{K}(\mathrm{TP}_k + \mathrm{TN}_k). \tag{A.2}$$

Note that Eqs. (A.1) and (A.2) are equivalent when the N_k are equal for all k. The problems of large variance in the estimated accuracy can be largely alleviated by K-fold cross-validation (CV) because the accuracy is now based on K estimates instead of one. Heuristically, the larger the size of the training dataset the better the accuracy. Consequently, as demonstrated by Figure A.1, the greater the value of K the better the accuracy. In particular, it has been demonstrated that CV is significantly better than holdout validation when the dataset size is small [84].

(iii) **Leave-one-out CV**. In this case, out of N samples, $N - 1$ are used for training and the lone remaining sample is used as the validation data. Leave-one-out CV is a special case of K-fold CV, in which $K = N$. Note that leave-one-out CV is better for estimating continuous errors, such as the mean-squared error. Its performance on discrete errors, such as misclassification counts, is generally poor [192]. In this respect, K-fold CV is generally preferred.

(iv) **Jackknife**. Jackknife [59, 60] is a resampling technique for estimating the bias and standard error in a statistic. It is easily confused with leave-one-out CV, primarily because both rely on the procedure that leaves one sample for validation and the remaining data for training. The difference from leave-one-out CV lies in the fact that jackknife computes some statistics (e.g. means, variances, and regression

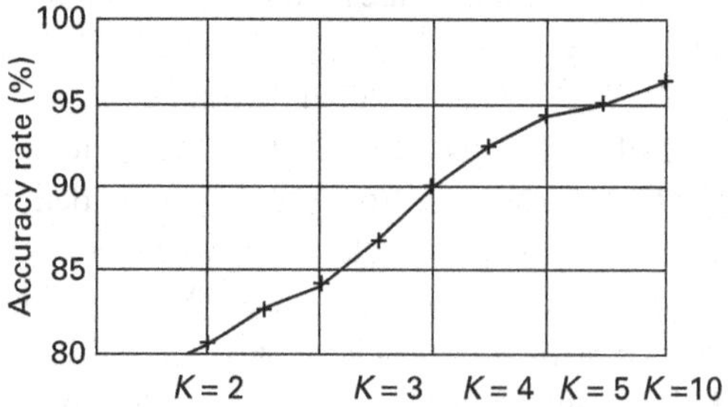

Fig. A.1. The performance of SVM classification on the image database 'http://wang.ist.psu.edu/docs/related/'. The dataset contains ten image classes, with 100 images in each class. It is evident that the greater K the better the accuracy.

Table A.1. Properties of different evaluation methods for estimating classification accuracy/error

Method	Bias	Variance	Computational cost
Re-substitution	High	Low	Low
Holdout validation	Low	High	Low
K-fold CV	Low	Medium	Medium
Leave-one-out CV	Low	Medium	High
Jackknife	Medium–low	Low	High
Bootstrap	Medium–low	Low	High

coefficients) of interest in each fold. At the end, the average of the statistics of all N folds is compared with the one computed using the entire dataset to estimate the bias that may be incurred when the whole dataset is used. For example, in [217], one accepts the fact that the estimated accuracy derived from the training set has bias and then attempts to estimate the bias (by using a resampling technique), which is then subsequently subtracted from the biased accuracy. Therefore, the resulting accuracy will be different from the one obtained from the leave-one-out CV.

(v) **Bootstrap**. Jackknife is a resampling procedure without replacement, whereas bootstrap [58] is a resampling procedure with replacement, meaning that every sample is returned to the pool after sampling. More precisely, given a dataset with N samples, a sample is randomly and sequentially drawn each time, with the drawn sample being returned to the pool before the next sample is taken. This process will be carried out N times, resulting in another set of N samples. (Because of the replacement procedure, some of the samples will be drawn multiple times and some might not be drawn at all.) The drawn samples will be used for training, whereas those samples which are skipped will be used for evaluation. This process is performed B times (typically $B = 25$–200 [60]) and the average of the B classification error rates will be used as the estimated error of the classification system. This procedure is known as the bootstrap zero estimator. It has been demonstrated in a microarray application that bootstrap provides the best performance in terms of the variance of the estimate, but at a high computational cost and some increase in bias (although much less than that of re-substitution) [28].

Table A.1 summarizes the properties of these evaluation methods.

A.2 Hypothesis testing and significance testing

In this section, two important test schemes will be explored.

(i) **Hypothesis testing.** This test requires prior knowledge on the statistical distributions of both the null hypothesis (H_0) and the alternative hypothesis (H_1), insofar as the decision depends on the likelihood ratio of the two hypotheses.

(ii) **Significance testing.** Such a test is based on the statistical distribution of the null hypothesis alone. Given an observation, this test helps assess how confidently one can hold on to the default hypothesis [171, 202].

A.2.1 Hypothesis testing based on the likelihood ratio

Assume that a test sample x is drawn from one of the two populations corresponding to two different hypotheses H_0 and H_1, with their density functions denoted by $p(x|H_0)$ and $p(x|H_1)$, respectively. The *Neyman–Pearson* test [193] is based on the likelihood ratio $\Lambda(x) \equiv p(x|H_0)/p(x|H_1)$:

$$\text{reject } H_0 \text{ if } \Lambda(x) \leq \eta, \tag{A.3}$$

where η is the ratio threshold to be specified. As discussed below, there are numerous ways to specify η.

Bayesian Test

In the basic Bayesian test, a very intuitive decision rule is as follows:

$$\text{reject } H_0 \text{ if } P(H_0|x) < P(H_1|x), \tag{A.4}$$

where $P(H_i|x)$, $i = 0, 1$, denotes the a-posteriori probability given the observation x. Put simply, the hypotheses with higher probability will be favored. According to the Bayesian theorem

$$P(H_i|x) = p(x|H_i)\pi_i/p(x) \text{ for } i = 0, 1, \tag{A.5}$$

where π_0 and π_1 denote the prior probabilities of the null and alternative hypotheses, respectively. Since $p(x)$ is the common factor, it may be dropped. This leads to the following Bayesian test:

$$\text{reject } H_0 \text{ if } p(x|H_0)\pi_0 < p(x|H_1)\pi_1. \tag{A.6}$$

Equivalently, in terms of the likelihood ratio,

$$\text{reject } H_0 \text{ if } \Lambda(x) < \frac{\pi_1}{\pi_0}. \tag{A.7}$$

In other words, the threshold on the ratio is $\eta = \pi_1/\pi_0$ in the basic Bayesian test.

Risk-adjusted Bayesian test

Let the positive and negative classes correspond to H_1 and H_0, respectively. The basic Bayesian test is based on the simple assumption that the false-negative and false-positive errors cause an identical cost. In practice, the two errors may suffer from very different costs. To take this situation into account, we denote C_{01} and C_{10}, respectively, as the costs associated with the false-negative and false-positive errors. This leads to the following risk-adjusted decision rule [308]:

$$\text{reject } H_0 \text{ if } P(H_0|x)C_{10} < P(H_1|x)C_{01}. \tag{A.8}$$

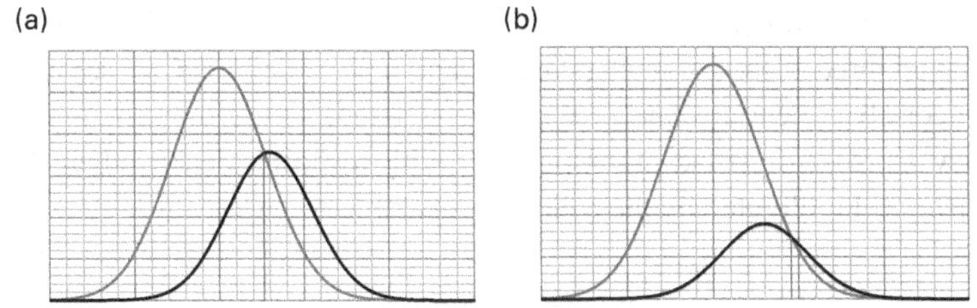

Fig. A.2. The effect of risk adjustment. (a) Here the distributions of the null hypothesis (H_0) and alternative hypothesis (H_1) correspond to the left and right Gaussian curves, respectively. Without risk adjustment, the hypothesis with the higher likelihood will be identified. (b) The risk-adjusted thresholds are determined by the relative prior likelihood and the penalty incurred by the error. Now the two curves show the distributions after the risk adjustment. In this case, the risk ration is 2, namely $C_{01} = 2C_{10}$, i.e. H_1 is now half-weighted in comparison with before. This results in a rightward shift of the cross-over point.

In terms of the likelihood ratio, the decision rule is

$$\text{reject } H_0 \text{ if } \Lambda(x) < \frac{\pi_1 C_{01}}{\pi_0 C_{10}}. \tag{A.9}$$

Namely, the decision threshold on the ratio becomes $\eta = \pi_1 C_{01}/\pi_0 C_{10}$ after the risk adjustment. Note that, if $C_{01} = 2C_{10}$, then the decision will be tilted towards favoring more H_0 than H_1. This is reflected by the fact that the cross-over point (i.e. the decision threshold) is shifted rightward on going from Figure A.2(a) to Figure A.2(b).

Decision threshold given a fixed identification rate

In some applications, there are other constraints dictating the decision. For example, a hospital may be overwhelmed by the number of incoming patients and thus can admit only a certain number of the most seriously ill patients. From the perspective of hypothesis testing, this means that only a pre-specified proportion, denoted by α^*, of the patients can be admitted. Here, by definition,

$$\alpha^* \equiv \frac{\mathrm{TP} + \mathrm{FP}}{P + N}, \tag{A.10}$$

Where the symbols have the same meanings as in Section 1.7. In this case, the ratio threshold η can be uniquely derived from α^* as follows:

$$\alpha^* = \frac{\mathrm{TP} + \mathrm{FP}}{P + N} = \Pr[\Lambda(x) \le \eta]. \tag{A.11}$$

Decision dictated by a false-discovery rate

For some other applications, the decision may be dictated by the maximum *false-discovery rate* (FDR) allowed, denoted as α'. For example, α' may represent the fraction of healthy patients among those identified as infected. Note that η can be uniquely determined once the maximum tolerable FDR has been pre-specified. More exactly, η can be derived from the following:

$$\alpha' = \frac{\mathrm{FP}}{\mathrm{TP} + \mathrm{FP}} = \frac{\Pr[\Lambda(x) \le \eta, H_0]}{\Pr[\Lambda(x) \le \eta, H_0] + \Pr[\Lambda(x) \le \eta, H_1]} = \frac{\Pr[\Lambda(x) \le \eta, H_0]}{\Pr[\Lambda(x) \le \eta]}. \tag{A.12}$$

The relationship among α', α^*, and η

Note that all three of the parameters α', α^*, and $\eta = \pi_1 C_{01}/(\pi_0 C_{10})$ are closely related. More precisely, when any one of the three is fixed, so are the remaining two. Actually, they increase/decrease monotonically with respect to each other. This intimate relationship is highlighted by the following example.

A case study

Assume that a somewhat premature medical test is designed for a specific infection. For an uninfected person (represented by H_0), there is a 50% probability of showing a reaction in a single test. When multiple tests are applied, the individual tests are assumed to be mutually independent of each other. (For example, a particular uninfected person has a 50% × 50% = 25% chance of two consecutive positive test results.) In comparison, for an infected person (represented by H_1) the likelihood of showing a positive reaction is only slightly higher, say, 60% per test.

The null hypothesis (H_0) can be conveniently modeled by a fair coin, with a 50% chance of showing a head per toss. On the other hand, the alternative hypothesis (H_1) can be modeled by an unfair coin with a 60% chance of showing a head. In order to judge whether an unknown coin is fair or unfair, a simple experiment can be done by tossing the coin N times to see whether the number of heads is unusually higher or lower than $N/2$. The statistic of the N tosses can be represented by

$$x = \frac{\sum_{i=1}^{N} x_i}{N},$$

where

$$x_i = \begin{cases} +1 \text{ if a head is shown} \\ -1 \text{ if a tail is shown} \end{cases} \tag{A.13}$$

in the ith toss.

Suppose that $N = 100$. Then, by the law of large numbers, the density function approaches a Gaussian distribution. The mean values are $\mu_0 = 0$ for H_0 and $\mu_1 = 0.2$ for H_1. The standard deviations are $\sigma_0 = 1.0$ for H_0 and $\sigma_1 = 0.98$ for H_1.

The hypothesis test described above may be used to assess whether the coin should be regarded as fair or unfair. Moreover, as shown below, the three thresholds ($\eta = 0.1$, α', and α^*) are closely related. More exactly, when any of them is known, then the other two are known too. This is illustrated by a numerical example.

Assume that the ratio of their prior probabilities is $\pi_1/\pi_0 = 0.1$ and the risk factor is $C_{01}/C_{10} = 1.0$. Then, $\eta = \pi_1 C_{01}/(\pi_0 C_{10}) = 0.1$. Since the distributions for H_0 and H_1 are represented by the fair and unfair coins, respectively, it follows that we can compute:

- $\alpha' = 0.267$ (see Eq. (A.12)) and
- $\alpha^* = 0.055$ (see Eq. (A.11)); and
- the decision threshold can be obtained as $\theta = 0.2141$, as shown in Figure A.3(a).

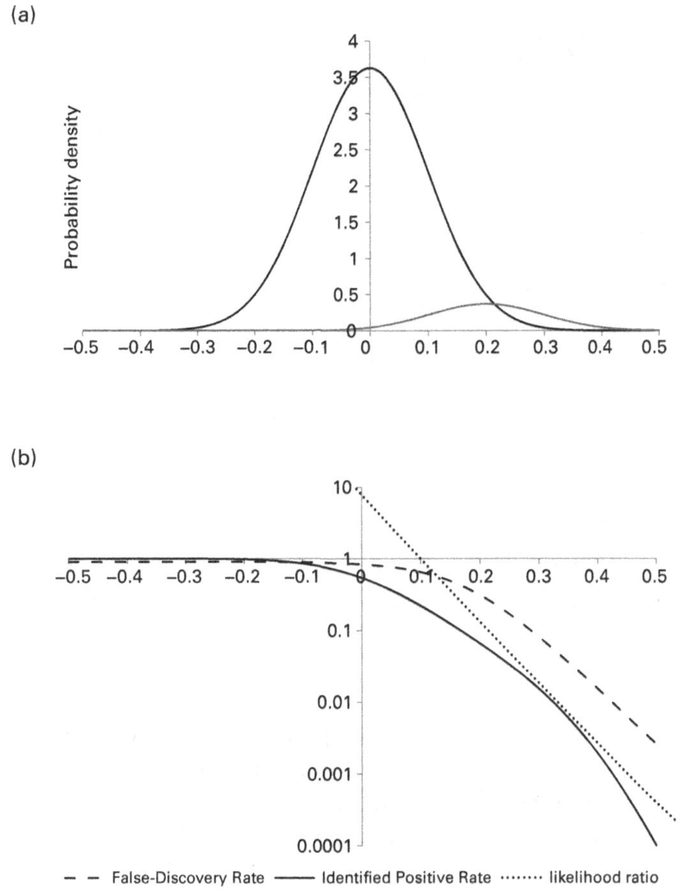

Fig. A.3. (a) For $\eta = 0.1$, the adjusted distributions for H_0 (lefthand curve) and H_1 (righthand curve). The decision threshold θ is determined by the cross-over point. In this case, $\theta = 0.2141$. (b) All four thresholds are closely related. The horizontal axis represents θ, while the corresponding values of α', α^*, and η are shown by the three curves. Note that all the curves are monotonically decreasing with respect to θ.

As shown in Figure A.3(b), all the values α', α^*, and η monotonically decrease with respect to θ, which effectively implies that θ plays the same role as the three thresholds.

A.2.2 Significance testing from the distribution of the null hypothesis

An important and practical scenario is when the average population is predominantly negative, i.e. $N \gg P$. Moreover, it is also a common scenario that only the statistical distribution of the null hypothesis H_0 is known. Normally, in this case, the default decision is H_0 unless a highly unusual event is observed. It is very possible that a seemingly abnormal event could take place merely by chance. In this case, the occurence of the

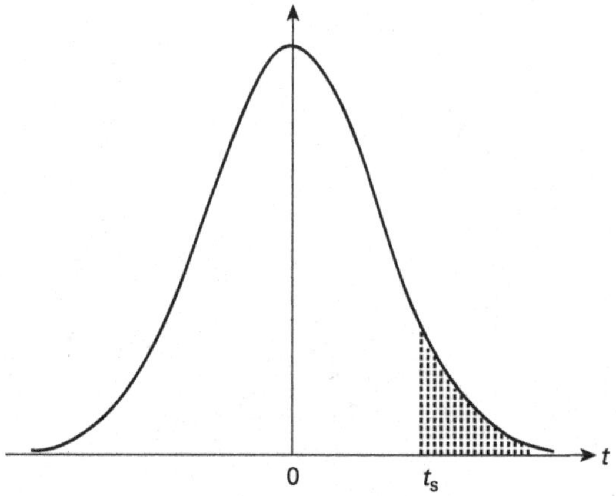

Fig. A.4. By the law of large numbers, for large N, the density function can be approximated by a Gaussian function. For one-sided tests the shaded area represents the p-value of the t-statistic t_s.

event itself is insufficient justification to reject H_0. The significance test offers a guideline to determine what kind of observation is considered significant enough to warrant the rejection of H_0.

The p-value

The p-value associated with the observation provides an effective metric for the significance test. The p-value is the likelihood of all events that are equal to or more extreme than the event observed. More importantly, the p-value of an observation can be obtained from the distribution of the null hypothesis alone. For example, as shown in the shaded area in Figure A.4, the p-value is the likelihood of an event that is at least as extreme as t_s (or x). For one-sided tests, the p-value is given by the area beyond t_s:

$$p = \Pr(t \geq t_s | H_0) = \int_{t_s}^{\infty} f(t) \mathrm{d}t, \tag{A.14}$$

where $f(t)$ is the probability distribution of t_s under the null hypothesis.

Maximum tolerable false-positive rate (FPR): α

The significance test hinges upon the comparison of the p-value with a pre-set FPR-related threshold denoted by α. (Two commonly adopted values are $\alpha = 1\%$ and $\alpha = 5\%$.) More precisely, the null hypothesis H_0 may be rejected only if the p-value becomes lower than α. In this case, it can be guaranteed that the rejection of H_0 will yield an FPR no higher than α. That is why α can be viewed as the maximum tolerable FPR.

The application of the significance test may be illustrated by a coin-tossing example.

Example A.1 (Coin-flipping test) *The null hypothesis (H_0) can be modeled by a fair coin, with 50% versus 50% chances of head and tail, while the alternative hypothesis (H_0) be modeled by an unfair coin which has 60% versus 40% chances of showing head and tail.*

In order to judge whether an unknown coin is fair or unfair, a simple experiment can be done by tossing the coin N times to see whether the number of heads is unusually higher or lower than N/2. As discussed previously, the null hypothesis (H_0) can be modeled by a fair coin, with a 50% chance of showing a head per toss. The Bernoulli trials will lead to the following binomial distribution. Let us denote HEAD as the number of heads observed in the N tosses. Under the null hypothesis, the probability of seeing exactly n heads is

$$\Pr(\text{HEAD} = n|H_0) = \binom{N}{n}\left(\frac{1}{2}\right)^n\left(1-\frac{1}{2}\right)^{N-n}.$$

It follows that the p-value corresponding to the event of seeing exactly n heads is

$$p\text{-value} = \Pr(\text{HEAD} \geq n|H_0) = \sum_{k=n}^{N}\binom{N}{k}\left(\frac{1}{2}\right)^k\left(\frac{1}{2}\right)^{N-k},$$

i.e. the p-value is the probability of seeing at least n heads (inclusive) in N tosses.

Now let us calculate the minimum integer n required so as to warrant the rejection of H_0 if the maximum FPR allowed is set to be $\alpha = 5\%$. Let us examine two examples: $N = 10$ and $N = 100$.

(i) **Case I:** $N = 10$. *If $n = 8$, then*

$$\Pr(\text{HEAD} \geq 8|H_0) = 5.5\% > 5\%.$$

On the other hand, if $n = 9$, then

$$\Pr(\text{HEAD} \geq 9|H_0) = 1.1\% < 5\%.$$

Therefore, there must be at least nine heads for us to confidently reject H_0.

(ii) **Case II:** $N = 100$. *If $n = 58$, then*

$$\Pr(\text{HEAD} \geq 58|H_0) = 6.66\% > 5\%.$$

On the other hand, if $n = 59$, then

$$\Pr(\text{HEAD} \geq 59|H_0) = 4.43\% < 5\%.$$

Therefore, we need to see at least 59 heads in order to declare that there is a sufficient evidence to reject H_0.

A.3 Problems

Problem A.1 *According to the significance test, when the p-value is higher than α, the test result will be regarded as normal (i.e. the hypothesis H_0 will not be rejected). Show that such a test scheme yields a specificity or true-negative rate (i.e. TNR) at least as high as $1 - \alpha$.*

Hint: *Recall that* FPR = 1 − specificity.

Problem A.2 (Significance test: coin-flipping experiments) *This problem is the same as Example A.1, except that the FPR threshold is now set to be* $\alpha = 1\%$. *How many heads out of* $N = 100$ *tosses are required in order to reject* H_0*?*

Problem A.3 *With reference to the case study above, cf. Figure A.3, let us now set* $\eta = 0.2$.

(a) *What are the corresponding values of FDR* α', α^*, *and* θ.

Hint: *When* $\eta = 0.2$, α' *is the false-discovery rate,* $\alpha' = \mathrm{FP}/(\mathrm{TP}+\mathrm{FP}) = 0.384$; α^* *is the identified positive rate,* $\alpha^* = \mathrm{IP}/(\mathrm{IP}+\mathrm{IN}) = 0.086$; *and the cutoff threshold is 0.1795.*

(b) *Repeat the same problem, except that the fake coin is now known to have 25% and 75% probabilities of showing head and tail, respectively.*

Problem A.4 (Coin-flipping test) *A minimum number of experiments is often required for a meaningful significance test.*

(a) *Show that, if* $N = 8$, *and* $\alpha = 2\%$, *then the fair-coin hypothesis (i.e.* H_0*) can never be rejected whatever the outcome of the* $N = 8$ *tosses.*

(b) *Given* $\alpha = 2\%$, *find the minimum value of* N *such that it is possible to show a sufficient number of heads so as to reject* H_0.

Appendix B *k*NN, PNN, and Bayes classifiers

There are two main learning strategies, namely *inductive* learning and *transductive* learning. These strategies are differentiated by their different ways of treating the (distribution of) testing data. The former adopts off-line learning models, see Figure B.1(a), but the latter usually adopts online learning models, see Figure B.1(b).

- *Inductive learning strategies.* The decision rule, trained under an *inductive* setting, must cover all the possible data in the entire vector space. More explicitly, the discriminant function $f(\mathbf{w}, \mathbf{x})$ can be trained by inductive learning. This approach can effectively distill the information inherent in the training dataset *off-line* into a simple set of decision parameters $\mathbf{w}$, thus enjoying the advantage of having a low classification complexity. As shown in Figure B.1(a), this approach contains two stages: (1) an off-line learning phase and (2) an on-field prediction phase. During the learning phase, the training dataset is used to learn the decision parameter $\mathbf{w}$, which dictates the decision boundary: $f(\mathbf{w}, \mathbf{x}) = 0$. In the prediction phase, no more learning is required, so the decision making can be made on-the-fly with minimum latency.
- *Transductive learning strategies.* In this case, the learner may explicitly make use of the structure and/or location of the putative test dataset in the decision process [281]. Hence, the discriminant function can be tailored to the specific test sample after it has been made known, presumably improving the prediction accuracy. It is intended for *online* learned models, implying that a great deal of learning will take place during the prediction phase, resulting in a prolonged on-the-fly processing time. As depicted in Figure B.1(b), the training dataset $[\mathcal{X}, \mathcal{Y}] = \{[\mathbf{x}_1, y_1], [\mathbf{x}_2, y_2], \ldots, [\mathbf{x}_N, y_N]\}$ will be provided on-the-fly and there is not any prior or off-line learning process. The main challenge lies in the ordeal that there will be no opportunity to conduct a preliminary learning process. In other words, the decision boundary will not be derived beforehand since the supervising information provided must be processed on-the-fly. Because there is no preliminary learning to form a simple decision rule, it will consume more real-time computation for decision making. Therefore, online classification is suitable only for applications with relatively low latency requirements. On the other hand, because the knowledge on the test sample $\mathbf{x}$ may now be used by the learner (in combination with the training dataset), this can be considered as a special case of transductive learning.

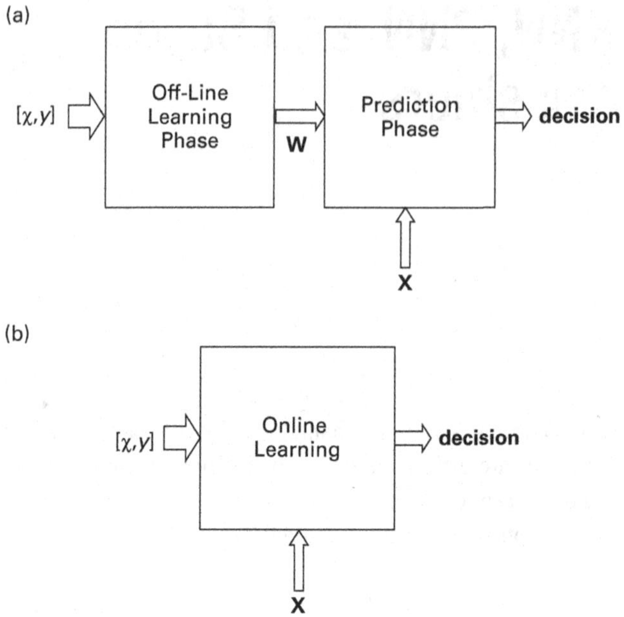

Fig. B.1. (a) The flowchart of supervised classification via explicit learning. It contains the following two phases. (1) The off-line learning (training) phase: training data are distilled into a relatively simple decision rule, parameterized by $\mathbf{w}$. The objective of the supervised learning is to find $\mathbf{w}$ from the training data $[\mathcal{X}, \mathcal{Y}]$, i.e. the learning process precludes any knowledge concerning the test sample $\mathbf{x}$. (2) The onfield prediction (retrieval) phase: the test sample $\mathbf{x}$ is known only during the retrieval phase. At that time both $\mathbf{x}$ and the learned parameter $\mathbf{w}$ are blended in the decision rule to obtain a prediction. (b) Online supervised classification. There is no preliminary learning phase. All the information, including the test sample $\mathbf{x}$ and training dataset $\mathcal{T} \equiv [\mathcal{X}, \mathcal{Y}] = \{[\mathbf{x}_1, y_1], [\mathbf{x}_2, y_2], \ldots, [\mathbf{x}_N, y_N]\}$, will be processed simultaneously for the purpose of identifying $\mathbf{x}$.

This appendix introduces several conventional supervised classification techniques, including some online-trained classifiers (with little learning) and some Bayesian classifiers (based on off-line learning).

(i) Section B.1 introduces two basic statistical inductive learning models: the Gaussian mixture model (GMM) and the normal Bayes classifier (NB). The Bayes classifier makes a decision that is based on the maximum a-posteriori (MAP) criterion [53].
(ii) Section B.2 introduces several transductive learning models suitable for supervised classification, including *k-nearest neighbors* (*k*NN), *probabilistic neural networks* (PNN), and the *log-likelihood classifier* (LLC).

B.1 Bayes classifiers

Online classifiers, such as PNN and LLC, circumvent any preliminary learning process, so the information provided by the training datasets has to be processed on-the-fly. The main disadvantage of online classification lies in its computational time in the prediction (or retrieval) phase. It is because the computational complexity is proportional to the number of subclasses (N_+ and N_-), which are usually very large. One solution is to simply have the original N training vectors represented by a smaller number of subclasses by an intra-class and off-line learning phase. More exactly, unsupervised clustering methods may be used to identify a (small) number of centroids to represent the positive (or negative) classes.

B.1.1 The GMM-based-classifier

GMM-based classification consists of the following two phases.

- **The learning phase.** The learning procedure involves finding GMMs to more concisely represent the positive or negative training datasets. The GMM models for positive and negative classes will be learned independently via the K-means or EM algorithm discussed in Section 5.3.

  Recall that $\Theta^+ = \{\mathbf{x}_1^+, \mathbf{x}_2^+, \ldots, \mathbf{x}_{N^+}^+\}$ was used to denote the positive training vectors and $\Theta^- = \{\mathbf{x}_1^-, \mathbf{x}_2^-, \ldots, \mathbf{x}_{N^-}^-\}$ for the negative training vectors. By the K-means clustering, they are regrouped into L^+ and L^- clusters respectively. Let $\tilde{\Theta}^+ = \{\mu_1^+, \mu_2^+, \ldots, \mu_{L^+}^+\}$ and $\tilde{\Theta}^- = \{\mu_1^-, \mu_2^-, \ldots, \mu_{L^-}^-\}$ denote the two sets of centroids discovered by the K-means clustering algorithm, such that the positive class C^+ contains all the clusters in $\tilde{\Theta}^+$, while the negative class C^- contains all the clusters in $\tilde{\Theta}^-$.
- **The prediction phase.** Following Eq. (B.12) (see later), we have two similar score functions for the GMM classifier:

$$f(\mathbf{x}, \tilde{\Theta}^+) = \sum_{i=1}^{L^+} h_i^+(x) \|\mathbf{x} - \vec{\mu}_i^{\,+}\|^2,$$

where

$$h_i^+(\mathbf{x}) = \frac{\exp\left\{-\|\mathbf{x} - \vec{\mu}_i^{\,+}\|^2/(2\sigma^2)\right\}}{\sum_{i=1}^{L^+} \exp\left\{-\|\mathbf{x} - \vec{\mu}_i^{\,+}\|^2/(2\sigma^2)\right\}};$$

and

$$f(\mathbf{x}, \tilde{\Theta}^-) = \sum_{i=1}^{L^-} h_i^-(x) \|\mathbf{x} - \vec{\mu}_i^{\,-}\|^2,$$

where

$$h_i^-(\mathbf{x}) = \frac{\exp\left\{-\|\mathbf{x} - \vec{\mu}_i^{\,-}\|^2/(2\sigma^2)\right\}}{\sum_{i=1}^{L^-} \exp\left\{-\|\mathbf{x} - \vec{\mu}_i^{\,-}\|^2/(2\sigma^2)\right\}}.$$

It then follows that the decision boundary is

$$f(\mathbf{x}) = f(\mathbf{x}, \tilde{\Theta}^{+}) - f(\mathbf{x}, \tilde{\Theta}^{-}) + \theta = 0, \tag{B.1}$$

where $\theta = \log P(C_+) - \log P(C_-)$.

B.1.2 The basic Bayes classifier

The basic Bayes classifier can be viewed as a special case of the GMM classifier, with $L^+ = 1$ and $L^- = 1$. In other words, all the positive training vectors are modeled after a simple Gaussian distribution. So are all the negative training vectors.

- **The learning phase.** The objective of the learning phase is to estimate the means and variances of the positive/negative datasets, denoted as $\{\vec{\mu}_+, \vec{\mu}_-\}$ and $\{\sigma_+^2, \sigma_-^2\}$, respectively. It is common to adopt the following estimation formula:

$$\vec{\mu}_+ = \frac{\mathbf{x}_1^+ + \mathbf{x}_2^+ + \cdots + \mathbf{x}_{N^+}^+}{N^+},$$
$$\vec{\mu}_- = \frac{\mathbf{x}_1^- + \mathbf{x}_2^- + \cdots + \mathbf{x}_{N^+}^-}{N^-},$$
$$\sigma_+ = \frac{(\mathbf{x}_1^+ - \vec{\mu}_+)^2 + (\mathbf{x}_2^+ - \vec{\mu}_+)^2 + \cdots + (\mathbf{x}_{N^+}^+ - \vec{\mu}_+)^2}{N^+},$$
$$\sigma_- = \frac{(\mathbf{x}_1^- - \vec{\mu}_-)^2 + (\mathbf{x}_2^- - \vec{\mu}_-)^2 + \cdots + (\mathbf{x}_{N^-}^- - \vec{\mu}_-)^2}{N^-}.$$

- **The prediction phase.** With the estimation results, the positive dataset can be statistically modeled by a normal distribution,

$$p(\mathbf{x}|C^+) = \frac{1}{\sqrt{2\pi}\sigma_+} \exp\left\{-\frac{\|\mathbf{x} - \vec{\mu}_+\|^2}{2\sigma_+^2}\right\},$$

and the negative dataset by another distribution:

$$p(\mathbf{x}|C^-) = \frac{1}{\sqrt{2\pi}\sigma_-} \exp - \left\{-\frac{\|\mathbf{x} - \vec{\mu}_-\|^2}{2\sigma_-^2}\right\}.$$

This leads to a basic normal Bayes (NB) classifier. In addition, the log-likelihood function (see Eq. (B.7) later) provides a computationally simpler decision rule. More exactly, the positive and negative score functions are

$$f(\mathbf{x}, C^+) = -\frac{\|\mathbf{x} - \vec{\mu}_+\|^2}{\sigma_+^2} + \frac{1}{2}\log\, \sigma_+ + \log\, P(C_+)$$

and

$$f(\mathbf{x}, C^-) = -\frac{\|\mathbf{x} - \vec{\mu}_-\|^2}{\sigma_-^2} + \frac{1}{2}\log\, \sigma_- + \log\, P(C_-).$$

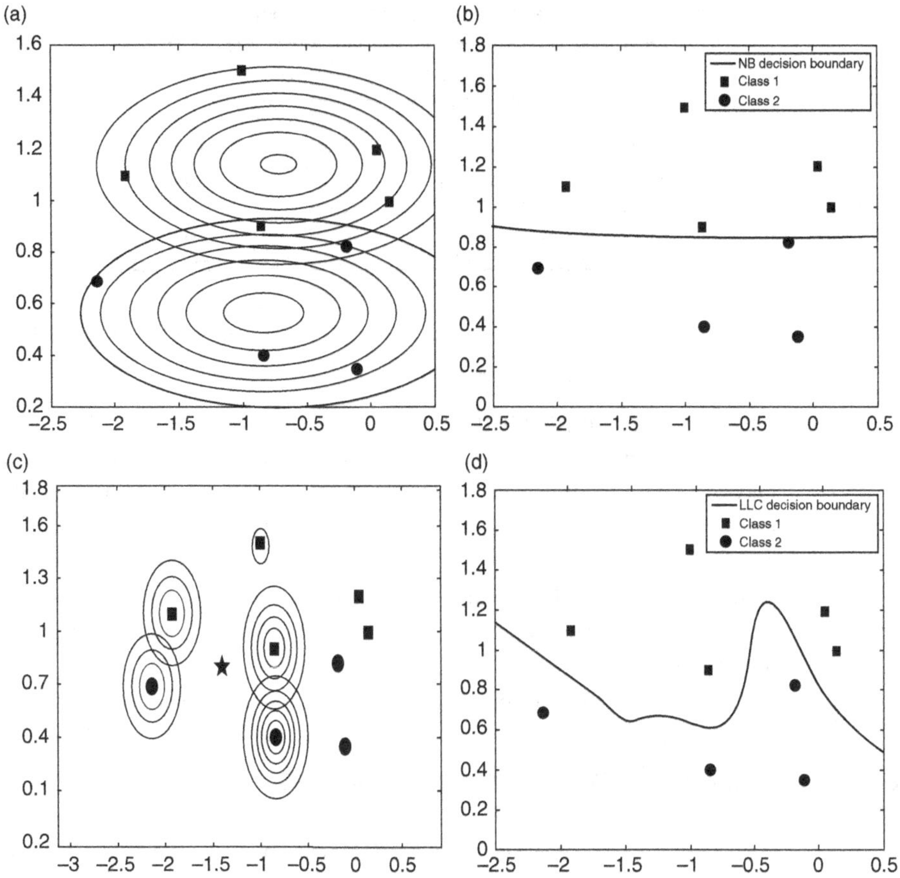

Fig. B.2. (a) The density function of the normal Bayes (NB) classifier. (b) The NB decision boundary. Note that the decision boundary is much smoother than the LLC's because each class is now modeled by a simple Gaussian distribution. (c) LLC examples. The training patterns and the corresponding probability density function contours after a test example (the star) has been observed are shown. Note that higher weights (i.e. h_i^+ and h_i^-) will be assigned to the subclasses around the squares and circles nearer to the test sample (marked by the asterisk). (d) The decision boundary of the LLC algorithm. (Adapted from Ref. [152].)

This leads to the following decision boundary:

$$\frac{\|\mathbf{x} - \vec{\boldsymbol{\mu}}_+\|^2}{\sigma_+^2} - \frac{\|\mathbf{x} - \vec{\boldsymbol{\mu}}_-\|^2}{\sigma_-^2} + \theta = 0, \tag{B.2}$$

where $\theta = \frac{1}{2}(\log\,\sigma_+ - \log\sigma_-) + \log P(C_+) - \log P(C_-)$.

Figure B.2 provides an illustration of a binary Bayes classifier. Note that the decision boundary is much smoother than the LLC's because each class is now modeled by a simple Gaussian distribution.

One special case of great interest is that, when $\sigma_+ = \sigma_-$, the NB becomes a linear classifier. Ironically, the LLC also becomes linear when $\sigma \to \infty$, because all the training samples within the same class will have equal weights, i.e. $h_i = 1/N^+$ and $h_i = 1/N^-$

Table B.1. Leave-one-out misclassification errors

	Training	Error rate
NB	Yes	20.73
GMM-BC (L=2, $\sigma = 1$)	Yes	18.90
GMM-BC (L=3, $\sigma = 1$)	Yes	20.01
LLC ($\sigma = 4, 5$)	No	18.29
LLC ($\sigma \geq 6$)	No	19.51

respectively for each of the positive and negative training vectors. In fact, these two *linear classifiers* happen to be identical.

Experiments on microarray data

Three classifiers are compared: the normal Bayes classifier, GMM Bayes classifier, and maximum log-likelihood classifier. A selected set of 82 (from a total of 104) genes from the cell-cycle database[257] are classified into five phase groups (G1, S, G2, M, and M/G1). In the normalization procedure, the mean expression value across the time points was subtracted from the un-normalized expression values in each gene profile. The mean normalized values were then divided by the standard deviation across the time points.

The leave-one-out misclassification error rates are summarized as in Table B.1.[1]

B.2 Classifiers with no prior learning process

With the teacher's supervision, two prominent online learned classifiers are k nearest neighbors (kNN) and probabilistic neural networks (PNN). Another alternative is the log-likelihood classifier (LLC). These three methods will be explored in this section.

B.2.1 k nearest neighbors (kNN)

By definition, there is no preliminary learning phase for online classifiers. The most prominent online classifier is arguably *k nearest neighbors* (kNN), which was proposed by Cover [44].

Given a test sample, from all the N training data, a pool of k vectors nearest to the test sample $\mathbf{x}$ is selected. Let k_+ and k_- denote the numbers of positive and negative vectors selected by the pool. Of course, we have $k = k_+ + k_-$. The heuristic justification of kNN is that the likelihood of the sample $\mathbf{x}$ belonging to positive (or negative) class can be reflected by the number of positive (or negative) nearest neighbors. Therefore, the test sample is identified with the class with the higher presence in the k neighbors. Let the positive score be $f_+(\mathbf{x}) = k_+$ while the negative score $f_-(\mathbf{x}) = k_-$. The sample $\mathbf{x}$ is identified as

$$\mathbf{x} \in \begin{cases} \mathcal{C}_+ & \text{if } k_+ \geq k_- \\ \mathcal{C}_- & \text{if } k_+ < k_-. \end{cases} \tag{B.3}$$

[1] After careful parameter adjustment, the LLC can deliver a better error rate of 13.4146%.

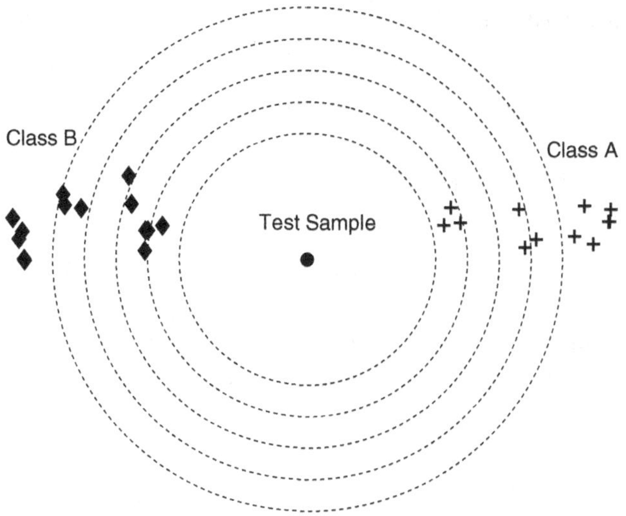

Fig. B.3. Classification by the kNN algorithm. The test sample (center) may be classified assigned to class A or to class B, depending on the value of k. For example, if $k = 3$, the sample is identified as belonging to class A. If $k = 7$, the same sample is identified as belonging to class B.

As exemplified by the dataset shown in Figure B.3, the classification results are highly dependent on k. For example, for the test sample, the decision is class A (positive) for $k = 3$, while it will become class B (negative) for $k = 7$. Note that the best integer k to be adopted in a kNN scheme is often determined by trial and error.

B.2.2 Probabilistic neural networks (PNN)

In addition to kNN, another example of online classification is the probabilistic neural network (PNN), which was proposed by Specht [256].

The maximum a-posteriori (MAP) decision rule.

In statistical learning, the score functions are derived from probabilistic models. For a new $\mathbf{x}$, its a-posteriori likelihood is $P(C_k|\mathbf{x})$ and, among the L possible classes, $\mathbf{x}$ is assigned to C_k if

$$k = \arg\max_j \; P(C_j|\mathbf{x}), \;\; C_j \in \{C_1, C_2, \ldots, C_L\}. \tag{B.4}$$

According to the Bayesian rule, the a-posteriori likelihood $P(C_j|\mathbf{x})$ can be obtained as

$$P(C_j|\mathbf{x}) = \frac{p(\mathbf{x}|C_j)P(C_j)}{p(\mathbf{x})}, \tag{B.5}$$

where $p(\mathbf{x}|C_k)$ denotes the conditional probability density function given the condition that $\mathbf{x}$ is known to belong to C_k.

The log-likelihood-based decision rule

Note that

$$\arg\max_j \; P(C_j|\mathbf{x}) = \arg\max_j \log P(C_j|\mathbf{x}). \tag{B.6}$$

By combining Eq. (B.5) and Eq. (B.6), we obtain the following log-likelihood-based decision rule:

$$\arg\max_j P(C_j|\mathbf{x}) = \arg\max_j \left(\log p(\mathbf{x}|C_j) + \log P(C_j)\right). \tag{B.7}$$

In this section, we shall focus on binary classification, i.e. $L = 2$. In this case, the training set can be subdivided into two disjoint subsets:

$$\mathcal{X} = \{\mathbf{x}_1, \mathbf{x}_2, \ldots, \mathbf{x}_N\} = \Theta^+ \cup \Theta^-,$$

where the positive subset $\Theta^+ = \{\mathbf{x}_1^+, \mathbf{x}_2^+, \ldots, \mathbf{x}_{N^+}^+\}$ denotes the set of N^+ positive training samples and the negative subset $\Theta^- = \{\mathbf{x}_1^-, \mathbf{x}_2^-, \ldots, \mathbf{x}_{N^-}^-\}$ denotes the set of N^- negative training samples. There are two (super-)classes: C^+ and C^-. The positive class $C^+ = \{C_1^+, C_2^+, \ldots, C_{N^+}^+\}$ contains all the subclasses associated with Θ^+, i.e. with each subclass modeled by a simple Gaussian distribution centered at a positive training vector. Likewise, the negative super-class $C^- = \{C_1^-, C_2^-, \ldots, C_{N^-}^-\}$ contains all the subclasses associated with Θ^-.

For derivation of the PNN, we introduce N subclasses $\{C_1, C_2, \ldots, C_N\}$, i.e. $L = N$, each with a Gaussian distribution centered at one of the training vectors $\{\mathbf{x}_1, \mathbf{x}_2, \ldots, \mathbf{x}_N\}$. In this case, the likelihood that $\mathbf{x}$ is associated with C_i can be expressed as

$$p(\mathbf{x}|C_i) = \frac{1}{\sqrt{2\pi}\,\sigma} \exp\left\{-\frac{\|\mathbf{x} - \mathbf{x}_i\|^2}{2\sigma^2}\right\}.$$

where the parameter σ is often pre-specified. Moreover, for simplicity, we shall assume that all the subclasses have an equal prior probability:

$$P(C_1) = P(C_2) = \ldots = P(C_N) = \frac{1}{N}.$$

According to the Bayesian rule (Eq. (B.5)), the a-posteriori likelihoods for the positive and negative classes are

$$P(C^+|\mathbf{x}) = \sum_{C_i \in C^+} P(C_i|\mathbf{x}) = \frac{\sum_{C_i \in C^+} p(\mathbf{x}|C_i)P(C_i)}{p(\mathbf{x})}$$

and

$$P(C^-|\mathbf{x}) = \sum_{C_i \in C^-} P(C_i|\mathbf{x}) = \frac{\sum_{C_i \in C^-} p(\mathbf{x}|C_i)P(C_i)}{p(\mathbf{x})}.$$

By dropping the common term $p(\mathbf{x})$ from the above, we can obtain the positive and negative score functions as follows:

$$f^{+}_{\mathrm{PNN}}(\mathbf{x}) = \sum_{C_i \in C^{+}} p(\mathbf{x}|C_i)P(C_i)$$
$$= \frac{1}{N\sqrt{2\pi}\sigma} \sum_{i=1}^{N^{+}} \exp\left\{-\frac{\|\mathbf{x}-\mathbf{x}_i^{+}\|^2}{2\sigma^2}\right\},$$

and

$$f^{-}_{\mathrm{PNN}}(\mathbf{x}) = \sum_{C_i \in C^{-}} p(\mathbf{x}|C_i)P(C_i)$$
$$= \frac{1}{N\sqrt{2\pi}\sigma} \sum_{i=1}^{N^{-}} \exp\left\{-\frac{\|\mathbf{x}-\mathbf{x}_i^{-}\|^2}{2\sigma^2}\right\}.$$

This leads to the following decision rule:

$$\mathbf{x} \in \begin{cases} C_{+} \text{ if } f^{+}_{\mathrm{PNN}}(\mathbf{x}) \geq f^{-}_{\mathrm{PNN}}(\mathbf{x}) \\ C_{-} \text{ if } f^{+}_{\mathrm{PNN}}(\mathbf{x}) < f^{-}_{\mathrm{PNN}}(\mathbf{x}). \end{cases} \tag{B.8}$$

B.2.3 The log-likelihood classifier (LLC)

Note that the derivation of the positive and negative scores in PNN is based on the implicit assumption that each of the training vectors is assigned the same prior probability: $1/N$. This means that the prior probability is proportional to the number of training vectors in each class, since the local scores from all the training vectors are equally weighted. It is desirable to allow that a flexible assignment of priors may be easily incorporated into other probabilistic models. One such example is the log-likelihood classifier (LLC).

Just like before, the LLC requires no preliminary training. Moreover, the distribution of the positive/negative class is again modeled as a weighted mixture of isotropic Gaussians centered at the positive/negative training vectors. For example, the positive conditional probability density function is

$$p(\mathbf{x}|C^{+}) = \sum_{i=1}^{N^{+}} P(C_i^{+}|C^{+})p(\mathbf{x}|C_i^{+}). \tag{B.9}$$

Let us denote

$$h_i^{+}(\mathbf{x}) \equiv \frac{\exp\left\{-\|\mathbf{x}-\mathbf{x}_i^{+}\|^2/(2\sigma^2)\right\}}{\sum_{i=1}^{N^{+}} \exp\left\{-\|\mathbf{x}-\mathbf{x}_i^{+}\|^2/(2\sigma^2)\right\}}.$$

Following the same weight assignment as that adopted in the EM algorithm, the conditional prior may be adjusted by taking advantage of the knowledge of the location of the test pattern, i.e. $P(C_i^{+}|C^{+}) = h_i^{+}(x)$. It follows that

$$p(\mathbf{x}|C^+) = \sum_{i=1}^{N^+} h_i^+(\mathbf{x}) p(\mathbf{x}|C_i^+). \tag{B.10}$$

Likewise,

$$p(\mathbf{x}|C^-) = \sum_{i=1}^{N^-} h_i^-(\mathbf{x}) p(\mathbf{x}|C_i^-). \tag{B.11}$$

Approximation of the log-likelihood function

Recall that an *approximation* of the log-likelihood function, which is critical to the development of the EM algorithm (see Section 5.17), is as follows:

$$\log\, p(\mathbf{x}|C^+) = \log \left(\sum_{i=1}^{N^+} h_i^+(\mathbf{x}) p(\mathbf{x}|C_i^+) \right) \approx \sum_{i=1}^{N^+} h_i^+(\mathbf{x}) \log\, p(\mathbf{x}|C_i^+).$$

Such an approximation may be adopted for deriving a simplified formula for the LLC score, More exactly, it leads to the following positive score function:

$$f_{\mathrm{LLC}}^+(\mathbf{x}) = -\sum_{i=1}^{N^+} h_i^+(\mathbf{x}) \|\mathbf{x} - \mathbf{x}_i^+\|^2 + \theta_+, \tag{B.12}$$

where

$$h_i^+(\mathbf{x}) = \frac{\exp\left\{-\|\mathbf{x} - \mathbf{x}_i^+\|^2/(2\sigma^2)\right\}}{\sum_{i=1}^{N^+} \exp\left\{-\|\mathbf{x} - \mathbf{x}_i^+\|^2/(2\sigma^2)\right\}}.$$

Likewise, the negative score function can be obtained as

$$f_{\mathrm{LLC}}^-(\mathbf{x}) = -\sum_{i=1}^{N^-} h_i^-(\mathbf{x}) \|\mathbf{x} - \mathbf{x}_i^-\|^2 + \theta_-$$

where

$$h_i^-(\mathbf{x}) = \frac{\exp\left\{-\|\mathbf{x} - \mathbf{x}_i^-\|^2/(2\sigma^2)\right\}}{\sum_{i=1}^{N^-} \exp\left\{-\|\mathbf{x} - \mathbf{x}_i^-\|^2/(2\sigma^2)\right\}}.$$

According to Eq. (B.7), we have

$$\theta_+ = \log P(C_+) \text{ and } \theta_- = \log\, P(C_-).$$

This leads to the following decision boundary:

$$f_{\mathrm{LLC}}^+(\mathbf{x}) - f_{\mathrm{LLC}}^-(\mathbf{x}) + \theta = 0,$$

where $\theta = \log\, P(C_+) - \log\, P(C_-)$. For many applications, it is convenient to assume that $P(C_+) = P(C_-)$, then the decision boundary is simply

$$f_{\mathrm{LLC}}^+(\mathbf{x}) - f_{\mathrm{LLC}}^-(\mathbf{x}) = 0.$$

The weight assignments used in the LLC are exemplified by Figure B.2(c), with the resulting decision boundary shown in Figure B.2(d).

B.3 Problems

Problem B.1 *Suppose that $\sigma_+ = \sigma_-$. Then the following normal Bayes classifier has a linear decision boundary:*

$$\|\mathbf{x} - \vec{\mu}_+\|^2 - \|\mathbf{x} - \vec{\mu}_-\|^2 = \mathbf{w}^{\mathrm{T}}\mathbf{x} + b = 0. \tag{B.13}$$

(a) *Find $\mathbf{w}$ and b.*

(b) *Show that such a linear classifier creates a maximal separation of centroids after being projected along the decision vector $\mathbf{w}$.*

Problem B.2 *Let $\mathbf{x}$ denote a sample vector in the feature space, and let C_j represent the jth class. Show that the maximum log-likelihood and maximum a-posteriori probability (MAP) criteria lead to the same result if all the clusters have the same a-priori probability.*

Hint: *Note that*

$$p(C_j|\mathcal{X}) = \frac{p(\mathcal{X}|C_j)P(C_j)}{p(\mathcal{X})}. \tag{B.14}$$

Problem B.3 *Show that*

$$\arg\max_j \log\left(P(C_j|\mathbf{x})\right) = \arg\max_j \left(\log\, p(\mathbf{x}|C_j) + \log P(C_j)\right).$$

Hint: *Use the Bayesian rule: $p(P(C_j)|\mathbf{x}) = p(\mathbf{x}|C_j)P(C_j)$.*

Problem B.4 *Express the posterior probability $p(C_k|\mathbf{x})$ in terms of the density function of $\mathbf{x}$ and the conditional density function $p(\mathbf{x}|C_k)$.*

Problem B.5 *The posterior probability of class C_k in a K-class problem is given by*

$$P(C_k|\mathbf{x}) = \frac{p(\mathbf{x}|C_k)P(C_k)}{p(\mathbf{x})},$$

where

$$p(\mathbf{x}|C_k) = \sum_{j=1}^{M} \pi_{kj} p(\mathbf{x}|\mu_{kj}, \Sigma_{kj}, C_k)$$

is a GMM, $P(C_k)$ is the prior probability of class C_k, and $p(\mathbf{x})$ is the density function of $\mathbf{x}$.

(a) *Express $p(\mathbf{x})$ in terms of $p(\mathbf{x}|C_k)$ and $P(C_k)$.*

(b) *Discuss the difference between $P(C_k)$ and π_{kj}.*

(c) *If* $P(C_k) \neq P(C_j)\ \forall k \neq j$, *explain how you would use K GMMs to classify a set of unknown pattern* $X = \{\mathbf{x}_1, \mathbf{x}_2, \ldots, \mathbf{x}_N\}$ *into K classes.*

Problem B.6 (Relationship among *k*NN, PNN, and LLC) *Show that there exists an intimate relationship among the three online classifiers kNN, PNN, and LLC.*

Hint: *Note that, when* $k = 1$, *the training sample nearest to the test sample* $\mathbf{x}$ *will dictate the classification result for the kNN classifier. On the other hand, in PNN or LLC, when* σ *is infinitesimal (i.e.* $\sigma \to 0$*) the same sole winner will dictate the decision making, i.e. the decision will again be dependent exclusively on the sole winner.*

Problem B.7 (MATLAB simulation on an image database) *An image database containing ten categories, each with 100 JPG images, can be found at http://wang.ist.psu.edu/docs/related/. Try online classifiers, kNN and LLC, and compare their performances.*

References

[1] C. C. Aggarwal and P. S. Yu. Outlier detection for high dimensional data. In *Proceedings of ACM SIGMOD*, pages 37–46, 2001.

[2] A. C. Aitken. On least squares and linear combinations of observations. *Proc. Royal Soc. Edinburgh*, 55:42–48, 1935.

[3] H. Akaike. A new look at the statistical model identification. *IEEE Trans. Automatic Control*, 19(6):716–723, 1974.

[4] A. A. Alizadeh, M. B. Eisen, R. E. Davis *et al.* Distinct types of diffuse large B-cell lymphoma identified by gene expression profiling. *Nature*, 403:503–511, 2000.

[5] U. Alon, N. Barkai, D. A. Notterman *et al.* Broad patterns of gene expression revealed by clustering analysis of tumor and normal colon tissues probed by oligonucleotide arrays. *Proc. Nat. Acad. Sci. USA*, 96(12):6745, 1999.

[6] P. Andras. Kernel-Kohonen networks. *Int. J. Neural Systems*, 12;117–135, 2002.

[7] S. A. Armstrong, J. E. Staunton, L. B. Silverman *et al.* MLL translocations specify a distinct gene expression profile that distinguishes a unique leukemia. *Nature Genetics*, 30(1):41–47, 2002.

[8] N. Aronszajn. Theory of reproducing kernels. *Trans. Am. Math. Soc.*, 68:337–404, 1950.

[9] P. Baldi and S. Brunak. *Bioinformatics: The Machine Learning Approach*, 2nd edition. Cambridge, MA: MIT Press, 2001.

[10] G. Baudat and F. Anouar. Generalized discriminant analysis using a kernel approach. *Neural Computation*, 12:2385–2404, 2000.

[11] D. G. Beer, S. L. R. Kardia, C.-C. Huang *et al.* Gene-expression profiles predict survival of patients with lung adenocarcinoma. *Nature Med.*, 8:816–824, 2002.

[12] R. Bellman. *Dynamic Programming*. Princeton, NJ: Princeton University Press, 1957.

[13] R. Bellman. *Adaptive Control Processes: A Guided Tour.* Princeton, NJ: Princeton University Press, 1961.

[14] S. Ben-David and M. Lindenbaum. Learning distributions by their density levels: A paradigm for learning without a teacher. *J. Computer System Sci.*, 55:171–182, 1997.

[15] A. Ben-Dor, L. Bruhn, N. Friedman *et al.* Tissue classification with gene expression profiles. *J. Computat. Biol.*, 7:559–583, 2000.

[16] A. Ben-Hur, D. Horn, H. Siegelmann, and V. Vapnik. A support vector method for hierarchical clustering. In T. K. Leen, T. G. Dietterich, and V. Tresp, editors, *Advances in Neural Information Processing Systems 13*. Cambridge, MA: MIT Press.

[17] D. P. Bertsekas. *Nonlinear Programming*. Belmont, MA: Athena Scientific, 1995.

[18] C. Bhattacharyya. Robust classification of noisy data using second order cone programming approach. In *Proceedings, International Conference on Intelligent Sensing and Information Processing*, pages 433–438, 2004.

[19] J. Bibby and H. Toutenburg. *Prediction and Improved Estimation in Linear Models*. New York: Wiley, 1977.

[20] C. M. Bishop. *Neural Networks for Pattern Recognition*. Oxford: Oxford University Press, 1995.

[21] C. M. Bishop. Training with noise is equivalent to Tikhonov regularization. *Neural Comput.*, 7:108–116, 1995.

[22] C. M. Bishop. *Pattern Recognition and Machine Learning*. Berlin: Springer, 2006.

[23] K. L. Blackmore, R. C. Williamson, I. M. Mareels, and W. A. Sethares. Online learning via congregational gradient descent. In *Proceedings of the 8th Annual Conference on Computational Learning Theory (COLT '95)*. New York: ACM Press, pages 265–272, 1995.

[24] B. E. Boser, I. M. Guyon, and V. N. Vapnik. A training algorithm for optimal margin classifiers. In D. Haussler, editor, *Proceedings of the 5th Annual ACM Workshop on Computational Learning Theory*, pages 144–152, 1992.

[25] R. Boulet, B. Jouve, F. Rossi, and N. Villa. Batch kernel SOM and related Laplacian methods for social network analysis. *Neurocomputing*, 71(7–9):1257–1273, 2008.

[26] M. Boutell, J. Luo, X. Shen, and C. Brown. Learning multi-label scene classification. *Pattern Recognition*, 37(9):1757–1771, 2004.

[27] P. S. Bradley and O. L. Mangasarian. Feature selection via concave minimization and support vector machines. In *International Conference on Machine Learning*, pages 82–90, 1998.

[28] U. M. Braga-Neto and E. R. Dougherty. Is cross-validation valid for small-sample microarray classification? *Bioinformatics*, 20(3):378–380, 2004.

[29] M. P. S. Brown, W. N. Grundy, D. Lin *et al.* Knowledge-based analysis of microarray gene expression data using support vector machines. *Proc. Nat. Acad. Sci. USA*, 97(1):262–267, 2000.

[30] C. J. C. Burges. A tutorial on support vector machines for pattern recognition. *Knowledge Discovery Data Mining*, 2(2):121–167, 1998.

[31] F. Camastra and A. Verri. A novel kernel method for clustering. *IEEE Trans. Pattern Anal. Machine Intell.*, 27(5):801–804, 2005.

[32] C. Campbell and K. P. Bennett. A linear programming approach to novelty detection. In *Advances in Neural Information Processing Systems 14*. Cambridge, MA: MIT press, 2001.

[33] H. Cao, T. Naito, and Y. Ninomiya. Approximate RBF kernel SVM and its applications in pedestrian classification. In *Proceedings, The 1st International Workshop on Machine Learning for Vision-based Motion Analysis – MLVMA08*, 2008.

[33b] J. Morris Chang, C. C. Fang, K. H. Ho *et al.* Capturing cognitive fingerprints from keystroke dynamics. *IT Professional*, 15(4):24–28, 2013.

[34] Chih-Chung Chang and Chih-Jen Lin. LIBSVM: A library for support vector machines. *ACM Trans. Intelligent Systems Technol.*, 2(27):1–27, 2011. Software available at http://www.csie.ntu.edu.tw/ cjlin/libsvm.

[35] O. Chapelle, P. Haffner, and V. N. Vapnik. Support vector machines for histogram-based image classification. *IEEE Trans. Neural Networks*, 10:1055–1064, 1999.

[36] O. Chapelle, V. Vapnik, O. Bousquet, and S. Mukhejee. Choosing kernel parameters for support vector machines. In *Machine Learning*, 46:131–159, 2002.

[37] P. H. Chen, C. J. Lin, and B. Schölkopf. A tutorial on ν-support vector machines, 2003 (http://www.kernel-machines.org).

[38] Y. Cheng and G. M. Church. Biclustering of expression data. In *Proceedings of the Eighth International Conference on Intelligent Systems for Molecular Biology (ISMB)*, volume 8, pages 93–103, 2000.

[39] V. Chercassky and P. Mullier. *Learning from Data, Concepts, Theory and Methods*. New York: John Wiley, 1998.

[40] A. Clare and R. D. King. Knowledge discovery in multi-label phenotype data. In *Proceedings of the 5th European Conference on Principles of Data Mining and Knowledge Discovery*, pages 42–53, 2001.

[41] C. Cortes and V. Vapnik. Support vector networks. *Machine Learning*, 20:273–297, 1995.

[42] R. Courant and D. Hilbert. *Methods of Mathematical Physics*. New York: Interscience, 1953.

[43] R. Courant and D. Hilbert. *Methods of Mathematical Physics*, volumes I and II. New York: Wiley Interscience, 1970.

[44] T. M. Cover. Geometrical and statistical properties of systems of linear inequalities with applications in pattern recognition. *IEEE Trans. Electron. Computers*, 14:326–334, 1965.

[44b] T. F. Cox and M. A. A. Cox. *Multidimensional Scaling*. London: Chapman and Hall, 1994.

[45] Data set provider. http://www.igi.tugraz.at/aschwaig.

[46] P. de Chazal, M. O'Dwyer, and R. B. Reilly Automatic classification of heartbeats using ECG morphology and heartbeat interval features. *IEEE Trans. Biomed. Eng.*, 51(7):1196–1206, 2004.

[47] A. P. Dempster, N. M. Laird, and D. B. Rubin. Maximum likelihood from incomplete data via the EM algorithm. *J. Royal Statist. Soc., Ser. B*, 39(1):1–38, 1977.

[48] I. S. Dhillon, Y. Guan, and B. Kulis. Kernel K-means, spectral clustering and normalized cuts. In *Proceedings of the 10th ACM KDD Conference*, Seattle, WA, 2004.

[49] K. Diamantaras and M. Kotti. Binary classification by minimizing the mean squared slack. In *Proceedings of the IEEE International Conference on Acoustics, Speech, Signal Processing (ICASSP-2012)*, Kyoto, pages 2057–2060, 2012.

[50] K. I. Diamantaras and S. Y. Kung. *Principal Component Neural Networks*. New York: Wiley, 1996.

[51] T. G. Dietterich and G. Bakiri. Solving multiclass learning problems via error-correcting output codes, *J. Artif. Intell. Res.*, 2:263–286, 1995.

[52] H. Drucker, C. J. C. Burges, L. Kaufman, Smola A., and V. Vapnik. Support vector regression machines. In *Advances in Neural Information Processing Systems (NIPS '96)*, Volume 9. Cambridge, MA: MIT Press, pages 155–161, 1997.

[53] R. O. Duda and P. E. Hart. *Pattern Classification and Scene Analysis*. New York: Wiley 1973.

[54] R. O. Duda, P. E. Hart, and D.G. Stork. *Pattern Classification, 2nd edition*. New York: Wiley, 2011.

[55] S. Dudoit, J. Fridlyand, and T. P. Speed. Comparison of discrimination methods for the classification of tumors using gene expression data. Technical Report 576, Department of Statistics, University of California, Berkeley, CA, 2000.

[56] S. Dudoit, J. Fridlyand, and T. P. Speed. Comparison of discrimination methods for the classification of tumors using gene expression data. *J. Am. Statist. Assoc.*, 97:77–88, 2002.

[57] R. Durbin and D. J. Willshaw. An analogue approach to the travelling salesman problem using an elastic net method. *Nature*, 326:689–691, 1987.

[58] B. Efron. Bootstrap methods: Another look at the jackknife. *Ann. Statist.*, 7:1–26, 1979.

[59] B. Efron. *The Jackknife, the Bootstrap and Other Resampling Plans*. Philadelphia, PA: Society for Industrial and Applied Mathematics, 1982.

[60] B. Efron. Estimating the error rate of a prediction rule: Improvement on cross-validation. *J. Am. Statist. Assoc.*, 78:316–331, 1983.

[61] M. B. Eisen, P. T. Spellman, P. O. Brown, and D. Botstein. Cluster analysis and display of genome-wide expression patterns. *Proc. Nat. Acad. Sci. USA*, 95:14863–14868, 1998.

[62] Y. Engel, S. Mannor, and R. Meir. The kernel recursive least-squares algorithm. *IEEE Trans. Signal Processing*, 52(8):2275–2285, 2004.

[63] B. Schölkopf, C. J. C. Burges, and A. J. Smola (editors). *Advances in Kernel Methods – Support Vector Learning*. Cambridge, MA: MIT Press, 1999.

[64] M. Aizerman, E. A. Braverman, and L. Rozonoer. Theoretical foundation of the potential function method in pattern recognition learning. *Automation Remote Control*, 25:821–837, 1964.

[65] T. Graepel, R. Herbrich, P. Bollman-Sdorra, and K. Obermayer. Classification on pairwise proximity data. *Advances in Neural Information Processing Systems 11*. Cambridge, MA: MIT Press, pages 438–444, 1999.

[66] T. R. Golub, D. K. Slonim, P. Tamayo *et al.* Molecular classification of cancer: Class discovery and class prediction by gene expression monitoring. *Science*, 286:531–537, 1999.

[67] M. Filippone, F. Camastra, F. Masulli, and S. Rosetta. A survey of kernel and spectral methods for clustering. *Pattern Recognition*, 41:176–190, 2008.

[68] R. A. Fisher. The use of multiple measurements in taxonomic problems. *Ann. Eugenics*, 7:179–188, 1936.

[69] R. Fletcher. *Practical Methods of Optimization*, 2nd edition. New York: Wiley, 1987.

[70] E. W. Forgy. Cluster analysis of multivariate data: Efficiency vs. interpretability of classifications. *Biometrics*, 21:768–769, 1965.

[71] R. J. Fox and M. W. Dimmic. A two-sample Bayesian t-test for microarray data. *BMC Bioinformatics*, 7(1):126, 2006.

[72] Y. Freund and R. Schapire. Large margin classification using the perceptron algorithm. *Machine Learning*, 37(3):277–296, 1999.

[73] K. Fukunaga. *Introduction to Statistical Pattern Recognition*, 2nd edition. Amsterdam: Elsevier, 1990.

[73b] G. Fung and O. L. Mangasarian. Proximal support vector machine classifiers. In *Proceedings, ACM KDD01*, San Francisco, 2001.

[74] T. S. Furey, N. Cristianini, N. Duffy *et al.* Support vector machine classification and validation of cancer tissue samples using microarray expression data. *Bioinformatics*, 16(10):906–914, 2000.

[75] I. Gat-Viks, R. Sharan, and R. Shamir. Scoring clustering solutions by their biological relevance. *Bioinformatics*, 19(18):2381–2389, 2003.

[76] T. V. Gestel, J. A. K Suykens, G. Lanckriet *et al.* Bayesian framework for least-squares support vector machine classifiers, Gaussian processes, and kernel Fisher discriminant analysis. *Neural Comput.*, 14(5):1115–1147, 2002.

[77] F. D. Gibbons and F. P. Roth. Judging the quality of gene expression-based clustering methods using gene annotation. *Genome Res.*, 12:1574–1581, 2002.

[78] M. Girolami. Mercer kernel based clustering in feature space. *IEEE Trans. Neural Networks*, 13(3):780–784, 2002.

[79] G. Golub and C. F. Van Loan. *Matrix Computations*, 3rd edition. Battimore, MD: Johns Hopkins University Press, 1996.

[80] G. H. Golub and W. Kahan. Calculating the singular values and pseudo-inverse of a matrix. *J. Soc. Industrial Appl. Math.: Ser. B, Numerical Anal.*, 2(2):205–224, 1965.

[81] G. Golub and C. van Loan. An analysis of the total least squares problem. *SIAM J. Numerical Anal.*, 17:883–893, 1980.

[82] T. R. Golub, D. K. Slonim, C. Huard *et al.* Molecular classification of cancer: Class discovery and class prediction by gene expression monitoring. *Science*, 286:531–537, 1999.

[83] G. Goodwin and K. Sin. *Adaptive Filtering: Prediction and Control.* Englewood Cliffs, NJ: Prentice Hall, 1984.

[84] C. Goutte. Note on free lunches and cross-validation. *Neural Comput.*, 9:1211–1215, 1997.

[85] T. Graepel and K. Obermayer. Fuzzy topographic kernel clustering. In W. Brauer, editor, *Proceedings of the Fifth GI Workshop Fuzzy Neuro Systems*, pages 90–97, 1998.

[86] Z. Griliches and V. Ringstad. Errors-in-the-variables bias in nonlinear contexts. *Econometrica*, 38(2):368–370, 1970.

[87] S. R. Gunn. Support vector machines for classification and regression. USC-ISIS Technical ISIS Technical Report, 1998.

[88] J. Guo, M. W. Mak, and S. Y. Kung. Eukaryotic protein subcellular localization based on local pairwise profile alignment SVM. *Proceedings, 2006 IEEE International Workshop on Machine Learning for Signal Processing (MLSP '06)*, pages 416–422, 2006.

[89] I. Guyon, J. Weston, S. Barnhill, and V. Vapnik. Gene selection for cancer classification using support vector machines. *Machine Learning*, 46:389–422, 2002.

[90] B. H. Juang, S. Y. Kung, and Kamm C. A. (Editors). *Proceedings of the 1991 IEEE Workshop on Neural Networks for Signal Processing*, Princeton, NJ, 1991.

[91] B. Hammer, A. Hasenfuss, F. Rossi, and M. Strickert. Topographic processing of relational data. In *Proceedings of the 6th Workshop on Self-Organizing Maps (WSOM 07)*, Bielefeld, 2007.

[92] J. A. Hartigan. Direct clustering of a data matrix. *J. Am. Statist. Assoc.*, 67(337):123–129, 1972.

[93] T. Hastie, R. Tibshirani, M. Eisen *et al.* "Gene shaving" as a method for identifying distinct sets of genes with similar expression patterns. *Genome Biol.*, 1(2):research0003.1–research0003.21, 2000.

[94] S. Haykin. *Adaptive Filter Theory*, 3rd edition. Englewood Cliffs, NJ: Prentice Hall, 1996.

[95] S. Haykin. *Neural Networks: A Comprehensive Foundation*, 2nd edition. Englewood Cliffs, NJ: Prentice Hall, 2004.

[96] X. He, D. Cai, and P. Niyogi. Laplacian score for feature selection. In *Advances in Neural Information Processing Systems 18*. Cambridge, MA: MIT Press, 2005.

[97] M. A. Hearst, B. Schölkopf, S. Dumais, E. Osuna, and J. Platt. Trends and controversies – support vector machines. *IEEE Intelligent Systems*, 13:18–28, 1998.

[98] V. J. Hodge and J. Austin. A survey of outlier detection methodologies. *Intell. Rev.*, 22:85–126, 2004.

[99] A. E. Hoerl and R. W. Kennard. Ridge regression: Biased estimation for nonorthogonal problems. *Technometrics*, 42(1):80–86, 1970.

[99b] T. Hofmann, B. Schölkopf, and A. J. Smola. Kernel methods in machine learning. *Ann. Statist.*, 36(3):1171–1220, 2008.

[100] H. Hotelling. Analysis of a complex of statistical variables into principal components. *J. Educational Psychol.*, 24:498–520, 1933.

[101] C. W. Hsu and C. J. Lin. A comparison of methods for multiclass support vector machines. *IEEE Trans. Neural Networks*, 13(2):415–425, 2002.

[102] D. Hsu, S. M. Kakade, J. Langford, and T. Zhang. Multi-label prediction via compressed sensing). In *Advances in Neural Information Processing Systems 22*, Cambridge, MA: MIT Press, pages 772–780, 2009.

[103] S. Hua and Z. Sun. A novel method of protein secondary structure prediction with high segment overlap measure: Support vector machine approach. *J. Molec. Biol.*, 308(2):397–407, 2001.

[104] Y. Huang and Y. D. Li. Prediction of protein subcellular locations using fuzzy *K*-NN method. *Bioinformatics*, 20(1):21–28, 2004.

[105] P. J. Huber. Robust statistics: A review. *Ann. Math. Statist.*, 43:1041–1067, 1972.

[106] P. J. Huber. *Robust Statistics*. New York: John Wiley and Sons, 1981.

[107] N. Iizuka, M. Oka, H. Yamada-Okabe *et al.* Oligonucleotide microarray for prediction of early intrahepatic recurrence of hepatocellular carcinoma after curative resection. *Lancet*, 361(9361):923–929, 2003.

[108] R. Inokuchi and S. Miyamoto. LVQ clustering and SOM using a kernel function. In *Proceedings of IEEE International Conference on Fuzzy Systems*, Volume 3, pages 1497–1500, 2004.

[109] L. B. Jack and A. K. Nandi. Fault detection using support vector machines and artificial neural networks, augmented by genetic algorithms. *Mechanical Systems Signal Processing*, 16:373–390, 2002.

[110] P. Jafari and F. Azuaje. An assessment of recently published gene expression data analyses: Reporting experimental design and statistical factors. *BMC Med. Inform.*, 6:27, 2006.

[111] A. K. Jain, M. N. Murty, and P. J. Flynn. Data clustering: A review. *ACM Comput. Surveys*, 31(3):264–323, 1999.

[112] W. James and C. Stein. Estimation with quadratic loss. In *Proceedings of the Fourth Berkeley Symposium on Mathematics, Statistics and Probability*, Volume 1. Berkeley, CA: University of California Press, pages 361–380, 1960.

[113] T. Joachims. Text categorization with support vector machines: Learning with many relevant features. *Proceedings of European Conference on Machine Learning*, Berlin: Springer, pages 137–142, 1997.

[114] T. Joachims. Making large-scale SVM learning practical. In B. Schölkopf, C. Burges, and A. Smola, editors, *Advances in Kernel Methods – Support Vector Learning*. Cambridge, MA: MIT Press, 1999.

[115] I. T. Jolliffe. *Principal Component Analysis*, 2nd edition. New York: Springer, 2002.

[116] E. M. Jordaan and G. F. Smits. Robust outlier detection using SVM regression. In *Proceedings of the 2004 IEEE International Joint Conference on Neural Networks*, volume 3, pages 2017–2022, 2004.

[117] M. I. Jordan and C. M. Bishop. *An Introduction to Probabilistic Graphical Models*. Cambridge, MA: MIT Press, 2002.

[118] B. H. Juang, S. Y. Kung, and C. A. Kamm. *IEEE Workshops on Neural Networks for Signal Processing*. New York: IEEE Press, 1991.

[119] T. Kailath. *Linear Systems*. Englewood Cliffs, NJ: Prentice Hall, 1980.

[120] T. Kailath, A. H. Sayed, and B. Hassibi. *Linear Esitmation*. Englewood Cliffs, NJ: Prentice Hall, 2000.

[121] M. Kass, A. Witkin, and D. Terzopoulos. Snakes: Active contour models. *Int. J. Computer Vision*, 1:321–331, 1987.

[122] S. S. Keerthi, S. K. Shevade, C. Bhattacharyya, and K. R. K. Murthy. Improvements to Platt's SMO algorithm for SVM classifier design. *Neural Comput.*, 13:637–649, 2001.

[123] J. Khan, J. S. Wei, M. Ringner *et al.* Classification and diagnostic prediction of cancers using gene expression profiling and artificial neural networks. *Nature Medicine*, 7(6):673–679, 2001.

[124] J. Khan, J. S. Wei, M. Ringner *et al.* Classification and diagnostic prediction of cancers using gene expression profiling and artificial neural networks. *Nature Medicine*, 7:673–679, 2001.

[125] K. I. Kim, K. Jung, S. H. Park, and H. J. Kim. Texture classification with kernel principal component analysis. *Electron. Lett.*, 36(12):1021–1022, 2000.

[126] G. S. Kimeldarf and G. Wahba. Some results on Tchebycheffian spline functions. *J. Math. Anal. Applications*, 33:82-95, 1971.

[127] S. Kirkpatrick, C. D. Gelat, and M. P. Vecchi. Optimization by simulated annealing. *Science*, 220:671–680, 1983.

[128] R. Kohavi and G. H. John. Wrappers for feature selection. *Artif. Intell.*, 97(1–2):273–324, 1997.

[129] T. Kohonen. Self-organized formation of topologically correct feature map. *Biol. Cybernet.*, 43:59–69, 1982.

[130] T. Kohonen. *Self-Organization and Associative Memory*. New York: Springer, 1984.

[131] T. Kohonen. *Self-Organizing Maps*, 2nd edition. Berlin: Springer, 1997.

[132] T. Kudo and Y. Matsumoto. Chunking with support vector machines. In *Proceedings, North American Chapter of the Association for Computational Linguistics*, 2001.

[133] H. T. Kung. Why systolic architectures? *IEEE Computer*, 15(1):37–46, 1982.

[134] S. Y. Kung. *VLSI Array Processors*. Englewood Cliffs, NJ: Prentice Hall, 1988.

[135] S. Y. Kung. *Digital Neural Networks*. Englewood Cliffs, NJ: Prentice Hall, 1993.

[136] S. Y. Kung. Kernel approaches to unsupervised and supervised machine learning. In *Proceedings of PCM 2009*, Bangkok, pages 1–32. Berlin: Springer-Verlag, 2009.

[137] S. Y. Kung, K. I. Diamantaras, and J. S. Taur. Adaptive principal component extraction (APEX) and applications. *IEEE Trans. Signal Processing*, 42(5):1202–1217, 1994.

[138] S. Y. Kung, F. Fallside, J. A. Sorensen, and C. A. Kamm (Editors). *Neural Networks for Signal Processing II*. Piscataway, NJ: IEEE, 1992.

[139] S. Y. Kung and Man-Wai Mak. PDA–SVM hybrid: A unified model for kernel-based supervised classification. *J. Signal Processing Systems*, 65(1):5–21, 2011.

[140] S. Y. Kung and M. W. Mak. Feature selection for self-supervised classification with applications to microarray and sequence data. *IEEE J. Selected Topics Signal Processing: Special Issue Genomic and Proteomic Signal Processing*, 2(3):297–309, 2008.

[141] S. Y. Kung, M. W. Mak, and S. H. Lin. *Biometric Authentication: A Machine Learning Approach*. Upper Saddle River, NJ: Prentice Hall, 2005.

[142] S. Y. Kung, M. W. Mak, and I. Tagkopoulos. Multi-metric and multi-substructure biclustering analysis for gene expression data. In *IEEE Computational Systems Bioinformatics Conference*, Stanford, CA, 2005.

[143] S. Y. Kung, M. W. Mak, and I. Tagkopoulos. Symmetric and asymmetric multimodality biclustering analysis for microarray data matrix. *J. Bioinformatics Comput. Biol.*, 4(3):275–298, 2006.

[144] S. Y. Kung and Peiyuan Wu. On efficient learning and classification kernel methods. In *Proceedings, IEEE International Conference on Acoustics, Speech, and Signal Processing (ICASSP '12)*, Kyoto, 2012.

[145] S. Y. Kung and Peiyuan Wu. Perturbation regulated kernel regressors for supervised machine learning. In *Proceedings, 2012 IEEE International Workshop on Machine Learning for Signal Processing (MLSP'12)*, 2012.

[146] S. Y. Kung and Yuhui Luo. Recursive kernel trick for network segmentation. *Int. J. Robust Nonlinear Control*, 21(15):1807–1822, 2011.

[147] N. Lawrence and B. Schölkopf. Estimating a kernel Fisher discriminant in the presence of label noise. In *Proceedings of the 18th International Conference on Machine Learning*, San Francisco. New York: Morgan Kaufman, 2001.

[148] L. Lazzeroni and A. B. Owen. Plaid models for gene expression data. Technical report, March, 2000 (www-stat.stanford.edu/owen/reports/plaid.pdf).

[149] K. H. Lee, S. Y. Kung, and N. Verma. Improving kernel-energy trade-offs for machine learning in implantable and wearable biomedical applications. In *Proceedings of ICASSP*, pages 1597–1600, 2011.

[150] K. H. Lee, S. Y. Kung, and N. Verma. Low-energy formulations of support vector machine kernel functions for biomedical sensor applications. *Journal of Signal Processing Systems*, Berlin: Springer, published online, 2012.

[151] B. Levy. *Principles of Signal Detection and Parameter Estimation.* Berlin: Springer, 2008.

[152] Dan Li. Performance Evaluation of Maximum Log-Likelihood Classification, ELE 571 Course Project Report, Princeton University, Princeton, NJ, 2010.

[153] L. Q. Li, Y. Zhang, L. Y. Zou, Y. Zhou, and X. Q. Zheng. Prediction of protein subcellular multi-localization based on the general form of Chou's pseudo amino acid composition. *Protein Peptide Lett.*, 19:375–387, 2012.

[154] T. Li and M. Ogihara. Toward intelligent music information retrieval. *IEEE Trans. Multimedia*, 8(3):564–574, 2006.

[155] Y. Liang, H. Wu, R. Lei *et al.* Transcriptional network analysis identifies BACH1 as a master regulator of breast cancer bone metastasis. *J. Biol. Chem.*, 287(40):33533–33544, 2012.

[156] Opensource EEG libraries and toolkit. http://www.goomedic.com/opensource-eeg-libraries-and-toolkits-for-developers.html.

[157] W. Liu, J. C. Principe, and S. Haykin. *Kernel Adaptive Filtering: A Comprehensive Introduction.* New York: Wiley, 2010.

[158] L. Ljung. *System Identification: Theory for the User.* Englewood Cliffs, NJ: Prentice Hall, 1999.

[159] Z.-P. Lo, M. Fujita, and B. Bavarian. Analysis of neighborhood interaction in Kohonen neural networks. In *Proceedings, 6th International Parallel Processing Symposium, Los Alamitos, CA*, pages 247–249, 1991.

[160] Z.-P. Lo, Y. Yu, and B. Bavarian. Analysis of the convergence properties of topology preserving neural networks. *IEEE Trans. Neural Networks*, 4:207–220, 1993.

[161] G. Lubec, L Afjehi-Sadat, J. W. Yang, and J. P. John. Searching for hypothetical proteins: Theory and practice based upon original data and literature. *Prog. Neurobiol.*, 77:90–127, 2005.

[162] S. Ma and J. Huang. Regularized ROC method for disease classification and biomarker selection with microarray data. *Bioinformatics*, 21(24):4356–4362, 2005.

[163] D. MacDonald and C. Fyfe. The kernel self organising map. In *Proceedings of 4th International Conference on Knowledge-Based Intelligence Engineering Systems and Applied Technologies*, 2000.

[164] M. MacQueen. Some methods for classification and analysis of multivariate observation. In *Proceedings of the 5th Berkeley Symposium on Mathematical Statistics and Probabilities* (L. M. LeCun and J. Neyman, editors, volume 1, pages 281–297. Berkeley, CA: University of California Press, 1967.

[165] P. C. Mahalanobis. On the generalised distance in statistics. *J. Proc. Asiatic Soc. Bengal*, 2:49–55, 1936.

[166] M. W. Mak, J. Guo, and S. Y. Kung. PairProSVM: Protein subcellular localization based on local pairwise profile alignment and SVM. *IEEE/ACM Trans. Comput. Biol. Bioinformatics*, 5(3):416–422, 2008.

[167] M. W. Mak and S. Y. Kung. A solution to the curse of dimensionality problem in pairwise scoring techniques. In *International Conference on Neural Information Processing*, pages 314–323, 2006.

[168] M. W. Mak and S. Y. Kung. Fusion of feature selection methods for pairwise scoring SVM. *Neurocomputing*, 71(16–18):3104–3113, 2008.

[169] M. W. Mak and S. Y. Kung. Low-power SVM classifiers for sound event classification on mobile devices. In *Proceedings of ICASSP*, Kyoto, 2012.

[170] O. L. Mangasarian, G. Fung, and J. W. Shavlik. Knowledge-based nonlinear kernel classifers. In *Learning Theory and Kernel Machines*. Berlin: Springer-Verlag, pages 102–113, 2003.

[171] H. B. Mann and D. R. Whitney. On a test whether one of two random variables is stochastically larger than the other. *Ann. Math. Statist.*, 18:50–60, 1947.

[172] Mathworks-SVM. Mathworks bioinformatics toolbox.

[173] M. Mavroforakis and S. Theodoridis. A geometric approach to support vector machine (SVM) classification. *IEEE Trans. Neural Networks*, 17(3):671–682, 2006.

[174] G. J. McLachlan. *Discriminant Analysis and Statistical Pattern Recognition*. New York: John Wiley & Sons, 1992.

[175] J. Mercer. Functions of positive and negative type, and their connection with the theory of integral equations. *Trans. London Phil. Soc.*, A209:415–446, 1909.

[176] S. Mika. *Kernel Fisher Discriminants*. PhD thesis, The Technical University of Berlin, Berlin, 2002.

[177] S. Mika, G. Ratsch, and K. R. Muller. A mathematical programming approach to the kernel Fisher algorithm. In *Advances in Neural Information Processing Systems 14*. Cambridge, MA: MIT press, pages 591–597, 2001.

[178] S. Mika, G. Ratsch, J. Weston, B. Schölkopf, and K. R. Mullers. Fisher discriminant analysis with kernels. In Y. H. Hu, J. Larsen, E. Wilson, and S. Douglas, editors, *Neural Networks for Signal Processing IX*, pages 41–48, 1999.

[179] S. Mika, A. J. Smola, and B. Schölkopf. An improved training algorithm for kernel Fisher discriminants. In T. Jaakkola and T. Richardson, editors, *Proceedings AISTATS*, San Francisco, CA, pages 98–104. New York: Morgan Kaufmann, 2001.

[180] B. Mirkin. *Mathematical Classification and Clustering*. Berlin: Springer, 1996.

[181] T. M. Mitchell. *Machine Learning*. New York: McGraw-Hill, 1997.

[182] P. J. Moreno, P. P. Ho, and N. Vasconcelos. A Kullback–Leibler divergence based kernel for SVM classification in multimedia applications. Technical Report, HP Laboratories Cambridge, 2004.

[183] MSPsim. http://www.sics.se/project/mspsim.

[184] S. Mukherjee, E. Osuna, and F. Girosi. Nonlinear prediction of chaotic time series using support vector machines. In J. Principe, L. Giles, N. Morgan, and E. Wilson, editors, *Proceedings, IEEE Workshop on Neural Networks for Signal Processing*, Amelia Island, FL, pages 276–285, 1997.

[185] K. R. Muller, S. Mika, G. Ratsch, K. Tsuda, and B. Schölkopf. An introduction to kernel-based learning algorithms. *IEEE Trans. Neural Networks*, 12(2):181–201, 2001.

[186] K. R. Muller, A. Smola, G. Ratsch *et al.* Predicting time series with support vector machines. In *Proceedings, International Conference on Artificial Neural Networks*, London: Springer-Verlag, pages 999–1004, 1997.

[187] K. R. Muller, S. Mika, G. Ratsch, K. Tsuda, and B. Schölkopf. An introduction to kernel-based learning algorithms. *IEEE Trans. Neural Networks*, 12(2):181–201, 2001.

[188] N. Murata, K. R. Muller, A. Ziehe, and S. Amari. Adaptive on-line learning in changing environments. In M. C. Mozer, M. I. Jordan, and T Petsche, editors, *Advances in Neural Information Processing Systems 9*. Cambridge, MA: MIT press, pages 599–605, 1997.

[189] C. L. Myers. Context-sensitive methods for learning from genomic data. Thesis, Department of Electrical Engineering, Princeton University, Princeton, NJ, 2007.

[190] C.L. Myers, M. Dunham, S.Y. Kung, and O. Troyanskaya. Accurate detection of aneuploidies in array cgh and gene expression microarray data. In *Bioinfomotics*. Published online, Oxford University Press, 2005.

[191] E. A. Nadaraya. On estimating regression. *Theory Probability Applicationss*, 9:141–142, 1964.

[192] Neural network frequently asked questions. http://www.faqs.org/faqs/ai-faq/neural-nets/part3/section-12.html.

[193] J. Neyman and E. S. Pearson. On the use and interpretation of certain test criteria for purposes of statistical inference. *Biometrika*, 20:175–240, 1928.

[194] S. Niijima and Y. Okuno. Laplacian linear discriminant analysis approach to unsupervised feature selection. *IEEE/ACM Trans. Comput. Biol. Bioinformatics*, 6(4):605–614, 2009.

[195] C. L. Nutt, D. R. Mani, R. A. Betensky *et al.* Gene expression-based classification of malignant gliomas correlates better with survival than histological classification. *Cancer Res.*, 63(7):1602–1607, 2003.

[196] E. Oja. A simplified neuron model as a principal component analyzer. *J. Math. Biol.*, 15:267–273, 1982.

[197] E. Osuna, R. Freund, and E. Girosi. An improved training algorithm for support vector machines. In J. Principe, L. Giles, N. Morgan, and E. Wilson, Editors, Proceedings, IEEE Workshop on Neural Networks for Signal Processing VII, Amelia Island, FL, pages 276–285, 1997.

[198] D. Parker. Learning logic. Technical Report TR-47, Center for Computational Research in Economics and Management Science, MIT, Cambridge, MA, 1985.

[199] E. Parzen. On estimation of a probability density function and mode. *Ann. Math. Statist.*, 33:1065–1076, 1962.

[200] P. Pavlidis, J. Weston, J. Cai, and W. N. Grundy. Gene functional classification from heterogeneous data. In *International Conference on Computational Biology*, Pittsburgh, PA, pages 249–255, 2001.

[201] K. Pearson. On lines and planes of closest fit to systems of points in space. *Phil. Mag. Ser. 6*, 2:559–572, 1901.

[202] M. S. Pepe. *The Statistical Evaluation of Medical Tests for Classification and Prediction*, Oxford: Oxford University Press, 2003.

[203] PhysioNet. http://www.physionet.org.

[204] J. C. Platt. Fast training of support vector machines using sequential minimal optimization. In B. Schölkopf, C. J. C. Burges, and A. J. Smola, editors, *Advances in Kernel Methods – Support Vector Learning*, Cambridge, MA: MIT Press, pages 185–208, 1999.

[205] J. C. Platt. Using analytic QP and sparseness to speed training of support vector machines. In *Advances in Neural Information Processing Systems 10*, 1998.

[206] N. Pochet, F. De Smet, J. A. K. Suykens, and B. L. R. De Moor. Systematic benchmarking of microarray data classification: Assessing the role of nonlinearity and dimensionality reduction. *Bioinformatics*, 20(17):3185–3195, 2004.

[207] T. Poggio and F. Girosi. Networks for approximation and learning. *Proc. IEEE*, 78(9):1481–1497, 1990.

[208] S. L. Pomeroy, P. Tamayo, M. Gaasenbeek *et al.* Prediction of central nervous system embryonal tumour outcome based on gene expression. *Nature*, 415(6870):436–442, 2002.

[209] M. Pontil and A. Verri. Support vector machines for 3D object recognition. *IEEE Trans. Pattern Analysis Machine Intell.*, 20:637–646, 1998.

[210] H. V. Poor. *An Introductionn to Signal Dection and Estimation*, 2nd edition, Berlin: Springer, 1994.

[211] D. M. Pozar. *Microwave Engineering*, 3rd edition. New York: Wiley, 2005.

[212] J. C. Rajapakse, K. B. Duan, and W. K. Yeo. Proteomic cancer classification with mass spectrometry data. *Am. J. Pharmacogenomics*, 5(5):281–292, 2005.

[213] S. Ramaswamy, P. Tamayo, R. Rifkin *et al.* Multiclass cancer diagnosis using tumor gene expression signatures. *PNAS*, 98(26):15149–15154, 2001.

[214] J. Read, B. Pfahringer, G. Holmes, and E. Frank. Classifier chains for multi-label classification. In *Proceedings of European Conference on Machine Learning and Principles and Practice of Knowledge Discovery in Databases*, pages 254–269, 2009.

[215] M. Reich, K. Ohm, M. Angelo, P. Tamayo, and J. P. Mesirov GeneCluster 2.0: An advanced toolset for bioarray analysis. *Bioinformatics*, 20(11):1797–1798, 2004.

[216] A. Reinhardt and T. Hubbard. Using neural networks for prediction of the subcellular location of proteins. *Nucl. Acids Res.*, 26:2230–2236, 1998.

[217] B. D. Ripley. *Pattern Recognition and Neural Networks*. Cambridge: Cambridge University Press, 1996.

[218] J. Rissanen. A universal prior for integers and estimation by minimum description length. *Ann. Statist.*, 11(2):416–431, 1983.

[219] H. Ritter, T. Martinetz, and K. Schulten. *Neural Computation and Self-Organizing Maps: An Introduction*. Reading, MA: Addison-Wesley, 1992.

[220] F. Rosenblatt. The perceptron: A probabilistic model for information storage and organization of the brain. *Psychol. Rev.*, 65:42–99, 1958.

[221] M. Rosenblatt. Remarks on some nonparametric estimates of a density function. *Ann. Math. Statist.*, 27:832–837, 1956.

[222] M. Rosenblatt. Density estimates and Markov sequences. In M. Puri, editor, *Nonparametric Techniques in Statistical Inference*. London: Cambridge University Press, pages 199–213, 1970.

[223] V. Roth, J. Laub, J. M. Buhmann, and K.-R. Muller. Going metric: Denoising pairwise data. In *Advances in Neural Information Processing Systems 15*. Cambridge, MA: MIT Press, pages 817–824, 2003.

[224] V. Roth and V. Steinhage. Nonlinear discriminant analysis using kernel functions. In S. A. Sola, T. K. Leen, and K. -R. Muller, editors, *Advances in Neural Information Processing Systems 12*. Cambridge, MA: MIT Press, pages 568–574, 2000.

[225] R. Rothe, Yinan Yu, and S. Y. Kung. Parameter design tradeoff between prediction performance and training time for ridge-SVM. In *Proceedings, 2013 IEEE International Workshop on Machine Learning For Signal Processing*, Southampton, 2013.

[226] D. E. Rumelhart, G. E. Hinton, and R. J. Williams. Learning internal representations by error propagation. In D. E. Rumelhart, J. L. McClelland, and the PDP Research Group, editors, *Parallel Distribution Processing: Explorations in the Microstruture of Cognition, Volume 1: Foundation*. Cambridge, MA: MIT Press/Bradford Books, 1986.

[227] T. D. Sanger. Optimal unsupervised learning in a single-layer linear feedforward neural network. *Neural Networks*, 12:459–473, 1989.

[228] A. Sayed. *Fundamentals of Adaptive Filtering*. New York: Wiley, 2003.

[229] A. Sayed and T. Kailath. A state space approach to adaptive RLS filtering. *IEEE Signal Processing Mag.*, 11:18–60, 1994.

[230] A. H. Sayed. *Fundamentals of Adaptive Filtering*. John Wiley, 2003 (see page 30).

[231] R. E. Schapire and Y. Singer. Boostexter: A boosting-based system for text categorization. *Machine Learning*, 39(2/3):135–168, 2000.

[232] L. Scharf. *Statistical Signal Processing*. Reading, MA: Addison-Wesley, 1991.

[233] S. M. Schennach. Nonparametric regression in the presence of measurement error. *Econometric Theory*, 20(6):1046–1093, 2004.

[234] B. Schölkopf. Statistical learning and kernel methods. Technical Report MSR-TR 2000-23, Microsoft Research, 2000.

[235] B. Schölkopf, C. Burges, and V. Vapnik. Incorporating invariances in support vector learning machines. In *Proceedings, International Conference on Artificial Neural Networks*, 1996.

[236] B. Schölkopf, R. Herbrich, A. Smola, and R. Williamson. A generalized representer theorem. NeuroCOLT2 Technical Report Series, NC2-TR-2000-82, 2000.

[237] B. Schölkopf, J. C. Platt, J. Shawe-Taylor, A. J. Smola, and R. C. Williamson. Estimating the support of a high-dimensional distribution. *Neural Computation*, 13:1443–1472, 2001.

[238] B. Schölkopf, A. Smola, and K.-R. Muller. Nonlinear component analysis as a kernel eigenvalue problem, *Neural Comput.*, 10:1299–1319, 1998.

[238b] B. Schölkopf, A. J. Smola, R. C. Williamson, and P. L. Bartlett. New support vector algorithms. *Neural Comput.*, 12:1207–1245, 2000.

[239] B. Schölkopf and A. J. Smola. *Learning with Kernels: Support Vector Machines, Regularization, Optimization, and Beyond*. Cambridge, MA: MIT Press, 2002.

[240] B. Schölkopf, R. C. Williamson, A. J. Smola, J. Shawe-Taylor, and J. C. Platt. Support vector method for novelty detection. In S. A. Sola, T. K. Leen, and K.-R. Muller, editors, *Advances in Neural Information Processing Systems 12*. Cambridge, MA: MIT Press, pages 568–574, 2000.

[241] A. Schwaighofer. SVM toolbox for MATLAB.

[242] G. Schwartz. Estimating the dimension of a model. Ann. Statist., 6(2):461–464, 1978.

[243] D. J. Sebald and J. A. Bucklew. Support vector machine techniques for nonlinear equalization. *IEEE Trans. Signal Processing*, 48(11):3217–3226, 2000.

[244] J. Shawe-Taylor and N. Cristianini. *Support Vector Machines and Other Kernel-Based Learning Methods*. Cambridge: Cambridge University Press, 2004.

[245] H. B. Shen and K. C. Chou. Virus-mPLoc: A fusion classifier for viral protein subcellular location prediction by incorporating multiple sites. *J. Biomol. Struct. Dyn.*, 26:175–186, 2010.

[246] P. Simard, A. Smola., B. Schölkopf, and V. Vapnik. Prior knowledge in support vector kernels. *Advances in Neural Information Processing Systems 10*. 640–646, 1998.

[247] D. Singh, P. G. Febbo, K. Ross *et al.* Gene expression correlates of clinical prostate cancer behavior. *Cancer Cell*, 1(2):203–209, 2002.

[248] I. Yamada, K. Slavakis, and S. Theodoridis. Online classification using kernels and projection-based adaptive algorithms. *IEEE Trans. Signal Processing*, 56(7):2781–2797, 2008.

[249] T. F. Smith and M. S. Waterman. Comparison of biosequences. *Adv. Appl. Math.*, 2:482–489, 1981.

[250] A. J. Smola, B. Schölkopf, and K. R. Müller. The connection between regularization operators and support vector kernels. *Neural Networks*, 11:637–649, 1998.

[251] A. J. Smola, P. L. Bartlett, B. Schölkopf, and D. Schuurmans. *Advances in Large Margin Classifiers*. Cambridge, MA: MIT Press, 2000.

[252] P. H. A. Sneath and R. R. Sokal. *Numerical taxonomy: The Principles and Practice of Numerical Classification*. San Francisco, CA: W. H. Freeman, 1973.

[253] M. Song, C. Breneman, J. Bi *et al.* Prediction of protein retention times in anion-exchange chromatography systems using support vector regression. *J. Chem. Information Computer Sci.*, 42:1347–1357, 2002.

[254] M. H. Song, J. Lee, S. P. Cho, K. J. Lee, and S. K. Yoo. Support vector machine based arrhythmia classification using reduced features. *Int. J. Control, Automation, Systems*, 3:571–579, 2005.

[255] T. Sørlie, R. Tibshirani, J. Parker *et al.* Repeated observation of breast tumor subtypes in independent gene expression data sets. *PNAS*, 100(14):8418–8423, 2003.

[256] D. F. Specht. Probabilistic neural networks. *Neural Networks*, 3:109–118, 1990.

[257] P. T. Spellman, G. Sherlock, M. Q. Zhang *et al.* Comprehensive identification of cell cycle-regulated genes of the yeast *Saccharomyces cerevisiae* by microarray hybridization. *Mol. Biol. Cell*, 9(12):3273–3297, 1998.

[258] M. O. Stitson and J. A. E. Weston. Implementational issues of support vector machines. Technical Report CSD-TR-96-18, Computational Intelligence Group, Royal Holloway, University of London, 1996.

[259] G. Strang. *Introduction to Linear Algebra*. Wellesley, MA: Wellesley Cambridge Press, 2003.

[260] J. A. K. Suykens and J. Vandewalle. Least squares support vector machine classifiers. *Neural Processing Lett.*, 9(3):293–300, 1999.

[261] SVMlight. http://svmlight.joachims.org/.

[262] I. Tagkopoulos, N. Slavov, and S. Y. Kung. Multi-class biclustering and classification based on modeling of gene regulatory networks. In *Proceedings, Fifth IEEE Symposium on Bioinformatics and Bioengineering (BIBE '05)*. Minneapolis, MN, pages 89–96, 2005.

[263] P. Tamayo, D. Slonim, J. Mesirov *et al.* Interpreting patterns of gene expression with self-organizing maps: Methods and application to hematopoietic differentiation. *Proc. Nat. Acad. Sci.* USA, 96:2907–2912, 1999.

[264] S. Tavazoie, D. Hughes, M. J. Campbell, R. J. Cho, and G. M. Church. Systematic determination of genetic network architecture. *Nature Genetics*, 22:281–285, 1999.

[265] D. M. J. Tax and R. P. W. Duin. Data domain description using support vectors. In M. Verleysen (Editor), *Proceedings of the European Symposium on Artificial Neural Networks, ESANN'99*, Brussels, pages 251–256, 1999.

[266] D. M. J. Tax and R. P. W. Duin. Support vector domain description. *Pattern Recognition Lett.*, 20:1191–1199, 1999.

[267] S. Theodoridis and K. Koutroumbas. *Pattern Recognition*, 4th edition. New York: Academic Press, 2008.

[268] R. Tibshirani. Regression shrinkage and selection via the LASSO. *J. Royal Statist. Soc. B*, 58:267–288, 1996.

[269] F. Tobar, D. Mandic, and S. Y. Kung. The multikernel least mean square algorithm. *IEEE Trans. Neural Networks Learning Systems*, 99 accepted for publication. 2013.

[270] C. Tong, V. Svetnik, B. Schölkopf *et al.* Novelty detection in mass spectral data using a support vector machine method. In *Advances in Neural Information Processing Systems 12*. Cambridge, MA: MIT Press, 2000.

[271] S. Tong and D. Koller. Support vector machine active learning with applications to text classification. *J. Machine Learning Res.*, 2:45–66, 2002.

[272] L. N. Trefethen and D Bau III. *Numerical Linear Algebra*. Philadelphia, PA: Society for Industrial and Applied Mathematics, 1997.

[273] G. Tsoumakas and I. Katakis. Multi-label classification: An overview. *Int. J. Data Warehousing Mining*, 3:1–13, 2007.

[274] G. Tsoumakas, I. Katakis, and I. Vlahavas. Mining multi-label data. In O. Maimon and L. Rokach (Editors), *Data Mining and Knowledge Discovery Handbook*, 2nd edition. Berlin: Springer, 2010.

[275] A. N. Tychonoff. On the stability of inverse problems. *Dokl. Akad. Nauk SSSR*, 39(5):195–198, 1943.

[276] I. Van Mechelen, H. H. Bock, and P. De Boeck. Two-mode clustering methods: A structured overview. *Statist. Methods Med. Res.*, 13(5):363–394, 2004.

[277] L. J. van 't Veer, Hongyue Dai, M. J. van de Vijver *et al.* Gene expression profiling predicts clinical outcome of breast cancer. *Nature*, 415:530–536, 2002.

[278] V. Vapnik. *Estimation of dependences based on empirical data* [in Russian]. Moscow, Nauka, 1979. (English translation New York: Springer, 1982.)

[279] V. Vapnik, S. Golowich, and A. Smola. Support vector method for function approximation, regression estimation, and signal processing. In M. Mozer, M. Jordan, and T. Petsche (editors), *Advances in Neural Information Processing Systems 9*. Cambridge, MA: MIT Press, pages 281–287, 1997.

[280] V. N. Vapnik. *The Nature of Statistical Learning Theory*. New York: Springer-Verlag, 1995.

[281] V. N. Vapnik. *Statistical Learning Theory*. New York: Wiley, 1998.

[282] C. Vens, J. Struyf, L. Schietgat, S. Dzeroski, and H. Blockeel. Decision trees for hierarchical multi-label classification. *Machine Learning*, 2(73):185–214, 2008.

[283] N. Villa and F. Rossi. A comparison between dissimilarity SOM and kernel SOM clustering the vertices of a graph. In *Proceedings of the 6th International Workshop on Self-Organizing Maps*. Bielefeld: Bielefeld University, 2007.

[284] G. Wahba. *Spline Models for Observational Data*. Philadelphia, PA: SIAM, 1990.

[285] Shibiao Wan, Man-Wai Mak, and S. Y. Kung. mGOASVM: Multi-label protein subcellular localization based on gene ontology and support vector machines. *BMC*

Bioinformatics, 13:290, 2012 (available at http://link.springer.com/article/10.1186/1471-2105-13-290/fulltext.html).

[286] Shibiao Wan, Man-Wai Mak, and S. Y. Kung. Adaptive thresholding for multi-label SVM classification with application to protein subcellular localization prediction. In *Proceedings of ICASSP '13*, Vancouver, pages 3547–3551, 2013.

[287] Jeen-Shing Wang and Jen-Chieh Chiang. A cluster validity measure with outlier detection for support vector clustering. *IEEE Trans. Systems, Man, Cybernet. B*, 38:78–89, 2008.

[288] L. Wang, J. Zhu, and H. Zou. The doubly regularized support vector machine. *Statist. Sinica*, 16:589–615, 2006.

[289] Y. Wang, A. Reibman, F. Juang, T. Chen, and S. Y. Kung. In *Proceedings of the IEEE Workshops on Multimedia Signal Processing*. Princeton, MA: IEEE Press, 1997.

[290] Z. Wang, S. Y. Kung, J. Zhang *et al.* Computational intelligence approach for gene expression data mining and classification. In *Proceedings of the IEEE International Conference on Multimedia & Expo*. Princeton, MA: IEEE Press, 2003.

[291] Z. Wang, Y. Wang, J. Lu *et al.* Discriminatory mining of gene expression microarray data. *J. Signal Processing Systems*, 35:255–272, 2003.

[292] J. H. Ward. Hierarchical grouping to optimize an objective function. *J. Am. Statist. Assoc.*, 58:236–244, 1963.

[293] G. S. Watson. Smooth regression analysis. *Sankhya: Indian J. Statist. Ser. A*, 26:359–372, 1964.

[294] P. J. Werbos. *Beyond Regression: New Tools for Prediction and Analysis in the Behavior Science*. PhD thesis, Harvard University, Cambridge, MA, 1974.

[295] J.Weston, A.Elisseeff, G.BakIr, and F. Sinz. http://www.kyb.tuebingen.mpg.de/bs/people/spider/main.html.

[296] J. Weston, A. Elisseeff, B. Schölkopf, and M. Tipping. Use of the zero-norm with linear models and kernel methods. *J. Machine Learning Res.*, 3:1439–1461, 2003.

[297] J. Weston and C. Watkins. Multi-class support vector machines. In *Proceedings of ESANN*, Brussels, 1999.

[298] B. Widrow and S. D. Stern. *Adaptive Signal Processing*. Englewood Cliffs, NJ: Prentice Hall, 1984.

[299] N. Wiener. *Interpolation and Smoothing of Stationary Time Series*. Cambridge, MA: MIT Press, 1949.

[299b] S. Winters-Hilt, A. Yelundur, C. McChesney, and M. Landry. Support vector machine implementations for classification clustering. *BMC Bioinformatics*, 7:S4, published online, 2006.

[300] L. Wolf and A. Shashua. Feature selection for unsupervised and supervised inference: The emergence of sparsity in a weight-based approach. *J. Machine Learning Res.*, 6:1855–1887, 2005.

[301] M. A. Woodbury. Inverting modified matrices. In Statistical Research Group Memorandum Report 42, MR38136, Princeton University, Princeton, NJ, 1950.

[302] Peiyuan Wu and S. Y. Kung. Kernel-induced optimal linear estimators and generalized Gauss–Markov theorems. Submitted 2013.

[302b] Peiyuan Wu, C. C. Fang, J. M. Chang, S. Gilbert, and S. Y. Kung. Cost-effective kernel ridge regression implementation for keystroke-based active authentication system. In *Proceedings of ICASSP '14*, Florence, Italy, 2014.

[303] Z. D. Wu, W. X. Xie, and J. P. Yu. Fuzzy *c*-means clustering algorithm based on kernel method. In *Proceedings of the Fifth International Conference on Computational Intelligence and Multimedia Applications*, pages 49–54, 2003.

[304] X. Xiao, Z. C. Wu, and K. C. Chou. iLoc-Virus: A multi-label learning classifier for identifying the subcellular localization of virus proteins with both single and multiple sites. *J. Theor. Biol.*, 284:42–51, 2011.

[305] E. P. Xing and R. M. Karp. CLIFF: Clustering of high-dimensional microarray data via iterative feature filtering using normalized cuts. *Bioinformatics*, 17(90001):306–315, 2001.

[306] H. Xu, C. Caramanis, and S. Mannor. Robust regression and LASSO. In *Advances in Neural Information Processing Systems 21*. Cambridge, MA: MIT Press, pages 1801–1808, 2009.

[307] Rui Xu and D. Wunsch II. Survey of clustering algorithms. *IEEE Trans. Neural Networks*, 16(3):645–678, 2005.

[308] L. Yan, R. Dodier, M. C. Mozer, and Wolniewicz R. Optimizing classifier performance via the Wilcoxon–Mann–Whitney statistics. In *Proceedings of the International Conference on Machine Learning*, pages 848–855, 2003.

[309] Haiqin Yang, Kaizhu Huang, Laiwan Chan, I. King, and M. R. Lyu. Outliers treatment in support vector regression for financial time series prediction. In *ICONIP '04*, pages 1260–1265, 2004.

[310] Yinan Yu, K. Diamantaras, T. McKelvey, and S. Y. Kung. Ridge-adjusted slack variable optimization for supervised classification. In *IEEE International Workshop on Machine Learning for Signal Processing*, Southampton, 2013.

[311] Yinan Yu, T. McKelvey, and S. Y. Kung. A classification scheme for "high-dimensional–small-sample-size" data using SODA and ridge-SVM with medical applications. In *Proceedings, 2013 International Conference on Acoustics, Speech, and Signal Processing*, 2013.

[311b] Yinan Yu, T. McKelvey, and S. Y. Kung. Kernel SODA: A feature reduction technique using kernel based analysis. In *Proceedings, 12th International Conference on Machine Learning and Applications (ICMLA'13)*, volume 4B, page 340.

[312] C.-H. Yuan, G.-X. Ho and C.-J. Lin. Recent advances of large-scale linear classification. *Proc. IEEE*, 100:2584–2603, 2012.

[313] M. Yukawa. Multikernel adaptive filtering. *IEEE Trans. Signal Processing*, 60(9):4672–4682, 2012.

[314] A. L. Yullie and N. M. Grzywacz. The motion coherence theory. In *Proceedings, International Conference on Computer Vision*, pages 344–353, 1988.

[315] D.-Q. Zhang and S.-C. Chen. A novel kernelized fuzzy *c*-means algorithm with application in medical image segmentation. *Artif. Intell. Med.*, 32:37–50, 2004.

[316] Lei Zhang, Fuzong Lin, and Bo Zhang. Support vector machine learning for image retrieval. In *Proceedings of the 2001 International Conference on Image Processing*, volume 2, pages 721–724, 2001.

[317] M. Q. Zhang. Computational prediction of eukaryotic protein-coding genes. *Nature Rev. Genetics*, 3(9):698–709, 2002.

[318] X. G. Zhang, X. Lu, Q. Shi *et al.* Recursive SVM feature selection and sample classification for mass-spectrometry and microarray data. *BMC Bioinformatics*, 7(197), 2006.

[319] Z. Zhang, X. D. Gu, and S. Y. Kung. Color–frequency–orientation histogram based image retrieval. In *Proceedings of ICASSP*, Kyoto, 2012.

[319b] Z. Zhang, G. Page, and H. Zhang. Applying classification separability analysis to microarray data. In S. M. Lin and K. F. Johnson, editors, *Methods of Microarray Data Analysis, CAMDA '00*. Boston, MA: Kluwer Academic Publishers, pages 125–136, 2001.

[320] J. Zhu, S. Rosset, T. Hastie, and R. Tibshirani. 1-norm SVMS. In *Advances in Neural Information Processing Systems 16*. Cambridge, MA: MIT press, 2004.

[321] H. Zou and T. Hastie. Regularization and variable selection via the elastic net. *J. Royal Statist. Soc., Ser. B*, 67(2):301–320, 2005.

Index

a-posteriori likelihood, 556
accession numbers of the genes, 133
  selected by signed-SNR, 133
  selected by SVM-RFE, 133
accuracies
  prediction accuracies, 21
  testing accuracies, 21
  training accuracies, 21
accuracy
  prediction, 251
  training, 251
acute lymphoblastic leukemia (ALL), 123
acute myeloid leukemia (AML), 123
additive coherence models, 171
adjacency matrix, 185
adjusted training error, 406
Aizerman M., E. A. Braverman, and L. Rozonoer, 564
algorithm and hardware co-design, 421
algorithm for FDA, 259
alignment of sequences, 184
annealing EM (AEM), 158–160
  inner loop: EM updating, 159
  outer loop: reduce temperature, 159
anti-support vectors, 303–305
application of feature selection, 131
  supervised gene selection, 132
  unsupervised gene pre-filtering, 131
application of KRR, 300
  cancer diagnosis, 301
  subcellular localization, 302
  UCI data, 300
application of Ridge-SVM, 300
  Ischemic Stroke Dataset, 415
  microarray cancer diagnosis, 413
  subcellular localization, 414, 415
  UCI data, 412
  using SODA, 415
applications of SNR tests, 121
applications of SOM
  executive summary, 166
  gene clustering, 168
  less sensitive to cluster size, 167
  tissue sample clustering analysis, 168
area under the curve (AUC)
  range of AUC, 42
Aronszajn N., 561
attributes, *see* features
auto-orthogonality, 472

back-propagation neural networks, 234
  architecture of, 234
  compared with KRR, 239
  error signals, 237
  gradient-descent, 237
  initial weights, 236
  lower layer, 234
  number of nodes, 240
  upper layer, 235
  weight updating rule, 238
backward elimination, 125
basis, 7
basis function
  kernel-induced, 462
  orthonormal, 463, 466, 480
Bayes classifiers, 550
Bayes' theorem, 542
Bayesian estimation, 458
Bayesian estimation and decision theory, *see* Bayesian test
Bayesian rule, 555, 556
Bayesian Test, 542
Bellman R., 561
between-class scatter matrix, 258
biclustering, 169
big data, 3, 393, 419, 422, 440
binary and multiple classification, 249
Bishop C. M., 562
bounded support vectors, *see* BSV
BSV, *see* OSV

"C&C" tradeoff, 421
  client versus cloud, 421
  computing versus communication, 425
cancer classification system, 131
Cartesian coordinates, 7
center-adjusted perturbational scatter matrix, 291
centroid-adjusted scatter matrix, 255, 259

centroid-adjusted training vectors, 255
centroid-update NJ methods, 206
  centroid update, 207
  node merger, 207
chunking, 404
  optimization subproblem, 404
  problem decomposition, 362
classification complexities
  RBF versus TRBF, 438
classification complexity
  empirical degree, 430
  intrinsic degree, 430
classifier architecture, 250
classifiers without prior learning, 554
closed-form optimal solution, 264
cloud computing, 421
cloud computing platforms, 423
  elastic hosting, 424
  extensive database, 423
  machines, 423
  storage space, 423
clustering criterion
  inter-cluster separation, 143
  intra-cluster compactness, 143
  log-likelihood, 144, 154
  maximum likelihood, 144
clustering quality score (CQS), 169
clustering strategy
  evaluation criterion, 144, 152
  inter-cluster separation, 143
  intra-cluster compactness, 143
  iterative learning/optimization, 143, 146
  node vectors, 143
  number of clusters, 143, 152
  objective function, 143
  topology of nodes, 143
co-clustering, *see* biclustering
co-expressed, 118
coefficients, 7
coherence models, 170
coin-flipping test, 544, 546
  fair coin, 544, 546, 548
  unfair coin, 544, 546
comparison of OCSVMs, 393
  equivalence, 391
  translation invariance, 380, 388
complexities
  classification, 430
  learning, 430
computational complexities, 193
computer cycles for training ECG data, 430
  KRR, 443
  RBF-SVM, 443
  scatter-matrix-based KRR, 443
conditional probability, 221, 555
consecutive search methods, 124
  backward elimination, 126
  forward search, 126
consecutive tensor operations, 436
convergent series, 47
  absolutely and uniformly, 47
conversion of representations, 61
  intrinsic to empirical, 58
  kernel trick, 64, 65
  kernelization, 58, 64
  LSP condition, 58
  representer theorem, 65
conversion to Mercer kernel, 189
  spectral-shift approach, 189
  spectral-truncation approach, 189
convex optimization, 345
coordinate system, 393
  coordinate-dependent, 74
correlation matrix of leukemia dataset, 132
  genes after pre-filtering, 132
  genes after signed-SNR selection, 132
  genes after SVM-RFE, 132
cost function, *see* objective function
cost-effective kernel functions, 424
Courant R. and D. Hilbert, 563
covariance matrix
  computing PCA, 82
  estimation of, 82
criteria for K-means on graph partition, 185
  combined association/cut criterion, 186
  ratio association: intra-cluster similarity, 185
  ratio cut: inter-cluster distance, 186
criteria for discriminant components
  OSNR, 322
  SNR, 313
  SoSNR, 313
  WOSNR, 329
criteria for network segmentation, 185
cross-covariance matrix, 83
cross-orthogonality, 473, 483, 491
cross-validation, 539
cross-validation techniques, 539
  K-fold cross-validation, 539
  bootstrap, 541
  holdout validation, 539
  jackknife, 540
  leave-one-out CV, 540

data
  big, 3, 393, 422
  graphic, 70
  non-vectorial, 14
  temporal, 6
  vectorial, 14
data analysis
  incomplete, 67
  nonvectorial, 14, 67
  vectorial, 14

data matrix, 80, 224
data-centroid similarity (DCS), 195
data-hyperplane, 265
  normal vector, 265
datasets
  eukaryotic protein, 119
  Ischemic stroke, 415
  leukemia, 132
  microarray cancer, 301
  subcellular localization, 302
  UCI, 300
DCA, 325, 326
  discriminant matrix, 326, 328
  extended applications, 333
  minor eigenvectors, 326
  noise subspace, 326
  numerical example, 329
  principal eigenvectors, 326
  projection matrix, 326, 328
  signal subspace, 326
  SNR of signal components, 326, 327
  trace-norm optimizer, 325
  twin optimizer, 326
  variance of noise components, 326, 327
DCA learning model, *see* DCA
DCA parameter ρ:
  choice of, 329
  wide dynamic range of, 328, 330
decision boundary, 558
decision components, 294
  center-adjustment, 297
  component magnitude and resilience, 298
  easy XOR dataset, 297
  hard XOR dataset, 297
  XOR dataset, 294
design freedom
  in empirical space, 63
  in intrinsic space, 63
  linear dependent basis functions, 63
  upper-bound of, 63
diagonal matrix, 82
Diamantaras K. I. and S. Y. Kung, 563
dimension reduction, 79
  computational cost, 79
  data over-fitting, 80
  feature selection, 80
  search space, 80
  subspace projection, 80
dimension reduction method, 8
  feature selection, 9
  subspace projection, 9
dimension-reduced vector, 85
direct kernelized K-means, 196
  updating of DCS, 197
  updating of SCN, 196
discriminant function, 249, 276
  in empirical representation, 432
  in intrinsic representation, 433
discriminant matrix, 328
  DCA, 320, 328
  MD-FDA, 328
  PC-DCA, 324, 328
  PCA, 328
distance
  Euclidean distance, 8, 69
  Mahalanobis distance, 69
distance axioms, 45
distribution
  Gaussian, 82
  independent, 144, 154
  independently and identically distributed (ii.d), 476
  isotropic, 259
  joint, 221
  non-isotropic, 259
  uniform, 477
dot product, *see* inner product
Doubly Woodbury Updating (DWU), 527
  decrement updating, 528
  finite-window EiV, 528
  increment updating, 531
  ZIP updating, 528
doubly-supervised supervised learning, 368
  nonvectorial data, 368
  vectorial data, 367
Duda R. O. and P. E. Hart, 563

E-step
  membership reproportion, 156
  monotonically decreasing property, 157
ECG processing system, 430
  arrhythmia detection, 438, 442
  computer cycles for training, 443
  low power budget, 431
  morphology features, 431
  RBF-SVM classifiers, 432
  training vectors, 431
eigenfunction, 47, 75
eigenvalue, 82, 83
eigenvalue decomposition, *see* spectral decomposition
eigenvector, 83
EiV, *see* errors-in-variables models
EiV estimator, *see* EiV regressor
  bias and variance, 514
  in empirical space, 515
  nonzero-mean, 514
EiV regressor, *see* EiV estimator
  kernelized formulation, 518
  with finite order, 518
  with Gaussian distribution, 517
elastic nets
  ℓ_1 elastic nets, 19

ℓ_2 elastic nets, 18
elementary set, 485
packed, 485
EM, *see* expectation-maximization
EM iterative algorithm, 155
E-step, 156
M-Step, 156
empirical approach, 58, 64
kernel trick, 64
prediction phase, 65
training phase, 64
empirical decision vector, 229
empirical KRR algorithm, 276
empirical learning models for nonvectorial data, 367
alignment score, 367
similarity score, 367
empirical learning models for vectorial and nonvectorial data analysis, 367
doubly-supervised supervised learning, 367
symmetric induced data matrix, 367, 368
empirical network
two-layer, 62
empirical space, 62, 225
decision vector, 106
decision vector in, 60
empirical degree of, 62
feature vector, 102, 104
feature vector in, 62, 222
training-data-dependent, 59
empirical vector, 62, 222
empirical vector space, *see* empirical space
empirical-space approach, *see* empirical approach
empirical-space approach to KPCA
center-adjusted kernel PCA: kernel-matrix based approach, 108
center-adjusted kernel PCA: XOR dataset, 107
center-adjusted versus unadjusted KPCAs, 106
center-unadjusted kernel PCA: XOR dataset, 106
empirical-space SVM for trimming of training vectors, 365
ℓ_1-Norm SVM in empirical space, 365
ℓ_2-Norm SVM in empirical space, 365
equal prior, 154, 556
equivalence between RR and PDA, 269, 281
equivalence of
K-means criteria, 182
BLE, BLP, and KRR, 502, 503
BLUE, BLUP, and LSE, 498
EiVE, EiVP, and EiV regressor, 513
intrinsic and empirical formulations, 289
KRR and PDA, 292
equivalence of FDAs, 260
equivalence of LSE and FDA, 261, 281
equivalent clustering criteria, 182
centroid-based criterion, 181, 182
centroid-free criterion in intrinsic space, 182, 183
kernelized or vector-free criterion, 182, 183
error analysis
KRR, 465
model-induced, 464
multivariate Hermite estimators, 481
two-projection, 486
error rates, 31
classification errors, 32
equal error rates (EER), 34
prediction errors, 449
testing errors, 416
training errors, 406
error vector, 256
error-free hyperplanes, 265
2-norm criterion, 263
maximal margin of separation, 265
error-order tradeoff, 475
errors-in-variables, 291, 293
errors-in-variables models, 459, 461, 510
estimation
error, 224
kernel-based, 468
linear, 461, 462, 468
linear-least-MSE, 223
MMSE, 221
non-parametric, 234
parametric, 234
estimation of the covariance matrix, 82
estimator, *see* estimation
eukaryotic protein dataset, 119
evaluation phase, 21
expectation, 83
expectation-maximization (EM), 153
Dempster, Laird, and Rubin, 153
log-likelihood, 153
monotonic convergence, 156
normalized membership, 155
simple example, 150
soft membership, 153
SSD-and-entropy criterion, 155
expectation-step, *see* E-step
explicit threshold, 245
exponential kernel, 73

false alarm, *see* false positive
false negatives (FN), 31
false positives (FP), 31
false-discovery rate (FDR), 545
false-negative rate (FNR), *see* miss probability, 32
fast KRR classification algorithm, 441
FDR, 121
accuracy comparison, 122
human genes, 122
feature representation, 4
feature selection, 9
feature vector, 6
column, 6

orthogonal, 6
row, 6
feature-weighted classifier, 122, 123
acute leukemias, 123
discriminant function, 123
local score, 123
SNR as weight, 123
features
isotropic, 26
mutually correlated, 27
mutually independent, 26
features selection, 119
accuracy, 119
Fisher method, 119
test time, 119
first-order gradient, 149, 224, 237, 255, 256, 267, 288, 345, 354
Fisher discriminant ratio, *see* FDR
Fisher R. A., 564
Fisher's discriminant analysis (FDA), 258
fist-order Gaussian distribution, *see* Gaussian distribution
flowcharts
K-means, 147
annealing EM (AEM), 160
EM, 156
kernelized NJ clustering, 147
on-line/off-line training, 574
recursive kernel trick, 199
RFE, 129
SOM, 163
forward search, 125
fraction of outliers, 380
Fukunaga K., 564
fusion of filter and wrapper, 373
over-selection phase, 374
pruning phase, 374
VIA-SVM+SD, 374, 375

Gauss-Markov generation models
conventional, 494
kernel-induced, 494, 496, 501
Gauss-Markov theorem, 224, 494, 498
best linear unbiased estimator (BLUE), 224, 228, 497, 498
best linear unbiased predictor (BLUP), 497, 498
equivalent (identical), 498
least-squares-error (LSE) regressor, 497, 498
Gauss-Markov theorem (EiV models), 510
EiV Estimator (EiVE), 512
EiV Predictor (EiVP), 513, 517
EiV regressor, 513, 516
equivalent (identical), 513
schematic diagram, 511
Gauss-Markov theorem (statistical models), 501, 502
best linear estimator (BLE), 505, 512
best linear predictor (BLP), 502
equivalence, 502, 503
kernel ridge regressor (KRR), 502
orthogonality, 502, 503
Gaussian distribution, 53, 509, 517
Gaussian mixture model (GMM), 550
gene ontology (GO), 169
generalization, 21
GMM-based-classifier, 551
learning phase, 551
prediction phase, 551
Golub G. and C. F. Van Loan, 565
green computing, 421

Haykin S., 565
Hermite estimators
error analysis, 474
high-order-Gaussian, 474
multivariate, 480
single-variate, 473
Hermite orthogonal polynomials, 463
Hermite polynomials, 463
Hermite regressors, 459
Hessian, 148
hierarchical cluster analysis, 204
agglomerative methods, 205
divisive methods, 204
hierarchical microarray data analysis, 212
high-order Gaussian distribution
*q*th-order, 477
second-order, 477
Hilbert space, 51, 62
empirical space, 62, 225
intrinsic space, 51, 222, 225
spectral vector space, 110
Hotelling H., 566
hybrid learning models
DCA and SODA, 331
DCA-SODA, 338
DCA: PCA and FDA, 325, 326
KRR and SVM, 401
Ridge-SVM: ridge regressor and SVM, 318
SODA: PCA and FDA, 313, 314
hyperplane-based one-class SVM, 385, 388
adaptive teacher value, 388
discriminant function, 388
dual optimizer in empirical space, 388
mirror-image of training vectors, 386
number of outliers, 388
outlier decision rule, 388
primal optimizer in intrinsic space, 387
virtual training vectors, 386
hypersphere-based one-class SVM, 389
discriminant function, 390
dual optimizer in empirical space, 390
learning model, 390
LSP condition, 390

number of outliers, 390, 391
outlier decision rule, 390
primal optimizer in intrinsic space, 389
radius R, 389
hypothesis, 34
alternative hypothesis (H_1), 541, 543, 546
cross-over point, 543
null hypothesis (H_0), 541, 543, 546
hypothesis testing, 542
Bayesian test, 542
decision threshold, 545
false-discovery rate (FDR), 543, 545
identification rate, 543, 545
likelihood ratio, 542, 545
relationship between, 544
risk-adjusted Bayesain test, 542, 543

identification rate, *see* identified positive rate
implanted pacemaker, 421
implementation cost, 66
choice of kernel functions, 67
in empirical approach, 67
in intrinsic approach, 66
implicit bias, 227
incremental learning, 458
inductive learning, 549
information preserving criteria, 81
maximum-entropy, 81
minimum reconstruction error, 81, 83, 84
information technologies (IT), 421
inner product
Euclidean inner product, 8
generalized inner product, 25
Mahalanobis inner product, 26, 142
input perturbation
random and additive, 291
statistically independent, 293
uncorrelated, 291
white and isotropic, 293
inter-feature redundancy, 118
internet-based IT era, 421
intrinsic approach, 58
compared with empirical approach, 230
computational complexities, 230
prediction phase, 57
training phase, 57
intrinsic data matrix, 54
intrinsic decision vector, 61
intrinsic degree, 48, 50
intrinsic learning models, 225
K-means, 180
hyperplane OCSVM, 385, 388
hypersphere OCSVM, 389
KPCA, 96
KRR, 228
SVM, 358
SVR, 381
time-adaptive recursive KRR, 447, 448, 522
intrinsic network
lower layer, 51
second-order example, 52, 53
two-layer, 51, 285
upper layer, 52
intrinsic representation, *see* intrinsic vector, 222
intrinsic space, 51, 222, 225
center-adjusted, 291
decision vector in, 111
expanded space, 53
feature vector in, 496
intrinsic degree of, 48, 50, 426
negative centroid, 291
positive centroid, 291
intrinsic vector, 496
intrinsic vector space, *see* intrinsic space
intrinsic-space approach to KPCA, 96
inversion lemma, *see* Sherman-Woodbury-Morrison formula
Ischemic Stroke Dataset
Fisher scores, 318
LASSO, 318
PCA, 318
rate of detection, 318
Ridge-SVM, 318
SODA, 317, 318

Jordan M. I. and C. M. Bishop, 566

K-means, 144
centroid, 145
clustering criterion, 144
computational cost, 147
evaluation criterion, 144, 152
gene clustering analysis, 152
hard membership, 153
joint optimization, 146
local optimum example, 151
log-likelihood, 144
monotonic convergence, 148
multiple trial, 152
simple example, 150
standard deviation, 145
sum-of-squared distances (SSD), 145
K-means algorithm, *see* K-means
K-means clustering criterion
in intrinsic space, 180
in kernel-matrix (empirical space), 181
K-means iterative optimization
addition/removal of a member, 148
centroid-update, 147
initialization, 146
membership-update, 146
winner-identification, 146
K-means learning model, *see* K-means
k nearest neighbors (kNN), 554

Kailath T., 566
Kailath T., A. H. Sayed, and B. Hassibi, 566
Karush-Kuhn-Tucker (KKT) condition, 348, 349
KDA, *see* kernel discriminant analysis
KDA versus KRR, 299
  Regression ratio, 299
KDCA learning model, 335
kernel K-means
  monotonic convergence condition, 189
kernel K-means for sparse networks, 197
  computational saving, 200
kernel K-means in intrinsic space, 180
  learning phase, 180
  prediction phase, 180
kernel discriminant analysis, 284
kernel discriminant matrix, 335
kernel function
  continuous, 46, 47
  factorizable, 47
  positive semi-definite, 47
  shift-invariance, 16, 50, 75, 428
  symmetric, 46, 47
  transformation-invariance, 75
kernel matrix, 63, 68, 140
  factorization of, 54, 55
  Mercer matrix, 140
  positive semi-definite, 140
  symmetric matrix, 140
kernel methods
  convergence, 187
  effective implementation, 30
  for cluster analysis, 36
  for green learning, 37
  for statistical estimation theory, 38
  numerical property, 140
kernel perceptron, 336
kernel principal component analysis (KPCA), 95
kernel regression analysis, 225
kernel ridge regression, *see* KRR
kernel ridge regressors (KRR)
  variants of, 36
kernel trick, *see* kernelization, 64, 65, 140
  Mercer condition, 46, 70
  nonvectorical data, 67
kernel, *see* kernel function, 44
kernel-based K-means learning models, 179
kernel-induced basis function, 462
kernel-induced intrinsic space, *see* intrinsic space
kernel-induced LSE estimator, 496
kernel-induced spaces, 111, 112
  Cholesky Space, 116
  empiric space, 111, 112
  intrinsic space, 111, 112
  spectral space, 111, 112
kernel-induced support vector machines, 358
  dual optimizer in empirical space, 359
  learning subspace property (LSP), 359
  primal optimizer in intrinsic space, 359
kernel-induced SVM in empirical space, 360
  discriminant function, 360
  empirical decision vector, 360
  learning algorithm, 360
  multiplier coefficients, 360
kernel-trick approach to KPCA, 100
kernelization, 58, 64
  LSP, 59
  necessary and sufficient condition, 14
kernelized ℓ_2 elastic nets, 18
kernelized K-means algorithms, 195
kernelized K-means learning models, 194
kernelized DCA (KDCA), 335
kernelized KPCA, 99, 100
kernelized learning models in empirical space
  linear kernels, 273
  nonlinear kernels, 287
kernelized models for under-determined systems, 273
kernelized NJ clustering methods, 207
  merger of the closest pair, 207
  update of DCS, 207
kernelized PC-DCA (KPC-DCA), 334, 335
kernelized SODA (KSODA), 333, 338
kernelized SOM, 202
kernels for SVM
  kernel matrix for SVM on the empirical space, 365, 367, 369
  linear kernel for original space, 365
  nonlinear kernel for intrinsic space, 365
KKT for Ridge-SVM
  subset selection, 402
  termination condition, 402
  working set, 403
Kohonen T., 567
KPCA on stroke dataset, 109
KRR, *see* kernel ridge regressors, 463
  multivariate, 467
KRR algorithm for big data (large N), 441
  classification complexity, 441
  learning complexity, 441
KRR and LS-SVM models, 287
KRR estimator, *see* KRR regressors
  bias and variance, 506
  nonzero-mean, 506
KRR learning complexities
  empirical models, 290
  intrinsic models, 290
  RBF versus TRBF, 440
KRR models in empirical-space
  decision rule, 289
  discriminant function, 289, 293
  empirical decision vector, 289
  learning algorithm, 289

KRR regressors
for EiV models, 510
in empirical space, 507
in kernelized formulation, 510
with Gaussian distribution, 53, 509
KRR versus SVM: application studies, 364
microarray cancer diagnosis, 364
subcellular protein sequence classification, 365
UCI data, 364

ℓ_1 norm learning models, 24
ℓ_2 norm learning models, 24
Lagrange multiplier, 263, 285, 345, 346, 354, 359, 382, 385
Lagrangian function, 158, 263, 285, 345, 346, 354, 359, 366
LASSO, 130
learning algorithm of LSE classifier, 256
matrix system, 256
learning complexities
empirical degree, 439
intrinsic degree, 439
KRR, 439
SVM, 439
learning from examples, 9
learning models
kernelization of, 13
optimization formulation, 10
supervised learning, 12
unsupervised learning, 12
learning models in empirical space, 225
learning phase, 20
learning separable SVM, 344
compared with LSE, 351, 352
compared with RR, 351, 352
error-free equality, 348
inequality, 348
Karush-Kuhn-Tucker (KKT) condition, 348, 349
non-support vectors, 349
optimizer in empirical space, 345
optimizer in original space, 345
support vectors, 349
learning subspace property, 59, 228, 288, 354
learning subspace property (LSP), 9, 11
learning subspace property of KPCA, 99
least absolute shrinkage and selection operator, *see* LASSO
least-squares SVM, 287
least-squares-error, *see* LSE
Legendre orthogonal polynomials, 489
Legendre polynomials, 489
Levy B., 568
linear and nonlinear models, 252
linear classification
decision boundary, 252, 257
decision hyperplane, *see* decision boundary
decision rule, 248, 250, 277
decision vector, 249
linear discriminant function, 250, 252
projection vector, 252, 258
why linear, 252
linear discriminant analysis (LDA), 258
linear kernel matrix, 91
linear least-squares-error (LLSE) analysis, 222
linear regression analysis
for approximation, 254
for classification, 254
linear ridge classifier
computational complexities, 278
invertible/nonsingular kernel-matrix, 274, 277
kernel-matrix-based, 276
scatter-matrix-based, 272
linear separable support vector machines, 344
decision boundary, 349
decision hyperplane, 344
decision threshold, 349
decision vector, 349
discriminant function, 350
marginal hyperplanes, 344, 349
safety zone/margin, 344
linear system of equations, 21
over-determined systems, 22
under-determined systems, 23, 65
linearly separability, 252
LLDA-RFE, 130
local or client computing, 423
local versus centralized processing, 424
log-likelihood classifier (LLC), 557
low power applications
brain-computer-interface, 423
health-care monitor, 423
pacemaker, 423
prosthesis, 423
therapeutics, 423
low power system requirements
constant recording, 423
implantability, 423
long battery usage, 423
no excessive heating, 423
signal processing, 423
LS-SVM, *see* least-squares SVM, 287
LSE solution
direct solution, 254
matrix formulation, 256
LSP, *see* learning subspace property (LSP), 9

M-Step
centroid update, 156
monotonically decreasing property, 158
machine learning systems, 4
Mahalanobis inner product, 26
Mahalanobis matrix, 45, 49
positive semi-definite, 49
symmetric, 49

Mahalanobis P. C., 569
major and minor subspaces, 85
MAP, *see* maximum a posteriori estimate, 550
marginal support vectors (MSV), 391
matrix inversion
  kernel-matrix, 278
  pseudo-inverse, 314
  scatter-matrix, 278
  within-class scatter-matrix, 258
  Woodbury identity, 290, 503, 522
maximization-step, *see* M-step
measurement errors
  input, 459
  output, 460
medial filtering, 69
Mercer condition, 46, 288
Mercer J., 569
Mercer kernel function, 27, 46
  construction of, 50
  Gaussian radial basis function (RBF), 16, 48, 55, 231
  induced, 73
  linear kernel function, 52
  Mercer condition, 46, 47
  necessary and sufficient condition, 47
  polynomial kernel function, 48, 52
  truncated RBF (TRBF), 56
Mercer matrix, *see* kernel matrix
Mercer's theorem, 47, 495
metric space, 45
microarray data analysis, 173
minimum mean-square-error, 461
  mean-square-error, *see* MSE
  MMSE, *see* minimum mean-square-error
  MSE, 221, 223
minimum variance, 225, 497, 498
miss probability, *see* false-negative rate (FNR)
mixed-component DCA (MC-DCA), *see* DCA
mobile device, 421
modified FDA, 260
  modified Fisher's score, 260
  signal-to-signal+noise ratio, 258
modified Fisher score, 291
modified polynomial kernel (POLY-TRBF), 428
mono-kernel function, 241
  linear combination of sub-kernels, 243
multi-class classification, 307
  one-on-one for all-pairs (AP), 307
  one-versus-all (OVA), 308
multi-class SVM, 361
  highest score, 362
multi-kernel KRR, 240
  equal factors, 240
  non-equal factors, 242
multi-kernel regression, 240, 242
  role of LSP, 242
multi-label classification, 307, 310
  learning formulation, 312
  modified one-of-N coding, 311
  teacher vector, 312
multinomial expansion, 48
multiplicative coherence models, 171

Nadaraya-Watson regression estimator (NWRE), 232, 233
  compared with KRR, 234
neighbor-joining (NJ) methods
  centroid-update approach, 206
  kernelized approach, 207
Neyman J. and E. S Pearson, 570
Neyman-Pearson test, 542
node vectors, 11
noise covariance matrix, 292
noise matrix, 258
noise-subspace, 322
  noise-power, 322
non-Mercel kernel
  sigmoid function, 73
nonvectorial data
  graphs, 184
  sequences, 184
  time series, 184
nonvectorial data analysis, 183
nonvectorical data analysis, 67, 68
  similarity metrics, 68
number of clusters, 152
  Akaike information criterion (AIC), 152
  Bayesian information criterion (BIC), 152
  minimum description length (MDL), 152
numerical methods for PCA, 89
  computational complexities, 94
  equivalence, 91
  spectral decomposition (of kernel matrix), 91
  spectral decomposition (of scatter matrix), 90
  SVD (of data matrix), 90

objective function of FDA, 258
  Fisher's score, 258
  signal-to-noise ratio, 258
off-line learning phase, 251
  inductive learning models, 251
OHP, *see* orthogonal hyperplane property
omnidirectional-SNR, *see* OSNR
on-line prediction phase, 251
  computing power, 251
  minimum latency, 251
optimal estimate of original vector, 83
optimal estimation
  order of estimator, 476
  projection, 469, 483, 489, 512
optimal subspace projection, 81
optimizer in empirical space, 354
  min-max formulation, 354, 359

optimum
global, 151
local, 151
original vector space
center-adjusted, 255
mass center, 255
negative centroid, 255
positive centroid, 255
orthogonal hyperplane property (OHP), 264–266, 285, 346, 397, 402
orthogonal polynomials, 459, 463
Cholesky decomposition, 490
Hermite, 463
Legendre, 489
OSNR, 322
2D visualization, 322
weighted (WOSNR), 329
outlier, 25, 380
outlier detection applications, 380
abnormal gene or sequences, 380
detection of imposters, 380
EEG/ECG monitoring, 380
personal/environmental safety detection, 380
outlier support vectors (OSV), 391, 392
OVA, 308
classification phase, 310
lower layer, 309
one-of-K coding, 308
two-layer network, 309
upper layer, 309
over-determined formulation, 253
overall-SNR, *see* OSNR

pairwise similarity, 140
alignment score, 367
Euclidean inner product, 8
generalized inner product, 25
kernel functions, 48
Mahalanobis inner product, 26, 142
similarity score, 367
parameters in WECs, 396
C in SVM, 397
ρ in KRR, 396, 397
ρ, C, and $C_{\min}$ in Ridge-SVM, 404, 413
complementary roles of ρ and C, 397
parameters of Ridge-SVM, 404, 414
location of ramp, 405
number of support vectors, 408
transition ramp, 404
tuning ρ, 409, 412
tuning C, 409
tuning $C_{\min}$, 409, 412
Parzen windows, 233
Parzen-Rosenblatt density estimator, 233
pattern recognition, 173
PC-DCA learning model, 324
relationship with DCA, 332
PCA
comparison with DCA and SODA, 315, 316, 318, 328, 331, 332
comparison with KPCA, 95
discriminant matrix, 328
subspace projection methods, 318
trace-norm optimizer, 318
PCA subspace projection
entropy, 81, 88
mean-square-error criterion, 81
mutual information, 81, 87, 88
reconstruction error, 83
PCA unsupervised learning model, 83
PCA versus KPCA, 95, 105, 106
supervised learning example, 105
unsupervised learning example, 105
PDA-SVM, *see* Ridge-SVM
performance metrics, 31
equal error rates (EER), 34
false-negative rate (FNR), 32
false-positive rate (FPR), 32
precision, 33
sensitivity, 32
specificity, 32
true-negative rate (TNR), 32
true-positive rate (TPR), 32
performance of Ridge-SVM, 413, 415
prediction accuracy, 408
training time, 408
perturbation
input, 459
output, 460
perturbation regulated regressor, *see* PRR
perturbational discriminant analysis (PDA), 268, 290
poly2 discriminant function, 434
decision matrix, 434
power saving, 434, 435
poly_*p* discriminant function
classification complexity, 437
tensor representation, 435, 436
polynomial kernel function, 48, 52
*p*th-order, 427
second-order, 52, 53
post-projection centroid-separation, 272
power consumption, 425
classification, 431
feature extraction, 431
PPDA, 304, 305
classification efficiency, 307
ECG arrhythmia detection, 306
learning complexity, 431
prediction performance, 306, 307
TRBF3-PPDA, 306
trimming training vectors, 303
pre-whitening, 328

precision matrix, 522
prediction complexity, *see* classification complexity
prediction errors, *see* classification errors
prediction performances w.r.t. size of training datasets, 364
  SVM-AP (one versus one), 364
  SVM-OVA (one versus all), 364
prediction phase, 21
primal optimizer in intrinsic space, 359
  dual optimizer in empirical space, 359
  learning subspace property (LSP), 359
principal component analysis, *see* PCA
principal components, 82, 83
prior model, 494, 500
probabilistic neural networks (PNN), 555
  MAP decision rule, 555
profile alignment SVM, 71
projection criteria, *see* criteria for discriminant components
PRR, 459, 467
  connection with LASSO, 488
  distinction from KRR, 471, 478
  Gaussian case, 472
  kernel-based, 471
  linear, 470
  two-projection, 486
pruned KRR, *see* (PPDA)
pruned PDA, *see* (PPDA)

quadratic programming, 345, 404

random variable, 81, 518
receiver operating characteristic (ROC), 33
  area under the curve (AUC), 34
  Conversion between ROCs, 34, 43
recovery of original data, 83
recursive EiV algorithms, 529
  in empirical space, 530
  in intrinsic space, 529
recursive feature elimination, *see* RFE
  Laplacian linear discriminant analysis-based (LLDA-RFE), 130
recursive kernel trick for K-Means, 199
  computational saving, 200
  updating of SOS, 198, 200
  updating of SSCN, 198, 200
recursive KRR algorithms, 521
  in empirical space, 524
  in intrinsic space, 522
  with a forgetting factor, 525, 527
regression function, 221, 464
regression model, 461
regularization parameterρ, 231
regularization via radial basis function (RBF) networks, 230
  back-propagation (BP) neural networks, 234
  Nadaraya-Watson regression estimator (NWRE), 232
  RBF approximation networks, 230
representer theorem, 65
reproducing kernel Hilbert space (RKHS), 28
ridge parameter ρ
  ill-conditioned, 270
  regularization effects, 270
  robustness of learned models, 272
ridge penalty, 225
ridge regression, 253, 266
ridge regression analysis, 459
ridge regressor
  kernel-based, 462
  linear least MSE, 462
  MMSE, 461
ridge regressor (RR), 221
ridge regularization, 225
Ridge-SVM, 399, 401
Ridge-SVM learning models, *see* Ridge-SVM
robust KRR classifier, 300
robust learning models, 253
  input-perturbation, 253, 266
  ridge regularization, 253, 266
robustness of learned classifiers, 273
RR, *see* ridge regressor
Rumelhart D. E., G. E. Hinton, and R. J. Williams, 572

scatter matrix, 22, 91, 224
  center-adjusted, 92
scatter-matrix-based KRR, 440
Scholkopf B. and A. J. Smola, 572
second-order statistics, 82
security, 423
selection strategy
  backward elimination, 126
  filtering approach, 126
  forward search, 126
  optimal selection, 126
self-organizing-map (SOM) learning models, 159
  k-dimensional grid/mesh, 162
  adjacent nodes, 161
  evaluation criterion, 165
  neighboring nodes (co-winners), 164
  node vectors, 162
  sensitivity function, 164, 165
  topological order, 160
  two-loop training procedure, 162
separation margin, 355
  compared with SNR, 272
  component, 271
  large C narrow margin, 355
  small C wide margin, 355, 372
Shawe-Taylor J. and N. Cristianini, 572
Sherman-Woodbury-Morrison formula, Woodbury's matrix identity, 261

signal matrix, 258
Signal-to-Noise ratio, *see* SBR
significance testing, 542
  p-value, 546
  t-statistic: t_S, 546
  false-positive rate (FPR), 32
  from null hypothesis, 545
significance tests, 34
similarity metric, 8, 68
similarity metrics, 15, 142
  network segmentation, 69
  sequences, 68
  temporal waveforms, 68
  time series, 68
simulated annealing, 158
singular value decomposition, *see* SVD
slack minimization, 378
slack variables, 353, 359
SNR, 120
  noise (intra-class) perturbation, 120
  signal (inter-class distinction), 120
SNR-type tests
  Fisher discriminant ratio (FDR), 121
  Signed-SNR, 120
  SNR, 121
  symmetric divergence (SD), 121
  two-sample t-statistics, 121
social network
  graphic representation, 70
  recursive segmentation, 199
SODA, 313
  algorithm, 314
  deflation method, 314, 338
  optimizer, 314
SOM iterative algorithm, 162
  inner loop: centroid updates, 202
  outer loop: shrinking of learning windows, 204
SOM iterative learning algorithm, 162
  inner loop: centroid updates, 163
  outer loop: shrinking of learning windows, 164
span, 7
special cases of Ridge-SVM, 400
  comparison, 402
  KDA, 397
  KRR, 401
  SVM, 401
specificity, *see* true-negative rate (TNR)
spectral K-means, 190
  learning phase, 190
  prediction phase, 191
spectral space, 295, 337
  basis functions, 295
  decision vector, 293, 294
  feature vector, 293, 294, 296
spectral vector space, 110
spectral-shift
  solution invariance of, 194
spectral-space
  decision vector, 104
  feature vector, 102, 104
squared-centroid-norm (SCN), 195
squarely integrable function, 47
static data, 4
statistical regression analysis, 221, 222, 459, 460
  kernel, 462
  linear, 462
  MMSE, 223, 461
  ridge, 459, 463
Strang G., 573
Student test, 121
subcelluar localization, 71
subspace, 8
  dimension of, 8
subspace projection methods
  commonality, 328
  comparison, 315, 316, 328, 331, 332
  DCA, 325, 326
  FDA, 319
  KDCA, 335
  KSODA, 333, 338
  MD-FDA, 319
  PCA, 318
  SODA, 313, 314
successively optimized discriminant analysis, *see* SODA
sum-of-SNR, *see* SoSNR
supervised classification, 248
supervised filtering criteria, 120
supervised learning models, 249
  over-determined formulation, 253
  under-determined formulation, 23, 59, 65, 263
supervised learning strategies, 252
  linear system of equation, 253
  robust models, 253
  separation margin, 253
supervised subspace projection methods, 313
supervised wrapper methods, 127
support vector clustering (SVC), 392
  cluster boundaries, 391
  outlier support vectors (OSV), 392
  separation between subclusters, 391
support vector machine (SVM)
  binary SVM, 343
  multi-class, 344
  variants of, 37
support vector machine (SVM), *see* Vapnik, V.N., 343
support vector regression (SVR), 381
  discriminant function, 382
  dual optimizer in empirical space, 382
  learning subspace property (LSP), 382
  primal optimizer in intrinsic space, 381

threshold value, 382
supporting hyperplanes, *see* marginal hyperplanes
surviving vectors, 305, 307
SVD, *see* singular value decomposition
SVM for cancer data analysis, 362
gene selections, 363
performance of SVM-OVA, 363
training and testing accuracies, 363
SVM learning softwares, 362
sequential minimal optimization (SMO), 362, 404
SVM with fuzzy separation
decision boundary, 355
decision threshold, 355
decision vector, 355
separation margin, 353, 355
SVM with weighted mitigation factor, 417
SVM's prediction scores, 133, 134
based on FDR features, 133
based on SVM-RFE features, 133
decision threshold, 133
varying numbers of genes, 134
SVM, *see* support vector machine, 343
SVM-RFE, 128, 129
SVR
error insensitivity, 381
grace interval, 381
SVR, *see* Vapnik, V.N., 343, 381
SVR, *see* support vector regression, 381
symmetric divergence (SD)
class-conditional means, 121
standard derivations, 121
symmetrical property, 85
system design, 421, 423
system variables
dependent, 221, 460
independent, 221, 460
input, 460
output, 460

t-test, 121
Taylor series expansion, 428
teacher value, 223, 224
temperature parameter, 160
temporal signals, 6
tensor product, 422, 435
testing phase, *see* evaluation phase
Theodoridis S. and K. Koutroumbas, 573
three phases in supervised learning, 250
evaluation and testing phase, 250
prediction phase, 251
training phase, 250
Tikhonov regularization, 463
ill-posed problem, 463
over-fitting problem, 463
time-adaptive algorithm, 458
time-adaptive KRR learning, 447, 448
intrinsic-space recursive algorithm, 449
with a forgetting factor, 452
time-course gene groups, 172
time-forgetting factor, 526
time-forgetting updating rule, 526
time-series predication, 458
time-varying variance, 526
total least-squares (TLS), 247
trace norm, 84, 319, 325
trace-norm maximizer/minimizer, 325
trace-norm optimization of KPCA, 96
optimal trace-norm, 96
trace-norm optimizers, 319
DCA, 325
FDA, 319
MD-FDA, 319
PC-DCA, 324
PCA, 318
tradeoff between
bias and variance, 487, 492, 532
order and error, 493
tradeoff between complexity and performance, 444, 446
PPDA Versus SVM, 446
RBF-SVM Versus RBF-KRR, 446
training SVM with fuzzy separation, 353
compared with LSE, 351, 352
compared with RR, 351, 352
error-free equality, 348
inequality, 348
Karush-Kuhn-Tucker (KKT) condition, 356
non-support vectors, 357
optimizer in empirical space, 354
optimizer in original space, 354
penalty factor, 354
support vectors, 357
training vectors, 11
transductive learning, 549
transformation, 82
transitiveness of orthogonality, 492
auto-orthogonality, 472
cross-orthogonality, 473, 483, 491
translation invariance, 380, 388, 392
TRBF discriminant function
tensor representation, 437
true negatives (TN), 31
true positives (PN), 31
true-negative rate (TNR), *see* specificity
truncated RBF (TRBF) kernel, 56, 422, 428
truncation discrepancy
implication of, 193
tightness of, 192
upper bound, 192
two-mode clustering, *see* biclustering
two-projection theorem, 460, 482, 483, 485, 486, 491
Tychonoff A. N., 574

ubiquity, 423
  any time, 423
  anyone, 423
  anywhere, 423
unbiased, 224, 228, 497, 498
unitary matrix, 82
unsupervised filtering, 124
  histogram of variances, 124
  variance, 124
unsupervised filtering criteria, 120
unsupervised wrapper methods, 129, 130

ν-SV, *see* ν-SVM classifiers
ν-SVM classifiers, 383
  adjustable teacher value, 383
  decision boundary, 385
  discriminant function, 385
  dual optimizer in empirical space, 383, 385
  margin separation, 383
  primal optimizer in intrinsic space, 383, 384
Vapnik V. N., 343, 381, 383, 392, 403, 574
variational principle, 231
vector function, 47
vector norm, 8
vector space, 6
  Cartesian coordinates, 7
  empirical space, 111, 112
  high-dimensional, 47
  infinite-dimension, 10
  intrinsic space, 111, 112
  kernel-induced space, 142
  oiginal space, 142
  orthogonality, 8
Venn-diagram, 126, 127, 135

WEC, 398, 400
  WEC for KDA, 397
  WEC for KRR, 303, 395
  WEC for Ridge-SVM, 395, 405, 406
  WEC for SVM, 357, 358, 398
WEC for KRR, 303
  a straight line, 304
  linearly proportional weight, 303
WEC for negative training vectors, 417
WEC of SVM, 357, 358
  flat region, 370
  vertical region, 370
weight-error-curve (WEC), *see* WEC
Wiener N., 575
within-class scatter matrix, 258
  isotropic, 259
  non-isotropic, 259
Wolfe dual optimization, 346, 354, 355, 358
Woodbury M. A., 575
Woodbury's matrix identity, 290, 503, 522
wrapper approach, 127, 128
  designated classifier, 128
  feature evaluation, 128
  feedback, 128
wrapper methods for empirical learning models, 369
  selection scheme based on distance to marginal hyperplane, 369
  SVM-RFE, 373–375
  VIA-SVM trimming scheme, 372–375
  wrapper methods for trimming training vectors, 369

XOR problem, 54, 102
XOR-dataset in intrinsic-space, 286

yeast cell cycle data, 124
  after filtering, 124
  before filtering, 124

zero gradient point, *see* first-order gradient, 158, 160, 223, 229, 258, 260, 263, 264, 285, 287, 288, 366, 462
zero-innovation-property (ZIP), 449, 523, 524

Printed in the United States
by Baker & Taylor Publisher Services